Sacred Darkness

SACRED DARKNESS

A GLOBAL PERSPECTIVE ON THE RITUAL USE OF CAVES

EDITED BY **Holley Moyes**

UNIVERSITY PRESS OF COLORADO
Boulder

© 2012 by University Press of Colorado

Published by University Press of Colorado
5589 Arapahoe Avenue, Suite 206C
Boulder, Colorado 80303

All rights reserved
Printed in the United States of America

 The University Press of Colorado is a proud member of
the Association of American University Presses.

The University Press of Colorado is a cooperative publishing enterprise supported, in part, by Adams State University, Colorado State University, Fort Lewis College, Metropolitan State University of Denver, Regis University, University of Colorado, University of Northern Colorado, Utah State University, and Western State Colorado University.

∞ This paper meets the requirements of the ANSI/NISO Z39.48-1992 (Permanence of Paper).

Library of Congress Cataloging-in-Publication Data

Sacred darkness : a global perspective on the ritual use of caves / edited by Holley Moyes.
  p. cm.
 Includes bibliographical references and index.
 ISBN 978-1-60732-177-4 (hardcover : alk. paper) — ISBN 978-1-60732-178-1 (ebook)
 1. Sacred space. 2. Caves—Religious aspects. 3. Caves—Cross-cultural studies. 4. Ritual. 5. Anthropology of religion. I. Moyes, Holley.
 BL580.S2293 2013
 203'.5—dc23
                    2012044578

Design by Daniel Pratt

21 20 19 18 17 16 15 14 13 12   10 9 8 7 6 5 4 3 2 1

To Charles H. Faulkner

for shedding light

on the dark zones.

Contents

List of Figures | ix

List of Tables | xiii

Preface | xv

Note on Radiocarbon Dating | xvii

Introduction | 1
    HOLLEY MOYES

Part I: Old World Ritual Cave Traditions

1. Ritual Cave Use in European Paleolithic Caves | 15
    JEAN CLOTTES

2. Constructed Caves: Transformations of the Underworld in Prehistoric Southeast Italy | 27
    ROBIN SKEATES

3. Caves of the Living, Caves of the Dead: Experiences Above and Below Ground in Prehistoric Malta | 45
    SIMON K.F. STODDART AND CAROLINE A.T. MALONE

4. Landscapes of Ritual, Identity, and Memory: Reconsidering Neolithic and Bronze Age Cave Use in Crete, Greece | 59
    PETER TOMKINS

5. Caves and the Funerary Landscape of Prehistoric Britain | 81
    ANDREW T. CHAMBERLAIN

6. The Subterranean Landscape of the Southern Levant during the Chalcolithic Period | 87
    YORKE M. ROWAN AND DAVID ILAN

7. The Chamber of Secrets: Grottoes, Caves, and the Underworld in Ancient Egyptian Religion | 109
    STUART TYSON SMITH

8. Caves as Sacred Spaces on the Tibetan Plateau | 125
    MARK ALDENDERFER

9. Differential Australian Cave and Rockshelter Use during the Pleistocene and Holocene | 135
    PAUL S.C. TAÇON, WAYNE BRENNAN, MATTHEW KELLEHER, AND DAVE PROSS

Part II: New World Ritual Cave Traditions

10. Caves as Sacred Space in Mesoamerica | 151
    HOLLEY MOYES AND JAMES E. BRADY

11. Footsteps in the Dark Zone: Ritual Cave Use in Southwest Prehistory | 171
    SCOTT NICOLAY

12. Forty Years' Pursuit of Human Prehistory in the World Underground | 185
    PATTY JO WATSON

13. A New Overview of Prehistoric Cave Art in the Southeast | 195
    JAN F. SIMEK, ALAN CRESSLER, AND JOSEPH DOUGLAS

14. Reevaluating Cave Records: The Case for Ritual Caves in the Eastern United States | 211
    CHERYL CLAASSEN

15. Ceremonial Use of Caves and Rockshelters in Ohio | 225
    OLAF H. PRUFER AND KEITH M. PRUFER

16. The Ritual Use of Caves and Rockshelters in Ozark Prehistory | 237
    GEORGE SABO III, JERRY E. HILLIARD, AND JAMI J. LOCKHART

Part III: Case Studies in Ritual Cave Use

17. The Prehistoric Funerary Archaeology of the Niah Caves, Sarawak (Malaysian Borneo) | 249
    GRAEME BARKER AND LINDSAY LLOYD-SMITH

18. Recognizing Ritual in the Dark: Nakovana Cave and the End of the Adriatic Iron Age | 263
    TIMOTHY KAISER AND STAŠO FORENBAHER

19. Sacred Spaces, Sacred Species: Zooarchaeological Perspectives on Ritual Uses of Caves | 275
    JOANNA E.P. APPLEBY AND PRESTON T. MIRACLE

20. Ritual Cave Use in the Bahamas | 285
    ROBERT S. CARR, WILLIAM C. SCHAFFER, JEFF B. RANSOM, AND MICHAEL P. PATEMAN

Part IV: Ethnographic and Ethnohistoric Studies

21. Caves in Ireland: Archaeology, Myth, and Folklore | 297
    PATRICK MCCAFFERTY

22. Caves in Black and White: The Case of Zimbabwe | 309
    TERENCE RANGER

23. Where the Wild Things Are: An Exploration of Sacrality, Danger, and Violence in Confined Spaces | 317
    SANDRA PANNELL AND SUE O'CONNOR

24. Ritual Uses of Caves in West Malaysia | 331
    JOSEPH J. HOBBS

25. A Quantitative Literature Survey Regarding the Uses and Perceptions of Caves among Nine Indigenous Andean Societies | 343
    NATHAN CRAIG

26. Caves and Related Sites in the Great Plains of North America | 353
    DONALD J. BLAKESLEE

Part V: New Approaches

27. Civilizing the Cave Man: Diachronic and Cross-Cultural Perspectives on Cave Ritual | 365
    ANDREA STONE

28. Caves and Spatial Constraint: The Prehistoric Implications | 371
    EZRA B.W. ZUBROW

29. Why Dark Zones Are Sacred: Turning to Behavioral and Cognitive Science for Answers | 385
    DANIEL R. MONTELLO AND HOLLEY MOYES

List of Contributors | 397

Index | 399

Figures

1.1. Map of the stone structures in the Bruniquel cave | **17**

1.2. Engraved flat sandstone pebble from Enlène | **18**

1.3. Cosquer cave, hand stencils at the brink of a deep shaft | **20**

1.4. Rhinoceros engraved as if issuing from a recess in the Chauvet cave | **21**

1.5. Natural hole in the Niaux cave identified as the head of a deer | **21**

1.6. Cougnac cave, fingers covered with paint applied to the walls | **22**

1.7. Chauvet cave, cave-bear humeri stuck into the ground | **23**

1.8. Chauvet cave strewn with cave-bear skulls | **24**

1.9. Cosquer cave, deliberately broken stalagmites | **24**

2.1. Sites mentioned in the text | **28**

2.2. Grotta Paglicci above the Valle di Settepende and the Tavoliere plain | **29**

2.3. Grotta Santa Maria on the Murge escarpment | **30**

2.4. Grotta delle Mura, located on the Adriatic coast | **33**

2.5. Mouth of Grotta Scaloria, filled by trees, with the Gargano uplands | **35**

2.6. Grottone di Manaccora and Punta Manaccore, on the Adriatic coast | **40**

3.1. Location of Malta and location of caves | **47**

3.2. Ggantija: the best-preserved aboveground cave | **48**

3.3. A comparison of the Hal Saflieni hypogeum and the Xaghra hypogeum | **49**

3.4. Bur Mghez, a natural burial cave | **50**

3.5. The intentionality of stratigraphy. Stacking of burials in Brochtorff Circle | **53**

3.6. The intentionality of stratigraphy. Destruction of large standing figure in Brochtorff Circle | **53**

3.7. Underground cave system of the Brochtorff Circle at Xaghra | **54**

3.8. Tarxien: an ideal plan of a cultural cave | **55**

4.1. Neolithic sites mentioned in the text | **60**

4.2. Early Minoan sites mentioned in the text | **60**

4.3. Aegean Neolithic and Early Bronze Age sites mentioned in the text | **61**

4.4. Knossos, subterranean chamber beneath the southeast corner of the Palace | **68**

5.1. Principal regions of Britain with outcrops of cavernous karst limestone | **82**

5.2. Distribution of Lateglacial and Holocene radiocarbon dates on human skeletal remains from British caves | **83**

5.3. Principal Components Analysis of finds from 100 archaeological caves in the Peak District and the Yorkshire Dales | **83**

5.4. Altitudes of burial caves in the Peak District of central Britain | **84**

5.5. Thor's Cave, Peak District | **85**

6.1. Selected Chalcolithic and mortuary sites | **88**

6.2. Chalcolithic ossuaries | **91**

6.3. Nahal Qanah Cave profile | **92**

6.4. Nahal Qanah Cave, karstic area with pottery churn fragment | **93**

6.5. Nahal Mishmar hoard as found in reed mat | **94**

6.6. Material items from mortuary cave contexts | **95**

6.7. Giva'tayim Caves 1 and 7, plan and section | **98**

6.8. Palmahim Cave, plan and section | **98**

6.9. Bir es-Safadi site plan | **100**

7.1. Sites mentioned in the text | **110**

7.2. Ancient Egyptian cosmology | **111**

7.3. Pyramid Texts and cosmological symbolism in the Pyramid of Unas | **111**

7.4. The sun sets along the Sphinx in line with Khafre's pyramid during equinoxes | **112**

7.5. At top column from the Chariot Hall, tomb of Ramses VI | **113**

7.6. Fourth hour of the Book of the Secret Chamber | **114**

7.7. Conceptual layout and placement of texts, tomb of Merneptah | **115**

7.8. The Osirion in back of Seti I's temple at Abydos | **116**

7.9. Anubis guards the burial chamber, tomb of Pashed | **117**

7.10. Small openings in the ceiling create twilight space, Hypostyle Hall of Osiris Temple, Abydos | **118**

7.11. Old Kingdom Temples: Montu at Medamoud and Satet on Elephantine Island | **119**

7.12. The temple as cosmos materialized: temple of Ramses III at Medinet Habu | **120**

7.13. Rameses II as Osiris, Abu Simbel | **121**

8.1. Ethnographic Tibet | **126**

8.2. Monastic habitation caves near Old Piyang; interior of habitation cave | **127**

8.3. Piyang mesa, showing the large number of excavated caves | **128**

8.4. Holley Moyes, negotiating a narrow crevice | **131**

8.5. An altar within a cave temple at Dungkar | **132**

9.1. Namorodo, depicted as a tall, thin giant | **137**

9.2. Rainbow Serpents figure prominently across Aboriginal Australia | **138**

9.3. Shelter above Twin Falls Creek, Northern Territory, Australia | **139**

9.4. Hundreds of images cover the shelter of Yuwunggayai, Deaf Adder Gorge, Northern Territory, Australia | **140**

9.5. Eagle's Reach is just below a ridgetop and is protected on three sides | **141**

9.6. Stencils and drawings at Eagle's Reach possibly span 4,000 years | **142**

9.7. Birds, Bird Ancestral Beings, and other creatures are common at Eagle's Reach | **142**

9.8. Dingo's Lair is next to a creek in a low valley | **143**

9.9. Dingos, quolls, and other creatures are frequent at Dingo's Lair | **144**

9.10. Emu Cave, New South Wales | **145**

10.1. Mesoamerica, showing selected caves mentioned in the text | **152**

10.2. Sixteenth-century depiction from the *Atlas de Duran* | **153**

10.3. The "El Rey" monument illustrating an important person within a cave | **153**

10.4. A Late Classic vase depicting Chac, the Maya rain god | **154**

10.5. Modern Naj Tunich cave ceremony | **155**

10.6. The Pyramid of the Sun at Teotihuacan | **156**

10.7. Large vessels from Chechem Ha Cave, Belize | **160**

10.8. "The Crystal Maiden" in Belize; Preclassic ossuary in Honduras | **162**

11.1. Major ritual caves and earth openings mentioned in the text | **172**

11.2. Entrance to Bear Creek Cave, Greenlee County, Arizona | **173**

11.3. Caver Robert S. Willis examines arrow offerings, Feather Cave, 1964 | **173**

11.4. Modified entrance to Spirit Bird Cave, Montezuma County, Utah | **174**

11.5. Mogollon "Tlaloc" effigies from New Mexico caves | **174**

11.6. Split-twig figurine in situ in a Grand Canyon Cave | **175**

11.7. Fragment of a grooved fending stick and a reed arrow in a ceremonial cave, south-central New Mexico | **177**

11.8. (A) Tourists and (B) flowstone basin in the grotto of Soda Dam | **180**

12.1. Cave archaeology crews in Salts Cave Sinks and Salts Cave Vestibule | **186**

12.2. Robert L. Hall in Upper Salts Cave, 1963 | **186**

12.3. Fragments of Early Woodland *Cucurbita pepo* in Lower Salts Cave | **186**

12.4. Fragments of prehistoric cane charcoal, Lower Salts Cave | **187**

12.5. Foot impression left by Late Archaic caver, Upper Crouchway, Floyd Collins Crystal Cave/Unknown Cave | **189**

13.1. Avian effigy images from Southeast Mississippian sites | **197**

13.2. Petroglyph, face effigy with "Toothy Mouth," 11th Unnamed Cave | **198**

13.3. Winged-warrior effigies from Southeast Mississippian sites | **204**

13.4. Avian effigy with human-warrior characteristics, 11th Unnamed Cave | **205**

13.5. Panel of three petroglyphs, 12th Unnamed Cave | **205**

13.6. Elements of panel composition shown in figure 13.5 | **206**

13.7. Triptych panel from 12th Unnamed Cave | **206**

13.8. Models for spatial structure of four Mississippian sites | **207**

14.1. Sites mentioned in the text | **212**

14.2. Russell Cave | **218**

14.3. Dust Cave | **219**

14.4. Austin Cave | **221**

15.1. Distribution of Ohio caves and rockshelters | **226**

15.2. Floor plan of Hendricks Cave | **226**

15.3. Hendricks Cave: human cranial bone and Laurentian projectile point | **227**

15.4. Stanhope Rockshelter: completeness chart of two skeletons | **228**

15.5. Stanhope Rockshelter: female skull with penetration impact wounds | **229**

15.6. Stow Rockshelter cache | **230**

15.7. Late Archaic cache from Rais Cave | **230**

15.8. Ceramic vessel from Stanhope Rockshelter | **231**

15.9. Gillie Rockshelter petroglyph, perhaps representing a turkey foot | **232**

15.10. Raven Rocks, general view (circa 1892) | **232**

15.11. White Rocks shell pendants | **233**

15.12. Krill Cave, descendants of veterans of the Grand Army of the Republic | **234**

16.1. Physiographic regions in Arkansas | **238**

16.2. Environmental similarity models for six archaeological type sites | **242**

17.1. Plan of the Niah Caves complex, Sarawak | **250**

17.2. The West Mouth of the Niah Great Cave | **251**

17.3. The archaeological zone of the West Mouth of the Niah Great Cave | **252**

17.4. Excavating a surviving balk in the Harrissons' Hell Trench, 2002 | **253**

17.5. An Early Holocene human burial excavated by the Harrisons, West Mouth | **254**

17.6. Looking into the archaeological zone of the West Mouth, Niah Great Cave | **255**

17.7. Spatial patterning, Neolithic cemetery, West Mouth, Niah Great Cave | **256**

17.8. Neolithic inhumation burial (B211) excavated by the Niah Cave Project, 2003 | **256**

17.9. Plan of intercutting burials, Neolithic cemetery, Niah Great Cave | **257**

17.10. Niah Great Cave, Neolithic cemetery: rattan matting on which a 3-year-old child was laid | **257**

17.11. Niah Great Cave, Neolithic cemetery: jar-burial atop earlier jar burial | **258**

18.1. Central Dalmatia, showing Nakovana Cave and other sites | **264**

18.2. Plan and section of Nakovana Cave, showing excavated areas | **265**

18.3. The middle chamber of Nakovana Cave | **266**

18.4. Stratigraphic context and dating of the stalagmite | **267**

18.5. Distribution of finewares and amphorae, middle chamber, Nakovana Cave | **268**

18.6. Cups and plates next to the stalagmite, middle chamber, Nakovana Cave | **269**

18.7. Gray ware relief-molded *phiale* with figurative motifs | **270**

19.1. Nakovana Cave and other major sites with Hellenistic pottery in Dalmatia | **278**

19.2. Distribution of fineware, amphorae, and faunal remains in Nakovana Cave | **279**

19.3. Minimum Animal Units and distribution of cut marks, Nakovana | **281**

20.1. Islands in the Bahama archipelago | **286**

20.2. Plan view of Eleuthera Island with inset of Preacher's Cave | **288**

20.3. Plan view of Individuals 1C–1E | **290**

20.4. Basketry-impressed left zygomatic (cheekbone) | **291**

21.1. Counties of Ireland and Northern Ireland | **298**

23.1. The *suco* of Tutuala in Timor-Leste | **318**

23.2. Ili Kérékéré: wall separating *Otoulumuha* ("stomach") from *Otoiriku* ("backside") | **319**

23.3. Anthropomorphs, holding objects above their heads, from Ili Kérékéré | **320**

23.4. Pedro Morais (seated center) at carved wooden post at the entrance to Ili Kérékéré | **321**

23.5. Agustu Mendes near the téi at Hiyo | **323**

23.6. Rafael Quimaraes addressing the téi at Léné Ara | **324**

23.7. Titiru, the president of all téi | **325**

23.8. Rafael Quimaraes and his son interacting with the téi at Lumuku | **326**

23.9. Téi structure combining a stone platform, wooden upright, forked stick, and stone upright at Mua Mimiraka | **327**

24.1. Malaysia: karst regions and principal cave temples | **332**

24.2. The Vairocana Buddha, flanked by Bodhisattvas of wisdom, knowledge, and virtue | **333**

24.3. Statue of Kwan Yin, cave temple of Kek Look Tong, Ipoh | **334**

24.4. Taoist figures, Goddess of Mercy and Eight Immortals Cave Temple, Ipoh | **335**

24.5. The karst aesthetic: popular Vietnamese miniature landscape | **336**

24.6. The Hindu faithful at Batu Caves | **336**

24.7. The stairway to Cathedral Cave, Batu Caves | **338**

24.8. Sister Mae Chee Piyachat in her cave | **338**

25.1. Results of the hierarchical cluster analysis applying the Ward's linkage method | **346**

25.2. Results of multidimensional scaling applying the Euclidean linkage method | **348**

26.1. Location of sites in the Great Plains mentioned in the text | **354**

26.2. The earth monster, as depicted at site 14OT4, Kansas | **355**

26.3. The Dragon's Mouth, Yellowstone Park | **355**

26.4. Meteorite fall and ribstone at the Star Site, southwestern Kansas | **357**

26.5. Animal lodge at Guide Rock, Nebraska | **359**

26.6. Pawnee sacred precinct at Pikes Peak | **359**

27.1. Drawing by Pachacuti Yamqui: three caves at Pacariqtambo | **368**

28.1. Spatial relationships redrawn from Frank (2006) | **374**

28.2. Four simple periodic movement patterns | **376**

28.3. Four more-complicated movement patterns | **377**

28.4. Four "two oscillating directions" periodic movement patterns | **378**

28.5. Four fractal periodic movement patterns | **379**

28.6. Four extended-function periodic movements with larger extended caves | **379**

28.7. Four extended activities reflecting periodic movements for caves with multiple functions | **380**

Tables

2.1. Chronological framework for prehistoric southeast Italy | **29**

3.1. Chronology of caves in Malta | **46**

3.2. Well-known caves in Malta | **50**

4.1. Chronological table | **59**

5.1. Comparison of numbers of individuals and sample composition, Neolithic–Early Bronze Age cave-burial sites and Neolithic long barrows | **84**

6.1. Chronology for Levantine sites | **89**

7.1. Egyptian dynastic chronology | **110**

10.1. Chronological periods for Mesoamerican archaeological cultures | **152**

10.2. Partial list of caves associated with Mesoamerican surface architecture | **157**

11.1. Chronology for cultures and eras of the Greater American Southwest | **172**

12.1. Dark-zone cave archaeological sites, midcontinental karst, United States | **188**

13.1. Uncalibrated radiocarbon age determinations for Southeastern cave-art sites | **199**

16.1. Mississippian site lists used in this study | **240**

16.2. Environmental-data layers created for GIS analysis | **240**

16.3. Example site-occurrence table, rockshelter sites with art | **241**

17.1. Simplified burial sequence in the West Mouth of Niah Great Cave | **259**

18.1. Pottery recovered from the middle chamber, Nakovana Cave | **267**

19.1. Burning and fracture type, faunal assemblages, Nakovana Cave | **279**

19.2. Minimum Numbers of Individuals, faunal assemblage, Nakovana Cave | **279**

20.1. Documented Bahamian caves and burial sites | **287**

20.2. Documented petroglyphs and pictographs in the Bahamas | **287**

20.3. Preacher's Cave radiocarbon samples | **289**

20.4. Age and sex distribution of prehistoric graves from Preacher's Cave | **289**

25.1. Abbreviations and textual references for nine indigenous groups | **347**

28.1. Popular techniques and methods in spatial data analysis | **372**

28.2. Location by figure number of results of simulations in this chapter's figures | **375**

Preface

This volume was conceived as part of a line of research that began while I was a graduate student at the University at Buffalo, where I became interested in how space is conceptualized by animals and humans. I had always been fascinated by caves, and my work in Mesoamerican cave archaeology illustrated that throughout the region, caves held a special place in indigenous consciousness. The literature suggested that this was not just a regional phenomenon but that caves were held in special regard in most, if not all cultures. However, compiling these data was a monumental task requiring specialized cultural and archaeological knowledge with a critical eye for interpretations in the archaeological record. In order to investigate the topic further, I organized a symposium titled *Journeys into the Darkness: A Cross-Cultural Perspective of Caves as Sacred Spaces* for the 69th Annual Meeting for the Society for American Archaeology (SAA) in Montreal, Canada, in 2004, a session that focused solely on the role of caves as sacred space and their use as ritual venues. Versions of thirteen of the following chapters were presented at the meeting. Over the last two years, SAA sessions organized by Scott Nicolay also helped to convince me that we needed to rethink our models of cave use. Since the 2004 session, I discovered more examples and more people interested in ritual caves both in the United States and Europe, so more chapters were added to the volume to broaden the geographic and temporal coverage.

I am grateful to all my authors and appreciative of their patience and diligence. They delighted me with their ideas, their cooperation, and professionalism. Additionally, the University Press of Colorado has been very supportive, patient, and helpful. I am particularly indebted to director Darrin Pratt, as well as Jessica d'Arbonne, Laura Furney, Daniel Pratt, and the press staff. Thanks are also extended to Wendy Ashmore and one anonymous reviewer for their thoughtful comments.

Conversations with many friends along the way helped focus my thoughts. In particular, I would like to thank my professor and friend Ezra Zubrow for his inspiration and for giving me the freedom to explore my ideas. Thanks to James Brady who encouraged this work and generously shared his library. I would also like to acknowledge my friend and colleague Jaime Awe for his support of my own research and for his mentorship. This line of research has also benefited from time spent at the University of California, Santa Barbara, where I established a valuable collaboration with Daniel Montello and spent many hours discussing my ideas with my lab partner and friend Nathan Craig. With academic and financial support from the University of California, Merced, I am happy to be able to partner with cognitive scientists Teenie Matlock and Michael Spivey in order to further interdisciplinary research in this area.

Although I mention them last, they are first—I appreciate my parents for indulging my obsession with caves and for their love and support. Finally but most importantly, I acknowledge my partner Mark Aldenderfer who has been my best friend, my harshest critic, and my biggest supporter throughout my professional career. Thank you, Mark.

Note on Radiocarbon Dating

The chapters in this volume report radiocarbon dates using a variety of acronyms. The choice of acronym depends largely on the scholarly traditions of the geographic region or temporal period under study. These may include BC/AD ("before Christ"/"in the year of our Lord"), or BCE/CE (Before Common Era/Common Era). CE is the same as AD and BC the same as BCE, but the BCE/CE designation avoids religious connotations. The term BP (bp) is often used when dating early time periods. The term "before present" avoids the BC/AD split altogether, and designates the number of years before 1950. These are uncalibrated dates unless they are reported as "Cal BP."

Sacred Darkness

Introduction

Holley Moyes

Caves are special places. They are mysterious. They captivate us. They draw us in. They can protect or entrap. Whether they fascinate or frighten, we recognize caves as otherworldly, transitional, or liminal. Archaeologists are interested in caves because many are data rich, containing keys to unlocking the human past. They are one of archaeology's most important resources, often having excellent artifact preservation and deep stratigraphic deposits (see Colcutt 1979; Farrand 1985; Ford and Williams 1989, 317; Sherwood and Goldberg 2001, 145; Straus 1990, 256; 1997; Woodward and Goldberg 2001, 328). In addition to containing well-preserved material, in contexts of deep antiquity, cave sites are often easily located, whereas open-air sites may be ephemeral or more difficult to find. No doubt differential preservation and accessibility led early archaeologists to believe that in the remote past dwelling in caves preceded living in open-air sites so people must have preferred to live in caves.

Despite the information that can be gleaned from the wealth of cave deposits, the sites themselves, their functions, and their contexts have often been misunderstood. As inside Plato's allegorical cave, archaeologists see only shadows of realities (in this case, the past) that are subject to interpretation. It has long been assumed that caves functioned primarily as domestic spaces, an idea so prevalent that it reached the status of an interpretive paradigm—one that seldom came into question. This work challenges that model and elucidates an underrepresented aspect of cave use.

The chapters in this volume focus on the ritual use of caves for sacred, religious, special, or cultic pursuits as a generalized cultural phenomenon, cross-cutting temporal and spatial boundaries. It is the first effort to address directly the role of caves in ritual practice, myth, and worldview from a cross-cultural global perspective. The chapters encompass six continents and span temporal periods ranging from the Paleolithic to the present. Despite their collective breadth, however, these offerings barely scratch the surface of the topic. With literally tens of thousands of ethnographic, historic, and archaeological reports that address the ritual use of caves, how does one begin to understand the phenomena of ritual cave use? In order to move this research agenda forward, those contributors working in areas with strong cave traditions have been asked to synthesize the current state of knowledge from a regional perspective, whereas those working in areas in which cave investigations are less developed were asked to present case studies. Also included are historical and ethnographic accounts that illuminate aspects of cave use that are difficult to detect in the archaeological record—such as the roles of caves as political space or in identity construction—and chapters that directly advance the methodology, comparative studies, and cognitive considerations of archaeological cave studies.

In this volume, major regional cave traditions spanning long temporal periods are separated into Old and New World traditions. Old World traditions begin with Paleolithic caves in Europe. In chapter 1, Jean Clottes reminds us that this tradition is not only the earliest but also the longest-lasting religious tradition in the history of the world. Robin Skeates examines changes in ritual cave use from the Upper Paleolithic through the Bronze Age in the Apulia region of Southeast Italy in chapter 2, followed by Simon Stoddart and Caroline Malone's discussion of natural and man-made caves in late Neolithic Malta. In chapter 4, Peter Tomkins contributes one of the first synthetic considerations of the Neolithic caves of Crete, and the Neolithic is again the period of focus in Andrew Chamberlain's report on mortuary caves in Britain in chapter 5. Next, Yorke Rowan and David Ilan examine Chalcolithic burial caves in the Levant. Stuart Tyson Smith analyzes the role of caves in ancient Egyptian cosmology in chapter 7, followed by Mark Aldenderfer's synthetic chapter on the use and meaning of caves in Tibetan Buddhist traditions. Concluding the section on Old World ritual cave traditions, Paul Taçon and his colleagues Wayne Brennan, Mathew Kelleher, and Dave Pross investigate cave use in Australia, focusing on changes in use between the Pleistocene and the Holocene.

Turning to the New World, James Brady and I provide a synthesis of Mesoamerican cave research that defines a 3,000-year tradition of ritual cave use that can still be found today (chapter 10). Scott Nicolay advances a long-overdue synthesis of ancient ritual cave use in the American Southwest in chapter 11, followed by Patty Jo Watson's discussion of the evolution of cave archaeology in the Eastern United States. In chapter 13, Jan Simek and his colleagues Alan Cressler and Joseph Douglas present a current synthesis of cave art in the Southeastern United States, while Cheryl Claassen offers fresh interpretations of archaeological assemblages from Southeastern caves in chapter 14. The late Olaf Prufer and Keith Prufer reconsider the use of prehistoric caves and rockshelters in Ohio (chapter 15), while George Sabo III and his colleagues Jerry Hilliard and Jami Lockhart evaluate spatial patterning of ritual caves and rockshelters in the Ozarks (chapter 16).

The four case studies in Part III on ritual cave use include a reevaluation of the Neolithic cemetery within Niah Cave in Borneo by Graeme Barker and Lindsay Lloyd-Smith (chapter 17). Two chapters address the spectacular Iron Age Adriatic site of Nakovana: Timothy Kaiser and Staško Forenbaher (chapter 18) describe and interpret this sealed site, while Joanna Appleby and Preston Miracle (chapter 19) present a methodological analysis of the faunal remains, offering insights into how this artifact class may generally contribute to examining ritual behavior. Finally, chapter 20, a case study of Preacher's Cave in the Bahamas by Robert Carr, William Schaffer, Jeff Ransom, and Michael Pateman breaks new ground in the interpretation of caves in the Caribbean.

Five chapters investigate historic or modern ritual use of caves. In chapter 21, Patrick McCafferty surveys Irish prehistoric and historic caves and examines their relationships to Irish folklore. Terence Ranger takes a deep historical perspective in describing the role of caves as power places in the construction of indigenous identity in Zimbabwe in chapter 22. Next, Sandra Pannell and Sue O'Connor discuss the political and social importance of caves in East Timor. Joseph Hobbs then focuses on how cave use both encourages social cohesion and reinforces ethnographic identity in modern Malaysian Hindu, Buddhist, and Taoist shrines (chapter 24). Nathan Craig in chapter 25 takes a quantitative ethnographic approach in his analyses of the uses and perceptions of caves among indigenous societies in the Andes. Donald Blakeslee then uses data gleaned from ethnographic reports to understand the cosmological implications of archaeological remains in and near caves of the Great Plains (chapter 26).

Some of the most forward-looking chapters in the volume present new ways to regard ritual caves, focusing on the cave space itself as a unit of analysis. Art historian Andrea Stone presents us with a synthetic piece that advances cross-cultural comparisons of ritual cave use and argues for emergent patterns based on levels of sociopolitical complexity and subsistence practice. Her chapter (27) also serves as a reminder of the importance of the changing relationships of humans to the landscape.

The final two chapters focus on how humans perceive the cave space itself. Ezra Zubrow (chapter 28) demonstrates the utility of spatial-constraint theory for intersite spatial analysis to examine the possible variations in the use of the cave space. His concern is to provide idealized models for comparing how a cave *can* be used as opposed to how it *is* used. This type of comparison highlights human behavioral patterns found in cave interiors, providing a unit of analysis that potentially addresses not only the behaviors themselves but the intentionality underlying behavioral patterns. This line of research is promising in looking at ritual practices in caves, and could aid in separating ritual from domestic usage.

In the concluding chapter (29), Daniel Montello and I examine the cross-cultural generality that caves—particularly their dark zones—are used as ritual spaces. We attempt to shed light on *why* this pattern is so robust by investigating shared human perceptions about caves or cave-like spaces using theories from environmental psychology and cognitive science. We hypothesize that shared perceptions of cave spaces lead to similar functions and meanings cross-culturally.

The chapters presented here illustrate the utility of both regional and case studies and represent a remarkable diversity in theoretical orientation. They demonstrate that data from caves may be employed not only in studies of cosmology, ritual, and religion, but in changing our understandings of ideologies and sociopolitical structures as well.

This volume may be counted as a success if it encourages researchers to critically evaluate and reevaluate archaeological and historical material from cave studies. The chapters collectively challenge early assumptions about the nature of cave use that lulled generations of archaeologists into an interpretive complacency. The following is a brief history of how caves initially and erroneously came to be thought of as domestic spaces.

THE ICONIC CAVE MAN

For over a century, the idea of living in caves has gripped the imagination of both scholars and the general public to the point that, in popular culture, the term *cave man* has become synonymous with early humans. This is not surprising when we consider that European caves produced some of archaeology's seminal finds. A short survey demonstrates that the popular notion of the cave man was well-entrenched by the late 1800s.

Much of the earliest evidence for the antiquity of man came from European caves in which Pleistocene mammal bones co-occurred with stone tools (see Daniel 1952). The cave man makes his appearance in early scholarly works such as Sir John Lubbock's *Pre-historic Times: As Illustrated by Ancient Remains, and the Manners and Customs of Modern Savages*, first printed in 1865. Lubbock devoted a chapter to "cave men" and noted in this early volume, "that some of the European caves were inhabited by man during the time of these extinct mammalia seems to be well established" (p. 257). A few years later, in his synthetic volume on European cave archaeology, *Cave Hunting: Researches on the Evidences of Caves Respecting the Early Inhabitants of Europe* (1874), W. Boyd Dawkins concluded that stone tools found in association with extinct mammal bones were the remains of "a hunting and fishing race of cave-dwellers" present in Europe during the Pleistocene (p. 430). The book was published only 15 years after Darwin's *On the Origin of Species* (1859) and only 3 years following *The Descent of Man, and Selection in Relation to Sex* (1871), which dealt with human evolution. The impact of such findings on a public that was only just coming to terms with the antiquity of humans (and for that matter, of the earth itself) had to have been considerable.

Given the early scholarship surrounding Paleolithic caves, it is hardly surprising that cave dwelling became the standard image of early man in popular culture. Images of our cave-dwelling ancestors have sparked the imaginations of the general public and raised the cave man to iconic status. As Bryan Hayden notes, the popular press often refers to prehistoric Europeans as "cave men" (2003, 100), and he goes on to observe that in prehistory, caves were not used as domestic spaces, though rockshelters were.

In a recent article, Judith Berman (1999) traces images of the cave man from the late 1800s to the present. The article features an 1873 artistic rendering from *Harper's Weekly* of a skin-clad couple camping in a rockshelter, labeled "The Neanderthal Man." The first Neanderthal discovery was in 1856 (Trinkaus and Shipman 1994, 4), so the illustration demonstrates that these kinds of images were in place soon after. By the 1870s, articles of archaeological interest were finding their way into popular magazines in Britain and the educated elite were expected to know something about the subject—so not only were these early finds popular among the general public, but they were part of the canon of knowledge for the well educated (Daniel 1952, 111–113).

Berman argues that the cave man image has a certain tenacity, and points out that some images are salient, taking on a life of their own that persist over time. Popular images with scientific merit can become galvanized, ceasing to be data dependent as scientific thought changes. The image of the cave man has this persistent quality and the distinction between the scientific models and popular culture have diverged only recently so that "the shaggy, grunting Cave Man, who fights dinosaurs, talks 'rock,' and woos prehistoric-bikini-clad Cave Women with a club, is firmly in place" (1999, 289).

Stereotypes of cavemen have been reinforced by over 150 films dating back to D. W. Griffith's 1912 silent movie *Man's Genesis*. More recent films like *The Clan of the Cave Bear* (1986), based on a 1980 novel by Jean M. Auel, and *Quest for Fire* (1981), based on the 1911 French novel by the brothers J.-H. Rosny, emphasize differences between Neanderthals and modern humans. The more primitive Neanderthals live in caves while the more advanced modern humans live in open-air sites. Although depictions of the cave man in the media are amusing, they are often quite racist, contrasting modern humans as more sophisticated and intelligent, less hairy, and possessing finer features, light skin, and blonde hair (e.g., Daryl Hannah in *The Clan of the Cave Bear*). Besides these skewed representations, popular culture not only reinforces but reinvents the stereotype that the preferred habitation for early man was the cave. It is interesting that even when spectacular cave art was discovered in Europe and became widely known in the early twentieth century, few images in popular culture depict ritual behavior or artistic expression as occurring in caves.

In 1910, in an address to the Anthropological Society of Washington titled "The Cave Dwellings of the Old and New Worlds," J. Walter Fewkes presented one of the first synthetic cross-cultural comparisons of human cave use. This and other early works focused on the evolutionary idea that people first lived in caves and that caves were the inspiration for later permanent structures. He concluded that caves were the "simplest kind of durable house" and that, as man's first form of habitation, provided the natural referent for the built environment. While he acknowledged that ritual and ceremony occurred in caves, these were minor considerations compared with the idea that, for early humans, caves were primarily dwellings.

The notion of the cave dweller did not easily die. It was revived by author David Kempe in 1988 in his volume *Living Underground*, which focused on cave dwelling from the past to the present. Though the work primarily expanded on Fewkes's 1910 paper, it is worth mentioning because it is one of the few volumes to examine cross-cultural cave use, and it included a short section on burial sites and ritual caves. However, Kempe introduced the book by parroting Fewkes's "cave first" model, stating that "for the first cave men, in the Stone Age, there was little option, unless one preferred to live in the open. Once the secret of fire had made cave dwelling so much safer and easier, it must indeed have been the first choice" (p. 7). In his final analysis, he relegated ritual use to a "secondary" status (p. 250). Kempe assumed that all caves were originally habitations and offered little explanation as to why caves transitioned to mortuary or ritual sites, other than to suggest that, due to superstitions about the dead, caves became places of fear once they were populated with burials.

Archaeologists are not immune to the appeal of the cave dweller. The legacy of early cave studies and the entrenched notion of the "cave man" in popular culture produced an interpretive climate in which archaeologists were willing to accept without question that caves were dwellings. They were rarely faulted. Archaeologists were rarely faulted when they assumed that cave deposits were the results of domestic behavior or storage, and the burden of proof typically lay in demonstrating that deposits were symbolic or ritual in nature. Nowhere is this better exemplified than in Mesoamerican archaeology. Although explorers and scholars found and recorded numerous deep caves for over 150 years, it was not until the 1970s that they were recognized as ritual spaces (Brady 1989; Brady and Prufer 2005; Moyes and Brady this volume). Artifacts found within caves were thought to be the result of habitation or storage, and this interpretation was not questioned until J. Eric S. Thompson published his 1959 article, "The Role of Caves in Maya Culture." Based on ethnographic analogy as well as his archaeological investigations, Thompson's article articulated a number of possible uses for caves that included their use as ritual venues. The 1959 piece was not originally well distributed, but it was reprinted in 1975 with a wider distribution. Partially because Thompson was the foremost Mayanist of his day, with great influence in the field, archaeologists began to recognize the significance of caves in Mesoamerican cosmology and worldview. However, it was not until the late 1990s, following archaeological investigations and reinterpretations of major cave sites, that the field widely accepted archaeological interpretations of caves as sacred space (see Brady 1989).

Mesoamericanists were not the only archaeologists to be affected by the paradigm of the cave dweller. Patty Jo Watson (this volume) discusses a similar shift in interpretive frameworks over the past 40 years of cave research in the Eastern United States and Peter Tomkins (this volume) makes a strong case for new interpretations for the caves of Neolithic Crete.

While interpretive frameworks are one of the challenges that have faced archaeologists, other issues include categorizing, describing, and defining the space itself. Exactly what do we mean by the word *cave*? The following is a good example of the problem of classification.

In his 1951 article, Robert Braidwood proposed a "cave stage"—a period during which people inhabited caves—as the earliest phase of Middle Eastern cultural development. In his model, cave dwelling transitioned into a stage in which people lived in open-air sites, and not until then did they begin to live in settled villages such as Jarmo. A few years later, in his discussion of general prehistoric cave use, Braidwood (1967, 48) clarified this position, suggesting that early people lived in open encampments as well as caves. He further states that they didn't actually live in caves but instead inhabited the *mouths* of caves. He goes on to say that they actually preferred rockshelters: "I'll go on using the term 'cave' since it is more familiar, but remember that I actually mean rock-shelter, as a place in which people actually lived."

The conclusion that caves are desirable dwellings can only be drawn when the term *cave* is employed in its most general usage. Likewise, the word *habitation* may further confuse the issue. For instance, to explain cave art in dark zones, Abbé Henri Breuil and Raymond Lantier (1965, 178–179) imagined that Paleolithic groups conducted weeks-long ceremonies while living underground. In this conceptualization, all cave use thus became "habitation." This example suggests that more-specific use of language needs to accompany shifts in interpretive frameworks.

In the few synthetic works on cave use, natural caves, man-made caves, and the many morphological cave types are all lumped together as functional equivalents. This lumping of ontological categories obscures potential patterns. As research on caves grows, it is becoming clear that subsuming all subterranean spaces under one term creates a methodological roadblock in comprehending patterns in human cave use. For instance, the notion of dwelling in caves is bolstered by modern and historical examples of people who live in man-made caverns and tunnels. In works aimed at understanding cave use as a cross-cultural phenomenon, Fewkes (1910), Kempe (1988), and later Clive Bonsall and Christopher Tolan-Smith (1997) offer many examples of constructed and architecturally modified caves from Europe, Asia, Africa, the Near East, and the New World. These include cliff dwellings and pit houses from the American Southwest, villages constructed into rock faces and in front of natural caves in the Loire and Dordogne Valleys in France, and dwellings excavated from loess or volcanic tuff. Some of the best-known examples of excavated sites are from Cappadocia, Turkey. The area was occupied as early as 2000 BC by the Hittites, but it is the Byzantine-aged structures created by early Christians that attract the most attention. Dwellings, hermitages, monasteries, chapels, and churches were carved into "fairy chimneys," the cone-shaped, soft-tuff deposits for which the area is noted (Kostof 1972). They are picturesque and currently part of a thriving tourist industry that features "cave hotels" with luxury suites that are both plumbed and well lit, reinforcing the notion that living in a cave is desirable. Dwellings excavated from volcanic tuffs and loess are also common in Europe, the Mideast, Africa, and Asia—anywhere that the soft material can be found. Mark Aldenderfer (this volume) points out that, similar to Cappadocia, early monastic institutions in Tibet constructed monks' quarters from loess deposits, but he cautions that these are not natural caves and therefore are not regarded as sacred spaces in and of themselves. In Buddhist tradition, it is natural caves that contain *gnas,* a spiritual presence, whereas man-made caves must be imbued with it through ritual action.

THE PROBLEMATIC TERM *CAVE*

For years scholars have used the term *cave* to mean any cavity in the earth. Ontologically caves are holes. Defining holes and examining what constitutes their "holeness" is a complicated exercise taken up by philosophers. The very existence of holes is questionable, as they cannot exist alone but are dependent on their hosts. Holes are not made of anything, but they are not always empty and they can be filled. They are not just regions in space, they can be moved. They are subject to whole–part relationships. They are morphologically complex and come in many different forms. Philosophers Alberto Casati and Achille Varzi (1994) describe three basic types of holes: superficial hollows dependent on surfaces; perforating tunnels through which a string can pass; and internal cavities, like holes in swiss cheese, wholly enclosed within three-dimensional objects and having no contact with the outside environment. Each of these types has its own set of problems in theories about holes, which impacts how we describe, analyze, understand, and talk about them (Casati and Varzi 1994). As holes, caves entail many of the problems that philosophers describe regarding their ontology. Therefore, definitions of caves are slippery and difficult to pin down.

While *cave* may be a noun used to describe certain kinds of spaces, the definitions of caves depend on human interaction. In the *Encyclopedia of Caves,* geoscientist William White defines a cave as "a natural opening in the Earth, large enough to admit a human being, and which some human beings choose to call a cave" (1988, 60; Culver and White 2004, 81). Similarly in the *Encyclopedia of Caves and Karst Science,* John Gunn (2003) notes that the term *cave* is "commonly applied to natural openings, usually in rocks, that are large enough to permit entry by humans" (vii). In both encyclopedias the authors stress the human–cave interaction as important to their very definition, suggesting that caves are partially defined by human perceptions of them and cannot be defined in terms of their geology alone. Therefore the word *cave* is generally considered a nonscientific term.

Because the definition of caves is so broad, it conveys little useful meaning and must be context specific. Geologists tend to classify caves by their formation processes, such as solution, volcanic, glacier, crevice, littoral, piping, and erosion caves (Klimchouk 2003, 204). These classifications are useful for the discipline but are only minimally useful in conveying possible human interactions—or, borrowing J. J. Gibson's terminology, "affordances" (see Montello and Moyes, this volume). For anthropologists and archaeologists, a typology needs to reflect human perception combined with the geomorphology of the feature, particularly in regard to the presence, absence, or quality of light. Natural light not only impacts the affordances of human usage, but of the biology of the cave as well.

One commonly recognized morphological distinction is between caves and rockshelters, and is a consequence of the functional and perceptual differences between them. A rockshelter is usually defined as "a cave, often at a cliff base, with a more or less level floor extending only a short distance so that no part is beyond daylight" (Jennings 1997). Thus, rockshelters are caves but caves are not necessarily rockshelters, and the terms should not be used interchangeably. In studies involving the human use of these spaces, the distinction between the two is critical to archaeological interpretations.

The quality of light in cavities may be divided into three zones: light, twilight, and dark (Faulkner 1988). When cavers refer to "caves," they are usually describing spaces that can be entered by humans and that contain a dark zone, as opposed to rockshelters, which are open and possess light or twilight areas. There are many combinations of the two, and geomorphology plays a large role in creating dark zones. For instance, a space may consist of a very long, narrow, straight tunnel enabling light to enter or it may have a relatively shallow tunnel whose passage makes an abrupt turn, creating a dark zone.

The myriad of morphological possibilities makes classification difficult, so archaeologists typically describe sites as best they can. Many archaeologists who work in caves have no background in spelunking or karst studies, making standardized description more difficult. In addition, though descriptive nomenclature developed by professional or avocational cavers is certainly the most systematic for describing cave features, it does not always include phenomena most useful to archaeologists. It is no wonder that there has been so much descriptive confusion, and that basic components of cave morphology as well as descriptions of light quality are often omitted in archaeological reports.

THE DARK ZONE

The distinction between caves and rockshelters and their quality of light is critical to understanding the cave context and to constructing plausible archaeological interpretations. Rockshelters containing light and twilight zones have often been used for habitation but these same sites may also contain ritual deposits, such as in cases presented from the North American Midwest by Prufer and Prufer in this volume. Changes in shelter function and use may also occur over time, complicating interpretive efforts.

Although shelters may be used in habitation, the use of cave dark zones as living spaces is rare. According to William Farrand (1985, 23), dark zones of true caves are useless for even temporary habitation except under extreme or desperate conditions. Examples could include refuge in times of war (see Ranger, this volume) or as shelters in extremely cold conditions. Paul Taçon and his colleagues (this volume) describe dark-zone habitation in Tasmania under brutally cold conditions about 30,000 BP. It is such a rare occurrence that if prehistoric people were living in dark zones, the question one should ask is, why?

The notion that dark zones served as ritual, symbolic, or liminal spaces in prehistory is not new. Many archaeologists have argued that Paleolithic people did not inhabit deep caves despite the early seductive interpretive paradigm of the "cave man." In 1933, Miles Burkitt wrote:

> The expression "cave man" is somewhat misleading; our prehistoric forerunners never lived in the depths of their caves. For one thing caves are very damp and rheumatism seems to have been as rife then as it is now; furthermore, they would have required perpetual artificial light. They did, however, frequently inhabit the mouths of caves where these were not too draughty, but seem to have preferred situations under overhanging cliffs where natural differential weathering had produced rockshelters. (1933:7)

Burkitt further suggested that Paleolithic deep caves were cult shrines (p. 174). This was echoed later by others (Faulkner 1988; Hole and Heizer 1965, 47) who contended that dark zones of caves were used most typically as ritual spaces. The notion was later elaborated by Brian Hayden,

> Rockshelters were far preferred for habitation areas since they were less damp and had much better lighting... they also acted to concentrate the warmth of the winter sun if they were south facing... [I]n the few instances when true caves were used for living at all, camps or structures were always made near the mouth of the cave, where there was both light and shelter... [T]he deep recesses of the caves were used only for sporadic ritual purposes. (2003, 100)

Chester Chard (1975, 171) suggested that, historically, most "caves" used for refuge were actually rockshelters. In their recent article on the geoarchaeology of caves, Paul Goldberg and Sarah C. Sherwood (2006, 15) also note that humans did not use cave interiors as habitation areas. This pattern is discussed and elaborated upon by many of the authors in this volume (e.g., Clottes, Craig, Moyes and Brady, Claassen, Watson). The data are particularly compelling in Mesoamerica (Moyes and Brady, this volume), where deep caves are abundant and well investigated. These tropical caves are dank, and often infested with bats and insects that carry a number of deadly diseases, including histoplasmosis, rabies, and chagas.

It is not only the physical conditions that prevent people from inhabiting dark zones, but the perceptions and concepts associated with them. Patrick McCafferty (this volume) points out that, historically in Ireland, caves are prominent in the mythical past and are depicted as the entrances to a magical, mysterious underworld that contains powerful beings, and as a result should be avoided. Throughout Mesoamerica these kinds of beliefs also underpin prohibitions against entering caves, which are thought to be entrances to the underworld and are traditionally considered spiritually dangerous (see Moyes and Brady, this volume). In ancient Eygpt, caves represented the entrance and exits to the Netherworld, a place of death, where the sun god Re made his daily descent to battle the forces of chaos and rise victorious every morning (see Smith, this volume).

Not only do real and imaginary beliefs about caves influence human interaction with them, but, as Daniel Montello and I argue (this volume), cave dark zones awaken something much more fundamental in the human psyche. We contend that the physical properties of caves have particular implications for human psychological responses and that our shared human perceptions of cave dark zones lead us to interpret these spaces in similar ways.

FINDING AND INTERPRETING RITUAL

Throughout this discussion I have referred to cave dark zones as "ritual," "sacred," "ceremonial," or "liminal" spaces—that is, as having "nonhabitational" use and thus standing in opposition to dwellings, which suggests a Durkheimian sacred–profane dichotomy. While this type of binary opposition may be attractive to the Western mind, many have argued that it is too static and does not express the complexity of religious or symbolic expression in many non-Western societies. Clottes (this volume) reminds us that in many cultures there is no dichotomy between the natural and a spirit world and we must keep in mind that what we call "ritual" is an etic construct.

There has been much recent debate about the definition of ritual (e.g., Kyriakidis 2007). Scholars tend to fall into two camps: those that limit ritual to religious rites and those that recognize nonreligious rituals, such as political ceremonies and rites. The logical extreme of the latter view is that any activity or performance, such as brushing your teeth, can be considered a ritual act. While Colin Renfrew (2007, 120–121) supports the broader view, he, like Clottes, reminds us that there is no separation between the religious and the secular in many societies, but that when "one begins to incorporate the cosmos within the equation," then the act must be designated religious. In many cases it is possible to demonstrate that cave dark zones are salient features of cosmology, and therefore activities enacted in them may be considered rituals in the religious sense, which is our interest here. Also, religious and political rites are often intertwined, particularly in transegalitarian or complex societies in which social hierarchies may be bolstered by control of the supernatural realm.

Archaeologists tend to talk about caves as "ritual" spaces because they can link the material remains to activities conducted in them, but cosmologies and beliefs underpin ritual practices and potentially may be inferred from them. While it has been argued that religious beliefs are the hardest inferences to attain in the archaeological record (Hawkes 1954), such inferences are not impossible, particularly among cultures with deciphered writing systems, well-studied iconography, and cultural continuity.

In archaeological cave sites, there are two circumstances in which ritual has traditionally been inferred unquestionably: in the presence of cave art and in mortuary contexts. It was not until the discovery of art in the Paleolithic caves in France and Spain that caves were recognized as ritual or symbolic venues, and this recognition remains a fundamental component in ritual interpretations. However, not every society created cave art. For instance, Clottes (this volume) argues for Neanderthal ritual cave use by noting the presence of a complete Neanderthal human burial containing bear and deer bone as well as other grave goods at the cave of Régourdou, in the Dordogne, France. This burial is so distinct that it could only have been placed by human agency.

Some major cave traditions are primarily defined by burial caves. This volume reports a number of major burial traditions during the Neolithic period. Andrew Chamberlain analyzes seventy-five burial caves in Britain, noting that their numbers rival constructed monuments as ritual places associated with the dead. Niah Cave in Borneo was used by foragers in the Late Pleistocene and Early Holocene but became a cemetery during the Neolithic (Barker and Lloyd-Smith, this volume). Skeates reports a similar regional trajectory for caves in the Apulia region of Italy, in which caves begin to be used as cemeteries in the Late Neolithic. He suggests that caves may have became tied to ancestors at this time. Peter Tomkins also notes that burials in caves became more common in the Late Neolithic and suggests that these practices relate to an increasingly elaborated social hierarchy and the control of symbolic natural resources.

It is much more difficult to infer ritual use from artifact assemblages alone, and as both Skeates (1997, 80) and Tomkins (this volume) note, archaeologists have not always been successful in defining ritual assemblages, particularly from early eras. This brings us back to the core issue of successfully dividing "ritual" from "domestic" uses that has plagued cave archaeology. For instance, Bonsall and Tolan-Smith (1997) suggest that caves fall into the categories of "economic" and "ritual." Their economic uses included long- and short-term residence, acquisition of raw materials, storage, and disposal of waste. However, some of these categories are not mutually exclusive of ritual practice. For instance, in the Americas and elsewhere there is considerable evidence that minerals were mined in caves in prehistory, but is this solely an "economic" activity? Brady and Rissolo (2006) argue that in Mesoamerica, cave mining was a ritual pursuit with little economic benefit. Material extracted from caves was likely considered "special" and used in the manufacture of sacred objects, in ritual architecture, or as curatives. In ancient Egypt in Sinai, temples devoted to the goddess Hathor were connected with mining copper and turquoise (Smith, this volume).

Waste disposal may also be a problematic characterization, as sites may contain "ceremonial trash" (Walker 1995). William Walker suggests that objects used in ceremonies or rituals are made sacred and must be disposed of in respectful ways. Many of us report finding broken objects in caves that may be the result of ritual activities occurring at the site, so broken votive offerings may be an imperative of ritual practice. Ethnohistorically we know that among the Maya, year-renewal offerings consist of old, worn out, or broken objects (Tozzer 1941). Ritual breakage is so common in ancient Maya caves that I have suggested elsewhere (Moyes 2006) that the practice is tied to the ancient creation myth recounted in the *Popol Vuh* (Tedlock 1996). In the myth, the beings living in the underworld are chastised for their bad behavior. The punishment comes in the form of placing limitations on ritual offerings they may receive to "scabrous nodules of sap" and "brittle things broken to pieces" (p. 138).

In older studies, Mesoamerican archaeologists misinterpreted artifacts in caves as domestic assemblages because they so often consisted of household objects. This is not an isolated problem but occurs elsewhere. Peter Tomkins (this volume) points out that one of the problems with cave interpretations in Neolithic Crete has been that ritual was traditionally treated as a polar opposite to domestic life. This notion asserts itself in the identification of ritual assemblages that are expected to differentiate themselves by containing specialized ritual equipment or votive objects. Rather than rest interpretations on the objects themselves, Tomkins argues that context cannot be ignored. Invoking Richard Bradley (1998), he notes that ritual time and space are understood to be distant from everyday life and that liminal spaces such as mountain peaks, rivers, monuments, tombs, and caves help to create this distance or otherness.

Another method of inferring ritual behavior in the archaeological record and understanding the meaning of caves as sacred space has been through the use of both formal and relational analogies. The debate surrounding the utility of analogs and what constitutes a good analogy has raged in archaeology since its inception (see Ormy 1981). The use of analogy fell into early disrepute based on its indiscriminant use by classical social evolutionists, who compared objects and artifacts across time and space with no regard to causal factors, resulting in weak or inappropriate analogies (Wylie 1985). Although analogy never completely disappeared, it was later invigorated by Waldo Wedel (1938) in his paper, "The Direct Historical Approach in Pawnee Archaeology." His direct historical approach was tailored to geographical areas demonstrated to have continuous occupations from historical to prehistoric times. Inferences were produced by working back in time from the ethnographically known to the archaeologically unknown using ethnographic, historical, and archaeological data. The strength of the method was that it concerned itself not only with continuities but with discontinuities as well. This particular approach is perhaps best suited to recent eras whose culture histories are more readily traced and migrations noted, as in many cultures of Mesoamerica. Other analogical approaches rely on cultural traits shared over regions, on generalities shared over time and space, or on cultures that share environmental or sociopolitical similarities.

Analogical approaches have been vitally important in understanding the function and meaning of ancient Maya caves sites (Brady 1989; Brady and Prufer 2005; Moyes and Brady, this volume), where cultural continuity and regional patterns can be demonstrated. In his ethnographic and ethnohistoric overview of Plains Indians, Donald Blakeslee (this volume) identifies patterns in beliefs about caves of the Great Plains and relates them to archaeological sites, suggesting that older cave interpretations warrant revisiting by archaeologists. In this volume, Cheryl Claassen brings analogy to bear on caves in the Eastern United States. She does the important work of revisiting older interpretations of cave assemblages in order to elaborate on ancient cave rites and find evidence for women's rituals.

In their comprehensive survey of dark-zone cave art in the Eastern Woodlands of the United States, Simek and his colleagues (this volume) shun the use of analogy, instead calling for analyses that focus on the archaeological record itself by using chronologies, spatial patterning, and the composition and structure of motifs. With this change in focus, different questions can be posed, such as why some sites are located far away from urban habitation and others are not. These sorts of data also lend themselves to a behavioral approach (Reid, Schiffer, and Rathje 1975; Schiffer 1995; Walker 1995) that shifts research efforts away from the interpretation of the meaning of artifacts to questions aimed at understanding the behaviors that created the site's depositional patterns.

As if to answer Simek's call, George Sabo and his colleagues (this volume) offer a spatial analysis of caves and rockshelters from the Ozark uplands of the American mid-South. This regional study takes a landscape approach, using Geographic Information Systems (GIS) to investigate the relationship between caves, rockshelters, and their associated communities. Their analysis reveals the presence of a ritual complex within an integrated cultural landscape, tying mound centers and rockshelters to other sites and natural features.

THE CONSTRUCTED CAVE

A testament to the deep meaning of caves within their cultural contexts is inferred by referents to these spaces in the constructed environment. Aldenderfer (this volume) poses the question, "How do caves influence the nature of monument construction and how do monuments evolve around them?" Moyes and Brady (this volume) note that in Mesoamerica, many site cores, palaces, temples, and (more recently) churches were built over natural caves. It is also well established that ancient Maya pyramids were representations of sacred mountains, while their interior chambers represented caves. Research suggests that natural and man-made caves are foundational to Mesoamerican rulership in that they provide the cosmic referents to the landscape that underlie the power of ancient earth-based religions, establishing and maintaining ties to the land and to earth deities.

In ancient Egypt, cosmology was materialized through the construction of dark sanctuaries in temples and by the excavation of deep underground tombs. According to Smith (this volume), pyramids represented the gateway to the Netherworld, and their underground burial chambers mimicked the sinking of the king-as-sun into this lower realm in order to defeat chaos and become reborn. Some temples were built around natural shallow grottoes or niches and some were excavated into mountains, but in general, constructions in temple architecture typically moved one from light into darkness, again mimicking the sun's journey through a cavernous underworld and reflecting Egyptian cosmology as part of ritual practice. What is extraordinary about Egyptian cosmology and temple architecture is that there are no deep caves in the Nile area, suggesting that the actual landscape referents came from elsewhere. Caves are an integral part of sacred landscapes, instrumental in shaping cosmological ideas, and even in their absence they have salient qualities that become embedded in cosmological traditions.

In cultures lacking epigraphic data, the architectural construction of metaphorical caves can provide a great deal of information about a culture's cosmology and the control of its associated power. Simon Stoddart and Caroline Malone (this volume) argue that Neolithic temples in Malta are synecdochical constructs that represent the island's landscape features. These large stone edifices emulated both the natural and man-made caves of the island with their tortuous underground chambers and passages. Over time, as the society moved away from an egalitarian system, temples became less accessible and penetrated deeper into the earth, suggesting greater social control of the ritual spaces by those in power.

Skeates similarly notes the construction of underground cave-like spaces in Apulia, Italy, beginning in the late Neolithic. The first of these, the Manfredi hypogeum, appeared to have functioned as both a ritual and a mortuary space. Later, these constructions were typically mortuary in nature though many have evidence of ritual feasting. As with the Maltese temples, access to the spaces became more restricted with the development of social inequality. This agrees with Tomkins, who sees a similar trend in the use of natural caves in Bronze Age Crete. He argues that caves, as power spaces important to the construction of identity and territoriality, were appropriated by emerging elites.

CAVES AS CONTEXTS

Lawrence Straus (1997) suggested that caves may be thought of as "convenient cavities" used opportunistically. This volume argues that caves are not simply conveniences but are ideologically charged spaces imbued with meaning. As Robin Skeates argues (this volume), caves are not just geographic features but are cultural constructs. We now think of cave use as a nuanced and culturally mediated phenomenon. As such, caves not only inform us about ancient religion and ritual practice, but also shed light on the social, economic, and political structures of which they are a part, at times elucidating their transformations (see Moyes 2006). These issues are explored in Peter Tomkins's analyses of the Neolithic caves on Crete (this volume), where caves are viewed as power places that are integral to the development of complexity, territoriality, and group identity. We see these themes also played out in Pannell and O'Connor's investigations of sacred sites in East Timor and in Ranger's examples from Africa, where sacred places become highly politicized in times of threat or war. They become highly charged symbols in identity construction and maintenance by creating deep historical connections and ties with the landscape under threat. These studies agree with David Lewis-Williams's (2002:229) extensive study of Paleolithic cave sites, in which he concluded that caves were "active instruments in both the propagation and the transformation of society."

It stands to reason that the very nature of the cave as a natural, chthonic, immovable cavity, carved in stone, can represent the earth itself, its associated deities, and its enduring presence. The only way to destroy a cave is to blow it up, a measure that was taken in colonial Africa (Ranger, this volume). This is in itself a testimony to the spiritual and political value that is often associated with caves. Pannell and O'Connor are the only archaeologists in the volume who were able to work directly with indigenous people in their archaeological investigations, but their contribution highlights the importance of the roles of caves in maintaining social memory. Caves can be the conduits for traditional values, active agents in identity construction, or focal spaces for revitalization movements and indigenous rights. This reminds archaeologists of the importance of partnering with indigenous people in their research and respecting the rights of other stakeholders in their investigations. In the case of East Timor, archaeological investigations were welcomed and valued by the indigenous community, but this may not always be the case. Depending on the culture, indigenous beliefs and ritual practices can be at odds with scientific archaeology. In these circumstances, investigations that are not condoned by or conducted in partnership with local communities may be construed as desecration of sacred sites. Therefore, researchers are responsible for maintaining ethical standards and articulating their research goals with the values of indigenous peoples.

While the chapters in this volume are diverse in their approaches, they all share a single vision—each author considers caves to be special contexts and each strives to deal with the place of caves within cosmology, religion, and sociopolitical structure. They clearly demonstrate that cave sites are potentially as fruitful as surface contexts in our understanding of both ancient and modern cultures. These contributions further our understandings of how humans think about caves by fostering new interpretations of cave artifacts and features, encouraging the inclusion of caves as part of the sociopolitical landscape, weaving cave use into the social fabric, and thinking about the cave itself as context. Finally, gaining a better understanding of caves as symbols and understanding their uses in ritual contexts promotes sensitivity in cave researchers that will be crucial in dealing with issues of heritage management involving indigenous people.

REFERENCES CITED

Berman, Judith. 1999. "Bad Hair Days in the Paleolithic: Modern (Re)Constructions of the Cave Man." *American Anthropologist* 101 (2): 288–304. http://dx.doi.org/10.1525/aa.1999.101.2.288.

Bonsall, Clive, and Christopher Tolan-Smith. 1997. "The Human Use of Caves." In *The Human Use of Caves*, ed. Clive Bonsall and Christopher Tolan-Smith, 217–219. BAR International Series 667. Oxford: Archaeopress.

Bradley, Richard. 1998. *The Significance of Monuments: On the Shaping of Human Experience in Neolithic and Bronze Age Europe*. London: Routledge.

Brady, James E. 1989. "Investigation of Maya Ritual Cave Use with Special Reference to Naj Tunich, Peten, Guatemala." PhD dissertation, Department of Anthropology, University of California, Los Angeles.

Brady, James E., and Keith M. Prufer. 2005. "Introduction: A History of Mesoamerican Cave Interpretation." In *In the Maw of the Earth Monster: Mesoamerican Ritual Cave Use*, ed. James E. Brady and Keith M. Prufer, 1–17. Austin: University of Texas Press.

Brady, James E., and Dominique Rissolo. 2006. "A Reappraisal of Ancient Maya Cave Mining." *Journal of Anthropological Research* 62 (4): 471–90.

Braidwood, Robert. 1951. "From Cave to Village in Prehistoric Iraq." *Bulletin of the American Schools of Oriental Research* 124: 12–18.

Braidwood, Robert. 1967. *Prehistoric Men*, 7th ed. Glenview, IL: Scott, Foresman and Company.

Breuil, Abbé Henri, and Raymond Lantier. 1965. *The Men of the Old Stone Age (Palaeolithic and Mesolithic)*. Trans. B. B. Rafter. New York: St. Martin's Press.

Burkitt, Miles. 1963 [1933]. *The Old Stone Age: A Study of Palaeolithic Times*, 4th ed. New York: Antheneum.

Casati, Roberto, and Achille C. Varzi. 1994. *Holes and Other Superficialities*. Cambridge, MA: MIT Press.

Chard, Chester S. 1975. *Man in Prehistory*. 2nd ed. New York: McGraw-Hill.

Collcutt, S. N. 1979. "The Analysis of Quaternary Cave Sediments." *World Archaeology* 10 (3): 290–301. http://dx.doi.org/10.1080/00438243.1979.9979738.

Culver, David C., and William B. White. 2004. *Encyclopedia of Caves*. Burlington, MA: Academic Press.

Daniel, Glynn E. 1952. *A Hundred Years of Archaeology*. London: Duckworth.

Dawkins, W. Boyd. 1874. *Cave Hunting: Researches on the Evidence of Caves Respecting the Early Inhabitants of Europe*. London: Macmillan and Co.

Farrand, William. 1985. "Rockshelter and Cave Sediments." In *Archaeological Sediments in Context*, ed. Julie K. Stein and William R. Farrand, 21–40. Orono, ME: Center for the Study of Early Man, Institute for Quarternary Studies.

Faulkner, Charles H. 1988. "Painters of the 'Dark Zone.'" *Archaeology* 41 (2): 30–8.

Fewkes, J. Walter. 1910. "The Cave Dwellings of the Old and New Worlds." *American Anthropologist* 12 (3): 390–416. http://dx.doi.org/10.1525/aa.1910.12.3.02a00040.

Ford, Derek C., and P. W. Williams. 1989. *Karst Geomorphology and Hydrology*. Boston: Unwin Hyman.

Goldberg, Paul, and Sarah C. Sherwood. 2006. "Deciphering Human Prehistory through the Geoarchaeological Study of Cave Sediments." *Evolutionary Anthropology* 15 (1): 20–36. http://dx.doi.org/10.1002/evan.20094.

Gunn, John. 2003. *Encyclopedia of Caves and Karst Science*. New York: Fitzroy Dearborn.

Hawkes, Christopher. 1954. "Archaeological Theory and Method: Some Suggestions from the Old World." *American Anthropologist* 56 (2): 155–68. http://dx.doi.org/10.1525/aa.1954.56.2.02a00020.

Hayden, Brian. 2003. *Shamans, Sorcerers and Saints: Prehistory of Religion*. Washington, DC: Smithsonian.

Hole, Frank, and Robert F. Heizer. 1965. *An Introduction to Prehistoric Archaeology*. New York: Holt, Rinehart, and Winston.

Jennings, J. N. 1997. "Cave and Karst Terminology, Australian Speleological Federation Inc. Administrative Handbook." http://home.mira.net/~gnb/caving/papers/jj-cakt.html (accessed August 1, 2009).

Kempe, David. 1988. *Living Underground: A History of Cave and Cliff Dwelling*. London: The Herbert Press.

Klimchouk, Alexander. 2003. "Caves." In *Encyclopedia of Cave and Karst Science*, ed. John Gunn, 203–205. Dearborn, NY: Fitzroy.

Kostof, Spiro. 1972. *Caves of God: The Monastic Environment of Byzantine Cappadocia*. Cambridge, MA: MIT Press.

Kyriakidis, Evangelos. 2007. "Archaeologies of Ritual." In *The Archaeology of Ritual*, ed. Evangelos Kyriakidis, 289–308. Los Angeles: Cotsen Institute of Archaeology, University of California.

Lewis-Williams, David. 2002. *The Mind in the Cave: Consciousness and the Origins of Art*. London: Thames and Hudson.

Lubbock, Sir John. 1865. *Pre-historic Times: As Illustrated by Ancient Remains, and the Manners and Customs of Modern Savages*. London: Williams and Norgate.

Moyes, Holley. 2006. "The Sacred Landscape as a Political Resource: A Case Study of Ancient Maya Cave Use at Chechem Ha Cave, Belize, Central America." PhD dissertation, Department of Anthropology, State University of New York at Buffalo.

Reid, Jefferson J., Michael B. Schiffer, and William J. Rathje. 1975. "Behavioral Archaeology: Four Strategies." *American Anthropologist* 77 (4): 864–9. http://dx.doi.org/10.1525/aa.1975.77.4.02a00090.

Renfrew, Colin. 2007. "The Archaeology of Ritual, of Cult, and of Religion." In *The Archaeology of Ritual*, ed. Evangelos Kyriakidis, 109–22. Los Angeles: Cotsen Institute of Archaeology, University of California.

Schiffer, Michael B. 1995. *Behavioral Archaeology First Principles*. Salt Lake City: University of Utah Press.

Sherwood, Sarah C., and Paul Goldberg. 2001. "A Geoarchaeological Framework for the Study of Karstic Cave Sites in the Eastern Woodlands." *Midcontinental Journal of Archaeology* 26 (2): 145–68.

Skeates, Robin. 1997. "The Human Uses of Caves in East-Central Italy during the Mesolithic, Neolithic and Copper Age." In *The Human Use of Caves*, ed. Clive Bonsall and Christopher Tolan Smith, 79–86. Oxford: British Archaeological Reports.

Straus, Lawrence Guy. 1990. "Underground Archaeology: Perspectives on Caves and Rockshelters." In *Archaeological Method and Theory*, vol. 2, ed. Michael B. Schiffer, 255–304. Tucson: University of Arizona Press.

Straus, Lawrence Guy. 1997. "Convenient Cavities: Some Human Uses of Caves and Rockshelters." In *The Human Use of Caves*, ed. Clive Bonsall and Christopher Tolan-Smith, 1–8. BAR International Series 667. Oxford: Archaeopress.

Tedlock, Dennis. 1996. *Popol Vuh: The Definitive Edition of the Mayan Book of the Dawn of Life and the Glories of the Gods and Kings*, rev. ed. New York: Simon and Schuster.

Thompson, J. Eric S. 1959. "The Role of Caves in Maya Culture." *Mitteilungen aus dem Museum für Völkerkunde im Hamburg* 25: 122–9.

Tozzer, Alfred M. 1941. *Landa's Relacion de las Cosas de Yucatan*. Papers of the Peabody Museum of American Archaeology and Ethnology, 18. Cambridge, MA: Harvard University.

Trinkaus, Erik, and Pat Shipman. 1994. *The Neanderthals: Of Skeletons, Scientists, and Scandals*. New York: Vintage Books.

Walker, William H. 1995. "Ceremonial Trash?" In *Expanding Archaeology*, ed. James M. Skibo, William H. Walker, and Axel E. Nielsen, 67–79. Salt Lake City: University of Utah Press.

Wedel, Waldo R. 1938. "The Direct-Historical Approach in Pawnee Archaeology." *Smithsonian Miscellaneous Collections* 97, no. 7. Washington, DC: Smithsonian Institution.

Woodward, Jamie C., and Paul Goldberg. 2001. "The Sedimentary Records in Mediterranean Rockshelters and Caves: Archives of Environmental Change." *Geoarchaeology* 16 (4): 327–54. http://dx.doi.org/10.1002/gea.1007.

Wylie, Alison. 1985. "The Reaction Against Analogy." *Advances in Archaeological Method and Theory* 8: 63–111.

Part I
Old World Ritual Cave Traditions

1

Ritual Cave Use in European Paleolithic Caves

Jean Clottes

This chapter examines evidence for ritual Paleolithic cave use in Europe. It begins with a case for limited ritual use of a deep cave by Neanderthals prior to the Upper Paleolithic and the arrival of modern humans in the area. Numerous examples of caves used for rock art by modern humans date from about 38,000 to 11,000 BP, and extend from the southern tip of the Iberian Peninsula to the Urals in Russia. Burials are rare at that time in painted or engraved caves (Cussac in the Dordogne, Vilhonneur in the Charente). On the other hand, many activities took place in caves and left abundant evidence that must be interpreted with caution to be able to work out whether they may be considered ritual behaviors, and to discover whatever additional information these data can bring us about the people who frequented the deep painted caves. Remains range from footprints on the ground to fires and their attendant debris (charcoal, burnt bones), from mobiliary art—which can be related (or not) to the wall art—to deliberate gestures and actions, such as breaking and using concretions, sticking bits of bones into cracks or cave-bear bones into cave floors, and making scratches on the walls. Such traces and remains are nowhere better preserved than in deep caves and are apt to bring invaluable information about ritual cave use tens of thousands of years ago.

A recent book on *The Human Use of Caves* (Bonsall and Tolan-Smith 1997) deals with many of the issues in point and presents a wealth of information and observations on which it will be necessary to dwell. First, we must explain precisely what we mean by *cave*. In the above-cited book, as in many other cases, the word *cave* is used indiscriminately by various authors. It can mean either rockshelters, where activities take place in the natural light of the day, or deep passages and chambers that truly pertain to the subterranean world. For clarity's sake, it is only the latter that should properly be called caves. To avoid misunderstandings, all cavities in the rock where in the daytime it is possible to see and to move about without the help of such artificial lighting as torches or grease lamps should and will be called *shelters*. Such a definition includes the entrances to deeper caves, often used as shelters.

Another central point is the definition of *ritual*. Actions evidenced as ritual in caves by Tolan-Smith and Bonsall include art, votive deposits, and burials. The authors also state that "some activities may be described, rather loosely, as economic. These include . . . the acquisition of raw materials such as workable stone, minerals, water and chemicals," while acknowledging that "we know from ethnography, ethnohistory and everyday experience that many aspects of economic behaviour have a ritual dimension, while ritual behaviour can often have an economic aspect." They add that "deep caves are rarely used at all and then only for ritual purposes" (Bonsall and Tolan-Smith 1997, 217).

Now, in traditional societies—such as those of hunter-gatherers—it could be argued that everything is ritual (or that nothing is). What *we* call the supernatural world is immanent to what *we* call the real, everyday world. In Australia, traditional Aranta hunters used to make drawings on rocks before going hunting. When asked why they were doing this by ethnologist Lewis Mountford, they were quite astounded at the silliness of the question and replied, "But how can we go hunting if we do not paint first?" Drawing an animal on the rock—which for us might be a ritual act—was obviously for them as much a part of the hunting process as preparing their weapons and stalking the game (Anati 1989, 10).

We must therefore be aware of the fact that the concept of "ritual" may well have been alien to the societies we are dealing with. It is the same with the concept of "art" and "artist" for which many traditional peoples did not even have a word at the time of Contact (Whitley 2001, 22). This being said, we should not be deterred from using those words—with provisos—whenever they prove useful to us and to our understanding of a particular phenomenon. Thus, an act may be called "ritual," perhaps provisionally, when it cannot be explained by any imaginable "practical" reason, while it may well have been felt to be entirely practical from the point of view of the authors of the act. This is all the more so when acts of the same ilk have been evidenced in many different cultural contexts and correspond to universal ways of thinking and acting (see examples below).

THE CAVE AS ANOTHER WORLD AND ITS USES

In order to attempt the difficult task of interpreting the uses of deep caves in Paleolithic times, it is necessary to consider the ways prehistoric and traditional people all over the planet have acted and felt about the subterranean world, whether they frequented it or not. In most cultures, deep caves have been shunned. In all of Africa, in South America, in Central India, and in most of Australia, for example, the traces of human activities are generally restricted to the entrances of caves or to shelters. When such a place has been painted or engraved, the rock art stops where the light no longer reaches. Among the available examples of people venturing into the depths of caves, in addition to the well-known European Paleolithic caves, Mesoamerica is prominent, in particular with the Mayas (Stone 1997; Moyes and Brady, this volume) but also with the rather late so-called Mudglyph Caves in the Southeast of the United States (Faulkner 1996; Simek, Cressler, and Douglas, this volume) and the Pleistocene limestone caves of southern Australia (Taçon et al., this volume). The latter are all the more interesting, because aboriginal feeling about what to do with caves has obviously changed with time (Bednarik 1986).

Everywhere in the world and at all times, people have had feelings of awe about caves. Caves are the realm of the supernatural powers, the spirits, the gods, and/or the dead. (See, for example, Charon and the Styx, a subterranean river in Greek mythology.) They can be highly respected places of emergence or of origin, as for the Incas who traced their origins from a cave 26 kilometers south of Cusco (Dransart 1997). It is only in our modern Western world that deep caves have lost their supernatural aura and are routinely explored by spelunkers for whom they are a challenge and an area of sport and study.

Traditional orientations to caves may entail one of two attitudes. They may be considered such spiritually dangerous places that people must keep away from them. Contemporary Aborigines have always felt that way, as do most Africans. Conversely, caves can be considered as providing a physical access to the other world and, as such, to constitute a valuable cultural resource that can be used whenever necessary. This might explain the deposition of the dead found in many different cultures, such as those of the Chalcolithic in Western Europe or of the Kalimantan people in Borneo (Chazine and Fage 2002).

Although their Pleistocene ancestors made use of deep caves, present-day and subcontemporary Australian Aborigines shun deep caves. In Mesoamerica, however, the tradition has continued until Contact and after, so that invaluable direct testimonies exist about the way deep caves are now viewed and probably were in the past. According to Andrea Stone:

> In Maya thought caves were a conduit into the bowels of the earth, a dangerous but supernaturally charged realm, often referred to as the "underworld" in current literature or by the Quiché term, *Xibalda*. Herein dwelt the ancestors, rain gods, various "owners" of the earth, culture heroes, nefarious death demons, animal and wind spirits. The Maya made pilgrimages to caves to propitiate these beings ... post-contact sources tell us that cave ceremonies usually concerned rain and other agricultural interests, hunting, ancestor worship, renewal/New Year rites and other calendrically-timed ceremonies, and petitions for various personal needs (e.g., health problems). Caves were also used by *brujos* (witches) to cast spells. (1997:202–3)

The two attitudes to caves (shunning them and going into them for particular ritual purposes) are not contradictory. They stem from the same beliefs and they can also be complementary, as access to caves may be restricted in various ways. For example, some sacred caves could only be accessed at particular periods or at very long intervals, sometimes spanning generations. Also there might have been all sorts of restrictions concerning the persons who went into them, depending on their age, sex, and status.

Finally, caves have occasionally been used for mining minerals. In southern Australia a number of examples have been evidenced and researched in the past 25 years, the best-known of them being Koonalda Cave (Bednarik 1986), where the mining is associated with a great number of finger tracings on the walls. Pleistocene people systematically extracted chert from those caves (in addition to Koonalda, see also Karlie-ngoinpool Cave and especially Gran Can Cave) (Bednarik 1992). As to the Maya, "some rather sketchy evidence indicates that Maya extracted clays and minerals from caves." For example, a "case of Prehispanic mining was discovered at Footprint Cave, Belize, where a stone mortar with a white mineral ground on the surface was found along with other Late to Terminal Classic artifacts" (Stone 1997, 202). It would be difficult to believe that all those activities would be "purely" economic and materialistic, especially considering the way the Maya felt about deep caves and behaved in them. Those observations will be particularly relevant when we address the activities of Paleolithic people in the deep painted caves.

RITUAL BEHAVIOR OF NEANDERTHALS IN THE DEEP CAVES

In the depths of the Bruniquel cave, in the Tarn-et-Garonne in France, broken stalactites and stalagmites were piled and arranged in a kind of oval roughly 5 meters by 5 meters, with a much smaller round structure next to it (figure 1.1). The nature of those structures and the conditions of the cave make it impossible for them to have been the consequence of animal or natural activities. They are indisputably human made.

The structures themselves cannot, of course, be directly dated, but a fire was made nearby, and a burnt fragment of bone from it was dated to more than 47,600 years BP. If this date also applies to the arrangement of stalagmites, as seems likely, it puts the structures well within the Mousterian, the local Neanderthal cultural period (Rouzaud, Soulier, and Lignereux 1995). Even though the cave was quite accessible before a collapse of the cliff blocked its entrance, and although it was by far the biggest in the area—where three smaller caves have been painted (Mayrière supérieure, Travers de Janoye) or engraved and carved (La Magdaleine) at various periods of the Upper Paleolithic—not a single painting or engraving was found on its walls. These conditions make it very unlikely that the Bruniquel cave was frequented by Cro-Magnons.

No practical purpose can be suggested for those constructions. The people who made them did not live that far inside the cave, as the absence of the kind of remains so common on habitation sites testifies. The hypothesis was made that the arrangements of stones could have been the

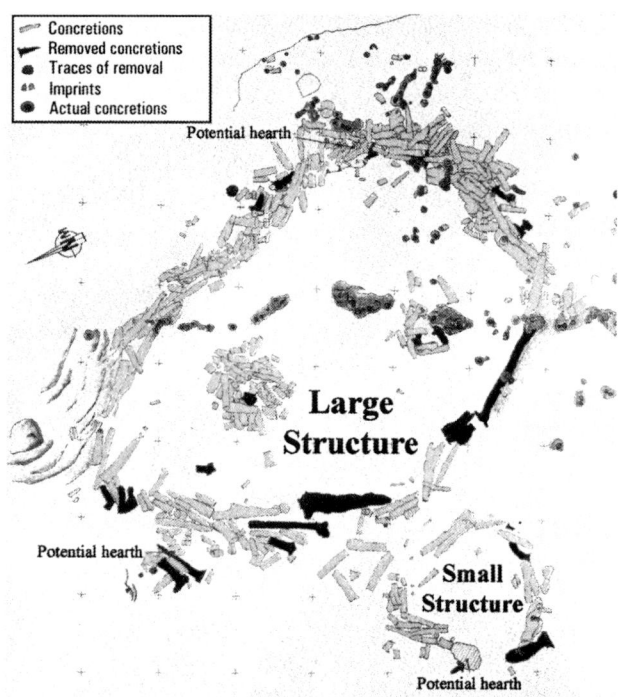

FIGURE 1.1 Map of the stone structures in the Bruniquel cave (Tarn-et-Garonne, France). The structures were made with an accumulation of stalactites and stalagmites. (From Rouzaud, Soulier, and Lignereux 1995.)

substructures of a tent (Rouzaud, Soulier, and Lignereux 1995). This would imply the construction of a superstructure consisting of poles and of hides arranged and tied onto them. The dimensions of the bigger structure would entail carrying a very heavy load of poles and of hides far into the cave. But if this were the case, why would physical protection be needed inside a deep cave, the climate of which is proverbially stable? In addition, building a big (perhaps 20 square meters) tent for practical purposes could only be done if prolonged stays in the cave were contemplated, and we have seen that the cave was never used as a habitation site. As a consequence, the only hypothesis that makes sense is the delimitation of a symbolic or ritual space well inside the subterranean world. This could thus be a valuable—if so far unique—testimony to Neanderthals' attitude to deep caves.

The cave of Régourdou, in the Dordogne (France), provides another unique example, this time of a complete Neanderthal human burial, with a stone wall separating it from a brown bear partially buried in a pit. Two bear legbones prolonged the human body that had been deposited on bear hides. Grave goods (bear bones and stone implements) had been left on top of a slab covering the body. A number of big stones protected the whole. Then a deer antler was put on top of the mound and covered with another layer of stones before a small fire was made. Other manmade structures with brown-bear remains were discovered nearby, some predating and others postdating the human burial (Bonifay 2002; Bonifay and Vandermeersch 1962). Those examples show the spiritual importance attached to bears by the Neanderthals.

Previous to the Neanderthals, we have no evidence that earlier humans went into caves for ritual purposes. In the Sima de los Huesos site at Atapuerca, in Spain, deep inside a cave, Juan Luis Arsuaga and his team did excavate the remains of more than thirty *Homo heidelbergensis*, found together with a spectacular biface which could well be the earliest "grave good" ever discovered. At the time of the burials, however, a 13-meter natural shaft existed and it is likely that the bodies were thrown into it and accumulated at its bottom. The site would certainly qualify as a burial place but not as a deep underground one.

ART IN THE DARK AND OTHER RITUAL ACTIVITIES DURING THE UPPER PALEOLITHIC

In the Upper Paleolithic—that is, when *Homo sapiens sapiens* inhabited Europe at the end of the last Ice Age—testimonies of human activities inside caves are plentiful. Contrary to a long-standing legend, however, the anatomically modern humans did not generally use deep caves as habitation sites. Like their Neanderthal predecessors they favored rockshelters (e.g., Le Placard in the Charente) or the entrances to bigger caves (e.g., Gargas in the Hautes-Pyrénées). For example, the enormous cavern of Niaux in the Ariège, one of the great painted caves in Europe, was never inhabited. The Magdalenians who frequented it lived at La Vache, a much smaller cave right across the valley, lower down and closer to the stream (Clottes and Delporte 2003).

Some exceptions are known of habitats far underground in the complete dark. Nearly always they are located in painted or engraved caves, such as Tito Bustillo in Asturias (Spain), Labastide in the Hautes-Pyrénées, and Bédeilhac in the Ariège. A case in point is Enlène, a cave in the Ariège which was long used as the entrance to the major painted and engraved cave of Les Trois-Frères during the Middle Magdalenian, about 14,000 years BP. An important Gravettian occupation site was discovered at the entrance to Enlène, as were Middle Magdalenian layers. Paleolithic remains in the depths of the cave, however, are Middle Magdalenian only and they are extremely abundant right to the end of the galleries, some 200 meters away from the entrance. At the bottom of the last chamber some red paint was smudged on the walls, and one big red dot and five vertical lines were also painted. Enlène is thus a

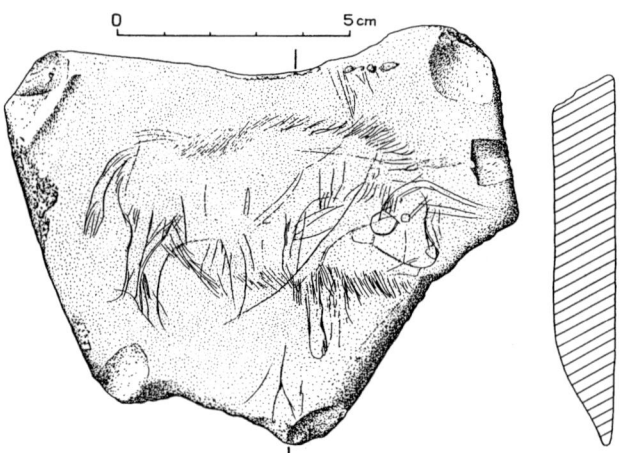

FIGURE 1.2 Engraved flat sandstone pebble from Enlène (Montesquieu-Avantès, Ariège, France), Middle Magdalenian. (Excavations by Jean Clottes, Robert Bégouën, Jean-Pierre Giraud, and François Rouzaud. Tracing by François Briois.)

minor painted cave, but its physical relation to Les Trois-Frères makes it unique, all the more so as the Magdalenian remains stop right at the end of the narrow gallery leading from Enlène to Les Trois-Frères, the latter being a major sanctuary and definitely not a habitation site. In Les Trois-Frères, some fires were built in the Chapelle de la Lionne and the Salle du Foyer during the Magdalenian, but there is no evidence for a long occupation at that time or before. The relation between the two is certain and so are their different roles (Bégouën and Clottes 1990; Clottes 1997).

Another distinct feature of such habitats in the depths is that they frequently evidence special characteristics, such as the abundance of portable art. In Enlène, more than 1,100 engraved plaquettes were discovered (figure 1.2) in addition to a wealth of art on bone and reindeer antler. The cave of Labastide (Hautes-Pyrénées) not only had dozens of engraved plaquettes, but also a series of nineteen *contours découpés* representing chamois found together (Simonnet, Simonnet, and Simonnet 1990). Labouiche, close to Foix in the Ariège, is one of the very rare Magdalenian habitation sites found in a cave devoid of any rock art. In it were discovered two exceptional objects: a plaquette with the engraving of a cave lion and a small sculpture of a bison modeled in clay (Méroc 1959). All this makes it likely that such prolonged stays in the dark were in close relation to the art and to ritual activities.

Few deep caves bear evidence of art. In fact, extrapolating from what we know in France, where a majority of sites are known (Clottes 1997), art in the complete dark is probably present in hardly more than 150 sites all over Europe. Compared to the immense duration of the period during which those caves were frequented (more than

20,000 years), this is very little. Roughly, this would mean one painted cave for every four generations for the whole of Europe.

The problem is compounded by the fact that most of the caves seem to have been in use for a restricted time and by a limited number of people. This can be observed from the study of the art itself, the number of images in relation to the available wall surfaces, the superimpositions and the different styles, but also from the remains and traces of human activities on the walls and on the ground. For example, in Lascaux, the Diverticule des Félins is a narrow winding gallery with soft wall surfaces right at the end of the cave where only two or three people can go at any given time. Despite the limited number of people who have had access to it since its discovery in 1940 and the precautions they took, there is evidence on the walls of accidental modern brushings with shoulders or touching with fingers, but very little ancient evidence of people touching those friable wall surfaces. The inescapable conclusion, given the fact that the wall surfaces have not changed with time, is that very few people went there in the Upper Paleolithic (Breuil 1952, 23; Leroi-Gourhan 1965, 123). Innumerable examples of the same sort could be given from many painted caves (Chauvet, Le Tuc d'Audoubert, Niaux, etc.).

About half the known sites with Paleolithic wall art were in often inhabited shelters or on rocks in the open (e.g., Foz Côa in Portugal; Siega Verde, Domingo Garcia, and others in Spain). Even if many painted caves have been destroyed or still remain undiscovered, the ritual use of caves must have been an exceptional phenomenon during the Upper Paleolithic. The most famous researchers in the twentieth century, Abbé Henri Breuil and André Leroi-Gourhan, recognized that fact a long time ago. "One fact struck prehistorians (most prominently the Abbé H. Breuil), it is that the cave sanctuaries were not all intensely frequented, as the traces found inside them show. . . . [S]ome—not the least elaborate, like Niaux—even seem to have had very few visits" (Leroi-Gourhan 1977, 23). This is exactly why Leroi-Gourhan logically came to a shamanic explanation for cave art. "Personally, I often wondered whether the mere knowledge that an organized world existed in the heart of the earth would not have been the most efficient role of the images, and if the competent (not to say initiated) man or men were not the ones who could visit them, either physically or in their minds [and from this to imagine shamanic travels would take but a step" (ibid., 23). But there Leroi-Gourhan added, characteristically, that such imagining would be a step "that it is better not to take in order not to conjure up a hodge-podge of the Amerindian mistress of the buffalos freeing the herds from her cavern, Sedna keeping the seals in her underwater retreat, Orpheus charming the animals and recovering Eurydice, Mithra and her sacrificed bull, the shaman and his female statuettes and so many parallel bits of information borrowed from the most diverse cultures" (ibid., 23). Most explicitly, Leroi-Gourhan was then denying the strong temptation of the shamanistic hypothesis to which he had arrived logically. He did so not because of the merits of the hypothesis itself nor because it would contradict in any way the Paleolithic data, but solely because of his real phobia against ethnographic analogies (Clottes and Lewis-Williams 2001, 215). Leroi-Gourhan's hypothesis about people projecting their minds far into the dark toward the sacred images in order to access their supernatural power can obviously never be proved but it would certainly explain our data better than any other hypotheses concerning the exceptional frequentation of the deeper caves.

Another surprising fact is that, despite the relative rarity of such occurrences, similar sophisticated forms of art in the depths are to be found not only all over Europe, from the southern tip of the Iberian Peninsula (see the caves of Pileta and Nerja in Andalucia) to the Urals in Russia (Kapovaya and Ignatievskaya) and in Rumania (Coliboaia painted cave, recently discovered), but also at all times in the Upper Paleolithic, from the Aurignacian (Chauvet) to the end of the Magdalenian (Niaux). For such a tradition to have gone on for so long, there must have been firmly rooted beliefs passed on from generation to generation and spreading over vast distances. In fact, Paleolithic art does evince an overall unity in various ways, not only in the themes represented in the art (mostly the bigger animals, few if any humans, many geometric signs) and the techniques used, but also in the use of caves and how they must have been considered at the time, as far as we can tell from the traces and remains discovered in them. We shall see a number of examples that can be construed as revealing the conceptions of Paleolithic people about the subterranean world.

Whether in the Aurignacian (Chauvet), in the Gravettian (Gargas, Cussac), in the Solutrean (Cosquer), or in the Magdalenian, for which we have over twenty examples, the creators of the art consistently explored extensive caves, sometimes more than a mile long (Niaux, Réseau Clastres, Montespan, Rouffignac, Cussac). In order to get as far as they could, they crawled along very narrow passages (Massat, Le Cheval at Arcy-sur-Cure, Cosquer, Gargas, Pergouset), climbed steep pitches, or avens (Le Tuc d'Audoubert, Bernifal), crossed precipitously narrow ledges (Les Trois-Frères, Etcheberri-ko-karbia, Cosquer), and even went down shafts several meters deep (Fontanet). These speleological feats (Rouzaud 1978) only make sense if they wanted to get to the deepest and farthest parts of the earth. It is far more probable that they did so to access the hidden powers of the underground than to achieve exploratory prowess.

FIGURE 1.3 In the Cosquer cave, near Marseille (France), a number of hand stencils were made at the very brink of a 60-foot-deep shaft. (Photograph by Jean Clottes.)

That the people of the Upper Paleolithic had a special way of considering the caves is obvious in their consistent use both of their topography and of their wall surfaces at all times during that very long period. They concentrated images around natural shafts. For example, in Rouffignac (Dordogne), the sixty-four Magdalenian animals of Le Grand Plafond were drawn on a ceiling immediately above and around a funnel-like hole leading to a deeper network of galleries (Plassard 1999). In Cosquer, the Gravettians made hand stencils next to a 60-foot-deep well (figure 1.3), a few inches away from the chasm (Clottes and Courtin 1996). In Niaux, most of the images were made in Le Salon Noir, at the end of a deep gallery and in the sole place in the cave where the voice resounds in a most impressive way (Clottes 1995). Many examples are known everywhere of animals painted or engraved as though they were issuing from the ends of passages or recesses (Covalanas, Chauvet [figure 1.4], Niaux) or, at times, disappearing into them (Lascaux).

The role of the cave as a place crawling with spirits in animal forms, where they were literally at hand, ready to emerge from the ends of galleries and from the walls themselves, is also apparent with the constant use of the natural outlines and reliefs on the wall surfaces. This is one of the main characteristics of art in the deep caves. The people who frequented them must have believed that the animal spirits were there inside the walls, hardly visible and half ready to come out (Lewis-Williams 2002, 210–14). Painting or engraving the missing outlines or details to complete the animals helped the people get in touch with the animals' power. That they systematically did so for thousands of years runs counter to the structuralist theories of Laming-Emperaire (1962) and Leroi-Gourhan (1965), who thought that the artists had brought an existing schema of the layout of an "ideal sanctuary" to the caves and had drawn animals and signs accordingly. Closely and constantly searching for natural outlines stems from a very different outlook, since the cave itself imposes the representation of a particular animal in a particular place on the wall, such as a bird at Altxerri or an upright bison and the head of a cervid at Niaux (figure 1.5) (Clottes and Lewis-Williams 1998, 56–7).

The deep galleries and passages, the vast underground chambers and the narrow recesses, and the walls and the ceilings were thus all felt to be places of power, a power that could be attained and made use of. This could be achieved in a variety of ways—through the images but also by touching and marking the walls—and this was done many times, with different techniques.

One of the possible procedures was making finger flutings or meanders on the soft-rock surfaces. They sometimes cover dozens of square meters (Cosquer, Pech-Merle, Rouffignac, Gargas, Les Trois-Frères) and are occasionally due to young children (Sharpe and Van Gelder 2003). They were perhaps also made by the uninitiated or the sick who were thus directly exposed to the supernatural power in the rock. Hand stencils and possibly handprints could have played a similar role, the paint facilitating contact through the wall. The oft-noted presence of children in the caves could thus be explained. In fact, whenever Paleolithic footprints have been found in deep caves, they include children's footprints. Several authors, such as Count Henri Bégouën, the Abbé Henri Breuil, and more lately John Pfeiffer (1982), have argued that this was for initiation ceremonies at their coming of age, an idea contradicted by the fact that some of these children were far too young: the footprints of a 3-year-old are preserved in Le Tuc d'Audoubert and the handprints of a 5- or 6-year-old in Fontanet. Children were most certainly not barred from the deep sanctuaries, but to assume that they were taken to the caves to be exposed to their power through finger-made meanders

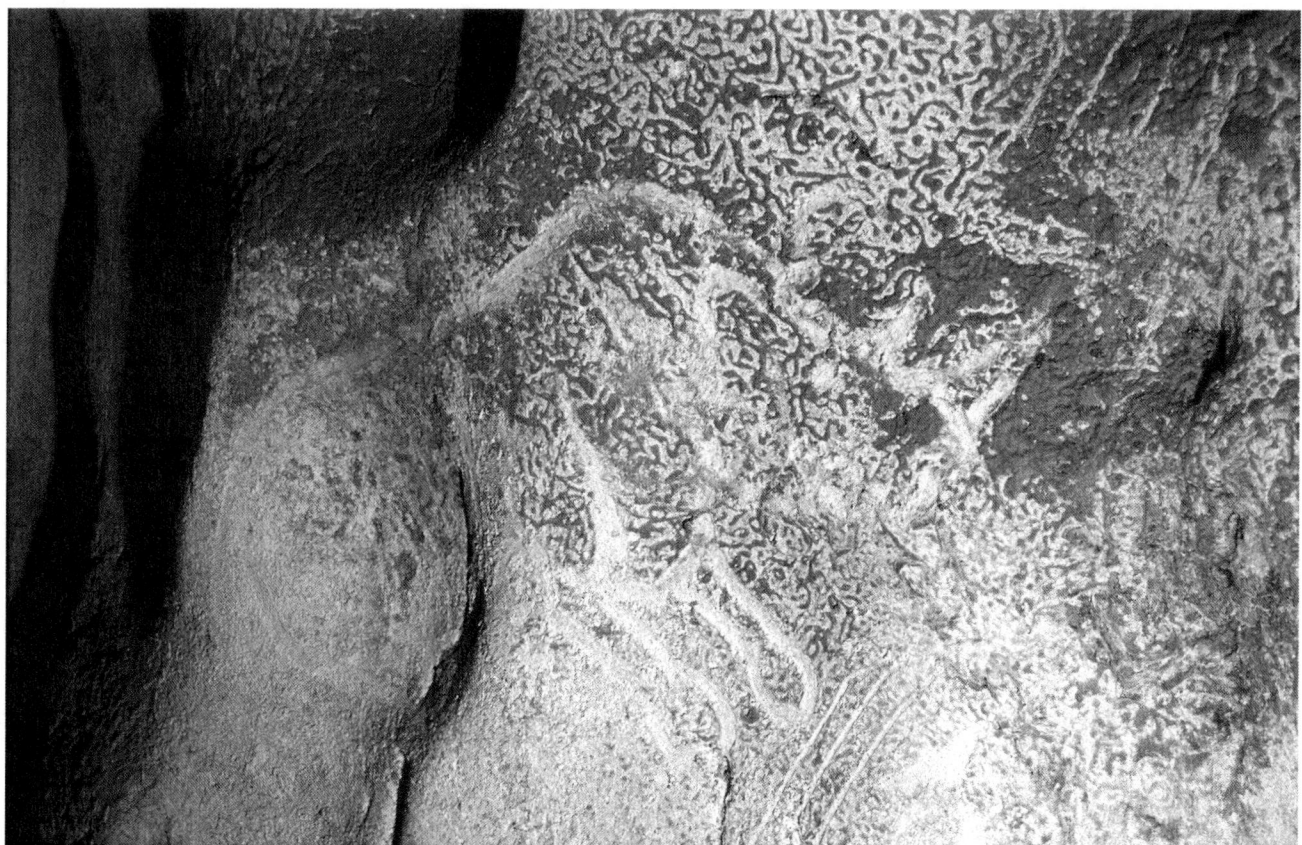

FIGURE 1.4 A rhinoceros was engraved as if issuing from a deep recess in the Chauvet cave (Vallon-Pont-d'Arc, France). (Photograph by Jean Clottes.)

and/or hand stencils (for which we have evidence)—and probably in other ways—is the hypothesis that makes the most sense (Clottes 1997).

Other sorts of evidence are available for actions that could be called "ritual" and that are best explained by a desire to access whatever supernatural power was believed to reside in the cave. The simplest is touching the walls with the tips of the fingers covered with paint. In the Cantabrian cave of La Garma, a whole panel is made with a great number of such marks. Black and red finger markings of the same sort are very numerous in Cougnac, both on stalactites and on the painted walls (figure 1.6), whereas in Cosquer, it is mostly stalactites and stalagmites that are marked in such a way (Clottes, Courtin, and Vanrell 2005).

Deposits of objects, valuable or not, in special places have always been made to placate spirits or gods or to draw their benevolence. Many such examples have long been known from the deep painted caves (Le Tuc d'Audoubert, Les Trois-Frères, Mas d'Azil, Bédeilhac, Labastide, etc.) (Bégouën and Clottes 1981) and more have been discovered lately (La Garma, Chauvet). Another Paleolithic ges-

FIGURE 1.5 A natural hole in the wall of the Niaux cave (Ariège, France) was identified by a Magdalenian as the head of a deer and was completed accordingly by adding the antlers. (Photograph by Jean Clottes.)

FIGURE 1.6 In the Cougnac cave (Lot, France), fingers covered with paint were often applied to the walls, sometimes next to paintings, as here close to an ibex head. (Photograph by Jean Clottes.)

ture has drawn less attention until recent times. It is the sticking of bits of animal bones, which apparently do not otherwise present any notable characteristics of their own, into the cracks and fissures of the walls. This was done in more than twenty painted or engraved caves of southern France and Spain (Clottes 2009). Planting bones into the ground can be construed as a related gesture. It was done less often, most times in the center of the Pyrenees (Enlène, Le Portel, Montespan, Fontanet, Labastide), except for Chauvet, where two cave-bear humeri were halfway stuck into the ground not far from the original entrance to the cave (figure 1.7). From the Aurignacian of Chauvet to the late Magdalenian of Troubat (Hautes-Pyrénées), that phenomenon lasted for most of the duration of the Upper Paleolithic and testifies to the same attitude of Ice Age people toward the caves.

The obvious reason for placing whole or fragmented bones in caves in these ways was a desire to reach beyond the ordinary world, that of the living, to pierce the veil (Lewis-Williams and Dowson 1990) barely separating it from the so-close supernatural forces and to touch them either directly or by means of an offering, however symbolic it might be. When they were sticking bones or their fragments into fissures or into the ground, it was not the object itself that was important—and this might explain why the splinters of bones are so commonplace—but rather the gesture, the will to bridge the gap and to contact the power hidden within the rock or the ground in that supernatural world of the dark and to bring away some of it in order to help with the eternal problems of everyday life. Innumerable examples of such actions are available all over the world and even nowadays in many different contexts (Clottes 2009).

Another manner of taking advantage of the particular power of the cave was to remove a small part of what it contained and to use it outside. This was done by the Magdalenians in Le Tuc d'Audoubert with the formidable incisors of cave bears that were forcibly removed and taken away. We must note that cave-bear remains and traces on the ground (footprints, lairs) and on the walls (scratches) must have felt extremely impressive to the Paleolithic people who went into the caves (see above about the

FIGURE 1.7 Not far from the entrance to the Chauvet cave, but well inside it, two cave-bear humeri, like this one, were forcibly stuck about half their length into the ground. (Photograph by Jean Clottes.)

Neanderthals.) Cave bears certainly played a particular part in their myths as, in addition to having bones that very much resemble human ones, they stood on their hind legs, they vanished into the caves at the beginning of winter, and they reemerged (i.e., resuscitated) in the spring. In Chauvet, we mentioned the two humeri stuck into the ground, but several other bones were displaced and marked with charcoal, and one cave-bear skull was prominently deposited on top of a big stone that had fallen from the ceiling into the middle of the central chamber (Clottes 2003; figure 1.8).

Flint "mining" has been observed in the painted Bara-Bahau cave (Dordogne) (Bednarik 1992, 14). It is possible that some of the nodules apparent in the walls of the cave were used in Paleolithic times. This would, however, be a very rare if not a single occurrence and would not necessarily mean that removing flint flakes was just a practical type of action. Two reasons explain these doubts: first, the quality of the flint inside the cave, Santonian in origin, is not very good and it is most times naturally broken, and, second, there is a surfeit of excellent flint sources in the immediate neighborhood on the plateau (Dr. Norbert Aujoulat,

personal communication). The flint could therefore have been removed for any number of reasons, including ritual ones. We will see more examples of such actions with other minerals, in particular from the Cosquer cave (Marseille).

In the deepest and highest chambers of Cosquer, the only ones that remained above sea level after the end of the Pleistocene, we have lately found many fascinating traces of the actions of the people who frequented them during two periods, the Gravettian (26,000 to 27,000 BP) and the local equivalent of the Solutrean (around 19,000 BP) (Clottes, Courtin, and Vanrell 2005). They consistently marked the walls with finger tracings on the soft white surface (a type of microcrystalline speleothem coating called *mondmilch* or *moonmilk*), they left sixty-five hand stencils and they made black marks on a great number of stalactites and stalagmites. All this can be construed as ritual, as we have just seen.

In addition, they broke the tops of many stalagmites and removed the pieces, as our in-depth study of the cave has shown lately (figure 1.9). The study of the cave began in 1991 and went on in 1992 and 1994. The study to which

FIGURE 1.8 The ground of the Chauvet cave is strewn with many cave-bear skulls. One of them was picked up and deposited on top of a big stone in the middle of a deep chamber. (Photograph by Jean Clottes.)

we have lately proceeded took place in 2002 and 2003. It could be carried out because the cave walls and ground are fairly well preserved. They also deeply scraped the wall surfaces and removed the moonmilk. Comparisons with similar practices well evidenced at much later times in other parts of the world led us to the conclusion that the most likely hypothesis was that those minerals could have been used for medicinal purposes. According to Trevor Shaw, "powdered calcite deposits from caves were widely used medicinally. It may be that virtue was originally ascribed to them because of their very strangeness, but the presence of calcium carbonate in a relatively pure form does provide real benefit in some cases" (Shaw 1997, 27). This would thus be the first example in the world of the use of a very specific medicine: calcium carbonate. It would have been effective in a number of conditions, as modern physicians can attest. In addition, rock powders coming from the deepest part of a painted cave would most probably have been thought to be quite potent and extraordinary. In a case like this, "ritual" elements and "practical" considerations must obviously be inextricably mixed. After making our discovery, we found evidence of breaking and removing Paleolithic stalagmites in several other painted caves of France (Gargas, Cougnac) and Spain (Hornos de la Peña, Las Monedas) (Clottes, Courtin, and Vanrell 2005).

Among the actions considered as "ritual," burials play a very special part, as we have seen (Bonsall and Tolan-Smith 1997, 217). Caves were widely used as burial places in the Neolithic and in the Bronze and Iron Ages (see Barker and Lloyd-Smith; Chamberlain; Rowan and Ilan; and Skeates, this volume). Until the end of the year 2000, however, no Upper Paleolithic burial had ever been found in a deep painted cave. The discovery of the Cussac cave, in the Dordogne, thus created quite a stir. The cave is about

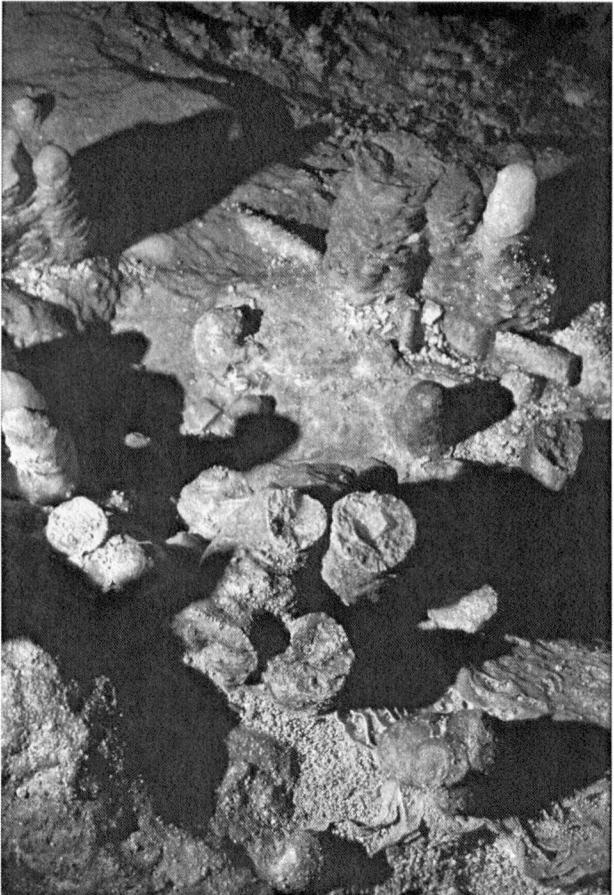

FIGURE 1.9 In the Cosquer cave, we have many examples of deliberately broken stalagmites and of the removal of their pieces. (Photograph by Jean Clottes.)

a mile long and its art, mostly consisting of engravings (horses, bison, cervids, rhino, mammoths, ibex, bird, fantastic animals), is abundant and stylistically homogeneous. It is entirely attributable to the Gravettian, because of some of its themes (e.g., figures of women similar to the ones in Pech-Merle) and techniques. The remains of seven human skeletons deep inside the cave were discovered in bear wallows and two radiocarbon dates were obtained from bones belonging to two of them. The analyses were carried out by Beta-Analitic, Miami, Florida. The first one gave an approximate date, "older than 20,000 BP." The other was 25,120 BP ± 120 (Aujoulat et al. 2001, 8). So far, those burials, covered with a fine film of silt, have not been excavated and we do not know whether grave goods or ochre were deposited with the bodies. The dates obtained suggest that the art and the skeletons could be roughly contemporaneous. That a deep cave—particularly one with hundreds of engravings—should be considered a place particularly fit for the deposit of the dead is quite understandable. But then, why should such an event be so exceptional? Were the people buried there special people in any way? Were they men and/or women? Were they related? As is so often the case, this new discovery brings far more questions than answers. Some of them may be answered when excavations and analyses (DNA comes to mind) have been carried out.

CONCLUSION

Before the Upper Paleolithic, the evidence of ritual use of caves is scanty and only attributable to Neanderthals (Bruniquel, Régourdou). Then, with the advent of modern humans in Europe, caves became more-often frequented and all the data we have point to ritual activities on the part of the Aurignacians and their successors. Considering the immensity of time (more than 20,000 years) and distances involved (from Iberia to the Urals), the 150 examples or so that we have—even if we are far from having discovered all the deep painted caves in Europe—are a relatively small number. They do testify to a common way of thinking and to ritual practices in the deep caves, but these may have been exceptional.

The fact that for more than 20,000 years some people went underground for their ceremonies is, however, the evidence of the longest-lasting religion in the history of the world. Deep caves and what they stood for played a major part in that religion. On the other hand, their particular conditions preserved not only the art but also the traces of many actions that took place there, thus allowing us to better understand the state of mind of those people and the way they considered the underworld as they discovered it under the fluttering light of their torches or their grease lamps, and also how they made use of its possibilities in so many different ways.

ACKNOWLEDGMENTS

I sincerely thank Mr. Michel Soulier, spelunker, and the owners of the Bruniquel cave for their permission to let me publish the map of the stone structures in that cave. I also thank Dr. Norbert Aujoulat and Dr. Eugène Bonifay for the information that they kindly provided; Holley Moyes for carrying out the project with enthusiasm and determination; and the two anonymous reviewers for their comments.

REFERENCES CITED

Anati, Emmanuel. 1989. *Les Origines de l'Art et la Formation de l'Esprit humain*. Paris: Editions Albin Michel.

Aujoulat, Norbert, Jean-Michel Geneste, Christian Archambeau, Dany Barraud, Marc Delluc, Henri Duday, and Dominique Gambier. 2001. "The Decorated Cave of Cussac." *International Newsletter on Rock Art* 30: 3–9.

Bednarik, Robert. 1986. "Cave Use by Australian Pleistocene Man." *Proc. Univ. Bristol Spelaeol. Soc.* 17 (3): 227–45.

Bednarik, Robert. 1992. "Early Subterranean Chert Mining." *Artefact* 15: 11–24.

Bégouën, Robert, and Jean Clottes. 1981. Apports mobiliers dans les cavernes du Volp (Enlène, Les Trois-Frères, Le Tuc-d'Audoubert). *Altamira Symposium*. Madrid, pp. 157–188.

Bégouën, Robert, and Jean Clottes. 1990. "Art mobilier et art pariétal dans les cavernes du Volp." In *L'Art des objets au Paléolithique*, vol. 1: *L'art mobilier et son contexte*, ed. Jean Clottes, 157–72. Colloque international Foix-Le Mas-d'Azil, November 16–21, 1987. Paris: Ministère de la Culture.

Bonifay, Eugène. 2002. "L'Homme de Néandertal et l'Ours (*Ursus arctos*) dans la grotte du Régourdou (Montignac-sur-Vézère, Dordogne, France)." In *L'Ours et l'Homme*, ed. Thierry Tillet and Lewis Binford, 247–254. Symposium d'Auberives-en-Royans-Isère-France, 1997. Liège: Université de Liège, ERAUL 100.

Bonifay, Eugène, and Bernard Vandermeersch. 1962. "Dépôts rituels d'ossements d'ours dans le gisement moustérien du Régourdou (Montignac, Dordogne)." *Comptes-rendus Académie des Sciences de Paris* 225: 1035–6.

Bonsall, Clive, and Christopher Tolan-Smith, eds. 1997. *The Human Use of Caves*. BAR International Series 667. Oxford: Archaeopress.

Breuil, Abbé Henri. 1952. *Four Hundred Centuries of Cave Art*. Montignac: Fernand Windels, Centre d'Etudes et de Documentation Préhistoriques.

Chazine, Jean-Michel, and Luc-Henri Fage. 2002. "New Discoveries in Borneo." *International Newsletter on Rock Art* 34: 1–7.

Clottes, Jean. 1995. *Les Cavernes de Niaux. Art préhistorique en Ariège*. Paris: Editions du Seuil.

Clottes, Jean. 1997. "Art of the Light and Art of the Depths." In *Beyond Art: Pleistocene Image and Symbol*, ed. Margaret Conkey, Olga Soffer, Deborah Stratmann, and Nina G. Jablonski, 203–16. Memoirs of the California Academy of Sciences 23. Berkeley: University of California Press.

Clottes, Jean, ed. 2003. *Chauvet Cave: The Art of Earliest Times*. Salt Lake City: University of Utah Press.

Clottes, Jean. 2009. "Sticking Bones into Cracks in the Upper Palaeolithic." In *Becoming Human: Innovation in Prehistoric Material and Spiritual Culture*, ed. Colin Renfrew and Ian Morley, 195–211. Cambridge: Cambridge University Press.

Clottes, Jean, and Jean Courtin. 1996. *The Cave beneath the Sea: Paleolithic Images at Cosquer*. New York: Harry N. Abrams.

Clottes, Jean, Jean Courtin, and Luc Vanrell. 2005. *Cosquer redécouvert*. Paris: Editions du Seuil.

Clottes, Jean, and Henri Delporte, eds. 2003. *La Grotte de La Vache (Ariège)*, vol. 1: *Les Occupations du Magdalénien*; vol. 2: *L'Art mobilier*. Éditions de la Réunion des Musées nationaux et du Comité des Travaux historiques et scientifiques. Paris. Vol. 1: 408 p., 293 figure; Vol. 2: 464.

Clottes, Jean, and David Lewis-Williams. 1998. *The Shamans of Prehistory: Trance and Magic in the Painted Caves*. New York: Harry N. Abrams.

Clottes, Jean, and David Lewis-Williams. 2001. *Les Chamanes de la Préhistoire. Transe et magie dans les grottes ornées. Suivi de Après Les Chamanes, polémique et réponses*. Paris: La maison des roches.

Dransart, Penny. 1997. "Rockshelters and Ritual Activities in the Atacama Desert of Northern Chile." In *The Human Use of Caves*, ed. Clive Bonsall and Christopher Tolan-Smith, 207–16. BAR International Series 667. Oxford: Archaeopress.

Faulkner, Charles H., ed. 1996. *Rock Art of the Eastern Woodlands*. San Miguel, CA: American Rock Art Association.

Hill, Carol A., and Paolo Forti. 1986. *Cave Minerals of the World*. Huntsville, AL: National Speleological Society.

Laming-Emperaire, Annette. 1962. *La Signification de l'Art Rupestre Paléolithique*. Paris: Picard.

Leroi-Gourhan, André. 1965. *Préhistoire de l'Art Occidental*. Paris: Mazenod.

Leroi-Gourhan, André. 1977. "Le Préhistorien et le Chamane." *L'Ethnographie* 74/75, numéro spécial *Etudes Chamaniques*: 19–25.

Lewis-Williams, David J. 2002. *The Mind in the Cave: Consciousness and the Origin of Art*. London: Thames & Hudson.

Lewis-Williams, David J., and Thomas Dowson. 1990. "Through the Veil: San Rock Paintings and the Rock Face." *South African Archaeological Bulletin* 45 (151): 5–16. http://dx.doi.org/10.2307/3887913.

Méroc, Louis. 1959. "Prémoustériens, Magdaléniens et Gallo-romains dans la caverne de Labouiche (Ariège)." *Gallia Préhistoire* 2 (1): 1–37. http://dx.doi.org/10.3406/galip.1959.1145.

Pfeiffer, John E. 1982. *The Creative Explosion: An Enquiry into the Origins of Art and Religion*. New York: Harper & Row.

Plassard, Jean. 1999. *Rouffignac: Le Sanctuaire des Mammouths*. Paris: Editions du Seuil.

Rouzaud, François. 1978. *La Paléospéléologie: L'Homme et le Milieu souterrain pyrénéen au Paléolithique supérieur*. Archives d'Ecologie Préhistorique 3. Toulouse: Ecole des Hautes Etudes en Sciences Sociales.

Rouzaud, François, Michel Soulier, and Yves Lignereux. 1995. "La Grotte de Bruniquel." *Spelunca* 60: 28–34.

Sharpe, Kevin, and Leslie Van Gelder. 2003. "Children and Palaeolithic "Art": Indications from Rouffignac Cave, France." *International Newsletter on Rock Art* 38: 9–17.

Shaw, Trevor R. 1997. "Historical Introduction." In *Cave Minerals of the World*, ed. Carol A. Hill and Paolo Forti, 27–43. Huntsville, AL: National Speleological Society.

Simonnet, Georges, Louise Simonnet, and Robert Simonnet. 1990. "Art mobilier et art pariétal à Labastide." In *L'Art des Objets au Paléolithique*, Tome 1: *L'art mobilier et son contexte*, ed. Jean Clottes, 173–87. Actes du Colloque de Foix-Le Mas d'Azil 1987, Colloques du Patrimoine. Paris: Ministère de la Culture.

Stone, Andrea. 1997. "Precolumbian Cave Utilization in the Maya Area." In *The Human Use of Caves*, ed. Clive Bonsall and Christopher Tolan-Smith, 201–6. BAR International Series 667. Oxford: Archaeopress.

Whitley, David S., ed. 2001. *Handbook of Rock Art Research*. Walnut Creek, CA: AltaMira Press.

2

Constructed Caves

Transformations of the Underworld in Prehistoric Southeast Italy

Robin Skeates

This chapter examines long-term transformations in the human use and perception of natural and artificial caves, particularly as sacred spaces, between the Upper Paleolithic and the Bronze Age in the Apulia region of Southeast Italy (ca. 34,000 BP–3000 BP/1300 BC) (figure 2.1, table 2.1). It focuses attention on the visual dimensions of the caves: not only their natural features (comprising, for example, durable stone structures in the landscape as well as complex underground formations) but also their cumulative, historically and culturally specific modifications (ranging from special deposits, to parietal art, dry-stone walling, and monumental entrances). In other words, it regards caves as cultural constructs, and, more specifically, as visually expressive and stimulating elements of visual culture, embedded in dynamic cultural processes.

From this perspective, a variety of questions are explored. These refer to the materials and techniques used in the modification and production of natural and artificial caves, the appearance of those caves, their uses and life histories, the social and aesthetic values ascribed to them, their phenomenological impact on viewers, and their contribution to processes of social interaction. More specifically, interpretations of the changing social and symbolic significance of these underground features, and of the ritual performances that led to their creation, are proposed, with reference to a broader cultural context of socioeconomic dynamics.

THE EARLY UPPER PALEOLITHIC: SOCIAL AGGREGATION AND VISUAL COMMUNICATION

The Early Upper Paleolithic dates in Apulia to between around 34,000 and 29,000 BP. This was an important period of transition, linked to the disappearance of the Neanderthals and the appearance of anatomically modern humans in Italy (e.g., Mussi 2001, 167–217). It is thought that the latter, who formed relatively dynamic and mobile hunting groups, but with a low population density, colonized the Italian peninsula from the north. Both populations established a predominantly coastal pattern of settlement, possibly linked to long-distance coastal communication routes. In particular, they occupied selected caves and rockshelters as base camps.

Some of these caves appear to have been established as key places of social aggregation and visual communication. An interesting archaeological contrast can be identified between the most intensively occupied caves, whose deposits contain the earliest sound evidence of the cultural use of visually attractive natural materials, and the less intensively frequented caves, which have so far not produced any "special artifacts." The "art objects" comprise small quantities of perforated seashells and colored iron oxide minerals. These have been found at a few cave sites near Nardò in South Apulia, and further inland at the Grotta del Cavallo (Borzatti von Löwenstern 1963, 1964, 1970; Palma di

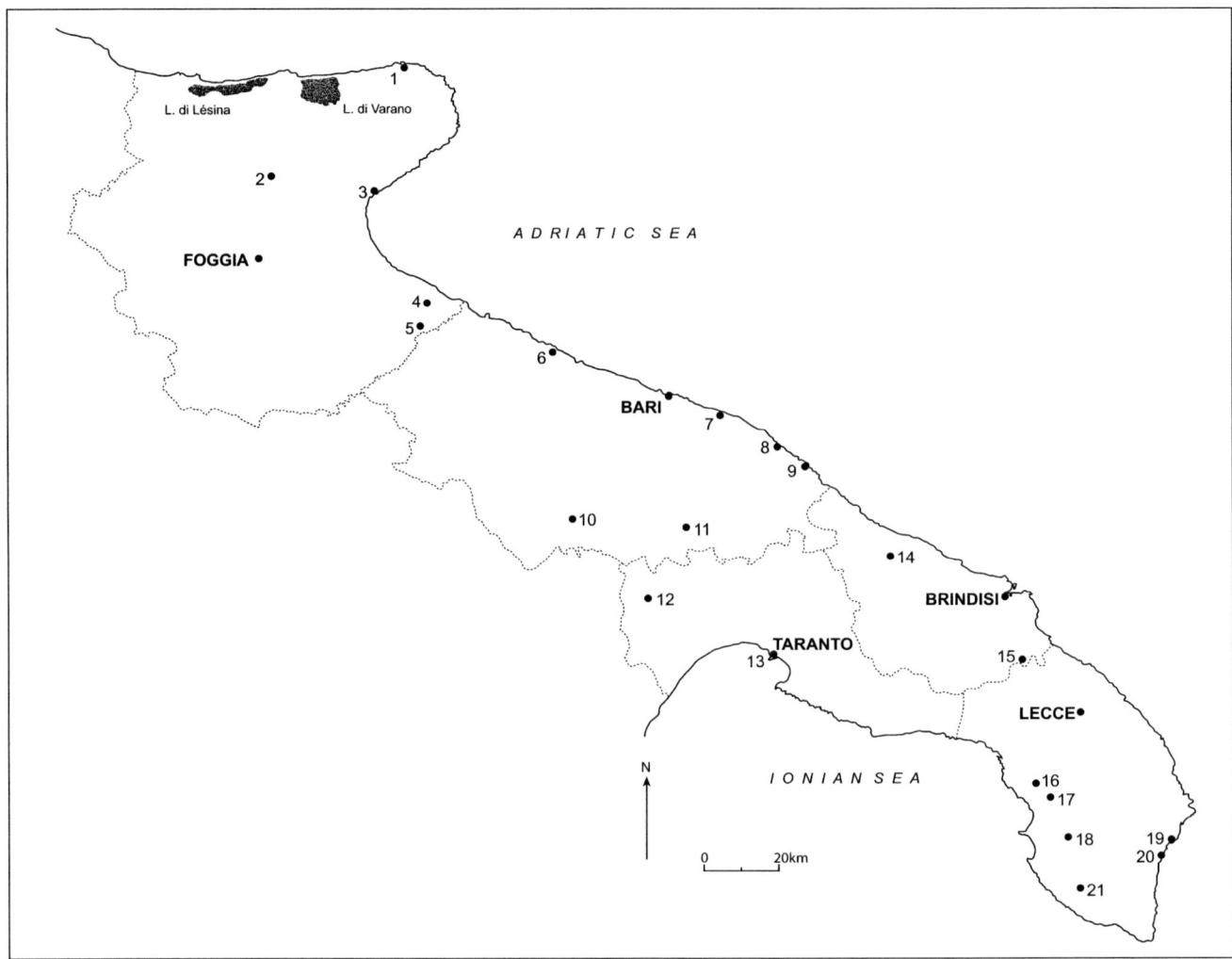

FIGURE 2.1 Sites mentioned in the text. 1. Valle Sbernia and Grottone di Manaccora (Peschici); 2. Grotta Paglicci (Rignano Garganico); 3. Grotta Scaloria (Manfredonia); 4. Madonna di Loreto (Trinitapoli); 5. Terra di Corte (San Ferdinando di Puglia); 6. Grotta di Santa Croce (Bisceglie); 7. Grotta di Cala Colombo and Grotta di Cala Scizzo (Torre a Mare); 8. Manfredi hypogeum, Grotta della Tartaruga and Madonna di Grottole (Polignano a Mare); 9. Grotta delle Mura (Monopoli); 10. Casal Sabini (Altamura); 11. Monte Sannace (Gioia del Colle); 12. Laterza; 13. Pizzone (Taranto); 14. Grotta Santa Maria di Agnano (Ostuni); 15. Cellino San Marco (S. Pietro Vernotico); 16. Grotta del Cavallo and Grotta di Uluzzo (Nardò); 17. Grotta Cappuccini (Galatone); 18. Grotta delle Veneri (Parabita); 19. Grotta di Porto Badisco (Santa Cesárea Terme); 20. Grotta Romanelli and Grotta della Zinzulusa (Castro); 21. Bocca Cesira, Fondo Focone (Ugento).

Cesnola 1965). Unfortunately, the published excavation reports only specify the vertical stratigraphic contexts of these objects, as opposed to their horizontal deposition contexts in relation to the plan of the caves and to other artifacts.

Nevertheless, it may be that these objects were mobilized as elements of body decoration during occasions of social aggregation at key caves, involving group activities and performances whose organization required greater nonverbal communication between members of normally dispersed social networks (Gamble 1999, 268–416). Over time, these caves may also have contributed to the cultural and symbolic construction of the landscape. In particular, generations of mobile and dispersed social groups, particularly colonizing groups of modern humans, may have perceived them as visible and durable shelters, vantage points, and landmarks.

THE MID UPPER PALEOLITHIC: PLACING THE DEAD

The following period is the Mid Upper Paleolithic, which dates in Apulia to between around 28,000 and 20,000 BP. This period saw the recolonization of the Italian peninsula

Period	Archaeological culture/style	Radiocarbon-dated age range
Early Upper Paleolithic	Aurignacian and Uluzzian	34,000–28,000 BP
Mid Upper Paleolithic	Gravettian	28,000–20,000 BP
Late Upper Paleolithic	Early and Evolved Epigravettian	20,000–15,000 BP
Final Upper Paleolithic	Final Epigravettian, Romanellian and Sauveterrian Mesolithic	15,000–7500 BP
Earliest Neolithic	Archaic impressed (and early painted) ware	6100–5800 cal BC
Later Neolithic	Impressed, incised, scratched, and painted wares	5800–4100 cal BC
Final Neolithic	Late Serra d'Alto painted and Diana-Bellavista ware	4100–3900 cal BC
Earlier Copper Age	Piano Conte ware	3900–3100 cal BC
Later Copper Age and Early Bronze Age	Piano Conte and Laterza (Protoapennine A) wares	3100–2300 cal BC
Middle Bronze Age	Protoapennine B, Myceanean Late Helladic II–IIIA and Apennine wares	2300–1200 cal BC

TABLE 2.1 Chronological framework for prehistoric southeast Italy.

FIGURE 2.2 Grotta Paglicci, located in the upper center of the photograph, above the Valle di Settepende and the Tavoliere plain.

by socioeconomically sophisticated human groups, who are thought to have spread southwards in small numbers (e.g., Mussi 2000). Subsistence strategies appear to have been flexibly focused on the hunting of local and migratory species of large mammals. A variety of strategically placed sites was established. At one extreme were small-scale activity sites, such as upland flint-procurement sites. At the other extreme were base camps, including caves with stratified deposits formed by repeated occupations, such as Grotta Paglicci, located on a boundary between the uplands and lowlands (figure 2.2). At the latter, dispersed and mobile groups may have congregated seasonally (possibly during the winter) to share in both everyday and ceremonial activities, as well as to exchange information, food, and partners (cf. Soffer 2000).

The social and symbolic significance of selected caves seems to have been enhanced during this period. In particular, what we now see, archaeologically, is the new formation of visually elaborate mortuary deposits, on different occasions, in selected cave sites also occupied intensively by the living. Good examples come from Grotta Paglicci in North Apulia, Grotta Santa Maria di Agnano in Central Apulia (figure 2.3), and the Grotta delle Veneri in the South (Coppola 1992; Cremonesi, Parenti, and Romano 1972; Mezzena and Palma di Cesnola 1972b, 1989–1990). The mortuary deposits found at these sites generally comprise articulated and intentionally placed bodies, deposited in the inner chambers of caves. They are generally accompanied by relatively large numbers of carefully placed body ornaments, including headdresses covered with ochre paste, deer canines, and seashells, as well as necklaces and bracelets. Some are also closely associated with flint tools. They were generally coated by large quantities of powdered red ochre.

These visually striking mortuary deposits were surely of cultural and symbolic significance. Within the caves, they could have contributed to the symbolic ordering of social space and social relations, by being placed, repeatedly, toward the back of some intensively occupied caves. In this way, they may have helped to put the dead, and more specifically the ancestors, in their place, in relation to the living and the landscape. The caves themselves may also have contributed to the recolonization and cultural reconstruction of the landscape, seen from afar and experienced close up (cf. Bradley 2000; Conkey 1984). They could have helped to generate a more symbolically structured landscape of culturally significant places and pathways, through being occupied and connected by generations of mobile and dispersed socioeconomic groups, and by being actively seen, through their intensive occupation and ritual elaboration, as visible, durable, and ancestral gathering places and resting places, vantage points, landmarks, monuments, and liminal points of contact with the supernatural.

FIGURE 2.3 Grotta Santa Maria di Agnano, located in the center left of the photograph, on the Murge escarpment.

THE LATE UPPER PALEOLITHIC: SYMBOLIC ELABORATION

The next period is the Late Upper Paleolithic, dated in Apulia to between around 20,000 and 15,000 BP. It coincides broadly with the relatively benign environmental context of the "last glacial maximum." This was a period of cultural consolidation and gradual expansion (e.g., Mussi 2001, 219–82). Settlement patterns can again be interpreted in terms of a system of logistical mobility. Certain cave sites were reoccupied. A good example is Grotta Paglicci, which continued to be frequented intensively throughout the Late Upper Paleolithic as a base for the strategic exploitation of local resources and for related symbolic activities.

During this period, the symbolic elaboration of selected caves was taken even further, to the extent that parts of them can now be defined as ritual spaces. For example, in Grotta Paglicci not only were a series of visually striking body ornaments and engraved objects deposited in the cave, but also the very walls of the cave began to be decorated with paintings and incisions (Mezzena and Palma di Cesnola 1972a, 1992). The most elaborate engraved artifact is a fragment of a horse pelvis with incisions clearly delineating the profiles of animals and projectiles. Some cave paintings can probably also be assigned to the same phase of the site's history. The best-dated of these is an exfoliated slab of limestone displaying part of a painted horse. Other paintings occur in situ, in one of the deepest and most inaccessible recesses of the cave complex, that is, in a niche, at the mouth of a small tunnel, in the terminal part of the cave. Details of at least three red and black painted horses have been identified here, together with at least five positive and negative red painted handprints.

As a consequence of these elaborate and primarily naturalistic artistic interventions in Grotta Paglicci, this cave may have taken on, exhibited, and framed additional, new, and more-explicit symbolic meanings, especially during the course of ritual performances in it. The accumulation of painted horses and handprints in this cave is particularly suggestive of repeated ritual practices, which might have addressed a central theme of cooperative large-game hunting. Their location in one of the deepest and most inaccessible recesses of the cave also suggests that, in this particular space, such practices involved a degree of secrecy, heightened sensory experience, and even ritual initiation into special knowledge (Zampetti and Mussi 1991, 154–7). Caves and the artworks displayed within them became, then, a malleable resource that individuals and groups embellished, manipulated, and drew upon (Lewis-Williams 2002).

THE FINAL UPPER PALEOLITHIC: RITUAL SPECIALIZATION

The Final Upper Paleolithic follows, dated in Apulia to between around 15,000 and 7500 BP. This period was associated with the onset of a warmer postglacial climate. It was a period of significant environmental and cultural change (e.g., Mussi 2001, 283–388). Human groups adapted well to new environmental niches, and consequently established more diversified patterns of settlement (Barker 1996). A variety of sites were occupied throughout Apulia. These range from upland caves on the Gargano promontory, to small campsites and rockshelters in the interior of the region, to more numerous and sometimes large open sites and cave sites around the coast. These sites were probably still occupied seasonally, but perhaps some for longer periods, by groups who gradually replaced their traditional specialized hunting economy with diversified systems of hunting, fishing, and gathering. Social networks of interaction, and even small-scale exchange, may also have developed.

During this period, the use of selected rockshelters and caves, both old and new, appears to have become even more specialized in nature. This is indicated by the accumulation within them of sometimes large quantities of artworks, particularly in special deposits, at sites such as Grotta Romanelli (Fabbri, Ingravallo, and Mangia 2003). Small quantities of traditional body ornaments occur. Engraved and painted artworks also appear in greater quantities. Some of these are decorated with naturalistic representations of animals but more frequently they carry abstract linear and geometric motifs, some of which are highly complex. Portable examples include decorated flint cores and cortical flakes, pebbles, pieces of limestone, and bone. A similar but locally specific type of decorated object is represented by some pieces of stalactite found in the Bocca Cesira at Fondo Focone (Segre Naldini and Bidditu 1992). Four fragments of engraved and painted stalactite were found here. In one case the entire surface of the stalactite is covered by groups of intersecting lines, forming a lattice or "weave" pattern that seems to "wrap" the entire stalactite. Parietal examples were generally incised but were occasionally also painted. A few human burials also reappear in the archaeological record.

It is clear that selected rockshelters and caves, both old and new, served as key repositories of visual culture during the Final Upper Paleolithic. Within them, sometimes large quantities of artworks were accumulated, particularly in special deposits. From this, it is tempting to suggest that their use became more specialized in nature, particularly as the number and variety of open sites increased throughout the region. However, the distinction between cave and open sites should not be overstated, particularly since examples of engraved cores and pebbles have been found at both. Instead, it seems appropriate, as in earlier periods, to regard the largest rockshelters and caves as seasonal aggregation sites, used as bases for the strategic exploitation of local resources and as arenas for related social and symbolic activities. On the other hand, all of these aspects probably now became more intensive, elaborate, and varied. This is particularly evident at Grotta Romanelli. Here, in addition to containing deep occupation deposits that provided good evidence of the broad-based strategic exploitation of local resources, the cave walls exhibit both seminaturalistic and abstract motifs, and the cave floors contain an accumulation of stones decorated with matching motifs and human burials.

The idea of ritual performance seems appropriate, particularly to the repeated production and consumption of the portable art objects, but also to the other specialized symbolic activities engaged in at the cave sites (Conkey 1985; Pluciennik 1994). The sheer number of engraved objects, and the repeated reinscribing of many of them—resulting in some deeply grooved lines, densely decorated surfaces, and superimposed motifs, particularly in the Epiromanellian phase (dating to around 8500–7300 BP or 7800–6100 BC)—seems both deliberate and meaningful. So too does their later fragmentation and cumulative deposition in large numbers, in special deposits, including piles, pits, and depressions in selected cave sites. Some of the human and animal remains found in Grotta Paglicci also appear to have been subject to a similar process, involving disarticulation, fragmentation, and selective redeposition. The portability of the decorated objects, indicated by their restricted size, shape, and weight, also seems relevant. It is possible to imagine that, in ritual performances; they were selected, decorated, handled, and inspected, as well as broken and placed in the ground. Furthermore, the making, manipulation, and breaking of visually expressive and stimulating "art," within the distinctive structure of caves and highlighted by engraved and painted parietal decoration, would have made the experience of this ritual process a highly visual one.

We can only guess at the symbolic meanings of such rituals, but the visual materials do provide us with some hints of at least four related themes. One theme, perhaps indicated by the portable art, may have been concerned with enhancing group membership and identity (Conkey

1980). In particular, the stylistic coherence of this material might have been maintained locally in order to emphasize the importance of contacts between members of increasingly separate social groups. The ritual fragmentation and burial of these portable objects might have served a similar purpose, by repeatedly emphasizing the threat of the fragmentation of social relations (Chapman 2000). Social distinctions, on the other hand, might have been pointed out with reference to some of the parietal art, notably the gendered "vulva" and "phallic" symbols.

A second theme, perhaps indicated by the installation art, may have been concerned with defining access to local resources. The ritual production of art at key sites in the landscape, which also served as bases for the exploitation of local resources and as places of social aggregation, might have highlighted the significance of those places to local kin groups. More specifically, the visible and repeated marking of those sites with parietal art, human burials, and other special deposits might have comprised part of a process in which groups increasingly defined and asserted territorial rights over local resources (Lewthwaite 1986, 61).

A third theme, perhaps indicated by the representation of animals, notably aurochs, in some cases associated with projectiles, may refer to hunting. This theme is likely to have had some historic, perhaps even mythical, significance, since it clearly developed out of the figurative art of the Late Upper Paleolithic, which may have remained visible in the painted interior of Grotta Paglicci. However, the meanings of the depicted animals and of hunting may now have been transformed, as their representation became more schematic in the Romanellian phase, and then disappeared, perhaps into abstraction, in the Epiromanellian phase. Perhaps this shift related to a redefinition of the status of large-game hunting, particularly within the context of the development of more diversified postglacial subsistence economies.

A fourth theme, possibly indicated by the band motifs, and in particular by the complex "ribbon" and "weave" motifs engraved on some stones and bones, and by the accumulation of these objects at certain sites, may have highlighted the importance of food gathering and storage. This hypothesis stems from an idea presented by Paolo Graziosi (1973, 36), who suggested that some of the "ribbon-shaped" engraved motifs with "fringes," "tufts," and "knots" might have been abstract representations of intertwined strings netting the stones. The "textile" motifs from the Grotta delle Venere, and the "weave" motif that "wraps" a stalactite from Bocca Cesira, are equally evocative. Could it be that these motifs represented organic containers, such as bags of string and woven textiles? If so, it may be significant that they were directly associated with special objects that were stored and accumulated in large numbers at key sites. Perhaps, then, their decoration and ritual use symbolized the increasingly important collaborative activities of food gathering and storage, particularly at key sites that served as bases for the exploitation of local resources and as foci for social aggregation.

THE EARLIEST NEOLITHIC: TRADITION AND ACCULTURATION

The earliest phase of the Neolithic period in Apulia can be dated to between around 6100 and 5800 BC. This was another period of significant cultural transformation. A degree of cultural continuity and evolution, including greater behavioral specialization, can be claimed to exist, particularly in hunting, fishing, and gathering practices and in related equipment identified at Earliest Neolithic sites. Traditional settlement patterns may also have been maintained, to judge from the continued concentration of sites along the coastal margins. At the same time, a wide range of novel elements of material culture is clearly present at Earliest Neolithic sites in Apulia. All of these can be related, in one way or another, to the appearance of a new cultural "package" of resources, socioeconomic practices, and knowledge relating to early agriculture. Ammerman and Cavalli Sforza (1971) explain this as a process of "demic diffusion," which would have seen small numbers of inherently expansive agricultural settlers advancing westward, carrying with them elements of their own culture. This model may be appropriate to the ditched enclosure sites of the Tavoliere plain in North Apulia. For other parts of Southeast Italy, however, it is possible to argue that the "transition to agriculture" was a gradual and selective process, characterized by at least a degree of cultural continuity between the last hunter-gatherers and the earliest farmers.

This would have involved the spread of new ideas and resources from neighboring groups in the Eastern Adriatic to indigenous groups in Apulia, who continued to adapt their lifestyle, adding stock herding, crop cultivation, and related equipment, when they became available, to their already broad-based and evolving subsistence economies (e.g., Donahue 1992; Whitehouse 1968b, 1971). This process could have taken place within a broader context of intensifying social networks of interaction and exchange, and growing maritime mobility and exploration, which enhanced connections between human groups based in different parts of the Southern Adriatic zone (e.g., Bass 1998).

These patterns of cultural continuity and change are also evident in the use of caves during the Earliest Neolithic, which can now be compared and contrasted with that of contemporary open sites as well as with Paleolithic caves.

FIGURE 2.4 Grotta delle Mura, located on the Adriatic coast.

On the one hand, stratigraphic continuity between Final Upper Paleolithic "Romanellian" and Earliest Neolithic deposits has been claimed by the excavators of some cave sites, such as Grotta delle Mura (figure 2.4) and Grotta di Uluzzo (Borzatti von Löwenstern 1964; Cornaggia Castiglioni and Menghi 1963). However, it is difficult to define just how "continuous" the occupation of these sites actually was. On the other hand, a wide range of novel elements of material culture are present at the cave sites. In addition, further novel elements have been found exclusively at open sites. These include: the carbonized remains of food plants; a wider range of novel tools and ornaments of stone, fired clay, and shell; and a variety of novel settlement features, including a few enclosure ditches, which now give the impression of relatively sedentary residential open sites (Skeates 2000, 176–7).

Furthermore, differences in site-specific practices are hinted at by differences in the deposition of early ceramics at the open and cave sites. At the former, ceramics are characteristically present in "living deposits," sometimes in large quantities, while in caves such as Grotta di Uluzzo relatively few sherds were deposited, notably in pits together with large quantities of mollusk shells. This filling of excavated features with mixed cultural deposits, including fragments of decorated artifacts, can be compared to earlier practices identified in certain Final Upper Paleolithic cave sites.

It is difficult to interpret these patterns, particularly due to the archaeological bias in the region toward the excavation of cave sites for the Upper Paleolithic and open sites for the Neolithic. It may again be possible to regard the large occupied coastal caves as seasonal aggregation sites. They may have continued to be used in a traditional manner, both as bases for the strategic exploitation of local resources and as arenas for related social and symbolic activities. At the same time, these cave-based practices selectively incorporated novel resources, socioeconomic practices, and knowledge relating to early agriculture. However, the use of caves as performative contexts appears to have become slightly less intensive, elaborate, and varied. Indeed, a shift may have occurred in the spatial context within which visual and ritual communication took place, with visual material—such as novel types of body ornaments, decorated ceramics, and special features—becoming more embedded within the fabric of daily life at open residential sites, rather than concentrated in ritual cave contexts.

THE LATER NEOLITHIC: LIMINALITY

The Later Neolithic dates to between around 5800 and 4100 BC in Apulia. Over this period, and in contrast to the Earliest Neolithic, a large body of archaeological data enables us to piece together a more comprehensive picture of socioeconomic practices and patterns in Apulia (e.g., Cremonesi 1979; Geniola 1987; Palma di Cesnola and Vigliardi 1984; Tinè and Simone 1984). The agricultural lifestyle and its material culture, introduced and adopted during the Earliest Neolithic, became fully established during the Later Neolithic. This is clearly reflected at the literally hundreds of Later Neolithic agricultural settlements identified across the region. They are particularly well represented on the Tavoliere plain in North Apulia, where extensive aerial and field survey has identified numerous sites characteristically enclosed by circular ditches (first seen during the Earliest Neolithic), and containing smaller C-shaped "compound" ditches (e.g., Jones 1987). This period also saw the continued intensification of social relations among members of agricultural communities. This is characterized by the development of slightly wider and more-intensive exchange and alliance networks, and of more elaborate and frequent ritual activities, compared to the Final Upper Paleolithic and Earliest Neolithic (Skeates 1993). Within these contexts, certain useful artifacts—such as obsidian blades, small polished serpentinite and jadeite axes, and painted fineware vessels, decorated in interregionally recognizable styles—appear to have been mobilized during the course of social and ceremonial performances, and to have consequently taken on added values. New types of symbolically rich artifacts were also produced, such as ceramic figurines, decorative ceramic stamps (or *pintaderas*), and "face-pots" decorated with anthropomorphic and zoomorphic motifs. New forms of institutionalized social control and power may also have developed at this time, based upon a principle of anteriority in social relations (Skeates 2000). Rituals, for example, may increasingly have involved the demonstration of links to ancestors. The social relations embedded in these activities were probably based, above all, on recognition of the benefits of mutual dependency and of social cohesion to groups that had adopted a fully agricultural lifestyle. However, clearer signs of social differentiation also began to appear in this period, both between communities and within them. In the densely settled northern half of the Tavoliere, for example, a picture of growing intercommunity differentiation is indicated by the formation of some very large residential communities through settlement nucleation, the multiplication and symbolic elaboration of boundary ditches, and the production of locally distinctive fineware styles. At the same time, hints of gender and age differences appear in the archaeological record.

Selected caves were a complementary component of this dynamic Later Neolithic socioeconomic system. These sites tend to be located on the margins of the agricultural landscape, around the edges of the Gargano uplands, along rocky coastlines, on the sides of karstic valleys, and in the Murge. However, they were never far removed, spatially and socially, from contemporary open sites and the mainstream of agricultural life (Skeates 1995b, 1997). Their use was complex and varied, although some general spatial regularities can be identified.

Around their entrances, deep occupation deposits often accumulated, which suggests that many of them served a convenient residential function as shelters, the seasonality of which still needs to be assessed scientifically. Cereals and domesticated animals were certainly consumed at them, if not actually produced in the immediate vicinity, but local resources were also exploited, including a greater range and number of wild fauna compared to open sites.

In the interiors of these caves, special deposits were also often formed. They are characterized by the presence of human remains, pits, hearths, large quantities of grain, animal bones, and pottery sherds, and significant numbers of artifacts with a high symbolic value. These seem to reflect the performance of mortuary rites accompanied by feasting, as well as the ritual "sacrifice" and accumulation of valued objects. They are comparable to the mortuary deposits identified at some contemporary open residential sites, save for the fact that infants and children, and possibly also women, appear to have been buried more commonly in the caves. A prime example is Grotta Scaloria (Quagliati 1936, 118–44; Tinè and Isetti 1975–1980; Winn and Shimabuku 1980). This cave is situated on a lowland plain between the Adriatic coast and the Gargano uplands, close to Grotta di Occhiopinto (figure 2.5). The cave system comprises two main chambers. Scaloria Alta (or Camerone Quagliati) is a large upper chamber lying adjacent to the cave entrance, extending over 80 by 100 meters, with a ceiling some 2 meters high. This space was repeatedly used as a burial chamber during the Later Neolithic. The remains of as many as 137 individuals have been found here, particularly in the deepest part of the chamber.

The deep interior spaces of the largest cave sites, with extensive underground complexes of chambers and corridors, were also visually elaborated by more specialized ritual structures and deposits. Here, human groups exploited and added to the existing natural and visually striking morphologies of the caves (including their walls, passages, floors, fissures, stalagmites, and water pools), inheriting and developing further a traditional way of seeing and ritually experiencing caves previously established in the Upper Paleolithic (Skeates 1991; Whitehouse 1992). Scaloria Bassa provides a unique example from North Apulia. It

FIGURE 2.5 Mouth of Grotta di Occhiopinto, filled by trees, with the Gargano uplands in the background.

comprises a wide lower chamber, which terminates in a small lake, situated beyond and below Scaloria Alta, and reached via a narrow and low gallery. This chamber was used in a more specialized way than the upper one, particularly for the collection of drip water. A hollowed rectangular basin was identified in the center of the sloping area of the chamber. This appears to have been used to collect the water dripping from the stalactites on the roof. Around this were found groups of pottery vessels, some still whole. All of these lay close to truncated stalagmites, some even on top of the base of the broken stalagmites. Traces of a large hearth, with the remains of partially burnt animal bones, were also found close to the basin, and a couple of human burials were also placed in natural fissures in the lower cave.

Another example is provided by the Grotta di Santa Croce near Bisceglie in Central Apulia (Boscato, Gambassini, and Ronchitelli 2002; Radina 2002). This large natural cave lies on the edge of a stream valley. It comprises a wide rockshelter and a long corridor. A small group of red painted starburst motifs are visible on the side wall, 3.4 meters above the present floor level, and 14 meters in from the entrance. Special deposits have also been identified deep inside the cave, about 60 meters along the corridor. A large, coil-built, woven basket, filled with burnt grains of barley, placed on the floor, looks like a ritual offering. Some broken vessels of elaborately impressed and incised ware, found nearby in a pair of small hollows, are also thought to have been used to collect stillicide water (as at Grotta Scaloria). Farther south, two much more elaborately decorated cave complexes have been found in the Salento peninsula, near Santa Cesárea Terme. The best known is the Grotta di Porto Badisco (or "Grotta dei Cervi") (Graziosi 1980; Guerri 1993; Lo Porto 1976). This site is today located on the top of a low hillslope, which overlooks a small coastal inlet. Like Grotta Scaloria, its location is visible and accessible, and it would have lain within easy reach of contemporary settlements (indicated by the presence of Later Neolithic pottery on the surrounding plateau). However, when entered, the great extent, complexity, and, in some parts, inaccessibility of this underground system is surprising, with its four main branching corridors extending over a total distance of around 850 meters. The morphology of these corridors varies from relatively large chambers (6–10 meters wide and 4–8 meters high), to restricted passages (1–3 meters high and 1–2 meters wide), some sections of which are only negotiable by crawling. This cave was first occupied and decorated during the Final Upper Paleolithic. It was then reoccupied during the Middle Neolithic, from around 5600 to about 5250 BC, through the Late Neolithic and up to the Copper Age.

During this period, and perhaps especially during the Late Neolithic, the cave complex was modified further, particularly by paintings, which have been identified in twelve morphologically distinctive zones along three of the main corridors. The paintings are colored black-brown and red. According to scientific analyses, the dark pigment is bat guano, a rich deposit of which exists in one part of the cave, while the red is derived from ochre materials (Cipriani and Magaldi 1979). The paintings combine schematic figures with abstract geometric and curvilinear motifs. They are dominated, numerically and spatially, by hunting scenes, some of which occupy central positions within particular decorated zones. However, the range of abstract motifs is wide and varied, and includes some distinctive geometric and curvilinear motifs. According to statistical analyses of the distribution of particular motifs along the corridors, some spatial contrasts and patterns were established within the cave complex (Albert 1982; Graziosi 1980; Whitehouse 1992).

Particular spaces in the cave were further elaborated and demarcated by carefully constructed special features and deposits. Part of the second corridor may have been artificially widened. Simple dry-stone walls were constructed. Steps were cut into the deposits filling the entrance passage. Some natural circular cavities in the floor of the cave appear to have been artificially widened, and many were refilled with numerous sherds of pottery. Stepping-stones were laid across the pool of stillicide water. Pits were dug just inside the entrance to the cave, and later filled and overlain by a layer of dark brown ashy soil, which contained some quite sizeable deposits of carbonized grain, a few bones, stone artifacts, and pottery sherds. Large quantities of pottery vessels and sherds were also deliberately deposited at the foot of the painted walls.

Such deep interior spaces still create an awe-inspiring sense of "otherness" and may well have been regarded as "liminal" places in the past, providing a point of contact between the lived-in and supernatural worlds. With the exception of the paintings placed relatively close to the entrance to the Grotta di Santa Croce, which may have alerted visitors to the ritual significance of the cave's interior, these special features were clearly not intended for open viewing, since they were situated in the most inaccessible (deepest, darkest, and most restricted) parts of the underground cave complexes in Grotta Scaloria and the Grotta di Porto Badisco. Indeed, a degree of ritual secrecy, characterized by socially restricted and controlled access to key symbolism and knowledge, is likely to have surrounded their production and consumption (Whitehouse 1990, 1992). More specifically, they may even have been associated with initiation rites, involving the induction of successive generations into different levels of secret, powerful, religious, ancestral knowledge. As part of this process, constraints may have been placed on women and children in terms of their access to the hidden interiors of these caves. This interpretation seems particularly appropriate to the painted Grotta di Porto Badisco, with its increasingly abstract symbolism the deeper one moves into the cave, and its group of painted juvenile handprints situated halfway along the second corridor.

Such features might be regarded, more generally, as characteristic elements of a distinctive "cave cult," which developed throughout the south-central Mediterranean during the Neolithic (Whitehouse 1992, 2–3). However, locally specific practices and meanings are also likely to have been expressed (Skeates 1995b). In Grotta Scaloria in the North, for example, specific ritual concerns with death and "abnormal" water may have been expressed. These might have related to specific agrarian concerns over the fertility, health, and productivity of people, crops, and stock on the adjacent densely settled Tavoliere plain. In the Grotta di Porto Badisco in the South, on the other hand, a slightly different set of ritual concerns may have been expressed through the reuse of a Paleolithic ritual cave, the recurrent representation of the male hunting of wild deer, the representation of animal–human hybrids, the repeated deposition of crops in the form of burnt offerings in the entrance to the cave, the confining of female symbols to the first decorated zone of the cave, and the group of juvenile handprints in the interior. These powerful images might have related to tensions within local indigenous groups with a hunter-gatherer ancestry surrounding their full transition to an agricultural way of life, including the gender- and age-based division of labor within this.

This period also saw the construction of what might be regarded as the earliest artificial cave in the region. The Manfredi hypogeum, at Santa Barbara near Polignano a Mare, is a unique Late Neolithic ritual feature, partly mortuary in nature (Geniola 1987, 1995). This artificial underground complex was dug into the inner side of a Late Neolithic settlement enclosure ditch, into the limestone bedrock. It is 9 meters long and has a symmetrical plan. A sloping access ramp (or *dromos*) leads to two underground chambers: a small elliptical "antechamber" and a large "back room," linked by a short central corridor with a square section and a step in the floor. Deer skulls were arranged along the walls of the dromos and first chamber, while small niches and a cross-shaped symbol were engraved in the walls of the second chamber. A small trench containing a deposit of human remains was also found in a lobe of the back room. The hypogeum also contained a stratified deposit, containing faunal and artifactual remains, possibly derived from ritual feasting.

An even more sophisticated pattern of cave use and perception was established, then, in the Later Neolithic, which incorporated as well as separated the underworld in relation to the landscape and local patterns of agricultural life. The entrance chambers of natural caves appear to have continued to be used in a traditional manner, as convenient shelters for the strategic exploitation of local resources. Cave interiors, on the other hand, appear to have been reestablished and further transformed—physically, symbolically, and conceptually—as powerful sacred spaces, during the course of increasingly elaborate and distinctive liminal ritual performances.

THE FINAL NEOLITHIC: THE REINVENTION OF TRADITION

The Final Neolithic period in Apulia dates to between around 4100 and 3900 BC. This phase is marked archaeologically by evidence of both cultural continuity and innovation in the region (e.g., Cremonesi 1979; Geniola 1979; Palma di Cesnola 1985; Palma di Cesnola and Vigliardi 1984). Site patterns indicate the continued but less-intensive occupation of the coastal lowlands, as well as an extension of settlement inland into hilly areas (Whitehouse 1984, 1114). Daily life appears to have generally followed a traditional pattern, although a few significant developments also took place. For example, it seems clear that the tradition of ditch digging ceased when the Later Neolithic ditched-enclosure sites were abandoned. Mixed farming continued to be practiced. A familiar range of tools were manufactured and used, with the addition of a few new projectile points. An increase in the quantity of imported obsidian and polished stone found at sites in Apulia, as well as the development of a greater degree of stylistic uniformity in potting and mortuary practices between sites, also indicate a strengthening and reorientation of long-distance interaction and exchange networks (e.g., Robb 1999; Skeates 1993).

In this context, caves continued to be used for a range of activities. Some large caves were again occupied as residential sites, particularly in the more traditional South. Other caves, situated close to contemporary residential sites, continued to be used as burial places for relatively large numbers of both adults and children. These are generally characterized by disturbed primary burials, accompanied by grave goods and other special deposits. They are similar in style and scale to the mortuary deposits found at open cemetery sites, but contain greater quantities of food-related remains, which probably derived from mortuary feasts. For example, Scaloria Alta continued to be used as a burial cave during the Final Neolithic. Another burial cave was newly established in Grotta di Cala Colombo, situated on the Adriatic coast near Torre a Mare (De Lucia et al. 1977). Here, the walls of a natural cave entrance appear to have been enlarged artificially to form an elaborate multicellular chamber. A few underground sites situated along the Adriatic coast were also used as special, nonmortuary structures, in which ritual performances involved the creation of some distinctive structural features and objects rather than human remains. For example, the elaborately decorated and structured Grotta di Porto Badisco may have been further transformed at this time. Grotta di Cala Scizzo, on the other hand, was first occupied in this period (Geniola and Tunzi 1980). The deep interior of this cave was transformed into a ritual space at an early stage through the modification of a natural hollow into an artificial basin, surrounded by a large dry-stone platform, within which were embedded some rare artworks.

The rock-cut Manfredi hypogeum continued to be used during the Final Neolithic. At the same time, a new kind of artificial underground mortuary structure was established. It is represented by an oven-shaped "rock-cut" tomb found at Arnesano (Lo Porto 1972). It comprised a small cylindrical chamber with an access pit, dug into the soft clay and sand terrain. The pit was sealed by a large limestone slab. Within the tomb, the body of an adult had been laid out on the floor of the chamber, in a crouched position. Grave goods were placed on one side of the body, including three plain pottery vessels and a stone "idol." The form of this oven-shaped tomb seems, on first impression, to be exotic (e.g., Walter 1988, 153). Nevertheless, it is not that different from earlier and contemporary mortuary structures found in Apulia. Regional precedents for it are provided by the burial cavities and hypogeum cut into the sides of ditches and the artificial caves of the Later Neolithic, not to mention the natural caves used for burials since the Upper Paleolithic (Whitehouse 1972). It is also comparable in size to the contemporary earth- and rock-cut pit and trench graves of the Taranto province.

These liminal underground places probably continued to be used for the performance of agrarian and initiation rituals, although their use as burial caves seems to have gradually increased at this time. Slightly more specialized assemblages of portable artifacts were also deposited at them. These mainly comprise either tools used in the preparation and serving of ritual feasts, ritual paraphernalia, or valuable objects of exchange and display "sacrificed" in special deposits. These transformations, introduced into traditional ritual performances in the caves, presumably by ritual leaders, may have been intended to establish even stronger reciprocal relations between members of living kin groups, their ancestors, and the supernatural.

THE COPPER AGE: SOCIAL AND RITUAL ELABORATION

The Copper Age remains a poorly defined period of Southeast Italian prehistory (Cazzella 1994). As a rough guide, the Earlier Copper Age may date to between around 3900 and 3100 BC, and the Later Copper Age and Early Bronze Age to between around 3100 and 2300 BC. The period as a whole is clearly characterized by continued cultural developments. Settlement and subsistence patterns expanded along similar lines to those established during the Final Neolithic. A growing number of aboveground special-purpose ritual sites developed, including statue stelae, menhirs, and rock engravings. Social dynamics also developed trends previously established during the Final Neolithic in Apulia (e.g., Skeates 1995a, 293–4; Whitehouse 1968a). For example, long-distance maritime and overland networks of interaction and exchange were maintained, expanded, and intensified. In particular, the use of a widely shared set of mortuary practices and symbols, and the circulation of some valuable artifacts (including some made of copper), reflect strengthened connections within the Mediterranean (Biancofiore 1987). Participation in a socioeconomic "tournament" may have lain at the heart of these developments. In this, prestige may have been won by leaders and their supporters through ceremonially advertising their control over local groups, territories, and resources, and their contacts with "exotic" (supernatural and distant) people, places, and things. It may be as a consequence of this tournament that the archaeological record provides growing signs of socioeconomic instability and competition, played out on different geographical and social scales between regional "cultures," territorially based communities, and kin-based burial groups.

In line with these developments, the human use of natural caves continued to evolve during the Copper Age. Some of these caves may have served as habitations, and in particular as base camps for herders and hunters. More commonly, however, they were used as places for the performance of rituals, including more visually elaborate funerary rites. These focused attention on the successive, collective, primary burial of relatives, especially adults but also some children (the latter sometimes spatially segregated). They were also accompanied by larger collections of valued goods. Particularly rich mortuary deposits were found in Grotta Cappuccini in South Apulia (Ingravallo 2002). This is a small natural cave, 11 meters long by 4 meters wide, located on the side of a large valley near Galatone. Spit 7, comprising the earliest and main cultural deposit in the cave, and containing human and animal bones, charcoal, a small flat stone smeared with red ochre, tools, ornaments, and ceramics. Three radiocarbon-dated samples of human bone provide a date range of around 2550 to 2350 BC. The human bones were found in a disarticulated, fragmented, and partially burnt state, partly as a result of old burials having been pushed toward the back to the cave to make space for new ones. A minimum of 311 individuals were buried there, comprising about two-thirds adults and one-third juveniles and children. These and other caves sometimes also contain special, possibly votive, deposits of valuable artifacts, not directly associated with burials, particularly in South Apulia. The most obvious example comes from the Grotta della Zinzulusa, which is well known today for its fantastic stalagmite and stalactite formations (Zecca 1984). Here, a special deposit of eleven ceramic vessels was recovered from one of the small lakes in the cave. They had been deposited along the edge of the natural basin. They have been interpreted as having been used in a water-related cult, like the Later Neolithic vessels placed under the stalactites in the Grotta Scaloria.

Artificial rock-cut tombs increased in number during the Copper Age, and especially during the Later Copper Age. Although they are normally described as "rock-cut," most were actually dug into soft bedrock, and a few were dug into compact sand and clay deposits. They have been found in small cemetery groups of between one and five tombs, at least some of which may have been situated close to settlement sites. The best-known Copper Age examples come from Central Apulia: at Monte Sannace near Gioia del Colle, Casal Sabini near Altamura, Cellino San Marco, Pizzone, and along the Valle delle Rose near Laterza (Biancofiore 1967, 1979; Biancofiore and Ponzetti 1957; Gervasio 1913, 77–94; Lo Porto 1962–1963). The forms of these tombs vary considerably, although some broadly shared features can be identified. They comprise artificially excavated, small, circular or oval, underground chambers. There is normally just one chamber. In section, some of these chambers have a flat floor and a domed roof. These spaces were accessible from above but sealed at their entrance, usually by a single square stone slab. A broad distinction can be drawn between those tombs accessed via a vertical "manhole" or steeply sloping cylindrical pit, and others accessed via a gently sloping passage (dromos). The number and disposition of human remains deposited within these tombs also varies, although general patterns can again be identified. Some chambers contained just one or two articulated bodies. Other tombs contained the remains of numerous individuals. At Cellino San Marco, for example, Chamber A contained thirty-five articulated skeletons, and Chamber B contained forty-one skeletons. These individuals appear to have been originally deposited in the form of primary inhumations. At Laterza, however, some of the bodies appear to have been disturbed by secondary burial practices, leading to the disarticulation of skeletons and the arrangement of some skulls along the end walls of the chamber. Each individual appears to have been accompanied by a few ornaments, tools, and pots. A few domesticated- and wild-animal bones and ashes, perhaps comprising the remains of mortuary feasts and food offerings, were also identified in some tombs. To this broad group of rock-cut tombs can also be added an abandoned flint mine reused in the Later Copper Age as a burial place, situated on a hillslope in the Valle Sbernia near Peschici on the Gragano promontory (Sublimi Saponetti 1991). Both the form of the mine and the nature of the mortuary deposits found within it are comparable to those of the rock-cut tombs.

Various meanings could have been expressed during the course of these underground rituals. The deposition of the dead away from settlements, in special-purpose mortuary sites, may reflect a strategic move by members of different families to bury their deceased relatives away from the *community*-based settlements within which they resided, in order to maintain and demonstrate their distinct *kin*-based identities (Skeates 1995c, 231–2). Successive burials in the same place may then have expressed the continuity and cohesion of members of the descent groups to whom those sites belonged, including their ancestors, the newly deceased, and their living relatives (Malone 1996, 54). At the same time, the prestigious social status, influence, wealth, and power of selected deceased individuals, and their mourners, may have been signaled through the public accumulation, display, and sacrifice of socially and symbolically valued portable grave goods (Skeates 1995a, 294–5; Whitehouse 1992, 171). Nonmortuary rituals performed in natural caves, which, like the burials at these sites, involved the votive deposition of valuable gifts, may also have expressed a desire to ensure the maintenance of beneficial reciprocal relations with spirits thought to dwell in the underworld.

THE MIDDLE BRONZE AGE: MONUMENTALIZATION

The Middle Bronze Age in Apulia dates to between around 2300 and 1200 BC. This period is characterized by patterns of continuity combined with significant developments. Settlement patterns in Apulia clearly exhibit these combined trends (e.g., Cazzella 1998; Gravina 1999; Tunzi Sisto 1996). In both coastal and inland zones, large settlements of long duration developed, situated in naturally defended positions, some augmented by artificial fortifications that dominated key communications routes and/or territories containing valued economic resources. Signs of growing settlement differentiation are also provided by new contrasts between some of the larger sedentary settlements supporting diversified economies, and smaller, shorter-lived sites situated in adjacent strategic but less-dominant locations and perhaps associated with more-restricted and possibly seasonal economic activities. Outside living areas, assemblages of relatively varied and valuable objects, accompanied by food and human remains, were deposited in increasingly monumental special-purpose ritual sites, including underground natural caves, artificial underground rock-cut tombs and hypogea, and aboveground tumuli covering dolmens or passage graves.

Social dynamics developed along similar lines to those established during the Final Neolithic and Copper Age in Apulia. However, they also became more intense, leading to greater extremes of socioeconomic integration and instability, competition, and violence, and at least a modest degree of social differentiation by the end of the period (Cazzella 1998; Malone, Soddart, and Whitehouse 1993; Moscoloni 1987). Arguably, an ever-expanding long-distance maritime and overland network of interaction, exchange, and social integration lay at the heart of these developments (e.g., Cazzella 1998, 18–19). Within this, local leaders and their supporters appear to have competed more aggressively to win prestige and power, particularly by advertising their control over local groups, territories, and resources, and their contacts with "exotic" (supernatural and distant) people, places, and things.

A few natural caves and rockshelters continued to be occupied throughout the region, and modified during the performance of rituals, but to a lesser extent than in the Copper Age. In the North, rich mortuary deposits have been found in a cave known as the Grottone di Manaccora near Peschici (Baumgärtel 1951, 1953). It is located at the western end of the Manaccore bay, at the base of a limestone promontory (the Punta Manaccore), and is protected from the sea by a high sand dune (figure 2.6). Given that a contemporary and (to judge from the ceramics found at both sites) clearly related settlement was located on this promontory, it may be that the underlying burial cave was perceived as a kind of liminal "underworld." It is a large cave, with a broad entrance, some 18 meters wide, and a main chamber leading to two smaller corridors, extending up to about 49 meters in depth. Mortuary deposits have so far been uncovered in four different areas along the cave walls, and especially toward the back of the cave. Access to the innermost "funerary cleft" appears to have been restricted by a wooden structure, indicated by numerous postholes, and by a dry-stone wall constructed at the entrance to

FIGURE 2.6 The Grottone di Manaccora (center left, at the end of the beach) and Punta Manaccore, on the Adriatic coast.

the passage. This area contained exclusively adult human remains, and also the richest grave goods found in the cave. In Central Apulia, the much smaller Grotta della Tartaruga provides an example of a previously occupied cave site that may have been architecturally elaborated during the Middle Bronze Age (Coppola and Radina 1985). Here, four small oval chambers were cut into the walls of the central natural cavity, which made the cave look more regular and monumental. The body of an infant was buried in the first of these chambers. Further south again, a special deposit of two bronze axes comes from the Grotta della Zinzulusa, one of which was decorated (Blanc 1958–1961).

Rock-cut tombs also continued to be constructed during the Middle Bronze Age, particularly in more-traditional Central and South Apulia (e.g., Drago 1954–1955; Orlando 1995). They are generally located in prominent positions in the landscape, within sight of the coast, and up to about 12 kilometers inland from it. In North Apulia, however, rock-cut tombs appear to have evolved into hypogea, with more marked entrances, elongated access corridors, and enlarged chambers. At Terra di Corte near San Ferdinando di Puglia, a complex of at least twelve Middle Bronze Age hypogea has been discovered (Tunzi Sisto 1999). The forms of these hypogea are varied, but share some general features. They tend to be linear in arrangement, varying in total length from around 11 to 29 meters. They may have been entered initially via some kind of wooden structure. They then continue with one or two long, narrow, access corridors. Their initial, steeply sloping sections are often revetted and covered by stone slabs. These corridors lead to a small entrance hole or chamber. This, in turn, leads to a large rectangular or subcircular chamber (5–15 meters long and 3 meters wide). The roof of this chamber, which sometimes comprises a barrel vault, is perforated by one or more circular pits, interpreted as ventilation shafts.

These chambers also appear to have been separated and divided by wooden structures, represented by postholes and, in one case, a small stone pillar. Special deposits were formed within these structures, as a result of a variety of ritual practices, which may have included secondary burial rites, ritual feasts, and rites of closure. The main chambers contained the richest and most varied deposits. Special deposits also sometimes accumulated in the access corridors. Piles of stones were eventually used to seal the entrances to the hypogea.

A similar complex of at least five Middle Bronze Age rock-cut hypogea has been found at Madonna di Loreto near Trinitapoli, not far from Terra di Corte (Tunzi Sisto 1999, 183–316). This was previously the site of a ditched settlement during the Later Neolithic. All of the hypogea appear to have followed the line of the original enclosure ditch, whose sunken surface presumably remained visible in the landscape. The elaborate "Hypogeum of the Bronzes" is the best known of these. It was first established as a non-mortuary ritual space, then sealed, and later reused and modified as a burial place throughout the Middle Bronze Age. It contained the remains of around 200 individuals. Their bodies were originally deposited as primary burials. Age- and gender-specific artifacts were often closely associated with these bodies, as well as large-animal bones interpreted as food offerings. Care was evidently taken not to disturb earlier burials. Burning torches, indicated by the presence of charcoal (and the absence of hearths and ashes), helped to illuminate this ritual process.

A series of contrasts can be identified between the mortuary deposits found in different parts of the hypogeum, which seem to have developed over space and time. Essentially, these patterns might be interpreted in terms of a shift in the social use of the hypogeum from the burial place of a kin-based group, to a burial place dominated by the bodies of a less-closely-related warrior class of men. Another underground structure, comprising an artificially modified natural cave at Madonna di Grottole near Polignano a Mare, might be regarded as a Southern relative of the North Apulian hypogea (Cardini 1948; Tunzi Sisto and Langella 1995). The main cave chamber has a trilobate plan, and is preceded by an access corridor with a shallow slope. The use of this site has been plausibly interpreted in terms of the ritual preparation and consumption of food, and compared to the evidence of ritual feasting at contemporary rock-cut tombs.

These underground structures may not have been particularly visible from a distance, but they do appear to have been ascribed a growing visual significance during the Middle Bronze Age. Grander entrances, comprising rock-cut façades, wooden doorways, and stone-lined access passages, were constructed at some of them. Their entrances were further elaborated during the course of mortuary rites, which led to the formation of symbolically rich deposits within them. Rituals appear to have commonly involved feasting and fragmentation, as well as occasional sacrifices of valuable artifacts. Mortuary rituals shared these features but also involved the incrementally collective deposition of the bodies of selected individuals, accompanied by a wide range of personal goods, presumably regarded as being of use to them in the afterlife. Rituals of closure were performed at some of these sites, particularly when they became filled with mortuary deposits. Many of these underground ritual sites were also located in prominent vantage points in the landscape. Views from them may therefore have played a part in the embodied rituals that were repeatedly performed at them. A variety of meanings could have been expressed at them. On the one hand, traditional but publicly visible ritual themes may have been expressed at them, through their establishment in liminal places and during successive gatherings and rituals enacted around their entrances. These may have made particular reference to: the power of the ancestors contained within their mortuary deposits; their membership of different kin-, gender-, and aged-based groups; their well-being and material wealth; the durability and strength of their living descent groups; and the history of their territories (Malone, Stoddart, and Whitehouse 1993, 186–8; Whitehouse 1995, 85). On the other hand, their dramatic mortuary rituals and architecture might have reinforced social distinctions between audiences positioned outside them and selected individuals allowed to enter and reorder their hidden and spatially structured interiors (cf. Thomas 1993).

CONCLUSION

Through this case-study of natural and artificial caves in prehistoric Southeast Italy, I have explored how successive generations selectively created, occupied, sacralized, and transformed the underworld in the process of constructing themselves. This process was culturally constrained by a respect for convention and tradition. However, through a variety of social and visual practices, caves were gradually ascribed old and new functions, meanings, and values, particularly at times of profound socioeconomic disruption, conflict, and change. In the Upper Paleolithic, they appear to have been established as bases for the exploitation of local resources and as key places of social aggregation and visual communication. Initially they may have been seen as durable residential shelters, vantage points, and landmarks, but later they may also have increasingly been perceived as performative ritual spaces, burial places, ancestral gathering places, monuments, and liminal points of contact with the supernatural. In the Neolithic, Copper, and Bronze Ages, these traditional values continued to be applied to natural caves, and also extended to a new range of elaborately modified and artificial caves, although access to their powerful ritual symbolism appears to have become increasingly socially restricted and controlled. In this way, these physically durable but conceptually malleable structures were actively used by people, across space and time, to perceive the world around them and to reproduce their social lives. They helped them to establish personal and collective boundaries, identities, and relationships, to acquire and exercise power, to promote ideologies, and to contest them, particularly in response to key social tensions. This was generally a subtle process, embedded in the routine experiences of life and landscape. However, on special occasions it was displayed and also concealed more overtly, marked by repeated ritual performances in culturally significant caves.

REFERENCES CITED

Albert, Eliette. 1982. "Étude statistique des figurations de la Grotte de Porto Badisco." *Rivista di Scienze Preistoriche* 37: 217–22.

Ammerman, Albert. J., and Luca L. Cavalli Sforza. 1971. "Measuring the Rate of Spread of Early Farming in Europe." *Man* 6 (4): 674–88. http://dx.doi.org/10.2307/2799190.

Barker, Graeme. 1996. "Early Holocene Environments and Subsistence Strategies in the Mediterranean Basin." In *International Union of Prehistoric and Protohistoric Sciences*, vol. 7: *The Mesolithic*, ed. Stefan K. Kozlowski and Carlo Tozzi, 105–12. Forli: ABACO.

Bass, Bryon. 1998. "Early Neolithic Offshore Accounts: Remote Islands, Maritime Exploitations, and the Trans-Adriatic Cultural Network." *Journal of Mediterranean Archaeology* 11: 165–90.

Baumgärtel, Elise J. 1951. "The Cave of Manaccora, Monte Gargano." *Papers of the British School at Rome* 19: 23–38.

Baumgärtel, Elise J. 1953. "The Cave of Manaccora, Monte Gargano, Part II: The Contents of the Three Archaeological Strata." *Papers of the British School at Rome* 21: 1–31.

Biancofiore, Franco. 1967. "La necropoli eneolitica di Laterza: origini e sviluppo dei gruppi 'protoappenninici' in Apulia." *Origini* 1:195–300.

Biancofiore, Franco. 1979. "La civiltà eneolitica di Laterza." In *La Puglia dal Paleolitico al Tardoromano*, ed. D. Adamesteanu, 128–49. Milano: Electa.

Biancofiore, Franco. 1987. "Per la storia delle comunità peucetiche tra il XX–XI Sec. a.Cr." In *Atti della XXV Riunione Scientifica dell'Istituto Italiano di Preistoria e Protostoria: Preistoria e Protostoria della Puglia Centrale*, ed. Anna Revedin, 87–108. Firenze: Istituto Italiano di Preistoria e Protostoria.

Biancofiore, Franco, and Francesco M. Ponzetti. 1957. "Tomba di tipo siculo con nuovo osso a globuli nel territorio di Altamura (Bari)." *Bullettino di Paletnologia Italiana* 66: 153–88.

Blanc, Alberto C. 1958–1961. "Relazione sulle osservazioni e ricerche stratigrafiche eseguite nella Grotta Zinzulusa (Castro Marina, Lecce) e sull'esito di alcuni sopraluoghi nel Salento: 22 dicembre 1958–5 gennaio 1959." *Quaternaria* 5: 330–4.

Borzatti von Löwenstern, Edoardo. 1963. "La Grotta di Uluzzo: Campagna di scavi 1963." *Rivista di Scienze Preistoriche* 18: 75–89.

Borzatti von Löwenstern, Edoardo. 1964. "La Grotta di Uluzzo: campagna di scavi 1964." *Rivista di Scienze Preistoriche* 19: 41–52.

Borzatti von Löwenstern, Edoardo. 1970. "Prima campagna di scavi nella grotta 'Mario Bernardini' (Nardò, Lecce)." *Rivista di Scienze Preistoriche* 25: 89–125.

Boscato, Paolo, Paolo Gambassini, and Annamaria Ronchitelli. 2002. "Una stuoia in fibre vegetali del Neolitico Antico nella Grotta Santa Croce." In *La Preistoria della Puglia: Paesaggi, Uomini e Tradizioni di 8,000 Anni Fa*, ed. Francesca Radina, 71–76. Bari: Mario Adda Editore.

Bradley, Richard. 2000. *An Archaeology of Natural Places*. London: Routledge.

Cardini, Luigi. 1948. "Abitati preistorici dei dintorni di Polignano a Mare (Bari)." *Rivista di Scienze Preistoriche* 3: 269.

Cazzella, Alberto. 1994. "Dating the 'Copper Age' in the Italian Peninsula and Adjacent Islands." *European Journal of Archaeology* 2(1): 1–19.

Cazzella, Alberto. 1998. "Il versante adriatico della Puglia durante l'Età del Bronzo: Appunti per una sintesi." In *Documenti dell'Età del Bronzo: Ricerche lungo il Versante Adriatico Pugliese*, ed. Angela Cinquepalmi and Francesca Radina, 17–22. London: Schena Editore.

Chapman, John C. 2000. *Fragmentation in Archaeology: People, Places and Broken Objects in the Prehistory of South Eastern Europe*. London: Routledge.

Cipriani, Niccolo and Donatello Magaldi. 1979. "Composizione mineralogica delle pitture della Grotta di Porto Badisco." *Rivista di Scienze Preistoriche* 34: 263–67.

Conkey, Margaret W. 1980. "Context, Structure and Efficacy in Palaeolithic Art and Design." In *Symbol as Sense: New Approaches to the Analysis of Meaning*, ed. Mary LeCron Foster and Stanley H. Brandes, 225–48. New York: Academic Press.

Conkey, Margaret W. 1984. "To Find Ourselves: Art and Social Geography of Prehistoric Hunter Gatherers." In *Past and Present in Hunter Gatherer Studies*, ed. Carmel Schrire, 253–76. New York: Academic Press.

Conkey, Margaret W. 1985. "Ritual Communication, Social Elaboration, and the Variable Trajectories of Palaeolithic Material Culture. In *Prehistoric Hunter-Gatherers: The Emergence of Cultural Complexity*, ed. T. Douglas Price and James A. Brown, 299–323. New York: Academic Press.

Coppola, Donato. 1992. "Nota preliminare sui rinvenimenti nella grotta di S. Maria di Agnano (Ostuni, Brindisi): I seppellimenti paleolitici ed il luogo di culto." *Rivista di Scienze Preistoriche* 44: 211–27.

Coppola, Donato, and Francesca Radina. 1985. "Grotta della Tartaruga di Lama Giotta (Torre a Mare–Bari) e la sequenza stratigrafica del Saggio A." *Taras* 5: 229–82.

Cornaggia Castiglioni, Luciano Ottavio, and Luciano Menghi. 1963. "Grotta delle Mura, Monopoli. II: paletnologia dei livelli olocenici." *Rivista di Scienze Preistoriche* 18: 117–54.

Cremonesi, Giuliano. 1979. "Il Neolitico e l'Inizio dei Metalli nel Salento." In *La Puglia dal Paleolitico al Tardoromano*, ed. Dinu Adamesteanu, 94–120. Milano: Electa.

Cremonesi, Giuliano, Raffaello Parenti, and Silvana Romano. 1972. "Scheletri paleolitici della Grotta delle Veneri presso Parabita (Lecce)." In *Atti della XIV Riunione Scientifica dell'Istituto Italiano di Preistoria e Protostoria in Puglia*, Istituto Italiano di Preistoria e Protostoria, 105–117. Firenze: Istituto Italiano di Preistoria e Protostoria.

De Lucia, A., D. Ferri, Alfredo Geniola, C. Giove, M. Maggiore, Nicola Melone, Vittorio Delfino Pesce, P. Pieri, and Vito Scattarella. 1977. *La Comunità Neolitica di Cala Colombo presso Torre a Mare (Bari)*. Bari: Società di Storia Patria per la Puglia.

Donahue, Randall E. 1992. "Desperately Seeking Ceres: A Critical Examination of Current Models for the Transition to Agriculture in Mediterranean Europe." In *Transitions to Agriculture in Prehistory*, ed. Anne B. Gebauer and T. Douglas Price, 73–80. Madison, WI: Prehistory Press.

Drago, Ciro. 1954–1955. "Specchie di Puglia." *Bullettino di Paletnologia Italiana* 64: 171–223.

Fabbri, Pier F., Elettra Ingravallo, and Antonio Mangia, eds. 2003. *Grotta Romanelli nel Centenario della sua Scoperta (1900–2000)*. Galatina: Congedo Editore.

Gamble, Clive. 1999. *The Palaeolithic Societies of Europe*. Cambridge: Cambridge University Press.

Geniola, Alfredo. 1979. "Il Neolitico nella Puglia settentrionale e centrale." In *La Puglia dal Paleolitico al Tardoromano*, ed. Dinu Adamesteanu, 52–121. Milano: Electa.

Geniola, Alfredo. 1987. "La cultura di Serra d'Alto nella Puglia centrale." In *Atti della XXVI Riunione Scientifica dell'Istituto Italiano di Preistoria e Protostoria: il Neolitico in Italia*, vol. 2, ed. Anna Revedin, 771–81. Firenze: Istituto Italiano di Preistoria e Protostoria.

Geniola, Alfredo. 1995. "Ipogeo Manfredi (Polignano a Mare, Bari)." In *Preistoria e Protostoria, Guide Archeologiche N. 11: Puglia e Basilicata; XIII Congresso Internazionale delle Scienze Preistoriche e Protostoriche*, ed. Renata Grifoni Cremonesi and Francesca Radina, 98–105. Forlì: ABACO Edizioni.

Geniola, Alfredo, and Anna-Maria Tunzi. 1980. "Espressioni cultuali e d'arte nella Grotta di Cala Scizzo presso Torre a Mare (Bari)." *Rivista di Scienze Preistoriche* 35: 125–46.

Gervasio, Michele. 1913. *I Dolmen e la Civiltà del Bronzo nelle Puglie*. Trani: Vecchi e C.

Gravina, Armando. 1999. "La Daunia centro-occidentale: Frequentazione, ambiente e territorio fra Neolitico Finale, Eneolitico ed Età del Bronzo." In *Atti del 19° Convegno Nazionale sulla Preistoria-Protostoria-Storia della Daunia*, ed. Armando Gravina, 83–141. San Severo: Archeoclub d'Italia, Sede di San Severo.

Graziosi, Paolo. 1973. *L'Arte Preistorica in Italia*. Firenze: Sansoni.

Graziosi, Paolo. 1980. *Le Pitture Preistoriche della Grotta di Porto Badisco*. Firenze: Istituto Italiano di Preistoria e Protostoria.

Guerri, Mara. 1993. "Grotta dei Cervi a Porto Badisco (Prov. di Lecce)." *Rivista di Scienze Preistoriche* 45: 270–1.

Ingravallo, Elettra. 2002. *Grotta Cappuccini (Galatone) tra Eneolitico e Primo Bronzo*. Dipartimento di Beni Culturali, Università degli Studi, Lecce.

Jones, G. D. Barri, ed. 1987. *Apulia*, vol. 1: *Neolithic Settlement in the Tavoliere*. London: Society of Antiquaries of London.

Lewis-Williams, David. 2002. *The Mind in the Cave: Consciousness and the Origins of Art*. London: Thames & Hudson.

Lewthwaite, James. 1986. "The Transition to Food Production: A Mediterranean Perspective." In *Hunters in Transition: Mesolithic Societies of Temperate Eurasia and their Transition to Farming*, ed. Marek Zvelebil, 53–66. Cambridge: Cambridge University Press.

Lo Porto, Felice. G. 1962–1963. "La tomba di Cellino San Marco e l'inizio della Civiltà del Bronzo in Puglia." *Bullettino di Paletnologia Italiana* 71–2: 191–225.

Lo Porto, Felice. 1972. "La tomba neolitica con idolo in pietra di Arnesano (Lecce)." *Rivista di Scienze Preistoriche* 27: 357–72.

Lo Porto, Felice. 1976. "L'attività archeologica in Puglia." In *Atti del 15° Convegno di Studi sulla Magna Grecia*, 635–44. Napoli: Arte Tipografica.

Malone, Caroline. 1996. "Cult and Burial in the Neolithic and Early Bronze Age Central Mediterranean: An Assessment of the Potential." In *Approaches to the Study of Ritual: Italy and the Ancient Mediterranean*, ed. John B. Wilkins, 31–54. London: Accordia Research Centre.

Malone, Caroline, Simon Stoddart, and Ruth Whitehouse. 1993. "The Bronze Age of Southern Italy, Sicily and Malta ca. 2000–800 BC." In *Development and Decline in the Mediterranean Bronze Age*, ed. Clay Mathers and Simon K.F. Stoddart, 167–94. Sheffield: John Collis Publications.

Mezzena, Franco, and Arturo Palma di Cesnola. 1972a. "Oggetti d'arte mobiliare di età gravettiana ed epigravettiana nella Grotta Paglicci (Foggia)." *Rivista di Scienze Preistoriche* 27: 211–24.

Mezzena, Franco, and Arturo Palma di Cesnola. 1972b. "Scoperta di una sepoltura gravettiana nella Grotta Paglicci (Rignano Garganico)." *Rivista di Scienze Preistoriche* 27: 27–50.

Mezzena, Franco, and Arturo Palma di Cesnola. 1989–1990. "Nuova sepoltura gravettiana nella Grotta Paglicci (Promontorio del Gargano)." *Rivista di Scienze Preistoriche* 42: 3–29.

Mezzena, Franco, and Arturo Palma di Cesnola. 1992. "Nuove manifestazioni d'arte Epigravettiana della Grotta Paglicci nel Gargano." In *Atti della XXVIII Riunione Scientifica dell'Istituto Italiano di Preistoria e Protostoria: l'Arte in Italia dal Paleolitico all'Età del Bronzo*, ed. Anna Revedin, 277–92. Firenze: Istituto Italiano di Preistoria e Protostoria.

Moscoloni, Maurizio. 1987. "Coppa Nevigata nell'ambito degli sviluppi culturali appenninici." In *Coppa Nevigata e il Suo Territorio: Testimonianze Archeologiche dal VII al II Millennio a.C*, ed. Selene M. Cassano, Alberto Cazzella, Alessandra Manfredini, and Maurizio Moscoloni, 121–30. Roma: Edizioni Quasar.

Mussi, Margherita. 2000. "Heading South: The Gravettian Colonisation of Italy." In *Hunters of the Golden Age: The Mid Upper Palaeolithic of Eurasia, 30,000–20,000 BP*, ed. Wil Roebroeks, Margherita Mussi, Josef Svoboda, and Kelly Fennema, 355–74. Leiden: University of Leiden.

Mussi, Margherita. 2001. *Earliest Italy: An Overview of the Italian Palaeolithic and Mesolithic*. New York: Kluwer Academic / Plenum Publishers.

Orlando, Medica A. 1995. "Presenze necropoliche e strutture funerarie nel Salento dal XVI al X sec. a.C.: Un tentativo di classificazione della documentazione esistente." *Studi di Antichità* 8 (2): 19–38.

Palma di Cesnola, Arturo. 1965. "Il Paleolitico superiore arcaico (facies uluzziana) della Grotta del Cavallo, Lecce." *Rivista di Scienze Preistoriche* 20: 33–62.

Palma di Cesnola, Arturo. 1985. "Lo sviluppo degli studi sul Neo-Eneolitico del Gargano." In *Studi di Paletnologia in Onore di Salvatore M. Puglisi*, ed. Mario Liverani, Alba Palmieri, and Renato Peroni, 767–79. Roma: Dipartimento di Scienze Storiche, Archeologiche e Antropologiche dell'Antichità, Università di Roma 'La Sapienza.'

Palma di Cesnola, Arturo, and Alda Vigliardi. 1984. "Il Neo-Eneolitico del promontorio del Gargano." In *La Daunia Antica: Dalla Preistoria all'Alto Medioevo*, ed. Marina Mazzei, 55–74. Milano: Electa.

Pluciennik, Mark Z. 1994. "Space, Time and Caves: Art in the Palaeolithic, Mesolithic and Neolithic of Southern Italy." *Accordia Research Papers* 5: 39–71.

Quagliati, Quintino. 1936. *La Puglia Preistorica*. Trani: Vecchi & C.

Radina, Francesca. 2002. "Il Neolitico a Grotta Santa Croce." In *La Preistoria della Puglia: Paesaggi, Uomini e Tradizioni di 8,000 Anni Fa*, ed. Francesca Radina, 77–83. Bari: Mario Adda Editore.

Robb, John. 1999. "Great Persons and Big Men in the Italian Neolithic." In *Social Dynamics of the Prehistoric Central Mediterranean*, ed. Robert H. Tykot, Jonathan Morter, and John E. Robb, 111–21. London: Accordia Research Institute.

Segre Naldini, Eugenia, and Italo Biddittu. 1992. "Rinvenimenti di arte mobiliare paleolitica ad Ugento (Lecce)." In *Atti della XXVIII Riunione Scientifica dell'Istituto Italiano di Preistoria e Protostoria: l'Arte in Italia dal Paleolitico all'Età del Bronzo*, ed. Anna Revedin, 341–45. Firenze: Istituto Italiano di Preistoria e Protostoria.

Skeates, Robin. 1991. "Caves, Cult and Children in Neolithic Abruzzo, Central Italy." In *Sacred and Profane: Proceedings of a Conference on Archaeology, Ritual and Religion*, ed. Paul Garwood, David Jennings, Robin Skeates, and Judith Toms, 122–34. Oxford: Oxford University Committee for Archaeology.

Skeates, Robin. 1993. "Neolithic Exchange in Central and Southern Italy." In *Trade and Exchange in Prehistoric Europe: Proceedings of a Conference Held at the University of Bristol*, ed. Christopher Scarre and Francis Healy, 109–14. Oxford: Oxbow Books.

Skeates, Robin. 1995a. "Animate Objects: A Biography of Prehistoric 'Axe-Amulets' in the Central Mediterranean Region." *Proceedings of the Prehistoric Society* 61: 279–301.

Skeates, Robin. 1995b. "Ritual, Context and Gender in Neolithic South-Eastern Italy." *European Journal of Archaeology* 2: 199–214.

Skeates, Robin. 1995c. "Transformations in Mortuary Practice and Meaning in the Neolithic and Copper Age of Lowland East-Central Italy." In *Ritual, Rites and Religion in Prehistory: Third Deià Conference of Prehistory*, vol. 1, ed. William H. Waldren, Josep A. Enseynat, and Rex C. Kennard, 211–37. Oxford: Tempus Reparatum.

Skeates, Robin. 1997. "The Human Uses of Caves in East-Central Italy during the Mesolithic, Neolithic and Copper Age." In *The Human Use of Caves*, ed. Clive Bonsall and Christopher Tolan Smith, 79–86. Oxford: British Archaeological Reports.

Skeates, Robin. 2000. "The Social Dynamics of Enclosure in the Neolithic of the Tavoliere, South-East Italy." *Journal of Mediterranean Archaeology* 13: 155–88.

Soffer, Olga. 2000. "Gravettian Technologies in Social Contexts." In *Hunters of the Golden Age: The Mid Upper Palaeolithic of Eurasia, 30,000–20,000 BP*, ed. Wil Roebroeks, Margherita Mussi, Josef Svoboda, and Kelly Fennema, 59–75. Leiden: University of Leiden.

Sublimi Saponetti, Sandro. 1991. "I resti scheletrici di Valle Sbernia–Peschici (FG)." In *Atti del 12° Convegno Nazionale sulla Preistoria-Protostoria-Storia della Daunia*, ed. Giuseppe Clemente, 79–84. San Severo: Archeoclub d'Italia, Sede di San Severo.

Thomas, Julian. 1993. "The Politics of Vision and the Archaeologies of Landscape." In *Landscape: Politics and Perspectives*, ed. Barbara Bender, 19–47. Oxford: Berg.

Tinè, Santo, and Eugenia Isetti. 1975–1980. "Culto neolitico delle acque e recenti scavi nella Grotta Scaloria." *Bullettino di Paletnologia Italiana* 82: 31–70.

Tinè, Santo, and Laura Simone. 1984. "Il Neolitico." In *La Daunia Antica: dalla Preistoria all'Alto Medioevo*, ed. Marina Mazzei, 75–100. Milano: Electa.

Tunzi Sisto, Anna-Maria. 1996. "Il Bronzo Antico nella Puglia settentrionale." In *L'Antica Età del Bronzo: Atti del Congresso di Viareggio*, ed. Daniella Cocchi Genick, 584–85. Firenze: Octavo.

Tunzi Sisto, Anna-Maria, ed. 1999. *Ipogei della Daunia: Preistoria di un Territorio*. Foggia: Claudio Grenzi Editore.

Tunzi Sisto, Anna-Maria, and Mario Langella. 1995. "La grotticella trilobata di Madonna di Grottole." *Taras* 15: 291–311.

Walter, Peter. 1988. "Shaft-Chambered Tombs of the Fourth Millennium B.C. in the Mediterranean." *Berytus* 36: 143–67.

Whitehouse, Ruth D. 1968a. "Settlement and Economy in Southern Italy in the Neothermal Period." *Proceedings of the Prehistoric Society* 34: 332–66.

Whitehouse, Ruth D. 1968b. "The Early Neolithic of Southern Italy." *Antiquity* 42: 188–93.

Whitehouse, Ruth D. 1971. "The Last Hunter-Gatherers in Southern Italy." *World Archaeology* 2 (3): 239–54. http://dx.doi.org/10.1080/00438243.1971.9979478.

Whitehouse, Ruth D. 1972. "The Rock-Cut Tombs of the Central Mediterranean." *Antiquity* 46: 275–81.

Whitehouse, Ruth D. 1984. "Social Organisation in the Neolithic of Southeast Italy." In *The Deya Conference of Prehistory: Early Settlement in the Western Mediterranean Islands and the Peripheral Areas*, ed. William H. Waldren, Robert Chapman, James Lewthwaite, and Rex C. Kennard, 1109–37. Oxford: British Archaeological Reports.

Whitehouse, Ruth D. 1990. "Caves and Cult in Neolithic Southern Italy." *Accordia Research Papers* 1: 19–37.

Whitehouse, Ruth D. 1992. *Underground Religion: Cult and Culture in Prehistoric Italy*. London: Accordia Research Centre.

Whitehouse, Ruth D. 1995. "From Secret Society to State Religion: Ritual and Social Organisation in Prehistoric and Protohistoric Italy." In *Settlement and Economy in Italy 1500 BC–AD 1500: Papers of the Fifth Conference of Italian Archaeology*, ed. Neil Christie, 83–88. Oxford: Oxbow Books.

Winn, Shan M.M., and Daniel M. Shimabuku. 1980. *The Heritage of Two Subsistence Strategies: Preliminary Report on the Excavations at Grotta Scaloria, Southeastern Italy, 1978*. Halifax: Department of Anthropology, St. Mary's University.

Zampetti, Daniela, and Margherita Mussi. 1991. "Segni di potere, simboli del potere: La problematica del Paleolitico Superiore italiano." In *Papers of the Fourth Conference of Italian Archaeology*, 2: *The Archaeology of Power*, Part 2, ed. Edward Herring, Ruth Whitehouse, and John Wilkins, 149–160. London: Accordia Research Centre.

Zecca, Maria G. 1984. "Vasi eneolitici dalla Grotta Zinzulusa di Castro (Lecce)." *I Quaderni* 2: 67–97.

3

Caves of the Living, Caves of the Dead

Experiences Above and Below Ground in Prehistoric Malta

Simon K.F. Stoddart and Caroline A.T. Malone

In the early prehistory of the Maltese islands, the construction of the ritualized use of caves and cave-like spaces above and below ground was an important materialized multiple metaphor for the rituals of the living and the dead, reproducing in miniature form the island itself. A further instance is the historical genesis of the cave from subterranean origins, above ground and then back below ground. Another is inherent in the qualities of cave materials. A further linked metaphor is that of the construction process using those materials. Once constructed, the cave formed a metaphorical process of physical constraint followed by infilling. A focal theme is the intentionality or nonintentionality of stratigraphy, as well as other construction. Ambiguity may have been deliberate, and the intention multivocal.

The analysis will proceed at two scales, the macro and the micro. At the macroscale, we ask: Are the rituals characterized by the closure of a stratigraphic cycle, with clearance followed by depositional and sometimes iconoclastic closure? There is evidence from the Brochtorff Circle at Xaghra that most of the deposits belong to one broad phase, which may have been preceded by clearance, and concluded by intense stratigraphy formation and iconoclasm. At a microscale, the Circle site includes a pit sequence in the entrance area that appears to be a deliberate male cultural construction of stratigraphy, probably assembled in reverse order of antiquity. At the base there is an intact male who appears to have been deliberately covered by the skulls of his male ancestors. At Hagar Qim, a series of corpulent images were deliberately placed under the threshold of the temple before the closure of the ritual process. The cave or enclosed space was a dominant ritual theme of Maltese prehistory. This chapter principally makes comparison between two caves culturally constructed underground for mortuary practices (Hal Saflieni and Brochtorff Circle at Xaghra) and several ritual structures culturally constructed above ground (most specifically the megalithic "temples" of Tarxien, Ggantija, Hagar Qim, and Mnajdra, which we reclass as aboveground caves for the present purposes).

THE MATERIALIZED METAPHOR

Materialized metaphors underwrite much of later European prehistory. One prominent example is that of the "house," which slips between the realms of the living and the dead. Ian Hodder is one main exponent of this idea (Hodder 1990), where he notes the metaphorical relationship between the houses of the living and the houses of the dead in the European Neolithic, building on observations that go back to the time of Sprockhoff (1938) and Childe (1949). This theme of the *longue durée* relationship between the living places of the living and the dead also has much currency in the European Iron Age, and, more specifically, has been frequently explored in the study of the

TABLE 3.1 Chronology of caves in Malta.

Phase	Date BC	Domestic Cave	Burial Cave	Monumental Cave
Ghar Dalam		Natural		
Skorba	4400–4100			
Zebbug	4100–3600	Unknown	Constructed below ground	
Ggantija	3600–3000	Unknown	Constructed below ground	Above ground
Saflieni Tarxien	3000–2400	Unknown	Natural and monumental below ground	Above and below ground
Tarxien Cemetery	2400–1500		Small-scale above ground	

Etruscans of central Italy (e.g., most recently Riva 2006), a society that developed multiple scales of house construction for the dead, from models to cities. In Etruria, the relationship was so apparently explicit that the cities of the dead once acted as a substitute for the study of the living city, until archaeological research changed direction and the living cities were investigated firsthand.

A less-explored materialized metaphor explored in this chapter is that of the constructed cave, which may act as a metaphorical substitute for the living house or even as a primordial dwelling place within other societies. In European prehistory, caves have been quite frequently explored as accumulations of domestic debris and as ritual locales (e.g., Malone 1986; Whitehouse 1992), but have been presented more rarely in the European sequence in the multiple metaphorical guises that are suggested here. Outside Europe, the Maya civilization provides numerous geographical cases of man-made caves located beneath structures (Brady 1997; Brady and Veni 1992; Moyes and Brady, this volume). This practice is demonstrated more widely in Mesoamerica at the site of Teotihuacan where a cave was deliberately constructed within the enormous Pyramid of the Sun (Manzanilla et al. 1994).

This gap in research within Europe is effectively filled by the prehistory of Malta (3600–2500 BC), where parallels between belowground caves for the dead and aboveground constructed caves for the living (generally characterized as "temples") can be readily identified (figure 3.1; table 3.1). This pattern contrasts with the remainder of the contemporary Mediterranean, where we may readily uncover caves for the dead, but can detect no transfer into a correspondingly elaborate format of caves for the living. A possible exception of the construction of an artificial cave above ground on a monumental scale is Monte d'Accoddi on Sardinia (Contu 2000; Tiné and Traverso 1992, 1999), but it constitutes a case where only special pleading can turn an artificial mountain of many phases into an artificial cave. The multiple construction of caves in Malta is so striking that it forms another component of the local construction of identity from local materials, lying at the extreme end of the spectrum of size, contrasting with and containing portable objects that are also principally made of local materials (Stoddart and Malone 2008).

Caves could have had a metonymic rather than metaphorical role. Maltese monumental constructions have already been considered metaphorical representations of the islands themselves (Robb 2001) or of a materialized cosmology that contains both islands and sea (Grima 2001). The symbolism could, however, be metonymical or more strictly synecdochical. What could be more symbolic of the islands themselves than an elaboration of a significant part of that very island, the cave, constructed out of, or containing, a redolent, suggestive combination of key island features: stone, sediment, and water, and peopled by vegetation, animals, and humans? Indeed one of the creative actions of the prehistoric Maltese was to create the so-called oracle rooms, which could be considered caves within caves.

This situation is not one of chance, since Malta is a limestone landscape rich in caves like that of the Yucatan, the Dordogne, or the karstic Balkans. In the case of Malta, the prominence of caves is promoted by the relative invisibility of domestic constructions, which were insubstantial (or hidden by later monumental constructions), as with so much Neolithic settlement evidence (for example the "tethered mobility" of Britain [Malone 2004; Whittle 1996]). The populations of Late Neolithic Malta appear to be tethered to substantial monumental constructions which, this chapter argues, comprise parallel cultural cave systems above and below ground, popularly called the Maltese Temples (a shorthand for significant monumental ritual places) (figure 3.2). These are immense stone-built and roofed structures of some considerable antiquity (fourth millennium BC), although no longer the oldest freestanding stone constructions in the world (Badischen Landesmuseum Karlsruhe 2007; Schmidt 2006). The temples have massive outer walls, restricted passage-like entrances, stacked shelves, and curvilinear spaces within, which emulate in many respects the natural and man-made caves below ground. The outward appearance of the aboveground caves may have been given an even more cave-like appearance if they were originally encased or embanked in earth or loose stones.

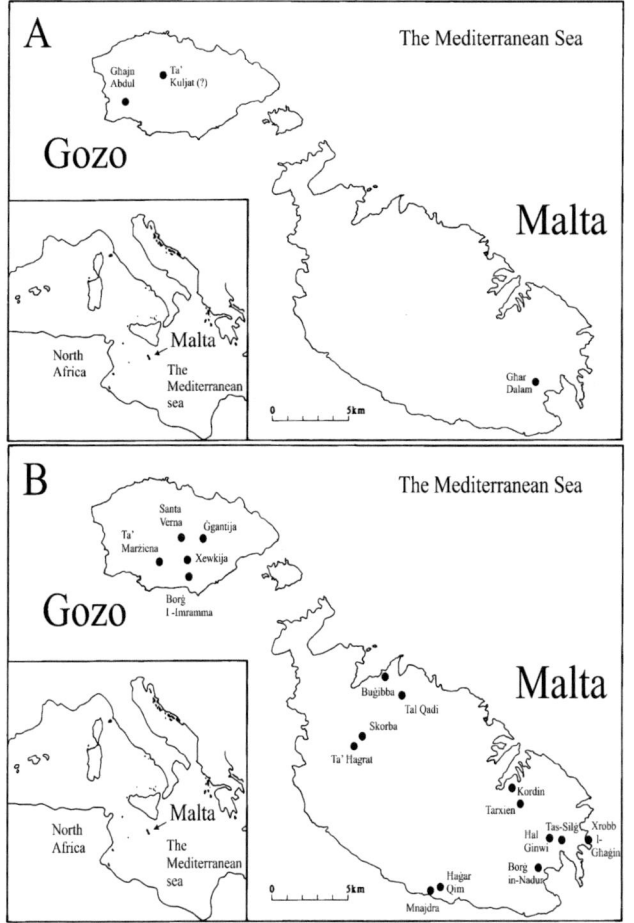
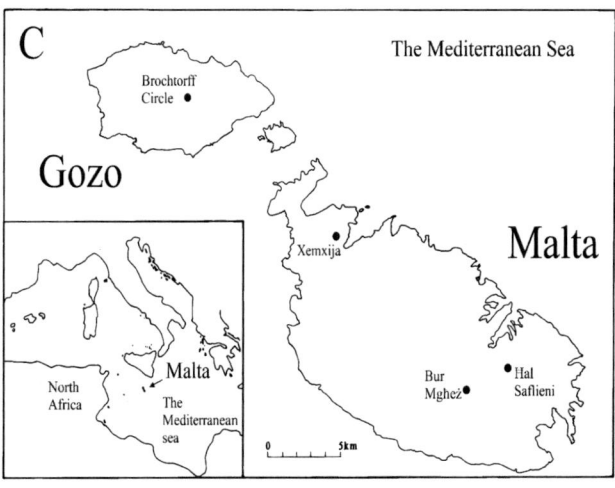

FIGURE 3.1 Location of Malta and location of caves: (A) "domestic"; (B) aboveground monumental; (C) belowground burial.

Caves are evocative underground constructions, which take humans away from the natural light and control or transform their visions of reality. This is the context in which caves have a powerful ritual role in early societies, a role that underlies contexts as widely distributed as the power of the rites of passage of transegalitarian societies (Owens and Hayden 1997), the allegory of the cave in Plato's *Republic*, and the architectural metaphor of the grotto of the Renaissance (Miller 1982). They are multiple places of passage that emphasize transition from one state to another, from life to death, from light to dark, and from land to earth (Hume 2007). As such, their transition parallels the passage of the day and the seasons. They are places for access to water and a refuge from the extremes of cold and heat. They are potentially stable refuges from the uncertainties of the fragile island world of Malta, whether real or imagined.

Much has been written recently on the nature of caves and the sensory experience that such places engender (e.g., Malone 1985, 1986, 2007; Whitehouse 1992; Skeates 2007). Studies of sound and senses generally have become de rigeur for monument and cave studies (e.g., Watson and Keating 1999; Watson 2001) and certainly have awakened archaeologists to the potential effects of the environment on peoples' experience of special spaces. Once constructed, these artificial caves may even have become wind chambers, evocatively resonating from the impact of forces from the outside maritime world, and yet providing protection. Caves may also have been special places for sensory transition in that they were locales where the effects of the smell of transitional states such as putrefaction (Howes 1987) may have been forcibly enclosed and concentrated.

A HISTORICAL METAPHOR?

A key question in the relationship between two states of a similar architectural form, be they houses or caves, is their historical relationship. In one cultural context, the different states may be constructed in parallel as different aspects of the same form. In another cultural context, one state may be the historical memory of the other. In the case of Northern Europe it appears that the long tombs are the materialized memory of the long houses (Hodder 1990, 141). In the Maltese cultural context there may be dynamic

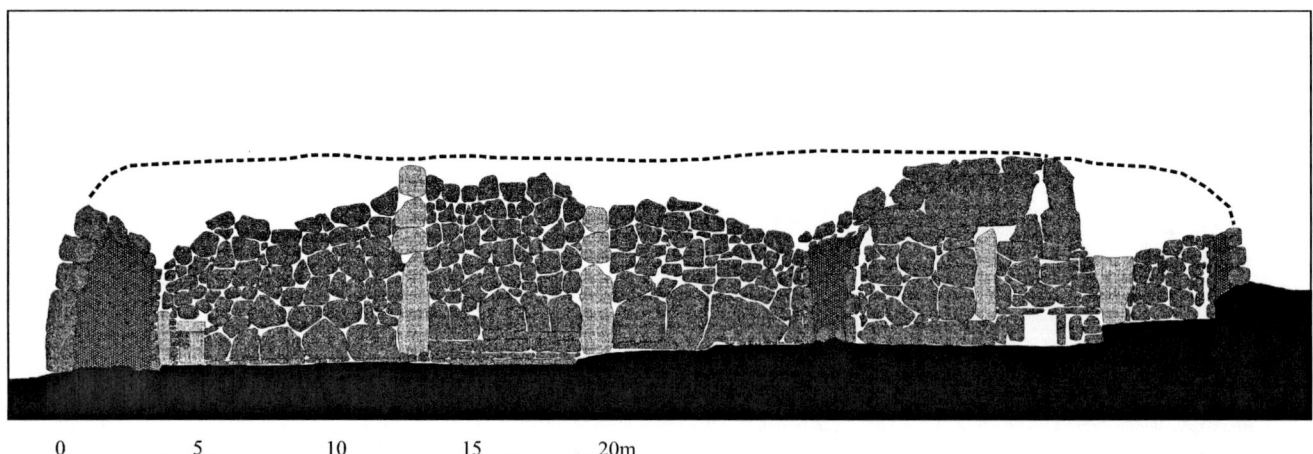

FIGURE 3.2 Ggantija, the best-preserved aboveground cave, in section.

developments from one form to another as well as parallel constructions, similarly exploring memories, in containers that we may class as memory caves or containers in which memories are unloaded and preserved.

In Malta, the linkage between the belowground mortuary constructions and the aboveground temples has already been made in an evolutionary perspective. Following his excavations at Zebbug (Baldacchino and Evans 1954) and Xemxija (Evans 1971), Evans made the intelligent historical linkage between architectural concepts associated with death ritual, and architectural concepts associated with life ritual (Evans 1959; Tilley 2004). He saw the practical possibilities of excavation in soft limestone (in the negative) transferred into the practical possibilities of constructing in hard and soft limestone (in the positive).

Historically, it has taken longer to move from an evolutionary linkage to explore the conceptual relationship between these two "cave-like" materializations (Stoddart 2002). If the historical reconstruction is correct, then, whereas in Northern Europe death rituals built on life inhabitation, in the island of Malta life rituals built on death rituals, most probably incorporating the outmoded domestic sites in their foundations (Trump 1966) and transcending their scale by elaboration based on belowground structures (figures 3.1, 3.3). It would be interesting to investigate if temples appropriated cave structures as well as more ancient domestic occupation in their foundations. The current situation is indicative if not yet proven. Certainly a number of temples from personal observation (e.g., Ggantija) have caves associated with them, and Grima (2005) has noticed an association with springs, which can be translated as water emerging from caves.

The immediate historical relationship of aboveground cultural caves (the temples) (figure 3.2) therefore, appears to have been with belowground caves employed for death rituals and burial, but the history of cave use in the Maltese islands is deeper in time and interconnects with the neighboring central Mediterranean. A tradition of cave use (both rockshelters and deeper caves) and an identity central to subsequent cultural activity was developed in the Maltese islands from the first Neolithic occupation, which probably derived from Sicily and southern Italy (figure 3.1; tables 3.1 and 3.2).

There, caves and more often rockshelters were commonly used for domestic shelter, burial, and ritual activity and were also reproduced as artificial rock-cut tombs over several millennia (Malone 1985, 1986; Whitehouse 1992). On Malta, the natural cliffside caves and deeper cavities, such as the habitation cave of Ghar Dalam, were formed from Coralline limestone and were often used as shelters during the primary settlement of the islands (Despott 1918, 1923). Some unmodified caves were employed for burial in parallel with more elaborate activities (figure 3.4). Recent surveys, particularly on Gozo by the Cambridge Gozo Project and other survey activity on the same island (Veen and Van der Blom 1992), has found many more open, domestic structures than subterranean sites, in spite of the ready availability of potential caves and rockshelters. The importance of caves in Malta lies in their monumental transformation. We can, therefore, suggest that uniquely in Malta and Gozo the role of the cave moved from a position of marginality (within the sphere of domesticity) to one of centrality (in the sphere of ritual) in the perception of the landscape by the prehistoric Maltese populations over this period, by the construction of a disproportionately large number of ritual caves both above and below ground (see figures 3.2 and 3.3).

From the Later Neolithic occupation of the Maltese islands, the builders of structures may have been attempt-

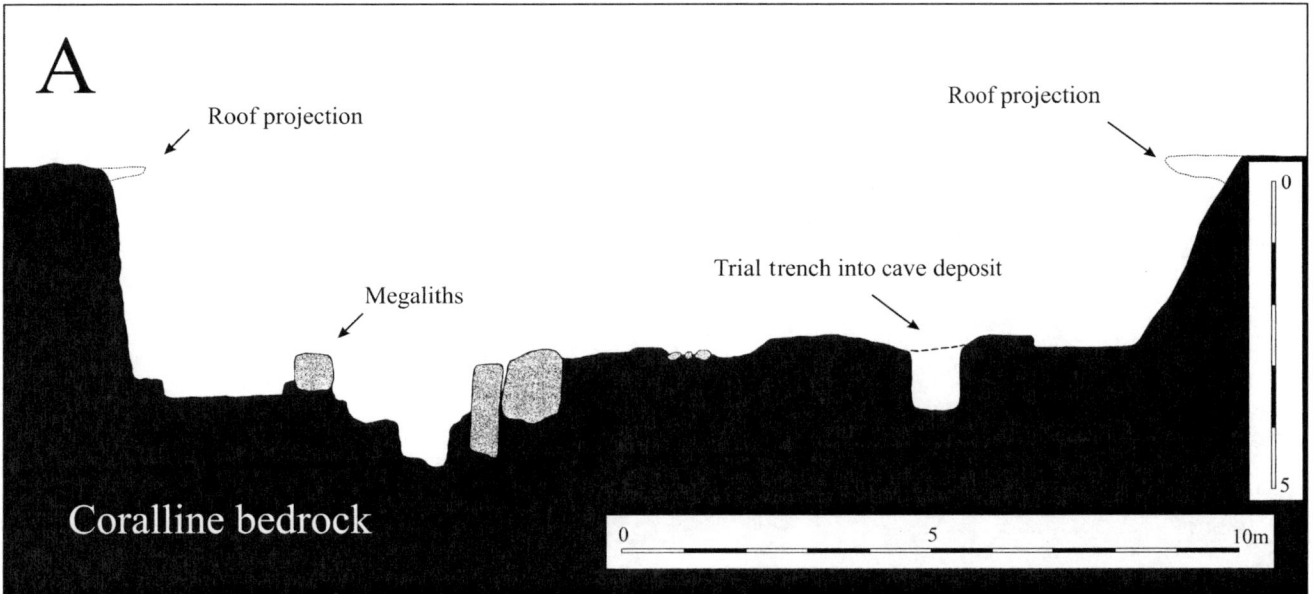

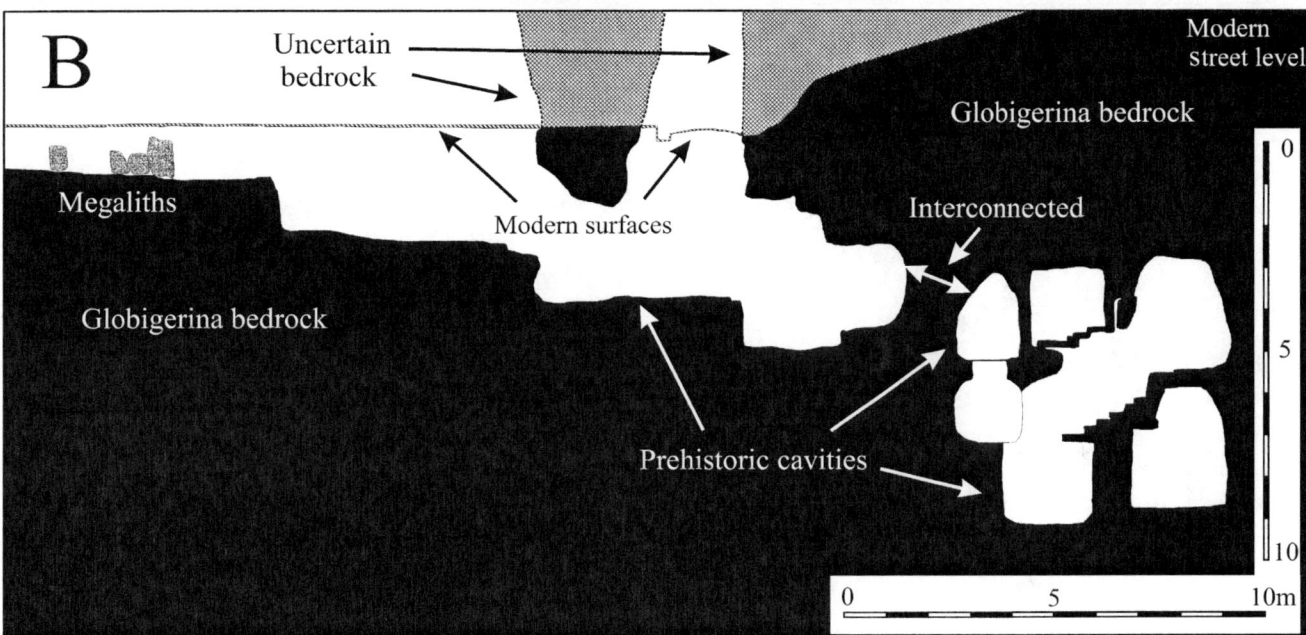

FIGURE 3.3 A comparison of (A) the Hal Saflieni hypogeum and (B) the Xaghra hypogeum, in section and with comparative scales.

ing to imitate caves above ground, or to attempt a mix of subterranean and terrestrial experience. The Skorba shrine at the temple site of Skorba (Trump 1966) had a sunken oval-shaped floor, carved from rock. Stone clearly made up some of the wall, but it is likely that mud brick, plaster, and timber provided the upper levels of the structure. There was apparently no doorway cut into the structure, so entry from above seems possible, and this structure too, could be seen as a metaphor for a cave-like, tomb-like space that was beginning to absorb notions of "dwelling house" alongside the cut rock of a cave and all that this represented.

In Malta, the form and scale of these spaces changes over time and between different locales, altering the sensory experience and creating a dynamic quality that the present authors see as an internalized imposition of control on a previously egalitarian system. Early monumental structures both above and below ground appear to be relatively shallow and open. Later monumental structures below ground penetrate deeper into the earth. Later monumental structures

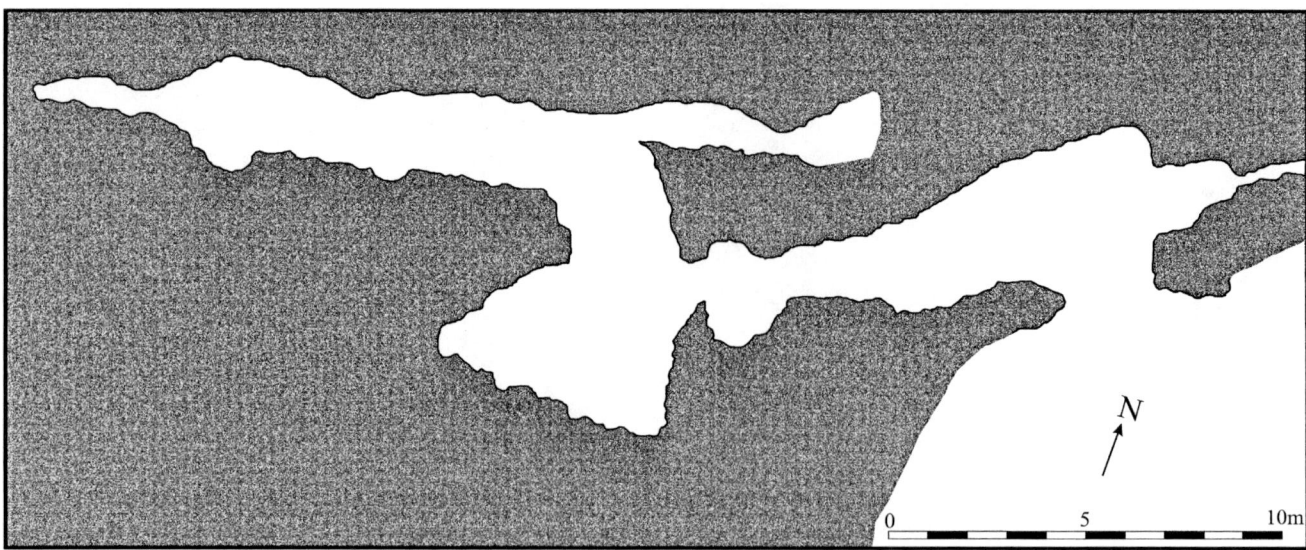

FIGURE 3.4 Bur Mghez, a natural burial cave.

above ground appear to have their entry points narrowed and demarcated. Both these trends reinforced the cave-like structure and facilitated greater social control.

METAPHORICAL PROPERTIES EMBEDDED IN RAW MATERIALS

The materials used in construction were suggestive of different metaphorical features (cf. Boivin 2004; Tilley 2004). Malta is formed mainly of two different limestones: one essentially hard (Coralline) and one essentially soft (Globigerina) (Pedley, Clarke, and Galea 2002). The permutations of these two essential qualities of the Maltese geology provided further conditions for the cave metaphors of the Maltese islands, namely two states of becoming: *additive* (such as seen in stalagmitic formation) and *reductive* (such as erosive action by the sea). Below ground, the Coralline limestone provided a good framework of natural cavities that could be embellished by an additive process of worked stone. Above ground, the Coralline limestone provided large slabs and rubble for construction, again by an additive process. Below ground, the Globigerina limestone offered fissures that could be readily excavated into organic and flexible forms by a reductive process. Above ground, Globigerina provided the potential of a soft material that could easily be shaped and manipulated to provide the finishing touches to cave constructions, once again by an additive process.

The softer components of geological strata, in both types of rock, permitted the easy excavation (often aided by

TABLE 3.2 Well-known caves in Malta.

Location	Form	Rock	Interior fitments	Scale
Below ground				
Ghar Dalam	Linear cave	Coralline	Natural deposits	Large
Xemxija	Artificial rock-cut tombs	Globigerina	Burial deposits	Small
Brochtorff	Natural cave system, enlarged caves/chambers	Coralline	Burial deposits and imported stones	Large
Hal Saflieni	Artificial cave system	Globigerina	Carved stone, imported stone, burial deposits	Large
Above ground				
Hagar Qim	Multistructured temple	Globigerina	Altars, thresholds, shrines, etc.	Large
Mnajdra	Three temples	Globigerina	Altars, thresholds, shrines	Large
Ggantija	Two temples	Coralline	Imported stone altars, thresholds, shrines	Large
Skorba	Two adjacent structures or shrines	Cut-stone floor; stone, plaster, and wood walls	Plaster floors	Small-medium

water action) of stable underground bedrock spaces. In the Coralline, this softer bedrock was a cream-white powder below the hard crust on the surface, and enabled deep fissures and cracks to be exposed. In the Globigerina bedrock, the consistently soft structure was often a honey-colored evocative material that could not only be excavated but also redeployed to decorate other caves, both cultural and natural, as structural and decorative panels. Some of these deep subterranean spaces were enhanced with stalagmites, passages, and water from hidden places, entered from the rock plateaus. In at least two cases the spaces were used as funerary caves, and in many more as simple tombs.

THE METAPHOR OF THE CONSTRUCTION PROCESS

The action of construction, both additive (above ground) and reductive (below ground), was an intentional action of construction of cave spaces within an island world, representative of that wider world. Below ground, the cave dwelt within the island itself. Above ground, the cave was almost a representation of the island itself with cliff-like façades, rising out of the land as the island rose out of the sea.

The subterranean sites were either modifications of natural cavities in rock, or were almost entirely man made. The natural cavities required little further change other than clearance of loose stone and deposit, and the insertion, over time, of new blocks of stone to form new cells and spaces. The only known elaborate example is the Brochtorff Circle at Xaghra (Malone et al. 2009; figure 3.3B), which provides detailed information on the modification of a natural, superficial funerary cave that included blocks inserted to support a crumbling cave roof and many man-made subdivisions. At this site, new spaces were also carved from seams of soft rock, sometimes breaking into earlier artificial rock-cut tombs.

Man-made caves were introduced from the Zebbug period (ca. 4000 BC) as *a forno* rock-cut tombs, very similar in form to those used in Sicily. Such sites were entered from the ground surface through vertical shafts that opened into one or more elliptical chambers, and that were used for multiple burials. Such sites were largely hidden, although probably marked on the surface by stone markers and carved heads (menhirs). Large man-made caves are represented only by the complex of Hal Saflieni (the Hypogeum) (figure 3.3B). This huge artificial space was carved from soft rock at a high point of a hill, and may, like the Brochtorff Circle, have been enclosed by a wall on the surface, thus marking the place. It appears to have started life as a series of seminatural cavities opening onto a natural hollow. This was then extended over three deep levels into more than thirty spaces, some echoing the simple elliptical tombs, but others carved in architectural detail with elements that are found in the built temples. Not all the spaces were intended for burial, with some "rooms" providing dramatic theatrical spaces with exits and entrances, viewpoints, hidden shelves, and display areas.

Terrestrial sites in the early settlement history of Malta were fragile affairs, built of insubstantial materials. At a stage yet to be firmly dated, domestic structures were transformed into stone-built monumental buildings, probably at the beginning of the so-called Ggantija phase about 3600 BC (see figure 3.2). Even then, the first stone structures were modest in scale but rapidly became immense monuments, on the same scale as the hypogea below ground. A key feature of the Temples of Malta is that they were built from high, impenetrable stone walls, often massive blocks, with only one or two ceremonial entrances into the interior. Thresholds of stone, sometimes of different heights, demarcated the passage from one zone to another, and corridors from the entrance led directly toward a semicircular end space filled by stone altars and display tables. Views from the exterior to the end altar were readily achieved, provided that the barriers that marked each separate space were lowered. However, the temples—if the models and recent research (Torpiano 2004) hold up in engineering terms—were fully roofed spaces, which implies they were dark, mysterious places, lit by fires, lamps, and shafts of daylight from the entrance. The curvilinear nature of the interior spaces, the corridors, the often low and restricted doorways (portholes), the decorated friezes of carved patterns and the many hidden secret spaces behind the more open, public areas, all echo the sense of a cave. Could it be that the builders were intentionally recreating a cave complex above ground?

THE METAPHOR OF THE PHYSICAL CONSTRAINT

Once constructed, the caves above and below ground formed profoundly physical constraints, not unlike the physical form of the island. Underground spaces are always constrained, difficult to access, dark, and often airless, and there is much that is unseen and unknown. In natural cavities, there are often sinkholes, lower galleries, dripping water, drafts, and in some parts of the Mediterranean, volcanic fumaroles, hot springs, and other natural curiosities (Malone 1986; Whitehouse 1992). Such places could be seen as dangerous, otherworldly, and liminal, although those used for settlement must, in part anyway, have been safe havens from the natural elements.

The building of monumental structures above ground in massive stones could potentially be seen as an attempt to recreate the solidity of subterranean space, whether as tombs or other structures. The construction of places with similar physical constraints to caves thus raises many questions about the metaphors that connect caves and architectural monuments. Were prehistoric people trying to recreate those dark spaces as alternative caves, into which to play out different versions of the rituals practiced in subterranean caves?

The internal structure of the caves also took the form of natural caves that are often naturally compartmentalized. Both aboveground and belowground caves consisted of a series of thresholds demarcating intervening space (Grima 2001). Access analysis has recently been combined with visibility analysis to show that the internal dynamics do not focus just on spaces but also on these thresholds. As a consequence, principles of revelation from one open space to another are crucial. That revelation is necessarily restricted by the relatively cramped conditions of the cave interior. Under these conditions there would have been a manipulated interplay of scales and modes of interpersonal communication from enforced intimate personal space (particularly in mortuary caves) through social space (1–2 meters) to public space (more than 4 meters) (Hall 1966). In some circumstances, in the close presence of the large image on the right of the Tarxien temple, the participant would be forced, on entering, to look up in an act of reverence by the constraints of space (Higuchi 1983, 46). The differential scale of the so-called oracle hole may also have played on these issues. Similarly, in the Brochtorff Circle at Xaghra, the celebrant would have been forced to crouch to enter a porthole into the area where specialist ritual objects were kept on the left of the entrance.

METAPHORS EMBEDDED IN THE STRATIGRAPHY OF THE INFILLING

The cave metaphor goes further than drawing attention to the combined effects of a natural and culturally constructed three-dimensional space. The process of "encavement" did not cease with their construction but continued with the performances within and the ultimate filling of the internal spaces, marked by "a succession of individual actions and events" (Grima 2001). Prehistoric caves have stratigraphy that is often considered to be a naturally formed fill, largely devoid of human intervention. However, as we argue here, stratigraphic buildup—that is, its layering and its modification—is very much a cultural construct. It becomes a key issue in both the culturally transformed natural spaces (below ground) and the naturally "transformed" cultural spaces (above ground). There are often identifiable levels of intentionality for filling the constructed space with material, fills, bodies, and objects, and then for the destruction of the space. Recent research on the belowground structures (Stoddart 2007) and the aboveground structures (Anderson and Stoddart 2007; Barrowclough 2007; Malone 2007) has investigated the possibility that some stratigraphies or layerings are more intentional, deliberate, and conscious, particularly in ritual circumstances, than others.

There appear to be three stages to the infilling of the caves. The first is the deliberate laying out of the liturgical furniture, which reaches full development in the final Tarxien phase. Many instances of this stage required some investment of infrastructure, and therefore survived any later action. The second phase is the preservation of the "deposits of performance," which are likely to be under-represented, most probably swamped by later intervention. Indeed, many rituals require the deliberate clearance of sacred refuse. Furthermore, ritual objects may have been stored for future use in much the same way as a Christian sacristy contains objects between different performances. The third phase is the backfilling, in part deliberate, of the caves at the end of the ritual cycle. Prominent concentrations of the object may be a product of permanent storage once ritual tradition was no longer current.

Can we propose a deliberate layout of liturgical furniture according to cave-like principles? Water ponding has been proposed by Grima (2001) as an island-like property, but could this not equally easily (and indeed compatibly with Grima's suggestion) be a cave-like property? One interpretation proposed by Grima is that the enclosed space is inverted to form a transition across open sea. The metaphor may not require such an inversion. It may form a reinforcement of the internalized island identities, which are prominent in terms of construction, drawing on the natural world of the islands themselves dominated by caves. An alternative to the island cosmology proposed by Grima is that these are caves filled with water, populated by fish, snakes, and other creatures of deep recesses, and ranging from land-based caves (containing snakes) to sea caves (containing fish and shells) (Malone 2008). Bowls, grinding stones, libation holes, and other containers may be evocative of pools within caves. At Tarxien, screens covered with spirals that border the central area may evoke reflections from pools on the walls of the cave.

The deposits of performance are more difficult to reconstruct. Liturgical furniture does not always seem to have been preserved literally at the place of action, although some fixed elements (libation holes, altars, etc.) are necessarily still in situ. There is evidence that caches of material were secreted away for later use in a number of key locations: an altar on the right when entering the first open space in Tarxien; axe amulets and a standing, skirted figure in a distant recess, also at Tarxien; a group of seated figures under a step at Hagar Qim; the sacristy

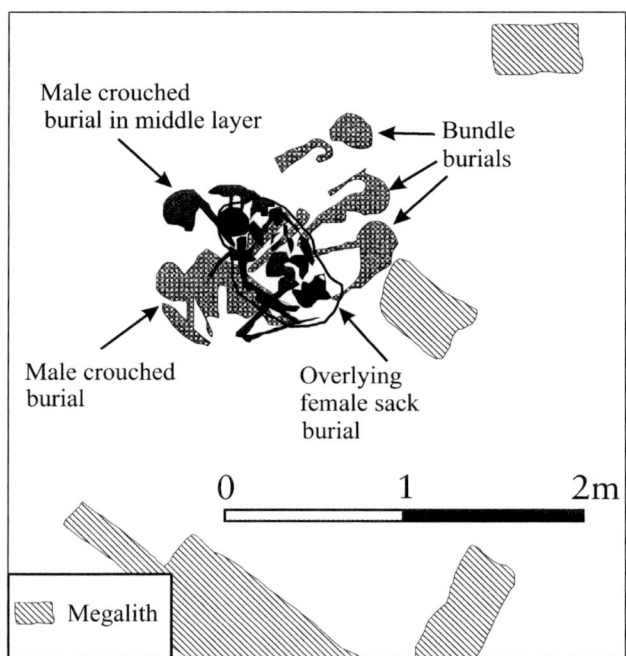

FIGURE 3.5 The intentionality of stratigraphy. Stacking of burials in the central part of the Brochtorff Circle.

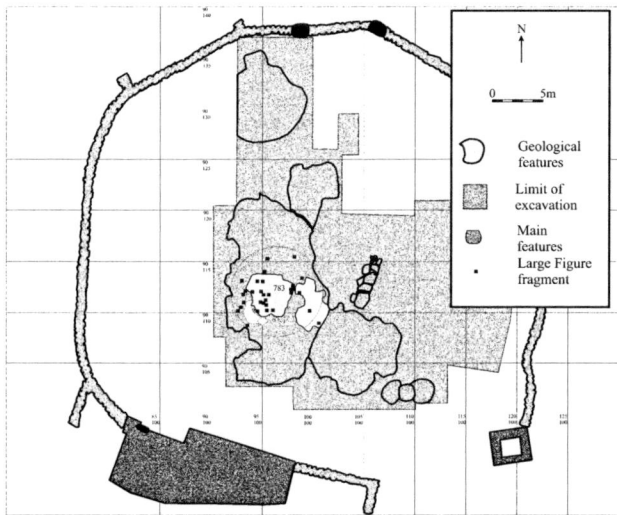

FIGURE 3.6 The intentionality of stratigraphy. Destruction of the large standing figure in the central part of the Brochtorff Circle.

shrine area at Brochtorff Circle at Xaghra; and many cavities at Hal Saflieni. GIS-based visibility analysis (Anderson and Stoddart 2007) suggests that objects were placed out of view, drawing on the common occlusive characteristics of caves.

In fact, there is some evidence of closure of the ritual process. In one case within the Brochtorff Circle at Xaghra, in the innermost recess so far uncovered of the cave system, the roof appears to have collapsed in prehistory, necessitating a closure of that sector of the site. However, elsewhere on the site there appears to have been the deliberate imposition of stratigraphy. First, there are several instances of stratigraphic constructions of human remains in pits, under the central shrine sacristy, and in the inner recesses of the cave system. In most instances, these sequences appear to have been led by intact male skeletons, followed by the insertion of overlying white sediment before the introduction of further skeletal material (figure 3.5).

Second, the site appears to have been deliberately closed down at the end of the ritual performances. Although the sacristy area may represent a deliberate storage of ritual paraphernalia, the quantity of overburden, collapsed cave roof, and megalithic remains may point to a deliberate infilling of the most significant central part of the site. An indication of the intentionality of this closure event is suggested by the destruction of a standing human image in a nearby related open area and the incorporation of its parts in the burial deposit (figure 3.6). At other sites, it is difficult to follow the same process with precision, since their stratigraphy is less well known, but some of the deliberate storage deposits at Tarxien, Hal Saflieni, and Hagar Qim may follow similar principles.

THE END RESULT

The final product of this speleogenesis, of these generative materializing metaphors, was a bipartite structure of monumental caves on the Maltese islands. This formal division of the island landscape into two types of monumental cave formation, accompanied by a limited number of small domestic structures, and a small number of less-developed burial caves of varying size (figure 3.4), was very particular to Malta during this period.

The subterranean hypogea (as opposed to simple rock-cut tombs) were spaces divided into a many separate zones, mostly accessed via one route (see figures 3.3 and 3.8). Thus the deepest places were only accessed after passing through many others and represent deep, secret, and hidden places, best demonstrated through the application of access theory (see Anderson and Stoddart 2007; Malone 2007). These spaces were intended to be filled by burials and deposits, and were thus made inaccessible over time. Only key routes through the hypogea were intended for continued access.

In sharp contrast, the built spaces on the ground surface (the constructed cave-temple) have far fewer but larger internal zones (figure 3.7), and generally these are accessed from one central corridor. Unlike the subterranean sites, these spaces were designed to remain clear and open for use. Some sites, such as Tarxien, which combine multiple temples, have greater depth, with one corridor leading to

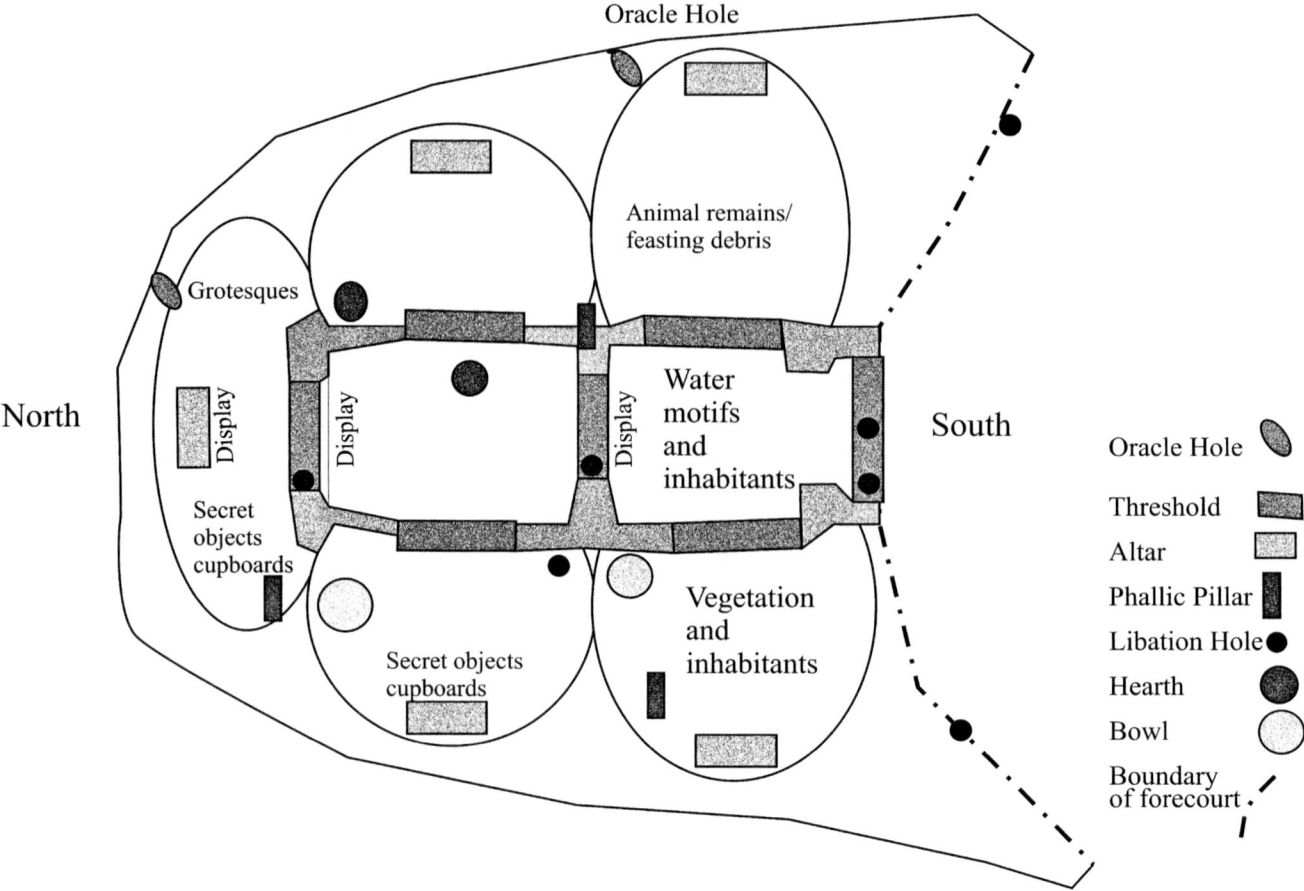

FIGURE 3.7 Underground cave system of the Brochtorff Circle at Xaghra. (C. Malone and Libby McQueeny.)

yet another, in order to access the deeper zones. In contrast to the subterranean sites, the surface temples include a complex and varied series of cupboards, hidden spaces (oracle holes), altars, and shelves that imply that space was bipartite—either large enough for activity and an audience, or small enough to obscure objects or a person from an audience. Areas for deposition were thus limited, given the paved or plastered floors, and the all-but-solid exterior walls.

Archaeologically, most objects or deposited waste from feasts and ritual seem to have been forced into cavities between stone structures, behind altars, and between the outer and inner walls of the buildings. Notable exceptions include the large stone figurines deposited below a stone step within Hagar Qim temple, and the cache of stone axes apparently fed through one of the exterior "oracle holes" on the east side of Tarxien. These deposits were clearly more than ritual waste, and give some ideas of the structuring of deposits that archaeologists need to note.

The accumulation of stratigraphy in burial sites is, at the simplest level of analysis, an inevitable part of the disposal of human remains. While bodies decompose, the skeletal structure remains and is compressed into the sediments. In the hypogea, there were two parallel processes of sedimentation: natural deposits falling from the cave walls and roof, together with rain-borne, washed-in sediment and the intentional placement of cultural material within these sediments. In temples, the accumulation is similar, with cultural placement combined with the blown- and washed-in dust and soil that plague a dry environment.

The archaeological process of excavation unravels aspects of the daily practice, the microstratigraphy, of the users of temples and hypogea, shown by the detailed buildup of stratigraphies of sediment, occupation, and structure. The process for subterranean sites is naturally better preserved than superficial sites, given the aggressive erosion of the rocky Mediterranean landscape of the Maltese islands, and thus stratigraphies have been fully recorded at the Brochtorff Xaghra circle to considerable depth. Similar records do not exist for the Hal Saflieni hypogeum, although the excavation notebooks of Zammit

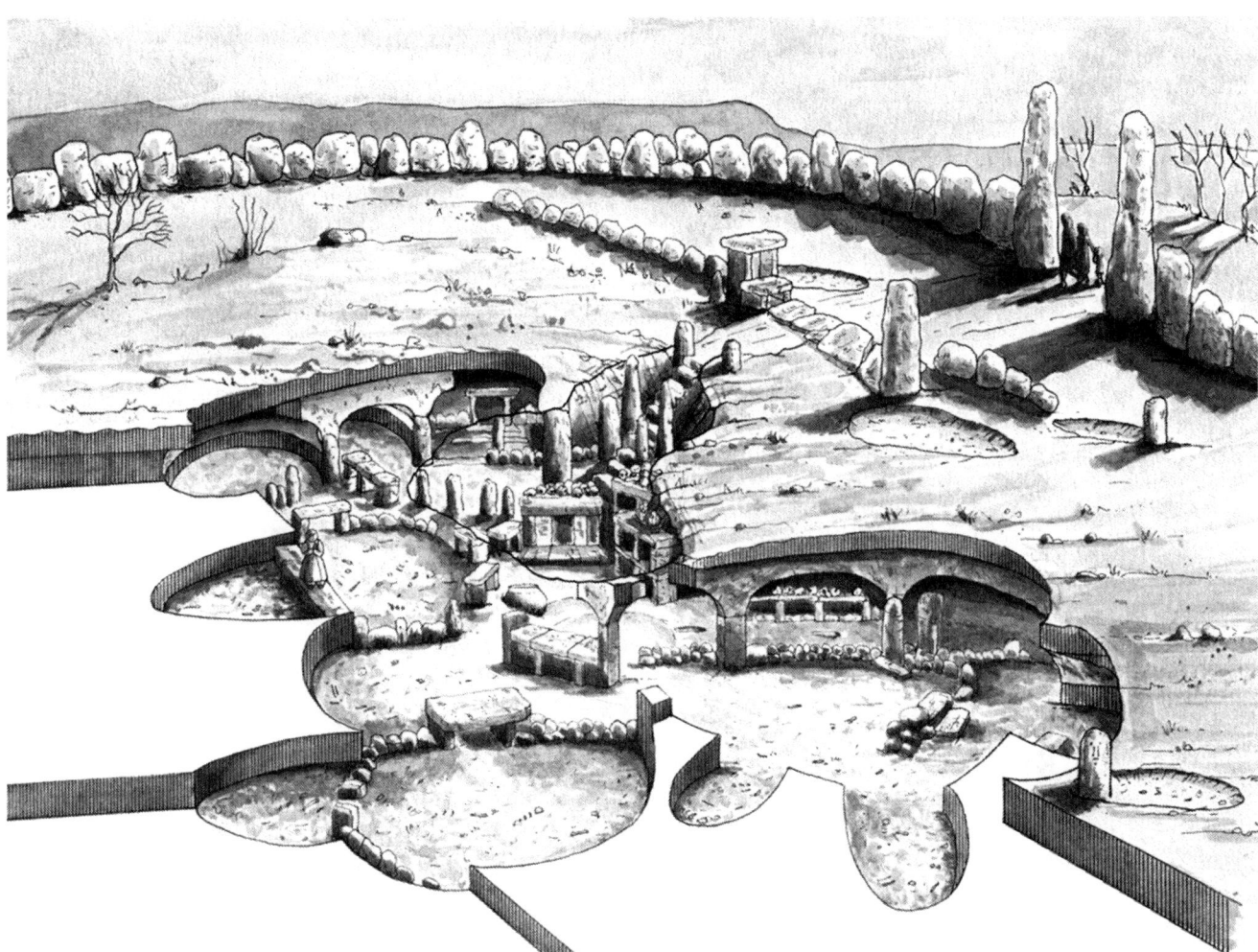

FIGURE 3.8 Tarxien: an ideal plan of a cultural cave.

(National Museum of Archaeology Archives) provide a graphic account of findspots of specific deposits, objects, and structures. In particular, certain categories of object (polished axes, animal bone, grotesque images, phallic objects, etc.) were sometimes found in unusual concentrations, suggesting that they had been placed, buried, heaped, or even posted through holes as part of elaborate ritual action. Similar detail was also important in the manner of arranging burials within the deep stratigraphies, with compartments, niches, pits, and zones demarcated for particular burials, as noted especially at the Brochtorff Circle, Xaghra. Over time, such compartments became muddled, mixed, and even obscured, so that additional burials were set into others, truncating earlier ritual arrangements and adding yet more complexity to individual actions recorded in the layers of accumulation.

Macrostratigraphy tends to be the outcome of major interventions, either naturally induced, such as collapse and flood, or through organized agency. In the case of Maltese sites, we can identify some moments of accumulation, change, and closure that might imply deliberate closure of sites. The temple sites appear to be modified and elaborated steadily through their use lives, eventually filling to the point of abandonment and change. These changes include structural additions and combinations, closure of access, internal divisions, decoration, reflooring and replastering episodes, accumulations of rubbish and artifacts, and perhaps also catastrophic collapse. Unfortunately, the early records of the stratigraphy and deposits found in all temples (other than Tarxien and Skorba) failed to record fallen stones or collapse, and later reconstruction and clearance has removed the possibility of reconstructing such damage. However, it is quite possible that closure, damage, destruction, and obscuration could have changed or hidden features.

In the hypogea, the likelihood of collapse was always a strong possibility, so the internal design of the two known sites employed various strategies to cope with instability.

In the Hypogeum, not only are the elaborate spaces carved deeply in the rock, but there are few areas where the roof span is greater than 4 to 5 meters, and numerous natural and, in some places, imported stone pillars provide vital support. In the Brochtorff Circle, though, the superficial rock roof of the natural cave, often little more than a meter in thickness, meant the subterranean space was liable to fracture, flaking, and catastrophic collapse. The span of the natural spaces is in excess of 7 to 8 meters, and it is thought that the site was largely covered by natural cave roof during its use life. The strategy employed was the use of large stones as "jacks" to support crumbling areas. Although evidence is now only partial, internal divisions with megaliths may have also have provided similar support.

The creative and destructive actions that eventually lead to the closure of a site, be it a temple or a burial hypogea, may be visible archaeologically. In the case of temples, iconoclasm may be identified, and we have some possible examples where large stone figures were irreparably damaged. One is the large figure in Tarxien, where the upper part of the figure, assuming it existed, was removed. Later ploughing is normally blamed, but it is also possible that damage and removal happened much earlier in history. The other example is the quite recently discovered relief figure from Tas Silg, where crisscross damage and removal of the head could be deliberate (Vella 1999). In the hypogea, only the Brochtorff Circle is well-enough known to suggest iconoclasm. In this case a medium-sized stone statue (probably at least one meter high originally) was apparently smashed and its pieces thrown across a wide area of the final burial deposits (see figure 3.6). Such destruction could possibly have been through the impact of falling rock, but the distribution of pieces, many of them embedded deeply among the skeletal remains, supports a more deliberate act of wanton iconoclasm, perhaps suggesting a local "regime" change or abandonment of former beliefs.

CONCLUSION

The Maltese islands provide a very different cave setting compared with the rest of the Mediterranean in the fourth and third millennia BC. The contemporaneous populations of North Africa remained substantially pastoral throughout this period (Nehren 1992), and thus natural caves remained principally employed in the context of these activities. In contemporaneous Sicily and Southern Italy, natural caves, often with liminal, potent, yet naturalistic qualities of water and gaseous venting, were depositories of redolent objects, but the attempts to construct cavernous environments were much less developed (Malone 1985, 1986; and subsequently Whitehouse 1992).

In the case of Malta, not only is identity constructed, but we contend that caves were constructed and elaborated in the support of identity, both above ground and below ground. Three-dimensional monumental ritual spaces adopted the models of the natural world that were readily available and which, through their intrinsic qualities, were suggestive of the permanence that failed to materialize in the human life cycle. Unfortunately even caves collapse—some spectacular examples are recorded in historical times in the Maltese islands—and the prehistoric peoples witnessed at least one at the Brochtorff Circle. In the same way as the caves collapsed, so did the stable ritual practices of the Tarxien period, which were formally closed and replaced by structures very different in kind.

ACKNOWLEDGMENTS

The first draft of this article was produced by the first author in the light-headed conditions of a transatlantic flight. We thank Holley Moyes and two anonymous reviewers for their positive critique, but any retained light-headedness remains the responsibility of the authors.

REFERENCES CITED

Anderson, Michael, and Simon Stoddart. 2007. "Mapping Cult Context: GIS Applications in Maltese Temples." In *Cult in Context*, ed. David Barrowclough and Caroline Malone, 41–44. Oxford: Oxbow.

Badischen Landesmuseum Karlsruhe, ed. 2007. *Die ältesten Monumente der Menschheit: Vor 12,000 Jahren in Anatolien*. Karlsruhe: Badisches Landesmuseum.

Baldacchino, Joseph G., and John D. Evans. 1954. "Prehistoric Tombs near Zebbug, Malta." *Papers of the British School at Rome* 22 (n.s. 9): 1–21.

Barrowclough, David. 2007. "Putting Cult in Context: Ritual, Religion and Cult in Temple Period Malta." In *Cult in Context*, ed. David Barrowclough and Caroline Malone, 45–53. Oxford: Oxbow.

Boivin, Nicole L. 2004. "Mind over Matter? Collapsing the Mind-Matter Dichotomy in Material Culture Studies." In *Rethinking Materiality: The Engagement of Mind with the Material World*, ed. Elizabeth DeMarrais, Christopher Gosden, and Colin Renfrew, 63–71. Cambridge: Cambridge University Press.

Brady, James E. 1997. "Settlement Configuration and Cosmology: The Role of Caves at Dos Pilas." *American Anthropologist* 99 (3): 602–18. http://dx.doi.org/10.1525/aa.1997.99.3.602.

Brady, James E., and George Veni. 1992. "Man-Made and Pseudo-Karst Caves: The Implications of Sub-surface Features within Maya Centers." *Geoarchaeology* 7 (2): 149–67. http://dx.doi.org/10.1002/gea.3340070205.

Childe, Vere Gordon. 1949. "The Origins of Neolithic Culture in Northern Europe." *Antiquity* 32: 129–35.

Contu, Ercole. 2000. *L'Altare preistorico di Monte D'Accoddi*. Sardegna archeologica. Guide e Itinerari 29. Sassari: Carlo Delfino editore.

Despott, Guiseppe. 1918. "Excavations Conducted at Ghar Dalam (Malta) in the Summer of 1917." *Journal of the Royal Anthropological Institute* 48: 214–21.
Despott, Guiseppe. 1923. "Excavations at Ghar Dalam (Dalam Cave)." *Journal of the Royal Anthropological Institute* 53: 18–35.
Evans, John D. 1959. *Malta*. Ancient People and Places. London: Thames and Hudson.
Evans, John D. 1971. *The Prehistoric Antiquities of the Maltese Islands: A Survey*. London: Athlone Press.
Grima, Reuben. 2001. "An Iconography of Insularity: A Cosmological Interpretation of Some Images and Spaces in the Late Neolithic Temples of Malta." *Papers from the Institute of Archaeology* 12: 48–65. http://dx.doi.org/10.5334/pia.164.
Grima, Reuben. 2005. "Monuments in Search of a Landscape: The Landscape Context of Monumentality in Late Neolithic Malta." PhD dissertation, University of London, London.
Hall, Edward T. 1966. *The Hidden Dimension*. Garden City, NY: Doubleday.
Higuchi, Tadahiko. 1983. *The Visual and Spatial Structure of Landscapes*. Cambridge, MA: MIT Press.
Hodder, Ian. 1990. *The Domestication of Europe*. Oxford: Blackwell.
Howes, David. 1987. "Olfaction and Transition: An Essay on the Ritual Uses of Smell." *Canadian Review of Anthropology and Sociology* 24 (3): 398–416. http://dx.doi.org/10.1111/j.1755-618X.1987.tb01103.x.
Hume, Lynne. 2007. *Portals: Opening Doorways to Other Realities through the Senses*. Oxford: Berg.
Malone, Caroline. 1985. "Pots, Prestige and Ritual in Neolithic Southern Italy." In *Papers in Italian Archaeology IV*, vol. 2: *Prehistory*, ed. Caroline Malone and Simon Stoddart, 118–51. BAR International Series 244. Oxford: British Archaeological Reports.
Malone, Caroline. 1986. "Exchange Systems and Style in the Central Mediterranean, 4500–1700 BC." PhD dissertation, University of Cambridge, Cambridge.
Malone, Caroline. 2004. *Neolithic Britain and Ireland*, rev. ed. Stroud: Tempus.
Malone, Caroline. 2007. "Access and Visibility in Prehistoric Malta." In *Recent Developments in the Research and Management at World Heritage Sites*, ed. Melanie Pomeroy-Kellinger and Ian Scott, 15–25. Oxford Archaeology Occasional Paper 16. Oxford: Oxford University Committee for Archaeology.
Malone, Caroline. 2008. "Metaphor and Maltese Art: Explorations in the Temple Period." *Journal of Mediterranean Archaeology* 21 (1): 81–108. http://dx.doi.org/10.1558/jmea.v21i1.81.
Malone, Caroline, Simon Stoddart, David Trump, Anthony Bonanno, and Anthony Pace. 2009. *Mortuary Ritual in Prehistoric Malta: The Brochtorff Circle Excavations (1987–1994)*. Cambridge: McDonald Institute.
Manzanilla, Linda, L. Barba, R. Chávez, A. Tejero, C. Cifuentes, and N. Peralta. 1994. "Caves and Geophysics: An Approximation to the Underworld of Teotihuacan, Mexico." *Archaeometry* 36: 141–57.
Miller, Naomi. 1982. *Heavenly Caves: Reflections on the Garden Grotto*. London: Allen & Unwin.
Nehren, Rudolf. 1992. *Zur Prähistorie Der Maghrebländer*. Marokko-Algerien-Tunesien 1–2. Teil. Mainz am Rhein: Phillipp von Zabern.
Owens, Dann A., and Brian Hayden. 1997. "Prehistoric Rites of Passage: A Comparative Study of Transegalitarian Hunter-Gatherers." *Journal of Anthropological Archaeology* 16 (2): 121–61. http://dx.doi.org/10.1006/jaar.1997.0307.
Pedley, Martyn, Michael Hughes Clarke, and Pauline Galea. 2002. *Limestone Isles in a Crystal Sea: The Geology of the Maltese Islands*. Malta: Publishers Enterprises Group.
Robb, John. 2001. "Island Identities: Ritual, Travel and the Creation of Difference in Neolithic Malta." *European Journal of Archaeology* 4 (2): 175–202. http://dx.doi.org/10.1177/146195710100400202.
Riva, Corinna. 2006. "The Orientalizing Period in Etruria: Sophisticated Communities." In *Debating Orientalization: Multidisciplinary Approaches to Change in the Ancient Mediterranean*, ed. Corinna Riva and Nicholas Vella, 110–134. Monographs in Mediterranean Archaeology 10. London: Equinox Press.
Schmidt, Klaus. 2006. *Sie bauten die ersten Tempel: Das rätselhafte Heiligtum der Steinzeitjäger*. Munich: C. H. Beck Verlag.
Skeates, Robin. 2007. "Religious Experience in the Prehistoric Maltese Underworld." In *Cult in Context*, ed. David A. Barrowclough and Caroline Ann Tuke Malone, 90–96. Oxford: Oxbow.
Sprockhoff, Ernst. 1938. *Die nordische Megalithkultur: Handbuch der Urgeschichte Deutschlands 3*. Berlin: W. de Gruyter & Co.
Stoddart, Simon. 2002. "The Xaghra Shaman." In *New Approaches to Medical Archaeology and Medical Anthropology: Practitioners, Practices and Patients*, ed. Gillian Carr and Patricia Anne Baker, 125–35. Oxford: Oxbow Books.
Stoddart, Simon. 2007. "The Maltese Death Cult in Context." In *Cult in Context*, ed. David A Barrowclough and Caroline Malone, 54–60. Oxford: Oxbow.
Stoddart, Simon, and Caroline Malone. 2008. "Changing Beliefs in the Maltese Body." In *Past Bodies*, ed. Dusan Boric and John Robb, 19–28. Oxford: Oxbow Books.
Tilley, Christopher Yates. 2004. "From Honey to Ochre: Maltese Temples, Stones, Substances and the Structuring Experience." In *The Materiality of Stone Explorations in Landscape Phenomenology*, ed. Christopher Tilley, 87–145. Oxford: Berg.
Tiné, Santo, and Antonella Traverso. 1999. *The Megalithic Altar in Monte d'Accoddi*. The Nurra Triangle: An Archaeological Tour of North-eastern Sardinia 3. Viterbo: Betagamma editrice.
Tiné, Vincenzo, and Antonella Traverso. 1992. *Monte d'Accoddi: 10 anni di nuovi scavi*. Genova: Istituto Italiano Archeologia Sperimentale.
Torpiano, Alex. 2004. "The Construction of the Megalithic Temples." In *Malta before History: The World's Oldest Free-standing Stone Architecture*, ed. Daniel Cilia, 347–65. Malta: Miranda.
Trump, David Hilary. 1966. *Skorba: Excavations Carried Out on behalf of the National Museum of Malta, 1961–3*. Research Reports of the Society of Antiquaries of London 22. London: Society of Antiquaries.
Veen, Veronica, and A. Van der Blom. 1992. *The First Maltese: Origins*. Malta: Fia.
Vella, Nicholas, 1999. "'Trunkess Legs of Stone': Debating Ritual Continuity at Tas-Silg, Malta." In *Facets of Maltese Prehistory*, ed. Anton Mifsud and Charles Savona-Ventura, 225–39. Malta: The Prehistoric Society of Malta.

Watson, Aaron. 2001. "The Sounds of Transformation: Acoustics, Monuments and Ritual in the British Neolithic." In *The Archaeology of Shamanism*, ed. Neil Price, 178–92. London: Routledge.

Watson, Aaron, and David Keating. 1999. "Architecture and Sound: An Acoustic Analysis of Megalithic Monuments in Prehistoric Britain." *Antiquity* 73: 325–36.

Whitehouse, Ruth D. 1992. *Underground Religion: Cult and Culture in Prehistoric Italy*. London: Accordia Research Centre.

Whittle, Alasdair William Richardson. 1996. *Neolithic Europe: The Creation of New Worlds*. Cambridge: Cambridge University Press.

4

Landscapes of Ritual, Identity, and Memory

Reconsidering Neolithic and Bronze Age Cave Use in Crete, Greece

Peter Tomkins

The island of Crete, lying on the southern border of the Aegean Sea, is rich in caves and rockshelters. One estimate, probably conservative, places the total at around 2,000 (Davaras 1976, 42), of which approximately 10 percent have produced material dating to phases of the Neolithic (ca. 7000–3100/3000 BC; Tomkins 2007b) or Bronze Ages (hereafter, Minoan; ca. 3100/3000–1100 BC; Warren and Hankey 1989) (see table 4.1, figures 4.1, 4.2, 4.3). The majority of these, including all Neolithic examples, host types of material culture, such as coarseware and fineware ceramics, that are essentially the same as those found at contemporary open-air sites. As a consequence, the default interpretation of Cretan prehistoric caves has been to treat them as domestic sites, whether refuges (Faure 1964, 30) or the seasonal homes of farmers or transhumant pastoralists (Davaras 1996, 93; Dickinson 1994, 37; Faure 1964, 189–97; Manteli 1993a, 191; Marinatos 1928, 100; 1950, 256; Nilsson 1950, 56; Papathanassopoulos 1996b; Pendlebury 1939, 384; Pendlebury, Pendlebury, Money-Coutts 1935–1936, 23; Sakellarakis 1989, 88; Tzedakis 1996; Watrous 1982, 10; 2001, 162–63). Exceptions to this rule are so-called "burial caves," defined by the presence of human skeletal material and mainly of Early Minoan (EM; ca. 3100/3000–2000 BC) date, or "sacred caves" of Middle Minoan (MM; ca. 2000–1600 BC) or Late Minoan date (LM; ca. 1600–1100 BC), the definition of the latter varying greatly in terms of stated

TABLE 4.1 Chronological table (after Tomkins 2007b, table 1.1).

Phase	Absolute Date Range
Mesolithic	ca. 8700–7000 BC
Initial Neolithic (IN)	ca. 7000–6500/6400 BC
Early Neolithic (EN)	ca. 6500/6400–6000/5900 BC
Middle Neolithic (MN)	ca. 6000/5900–5500/5300 BC
Late Neolithic I (LN I)	ca. 5500/5300–4900 BC
Late Neolithic II (LN II)	ca. 4900–4500 BC
Final Neolithic IA (FN IA)	ca. 4500–4200 BC
Final Neolithic IB (FN IB)	ca. 4200–3900 BC
Final Neolithic II (FN II)	ca. 3900–3600 BC
Final Neolithic IIII (FN III)	ca. 3600–3300 BC
Final Neolithic IV (FN IV)	ca. 3300–3100/3000 BC
Early Minoan I-III	ca. 3100/3000–2000 BC
Middle Minoan I-III	ca. 2000–1600 BC
Late Minoan I-III	ca. 1600–1100 BC

degrees of certainty (Rutkowski and Nowicki 1996, 4–5). Although the incidence of their usage varies from period to period across Crete and the wider Aegean, caves are always a rare site-type when compared to open-air sites and especially to the total number of caves available for use. Even though caves dominate the list of known Neolithic sites in certain regions (e.g., western Crete), this is an artifact

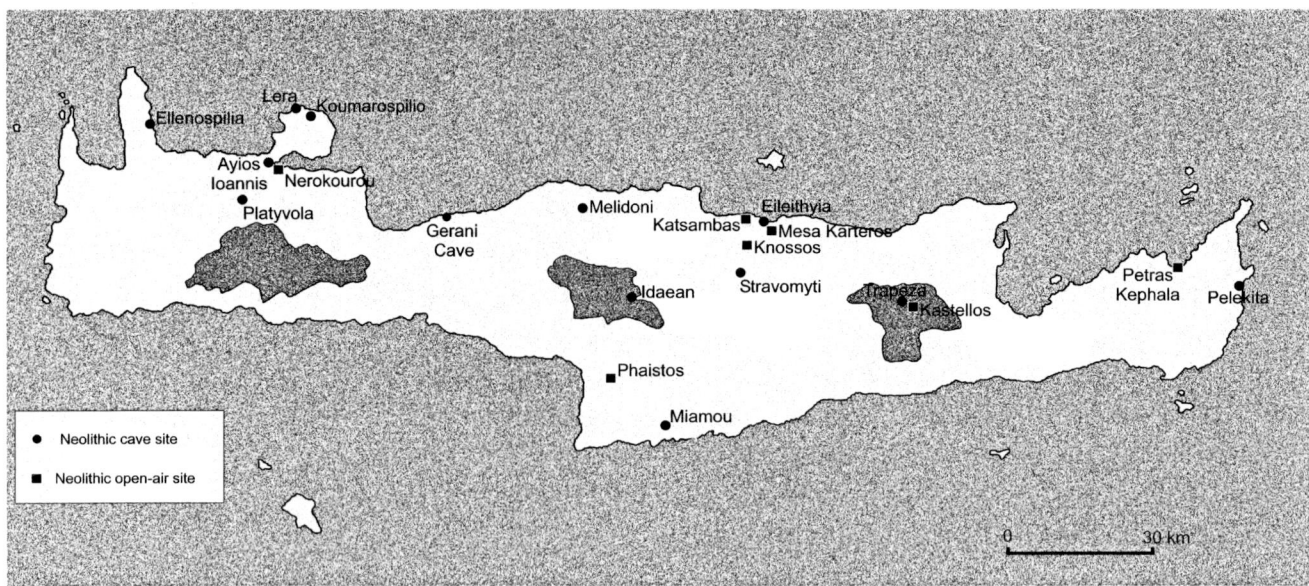

FIGURE 4.1 Neolithic sites mentioned in the text.

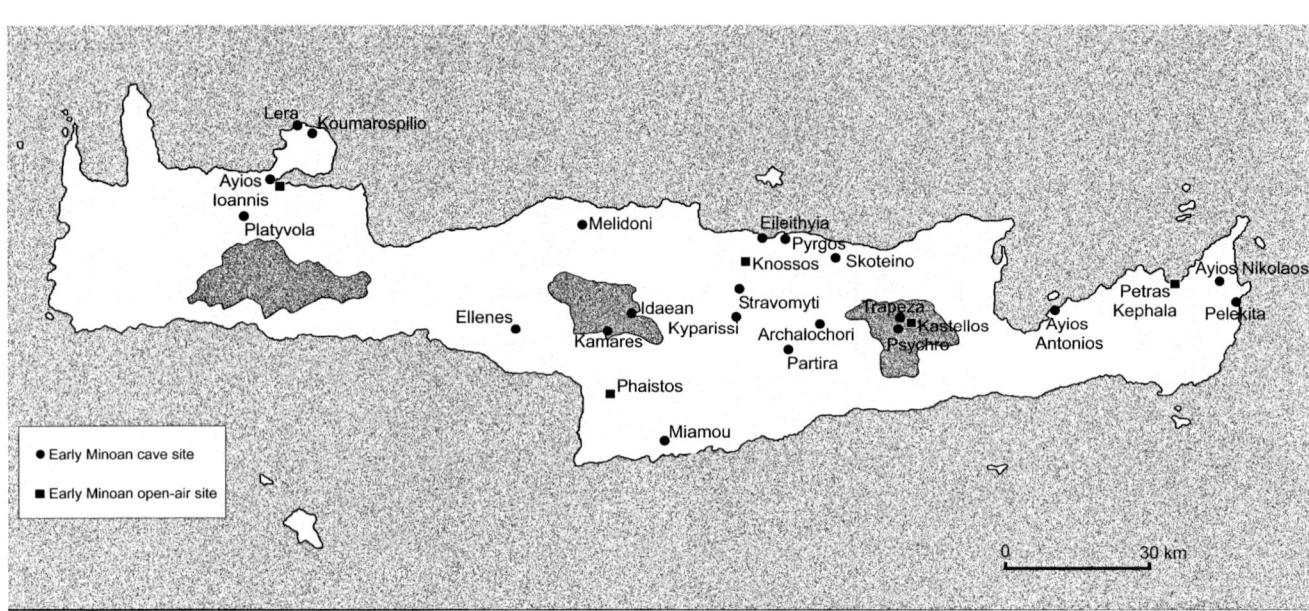

FIGURE 4.2 Early Minoan sites mentioned in the text.

of methodologies of investigation in which caves were prioritized for investigation by early field workers (e.g., Faure 1964; Marinatos 1928, 1950; Taramelli 1897, 1901).

Structuring interpretations of function has been the presumption that domesticity represents the natural and self-evident interpretation of prehistoric cave usage—a belief held most strongly for the Neolithic period. In this way the onus of proof is placed firmly on those seeking alternative, usually ritual, interpretations. In this chapter I argue that this presumption should be reversed, that Neolithic and Minoan cave use on Crete was primarily if not entirely ritual in nature and, moreover, that Middle and Late Minoan cave sanctuaries developed directly out of an earlier tradition of ritual usage during the Neolithic and Early Minoan periods. Key elements of this argument have been developed in detail elsewhere with specific reference to Neolithic caves in the Aegean (Tomkins 2009). In this chapter the focus is on cave use on Crete during the Neolithic and Early Minoan periods and the transition to Middle Minoan (ca. 7000–2000 BC).

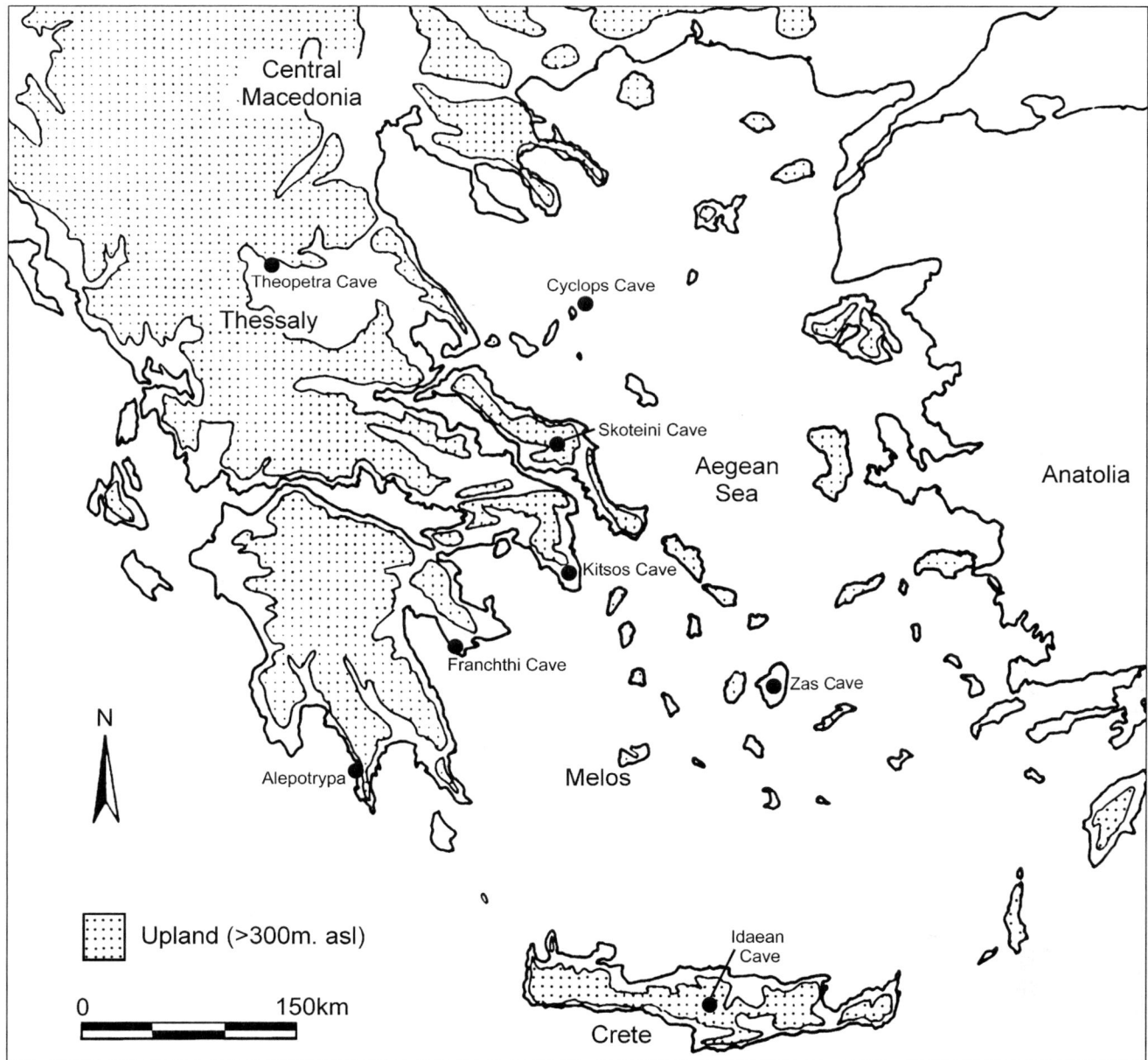

FIGURE 4.3 Aegean Neolithic and Early Bronze Age sites mentioned in the text.

DOMESTICITY RECONSIDERED

One of the reasons that domesticity has seemed such a safe and uncontroversial interpretation is that it accords with the popular myth that prehistoric people, but particularly those of the Stone Age, were cave dwellers by preference. In fact, during the Upper Paleolithic and Mesolithic in the Aegean, both cave and open-air dwelling coexisted as logical parts of a strategy of seasonal foraging where specific caves offered convenient shelter close to important subsistence resources (e.g., Bailey 1992; Runnels 2001, 236–7, 239, 241, 244–5, 253). In the case of agriculture, however, with its very different regimes of subsistence and mobility, the logic of an adaptive, domestic use of caves is rather more difficult to envisage (Tomkins 2009 for a discussion). The modal form of agricultural production in the regions of the Aegean during the Neolithic and Bronze Age was small-scale and horticultural in the sense that it took the form of an intensive cultivation of plant and animal domesticates (Halstead 1989, 70–1; 1996a, 301–3). Proximity of habitation was a critical part of this subsistence strategy, minimizing costs of security, time, and labor (G. Jones 2005). It is thus entirely logical that the principal forms of

Neolithic and Bronze Age habitation in the Aegean should be the open-air dwelling, hamlet, village, or city located directly adjacent to the areas of arable land that formed the foci of subsistence production (Halstead 1994, 198, 200).

In contrast, the kinds of caves frequented during the Neolithic and Bronze Age tend to lie at or beyond the margins of agricultural production, often on high hills and steep slopes, and can thus never compete with the proximity, locational flexibility, and efficiency offered by open-air forms of habitation. Moreover, it should not simply be assumed that areas of modern or historic cultivation that lie in the vicinity of these cave sites were always deemed cultivable in the past, agricultural strategies being no more universal than other cultural constructs. The agricultural colonization of agriculturally marginal upland regions in Crete begins only in the final few centuries of the Neolithic (i.e., FN IV; ca. 3300–3100/3000 BC; Tomkins 2007b, 44) or else at the beginning of the Bronze Age (i.e., EM I), depending on the particular region concerned (Tomkins 2008, 37–42), while the introduction of agricultural terracing on steeper slopes in the Aegean is currently placed no earlier than the Middle Bronze Age (French and Whitelaw 1999, 173–75). In this way, it is difficult to see how caves might have formed a logical element within an agricultural subsistence strategy as they typically lie beyond the diurnal sphere of production.

Domestic explanations are further called into question by some of the specific characteristics of caves known to have been frequented during the Neolithic or Bronze Age. Often Cretan prehistoric cave sites comprise features that would seem to render them poorly suited for habitation, whether through excessive darkness (e.g., Trapeza, Ellenes, Eileithyia), dampness (e.g., Trapeza, Pelekita, Ellenes), cold (e.g., the Idaean and Kamares caves), or through difficulties of access (e.g., Stravomyti) (Faure 1964, 55–6, 72; Hall 1999, 128, 131; Tyree 1974, 34–6; Zois 1973, 176–7). Thus the small entrance of the Eileithyia cave restricts ventilation to such an extent that at on at least one occasion its excavation was brought to a halt (Faure 1964, 55); and workers excavating in the narrow, awkward passageways of the Stravomyti cave are said to have panicked on at least one occasion (Marinatos 1950, 252). Movement inside many caves is also restricted by fallen boulders and gaping chasms (e.g., Platyvola; Hall 1999, 118–19). Moreover, in several cases the principal area of prehistoric deposition actually seems to have been focused in the darkest parts of the cave. In these characteristics Cretan prehistoric caves closely parallel those frequented elsewhere in the Aegean (Tomkins 2009; Wickens 1986).

Equally challenging to the domestic model is the relatively frequent presence of human skeletal material. It has been suggested that examples of articulated skeletons found on the surface inside some Cretan caves, such as the three from the entrance to the Gerani cave, represent the remains of inhabitants who were trapped by a rockfall (Godart and Tzedakis 1992: 77–8; cf. also Papathanassopoulos 1996c, 82; Weinberg 1970, 579) or who were victims of violence (Faure 1964, 30; 1969a; 1969b). However, articulated skeletal material has also been found stratified below these final use-surfaces (e.g., Ayios Ioannis; French 1990, 79). This suggests instead a deliberate form of primary corporal deposition, parallels for which occur at other Neolithic caves in the Aegean (e.g., Alepotrypa; Papathanassopoulos 1996d; more generally, see Tomkins 2009). More frequently, however, human skeletal material in Neolithic caves in Crete and the Aegean is disarticulated and associated with different stratigraphic units. It has often been assumed that this juxtaposition and intermingling of activity areas with mortuary space was standard Neolithic practice (e.g., Papathanassopoulos 1996b, 1996c). In fact, the relationship between the two appears to have been structured and clearly defined. Human skeletal material is typically absent from active domestic living spaces in Neolithic villages, such as the Cretan site of Knossos, but does occur occasionally sealed in pits, walls, ditches, and cemeteries (Perlès 2001, 273, 281; Triantaphyllou 1999, 128–30; 2008, 142–47). The only exceptions are rare isolated fragments, which appear to have circulated above ground as valued items in their own right. On Crete this separation is further enhanced and formalized with the emergence of specific burial foci, certainly from the beginning of EM I, if not the preceding FN IV period (see below).

And so, at the heart of the domestic model of prehistoric cave use lies a paradox. Why would prehistoric farmers periodically use caves as habitation sites when those caves that are known to have been frequented are less conveniently situated in relation to agricultural land than are open-air locations, and they often lie in landscapes where agriculture may not have been practiced until long after such caves were first frequented? For domestic explanations to remain valid, they need to explain not only how and why certain caves might have been viable and advantageous domestic sites for farmers, but also how domestic usage might account for all aspects of the prehistoric assemblages found within them.

One much favored domestic explanation for cave use posits that prehistoric caves in Crete and elsewhere in the Aegean served as the seasonal dwellings of mobile pastoralist groups (e.g., Jacobsen 1984; Moody 1987, 288–91; Watrous 1982, 10; 2001, 166). This seemingly attractive theory is, however, actually very difficult to sustain both theoretically and empirically, particularly so in the case of the Neolithic (Halstead 2008; Tomkins 2009). Studies of faunal and botanical assemblages from Neolithic–Early

Bronze Age caves around the Aegean consistently indicate a mixed-farming mode of subsistence, essentially the same as that practiced at lowland open-air villages (Halstead 2008, 241–43; Halstead and Jones 1987, 144–5). Domesticated animals do not appear to have been managed to maximize their calorific yield via dairying, but were instead kept in small numbers and culled periodically for their meat (Halstead 1996a; 2008, 241–44). Stable-isotope analysis of human skeletal material from Neolithic caves elsewhere in Greece confirms this picture, suggesting that the users of caves ate mainly cereals and legumes, with no evidence for a significant intake of red meat (Papathanasiou 2001, 24–6, 38–40, 44). The earliest evidence for a coherent system of upland sites on Crete dates to the final phase of FN (i.e., FN IV: e.g., east Cretan uplands), but here caves still remain a minority site in a landscape that consists almost entirely of small, dispersed, open-air sites located next to small stands of cultivable arable land and with surface assemblages that include mortars (Tomkins 2008, 37–42). Although none of these sites has yet been excavated, current evidence suggests a form of mixed farming (Halstead 2008; Tomkins 2008, 40, 42). It is perhaps also worth noting that the distribution of a FN IV vessel type known as the "cheesepot" (if, that is, it had anything to do with cheese production) is almost entirely confined to FN IV coastal sites, such as Petras Kephala, and is absent from the Cretan upland interior (Tomkins 2007b, 44; 2008, 42).

Problematic also is the way domestic explanations draw support from modern Greek traditions and ethnographies of cave use, thus assuming a series of questionable socioeconomic constants—such as attitudes to landscape, subsistence practices, or mobility—with time as the only variable (Halstead 1996b; Nixon and Price 2001, 395–7). In reality the traditional Mediterranean rural economy, within which pastoralism has historically operated, is the product of specific socioeconomic conditions (e.g., global market economy, extensive agriculture) that are unlikely to have been in place before the Middle Bronze Age, if not later (Cherry 1988; Halstead 1996a, 301–2; Nixon and Price 2001). Similarly anachronistic is the notion that Neolithic caves on Crete served as refuges under similar geopolitical conditions of domination and resistance as obtained in the nineteenth century AD (Faure 1964, 30; Hall 1999, 104–5 for a critique).

In the last decade or so several scholars have suggested that the use of some Neolithic caves on Crete and elsewhere in the Aegean may have been ritual in nature (Broodbank 2000, 165; Demoule and Perlès 1993, 404–5; Dickinson 1994, 34, 40–41; Hall 1999, 105–7; Nakou 1995, 21–2; Whitehouse 1992, 194). In most cases these are brief statements, couched in cautious language, and confined only to caves that stand out by virtue of their distance from arable land, their difficulty of access, and/or the nature of their finds (e.g., metal objects; Nakou 1995). Even in such cases the idea that they might have been ritual sites has met with resistance (e.g., Zachos 1999, 158–61). In general the continued attractiveness of domestic explanations of cave use may be understood to derive from a failure fully to comprehend Neolithic ritual and develop methodologies for its identification, a situation which in turn has prevented the development of a ritual model of Aegean prehistoric cave use that might challenge the dominance of domestic explanations (Tomkins 2009).

DEFINING AND IDENTIFYING PREHISTORIC RITUAL

Ritual is generally understood to denote something deliberately odd, in the sense that it belies functional or economic explanation and is unusual, striking, and symbolic when placed within its temporal and spatial context (Hodder 1982, 164). Most approaches to prehistoric ritual in the Aegean have treated it as a separate domain of activity, in isolation from and often in polar opposition to the domestic or that which is daily, familiar, and habitual. The conventional methodology for the identification of prehistoric ritual in the Aegean has been to rely on the presence of material signifiers that are interdependent and defy explanation in domestic terms (e.g., Renfrew 1985, 19–20; 1994, 51–2). Central to this approach is the notion that ritual practices and places will identify themselves through their distinctively different and unusual formal characteristics (e.g., specialized shrine architecture; dedicated "ritual assemblages" of specialized equipment, or votives).

This approach lends itself well to cases when ritual is marked in such unambiguous terms. In the case of MM and LM Crete, the presence of votives (e.g., figurines, body parts, miniature vases) and/or specialist shrine equipment (e.g., offering tables, altars) in distinctive natural locations, such as hilltops, peaks, caves, and springs, provides the basis for their identification as sacred sites (Peatfield 1983, 1987, 1990; Rutkowski and Nowicki 1996; Tyree 1974, 6; Watrous 1996, 28–9, 73–96). However, the effectiveness of this approach is predicated on the incidence of such strong indicators, which varies from site to site. This is less of an issue for peak and spring sanctuaries, where unambiguous ritual assemblages are a consistent feature from the beginning of the Middle Minoan period onwards. In the case of caves, however, their incidence is much more infrequent. For MM I–II, only Trapeza and Psychro have produced bronze objects, clay figurines, stone offering tables, or seals that secure a ritual identification by this method (Jones 1999, 5–6, 23–4, 69–72, 80; Watrous 1996, 33). For the Late Minoan period (MM III–LM III), they are present in only eleven caves from a much larger total of known LM cave sites (Jones 1999, 5–12, 23–4; Rutkowski and Nowicki 1996; Tyree 1974).

In this way the vast majority of Neolithic and Bronze Age cave sites on Crete lack the sort of "ritual assemblages" upon which the conventional methodology for identification depends. Interestingly, however, this has not prevented some of them from being identified as sacred through a broadening of the criteria for identification to include aspects such as location. Central to this process was the early identification of the mainly MM Kamares cave as a sacred site on the basis of its restricted range of ceramic forms (including decorated finewares), an absence of lithic material or other sorts of the debris one would expect from a habitation site, and its unsuitability for habitation (i.e., so high on Mount Ida as to be blocked by snow for half the year; Dawkins and Laistner 1913, 1–34; Taramelli 1901). As a result of an early and wide acceptance of this identification, Kamares quickly became the model for the identification of other MM caves as sacred sites, where aspects of location and topography were taken into account (e.g., Faure 1994, 77–83; Rutkowski and Nowicki 1996). This loosening and broadening of the methodology for identification has not, however, been consistently applied to all MM and LM cave sites, nor has it been extended to the Neolithic or Early Minoan periods, when cave assemblages are also, like Kamares, composed mainly of pottery.

Neolithic ritual, and to a lesser extent that of the Early Minoan period (Warren 1973), has long been an area of difficulty in Aegean archaeology, the pursuit of which might be characterized as an ultimately fruitless search for a special class of ritual objects (Whitehouse 1996, 28, for a discussion). Neolithic material culture has long suffered from being forced into modern functional categories, despite the fact that its formal characteristics consistently fail to conform to expectations aroused by terms such as *domestic* or *ritual*. Common forms, such as ceramic containers or lithic tools, have repeatedly been glossed as "utilitarian" or "domestic" in function (e.g., Hall 1999, 104; Papathanassopoulos 1996b, 1996c; Perlès 1992, 148–49; Sampson 1992, 95; Watrous 1996, 57–73), rather than treated more neutrally as objects no less subject to esteem and fluctuating value than other rarer types, such as beads or pendants (Appadurai 1986; Tomkins 2009). Figurines, in contrast, have long been privileged, fetishized even, as sacred objects, whether considered as votives or representations of the divine (e.g., Gimbutas 1991; Mellaart 1967), and have long been treated as our only source for Neolithic or Early Bronze Age ritual (Evans 1901; Nilsson 1950, 291–3; Sampson 1992, 96; Watrous 2001, 162). Such an approach is, however, anachronistic in assuming that such figurines functioned in similar ways to the votive or cult representations of the human form found at later Greek sanctuaries. Moreover, recent contextual studies of Neolithic figurines in Crete, the Aegean, the Balkans, and Anatolia have tended to suggest that figurines did not specifically serve as specialized cult items nor did dense accumulations of them demarcate shrines, but rather that they were bound up in the practice and negotiation of everyday life (Bailey 2005; Hodder 1996; Meskell et al. 2008, 143–5; Mina 2008). It would appear, therefore, that there is nothing intrinsic to categories of Neolithic or Early Minoan material culture that might indicate where or indeed if a boundary between domestic and ritual deployment might be drawn.

The origin of these issues of recognition and interpretation can be traced back to the misplaced notion that rituality and domesticity were always the seemingly opposing and separable domains of behavior that they are in modern Western society. In fact many small-scale societies lack a conception of ritual as a distinct and separate domain of activity. In view of this, it makes better sense to define prehistoric ritual in broader terms as a particular form of practice or performance, described by its own conventions and occupying a continuum between the local and informal and the public and highly structured (Barrett 1988; Bradley 2005, 29–30, 119; Brück 1999, 314–18). In this way the apparent ambiguity of prehistoric ritual, at least to modern outsiders, is its crucial element, deriving from a close relationship with the domestic. Ritual offered a different way of experiencing the domestic and through it people were able to develop an understanding of their world that connected the everyday with the cosmological. This plays out at an active material level in the process of ritualization, where objects symbolic of the everyday are transformed into important statements about human existence through their juxtaposition with distinctive kinds of performance and context (Barrett 1988, 31–2; Bradley 2005; Hodder 1982, 172).

In this way it is ritualization, expressed in aspects of performance and context rather than ritual objects, that is most critical to the identification and interpretation of Neolithic and Bronze Age ritual (Bradley 2005; Tomkins 2009). Time and space are key components of ritualization, not just in the sense that rituals may occur in specific places or at specific times, but also in the sense that in ritual time and space are experienced in very different ways, which create distance from the everyday (Bradley 1998, 88–90). In nonindustrial societies, locales that are in some way liminal to the domestic may come to evoke qualities associated with the supernatural realm (Helms 1993; Renfrew 1985, 16–20). This is usually clearest in cases when foci that are spatially separate from habitation—whether natural places, such as caves, mountain peaks, or rivers, or constructed monuments, such as built tombs—become the focus for ritual practice and deposition (Bradley 1998). However, liminality also operates at smaller scales, as illustrated by ritual contexts that are adjacent to or overlap with domestic space, such as examples of structured depositions in pits or in the fabric of buildings at Neolithic Knossos (Tomkins 2007a, 187–90; Triantaphyllou 2008). Distance from the everyday may also be invoked by enlarging or miniaturizing familiar subjects.

It is important also to be sensitive to different regimes of value operating within and between different forms and media, and to how their selective deployment may serve to raise an everyday activity to the level of ritual performance. During the Neolithic, ceramic containers were highly valued and their use seemingly restricted to special occasions, with the daily burden of container usage being borne by a range of more durable nonceramic containers (Tomkins 2007a; Vitelli 1993, 213–16). Regimes of value may also be glimpsed operating within object-substance categories, such as pottery, where preferential use and deposition of finewares or vessels from nonlocal sources may serve to mark unusual contexts of deposition, examples of which may be noted at the Neolithic Cretan sites of Knossos and Katsambas (Tomkins 2007a, 2012, n.d.a, n.d.b). Moving from containers to their contents, food consumption may be ritualized by consuming everyday food in association with special or high-value object types, by consuming unusual forms of food, or by preparing food in special ways. The main dietary staples of Neolithic and Early Bronze Age communities appear to have been cultivated cereals and pulses, while all evidence, including bioarchaeological and stable-isotope analyses of human bone, suggests that meat was consumed very infrequently, probably only on special occasions (Halstead 2007; Papathanasiou 2001, 24–6, 38–40, 44). Meat consumption not only had a simple rarity value, but also carried with it certain ideological and social implications in that it involved the killing of livestock, the possession of which is likely to have been a source of status. Generally the carcasses of large animals spoil easily and are thus most amenable to short-term, larger-scale consumption by groups larger than a single household (Halstead 2007, 27, 39, 41–43).

Rituals, such as floor cleaning, the deposition of complete vessels, and deliberate destruction by burning, may accompany the abandonment of Neolithic houses at Knossos and elsewhere in the Aegean (e.g., Stevanović 1997; Tomkins 2007a). Other forms of ritual performance, such as fragmentation and accumulation, play out more explicitly at the level of objects. Fragmentation refers to the deliberate breakage or division of something and the distribution of its parts in order to construct and represent relations between people and objects (Chapman and Gaydarska 2007; Gamble 2007, 132–52). These parts might circulate as part of everyday existence, serving as "material citations" of the ritual act (A. Jones 2005). Such forms of ritual fragmentation and circulation may, for example, help to explain the presence at Knossos and other Neolithic village sites of small, worked sherd disks that are often pierced. Such disks may have served as material citations of specific object-person relationships, which might be strung together and thus accumulated and displayed. In this way such part-whole relationships may serve as metaphors for social relations through processes of accumulation, where parts or wholes are collected together as sets, or enchainment, where a chain of social relations is achieved through exchange. A related form of performance, which might be termed curation, involves the deliberate deposition of complete, unfragmented objects in such a way as to divert them from normal patterns of circulation and access.

Recent studies have demonstrated that through the characterization and contextualization of these techniques of ritualization it is possible to gain important insights into social categorization and social relations (e.g., Bradley 2005, 145–64; Chapman and Gaydarska 2007, 53–112). In Neolithic Crete, as well as the wider Aegean, examples of these techniques abound wherever forms of deposition are structured and spatially restricted (e.g., pits, caves), and where there has been a commitment to contextual study (Tomkins 2007a, 185–91; 2009). Fragmentation practices may also extend to include the human body or what has been termed corporal culture (for the distinction between corporal and material culture see Gamble 2007, 87–110), good examples of which are the isolated human skeletal fragments in Cretan settlement contexts, such as Knossos, that seem to have circulated among the living as expressions of relationships with the dead (Triantaphyllou 1999, 2008).

CRETAN NEOLITHIC CAVES AS RITUAL PLACES

Issues of Data and Interpretation

With a handful of notable Bronze Age exceptions (e.g., Ida, Kamares, Psychro), prehistoric cave use on Crete is a neglected area of study (see Hall 1999 10–18; Strasser 1992, 39–89, for discussions of the problem). The very recent identification of twenty-eight Paleolithic and Mesolithic sites in the Plakias region of southern Crete (Strasser et al. 2010) demonstrates that the human use of caves and rockshelters on the island may now be pushed back well into the Pleistocene. Elsewhere on the island clear evidence for pre-Neolithic usage is currently lacking, although mention of bone fishhooks in preliminary reports of excavations at the large coastal cave of Pelekita in east Crete (Papadakis 1987) hints at possible Mesolithic usage, given that bone hooks are entirely unknown at Neolithic sites on Crete but are characteristic of Aegean Mesolithic coastal cave assemblages (e.g., Cyclops Cave, Yioura; Sampson 1999). At least 100 caves are known to have produced Neolithic–EM material, around half of which have seen some form of excavation; but only in the case of a quarter or less has this been more than a small sounding (Hall 1999, 10–12). Almost all of these excavations are either unpublished or accessible only in the form of preliminary reports. Certainly no cave has yet been investigated or published to the standards set by the work at Franchthi (e.g., Jacobsen and Farrand 1988) and Kitsos (Lambert 1981) on the Greek mainland.

Complicating understanding further have been a series of long-standing problems of Neolithic and EM I phasing and chronology, problems which have only very recently been resolved (Di Tonto and Todaro 2008; Todaro 2005; Tomkins 2007b). Naturally, the available literature on caves, formed during the course of more than a century of investigation (for useful summaries see Hall 1999, 98–146; Strasser 1992, 193–265), reflects older confusions over phasing or terminology and thus considerable caution must be exercised in using chronological attributions that are not well corroborated by illustration. This chapter focuses primarily on caves that satisfy this criterion and may thus be more securely linked to a newly revised Neolithic chronology for Crete (Tomkins 2007b).

At present the earliest dated pottery from a Cretan cave takes the form of a dipper with a double-horned wishbone handle from Gerani that finds close parallels in Middle Neolithic (MN) levels from Knossos (Tomkins 2007b, figure 1.4, 21). In advance of full publication of the Gerani excavations the possibility of still-earlier ceramic material cannot be ruled out, although the original claim of an Initial Neolithic (IN) stratum has been discredited (Jarman 1996, 215–16). Although there have been uncorroborated claims of pottery of Late Neolithic (LN) type from Ayios Ioannis and Pelekita (Godart and Tzedakis 1992, 44; Papadakis 1987; Tomkins 2007b, 27–32), the only illustrated material of this type comes from Gerani (for references, see Tomkins 2007b, 29), Miamou (Taramelli 1897, figures 10, 16), and possibly Koumarospilio (Manteli 1993b, figure 72, 6). However, future study and publication of excavated cave assemblages and further deep soundings will surely increase this number. All other known Cretan Neolithic cave assemblages appear to date to one or more subphases within the long Final Neolithic period (FN I–IV; ca. 4500–3100/3000 BC). Until very recently (i.e., Todaro 2005; Tomkins 2007b: 41–48; Warren 2004), confusion has reigned over the precise sequencing of deposits between the end of FN and the beginning of EM, such that early EM I assemblages from caves or rockshelters, such as Ayios Nikolaos, Eileithyia, and Partira, were mistakenly dated to the Neolithic (e.g., Renfrew 1964; Vagnetti and Belli 1978).

Temporality and Spatiality

At present a lack of detailed study and publication restricts what can be said about how and over what time scales Neolithic cave deposits were formed. Analogy with better-known Neolithic cave sequences from other Aegean regions would suggest that cave use was episodic and punctuated by frequent and sometimes long periods of hiatus (e.g., Tomkins 2009; Vitelli 1999, 12, 15, 61–62, 96). Indirect support for this in Cretan caves is provided by the presence of ceramic material belonging to multiple phases of the Neolithic. For example, the mixed deposits from Lera have produced material belonging to FN II–IV as well as later Minoan phases (Manteli 1993b, 169–76; Tomkins 2007b, 35–44). At Platyvola, the vast majority of the Neolithic pottery dates no earlier than FN IV (i.e., dull burnish; bowls with incurved rim; deep bowls with convex base; high-necked jars; s-profile bowls; bowls with horizontal tubular lug; Manteli 1993a, 124–5, 200; Tomkins 2007b, 41–44). Nonetheless, small amounts of FN I (e.g., ripple decoration) and FN II–III (Manteli 1993b, 125, figure 82) are also present. Likewise at Koumarospilio, the majority of the Neolithic pottery, including all illustrated semicomplete vessels, appears to be no earlier than FN IV in date (e.g., granulation decoration; deep bowls with convex base; low pedestal bases; cheesepots; bowl with horizontal tubular lug; Manteli 1993a, 163; 1993b, 180–82; figures 73.6, 9; 73b.8). However, there is also sherd material that appears to date to earlier phases, namely LN (i.e., carinated bowl with pellet decoration; Manteli 1993b, figure 72, 6), FN I (Tzedakis 1973, 583), and FN III (circular and triangular jabbed decoration; Manteli 1993b, figure 74, 6). In these examples the material from earlier FN phases is scarce, usually highly fragmented, and sufficient only to suggest periodic visitation.

The episodic nature of Cretan cave use is most clearly demonstrated by the sequences from Miamou and Gerani. At Miamou lower (LN II–EM IA) and upper (mainly EM I–II) strata of deposition are separated by a hard layer of calcitic concretion (Taramelli 1897, 289–303, figures 11, 14, 15). However, the presence of EM I material in both levels suggests that the break in use lasted no more than a few generations. At Gerani deposits of MN–LN I, LN II, and FN I date are similarly separated by thin (1–3 centimeters) calcified layers, each of which would have taken at least 80 years to have formed (Godart and Tzedakis 1992, pls. xciv–xcvi; Manteli 1993b, 159, 167; Tzedakis

1980). Despite the episodic nature of their formation, the individual components of the Gerani sequence are, like Miamou, chronologically proximate and demonstrate clear continuities in depositional practice. It would thus appear that, unlike at open-air village sites, where structured forms of deposition (e.g., pits) suggest a need for direct physical concealment, in caves items of material or corporal culture might be left exposed on the surface, often for long periods, safe from unsanctioned removal. Such a practice enhanced the potential for the accumulation and periodic reorganization of sets of objects, which, in remaining visible, actively contributed to the ongoing significance of the cave (Tomkins 2009; cf. Briault 2007, 134–5 for MM–LM peak sanctuaries). In this way caves could function as single depositional contexts, which, in remaining open, allowed activities to play out over different time scales involving multiple visits (Tomkins 2009).

Long-term continuities in practice suggest that the significance of a cave, such as Gerani, and the nature of the practices that took place within it were codified and maintained at permanently settled, open-air village locations beyond the cave, where they were successfully transmitted over centuries or even millennia before the next phase of cave deposition might begin. In this way oral traditions of place, reinforced and perpetuated by the ongoing landscape presence of caves, are likely to have ensured that caves remained candidates for further activity. This aspect of caves is crucial to an understanding of subsequent phases of cave use during the Neolithic and Bronze Age.

The main built features noted in reports on Cretan Neolithic caves, such as Miamou, Gerani, and Ayios Ioannis, are hearths and floors (Manteli 1993b: 159; Taramelli 1897, 295–96; Tzedakis 1980; 1981, 395). Such features are typical of Neolithic caves in general around the Aegean, which, like the Cretan caves, also appear to lack the complex spatial subdivisions thought to demarcate separate household groups at open-air village sites (Halstead 1999, 79–81; Tomkins 2009). Rather access and deposition in caves seems to have been structured by natural features of internal physical topography, such as niches, passageways, chambers, and pools, as well as the distribution and degree of light. At Ellenospilia human bones and Neolithic finewares were noted as clustering around a prominent stalagmite in the central hall, while the dark back chambers appear to have been the focus for more than a meter of dark ashy deposit (Faure 1956, 99; 1964, 53). At Eileithyia, the bulk of the Neolithic material was excavated at the very back of a long chamber and in a small, low, and nearly inaccessible chamber (Marinatos 1932). At Koumarospilio the main focus of Neolithic and Bronze Age deposition appears to have been a massive rock in the upper chamber, from where a small opening leads via a twisting passage to a lower chamber (Jantzen 1951; Manteli 1993b, 178).

Liminality

Currently the number of known or suspected Neolithic cave sites represents less than 5 percent of the estimated total number of caves on Crete. This would seem to suggest that cave users were highly selective in the caves they chose to frequent and thus that aspects of cave morphology or location are likely to have been significant for function. When compared to the open-air village—the modal form of Neolithic settlement in the Aegean—all Cretan Neolithic caves emerge as liminal places, entry into which involves dramatic changes in light, sound, smell, and freedom of movement that force visitors momentarily to reorient themselves. Aspects of topography, such as steep rock-faces, may further complicate access. For example, the Stravomyti cave is situated in a cliff with multiple, mostly inaccessible openings and comprises two separate but connected cave systems with chambers and narrow passages that weave around each other (Hall 1999, 127–29).

In many of the Cretan Neolithic caves this quality of liminality also seems to operate at the level of the wider landscape (Hall 1999; cf. Tomkins 2009). The large cave of Ellenospilia lies near a small bay, on the east coast of the rocky and arid Rhodhopi peninsula in West Crete and at a considerable distance from the nearest zone of fertile arable land (Marinatos 1928, 100). Miamou lies high above the agricultural plain of the Mesara in the hills of the Asterousia. Even further removed from the diurnal sphere of Neolithic production is the Idaean cave, located above the snow line high in the mountains of central Crete. Koumarospilio lies in an arid, rocky, mountainous landscape unsuitable for agriculture on the north coast of the Akrotiri peninsula (Moody 1987, 287). Pelekita is located on a rocky, steep, and arid stretch of the east Cretan coast, at least 5 kilometers from the fertile river valleys of Zakros and Palaikastro.

Exceptions to the trend toward geographical liminality include a group of caves or artificially enhanced subterranean chambers in locations proximate to permanent open-air Neolithic settlement and fertile arable land. In such cases, liminality is evoked more obviously by the qualities of the actual cave or chamber as a separate space of activity than by its geographical distance from the everyday. For example, immediately to the west of the FN III–IV settlement site of Kastellos on the Lasithi Plain lie the caves of Trapeza, Grymani, Skaphidhia, and Meskine, all of which have produced evidence of use during FN and/or EM (Pendlebury, Pendlebury, Money-Coutts 1937–

1938, 6). The FN–EM Eileithyia cave lies in rocky terrain, just above the Bronze Age coastal settlement of Amnisos, not far from the FN IV open-air site of Mesa Karteros (Karetsou 1976; Tomkins 2007b, 44). The cave of Ayios Ioannis is easily accessible from the fertile agricultural plain east of Chania, and Platyvola, although located in steeply sloping terrain, is only a kilometer from a suspected FN open-air site (Tzedakis 1966: 429; Godart and Tzedakis 1992, 50).

In addition a number of artificial or artificially enhanced subterranean chambers, apparently in use during MN and LN, have been brought to light on the immediate periphery of the open-air habitation sites of Knossos and Katsambas in north-central Crete (Tomkins n.d.a, n.d.b). At Knossos (figure 4.4) excavations early in the twentieth century on the south slope of the Neolithic settlement revealed a series of artificial subterranean chambers, clearly anterior to the Middle and Late Bronze Age structures above them (e.g., Evans 1921, 103–7, 427–30; 1928, 289–96). Although most of these chambers now lack positive dating evidence, more-recent excavations on the south slope have brought to light the entrance to a subterranean chamber, the mouth of which was filled with a mixed MN–LN I deposit (Trench Z; Evans 1994; Tomkins 2007b). Elsewhere in this area modern tests have produced indirect evidence for digging in the form of earlier Neolithic material redeposited in LN I levels (Tomkins n.d.b). At Katsambas, around 10 meters to the south of a LN I house, a series of connected subterranean chambers up to 4.5 meters in length were excavated, the roof of which appears to have collapsed at some point after the Neolithic (Alexiou 1953). Contemporary reports mention the presence of burnt human bone in the chambers (Cook and Boardman 1953, 50; Courbin 1954, 152; Faure 1964, 78). Study of the pottery by the author suggests that the original in situ deposit in these chambers was MN and LN (mainly LN I) in date and was unusual, with respect to MN and LN assemblages from houses at Katsambas, in being dominated by pottery in fabrics of nonlocal (> 7 kilometers) origin (Tomkins n.d.a). Recent rescue excavations in the immediate vicinity of this chamber have revealed additional, artificially enhanced subterranean chambers and Neolithic ceramic assemblages. Therefore, it would appear that in the case of Knossos and Katsambas, our two earliest known Neolithic open-air sites on Crete, ritual deposition, probably in association with human skeletal material, also took place within the immediate vicinity of habitation, but in a zone set aside for special purpose (i.e., the south slope at Knossos, and the hilltop at Katsambas) and specifically focused on subterranean, dark places, specially created or modified so to function as concealed, intimate ritual spaces.

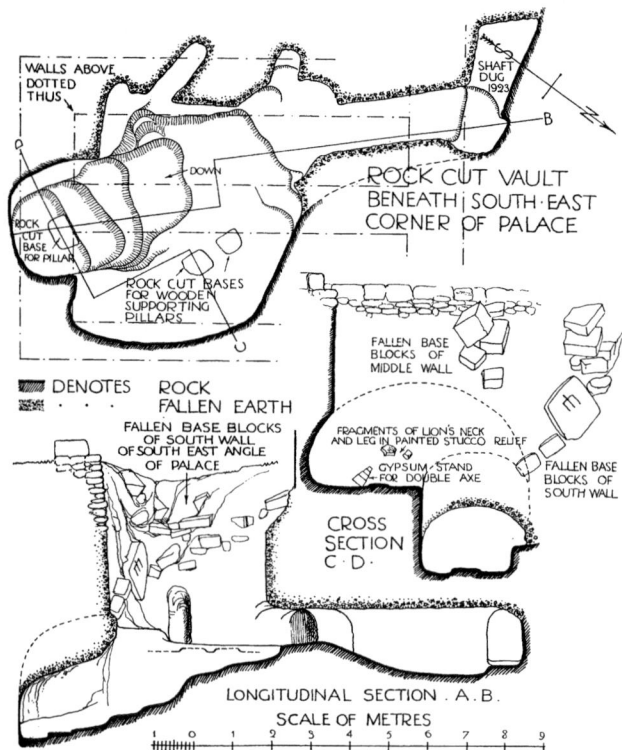

FIGURE 4.4 Knossos, subterranean chamber beneath the southeast corner of the Palace. (Evans 1928, figure 171.)

Centrality

In many cases the significance of a cave may also have been informed by its centrality in relation to other prominent natural features in the landscape (see Tomkins 2009). Examples include Stravomyti, located in the western flank of Mount Iuktas, which dominates the landscape of north-central Crete and whose peak was the site of a Bronze Age peak sanctuary (Karetsou 1981); the Idaean cave, on the northern slope of Mount Ida, which is visible from much of the island; and Pelekita on the eastern flank of Mount Traostalos. Such caves are conspicuous for being the largest in their respective regions and may have served as focal points, or *axes mundi*, within wider sacred landscapes, where other natural features, such as rocks, rivers, or mountains, were invested with special meanings. Ritual cave use would thus have been one of the ways in which the significance of wider sacred landscapes could have been perpetuated or contested. In this way evidence for changes in depositional practice in caves, such as those that occur in FN IV–EM I and MM I (see below), might then be read as deliberate attempts to alter the significance of or otherwise appropriate wider areas of landscape. In contrast, the continuities in depositional practice that typify Neolithic caves, which often bridge long periods of hiatus, are suggestive of periods of continuity in significance, where landscape provides a stable structure upon which to hang oral traditions. In this respect, the fact that the peaks of Iuktas and Traostalos were the sites of later Bronze Age sanctuaries, while Mount Ida was a focus of veneration via the Bronze Age cave sanctuaries at Kamares and the Idaean cave, suggests the likelihood that Bronze Age ritual in natural locations, such as peaks, caves, and springs, was informed by much deeper traditions of knowledge and practice and linked to far older sacred landscapes.

The location of MN–FN I Gerani on the rocky coast of northwest Crete, at the mouth of a small river but away from the fertile locations favored by early farmers, fits a pattern of earlier Neolithic cave usage around the Aegean characterized by a preference for locations close to the sea along routes of long-range, marine-based movement (Tomkins 2009). Combined stylistic and petrographic study of EN and MN pottery from Knossos has demonstrated intense local circulation of ceramic vessels as well as evidence, in the form of imported vessels, for longer journeys made along the north coast to the western and eastern extremes of the island, as well as to still more distant regions of the Greek and Anatolian mainlands (Tomkins 2004; Tomkins and Day 2001; Tomkins, Day, and Kilikolou 2004). Taken together this suggests that Gerani and other coastal Neolithic caves, such as Lera, Ellenospilia, or Pelekita, could have been frequented as much because they were nodal points or landmarks on longer journeys as for their distance from the everyday. Such caves were thus well qualified to act as places for interaction between everyday and outside worlds—*outside* denoting not just the divine but also, via the equation of geographical distance with supernatural distance, individuals and groups from distant places (Helms 1993). Any such organized encounters at caves between different allochthonous groups are likely to have been ritualized, with participation in them indexed by identity and status.

Material and Corporal Fragmentation and Accumulation

A feature of Neolithic cave assemblages on Crete, and one that has been used to argue in favor of a domestic function, is the presence of animal bone together with items of material culture (e.g., stone tools, pottery) identical to that encountered at open-air sites. However, if one accepts that the function of Neolithic material culture is not intrinsically domestic or ritual but is determined by aspects of context and performance, then different avenues of interpretation are opened up. While too little is currently known to be able to draw any meaningful conclusions about the depositional context of rarer items of material culture—such as spindle whorls, axes, quernstones, pendants, or clay beads (e.g., Godart and Tzedakis 1992, pls. c–ciii; Taramelli 1897, 296–98)—reconsideration of some of the more common items is instructive.

In view of the special nature of meat consumption, which took place rarely, presumably on special occasions, and which implies a participating group larger than a single nuclear household (Halstead 2008), the presence in caves, often, of large quantities of domesticated-animal bone most likely marks a ritualized form of communal food consumption. Evidence from Aegean Neolithic caves beyond Crete suggests that animal domesticates were most likely slaughtered and butchered close to but probably not within caves (Halstead and Jones 1987, 139). They were most likely driven there for special purpose from village locations. Thus the nearest source for the domesticated-animal bone (cows, ovicaprids) found in the lower (LN II–EM IA) level at Miamou (Taramelli 1897, 296–97), lay quite some distance below and to the north of the cave at open-air settlements on the Mesara plain. Similarly distant to the south is the closest source of the shellfish, sea crab, and lobster also found in this level (Taramelli 1897, 297). The transportation of these resources to a distant location far from their areas of procurement or production may be understood in terms of the special investment expected of sacred places (Renfrew 1985).

Similarly suggestive of special investment are the unusually large amounts of obsidian tools reported from MN–FN I Gerani, LN(?)–FN Pelekita, and the late FN deposits from the Idaean cave (Papadakis 1987, 404; Sakellarakis 1985, 80; Tzedakis 1967, 1970, 1980). The closest obsidian sources to Crete are those on the Aegean islands of Melos and Yiali, with the former the source for the very large majority of the Neolithic obsidian tools from Crete. At Neolithic Knossos obsidian tools are characterized by a high intensity of reworking, suggestive of resource scarcity, and are most common during IN–LN I, after which they become considerably scarcer (Conolly 2008). During FN IV it is now clear that there was significant disparity in access to obsidian between coastal and inland sites, sufficient to suggest that obsidian procurement, working, and distribution were controlled by coastal "gateway" communities, such as Petras Kephala and Nerokourou (Carter 1998; Papadatos et al. n.d.; Tomkins 2008, 40; Tomkins and Schoep 2010). Thus the presence of sixty-eight obsidian flakes together with debitage and cores in a single late FN context from the Idaean cave (Catling 1987, 57–8; Sakellarakis 1985, 80) indicates a deposit that is as rich as it is unusual. The considerable distance of the cave from the coast and from the nearest lowland settlement further contributes to the impression that this reflects a special form of investment. Such tools could have played a part in a variety of ritual acts associated with their production and consumption. From shaving or corporal inscription to the processing of animal carcasses for consumption, the use of obsidian—a more scarce, more effective, and thus high-value material—may have served as an additional form of ritualization. The relatively large amounts of obsidian in the MN–FN I Gerani cave—but above all the presence of unbroken, high-quality, leaf-shaped spear points from an early FN level (Tzedakis 1970, pl. 416, e), of a type unknown on Crete but present at other Aegean cave sites (e.g., Zas: Zachos 1990, 38; Alepotrypa: Papathanassopoulos 1996a, no. 39)—suggests deliberate curation as well as a preference for the deposition of high-value objects, especially those whose raw material and/or style of production demonstrates connections with regions beyond the island. Notable also in this regard are two figurines at Gerani of types that are rare or unparalleled in the corpus of Cretan Neolithic figurines (i.e., Godart and Tzedakis 1992, pl. c, 2–3; Tzedakis 1970: 475; Ucko 1968), Rare, too, is the series of phallic "idols" from Pelekita (FN), Trapeza (mixed FN/EM), and Stravomyti (FN?) (Marinatos 1950, 255–6; Papadakis 1987, 404; Pendlebury, Pendlebury, and Money-Coutts 1935–1936, 116; Strasser 1992, 256), which lack comparanda from most Cretan open-air sites (FN IV Petras Kephala for an exception), but may be related to examples from the Anatolian Chalcolithic and, more generally, to the phallus imagery that occurs at other FN caves in the Aegean (e.g., Skoteini: Sampson 1992, figures 24–28; Kitsos: Lambert 1981, 412, figure 284; Tomkins 2009).

Equally unusual is the frequency with which complete or semicomplete vessels occur in cave assemblages, a feature also, it should be remembered, of the MM Kamares cave sanctuary. The complete or semicomplete MN–FN I vessels from Gerani are significant for providing our most complete view of several form types (Godart and Tzedakis 1992, pls. xcvii–xcix, ciii–iv; Tzedakis and Martlew 1999, 82–84, nos. 45–51) that are otherwise only present in fragments in the much more extensively excavated and studied deposits from Knossos. The dipper form is particularly common at Knossos but is always found in fragments, the wishbone handles being especially prone to breakage at their point of attachment, the legacy of the probable origins of the form in a different medium (wood) (Tomkins 2007a, 186). Although there are as yet no details of the precise depositional context of the vessels from Gerani, their degree of completeness is suggestive of some form of deliberate, ritualized deposition. Other examples of this would include the intact FN I ripple-burnished bowls from Platyvola and probably also Ellenospilia (Marinatos 1928, 100–1; Warren and Tzedakis 1974, 337), a FN III vessel containing the bones and part of a skull of a neonate from Stravomyti (Marinatos 1950, 255–6; Sakellarakis and Sapouna-Sakellarakis 1997, figure 329, far left), and the complete or semicomplete FN IV–EM IA jugs with v-shaped spouts from the Melidoni and Idaean caves (Godart and Tzedakis 1992, pl. cv). The presence of these jugs at cave sites is particularly striking, not just because they are normally only found at large FN III–IV villages in lowland locations (Manteli 1993a, 162), but also because at Phaistos and Knossos they occur mainly in contexts of consumption and deposition that appear themselves to be unusual and seemingly ritual in nature (Di Tonto and Todaro 2008; Tomkins 2007b, 38, 41–42). The quantity of complete vessels from caves is made all the more remarkable by the fact that vessels and profiles, owing to homogeneities in form and finish, are notoriously difficult to mend up in Neolithic ceramic assemblages, especially those that are as fragmented and mixed as tends to be the rule for cave assemblages. This suggests the likelihood that the complete and semicomplete Neolithic vessels known from the literature were actually found in situ, either complete or in a fragmented but undispersed state.

Notable also is a marked preference for the consumption and deposition of a range of open-bowl forms at cave sites, primarily in finewares, to the near exclusion of the types of closed vessel that make up the remainder of ceramic assemblages at open-air sites. For example, at MN-FN I Gerani all the form types illustrated are bowls, including the few listed closed-jar forms, which appear to be bowl forms that have been incorrectly oriented and illustrated (Manteli 1993a, 119; Tzedakis 1980). Certainly none of the necked- or collared-jar forms present in the MN–FN I assemblages at Knossos are illustrated as present. This focus on bowls suggests a structured form of consumption and deposition, in which both the container *and* its contents, whether containing the remains of a meal or, as at Stravomyti, the bones of a neonate, were important, visible elements.

A feature of many Cretan Neolithic cave assemblages is the presence of human skeletal material. In several caves, such as Gerani, Ellenospilia, and Ayios Ioannis, fully or partially articulated human skeletons are reported to have been found on the surface of Neolithic strata (Faure 1962, 45; Godart and Tzedakis 1992, 77–8; Marinatos 1928). A skeleton in a crouched position from an FN level at Ayios Ioannis and subsequently damaged by a rockfall was probably also originally deposited in a similar way (Godart and Tzedakis 1992, 44; Tzedakis 1981, 395). A second skeleton from a lower stratum appears to have been associated with a schist flake (found at its feet) and some animal bones, suggesting the burial was accompanied by some form of material deposition and food consumption or deposition. These and other Neolithic examples from Aegean caves testify to a practice of excarnation, in which bodies were laid out to decompose in caves, after which they might be subjected to secondary forms of funerary performance, such as fragmentation and accumulation (Tomkins 2009). A good example of such secondary forms of corporal manipulation are the five crania found together in an FN level at Koumarospilio and the small pile of human skeletal material, comprising a minimum of seven individuals, that was found nearby (Jantzen 1951, 2–3).

Although no full study of human skeletal material from a Cretan Neolithic cave is yet available, reported quantities are generally low—perhaps the one exception to this being the large quantity of human bone reported from Ellenospilia (Marinatos 1928, 100–1). Similarly low quantities characterize other Neolithic caves around the Aegean, with only Alepotrypa, situated not far from Ellenospilia, opposite Crete on the southern coast of Greece, producing a much larger assemblage (Tomkins 2009, table 2). The relatively small size of corporal assemblages and the generally long histories of individual cave use suggest that a significant degree of selection was in operation, with archaeologically visible forms of corporal deposition very much the exception (Perlès 2001, 274; Tomkins 2009). The infrequency of this form of treatment and the effort required to transport a body to a cave strongly suggest that selection may have been linked to status.

Although the presence of human skeletal material in Neolithic cave assemblages on Crete has encouraged some to categorize them separately as "burial caves" (e.g., Dickinson 1994, 42; Strasser 1992, 61, 74; Vagnetti and Belli 1978, 150; Watrous 2001, 162–63), such a term implies a degree of intensity and a form of functional specialization that seems inappropriate and overly simplifies a wider range of ritual behaviors. Typically corporal deposition at Neolithic caves occurs alongside evidence for a variety of other ritual activities, most notably the preparation and consumption of food (i.e., animal bone, hearths; e.g., Ayios Ioannis; Tzedakis 1981, 395), and the deposition of valued items of material culture. Since corporal deposition itself represents a specific type of ritualization, it is perhaps better to accommodate "burial sites" and "sacred sites" within a single category of ritual places.

The first hints of a development in this pattern of Neolithic cave use may be detected in the very final phase of FN (FN IV). At Trapeza a small but seemingly undisturbed deposit at the bottom of the inner chamber contained pottery, probably no later than FN III in date (incised decoration; slashed rims; Tomkins 2007b, 39–41), and animal bone, but no trace of human bone or stone tools (Pendlebury, Pendlebury, and Money-Coutts 1935–1936, 17–8). In the mixed, mainly FN IV–EM II level above this, large quantities of human bone representing a minimum of 110 individuals were found (Pendlebury, Pendlebury, and Money-Coutts 1935–1936, 102–27). A similar pattern can be detected at Koumarospilio, where a long earlier phase of low-intensity cave use represented entirely by sherd material (LN–FN III) appears to be succeeded by a more-intense phase of FN IV deposition comprising ceramic containers and human skeletal material but lacking the animal bone, dark organic material, and hearths that normally characterize Neolithic cave use (Jantzen 1951, 3–4). Other caves that have produced evidence for an earlier phase of lower-intensity deposition (Tomkins 2007b, 32–35) followed by larger FN IV–EM assemblages of human bone and material culture, such as Eileithyia and Skaphidia, may also fit this pattern. Although further detailed study is required in order to clarify this picture, it seems likely that the functional diversification and specialization that typifies ritual cave use during EM I–II (see below) may have first begun at some caves during the preceding FN IV phase. It is perhaps significant that this shift is first apparent at caves that have an earlier history of significance and either had always been close to open-air settlement (e.g., Trapeza to Kastellos) or had become close to settlement in FN IV as a result of the agricultural colonization of the more marginal areas in which they were located (Tomkins 2008, 37–42). More-intensive forms of material and corporal deposition of this sort represent a departure from Neolithic practice and may be related to a more fundamental transformation in society that appears to take place at this time (Tomkins 2010 for a discussion). During the late FN in Crete and the wider Aegean, a variety of ritual contexts, of which caves may form part, exhibit evidence for a process of communal appropriation whereby specific interest groups seek to appropriate control over what had previously been communally controlled resources (Tomkins 2010, 2012a; Tomkins and Schoep 2010).

RECONSIDERING CAVE USE IN THE BRONZE AGE

The changes in cave use hinted at in FN IV become much clearer from the beginning of EM I, when many more caves, rockshelters, and crevices become the focus for depositional activity for the first time. Broadly these may be grouped into two categories:

(1) *Burial Caves*: this group includes crevices, rockshelters, and mainly small caves with restricted entrances, usually situated in the vicinity of permanent, open-air habitation. Assemblages of this group combine frequently dense accumulations of human skeletal material with valued items of material culture. Examples of this type occur throughout the island, with the notable exception of south-central Crete (Branigan 1993, 152–54; Haggis 1993, 13, 15), and include Ayios Antonios, Ayios

Nikolaos, Ellenes, Grymani, and Partira (Béguignon 1931, 517; Haggis 1993; Marinatos 1933, 296; Mortzos 1972; Pendlebury, Pendlebury, and Money-Coutts 1935–1936, 13; 1937–1938, 3, 16–17; Platon 1953, 491; Tod 1902–1903; Tomkins 2007b, 20, table 1.6, 44–48).

(2) *Nonburial Caves*: this second and much less-discussed group of EM caves is primarily defined by an apparent absence of human skeletal material. Caves in this group are mainly larger and are often associated with prominent natural landmarks in a region, such as mountains (e.g., Kamares) or hilltops (e.g., Archalochori). Several of these (e.g., Archalochori, Kamares, Psychro, and Skoteino; Dawkins and Laistner 1912, 12–13; Hazzidakis 1913, 38–43; Vagnetti and Belli 1978), are accepted to be foci for ritual activity during subsequent phases of the Middle and Late Bronze Age. In the case of Psychro (upper chamber), a lower stratum with domesticated-animal bone and "bucchero" (burnished) pottery is mentioned (Hogarth 1900, 96), which, on the basis of the small group of burnished pottery published from the site (Watrous 2004, nos. 144–45, 142), would appear to be no earlier than EM I in date. For other caves in this group, such as Ida, Lera, Pelekita, and Stravomyti (Manteli 1993b, 169–76), EM activity represents a continuation of a pattern of material deposition that stretches back into the Neolithic, as well as forward into the Middle and Late Bronze Age, when these caves are accepted as "cult sites" (Rutkowski and Nowicki 1996, 21–40).

In none of the examples of this second group does EM deposition appear to be extensive, yet its presence is significant for marking the continuation of an essentially Neolithic form of episodic, low-intensity ritualized deposition involving ceramic vessels and other valued items of material culture. The presence of particularly valued items of EM date at some caves, such as the Idaean cave (EM II/III seals; Sakellarakis 1985, 1988); the Psychro cave (EM cutters, tweezers, and diadem; Boardman 1961, 4–5), and possibly some of the votive metal objects from Archalochori (Hazzidakis 1913, figure 8, 44–46; cf. Branigan 1993, 129, 133–5) is notable and finds parallels in the Early Bronze Age deposition of sealings and metal objects at prominent Neolithic cave sites elsewhere in the rest of the Aegean (e.g., Skoteini: Sampson 1992, 66, 68; Zas: Zachos 1999, 153).

In this way, while the intensity of deposition at caves may vary through time and space, the most striking feature of these Neolithic, EM, and indeed MM caves is the generally similar character of their assemblages, consisting in the main of a range of coarse and fine ceramic forms identical to those in use at contemporary open-air habitation sites. Recognition of this emphasizes the illogicality and inconsistency of confining identifications of prehistoric ritual usage solely to MM caves, as is presently the case (e.g., Watrous 1996, 47–48, 73–75). Rather, a more consistent reading of the evidence would suggest a continuity in the ritual use of caves stretching back deep into the Neolithic. The juxtaposition of domestic forms with the nondomestic environment of a cave, often located at great distance from habitation and/or in a prominent landscape feature, ritualized their deployment, which offered a means of commenting upon and situating the domestic within a wider cosmological context.

While the shift toward more intensive corporal deposition at caves seems to have begun in some northern areas of Crete (e.g., north coast; Lasithi plain) already by FN IV, in others, such as south-central Crete, this seems only to begin in EM I. For example, the upper layer from Miamou clearly evidences a shift to more-intense corporal and material deposition, a shift which appears to have taken place during the course of EM I after a relatively short hiatus in the use of the cave. Significantly this appropriation in EM I of what had hitherto been a liminal resource of communal significance coincides with the first wave of open-air settlement along the valleys and coast of the Asterousia region in which the cave is situated (Tomkins 2008, 37–42; Watrous 2001, 163, 168). Associated with this new wave of settlement in the Asterousia and with other EM settlements spread across the Mesara plain of south-central Crete are built circular tombs, known as *tholoi* (sing. *tholos*), the earliest of which date no earlier than EM IA (Branigan 1993, 127; Tomkins 2007b, 20, table 1.6, 46–48; Warren 2004). These tombs enclosed round, dark, and in some cases vaulted chambers, accessed via a small opening. The morphological link between these artificial caves and EM burial caves is obvious and is reinforced by similar forms of corporal and material deposition (Branigan 1970, 146–7; 1993, 39–45). During EM and MM cave and tomb assemblages comprise cups, bowls, jugs, and "fruitstands," while a piece of stalagmite deposited in one of the side chambers at the Apesokari tholos (Davaras 1976, 43) represents an example of the fragmentation of the fabric of a cave itself and its return deposition in a tomb. In this way tholos tombs might best be understood to have originated as an artificial type of proximate cave and should be interpreted, at least in their earliest phase of use, as a regional variant of the EM burial caves. If correct, this would serve further to underline the importance of proximity to habitation in the selection of caves, rockshelters, and crevices as foci for the intensive deposition of corporal and material culture.

Corporal deposition in caves, rockshelters, and round tombs seems to have been most intense during EM I–II, after which deposition ceases or changes in intensity and perhaps nature. At Pyrgos, Kyparissi, and Eileithyia in north-central Crete it appears to cease after EM IIA, with material deposition recommencing only at Eileithyia from MM I, from which period it is considered to serve as a sacred cave (Betancourt and Marinatos 2001, 232–33;

Warren 1980, 490). Similarly, although the date range of Ayios Antonios is EM I–MM I, broadly that of the nearby settlement of Alykomouri, the majority of the material is EM I–II (Haggis 1993, 15–28). At Trapeza, although the stratigraphy was mixed, the excavator was sure that burials continued until EM III, after which and up until MM II it became a sacred cave receiving only depositions of pottery and high-value votives in a manner similar to the nearby Psychro cave (Pendlebury, Pendlebury, and Money-Coutts 1937–1938, 23). A similar trajectory of intense corporal deposition during the earlier EM followed thereafter by a shift toward purely material deposition has similarly been suggested for the Mesara round tombs. From EM II these and other built tombs gain additional chambers that served to accommodate discarded bones and offerings and, in some cases, also altars, niches, or paved courtyards (Branigan 1970, 170; 1993, 127–36; Peatfield 1990, 124–5). It would thus appear that, from the latter part of EM, burial caves and tholoi entered new cycles of use, either ceasing to be foci for deposition (but probably remaining important places in the collective memory) or else becoming foci for ritualized material deposition of a form essentially the same as that of the second, nonburial group of EM caves.

This convergence of practice at burial caves, nonburial caves, and tholos tombs suggests a later EM ritual landscape rich in ritual sites, but ones with differing identities, biographies of significance, and scales of influence. The proximity of tholoi and burial caves to settlement suggests that they served as ritual foci for a local community, but in ways that differed from Neolithic proximate caves through their personalization and appropriation by one or more local lineages through corporal deposition. Here the strategy of intensive corporal deposition during FN IV–EM II may be understood to represent a high-cost, high-energy form of symbolic investment, most appropriate to a formative period when emergent elite groups are first seeking to define themselves as qualitatively different. Consequently, the decline of this practice at proximate caves and built tombs after EM II reflects a situation where the social position of elite groups is more established and investment may take a more purely material form, but with a continued emphasis on high-value items, at least until MM I.

The significant distance from habitation of other more liminal places of deposition, whether nonburial caves, springs, hilltops, or peaks, suggests a second type of EM–MM ritual focus, one that was more regional in influence and whose significance was embedded within far-older sacred landscapes and, in many cases, rooted in deep, local continuities in ritual practice stretching back into the Neolithic. Although the significance and location of these regional ritual sites may have put them initially beyond the control of local elites during EM I–II, changes in the nature and scale of elite activity and political organization after EM III increasingly brought these more distant regional ritual places and the sacred landscapes within which they were situated into play. Their regional ritual significance, particularly as *axes mundi* within wider regional sacred landscapes, and the visibility they enjoy over agricultural resources and their location, often straddling the boundaries between different agricultural regions, made them ideal sites at which elites might contest or maintain sovereignty and influence. In this way the changing cycles of deposition at such caves during the late Early, Middle, and Late Bronze Age may be read in terms of the changing political geography of Crete, in much the same way as depositional behavior at extraurban sanctuaries has been read as an index of the geopolitics of Iron Age Greece (de Polignac 1984, 1994; Tomkins 1996; Watrous 1996, 78–81).

CONCLUSION

Traditionally, interpretation of the function of Neolithic and Early Bronze Age caves on Crete has been structured by the belief that domesticity represents a more natural, self-evident form of cave usage than rituality. This chapter has argued for a reversal of this presumption, namely that key aspects of the location and material records of cave sites can only be adequately explained if Neolithic and Bronze Age cave use on Crete is understood as having been essentially ritual in nature. It was also suggested that methodologies for the identification of prehistoric ritual that rely solely on the presence of ritual assemblages are structured by an overly narrow and exclusive understanding of ritual and ritualization, and of the relationship of both to the domestic. Although insights are currently restricted by a lack of detailed information from Cretan prehistoric caves, forms of ritualization may be glimpsed in the temporality and spatiality of Cretan cave use as well as in aspects of their depositional records. It is, however, in the liminal nature of Neolithic cave sites that ritualization is presently most clear. In many instances caves appear to have been selected for use because of their distance from the diurnal sphere. In others, where caves are more proximate to settlement, liminality plays out more specifically through the very different locational characteristics of the cave. It may be suggested that within agricultural landscapes, such as those of Crete during the Neolithic and Bronze Age, the very act of traveling to and conducting activity in a cave served itself as a form of ritualization.

From the perspective advanced here, ritual activity at caves and the existence of sacred landscapes do not emerge suddenly around MM I (*contra* Watrous 1996, 47, 57–60, 73–4) but may be pushed back deep into the Neolithic (cf. also Dickinson 1994, 258; Whitehouse 1992, 194). The intense MM I horizon of ritual deposition at certain cave and peaks is thus simultaneously real, reflecting a shift in depositional intensity that may be plausibly linked to territorial expansion at this time (Watrous 1996, 77–80; Whitelaw 2004, 243, figure 13.8, 245), and artificial, created by a latent circularity in traditional methodologies of ritual identification. By confining our definition of ritual to the presence or absence of special classes of ritual object, such as shrine equipment and votive, we confine our window on ritual solely to periods when such specialized forms were in use. Such ritual objects are not, however, culturally universal but denote a specific form of ritual signification. The MM I ritual horizon on peaks and at certain caves (e.g., Psychro) thus reflects an extension to the materiality of ritual on Crete, manifest in more elaborate or specialized ritual equipment, but not the origins of the ritual significance of natural places. It may be suggested that the development of specialized categories of ritual object reflects increased specialization in ritual practice and perhaps offered more sophisticated ways of marking social heterogeneity and hierarchy. That such objects were not an essential element of ritual usage is shown, above all, by their absence from the MM and LM assemblages from the Idaean and Kamares caves, and indeed from the vast majority of MM and LM cave sites on Crete.

While the traditional technique of grouping and separating prehistoric ritual activity via typologies of place (e.g., cave, peak, hilltop) retains an analytical usefulness, it is important also to appreciate how different ritual places at different times interrelate and how they articulate wider sacred landscapes. During EM and MM there are clear links in the nature of depositional activity at built tombs and caves, but less so between built tombs, caves, and peak sites (Tomkins 1996, 30–33; Watrous 1996, 74–5). Offerings at tombs, as at caves, consist primarily of open ceramic forms, such as cups, bowls, and jugs (Branigan 1993, 129, 133–5), and while these also occur at peaks, human and animal figurines predominate in a manner quite unlike at caves. Attempts to force these data into a compressed, linear narrative of Minoan ritual development from cave to tomb to peak and palace (e.g., Peatfield 1987, 89–93; 1990, 123–6) distort and oversimplify a much broader and complex picture of coexisting forms and scales of ritual practice.

Crucial to an understanding of the history and significance of prehistoric cave use on Crete is the recognition that the significance of distinctive features of the landscape may endure long after it stopped being actively constructed through visitation and deposition. Through the retelling of narratives of place and origin over successive generations, locales in the landscape retained their importance and presented themselves for future activity, while episodes of sometimes intense deposition represent periods in which the significance of caves and wider sacred landscapes was being more actively negotiated.

Throughout Cretan prehistory, caves provide glimpses of continuity across centuries of hiatus, suggesting that they remained constants in an otherwise changing social landscape. In the Neolithic they were ritual foci, operating at different scales of proximity to the everyday, reproducing differing scales of community and identity, and referencing wider sacred landscapes. This role and significance continued into the Bronze Age, where it became more obviously subject to manipulation and usurpation by specific, special-interest groups. From the end of the Neolithic (FN IV) notably more-intense deposition of human skeletal material and material culture at certain caves is interpreted here as early attempts by specific groups to appropriate existing communal resources, a process of appropriation sustained by emerging social inequality (Tomkins 2010), which by EM I had extended to include also places (i.e., other caves, rockshelters, crevices, and perhaps even artificial caves or tholoi) that had not previously been ritual foci but which had the virtue of being proximate to settlement. It has been suggested that changes in the nature and intensity of deposition at prehistoric cave sites are perhaps best interpreted as attempts to contest, alter, or even appropriate the significance of ritual places and the wider sacred landscapes in which they sit. Through such interventions groups could edit the cultural hard-drive of their society, rewriting histories of place and cosmological origins to include or exclude specific elements. In this way future, more-detailed studies of continuity and change in depositional practice at Cretan prehistoric caves and other ritual sites hold the potential to bring insights into the configuration and scale of social identities and territoriality, and into the ways in which these became transformed during the Neolithic and Bronze Age.

ACKNOWLEDGMENTS

The author thanks Camilla Briault for providing comments on an earlier version of this chapter.

REFERENCES CITED

Appadurai, Arjun. 1986. *The Social Life of Things*. Cambridge: Cambridge University Press.

Alexiou, Stylianos. 1953. "Anaskaphai en Katsamba." *Praktika tis en Athenais Archaiologikis Etaireias* (1953): 305–8.

Bailey, Douglass. 2005. *Prehistoric Figurines: Representation and Corporeality in the Neolithic*. New York: Routledge. http://dx.doi.org/10.4324/9780203392454.

Bailey, Geoff. 1992. "The Palaeolithic of Klithi in Its Wider Context." *Annual of the British School at Athens* 87: 1–28.

Barrett, John. 1988. "The Living, the Dead and the Ancestors: Neolithic and Early Bronze Age Mortuary Practices." In *The Archaeology of Context in the Neolithic and Bronze Age Recent Trends*, ed. John Barrett and Ian Kinnes, 30–41. Sheffield: Sheffield Academic Press.

Béguignon, Yves. 1931. "Chronique des fouilles et découvertes archéologiques en Grèce en 1930." *Bulletin de Correspondance Hellenique* 55: 450–522.

Betancourt, Philip, and Nanno Marinatos. 2001. "To Spilaio tis Amnisou: I Ereuna tou 1992." *Archaiologiki Ephemeris* (2000) 139: 179–236.

Boardman, John. 1961. *The Cretan Collection in Oxford*. Oxford: Oxford University Press.

Bradley, Richard. 1998. *The Significance of Monuments: On the Shaping of Human Experience in Neolithic and Bronze Age Europe*. London: Routledge.

Bradley, Richard. 2005. *Ritual and Domestic Life in Prehistoric Europe*. London: Routledge.

Branigan, Keith. 1970. *The Foundations of Palatial Crete: A Survey of Crete in the Early Bronze Age*. London: Routledge.

Branigan, Keith. 1993. *Dancing with Death: Life and Death in Southern Crete, ca. 3000–2000 BC*. Amsterdam: A. M. Hakkert.

Briault, Camilla. 2007. "Making Mountains Out of Molehills in the Bronze Age Aegean: Visibility, Ritual Kits, and the Idea of a Peak Sanctuary." *World Archaeology* 39 (1): 122–41. http://dx.doi.org/10.1080/00438240601136355.

Broodbank, Cyprian. 2000. *An Island Archaeology of the Early Cyclades*. Cambridge: Cambridge University Press.

Brück, Joanna. 1999. "Ritual and Rationality: Some Problems of Interpretation in European Archaeology." *European Journal of Archaeology* 2 (3): 313–44. http://dx.doi.org/10.1177/146195719900200303.

Carter, Tristram. 1998. "The Chipped Stone." *Annual of the British School at Athens* 93: 47–50.

Catling, Hector. 1987. "Archaeology in Greece, 1986–87." *Archaeological Reports* 33: 3–61.

Chapman, John, and Bisserka Gaydarska. 2007. *Parts and Wholes: Fragmentation in Prehistoric Context*. Oxford: Oxbow Books.

Cherry, John. 1988. "Pastoralism and the Role of Animals in the Pre- and Protohistoric Periods of the Aegean." In *Pastoral Economies in Classical Antiquity*, ed. Charles Whittaker, 6–34. Cambridge: Cambridge University Press.

Conolly, James. 2008. "The Knapped Stone Technology of the First Occupants at Knossos." In *Escaping the Labyrinth: The Cretan Neolithic in Context*, ed. Valasia Isaakidou and Peter Tomkins, 75–92. Sheffield Studies in Aegean Archaeology 8. Oxford: Oxbow Books.

Cook, John, and John Boardman. 1953. "Archaeology in Greece 1952." *Archaeological Reports* 1: 142–149.

Courbin, Paul. 1954. "Chronique des fouilles et découvertes archéologiques en Grèce en 1953." *Bulletin de Correpsondance Hellenique* 78: 95–157.

Davaras, Costas. 1976. *Guide to Cretan Antiquities*. Athens: Eptalofos S.A.

Davaras, Costas. 1996. "Crete (Settlement)." In *Neolithic Culture in Greece*, ed. George Papathanassopoulos, 92–93. Athens: Greek Ministry of Culture.

Dawkins, Richard, and Max Laistner. 1913. "The Excavation of the Kamares Cave in Crete." *Annual of the British School at Athens* 19: 1–34.

Demoule, Jean-Pierre, and Catherine Perlès. 1993. "The Greek Neolithic: A New Review." *Journal of World Prehistory* 7 (4): 355–416. http://dx.doi.org/10.1007/BF00997801.

De Polignac, François. 1984. *La Naissance de la Cité Grecque*. Paris: Editions la Découverte.

De Polignac, François. 1994. "Mediation, Competition, and Sovereignty: The Evolution of Rural Sanctuaries in Geometric Greece." In *Placing the Gods: Sanctuaries and Sacred Space in Ancient Greece*, ed. Susan Alcock and Robin Osborne, 3–18. Oxford: Clarendon Press.

Dickinson, Oliver. 1994. *The Aegean Bronze Age*. Cambridge: Cambridge University Press.

Di Tonto, Serena, and Simona Todaro. 2008. "The Neolithic Settlement at Phaistos Revisited: Evidence for Ceremonial Activity on the Eve of the Bronze Age." In *Escaping the Labyrinth: The Cretan Neolithic in Context*, ed. Valasia Isaakidou and Peter Tomkins, 180–93. Sheffield Studies in Aegean Archaeology 8. Oxford: Oxbow Books.

Evans, Arthur. 1901. "The Neolithic Settlement at Knossos and Its Place in the History of Early Aegean Culture." *Man* 1: 184–6. http://dx.doi.org/10.2307/2839523.

Evans, Arthur. 1921. *The Palace of Minos*, vol. 1. London: Macmillan.

Evans, Arthur. 1928. *The Palace of Minos*, vol. 2: I. London: Macmillan.

Evans, John. 1994. "The Early Millennia: Continuity and Change in a Farming Settlement." In *Knossos: A Labyrinth of History; Papers Presented in Honour of Sinclair Hood*, ed. Don Evely, Helen Hughes-Brock, and Nicoletta Momigliano, 1–22. Oxford: Oxbow.

Faure, Paul. 1956. "Grottes Crétoises." *Bulletin de Correspondance Hellenique* 80 (1): 95–103. http://dx.doi.org/10.3406/bch.1956.2412.

Faure, Paul. 1962. "Cavernes et Sites aux Deux Extrémités de la Crète." *Bulletin de Correspondance Hellenique* 86 (1): 36–56. http://dx.doi.org/10.3406/bch.1962.2302.

Faure, Paul. 1964. *Fonctions des Cavernes Crétoises*. Paris: Éditions de Bocard.

Faure, Paul. 1969a. "Antiques Cavernes de Refuge dans la Crète de l'Ouest." *Athens Annals of Archaeology* 2: 213–6.

Faure, Paul. 1969b. "Sur trois sortes de Sanctuaires Crétois." *Bulletin de Correspondance Hellenique* 93 (1): 174–213. http://dx.doi.org/10.3406/bch.1969.2184.

Faure, Paul. 1994. "Cavernes sacrées de la Crète antique." *Cretan Studies* 4: 77–83.

French, Charles, and Todd Whitelaw. 1999. "Soil Erosion, Agricultural Terracing and Site Formation Processes at Markiani, Amorgos, Greece: The Micromorphological Perspective." *Geoarchaeology* 14 (2): 151–89. http://dx.doi.org/10.1002/(SICI)1520-6548(199902)14:2<151::AID-GEA3>3.0.CO;2-R.

French, Elisabeth. 1990. "Archaeology in Greece, 1989–90." *Archaeological Reports* 36: 3–82.

Gamble, Clive. 2007. *Origins and Revolutions: Human Identity in Earliest Prehistory*. Cambridge: Cambridge University Press. http://dx.doi.org/10.1017/CBO9780511618598.

Gimbutas, Marija. 1991. *The Civilization of the Goddess*. San Francisco: Harper.

Godart, Louis, and Yiannis Tzedakis. 1992. *Témoignages Archéologiques et Épigraphiques en Crète Occidentale du Néolithique au Minoen Récent IIIB*. Incunabula Graeca 93, Rome: Edizioni dell' Ateneo.

Haggis, Donald. 1993. "The Early Minoan Burial Cave at Ayios Antonios and Some Problems in Early Bronze Age Chronology." *Studi Micenei ed Egeo-Anatolici* 31: 7–33.

Hall, Heinrich. 1999. "Ritual in Neolithic Crete." MA thesis. University College Dublin, National University of Ireland, Dublin.

Halstead, Paul. 1989. "The Economy Has a Normal Surplus: Economic Stability and Social Change among Early Farming Communities of Thessaly Greece." In *Bad Year Economics*, ed. Paul Halstead and John O'Shea, 68–80. Cambridge: Cambridge University Press. http://dx.doi.org/10.1017/CBO9780511521218.006.

Halstead, Paul. 1994. "The North-South Divide: Regional Paths to Complexity in Prehistoric Greece." In *Development and Decline in the Mediterranean Bronze Age*, ed. Clay Mathers and Simon Stoddart, 195–219. Sheffield: John Collis.

Halstead, Paul. 1996a. "The Development of Agriculture and Pastoralism in Greece: When, How, Who, What?" In *The Origins and Spread of Agriculture and Pastoralism in Eurasia*, ed. David Harris, 296–309. London: UCL Press.

Halstead, Paul. 1996b. "Review of *Skoteini, Tharrounia: The Cave, The Settlement and the Cemetery*, by Adamantios Sampson." *American Journal of Archaeology* 100 (1): 179–80. http://dx.doi.org/10.2307/506312.

Halstead, Paul. 1999. "'Neighbours from Hell'? The Household in Neolithic Greece." In *Neolithic Society in Greece*, ed. Paul Halstead, 77–95. Sheffield Studies of Aegean Archaeology 2. Sheffield: Sheffield Academic Press.

Halstead, Paul. 2007. "Carcasses and Commensality: Investigating the Social Context of Meat Consumption in Neolithic and Early Bronze Greece." In *Cooking Up the Past: Food and Culinary Practices in the Neolithic and Bronze Age Aegean*, ed. Chris Mee and Josette Renard, 25–48. Oxford: Oxbow Books.

Halstead, Paul. 2008. "Between a Rock and a Hard Place: Coping with Marginal Colonization in the Later Neolithic and Early Bronze Age of Crete and the Aegean." In *Escaping the Labyrinth: The Cretan Neolithic in Context*, ed. Valasia Isaakidou and Peter Tomkins, 232–60. Sheffield Studies in Aegean Archaeology 8. Oxford: Oxbow Books.

Halstead, Paul, and Glynis Jones. 1987. "Bioarchaeological Remains from Kalythies Cave, Rhodes." In *I Neolithiki Periodos sta Dodekanisa*, ed. Adamantios Sampson, 135–52. Athens: Tamio Archaiologikon Poron kai Apalothriseon.

Hazzidakis, Joseph. 1913. "An Early Minoan Sacred Cave at Archalohori in Crete." *Annual of the British School at Athens* 19: 35–48.

Helms, Mary. 1993. *Craft and the Kingly Ideal: Art, Trade and Power*. Austin: University of Texas Press.

Hodder, Ian. 1982. *The Present Past*. London: Batsford.

Hodder, Ian, ed. 1996. *On the Surface: Çatal Höyük 1993–1995*. Macdonald Institute Monographs / BIAA Monograph 22. London: McDonald Institute for Archaeological Research, Cambridge/British Institute at Ankara.

Hogarth, David. 1900. "The Dictaean Cave." *Annual of the British School at Athens* 6: 94–116.

Jacobsen, Thomas. 1984. "Seasonal Pastoralism in Southern Greece: A Consideration of the Ecology of Neolithic Urfirnis Pottery." In *Pots and Potters: Current Approaches in Ceramic Archaeology*, ed. Prudence M. Rice, 27–43. Los Angeles: Institute of Archaeology, University of California.

Jacobsen, Thomas, and William Farrand. 1988. *Franchthi Cave and Paralia: Maps, Plans, and Sections*. Excavations at Franchthi Cave, Greece, Fascicle 1. Bloomington: Indiana University Press.

Jantzen, Ulf. 1951. "Die Kumaro-Höhle." In *Forschungen auf Kreta 1942*, ed. Friedrich Matz, 1–12. Berlin: De Gruyter.

Jarman, Michael. 1996. "Human Influence in the Development of Cretan Mammalian Fauna." In *Pleistocene and Holocene Fauna of Crete and its First Settlers*, ed. David Reece, 211–29. Monographs in World Archaeology 28. Philadelphia: University of Pennsylvania Museum of Archaeology and Anthropology.

Jones, Andy. 2005. "Lives in Fragments? Personhood and the European Neolithic." *Journal of Social Archaeology* 5 (2): 193–224. http://dx.doi.org/10.1177/1469605305053367.

Jones, Donald. 1999. *Peak Sanctuaries and Sacred Caves in Minoan Crete: Comparison of Artifacts*. Sävedalen: Paul Åströms Förlag.

Jones, Glynis. 2005. "Garden Cultivation of Staple Crops and Its Implications for Settlement Location and Continuity." *World Archaeology* 37 (2): 164–76. http://dx.doi.org/10.1080/00438240500094564.

Karetsou, Alexandra. 1976. "Kentriki Kriti." *Praktika tis en Athenais Archaiologikis Etaireias* (1974): 240–6.

Karetsou, Alexandra. 1981. "The Peak Sanctuary of Mt. Juktas." In *Sanctuaries and Cults in the Aegean Bronze Age*, ed. Robin Hägg and Nanno Marinatos, 137–53. Stockholm: Swedish Institute at Athens/Paul Åströms Förlag.

Lambert, Nicole, ed. 1981. *La Grotte Préhistorique de Kitsos (Attique). Missions 1968–1978*, vols. I–II: *L'occupation néolithique les vestiges des temps paléolithiques, de l'antiquité et d'histoire récente*. Paris: Editions Bocard.

Manteli, Katya. 1993a. "The Transition from the Neolithic to the Early Bronze Age in Crete, with Special Reference to Pottery, Volume I." PhD thesis, University of London, London.

Manteli, Katya. 1993b. "The Transition from the Neolithic to the Early Bronze Age in Crete, with special reference to pottery, Volume II." PhD thesis, University of London, London.

Marinatos, Spyridon. 1928. "Höhlenforschungen in Kreta." *Mitteilungen über Höhlen- und Karstforschung, Zeitschrift des Hauptverbandes Deutscher Höhlenforscher* 4: 97–107. Berlin.

Marinatos, Spyridon. 1932. "Anaskaphai en Kriti." *Praktika tis en Athenais Archaiologikis Etaireias* (1930): 91–99.

Marinatos, Spyridon. 1933. "Funde und Forschungen auf Kreta." *Archaologischer Anzeiger* 48:295–7.

Marinatos, Spyridon. 1950. "To Megaron Vathypetrou." *Praktika tis en Athenais Archaiologikis Etaireias* (1950): 242–57.

Mellaart, James. 1967. *Çatal Hüyük: A Neolithic Town in Anatolia*. London: Thames and Hudson.

Meskell, Lynn, Carolyn Nakamura, Rachel King, and Shahina Farid. 2008. "Figured Lifeworlds and Depositional Practices at Çatalhöyük." *Cambridge Archaeological Journal* 18 (2): 139–61. http://dx.doi.org/10.1017/S095977430800022X.

Mina, Maria. 2008. "Figurin' out Cretan Neolithic Society: Anthropomorphic Figurines, Symbolism and Gender Dialectics." In *Escaping the Labyrinth: The Cretan Neolithic in Context*, ed. Valasia Isaakidou and Peter Tomkins, 118–38. Sheffield Studies in Aegean Archaeology 8. Oxford: Oxbow Books.

Moody, Jenny. 1987. "The Environmental and Cultural Prehistory of the Khania Region of West Crete: Neolithic through Late Minoan III." PhD thesis, University of Minnesota, Minneapolis.

Mortzos, Christos. 1972. "Partira: Mia Proimos Minoiki Kerameiki Omas." *Epetiris Epistimonikon Erevnon tou Panepistimiou Athinon* 3: 386–421.

Nakou, Georgia. 1995. "The Cutting Edge: A New Look at Early Aegean Metallurgy." *Journal of Mediterranean Archaeology* 8: 1–32.

Nilsson, Martin. 1950. *The Minoan-Mycenaean Religion and Its Survival in Greek Religion*. Lund: W. K. Glarup.

Nixon, Lucia, and Simon Price. 2001. "The Diachronic Analysis of Pastoralism through Comparative Variables." *Annual of the British School at Athens* 96: 395–424.

Papadakis, Nikos. 1987. "Archaiotites kai mnimeia Anatolikis Kritis." *Archaiologikon Deltion Chronika* 34 (B2): 402–10.

Papadatos, Yiannis, Peter Tomkins, Eleni Nodarou, and Yiannis Iliopoulos. N.d. "The Beginning of the Early Bronze Age in Crete: Continuities and Discontinuities in the Ceramic Assemblage at Kephala Petras, Siteia." In *The Aegean Early Bronze Age: New Evidence*, ed. Christos Doumas, Colin Renfrew, and Ourania Koukou. Athens. Forthcoming.

Papathanasiou, Anastasia. 2001. *A Bioarchaeological Analysis of Neolithic Alepotrypa Cave, Greece*. British Archaeological Reports, International Series 961. Oxford: BAR.

Papathanassopoulos, George, ed. 1996a. *Neolithic Culture in Greece*. Athens: Greek Ministry of Culture.

Papathanassopoulos, George. 1996b. "Habitation in Caves." In *Neolithic Culture in Greece*, ed. George Papathanassopoulos, 38–40. Athens: Greek Ministry of Culture.

Papathanassopoulos, George. 1996c. "Neolithic Diros: The Alepotrypa Cave." In *Neolithic Culture in Greece*, ed. George Papathanassopoulos, 80–84. Athens: Greek Ministry of Culture.

Papathanassopoulos, George. 1996d. "Burial Customs at Diros." In *Neolithic Culture in Greece*, ed. George Papathanassopoulos, 175–77. Athens: Greek Ministry of Culture.

Peatfield, Alan. 1983. "The Topography of Minoan Peak Sanctuaries." *Annual of the British School at Athens* 78: 273–80.

Peatfield, Alan. 1987. "Palace and Peak: The Political and Religious Relationship between Palaces and Peak Sanctuaries." In *The Function of the Minoan Palaces*, ed. Robin Hägg and Nanno, 89–93. Stockholm: Paul Astrom Forlag.

Peatfield, Alan. 1990. "Minoan Peak Sanctuaries: History and Society." *Opuscula Atheniensia* 17: 117–31.

Pendlebury, John. 1939. *The Archaeology of Crete*. London: Methuen.

Pendlebury, Hilda, John Pendlebury, and Mercy Money-Coutts. 1935–1936. "Excavations in the Plain of Lasithi, I." *Annual of the British School at Athens* 36: 5–131.

Pendlebury, Hilda, John Pendlebury, and Mercy Money-Coutts. 1937–1938. "Excavations in the Plain of Lasithi, II." *Annual of the British School at Athens* 38: 1–56.

Perlès, Catherine. 1992. "Systems of Exchange and Organization in Neolithic Greece." *Journal of Mediterranean Studies* 5 (2): 115–64.

Perlès, Catherine. 2001. *The Early Neolithic in Greece*. Cambridge: Cambridge University Press. http://dx.doi.org/10.1017/CBO9780511612855.

Platon, Nikolas. 1953. "I Archaiologiki Kinisis en Kriti kata to etos 1953." *Kritika Chronika* 7: 478–92.

Renfrew, Colin. 1964. "Crete and the Cyclades before Rhadamanthus." *Kritika Chronika* 18: 107–41.

Renfrew, Colin. 1985. *The Archaeology of Cult: The Sanctuary at Phylakopi*. British School at Athens Supplement 18. London: Thames and Hudson.

Renfrew, Colin. 1994. "The Archaeology of Religion." In *The Ancient Mind: Elements of Cognitive Archaeology*, ed. Colin Renfrew and Ezra Zubrow, 47–54. Cambridge: Cambridge University Press. http://dx.doi.org/10.1017/CBO9780511598388.007.

Runnels, Curtis. 2001. "Review of Aegean Prehistory IV: The Stone Age of Greece from the Palaeolithic to the Advent of the Neolithic." In *Aegean Prehistory: A Review*, ed. Tracey Cullen, 225–254. American Journal of Archaeology Supplement 1. Boston: Archaeological Institute of America.

Rutkowski, Bogdan, and Krzystof Nowicki. 1996. *The Psychro Cave and Other Sacred Grottoes in Crete*. Warsaw: Art and Archaeology.

Sakellarakis, Yiannis. 1985. "Idaion Antron." *Ergon* 83–86.

Sakellarakis, Yiannis. 1988. "The Idaean Cave: Minoan and Greek worship." *Kernos* 1: 207–14.

Sakellarakis, Yiannis. 1989. "Hundert Jahre Erforschung der Ida-Höhle." *Hellenika: Jahrbuch für die Freunde Griechenlands* 25: 83–97.

Sakellarakis, Y., and E. Sapouna-Sakellaraki. 1997. *Archanes: Minoan Crete in a New Light*. Athens: Ammos.

Sampson, Adamantios. 1992. "Late Neolithic Remains at Tharrounia, Euboea: A Model for the Seasonal Use of Settlements and Caves." *Annual of the British School at Athens* 87: 61–101.

Sampson, Adamantios. 1999. "The Neolithic and Mesolithic Occupation of the Cave of Cyclope, Youra, Alonnessos, Greece." *Annual of the British School at Athens* 94: 1–22.

Stevanović, Mirjana. 1997. "The Age of Clay: The Social Dynamics of House Destruction." *Journal of Anthropological Archaeology* 16 (4): 334–95. http://dx.doi.org/10.1006/jaar.1997.0310.

Strasser, Thomas. 1992. "Neolithic Settlement and Land-use on Crete." PhD thesis, Indiana University, Bloomington.

Strasser, Thomas, Eleni Panagopoulou, Curtis Runnels, Priscilla Murray, Nicholas Thompson, Panayiotis Karkanas, Floyd McCoy, and Karl Wegmann. 2010. "Stone Age Seafaring in the Mediterranean: Evidence from the Plakias Region for Lower Palaeolithic and Mesolithic Habitation of Crete." *Hesperia* 79 (2): 145–90. http://dx.doi.org/10.2972/hesp.79.2.145.

Taramelli, Antonio. 1897. "Cretan Expedition VIII: The Prehistoric Grotto at Miamu." *American Journal of Archaeology* 1 (4/5): 287–312. http://dx.doi.org/10.2307/496717.

Taramelli, Antonio. 1901. "Cretan Expedition XX: A Visit to the Grotto of Camares." *American Journal of Archaeology* 5 (4): 437–51. http://dx.doi.org/10.2307/496585.

Tod, Marcus. 1902–1903. "Hagios Nikolaos." *Annual of the British School at Athens* 9: 336–43.

Todaro, Simona. 2005. "EM I-MM IA Ceramic Groups at Phaistos: Towards the Definition of a Prepalatial Ceramic Sequence in South Central Crete." *Creta Antica* 6: 11–46.

Tomkins, Peter. 1996. "Minoan Cave Cult: Sanctity and Society." MA thesis, Institute of Archaeology, University College London, London.

Tomkins, Peter. 2004. "Filling in the 'Neolithic Background': Social Life and Social Transformation in the Aegean before the Bronze Age." In *The Emergence of Civilization Revisited*, ed. John Barrett and Paul Halstead, 38–63. Sheffield Studies in Aegean Archaeology 5. Sheffield: Continuum Press.

Tomkins, Peter. 2007a. "Communality and Competition: The Social Life of Food and Containers at Aceramic and Early Neolithic Knossos, Crete." In *Cooking up the Past: Food and Culinary Practices in the Neolithic and Bronze Age Aegean*, ed. Chris Mee and Josette Renard, 174–99. Oxford: Oxbow Books.

Tomkins, Peter. 2007b. "Neolithic: Strata IX–VIII, VII–VIB, VIA–V, IV, IIIB, IIIA, IIB, IIA and IC Groups." In *Knossos Pottery Handbook*, Vol. I: *Neolithic and Bronze Age (Minoan)*, ed. Nicoletta Momigliano, 9–48. British School at Athens Special Studies 14. London: British School at Athens.

Tomkins, Peter. 2008. "Time, Space and the Reinvention of the Cretan Neolithic." In *Escaping the Labyrinth: The Cretan Neolithic in Context*, ed. Valasia Isaakidou and Peter Tomkins, 22–51. Sheffield Studies in Aegean Archaeology 8. Oxford: Oxbow Books.

Tomkins, Peter. 2009. "Domesticity by Default: Ritual, Ritualization and Cave-use in the Neolithic Aegean." *Oxford Journal of Archaeology* 28 (2): 125–53. http://dx.doi.org/10.1111/j.1468-0092.2009.00322.x.

Tomkins, Peter. 2010. "Neolithic Antecendents." In *The Oxford Handbook for the Bronze Age Aegean*, ed. Eric Cline, 31–49. Oxford: Oxford University Press.

Tomkins, Peter. 2012. "Behind the Horizon: Reconsidering the Genesis and Function of the 'First Palace' at Knossos (Final Neolithic IV–Middle Minoan IB)." In *Back to the Beginning: Reconsidering Social and Political Complexity on Crete during the Early and Middle Bronze Age*, ed. Ilse Schoep, Peter Tomkins, and Jan Driessen. Oxford: Oxbow. Forthcoming

Tomkins, Peter. N.d.a. "Ceramic Perspectives on Stratigraphy, Taphonomy, Deposition and Consumption at Neolithic Katsamba." In *Katsambas: A Neolithic Settlement by the Kairatos*, ed. Nena Galanidou. Philadelphia: INSTAP Press. Forthcoming.

Tomkins, Peter. N.d.b. "Dark Places and Open Spaces: Hypogaea and Ritual Practice on the South Slope at Knossos during the Neolithic." Submitted to *Annual of the British School at Athens*.

Tomkins, Peter, and Peter Day. 2001. "Production and Exchange of the Earliest Ceramic Vessels in the Aegean: A View from Early Neolithic Knossos, Crete." *Antiquity* 75: 259–60.

Tomkins, Peter, Peter Day, and Vasilis Kilikoglou. 2004. "Knossos and the Early Neolithic Landscape of the Herakleion Basin." In *Knossos: Palace, City, State*, ed. Gerald Cadogan, Eleni Hatzaki, and Andonis Vasilakis, 51–9. British School at Athens Studies 12. London: British School at Athens.

Tomkins, Peter, and Ilse Schoep. 2010. "The Early Bronze Age in Crete." In *The Oxford Handbook for the Bronze Age Aegean*, ed. Eric Cline, 66–82. Oxford: Oxford University Press.

Triantaphyllou, Sevi. 1999. "Prehistoric Makriyialos: A Story from the Fragments." In *Neolithic Society in Greece*, ed. Paul Halstead, 128–35. Sheffield Studies in Aegean Archaeology 2. Sheffield: Sheffield Academic Press.

Triantaphyllou, Sevi. 2008. "Living with the Dead: A Re-Consideration of Mortuary Practices in the Greek Neolithic." In *Escaping the Labyrinth: The Cretan Neolithic in Context*, ed. Valasia Isaakidou and Peter Tomkins, 139–57. Sheffield Studies in Aegean Archaeology 8. Oxford: Oxbow Books.

Tyree, Loeta. 1974. "Cretan Sacred Caves: Archaeological Evidence." PhD thesis, University of Missouri, Columbia.

Tzedakis, Yiannis. 1966. "Archaoitites kai mnimeia Dytkis Kritis." *Archaiologikon Deltion Chronika* 21 (B2): 425–9.

Tzedakis, Yiannis. 1967. "Archaoitites kai mnimeia Dytkis Kritis." *Archaiologikon Deltion Chronika* 22 (B2): 501–6.

Tzedakis, Yiannis. 1970. "Archaoitites kai mnimeia Dytkis Kritis." *Archaiologikon Deltion Chronika* 25 (B2): 465–78.

Tzedakis, Yiannis. 1973. "Archaoitites kai mnimeia Dytkis Kritis." *Archaiologikon Deltion Chronika* 28 (B2): 581–3.

Tzedakis, Yiannis. 1980. "La Grotte de Gerani et la céramique néolithique en Crète occidentale." PhD thesis, Université de Paris I, Paris.

Tzedakis, Yiannis. 1981. "Spilia Ayiou Iannou." *Archaiologikon Deltion Chronika* 36 (B2): 395–6.

Tzedakis, Yiannis. 1996. "Caves of Western Crete." In *Neolithic Culture in Greece*, ed. George Papathanassopoulos, 94. Athens: Greek Ministry of Culture.

Tzedakis, Yiannis, and Holly Martlew. 1999. *Minoans and Myceneans Flavours of Their Time*. Athens: Greek Ministry of Culture.

Ucko, Peter. 1968. *Anthropomorphic Figurines of Predynastic Egypt and Neolithic Crete with Comparative Material from the Prehistoric Near East and Mainland Greece*. London: Andrew Szmidla.

Vagnetti, Lucia, and Paolo Belli. 1978. Characters and Problems of the Final Neolithic in Crete. *Studi Micenei ed Egeo Anatolici* 19: 125–63.

Vitelli, Karen. 1993. *Franchthi Neolithic Pottery: Classification and Ceramic Phases 1 and 2*. Excavations at the Franchthi Cave, Greece, Fascicle 8. Bloomington: Indiana University Press.

Vitelli, Karen. 1999. *Franchthi Neolithic Pottery*, Vol. 2: *The Later Neolithic Ceramic Phases 3 to 5*. Excavations at the Franchthi Cave, Greece, Fascicle 10. Bloomington: Indiana University Press.

Warren, Peter. 1973. "The Beginnings of Minoan Religion." *Antichità Cretesi, Studi in Onore di Doro Levi* 1: 137–47. Istituto di Archeologia, Catania.

Warren, Peter. 1980. "Problems of Chronology in Crete and the Aegean in the Third and Earlier Second Millennium B.C." *American Journal of Archaeology* 84 (4): 487–99. http://dx.doi.org/10.2307/504077.

Warren, Peter. 2004. "Part II: The Contents of the Tombs." In *The Early Minoan Tombs of Lebena, Southern Crete*, ed. Stylianos Alexiou and Peter Warren, 23–218. Studies in Mediterranean Archaeology vol. 30. Sävedalen: Paul Åströms Förlag.

Warren, Peter, and Yiannis Tzedakis. 1974. "Debla: An Early Minoan Settlement in Western Crete." *Annual of the British School at Athens* 69: 249–342.

Warren, Peter, and Vronwy Hankey. 1989. *Aegean Bronze Age Chronology*. Bristol: Bristol Classical Press.

Watrous, L. Vance. 1982. *Lasithi: A History of Settlement on a Highland Plain in Crete*. Hesperia supplement 18.

Watrous, L. Vance. 1996. *The Cave Sanctuary of Zeus at Psychro: A Study of Extra-Urban Sanctuaries in Minoan and Early Iron Age Crete*. Aegaeum 15. Liege: Université de Liège / Austin: University of Texas.

Watrous, L. Vance. 2001. "Review of Aegean Prehistory III: Crete from the Earliest Prehistory through the Protopalatial Period." In *Aegean Prehistory: A Review*, ed. Tracey Cullen, 157–223. American Journal of Archaeology Supplement 1. Boston: Archaeological Institute of America.

Watrous, L. Vance. 2004. "New Pottery from the Psychro Cave and Its Implications for Minoan Crete." *Annual of the British School at Athens* 99: 129–47.

Weinberg, Saul. 1970. "The Stone Age in the Aegean." In *Cambridge Ancient History*, Volume I, Part 1: *Prolegomena and Prehistory*, ed. Iorwerth Edwards, Cyril Gadd, and Nicholas Hammond, 557–618. Cambridge: Cambridge University Press.

Whitehouse, Ruth. 1992. *Underground Religion, Cult and Culture in Prehistoric Italy: Specialist Studies on Italy 1*. London: Accordia Research Centre.

Ruth, Whitehouse. 1996. "Ritual Objects: Archaeological Joke or Neglected Evidence." In *Approaches to the Study of Ritual, Italy and the Ancient Mediterranean*, ed. John Wilkins, 9–30. Accordia Specialist studies on the Mediterranean 2. London: Accordia Research Centre.

Whitelaw, Todd. 2004. "Alternative Pathways to Complexity in the Southern Aegean." In *The Emergence of Civilisation Revisited (SSAA 5)*, ed. John Barrett and Paul Halstead, 232–56. Oxford: Oxbow.

Wickens, Jere. 1986. "The Archaeology and History of Cave Use in Attica, Greece from Prehistoric through Late Roman Times." PhD thesis, Indiana University, Bloomington.

Zachos, Kostas. 1990. "The Neolithic Period in Naxos." In *Cycladic Culture: Naxos in the 3rd Millennium BC*, ed. Lila Marangou, 29–38. Athens: Nicholas P. Goulandris Foundation.

Zachos, Kostas. 1999. "Zas Cave on Naxos and the Role of Caves in the Aegean Late Neolithic." In *Neolithic Society in Greece*, ed. Paul Halstead, 153–63. Sheffield Studies in Aegean Archaeology 2. Sheffield: Sheffield Academic Press.

Zois, Antonis. 1973. *Kriti: Epochi tou Lithou*. Ancient Greek Cities 18. Athens: Athens Center of Ekistics.

5

Caves and the Funerary Landscape of Prehistoric Britain

Andrew T. Chamberlain

The extensive tradition of archaeological research in Britain has focused mainly on monuments, stratified occupation sites, and humanly modified landscapes, and only in the past two decades has an awareness of natural-place archaeology become salient in intellectual and curatorial approaches to the archaeological record (Bradley 2000; Tilley 1994). As is the case with other elements of the natural landscape, the aesthetic and natural-history values of caves are well established and appreciated, but the archaeological properties of caves are difficult to characterize and control within existing cultural resource management frameworks. The archaeological significance of a cave site is normally recognized only at the point when cave deposits and their contents are intrusively and destructively investigated, and most caves in Britain have never been visited by a professional archaeologist, thus even disturbed or eroding archaeological deposits at these sites may not be recorded as having archaeological significance. Coupled with the logistical difficulties and stratigraphic complexities that hinder traditional excavation methods inside caves, our knowledge of archaeological caves tends to be less complete and less reliable than is the case for equivalent archaeological sites at open locations.

The purpose of this contribution is to draw attention to the results of recent and ongoing field survey work and synthetic analysis of data from archaeological caves in Britain, with the particular aim of elucidating prehistoric funerary activities. The sites under consideration include classical caves (defined as accessible natural voids within rock formations), together with rockshelters (caves of limited depth, typically with absent or poorly defined side walls), fissures (natural cavities that lack a well-defined roof), and potholes (vertical cave systems with limited horizontal passage development). Excluded are artificial caves and grottoes, as well as hydraulically active cave systems that are normally accessible only with diving equipment. The term *cave burial* is used here in a generic sense to mean the emplacement of human remains within a cave, including the deposition of disarticulated remains as well as intact cadavers.

INTERPRETATION OF CAVE ARCHAEOLOGICAL DATA

The most recent all-period review of cave archaeology in Britain was published half a century ago (Jackson 1962) and since that time only a few audits of the cave archaeological resource have been carried out, all of which are specific to particular time periods, regions, or categories of material (Barton and Colcutt 1986; Branigan and Dearne 1991; Chamberlain and Ray 1994; Ford 1989; Holderness et al. 2007; Tolan-Smith 2001; Trent and Peak Archaeological Trust 1993; see also gazetteers of archaeological and paleontological cave sites in Britain published at www.capra.group.shef.ac.uk).

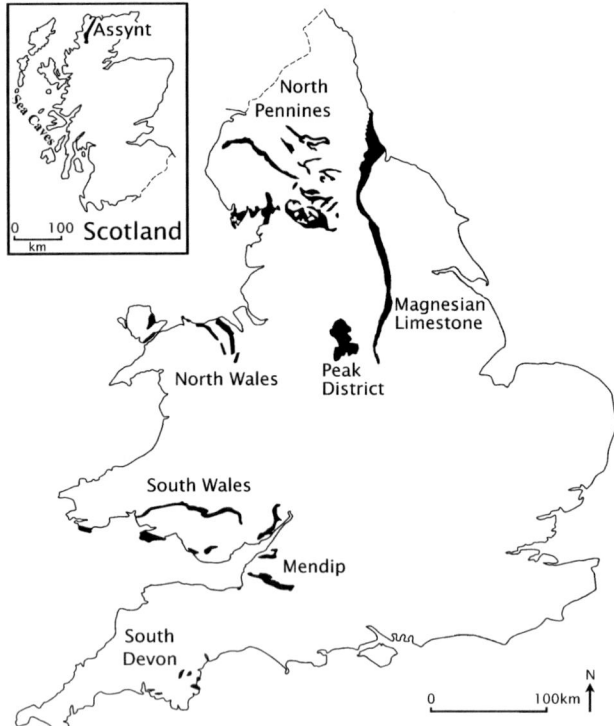

FIGURE 5.1 Principal regions of Britain with outcrops of cavernous karst limestone. Most of the karst is formed in limestones of Carboniferous or Permian (Magnesian Limestone) age, but the caves of South Devon are in Devonian limestone, and those of Assynt (Scotland) are in Cambro-Ordovician limestones. Sea caves are also common along the western coastline of Britain.

Although these audits have provided a measure of the wealth and potential of cultural data from cave sites in Britain, much of the primary information for archaeological caves exists in an unpublished and relatively poorly cataloged archival form. This, together with the marginal location of many caves in upland and western coastal areas of Britain (figure 5.1), has probably hindered the extent to which syntheses of British prehistory have recognized the importance of cave sites as loci for past human activities.

Previous studies of cave usage in antiquity have categorized activities at cave sites as either *ritual*, such as art, human burial, and votive deposition, or as *subsistence related*, for instance domestic occupation, storage, industrial activities, and refuge. While there is copious historical and anthropological evidence that can justify such categorizations (e.g., Bonsall and Tolan Smith 1997; Galanidou 2000), it is often difficult to elucidate patterns of usage from the cultural evidence preserved at specific cave sites. The nature and quality of the archaeological evidence recorded from earlier excavations, the frequent lack of structural modifications within cave sites, and the ephemeral and palimpsest nature of the activities themselves all serve to render interpretations of past activities imprecise. Furthermore, such approaches tend to portray caves as the serendipitous but passive receptacles of human activity, as "convenient cavities" in the memorable expression of Lawrence Straus (1997), rather than as the "supernatural places" that caves may have been viewed as by prehistoric communities (cf. Tilley and Bennett 2001).

The challenge of proceeding beyond the utilitarian view of caves as neutral arenas for mundane human activities has been posed succinctly by Richard Bradley, "Is it possible to discuss the role of entirely unaltered features of the natural landscape? Can such places be studied to any purpose in areas where monuments are absent?" (Bradley 2000, 43). Bradley answered these questions in the conditional affirmative, with the proviso that prospective studies should be based on archaeological material closely and purposefully associated with the landscape features in question. The onus, therefore, is on the archaeologist to demonstrate that a natural cave was once a symbolic or sacred space. This is an interpretive burden that contrasts markedly with the manner in which we achieve an understanding of other prehistoric sites such as barrows, stone and timber circles, pit alignments, and earthwork enclosures, where the default presumption is that these manifestly constructed sites served a ritual function even where material cultural evidence for such activity is totally lacking.

PREHISTORIC CAVE BURIALS

Although the contextual evidence is often insufficient to establish the precise date of human remains in cave deposits, John Gilks was prescient in drawing attention to a widespread tradition of prehistoric cave burial in Britain, noting the frequent association of human skeletal remains and prehistoric artifacts in the caves of Northern England (Gilks 1989). The advent of the use of accelerator mass spectrometry for direct radiocarbon dating of human bones dramatically confirmed the extent to which caves were used as burial sites in the Neolithic period from 4000 to 2000 BC (Chamberlain 1996). Over 160 radiocarbon determinations on human remains from eighty-one caves in Britain are currently available—these provide evidence for 102 phases of funerary activity in this sample of caves from the Lateglacial period onwards (figure 5.2).

The chronological pattern of deposition of human remains in caves shows some initial activity associated with successive recolonizations of Britain by hunter-gatherers during the Lateglacial Interstadial and Early Holocene periods, tailing off into the Late Mesolithic (seventh to fifth millennia BC). This is followed by a marked peak of burial activity during the Early Neolithic (fourth millennium

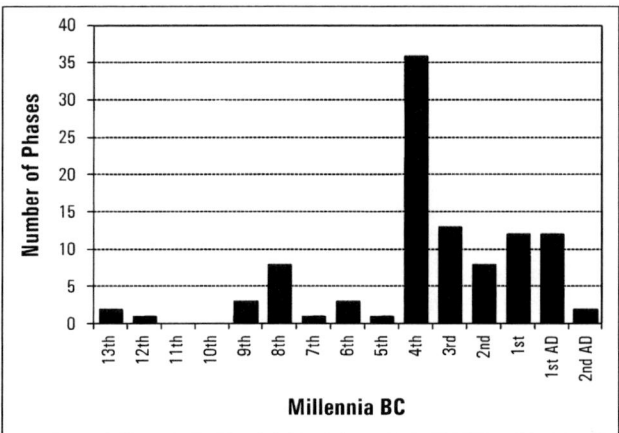

FIGURE 5.2 Distribution of Lateglacial and Holocene radiocarbon dates on human skeletal remains from British caves. Data are for 102 phases of burial in eighty-one caves (some phases are represented by multiple dates, a total of 160 radiocarbon dates were included in the analysis). Dates have been calibrated using the calibration curve of Stuiver, Long, and Kra 1993, but estimated dating errors have been ignored as these are considerably smaller than the 1000-year categories into which the calibrated data have been aggregated. Three much earlier cave burials from the British Lateglacial have been omitted: these are at Eel Point Cave (ca. 24,500 radiocarbon years BP), Paviland Cave (ca. 26,000 radiocarbon years BP), and Kent's Cavern (ca. 30,000 radiocarbon years BP).

BC). Cave burial in Britain appears to have continued through later prehistory and into the early historic period (first millennium AD), but it is significant that there are only two instances of cave sites in Britain with direct radiocarbon determinations on skeletal remains that postdate the arrival of Christianity at about AD 600. In this respect Britain contrasts with the neighboring island of Ireland, where caves and other places in the natural landscape continued to be used as burial sites even after Christian burial traditions became established (Connolly and Coyne 2000; Dunnington and Coleman 1950; Edwards 1990). The direct radiocarbon dating evidence is also useful in demonstrating that the prehistoric deposition of human remains in caves was a deliberate act rather than the consequence of accidental or natural depositional processes. If the presence of human remains in cave deposits were the result of accidental deaths, or the consequence of secondary deposition arising from colluviation or from carnivore activity, then the absence of human remains from any periods after AD 1500 (when population numbers were much higher than in prehistory) would be inexplicable.

Even without the clear evidence provided by direct radiocarbon dating, the association of human remains with prehistoric material culture is evident from a wider sample of archaeological caves. Figure 5.3 displays the results of a multivariate analysis of finds from 100 archaeological caves in the Carboniferous Limestone region of the Peak District and Yorkshire Dales regions of central Britain (Holderness et al. 2007). The chart shows the loadings of the eleven categories of finds on rotated principal components, which account for 48 percent (component 1) and 13 percent (component 2) of the variation in the data set. The analysis shows that finds of human skeletal remains are associated with the presence of faunal remains and with prehistoric artifacts including pottery and stone tools. A separate, divergent cluster of variables represents finds of historical-period artifacts, including Roman and post-Roman pottery, glass, metalwork, worked bone, and coins. This indicates how the deposition of cultural material in British caves continues into the historical period but with a change of character, as human remains become a less-frequent and eventually absent component of the depositional assemblages.

Archaeological survey within the Peak District region of limestone karst topography suggests that caves with human remains (burial caves) may be preferentially located at higher altitudes, compared to caves without evidence of burial (the latter category includes mainly unexcavated

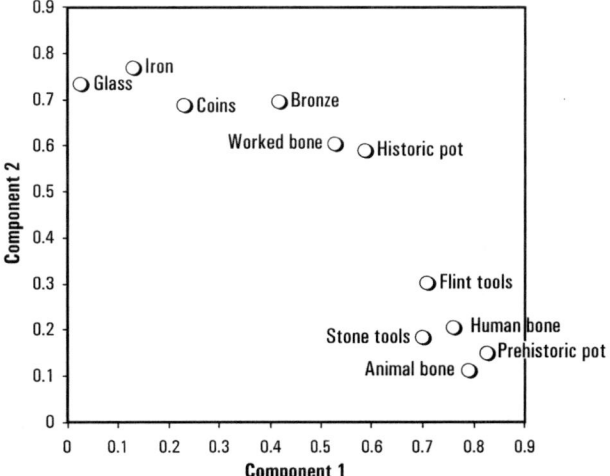

FIGURE 5.3 Principal Components Analysis of finds from 100 archaeological caves in the Peak District and the Yorkshire Dales. The chart shows the loadings of the variables on rotated principal components which account for 48 percent (component 1) and 13 percent (component 2) of the variation in the data set. The analysis shows that finds of human skeletal remains are associated with faunal remains and prehistoric artifacts, including pottery and stone tools. A separate cluster of variables represents finds of historical-period artifacts, including Roman and post-Roman pottery, glass, metalwork, worked bone, and coins.

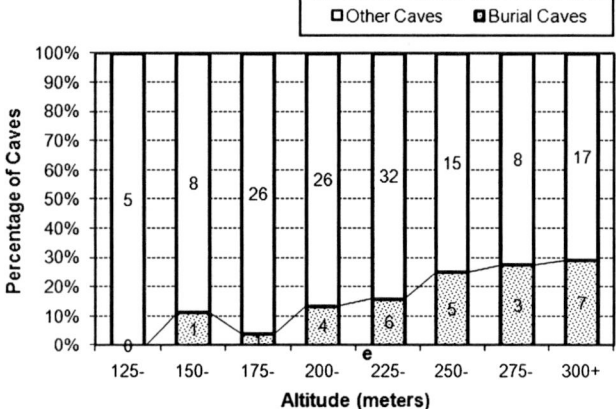

FIGURE 5.4 Altitudes of burial caves in the Peak District of central Britain. (Numbers on the columns indicate sample sizes for each category.) The proportion of caves containing burials increases with altitude. In part this reflects a general higher frequency of archaeological caves at higher altitudes, but it may also reflect the selection of prominent visual locations, which is also a pattern found in the location of prehistoric surface-burial sites in the region.

TABLE 5.1 Comparison of numbers of individuals and sample composition in Neolithic–Early Bronze Age (ca. 4000 to 2000 BC) cave-burial sites and in Neolithic nonmegalithic long barrows. (Data from Kinnes 1992.)

	No. of sites with human remains	Minimum no. of individuals (MNI)	Average MNI per site	Proportion of immatures
Cave-Burial Sites	89	407	4.6	38%
Neolithic Long Barrows	60	604	10.1	26%

caves together with archaeologically excavated caves where human remains were not discovered). Figure 5.4 shows the association of cave burial with altitude, but it is not yet clear whether the pattern is a true reflection of a preference among prehistoric communities for selecting higher and thus more prominent locations for cave burial, or whether it is influenced by the choice of these prominent caves for invasive archaeological investigation by modern antiquarians. The fact that prehistoric burials at surface sites in the same region are also concentrated at higher altitudes (Barnatt 1996) suggests that the apparent preference for burial at topographically prominent locations may have been a real one (figure 5.5).

Comparison of the assemblages of human remains recovered from Neolithic–Early Bronze Age cave burials in Britain with those from Neolithic long-barrow burials (a major category of surface mortuary site in the British Neolithic: Kinnes 1992) reveals some interesting distinctions (table 5.1). The cave-burial sites contain significantly fewer individuals per site, and a significantly higher proportion of immature individuals (infants, children, and juveniles) when compared to the burials in long barrows. The smaller groups of individuals represented in the cave-burial assemblages may in part arise from the fact that in many instances the cave archaeological sites were not totally excavated, so the original number of individuals interred in these caves may have been higher than is represented by the reported sizes of the skeletal assemblages. The higher proportion of immature individuals in the cave-burial sites (38 percent) is closer to the proportion expected for prehistoric populations with moderate to high rates of mortality (Chamberlain 2000), and this may indicate that caves received a representative sample of the dead, whereas the monumental Neolithic burial sites received a more selected sample of the deaths from the communities that they served.

Another notable feature of the prehistoric cave-burial sites is that in many instances there have been multiple phases of mortuary activity, often separated by extensive time intervals. Where multiple radiocarbon determinations have been undertaken on assemblages of human remains from cave sites, in half of the cases the dates are sufficiently dispersed to support a hypothesis of multiple burial phases. Multiple secondary burials are commonly found at barrow sites during the Neolithic and Bronze Age in Britain (Parker Pearson 1993; Woodward 2000), so it is perhaps reasonable to suggest that the continued accessibility of many caves would have facilitated their long-term use as burial sites. Despite this indirect evidence for continuity of prehistoric burial activities in caves, there is relatively infrequent evidence for structural modifications within the caves themselves, and in many instances the entrances to burial caves are small and may be located in secluded positions within the wider landscape (cf. Barnatt and Edmonds 2002).

CONCLUSIONS

In terms of frequency of usage, caves were important localities in Neolithic Britain for the deposition of assemblages of human remains and other cultural material, and they rivaled constructed monuments as significant foci for rites associated with the dead. To what extent is it possible to extrapolate this statement to the broader natural landscape? Caves are unusual in providing localized, protected natural environments where the potential for survival of organic remains and artifacts is enhanced relative to other depositional environments. Deposition of human remains may have occurred at other focal points in the British land-

FIGURE 5.5 Thor's Cave, a large archaeological cave in the Peak District of England. The visual prominence of the entrance to the cave in a sheer limestone crag that rises above the wooded valley may have attracted prehistoric activities as well as early antiquarian interest (the cave was excavated in 1864).

scape, and there is evidence that major rivers (Bradley and Gordon 1988) and upland and lowland peat bogs (Turner 1995) may have been further examples of such localities. However, most terrestrial natural environments are erosional rather than accretional, so the material evidence for deposition of human remains and other cultural material at unmodified locations in the landscape is likely to have disappeared in the majority of instances. This taphonomic consideration, together with our limited understanding of past perceptions of the natural landscape, continues to pose obstacles to a fuller appreciation of the range and diversity of prehistoric mortuary ritual in Britain. From spatially restricted studies it is apparent that about 20 percent of caves in Britain are likely to preserve archaeological material, but we currently lack a predictive model for assessing the archaeological potential of unexcavated cave sites. In the absence of such a model it is impossible to quantify the archaeological potential of most of our caves, or to incorporate archaeology effectively within cave-conservation strategies except in a very broad and general sense. Further research on this issue is in progress, and continuing advances in our understanding of the usage and significance of caves in prehistory are anticipated.

ACKNOWLEDGMENTS

Helen Holderness collected some of the data used in this study as part of a research project funded by English Heritage and codirected by the author with Dr. Randolph Donahue of the University of Bradford. The support of the Arts and Humanities Research Council is also gratefully acknowledged.

REFERENCES CITED

Barnatt, John. 1996. "Barrows in the Peak District: A Review and Interpretation of Extant Sites and Past Excavations." In *Barrows in the Peak District: Recent Research*, ed. John Barnatt and John Collis, 3–94. Sheffield: Sheffield Academic Press.

Barnatt, John, and Mark Edmonds. 2002. "Places Apart? Caves and Monuments in Neolithic and Earlier Bronze Age Britain." *Cambridge Archaeological Journal* 12 (1): 113–29. http://dx.doi.org/10.1017/S0959774302000069.

Barton, R.E. Nicholas, and Simon N. Colcutt. 1986. "A Survey of Palaeolithic Cave Sites in England and Wales." Unpublished report. London: English Heritage.

Bonsall, Clive, and Christopher Tolan-Smith, eds. 1997. *The Human Use of Caves*. BAR International Series 667. Oxford: Archaeopress.

Bradley, Richard. 2000. *An Archaeology of Natural Places*. London: Routledge.

Bradley, Richard, and Ken Gordon. 1988. "Human Skulls from the River Thames, Their Dating and Significance." *Antiquity* 62: 503–9.

Branigan, Keith, and Martin J. Dearne. 1991. *A Gazetteer of Romano-British Cave Sites and Their Finds*. Department of Archaeology and Prehistory, University of Sheffield.

Chamberlain, Andrew T. 1996. "More Dating Evidence for Human Remains in British Caves." *Antiquity* 70: 950–3.

Chamberlain, Andrew T. 2000. "Minor Concerns: A Demographic Perspective on Children in Past Societies." In *Children and Material Culture*, ed. Joanna Sofaer Derevenski, 206–12. London: Routledge.

Chamberlain, Andrew T., and Keith Ray. 1994. *A Catalogue of Quaternary Fossil-Bearing Cave Sites in the Plymouth Area*. Plymouth, UK: City Museum.

Connolly, Michael, and Frank Coyne. 2000. "Cloghermore Cave: The Lee Valhalla." *Archaeology Ireland* 14: 16–9.

Dunnington, N. J., and J. C. Coleman. 1950. "Dunmore Cave, Co. Kilkenny." *Proceedings of the Royal Irish Academy* 53B: 15–24.

Edwards, Nancy. 1990. *The Archaeology of Early Medieval Ireland*. London: Batsford.

Ford, Trevor D., ed. 1989. *Limestones and Caves of Wales*. Cambridge: Cambridge University Press.

Galanidou, Nena. 2000. "Patterns in Caves: Foragers, Horticulturalists, and the Use of Space." *Journal of Anthropological Archaeology* 19 (3): 243–75. http://dx.doi.org/10.1006/jaar.1999.0362.

Gilks, John. 1989. "Cave Burials of Northern England." *British Archaeology* 11: 11–5.

Holderness, Helen, Glyn Davies, Randolph Donahue, and Andrew T. Chamberlain. 2007. "A Conservation Audit of Archaeological Caves in the Peak District and Yorkshire Dales: Research Report." ARCUS Report 743.1. *Cave Archaeology and Palaeontology Research Archive* 7. http://capra.group.shef.ac.uk/~capra/7/.

Jackson, J. W. 1962. "Archaeology and Palaeontology." In *British Caving*, ed. C.H.D. Cullingford, 252–346. London: Routledge.

Kinnes, Ian. 1992. *Non-Megalithic Long Barrows and Allied Structures in the British Neolithic*. London: British Museum.

Parker Pearson, Michael. 1993. *Bronze Age Britain*. London: Batsford.

Straus, Lawrence Guy. 1997. "Convenient Cavities: Some Human Uses of Caves and Rockshelters." In *The Human Use of Caves*, ed. Clive Bonsall and Christopher Tolan-Smith, 1–8. BAR International Series 667. Oxford: Archaeopress.

Stuiver, Minze, A. Long, and R. S. Kra, eds. 1993. "Calibration 1993." *Radiocarbon* 35 (1): 1–244.

Tilley, Christopher. 1994. *A Phenomenology of Landscape*. Oxford: Berg.

Tilley, Christopher, and Wayne Bennett. 2001. "An Archaeology of Supernatural Places: The Case of West Penwith." *Journal of the Royal Anthropological Institute* 7 (2): 335–62. http://dx.doi.org/10.1111/1467-9655.00066.

Tolan-Smith, Christopher. 2001. *The Caves of Mid Argyll: An Archaeology of Human Use*. Edinburgh: Society of Antiquaries of Scotland.

Trent and Peak Archaeological Trust. 1993. "Manifold Valley, Staffordshire, Cave Survey." Unpublished Report. Nottingham: Trent and Peak Archaeological Trust.

Turner, Richard C. 1995. "Recent Research into British Bog Bodies." In *Bog Bodies: New Discoveries and New Perspectives*, ed. Richard C. Turner and Robert G. Scaife, 109–22. London: British Museum Press.

Woodward, Anne. 2000. *British Barrows: A Matter of Life and Death*. Stroud: Tempus.

6

The Subterranean Landscape of the Southern Levant during the Chalcolithic Period

Yorke M. Rowan and David Ilan

> Hence, loathèd Melancholy
> Of Cerberus and blackest Midnight born
> In Stygian cave forlorn
> 'Mongst horrid shapes, and shrieks, and sights unholy!
> Find out some uncouth cell
> Where brooding Darkness spreads his jealous wings
> And the night-raven sings;
> There under ebon shades, and low-brow'd rocks
> As ragged as thy locks,
> In dark Cimmerian desert ever dwell!
>
> **John Milton, "L'Allegro"**

Human beings find caves, and the subterranean dimension in general, alluring. But the subterranean is also viewed with trepidation, the locus of unknown dangers and mysteries. The idea of the cave as a place of divine immanence, a zone of contact with "otherworldliness," is one that extends across millennia and continents, and one that is significant in many cultures, societies, and religions. The first divine messages received by Mohammed were received in a cave; the Dome of the Rock in Jerusalem, sacred as the place where Mohammed ascended to heaven and the location of the Jewish Temple, was established over a cave. According to some traditions, Christ was born in a manger—in a cave. Oracles and ascetic hermits have often been associated with caves believed to contain special powers, provide entrance to other worlds, allow contact with the numinous, and provide optimal conditions for rites of passage.

In the Levant, cave habitation and mortuary use dates from as early as the Paleolithic. The Amud, Kebara, Qafzeh, Skhul, and Tabun caves include evidence for intentional burial of the dead from as early as the Mousterian (Bar-Yosef et al. 1992; Garrod and Bate 1937; McCown 1937; Rak, Kimbel, and Hovers 1994; Suzuki and Takai 1970; Tillier et al. 1988; Vandermeersch 1982). The intentional inclusion of animal mandibles, maxillae, and antlers (Kaufman 1999), and the missing skull from an otherwise articulated skeleton at Kebara Cave (Bar Yosef et al. 1992), suggest symbolic behavior. Although there are few cave burials from the Upper Paleolithic (Gilead 1998, 136), many have been documented from the Natufian, when manipulation of human remains becomes more common and unambiguous. During the Natufian, people inhabited caves and buried their dead within, both singly and in multiples. By the end of the Natufian, skull removal—best known from the subsequent Neolithic—became more common, as exemplified by the burials found at Hayonim Cave (Valla 1998). Throughout the subsequent Neolithic phases, caves were only rarely used for habitation (e.g., Kuijt, Mabry, and Palumbo 1991), but their ritual use is clearly in evidence (e.g., Nahal Hemar: Bar-Yosef and Alon 1988; Qana Cave: Gopher 1996, 53–82).

It seems to be during the Chalcolithic period, however, that the ritual use of caves became customary (figure 6.1), most prominently with regard to inhumation. For the first

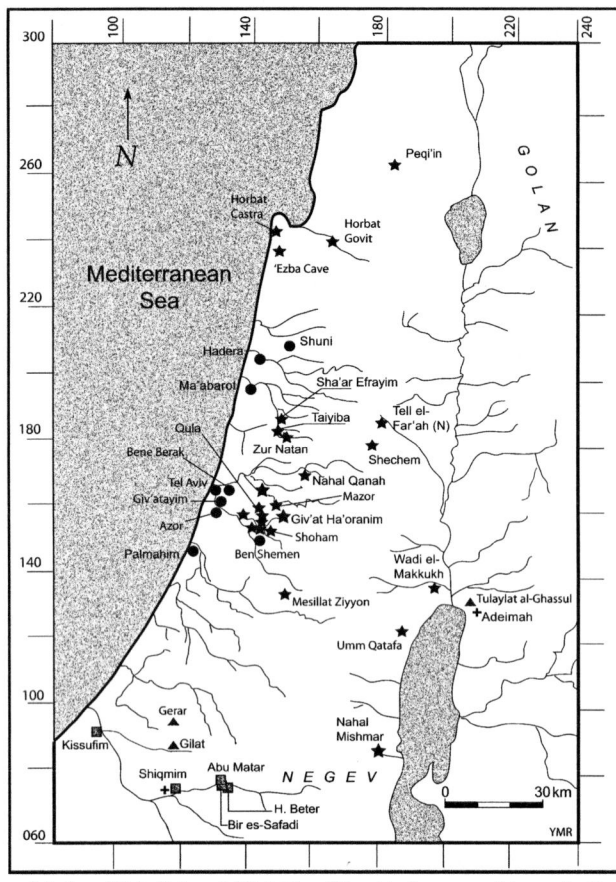

FIGURE 6.1 Selected Chalcolithic cave and mortuary sites.

time, artificial caves—mainly tombs—were carved into bedrock and loess. Ritual and symbolic activity that took place within caves was referenced by rituals and symbols above ground as well. Hidden from view, caves are nevertheless a part of the landscape. The theme of landscape as inhabited space and arena for ritual practice is now prominent in archaeological studies (Alcock 1993; Ashmore and Knapp 2000; Bradley 1991, 2002; Buikstra and Charles 2000; Crumley 2000; Derks 1997; Taçon 2000; Thomas 1993) and is particularly relevant to the Chalcolithic period. Burial grounds, promontories, springs, seasonal pastureland, and other features had chthonic or cosmological associations that induced people to modify the landscape. Continuity was one motif but reinterpretation was certainly another. Chalcolithic caves show both.

In this chapter, we examine the ways in which Chalcolithic people exploited underground spaces. We first survey the variety of subterranean forms, ranging from the extensive karstic formations of the western highlands to the artificial subterranean rooms and tunnels of the northern Negev. We then examine the material-culture assemblages found in these subterranean contexts. In conclusion, we argue that intensive exploitation, creation, and modification of these spaces reflect a central pillar of Chalcolithic cosmology and worldview. Storage, habitation, and possibly safe haven are possibilities in a few instances, particularly in rockshelters and semisubterranean areas, but mortuary practices were the dominant motif for much of subterranean space. We suggest that the manipulation of the dead complements a broader belief system that emphasizes ancestors, the regeneration of life, and the life cycle in general.

THE LEVANTINE CHALCOLITHIC: A SYNOPSIS

The Chalcolithic period (ca. 4500–3600 BC) marks an era of later southern Levantine prehistory (see table 6.1 for general chronology) when a number of fundamental changes occur (Levy 1986a, 1986b; Rowan and Golden 2009). Sedentary populations expand and settlements are established in areas previously only sparsely occupied during the Late Neolithic. Different lines of evidence indicate intensification of agricultural production, with cereal cultivation complemented by an increased reliance on fruits and olives in particular. Secondary animal products play a key role in this expansion of production. Craft activity increases in volume, together with evidence for innovation, technological sophistication, and the utilization of exotic materials. Ceramics, stone working, and ivory carving comprise the more visible evidence of this attention to craft production, but the rare preservation of textiles and wall murals underscores the elaborate nature of material culture. Metallurgy, unknown in the Neolithic, is perhaps the most critical technological leap, showing smelting techniques sophisticated beyond those practiced in Egypt and Mesopotamia during the same period. All these developments appear to correspond to changes in the configuration of more-complex sociopolitical structures, though just what these structures were is the subject of debate (Levy 1986a, 1986b, 1998, 2006 vs. Gilead 1988).

CHALCOLITHIC MORTUARY PRACTICES

In the following section it is shown that much of the subterranean dimension can be associated with burial, burial rites, and perhaps chthonic cosmology. This being the case, it is worthwhile summarizing what we know about the diversity of Chalcolithic mortuary practices. As in the Natufian and Neolithic periods, intramural burials are well attested in the Chalcolithic, in the form of both single primary burials—for example, at Gerar (Gilead 1995) and Shiqmim (Levy et al. 1991a, figure 17)—and multiple, primary interments—mainly at Gilat (Levy et al. 2006; Smith

TABLE 6.1 Chronology for Levantine sites.

Period	Key entities (phases or cultures)	Radiometric dates (cal BC)
Late Neolithic	Yarmukian, Jericho IX, Wadi Rabah, Qatifian, Tsafian, Besorian	ca. 6400–4600/4500
Chalcolithic	Ghassulian, Beershevan, Golan	ca. 4600/4500–3700/3600
Early Bronze Age (I)	A, B	ca. 3700/3600–3200/3100

et al. 2006) and at Shiqmim (Levy and Alon 1987, figures 6.17a, b; figure 6.1). Intramural burials include both sexes and all age groups (Smith et al. 2006). Fetuses and infants buried in jars constitute one phenomenon that appears to continue an earlier practice (Gopher and Orrelle 1995). Chalcolithic examples come from Ghassul (Mallon, Koeppel, and Neuville 1934) and Gilat (Smith et al. 2006, 335, 338–39).

But the Chalcolithic period introduced changes in mortuary behavior that are even more significant. Chalcolithic burials are more frequent relative to the period's duration of about 800 to 1,000 years. Mortuary remains are found in regions where they were rare or nonexistent in earlier periods (the northern Negev, the central highlands, and the central coastal plain, for example). The utilization of natural caves was supplemented by the carving of artificial tombs. Separate cemeteries became normative.

Extramural cemeteries may occur as early as the Late Neolithic (Avner 1989; Avner, Carmi, and Segal 1994) but the Chalcolithic has many of them. Perhaps the best example of a formal extramural Chalcolithic cemetery is that of Shiqmim (Levy 1998; Levy and Alon 1979, 1982, 1985, 1987; Levy, Alon, Grigson, et al. 1991a; Levy, Grigson, et al. 1991b; Levy, Alon, Goldberg, et al. 1994), where the cemetery lies on a ridge above the settlement. Here we find rock-hewn cists and aboveground, circular stone structures containing secondary remains, albeit poorly preserved and in small quantities. (We shall return to the Shiqmim assemblage at a later point in this chapter.) Other examples of extramural, formal cemeteries in the arid Negev come from the unpublished sites at Nahal Sekher (Gilead and Goren 1986).

The tumuli (rock piles) and burial chambers at Adeimah, near Tulaylat al-Ghassul would also appear to be Chalcolithic (Stekelis 1935), at least in part, as may be the *nawamis* grave circles of northern Sinai (Bar-Yosef, Belfer, et al. 1977; Bar-Yosef, Belfer-Cohen, et al. 1986). Stone circles or "cairns," similar to those at Shiqmim, were recorded at a cemetery near Bab edh-Dhraᶜ, on the eastern escarpment above the Dead Sea. These contained little in the way of human remains and artifacts but they, too, may well be Chalcolithic (Clark 1979). All told, grave circles and tumuli-over-cist structures seem to concentrate in the arid Negev and Sinai, on the southern margins of the Levant.

Farther to the north, but mainly east of the Jordan River, dolmens seem to be the dominant burial feature. Dolmens tend to exist in groups and today they appear as an above-surface phenomenon, but there is some evidence that they were covered by tumuli. Exposed as they are, dolmens are usually empty of finds, having been robbed, reused, or in some cases perhaps poorly excavated and documented. As a result, their dating is usually equivocal. There is no doubt that they were already in use by the Early Bronze Age (Vinitzky 1992). Though no dolmens have been found to contain Chalcolithic remains in the Golan Heights, their close proximity to Chalcolithic sites suggests that they were perhaps introduced in this period.

The greatest concentration of cave interments is found on the central coastal plain of Israel (van den Brink 1998) and inland as far east as the Nablus–Tell Balatah region in the Palestinian National Authority (e.g., Clamer 1977; Clamer 1981). A recent survey of caves in the northern highlands of Jordan has produced scant evidence for Chalcolithic mortuary remains (Lovell 2009). No similar mortuary finds from this period are in evidence from Lebanon or Syria.

Chalcolithic mortuary rites are apparent in the variety of secondary treatment of the human bones. The caves and carved tombs of the central coastal plain and the central highlands contain perhaps the richest burial assemblages. These assemblages display a burst of symbolic, artistic representation, especially in the form and decoration of ceramic ossuaries containing secondary burials (figure 6.2). Ossuaries, however, come in other forms as well. Perrot and Ladiray (1980) have identified three types of Chalcolithic ossuary: boxes (or "tubs") (figure 6.2E), structures (figure 6.2B, D), and jars (figure 6.2A); the first can be stone or ceramic and the latter two are ceramic. Most frequent are those termed structural or "house ossuaries," due to the peaked roofs and occasional modeled features that appear to be beams and poles (though such features are not known from the architectural corpus of the period). Other modeled features include tools. Structural ossuaries are almost always painted, often with prominent eyes and noses. The recent discoveries at Peqi'in included mouths for the first time (Gal, Smithline, and Shalem 1997, figure 4; 1999, figures 4–6, 9). Other, more-elaborate features recently discovered at the Peqi'in cave include modeled, painted ears (figure 6.2B), painted hair, and modeled arms and hands (Gal, Smithline, and Shalem 1999, figures 1, 4, 6). A few ossuaries include modeled breasts (figure 6.2C), and these, at least, must have been intended to be female in essence.

Jar ossuaries (figure 6.2A), on the other hand, may be representations of grain silos (Bar-Yosef and Ayalon 2001) or chrysalises (Nativ 2008). But whatever the variant, ossuaries seem to share the idea of expediting metamorphosis or rebirth.

In contrast to the dearth of grave goods characteristic of Late Neolithic burials (Gopher and Orrelle 1995), mortuary goods are markedly more common in the Chalcolithic, though interments with few or no associated finds are not unusual. The inclusion of burial goods is generally associated with secondary-burial contexts, most often in caves. However, primary burials may also be associated with offerings placed farther away, in locations and positions less obviously related. While the quantity and quality of burial goods varies widely and may reflect some element of social status, in most cases specific goods cannot be associated with an individual interment, whether in a cave or not.

SUBTERRANEAN CATEGORIES

The caves exploited by Chalcolithic people along the eastern Mediterranean littoral can be divided into three categories:

(1) Natural karstic caves. These occur in the limestones of the Mt. Carmel range and the central hill country on both flanks of the Judea-Samaria-Galilee Anticline (the west, maritime flank has a Mediterranean climate and maquis vegetation while the east flank lies mostly in a rain-shadow desert). Such caves exist east of the Jordan River, in modern Jordan as well, but thus far no Chalcolithic mortuary material has been recovered in the caves of Jordan (though a recent project is seeking them out: Lovell 2009). Karstic caves were generally modified to some extent.

(2) Artificial caves in soft bedrock. These are found primarily in the piedmont zone between the limestone central hills and the coastal plain. Closer to the central hills we find Senonian chalk, which, when exposed to the elements over time, forms a 0.5–1.5-meter-thick crust of hard minerals, called *nari*. Nari is frequently used as a building stone (the underlying chalk is too soft), but it also forms the "encasement" when a cavity is hollowed out of the softer chalk. The second, and more frequent type of rock used to carve tombs is aeolian calcareous sandstone, locally termed *kurkar*. This rock type is found along the Mediterranean coast in a series of four ridges that represent sand-dune formation along four different Pleistocene shorelines. These fossilized dune belts correspond to changing sea levels affected by periodic glaciation.

(3) Artificial caves and sunken chambers in loess. Loess—a silty, windblown deposit—is characteristic of the northern section of the Negev desert in Israel. While susceptible to erosion, it is also compact and amenable to the excavation of cavities.

Below, we introduce what are perhaps the best exemplars of the Chalcolithic caves of southern Levant, organized by rock type. It will become clear that most of the artificial features occur across the different cave types, whether natural or hewn by humans. Indeed, certain aspects of natural, karstic caves were copied by people who carved artificial caves.

KARSTIC CAVES

Karstic caves run the gamut from active caves in the wetter highland zone to drier, fairly inactive caves in the desert and piedmont zones. Both desert- and Mediterranean-zone caves were modified in antiquity but the latter, being more active, show more evidence for attention to speleothems. Active karstic caves are best represented by two illustrious examples: the Nahal Qanah Cave and the Peqi'in Cave. The striking thing about these two caves is the effect that active karst has on archaeological deposits. Artifacts, such as ossuaries and ceramic vessels, and human skeletal material are sometimes coated or covered by carbonate deposits, and the dampness causes the decomposition of human bones. At the same time, the active karstic caves contain some of the richest finds precisely because they are still active and not exposed to the open air.

Nahal Qanah Cave

The Nahal Qanah Cave is located in the maquis-covered limestone hills of the western highlands (see figure 6.1). Spread out over five levels, this cave complex achieves maximums (to the best of our knowledge) of approximately 25 meters in depth and about 90 meters in length (figure 6.3). A narrow tunnel leads to the uppermost level and the Main Hall (ca. 500 m²) from which extend additional passages, crevices, and tunnels (Gopher and Tsuk 1996a, 13–52). One tunnel provides access to the deeper areas where several galleries are interconnected by narrow passages. The chambers and passages contained cultural material dated to the Pottery Neolithic (6000–4500 BCE), Chalcolithic (4500–3600 BCE), and the Early Bronze Age I (3600–3100 BCE). The majority of finds date to the Chalcolithic. Excavation was challenging and one cannot expect total retrieval (Gopher and Tsuk 1996a, 7–12).

Nahal Qanah included Neolithic and Early Bronze Age material, but context and find associations—particularly with ossuary fragments—suggested to the excavators that all of the human remains should be attributed to the Chalcolithic period (Hershkovitz and Gopher 1996, 175). Human skeletal remains were estimated at twenty-three individuals and nearly as many ossuaries (ca. twenty-two).

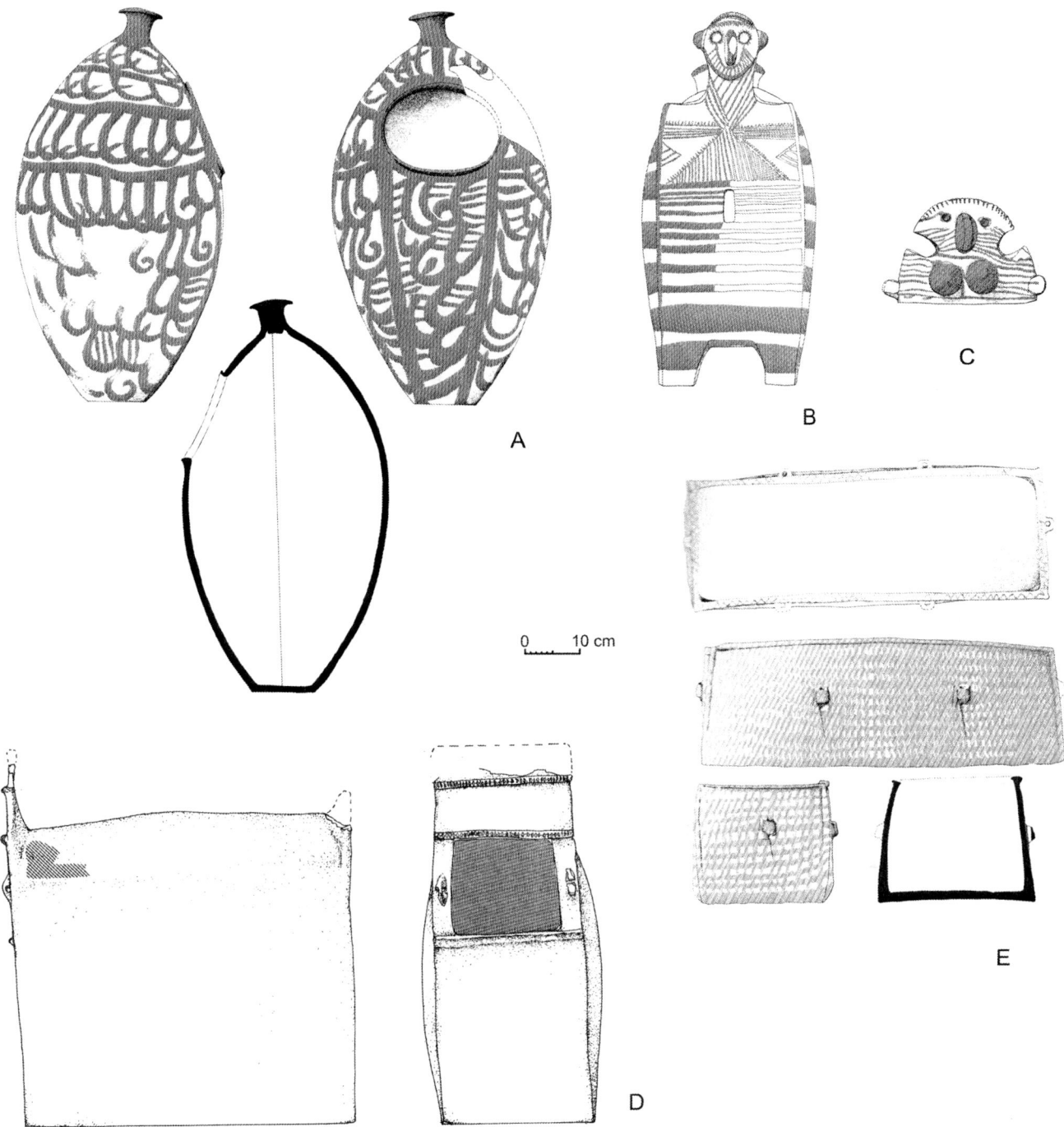

FIGURE 6.2 Chalcolithic ossuaries: (A) Kissufim mortuary urn (from Goren 2002, figure 4.12); (B, C) ossuary façades from Peqi'in Cave (from Gal, Smithline, and Shalem 1999, figures 1, 7); (D) structural ("house") ossuary from Shoham (N), Cave 2 (from van den Brink 2005b, figure 4.5); and (E) box ossuary from et-Taiyiba (from Yannai and Porath 2006, Ossuary No. 4).

Despite careful excavation and recording methods, extraction of bones from the travertine deposits was complicated by their prolonged exposure to moisture and their fragmentary nature after crushing by rockfalls. At least ten individuals and twenty ossuaries were found in the Main Hall, the Passage, the Copper Room, the corridor leading

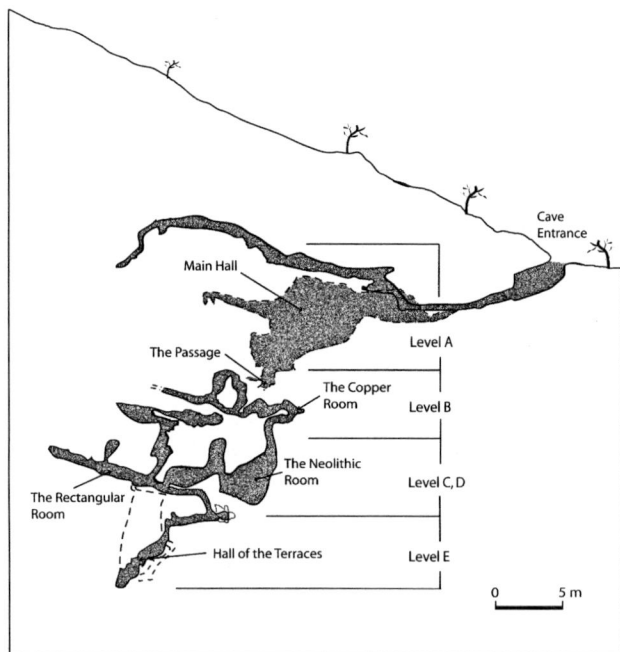

FIGURE 6.3 Nahal Qanah Cave profile, showing five levels. (Adapted from Gopher and Tsuk 1996a, figure 2.1.)

from the Copper Room to the Rectangular Room, and possibly the Hall of the Terraces (Gopher and Tsuk 1996c, 218). In these galleries, stepped terraces were built.

In virtually every context where human remains were found, ossuary fragments were also discovered, indicating secondary burial. The reverse, however, was not observed, possibly because some bones have simply dissolved in the damp karstic environment (figure 6.4). The state of the skeletal remains precluded determining whether bone selection was intentional (Hershkovitz and Gopher 1996, 176). Despite their poor condition, the bones indicate (1) an absence of adult crania, (2) that most individuals interred in the cave were under the age of 20 years old (ca. 60 percent: Hershkovitz and Gopher 1996, figure 8.2), and (3) that, with the exception of signs of anemia in the bones of a child, few pathologies were evident. Usually only one side of an individual was represented, vertebrae are entirely missing from the cave, and major parts of skeletons are underrepresented (ibid., 176; table 8.1). It is unfortunate that such data are not available from most other cave sites, for these patterns are intriguing and open to interpretation. Such an endeavor is beyond the purview of this chapter, however.

A strikingly rich material culture repertoire was discovered, including three piriform hematite maceheads, a standard, an axe or adze, and wire—all of copper—as well as a "greenstone" pendant, a decorated turquoise bead, and other beads made of carnelian and other stone as well as dentalium shell. Most surprising, and still unique for the southern Levantine Chalcolithic, were eight gold and electrum rings discovered in close proximity to one another (see figure 6.6C). These are clearly prestige items previously unknown for this period in the ancient Near East (Gopher et al. 1990). The gold and electrum must have traveled a great distance (Nubia is the best candidate for the source) and the ring's shape and purity argue for technological sophistication.

Other important artifacts include 101 basalt vessel fragments (Gopher and Tsuk 1996b, 109–112), estimated to represent at least ten individual vessels, four open-form bowls, and six fenestrated stands (Rowan 1998). Parallels to these large vessels have been found at other burial sites such as Peqi'in (figure 6.6B), Shoham, and Yehud (van den Brink, Rowan, and Braun 1999), and in the subterranean chambers at Giv'at ha-Oranim (Scheftolowitz and Oren 2004, and see below). That these were prestige goods related to ritual activities is evident from the great labor investment into their intricate form, using nonlocal, hard materials. Other special equipment includes a ceramic basket handle similar to one from Kissufim (Goren and Fabian 2002) and a copper exemplar from Nahal Mishmar (Bar-Adon 1980, 108–109), and perforated hippopotamus tusks like those found at Shiqmim (Levy and Alon 1992) and Nahal Mishmar (fig. 6.6D; Bar-Adon 1980, 16–23). Other artifacts include pedestaled and fenestrated ceramic vessels (Gopher and Tsuk 1996b, figures 4.2:3–9) as well as standard ceramic forms such as V-shaped bowls, holemouth jars, and churns. Very little flint was found, although a perforated, circular, tabular piece is a form best known from the Jordan Valley, the Galilee, and the Golan (Noy 1998, 277–283; Rosen 1997, 84–85). Based on parallels known from other Chalcolithic mortuary contexts (Gopher and Tsuk 1996b, 218), the excavators suggest that the Nahal Qanah ceramic vessels are grave goods.

Peqi'in Cave

Discovered during road construction in 1995, Peqi'in Cave is located in the northern Galilee, Israel (figure 6.1). The cave comprises three units situated on three different levels that slope from east to west (17 meters in length, 5–7 meters in width: Gal, Smithline, and Shalem 1997, 145). Following abandonment and ancient disturbance or robbery, karstic activity increased, covering the ossuaries and other finds with travertine. Using the $^{230}Th/^{234}U$ disequilibrium method, a date of 6780 years BP was derived from the base of a stalagmite that sealed an ossuary, consistent with radiocarbon dates from this cave and other Chalcolithic sites (Bar-Yosef Mayer et al. 2004, 495; Segal et al. 1998). The cave may have had an earlier, pre-Chalcolithic, non-

FIGURE 6.4 Nahal Qanah Cave, karstic area with pottery churn fragment in situ. (Photograph courtesy of Tsvika Tsuk.)

mortuary phase, but the main phase features ossuary and jar burials. Although the deposits are probably disturbed (Gal, Smithline, and Shalem 1997, 147), the assemblage is a rich one, including dozens of ceramic ossuaries in a variety of shapes and sizes.

Peqi'in replicates many features observed in the Nahal Mishmar and Nahal Qanah assemblages: evidence for mortuary behavior (skeletal material, ossuaries); offerings of wealth in the form of metal objects, some in the form of weapons or tools; motifs that include aspects of female sexuality—and new variations of typical Chalcolithic facial features. The surprising discovery of Peqi'in greatly extends the reach of what has been termed the Ghassulian (southern Chalcolithic) culture much farther north than was previously known. As a result of the discoveries at Peqi'in, Nahal Qanah, and Shoham (north), it is clear that metals are not limited to Negev Chalcolithic entities. Moreover, the well-known Ghassulian motifs of eyes, elongated noses, knobs, and beams find their greatest elaboration on the ossuaries from Peqi'in cave. Ossuaries with façades or lids with painted faces, human facial features applied to plaques, and modeled three-dimensional human heads (figure 6.2B) extend the range of known ossuary decoration beyond anything previously recovered. Finds included not only mortuary jars and ossuaries but also an ivory figurine, steatite beads, objects of copper (and "bronze" according to Bar-Yosef Mayer et al. 2004, 495), and basalt bowls.

The final publication of the Peqi'in assemblage is not yet available. Preliminary publication has emphasized mainly the ornamental aspects of selected ossuaries. The total number of ossuaries is probably in the hundreds (Gal, Smithline, and Shalem 1999). New anthropomorphic elements from Peqi'in elaborate and expand the classic Ghassulian repertoire of exaggerated noses and round eyes (rare beards or ears are known from the Golan basalt pillar figurines). Novelties of the Peqi'in assemblage include ossuaries portraying mouths, teeth, hair, and hands. Although the prevalence of the prominent nose is a standard in the Chalcolithic repertoire, the presence of nostrils is very rare and, again, their existence at Peqi'in is notable.

FIGURE 6.5 Nahal Mishmar hoard as found in reed mat.

Nahal Mishmar (The Cave of the Treasure)

Since its 1961 discovery (Bar-Adon 1980) the Chalcolithic deposit from Nahal Mishmar in Israel has dazzled both the scholarly community and lay people. Found in a small cave (Cave 1) near the Dead Sea and perched dramatically in a sheer cliff face 250 meters above the wadi bottom, the deposit included 442 objects—mostly fashioned in copper, but some in ivory—wrapped in a reed mat (figure 6.5). It is, without doubt, the most intensely scrutinized Chalcolithic assemblage of all, and perhaps the richest iconographically.

A number of scholars have ventured various interpretations as to the deposit's implications. The excavator surmised a cultic function for the deposit and suggested that it came from a temple in the vicinity (Bar-Adon 1980, 202). Ussishkin (1971, 1980) proposed that the objects were transported from the contemporary sanctuary at En Gedi, 10.5 kilometers to the north. Moorey (1988) understood it as a utilitarian hoard originating in the treasury of a shrine (probably the structure located at the top of the cliff, above Cave 1). Two other contributions emphasized socioeconomic implications over cultic aspects, viewing the artifacts as commodities originating from the realm of private enterprise (Gates 1992; Tadmor 1989). Iconography is accented in other studies (e.g., Beck 1989; Elliot 1977; Epstein 1978; and most effectively, Merhav 1993). More recently, Garfinkel (1994) has suggested that the deposit comprises the ritual burial of "worn out" or otherwise "unsuitable" cult objects.

Oddly, these interpretations have largely ignored the human skeletal remains found in the cave—remains of five individuals, to be precise. The final report is somewhat inconsistent and vague about the precise location of the "treasure" and the burials (Bar Adon 1980, 5–8, 198) but a physical anthropology report (Haas and Nathan 1973) makes it clear that the burials were primary and intentional.

Evidence for weaving, spinning, food storage, and cooking in Stratum III of Cave 1 led Bar-Adon (and most subsequent researchers) to infer the prosaic activities of between this region and the coastal–piedmont zone to the west. In the Judean Desert, primary inhumation was apparently final, without recourse to secondary mortuary treatment. (For other Chalcolithic burials of the Judean Desert see, for example, Eshel and Zissu 1995; Haas and Nathan 1973; Schick 1998.)

SHOHAM (NORTH)

Shoham is located approximately 20 kilometers southeast of Tel Aviv at the foothills of the Shomeron anticline. Salvage excavations concentrated on four interconnected karstic caves used, according to the excavators (van den Brink and Gophna 2005), for both burial and habitation, beginning in the Chalcolithic. Subsequent reoccupation and burial in later periods—Early Bronze Age I (EBI) and Intermediate Bronze Age—introduced contamination and prejudiced Chalcolithic context in places.

In parts of the system, roofs had collapsed with attendant damage; in other places, particularly around natural pillars, the assemblage was better preserved. Cave 1 was irregularly shaped, measuring about 12 meters (north-south) by 11 meters (east-west), with a maximum height ranging from 1.5 to 2.0 meters. Where the roof had not collapsed, six ossuary jars containing secondary burials were found on stones placed over the bedrock. Next to these jars, two other secondary burials were placed in a basin and large bowl.

Located immediately to the northwest, Cave 2 (12 meters by 5 meters, maximum height 1.8 meters) was accessed via five steps cut into the bedrock, leading down about 2 meters into the cave. Also irregular in shape, Cave 2 had two natural niches in the rear. The bottom layer (ca. 50 centimeters) in the cave included Chalcolithic burial remains and approximately thirty-nine box and jar ossuaries under the collapsed ceiling. Many larger ossuary fragments were recovered from a deep pit in the bedrock in front of one niche. A natural crevice led from behind this pit into Cave 4.

Divided into two sections by a natural supporting pillar, Cave 4 measured about 15 meters by 12 meters and had an intact roof up to 3.5 meters in height. The excavators interpreted pottery scattered on the bedrock in one part of the cave as an "early Chalcolithic" occupation. In their view, the cave was then reused for mortuary purposes, including at least twenty-two ossuaries (box and jar types) and other artifacts. Many of the ossuary fragments and pedestaled, fenestrated, basalt bowl fragments were recovered from two pits in the bedrock, while the few in situ burials were limited to areas around the natural pillar. A heavy stone collapse sealed the mortuary stratum, and on top of this collapse a superseding Chalcolithic occupation

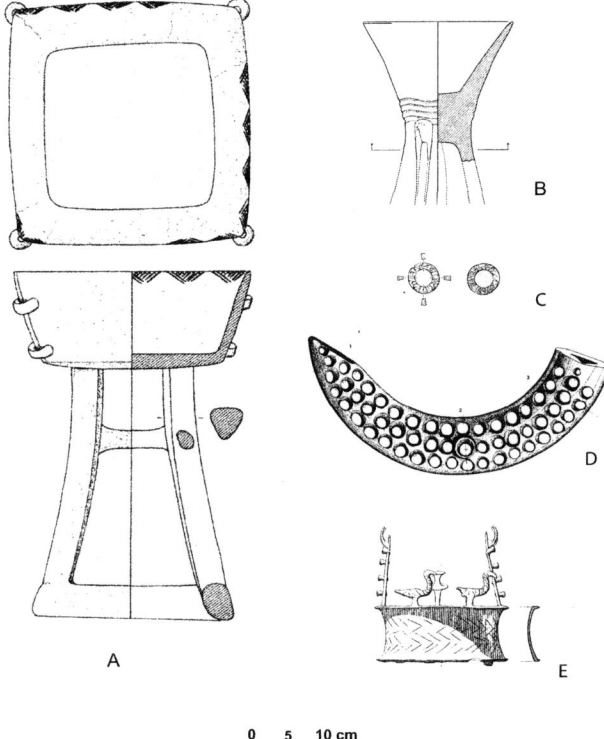

FIGURE 6.6 Material items from mortuary cave contexts: (A) unique, pedestaled, square, basalt vessel from Giv'at ha-Oranim (from Scheftelowitz 2004, figure 4.7:3); (B) pedestaled basalt vessel from Peqi'in (after van den Brink, Rowan, and Braun 1999, figure 9); (C) gold and electrum ring from Nahal Qanah (Gopher and Tsuk 1996b, figure 4.24:5); (D) perforated hippopotamus-ivory tusk from Nahal Mishmar (adapted from Bar-Adon 1980, No. 1); and (E) copper "crown" from Nahal Mishmar (Bar-Adon 1980, No. 7).

everyday life over a prolonged period of time. Following this line of thinking, the burials were attributed to people who actually dwelt in the caves, despite the inaccessibility of the cave in a sheer cliff. For parallel behavior Bar-Adon drew upon subterranean or troglodyte habitations identified at Lachish, Beersheba, and Wadi Muraba'at (Bar-Adon 1980, 202–203) as a basis for contending that the treasure was deposited in response to a crisis relating to Egyptian incursions (1980, 7, 14, 204).

Our own analysis (Rowan and Ilan, n.d.) has shown that at least one burial must be coeval with the so-called treasure. Moreover, given the parallels from other mortuary contexts—karstic and nonkarstic, contextual and iconographic—it seems clear that the Nahal Mishmar treasure should be associated with mortuary ritual, as such deposits are in the Nahal Qanah and Peqi'in caves. The lack of ossuaries reflects, we believe, a more general Judean Desert–Rift Valley dearth of ossuaries, that is, a cultural difference was radiometrically dated to about 4000 BC based on two samples (oak and olive: van den Brink and Gophna 2005; Carmi and Segal 2005). The reuse of this cave was marked by large quantities of sherds, a few flint tools, and many animal bones. The virtual absence of human remains during this phase suggests it was probably cleared. Additional, later phases of reuse are dated to early EBI and Intermediate Bronze Age.

Artifacts recovered from Shoham are similar to those recovered at other cave-burial sites. Eighty-five ossuaries were tabulated (many fragmentary) and included all three types identified by Perrot and Ladiray (1980; van den Brink 2005b). Some of the ossuary jars were decorated with modeled ruminant (ibex?) horns, a well-known motif in the funerary iconography of the Chalcolithic. Some ground-stone vessels were gleaned from the caves, and the basalt vessels include forms of greater intricacy, similar to examples from burial contexts such as Nahal Qanah and Giv'at ha-Oranim (Rowan 2005, figures 9.11, 9.15; van den Brink, Rowan, and Braun 1999, 174–178). A number of palette fragments were also found (Rowan 2005, figure 9.1:1–4), similar to one found at the mortuary installation at Kissufim (Fabian and Goren 2002, figure 6.6; and see below).

The Shoham excavation report includes the most thorough ceramic analysis of any assemblage from a mortuary context. Summarizing this assemblage, Commenge (2005, 60) concludes that vessels with more-complex morphological forms, such as fenestrated pedestal bowls and miniature churns are typically associated with ossuaries and are rare at settlement sites. Their high frequency at the Gilat sanctuary reaffirms their ritual association (Commenge 2006, 425–43). Pottery assemblages from the Shoham caves include higher quantities of basins, jars, and pedestal bowls than are typically found at settlement sites in household contexts (Commenge 2005, 61, figure 6.38).

CAVES CARVED IN CHALK AND NARI

The Senonian chalk outcroppings of the lower piedmont are found near and interspersed among the lower western reaches of the Cenomanian and Turonian limestone and dolomites of the Samarian and Judean anticlines (Orni and Ephrat 1973, 53–79). The outer nari layer is protective, but once the nari is breached, the underlying chalk is easily eroded. All the reported sites were damaged both in antiquity and in the process of modern construction, and as a result all were excavated as part of rescue operations. The finds most likely represent only those items not affected by plunder; most metal artifacts presumably had been removed prior to the salvage efforts. Here we have chosen to focus on one illustrative example—the Giv'at ha-Oranim complex—followed by a brief account of two other examples at et-Taiyiba and Ben Shemen.

GIV'AT HA'ORANIM

Giv'at Ha'oranim lies 15 kilometers northeast of Ben Gurion International Airport and 3 kilometers east of the modern town of Shoham (Scheftelowitz and Oren 2004a). Earlier survey in the area identified Byzantine quarries, basins, a wine press, and agricultural terraces. The site extends over approximately 8,250 square meters. Salvage excavations were conducted in 1996 and 1997 after severe damage to the site by roadwork revealed eight multichambered cave complexes. The complexes were excavated into the bedrock and were sometimes interconnected by narrow horizontal shafts. At least fifteen installations—basins and cup marks—were carved into the outer nari bedrock. Similar installations, probably for food and oil production, are known from a variety of Chalcolithic sites, including the nearby site of Nevellat (van den Brink et al. 2001).

Due to the meager and sporadic nature of the human remains, five of the eight cave complexes are regarded by the excavators as habitations. The rest are considered storage or industrial facilities (Scheftelowitz and Oren 2004a). Cave complex 1780 included seven chambers. The largest chamber (ca. 3.5 meters in diameter, 1.6 meters in height) contained a depression in the leveled floor, near which was found a cache of six maceheads (three of copper and three of stone), a copper adze, a copper axe, and a unique spatula-shaped copper item. The excavators note that the frequency of fenestrated ceramic vessels and basins was exceptional—higher than the "repertoire common to the habitable caves" (Scheftelowitz and Oren 2004a, 10). These vessels, taken together with the cache of copper objects, the maceheads, and the absence of typical domestic features (e.g., hearths, grinding stones, and flint debris) seem to suggest something more in the way of ceremonial activity.

Cave 1595 (12–14 meters in diameter) had pits in the floor containing caches of open form and fenestrated basalt bowls, a copper axe, a copper standard, and two hematite maceheads. The copper standard is decorated with ibex and parallels one from Nahal Mishmar (see above). Another pit held a vessel cache of five bowls. An access shaft included a single human phalange (Scheftelowitz and Oren 2004a, 15). Another chamber in Cave 1595, reached through a 3-meter-deep, stepped shaft included the remains of a 40-year-old female and a 2–4-year-old child, surrounded by sixteen large storage jars and smaller vessels. The fill of the shaft also included a pedestaled basalt bowl. Once again, this evidence, along with the complete absence of hearths, grinding slabs, or domestic utensils, argues against a typical domestic habitation area.

Cave 1597 included eight small loci connected by apertures. It is also considered a habitation area by the excavators, based on the pottery, flint-tool assemblage, and two hematite maceheads (Scheftelowitz and Oren 2004a, 17). Two flexed burials were found in one of its bell-shaped chambers (L1309)—an adult (25–35-years-old, no sex provided) and a 12–15-year-old boy. Associated with these burials were two fenestrated basalt vessels (Scheftelowitz and Oren 2004a, figures 2.25, 2.56), one of which is perhaps the most impressive Chalcolithic basalt vessel known (see figure 6.6A). This unique item, nearly half a meter high, has a square receptacle with two small loop "handles" at each of its four corners. The interconnected stems are similar to forms recognized recently in the burial caves of Shoham, Nahal Qanah, and Peqi'in (van den Brink, Rowan, and Braun 1999). Four other basalt bowls, a copper standard fragment, and a fragment of mother-of-pearl were also found near the burial. An additional burial (L1310) produced an infant's ulna.

Caves 1185 and 1186 are two cave complexes considered uninhabitable by the excavators. The latter included a main chamber and subsidiary chamber, with a series of pits as well as stairs leading down to another oval inner room 1 meter below the central room. Cave 1185 was the longest at the site, extending 25 meters (east–west) and ranging in width from 6 meters to as little as 0.7 meters. Four areas were defined: an entrance hall, anteroom, corridor, and inner hall. The few ossuary fragments from the site were found in this area, as were flat stones that may have been paving or stelae, and a copper macehead. At the west end of the tapering corridor human remains were encountered. A large basalt bowl was found set into the cave floor (Scheftelowitz and Oren 2004a, figure 2.30). Few sherds ($n = 193$) were found in this cave complex; more than half were concentrated at the entrance, probably an indication of later disturbance, perhaps plunder.

The Giv'at Ha'oranim cave complexes contain far more metal artifacts and basalt vessels than other cave burial sites. Twenty-five copper artifacts were recovered, all but one dated to the Chalcolithic. Quantitatively, this metal collection is second only to the Nahal Mishmar assemblage, and, like Nahal Mishmar, it includes maceheads and standards, chisels, awls, and axes. The basalt-vessel assemblage is also remarkable for its quantity, variety, and elaboration. Seventy-four fenestrated basalt bowls are noted (Scheftelowitz and Oren 2004a, 61), perhaps the largest and best-crafted collection from a Chalcolithic site. A perforated ivory fragment (Scheftelowitz and Oren 2004b, figure 6.1) has parallels from mortuary contexts at Nahal Mishmar (see figure 6.6D), Nahal Qanah, and Shiqmim.

Preservation of the human remains is poor, and only a few ossuary fragments are reported, but a mortuary interpretation must be entertained for much of the Giv'at ha-Oranim assemblage. The minimum number of individuals was fifteen, but once skeletal remains were exposed, bone-eating carnivores (hyenas and porcupines in particular) and the natural elements would have combined to eliminate much of these remains. The excavators suggest that the burials were primary, probably based on (1) the two partially articulated, flexed skeletons and (2) the lack of ossuaries. But several ossuary fragments were found, and vessels other than ossuaries may have served as burial containers, as they often did at other sites (e.g., Ben Shemen, Shoham, and the recent cemetery at Palmahim). The Giv'at ha-Oranim assemblage is similar to the finds from the subterranean chambers of the northern Negev sites—Shiqmim, Horvat Beter, Horvat Hor, and Bir Safadi—as well as those from the Nahal Mishmar cave, which in our estimation were used for at least primary inhumation (see below).

Taiyiba

Quarried into Eocene chalk, Taiyiba was an irregular oval cave (4.5 meters by 6.0 meters, up to 1.5 meters high), with a pillar left on the southern side of the cave (Yannai and Porath 2006). The margins of the cave may have been left elevated as benches, and a number of the ossuaries were placed on flat stone slabs. Modern construction damaged the cave and it was heavily looted prior to salvage excavations. As a result, few human remains were recovered and the recovered artifacts were limited to ossuary and pottery fragments. The ossuaries from Taiyiba were more carefully and intricately decorated than those recovered from most other caves, although the style and motifs are essentially the same. The more extensive plastic modeling of anthropomorphic features, known from the site of Peqi'in, is not in evidence at Taiyiba.

Ben Shemen

The six caves at Ben Shemen were quarried in Senonian chalk, with nari forming the roof (Perrot 1967; Perrot and Ladiray 1980). These, too, were collapsed and then severely damaged by road construction. Ceramic vessels and ossuaries of pottery or stone make up almost the entire inventory of artifacts. Moreover, there is a great deal of Early Bronze Age (i.e., later) pottery among the finds and the Early Bronze Age people appear to have continued to bury their dead here. Overall, the picture is, once again, one of a disturbed (probably robbed) context.

Among the remarkable characteristics were the stelae (vertical erected stones; Perrot and Ladiray 1980, figures 117, 134:3). Perrot estimated that a minimum of sixty

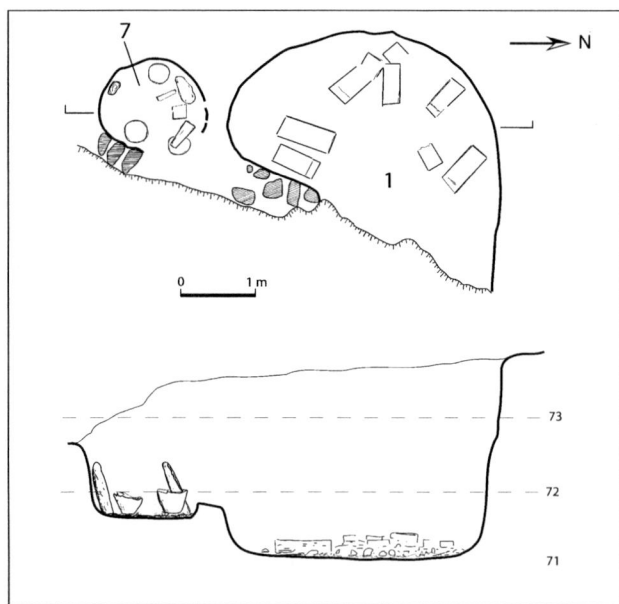

FIGURE 6.7 Giv'atayim Caves 1 and 7, (top) plan and (bottom) section. (After Sussman and Ben-Arieh 1966, figure 3.)

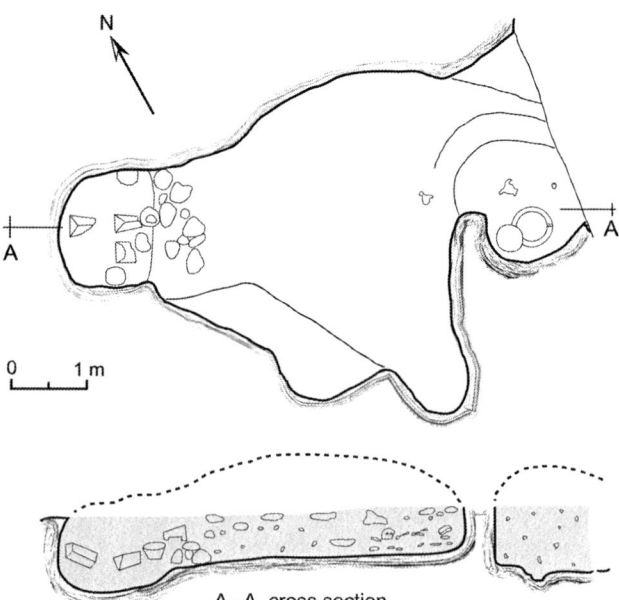

FIGURE 6.8 Palmahim Cave, (top) plan and (bottom) section. (After Gophna and Lifshitz 1980, figure 2.)

individuals were recovered in excavation and a figure of double this was more likely. No articulated skeletons were discerned; most of the intact osteological material was clearly the result of secondary placement in ossuaries or in sorted and arranged piles on the floors (Perrot and Ladiray 1980).

CAVES CARVED IN CALCAREOUS SANDSTONE (KURKAR) RIDGES

The only available rock near the coastline of the southern Levant is calcareous aeolian sandstone, or *kurkar*, which forms ridges that are essentially lithified sand dunes. Good examples of cave tombs carved out of this rock are at Bene Brak (Ory 1946), Giv'atayim (Kaplan 1993b, 520; see figure 6.7), Haderah (Sukenik 1937), Ma'abarot (Porath 2006), Palmahim (figure 6.8), Tel Aviv, and Tel Ifshar. The northernmost group is from Horbat Castra, just south of Haifa (van den Brink 2000a), and the farthest south is Palmahim (van den Brink 2005a). Kurkar caves often come in groups—for example, Palmahim ($n = 11$), Bene Berak ($n = 9$), Giv'atayim ($n = 13?$; Kaplan 1963, 1993b, 520), and Tel Aviv ($n = 2?$; Kaplan and Ritter-Kaplan 1993). They are usually carved into hillslopes (rather than via a shaft from above), working to the left and the right in order to leave a central pillar (e.g., at Ma'abarot, Giv'atayim, Tel Aviv, and Palmahim Tombs 2 and 9). Similar constructions are also known from the chalk caves described above (van den Brink 2005a, 175).

Kurkar tombs are not standardized in size or shape, varying from rectilinear to ovoid, though never very symmetrical nor well smoothed. In some cases chambers were carved branching off from each other, such as those at Azor and Giv'atayim (figure 6.7), similar to some of the caves at Shoham and Giv'at ha-Oranim as well as the subterranean complexes uncovered at the Beersheba Valley sites (discussed further below).

In some cases, interior floor surfaces are apparently leveled by quarrying debris. Similar to karstic and chalk-carved caves, shelves and platforms were sometimes constructed and objects placed on them—particularly ossuaries and other grave goods. Such was the case at Giv'atayim (Sussman and Ben-Arieh 1966, pl. IX.1). In Tomb A at Bene Berak, the floor was bordered by a bench that held an ossuary, placed with its opening facing the center of the tomb. Benches or no benches, ossuaries were typically placed along the walls of caves. Where caves are sufficiently intact, it seems that the ossuaries were often placed on kurkar or limestone slabs, such as at Giv'atayim (Sussman and Ben-Arieh 1966, pl. IX.1). In similar fashion, seven ossuaries were placed on a wide stone bench in front of three shallow niches at Azor (Perrot 1993b, 125). Niches too, are not uncommon in caves (and see the subterranean structure at Kissufim, below). The ossuaries at Giv'at Ha-Radar (Hadera) were placed on stone slabs in the corners of the caves, but the ceramics were placed in the center of the cave (Kaplan 1993a, 187). Associated mortuary goods were apparently placed near the ossuaries, and never inside. An interesting exception is the figurine from Quleh, which was found inside of an ossuary (Milevski 2002, 134, figures 3, 7).

STELAE IN CAVE TOMBS

Stelae are a widespread phenomenon. They have been documented, for example, at Azor, Ben Shemen, Bene Berak, Giv'atayim, Quleh, and Shoham. One kurkar example is known from Azor (Perrot and Ladiray 1980, 77.5), but stelae are generally elongated and rectangular or oval slabs manufactured of limestone or chalk, varying from heavily flaked and modified examples to natural cobbles with minimal flaking or modification. Larger examples, such as two discovered from Cave 4 at Shoham (Rowan 2005, 116–117, figures 9.19–20) are over a meter long (1.25 meters and 1.5 meters). At Giv'atayim four stelae were found in Cave 7, two in situ flanking an ossuary (see figure 6.7), one in the middle of the cave, and one on the floor (Sussman and Ben-Arieh 1966, 4*). One of the Giv'atayim stelae was painted red.

Prior to their discovery at Shoham, stelae were unknown in karstic cave systems. Parallels are found at noncave sites as well, both in mortuary contexts such as Kissufim and Shiqmim (Alon and Levy 1989, 183, and see below) as well as ostensibly nonmortuary sites such as Gilat (Levy et al. 2006, pl. 5.64). The strong correlation between stelae and mortuary contexts suggests to us that they have a mortuary function at these sites as well, albeit a less apparent one (Rowan and Ilan, n.d.).

SUBTERRANEAN FEATURES EXCAVATED IN LOESS SOILS

The Kissufim Charnel House

Although not a cave, Kissufim is a carefully constructed subterranean chamber, with features similar to some caves (Goren and Fabian 2002). Built inside of a large semisubterranean, rectangular pit, the primary feature was a rectangular mudbrick chamber with walls preserved up to 1 meter in height (Goren and Fabian 2002, plans 2.2–2.5, figure 2.5). Measuring 4 meters by 2.5 meters, the chamber resembles typical broadroom structures of Chalcolithic sites (ibid., 7). The lack of a doorway suggests that access was from above, and the excavators speculate that wooden logs anchored by large kurkar slabs may have covered the structure. Benches were constructed along the interior walls for burial goods, reminiscent of benches discovered in the cave tombs of the coastal plain (see above). Shallow pits in the earthen floor contained ossuaries, urns, burial tubs, kraters, and other smaller vessels; two niches were found in the walls (Goren and Fabian 2002, figures 2.5, 2.6). Various vessels such as bottles, kraters, jars, and many V-shaped bowls with traces of burning or organic matter were scattered across the floor (Goren 2002).

Burials placed in pits outside of the mortuary chamber were found with few finds. In one pit (L510) eleven individuals were found; several stone tubs apparently came from nearby. Another stone tub containing six individuals was found in situ at the bottom of this stone-lined pit, along with V-shaped bowls, a miniature churn, and other vessels. Less than 1 meter to the south, at least six modified chalk slabs and pebbles were erected in two groups of stelae with additional ceramic vessels placed among them. According to the excavators, funerary offerings differ according to their location inside or outside of the main chamber. For instance, various ceramic containers served as ossuaries (boxes, jars, tubs) within the funerary chamber, but stone tubs were related to the collective burial outside the chamber (Goren and Fabian 2002, 83). A number of shell pendants were probably associated originally with the exterior collective burials, while the unique and rare ceramic forms were primarily in the funerary chamber.

The pottery assemblage included both typical Chalcolithic forms and other, more unusual forms, some typically associated with mortuary and ritual deposits. These included goblets (Goren 2002, figure 4.1:9–15); pedestaled forms (ibid., figure 4.2:1, 3, 6), including one with a basket handle (ibid., figure 4.2:2, 4–5); and a high-necked bottle, known only from a vessel cache at Shiqmim (see Levy and Alon 1987, pl. 11.a, b; figure 12.15:3) and the burial cave at Palmahim (Gophna and Lifshitz 1980, figure 4:6). Two ceramic rings were found, similar to one from a burial at Shiqmim (Levy and Alon 1987, figure 13.16:10) and a few other sites (e.g., Pella, Hanbury-Tenison 1986, figure 26.8).

Burial containers consisted of oval ceramic tubs, box ossuaries, jar ossuaries, and a krater—quite a diverse array for such a small assemblage. Burial tubs included the remains of more than one individual. Although tubs are much less common, the inclusion of more than one individual in tubs is typical (e.g., Ben Shemen, Bene Berak, Giv'atayim Kissufim, Palmahim, and Qulah), but no correlation has been established between tubs and age, sex, or status. Jar ossuaries feature red-painted geometric and vegetal motifs and are more elaborately decorated than is usual in the coastal plain burial sites (figure 6.2A). Other finds include a bird figurine made from a lion's tooth (Poplin 2002, 53–4; figure 8.1), a palette (Fabian and Goren 2002, 48; see figure 6.6), and fifteen shell pendants (Bar-Yosef-Mayer 2002, 49–52; figures 7.1:1–11).

Most of the estimated fifty-four individuals were secondary burials and included both sexes and children

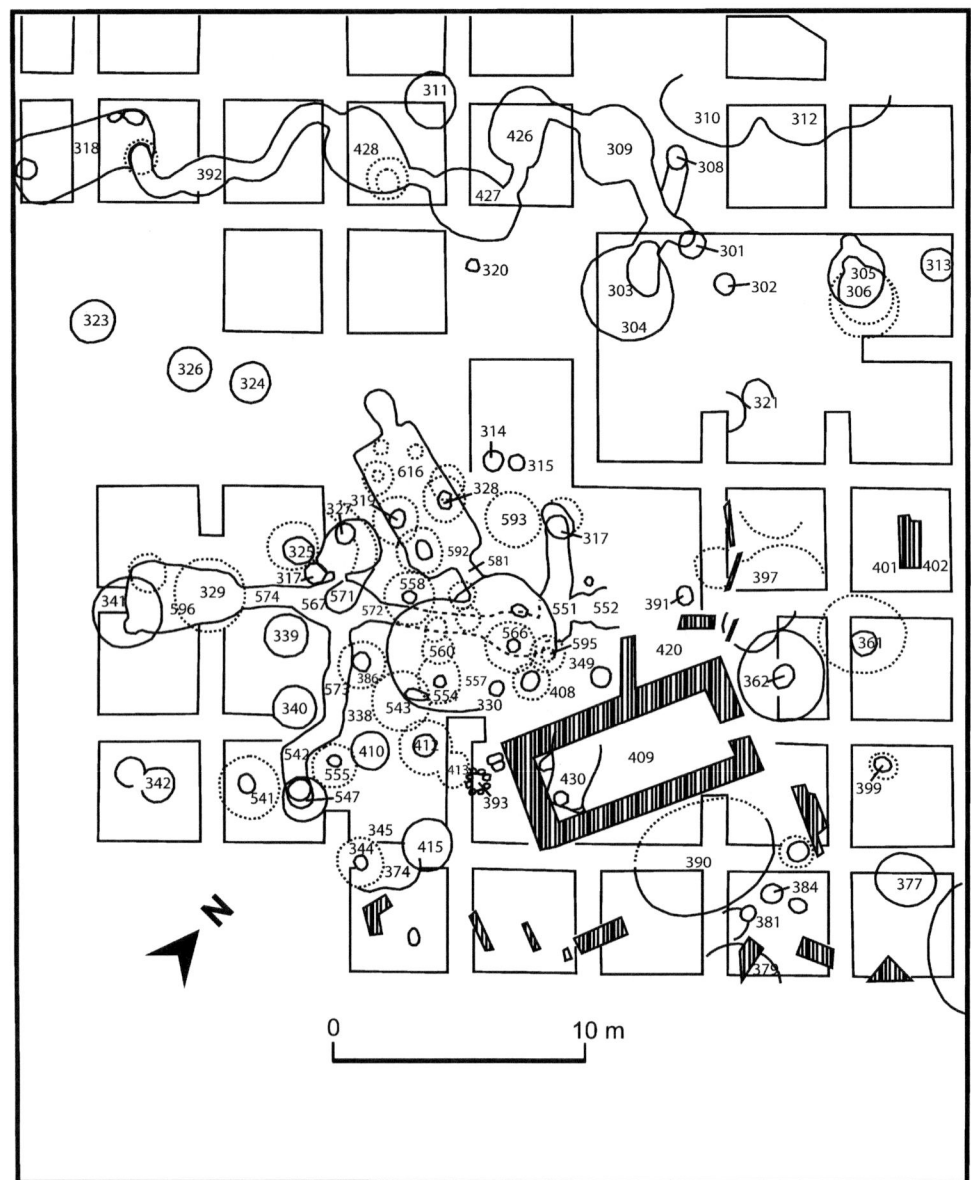

FIGURE 6.9 Bir es-Safadi site plan, southern section. Dark shading represents rectilinear surface architecture; curvilinear lines represent subterranean features. (Adapted from Commenge-Pellerin 1990, figure 2a.)

(Zagerson and Smith 2002, 57–65). Within the mudbrick burial chamber itself, however, only two children were included, in separate vessels. As noted above, low frequencies of infants and juveniles are typical of secondary burial contexts, and Kissufim resembles these most closely (Zagerson and Smith 2002, 61–2; table 10.2). Taphonomic analyses revealed carnivore modification of the skeletal remains prior to collection and reburial in mortuary vessels (Le Mort and Rabinovich 2002), an interesting contrast to the artificial defleshing documented at Ben Shemen (Le Mort and Rabinovich 1994).

THE NORTHERN NEGEV DESERT: SUBTERRANEAN LIVING SPACES OR MORTUARY COMPLEXES?

Settlements in the Negev exhibit both aboveground and subterranean features. Underground complexes were discovered through the pioneering work of Jean Perrot in the Beersheba Valley of the Negev desert of Israel (specifically the sites of Abu Matar and Bir es-Safadi; figure 6.9). They were initially thought to represent a "pioneer phase" of architecture fashioned by pastoral seminomads as an adaptation to a hot, arid environment (e.g., Levy 1986a; Perrot

1955, 1984). These subterranean chambers were dug into the loess, a compact, silty soil typical of the northern Negev desert region. Although not as sturdy as chalk and limestone deposits, the loess is sufficiently compact to support the weight of a roof. According to Perrot's reconstruction, the subsequent settlement phase consisted of semisubterranean, then aboveground habitation, with the subterranean spaces remaining in partial use.

With the discovery of similar subterranean chambers and tunnels at Shiqmim, Levy then suggested that they served as storage facilities and as defensive measures, similar to the underground hideouts constructed by rebels during the Bar Kokhba Revolt of the Roman period (Levy 1993, 66; Levy et al. 1991a). Gilead (1994) posits that the subterranean systems of the Beersheba Valley are contemporaneous with aboveground construction and functioned mainly as storage space. Levy (1993, 68) notes that the main occupation phase at Shiqmim includes both subterranean and aboveground features.

Perrot's excavations in the 1950s revealed no formal cemetery, only a few skeletons and isolated human bones in the fills and pits of the subterranean chambers (Perrot 1955, 23–26, 76–77, 173–174, pl. 23; 1984). At Shiqmim, on the other hand, a cemetery was found and excavated on the hills above the site (Levy and Alon 1979, 1982, 1985). This cemetery contained fragmentary but clear evidence for secondary burials. Down in the village below, several articulated skeletons and a number of stray bones were recovered, similar to the Beersheba Valley sites excavated by Perrot (e.g., Levy et al. 1991a). Some of this material was discovered in the subterranean chambers. The results of these excavations are currently being finalized for publication (Levy et al., forthcoming) and can be treated only briefly here.

The human remains discovered in the subterranean rooms tend to be fragmentary, often pushed to the sides of the chambers or in pits dug into the chamber floors (much like the cave tombs of the coast and piedmont). When skeletal remains are found in the pits, it is difficult to know whether disarticulated human remains are intentional deposits or the result of site-formation processes and part of the rubbish swept in from elsewhere. In some cases, however, initial burial in the subterranean context is clear, such as the human bones found near or at the floor level in Subterranean Room (SR) 1 in association with a basalt bowl and several ceramic bowls. Disarrayed human bones were also found on the surface of SR 8. In SR 16–17, a series of successive chambers included small bell-shaped pits in the floor, with the remains of at least five individuals scattered across the surface (L. 4201, 4202). Walls were sometimes constructed in the subterranean chambers to "fence off" a burial. In SR 15, a cranium and other bones were buried in a raised platform over 1 meter above the surface of the chamber floor, behind a separating wall.

SR 16 Locus 4084 was in a fill (Chamber 4141) that contained human skeletal material and a number of finds: three V-shaped bowls, some copper fragments, a stone macehead, a spindle-whorl fragment, a bead, and a mother-of-pearl pendant. Two burials were uncovered: an articulated infant, located against the northwest side of the chamber, and cranial fragments of a neonate found against the central west side of the chamber. A possible mudbrick lining was discerned associated with a copper fragment (Levy et al., forthcoming).

This evidence, and that of other sites in the northern Negev not discussed here, argues for a mortuary function for at least some of the subterranean features found in the northern Negev loess environment (cf. Horvat Hor in particular: Smith and Sabari 1995). This mortuary function may have involved the initial primary inhumation prior to secondary reburial in extramural cemeteries. Remains reburied in the cemetery show no restriction in age or sex categories in comparison to village burials, although no infant remains were recovered from the cemetery complex, where the only grave offerings were found (Levy et al. 1991a, 410).

CHALCOLITHIC CAVES: CONCLUDING REMARKS

At first glance, the various manifestations of subterranean space in the Chalcolithic period of the southern Levant appear to represent different functions and different cultural preferences. While many caves are easily recognized as burial chambers and the locus of mortuary rituals, other caves and spaces are subject to widely divergent interpretations. At the risk of seeming reductionist, we propose that most of these subterranean spaces are funerary in nature. There is a clear sense of pattern and redundancy in the spatial organization, componential composition, and iconographic representation.

The practice of interring the dead in caves is an old one. But the number of burials encountered in caves is quite small. This discrepancy is particularly conspicuous in the Neolithic period, when burials are most often found in settlements, though never in numbers that would correspond to settlement size and density. The Neolithic, however, appears to be the first period, in the Levant at least, in which caves become the locus of intense ritual behavior with a mortuary emphasis. The Nahal Qanah and Peqi'in caves, containing some of the most evocative Chalcolithic burial assemblages, also contain Late Neolithic material that appears, to the present writers, to be funerary in nature as well. In our estimation, there are probably many more caves, karstic ones especially, containing Late Neolithic and Early Chalcolithic mortuary assemblages.

The Neolithic cemetery at Eilat (Avner 1989) presages the establishment of separate cemeteries. It is the only one of its kind for the Neolithic, but by the succeeding Chalcolithic period people were constructing, or carving, cemeteries outside their settlements in a systematic way. The first tombs—artificial caves—were hewn during this time. One might hypothesize that the first foray into artificial-cavity creation began with the modification of existing karstic chambers, especially inactive ones, such as Shoham, Giv'at ha-Oranim, and Quleh. The next step was the hewing of completely new cavities in either the calcareous sandstone of the coastal plain, in the nari-covered chalk in the lower piedmont (e.g., at Taiyibeh and Ben Shemen), or in the loess of the northern Negev (e.g., Shiqmim and Bir es-Safadi, see figure 6.9). From this point on, the carved cave-tomb was normative for many periods (Early Bronze Age I, Intermediate Bronze Age, Middle and Late Bronze Ages, Iron Age II), at least for part of the population (Early Bronze Age II and Iron Age I burials are rare in general). Of course, certain regions (the Golan Heights, the Negev and Sinai Deserts) show little in the way of cave tombs, simply because karstic formations are less accessible or absent. In these regions Chalcolithic (and later) people buried their dead in aboveground tombs—tumuli, dolmens, and *nawamis* (e.g., Ilan 2002).

One of the most striking burial practices of the fifth and fourth millennia is that of secondary ossuary interment. While ossuaries are sometimes found in aboveground contexts, the vast majority are known from the central coastal plain and the piedmont of Israel/Palestine. The easternmost (i.e., furthest inland) occurrences of ossuaries come from the tombs at Shechem in the Palestinian Autonomous Area (Clamer 1981) and the village of Abu Hamid on the Jordanian side of the Jordan River (Lovell, personal communication). The northernmost ossuary group is that of Peqi'in.

Funerary assemblages found in association with subterranean secondary burials are fairly standardized. Associated ceramics were generally open-form ceramic vessels— V-shaped bowls (larger examples sometimes containing human bones), basins, holemouth and necked jars, and pedestaled, fenestrated stands. Much less frequently, cornets are also found in association with burials. Groundstone vessels are also part of the mortuary kit—finely crafted basalt bowls are frequent and limestone vessels less so (Rowan 2005). These vessels and other burial goods were generally placed toward the center of the chamber and not inside the ossuaries themselves.

In the region where most of the caves and burials are found (mainly in the central coast and piedmont), clear-cut examples of primary interment in caves are few. But some cases of primary burial in caves are known, especially in the Judean Desert, where, conversely, almost no ossuaries are found. An interment was found in what is now known as the "Cave of the Warrior," just to the west of Jericho in Wadi el-Makkukh (Schick 1998) and dated from the mid-fifth millennium to the early fourth millennium (Jull et al. 1998, 110–11). Wrapped in a well-preserved linen shroud (7 meters by 2 meters) and resting on a woven mat, this articulated, flexed adult male was accompanied by well-preserved organic remains, including a reed basket, a wooden bowl (of oak), a broken wooden bow, wooden reed fragments (arrows?), and leather sandals. A few skeletal remains of a child were also found (Nagar 1998, 68). Many of the finds were treated with ground-ochre powder, including the exceptionally large prismatic blade just under the skeleton (Oshri and Schick 1998). This primary burial, along with those from the Nahal Mishmar cave and Horbat Govit (van den Brink 2000b), and a few examples from the loess chambers of the northern Negev, are the rare instances of primary interments in caves. In the Levantine Chalcolithic, primary burials without secondary interment may have been normative only in the Judean Desert, but it is quite possible that primary interment in caves was normative in many other parts of the country too.

Drawing broader demographic conclusions is difficult because so few paleoanthropological reports are available, but recent reports provide intriguing glimpses. For example, the population from the Ma'abarot cave, estimated at approximately fifty-eight individuals, is postulated to be at least 90 percent, and possibly as much as 100 percent, male (Agelarakis et al. 1998, 439). This stands in striking contrast to other physical anthropological reports of mortuary remains from Chalcolithic burial grounds. Most burial grounds with secondary remains include low frequencies of infants and very young children (Smith 1989; Zagerson and Smith 2002). This is particularly evident in the recent preliminary analysis of an estimated 453 individuals from Peqi'in cave where no individuals under the age of 3 to 4 years old were included. Eighty percent of the sample was aged 15 or older (Nagar and Eshed 2001, table 1). Kissufim showed similar patterns, with infants and children appearing mainly outside the burial structure. On the other hand, cave assemblages in the northern Negev and at Giv'at ha-Oranim, for example, do contain some infants and children.

The modification of caves and the creation of artificial caves, some with interior terraces or benches, the use of ornamented ossuaries, and the occasional inclusion of symbolically loaded objects such as maceheads, maces, ivory, and basalt vessels all represent the investment of energy and the consumption of valuable resources. Increased deposition of valuable resources suggests their increased accumulation by lineages, or individuals, the encouraging of participation in alliances, and exchange opportunities of increased scope. The rare inclusion of exotic goods suggests nonegalitarian forms of organization, yet this need not indicate categorically permanent forms of inherited power. The iconography of the Chalcolithic in general, and that of mortuary contexts in particular, indicate the actions of ritual specialists. Elsewhere, we have made the case for the coexistence of both shamanistic and priestly practitioners (Rowan and Ilan, 2007).

Why place the remains of former community members deep in a cave? Why go to the trouble of retrieving the remains later in order to manipulate them and reinter them in a specialized, symbol-laden container? As we have intimated above, there is much in Chalcolithic mortuary iconography that is sexual or reproductive in nature. This theme is well documented in the literature and we expand upon it elsewhere, especially in that we assign mortuary-related functions to objects and contexts not interpreted as such until now (Ilan and Rowan 2012: 105–106; Rowan and Ilan, n.d.). If we are to speculate, the cave—whether natural or artificial—was also conceived of as the womb, part of the mother, who is the earth itself. The dead will be reborn and burial in the tomb, a multiphased process that was perhaps conceived as a sort of midwifery. In this framework, we also consider ossuaries to be the vehicle or container of metamorphosis. A certain compactness and separation of bones may have been required to expedite rebirth, at least in some circumstances. Secondary burial in containers represents one of the later phases in an extended rite of passage. In the Chalcolithic, then, the cave was the locus of contact with the chthonic forces of death that expedite rebirth. As such, the cave was a place of power, frightening yet crucial—the essential link that perpetuated the cycle of life, death, and life again.

ACKNOWLEDGMENTS

The authors offer their thanks to Holley Moyes for her invitation to join this volume. Tom Levy and Jaimie Lovell read earlier drafts and offered valuable insights. In particular, we thank Tom Levy for permission to include some data from Shiqmim prior to the appearance of the final publication. We also thank the institutions that supported Rowan while this manuscript was completed, in particular the Binational Fulbright Commission in Jordan for financial support and the American Center for Oriental Research in Amman, Jordan.

REFERENCES CITED

Agelarakis, Anagnostis P., Samuel Paley, Yosef Porath, and Jennifer Winik. 1998. "The Chalcolithic Burial Cave in Ma'avarot, Israel, and Its Paleoanthropological Implications." *International Journal of Osteoarchaeology* 8 (6): 431–43. http://dx.doi.org/10.1002/(SICI)1099-1212(199811/12)8:6<431::AID-OA439>3.0.CO;2-8.

Alcock, Susan. 1993. *Graecia Capta: The Landscapes of Roman Greece*. Cambridge: Cambridge University Press.

Alon, David, and Thomas E. Levy. 1989. "The Archeology of Cult and Chalcolithic Sanctuary at Gilat." *Journal of Mediterranean Archaeology* 2: 163–22.

Ashmore, Wendy, and A. Bernard Knapp, eds. 2000. *Archaeologies of Landscape*. Oxford: Blackwell.

Avner, Uzi. 1989. "Eilat-tumuli." *Hadashot Arkheologiyot* 94: 64–5.

Avner, Uzi, Israel Carmi, and Dror Segal. 1994. "Neolithic to Bronze Age Settlement of the Negev and Sinai in Light of Radiocarbon Dating: A View from the Southern Negev." In *Late Quaternary Chronology and Paleoclimates of the Eastern Mediterranean*, ed. O. Bar-Yosef and R. S. Kra, 265–300. Tucson: University of Arizona Press.

Bar-Adon, Pessah. 1980. *The Cave of the Treasure*. Jerusalem: Israel Exploration Society.

Bar-Yosef, Ofer, and David Alon. 1988. "Nahal Hemar Cave." *Atiqot* 18: 1–30.

Bar-Yosef, Ofer, and E. Ayalon. 2001. "Chalcolithic Ossuaries: What Do They Imitate and Why?" (Hebrew) *Kadmoniyot* 343: 34–43.

Bar-Yosef, Ofer, Anna Belfer, Avner Goren, and Patricia Smith. 1977. "The *Nawamis* near 'Ein Huderah (Eastern Sinai)." *Israel Exploration Journal* 27: 65–88.

Bar-Yosef, Ofer, Anna Belfer-Cohen, Avner Goren, Israel Hershkovitz, Ornit Ilan, Henk K. Mienis, and Benjamin Sass. 1986. "Nawamis and Habitation Sites near Gebel Gunna, Southern Sinai." *Israel Exploration Journal* 36: 121–67.

Bar-Yosef, Ofer, Bernard Vandermeersch, Baruch Arensburg, Anna Belfer-Cohen, Paul Goldberg, H. Laville, L. Meignen, Yoel Rak, John D. Speth, Eitan Tchernov, et al. 1992. "Excavations in Kebara Cave, Mt. Carmel." *Current Anthropology* 33 (5): 497–550. http://dx.doi.org/10.1086/204112.

Bar-Yosef Mayer, Daniella. 2002. "The Shell Pendants." In *Kissufim Road: A Chalcolithic Mortuary Site*, ed. Y. Goren and P. Fabian, 49–52. Israel Antiquities Authority Reports No. 16. Jerusalem: Israel Antiquities Authority.

Bar-Yosef Mayer, Daniella E., Naomi Porat, Zvi Gal, Dina Shalem, and Howard Smithline. 2004. "Steatite Beads at Peqi'in: Long Distance Trade and Pyro-Technology during the Chalcolithic of the Levant." *Journal of Archaeological Science* 31 (4): 493–502. http://dx.doi.org/10.1016/j.jas.2003.10.007.

Beck, Pirhiya. 1989. "Notes on the Style and Iconography of the Chalcolithic Hoard from Nahal Mishmar." In *Essays in Ancient Civilization presented to Helene J. Kantor*, ed. A. Leonard and B. B. Williams, 39–54. Chicago: The Oriental Institute.

Bradley, Richard. 1991. "Rock Art and the Perception of Landscape." *Cambridge Archaeological Journal* 1 (01): 77–101. http://dx.doi.org/10.1017/S0959774300000263.

Bradley, Richard. 2002. *An Archaeology of Natural Places*. London: Routledge.

Buikstra, Jane E., and Douglas K. Charles. 2000. "Centering the Ancestors: Cemeteries, Mounds, and Sacred Landscapes of the Ancient North American Midcontinent." In *Archaeologies of Landscape*, ed. W. Ashmore and A. B. Knapp, 201–28. Oxford: Blackwell.

Carmi, Isaac, and Dror Segal. 2005. "The Radiocarbon Dates." In *Shoham (North) Late Chalcolithic Burial Caves in the Lod Valley, Israel*, ed. E.C.M. van den Brink and R. Gophna, 163. IAA Reports No. 27. Jerusalem: Israel Antiquities Authority.

Clamer, Christa. 1977. "A Burial Cave near Nablus (Tel Balata)." *Israel Exploration Journal* 27: 48.

Clamer, Christa. 1981. "A Burial Cave of the Late Bronze Age near Shechem." (Hebrew) *Qadmoniot* 14: 30–4.

Clark, V. A. 1979. "Investigations in a Prehistoric Necropolis near Bab edh-Dhra'." *Annual of the Department of Antiquities of Jordan* 23: 57–78.

Commenge, Catherine. 2005. "The Late Chalcolithic Pottery." In *Shoham (North), Lod Valley, Israel: Excavations of Three Late Chalcolithic Burial Caves*, ed. E.C.M. van den Brink and R. Gophna, 52–97. Jerusalem: Israel Antiquities Authority Reports.

Commenge, Catherine. 2006. "Gilat's Ceramics: Cognitive Dimensions of Pottery Production." In *Archaeology, Anthropology and Cult: The Sanctuary at Gilat, Israel*, ed. Tom E. Levy, 394–506. London: Equinox.

Commenge-Pellerin, C. 1990. *La Potterie de Safadi (Beersheva) au IVe millenaire avant l'ere chretienne*. Paris: Association Paleorient.

Crumley, Carol L. 2000. "Sacred Landscapes: Constructed and Conceptualized." In *Archaeologies of Landscape*, ed. W. Ashmore and A. B. Knapp, 269–76. Oxford: Blackwell.

Derks, Ton. 1997. "The Transformation of Landscape and Religious Representation in Roman Gaul." *Archaeological Dialogues* 4 (02): 126–47. http://dx.doi.org/10.1017/S1380203800000982.

Elliot, Carolyn. 1977. "The Religious Beliefs of the Ghassulians, ca. 4000–3100 BC." *Palestine Exploration Quarterly* 109: 3–25.

Epstein, Clare. 1978. "Aspects of Symbolism in Chalcolithic Palestine." In *Archaeology in the Levant: Essays in Honour of Kathleen Kenyon*, ed. R. Moorey and P. Parr, 23–35. Warminster, England: Aris & Phillips.

Eshel, Hanan, and Boaz Zissu. 1995. "Ketef Jericho, 1993." *Israel Exploration Journal* 45 (4): 292–8.

Fabian, Peter, and Yuval Goren. 2002. "The Stone Artifacts." In *Kissufim Road: A Chalcolithic Mortuary Site*, ed. Y. Goren and P. Fabian, 44–48. IAA Reports 16. Jerusalem: Israel Antiquities Authority.

Gal, Zvi, Howard Smithline, and Dina Shalem. 1997. "A Chalcolithic Burial Cave in Peqi'in, Upper Galilee." *Israel Exploration Journal* 47: 145–54.

Gal, Zvi, Howard Smithline, and Dina Shalem. 1999 "New Iconographic Aspects of Chalcolithic Art: Preliminary Observations on Finds from the Peqi'in Cave." *Atiqot* 37: 1–16.

Garfinkel, Yosef. 1994. "Ritual Burial of Cultic Objects: The Earliest Evidence." *Cambridge Archaeological Journal* 4 (02): 159–88. http://dx.doi.org/10.1017/S0959774300001062.

Garrod, Dorothy A.E., and Dorothea M. Bate. 1937. *The Stone Age of Mount Carmel*. Oxford: Clarendon Press.

Gates, Marie-Henrietta. 1992. "Nomadic Pastoralists and the Chalcolithic Hoard from Nahal Mishmar." *Levant* 24: 131–9.

Gilead, Isaac. 1988. "The Chalcolithic Period in the Levant." *Journal of World Prehistory* 2 (4): 397–443. http://dx.doi.org/10.1007/BF00976197.

Gilead, Isaac. 1994. "The History of the Chalcolithic Settlement in the Nahal Beer Sheva Area: The Radiocarbon Aspect." *Bulletin of the American Schools of Oriental Research. American Schools of Oriental Research* 296 (296): 1–13. http://dx.doi.org/10.2307/1357176.

Gilead, Isaac. 1995. *Grar: A Chalcolithic Site in the Northern Negev*. Ben Gurion, Beer Sheva: University of the Negev Press.

Gilead, Isaac. 1998. "The Foragers of the Upper Paleolithic Period." In *The Archaeology of Society in the Holy Land*, ed. T. E. Levy, 124–40. London: Leicester University Press.

Gilead, Isaac, and Yuval Goren. 1986. "Stations of the Chalcolithic Period in Nahal Sekher, Northern Negev." *Paléorient* 12 (1): 83–90. http://dx.doi.org/10.3406/paleo.1986.4402.

Gopher, A. 1996. "The Neolithic Assemblage." In *The Nahal Qanah Cave: Earliest Gold in the Southern Levant*, ed. A. Gopher, 53–82. Monograph Series of the Institute of Archaeology, No. 12. Tel Aviv: Tel Aviv University.

Gopher, Avi, and Erella Orrelle. 1995. "New Data on Burials from the Pottery Neolithic Period (Sixth-millennium BC) in Israel." In *The Archaeology of Death in the Ancient Near East*, ed. G. S. Campbell and A. Green, 24–48. Oxford: Oxbow.

Gopher, Avi, and Tvika Tsuk. 1996a. "Description of the Cave and Excavation Areas." In *The Nahal Qanah Cave: Earliest Gold in the Southern Levant*, ed. A. Gopher, 13–52. Monograph Series of the Institute of Archaeology, No. 12. Tel Aviv: Tel Aviv University.

Gopher, Avi, and Tvika Tsuk. 1996b. "The Chalcolithic Assemblages." In *The Nahal Qanah Cave: Earliest Gold in the Southern Levant*, ed. A. Gopher, 91–138. Monograph Series of the Institute of Archaeology, No. 12. Tel Aviv: Tel Aviv University.

Gopher, Avi, and Tvika Tsuk. 1996c. "Conclusion." In *The Nahal Qanah Cave: Earliest Gold in the Southern Levant*, ed. A. Gopher, 209–43. Monograph Series of the Institute of Archaeology, No. 12. Tel Aviv: Tel Aviv University.

Gopher, Avi, Tsvika Tsuk, Sariel Shalev, and Ram Gophna. 1990. "Earliest Gold Artifacts in the Levant." *Current Anthropology* 31 (4): 436–43. http://dx.doi.org/10.1086/203868.

Gophna, Ram, and Nilli Lifshitz. 1980. A Chalcolithic Burial Cave at Palmahim. *Atiqot* 14(ES): 1–8.

Goren, Yuval. 2002. "The Pottery Assemblage." In *Kissufim Road: A Chalcolithic Mortuary Site*, ed. Y. Goren and P. Fabian, 21–41. IAA Reports No. 16. Jerusalem: Israel Antiquities Authority.

Goren, Yuval, and Peter Fabian. 2002. *Kissufim Road: A Chalcolithic Mortuary Site*. IAA Reports No. 16. Jerusalem: Israel Antiquities Authority.

Hanbury-Tenison, Jack W. 1986. *The Late Chalcolithic to Early Bronze I Transition in Palestine and Transjordan*. BAR International Series 311. Oxford: British Archaeological Reports.

Haas, Nico and Nathan, H. 1973. "An Attempt at Social Interpretation of the Chalcolithic Burials in the Nahal Mishmar Caves." *Excavations and Studies*, ed. A. Aharoni, 144–53. Tel Aviv: Tel Aviv University. (Hebrew with English summary on pp. xvii–xviii.)

Hershkovitz, Israel, and Avi Gopher. 1996. "Human Skeletal Remains." In *The Nahal Qanah Cave: Earliest Gold in the Southern Levant, Monograph Series of the Institute of Archaeology*, ed. A. Gopher, 175–80. Tel Aviv: Tel Aviv University.

Ilan, David. 2002. "Mortuary Practices in Early Bronze Age

Canaan." *Near Eastern Archaeology* 65 (2): 92–104. http://dx.doi.org/10.2307/3210870.

Ilan, David and Yorke M. Rowan. 2012. "Deconstructing and Recomposing the Narrative of Spiritual Life in the Chalcolithic of the Southern Levant (4500–3600 B.C.E.)." In *Beyond Belief: The Archaeology of Religion and Ritual*, ed. Y. M. Rowan, 89–113. Archeological Papers of the American Anthropological Association, No. 21. Hoboken, NJ: Wiley.

Jull, A. J. Timothy, D. J. Donahue, Israel Carmi, and Dror Segal. 1998. "Radiocarbon Dating of Finds." In *The Cave of the Warrior: A Fourth Millennium Burial in the Judean Desert*, ed. T. Schick, 110–12. Israel Antiquities Authority Reports 5. Jerusalem: Israel Antiquities Authority.

Kaplan, Jacob. 1963. "Excavations at Benei Beraq, 1951." *Israel Exploration Journal* 13: 300–12.

Kaplan, Jacob. 1993a. "Bene Berak." *New Encyclopedia of Archaeological Excavations in the Holy Land* 1: 186–87.

Kaplan, Jacob. 1993b. "Giv'atayim." *New Encyclopedia of Archaeological Excavations in the Holy Land* 2: 520–21.

Kaplan, Jacob, and Haya Ritter-Kaplan. 1993. "Tel Aviv." *New Encyclopedia of Archaeological Excavations in the Holy Land* 4: 1451–57.

Kaufman, Daniel. 1999. *Archaeological Perspectives on the Origins of Modern Humans: View from the Levant*. London: Bergin and Garvey.

Kuijt, Ian, Jonathan Mabry, and Gaetano Palumbo. 1991. "Early Neolithic Use of Upland Areas of Wadi el-Yabis: Preliminary Evidence from the Excavations of 'Iraq ed-Dubb, Jordan." *Paléorient* 17 (1): 99–108. http://dx.doi.org/10.3406/paleo.1991.4543.

Le Mort, Françoise, and Rivka Rabinovich. 1994. "L'apport de l'étude taphonomique des restes humains à la connaissance des pratiques funéraires: Exemple du site chalcolithique de Ben-Shemen (Israel)." *Paléorient* 20 (1): 69–98. http://dx.doi.org/10.3406/paleo.1994.4603.

Le Mort, Françoise, and Rivka Rabinovich. 2002. "Taphonomy and Mortuary Practices." In *Kissufim Road: A Chalcolithic Mortuary Site*, ed. Y. Goren and P. Fabian, 66–81. Israel Antiquities Authority Reports No. 16. Jerusalem: Israel Antiquities Authority.

Levy, Thomas E. 1986a. "Archaeological Sources for the History of Palestine: The Chalcolithic Period." *Biblical Archaeologist* 49 (2):82–108. http://dx.doi.org/10.2307/3210005.

Levy, Thomas E. 1986b. "Social Archaeology and the Chalcolithic Period: Explaining Social Organizational Change during the 4th Millennium in Israel." *Michmanim* 2: 5–20.

Levy, Thomas E. 1993. "Production, Space and Social Change in Prehistoric Palestine." In *Spatial Boundaries and Social Dynamics*, ed. A. Holl and T. E. Levy, 63–81. Ann Arbor, MI: International Monographs in Prehistory.

Levy, Thomas E., ed. 1998. *The Archaeology of Society in the Holy Land*. London: Leicester University Press.

Levy, Thomas E., ed. 2006. *Archaeology, Anthropology and Cult: The Sanctuary at Gilat, Israel*. London: Equinox.

Levy, Thomas E., and David Alon. 1979. "A Preliminary Note on the Chalcolithic Cemeteries at Shiqmim, Northern Negev, Israel." *Mitekufat Haeven* 16: 109–17.

Levy, Thomas E., and David Alon. 1982. "The Chalcolithic Mortuary Site near Mezad Aluf, Northern Negev Desert: A Preliminary Study." *Bulletin of the American Schools of Oriental Research: American Schools of Oriental Research* 248: 37–59. http://dx.doi.org/10.2307/1356673.

Levy, Thomas E., and David Alon. 1985. "The Chalcolithic Mortuary Site near Mezad Aluf, Northern Negev Desert: Third Preliminary Report, 1982 Season." *Bulletin of the American Schools of Oriental Research*, Supplement no. 23: 121–35.

Levy, Thomas E., and David Alon. 1987. "Excavations in Shiqmim Cemetery 3: Final Report on the 1982 Excavations." In *Shiqmim I*, ed. T. E. Levy, 333–55. BAR International Series 356. Oxford: British Archaeological Reports.

Levy, Thomas E., and David Alon. 1992. "A Corpus of Ivories from Shiqmim." (Hebrew) *Eretz Israel* 23: 65–71.

Levy, Thomas E., David Alon, Caroline Grigson, Augustin Holl, Paul Goldberg, Yorke Rowan, and Patricia Smith. 1991a. "Subterranean Negev Settlement." *National Geographic Research and Exploration* 7: 394–413.

Levy, Thomas E., Caroline Grigson, Augustin Holl, Paul Goldberg, Yorke Rowan, and Patricia Smith. 1991b. "Protohistoric Investigations at the Shiqmim Chalcolithic Village and Cemetery: Interim Report on the 1987 Season." *Bulletin of the American Schools of Oriental Research: American Schools of Oriental Research* 27 (Supplement): 29–45.

Levy, Thomas E., David Alon, Paul Goldberg, Caroline Grigson, Patricia Smith, Jane Buikstra, Augustin Holl, Yorke M. Rowan, and Pamela Sabari. 1994. "Protohistoric Investigations at the Shiqmim Chalcolithic Village and Cemetery: Interim Report on the 1988 Season." *Annual of the American Schools of Oriental Research* 51: 87–106.

Levy, Thomas E., David Alon, Yorke M. Rowan, and Morag Kersel. 2006. "The Sanctuary Sequence: Excavations at Gilat: 1975–77, 1989, 1990–92." In *Archaeology, Anthropology and Cult: The Sanctuary at Gilat, Israel*, ed. T. E. Levy, 95–212. London: Equinox.

Levy, Thomas E., Yorke M. Rowan, James D. Anderson, and Morag M. Kersel. Forthcoming. "The Settlement Center: Phase II Excavations in the Shiqmim Village—Stratigraphy, Architecture, and Social Change." In *Desert Chiefdom: Dimensions of Subterranean Settlement and Society in the Israel's Negev Desert (ca. 4500–3600 BC) Based on New Data from Shiqmim*, ed. T. E. Levy, Y. M. Rowan, and M. Burton. London: Equinox.

Levy, Thomas E., Yorke M. Rowan, and Margie Burton, eds. Forthcoming. *Desert Chiefdom: Dimensions of Subterranean Settlement and Society in the Israel's Negev Desert (ca. 4500–3600 BC)*. London: Equinox.

Lovell, Jaimie L. 2009. "Chalcolithic Caves Discovered East of the River Jordan." (Project Gallery) *Antiquity* 83. http://antiquity.ac.uk/projgall/lovell322/.

Mallon, Alexis, Robert Koeppel, and Rene Neuville. 1934. *Teleilat Ghassul I, 1929–32*. Rome: Pontifical Biblical Institute.

McCown, Theodore D. 1937. "Mugharet es-Skhul: Description and Excavations." In *The Stone Age of Mount Carmel*, ed. D.A.E. Garrod and D.M.A. Bate, 91–107. Oxford: Clarendon Press.

Merhav, Rivka. 1993. "Sceptres of the Divine from the Cave of the Treasure at Nahal Mishmar." *Studies in the Archaeology and History of Ancient Israel in Honour of Moshe Dothan*, ed. M. Heltzer, A. Segal, and D. Kaufman, 21–42. Haifa: Haifa University Press. (Hebrew).

Milevski, Ianir. 2002. "A New Fertility Figurine and New Animal Motifs from the Chalcolithic in the Southern Levant: Finds from Cave K-1 at Quleh, Israel." *Paleorient* 28 (2): 133–41. http://dx.doi.org/10.3406/paleo.2002.4751.

Moorey, Peter Roger Stuart. 1988. "The Chalcolithic Hoard from Nahal Mishmar, Israel, in Context." *World Archaeology* 20 (2): 171–89. http://dx.doi.org/10.1080/00438243.1988.9980066.

Nagar, Y. 1998. The human skeleton. In "The cave of the Warrior" (T. Schick, ed.). IAA Reports 5. pp. 65-72.

Nagar, Yossi, and Vered Eshed. 2001. "Where Are the Children? Age-Dependent Burial Practices in Peqi'in." *Israel Exploration Journal* 51 (1): 27–35.

Nativ, Assaf. 2008. "A Note on Chalcolithic Ossuary Jars: A Metaphor for Metamorphosis." *Tel Aviv* 35: 209–14.

Noy, Tamar. 1998. "The Flint Artifacts." In *The Chalcolithic Culture of the Golan*, ed. C. Epstein, 269–99. Israel Antiquities Authority Report No. 4. Jerusalem: Israel Antiquities Authority.

Orni, Ephraim, and Elisha Ephrat. 1973. *Geography of Israel*. Rev., 3rd ed. Jerusalem: Israel Program for Scientific Translations.

Ory, J. 1946. "A Chalcolithic Necropolis at Bnei Beraq." *Quarterly of the Department of Antiquities of Palestine* 12: 43–57.

Oshri, Aviram, and Tamar Schick. 1998. "The Lithics." In *The Cave of the Warrior: A Fourth Millennium Burial in the Judean Desert*, ed. T. Schick, 59–62. Jerusalem: Israel Antiquities Authority.

Perrot, Jean. 1955. "The Excavations at Tell Abu Matar, Near Beersheba." *Israel Exploration Journal* 5: 17–41, 73–84, 167–89.

Perrot, Jean. 1967. "Les ossuaries de Ben Shemen." *Eretz Israel* 8: 46*–49*.

Perrot, Jean. 1984. "Structures d'habitat mode de vie et environnement: Les villages souterrains des pasteurs de Beersheva, dans le sud d'Israel, au IVe millenaire avant L'ere chretienne." *Paléorient* 10 (1): 75–96. http://dx.doi.org/10.3406/paleo.1984.4351.

Perrot, Jean. 1993a. "Umm Qatafa and Umm Qala'a: Two Ghassulian Caves in the Judean Desert." *Eretz Israel* 23: 100–11.

Perrot, Jean. 1993b. "Azor." In *New Encyclopedia of Archaeological Excavations of the Holy Land*. Jerusalem: Israel Exploration Society and Carta.

Perrot, Jean, and Daniel Ladiray. 1980. *Tombes A Ossuaires de la Region Cotiere Palestinienne, Au IVe Millenaire Avant L'ere Chretienne*. Paris: Association Paléorient.

Poplin, François. 2002. "The Bird Figurine." In *Kissufim Road: A Chalcolithic Mortuary Site*, ed. Y. Goren and P. Fabian, 53–54. Israel Antiquities Authority Reports No. 14. Jerusalem: Israel Antiquities Society.

Porath, Yosef. 2006. "Chalcolithic Burial Sites at Ma'abarot and Tel Ifshar." *Atiqot* 53: 45–63.

Rak, Yoel, W. H. Kimbel, and Erella Hovers. 1994. "A Neandertal Infant from Amud Cave, Israel." *Journal of Human Evolution* 26 (4): 313–24. http://dx.doi.org/10.1006/jhev.1994.1019.

Rosen, Steven A. 1997. *Lithics after the Stone Age*. Walnut Creek, CA: AltaMira.

Rowan, Yorke M. 1998. "Ancient Distribution and Deposition of Prestige Objects: Basalt Vessels during Late Prehistory in the Southern Levant." PhD dissertation, University of Texas, Austin.

Rowan, Yorke M. 2005. "The Groundstone Assemblages." In *Shoham (North), Lod Valley, Israel: Excavations of Three Late Chalcolithic Burial Caves*, ed. E.C.M. van den Brink and R. Gophna, 113–39. IAA Reports 27. Jerusalem: Israel Antiquities Authority.

Rowan, Yorke M., and Jonathan Golden. 2009. "The Chalcolithic Period of the Southern Levant: A Synthetic Review." *Journal of World Prehistory* 22 (1): 1–92. http://dx.doi.org/10.1007/s10963-009-9016-4.

Rowan, Yorke M., and David Ilan. 2007. "The Meaning of Ritual Diversity in the Chalcolithic of the Southern Levant." In *Cult in Context, Conference Proceedings*, ed. D. Barrowclough, C. Malone, and S. Stoddart, 249–56. Oxford: Oxbow.

Rowan, Yorke M., and David Ilan. N.d. "Cult, Cache and the Subterranean: Death's Dominion in the Chalcolithic of the Southern Levant." In preparation.

Scheftelowitz, Na'ama. 2004. "Stone Artefacts." In *Giv'at Ha-Oranim: A Chalcolithic Site*, ed. N. Scheftelowitz and R. Oren, 59–67. Tel Aviv: Tel Aviv University.

Scheftelowitz, Na'ama, and Ronit Oren, eds. 2004a. *Giv'at Ha-Oranim: A Chalcolithic Site*. Tel Aviv: Tel Aviv University.

Scheftelowitz, Na'ama, and Ronit Oren. 2004b. "Miscellaneous Small Finds." In *Giv'at Ha-Oranim: A Chalcolithic Site*, ed. N. Scheftelowitz and R. Oren, 84–86. Tel Aviv: Tel Aviv University.

Schick, Tamar. 1998. *The Cave of the Warrior: A Fourth Millennium Burial in the Judean Desert*. Jerusalem: Israel Antiquities Authority.

Segal, Dror, Israel Carmi, Zvi Gal, Howard Smithline, and Dina Shalem. 1998. "Dating a Chalcolithic Burial Cave in Peqi'in, Upper Galilee, Israel." *Radiocarbon* 40 (2): 707–12.

Smith, Patricia. 1989. "Skeletal Biology and Paleopathology of Early Bronze Age Populations in the Levant." In *L'urbanisation de la Palestine a l'age du Bronze Ancien*, ed. P. de Miroschedji, 297–316. BAR International Series 527(ii). Oxford: British Archaeological Reports.

Smith, Patricia, and Pamela Sabari. 1995. "The Chalcolithic Skeletal Remains from Horvat Hor." *Israel Exploration Journal* 45: 128–35.

Smith, Patricia, Tania Zagerson, Pamela Sabari, Jonathan Golden, Thomas E. Levy, and Leslie Dawson. 2006. "Death and the Sanctuary: The Human Remains from Gilat." In *Archaeology, Anthropology and Cult: The Sanctuary at Gilat, Israel*, ed. T. E. Levy, 327–66. London: Equinox.

Stekelis, Moshe. 1935. *Les Monuments Megalithiques de Palestine*. Archives de l'Institute de Paleontonlogie Humaine, Memoire 15. Paris: Masson et Cie.

Sukenik, Eliezer L. 1937. "A Chalcolithic Necropolis at Hederah." *Journal of the Palestine Oriental Society* 17: 15–30.

Sussman, Varda, and Sarah Ben-Arieh. 1966. "Ancient Burials in Giv'atayim." *'Atiqot* 3: 27–39 (Hebrew; Eng. Summary 4).

Suzuki, Hisashi, and Fuyuji Takai, eds. 1970. *The Amud Man and His Cave Site*. Tokyo: University of Tokyo Press.

Taçon, Paul S.C. 2000. "Identifying Ancient Sacred Landscapes in Australia: From Physical to Social." In *Archaeologies of Landscape*, ed. W. Ashmore and A. B. Knapp, 33–57. Oxford: Blackwell.

Tadmor, Miriam. 1989. "The Judean Desert Treasure from Nahal Mishmar: A Chalcolithic Traders' Hoard." In *Essays in Ancient Civilization presented to Helene J. Kantor*, ed. A. Leonard and B. B. Williams, 251–61. Chicago: The Oriental Institute of the University of Chicago.

Thomas, Julian. 1993. "The Politics of Vision and the Archaeologies of Landscape." In *Landscape: Politics and Perspectives*, ed. B. Bender, 19–48. Oxford: Berg.

Tillier, Anne-Marie, Baruch Arensburg, Yoel Rak, and Bernard Vandermeersch. 1988. "Les sépultures néandertaliennes du Proche Orient: état de la question." *Paléorient* 14 (2): 130–36. http://dx.doi.org/10.3406/paleo.1988.4462.

Ussishkin, David. 1971. "The Ghassulian Temple in Ein Gedi and the Origin of the Hoard from Nahal Mishmar." *Biblical Archaeologist* 34 (1): 23–39. http://dx.doi.org/10.2307/3210951.

Ussishkin, David. 1980. "The Ghassulian Shrine at Ein Gedi." *Tel Aviv* 7 (1): 1–44. http://dx.doi.org/10.1179/033443580788441071.

Valla, Francois. 1998. "First Settled Societies—Natufian (12,500–10,200 BP)." In *The Archaeology of Society in the Holy Land*, ed. T. E. Levy, 169–87. London: Leicester University Press.

van den Brink, Edwin C.M. 1998. "An Index to Chalcolithic Mortuary Caves in Israel." *Israel Exploration Journal* 48:165–73.

van den Brink, Edwin C.M. 2000a. "Horbat Castra." *Hadashot Arkheologiyot: Excavations and Surveys in Israel* 111: 17.

van den Brink, Edwin C.M. 2000b. "Horbat Govit." *Hadashot Arkheologiyot: Excavations and Surveys in Israel* 112: 117.

van den Brink, Edwin C.M. 2005a. "Chalcolithic Burial Caves in Coastal and Inland Israel." In *Shoham (North) Late Chalcolithic Burial Caves in the Lod Valley, Israel*, ed. E.C.M van den Brink and R. Gophna, 175–89. IAA Reports No. 27. Jerusalem: Israel Antiquities Authority.

van den Brink, Edwin C.M. van den. 2005b. "The Ceramic Ossuaries." In *Shoham (North) Late Chalcolithic Burial Caves in the Lod Valley, Israel*, ed. E.C.M. van den Brink and R. Gophna, 27–46. Jerusalem: Israel Antiquities Authority.

van den Brink, Edwin C.M., and Ram Gophna. 2005. *Shoham (North) Late Chalcolithic Burial Caves in the Lod Valley, Israel*. IAA Reports No. 27. Jerusalem: Israel Antiquities Authority.

van den Brink, Edwin C.M., Yorke M. Rowan, and Eliot Braun. 1999. "Pedestalled Basalt Bowls of the Chalcolithic: New Variations." *Israel Exploration Journal* 49 (3–4): 161–83.

van den Brink, Edwin C.M., Nili Liphschits, Dorit Lazar, and G. Bonani. 2001. "Chalcolithic Dwelling Remains, Cup Marks and Olive (Olea europea) stones at Nevallat." *Israel Exploration Journal* 51: 36–45.

Vandermeersch, Bernard. 1982 "The First *Homo sapiens sapiens* in the Near East." In *The Transition from Lower to Middle Paleolithic and the Origin of Modern Man*, ed. A. Ronene. Oxford: BAR International Series, 151, 297–99. Oxford: British Archaeological Reports.

Vinitzky, Lipaz. 1992. "The Date of the Dolmens in the Golan and Galilee: A Reassesment." *Tel Aviv* 19: 100–12.

Yannai, Eli, and Yosef Porath. 2006. "A Chalcolithic Burial Cave at Et-Taiyiba." *'Atiqot* 53: 1–44.

Zagerson, Tania, and Patricia Smith. 2002. "The Human Remains." In *Kissufim Road: A Chalcolithic Mortuary Site*, ed. Y. Goren and P. Fabian, 57–65. Israel Antiquities Authority Reports No. 16. Jerusalem: Israel Antiquities Authority.

7

The Chamber of Secrets

Grottoes, Caves, and the Underworld in Ancient Egyptian Religion

Stuart Tyson Smith

> Hail to you, gods of the caverns which are in the West!
> Hail to you, door-keepers of the Duat who guard this
> god and who bring news to the presence of Osiris.
> May you be alert, may you have power, may you
> destroy the enemies of Re, may you make brightness,
> may you dispel your darkness . . . may you guide [the
> deceased] to your doors. May his soul pass by your
> hidden things, for he is one of you.
>
> **The Book of Going Forth by Day** (Faulkner 1990, 115)

Ancient Egypt provides the curious case of a theology in which deep caverns play a central role, but without the presence of natural caves upon which theologians could draw for inspiration. Egyptian cosmology is filled with cave symbolism. For example, Egyptians believed that the life-giving annual flood, personified by the androgynous god Hapy, flowed forth from a cave located among the granite outcrops of the first cataract of the Nile (figure 7.1). Caves and grottoes play a central role in Egyptian solar cosmology and funerary theology, providing secretive, hidden realms where the divine was made manifest and the dead journeyed toward immortality. Each day the sun god Re set in the west to enter a dark Underworld where he lit the land of the dead and battled and defeated the forces of chaos, to be reborn again with each sunrise in a continual cycle of renewal. This theology was materialized through the construction of dark and mysterious sanctuaries in temples and through the excavation of deep underground tombs that symbolized the Underworld. This chapter examines the role of caves in Egyptian theology, starting with a discussion of the central role that caves play in Egyptian cosmology. A discussion of the cave symbolism of tombs follows, focusing first on the artificial cave-horizon embodied in Old Kingdom pyramids (for chronology, see table 7.1), moving on to the cavernous New Kingdom royal burials in the Valley of the Kings, and finishing with the less-elaborate underground complexes of private tombs. I then continue with a consideration of the intersection of cosmology, lightness, and darkness in Egyptian temples, including their evolution from the more idiosyncratic layouts of select Old Kingdom sanctuaries to highly standardized formal plans of the New Kingdom that embody a transition from light to twilight to darkness. An exploration of the possible origins of this deep-cave symbolism in the Saharan Neolithic rounds out the discussion.

CAVES AND EGYPTIAN COSMOLOGY

> Hail to thee, Re, supreme power, who makes the earth
> visible, who gives light to those Westerners [the dead].
>
> *The Litany of Re* (Piankoff 1964, 22, Pl. 3)

The Egyptian cosmos was centered on the daily journey of Re upon his Solar Bark (figure 7.2). The sun god traveled each day across the sky, giving life to those who lived on earth. As the day wore on, Re approached the Akhet

FIGURE 7.1 Sites mentioned in the text.

TABLE 7.1 Egyptian dynastic chronology.	
Date BC	Phase (Dynasty)
6500–4350	Badari—Middle Neolithic
4350–3050	Naqada—Late Neolithic (0)
3050–2180	Early Dynastic–Archaic (1–3)
2680–2180	Old Kingdom (4–6)
2180–2040	First Intermediate Period (7–11)
2050–1650	Middle Kingdom (11–13)
1650–1550	Second Intermediate Period (14–17)
1550–1050	New Kingdom (18–20)
1050–650	Third Intermediate Period (21–25)
650–332	Late Period (26–31)

(horizon), symbolized by two mountains and a sun disk. The Egyptians believed that Re slipped into the west at sunset through a door leading into a vast Underworld, called the Duat, where he fought the forces of evil and brought the dead to life before being reborn into the world through the east at sunrise. The Egyptian theology of Ma'at embodied the cosmological moral struggle of Re with the evil snake god Apophis. Ma'at (order, righteousness) existed in opposition to Isfet (chaos, evil). Re embodied Ma'at, while Apophis embodied its opposite, Isfet.

The struggle between two gods over the fate of the cosmos took place in the Netherworld over the twelve hours of the night. Re always triumphed in the end, emerging from the horizon to sail across the sky another day. We tend to think of Egyptian theology as very static—a legacy of the Hellenistic encounter with Egypt (Assmann 2002)—but Egyptian cosmology was in reality highly dynamic. Each new dawn was a renewal—a bit like the moment of the first creation, since the god taps into the same magic in order to triumph over death and be born again every day. In the end, however, the Egyptians believed that Apophis would finally triumph, undoing creation and swimming away into a watery chaos like the primordial waters that existed before creation (Hornung 1992, 39–54).

Geography tied the Underworld to the land of living. The hill-countries provided both an entrance and exit to the Netherworld and a symbol of earthly chaos connected with foreigners. Thus, the Nile Valley of Egypt provided the earthly expression of Ma'at, but was surrounded by a mountainous desert filled with foreigners who constantly sought to overthrow the earthly order, just as Apophis sought to destroy the divine order through his attacks on the Sun Bark in the Underworld. Egyptian theology therefore created a self–other ethnic opposition between Egyptians and a group of three archetypical foreigners: Libyans to the west, Asiatics to the northeast, and Nubians to the south (Smith 2003). The king's struggle with these earthly enemies connected him to Re's struggles against Apophis. The theology of Ma'at explicitly connected kingship with the cosmological struggle. Earthly order was decreed by Re but established by Pharaoh (Assmann 1989).

The living king was the incarnation of the falcon-sky god Horus, while the deceased king became Osiris, descending into the Duat to rule over the dead and assist Re in his nightly rejuvenation and triumph over Isfet (Assmann 2001, 83–147). As a result, the liminal spaces where divine and mundane met—temples and tombs, especially royal ones—came to symbolize the Duat. Keeping this theological and ideological background in mind, the next sections examine the link between tombs, temples, and the Underworld.

CHAMBER OF SECRETS: TOMBS AND UNDERWORLD SYMBOLISM

> I inspected the excavation of the cliff-tomb of his majesty, alone, no one seeing, no one hearing.
>
> **Ineni, architect of Thutmose I (Breasted 1906, 43)**

As the entrance to the Underworld (figures 7.1 and 7.2), the western hills bordering the Nile became a symbol for death and the idealized, but not always realized, location for tombs that increasingly provided a direct analog to Underworld geography. Indeed, the burial chambers of both royal and private tombs were known as the Duat. The

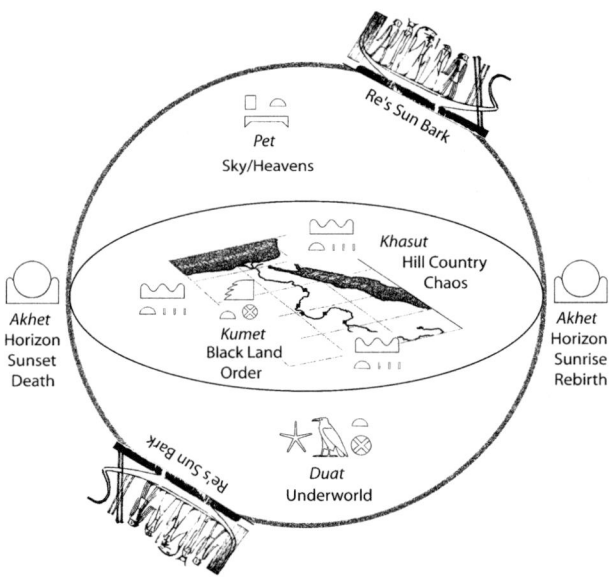

FIGURE 7.2 Ancient Egyptian cosmology.

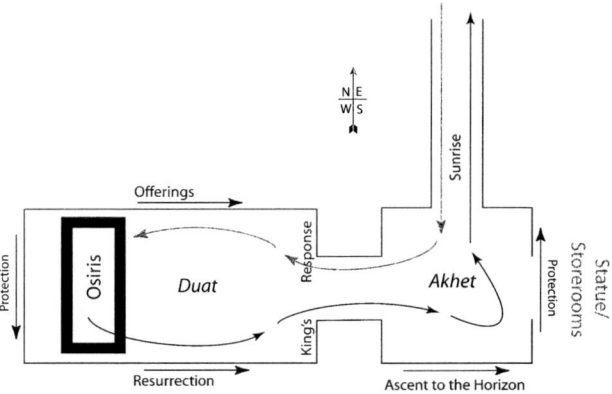

FIGURE 7.3 Pyramid Texts and cosmological symbolism in the Pyramid of Unas, ca. 2350 BC. (After Allen 1993.)

link between the king's journey through the afterlife and the sun's daily descent through the Underworld was codified explicitly during the New Kingdom (ca. 1550–1070 BC) in the Book of the Secret Chamber, an allusion to the mysterious underground realm of the Netherworld through which the sun journeyed every night. This illustrated book is more commonly known as the Am Duat, or "that which is in the Netherworld," but the Egyptians used this term to refer to the entire corpus of Underworld texts, not just the Book of the Secret Chamber. Earlier funerary books like the Pyramid Texts and its successors the Coffin Texts and the Book of Going Forth by Day, more commonly known as the Book of the Dead, are not set in an underground realm like the later books of the Am Duat, but rather describe the king's journey to a celestial realm where he joins the immortal gods and goddesses (Hornung 1999, 1–12). Nevertheless, Arnold (1997, 71) notes that parts of the Pyramid Texts reflect the king's descent into the Netherworld and conflate his journey with the daily journey of Re. Allen (1993) argues persuasively that the placement of the different components of the Pyramid Texts within the burial chambers make for a setting that is "conceptually identical to the cosmic geography of the sun's nightly journey described in the Amduat and similar New Kingdom creations." In this section, I examine the Duat-cavern symbolism of pyramids as reflected in the Pyramid Texts, then move on to a consideration of the books of the Am Duat in the royal burials of the Valley of the Kings, and finish with the evolution of Netherworld symbolism in private tombs.

Starting with the reign of Unas in the Fifth Dynasty (ca. 2350 BC), the Pyramid Texts were carved onto the walls of the burial chambers inside pyramids, although the spells, which make up Egypt's oldest religious literature, probably date much earlier (Hornung 1999). Theologically, the Pyramid Texts directly link the king to the sun god. He enters the tomb at sunset as Re-Atum, the evening sun; spends the night in the tomb as Osiris; emerges into the antechamber reborn as Khepri, the infant sun; and finally ascends into the morning sky as Re-Horakhti, the sun-falcon who courses across the sky (Arnold 1997, 71). Looking carefully at the placement of each spell, James Allen (1993) argues that the burial chamber itself represents the Duat, where the sun unites with Osiris (i.e., the king's mummy). The antechamber represents the Akhet, horizon-gateway, and the entrance passage represents the route of the Sun Bark's ascent into the sky at dawn (figure 7.3). As in the Am Duat, the king passes through the night, descending into the Duat (burial chamber) through the entrance passage of the pyramid, like the sun sinking into the western hills. He unites with Osiris at midnight in the depths of the tomb (as a mummy). Allen observes that the arrangement of the Pyramid Texts literally lead the king's spirit out of the burial chamber-Duat into the antechamber-Akhet to be reborn again and exit back out the main passage with the new dawn.

Pyramids thus represent an artificial horizon and gateway to the Duat or Netherworld, the burial chambers that lay within or below these massive funerary monuments (see figure 7.3 and 7.4). The Great Pyramid itself was called Akhet Khufu, "Horizon of Khufu." Moreover, the monuments at Giza are linked together in a grand materialization of Akhet. The three pyramids make two sets of horizons, conceived as mountains with valleys in between. Mark Lehner (1997, 126–130) discovered that the sun

FIGURE 7.4 The sun sets along the left side of the Sphinx (ca. 2500 BC) in line with Khafre's pyramid during the equinoxes. Menkaure's smaller pyramid lies to the left and Khufu's larger pyramid is out of the picture to the right.

sets exactly between Khafre's pyramid and Khufu's Great Pyramid for three days running during the summer solstice when viewed from the Sphinx temple, making a gigantic horizon symbol. He goes on to observe that the Sphinx complex was laid out so that the sun sets at the southern foot of Khafre's pyramid in line with the Sphinx temple's axis (along the left side of the Sphinx, see figure 7.4) on the equinoxes (approximately March 20 and September 22 each year), after which it continues southwards, setting between Khafre's pyramid and Menkaure's smaller pyramid. The Sphinx itself was called Hor-em-Akhet, "Horus on the Horizon," a reference to the rising and setting sun. The temple at its feet has eastern and western niches for each horizon and twelve columns within a central courtyard that symbolize the twelve hours of the day and night. The rising and setting sun would have illuminated any cult image in the niches during the equinoxes. Even at other times of the year, each evening the pyramids and sphinx would provide a dramatic backdrop to the sunset when viewed from the temple or its environs.

Thutmose I and his architect, Ineni, abandoned the pyramid in favor of hidden burial places in the Valley of the Kings around 1500 BC (figures 7.5, 7.6, 7.7), as the quotation above from Ineni's autobiography specifies. Originally this passage was interpreted as an indication that Thutmose and Ineni wanted greater security for the royal burial, since pyramids were an obvious lure to looters (e.g., Breasted 1906, 43, note g). But why would we expect a sudden interest in security after over a millennium of pyramid construction? Instead, we can see this radical shift in royal tomb plan as a major theological innovation. It is no coincidence that Thutmose I and Ineni also inaugurated the use of the Book of the Secret Chamber for royal burials, placing the illustrated book on stone panels that originally lined the burial chamber of the new sepulcher. New Kingdom and later royal tombs were therefore con-

FIGURE 7.5 At the top of the column from the Chariot Hall in the Valley of the Kings tomb of Ramses VI (ca. 1150 BC), Re-Horakhti leads a group of deities, including Amun and the dead king, above a large image of the sun god. This chamber is decorated with divine figures, the Book of Gates, the Book of Caverns, an Osiris shrine, and an astronomical ceiling.

structed as direct analogs to the Netherworld, with security at best a secondary consideration. These new "hidden" tombs in the Valley of the Kings created cavernous darkzone spaces and passages that mimic the "secret chambers" of the sun god's daily journey through the Underworld. A new kind of mortuary temple in the Nile Valley opposite provided a connection between the royal and divine cults and a gateway between this world and the Duat (see below, figure 7.13). The Book of the Secret Chamber decorated the walls of the royal burial chamber for the next 200 years, after which it spread to various other parts of the royal sepulcher. It may also have appeared on the golden shrines that surrounded the king's sarcophagus, which survive only for Tutankhamen (Piankoff 1955). New Kingdom theologians elaborated upon the Underworld theme in a series of new books, including the Book of Gates (ca. 1300 BC), the Book of Caverns (ca. 1200 BC), and the Book of the Earth (ca. 1200 BC). Each of these illustrated books describes the journey of the sun god through the night, conceived of as a cavernous realm that lay beneath Egypt. Like the Pyramid Texts during the Old Kingdom, the books of the Am Duat were restricted almost exclusively to kings during the New Kingdom, but spread afterwards to anyone who could afford a papyrus copy.

The Book of the Secret Chamber provided the basis for all of the other Netherworld books. Combining texts and representations, it describes the nocturnal travels and travails of the sun god as a Ba, or soul, passing through an explicitly subterranean inner cosmos. It is divided into twelve sections, each representing an hour of the night. The first three hours describe the denizens of the Underworld and the Waters of Wernes and Osiris, a realm of plenty where the dead live. In the fourth hour, Re enters into the dark and forbidding realm of Ro-Setau, where the falcon-headed god Sokar rules, a desert teeming with snakes that have legs and wings. With the help of towing bargemen, the

FIGURE 7.6 In the fourth hour of the Book of the Secret Chamber, Horus and Sokar protect and renew the Solar Eye as the sun god travels a weaving road blocked by doors running through the forbidding desert of Ro-Setau. Depicted in this scene from left to right: Osiris (behind him is a door), followed by Thoth, who presents the Eye to Sokar, behind whom is a deity named "Crowned Brow" with Thutmose III striding ahead of him with mace and staff in hand. (From the Valley of the Kings tomb of Thutmose III, ca. 1450 BC.)

Sun Bark makes a difficult passage through a zigzag channel and past a lake of fire where the wicked are punished. Re continues through Sokar's realm in the fifth hour, passing by the tomb of Osiris and a group of menacing demons. Then the bark arrives at the Cave of Sokar where the mysterious union between Osiris and Re takes place (see figure 7.6). In the sixth hour, the Sun Bark leaves Ro-Setau and reaches the deepest part of the Underworld, where the primordial, regenerative waters of Nun allow Re to reunite with his body and the sun to shine again.

The seventh hour marks the beginning of the sun god's struggle to reach the eastern horizon, battling past the evil snake god Apophis and his minions. Helpful deities, who restrain Apophis and destroy the enemies of Ma'at, protect Re. From now on a divine bodyguard protects the sun god. Re's travels through the eighth and ninth hours deal with the provisioning of the dead with clothing and food.

Using the regenerating waters of Nun in the tenth hour, Re as Horus of the Netherworld revives the drowned, whose souls were in jeopardy because their bodies did not survive to be mummified. Re's enemies are again defeated in the eleventh hour, to be destroyed by the Serpent Who Burns Millions and then be cast into fiery pits. Apophis makes a final attempt to sink the Sun Bark in the twelfth hour, but a group of fearsome goddesses with fire-spitting serpents repel him. Rejoicing deities welcome the rebirth of both Re and Osiris. The sun god flies out of the Underworld as the scarab god Khepri, but Osiris remains as ruler of the Netherworld. With the new dawn comes the renewal of the world as the sky god Shu reseals the eastern entrance to the Underworld.

The advent of Book of Gates and the Book of Caverns coincided with the expansion of royal tombs into a long series of elaborately decorated corridors and chambers

Passage of Re, praising the sun god's many manifestations as he enters and exits the tomb-Underworld. Chapters from the Book of the Secret Chamber and the Book of Gates dominate the upper part of the tomb as one passes through several doorways. The Doorkeeper's Rooms provide a symbolic place for the guardians who block doorways, starting in the books of the Am Duat and in the Book of Going Forth by Day, as seen in the epigraph at the beginning of this chapter.

The Hall of Hindering provides the most explicit connection between architecture and cosmology (see figure 7.7). Early Egyptologists characterized the pit chamber as a security measure against thieves and/or as a well for the periodic flooding that hits Upper Egypt once every 80 years or so. As Erik Hornung (1990, 27) points out, however, it is a mistake to look to practical reasons to explain changes that are more likely theological. The pits would hardly have fooled thieves, and once a tomb was sealed it would have no need for flood protection (Weeks 2004). Thus we must look to the texts found for an explanation of this architectural feature. Starting with the tomb of Seti I (ca. 1290 BC), the fourth and fifth hours of the Book of the Secret Chamber consistently appear on the walls of the corridor approaching the pit chamber. The pit itself thus materializes the obstacles that Re faces in his journey through the forbidding land of Ro-Setau. Moreover, in three of the eight royal tombs with an actual pit, there is a room at the bottom that almost certainly symbolizes the cave of Sokar mentioned in the fourth hour. (Four more pits remain unexcavated and may also have rooms; see Hornung 1990; Weeks 2004.) An Osiris shrine consistently appears in the Chariot Hall and its annex (see figure 7.5), resonating with the sun's journey in the sixth hour, when the Ba of Re reunites with his body-mummy-Osiris. Hornung (1990, 27) argues that this room also served as a kind of cenotaph, or symbolic burial chamber, which would further cement the connection between this series of chambers and the fourth through sixth hours of the sun's journey into the Netherworld.

The Opening of Dragging may simply refer to dragging the sarcophagus into the burial chamber (see figure 7.7), but Re's celestial boat is also dragged through the desert land of Ro-Setau, just before reaching the deepest part of the Netherworld in hour six (Hornung 1990, 36–38). The Books of Gates, Caverns, and the Earth commonly decorate the burial chamber—the deepest part of the tomb where, as in the pyramid complexes before, Osiris and Re symbolically unite in the form of the king's mummy. The sarcophagus sometimes sits in a well upon a stone platform, symbolizing the primordial mound of creation emerging from the waters of Nun. This matches midnight in the Netherworld, the sixth hour when the Ba of Re reunites

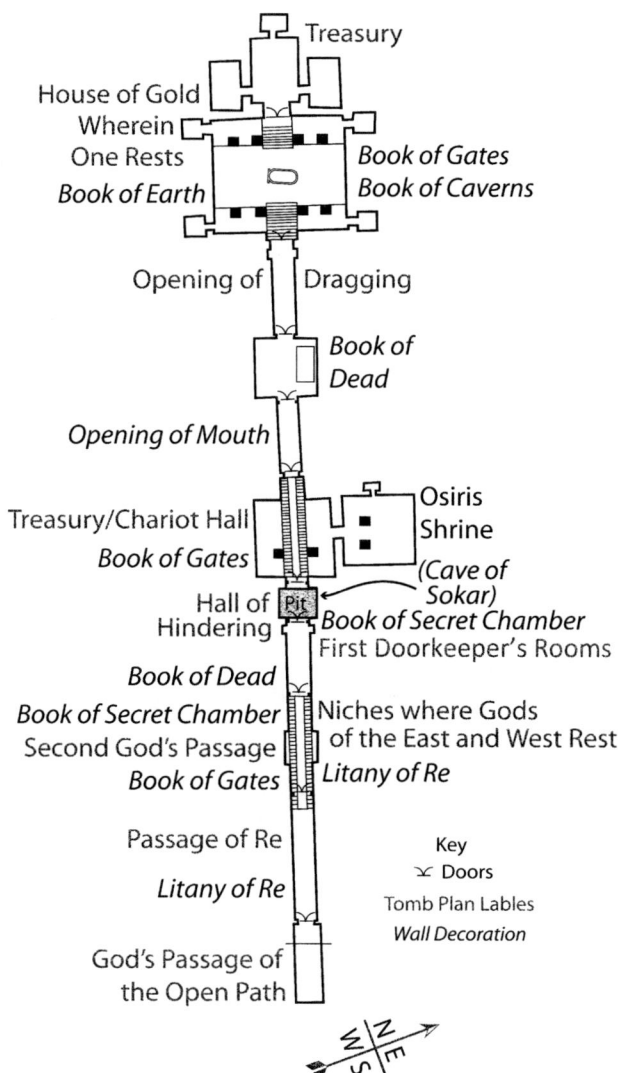

FIGURE 7.7 Conceptual layout and placement of texts in the Valley of the Kings tomb of Merneptah (ca. 1214 BC).

separated by doorways that symbolically represented the gates that lay between the hours or divisions of the sun's journey (see figures 7.5 and 7.7). This architectural innovation materialized the more formal division of the Netherworld found in each text, although there is not necessarily an exact correlation between text and architecture. There are also two surviving plans of royal tombs from the same period that name the different rooms and corridors, which again resonate with the sun god's journey into the Netherworld without matching its stages exactly. For example, while the various books of the Am Duat are scattered throughout the tomb of Merneptah (see Figure 7.7; ca. 1200 BC), the layout of the tomb's gated passageways clearly echo the stages of the journey of Re through the Underworld. The Litany of Re lines the walls of the

FIGURE 7.8 Perhaps employed in the funerals of kings, the Osirion in back of Seti I's temple at Abydos mimics a New Kingdom royal burial chamber (ca. 1290 BC).

with his body and shines again thanks to the rejuvenating powers of Nun, god of the primeval waters. This imagery is even more explicit in the Osirion, a subterranean complex that lies behind the Osiris temple of Seti I at Abydos (Wilkinson 2000, 146–48). A sloping and winding passage leads down into a large pillared chamber reminiscent of New Kingdom royal tombs (figure 7.8). A platform sits upon an island surrounded by canals filled with groundwater. Seti's burial party may have used the underground structure as an important stage in the funeral procession after the mummification of the king, since Abydos is the cult center of Osiris (Clayton 1994, 144). Although Seti I originally commissioned the Osirion, Merneptah, who ruled around a hundred years after Seti, added the Books of Gates, Caverns, and the Earth, along with the Spell of Twelve Caves from the Book of Going Forth by Day (Hornung 1999). A similar smaller structure dating from the New Kingdom was found recently down a deep shaft beneath the causeway of Khafre's pyramid at Giza. Hawass (2005) argues persuasively that like the Abydos Osirion, it represents the tomb of Osiris in Ro-Setau.

Private tombs also represented a passage from this world and the Netherworld (Assmann 1984; Seyfried 1987). At least to begin, the connection was not as explicit as in royal tombs. Although they consisted of enclosed twilight spaces, tomb chapels during the Old Kingdom represented a house for the deceased, consisting of a built structure called a *mastaba* that often mimicked the layout of an actual house. The decoration emphasized the commemoration of the deceased in life and the offering cult—a form of ancestor veneration. False doors located near the tomb shaft, however, allowed the soul to emerge from the deep and dark burial chamber and by implication from the Netherworld (Assmann 2003). Seyfried (1998, 389) argues that the burial complex itself actually represented the Duat. The cave symbolism of private tombs became even more explicit once rock-cut tombs became popular at places like Aswan at the end of the Old Kingdom (Sixth Dynasty, ca. 2300 BC). By the Middle Kingdom, the Coffin Texts put an end to the royal monopoly on immortality in the afterlife, adapting the exclusively royal Pyramid Texts for private use. Anyone could now be associated with Osiris

FIGURE 7.9 Anubis guards the entrance to the burial chamber in the tomb of Pashed at the artisans' village of Deir el-Medina (ca. 1250 BC). Osiris and other Netherworld deities decorate the burial chamber, connecting it directly with the Duat.

and journey from the tomb toward the night sky, and even share in the daily journey of the sun. Mythical creatures reminiscent of the denizens of the Duat begin to appear in tomb chapels, although the overall decoration is still dominated by scenes of the tomb owner in daily life. Although more idealized, the layout retains some elements of a real house (Shedid 1994). The Book of the Two Ways presents the first real guide to the Netherworld, including the forbidding snake-infested land of Ro-Setau, where the tomb of Osiris lay. Like the Pyramid Texts, however, the imagery is more sky than cavern oriented, although elements of the Am Duat are presaged here, including connections with the solar cycle and the introduction of a series of portals with gatekeepers that present a challenging obstacle to the deceased (Hornung 1999, 7–12).

An important shift takes place during the New Kingdom. The image of a cavernous Underworld is more explicit in the Book of Going Forth by Day, as is apparent in the quotations at the beginning and end of this chapter. Spell 168 describes the Netherworld as twelve caves, each containing a number of deities. Unlike the struggle between good and evil that sits at the heart of the Am Duat, here the denizens of the Duat grant favors to the deceased, including sight, free movement in the afterlife, passage through the gates of the Netherworld, light and sustenance, and protection against all enemies (Hornung 1999, 54–55). Toward the end of the Eighteenth Dynasty (ca. 1350 BC), two fundamental changes align private tombs with Underworld symbolism: a change in plan, and the abandonment of scenes of daily life in favor of religious scenes from the Book of Going Forth by Day and other sources. The use of solar hymns at the entrance, temple-like plans, and pyramids cement the private tomb's shift away from commemoration and toward the creation of a solar chapel akin to the much grander temple-tomb complexes dedicated to contemporary pharaohs. Like the tombs in the Valley of the Kings, a sometimes winding, sloping passage leads underground, replacing the tomb shafts of the Old and Middle Kingdoms. The underground chambers are now sometimes decorated with scenes of the deceased in the afterlife with an emphasis on solar imagery and Netherworld deities like Osiris and Anubis (figure 7.9; Assmann 2003; Martin 1991). Seyfried (1998, 389) argues that the burial complex now represents the cavernous passage through Ro-Setau in hours four and five of the Am Duat. Assmann (2003, 50) extends this idea, making a convincing case that the underground part of the tomb corresponds specifically to the Cave of Sokar. He supports this notion by analogy to a Sokar-based grain-mummy ritual attested to in the New Kingdom Necropolis at Saqqara. A procession goes to the tomb and descends down to the "Secret Place"—surely a reference to the Secret Chamber of the Netherworld, and specifically the Cave of Sokar, where Osiris and Re have their mystical union.

HIDDEN REALMS: TEMPLES AS DARK SPACES

> Hail to thee, O Nile!
> Who manifesteth thyself over this land
> And comest to give life to Egypt!
> Mysterious is thy issuing forth from the darkness,
> On this day whereon it is celebrated!...
> None knows the place where he dwells,
> None discovers his retreat by the
> power of a written spell.
>
> Khety, "Hymn to the Nile,"
> (Thatcher 1907, 79, 80)

FIGURE 7.10 Small openings in the ceiling create a twilight space in the Hypostyle Hall of the Osiris Temple of Seti I at Abydos (ca. 1290 BC).

The archetypical Egyptian temple also employed cave symbolism, reflecting a materialization of Egyptian cosmology that combined the solar cycle with the creation myth (Assmann 2001, 35–40; Hornung 1990, 115–129). Temples linked heaven, earth, and the Netherworld through mystical and magical connections (Bell 1997, 132). Shallow grottoes appear in a variety of local cults, particularly shrines dedicated to the Goddess Hathor, whose temple at Dendara also had an underground component (Wilkinson 2000, 148–51). The ideal temple plan moves from open to restricted, and from light to dark space. A bright courtyard is followed by the twilight of the hypostyle Hall of Appearances, which is in turn followed by a series of inner rooms of increasing darkness, with only a few openings in the ceilings and walls casting mysterious, isolated shafts of light (Assmann 2001, 31; figures 7.10; see also figures 7.12, and 7.13). Although this standardized temple layout evolved over a long period of time, the connection between temples and caves goes back at least to the foundations of the Egyptian state. Few temples survive from the Old Kingdom, and those monuments show a considerable diversity of plan that Kemp (1989) characterizes as "Preformal." I discuss here two of the earliest attested Egyptian temples that incorporate cave imagery: the sanctuaries of Montu at Medamoud, and Satet on Elephantine Island. Both of these temples incorporate a transition from light to dark spaces, what Kemp characterizes as the "Hidden" and "Revealed." Although the layout becomes more axial and standardized, Kemp's "Formal" temple layout incorporates the same symbolism that I explore using the temple of Ramses III at Medinet Habu, one of the best preserved in Egypt. Egyptian temples sometimes incorporated built caverns, including the sanctuary of Amun-Re at Hatsheptsut's Deir el-Bahari mortuary temple (Wilkinson 2000, 178). I use the famous temples at Abu Simbel and the cave shrines to Hathor in the Sinai to illustrate this more direct connection between temples and cave symbolism.

The Satet Temple lies on Elephantine Island at the first cataract of the Nile, where the river was thought to emerge from secret deep caverns. The inundation was thought to emerge from secret deep caverns on nearby Bigeh Island. Khety indicates in the Hymn to the Nile that Hapy, god of the inundation, presided over this hidden place. Perhaps resonating with this myth, a natural cave-like niche-grotto provides the focus for the earliest temple to the goddess (figure 7.11).

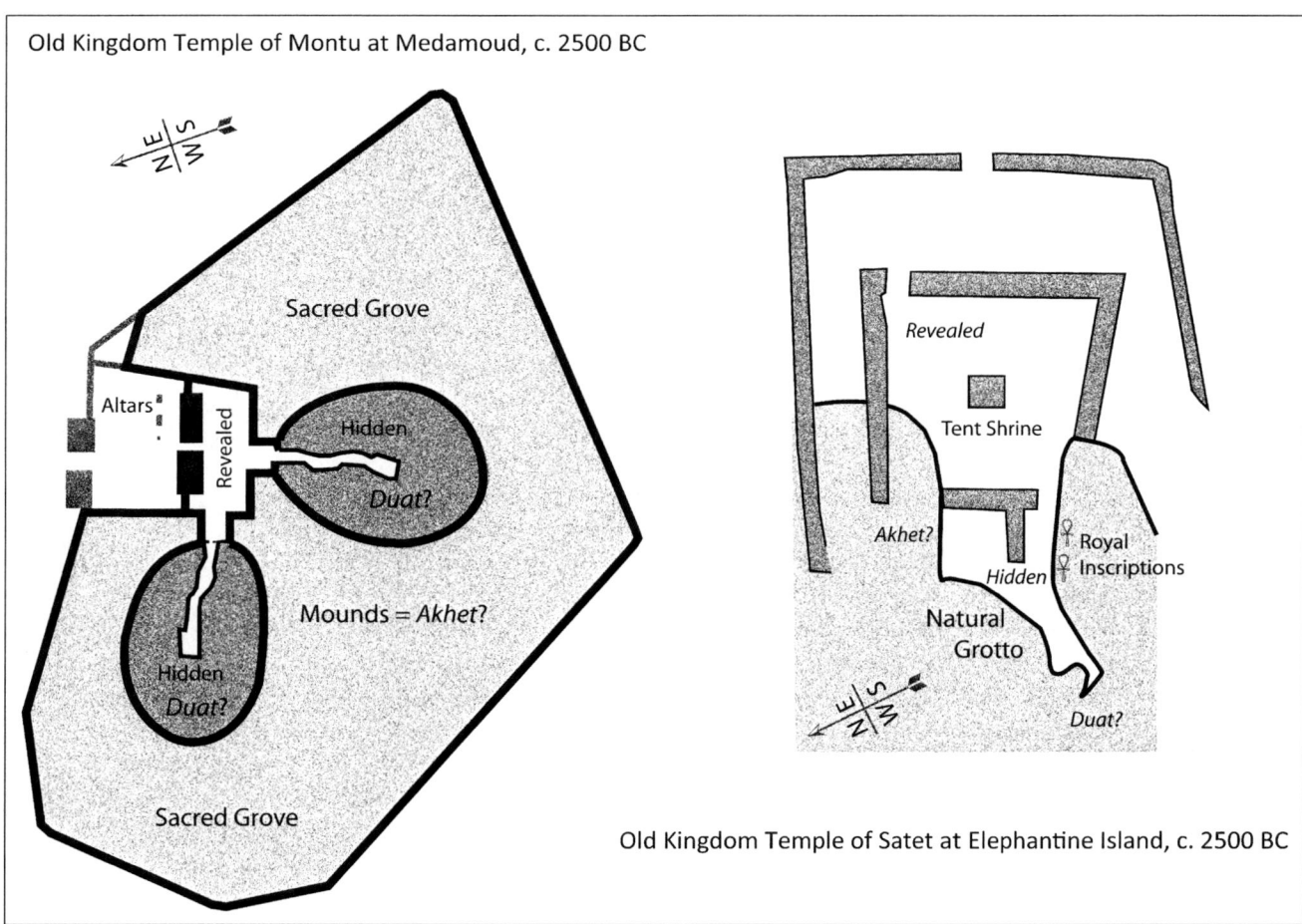

FIGURE 7.11 Old Kingdom Temples: (Left) Montu at Medamoud and (Right) Satet on Elephantine Island (ca. 2600–2150 BC).

Archaeological evidence demonstrates that the earliest structure at the rocky site goes back to the Early Dynastic Period (3050–2180 BC). In the outer chambers, Kemp (1989) sees a Revealed Realm of the goddess, which people could approach and where they could deposit the many votive offerings found at the site (Dreyer 1986). The inner part of the shrine—the grotto itself—was the Hidden Realm of the Goddess, technically accessible only to the king as the incarnation of the god Horus and high priest of all the gods of Egypt, but in practice visited daily by ritually purified priests who substituted for the king in the daily offering cult. This arrangement produced a juxtaposition of accessible, light spaces and mysterious, hidden, dark spaces that becomes the hallmark of Egyptian temple plans. The niche-grotto's entrance is also oriented east-west, with the deepest part to the west, where the sun would set on the equinoxes. Perhaps here the boulders symbolized the Akhet, where the god is made manifest, while the grotto represents the entrance to the Duat—the Secret Chamber where mortals could not travel.

Unlike the Satet Temple's use of a natural feature, the Old Kingdom Temple of Montu at Medamoud created artificial mountains with underground spaces (see figure 7.11). The earliest temple at the site has a series of open courtyards leading to a sacred grove dominated by two built mounds (Kemp 1989; Robichon and Varille 1940). Each mound had a winding underground passage leading to a central chamber-sanctuary that presumably would be plunged into complete darkness in the absence of artificial lighting. Since the gap between the mounds is oriented nearly east-west, it is tempting to read an Akhet in them, in which case the chambers underneath each would represent a kind of dual Duat. The similarity to the pyramids at Giza is striking (particularly before Menkaure's pyramid was constructed), although this theory is impossible to prove on the existing evidence. Regardless, there is clearly a contrast between relatively accessible light space with altars and a difficult-to-access, hidden, dark space, with the chambers beneath the mounds very likely representing some notion of Duat.

The Formal temples that replaced these earlier structures more explicitly embodied the symbolism of Akhet and Duat, acting as a materialization of the cosmos and a bridge between divine and mundane (Assmann 2001, 35–40; Hornung 1990, 115–29). The mortuary temple of Ramses III at Medinet Habu illustrates this cosmology of temple planning (figure 7.12). Here the pylons explicitly represent the Akhet, in spite of the fact that the temple is really oriented more nearly north-south than east-west. Here the Nile becomes the main compass referent, as is often the case with Egyptian temples. In keeping with the theological shift in royal burial practice, Medinet Habu is laid out along the lines of a temple for the living, and actually served as an important cult place for Amun-Re. The Formal temple plan expands on the theme of transition from light to dark, and from revealed to hidden, that is found in the earlier temples at Medamoud and Elephantine Island. The space before the entrance pylon and the large porticoed courtyards that followed were accessible to the ordinary worshipper, explicitly indicated by inscriptions naming the Rekhit "masses" who praised the god in these locations. The Rekhit are symbolized in hieroglyphs and iconographically in temple decoration by the lapwing, a plentiful, small, and very noisy bird. The Rekhit still had access to a kind of twilight space in the large hypostyle hall with a clerestory running down the central aisle, supplemented by holes in the roof for subdued lighting (see Figure 7.10). Darker still and more restricted of access were the offering chambers that lay before the shrine wherein the god resided, which only the king or a purified priest could approach.

Regardless of the deity worshipped, the temple's layout materialized the solar cycle through a combination of art and architecture (cf. figures 7.2 and 7.12). The exterior was decorated with scenes of battle and the subduing of foreign enemies, symbolizing the king's triumph over Isfet and, by analogy, Re's battle with Apophis. The temple is surrounded by representations of Isfet, the scenes of battle symbolically and magically protecting Ma'at, which lies inside (Finnestad 1997; Hornung 1992). In order to represent creation surrounded by chaos, the Formal temple lies on a slope, gently ascending to the sanctuary, where the deity sits in his or her shrine upon an artificial rise symbolizing the mound of creation that arose from the primordial waters of Nun. Column capitals that mimic papyrus and lotus blossoms denote the fertile creative forces that surround the primordial mound, where all life began. The sanctuary itself represents the Duat. The temple rituals enact the daily journey of the sun, with the god or goddess emerging from the sanctuary-Duat toward the pylon-Akhet at dawn and returning each night. Like royal crypts going back to the Old Kingdom pyramids, the inner ceilings of temples were decorated with stars symbolizing the

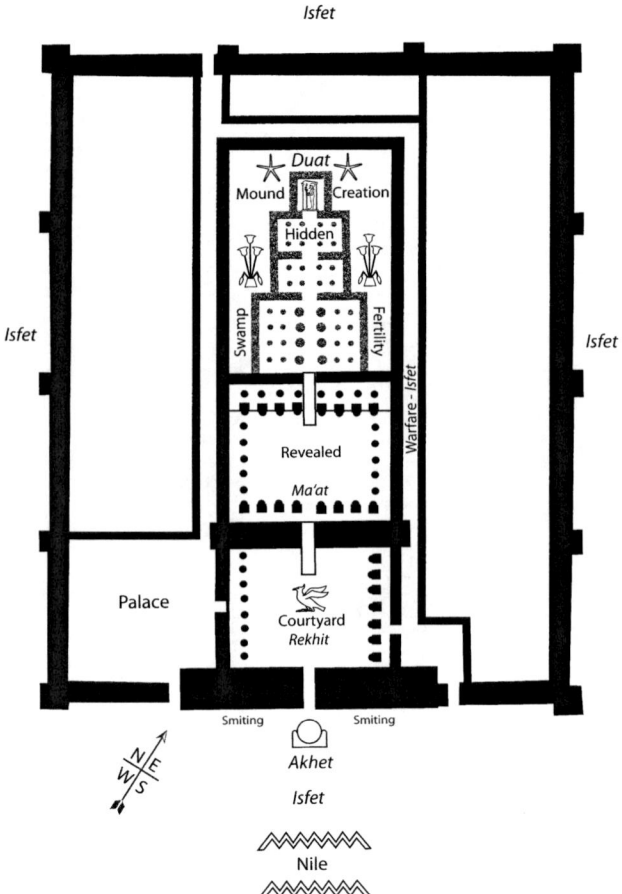

FIGURE 7.12 The temple as cosmos materialized: the New Kingdom mortuary temple of Ramses III at Medinet Habu (ca. 1163 BC).

dark realm of the Duat. Egyptian theologians named the entrance to the sanctuary the "Doors of Heaven" (Bell 1997, 134). The innermost shrine itself was called the Duat-en-Ba, a Netherworld for (the divine) Ba. Each day the god arose in the morning rituals as a regenerated Ba emerging from the Duat (Finnestad 1997, 210–12).

Mainly but not exclusively in Nubia, New Kingdom pharaohs commissioned rock-cut temples that created artificial cave-Duats in the cliffs bordering the Nile Valley (Wilkinson 2000). The most famous of these is the temple of Ramses II at Abu Simbel (ca. 1250 BC). Cut out of dramatic Nubian sandstone cliffs, the temple and another nearby dedicated to his wife were moved 60 feet above their original level in order to save them from the waters of Lake Nasser between 1963 and 1968. The first rock-cut temples in the area were dedicated to the goddess Hathor and were built by Ay and Horemheb (ca. 1323–1307 BC). Ramses II built seven rock-cut temples in Nubia, but Abu Simbel is without doubt the most impressive ever built in Nubia or Egypt. Called the "Estate of Ramses," the huge

FIGURE 7.13 Ramses II appears as Osiris on columns at Abu Simbel in Nubia (ca. 1250 BC).

complex, with its four 69-foot-high statues took 35 years to complete. In keeping with the standard temple plan discussed above, the cliff face slopes like a pylon-horizon, and the complex of rooms gradually slopes over the 200 feet that it extends into the mountain (Kitchen 1990, 64–67; Wilkinson 2000, 223–28). After passing through the entrance, one reaches a grand hypostyle hall with scenes of the defeat of Egypt's iconic ethnic enemies—Nubians, Syrians and Libyans—symbolizing earthly Isfet. Each column along the main aisle has a statue of the king as Osiris (figure 7.13). When the doors of temple were open, this would have been twilight space, with inner rooms becoming increasingly darker. Two smaller inner halls with offering scenes to Amun-Re and Re-Horakhti follow, also in keeping with ideal plan representing the Ramses's establishment of Ma'at in Egypt. The sanctuary contains rock-cut statues of Ptah, Amun-Re, Ramses, and Re-Horakhti. This is one of the few temples in which a living king was actually worshipped like a god. In an impressive feat of engineering and astronomy, the sun lights the statues of Amun-Re, Ramses, and Re-Horakhti every February 22 and October 22, the dates of Ramses's birthday and coronation. The reconstructed temples were sited so that this event still occurs, just as it has for the past 3,200 years.

A smaller but nonetheless impressive Hathor temple next to Ramses's grand monument was dedicated to Queen Nefertari. An inscription over the entrance states: "Ramesses II, he has made a temple, excavated in the mountain, of eternal workmanship, for the Great Royal Wife Nefertari, beloved of Mut, in Nubia, forever and ever, Nefertari for whose sake the very sun shines" (Kitchen 1990, 99). Here Hathor appears in her Netherworld guise as Mistress of the West. Her image is carved as a cow literally emerging from rock—the back wall of the sanctuary. Similar imagery is common at Thebes in both royal and private tombs. Hathor has cave or rockshelter temples elsewhere, particularly connected with copper and turquoise mining in Sinai. The temple at Timna was built during the New Kingdom in a natural-rock overhang along a dramatic wadi (dry wash) of the Negev desert (Rothenberg 1972). The Middle to New Kingdom temple at Serabit el-Khadim sits on top of a mountain overlooking the rugged terrain of the southwestern Sinai (Valbelle and Bonnet 1996). Several caves were incorporated into the complex layout. The main rock-cut dual sanctuaries were fronted by an extensive set of antechambers, pylons, and courtyards, creating dramatic alternating sequence of light, twilight, and dark spaces. This symbolism of goddess in the mountain clearly plays off of Hathor's roles as Mistress of Turquoise and Mistress of the West. The layout of these temples also suggests an Akhet-Duat symbolism found in her main sanctuary at Dendara. A series of crypts below the temple held a statue of the Ba of Hathor that was taken out to the roof of the temple during New Year's in a festival of renewal connected with Osiris and the Netherworld (Wilkinson 2000, 148–51).

"SWALLOWER OF ALL": THE ORIGINS OF EGYPTIAN CAVE SYMBOLISM

> They entered the seventh hall, and Setne saw the mysterious form of Osiris, the great god, seated on his throne of fine gold, crowned with the atef-crown. Anubis, the great god, was on his left, the great god Thoth was on his right, and the gods of the tribunal of the inhabitants of the netherworld stood on his left and right. The balance stood in the center before them, and they weighed the good deeds against the misdeeds.
>
> "Prince Khamwas and Si-Osire" (Lichtheim 1980, 140)

The entrance to the Underworld was known simply as the "Swallower of All," referring to the fact that everyone would eventually pass through its portal. The origins of this underground imagery are not clear, since the Nile Valley contains no deep caves, although some small caves and shallow grottoes do exist. Some early sanctuaries like the Satet Temple took advantage of these natural features, but how could the notion of extensive caverns like the underground realm that Re journeyed through each night have originated? Although there are none in the Nile Valley proper, there are caves in the Egyptian, Libyan, and Sudanese Sahara that were used for some kind of rituals during the Neolithic. The most famous of these are the rock-art-filled caves at Gebel Uweinat and the Gilf Kebir (figure 7.1). The latter is the home of the famous "Cave of Swimmers" (Almásy 1936, 1998), popularized by the novel and film *The English Patient* (1996; Ondaatje 1992), but there are many other cave sites with rock art in the eastern Sahara (Hinkel 1979; Rhotert 1952; Winkler 1939; Zboray 2003, 2004). Today's formidable landscape is very different from conditions in the distant past. Summer monsoon rains coming off of the Indian Ocean reached north into Egyptian Nubia and southern Egypt during the Neolithic Wet Phase, which lasted from the middle seventh to middle fourth millennium BC (Kuper 1989; Kuper and Kröpelin 2006; Schön 1994). This led to the formation of temporary lakes like Nabta Playa that attracted seasonal and even perhaps some permanent human settlement, particularly during the Middle and Late Neolithic (ca. 6500–3500 BC; Wendorf, Close, and Schild 1992–93).

The painted caves at the Gilf Kebir and Gebel Uweinat are not particularly deep—more twilight than dark zone. At Djara to the north, however, there is a remarkable deep dripstone cave with evidence of ritual use (Claßen et al. 2001; Kuper 1996). The underground complex has spectacular, glittering stalactites and stalagmites and includes a large hall almost 50 meters in length and 15 meters high. Some of the stalagmites are covered with engraved and/or pecked petroglyphs arranged in dense panels with depictions of people and animals, including gazelles, ostriches, antelope, possible oryx, goats, and bovids. The site, also known as Rohlfs Cave, sits in the middle of the Egyptian limestone plateau upon a more recent caravan route connecting Farafra Oasis to Asyut (see figure 7.1), a route that was probably also used in antiquity, since flint bifacial knives and circular scrapers show similarities in technique to contemporary Nilotic examples. Good flint sources would have made the area particularly attractive to Neolithic settlement. Archaeological surveys have established an occupation at Djara during the Middle Neolithic, from about 6500 to 5360 BC. Occupation at the specific site seems to have ended (though investigative work is ongoing), but it forms the core of a settlement area of 5 by 10 kilometers that may span the entire Neolithic Wet Phase.

The late Michael Hoffman (1979) argued for the interrelationships and importance of peoples living in the Sahara and especially the Red Sea Hills to the emergence of Pharaonic civilization. Robert Carneiro and Kathryn Bard (1989) have suggested more recently that the influx of people from Egypt's deserts during a period of hyperaridity in the Sahara around 3500 BC created densities of population and competition over scarcer resources that ultimately drove an accelerated cultural evolution toward complexity. Regardless, a number of links including artifact types, technological features, and artistic motifs suggest contacts between the Neolithic in the Western Desert and Predynastic, Naqada period Egypt, perhaps in a system of transhumance connected to the seasonal nature of the Neolithic Wet Phase (Kuper 1996; Wendorf, Close, and Schild 1992–1993; Wilkinson 2003). In particular, the remarkable discoveries by Fred Wendorf and his team in the Egyptian Nubian Sahara have engendered a new interest in the early contributions of pastoralists to the rise of the pharaohs. Excavation at key sites like Nabta Playa that date to the Neolithic Wet Phase revealed a highly sophisticated cattle culture with evidence for elaborate ritual practice, large-scale feasting, monolithic tomb construction, and astronomical "calculators" that pointed toward the circumpolar stars and may have helped with the timing of seasonal events. Wendorf and his collaborators suggest tentatively that the tighter, hierarchical organization that appears first as an adaptation to the sometimes unpredictable and dangerous conditions of these desert grasslands was ultimately transported to the Nile when the summer rains stopped and the grasslands retreated south. Toby Wilkinson (2003) echoes these arguments in support of an Eastern Desert origin for Pharaonic civilization, taking a somewhat uncritical and therefore problematic diffusionist stance, and curiously underplaying the importance of Saharan peoples (Smith 2004). Fekri Hassan (1997; cf. Frankfort 1948) adopts the most explicit ideological approach, noting early similarities between the imagery of desert rock art and Pharaonic royal and religious iconography.

CONCLUSIONS: DUAT AS DARK ZONE

> The cavern is opened for those who are in the Abyss, and those who are in the sunshine are released; the cavern is opened for Shu, and if he comes out, I will come out. I will go down into the earth-opening.... I will go down to my seat which is in the Bark of Re ... the great [one] who rises and shines in the waterway of the lake.
>
> The Book of Going Forth by Day
> (Faulkner 1990, 69)

As Holley Moyes (introduction, this volume) points out, the quality of light affects the ritual and mundane use of caves, whether they are natural or constructed. The Egyptians built ritual spaces that created light, twilight, and dark zones. In keeping with other cultures like the Maya, the dark zone, whether sanctuary or burial chamber, represented the most sacred and secret space—the Duat—where esoteric rituals before divine images or mummified bodies took place. In temples, twilight space represented a liminal zone between the mundane and the divine, where people could approach, petition, and adulate their gods. Theologically the imagery of the sun's journey through a cavernous Underworld corresponds to these built spaces. The penitents travel from light to twilight to darkness in order to approach their god. The dead travel from light to night when they descended into the tomb. The subterranean components of both royal and private tombs provide a direct analogy to the cavernous Duat. But the Ba of each of the deceased can fly back out of the dark and into the light, aided by the spell from the Book of Going Forth by Day. Similarly, the divine Ba emerges from the Duat to inhabit the divine statue each morning, and even exits the dark zone and comes into the light in processions during the great festivals that marked Egypt's religious calendar.

What was the origin of this dark-zone symbolism? Natural caves along the Nile were confined to twilight spaces—small, shallow caves and grottoes. Could the imagery of deep, sacred caves that became such a fundamental part of Egyptian mythology also have come from the Neolithic pastoralists who moved from the Sahara into the Nile valley? We can at least establish a tentative chain of connections, from Neolithic desert caves with associated motifs and artifacts that connect them to the Nile Valley, to the emergence of Pharaonic culture and the solar theology described above and coinciding with the end of the Neolithic Wet Phase, through pyramids and early temples, and on to the Valley of the Kings and the grand formal temples of the New Kingdom that provided portals into the Chamber of Secrets where Re journeyed during the night to be reborn again each morning.

REFERENCES CITED

Allen, James P. 1993. "Reading a Pyramid." *Bibliotheque d'Égypte* 106 (1): 5–28.

Almásy, László. 1936. *Recentes Explorations dans le Desert Libyque*. Cairo: Royal Geographical Society of Egypt.

Almásy, László. 1998. *Schwimmer in der Wüste: Auf der Suche nach der Oase Zarzura*. Munich: DTV.

Arnold, Dieter. 1997. "Royal Cult Complexes of the Old and Middle Kingdoms." In *Temples of Ancient Egypt*, ed. Byron E. Shafer, 31–85. Ithaca, NY: Cornell University Press.

Assmann, Jan. 1984. "Das Grab mit gewundenem Abstieg: Zum Typenwandel des Privatgrabes im Neuen Reich." *Mitteilungen des Deutschen archäologischen Instituts, Abteilung Kairo* 40: 277–90.

Assmann, Jan. 1989. "State and Religion in the New Kingdom." In *Religion and Philosophy in Ancient Egypt*, ed. William Kelley Simpson, 55–88. New Haven, CT: Yale University Press.

Assmann, Jan. 2001. *The Search for God in Ancient Egypt*. Trans. David Lorton. Ithaca, NY: Cornell University Press.

Assmann, Jan. 2002. *The Mind of Egypt: History and Meaning in the Time of the Pharaohs*. Trans Andrew Jenkins. New York: Metropolitan Books.

Assmann, Jan. 2003. *The Theban Necropolis: Past, Present, and Future*. Ed. Nigel Strudwick and John H. Taylor, 46–52. London: British Museum Press.

Bell, Lanny. 1997. "The New Kingdom 'Divine' Temple: The Example of Luxor." In *Temples of Ancient Egypt*, ed. Byron E. Shafer, 127–84. Ithaca, NY: Cornell University Press.

Breasted, James Henry. 1906. *Ancient Records of Egypt*, vol. 2: *The Eighteenth Dynasty*. Chicago: University of Chicago Press.

Carneiro, Robert, and Kathryn Bard. 1989. "Patterns of Predynastic Settlement Location, Social Evolution, and the Circumscription Theory." *Cahiers de Recherches de l'Institut de Papyrologie et d'Egyptologie de Lille* 11: 15–24.

Claßen, Erich, Karin Kindermann, Andreas Pastoors, and Heiko Riemer. 2001. "Djara 90/1-Felsbildhöhle und Fundplatz eines holozänen Gunstraums der Nordost-Sahara (Ägypten)." *Archäologisches Korrespondenzblatt* 31: 349–64.

Clayton, Peter. 1994. *Chronicle of the Pharaohs: The Reign-by-Reign Record of the Rulers and Dynasties of Ancient Egypt*. London: Thames and Hudson.

Dreyer, Günter. 1986. *Der Tempel der Satet: Die Funde der Frühzeit und des Alten Reiches*. Mainz am Rhein: Von Zabern.

Finnestad, Ragnhild B. 1997. "Temples of the Ptolemaic and Roman Periods: Ancient Traditions in New Contexts." In *Temples of Ancient Egypt*, ed. Byron E. Shafer, 185–238. Ithaca, NY: Cornell University Press.

Frankfort, Henri. 1948. *Kingship and the Gods: A Study of Ancient Near Eastern Religion as the Integration of Society & Nature*. Chicago: University of Chicago Press.

Hassan, Fekri. 1997. "Primeval Goddess to Divine King." In *The Followers of Horus: Studies Dedicated to Michael Allen Hoffman*, ed. Renée Friedman and Barbara Adams, 307–22. Oxford: Oxbow.

Hawass, Zahi. 2005. *The Osiris Shaft*. Electronic Document. http://www.guardians.net/hawass/osiris1.htm, accessed August 31, 2005.

Hinkel, Friedrich W. 1979. *The Archaeological Map of the Sudan II: The Area of the South Libyan Desert*. Berlin: Akademie Verlag.

Hoffman, Michael A. 1979. *Egypt before the Pharaohs: The Prehistoric Foundations of Egyptian Civilization*. New York: Knopf.

Hornung, Erik. 1990. *The Valley of the Kings: Horizon of Eternity*. Trans. David Warburton. New York: Timkin.

Hornung, Erik. 1992. *Idea into Image: Essays on Ancient Egyptian Thought*. Trans. Elizabeth Bredeck. New York: Timkin.

Hornung, Erik. 1999. *The Ancient Egyptian Books of the Afterlife*. Trans. David Lorton. Ithaca, NY: Cornell University Press.

Kemp, Barry J. 1989. *Ancient Egypt: Anatomy of a Civilization*. London: Routledge.

Kitchen, Kenneth A. 1990. *Pharaoh Triumphant: The Life and Times of Ramesses II*. Cairo: American University in Cairo Press.

Kuper, Rudolf, ed. 1989. *Forschungen zur Umweltgeschichte der Ostsahara: Africa Praehistorica 2*. Cologne: Heinrich Barth Institut.

Kuper, Rudolf. 1996. "Between the Oases and the Nile—Djara: Rohlfs' Cave in the Western Desert." In *Interregional Contacts in the Later Prehistory of Northeastern Africa*, ed. Lech Krzyzaniak, Karla Kroeper, and Michal Kobusiewicz, 81–91. Studies in African Archaeology 5. Poznan: Poznan Archaeological Museum.

Kuper, Rudolf, and Stefan Kröpelin. 2006. "Climate-Controlled Holocene Occupation in the Sahara: Motor of Africa's Evolution." *Science* 313, no. 5788 (August 11): 803–7. http://dx.doi.org/10.1126/science.1130989. Medline:16857900.

Lehner, Mark. 1997. *The Complete Pyramids*. London: Thames and Hudson.

Lichtheim, Miriam. 1980. *Ancient Egyptian Literature III: The Late Period*. Berkeley: University of California Press.

Martin, Geoffrey T. 1991. *The Hidden Tombs of Memphis: New Discoveries from the Time of Tutankhamun and Ramesses the Great*. London: Thames and Hudson.

Ondaatje, Michael. 1992. *The English Patient*. New York: Knopf.

Piankoff, Alexandre. 1955. *The Shrines of Tut-Ankh-Amon*. Ed. N. Rambova. Bollingen series 40:2; Egyptian Religious Texts and Representations 2. New York: Pantheon Books.

Piankoff, Alexandre. 1964. *The Litany of Re*. Bollingen series 40:4; Egyptian Religious Texts and Representations 4. New York: Pantheon Books.

Rhotert, Hans. 1952. *Libysche Felsbilder: Ergebnisse der XI und XII Deutschen Inner-afrikanischen Forschungs-Expedition (DIAFE) 1933/1934/1935*. Darmstadt: Wittich.

Robichon, Clément, and A. Varille. 1940. *Description sommaire du temple primitif de Médamoud: Recherches d'archéologie, de philologie et d'histoire, t. 11*. Cairo: l'Institut français d'archéologie orientale.

Rothenberg, Benno. 1972. *Were These King Solomon's Mines? Excavations in the Timna Valley*. London: Thames and Hudson.

Schön, Werner. 1994. "The Late Neolithic of Wadi el Akhdar (Gilf Kebir) and the Eastern Sahara." *Archéologie du Nil moyen* 6: 131–75.

Seyfried, Karl-Joachim. 1987. "Entwicklung in der Grabarchitektur des Neuen Reichs al seine weiterer Quelle für theologische Konzeptionen der Ramessidenzeit." In *Problems and Priorities in Egyptian Archaeology*, ed. Jan Assmann, G. Burkhard, and Vivian Davies, 219–254. London: Keagan-Paul.

Seyfried, Karl-Joachim. 1998. "Kammern, Nischen und Passagen in Fels gräbern des Neuen Reiches." In *Stationen, Festschrift R. Stadelmann*, ed. Heika Guksch and Daniel Polz, 389–406. Mainz am Rhein: Von Zabern.

Shedid, Abdel Ghaffar. 1994. *Die Felsgraäber von Beni Hassan in Mittelägypten*. Zaberns Bildbände zur Archäologie 16. Mainz am Rhein: Von Zabern.

Smith, Stuart Tyson. 2003. *Wretched Kush: Ethnic Identities and Boundaries in Egypt's Nubian Empire*. London: Routledge.

Smith, Stuart Tyson. 2004. "Review of Genesis of the Pharaohs by Toby Wilkinson." *American Journal of Archaeology* 108: 284–5.

Thatcher, Oliver J., ed. 1907. *The Library of Original Sources*, vol. 1: *The Ancient World*. Milwaukee: University Research Extension Co.

Valbelle, Dominique, and Charles Bonnet. 1996. *Le sanctuaire d'Hathor maîtress de la turquoise: Sérabit el-Khadim au Moyen Empire*. Paris: Picard.

Weeks, Kent. 2004. *Anatomy of a Tomb: Modern Tomb Designations*. Electronic Document. http://www.thebanmappingproject.com/articles/article_4.4a_1.html, accessed August 23, 2005.

Wendorf, Fred, Angela E. Close, and Romuald Schild. 1992–1993. "Megaliths in the Egyptian Sahara." *Sahara* 5 (1992–1993): 7–16.

Wilkinson, Richard H. 2000. *The Complete Temples of Ancient Egypt*. New York: Thames and Hudson.

Wilkinson, Toby. 2003. *Genesis of the Pharaohs: Dramatic New Discoveries Rewrite the Origins of Ancient Egypt*. London: Thames and Hudson.

Winkler, Hans A. 1939. *The Rock Drawings of Southern Upper Egypt II*. London: Egypt Exploration Society.

Zboray, András. 2003. "New Rock Art Findings at Jebel Uweinat and the Gilf Kebir." *Sahara* 14: 111–27.

Zboray, András. 2004. "Rock Art Finds on the 'Hassanein Plateau,' Jebel Uweinat." *Sahara* 15: 134–6.

8

Caves as Sacred Spaces on the Tibetan Plateau

Mark Aldenderfer

Caves—both natural and created by excavation—are common on the Tibetan plateau. Although the beginnings of cave use on the plateau are currently unknown, caves became especially important with the advent of Buddhism in the seventh century AD. Today, caves continue to be used in both secular and sacred contexts. In this chapter, although my focus is primarily upon the use of caves within a religious or ritual context, it is necessary to identify and define the material indicators of caves used primarily as dwellings or habitations. Using historical, literary, and anthropological warrants, I then turn to a discussion of why some caves have sacred connotations on the plateau. Finally, I examine two specific manifestations of the sacred: the use of caves as symbolic foundations for temples, shrines, and so-called power places, and the meaning and use of caves within the context of pilgrimage.

CAVES: CONSTRUCTED AND NATURAL

There are natural caves on the plateau, especially in the karstic zone in central Tibet near Lhasa (figure 8.1). Many, but not all, of these caves have natural dark zones and extensive subterranean chambers. A large number of these natural caves were used in the past as well as today in the practice of Tibetan Buddhism. But by far, most caves on the plateau are better described as chambers and have been excavated by people. Many of these chambers are small and simple, and consist of a single room. Others are far more complex and are connected by shafts, passageways, and tunnels. These more complex chambers can be said to have dark zones in the sense that most have no way for natural light to enter. Chambers are used for both secular and religious purposes. In still other instances, rockshelter-like locations have been turned into chambers by the addition of rock walls designed to enclose the natural space more completely. To avoid confusion, in this chapter I use the term *chamber* to describe excavated caves, and will reserve the term *cave* for natural landscape features that have true dark zones.

THE ANTIQUITY OF CAVE USE ON THE TIBETAN PLATEAU

Unfortunately, data regarding the use of caves in prehistory on the plateau are essentially nonexistent. Although anecdotal information about the presence of lithic materials in caves in the Lhasa area has been reported, none of these materials has been described in a systematic manner. This situation is not surprising since archaeological research on the plateau only began in earnest in the late 1970s, and most of what has been done has focused upon later, usually Buddhist, eras of prehistory and history (Aldenderfer and Zhang 2004).

Although John Bellezza (1997, 2001, 2002) asserts that many of the caves and chambers he has documented

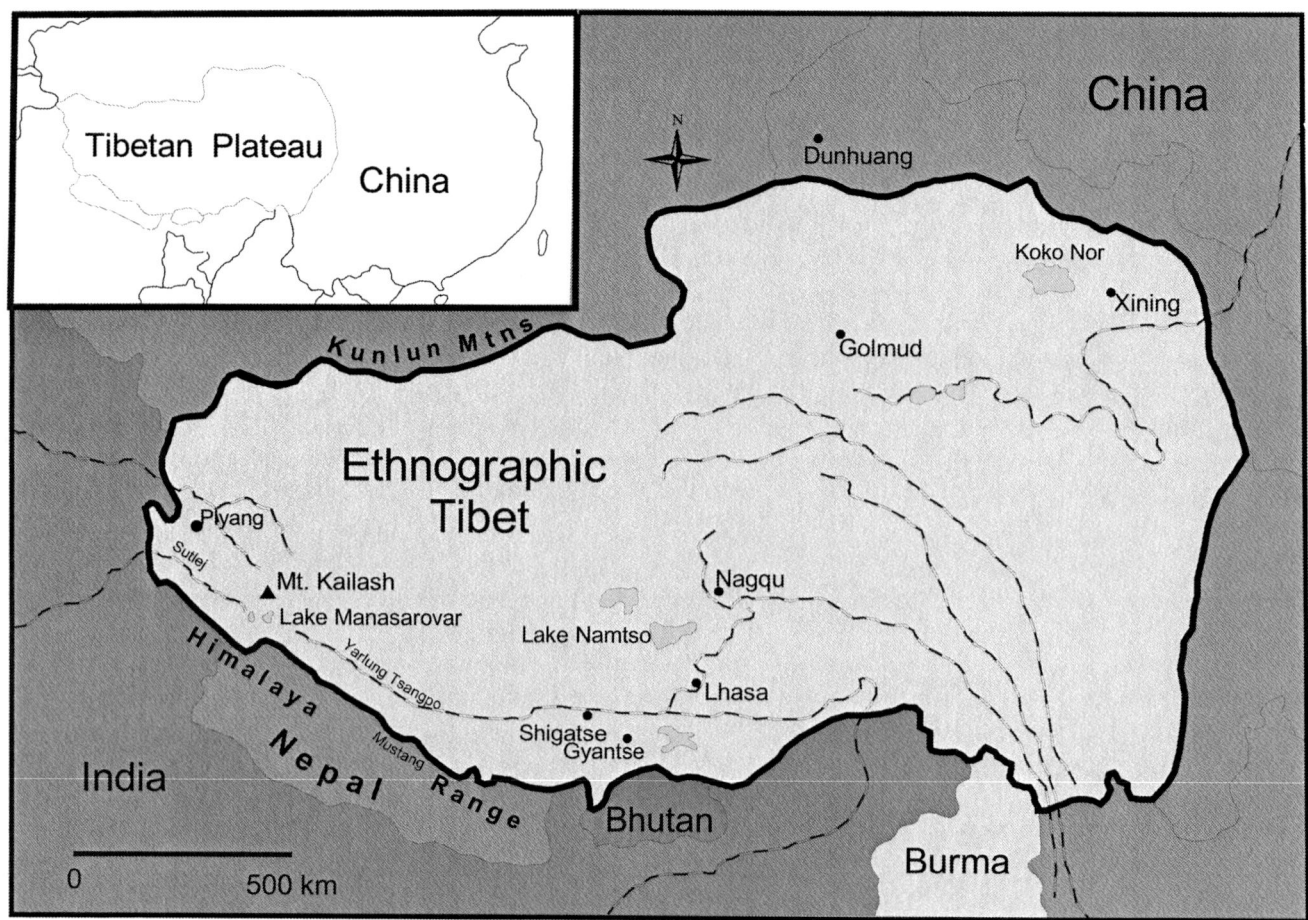

FIGURE 8.1 Ethnographic Tibet. (Map drawn by Holley Moyes.)

in northern Tibet on the Chang Tang were occupied in pre-Buddhist times, he is able to offer only indirect support for his hypothesis by using the oral traditions of modern inhabitants and undated rock art. No archaeological research has been done in any of these sites, so his contentions, while plausible, remain unverified. Research on the southern margin of the plateau offers some insights into what might be expected to be discovered in some Tibetan chambers. Data have been recovered by the Nepal-German Project on High Mountain Archaeology sponsored by the Institute of Prehistory and Early History (Institut für Ur- und Frühgeschichte) of the University of Cologne. The project was conducted in the Upper Mustang district in the Kaligandaki and Muktinath Valley systems during the late 1980s and early 1990s. At three major sites—Chokhopani, Mebrak, and Phuzdeling—the project recovered cultural materials ranging in date from approximately 1200 BCE to the present (Alt et al. 2003; Simons and Schön 1998; Simons, Schön, and Shrestha 1994a, 1994b). They dated a number of contexts from these sites, and tentatively identified six occupational periods: Chokhopani (1200–450 BC), Mebrak (450 BC–AD 100), Third (AD 200–700), Fourth (AD 900–1450), Fifth (AD 1450–1600), and Sixth (AD 1600-present). Chambers, all quarried, were used as mortuary facilities in the Chokhopani, Mebrak, and Third periods, while in the Fourth and Fifth periods chambers were used exclusively as dwellings. Modern, post–AD 1600 use is sporadic at best, and reflects storage and temporary shelter.

In periods of the most intensive utilization, the chambers form complexes that dot the cliff faces above the valley floor. Many of these chambers could only be reached by rope, ladders, or external staircases, but others could be accessed by complex tunnels that led to lower-elevation entrances. Dwellings consisted of chambers with multiple rooms connected by vertical and horizontal passages. Some of these chambers had mud-brick walls within them that created rooms. Mortuary chambers contained significant quantities of ceramics, wooden artifacts, and metal, as well as human remains. These chambers were also connected by tunnels and shafts. One chamber (Mebrak 63) dating to the Mebrak phase is of particular interest. It was most likely a community mortuary facility that housed more than thirty mummified human remains on bedlike wood coffins, as well as the remains of mummified domesticated animals. Furs, textiles, ceramics, wooden objects, and other artifacts were found with the dead. An attempt was made to recover DNA from the human remains, but despite the excellent preservation conditions, the DNA was contaminated and degraded by bird droppings. However, an analysis of skeletal remains led the team who discovered the cave to label the remains as ethnically Mongolian, suggesting an origin from the central Asian plains (Alt et al. 2003, 1533).

The chambers of Upper Mustang offer a useful model for what may be encountered when research is directed toward chamber systems on the plateau. Very similar, probably pre-Buddhist chamber systems are known primarily from far western Tibet in the modern province of Ngari along the Sutlej (Langchen Kebab) River and its tributary systems. These systems are often ascribed to a "Bon" or pre-Buddhist cultural tradition by local inhabitants and monks resident in nearby monasteries. Like the situation on the Chang Tang, direct evidence for such an affiliation remains speculative at best. However, archaeologists should be prepared to find both dwellings and mortuary facilities when these sites are finally examined in detail.

CAVES AND CHAMBERS AS DWELLINGS OR HABITATIONS

Much more is known about cave and chamber use after the seventh century AD. Buddhism was introduced onto the plateau at this time, and was sponsored first by a series of secular rulers of the expanding Tibetan empire who moved to establish it as one of a number of competing court religions. Over the next 200 years, Buddhism became the dominant form of religious practice on the plateau and was extensively and lavishly sponsored by secular rulers at all levels. Numerous temples, monasteries, and other religious complexes were built, and many of these attracted large numbers of lay and religious followers who required housing. Depending on local conditions, chambers were the favored type of habitation in many instances.

A good example of the quarrying of chambers for dwellings can be found at Piyang, a temple and monastic complex in far western Tibet (Aldenderfer 2001). The first construction at Piyang was a simple chapel built in the late tenth century AD as a part of the resurgence of Buddhism following its decline in the middle of the eighth century AD. Within 30 years, a temple was constructed, and a small community of monks was present (Aldenderfer 2008). These monks lived in small chambers quarried from the soft conglomerate rock of the region (figure 8.2a). Although some of these had multiple rooms, most were

FIGURE 8.2 (a) Monastic habitation caves near Old Piyang, far western Tibet. (b) Interior of one of the monastic habitation caves at Old Piyang. (Photographs by Mark Aldenderfer.)

simple and consisted of a single room, a series of shelves, basins for the storage of fuel, and a firepit or hearth (figure 8.2b). Some chambers were even simpler, consisting of a single room and small surface hearth in the center of the structure. Almost no cultural material is found in such monastic chambers, which is consistent with the ascetic life that monks were enjoined to follow.

In contrast, chambers created by secular peoples tend to be far more complex. Once Piyang was established as a major ritual center by the twelfth century AD, large numbers of people were attracted to it, and over the next 300 years, more than 1,500 secular dwellings were dug into a mesa to the west of the monastic complex (figure 8.3). Some were used as storage facilities while others had kitchens and sleeping areas. Many had multiple rooms, as many as six in the most complex, and some were networked by tunnels and, presumably, ladders. These complexes are often full of quotidian debris, including broken ceramics, food remains, scraps of cloth, metal, and basketry, as well as raw materials such as wood and bone. Deep and extensive middens are

FIGURE 8.3 Piyang mesa, showing the large number of excavated caves. (Photograph by Mark Aldenderfer.)

often found below the mouths of these chambers. Such systems are common through western Tibet. Although details of construction are different, as are the contents, they are similar to those seen used in the Fourth and Fifth periods of Upper Mustang when Tibetan-speaking peoples are known to have occupied this region.

A special kind of dwelling or habitation spans the boundary between the sacred and the secular—the hermitage. Hermitages are places where lamas, yogis, monks, and other holy figures resided for a period of time, engaging in meditation. Although the notion of a hermitage conjures up a sense of isolation and avoidance, there is surprising variability in their placement upon the landscape and in details of their construction. Some hermitages are truly isolated and are found on almost inaccessible cliff faces and mountain peaks. Others, however, are found near or even within monastic complexes. A hermitage may be situated in a place with an extraordinary viewshed of "empty sky" or "wilderness." But others may be in locations suitable for closure, thus creating a dark interior space with no light permitted to enter. Some hermitages have small hearths that suggest the resident cooked food brought to the hermitage by local villagers. Others are simply stark, empty spaces that were exposed to light only when food was brought to the resident. Still others resemble relatively comfortable monastic dwellings. The hermitage, then, varied in its location, form, and contents according to the wishes of the resident as well as his style and motivation for reflection and meditation. This makes it difficult to distinguish hermitages from monastic residences.

A feature contained in some hermitages is a physical manifestation of one of its residents, such as a hand- or footprint. These are usually some sort of depression or irregularity in a surface feature of the wall, ceiling, or floor and are said to be created by the mystical powers of important religious figures as they touch these places and move about. Some such manifestations are often inadvertent, such as when a yogi or lama bumps his head on the ceiling, whereas others are said to be deliberately made to create a "power place" in that location. However, recognizing such manifestations is nearly impossible without some sort of historical documentation of the place or oral tradition that speaks to the event that created the manifestation in the first place.

WHAT MAKES A CAVE OR CHAMBER SACRED?

Two scholarly threads dominate our understanding of religious phenomena on the Tibetan plateau: the use of canonical Indic Buddhism and its extensive literature in both Sanskrit and Tibetan, and scholarship on what is deemed to reflect "indigenous" or "pre-Buddhist" religion. Not surprisingly, the canonical tradition has dominated much of this scholarship. Tibetan Buddhism has a vast and impressive literature, and it has been used over the course of the past 1,300 years to interpret both historical and contemporary religious practice. There is no question that modern Tibetans interpret much of their practice within Indic Buddhist metaphysical language. However, as Huber (1999a, 78) notes, the dominance of the canonical approach to the interpretation of Tibetan religious phenomena comes with a cost, that being the submersion of possible indigenous motivations and traces of origins of these practices.

The search for indigenous beliefs and practices takes two forms: the review of the extensive literature of Bon, and anthropological studies of contemporary forms of religious practice. Although contemporary Bon practice has elements of folk beliefs, it is better known from textual sources as a more structured, heterodox, and ecclesiastical form of religious practice that at least today shows marked affinities to Tibetan Buddhism (Karmay and Watt 2007; Kvaerne 1985; Samuel 1993; Tucci 1988). Kvaerne (1995, 9–10) observes that Bon has at least three general meanings to Western scholars, the first of which is of interest to us here: it is said to be the indigenous, pre-Buddhist religion of Tibet, especially as regards its manifestation as the court religion of the early elites that came before the Yarlung clans that formed the nascent Tibetan empire in the seventh century AD. As such, much emphasis was placed upon burial rites, complex rituals, and animal sacrifice. The evidence for a deep antiquity of Bon resides primarily in texts and to a lesser extent in oral tradition. No archaeological evidence for Bon is widely accepted, although scholars such as John Bellezza (2001, 2002) have argued that many of the mortuary and village sites found on the Chang Tang (the northern part of the Tibetan plateau) reflect Bon religious traditions. More recently, I have evaluated the archaeological evidence for pre-Buddhist religious practice in far western Tibet (Aldenderfer 2011), and have arrived at the not-so-surprising conclusion that while pre-Buddhist religious architecture and other features dating to as early as 500 BC exist, it is not possible at this time to associate them with Bon. They are indigenous but they speak little about practice and belief.

Bon illustrative art does present the use of caves or possibly chambers by some of its key figures, notably Drenpa Namkha, a historical figure who contested the introduction of Buddhism into Tibet in the seventh century AD (Kvaerne 1995, 119; see also plate 43). Whether this is an indigenous representation of Bon tradition or a borrowing of Buddhist iconography is far from clear. Indeed, what little is known of the massive Bon literature does not privilege caves as special places on the landscape in a manner that is significantly different from that seen in the Indic Buddhist tradition (Henk Blezer, personal communication, 2007).

The anthropology of contemporary religious practice offers insights into a set of beliefs that appear to have a deep history on the plateau. Following Toni Huber's (1999a, 1999b) discussion of pilgrimage in Tibet, three terms are of relevance in the search for indigenous sacred warrants for caves: *gnas, sgrib*, and *byin. Gnas* (pronounced *né*) glosses as "place," but as Toni Huber (1999b, 91) and others, such as Katia Buffetrille (1998, 19), have noted, it has a more active sense of "abide." That is, landscape features, urban centers, monuments, and other physical features of the world are the "abodes" of spiritual power. This power may be associated with an animistic entity, spirits, or deities, but also, as I discuss below, with Buddhist traditions. *Sgrib* is a term variously glossed as "stain," "impurity," or "shadow." Sgrib is created by negative interactions with people, deities, and places that possess gnas, and must be cleansed by appropriate ritual action (Huber 1999b, 90). Finally, the term *byin* translates roughly into "blessing," or "empowerment" in the sense of personal power to overcome sgrib or other manifestations of personal impurity. Of note is that the term *byin* was used in the pre-Buddhist royal religious cult to denote the power and status of the divine king of this era (Huber 1999b, 90). This association suggests a deep antiquity of the concept in indigenous Tibetan worldview.

To purge the body (or mind) of sgrib, one must encounter a location that possesses gnas, or in Tibetan, a *gnas-chen*, which Huber (1999b, 91) labels a "power place." Actual physical locations become saturated with gnas, including plants, rocks, water, and other materials found associated with it, and to that end, a sufferer of sgrib seeks an encounter—a *gnas-mjal*—with a gnas-chen. This encounter is how Tibetans describe the process of pilgrimage, which is termed *gnas-khor* (Huber 1999b, 83). Byin is the empowerment of the individual that one receives from the encounter of gnas at the gnas-chen, resulting in the cleansing of sgrib.

In indigenous belief, a place becomes saturated with gnas by association with an animistic spirit, deities, or some other religious figure. As noted above, almost any landscape feature can become a gnas-chen. The most prominent of these gnas-chen landscape features are mountains. Much of what is described as indigenous religious practice on the plateau and the surrounding high Himalayan valleys today is associated with the veneration of various kinds of mountain deities (Blondeau 1998). Mountains have varied meanings, and over time these meanings were assimilated and absorbed into Tibetan Buddhist religious ideology and terminology. At the core, mountains were associated with clan divinities—*pho lha*—and their associated lineages. At a more regional level, such deities may represent territorial divinities—*yul lha*—that have responsibility for the protection of multiple valleys, villages, and regions. And as absorbed by Tibetan Buddhism, these deities become known as "Protectors of the doctrine," or *chos kyong* (Blondeau 1998, 9). Shrines are constructed near and on these mountains, and they are the scenes of pilgrimages at varying scales and ritual events.

Many caves and chambers are gnas-chen. Undoubtedly, some of these caves, especially those in central Tibet with extensive dark zones, such as the Guru Rinpoche Caves in the Yarlung Tsangpo Valley 30 kilometers southeast of Lhasa, or the Cave of the Subjugation of Mara in Lapchi of south-central Tibet, were gnas-chen before Buddhist connotations were overlaid upon them. Indeed, it is quite probable that many caves now associated with the activities of the founders of Buddhism on the plateau, especially those who were involved the subjugation of the "demons" of the indigenous religion, were important to the followers of Bon or whatever was the pre-Buddhist religion of the central plateau.

However, it remains the case that most caves and chambers on the plateau are directly associated with Indic Buddhist traditions and the yogis and scholars who brought Buddhism to the plateau. Barnes (1999, 119–20) notes that caves are of special interest to Buddhists, for it is within a cave that the historical Buddha meditated for 6 years in his search for enlightenment, which he achieved only after his emergence from it. In the Vinaya Pitaka, or the Book of Discipline for Buddhist monks, the historical Buddha observes that caves (as well as chambers or more informal shelters) are one of the suitable locations for habitation and meditation, thus underlining their importance in the Buddhist tradition. Indeed, many of the most important early Indian monastic communities were massive rock-cut cave complexes best represented by the Ajanta and Ellora sites.

The Guru Rinpoche cave complex illustrates this identification nicely. The caves in this complex range from small chambers that served as hermitage or meditation sites, to large, deep, and natural subterranean passageways that contain altars, statues, and wall paintings executed over the past 800 years. Guru Rinpoche, also known as Padmasambhava, was an Indian tantric master invited to Tibet in the eighth century AD by the Tibetan king Trisong Detsen. Tibetan Buddhist tradition relates that Guru Rinpoche was asked to subdue the demons of the plateau, thus preparing it for the establishment of Buddhism. Indeed, he is said to have created the caves of the complex as he pursued a demon. Using their magical powers, both tunneled through a sheer rock face, thus creating the labyrinthine caverns, until the demon was finally destroyed.

Caves and chambers may also obtain gnas by association with the "birth" or emanation of a powerful religious figure (Tucci 1988, 217). As noted above, Sakyamuni, the historical Buddha, sought enlightenment (*nirvana*) in a cave, and in a sense, was reborn through this process. Monks and lamas seeking nirvana have emulated this tradition for centuries, and their meditation caves, especially those of the most famous, are saturated with gnas. These caves are often revisited by later generations of yogis and monks who wish to absorb the gnas of these places to assist them toward their goals. These caves thus take on genealogies based on these historical traditions.

CAVES AND CHAMBERS AS SYMBOLIC FOUNDATIONS

Caves and chambers often serve as foundational elements of major temple and monastic complexes. For example, the Potala Palace, one of Tibet's most sacred sites and the winter residence of the Dalai Lamas, is said to have been founded upon a meditation cave used by Songsten Gampo, the first Buddhist king of Tibet. His presence there created a gnas-chen. Although there is a hagiographic tone to this story, it illustrates nicely the way in which a natural landscape feature is believed to possess gnas, and how this association is then used to justify the placement of monuments on the landscape. This has clear connections to Tibetan theories of geomancy, which rely in part upon understanding the presence, distribution, and potency of gnas on the landscape (Mills 2007; Stutchbury 1999).

Lamayuru in Ladakh is an example of a more humble but still important Tibetan Buddhist temple and monastery. It is built around the reputed (but not verified) meditation cave of Naropa, an Indian tantric master who was the guru of Marpa, one of the major Tibetan translators of the Dharma and one of the founders of the Kagyupa tradition (Vanquaille and Vets 2003, 87). It is said that before the complex was constructed, the cave was a stop on the pilgrimage route of this part of Ladakh. This leads us to a consideration of the relationship of caves and pilgrimage.

CAVES, CHAMBERS, AND PILGRIMAGE

According to Toni Huber (1999a, 12), there is no direct or compelling evidence from the Tibetan plateau for "any ancient ritual form resembling pilgrimage as we know it existed before the systematic introduction of Indian Buddhism." Indian Buddhism, of course, has a long and well-established tradition of pilgrimage that was sanctioned by the historical Buddha himself, who advocated pilgrimage to four important sites: Lumbini, his birthplace; Bodhgaya, the place of his enlightenment; Sarnath, where he delivered his first sermon; and Kusinara, where he died (San 2001). Once Buddhism was established on the plateau, however, pilgrimage became an essential element of ritual practice. The best-known pilgrimage journey (or *khora*) is that to Mt. Kailash in far western Tibet, and every devout Tibetan is enjoined to complete one visit to, and circuit around, the mountain in his or her lifetime. Many other mountains on the plateau are major pilgrimage sites, as are Lhasa and other major centers of Buddhist thought and practice (Huber 1999a).

Contemporary Tibetan pilgrims describe their motivations for pilgrimage in terms of canonical Indic Buddhism: the journey is undertaken to obtain merit (Sanskrit: *punya*) so as to obtain a more favorable rebirth in the cycle of life (Sanskrit: *samsara*), with the eventual goal of achieving liberation from this cycle (Sanskrit: *nirvana*) (Huber 1999a, 12). However, this motivation can also be expressed in terms of gnas and the journey to a gnas-chen to obtain a blessing for the cleansing of impurity or stain. That is, while pilgrims may use terms from Indian Buddhism to describe their motivations, their practice is deeply rooted in indigenous conceptions of the sacred for Tibetans. Thus caves and chambers, as potential gnas-chen, may be fixtures on a pilgrimage route. It is important to stress, however, that many such journeys may be more local when compared to the major pilgrimage cycles to sacred mountains or other holy sites. In other words, pilgrims may be seeking encounter—gnas-mjel—with the gnas-chen.

Caves and chambers, particularly those with narrow passageways or entrances, are especially significant places both as freestanding gnas-chen and as important features of pilgrimage destinations. Pilgrims are enjoined to try to get their bodies through these tight squeezes. Huber (1999a, 233n28) likens this process to *bardo tranglam*, which is in Tibetan religion the perilous state between death and rebirth. The successful passage through the squeeze predicts a successful rebirth for the virtuous (figure 8.4).

FIGURE 8.4 Holley Moyes, negotiating a narrow crevice used to gauge merit toward a good rebirth along the khora (pilgrimage) around Ganden monastery. Such squeezes are used in caves for similar purposes. (Photograph by Mark Aldenderfer.)

Many of the largest pilgrimage caves, especially those associated with very significant or important lamas, yogis, or other religious figures, have substantial architecture embellishments. Some have whole temples constructed within them, while other have various types of structures, most typically *chortens* (reliquaries) or incense burners,

FIGURE 8.5 An altar within a cave temple at Dungkar, far western Tibet. Note the offerings left behind. (Photograph by Holley Moyes.)

placed at their entrances. Constructions of this kind were created by wealthy monastic institutions or lay patrons. Aside from architectural components, many cave temple-complexes are believed to be the sites of "hidden treasures" placed there by saints and yogis. Sometimes these treasures are real objects, such as texts, but may also be "jewels of realization" or insight into the nature of reality. Hermitages may also contain such treasures.

One of the most interesting outcomes of pilgrimage to any gnas-chen, including caves, is the removal of material from the location, and the discard of some personal object or other offering at the site. As Huber (1999a, 15–16) notes, pilgrims will take earth, stones, bits of vegetation, and other materials from a gnes-chen since it is understood that they are saturated with power. These items are taken back to the pilgrim's residence, where they can be transformed into objects, such as *tsa-tsa* (clay medallions),

embedded in the foundation of a new house, or placed on the family altar. Monasteries also recover items from gnas-chen, and there is a formal economy of these items that are bought and exchanged by individuals seeking special benefits from specific locations. Pilgrims often leave personal objects behind at gnas-chen, such as articles of clothing, glasses, shoes, bank notes, coins, and other similar objects. So doing creates a personal relationship with the source of the gnas at the location (figure 8.5).

CONCLUDING REMARKS

This brief examination has shown that caves and chambers have a special meaning in the sacred geography of the Tibetan plateau. It appears that this appreciation has a deep but as yet unverified antiquity. Although Indian Buddhism overlies much of the historical and modern discourse on the use of caves and chambers, there is a strong and detectable signature of the indigenous that offers an alternative interpretation of their meaning within Tibetan religious and ritual practice. The concept of gnas—to abide—connects physical locations on the landscape to autochthonous spirit entities that may provide protection or benefit to the individual who seeks them out. Landscape features, in this case caves, are not simply symbols of these entities, but the abode of their immanence, and their power pervades their surroundings.

This indigenous understanding is reinforced by the traditions of Indian Buddhism. Instead of spirit entities, we see that caves and chambers, as they are used by lamas, yogis, teachers, and powerful secular rulers, take on ancient roles and obtain gnas within the Buddhist tradition. These sites become venues for pilgrimage and take on genealogies of the prominent sages who used them.

It can be argued that caves and chambers are no more special than other landscape features, such as mountains, lakes, rivers, and boulders. This may be true, but there seems to be no question that there is a kind of chthonic sensibility within Tibetan religious traditions of all kinds. Caves are places of origin, and powerful spirits and religious artifacts emerge from them. Although this has yet to be demonstrated via text or excavation, given their association with origins, it is likely that they may well serve secular ends as ways in which landholding groups may assert lineage and identity. It is not that caves or chambers are likely to be owned, but they may, like sacred mountains, be associated with human-built places on the landscape and the social groups that lived within them.

We also have seen that caves serve a powerful foundational role. Richard Bradley (2000, 104) asks, "What do monuments do to the places where they are built?" With regard to caves and chambers on the plateau, one might reverse the question slightly and ask, "How do caves influence the nature of monument construction and how do monuments evolve around them?" This ties in nicely with ideas like geomancy and how landscapes are conceived by those who live upon them. Caves, chambers, and their gnas provide powerful arguments for the creation of monuments in them and near them, either to glorify the memory of the place or to control access to it and the benefits that the power places offer. Caves and chambers on the Tibetan plateau, then, are tied closely and intimately to memory, identity, and religious sensibility. Further work will serve to deepen our understanding of these special places, and help to gauge the antiquity of these practices and beliefs.

REFERENCES CITED

Aldenderfer, Mark S. 2001. "Piyang: A 10th/11th C A.D. Tibetan Buddhist Temple and Monastic Complex in Far Western Tibet." *Archaeology, Ethnology & Anthropology of Eurasia* 4 (8): 138–46.

Aldenderfer, Mark S. 2008. "On Text, Materiality, and the Tibetan Buddhist Religious Architecture at Piyang: 900–1500 CE." In *Religion in the Material World*, ed. Lars Fogelin, 339–58. Carbondale: Center for Archaeological Investigations, Southern Illinois University.

Aldenderfer, Mark S. 2011. "The Material Correlates of Religious Practice in Far Western Tibet: 500 BCE–500 CE." In *Emerging Bob: The Formation of Bon Traditions in Tibet at the Turn of the First Millennium AD, PIATS 2006; Tibetan Studies*, ed. Henk W.A. Blezer, 13–33. Halle: International Institute of Tibetan and Buddhist Studies.

Aldenderfer, Mark S., and Zhang Yinong. 2004. "The Prehistory of the Tibetan Plateau to the Seventh Century AD: Perspectives and Research from China and the West since 1950." *Journal of World Prehistory* 18 (1): 1–55. http://dx.doi.org/10.1023/B:JOWO.0000038657.79035.9e.

Alt, K., J. Burger, A. Simons, W. Schön, G. Grupe, S. Hummel, B. Grosskopf, W. Vach, C. Téllez, C.-H. Fischer, et al. 2003. "Climbing into the Past—First Himalayan Mummies Discovered in Nepal." *Journal of Archaeological Science* 30 (11): 1529–35. http://dx.doi.org/10.1016/S0305-4403(03)00056-6.

Barnes, Gina. 1999. "Buddhist Landscapes of East Asia." In *Archaeologies of Landscape*, ed. Wendy Ashmore and A. Bernard Knapp, 101–23. London: Blackwell.

Bellezza, John. 1997. *Divine Dyads: Ancient Civilization in Tibet*. Dharamsala: Library of Tibetan Works and Archives.

Bellezza, John. 2001. *Antiquities of Northern Tibet, Pre-Buddhist Archeological Discoveries on the High Plateau, Findings of the Changthang Circuit Expedition, 1999*. Delhi: Adroit Publishers.

Bellezza, John. 2002. *Antiquities of Upper Tibet: Pre-Buddhist Archaeological Sites on the High Plateau; Findings of the Upper Tibet Circumnavigation Expedition 2000*. Delhi: Adroit Publishers.

Blondeau, Anne-Marie. 1998. "Foreword." In *Tibetan Mountain Deities: Their Cults and Representations*, ed. Anne-Marie Blondeau, 1–9. Vienna: Verlag de Österreichischen Akademie der Wissenschaften.

Bradley, Richard. 2000. *An Archaeology of Natural Places*. London: Routledge.

Buffetrille, Katia. 1998. "Reflections on Pilgrimages to Sacred Mountains, Lakes, and Caves." In *Pilgrimage in Tibet*, ed. Alex McKay, 18–34. Richmond, Surrey, UK: Curzon.

Huber, Toni. 1999a. *The Cult of Pure Crystal Mountain: Popular Pilgrimage and Visionary Landscape in Southeast Tibet*. New York: Oxford University Press.

Huber, Toni. 1999b. "Putting the *Gnas* Back into *Gnas-khor*: Rethinking Tibetan Pilgrimage Practice." In *Sacred Spaces and Powerful Places in Tibetan Culture: A Collection of Essays*, ed. Toni Huber, 77–104. Dharamasla: Library of Tibetan Works and Archives.

Karmay, Samten, and Jeff Watt, eds. 2007. *Bon: The Magic Word*. New York: Rubin Museum of Art.

Kvaerne, Per. 1985. *The Bön Religion: A Death Ritual of the Tibetan Bön pos*. Leiden: Brill.

Kvaerne, Per. 1995. *The Bön Religion of Tibet: The Iconography of a Living Tradition*. London: Serindia.

Mills, Martin A. 2007. "Re-Assessing the Supine Demoness: Royal Buddhist Geomancy in the Srong btsan sgam po Mythology."

Journal of the International Association of Tibetan Studies 3: 1–47. http://www.thlib.org/collections/texts/jiats/#!jiats=/03/mills/.

Samuel, Geoffrey. 1993. *Civilized Shamans: Buddhism in Tibetan Societies*. Washington, DC: Smithsonian Institution Press.

San, Chan Khoon. 2001. *Buddhist Pilgrimage*. Kuala Lumpur, Malaysia: Buddha Dharma Education Association.

Simons, Angela, and Werner Schön. 1998. "Cave Systems and Terrace Settlements in Mustang, Nepal: Settlement Periods from Prehistoric Times up to the Present Day." *Beitrage zur Allgemeinen und Vergleichenden Archaeologie* 18: 27–47.

Simons, Angela, Werner Schön, and Sukra Shrestha. 1994a. "Preliminary Report on the 1992 Campaign of the Institute of Prehistory of the University of Cologne." *Ancient Nepal* 136: 51–75.

Simons, Angela, Werner Schön, and Sukra Shrestha. 1994b. "The Prehistoric Settlement of Mustang: First Results of the 1993 Archaeological Investigations in Cave Systems and Connected Ruined Sites." *Ancient Nepal* 137: 93–129.

Stutchbury, Elizabeth. 1999. "Perceptions of Landscape in Karzha: 'Sacred' Geography and the Tibetan System of 'Geomancy.'" In *Sacred Spaces and Powerful Place in Tibetan Culture: A Collection of Essays*, ed. Toni Huber, 154–86. Dharamasla: Library of Tibetan Works and Archives.

Tucci, Giuseppe. 1988. *The Religions of Tibet*. Berkeley: University of California Press.

Vanquaille, Amandus, and Hilde Vets. 2003. "Lamayuru: The Symbolic Architecture of Light." In *Sacred Landscapes of the Himalaya*, ed. Niels Gutschow, Axel Michaels, Charles Ramble, and Ernst Steinkeller, 85–94. Vienna: Austrian Academy of Sciences Press.

9

Differential Australian Cave and Rockshelter Use during the Pleistocene and Holocene

Paul S.C. Taçon, Wayne Brennan, Matthew Kelleher, and Dave Pross

Many researchers have noted local changes in cave and rockshelter use in different parts of Australia from the Late Pleistocene to the Middle and Late Holocene. In many parts of the country rockshelters in more-remote and/or less-accessible locations were adorned with rock art in the Pleistocene, while in the Holocene more-accessible shelters were frequently chosen for art making and for occupation. In southern Australia, deep caves such as those found on the Nullarbor were visited primarily in the Pleistocene. Many were abandoned in the Holocene, and in ethnographic times there were prohibitions against venturing deep inside. In many parts of Australia, rockshelters were used as burial or secondary-burial sites in the Holocene, sometimes in conjunction with occupation and rock-art activity, but surviving Pleistocene burials are mostly from outside caves and shelters. This chapter argues that the changes in cave and rockshelter use are not simply a reflection of the taphonomic record or environmental change. Rather it was social processes and new forms of social interaction that most likely led to new ways of relating to landscapes and places of stone.

A FASCINATION WITH CAVES

What is it about caves? Why are we, our ancestors, and people worldwide so attracted to them? Were they places where special forms of art and ritual were practiced? Were they centers of ancient religions, places of worship, burial sites, and/or landscape locations where one could most easily enter into some supernatural world? How did activities within caves and rockshelters differ from those outside? And what differences in the archaeological record are there between different parts of caves? Did cave and rockshelter use change over time in various locations or have people always related to such rocky and subterranean locations in similar ways? This chapter examines the use of caves by Aboriginal Australians, not only to provide some recent ethnographic insight but also to demonstrate long-term change in relationships to place. But before this is discussed in detail it is important to be aware of biases in archaeological research, the impact of taphonomic forces on the archaeological record, and other factors that might influence interpretation.

According to most dictionaries, a cave is essentially a hollow in the earth, especially one opening horizontally into a hill or mountain, though caves can also open vertically, through shafts. The key is that they are usually relatively deep in comparison to rockshelters, and it is this quality that almost universally makes them special and/or sacred landscape features. But as many authors in this volume emphasize, there are other types of places—such as water bodies, mountain peaks, and even woodland or forest groves—that are also sacred for some peoples, and this is certainly widespread in Aboriginal Australia (see

Taçon 1999 for a review). What is similar among all these places is that they represent limen, or a break from the surrounding mundane environment (see Kelleher 2003). However, caves represent a special type of limen because they are inside rather than on or outside of the earth. This womblike quality appears to have conjured up similar notions among many different peoples widely separated in time and space. In this sense, it is interesting to note the somewhat narrow range of human responses to caves and other geographic features, as the chapters of this volume attest. It is also important to keep in mind that in many parts of Australia and in many other parts of the world (especially southern Africa) rockshelters were often seen as openings into other worlds, as evidenced by both oral history and certain forms of rock-art imagery (e.g., Lewis-Williams and Dowson 1990; Taçon and Ouzman 2004). Rock art, rockshelters, and cave entrances were also used as "signposts," "beacons," and meeting places when journeying across country.

An essential aspect of caves to note in any discussion of their meaning and use is the nature or quality of darkness. The intense darkness of a cave enhances its ability to isolate or separate the occupants of the cave from other parts of the environment. Thus it is important for cave research to distinguish between caves and rockshelters and to specify the quality of the light. Unfortunately, this is rarely done, and in many archaeological reports the term *cave* is often used for something more properly described as a *rockshelter*. Another concern is that there is a bias in the archaeological record toward the excavation of rockshelters and caves rather than nearby open sites (see Attenbrow 2004, 111–12 for the Sydney region). "While rockshelters offer a bonanza for archaeologists, they were not necessarily commonly used camp sites. In some desert areas rockshelters were normally used only during rain or dust storms, and over a period of thousands of years visited only occasionally" (Mulvaney and Kamminga 1999, 23).

This is true not only of Australia but also of the world in general, leading to the misleading impression that ancient and some recent peoples spent much, if not most, of their time in rocky areas, often in caves and rockshelters. Indeed, early finds of art in the deep caves of Europe as well as stone tools and skeletal remains of Neanderthal led to a "cave man" mythology that is very much alive today, with expression in cartoons, books, movies, and many other media. Of course, much of our interpretation of the past has resulted from the excavation of such places, as well as recordings of the symbolic marks or "art" that people left behind. But what we find in caves and shelters is only a small part of the picture. As noted by Mulvaney and Kamminga (1999, 23), "There is a common misconception about prehistoric cave occupancy. As a general rule, Aborigines did not live in the deep and dark recesses of caves, but camped at the entrance and only ventured into the passages for special purposes."

Recent work in the Keep River region of northern Australia, for instance, has highlighted significant differences between the nature and age of deposits outside rockshelters and those within. Deposits outside are often deeper, older, and richer, suggesting people situated themselves outside but near shelters much of the time (Ward 2004; Ward et al. 2006), and ventured in for art or to escape the heat of the afternoon or a passing storm (e.g., see Mulvaney 1996). Across Australia, if not hunting and gathering, people were often eating, socializing, or relaxing in the open, sometimes near bodies of water or in-season food resources, sometimes not far from rockshelters, but not always in shelters (see Koettig 1976, 142–60 for the historic, early-Contact period). This appears especially true of the Pleistocene and Early Holocene when rockshelters were used less intensively than in the past few thousand years, even when differential preservation and other aspects of taphonomy are taken into account (e.g., see Stockton and Holland 1974 for the Blue Mountains, NSW). Both environmental and cultural factors influenced changing relationships to rockshelters (including population change and behavioral change; see Attenbrow 2004, 11–36 for an extensive Australia-wide review), with more-intensive rock-marking activity and the establishment of fruit-seed processing near shelters 3,500 to 4,000 years ago as major developments (Atchison 2000; Taçon et al. 2003).

In terms of ceremonial activity, this also varied between open sites on one hand and caves and rockshelters on the other, for both men and women. Indeed, much activity occurred at sacred sites or other areas in the open, rather than deep inside or under cover of rock (e.g., Kelleher 2003 for the Blue Mountains, NSW). If we look more specifically at rock art, we find much variation between open sites (platforms, boulders, etc.) and shelters, even within the same region. In the greater Sydney region of southeast Australia, for instance, significant differences between the rock art of shelters and rock platforms are readily seen in terms of homogeneity, subject matter, and motivation (McDonald 1998, 1999, 2000, 2008). Interestingly, formal analysis of the iconography, early (albeit scant) ethnographic evidence recorded in the southeast (e.g., Mathews 1897a, 1897b, 1897c, 1903), and site location in relation to landscape features (Kelleher 2003) all suggest it was the open sites rather than the shelters that were used for large ceremonial gatherings and the more significant religious rituals and activities. However, deep shelters that can more properly be considered caves did receive some special status, as recent research in various parts of Australia has revealed.

AUSTRALIAN CAVES

In Australia much of the surface geology consists primarily of various types of sandstone, quartzite, granite, basaltic outcrops, and patches of limestone. All of these types of rocky landscapes were inhabited and exploited by Aboriginal people for tens of thousands of years and at least in recent times were given elaborate mythological meaning associated with great acts of creation or destruction by powerful Ancestral Beings (e.g., see Taçon 1999). They also were marked with a vast array of engraved, stenciled, painted, and drawn designs. At some locations quarries were not only functional but also played elaborate roles in stories about Ancestral Beings, in trade and social systems, and as places of great spiritual power (Brumm 2004; Jones and White 1988; Taçon 1991). There are many hundreds of thousands of rockshelters scattered across Australia and at least 100,000 rock-art sites (Flood 1997). However, deep limestone caves are somewhat rare, with most of them concentrated in southern and southeastern Australia, including Tasmania. Occasionally, deep cave-like sandstone shelters are found in various parts of the country, including both northern and southern Australia. Small limestone shelters are found in northern Queensland (e.g., Riversleigh in the west, Cape York in the east) but most are not true caves in that they are open to the light. As Mulvaney and Kamminga (1999, 23) highlight:

> True caves, created by water action and dissolution, are commonly found in limestone country, and large ones occur along the southern coast from Victoria to southwest Western Australia, and others in Cape York Peninsula and southern Tasmania. Rockshelters are the result of cavernous weathering of sandstone or quartzite formations by wind and water, or of large rocks broken from a cliff face which lean over and serve to shelter or shade the ground.

Northern Australia

Although proper caves are generally rare in northern Australia, there are many stories about worlds that exist inside rock (Taçon and Ouzman 2004). Indeed, this is where Mimi spirits normally reside and it is said the tall, thin Mimi were the ones who first taught the ancestors of Aboriginal people of western Arnhem Land how to paint on rock. Inside the rock it is believed the world is much like that outside, except all creatures exist as spirits. There are also stories about groups of Aboriginal people who once lived in large caves but did not follow proper modes of behavior. It is believed powerful Ancestral Beings, such as Namorodo (figure 9.1), infuriated by the breaking of rules of conduct, sealed the entrances to these caves, imprisoning everyone inside. At a number of locations, contempo-

FIGURE 9.1 Namorodo was sometimes depicted as a tall, thin giant. In this rock painting from Ubirr, Kakadu National Park, Australia, he is shown holding a line of recently caught fish. In the oral history of the area it is said he punished people who stole his fish by blocking their caves, thus banishing them to a prison inside rock. (© Paul S.C. Taçon.)

rary elders claim one can still hear the people banging on the wall, trying to get out of the darkness (Taçon 1989, 1992, 2005). Elsewhere, caves and tunnels through rock are attributed to the all-powerful Rainbow Serpent, and at some locations versions of this being reside in prominent rocky features. Where the creature passed through rock it sometimes left its image behind (figure 9.2). The buzz of rock-nesting bees signals where these might be. In some rockshelters and rock hollows the bones of the dead, sometimes painted with ochre, were placed as part of the final phase of secondary-burial practices. In the Hopevale area of southeast Cape York, the Havilands have noted that the paintings on cave walls only became sacred once a burial was placed deep inside the cave (Haviland and Haviland 1979). Once the cave paintings had been sanctified, the place was not to be approached by the uninitiated. All of these are

FIGURE 9.2 Rainbow Serpents figure prominently in art, stories, and ceremony right across Aboriginal Australia. At some locations they reside in rock, or made caves and tunnels through it. Sometimes when they entered a rock wall they left their images behind, such as at this location near the East Alligator River in Kakadu National Park. (© Paul S.C. Taçon.)

recent, from the Late Holocene, but if people engaged in such activity in the Pleistocene or Early Holocene we will likely never know because the acidic soils and harsh climate have precluded their survival.

In the Kimberley, Kakadu-Arnhem Land, and parts of northern Queensland there are lengthy rock-art records extending back well into the Pleistocene. Most of the art is found in rockshelters with very little in the open. When caves are adorned, the marks are invariably near the entrance and most appear to be Late Holocene. Occasionally, relatively deep caves are found with marks farther inside, but these are rare and usually are associated with restricted initiated men's business (e.g., at Riversleigh, Queensland, where it is not permissible to photograph such rock art; personal observation 2002). Across much of northern Australia, especially in the Kimberley region and Kakadu-Arnhem Land, there is a noticeable landscape difference between recent and early rock art. The oldest surviving pigment rock art is located in less-accessible, smaller, and more problematic locations for habitation than is Mid- to Late Holocene art (e.g., figure 9.3; Chaloupka 1993; Taçon 1989; Walsh 2000). This pronounced physical separation of the oldest art from the outside world suggests that this art may be associated with sacred behavior (e.g., Chippindale et al. 2000).

During the past 4,000 years, Aboriginal people were using larger shelters located on the edges of plains more frequently than the shelters high above escarpments, as had been the case in earlier times (figure 9.4). This process accelerated during the past 1,500 years, correlating with environmental change, but also with social change. Much of this was expressed in new styles and forms of art (Chaloupka 1993; Lewis 1988; Taçon and Chippindale 2008; Taçon et al. 2003; Walsh 2000) and in new relationships to land that included the development of totemic systems (Taçon and Chippindale 2008).

VICTORIA AND NEW SOUTH WALES

One of the outstanding archaeological cave sites dating to the Australian Pleistocene is Cloggs Cave, Victoria, in southeast Australia. It was first used 17,700 years ago

FIGURE 9.3 This shelter above Twin Falls Creek, Northern Territory, Australia, is located on the Arnhem Land plateau. It does not have a good floor or any comfortable living space but it does have several layers of images in various Late Pleistocene and Early to Mid-Holocene styles. (© Paul S.C. Taçon/Australian Museum.)

and is the best Pleistocene site for preserved bone and bone tools (see Flood 1980). It has both a more-exposed outer cave and a dimly lit inner area. It was initially occupied by various species of now extinct animals, such as the Tasmanian tiger, as well as rock wallabies. As Flood notes, things changed when Aborigines arrived at the site almost 18,000 years ago:

> At first they used simple flakes and pebble tools of local quartz, but gradually their toolkit expanded to include scrapers of finer-grained rock like chert and jasper. They paid only small visits to the cave ... As it became warmer at the end of the last glaciation between 13,000 and 9,000 years ago, use of the cave increased. In daytime the rockshelter was used, the north-facing ledges providing warm sitting places and a good vantage point out over the valley. At night fires were lit on the cave floor from *Eucalyptus* wood ... The inner chamber of the cave was not used after 8,500 years ago, and the site seems to have been vacated until a thousand years ago. (1990, 238–39)

Cloggs Cave is an exceptional site as deep caves that were used by Aboriginal people are rare in Victoria and New South Wales. However, it has no dark zone, as the inner part of the cave is dimly lit (Flood 1990, 238). And as Flood (1990, 272) notes for New South Wales, deep caves are more often associated with ancient animal remains rather than old or recent signs of Aboriginal activity:

> Limestone caves with impressive formations can be seen at Yarrangobilly in the Kosciusko National Park, where there is also a large thermal pool, Carey's Cave at Wee Jasper, near Yass, and in the Blue Mountains region, Jenolan, Abercrombie, Wombeyan and Wellington Caves. At most of these the bones of extinct animals such as giant kangaroos and diprotodontids have been found.

However, recently some cave-like sandstone rockshelters have revealed startling rock-art activity, as well as archaeological deposits with charcoal, stone flakes, and stone tools. Since early 2001 we have been working with a range of Aboriginal people from several communities, as well as archaeologists, students, and members of the bushwalking community, to locate and record rock-art sites in the rugged, wild Wollemi region (Taçon, Brennan, et al. 2005;

FIGURE 9.4 Hundreds of images and other marks cover the lengthy shelter of Yuwunggayai in Deaf Adder Gorge, Northern Territory, Australia. The painted art covers much-earlier cupule engravings. The cupules were deliberately positioned up to where there is a slight change in the slope of the wall surface, whereas the paintings continue over and above to make full use of the surface. The cupules are likely Late Pleistocene or Early Holocene, while the painted art is Late Holocene. The shelter is located at the junction of plain and escarpment, not far from a wide variety of food resources. It has an extensive living floor and is in a location typical of Late Holocene north Australian rock-art sites. (© Paul S.C. Taçon.)

Taçon, Kelleher, Brennan, et al. 2006; Taçon, Kelleher, King, et al. 2008; Taçon, Chapple, et al., 2010). This is the first project of its sort as until now most people thought very little evidence of past Aboriginal activity would be found in the Wollemi. Hundreds of sites have been found but survey has barely scratched the surface of the over-5,000-square-kilometer area. Significantly, among the many rockshelters adorned with rock art there are three that can be considered small caves because of their size, and especially their depth, and the fact they do not receive direct sunlight. Although they differ from each other in terms of the nature of the marking activity that took place and the subject matter depicted, they are all adorned in a much more extensive and dramatic way than most of the rockshelters of the region.

The three caves were used at different times, although the first, Eagle's Reach (figure 9.5), has a dozen layers of imagery possibly spanning as much as 4,000 years (figure 9.6). Indeed, Eagle's Reach has more pigment art than most sites across the Sydney region, with only three sites out of several thousand having more drawings. The site is located high up in the landscape, on an 18-square-kilometer plateau. In layers thought to be less than 1,600 years of age, there are dozens of birds (figure 9.7) and other creatures, such as gliders, that one expects to see up high, and also several depictions of supernatural beings. On the other hand, the second cave, Dingo's Lair (figure 9.8), is low in a valley, on the edge of a creek. It mostly has detailed charcoal drawings arranged across the back of the cave. There are many dingos (figure 9.9) and quolls (marsupial ferret-like predators related to Tasmanian devils), as well as other creatures typical of an area low in the landscape. Creatures are animated and naturalistic but are hard to see because of the cave's darkness. Most of this figurative art is thought to

FIGURE 9.5 Eagle's Reach is just below a ridgetop and is protected on three sides. The ceiling and back wall never receive direct sunlight. (© Paul S.C. Taçon/Australian Museum.)

have been made between 1,600 and 200 years ago, as with Eagle's Reach. The third site, Emu Cave, is the only known place within the larger region that has an extensive panel of engraved tracks, mostly bird (figure 9.10). There are 172 vertical engravings, along with a few ancient-looking stencils and red lines. A sample of crust that formed over one of the engravings was amenable to AMS radiocarbon dating, giving a minimum age of 2,000 years (Taçon et al. 2006). Like Eagle's Reach, Emu Cave is located high up, on the side of a ridge.

All of the evidence to date suggests these three sites were considered extra special as places for rock art and other activities (compare Kelleher 2003). The imagery left behind was not randomly placed. It was purposely positioned with much thought going into what should be where, unlike marks in most of the rockshelters near these sites, which appear less organized and less symbolic. This illustrates that even within a region where much ceremonial activity took place out in the open, small caves were also considered special and thus were marked differently than nearby and more-exposed rockshelters. Undoubtedly, certain criteria were used to select which shelters would become most important. For instance, a direct relationship between ridgetops and shelter selection can be observed across the Wollemi. Practical factors, such as level floors, sufficient protection from the elements, and good surfaces to draw and paint on would have played a role in determining which shelters would be inhabited and/or adorned with art. Yet, across Australia, including the Wollemi, there are also hundreds of what appear to us to be perfectly good places for habitation and/or art making that nonetheless were never used. Thus there must also have been a bigger picture of the landscape that affected shelter selection, including a whole range of variables such as religious, spatial, social, political, resource access, and other concerns.

The contemporary Indigenous interpretation of the three Wollemi caves by Darkingjung, Darug, and Wiradjeri peoples, in whose traditional country the small caves are found, is that because of many of these variables they were selected as teaching sites (Taçon et al. 2008). For them, art

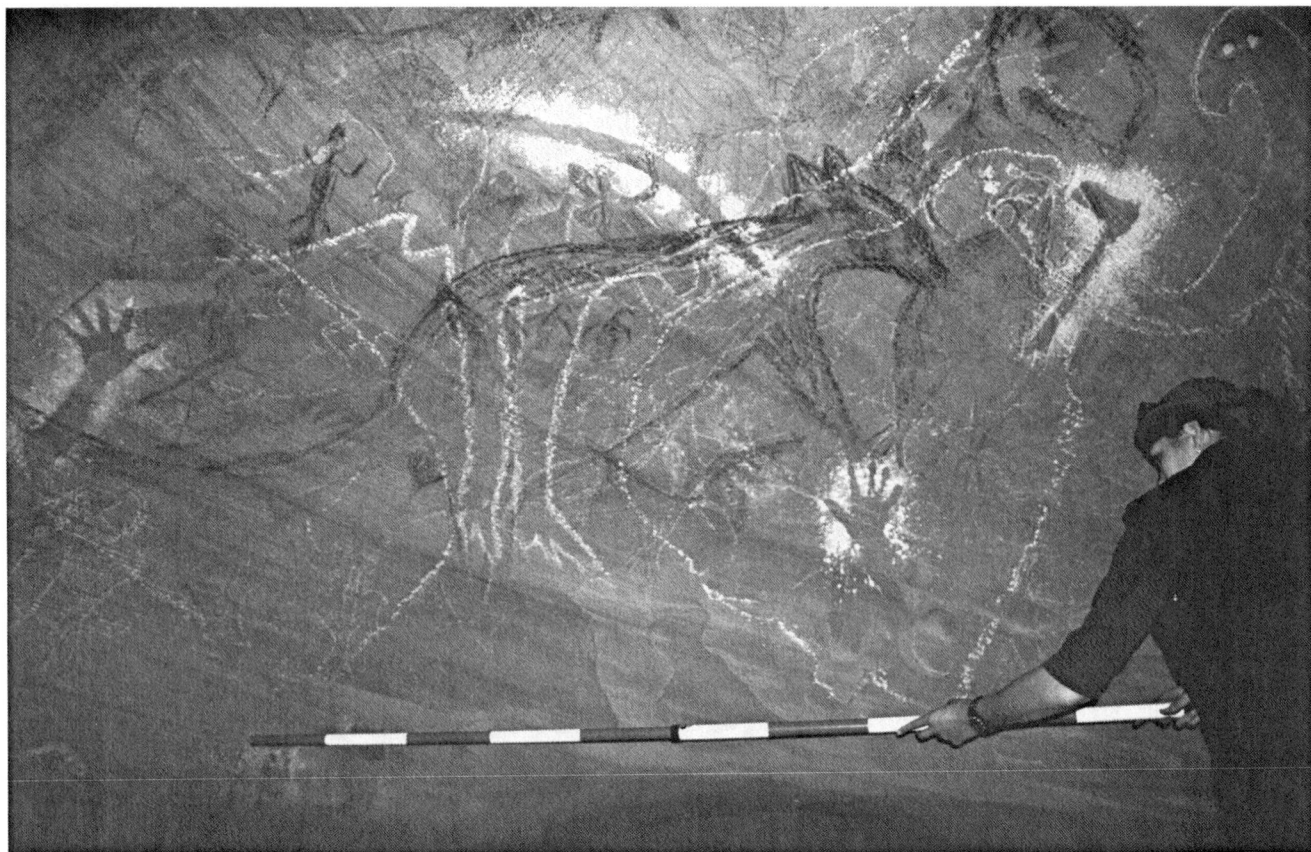

FIGURE 9.6 (above) The twelve layers of stencils and drawings at Eagle's Reach possibly span 4,000 years. Art activity appears particularly intensive from about 1,600 to 200 years ago. (© Paul S.C. Taçon/Australian Museum.)

FIGURE 9.7 (right) Birds, Bird Ancestral Beings, and other creatures of higher altitudes are common at Eagle's Reach but rare elsewhere. Several can be seen in this photograph but the large white eagle was deliberately placed in association with stencils of a boomerang and hafted stone axe, suggesting it is holding these artifacts. It is likely a depiction of the Eagle Ancestor associated with the larger region. (© Paul S.C. Taçon/Australian Museum.)

was and is the oldest "language," with pictures in caves and rockshelters conveying a vast array of meaning and history. After visiting the three caves described above, a number of elders suggested they were likely used in a number of education-related ways, illustrating and confirming important aspects of landscape origins, Dreamtime Beings and events, social relations, hunting practices, history, and so forth. In a sense, the pictures acted as memory prompts but also they inspired new oral and visual expressions of individual and group identity and experience.

FIGURE 9.8 Dingo's Lair is located next to a creek in a low valley. It is similar in size to Eagle's Reach and is likewise well protected. Drawings are located at the back of the shelter where it is very dark. (© Paul S.C. Taçon/Australian Museum.)

South Australia, Southwestern Western Australia, and Tasmania

In the south of South Australia and along the Nullarbor plain, some deep limestone caves were used as much as 34,000 years ago (Allen's Cave). In others, Aboriginal people created various forms of art, including finger-fluting designs and petroglyphs. Both flint and chert were quarried as much as 20,000 years ago at places such as Koonalda Cave and more recently in thirty-five small limestone caves in the Mt. Gambier area (see Bednarik 1986; Bednarik, Aslin, and Bednarik 2003; Flood 1997, 25–72; Wright 1971 for reviews). It has been argued that some caves have symbolically arranged stones inside them (Sharpe and Fawbert 2000). Much of this activity seems to have occurred in the Pleistocene, although some Mt. Gambier sites have petroglyphs dated to the Mid-Holocene (Bednarik 1998). As Flood (1990, 186–87) describes,

> About forty Aboriginal sites associated with caves or dolines (conical depressions in limestone which may be many meters in diameter) have been found on the Nullarbor. Hand stencils occur in twenty, stone artifacts or other evidence of occupation in nine, stone arrangements in nine and flint mining in two. One cave has a stone arrangement with a substantial growth of stalagmite on top of the cairns, evidence of their considerable antiquity.

At Koonalda Cave, habitational remains are found in the twilight zone while scratches, finger markings, and incised lines believed to be up to 20,000 years of age, and interpreted by Flood as of ritual/symbolic origin, are found in the dark zone, along with charcoal from torches:

> One of the most remarkable discoveries in Koonalda Cave was the presence of Pleistocene engravings in complete darkness in deep inner passages, some 300 metres inside the entrance. These vary from finger markings where the rock surface is soft to lines incised with a stone or stick in the harder surfaces. The lines resemble the so-called macaroni style of European cave art. Some appear to be random criss-crossing

FIGURE 9.9 Dingos, quolls, and other creatures common to lower altitudes are frequent at Dingo's Lair, while the only bird depicted is the flightless emu. (© Paul S.C. Taçon/Australian Museum.)

lines, but definite patterns occur, such as grids, lattices and concentric circles. One interesting design is a herringbone consisting of 74 short diagonal lines incised in a row below 37 similar finger markings. The fact that 37 is exactly half of 74 can hardly be coincidence, and suggests that these marks had some purpose and significance . . . These engravings were the first evidence in Australia that Aboriginal people carried out artistic activity in totally dark caves, and they demonstrate the considerable antiquity of Aboriginal art, which is comparable with that of cave art of France and Spain. (Flood 1990, 190-1)

In the southwest of Western Australia there are many limestone caves with the remains of extinct animals. Some also have evidence of various forms of human activity, including Orchestra Shell Cave with occupation going back at least 6,500 years and bearing the remains of faint, possibly Pleistocene engraved designs. "There are at least four different 'designs'—a set of grooves splaying out from a single stem, sets of wide-spaced straight parallel grooves, short very deep individual cuts, and curving crisscrossing sets of usually fivefold narrow-spaced parallel grooves . . . Orchestra Shell Cave is one of only two similar engraving sites so far discovered in West Australia" (Flood 1990, 46). Some of the markings are in a dark, narrow fissure while others are on the walls of a dark chimneylike crevice at the western end:

> This is a confined, inaccessible spot, but an entire wall of almost 7 square metres (75 square feet) is completely covered with markings, the majority of human origin. They are very difficult to photograph, but hundreds of finger marks have been preserved in near-pristine condition, together with tool marks . . . Others are definitely animal scratch marks, the individual claw incisions never exceeding one millimeter. (Flood 1997, 62; see also Bednarik 1987)

Another impressive cave in the region is Devil's Lair, a limestone cave that is one of Australia's oldest and most important archaeological sites (Dortch 1979a, 1979b, 1984; Dortch and Dortch 1996). Recent new dating attempts suggest it is up to 50,000 years of age (Turney

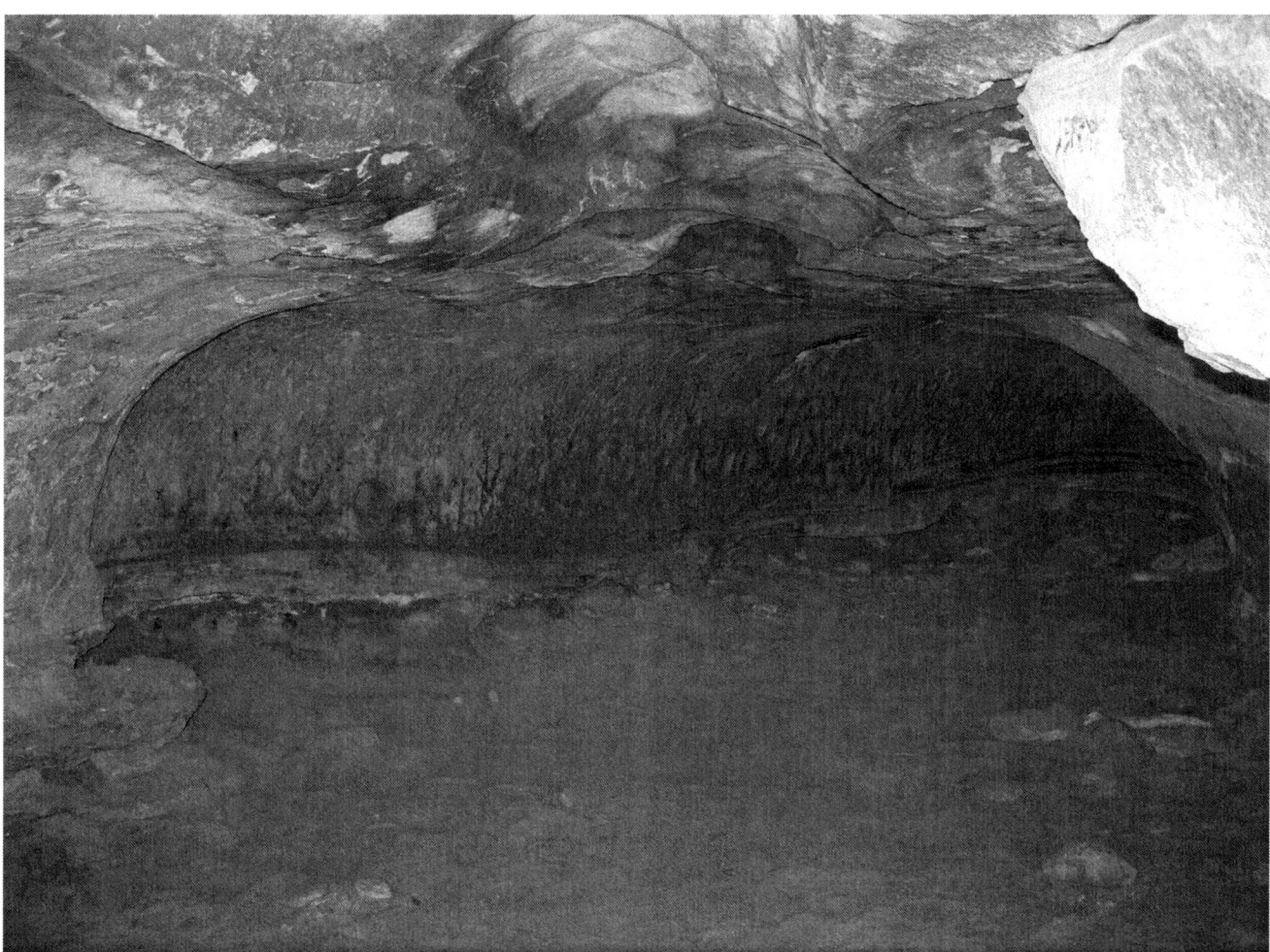

FIGURE 9.10 Emu Cave, New South Wales, has 172 engravings, mostly bird tracks, on the western wall as well as in the deepest recess. (Photograph by Paul S.C. Taçon.)

et al. 2001) and there is a wide range of occupational debris, bone and stone tools, hearths, and even symbolic objects, including beads of 12,000 to 15,000 years of age. Interestingly, two small carved-limestone plaques were recovered from excavations. They have incised straight lines that Dortch interprets as of artistic or ritual origin. The plaque is reminiscent of designs on the walls of Orchestra Shell Cave, Koonalda Cave, and various caves of the Mt. Gambier region of South Australia (see Bednarik, Aslin, and Bednarik 2003). However, after microscopic study, Bednarik (2001, 179) concludes that "none of the six limestone pieces, two of which had been published as engraved plaques, were found to bear any intentional anthropic marks." Furthermore, there is no proper dark zone at Devil's Lair, and as Mulvaney and Kamminga (1999, 178) note, "Although the excavation at Devil's Lair provided some of Australia's earliest bone implements and ornaments, the artifact density is surprisingly low, and human visits, made over a period of twenty millennia, were probably infrequent and of short duration."

In Tasmania, Aboriginal people generally avoided occupying areas higher than 1,200 meters but lower areas of rocky terrain were frequently used, including those with significant caves. Tasmania has extensive areas of limestone caves with many repeatedly used for habitation in the Pleistocene. Indeed, surviving the Ice Age that gripped much of Tasmania was made possible by exploiting both caves and food resources associated with the protected gorges they are found in. Pleistocene-occupied caves include Warreen Cave (35,000–16,000 BP), Nunamira Cave (30,000 BP), Palewardia Walana Lanola (29,800 BP), Bone Cave (29,000 BP), Kutikina Cave (19,970–15,000 BP), Wargata Mina (with hand stencils well over 12,000 years of age), and Ballawinne (with pigment art and a small occupation deposit at least 14,000 years old). Ballawine, on the Maxwell River, is particularly intriguing as there are at least sixteen hand stencils on the walls of a chamber and patches of red ochre on the ceiling. Other patches of ochre can be found in various places near the entrance but the gallery of red hand stencils is in complete darkness. "This is extremely rare among Australian art sites, but more nearly parallels decorated caves of the Upper Palaeolithic in Europe" (Flood 1997, 225). In this regard, Wargata Mina (formerly Judd's Cavern) is also noteworthy in that it contains a chamber filled with faint red hand stencils "some 35 meters (115 feet) from the entrance and at the very last glimmer of daylight penetration" (Flood 1997, 226).

Significantly, all caves in southwest Tasmania were abandoned by 13,500 BP "when dense forest and scrub colonized much of the region" (Mulvaney and Kamminga 1999, 182). Some caves in other parts of Tasmania were occupied during various periods of the Holocene but most do not have great depth or darkness. More generally, there was an expansion of settlement throughout Tasmania from 4,000 to 3,000 years ago, with the colonization of new areas and occupation of a range of environments and site types (Mulvaney and Kamminga 1999, 345). Although Tasmania had been cut off from mainland Australia for thousands of years, the archaeological record of the region indicates it underwent major social changes about the same time as many parts of the Australian continent, especially the far north.

CONCLUSION

True caves, places of darkness, with evidence of ancient human activity are rare in Australia; rockshelters are much more common. Where they occur, really extensive, deep caves like those of Europe or the Americas were not usually adorned or used much in symbolic ways in recent times. However, in the Pleistocene, some deep caves in southern Australia were used and marked, mainly with hand stencils, ochre smears and streaks, finger-fluting designs, and engraved-line complexes, often in the dark or darkest zones. Exceptional examples can be found in Tasmania, along the Nullarbor of South Australia, and at Orchestra Shell Cave, Western Australia. This suggests the marks were not only purposefully placed but had ritual intent, as has been argued for similar designs in deep-cave dark zones of other continents.

More recently, some small caves with twilight zones were treated in special ways, for example in Wollemi National Park of New South Wales, and rockshelters across the continent were adorned with elaborate imagery that resulted from a range of motivations. Indeed, in Holocene Australia it was rockshelters and open sites that experienced the preponderance of ritual, symbolic, and art activity. The general rule during the Holocene for much of Australia was that one did not journey into the really deep, dark caves—that they were places to be avoided if at all possible. And in much of Tasmania they were completely abandoned. This is important as it suggests different religious orientations in terms of landscape between the Pleistocene and Holocene. Studies of long-term changes in rock art support this idea, with a move from more-shamanistic themes to the dominance of Ancestral Beings and totemism in many regions, especially northern Australia (Layton 1992; Taçon and Chippindale 2008), as well as a continent-wide florescence in shelter and open-site rock-art activity after about 4,000 to 6,000 years ago. From the Mid-Holocene onward there were many other changes to the ways people oriented themselves to, expressed relations to, and marked rocky landscapes. For instance, there was a shift in landscape preference for the placement of rock art, especially in northern Australia, associated with various other cultural and environmental changes.

In historic times, for most Aboriginal people deep caves were considered dangerous places, associated with a range of spirits and Ancestral Beings. One could get into trouble if one went too far inside. This is one of the reasons why there was much symbolic activity, including associated art, conducted in open areas across the country—with engraved rock-art on boulders, the sand drawings of central Australia, and mud and earth sculptures included among the many resulting ceremonial art forms documented by Europeans. Deep caves were mainly left to Ancestral Beings and spirits in very recent times. However, worlds within rock figured prominently—and continue to do so—in Dreamtime stories and other aspects of oral history.

At no time did people inhabit the dark zones of caves, and visits to these areas were fleeting and infrequent. In most cases visits likely related to ritual activity. Cave habitation in the Pleistocene was infrequent, when it occurred at all, and it was confined to areas with light. Increasingly, archaeological evidence also suggests the habitation of rockshelters across Australia was much less frequent and/or extensive than previously believed. The use of shelters for habitation in the Holocene is more common than in the Pleistocene but in both eras it must have been more usual for people to camp in the open. In historic times, people sometimes camped close to shelters and often in bark huts. Shelters were extensively used for rock art in both the Pleistocene and Holocene, although different locations were preferred in each era. Shelters thus may always have been primarily places for symbolic storage, ritual, teaching, relating history, expressing experience, and so forth, with habitation more usually resulting from and in relation to these sorts of purposeful visits. Shelters may also have been occupied briefly during bad weather or as an overnight stop when traveling through the country.

More generally, rockshelters and caves, along with the art they hold, likely operated on various levels within social systems in both the Pleistocene and Holocene. They were more than just places of habitation, visitation, storytelling, art, or ceremony. In most parts of Australia they also functioned as landscape signposts or beacons, or meeting places, when moving through country. In this and other ways they are intrinsically tied to the stories of landscape. The knowledge of these stories, and an understanding of the link between land and the art in shelters and caves, would be very important for being able to move through both a physical and spiritual landscape confidently and in appropriate fashion.

REFERENCES CITED

Atchison, Jenny. 2000. "Continuity and Change: A Late Holocene and Post-Contact History of Aboriginal Environmental Interaction and Vegetation Process from the Keep River Region, Northern Territory." PhD dissertation. University of Wollongong, Wollongong, New South Wales.

Attenbrow, Val J. 2004. *What's Changing? Population Size or Land-Use Patterns? The Archaeology of Upper Mangrove Creek, Sydney Basin*. Terra australis 21. Canberra: Pandanus Press.

Bednarik, Robert G. 1986. "Cave Use by Australian Pleistocene Man." *Proceedings of the University of Bristol Spelaeological Society* 17 (3): 227–45.

Bednarik, Robert G. 1987. "The Cave Art of Western Australia." *Artefact* 12: 1–16.

Bednarik, Robert G. 1998. "Direct Dating Results from Australian Cave Petroglyphs." *Geoarchaeology* 13(4): 411–18.

Bednarik, Robert G. 2001. *Rock Art Science: The Scientific Study of Palaeoart*. Turnhout, Belgium: Brepols.

Bednarik, Robert G., Geoffrey D. Aslin, and Elfriede Bednarik. 2003. "The Cave Petroglyphs of Australia." *Cave Research* 3: 1–7.

Brumm, Adam. 2004. "An Axe to Grind: Symbolic Considerations of Stone Axe Use in Ancient Australia." In *Soils, Stones and Symbols: Cultural Perceptions of the Mineral World*, ed. Nicole Boivin and Mary Ann Owoc, 143–63. London: UCL Press.

Chaloupka, George. 1993. *Journey in Time: The World's Longest Continuing Art Tradition*. Chatswood, NSW: Reed Books.

Chippindale, Christopher, Ben Smith, and Paul S.C. Taçon. 2000. "Visions of Dynamic Power: Archaic Rock-Paintings, Altered States of Consciousness and 'Clever Men' in Western Arnhem Lane (NT), Australia." *Cambridge Archaeological Journal* 10 (1): 63–101. http://dx.doi.org/10.1017/S0959774300000032.

Dortch, Charles E. 1979a. "Devil's Lair: An Example of Prolonged Cave Use in Southwestern Australia." *World Archaeology* 10 (3): 258–79. http://dx.doi.org/10.1080/00438243.1979.9979736.

Dortch, Charles E. 1979b. "33,000 Year Old Stone and Bone Artifacts from Devil's Lair, Western Australia." *Records of the Western Australian Museum* 7: 329–67.

Dortch, Charles E. 1984. *Devil's Lair: A Study in Prehistory*. Perth: Western Australian Museum.

Dortch, Charles E., and Joe Dortch. 1996. "Review of Devil's Lair Artefact Classification and Radiocarbon Chronology." *Australian Archaeology* 43: 28–32.

Flood, Josephine. 1980. *The Moth Hunters: Aboriginal Prehistory of the Australian Alps*. Canberra: Australian Institute of Aboriginal Studies.

Flood, Josephine. 1990. *The Riches of Ancient Australia*. St. Lucia: University of Queensland Press.

Flood, Josephine. 1997. *Rock-Art of the Dreamtime*. Sydney: Angus and Robertson.

Haviland, J., and L. Haviland. 1979. "Report on fieldwork at Hopevale 1979." Unpublished report, 3185. Australian Institute of Aboriginal Studies, Canberra.

Jones, Rhys, and Neville White. 1988. "Point Blank: Stone Tool Manufacture at the Ngilipitji Quarry, Arnhem Land, 1981." In *Archaeology with Ethnography: An Australian Perspective*, ed. B. Meehan and R. Jones, 51–87. Canberra: Australia National University.

Kelleher, Matthew. 2003. "Archaeology of Sacred Space: The Spiritual Nature of Religious Behaviour in the Blue Mountains National Park Australia." PhD dissertation, University of Sydney, Sydney.

Koettig, Margit. 1976. "Rising Damp: Aboriginal Structures in Perspective." MA Qual. thesis, University of Sydney, Sydney.

Layton, Robert. 1992. *Australian Rock-Art: A New Synthesis*. Cambridge: Cambridge University Press.

Lewis, Darrell. 1988. *The Rock Paintings of Arnhem Land, Australia: Social, Ecological and Material Culture Change in the Post-Glacial Period*. British Archaeological Reports, International Series S415. Oxford: Archaeopress.

Lewis-Williams, J. David, and Thomas Dowson. 1990. "Through the Veil: San Rock Paintings and the Rock Face." *South African Archaeological Bulletin* 45 (151): 5–16. http://dx.doi.org/10.2307/3887913.

Mathews, R. H. 1897a. "The Burbung of the Darkinung Tribes." *Proceedings of the Royal Society of Victoria* 10: 1–12.

Mathews, R. H. 1897b. "Rock Carving by the Australian Aborigines." *Proceedings of the Royal Society of Queensland* 12: 96–8.

Mathews, R. H. 1897c. "The Totemic Divisions of Australian Tribes." *Journal and Proceedings of the Royal Society of New South Wales* 31: 154–76.

Mathews, R. H. 1903. "Languages of the Kamilaroi and Other Aboriginal Tribes of New South Wales." *Journal of the Anthropological Institute of Great Britain and Ireland* 33 (2): 259–83. http://dx.doi.org/10.2307/2842812.

McDonald, Josephine. 1998. "Shelter Rock-art in the Sydney Basin: A Space-Time continuum; Exploring Different Influences on Stylistic Change." In *The Archaeology of Rock-Art*, ed. Christopher Chippindale and Paul S.C. Taçon, 319–35. Cambridge: Cambridge University Press.

McDonald, Josephine. 1999. "Bedrock Notions and Isochrestic Choice: Evidence for Localised Stylistic Patterning in the Engravings of the Sydney Region." *Archaeology in Oceania* 34 (3): 145–60.

McDonald, Josephine. 2000. "Media and Social Context: Influences on Stylistic Communication Networks in Prehistoric Sydney." *Australian Archaeology* 51: 54–63.

McDonald, Josephine. 2008. *Dreamtime Superhighway: Sydney Basin Rock Art and Prehistoric Information Exchange*. Terra Australis 27. Canberra: ANU E Press.

Mulvaney, D. John, and Johan Kamminga. 1999. *Prehistory of Australia*. Sydney: Allen and Unwin.

Mulvaney, Ken. 1996. "What to Do on a Rainy Day: Reminiscences of Mirriuwung and Gadjerog Artists." *Rock Art Research* 13: 3–20.

Sharpe, K., and H. Fawbert. 2000. "The Smoothing and Rounding of the Boulders in the Upper Chamber of Koonalda Cave, South Australia." Paper presented at the Third AURA Congress, Alice Springs, July 13, 2000.

Stockton, E. D., and W. Holland. 1974. "Cultural Sites and Their Environment in the Blue Mountains." *Archaeology and Physical Anthropology in Oceania* 9 (1): 36–65.

Taçon, Paul S.C. 1989. "From Rainbow Snakes to 'X-Ray' Fish: The Nature of the Recent Rock Painting Tradition of Western Arnhem Land, Australia." PhD dissertation, Australian National University, Canberra.

Taçon, Paul S.C. 1991. "The Power of Stone: Symbolic Aspects of Stone Use and Tool Development in Western Arnhem Land, Australia." *Antiquity* 65: 192–207.

Taçon, Paul S.C. 1992. "'If You Miss All This Story, Well Bad Luck': Rock Art and the Validity of Ethnographic Interpretation in Western Arnhem Land, Australia." In *Rock Art and Ethnography*, ed. Michael J. Morwood and Douglas R. Hobbs, 11–18. Occasional AURA Publication No. 5. Melbourne: Australian Rock Art Research Association.

Taçon, Paul S.C. 1999. "Identifying Ancient Sacred Landscapes in Australia: From Physical to Social." In *Archaeologies of Landscape: Contemporary Perspectives*, ed. Wendy Ashmore and A. Bernie Knapp, 33–57. Oxford: Blackwell Publishers.

Taçon, P.S.C. 2005. "The World of Ancient Ancestors: Australian Aboriginal Caves and Other Realms within Rock." *Expedition* 47(3): 37–42.

Taçon, P.S.C., W. Brennan, S. Hooper, M. Kelleher, and D. Pross. 2005. "Greater Wollemi: A New Australian Rock-Art Area Bordering Sydney." *International Organisation of Rock Art (INORA) Newsletter* 43: 1–6.

Taçon, Paul S.C., R. Chapple, J. Merson, D. Ramp, W. Brennan, G. King, and A. Taisire. 2010. "Aboriginal Rock Art Depictions of Fauna: What Can They Tell Us about the Natural History of the Greater Blue Mountains World Heritage Area?" In *The Natural History of Sydney*, ed. D. Lunney and P. Hutchings, 58–73. Sydney: Royal Zoological Society of New South Wales.

Taçon, Paul S.C., and C. Chippindale. 2008. "Changing Places: Ten Thousand Years of North Australian Rock-Art Transformation." In *Time and Change: Archaeological and Anthropological Perspectives on the Long-Term in Hunter-Gatherer Societies*, ed. D. Papagianni, H. Maschner, and R. Layton, 73–94. Oxford: Oxbow Books.

Taçon, P.S.C., M. Kelleher, W. Brennan, S. Hooper, and D. Pross. 2006. "Wollemi Petroglyphs, NSW, Australia: An Unusual Assemblage with Rare Motifs." *Rock Art Research* 227–238.

Taçon, P.S.C., M. Kelleher, G. King, and W. Brennan. 2008. "Eagle's Reach: A Focal Point for Past and Present Social Identity within the Northern Blue Mountains World Heritage Area, New South Wales, Australia." In *Archaeologies of Art: Time, Place and Identity*, ed. I. Sanz, D. Fiore, and S. K. May, 195–214. Walnut Creek, CA: Left Coast Press.

Taçon, Paul S.C., Ken Mulvaney, Sven Ouzman, Richard Fullagar, Lesley Head, and Paddy Carlton. 2003. "Changing Ecological Concerns in Rock-Art Subject Matter of North Australia's Keep River Region." *Before Farming* 2003/3 (4): 354–66.

Taçon, Paul S.C., and Sven Ouzman. 2004. "Worlds within Stone: The Inner and Outer Rock-Art Landscapes of Northern Australia and Southern Africa." In *The Figured Landscapes of Rock-Art*, ed. Christopher Chippindale and George Nash, 39–68. Cambridge: Cambridge University Press.

Turney, C.S.M., M. Bird, L. K. Fifield, R. G. Roberts, M. Smith, C. E. Dortch, R. Grün, E. Lawson, L. K. Ayliffe, G. H. Miller, et al. 2001. "Early Human Occupation at Devil's Lair, Southwestern Australia, 50,000 Years Ago." *Quaternary Research* 55 (1): 3–13. http://dx.doi.org/10.1006/qres.2000.2195.

Walsh, Graeme. 2000. *Bradshaw Art of the Kimberley*. Melbourne: Takarakka Nowan Kas.

Ward, Ingrid A.K. 2004. "Comparative Records of Occupation in the Keep River Region of the Eastern Kimberley, Northwestern Australia." *Australian Archaeology* 59: 1–9.

Ward, Ingrid A.K., Richard Fullagar, Tessa Boer-Mah, Lesley Head, Paul S.C. Taçon, and Ken Mulvaney. 2006. "Comparison of Sedimentation and Occupation Histories Inside and Outside Rock Shelters, Keep River Region, Northwestern Australia." *Geoarchaeology* 21 (1): 1–27. http://dx.doi.org/10.1002/gea.20087.

Wright, Richard V.S., ed. 1971. *Archaeology of the Galus Site*. Canberra: Australian Institute of Aboriginal Studies.

Part II

New World Ritual Cave Traditions

10

Caves as Sacred Space in Mesoamerica

Holley Moyes and James E. Brady

Mesoamerica is a term coined by Paul Kirchhoff (1943) to describe a geographical region that includes most of Mexico, all of Guatemala, Belize, and El Salvador, and parts of Honduras, Nicaragua, and northern Costa Rica (figure 10.1, table 10.1). Using ethnohistoric and linguistic data gathered at the time of the Spanish Conquest in 1521, Kirchhoff argued that the region constituted a "culture area" based on its cultural unity and similar religious principles. The shared traits included similar farming techniques, crop types, food-preparation techniques, body decorations, uses of obsidian, stepped pyramids, ballcourts, hieroglyphic writing on screenfold books, calendrical systems, religious practices such as bloodletting and human sacrifice, and ritual warfare.

Much of Mesoamerica consists of a karstic landscape, dotted with limestone caves and rockshelters. Their use by both ancient and modern people is documented in archaeological, ethnohistoric, and ethnographic contexts, yet it is only within the past 30 years that the nature of these sites has become well understood. In this chapter we examine conceptualizations of caves by Mesoamerican indigenous people. We review the historic development of the archaeology of caves in tandem with the contributions that allowed us to reach a sophisticated understanding of these sites. We discuss how various lines of inquiry have contributed to our knowledge of cave function and meaning in prehistory, and conclude by reviewing recent archaeological trends and agendas for future research.

WHAT IS A "CAVE"?

For most Westerners the word *cave* has a fairly narrow range of meaning and generally calls up an image of a large, deep, dark hole. Not surprisingly, indigenous conceptualizations differ from our own. The Maya word *ch'en* or *ch'een,* for instance, can be translated as "cave" but it also includes springs, water holes, sinkholes, crevices, rockshelters, and virtually any hole within the earth (Brady 1997, 603; Laughlin 1975, 132; Rissolo 2005, 354–356; Vogt and Stuart 2005), be they natural (e.g., Ishihara 2008) or man made. As an example, Ann Scott and Walter E. Little (2003) reported that they were taken to a cave ceremony at Tikal by a Kaqchikel Maya shaman. The "cave" turned out to be an abandoned tunnel excavated by University of Pennsylvania archaeologists in the 1960s. In this chapter we employ the indigenous definition of *cave* but for heuristic purposes we use the Western distinction of *caves* (entities that contain light, twilight, and dark zones), from *rockshelters* (natural overhangs that contain only light and twilight areas).

THE MEANING OF CAVES IN MESOAMERICAN CULTURE

To understand how caves are culturally constructed, one must first explore Mesoamerican thought and worldview. Throughout the Americas, indigenous people believe that

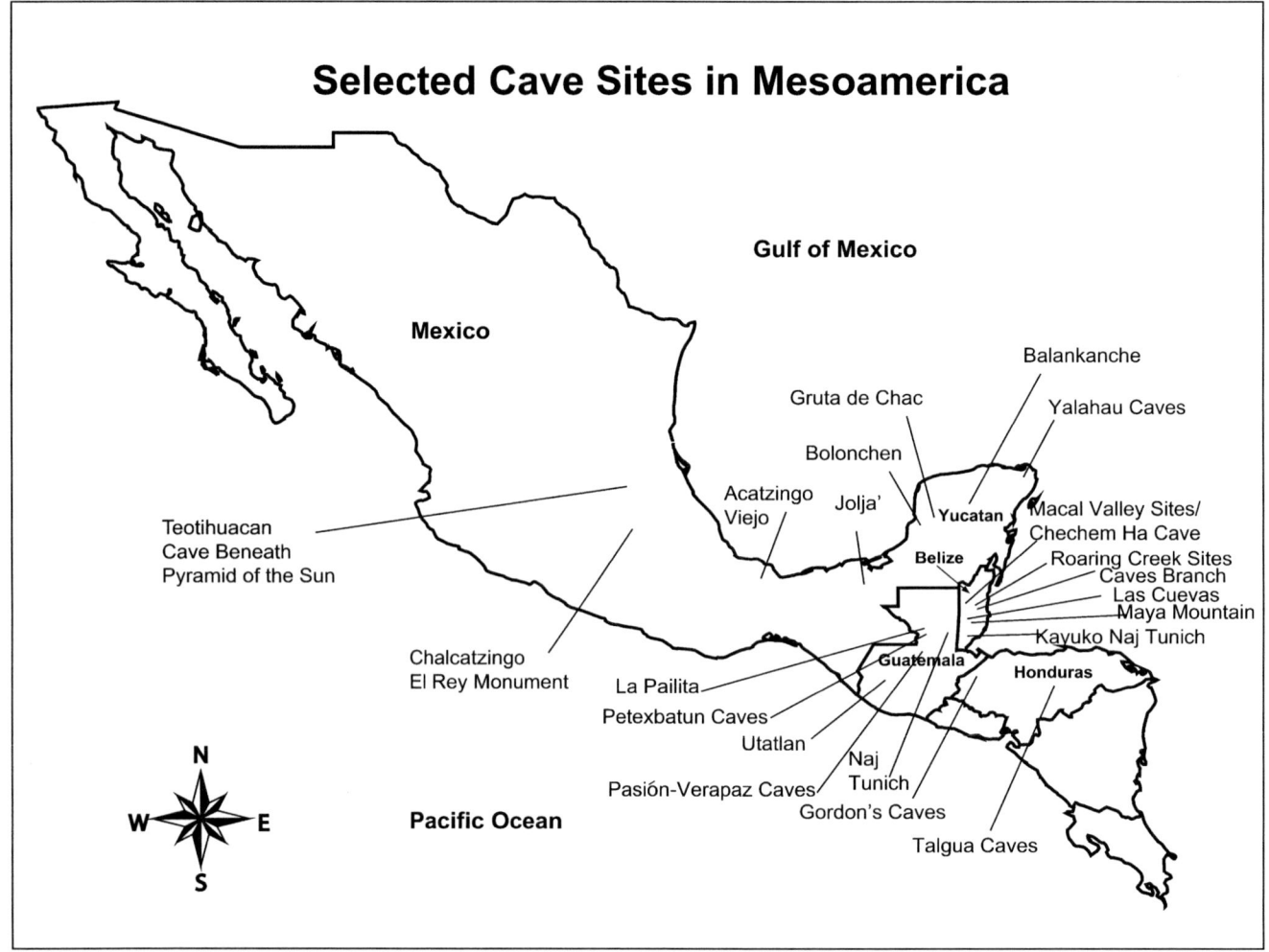

FIGURE 10.1 Mesoamerica, showing selected caves mentioned in the text.

the earth is animate and populated with spirits or deities that dwell within landscape features such as mountains, rocks, trees, springs, lakes, rivers, and caves. The earth itself constitutes one of the most revered elements in indigenous cosmology, assuming the role of the universal creator of life (Eliade and Sullivan 1987, 534–41).

We find evidence of the antiquity of this belief in central Mexico, where the earth is represented by the deity Tlaltecuhtli, from whose body springs all life, water, and vegetation (Bernal-García 2001, 332–33). In the ethnohistoric text *Historia de los Mexicanos por sus pinturas (History of the Mexicans as Told by Their Paintings)* it is explained that from the deity's hair grow trees, flowers, and grasses; from the skin, fine herbs and little flowers; from the nose, valleys and mountains; from the eyes, wells, fountains, and small caves; and from the mouth, rivers and caverns.

Caves are also intricately involved in Mesoamerican creation myths. In these narratives, caves are the place of

TABLE 10.1 Chronological periods for Mesoamerican archaeological cultures mentioned in the text.

Culture	Estimated Dates
Olmec	1600–400 BC
Maya	
Early Preclassic	2000–1000 BC
Middle Preclassic	1000–400 BC
Late Preclassic	400 BC–AD 100
Terminal Preclassic	AD 100–250
Early Classic	AD 250–600
Late Classic	AD 600–800
Terminal Classic	AD 800–900/1000
Postclassic	AD 900/1000–1500
Teotihuacan	AD 100–500
Aztec	AD 1200–1521

FIGURE 10.2 Sixteenth-century depiction from the *Atlas de Duran* illustrating primordial humans emerging from an earth-monster cave mouth. (Durán 1994 [1588?], plate 3.)

origin for human creation or they mark the place of human emergence from the earth onto its surface. It is a prominent theme in ancient central Mexican mythology that ethnic groups sprang from a cavern or series of caverns known as *Chicomostoc* meaning "Place of the Seven Caves" (Heyden 1975, 134). The event is well illustrated in the *Atlas de Duran,* in which we see humans walking out from the mouth of the earth monster or theriomorphic cave (figure 10.2). A similar motif is also found in vessels from Honduras (Nielsen and Brady 2006) in which the primordial couple sits within a cave.

Primordial scenes are also found on the Preclassic Maya murals from the site of San Bartolo dating to the first century BC. The north wall illustrates a creation event in which maize tamales and a gourd of water are being handed out of the entrance of a cave thought to be the cave of origin (Saturno et al. 2005). An early representation of the ancient Maya Maize God is depicted at the mouth of the cave accepting the offerings. The association suggests that both primordial water and the first maize issued from the cave, and it explains its importance in later water and fertility rites.

Throughout the region, indigenous people consider rain to be a terrestrial phenomenon originating in caves (see Adams and Brady 2005, 305, for discussion). The belief is well reported ethnographically, and it is not difficult to infer its origin based on empirical observations—clouds appear to sit on top of mountains, and caves can be seen emitting fog after rains. For instance, John Monaghan (1995, 107) noted that among the Mixtec of Oaxaca, caves are considered to be "rain houses" that people treat as shrines. Water dripping from the walls of the cave is considered to be "raindrops," and rain clouds are thought to pour from the cave before storms. Working among the Tzotzil Maya of highland Chiapas, Vogt reported having a number of conversations in which he tried to convince local people

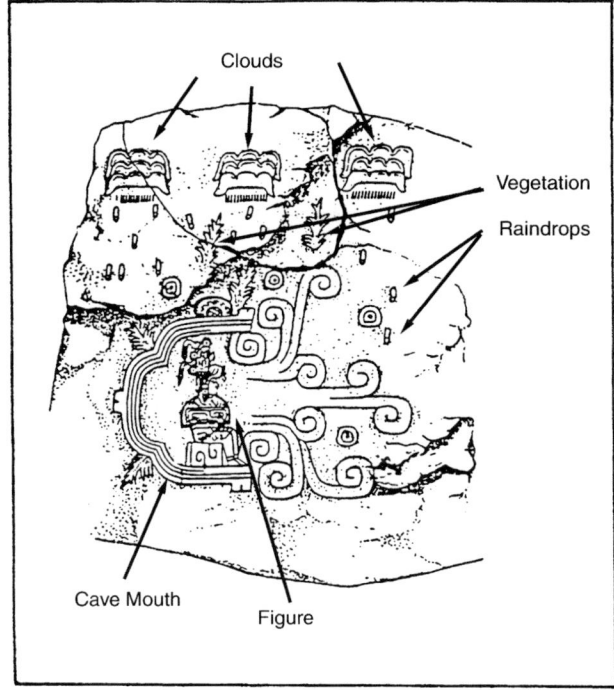

FIGURE 10.3 The "El Rey" monument is a bas-relief illustrating an important person sitting within a cave. Clouds rain on top of the cave and plants are shown growing on the surface. (After Reilly 1994, 85.)

that clouds formed in the air, not in caves (1969, 387; Vogt and Stuart 2005, 164–65). Watching the storm clouds in the Grijalva River lowlands stream over the highland ridges, he had to admit that, based on the empirical information, the belief was understandable. This is most likely an old tradition illustrated in the "El Rey" monument from Chalcatzingo (figure 10.3) that dates to the Olmec period (1200–200 BC). The monument is a huge bas-relief design carved into a large boulder and situated on a mountainside adjacent to the main rainwater runoff channel. In the carving, a personage is shown sitting on a cloud scroll within a cave. Mist or smoke emanates from the entrance and clouds rain on the scene (Angulo 1987, 133–58; Grove and Gillespie 1984, 32–33; Reilly 1994, 78–79; 1995).

Rain deities such as the Maya Chac, the Zapotec Cocijo, and the Central Mexican Tlaloc (Miller and Taube 1993, 184) are thought to dwell in caves (Bassie-Sweet 1991, 1996; Brady 1989; Stone 1995). There are iconographic depictions from the Maya Classic and Postclassic periods that illustrate Chac, the rain god, sitting in his cave or its functional equivalent, a *cenote* (sinkhole). Depictions of Chac seated in his cave are found in the Dresden Codex (pages 30a and 67b: Bassie-Sweet 1991, 91–95) and the Madrid Codex (pages 29 and 73: Bassie-Sweet 1996,

FIGURE 10.4 An illustration from a painted Late Classic vase depicting Chac, the Maya rain god, sitting in his cave house, drawn as a building in profile. (After Stone 1995, figure 3-1, adapted from Coe 1978, 78, no. 11.)

98–103). In addition, there are iconographic depictions from the Maya Classic Period that illustrate Chac, the rain god, sitting in his cave (figure 10.4). The images are reified at the cave of La Pailita in Guatemala where a life-size sculpture of Chac sits on his throne in the cave's interior (Graham 1997). Similarly, the Aztec god Tlaloc lived in caves or on mountaintops and was described by ethnohistorian Diego Durán as the "God of Rain, Thunder, and Lightning . . . The name means Path under the Earth or Long Cave" (in Heyden 1975, 134).

Caves also serve as fundamental anchoring points for Mesoamerican communities and play important roles in settlement patterns. Work by ethnohistorian Angel García-Zambrano (1994) demonstrated that caves and water holes functioned as salient geopolitical entities. In his study of mid-sixteenth-century town land titles (*títulos de pueblos y tierras*) housed in the National Archives in Mexico City, he discussed models of ideal landscapes that immigrants used to make decisions on where to settle. The ideal location was based on a quincuncial model of the cosmos of four cardinal directions and a central point. The model was reified in the natural environment by a group of four mountains, which functioned as the peripheries of the community, with a fifth and centrally located mountain representing the center point, or *axis mundi*.

The central mountain was ideally dotted with caves and springs. Caves with water emitting from their interiors were favored, but man-made substitutes or modified crevices could be created to fit the model. A chosen cave would then function as the mythological place of origin of the people and as the sacred core of the community that provided the "cosmogonic referents that legitimized the settler's rights for occupying that space and for the ruler's authority over that site" (García-Zambrano 1994, 217–18). The leader or ruler of the group conducted rituals in the cave to petition local deities.

If the local environment failed to naturally mimic the ideological model, modifications could be undertaken. For instance, pyramids could be constructed to represent mountains. Dams and/or aqueducts could be used to channel water to the site core. In the absence of a natural cave, an artificial cave could be excavated or a large clay water jar could be interred in the town plaza to represent the cave.

Once an area was settled, peripheries were drawn and ritually sanctified by ceremonially circumambulating and beating the boundaries. Reification of the agreed-upon periphery was provided by boundary markers, including stones that could be moved into place, or natural features such as boulders, trees, water holes, wells, or caves. This information agrees with ethnographic accounts from the Maya area reported by Evon Vogt (1976, 111–15; 1969, 690–95). In Zinacantecan, *K'in Krus* rites or water-hole ceremonies were community renewal rites that beat the boundaries of the community. Their execution encircled the culturally used parts of the local environment associated with particular lineage groups. Prayers and offerings to compensate the earth deity for the use of natural resources were made at particular stations that served as boundary markers, which included natural landscape features such as caves, waterholes, and rocks. Vogt (1969, 391) noted that the definition of territorial geographic space remained an important feature of modern Maya spatial cognition.

Because of the widespread belief that they are the place of origin or emergence of ancestral people, caves function as territorial markers and play a role in ethnic identity. Ethnographically this has been demonstrated among the Tzotzil Maya of Guatemala (Guiteras-Holmes 1947, 1). Tzotzil lineages are formed into clans that are associated with particular caves. The cave represents both the place of emergence of the lineage ancestors and the place where one returns at death. Vogt (1976, 99) noted a similar attachment in which lineages take their names from the cave or spring around which they live. Villa Rojas (1969, 215) observed that distinguished members of each lineage were buried in their respective caves. Patricia McAnany (1995,

FIGURE 10.5 Modern Naj Tunich cave ceremony. (Photograph by James E. Brady.)

159) relates this notion to the past, arguing that Maya lineages were intimately connected to the land they inhabited. The close identification of caves with the sacred earth and their function as residences of the earth "owners" explain why caves are salient ritual venues (figure 10.5). Rituals today include obtaining permission to utilize the earth and its resources, petitions for rain, calendrical rites, and rites for divination, hunting, and curing. Caves may also contain oracles and may be used in rites of sorcery and witchcraft.

CAVE ARCHAEOLOGY

Much of our knowledge concerning Mesoamerican concepts about caves derives from textual, iconographic, or ethnographic information, but it is the archaeology of caves that has contributed most to our understanding of caves as ritual venues among ancient people. Archaeological cave sites have yielded enormous artifact assemblages that often include organic remains. Excellent preservation in caves and an almost exclusively ritual context has allowed archaeologists to develop a fresh view of ancient Mesoamerican religion.

Although the utilization of caves was noted in the mid-nineteenth century explorations of John Lloyd Stephens and Frederick Catherwood (Stephens 1963 [1843]), it has only been since the mid-1970s that caves have been recognized as ritual spaces (Brady 1989; Brady and Prufer 2005). In their journeys through Yucatan, Stephens was taken to various "caves" by local people. These sometimes turned out to be man-made subterranean passages beneath ancient architecture. His guides consistently refused to enter these tunnels. Stephens found this curious but never discovered the cause. He noted that, while exploring the deep passages of the natural cave of Bolonchen, his local guides disappeared, suggesting that there may have been overriding reasons for not entering particular parts of the cave. Women may also have been proscribed from entering the cave near the "rancho of Chaak" (Chac). This was made apparent because, as Stephens (1963 [1843], 2: 16) reported, water collection was usually the domain of women but, curiously, only men entered the cave. He concluded that natural caves such as the large Bolonchen were used as emergency water sources during dry seasons and that in general caves served as wells.

Stephens's observations set the stage for attributions of cave use for quite some time and seriously affected early archaeological thinking (Rissolo 2005, 345). It was not until much later that water collection was recognized as a function of survival particular to the arid, low-lying areas of the Yucatan Peninsula where the water table was accessible only in deep caves and water holes during the driest of times. Later archaeological studies by Dominique Rissolo (2005) in the Yalahau region of Yucatan demonstrated that, where wells provided an ample water supply, both caves and rockshelters took on a strictly ceremonial and sacred nature.

One of the first studies to prompt archaeological interest in caves was Doris Heyden's interpretation of the cave beneath the second-largest structure in Mesoamerica, Teotihuacan's Pyramid of the Sun, located in central Mexico. Her seminal studies were among the first to suggest that caves functioned as ritual spaces (Brady 1989; Brady and Prufer 2005). Using ethnohistoric textual information, Heyden (1973, 1975) inferred the ritual function and cosmological significance of the pyramid's cave. Although the cave dated to the first century AD, she argued that its spatial configuration resembled ethnohistoric iconographic depictions of *Chicomostoc,* the primordial cave of emergence of the later Aztec people. Heyden was not aware that the cave was man made, but later research demonstrated that the design was in fact deliberate (Manzanilla 2000; Manzanilla et al. 1994). The man-made tunnel or

FIGURE 10.6 The Pyramid of the Sun at Teotihuacan. The inset illustrates the location of the cave beneath the structure.

"cave" stretches from the base of the central stairway to beneath the center of the pyramid (Manzanilla 2000, 98; figure 10.6). In antiquity, water was channeled through a system of drains into the tunnel so that it flowed out of the entrance—the "cave's mouth"—completing the image of a fertile sacred mountain with water flowing from its interior (Heyden 1973, 1975; Millon 1981).

Using a landscape approach, James Brady later identified this mountain/cave/water complex in the Maya Classic period at the site of Dos Pilas, Guatemala (Brady et al. 1997a). The royal palace complex was built above the Cave of the Bats (*Cueva de Murciélagos*) that served as an outlet for an entire drainage system of the site. To this day, during heavy rains, water gushes from the mouth of the cave with such force that the roar can be heard half a kilometer away. Brady and his colleagues suggested that this was a sensory cue that announced the beginning of the rainy season, the purpose of which was to reify the power and control of the king over life-giving water.

The mountain/cave/water complex is also manifest at the Classic period site of Las Cuevas in the Mountain Pine Ridge area of Belize. Here a temple construction sits directly atop a large natural cave whose cathedral-like entrance contains a spring (Digby 1958; Moyes et al. 2011; Thompson 1959). Monumental architecture including rooms and terraces surround the spring, blocks of cut stone line the water hole, and stairs descend to the pool at its base. The cave entrance was clearly a theatrical venue for public performance. The constructions surrounding this natural feature create a strong cosmological statement referencing the three-tiered universe and reifying the mountain/cave/water complex.

CAVES AND COMMUNITY

The archaeological record demonstrates that geospatial models used in Mesoamerican community foundation as described by García-Zambrano (1994) were in place by the Preclassic period. This appears to be a pattern in the Maya area where cave sites date either earlier than or contemporaneous with the earliest local settlements. For instance, Chechem Ha Cave in western Belize produced the earliest radiocarbon dates from a cave in the Maya Lowlands, documenting use as early as 1100–1200 BC, contemporaneous with the earliest known settlement in the region (Moyes 2006, 2007a, 2008; Moyes et al. 2009). Recently an Early Classic cave shrine with a viewshed to the site of Uxbenká in southern Belize was found to be contemporaneous with the site's earliest architectural construction phase (Moyes 2007a; Moyes and Prufer 2009). Rissolo (2001) noted the early use of caves in his survey of Yalahau in the Yucatan and Keith Prufer's (2002) survey of ninety caves in the

Maya Mountains of Belize found that the use of caves appeared to precede the area's settlement.

In addition to natural caves directly associated with site cores, artificial caves are excavated into hillsides below architecture. Table 10.2 is a partial list, but numerous others are known to exist. Artificial caves document that the placement of structures over caves was deliberate. Furthermore it suggests that in areas where caves do not naturally form, these features are so important that they are constructed. James Brady (Brady 1991, 2004; Brady and Veni 1992) recorded a number of man-made caves in Guatemala, most notably at Mixco Viejo, Esquipulas, and Utatlan. The spatial configuration of Utatlan cave in the highlands is of particular interest. The passage exhibits a number of lobes or alcoves similar to the cave beneath the Pyramid of the Sun at Teotihuacan. Brady speculates that the cave may represent the place of emergence described in the Popol Vuh. Additionally, on a hillside beneath the site of Acatzingo Viejo in central Mexico, Manuel Aguilar and his colleagues (Aguilar et al. 2005) describe seven man-made caves mimicking iconographic representations of *Chicomostoc*, the Aztec seven-lobed cave of emergence. These examples demonstrate the importance of caves in establishing identity and a sense of place in the archaeological record.

Epigraphic and iconographic evidence also corroborates the importance of caves in the establishment of communities. David Stuart (1999) first recognized the Maya hieroglyph for *cave*. In the Classic period the glyph is often associated with place names or emblem glyphs denoting polities. The term *chan ch'een*, or "sky cave," is often found in association with local toponyms, suggesting a universal term for the community or the world (Vogt and Stuart 2005). In Central Mexico, the Nahuatl term for community, *altepetl*, literally means "water-filled mountain," while the Aztec glyph for a community was a hill with the specific name at the top. This suggests that throughout Mesoamerica indigenous peoples saw these sacred landmarks as the truly important symbols of the polity. Clearly, by the Classic period, caves had taken on a political significance. Epigraphy found within caves strengthens this evidence.

While some caves are located within site cores, many caves are found in remote locations. In one instance we are able to link a cave directly to the polities that visited the site. Naj Tunich cave in Guatemala is one of the largest and best-documented pilgrimage caves in Mesoamerica. Not only does the site contain architecture, tombs, and numerous artifacts, but it was also a venue for numerous cave paintings and panels of hieroglyphs. Some of the inscriptions contain emblem glyphs from distant polities (Brady 1989; Colas 1998; Stone 1995), indicating that the cave was a pilgrimage site for numerous groups. Pierre Colas has argued that some of the rituals conducted at Naj Tunich were political in nature, recording war-related events.

This suggests that caves may have had specific functions in intersite interactions. In a separate study, Brady and Colas (2005) argue that inscriptions from looted hieroglyphic panels thought to come from the area around

TABLE 10.2 Partial list of caves directly associated with Mesoamerican surface architecture.

Site	Natural/ Artificial	Country	Publication
Atcatzingo Viejo	Artificial	Mexico	Aguilar et al. 2005
Cahal Witz Na	Natural	Belize	Awe and Helmke 1998; Halperin 2005
Chichen Itza	Artificial	Mexico	Thompson 1938
Cholula	Natural	Mexico	McCafferty 1996
Chuncanol	Natural	Mexico	Carter 1935
Cozumel	Natural	Mexico	Mason 1927; Patel 2005; Sanders 1955
Dos Pilas	Natural	Guatemala	Brady 1997; Demarest et al. 2003
El Cayo	Natural	Mexico	Lee and Hayden 1988
Esquipulas	Artificial	Guatemala	Brady and Veni 1992
Ix Chel	Natural	Belize	Reeder 1993; Webster 2000
Jamasquire	Natural	Honduras	Dixon et al. 1998; Stone 1941
La Lagunita	Artificial	Guatemala	Ichon and Arnauld 1985
Las Cuevas	Natural	Belize	Digby 1958
Ma'ax Na	Natural	Belize	King and Shaw 2003
Malinalco	Artificial	Mexico	Townsend 1982
Mayapan	Natural	Mexico	Pugh 2001
Mixo Viejo	Artificial	Guatemala	Brady and Veni 1992
Pusilha	Natural	Belize	Joyce 1929; Joyce et al. 1928
Quen Santo	Natural	Guatemala	Brady 2009; Seler 2003
Tenampua	Artificial	Honduras	Popenoe 1936
Teotihuacan	Artificial	Mexico	Heyden 1975; Manzanilla 2000
Totimehuacan	Artificial	Mexico	Spranz 1967
Tulum	Natural	Mexico	Lothrop 1924
Utatlan	Artificial	Guatemala	Brady and Veni 1992; Fox 1978, 1991, 1993
Uxbenka	Natural	Belize	Moyes 2007a; Moyes and Prufer 2009
Xabaj	Artificial	Guatemala	Smith 1955
Xochicalco	Artificial	Mexico	Hirth 2000

Piedras Negras record "throwing fire" or burning events occurring in caves as acts of war. According to the authors, these may include not only burning but desecration or destruction of the site. This suggests that there were significant political aspects associated with cave use that are only beginning to be understood.

One of the problems that has plagued cave archaeology is, Who is using the caves? Sites such as Naj Tunich or Jolja Cave in Chiapas, Mexico, contain hieroglyphic writing recording "arrivals," suggesting that they are elite pilgrimage sites (Bassie-Sweet, Perez de Lara, and Zender 2000; Stone 1995; Vogt and Stuart 2005), but these are rare examples. Were all caves used by elites? Awe, Griffith, and Gibbs (2005) argue from the presence of uncarved stelae or standing stones in caves in western Belize that cave rites were the prerogative of elites.

Research by Christophe Helmke and Dorie Reents-Budet suggests that lesser elites were using caves during the Late to Terminal Classic period. Helmke studied Late to Terminal Classic molded-carved censers that are typically found in cave deposits. In a spatial analysis of their distribution in surface contexts surrounding the site of Altun Ha, he found that these vessels were most commonly excavated from structures belonging to lesser elites. He and Reents-Budet further argued that these vessels represented the "restructuring of social negotiations—from the hands of paramount royalty during the Late Classic period to the hands of lesser nobles . . . in Terminal Classic times" (2008, 47). This suggests that rites in caves became connected to these lesser elites. .

CAVE ARCHAEOLOGY

Archaeologist J. Eric S. Thompson (1959) was the first to publish a synthetic article using archaeology, ethnohistory, and ethnography to suggest that ancient Maya caves had ritual uses. Although Thompson was one of the most important Maya scholars of his day, "The Role of Caves in Maya Culture" was not well circulated and received little attention. In 1975, about the time that Doris Heyden was writing about the cave beneath the Pyramid of the Sun, Thompson elaborated on the original article and published it as an introduction to the reprint edition of *The Hill-Caves of Yucatan* (Mercer 2005 [1896]) and archaeologists began to take note. Thompson's uses included (1) sources of drinking water, (2) sources of "virgin" water, (3) venues of religious rites, (4) places for burials, ossuaries, and cremations, (5) art galleries, (6) deposition of ceremonially discarded utensils, (7) places of refuge, and (8) other uses (which included mining).

Thompson placed particular emphasis on the collection of "virgin" water, or *zuhuy ha,* to be used in ceremonies. Barbara Tedlock (personal communication, 2000) suggested that the correct spelling is *suhuy,* which translates as "pure," as distinct from "virgin." Pure water used in rituals is caught and never touches the ground. It may be rainwater or dew, or may be collected from a spring or cave. It was noted by Aramoni (Heyden 2005), that in Tzinacapan, water coming from caves in the area is believed to be pure because it originates in Talocan (the underworld). While water collection surely occurred in the past, many archaeologists have systematically interpreted the large jars that make up the bulk of cave assemblages as vessels for water collection. In a few rare instances jars were in fact placed beneath dripping stalactites, but this does not appear to be a common pattern. Most vessels exhibit ritual breakage and are ill-suited to contain either liquid or solid material, suggesting that the vessel itself was an offering. Moyes and her colleagues (2009) argued that jars found in caves were appropriate gifts for rain deities. Broken sherds could also serve as gifts for earth or underworld deities (Moyes 2001).

Although Thompson's list was not without flaws (see Brady in Mercer 2005), it became the new bible for cave interpretation for many years. Scholars today still grapple with his categories. Though some uses would be considered minor, others are more common than originally conceived, and some such as "art galleries" are clearly Western constructs. For instance, Thompson himself (1975, xli) noted that evidence for "places of refuge" is "scant," but he nonetheless adduces a few isolated modern examples in which caves were temporary shelters under adverse conditions. Henry Mercer (1975, 141) was told that people hid in caves during wartime, and Hatt and his colleagues (1953, 21) reported that farmers lived in caves close to their fields in times of peril. Neither of these scholars actually witnessed people living in caves, even temporarily, but Moyes has witnessed farmers in western Belize camping in the mouth of Stela Cave to watch over their fields and prevent looting. It is of note that the farmers did not use the dark zone of the cave. She was also told that small caves provided shelter during hurricanes for people living in the Macal Valley and that hunting blinds were sometimes erected at the mouths of caves to stalk the elusive *Agouti paca* (known by a variety of names, including gibnut and tepezquintle). It is important to note here that people in this area are immigrants with few or no ties to Maya communities and little knowledge of traditional religious traditions. So, while there is some precedent for the use of caves as temporary shelters, even in nontraditional communities this is a rare occurrence.

Thompson may have underestimated the prevalence of cave mining. Brady and Rissolo (2006) produce examples of mining *kancab* (red earth), *sahkab* (white earth), gypsum, rock for ceramic temper, and palygorskite (a clay used for making blue pigment and as an antidiarrheal medication). Mining pits in caves are often located in the deepest recesses or in dark zones even when other more-accessible areas are available for extraction of materials. This impractical practice argues that cave-specific contextual extraction has a ritual component due to ancient belief systems that regard the earth as sacred and animated, and cave dark zones as magic or supernatural places. In addition, because only small amounts of material are extracted from these sites, it is unlikely that there is an economic benefit to cave mining. Material extracted from caves sites may be used in the manufacture of sacred objects, in the creation of architectural features in ritual spaces, or as powerful medicines used in curing. The authors also suggest that large quarrying sites such as a group of tunnels located behind the Pyramid of the Sun at Teotihuacan were excavated not only for construction material but also to create man-made caves.

However, history has shown that Thompson was entirely correct in some respects. Nearly 50 years after Thompson's original article, archaeology in caves has demonstrated that they were indeed ritual venues that were sometimes used as burial places and ossuaries.

Some early studies are notable. In the late 1970s Dorie Reents-Budet and Barbara MacLeod conducted a major study at Petroglyph Cave in Belize (Reents 1980; Reents-Budet and MacLeod 1997). With the help of cavers they made detailed maps, collected surface finds, conducted limited excavations, and recorded artifacts. Their interpretations were based heavily on iconographic as well as textual sources.

Work at Naj Tunich cave was another early case study that involved a team approach that integrated archaeology, art history, and professional cavers (Brady 1989; Stone 1995). In his early work Brady not only recorded, mapped, and excavated the site but also created models of cave use based on the comprehensive synthesis of hundreds of ethnographic and ethnohistoric documents as well as archaeological accounts. This synthetic approach clearly demonstrated to the archaeological community that most caves were exclusively used for ritual purposes.

Andrea Stone recorded the Naj Tunich cave art, later producing a synthetic document that detailed and interpreted the paintings and hieroglyphs, comparing the material with art documented at other Maya cave sites. Other early case studies provided a solid exploratory basis for future efforts and many resulted in well-executed reports (Andrews 1970; Graham, McNatt, and Gutchen 1980; Pendergast 1969, 1970, 1971, 1974). Once patterns in artifact assemblages could be established, scholars began to understand the nature of the ritual assemblages in caves.

While some objects found in caves, such as appliquéd incense burners, are clearly ritual artifacts, others are less obvious. For instance, caves throughout the Maya area exhibit speleothem breakage, movement, caching, and removal (Brady et al. 1997b). Brady argues that these are objects of power that contain a powerful essence similar to Polynesian *mana*. This is hardly surprising considering that the Yucatec term for speleothems is *xix ha tunich* or "dripwater stone" (Barrera Vásquez 2007, 946), indicating that the Maya conceived of stalactites and stalagmites as having been formed from water that was *suhuy* or ritually pure.

Speleothems such as stalactites and stalagmites could be used to construct features in caves such as hearths, platforms, and altars (Brady 1989; Moyes 2000, 2001) or they might accompany ritual deposits. For instance, a spatial analysis of artifacts at Actun Tunichil Muknal (Moyes 2001, 2003, 2005a; Moyes and Awe 1998, 2000) indicated that speleothems comprised 16 percent of the total assemblage and occurred in 23 percent of the 252 artifact groupings. Speleothems were also removed from caves and have been found at numerous surface sites throughout the Maya realm in a variety of contexts, such as atop platforms, as substela caches, and in ballcourts, shrines, middens, and burials (Brady et al. 1997b; Moyes, Awe, and Schwarcz 2006; Peterson, McAnany, and Cobb 2005; Strómsvik 1942).

Despite the number of exotic items that may be associated with caves, the bulk of cave assemblages are composed of household items, such as unslipped ceramics, grinding stones, spindle whorls, chipped stone, animal bones, or unmodified stone. The use of household objects in ritual contexts is one of the major reasons that early studies attributed cave use to habitation. Despite this, cave assemblages possess unique properties. First, most objects in caves are highly fragmentary and may have been ritually smashed. Ceramics left in caves have usually been broken and the pieces stacked or scattered within a small area. This has been well documented in the systematic study at Actun Tunichil Muknal (Moyes 2001), a cave with little subsurface sedimentation. In situ refitting demonstrated that the farthest a sherd fell from its associated sherds was within 5 meters. In many cases, sherds were stacked together and placed in niches or small alcoves (Moyes 2001, 73–75; 2005a). Although many vessels could be refitted, they were invariably missing fragments, which suggests that some sherds were removed from the cave. Also, single sherds were brought into the cave as offerings in and of themselves. Brady (1989, 86) similarly noted that, when refitting vessels at Naj Tunich, some portion of the vessel was always missing.

Artifact classes in caves vary from cave to cave and no two are identical. Ceramic sherds are present at all sites used after about 1000 BC, but there is variability in temporal and modal patterning within assemblages as well as

FIGURE 10.7 Large vessels from Chechem Ha Cave, Belize. (Photograph by Holley Moyes.)

among other artifact classes. While there appear to be a number of thematic similarities in the overall function and meaning of caves, variability in artifact assemblages and architectural modifications suggest that caves were used in different and possibly unique ways. Some caves have petroglyphs or paintings, whereas others do not. Some caves contain spindle whorls, celts, stingray spines, lithics, or other artifact classes, while others are completely devoid of these objects (Moyes 2001, 2002; Prufer 2002, 626–27). Caves also contain unique finds. For instance, in Petroglyph Cave, a snake skeleton was found propped up on a speleothem, possibly the only occurrence of its kind (Reents-Budet and MacLeod 1997).

Miniatures or oversized objects may also be found in caves. At Balankanche in Yucatan, Wyllys Andrews (1970) discovered hundreds of tiny metates or grinding stones. At Chechem Ha Cave in Belize, a small passage was filled with huge water jars with rim diameters up to half a meter (figure 10.7). Also, many caves contain unique feature constructions. At Actun Tunichil Muknal, a crevice in the floor was in-filled with at least forty-eight broken speleothems. The construction, located deep within the cave, had to be stepped over to move from one area to another. The crevice only measured 30 centimeters wide and provided no real obstacle, so the construction's function appears to have been esoteric (Moyes 2001, 2003). Such instances suggest that either there is variation on common ritual themes or that unique rites occurred in caves.

Based on iconographic or epigraphic evidence, researchers have tried to define the types of rites that may have taken place, but isolating these ceremonies in the archaeological record is difficult. For instance, Mary Pohl (1981) makes a good argument based on ethnohistorical, ethnographic, and iconographic data that *cuch,* or renewal rites related to the accession of rulers, may have occurred in caves and she suggests that such rites are evidenced by deer bones found in some assemblages. However, one might argue that the bones are a result of hunting rites (Brown 2005). Without a clear pattern of material correlates, it is difficult to establish unambiguous connections.

Members of the Western Belize Regional Cave Project (WBRCP), under the direction of Jaime Awe, have produced a number of studies that have focused most heavily on the archaeological record itself. For instance, in their research at Handprint Cave (*Actun Uayazba Kab*), Christophe Helmke and Awe (1998) use an iconographic approach to compare the cave's petroglyphs to iconography on Classic period stelae. The presence of similar sets of motifs suggests that the cave was the focus of elite accession rites. This reinforces a wider body of evidence that caves took on a political functions in the Classic period.

In his work on ethnobotanical remains, Christopher Morehart (2002a, 2002b) argued that caves were the venues of fertility rites and agricultural rituals that included first-fruit and harvest rites. Other studies support these findings. At Chechem Ha Cave, constructions, features, and the artifact assemblage of Crawl 3, a small side-tunnel in the cave system, suggest that it was a ritual sweat bath (Moyes 2005b). Not only was its construction morphologically similar to known sweat baths, but a fire was lit in the tunnel, suggesting that it actually heated up. In Mesoamerican thought, sweat baths are strongly associated with aspects of fertility and Earth deities—denizens of caves and sweat baths are associated with creation, birth, and renewal. The artifact assemblage in Crawl 3 was consistent with fertility and renewal rites dedicated to Earth gods.

Highly detailed mapping programs, coupled with excellent artifact preservation, allowed the project to evaluate the use of space in the Main Chamber at Actun Tunichil Muknal (Moyes 2001, 2005a; Moyes and Awe 1998, 2000). The study showed that caves were ritually bounded spaces. Ritual pathways in caves suggested that boundaries were beaten and ritual stations were visited within the cave, similar to rites of foundation at site cores as detailed by García-Zambrano (1994).

The study also demonstrated that 51 percent of the artifact assemblage was deposited in intermittent pools, which suggests that water-related rites were prevalent. This agrees well with growing evidence that caves were important venues for propitiating rain deities. Dominique Rissolo (2001, 2005) noted that many of the caves in his survey of forty-eight caves in the Yalahau area of Quintana Roo, Yucatan, contained interior water features. Both rock art and architectural modifications tended to be associated with these features, and art from the cave of Pak Che'n contained rain-god motifs. At the cave of Balankanche, also in Yucatan, large anthropomorphic censers were scattered around a stalagmitic column (Andrews 1970, 69). Most of the censers were modeled with images of the central Mexican rain god, Tlaloc. Similarly, at the site of the Gruta de Chac, Andrews (1965, 14) reported finding large numbers of painted globular jars with water motifs, such as stylized frogs and water birds. These were located throughout a passage that led to an underground pool. Because of the motifs on the jars and their spatial proximity to the underground water source, Michael Smyth (2000) argued that they were offerings to rain deities.

HUMAN REMAINS IN CAVES

Human remains are prevalent in caves, rockshelters, and sinkholes. Although their presence has been noted for years, there has been little systematic research beyond reports. Remains may be classified as burials, sacrifices, or problematic deposits, and burials may be single or multiple, elite or nonelite (Scott and Brady 2005). There are relatively few apical-elite burials in caves and few formal tomb constructions with some notable exceptions. Looted masonry tombs found at Naj Tunich contained pieces of bone, jades, and polychrome vessels, suggesting that elites were once interred in these structures. Recently another elaborate masonry tomb was reported from Quen Santo (Kieffer 2008). A number of burials in walled-off cave alcoves were found that dated to the Late Preclassic period (300 BC–AD 250). The burials had been looted but still contained jade and pyrite beads, implying that the individuals had held high status (Garza, Brady, and Christensen 2001). Outside of the Maya area, another example is found in Oaxaca where Christopher Moser (1975, 1976, 1983) discovered forty masonry tombs in a cave. Also, elite cave burial has been mentioned in ethnohistorical sources from Oaxaca (Burgoa 1934, 2: 121). Researchers have long thought that tombs placed within pyramids represented symbolic caves, so perhaps this accounts for the lack of more elite burials in the natural landscape.

Cave sites with multiple burials are usually referred to as *ossuaries*, a general term for places or receptacles for the bones of the dead. One well-reported example is Gordon's Cave 3, located at the site of Copan in Honduras. The cave was originally discovered by George Gordon in 1893 and later investigated by James Brady (Brady 1995; Gordon 1898). The cave contains 600 to 700 skeletons and most likely dates to the Early to Middle Preclassic period (1100–800 BC). Similar sites with Early to Middle Preclassic date ranges found in the Talgua region (figure 10.8) suggest that this is an early pattern (Scott and Brady 2005). Ossuary sites dating to the Postclassic period (AD 900–1500) are found in Guatemalan highlands (Blom 1954; O'Neale 1942; Wauchope 1942).

A number of rockshelters appear to have been used as cemeteries primarily for local nonapical elites or for commoners. Caves Branch Rock Shelter in Belize is part of an ongoing, multiyear study. At the back of the rockshelter is a small cave with a dark zone. The first excavation of the rockshelter area was carried out by Juan Luis Bonor Villarejo, with laboratory analysis conducted by David Glassman (Glassman and Bonor Villarejo 2005). Bonor

FIGURE 10.8 (Left) "The Crystal Maiden" from Actun Tunichil Muknal in Belize may be a sacrificial victim. (Photograph by John Lyle.) (Right) Preclassic ossuary in the Cave of the Glowing Skulls in the Talgua region of Honduras. (Photograph by James Brady.)

excavated thirty-two individuals from the shelter, including males and females of all ages, but estimated that there were at least 100 more. Glassman and Bonor found that the site was a cemetery for the local community, and they argued that the rockshelter functioned as a "cave" for those of lesser status. Later work by Gabriel Wroebel uncovered another ninety-seven interments and determined (based on 2-sigma AMS dates) that the shelter was used more or less continuously between AD 80 and 950 (Wroebel 2008). By excavating both the cave dark zone and the outer rockshelter, Wroebel demonstrated that burials only occurred in the rockshelter area.

Caves Branch Rock Shelter does not appear to be an isolated occurrence. Handprint Cave in western Belize is morphologically similar to the Caves Branch site in that a cave is present at the rear of the rockshelter. Working with the WBRCP, Josalyn Ferguson and Sherry Gibbs (Ferguson and Gibbs 1999; Gibbs 1998, 2000) excavated eleven interments complete with grave goods in a lighted alcove of the rockshelter area. Like Caves Branch, the cave dark zone contained no burials. As at Caves Branch, burials were layered one on top of another and appeared to span a long temporal period, which led Gibbs to suggest that the individuals may have represented a lineage group, an idea posited years ago by J. Eric S. Thompson (1975, xxxiii). Working on the Maya Mountains Archaeological Project, Keith Prufer (2002; Saul, Prufer, and Saul 2005) also excavated three rockshelters containing human remains of lower-status individuals.

Aside from multiple burials in rockshelters, Prufer discovered a small site, Bats'ub Cave, whose terminus was walled off, serving as a tomb (Prufer 2002; Prufer and Hurst 2007). (Similar looted constructions were recorded by Brady [2005] at Naj Tunich.) Behind the wall was a burial that was relatively intact, despite looting. The burial was unusual in that the head had been removed and replaced by a broken pottery vessel containing a single jade bead. A cranium, possibly of the interred individual, was placed to the left of the pelvis, and a bowl containing cocoa seeds was placed on top. Based on the decapitated cranium and presence of cacao, Prufer suggests that the interred individual may have been a ritual specialist.

Unlike the above instance, individual skeletons found in caves are often much more difficult to classify and are often attributed to human sacrifice rather than interments, particularly when they are not buried. Ethnohistoric evidence linking caves and cenotes to human sacrifice abounds. In Yucatan children were drowned in the Cenote of Sacrifice at Chichen Itza, a practice that was documented both ethnohistorically (Tozzer 1941, 44n) and archaeologically (Hooton 1940; Tiesler 2005). In the Guatemalan highlands, children have been reported to have been sacrificed in a cave near Mixco Viejo as part of a rain ceremony (Fuentes y Guzmán 1932, 36). Toribio de Benavente Motolinía (1971 [1555], 50) records sacrificial rituals involving caves performed in central Mexico in honor of Tlaloc, the rain deity.

Iconography from the Maya area also suggests that sacrifice occurred in caves. At Caracol in Western Belize, Altar 13 portrays a male figure that stands next to a kneeling, decapitated figure while a third watches the event. This scene is set within a quatrefoil frame, indicating that it took place in an underworld or cave setting (Beetz and Satterthwaite 1981, figure 24). Pictured on Tikal Altar 8 is a bound captive, presumably about to be sacrificed. Vogt and Stuart (2005, 162) note that in the accompanying inscription the cave glyph is present in the place name *Yax Mutul*, suggesting that the event took place in a cave.

It has been argued that the Main Chamber of Actun Tunichil Muknal in western Belize is a place of sacrifice (Gibbs 1998, 2000; Lucero and Gibbs 2007; Moyes 2001; Moyes and Awe 1998, 2000; Moyes and Gibbs 2000). The site was investigated in the late 1990s by the WBRCP and is now a major tourist destination. The cave contains an interior water source, and a river must be traversed to reach the chamber, which is located over 500 meters from the cave entrance. The chamber dates to the end of the Late Classic period based on two almost identical AMS dates (2-sigma calibration: AD 710–950 and AD 720–960). Distributed throughout the 4,450-square-meter chamber are thirteen skeletons and several unarticulated bones that are likely a secondary burial representing a fourteenth individual. Due to the cave's high humidity, the bones were in poor condition but did allow for some analyses by Sherry Gibbs (1998, 2000). Of the thirteen, five are children under the age of 3 years, two are subadults, and the remaining six are adults ranging from their early twenties to approximately 40 years of age. Of the adults, two are likely to be female and three, possibly four, are male. Not one of the thirteen individuals was buried but all were located on the surface. Eleven of the thirteen were placed in intermittent pools.

The "Crystal Maiden" made famous in tourist lore is located in a high alcove that must be accessed by ladder (see figure 10.8). The remains are of a woman approximately 20 to 23 years old. She was placed in an intermittent pool where the filling and draining of the calcitic water had left a crystalline crust on the bones, cementing them in her final resting position. The woman appears to have been thrown down and her right arm is extended over her head. The context and lack of grave goods suggest that the remains in Actun Tunichil Muknal are sacrificial victims. Lisa Lucero and Gibbs (2007) have taken this a step further in suggesting that the victims were condemned witches, though there is no direct evidence for that supposition. A considerable amount of data collection and methodological development will be necessary to further address issues of sacrifice in caves.

Finally, problematic deposits usually refer to single bones or teeth found in caves. For instance, working at the Cueva de Sangre in Guatemala, Brady (in Scott and Brady 2005) located a vessel that he believed to have been specially commissioned for a cave ceremony. A painted vessel lay inverted over a broken human tibia. The scene on the vessel depicted a spear piercing the left leg of a man at approximately the point where the accompanying bone was broken. This led Brady to conclude that the scene represented the taking of a captive who was later sacrificed. The offering commemorated the event and the bone of the victim was used in the ceremony. Other less spectacular finds of single bones may be relics of ancestors or sacrificial victims, as the Cueva de Sangre example suggests.

RECENT RESEARCH TRENDS

Due to the efforts of many researchers over the past 30 years, Mesoamerican caves are becoming widely accepted as ritual spaces. This interpretive paradigm has allowed the field to move forward and begin to formulate new questions. There have been recent changes in the way that we are thinking about the sites themselves. Rather than viewing caves as single entities, or "containers," as has been the case in most early work, archaeologists are contextualizing caves within larger settlement networks. The WBRCP was one of the first projects to investigate both cave and surface sites within the same project, articulating their chronologies and evaluating their spatial distributions (Awe 1998). Other projects conducted in the 1990s—such as the Petexbatun Regional Archaeological Project in Guatemala and the Maya Mountains Cave Project in southern Belize, and more recently the Vanderbilt Cancuen Project and the Uxbenká Archaeological Project—have incorporated a cave-survey component aimed at better understanding settlement patterns.

With increased radiocarbon dating in caves, it has become apparent that the sites are even older than once thought. Because ritual cave use can be traced into a remote past, archaeologists have begun to question how ritual use has changed over time and to ponder what those changes might mean in broader sociopolitical contexts. In his study of ceramics from caves in the Pasion-Verapaz Region of Guatemala, Brent Woodfill (2007) examined changing spheres of influence between highland and lowland Maya populations by studying the variation in ceramic assemblages. He argued that artifacts in caves function not only as ritual objects, but in economic and social arenas as well.

Moyes's (2006) work with the WBRCP at Chechem Ha Cave in western Belize traced ritual use of the site over 2,000 years, from the Early Middle Preclassic to the Terminal Classic (1200 BC to AD 950). Her case study uncovered spatiotemporal patterning in ritual deposits, demonstrating that dramatic changes in ritual behavior occurred over time. She further argued that changes in cave ritual should be understood within broader social contexts. By articulating patterns of cave use with local social, political, and environmental histories, it was possible to demonstrate that a Late Classic drought cult accompanied environmental changes just prior to the Maya collapse (Moyes 2006, 2007b, 2008; Moyes et al. 2009).

Finally, new questions require new research methods and new methods. Geochemical analyses permit the sourcing of artifacts in caves, which allows us to pair caves with particular surface sites or larger regions, and to conduct catchment studies. This is one of the most direct methods for inferring the place of origin of cave users, though trade patterns can affect results. This method is particularly useful when we consider patterns of pilgrimage or attempt to infer polity boundaries from cave use. Woodfill (2007) used Instrumental Neutron Activation Analysis (INAA) to source ceramics found at his sites to determine their origins. Michael Smyth (2000) used INAA to compare the clay used in cave ceramics with cave clays to find out whether cave clays were the sources for pastes and slips.

These new analytical tools open the possibility of addressing some fundamental questions in cave archaeology. In instances in which caves are not located in close proximity to surface site cores, we have very little idea of which group or groups were using them. Were the caves used by people from only one polity or were they features that saw visitation from multiple sites in the area? Some of these questions could be answered by comparing the chemical signatures of cave pottery derived from INAA or inductively coupled plasma mass spectrometry (ICP-MS) with the signatures of pottery from surrounding surface sites.

While we have argued that caves are primarily ritual features, they nevertheless offer opportunities to address other questions. Archaeologists want to find the political boundaries of polities but have not been particularly successful in establishing them, perhaps because they have little idea of what may constitute boundaries. As we noted earlier, modern Maya community boundaries are drawn as lines between sacred landmarks and they are regularly revalidated through ritual circuits that pass from one to another sacred landmark. If we recognize that politically important issues are often expressed and celebrated in religion, then methodology may be developed to allow us to answer some larger political questions beyond simply who is using a cave.

Preliminary studies suggest that speleothems from caves may carry a signature of that site. Using INAA in their study of speleothems in the Copan Valley, Honduras, James Brady and his colleagues (1997) found that they exhibited chemical elemental signatures specific to their site of origin, suggesting that a speleothem could be traced to a specific cave. They demonstrated that chemical variability between caves was greater than within-source variation. More recently, ICP-MS is being used to measure quantities of rare earths in speleothems collected in both cave and surface contexts in the Belize Valley in hopes of pairing sites with caves (Moyes, Awe, and Schwarcz 2006).

Cave stalagmites can be a valuable source of high-resolution, local climate data and most importantly can be very accurately dated by ICP-MS Uranium-series (e.g., Ford and Williams 1989; Hill and Forti 1997; Schwarcz and Rink 2001). In tropical environments with seasonal rainfall patterns, speleothems produce annual rings, much like tree rings. Variations in stalagmite petrography, oxygen and carbon isotopes, color, and UV-stimulated luminescence may be used as climate proxies to estimate rainfall abundance. James Webster, George Brook, and their colleagues (2007) produced the first paleoenvironmental reconstruction in Mesoamerica using a stalagmite collected from the Vaca Plateau in western Belize. The paleoclimate reconstruction provided sufficient resolution to compare archaeological events to climatic correlates (Moyes et al. 2009). This method opens up new avenues of research into human and environmental interactions.

Although there is now solid evidence for elite cave use among the Classic Maya, the majority of caves that have been studied contain much more modest remains. Caves and rockshelters located in rural or remote areas are difficult to access and many have little material associated with them. While these may be nonelite sites, no one has developed methodology to examine this issue. Starting in the 1990s, cave surveys that examined multiple caves in and around surface sites have been carried out. Most of these have tended to focus on caves closest to site cores and so have an elite bias. We would suggest that what is needed are cave surveys carried out along a transect that would provide comparative data on both core-area and rural caves, and which would consciously sample both large and modest-sized caves.

As cave studies progress, we expect that researchers will increasingly employ scientific methods to complex and difficult questions. New mapping techniques such as Light Detection and Ranging (LIDAR) are expected to improve accuracy. It is an optical remote-sensing technology that measures properties of scattered light to find range and/or other information of a distant target using laser pulses. This method produces highly detailed three-dimensional images. Increased use of Geographic Information Systems (GIS) will encourage more systematic spatial analyses and create searchable databases for cross-site comparison (see Moyes 2002; Moyes and Awe 2000).

Studies of site-formation processes in tropical caves are in their infancy (see Barker for an exception, this volume; Moyes 2006), but greater appreciation and study of micromorphology, soil chemistry, guano diagenesis, and mineral formation in soils can be expected to contribute to our future understanding of the cave deposits. These and other scientific methods are the keys to advancing cave studies.

CONCLUSION

This chapter has presented an overview of the history of Mesoamerican cave research, though it is by no means comprehensive. We have been able to highlight only a few of the innovative studies that have led to our current understanding of caves and the roles that they have played in Mesoamerican societies. This overview demonstrates that caves functioned as ritual spaces for the earliest settlers, and that, as complex societies developed, caves were appropriated by emerging elites as powerful symbols of legitimacy. The indigenous conceptualization of caves as entrances to the underworld and the home of earth deities forms a foundation for the use of caves as multipurpose ritual venues ideally suited for earth-based rites such as rain, fertility, and renewal ceremonies. They also form the bases for the reification of Mesoamerican cosmological principles and the embodiment of mythological narratives. Rather than thinking of caves as encapsulated entities, archaeologists are beginning to appreciate how they are integrated into the fabric of Mesoamerican culture. Looking at the sheer number of ritual caves, their geographic expanse, and their long temporal spans, it becomes clear that this is one of the strongest cave traditions in the history of the world.

While ethnographic analogy has been indispensible in establishing the place of caves in Mesoamerican cosmology and thought, new questions are emerging that can only be addressed by the archaeological record itself. Changes in ritual practice and disjunctions between the Classic period and today remind us of the importance of testing ethnographic analogies and recognizing that many behaviors in the past may be without ethnohistoric or modern correlates. By tracing the trajectory of Mesoamerican cave research, it becomes apparent that cave studies not only contribute to understanding ritual and religion, but also are barometers of many aspects of the broader culture. As research programs become more sophisticated and new methodologies develop, we expect that cave studies will continue to contribute to the overall understanding of Mesoamerican histories, cultures, and cultural processes.

REFERENCES CITED

Adams, Abigail E., and James E. Brady. 2005. "Ethnographic Notes on Maya Q'eqchi' Cave Rituals: Implications for Archaeological Interpretation." In *In the Maw of the Earth Monster: Mesoamerican Ritual Cave Use*, ed. James E. Brady and Keith M. Prufer, 301–27. Austin: University of Texas Press.

Aguilar, Manuel, Miguel Medina Jaen, Tim M. Tucker, and James E. Brady. 2005. "The Significance of a Chicomoztoc Complex at Acatzingo Viejo." In *In the Maw of the Earth Monster: Mesoamerican Ritual Cave Use*, ed. James E. Brady and Keith M. Prufer, 69–87. Austin: University of Texas Press.

Andrews, E. Wyllys, IV. 1965. *Explorations in the Gruta de Chac*. Middle American Research Institute Publication 31: 1–21. New Orleans: Middle American Research Institute, Tulane University.

Andrews, E. Wyllys, IV. 1970. *Balankanche: Throne of the Tiger Priest*. Middle American Research Institute Publication 32. New Orleans: Middle American Research Institute, Tulane University.

Angulo, Jorge V. 1987. "The Chalcatzingo Reliefs: An Iconographic Analysis." In *Ancient Chalcatzingo*, ed. David C. Grove, 133–58. Austin: University of Texas Press.

Awe, Jaime J., Cameron Griffith, and Sherry Gibbs. 2005. "Cave Stelae and Megalithic Monuments in Western Belize." In *In the Maw of the Earth Monster: Mesoamerican Ritual Cave Use*, ed. James E. Brady and Keith M. Prufer, 223–48. Austin: University of Texas Press.

Awe, Jaime J., and Christophe G.B. Helmke. 1998. "Preliminary Report on the Reconnaissance of Cahal Uitz Na, Roaring Creek Valley, Cayo District, Belize." In *The Western Belize Regional Cave Project: A Report of the 1997 Field Season*, ed. J. J. Awe, 200–15. Department of Anthropology, Occasional Paper No. 1. Durham: University of New Hampshire.

Bassie-Sweet, Karen. 1991. *From the Mouth of the Dark Cave: Commemorative Sculpture of the Late Classic Maya*. Norman: University of Oklahoma Press.

Bassie-Sweet, Karen. 1996. *At the Edge of the World: Caves and Late Classic Maya World View*. Norman: University of Oklahoma Press.

Bassie-Sweet, Karen, Jorge Perez de Lara, and Marc Zender. 2000. "Jolja' Cave." *PARI Journal* 1 (1): 5–10.

Beetz, Carl P., and Linton Satterthwaite. 1981. *The Monuments and Inscriptions at Caracol, Belize*. University Museum Monograph 45. Philadelphia: University of Pennsylvania Museum.

Bernal-García, Maria Elena. 2001. "The Life and Bounty of the Mesoamerican Sacred Mountain." In *Indigenous Traditions and Ecology*, ed. John Grimm, 325–50. Cambridge, MA: Harvard University, Center for the Study of World Religions.

Blom, Frans. 1954. "Ossuaries, Creamation and Secondary Burials among the Maya of Chiapas, Mexico." *Journal de la Société des Americanistes* 43 (1): 123–36. http://dx.doi.org/10.3406/jsa.1954.2418.

Bonor, Juan Luis. 1995. "Excavación de Salvamento en 'Caves Branch Rock Shelter,' Cayo District, Belize." *IV Encuento Internacional Investigadores de la Cultura Maya* 1: 46–70.

Brady, James E. 1989. "An Investigation of Maya Ritual Cave Use with Special Reference to Naj Tunich, Peten, Guatemala." PhD dissertation, Archaeology Program, University of California, Los Angeles.

Brady, James E. 1991. "Caves and Cosmovision at Utatlan." *California Anthropologist* 18 (1): 1–10.

Brady, James E. 1995. "A Reassessment of the Chronology and Function of Gordon's Cave #3, Copan, Honduras." *Ancient Mesoamerica* 6: 29–38. http://dx.doi.org/10.1017/S095653610000208X.

Brady, James E. 1997. "Settlement Configuration and Cosmology: The Role of Caves at Dos Pilas." *American Anthropologist* 99 (3): 602–18. http://dx.doi.org/10.1525/aa.1997.99.3.602.

Brady, James E. 2004. "Constructed Landscapes: Exploring the Meaning and Significance of Recent Discoveries of Artificial Caves." *Ketzalcalli* 1: 2–17.

Brady, James E. 2005. "Foreword." In *The Hill-Caves of Yucatan*, by Henry C. Mercer, f-1–f-23. Austin: Association for Mexican Cave Studies.

Brady, James E. 2009. *Exploring Highland Maya Ritual Cave Use: Archaeology and Ethnography in Huehuetenango, Guatemala*. Association for Mexican Cave Studies, Bulletin 20, Austin, TX.

Brady, James E., and Pierre R. Colas. 2005. "Nikte Mo' Scattered Fire in the Cave of K'ab Chante: Epigraphic and Archaeological Evidence for Cave Desecration in Ancient Maya Warfare." In *Stone Houses and Earth Lords: Maya Religion in the Cave Context*, ed. Keith M. Prufer and James E. Brady, 149–66. Boulder: University Press of Colorado.

Brady, James E., and Keith M. Prufer. 2005. "Introduction: A History of Mesoamerican Cave Interpretation." In *In the Maw of the Earth Monster: Mesoamerican Ritual Cave Use*, ed. James E. Brady and Keith M. Prufer, 1–17. Austin: University of Texas Press.

Brady, James E., and Dominique Rissolo. 2006. "A Reappraisal of Ancient Maya Cave Mining." *Journal of Anthropological Research* 62 (4): 471–90.

Brady, James E., Ann Scott, Allan Cobb, Irma Rodas, John Fogarty, and Monica Urquizú Sánchez. 1997a. "Glimpses of the Dark Side of the Petexbatun Project: The Petexbatun Regional Cave Survey." *Ancient Mesoamerica* 8 (2): 353–64. http://dx.doi.org/10.1017/S0956536100001784.

Brady, James E., Ann Scott, Hector Neff, and Michael Glascock. 1997b. "Speleothem Breakage, Movement, Removal, and Caching: An Aspect of Ancient Maya Cave Modification." *Geoarchaeology* 12 (6): 725–50. http://dx.doi.org/10.1002/(SICI)1520-6548(199709)12:6<725::AID-GEA10>3.0.CO;2-D.

Brady, James E., and George Veni. 1992. "Man-Made and Pseudo-Karst Caves: The Implications of Sub-Surface Features within Maya Centers." *Geoarchaeology* 7 (2): 149–67. http://dx.doi.org/10.1002/gea.3340070205.

Brown, Linda A. 2005. "Planting the Bones: Hunting Ceremonialism at Contemporary and Nineteenth-Century Shrines in the Guatemalan Highlands." *Latin American Antiquity* 16 (2): 131–46. http://dx.doi.org/10.2307/30042808.

Burgoa, Francisco de. 1934 [1674]. *Geográfica Descripción*. Mexico: Talleres Graficos de la Nación, Mexico.

Carter, James B. 1935. "A Brief Description of the Ruins of Chucanob." *Maya Research* 2 (1): 36–59.

Coe, Michael. 1978. *Lords of the Underworld*. Princeton, NJ: Princeton University Press.

Colas, Pierre Robert. 1998. "Ritual and Politics in the Underworld." *Mexicon* 20 (5): 99–104.

Demarest, Arthur, Kim Morgan, Claudia Wooley, and Héctor Escobedo. 2003. "The Political Acquisition of Sacred Geography." In *Maya Palaces and Elite Residences: An Interdisciplinary Approach*, ed. Jessica Joyce Christie, 120–53. Austin: University of Texas Press.

Digby, Adrian. 1958. "A New Maya City Discovered in British Honduras at Las Cuevas and an Underground Necropolis Revealed." *London Illustrated News* 232: 274–5.

Dixon, Boyd, George Hasemann, James Brady, Pastor Gomez, and Marilyn Beaudry-Corbett. 1998. "Multi-Ethnicity or Multiple Enigma: Archaeological Survey in the Rio Talgua Drainage, Department of Olancho, Honduras." *Ancient Mesoamerica* 9: 327–40.

Durán, Fray Diego. 1994 [1588?]. *The History of the Indies of New Spain*. Trans. Doris Heyden. Norman: University of Oklahoma Press.

Eliade, Mircea, and Lawrence E. Sullivan. 1987. "Center of the World." In *The Encyclopedia of Religion*, ed. Mircea Eliade, 166–71. New York: Macmillan.

Ferguson, Josalyn M., and Sherry Gibbs. 1999. "Report on the 1998 Excavations at Actun Uayazba Kab, Roaring Creek Valley, Belize." In *The Western Belize Regional Cave Project: A Report of the 1998 Field Season*, ed. Jaime J. Awe, 112–45. Department of Anthropology Occasional Paper No. 2. Durham: University of New Hampshire.

Ford, Derek C., and Paul W. Williams. 1989. *Karst Geomorphology and Hydrology*. Boston: Unwin Hyman.

Fox, John W. 1978. *Quiche Conquest: Centralism and Regionalism in Highland Guatemalan State Development*. Albuquerque: University of New Mexico Press.

Fox, John W. 1991. "The Lords of Light Versus the Lords of Dark: The Postclassic Highland Maya Ballgame." In *The Mesoamerican Ballgame*, ed. Vernon Scarborough and David R. Wilcox, 213–38. Tucson: University of Arizona Press.

Fox, John W. 1993. "Political Cosmology among the Quiche Maya." In *Factional Competition and Political Development in the New World*, ed. Elizabeth Brumfiel and John W. Fox, 158–70. Cambridge: Cambridge University Press.

Fuentes y Guzmán, Francisco Antonio de. 1932. *Recordación Florida: Discurso Historical y Demostración Natural, Material, Militar y Politica del Reyno de Goathemala*. Biblioteca Goathemala Vols. 6–8. Guatemala: Biblioteca Goathemala.

García-Zambrano, Angel J. 1994. "Early Colonial Evidence of Pre-Columbian Rituals of Foundation." In *Seventh Palenque Round Table, 1989*, ed. Merle Greene Robertson and Virginia Field, 217–27. San Francisco: Pre-Columbian Art Research Institute.

Garza, Sergio, James E. Brady, and Christian Christensen. 2001. "Balam Na Cave 4: Implications for Understanding Preclassic Cave Mortuary Practices." *California Anthropologist* 28 (1): 15–21.

Gibbs, Sherry A. 1998. "Human Skeletal Remains from Actun Tunichil Muknal and Actun Uayazba Kab." In *The Western Belize Regional Cave Project: A Report of the 1997 Field Season,* ed. Jaime J. Awe, 71–92. Department of Anthropology Occasional Paper No. 1. Durham: University of New Hampshire.

Gibbs, Sherry A. 2000. "An Interpretation of the Significance of Human Remains from the Caves of the Southern Maya Lowlands." MA thesis, Department of Anthropology, Trent University, Peterborough, Ontario.

Glassman, David M., and Juan Luis Bonor Villarejo. 2005. "Mortuary Practices of the Prehistoric Maya from Caves Branch Rock Shelter, Belize." In *Stone Houses and Earth Lords: Maya Religion in the Cave Context,* ed. Keith M. Prufer and James E. Brady, 285–96. Boulder: University Press of Colorado.

Gordon, George Byron. 1898. "Caverns of Copan, Honduras." *Peabody Museum of Archaeology and Ethnology Memoirs* 1: 137–48.

Graham, Elizabeth, Logan McNatt, and Mark A. Gutchen. 1980. "Excavations in Footprint Cave, Belize." *Journal of Field Archaeology* 7: 153–72.

Graham, Ian. 1997. "Discovery of a Maya Ritual Cave in Peten, Guatemala." *Symbols* (Spring): 28–31.

Grove, David C., and Susan Gillespie. 1984. "Chalcatzingo's Portrait Figurines and the Cult of the Ruler." *Archaeology* 37 (4): 27–33.

Guiteras Holmes, C. 1947. "Clanes y Sistema de Parantesco de Cancuc (México)." *Acta Americana* 5: 1–17.

Halperin, Christina. 2005. "Social Power and Sacred Space at Actun Nak Beh, Belize." In *Stone Houses and Earth Lords: Maya Religion in the Cave Context,* ed. Keith M. Prufer and James E. Brady, 71–90. Boulder: University Press of Colorado.

Hatt, Robert T., Harvey I. Fisher, Dave A. Langebartel, and George W. Brainerd. 1953. "Faunal and Archaeological Researches in Yucatan Caves." *Cranbrook Institute of Science Bulletin* 33.

Helmke, Christophe G.B. 1999. "Exploration and Investigations of the Sinkhole Tunnels, Actun Tunichil Muknal, Belize." In *The Western Belize Regional Cave Project: A Report of the 1998 Field Season,* ed. Jaime J. Awe, 146–65. Department of Anthropology, Occasional Paper No. 2. Durham: University of New Hampshire.

Helmke, Christophe G.B., and Jaime J. Awe. 1998. "Preliminary Analysis of the Pictographs, Petroglyphs and Sculptures of Actun Uayazba Kab, Cayo District, Belize." In *The Western Belize Regional Cave Project: A Report of the 1997 Field Season,* ed. Jaime J. Awe, 141–99. Department of Anthropology, Occasional Paper No. 1. Durham: University of New Hampshire.

Helmke, C., and D. Reents-Budet. 2008. "A Terminal Classic Molded-Carved Ceramic Tradition of the Eastern Maya Lowlands: Character and Identity." In *Research Reports in Belizean Archaeology,* vol. 5, ed. J. Morries, J. J. Awe, S. Jones, and C. Helmke, 37–49. Belmopan: Institute of Archaeology, National Institute of Culture and History.

Heyden, Doris. 1973. "¿Un Chicomostoc en Teotihuacan? La Cueva Bajo la Pirámide del Sol." *Boletín del Instituto Nacional de Antropología e Historia,* Época II (6): 3–18.

Heyden, Doris. 1975. "An Interpretation of the Cave underneath the Pyramid of the Sun in Teotihuacan, Mexico." *American Antiquity* 40 (2): 131–47. http://dx.doi.org/10.2307/279609.

Heyden, Doris. 2005. "Rites of Passage and Other Ceremonies in Caves." In *In the Maw of the Earth Monster: Mesoamerican Ritual Cave Use,* ed. James E. Brady and Keith M. Prufer, 21–34. Austin: University of Texas Press.

Hill, Carol A., and Paolo Forti. 1997. *Cave Minerals of the World,* 2nd ed. Huntsville, AL: National Speleological Society.

Hirth, Kenneth. 2000. *Archaeological Research at Xochicalco,* Volume 2: *The Xochicalco Mapping Project.* Salt Lake City: University of Utah Press.

Hooton, Earnest A. 1940. "Skeletons from the Cenote of Sacrifice at Chichen Itzá." In *The Maya and Their Neighbors: Essays on Middle American Anthropology and Archaeology,* ed. Clarence L. Hay, Ralph L. Linton, Samuel K. Lothrop, Harry L. Shapiro, and George C. Vaillant, 272–80. New York: D. Appleton-Century Company.

Ichon, Alain, and Marie Charlotte Arnauld. 1985. *Le Protoclassique á La Lagunita, El Quiché Guatemala.* Centre National de la Recherche Scientifique/R.C.P. 294 et 500. Piedra Santa, Guatemala: Institut d'Ethnologie, Paris.

Ishihara, Reiko. 2008. "Rising Clouds, Blowing Winds: Late Classic Maya Rain Rituals in the Main Chasm, Aguateca, Guatemala." *World Archaeology* 40 (2): 169–89. http://dx.doi.org/10.1080/00438240802030001.

Joyce, T. A. 1929. "Report on the British Museum Expedition to British Honduras, 1929." *Journal of the Royal Anthropological Institute* 59: 439–59.

Joyce, T. A., T. Gann, E. L. Gruning, and R.C.E. Long. 1928. "Report on the British Museum Expedition to British Honduras, 1928." *Journal of the Royal Anthropological Society* 58: 323–49.

Kieffer, C. L. 2008. "New Cave Discoveries at Quen Santo, Huehuetenango." Paper presented at the 73rd Annual Meeting of the Society for American Archaeology, Vancouver, British Columbia, Canada, March 26–30.

King, Eleanor M., and Leslie C. Shaw. 2003. "A Heterarchical Approach to Site Variability." In *Heterarchy, Political Economy, and the Ancient Maya,* ed. Vernon L. Scarborough, Fred Valdez Jr., and Nicholas Dunning, 64–76. Tucson: University of Arizona Press.

Kirchhoff, Paul. 1943. "Mesoamérica: Sus Límites Geográficos, Composición Étnica y Caracteres Culturales." *Acta Americana* 1 (1): 92–107.

Laughlin, Robert M. 1975. *The Great Tzotzil Dictionary of San Lorenzo Zinacantan.* Smithsonian Contributions to Anthropology, No. 19. Washington, DC: Smithsonian Institution Press.

Lee, Thomas A., and Brian Hayden. 1988. *San Pablo Cave and El Cayo on the Usumacinta River, Chiapas, Mexico.* Papers of the New World Archaeological Foundation No. 53. Provo: New World Archaeological foundation.

Lothrop, Samuel Kirkland. 1924. *Tulum: An Archaeological Study of the East Coast of Yucatan.* Carnegie Institution of Washington, Publication No. 335. Washington, DC.

Lucero, Lisa J., and Sherry A. Gibbs. 2007. "The Creation and Sacrifice of Witches in Classic Maya Society." In *New Perspectives on Human Ritual Sacrifice and Ritual Body Treatments in Ancient Maya Society,* ed. Vera Tiesler and Andrea Cucina, 45–73. New York: Springer.

Manzanilla, Linda. 2000. "The Construction of the Underworld of the Underworld in Central Mexico." In *Mesoamerica's Classic Heritage: From Teotihuacan to the Aztecs,* ed. David

Carrasco, Lindsay Jones, and Scott Sessions, 87–116. Boulder: University Press of Colorado.

Manzanilla, L., L. Barba, R. Chávez, A. Tejero, C. Cifuentes, and N. Peralta. 1994. "Caves and Geophysics: An Approximation to the Underworld of Teotihuacan, Mexico." *Archaeometry* 36: 141–57.

Mason, Gregory. 1927. *Silver Cities of Yucatan*. New York: G. P. Putnam's Sons.

McAnany, Patricia A. 1995. *Living with the Ancestors*. Austin: University of Texas Press.

McCafferty, Geoffrey G. 1996. "Reinterpreting the Great Pyramid of Cholula, Mexico." *Ancient Mesoamerica* 7 (01): 1–17. http://dx.doi.org/10.1017/S0956536100001255.

Mercer, Henry C. 1975 [1896]. *The Hill-Caves of Yucatan*. Norman: University of Oklahoma Press.

Mercer, Henry. 2005 [1996]. *The Hill-Caves of Yucatan*. AMCS Reprint Series 7. Foreword by James Brady. Austin, TX: Association for Mexican Cave Studies.

Miller, Mary, and Karl Taube. 1993. *The Gods and Symbols of Ancient Mexico and the Maya*. New York: Thanes and Hudson.

Millon, René. 1981. "Teotihuacan: City, State, and Civilization." In *Supplement to the Handbook of Middle American Indians*, Vol. 1: *Archaeology*, ed. Jeremy A. Sabloff, 198–243. Austin: University of Texas Press.

Monaghan, John. 1995. *The Covenant with Earth and Rain: Exchange, Sacrifice, and Revelation in Mixtec Sociality*. Norman: University of Oklahoma Press.

Morehart, Christopher T. 2002a. "Ancient Maya Ritual Cave Utilization: A Paleoethnobotanical Perspective." Master's Thesis, Department of Anthropology, Florida State University, Tallahassee.

Morehart, Christopher T. 2002b. "Plants of the Underworld: Ritual Plant Use in Ancient Maya Cave Ceremonies." Report submitted to the Foundation for the Advancement of Mesoamerican Studies, Crystal River, FL.

Moser, Christopher L. 1975. "Cueva de Ejutla: ¿Una Cueva Funeraria Postclásca?" *Boletín del Instituto Nacional de Antropología e Historia* 14 (Época II, July/September): 25–36.

Moser, Christopher L. 1976. "Cueva de Ejutla: A Postclassic Burial Cave?" *Katunob* 9 (1): 22–7.

Moser, Christopher L. 1983. "A Postclassic Burial Cave in the Southern Cañada." In *The Cloud People*, ed. Kent V. Flannery and Joyce Marcus, 270–72. New York: Academic Press.

Motolinía, Toribio de Benavente. 1971 [1555]. *Memoriales o Libro de las Cosas de la Nueva España y de los Naturales de ella*. Mexico: Universidad Nacional Autónoma de México.

Moyes, Holley. 2000. "The Cave as a Cosmogram: Function and Meaning of Maya Speleothem Use." In *The Sacred and the Profane: Architecture and Identity in the Maya Lowlands*, ed. Pierre Robert Colas, Kai Delvendahl, Marcus Kuhnert, Annette Schubart, 137–48. Acta Mesoamericana 10. Markt Schwaben, Germany: Verlag Anton Saurwein.

Moyes, Holley. 2001. "The Cave as a Cosmogram: The Use of GIS in an Intrasite Spatial Analysis of the Main Chamber of Actun Tunichil Muknal; A Maya Ceremonial Cave in Western Belize." MA thesis, Department of Anthropology, Florida Atlantic University, Boca Raton.

Moyes, Holley. 2002. "The Use of GIS in the Spatial Analysis of an Archaeological Cave Site." *Journal of Caves and Karst Studies* 64 (1): 9–16.

Moyes, Holley. 2003. "Changes and Continuities in Ritual Practice at Chechen Ha cave, Belize: Report on Excavations Conducted in the 2003 Field Season." Electronic document, http://www.famsi.org/reports/02086/index.html. Accessed January 29, 2005.

Moyes, Holley. 2005a. "Cluster Concentrations, Boundary Markers, and Ritual Pathways: A GIS Analysis of Artifact Cluster Patterns at Actun Tunichil Muknal, Belize." In *In the Maw of the Earth Monster: Mesoamerican Ritual Cave Use*, ed. James E. Brady and Keith M. Prufer, 269–300. Austin: University of Texas Press.

Moyes, Holley. 2005b. "The Sweatbath in the Cave: A Modified Passage in Chechem Ha Cave, Belize." In *Stone Houses and Earth Lords: Maya Religion in the Cave Context*, ed. Keith M. Prufer and James E. Brady, 187–211. Boulder: University Press of Colorado.

Moyes, Holley. 2006. "The Sacred Landscape as a Political Resource: A Case Study of Ancient Maya Cave Use at Chechem Ha Cave, Belize, Central America." PhD dissertation, Department of Anthropology, State University of New York at Buffalo, Buffalo.

Moyes, Holley. 2007a. "The Canoe in the Cave: A Foundational Shrine at Uxbenká?" Interim Report submitted to the Foundation for the Advancement of Mesoamerican Studies, Inc. http://www.famsi.org/reports/07068/index.html.

Moyes, Holley. 2007b. "The Late Classic Drought Cult: Ritual Activity as a Response to Environmental Stress among the Ancient Maya." *Cult in Context: Reconsidering Ritual in Archaeology*, ed. David Barrowclough, Caroline Malone, and Simon Stoddard, 217–28. Oxford: Oxbow Books.

Moyes, Holley. 2008. "Charcoal as a Proxy for Use-Intensity in Ancient Maya Cave Ritual." In *Religion, Archaeology, and the Material World*, ed. Lars Fogelin, 139–58. Carbondale, IL: Center for Archaeological Investigations.

Moyes, Holley, and Jaime J. Awe. 1998. "Spatial Analysis of Artifacts in the Main Chamber of Actun Tunichil Muknal, Belize: Preliminary Results." In *The Western Belize Regional Cave Project: A Report of the 1997 Field Season*, ed. Jaime J. Awe, 22–38. Department of Anthropology Occasional Paper No. 1. Durham: University of New Hampshire.

Moyes, Holley, and Jaime J. Awe. 2000. "Spatial Analysis of an Ancient Cave Site." *ArcUser: The Magazine for ESRI Software Users* 3 (4): 64–7.

Moyes, Holley, Jaime J. Awe, George Brook, and James Webster. 2009. "The Ancient Maya Drought Cult: Late Classic Cave Use in Belize." *Latin American Antiquity* 20 (1): 175–206.

Moyes, Holley, Jaime J. Awe, and Henry Schwarcz. 2006. "Tracing the Origin of Speleothems at Ancient Maya Archaeological Sites in Belize, Central America." Report on file with the Institute of Archaeology, National Institute of Culture and History, Belmopan, Belize.

Moyes, Holley, Mark Robinson, Laura Kosakowsky, and Barbara Voorhies. 2012. "Better Late than Never: Preliminary Investigations at Las Cuevas," *Research Reports in Belizean Archaeology*, 9. Institute of Archaeology, NICH, Belmopan, Belize.

Moyes, Holley, and Sherry Gibbs. 2000. "Sacrifice in the Underworld: The Human Remains from Actun Tunichil Muknal, An Ancient Maya Cave Site in Western Belize." 99th Annual Meeting of the American Anthropological Association, San Francisco, CA.

Moyes, Holley, and Keith M. Prufer. 2009. "Kayuko Naj Tunich: A Foundational Shrine at Uxbenká." *Research Reports in Belizean Archaeology* 6 Belmopan, Belize.

Nielsen, Jesper, and James E. Brady. 2006. "The Couple in the Cave: Origin Iconography on a Ceramic Vessel from Los Naranjos, Honduras." *Ancient Mesoamerica* 17 (02): 203–17. http://dx.doi.org/10.1017/S0956536106060123.

O'Neale, Lila M. 1942. "Early Textiles from Chiapas, Mexico." *Middle American Research Records* 1 (1): 1–6. Middle American Research Institute, New Orleans.

Patel, Shankari. 2005. "Pilgrimage and Caves on Cozumel." In *Stone Houses and Earth Lords: Maya Religion in the Cave Context*, ed. Keith M. Prufer and James E. Brady, 91–112. Boulder: University Press of Colorado.

Pendergast, David M. 1969. *The Prehistory of Actun Balam, British Honduras*. Art and Archaeology Occasional Paper No. 16. Toronto: Royal Ontario Museum.

Pendergast, David M. 1970. *A. H. Anderson's Excavations at Rio Frio Cave E, British Honduras (Belize)*. Art and Archaeology Occasional Paper No. 20. Toronto: Royal Ontario Museum.

Pendergast, David M. 1971. *Excavations at Eduardo Quiroz Cave, British Honduras (Belize)*. Art and Archaeology Occasional Paper No. 21. Toronto: Royal Ontario Museum.

Pendergast, David M. 1974. *Excavations at Actun Polbilche, Belize*. Royal Ontario Museum Monograph 1. Toronto: Royal Ontario Museum.

Peterson, Polly A., Patricia A. McAnany, and Allan B. Cobb. 2005. "De-fanging the Earth Monster: Speleothem Transport to Surface Sites in the Sibun Valley." In *Stone Houses and Earth Lords: Maya Religion in the Cave Context*, ed. Keith M. Prufer and James E. Brady, 225–47. Boulder: University Press of Colorado.

Pohl, Mary. 1981. "Ritual Continuity and Transformation in Mesoamerica: Reconstructing the Ancient Maya Cuch Ritual." *American Antiquity* 46 (3): 513–29. http://dx.doi.org/10.2307/280598.

Popenoe, Dorothy H. 1936. "The Ruins of Tenampua, Honduras." *Annual Report of the Smithsonian Institution* 1935: 559–72. Washington, DC.

Prufer, Keith M. 2002. "Communities, Caves and Ritual Specialists: A Study of Sacred Space in the Maya Mountains of Southern Belize." PhD dissertation, Department of Anthropology, Southern Illinois University, Carbondale.

Prufer, Keith M., and W. Jeffrey Hurst. 2007. "Chocolate in the Underworld Space of Death: Cacao Seeds from an Early Classic Mortuary Cave." *Ethnohistory (Columbus, Ohio)* 54 (2): 273–301. http://dx.doi.org/10.1215/00141801-2006-063.

Pugh, Timothy W. 2001. "Flood Reptiles, Serpent Temples, and the Quadripartite Universe: The *Imago Mundi* of Late Postclassic Mayapan." *Ancient Mesoamerica* 12 (02): 247–58. http://dx.doi.org/10.1017/S0956536101122042.

Reeder, Phillip. 1993. "Cave Exploration and Mapping on the Northern Vaca Plateau." *NSS News* 51 (11): 296–300.

Reents, Doris Jane. 1980. "The Prehistoric Pottery from Petroglyph Cave, Caves Branch Valley, El Cayo District, Belize, Central America." MA thesis, University of Texas, Austin.

Reents-Budet, Dorie, and Barbara MacLeod. 1997. "The Archaeology of Petroglyph Cave, Cayo District, Belize." Unpublished manuscript, on file with the Institute of Archaeology, Belmopan, Belize.

Reilly, F. Kent, III. 1994. "Visions to Another World: Art, Shamanism, and Political Power in Middle Formative Mesoamerica." PhD dissertation, Department of Art History, University of Texas, Austin.

Reilly, F. Kent, III. 1995. "Art, Ritual, and Rulership in the Olmec World." In *The Olmec World: Ritual and Rulership*, ed. Art Museum of Princeton University, 27–46. New York: Harry N. Abrams.

Rissolo, Dominique A. 2001. "Ancient Maya Cave Use in the Yalahau Region, Northern Quintana Roo, Mexico." PhD dissertation, Department of Anthropology, University of California, Riverside.

Rissolo, Dominique A. 2005. "Beneath the Yalahau: Emerging Patterns of Ancient Maya Ritual Cave Use from Northern Quintana Roo, Mexico." In *In the Maw of the Earth Monster: Mesoamerican Ritual Cave Use*, ed. James E. Brady and Keith M. Prufer, 342–72. Austin: University of Texas Press.

Sanders, William T. 1955. *An Archaeological Reconnaissance of Northern Quintana Roo*. Carnegie Institution of Washington, Current Report No. 24. Washington, DC.

Saturno, William A., Karl A. Taube, David Stuart, and Heather Hurst. 2005. "The Murals of San Bartolo, El Petén, Guatemala, Part 1: The North Wall." *Ancient America* 7.

Saul, Julie Mather, Keith M. Prufer, and Frank P. Saul. 2005. "Nearer to the Gods: Rockshelter Burials from the Ek Xux Valley, Belize." In *Stone Houses and Earth Lords: Maya Religion in the Cave Context*, ed. Keith M. Prufer and James E. Brady, 297–322. Boulder: University Press of Colorado.

Schwarcz, Henry P., and W. J. Rink. 2001. "Dating Methods for Sediments of Caves and Rockshelters with Examples from the Mediterranean Region." *Geoarchaeology* 16 (4): 355–71. http://dx.doi.org/10.1002/gea.1008.

Scott, Ann M., and James E. Brady. 2005. "Human Remains in Lowland Maya Caves: Problems of Interpretation." In *Stone Houses and Earth Lords: Maya Religion in the Cave Context*, ed. Keith M. Prufer and James E. Brady, 263–84. Boulder: University Press of Colorado.

Scott, Ann M., and Walter E. Little. 2003. "Contemporary Maya Beliefs and Cave Utilization: Implications for Archaeological Interpretations." Paper presented at the 68th Annual Meeting of the Society for American Archaeology, Milwaukee, April 9–13.

Seler, Eduard. 2003. *The Ancient Settlements of Chaculá in the Nentón District of the Department of Huehuetenango, Republic of Guatemala*. Lancaster, CA: Labyrinthos.

Smith, A. Ledyard. 1955. *Archaeological Reconnaissance in Central Guatemala*. Carnegie Institution of Washington, Publication 608. Washington, DC.

Smyth, Michael P. 2000. "A New Study of the Gruta de Chac, Yucatán, México." Submitted to the Foundation for the Advancement of Mesoamerica Studies, Inc., http://www.famsi.org/reports/97011.

Spranz, Bodo. 1967. "Descubrimiento en Totimehuacan, Puebla." *Boletín del Instituto Nacional de Antropología e Historia* 27: 19–22.

Stephens, John Lloyd. 1963 [1843]. *Incidents of Travel in Yucatan*. Norman: University of Oklahoma Press.

Stone, Andrea J. 1995. *Images from the Underworld: Naj Tunich and the Tradition of Maya Cave Painting*. Austin: University of Texas Press.

Stone, Doris. 1941. *The Archaeology of the North Coast of Honduras*. Memoirs of the Peabody Museum of American Archaeology and Ethnology, Harvard University, Vol. 9, No. 1. Cambridge, MA: Harvard University.

Strómsvik, Gustav. 1942. *Substela Caches and Stela Foundations at Copan and Quirigua*. Contributions to American Anthropology and History, No. 37. Carnegie Institution of Washington Publication 528. Washington, DC: Carnegie Institution of Washington.

Stuart, David S. 1999. "Cave References in Maya Inscriptions." Manuscript on file. Department of Anthropology, Harvard University, Cambridge, MA.

Thompson, Edward H. 1938. *The High Priest's Grave, Chichen Itza, Yucatan, Mexico*. Prepared for publication, with notes and introduction by J. Eric Thompson. Anthropology Series 27, No.1. Chicago: Field Museum of Natural History.

Thompson, J. Eric S. 1959. "The Role of Caves in Maya Culture." *Mitteilungen aus dem Museum für Völkerkunde im Hamburg* 25: 122–9.

Thompson, J. Eric S. 1975. "Introduction to the Reprint Edition." In *The Hill-Caves of Yucatan*, by Henry C. Mercer, vii–xliv. Norman: University of Oklahoma Press.

Tiesler, Vera. 2005. "What Can Bones Really Tell Us? The Study of Human Skeletal Remains from Cenotes." In *Stone Houses and Earth Lords: Maya Religion in the Cave Context*, ed. Keith M. Prufer and James E. Brady, 341–63. Boulder: University Press of Colorado.

Townsend, Richard F. 1982. "Pyramid and Sacred Mountain." In *Ethnoastronomy and Archaeoastronomy in the American Tropics*, ed. Anthony F. Aveni and Gary Urton, 37–62. Annals of the New York Academy of Sciences, Vol. 385. New York: New York Academy of Sciences.

Tozzer, Alfred M. 1941. *Landa's Relación de las Cosas de Yucatan*. Papers of the Peabody Museum of American Archaeology and Ethnology, Vol. 18. Cambridge: Harvard University.

Vásquez, Alfredo Barrera. 2007. *Diccionario Maya*, 5th ed. Mexico City: Editorial Porrúa.

Villa Rojas, Alfonso. 1969. "The Tzeltal." In *Handbook of Middle American Indians*, Vol. 7: *Ethnology*, ed. Evon Z. Vogt, 195–225. Austin: University of Texas Press.

Vogt, Evon Z. 1969. *Zinacantan: A Maya Community in the Highlands of Chiapas*. Cambridge, MA: Harvard University Press.

Vogt, Evon Z. 1976. *Tortillas for the Gods: A Symbolic Analysis of Zinacanteco Rituals*. Cambridge, MA: Harvard University Press.

Vogt, Evon Z., and David Stuart. 2005. "Some Notes on Ritual Caves among the Ancient and Modern Maya." In *In the Maw of the Earth Monster: Mesoamerican Ritual Cave Use*, ed. James E. Brady and Keith Prufer, 155–85. Austin: University of Texas Press.

Wauchope, Robert. 1942. "Notes on the Age of the Cineguilla Cave Textiles from Chiapas." Middle American Research Institute, *Middle American Research Records* 1 (2): 7–8.

Webster, James W. 2000. "Speleothem Evidence of Late Holocene Climate Variation in the Maya Lowlands of Belize Central America and Archaeological Implications." PhD dissertation, Department of Geology, University of Georgia, Athens.

Webster, James W., George A. Brook, L. Bruce Railsback, Hai Cheng, R. Lawrence Edwards, Clark Alexander, and Philip P. Reeder. 2007. "Stalagmite Evidence from Belize Indicating Significant Droughts at the Time of Preclassic Abandonment, the Maya Hiatus, and the Classic Maya Collapse." *Palaeogeography, Palaeoclimatology, Palaeoecology* 250 (1-4): 1–17. http://dx.doi.org/10.1016/j.palaeo.2007.02.022.

Woodfill, Brent Kerry Skoy. 2007. "Shrines of the Pasion-Verapaz Region, Guatemala: Ritual and Exchange along an Ancient Trade Route." PhD dissertation, Department of Anthropology, Vanderbilt University, Nashville.

Wroebel, Gabriel D. 2008. "Report on the Caves Branch Rockshelter Excavations: 2006 and 2007 Fields Seasons." In *The Belize Valley Archaeological Reconnaissance Project: A Report of the 2007 Field Season*, ed. Christophe G.B. Helmke and Jaime J. Awe. Belmopan, Belize: Institute of Archaeology and National Institute of Culture and History.

11

Footsteps in the Dark Zone

Ritual Cave Use in Southwest Prehistory

Scott Nicolay

Published studies describe numerous caves in the Southwest as shrines or ceremonial sites. Despite this recognition, there has been little attempt to explore what Walter Hough (1914, 91) described almost a century ago as a "cave cult" that "has survived to the present." The purpose of the present study is to present an initial synthesis of the widely scattered information about ritual cave use in Southwest prehistory, to place both the archaeological record and its study in context, and to suggest avenues for future research.

The dry caves and rockshelters of the Southwestern United States have long attracted the attention of archaeologists due to their extraordinary preservation of perishable artifacts (figure 11.1, table 11.1). As a result, we have a number of early reports of cave investigations, often as part of regional surveys including related surface sites (Alexander and Reiter 1935; Alves 1929, 1932; Coffin 1932; Cosgrove 1947; Crimmins 1929; Ferdon 1946; Fulton 1941; Guernsey 1931; Guernsey and Kidder 1921; Harrington 1933; Haury 1945; Holden 1937; Hough 1907, 1914; Howard 1932, 1935; Hurst 1947; Jeancon 1929; Kidder and Guernsey 1919; Martin, Rinaldo, and Bluhm 1954; Martin et al. 1952; Mera 1938; Nusbaum 1922; Sayles 1930; Steward 1937; Wheeler 1935; Woolsey 1936). Interestingly, many of these caves were recognized as early as the late nineteenth century as having ritual significance due to the presence of artifacts known from contemporary Pueblo ceremonialism, such as *pahos* (prayer sticks) and cane cigarettes (Fewkes 1898, 1971 [1898]). Despite this early awareness of caves as ritual sites, there have been few attempts to investigate the overall importance of caves within the religion and cosmology of the ancient peoples of the Southwest or their successors and descendants. Most studies of ritual cave sites have focused primarily on descriptions of material culture, and the few notable exceptions that have explored the nature of ritual cave use have been primarily site-specific analyses (B. Bilbo 1997; M. Bilbo 1997; Creel 1997; Ellis and Hammack 1968; Ferg and Mead 1993; Greer and Greer 1995, 1996, 1997, 1999, 2002; Lambert and Ambler 1961; Lekson, Ross, and Fitting 1971; O'Laughlin 2003).

Archaeologists studying cave use in Mesoamerica have faced difficulty in achieving recognition for caves in that region as ritual sites. The situation in the Southwest has been somewhat different. As early as 1898, J. Walter Fewkes recognized the ritual significance of caves in the Southwest, when he wrote:

> Many caves in this region have narrow entrance into passages which extend with many ramifications into the bowels of the earth. Most of these were used in ancient times for religious purposes, and still contain relics left on former visits by the Indians. The nature of the objects found in them shows that the caves were not inhabited, but were resorted to for purposes of prayer and sacrifice. (1971 [1898], 166)

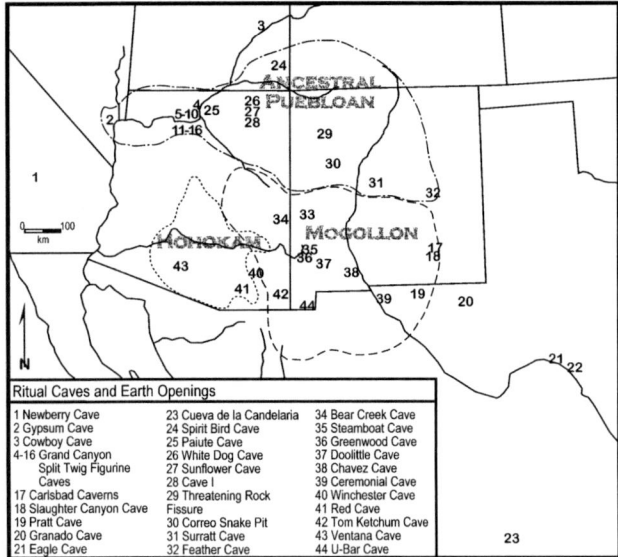

FIGURE 11.1 Major ritual caves and earth openings mentioned in the text. Sites 1–23 contained significant Archaic components.

Hough (1914), like Fewkes, working in the Upper Gila River Valley, could write casually of a typical ceremonial cave assemblage and even refer to a "cave cult," which was "responsible for the preservation of perishable objects connected with the religious beliefs of the ancient Pueblos," adding "this cult has survived to the present." He also identified caves as "essentially a place for the worship of the beings of the underworld" (p. 91).

Unfortunately, there has been little further mention of this "cave cult" since Hough first identified it. In fact, early reporting of spectacular ritual cave sites—such as Bear Creek Cave (Hough 1907, 1914) (figure 11.2), in which "Immense quantities of objects had been deposited . . . the whole mass of débris averaging 2 feet in depth" (Hough 1907, 51) or another cave on Pueblo Creek in Socorro County, New Mexico, whose discoverer "found bows, arrows, painted tablets, and other objects arranged . . . in orderly manner around the walls of the cavern" (Hough 1907, 57)—may have led later researchers to take such sites for granted, and perhaps even hindered them from recognizing other caves as ritual sites if they did not present such extensive cultural deposits. Even in Hough's time extensive looting, guano mining, and wanton destruction of artifacts (some visitors used bundles of artifacts as torches to light their way in the caves [Hough 1907, 52]) were already serious problems, and soon the cultural deposits in most such sites would be seriously reduced. By the mid-twentieth century all known ritual cave sites in the Southwest had been decimated, and it was not until the rediscovery of the Arrow Grotto of Feather Cave in 1964 (Ellis and Hammack 1968) that any researcher would have the opportunity to study an intact cave shrine (figure 11.3).

Most of the early reports were more concerned with cave sites for the windows they provided on the cultural history of the Southwest than with any analysis of ritual cave use, and with the lack of undisturbed sites, the topic has attracted only sporadic attention since. Ethnographic data, though not totally lacking, are limited to scattered references as well. As Ellis and Hammack (1968, 30) point out, "The significance of caves in this pattern has been little recognized by anthropologists because Pueblos are secretive about the subject, even native nonceremonialists being excluded from much information."

In reviewing the literature, it is clear that the term *cave* has been applied rather inconsistently to a variety of features, many of which would now be classified as rockshelters, that is, features lacking a "dark zone." This is particularly true in the Ancestral Puebloan region of the Colorado Plateau, which is largely composed of sandstone. Sandstone rockshelters and overhangs of varying depth often served as habitation sites, some of them, such as those at Mesa Verde and Cañon de Chelly, of quite spectacular size and often containing equally spectacular architecture. Most of the sites in this region identified as caves, some of them quite famous, are of this type (Gifford 1980; Guernsey 1931; Guernsey and Kidder 1921; Hargrave 1970; Haury 1945; Hays-Gilpin, Deegan, and Morris 1998; Hurst 1947; Kidder and Guernsey 1923; Lockett and Hargrave 1953; Nusbaum 1922; Van Valkenburgh 1940).

However, Scott and Little (2003) emphasize the need for Maya cave archaeologists to recognize that virtually any opening into the earth, natural or artificial, might be identified as a cave (and thoroughly imbued with all the sacred connotations thereof), and it is entirely possible that a sim-

TABLE 11.1. Chronology for archaeological cultures and eras of the Greater American Southwest mentioned in the text.

Paleoindian Period	12,000/20,0000–8000 BC
Archaic Period	8000–2000 BC
Basketmaker II (Pecos)	AD 1–500
Basketmaker III (Pecos)	AD 500–700
Pueblo I (Pecos)	AD 700–900
Pueblo II (Pecos)	AD 900–1100
Pueblo III (Pecos)	AD 1100–1300
Pueblo IV (Pecos)	AD 1300–1600
Pueblo V (Pecos)	AD 1600–1800
Anasazi	AD 500–1300
Hohokam	AD 200–1450
Mogollon	AD 200–1450

FIGURE 11.2 Entrance to Bear Creek Cave, Greenlee County, Arizona, described by Walter Hough as "the greatest of all known ceremonial caves in the Southwest" (1907, 52).

FIGURE 11.3 Caver Robert S. Willis examines an in situ assemblage of arrow offerings in the Arrow Grotto of Feather Cave, 1964. At least thirty-six reed arrows had been inserted into a crevice in this area (Ellis and Hammack, 1968, 26–27). (Photograph by Laurens Hammack. Author's collection.)

ilar perspective may have existed among the peoples of the Southwest. Parsons (1996, 308), in her study of modern Pueblo Indian religion, reports that these beliefs may still exist: "Any available cave or near-cave like a rock shelf will be used as a shrine."

Nonetheless, dark-zone sites may have been particularly important, especially those with naturally restricted entrances requiring entrants to pass through a crawlway and/or a keyhole, such as the Arrow Grotto of Feather Cave (Ellis and Hammack 1968), Chavez Cave (Cosgrove 1947; O'Laughlin 2003), Red Cave (Ferg and Mead 1993), Spirit Bird Cave (Cutrone 2003), Surratt Cave (Caperton 1981; Greer and Greer 1995, 1996, 1997, 1998, 2002), and U-Bar Cave (Greer and Greer 1999; Harris 1985; Lambert and Ambler 1961). Similarly, in Red Bow Cliff Dwelling, Gifford (1980, 24) identified a ceremonial area that was partially blocked by two large boulders and that could not have accommodated more than three people at once. This ceremonial area contained pahos, miniature bows and arrows, and hundreds of cane cigarettes.

The importance of a restricted entrance as a ceremonial feature can be seen in Spirit Bird Cave (Cutrone 2003), a culturally modified cliffside slump-fissure cave near the Nancy Patterson site, a large Ancestral Puebloan village in Montezuma Canyon, Utah. The cave was probably a major shrine, perhaps even the *sipapu* (emergence shrine) for the community in the valley below, and perhaps a pilgrimage site for the smaller surrounding communities. Spirit Bird Cave features an outer room with a small, carefully made doorway, which leads in turn to a platform with a culturally modified keyhole that provides access to an inner area (figure 11.4). Fewkes (1971, 620–21, figure 259 [1898]) describes and illustrates a similar, though apparently less elaborate, shrine associated with a deep crack atop a cliff at Awatovi, an abandoned Hopi village. Perhaps the most important such feature in the region was Threatening Rock Fissure behind Pueblo Bonito in Chaco Canyon. This earth opening may actually have been a focus of settlement in the canyon (Marshall 2003; Nicolay 2005). Although the Chacoans did not modify the opening of the fissure, they restricted access to it by surrounding it with a series of walls and a plaza that together comprise the North Terrace (Stein, Ford, and Friedman 2003).

FIGURE 11.4 Modified entrance to Spirit Bird Cave, Montezuma County, Utah. (Author's photograph.)

CAVE RITUAL IN THE SOUTHWEST

Shrines on hills and mountaintops, at lakes and springs, and in caves have tremendous importance in contemporary Pueblo cosmology as places to communicate with the wide array of subterranean supernaturals (Ortiz 1969, 19; Stevenson 1904, 23). Prehistoric sites appear to reflect similar practices and concerns. The use of caves as shrines relates directly to the emergence myth that is shared by all the Pueblos, in which the portal back into the underworld is known as the sipapu, or some variation thereof. "Specific caves and small lakes are revered by various pueblos as the Shipap opening, and all springs are assumed to connect with that underworld lake whence emerge the katcina rain spirits" (Ellis and Hammack 1968, 31).

There appears to be a division of cultural materials from ritual cave sites into three general themes: rain/fertility, warfare/hunting, and gaming. Mesoamerican caves are well recognized as the loci of fertility rituals associated with rain and maize agriculture. Schaafsma and Taube (2006) argue for the Southwest's participation in this Mesoamerican ritual complex, and there is evidence that some types of ritual cave use in the prehistoric Southwest, particularly among the Mogollon and Hohokam, reflect this type of ritual. Perhaps the most powerful evidence comes from three figurines of the Mesoamerican rain god Tlaloc found in caves in southern New Mexico (Lambert and Ambler 1961; O'Laughlin 2003; Schaafsma 1997) (figure 11.5). Surratt Cave, a deep cave in Socorro County, New Mexico, near the Pueblo V site of Gran Quivira, contains dark-zone pictographs of both cloud terraces and lightning serpents, imagery intimately associated with rain ritual (Caperton 1981; Greer and Greer 1995, 1996, 1997, 1998, 2002). Above all, the abundance in cave sites of ritual items related to rain/maize ceremonialism, such as prayer sticks (pahos), cloud blowers, tablitas, cane cigarettes, and ears of corn, argues strongly for this type of activity.

At least some of the gaming equipment (such as balls, dice, kick sticks, and possibly sandals) found in so many caves may also relate to this ritual complex. Ellis and

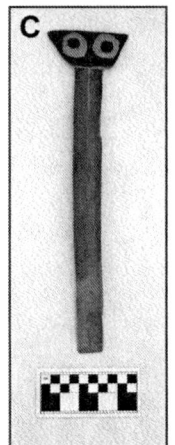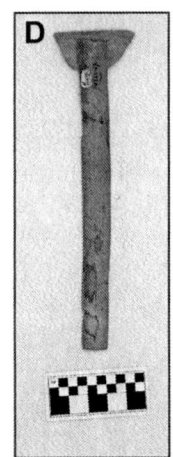

FIGURE 11.5 Mogollon "Tlaloc" effigies from New Mexico caves. (A–B) U-Bar Cave, Hidalgo County; height 13.84 cm. (Courtesy of the Museum of New Mexico.) (C–D) Lincoln County, exact provenience unknown, probably Feather Cave; height 34.85 cm. (Courtesy of the Museum of New Mexico.) (E) Chavez Cave, Doña Ana County; height 8.9 cm. (Courtesy of the New Mexico Archaeological Society.)

Hammack (1968, 330) discuss this connection: "Miniature or full-size kick balls or kick sticks are left for the katcinas by all the Pueblos, in hope that as those beings race across the sky playing their favorite kick stick game they will bring rain."

Lambert and Ambler (1961, 83) suggest that U-Bar Cave, an Animas phase Casas Grandes site in Hidalgo County, New Mexico, was primarily a hunting shrine, and Ferg and Mead (1993, 59–61) consider Red Cave, a Hohokam cave shrine near Tucson, as a probable "dual purpose shrine" that was used for both fertility and hunting ritual. Despite the wealth of artifacts related to hunting from these and other ritual cave sites, which includes atlatls and darts, fending sticks, full-size and miniature bows and arrows, and nets, less ethnographic support exists for the use of caves in the Southwest as hunting shrines. Brown (2005, 131–146) has documented archaeological evidence for hunting ritual in caves in Mesoamerica, based primarily on a faunal assemblage, but we must note that the artifacts indicative of such activity in the Southwest, other than faunal remains, whether from the Archaic period or later, are largely of a perishable nature, and the sort that do not survive in the wet caves of Central America. Ellis and Hammack (1968, 32–33) identify "miniature—and sometimes full size—bows and arrows, rabbit sticks, lightning sticks, prayer sticks . . . such items as the netted shield of the War gods, and images of plants and animals for which increase is desired" as "winter offerings . . . addressed to supernaturals concerned with warfare and hunting."

Although this chapter focuses on ritual cave use among the three major agricultural civilizations of the Southwest—the Pueblo, Hohokam, Mogollon, and their descendants—there does appear to be an even earlier period of ritual cave use in the region, one which clearly seems related to hunting, and which predates virtually all evidence of strong connections with Mesoamerica. This is the tradition of split-twig figurines, found primarily in caves and rockshelters in four states (Arizona, California, Nevada, and Utah) (figure 11.6), but most extensively in the Grand Canyon (Coulam and Schroedl 2004; Davis and Smith 1981; Emslie, Mead, and Coats 1995; Emslie, Euler, and Mead 1987; Euler 1984; Farmer and deSaussure 1955; Geib and Keller 2003; Jett 1962, 1987; Schroedl 1977; Schwartz, Lange, and deSaussure 1958). The figurines date to the Late Archaic, from 2900 to 1250 BC (Coulam and Schroedl 2004, 41). Though no clear ethnographic analogies exist for items of such antiquity, these figurines strongly suggest hunting rituals: they appear to represent game animals exclusively, some examples are pierced with a small "spear," and some contain a small pellet of animal dung. The figurines may be the material correlates of assemblages related to hunting ritual from later sites. Davis and

FIGURE 11.6 Split-twig figurine in situ in a Grand Canyon Cave. (Photograph courtesy of Steve Emslie.)

Smith (1981, 89–90) interpret materials from Newberry Cave in southern California, which included split-twig figurines in association with atlatl darts and pictographs of game animals, as a "magico-religious hunting assemblage."

The Archaic peoples who fabricated the split-twig figurines in the Grand Canyon usually left them in association with rock cairns. Other than a few sticks, sometimes split like those used in the fabrication of the figurines, and some clumps of dried grass, almost no other cultural materials appear in association with the figurines. The typical Grand Canyon figurine site is a deep limestone cave, but the figurines are always near the entrance, not in the dark zone (Emslie, Mead, and Coats 1995, 170). Many Southwest tribes hold a belief that game animals come from a corral inside a hollow mountain where they live with a deity who is their keeper; offerings left by Archaic hunters in the mouth of the cave may represent offerings to such a figure. This is very similar to Mesoamerican beliefs regarding chthonic deities. Coulam and Schroedl (2004) argue that the figurines originally functioned as "increase totems" and later as "social totems." They also point to different construction techniques for the later figurines, and the fact that these appear in rockshelters rather than caves. However, they fail to recognize that dark-zone caves are almost nonexistent on the Colorado Plateau outside the Grand Canyon. Parsons (1996, 335) records the modern use of animal images at Zuni "in the hunt and by warriors" and adds that they also served as "altar or house guardians."

Many of the artifacts that suggest hunting ritual could equally well relate to warfare, and there is also a definite connection between warfare and rainmaking in Pueblo ceremonialism. Parsons (1924, 6) writes that the Zuni Scalp Dance was used to transform a scalp into a rainmaking supernatural. The inhabitants of Laguna Pueblo kept their scalps in a cave (Parsons 1996, 311), and at other pueblos, scalps are "kept in small stone houses or 'scalp houses,' in kiva niches, or in caves, as are at Zuni the skulls of prey animals" (Parsons 1996, 200).

The most famous scalp documented in an archaeological context is one described by Kidder and Guernsey (1919, 190–92) from Cave I, a rockshelter in Kinboko Canyon near Kayenta, Arizona. The elaborately painted scalp (actually the complete head and face skin) was found as a grave offering in a cyst burial. Lambert and Ambler (1961) reported a cache in U-Bar Cave containing four hanks of human hair, possibly scalp trophies, wrapped in thirty snares, together with an extraordinary 151-foot hunting net of human hair. Both the snares and the hunting net, despite the enormous amount of labor invested in the latter, appeared to be unused. Associated with the net was a coiled netted bag containing a stone "cloud blower" pipe. Schaafsma (2000, 126) identifies nets and depictions of netting as associated with both war and rain clouds. Many other caves also contained nets or netting (Clark 1967; Kaemlein 1971), including a spectacular 240-foot specimen from White Dog Cave (Guernsey and Kidder 1921, 77–79, plate 31). It is possible that the ubiquitous offerings of fending sticks, atlatls and darts, and full-size and miniature bows and arrows in caves may have a connection to warfare as well as to hunting, possibilities which are not mutually exclusive.

The Correo Snake Pit, an ethnographically identified Laguna war shrine, first documented by Parsons (1924) and later excavated by Sandberg (1950), contained prayer sticks, bows and arrows, darts, fending sticks, and sandals. The site is cave-like but not a cave: it is an open pit atop a small hill left by an extinct hot spring or geyser. More importantly, there is no evidence that it was ever a habitation site, and the recovered assemblage consisted exclusively of ritual items (Sandberg 1950, 178–180). Although the site did not contain examples of most of the artifacts associated directly with rain/fertility ritual such as cane cigarettes, cloud blowers, and tablitas, Sandberg (1950, 170) postulates a period of agricultural emphasis based on the presence of two miniature pots of a type associated with agricultural ritual. Miniature or votive offerings in ritual cave sites, including miniature rabbit sticks, bows and arrows, and clothing, as well as pottery, are common in both Mesoamerica and the Southwest. Schaafsma and Taube (2006, 30) write that, "In both the Southwest and Mexico, miniature offerings and caches were dedicated to the deities of rain, and small clay vessels were utilized in many rain rituals." Ellis and Hammack (1968, 32) provide one of the few explanations for these miniature offerings, explaining that "Miniature offerings of any type are believed to enlarge to the correct size for use of the supernatural who receives them."

One type of artifact that deserves special mention in the context of both hunting and warfare is the grooved fending stick, or rabbit stick (figure 11.7)—a flat, curved, boomerang-like club or throwing stick, usually with three or four grooves along one side. Examples of fending sticks occur in many of the sites discussed in this chaper that date from the last 2,000 years. Heizer (1942) explores the origin and function of this artifact at length, but does not suggest any nonutilitarian usage. Clear evidence that these sticks were important ceremonial offerings comes from the large numbers recovered from the Correo Snake Pit (284 whole or fragmentary) (Sandberg 1950, 53–60), the presence of a miniature example in the Arrow Grotto of Feather Cave (Ellis and Hammack 1968, 28), and the stenciled pictograph of one in the terminal room of Surratt Cave (Greer and Greer 1996, 20–21, 1998, figure 38). All of these were purely ritual sites with no evidence of habitation.

An important but neglected element of cave ritual is witchcraft or sorcery. In a semifictionalized account of his ethnobotanical research among contemporary Nahua speakers in Mexico, Timothy Knab (1995) describes ceremonialists who make offerings at a cave shrine for purposes of both blessing and witchcraft. In both cases, the offerings are directed toward deities believed to reside in a complex underworld to which the cave is the entrance. The author has encountered concern from Diné (Navajo) informants, not least among them his wife, over his involvement with caves, which to many traditional Diné are places firmly associated with witchcraft and not to be visited under any circumstances. One informant, a traditional Diné employed by the US Forest Service, politely refused to share the locations of mountain caves on the Diné Nation due to the concern that the families of both author and informant would be subject to catastrophic illness. According to Kluckhohn (1989, 27), the Diné believe that witches hold their secret meetings in caves. Reilly (1973, 46) notes that the Diné "regarded caverns with aversion and fear."

The presence of owl feathers (from non-trogloxenic species) in sites such as Sand Dune Cave (Hargrave 1970) also suggests witchcraft. For many Southwest tribes, owl feathers are used only for witchcraft (Hough 1914, 103). Hurst (1947, 15, plate I, figure 24, plate III) recovered a medicine bundle from Dolores Cave in southwest Colorado that contained a bundle of horned owl feathers. Sandberg (1950, 124, 171) considers the possibility that some of the prayer sticks in Correo Snake Pit may be witchcraft related. Martin, Rinaldo, and Bluhm (1954, 153–154) speculate that small human figurines of unfired clay found in Tularosa and O-Block Caves may have been associated with witchcraft. Morris (1980, 141–142, fig-

FIGURE 11.7 Fragment of a grooved fending stick (lower left) and a reed arrow (center) in situ in a ceremonial cave in south-central New Mexico. (Photograph courtesy of Joel Craig Williams.)

ure 92) provides an illustration of a human-head figurine stuck with numerous cactus spines and suggests that it may represent witchcraft. Human figurines dating to the Early Archaic were also part of the assemblage in Cowboy Cave (Coulam and Schroedl 1996; Hull and White 1980, 122–24), a site with many split-twig figurines.

Witchcraft in Zuni tradition is explicitly linked to both maize agriculture and the underworld via the traditional emergence story, in which the first witches are allowed to ascend into this world only because they have brought seeds of maize (Stevenson 1904, 30–32; Tedlock 1972, 258–63). Upon entering this world, the witches demand child sacrifice, saying: "We wish to kill the children that the rains may come" (Stevenson 1904, 30). The sacrifice of children in caves as part of the rain/maize cult is well known in Mesoamerica.

Perhaps the only artifacts that do not have a clear association with either rainmaking, hunting and war, or witchcraft are the numerous sandals found in almost every ritual cave site in the region. Sandals are found in a variety of sites, and by themselves their presence is not indicative of ritual activity, but in conjunction with other ceremonial artifacts, they appear to represent part of a ritual complex. The enormous numbers of sandals in some sites, and their presence in known shrine sites, such as the Correo Snake Pit, makes it clear that they do have a ritual significance in some contexts. Mera (1938, 54) reports that in the Guadalupe Mountains caves he studied, "Sandals by far outnumbered all other kinds of woven objects obtained during both excavation and reconnaissance." Cosgrove (1947, 92) recovered 923 whole and fragmentary sandals from Ceremonial Cave in the Hueco Mountains of West Texas, and this was after extensive looting. Cosgrove (1947, 97) interprets these as evidence for a "custom of leaving worn-out footgear in shrines." Ellis and Hammack (1968, 34) suggest that "Sandals found in the outer room of Feather Cave could have been those worn by participants in these ceremonial races and then left as offerings, evidence of religious zeal." Moccasins used in the Diné shoe game, a socioceremonial activity, are afterwards considered sacred and cannot be used as footgear. Brady (n.d.; Moyes and Brady, chapter 10, this volume) discusses the importance of Maya cave shrines as pilgrimage sites, and sandal offerings may well reflect a similar function for cave shrines in the Southwest.

In addition to the aspects of cave ritual evidenced by these artifact categories, caves in the Southwest also served as mortuary sites. Some might argue that the disposal of the dead in this context is a purely utilitarian activity; however, ethnographic sources are consistent throughout the region in describing the dead as returning to the underworld. Boyd is explicit in identifying mortuary practice in the Chihuahuan Desert and nearby areas as reflecting such beliefs: "The use of vertical shaft caves as mortuary sites in the lower Pecos was a means of returning the dead to the place of origin" (2003, 63). Among the sites that show evidence of mortuary activity is the region's most famous cave, Carlsbad Caverns. Early explorer Jim White described a calcite-covered skeleton in the Big Room (1940, 9–10). Abijah Long, who supervised the excavation of the massive guano deposit inside the natural entrance, described other burials: "What is more, skeletons have been found in the cave, some buried in baskets! These were found on shelves in the walls. Other skeletons were found buried beneath piles of guano far back in the cave, together with bits of pottery and broken arrow points . . . Some archaeologists believe the cave was used mostly as a tomb" (Long and Long 1956, 72). Basket burials are generally Archaic, but the presence of pottery clearly points to an additional later period of use. Other caves in the Guadalupe Mountains also show evidence of mortuary activity (Howard 1932, 1935; Mera 1938; Schroeder 1983). Sadly, looting in this area appears to have been systematic and thorough since the latter half of the nineteenth century. Mera (1938, 10) reports the case of a local settler who looted a burial cave and "decorated the fence posts surrounding his house with skulls." Casa Malpais, a western Mogollon site in Arizona may have contained hundreds of burials in "catacombs" formed by the interstices between fractured basalt columns beneath the settlement (Hohmann 1990). An especially well-documented mortuary site on the periphery of the Southwest is Cueva de la Candelaria in Coahuila, Mexico (Aveleyra, Maldonado, and Martinez del Rio 1956). Burials in this site contained elaborate ceremonial artifacts, including some similar to those reported from the Shumla Caves in the Lower Pecos region of Texas. All this suggests that beliefs about the underworld have a considerable time depth throughout the Southwest.

GEOGRAPHIC DISTRIBUTION OF CAVE SITES

The majority of ritual cave sites in the Southwest have been reported south of the Colorado Plateau (see figure 11.1). This may have more to do with geology and politics than with cultural differences, given the presence of more karst features in this region, as opposed to the Ancestral Puebloan region on the Colorado Plateau, which is composed almost entirely of sandstone. The few significant cave, karst, and pseudokarst areas of this region, such as the Grand Canyon and the lava flows of El Malpais near Grants, New Mexico, are underreported in this regard. Limited reporting of Grand Canyon and Hohokam sites may also reflect the famous secretiveness of Arizona cavers, whose stock reply to any question related to caves is, "Arizona has no caves to speak of."

One of the most important cave shrines in the Southwest is the Arrow Grotto of Feather Cave, a Mogollon IV–V site. Ellis and Hammack's (1968) report and interpretation of this site is widely recognized and is the cornerstone on which the developing study of ritual cave use in the Southwest rests. In their exploration of the prehistoric significance of the site, the authors incorporate large amounts of primary informant data, most of which would be difficult or impossible to replicate today. However, their paper contains only limited information about the cultural materials from Feather Cave and not all of the information about other sites is accurate (Creel 1997, 85). The Field School of the University of New Mexico excavated the outer area of Feather Cave in 1950 and 1951, but the only materials reported were large numbers of sandals (Roosa 1952). Other materials remain unreported. A collection acquired by a looter in the main chamber of Feather Cave, now in the Laboratory of Anthropology, contains many ritual artifacts, including prayer sticks and tablita fragments.

Most of the dozens of Ancestral Puebloan sites identified as caves are actually rockshelters, and they do not appear to show the same kind of ritual use as deep caves in the Mogollon and Hohokam regions. They do, however, contain a great number of burials, as many as ninety-six in one site (Palmer 2001, 117). Like those of the Chihuahuan Desert sites, many of these burials included important ceremonial items. In other cases, ceremonial items were cached separately in rockshelters, often in carefully constructed stone-lined cysts. The most noteworthy of these caches came from Sunflower Cave (Guernsey and Kidder 1921, 3–7; Kidder and Guernsey 1919, 92–97), so-named because of the cached pot found there that contained wooden and leather flowers along with cone-shaped objects and a carved bird figurine. Wasley (1962) reports a similar cache from a cave on Bonita Creek, Arizona. The contents of both caches appear to be materials from Puebloan altars.

Such caches may themselves have a ritual dimension, as Ellis and Hammack (1968, 30) point out: "The Pueblos feel that persons more closely approach the underworld when they meet, store paraphernalia, or deposit offerings in caves." In addition to Spirit Bird Cave (described above), another likely Ancestral Puebloan ritual cave is Paiute Cave (Reilly 1973) located between the Echo Cliffs and Marble Canyon in northeastern Arizona. Pottery from this site dates at least as far back as Pueblo II, if not earlier (Reilly 1973, 53). A lava tube in the Arizona Strip, also known as "Paiute Cave," contains rock art in the Cave Valley Style, which dates to the Basketmaker III–Pueblo II periods (Slifer 2000, 32–34, 160–161, plates 19–20). Slifer suggests that, "perhaps this site was a shrine to spirits of the underworld or was recognized as a place of ancestral origin" (2000, 161).

In the Hohokam region, Ventana Cave, a rockshelter described by Haury (1950) as a type site for Hohokam culture, shows signs of ritual use in the presence of prayer sticks, grooved fending sticks, cane cigarettes, and gaming pieces. The best-documented Hohokam ritual cave site, however, is Red Cave (Ferg and Mead 1993). The site is an interesting example of a Southwest ritual cave assemblage exposed to wet cave conditions. It provides some suggestion of what might be missing in other areas where cultural materials are generally limited to lithics, ceramics, and bone. To provide a context for their analysis, Ferg and Mead (1993, 59–60) explore the literature of other ritual sites, both cave and surface. In the process, they touch on an important division in artifact assemblages which suggests a valid method for interpreting sites as either hunting shrines, emergence/fertility shrines, or "dual purpose shrines" based on the assemblage of artifacts. Given, however, the consideration that many artifacts associated with hunting may also relate to war, and the possible interrelation of war ritual to rain/maize ceremonialism, this distinction between these two realms of activity may not have not have been clearly defined among the prehistoric peoples who used these caves.

The actual boundaries for the Southwest cave ritual complex are difficult to define, but clearly extend beyond the generally accepted limits of the region. The Archaic split-twig figurine complex extends into southern California (Davis and Smith 1981), and the later warfare/hunting ritual complex described above, as represented by offerings of grooved fending sticks and arrows, extends as far west as southern Nevada, most notably in Gypsum Cave (Harrington 1933; Wheeler 1935). To the south there are a number of sites in Trans-Pecos Texas (Coffin 1932; Epstein 1963; Hamilton 2001; Martin 1933; Ross 1965; Word and Douglas 1970). The assemblage in many of these sites is marked by engraved and painted pebbles, which may date to the Early Archaic, perhaps representing a distinct ritual complex (Parsons 1965, 146). Lister (1958, 90–92) recovered arrows, a miniature bow, reed cigarettes, and a possible offering of corncobs on a string in caves in the northern Sierra Madre Occidental. Cueva de la Candelaria in Coahuila, Mexico, contained a wide variety of ceremonial paraphernalia, mostly as grave goods, some identical to materials from the Lower Pecos (Aveleyra, Maldonado, and Martinez del Rio 1956; Boyd 2005). Boyd (1996) describes rock art from northern Mexico dating to the Late Archaic that depicts shamanic ritual in conjunction with cave entrances. Even farther to the south, Lumholtz (1902, 159–63, 174–77, 199) reports both hunting and water-related cave ritual among the Huichol, including the offering of arrows and prayer sticks in caves.

CHRONOLOGY OF RITUAL CAVE USAGE

Cave ritual in the Southwest extends at least as far back as the Late Archaic, as represented by the Grand Canyon split-twig figurines, the oldest of which date to 2900 BC. This ritual complex continued until at least 1250 BC. If the nonutilitarian painted/incised pebbles from the Trans-Pecos and northern Mexico and/or the unfired clay-figurine tradition from Cowboy Cave in Utah represent ritual activity in adjacent regions, then cave ritual in the Southwest may also date back to the Early Archaic. A much more extensive and diverse cave ritual complex developed with the appearance of the agricultural Basketmaker–Puebloan, Hohokam, and Mogollon cultures shortly before the beginning of the Christian Era, and despite gaps in the record, this appears to continue to the present, with several sites documented for the current Pueblo VI period beginning about AD 1300.

One of the best-documented Pueblo VI sites is Jemez Cave (Alexander and Reiter 1935), which appears to have been a secondary ritual site for Jemez Pueblo, associated with a smaller cave beneath the nearby Soda Dam, which had greater ritual significance (figure 11.8). Alexander and Reiter (1935, 65) conclude that the initial use of Jemez Cave was as a temporary shelter, but add, "It may, even during this early period, have had ritual significance." After a period of more permanent occupation (AD 1250–1300), the cave returns to its use as a temporary shelter. However, they also note that the Jemez people "may also establish a secondary, ceremonial use for the site" (p. 67) because the natural dam located there was recognized as being of ceremonial importance. A more recent study of Jemez Cave identified it as an ancient maize site with a date range of 2440 +/-250 BP (Ford 1975, 22). Conversely, Bat Cave, one of the best-known ancient maize sites in the Southwest, yielded arrows, cane cigarettes, pipes, and gaming pieces in the higher levels of the excavation, which dated to the Mogollon I period (Dick 1965, 81).

Stevenson (1904, 234) identifies He'patina, a cave near the top of a high rock outcropping, as the emergence shrine for the Zuni. Despite the importance of this shrine, Stevenson writes that only expert climbers could reach it. Jeancon (1929, 7) describes a cave near Taos as a ceremonial cave used by the inhabitants of Taos Pueblo until the founding of the Hispanic town of Arroyo Seco nearby. Although it had been abandoned and contained no artifacts, Devereux (1966) relocated a shipap shrine ethnographically attributed to the Eastern Keresan Pueblos. Sandberg (1950, 180) reported that when he revisited the Correo Snake Pit after his excavations were complete, it contained fresh offerings. Laurens Hammack reports seeing offerings of canned goods, paper money, and loaves of bread there in 1957 or 1958 (personal communication, 2005). Woods (1945) suggests a continuity of ritual cave use from the Hohokam to the contemporary Pima, but as noted earlier, more reporting is needed from this area for all periods.

CONCLUSIONS

Whether undertaken for success in agriculture, hunting, witchcraft, or war (all of which may be interrelated), much or all cave ritual in the prehistoric Southwest receives its context from a belief in caves as gateways between this world and another beneath or within the earth, one which is the home of powerful supernaturals whose intervention is needed for the success of endeavors in this world, whether the support of oneself and one's relations or the destruction of one's enemies. Good things—rain, grain, and game—all are stored within the earth, and can only be obtained through supplication of the beings who control the portals of the cave-mountains. In this aspect, cave ritual in the Southwest appears to be much like that in Mesoamerica.

Although all of the known ritual cave sites in the Southwest have been heavily disturbed, many are still worthy of further study. Recent work by O'Laughlin in Chavez Cave (2003) yielded a new Tlaloc figurine (and the first painted-stone example) despite extensive looting and several earlier excavations. Some understudied areas may still hold intact shrines. There is a great need for more work in northern Mexico. Further study and reporting of existing museum collections, often scattered, would be of considerable value. Ultimately, ritual cave sites represent important resources for the understanding of prehistoric ritual practices in the Southwest. Combined with ethnographic sources, the careful study of these sites provides the opportunity to reconstruct significant portions of a record of religious practices that spans five millennia or more.

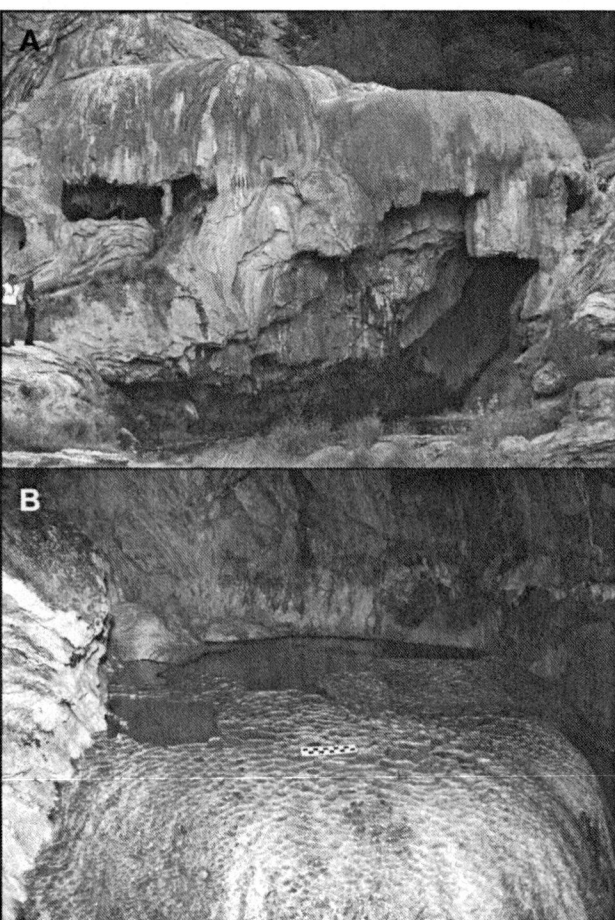

FIGURE 11.8 (A) Tourists in the grotto of the Soda Dam, an important shrine for the people of Jemez Pueblo. Before this part of the dam was dynamited during highway construction, a waterfall ran over it. (B) Flowstone basin inside the grotto of the Soda Dam, once the focus of ceremonial activities. (Author's photographs.)

REFERENCES CITED

Alexander, Herbert G., and Paul Reiter. 1935. *Report on the Excavation of Jemez Cave, New Mexico*. The University of New Mexico Bulletin, Monograph Series, Vol. 1, No. 3. Albuquerque: University of New Mexico Press.

Alves, E. 1929. "Caves of the El Paso District." *Bulletin of the Texas Archeological and Paleontological Society* 2: 64–9.

Alves, E. 1932. *Perishable Artifacts of the Hueco Caves*. West Texas Historical and Scientific Society: Publications. No. 4. Alpine, TX: Sul Ross State Teachers College.

Aveleyra Arroyo de Anda, Luis, Manuel Maldonado, and Pablo Martinez del Rio. 1956. *Cueva de la Candelaria*. Memorias del Instituto Nacional de Antropologia e Historia V. Mexico: INAH.

Bilbo, Barbara. 1997. "The Slaughter Canyon (New) Cave Pictograph Site, Carlsbad Caverns National Park, New Mexico." In *American Indian Rock Art* 23, ed. Stephen Freers, 49–56. San Miguel: American Rock Art Research Association.

Bilbo, Michael. 1997. "Carlsbad Caverns Natural Entrance Pictograph Sites 1 and 2, Carlsbad Caverns National Park, New Mexico." In *American Indian Rock Art 23*, ed. Stephen Freers, 41–47. San Miguel: American Rock Art Research Association.

Boyd, Carolyn E. 1996. "Shamanistic Journeys into the Otherworld of the Archaic Chichimec." *Latin American Antiquity* 7 (2): 152–64. http://dx.doi.org/10.2307/971615.

Boyd, Carolyn E. 2003. *Rock Art of the Lower Pecos*. College Station: Texas A&M University.

Boyd, Carolyn E. 2005. "Tools of the Shaman or the Hunter? A Review of Material Culture in the Lower Pecos Region of Texas and Mexico." Paper presented at the 70th Annual Meeting of the Society for American Archaeology, Salt Lake City.

Brady, James. N.d. "Caves as Ancient Maya Pilgrimage Centers: Archaeological Evidence of a Multifaceted Role." In *Pilgrimage and the Ritual Landscape in Pre-Columbian America*, ed. John Carlson. Washington, DC: Dumbarton Oaks Research Library and Collection. In press.

Brown, Linda A. 2005. "Planting the Bones: Hunting Ceremonialism at Contemporary and Nineteenth-Century Shrines in the Guatemalan Highlands." *Latin American Antiquity* 16: 131–46.

Caperton, Thomas J. 1981. "An Archaeological Reconnaissance." In *Contributions to Gran Quivira Archaeology*, ed. Alden C. Hayes, 4–11. Publications in Archaeology 17. Washington, DC: National Park Service, US Department of the Interior.

Clark, Darrell F. 1967. "A Net From Chihuahua, Mexico." *Kiva* 32 (4): 121–7.

Coffin, Edwin F. 1932. *Archaeological Exploration of a Rock Shelter in Brewster County, Texas*. Museum of the American Indian, Indian Notes and Monographs, No. 48 New York: Heye Foundation.

Cosgrove, C. B. 1947. *Caves of the Upper Gila and Hueco Areas in New Mexico and Texas*. Papers of the Peabody Museum of American Archaeology and Ethnology 24(2). Cambridge, MA: Harvard University. Reprint; New York: Kraus Reprint Corporation, 1968.

Coulam, Nancy J., and Alan R. Schroedl. 1996. "Early Archaic Clay Figurines from Cowboy and Walters Caves in Southeastern Utah." *Kiva* 61 (4): 4-1–12.

Coulam, Nancy J., and Alan R. Schroedl. 2004. "Late Archaic Totemism in the Greater American Southwest." *American Antiquity* 69 (1): 41–62. http://dx.doi.org/10.2307/4128347.

Creel, Darrell G. 1997. "Ceremonial Cave: An Overview of Investigations and Contents, Appendix A." In *The Hueco Mountain Cave and Shelter Survey: A Phase I Baseline Inventory in Maneuver Area 2D on Fort Bliss, Texas*, by Federico A. Almarez and Jeff D. Leach. Archaeological Technical Reports 10. El Paso: Anthropology Research Center, University of Texas at El Paso.

Crimmins, M. L. 1929. "An Archaeological Survey of the El Paso District." *Bulletin of the Texas Archaeological and Paleontological Society* 1: 36–42.

Cutrone, Daniel. 2003. "Cave and Ritual in the Southwest." Paper presented at the 68th Annual Meeting of the Society for American Archaeology, Milwaukee.

Davis, C. Allan, and Gerald C. Smith. 1981. *Newberry Cave*. Redlands, CA: San Bernardino County Museum Association.

Devereux, Don. 1966. "The Relocation of a Pueblo Emergence Shrine." *El Palacio* 73(4): 21–26.

Dick, Herbert W. 1965. *Bat Cave*. School of American Research Monograph No. 27. Santa Fe, NM: School of American Research.

Ellis, Florence Hawley, and Laurens Hammack. 1968. "The Inner Sanctum of Feather Cave: A Mogollon Sun and Earth Shrine Linking Mexico and the Southwest." *American Antiquity* 33 (1): 25–44. http://dx.doi.org/10.2307/277771.

Emslie, Steven D., Robert C. Euler, and Jim I Mead. 1987. "A Desert Culture Shrine in Grand Canyon, Arizona, and the Role of Split-Twig Figurines." *National Geographic Research* 3: 511–6.

Emslie, Steven D., Jim I. Mead, and Larry Coats. 1995. "Split-Twig Figurines in Grand Canyon, Arizona: New Discoveries and Interpretations." *Kiva* 61 (2): 145–73.

Epstein, Jeremiah F. 1963. *Centipede and Damp Caves: Excavations in Val Verde County, Texas, 1958*. Bulletin of the Texas Archaeological Society, Vol. 33 (for 1962).

Euler, Robert C., ed. 1984. *The Archaeology, Geology, and Paleobiology of Stanton's Cave, Grand Canyon National Park, Arizona*. Grand Canyon Natural History Monograph No. 6. Grand Canyon, AZ: Grand Canyon Natural History Association.

Farmer, Malcolm F., and Raymond deSaussure. 1955. "Split-Twig Animal Figurines." *Plateau* 27 (4): 13–23.

Ferdon, Edwin N., Jr. 1946. *An Excavation of Hermit's Cave, New Mexico*. School of American Research, Monograph No. 10. Albuquerque: University of New Mexico Press.

Ferg, Alan, and Jim I. Mead. 1993. *Red Cave: A Prehistoric Cave Shrine in Southeastern Arizona*. The Arizona Archaeologist No. 26. Phoenix: Arizona Archaeological Society.

Fewkes, Jesse Walter. 1898. "An Ancient Human Effigy Vase from Arizona." *American Anthropologist* 11 (6): 165–70. http://dx.doi.org/10.1525/aa.1898.11.6.02a00000.

Fewkes, Jesse Walter. 1971 [1898]. *Archaeological Expedition to Arizona in 1895: 17th Annual Report of the Bureau of American Ethnology, 1895–1896, Part II*. Glorieta, NM: Rio Grande Press.

Ford, Richard I. 1975. "Re-excavation of Jemez Cave, New Mexico." *Awanyu: Archaeological Society of New Mexico* 1 (3): 13–26.

Fulton, William S. 1941. *A Ceremonial Cave in the Winchester Mountains, Arizona*. Amerind Foundation Technical Report, No. 2. Dragoon, AZ: Amerind Foundation.

Geib, Phil R., and Donald R. Keller, eds. 2003. *Bighorn Cave: Test Excavations of a Stratified Dry Shelter*. Mohave County, AZ: Bilby Research Center, NAU.

Gifford, James C. 1980. *Archaeological Explorations in Caves of the Point of Pines Region Arizona*. Anthropological Papers of the University of Arizona No. 36. Tucson: University of Arizona Press.

Greer, John, and Mavis Greer. 1995. "Preliminary Observations on Dark Zone Pictographs at Surratt Cave (LA 9045), Lincoln County, New Mexico." Report prepared for Rick Surratt, San Antonio, Texas. On file with the Archaeological Records Management Section (ARMS), Museum of New Mexico, Santa Fe.

Greer, John, and Mavis Greer. 1996. "Dark Zone Rock Art in Surratt Cave, A Ceremonial Site in Central New Mexico." Report prepared for Rick Surratt, San Antonio, Texas. On file with the Archaeological Records Management Section (ARMS), Museum of New Mexico, Santa Fe.

Greer, John, and Mavis Greer. 1997. "Dark Zone Rock Art in Surratt Cave, a Deep Cavern in Central New Mexico." In *American Indian Rock Art 23*, ed. Stephen Freers, 25–40. San Miguel, CA: American Rock Art Research Association.

Greer, John, and Mavis Greer. 1998. "Dark Zone Rock Art in North America." In *Rock Art Papers*, vol. 13, ed. Ken Hedges, 135–44. San Diego Museum Papers 35. San Diego, CA: San Diego Museum of Man.

Greer, John, and Mavis Greer. 1999. "Dark Zone and Twilight Zone Pictographs in U-Bar Cave, Southwestern New Mexico." In *Rock Art Papers*, vol. 14, ed. Ken Hedges, 11–19. San Diego Museum Papers 36. San Diego, CA: San Diego Museum of Man.

Greer, John, and Mavis Greer. 2002. "Dark Zone Pictographs at Surratt Cave, Central New Mexico." In *Forward into the Past: Papers in Honor of Teddy Lou and Francis Stickney*, ed. Regge Wiseman, Thomas C. O'Laughlin, and Cordelia T. Snow, 37–46. Archaeological Society of New Mexico 28. Albuquerque: Archeological Society of New Mexico.

Guernsey, Samuel James. 1931. *Explorations in Northeastern Arizona: Report on the Archaeological Fieldwork, 1920–23*. Papers of the Peabody Museum of American Archaeology and Ethnology, 12(1). Cambridge, MA: Harvard University.

Guernsey, Samuel J., and Alfred V. Kidder. 1921. *Basketmaker Caves of Northeastern Arizona: Report on the Explorations, 1916–17*. Papers of the Peabody Museum of American Archaeology and Ethnology, 8(2). Cambridge, MA: Harvard University.

Hamilton, Donny L. 2001. *Prehistory of the Rustler Hills: Granado Cave*. Austin: University of Texas Press.

Hargrave, Lyndon L. 1970. *Feathers from Sand Dune Cave: A Basketmaker Cave Near Navajo Mountain, Utah*. Technical Series No. 9. Flagstaff, AZ: Museum of Northern Arizona.

Harrington, Mark Raymond. 1933. *Gypsum Cave, Nevada*. Southwest Museum Papers, No. 8. Highland Park, CA: Southwest Museum.

Harris, Arthur H. 1985. "Preliminary Report on the Vertebrate Fauna of U-Bar Cave, Hidalgo County, New Mexico." *New Mexico Geology* 7: 74–77, 84.

Haury, Emil W. 1945. *Painted Cave, Northeastern Arizona*. Amerind Foundation Technical Report, No.3. Dragoon, AZ: Amerind Foundation.

Haury, Emil W. 1950. *The Stratigraphy and Archaeology of Ventana Cave, Arizona*. Tucson: University of Arizona Press; Albuquerque: University of New Mexico Press.

Hays-Gilpin, Kelley Ann, Ann Cordy Deegan, and Elizabeth Ann Morris. 1998. *Prehistoric Sandals from Northeastern Arizona: The Earl H. Morris and Ann Axtel Morris Research*. Anthropological Papers of the University of Arizona No. 62. Tucson: University of Arizona Press.

Heizer, Robert F. 1942. "Ancient Grooved Clubs and Modern Rabbit Sticks." *American Antiquity* 8 (1): 41–56. http://dx.doi.org/10.2307/275634.

Hohmann, John W.A. 1990. *Master Stabilization and Development Plan for the Casa Malpais National Historic Landmark Site*. Phoenix: Louis Berger.

Holden, W. C. 1937. "Excavation of Murrah Cave." *Bulletin of the Texas Archaeological and Paleontological Society* 9: 48–73.

Hough, Walter. 1907. *Antiquities of the Upper Gila and Salt River Valleys in Arizona and New Mexico*. Bureau of American Ethnology, Bulletin 35. Washington, DC: US Government Printing Office.

Hough, Walter. 1914. *Culture of the Ancient Pueblos of the Upper Gila Region, New Mexico and Arizona*. United States National Museum, Bulletin 87. Washington, DC.

Howard, Edgar B. 1932. "Caves along the Slopes of the Guadalupe Mountains." *Bulletin of the Texas Archaeological and Paleontological Society* 4: 7–19. Abilene.

Howard, Edgar B. 1935. "Evidence of Early Man in North America." The Museum Journal, University of Pennsylvania Museum 24: 61–175. Philadelphia: University of Pennsylvania Museum.

Hull, Frank W., and Nancy M. White. 1980. "Spindle Whorls, Incised and Painted Stone, and Unfired Clay Objects." In *Cowboy Cave*, ed. Jesse D. Jennings, 117–25. University of Utah Anthropological Papers, No 104. Salt Lake City: University of Utah Press.

Hurst, C. T. 1947. "Excavation of Dolores Cave—1946." *Southwestern Lore* 13 (1): 8–17.

Jeancon, J. A. 1929. *Archaeological Investigations in the Taos Valley, New Mexico*. Smithsonian Miscellaneous Collections 81(12). Washington, DC: Smithsonian Institute.

Jett, Stephen C. 1968. "Grand Canyon Dams, Split-Twig Figurines, and 'Hit and Run' Archaeology." *American Antiquity* 33 (3): 341–51. http://dx.doi.org/10.2307/278702.

Jett, Stephen C. 1987. "Additional Information on Split-Twig and Other Willow Figurines from the Greater Southwest." *American Antiquity* 52 (2): 392–6. http://dx.doi.org/10.2307/281792.

Kaemlein, Wilma. 1971. "Large Hunting Nets in the Collections of the Arizona State Museum." *Kiva* 36 (3): 21–52.

Kidder, A. V., and S. J. Guernsey. 1919. *Archaeological Explorations in Northeastern Arizona*. Bureau of American Ethnology Bulletin 65. Washington, DC: US Government Printing Office.

Kluckhohn, Clyde. 1989. *Navajo Witchcraft*. Boston: Beacon Press.

Knab, Timothy. 1995. *A War of the Witches: A Journey Into the Underworld of the Contemporary Aztecs*. San Francisco: Harper.

Lambert, M. E., and J. R. Ambler. 1961. *A Survey and Excavation of Caves in Hidalgo County, New Mexico*. School of American Research Monograph No. 25: 1–107. Santa Fe, NM: School of American Research.

Lekson, Stephen, James L. Ross, and James E. Fitting. 1971. *The Stailey Cave Collection*. Southwestern New Mexico Research Reports No 6. Cleveland: Case Western Reserve University.

Lister, Robert H. 1958. "Archaeological Excavations in the Northern Sierra Madre Occidental, Chihuahua and Sonora, Mexico." With reports by Paul C. Mangelsdorf and Kate Peck Kent. University of Colorado Studies, Series in Anthropology, No. 7. Boulder, CO: University of Colorado Press.

Lockett, H. Claiborne, and Lyndon L. Hargrave. 1953. *Woodchuck Cave: A Basketmaker II Site in Tsegi Canyon, Arizona*, ed. Harold S. Colton and Robert C. Euler. Museum of Northern Arizona Bulletin 2. Flagstaff, AZ: Museum of Northern Arizona.

Long, Abijah, and Joe N. Long. 1956. *The Big Cave*. Long Beach, CA: Cushman Publications.

Lumholtz, Carl. 1902. *Unknown Mexico*. Vol. 1. New York: Scribners.

Marshall, Anne Lawrason. 2003. "The Siting of Pueblo Bonito." In *Pueblo Bonito: Center of the Chacoan World*, ed. Jill E. Neitzel, 10–13. Washington, DC: Smithsonian Books.

Martin, George C. 1933. *Archaeological Exploration of the Shumla Caves.* Witte Memorial Museum Bulletin, No. 3. San Antonio, TX: Southwest Texas Archaeological Society.

Martin, Paul S., John B. Rinaldo, and Elaine Bluhm. 1954. *Caves of the Reserve Area.* Fieldiana: Anthropology, Vol. 42. Chicago: Field Museum of Natural History.

Martin, Paul S., John B. Rinaldo, Elaine Bluhm, Hugh C. Cutler, and Roger Grange Jr. 1952. *Mogollon Continuity and Change: The Stratigraphic Analysis of Tularosa and Cordova Caves.* Fieldiana: Anthropology, Vol. 40. Chicago: Field Musaeum of Natural History.

Mera, H. P. 1938. *Reconnaissance and Excavation in Southeastern New Mexico.* Memoirs of the American Anthropological Association, No. 51. Menasha, WI: American Anthropological Association.

Morris, Elizabeth Ann. 1980. *Basketmaker Caves in the Prayer Rock District, Northeastern Arizona.* Anthropological Papers of the University of Arizona 35. Tucson: University of Arizona Press.

Nicolay, Scott. 2005. "The Grand Opening: A New Perspective on the Location of Pueblo Bonito in Chaco Canyon, New Mexico." Paper presented at the 70th Annual Meeting of the Society for American Archaeology, Salt Lake City.

Nusbaum, Jesse L. 1922. *A Basket-maker Cave in Kane County, Utah.* Museum of the American Indian, Heye Foundation, Indian Notes and Monographs, Miscellaneous Series, No. 29. New York: Museum of the American Indian, Heye Foundation.

O'Laughlin, Thomas C. 2003. "A Possible Dark Area Shrine in Chavez Cave, Doña Ana County, New Mexico." In *Climbing the Rocks: Papers in Honor of Helen and Jay Crotty,* ed. Regge N. Wiseman, Thomas C. O'Laughlin, and Cordelia T. Snow, 137–46. The Archaeological Society of New Mexico 29. Santa Fe: Archaeological Society of New Mexico.

Ortiz, Alfonso. 1969. *The Tewa World: Space, Time and Becoming in a Pueblo Society.* Chicago: University of Chicago Press.

Palmer, Jay W. 2001. "A Basketmaker II Massacre Revisited." *North American Archaeologist* 22 (2): 117–41. http://dx.doi.org/10.2190/N2PN-JKDL-BV03-V61W.

Parsons, Elsie Clews. 1918. "War God Shrines of Laguna and Zuñi." Lancaster. *American Anthropologist* 20 (4): 381–405. http://dx.doi.org/10.1525/aa.1918.20.4.02a00030.

Parsons, Elsie Clews. 1924. *The Scalp Ceremonial of the Zuni.* Memoirs of the American Anthropological Association 31. Menasha, WI: American Anthropological Association.

Parsons, Elsie Clews. 1996. *Pueblo Indian Religion.* 2 vols. Lincoln: University of Nebraska Press.

Parsons, Mark L. 1965. "Painted and Engraved Pebbles: Appendix I." In *The Archeology of Eagle Cave,* ed. Richard E. Ross, 146–59. Papers of the Texas Archaeological Salvage Project. No 7. Austin: Texas Archeological Salvage Project.

Reilly, P. T. 1973. "The Refuge Cave." *Masterkey* 47 (2): 46–54.

Roosa, William B. 1952. Sandals of Feather Cave." *Texas Archaeological and Paleontological Society, Bulletin,* Vol. 23: 133–46. Lubbock: Texas Archaeological and Paleontological Society.

Ross, Richard E. 1965. *The Archeology of Eagle Cave.* Papers of the Texas Archaeological Salvage Project. No 7. Austin: Texas Archeologicasl Salvage Project.

Sandberg, Sigfred. 1950. "An Archaeological Investigation of Correo Snake Pit." MA thesis, University of New Mexico, Albuquerque.

Sayles, E. B. 1930. "A Rock Shelter in Coke County." *Bulletin of the Texas Archaeological and Paleontological Society* 2: 33–40.

Schaafsma, Polly. 1997. "Tlalocs, Kachinas, Sacred Bundles, and Related Symbolism in the Southwest and Mesoamerica." In *The Casas Grandes World,* ed. C. F. Schaafsma and C. L. Riley, 164–92. Salt Lake City: University of Utah Press.

Schaafsma, Polly. 2000. *Warrior, Shield, and Star: Imagery and Ideology of Pueblo Warfare.* Santa Fe, NM: Western Edge Press.

Schaafsma, Polly, and Karl Taube. 2006. "Bringing the Rain: An Ideology of Rain Making in the Pueblo Southwest and Mesoamerica." In *A Pre-Columbian World,* ed. Jeffrey Quilter and Mary Miller, 231–85. Washington, DC: Dumbarton Oaks.

Schroeder, Alan R., comp. 1983. "The Pratt Cave Studies." G. X. Fitzgerald, ed. *The Artifact* 21: 1, 2, 3, and 4.

Schroedl, Albert H. 1977. "The Grand Canyon Figurine Complex." *American Antiquity* 42 (2): 254–64. http://dx.doi.org/10.2307/278988.

Schwartz, Douglas W., Arthur R. Lange, and Raymond deSaussure. 1958. "Split-Twig Figurines in the Grand Canyon." *American Antiquity* 23 (3): 264–73. http://dx.doi.org/10.2307/276308.

Scott, Ann M., and Walter E. Little. 2003. "Contemporary Maya Beliefs and Cave Utilization: Implications for Archaeological Interpretations." Paper presented at the 68th Annual Meeting of the Society for American Archaeology, Milwaukee.

Slifer, Dennis. 2000. *Guide to Rock Art of the Utah Region.* Santa Fe, NM: Ancient City Press.

Stein, John R., Dabney Ford, and Richard Friedman. 2003. "Reconstructing Pueblo Bonito." In *Pueblo Bonito: Center of the Chacoan World,* ed. Jill E. Neitzel, 33–60. Washington, DC: Smithsonian Books.

Stevenson, Matilda Coxe. 1904. *The Zuñi Indians: Their Mythology, Esoteric Fraternities, and Ceremonies.* Twenty-Third Annual Report of the Bureau of American Ethnology, 1901–1902. Washington, DC: US Government Printing Office.

Steward, Julian H. 1937. *Ancient Caves of the Great Salt Lake Region.* Bureau of American Ethnology, Bulletin 116. Washington, DC: US Government Printing Office.

Tedlock, Dennis, trans. 1972. *Finding the Center: Narrative Poetry of the Zuni Indians.* New York: Dial Press.

Van Valkenburgh, Richard. 1940. "Tsosi Tells the Story of Massacre Cave." *Desert Magazine* 3 (4): 22–5.

Wasley, William W. 1962. "A Ceremonial Cave on Bonita Creek, Arizona." *American Antiquity* 27 (3): 380–94. http://dx.doi.org/10.2307/277803.

Wheeler, S. M. 1935. "A Dry Cave in Southern Nevada." *Masterkey* 9: 5–12.

White, Jim. 1940. *The Discovery and History of Carlsbad Caverns New Mexico.* Carlsbad, NM: Jim White and Charley Lee White.

Woods, Clee. 1945. "I Found the Cave of a Pima God." *Desert Magazine* 8 (9): 8–10.

Woolsey, A. M. 1936. "Reconnaissance in El Paso County, March 15 to March 27, 1936." Manuscript in El Paso County Miscellaneous File, Texas Archaeological Research Laboratory, University of Texas at Austin.

Word, James H., and Charles L. Douglas. 1970. *Excavations at Baker Cave, Val Verde County, Texas.* Bulletin of the Texas Memorial Museum 16. Austin: University of Texas Press.

12

Forty Years' Pursuit of Human Prehistory in the World Underground

Patty Jo Watson

In Eastern North America, systematic archaeology in big caves with miles of dark zone began during the 1960s. Research goals, research techniques, and interpretative frameworks have changed significantly over the past 50 years. The 50 years began in 1963 when Joe Caldwell—then Head Curator of Anthropology at the Illinois State Museum—refused to undertake an archaeological study of Salts Cave, Mammoth Cave National Park, Kentucky. Instead he offered me $300 from the Museum Society and the help of his Assistant Curator, Bob Hall, if I would direct the work myself (Watson 1999, 288–89). So the Cave Research Foundation Archeological Project was born (figure 12.1). Bob Hall was a wonderful colleague, and a natural-born caver. He arrived at the Cave Research Foundation field station with all his own equipment (hardhat, carbide lamp, knee crawlers, cave pack), and spent any spare moments underground looking for leads in the Upper Salts breakdown (Hall 1967).

Bob supervised test excavations in one of the few places within Upper Salts where there is sufficient sediment to make digging possible (figure 12.2). In addition he collected representative items for the Illinois State Museum: fragments of vegetal-fiber artifacts (cordage, footwear), remnants of bottle gourd and hard-shelled squash containers, cane, and other prehistoric torch materials (figures 12.3, 12.4). Meanwhile, I led small crews in surveying and recording in situ remains in Indian Avenue of Lower Salts.

That first field season was sufficiently successful to interest the National Geographic Society Research Committee, which helped fund the Salts Cave project for several years, as did a couple of grants from the National Endowment for the Humanities and National Science Foundation, but the crucial logistical support aboveground and below came—first, last, and always—from the Cave Research Foundation (CRF).

From its 1963 beginnings in Salts Cave (Watson 1969), the CRF Archeological Project expanded to Mammoth Cave in 1969 and to Lee Cave (in Mammoth Cave National Park) in the early 1970s (Freeman et al. 1973). In 1976, Ron Wilson (paleontologist and archaeozoologist), Louise Robbins (physical anthropologist), and I began work at Jaguar Cave, Tennessee (Robbins, Wilson, and Watson 1981; Watson et al. 2005; Willey, Stolen, et al. 2005; Willey, Watson, et al. 2009). A year later, National Speleological Society (NSS) cavers exploring another Tennessee cave (now known as 3rd Unnamed Cave) told us about archaeological remains they had found there, and we undertook some preliminary documentation in 1977 and 1981 (Franklin 2008).

Back in Mammoth Cave National Park, still during the 1970s, one of my Washington University graduate students, Ken Carstens, initiated a dissertation project surveying rockshelters and open sites to build a chronology of the park's prehistory, and to provide context for the dark-zone

FIGURE 12.1 (a) 1960s cave archaeology crew in Salts Cave Sink, walking down to Salts Cave entrance. (Cave Research Foundation photograph by William T. Austin; Watson 1969, pl. 1, reproduced here with permission from the Cave Research Foundation and the Illinois State Museum, Springfield.) (b) 1960s cave archaeology crew entering Salts Cave Vestibule. (Cave Research Foundation photo by William T. Austin; Dye 2008, figure 0.1, reproduced here with permission from the Cave Research Foundation and the University of Tennessee Press, Knoxville.)

FIGURE 12.2 Robert L. Hall at work in Test A, Upper Salts Cave, August 1963. (Cave Research Foundation photograph by William Curtsinger.)

FIGURE 12.3 Fragments of Early Woodland *Cucurbita pepo* var. *ovifera* in situ in Lower Salts Cave. (Cave Research Foundation photograph by Pete Lindsley.)

cave archaeology (Carstens 1980). This was quite important, and something I had ignored for far too long. Also in the 1970s, another Washington University grad student—Bill Marquardt—and I began a long-term effort (the Shell Mound Archaeological Project, SMAP) in the Big Bend of Green River, 40 miles downstream of Mammoth Cave National Park (Marquardt and Watson 2005). My involvement in SMAP grew out of the work by Dick Yarnell on plant remains from Salts Cave, including those he retrieved from a series of ancient human fecal deposits (Yarnell 1969, 1974a, 1974b).

During the period of the 1960s and 1970s, the CRF Archeological Project was unique in Eastern North American archaeology. No one else was persistently investigating prehistoric human activities far into the dark zones of caves that were dozens of miles long. Approximately 15–20 miles of Mammoth and Salts Caves were known to prehistoric people, the total length of the system containing these two and several other connected caves now being in excess of 390 mapped miles and still going. In 1980, however, Patrick and Cheryl Munson began archaeological research in another big midcontinental cave, Wyandotte (5.2 miles long), in southern Indiana (Munson and Munson 1990).

A second significant breakthrough also came in 1980 when University of Tennessee archaeologist Charles Faulkner was told about a cave in central Tennessee (soon named Mud Glyph) that had unusual markings on the sediment-coated passage walls (Faulkner 1986, 2008). By 1986, there was sufficient work in subterranean locales of the Eastern Woodlands to enable a half-day session at the Society for American Archaeology's (SAA) 51st Annual Meeting in New Orleans (Session 75, April 27). The ses-

FIGURE 12.4 Fragments of prehistoric cane charcoal in situ on the floor of Indian Avenue, Lower Salts Cave. (Cave Research Foundation photograph by Pete Lindsley.)

sion was organized and chaired by Patrick Munson. Cave archaeology in the Midwest, Midsouth, and Southeast continued to grow slowly during the 1990s. By the end of the decade, enough research had either been completed or was ongoing that one entire issue of *Midcontinental Journal of Archaeology* (volume 26, number 2, edited by Sarah Sherwood and Jan Simek) was dedicated to cave archaeology. In 2002, an authoritative synthesis, *The Woodland Southeast* (Anderson and Mainfort editors), was published, containing a chapter on "Woodland Cave Archaeology in Eastern North America" (Crothers et al. 2002). Beginning in 2007, sessions on cave archaeology appeared yearly in the SAA Annual Meeting programs. Given all that, what do we now know about ancient cavers in Eastern North America?

PREHISTORIC CAVERS IN THE EASTERN WOODLANDS

Archaic Period

We know that people began exploring big caves in Tennessee (Jaguar, 48th Unnamed, 3rd Unnamed) well before 5,000 years ago (table 12.1). The evidence so far clearly indicates that at least some Archaic people were as capable and competent belowground as they were in moving around the deciduous forest on the surface. Together with well-documented activities more than 4,500 years ago by eight or nine people far back in Jaguar Cave, Tennessee (Watson et al. 2005), the best demonstration I know of ancient cavers as undaunted explorers of the dark zone is provided by a 3,670-year-old trail left by two people in a mud-floored passage called the Upper Crouchway (figure 12.5). This passage connects a portion of Floyd Collins Crystal Cave with Unknown Cave, which links to the far end of Indian Avenue in Lower Salts Cave. The footprint trail was discovered in 1954 by William Austin and Jack Lehrberger. For more than 50 years the foot impressions were thought to have been created by two prehistoric cavers who had entered the Upper Crouchway via Unknown Cave and Indian Avenue in Lower Salts (Brucker and Watson 1976, 259–63; Watson 1969, 62–64; Willey et al. 2009, 73). Recent cartographic work in this part of Unknown and Crystal Cave, however, indicates that a more likely entry point for the two ancient explorers was not from Lower Salts into Unknown Cave (and beyond it to the Upper Crouchway that connects Unknown to Floyd Collins Crystal Cave), but rather via a much earlier configuration of the breakdown and sinkhole complex now known as Unknown Cave. Cave Research Foundation cartographer Paul Hauck says,

> We know that both Upper Crouchway and Lower Crouchway end in breakdown [at the Unknown Cave sinkhole/passageway complex] as does Upper Upper Crouchway. Judging from the [newest] map, it's all the same breakdown. Many of these breakdowns occur when a surface valley downcuts through the sandstone caprock and surface water begins to seep its way down through the underlying limestone, creating many of the shaft complexes we see so often in the Flint Ridge cave system. As downcutting continues, breakdown begins to fill them up. I think that at one time there was an entry into this breakdown from the surface, maybe a passage like the Unknown Entrance, which was then filled in by surface detritus, a process taking place at the Unknown Entrance right now. I think [the ancient cave explorers] managed to find a way down through that breakdown, came out in Upper Upper Crouchway or Upper Crouchway, and made their way on out to Smith Avenue [in Crystal Cave], perhaps as far as Foundation Hall. (Paul Hauck, letter to P.J. Watson dated August 3, 2008)

It certainly appears that some Archaic folk in some big caves (e.g., Lee Cave in Mammoth Cave National Park, Jessup Avenue in Lower Mammoth Cave, Indian Avenue in Lower Salts, as well as Jaguar Cave and the Upper Crouchway of Unknown/Crystal Cave) were primarily engaged simply in exploring the world underground. This inference about motivations of the ancient cavers is based on the fact that the only Archaic-age evidence known so far from the caves and passages just listed consists solely of torch fragments, torch smudges, and/or footprints. No pictographs or petroglyphs like those in Adair Glyph Cave, Mud Glyph Cave, and numerous other caves now documented elsewhere (see discussion below) have been reported from Jaguar, Lee, Jessup Avenue in Mammoth Cave, the Upper Crouchway in Unknown/Crystal Cave, or Indian Avenue in Lower Salts Cave. In contrast to the original explorers of those caves and passages, ancient cavers in 3rd Unnamed Cave, Adair Glyph Cave, and Fisher Ridge Cave—whatever else they were doing—seem to have been mindful of caves as portals to a special underworld locale where supernatural forces or entities might be encountered. I include Upper Salts Cave in this group on the strength of resemblance between an incised petroglyph in the Late Archaic chert quarry of 3rd Unnamed Cave with two charcoal pictographs on a breakdown block in Upper Salts (compare Simek, Franklin, and Sherwood

TABLE 12.1 Dark-zone cave archaeological sites in the midcontinental karst of the United States. (This list is representative but not exhaustive.)

5000–4000 calibrated age BP (top to bottom roughly in order of earlier to later)
48th Unnamed, TN (Creswell 2007)
3rd Unnamed, TN (Crothers et al. 2002; Franklin 2008)
Jaguar, TN (Crothers et al. 2002; Franklin 2008)
Lee, KY (Crothers et al. 2002)
Wyandotte, IN (Munson and Munson 1990)
Mammoth, KY (Crothers et al. 2002)

4000–3000 calibrated age BP (top to bottom roughly in order of earlier to later)
Wyandotte, IN (Munson and Munson 1990)
Mammoth, KY (Crothers et al. 2002)
Unknown/Floyd Collins Crystal, KY (Crothers et al. 2002)
Adair, KY (DiBlasi 1996)
Fisher Ridge, KY (Crothers et al. 2002)
Salts, KY (Crothers et al. 2002)
3rd Unnamed, TN (Crothers et al. 2002; Franklin 2008)
Short, KY (Horton 2003)

3000–500 calibrated age BP (top to bottom roughly in order of earlier to later)
Wyandotte, IN (Munson and Munson 1990)
Mammoth, KY (Crothers et al. 2002)
Salts, KY (Crothers et al. 2002)
Indian Salts, KY (Barrier and Byrd 2008)
Big Bone, TN (Crothers et al. 2002)
Hubbards, TN (Pritchard 2008)
Crystal Onyx, KY (Crothers et al. 2002)
Crumps, KY (Crothers et al. 2002; Davis 1996)
3rd Unnamed, TN (Franklin 2008)
5th Unnamed, TN (Crothers et al. 2002)
6th Unnamed, TN (Crothers et al. 2002)
2nd Unnamed, TN (Crothers et al. 2002)
19th Unnamed, AL (Crothers et al. 2002)
7th Unnamed, TN (Crothers et al. 2002)
Picture Cave, MO (Diaz-Granados 2008)
22nd Unnamed, TN (Franklin 2008)
Mud Glyph, TN (Crothers et al. 2002; Faulkner 2008)
Xanadu, TN (Franklin 2008)
Jaguar, TN (Franklin 2008)
Hubble Post Office, TN (Douglas, Roebuck, and Roebuck 2008)
Mountain Eye, TN (Franklin 2008)

1998, figure 10d, with DiBlasi 1996, figure 5.1, lower right).

Images created in Adair Glyph Cave, Kentucky (DiBlasi 1996), on the mud floor of a room well back in

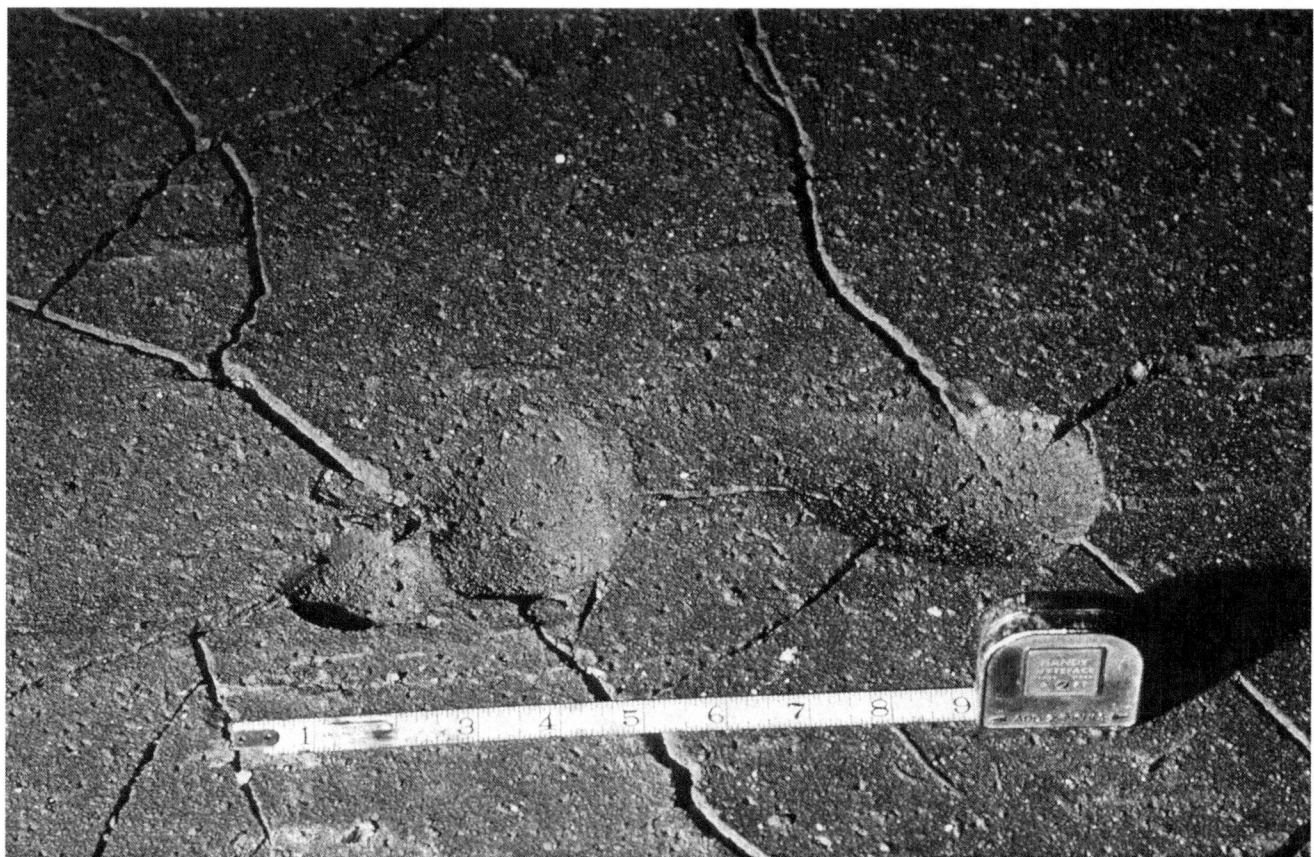

FIGURE 12.5 Foot impression left by a Late Archaic caver in the Upper Crouchway of Floyd Collins Crystal Cave/Unknown Cave, Kentucky. The associated radiocarbon determination is 3670 +/–50 BP, Beta-96145, 1950 half-life, uncalibrated (Crothers et al. 2002: table 23.1). (Cave Research Foundation photograph by William T. Austin; Watson 1969, pl. 14 Lower; reproduced here with permission from the Cave Research Foundation and the Illinois State Museum, Springfield.)

the dark zone indicate Archaic antecedents to late prehistoric Mud Glyph Cave, Tennessee (Faulkner 1986). Both certainly appear to have been sacred spaces, as does the 90-meter Glyph Passage in Crumps Cave, Kentucky, whose glyphs are nearly 2000 years old (two uncalibrated dates: 1960 +/–60 BP and 1840 +/–80 BP; Crothers et al. 2002; Davis 1996, 349; Simek and Cressler 2005, 104–106).

Woodland Period: Early to Middle Woodland

Third Unnamed Cave, Tennessee, and Salts and Mammoth Caves in Kentucky contain clear evidence of mining (chert in 3rd Unnamed and gypsum in Salts and Mammoth), as well as pictographs and petroglyphs seemingly evocative of a spirit world. These include straight and curvilinear lines, rayed circles, and zoomorphic shapes. Some of the latter might be Archaic–Early Woodland references to a supernatural subterranean creature analogous to the ethnographically described earth-serpent/water-panther/long-tailed-monster called the Uktena in the Southeast, and Mishi Bizi in the Northeast (Diaz-Granados 2008, 207–10; Martin 1999, 199–210). Crosshatching or latticework is also common, one ethnographic analog for which comes from the Great Lakes region where lattices are boundary markers between land and water, or between This World and The World Below (Martin 1999, 206).

There are also several examples of caves that were mined for gypsum, aragonite, and/or chert but that are not known to contain pictographs or petroglyphs: Big Bone, Tennessee (Late Archaic to Late Woodland); Wyandotte, Indiana (early Late Archaic to Late Woodland); Hubbards, Tennessee (Early Woodland to Late Woodland); and Indian Salts Cave, Kentucky (Early Woodland). The seeming absence of prehistoric imagery in these caves may be due to historic disturbance and destruction (especially saltpeter mining and casual or systematic looting), or to lack of careful examination by latter-day cavers and archaeologists.

LATE WOODLAND–MISSISSIPPIAN

Cave sites dating to the late prehistoric period include the two best-known cases of ceremonial locales: Mud Glyph, Tennessee, and Picture Cave, Missouri. Other examples are continually being added to the list (Simek and Cressler 2009), but ceremonial or art caves are still somewhat unusual. Even more uncommon are caves with clear evidence of prehistoric mineral mining, an activity I once thought to be the major reason for extended visits to big-cave dark zones (like those of Salts and Mammoth) by generations of prehistoric cavers. One of my other suggestions (Watson 1986) that ritual caves are late and "footprint caves" are early has also been proven wrong. Footprint caves are those like Jaguar containing no evidence for any activity except exploration. It is now clear that some caves (e.g., Adair, Fisher Ridge, Mammoth, Salts, 3rd Unnamed) were thought of as special places by Archaic and Early Woodland cave explorers and cave miners (e.g. Crothers 2012), and that some Mississippian people were accomplished explorers of caves where no ritual or extractive activity is evidenced (Douglas 2008; Douglas, Roebuck, and Roebuck 2008, 164–66; Franklin 2008, 150; Simek and Cressler 2009).

Finally, at least as early as 3000 BP, pits and caves were being used as mortuary facilities. Some were cemeteries where bodies were interred (e.g., Terminal Archaic–Early Woodland Short Cave in Kentucky [Horton 2003], Middle Woodland Copena burial caves in Alabama [Walthall and DeJarnette 1974], and several Middle Woodland and late prehistoric burial caves in Tennessee [Crothers and Willey 2009; Franklin 2008, 151–52; Simek, Cressler, and Pope 2004]). Others (Ausmus in Tennessee; Crystal Onyx and Pit of the Skulls in Kentucky; Pinson Cave, Alabama; and several sites in Virginia) are sinkholes into which bodies were lowered, dropped, or thrown (Crothers and Willey 2009; Haskins 1988; Hemberger 1989, 48–66).

CHANGING PERSPECTIVES: 1960s TO 2000s

When the CRF Archeological Project began fieldwork in Salts Cave 50 years ago, our objectives were quite particularistic, basic time-space systematics being a major focus. When was the ancient caver activity, what was it, and where was it? More general concerns were also present, however. Archaeobotany (paleoethnobotany), archaeozoology, and biological anthropology were represented by Dick Yarnell, Lathel Duffield, and Louise Robbins, respectively. My own primary interest was in the plant remains, once we began to accumulate radiocarbon dates, and Yarnell (Watson and Yarnell 1969; Yarnell 1969, 1974a, 1974b) began to define a pattern of early cultigen use combining two species, pepo gourd (*Cucurbita pepo*) and bottle gourd (*Lagenaria sicer-aria*)—then thought to have been domesticated in Latin America but later shown to be indigenous—with several native crop plants (sunflower, sumpweed, chenopod, maygrass). That research focus proved to be very productive, and was central to a new body of data documenting Eastern North America as one of the few world areas where an indigenous agricultural system was independently created (ca. 4000 BP) and sustained for many millennia (Browman et al. 2009; Smith and Yarnell 2009). Key evidence was furnished during the 1960s-1970s by the wealth of human paleofecal deposits perfectly preserved in the dry passages of Salts and Mammoth Caves (Yarnell 1969, 1974b). Many other dry caves and rockshelters have now added much more information, as have open sites where flotation techniques have been used to recover charred plant remains (Browman et al. 2009; Chapman and Watson 1993; Fritz 1990; Gremillion 2002; Smith 2002; Smith and Yarnell 2009; Watson 1976, 1997). This early-agriculture theme continues to be prominent, and evidence from dry caves and rockshelters is still extremely important.

Another central focus in the 1960s and 1970s was that of caves as sources of valued materials: for example, chert (Wyandotte, 3rd Unnamed), gypsum and other sulfate minerals (Salts and Mammoth Caves, Hubbards Cave, Indian Salts Cave, Big Bone Cave), and flowstone (Wyandotte Pillar of the Constitution [Munson and Munson 1990; Tankersley et al. 1990; Tankersley et al. 1997])—in other words, caves as mines and quarries. That was pretty much my attitude about Salts and Mammoth for some 20 years (Munson et al. 1989; Watson 1969, 1974). By the mid- to late 1980s, however, the picture began to change. The discovery of Mud Glyph Cave, Tennessee, in 1980 (Faulkner 1986, 2008) followed by that of Adair Glyph Cave, Kentucky, in 1986 (DiBlasi 1996) and Picture Cave, Missouri, in 1991 (Diaz-Granados 2008), marked the dawn of a new era wherein ceremonial or ritual sites were widely recognized. They are more numerous than mine and quarry caves, and they are highly significant. Moreover, the signatures (petroglyphs and pictographs) indicating concern for supernatural entities and the spirit world began to be noticed more widely in caves previously classed as solely mines and quarries (Salts, Mammoth, 3rd Unnamed), or as sites of exploration only (Fisher Ridge). This is partly a result of having more people—archaeologists and cavers—looking more carefully, and partly a result of knowledge about what to look for as demonstrated by exemplar sites such as Mud Glyph, Adair Glyph, Picture Cave, and other art caves in Alabama, Tennessee, and Virginia (DiBlasi 1996; Diaz-Granados 2008; Faulkner 1986, 1988; Simek and Cressler 2005, 2008, 2009; Simek, Faulkner, Ahlman, et al. 2001; Simek, Faulkner, Fankenberg, et al. 1997).

Another major trend in dark-zone cave archaeology is improvement in recording and analytical procedures. Back in the 1960s, our primary technique was to move slowly from survey station to survey station, locating and recording prehistoric materials (e.g., Watson 1969, 25–31). In 1969, Charles Redman suggested we experiment with quantified surface survey techniques (see Redman and Watson 1970) in a portion of Upper Salts Cave. We did try, but we failed. The issues of precise find-spotting plus standardized categorization and quantification were too time-consuming and/or just too intractable. Now, however, new technology—including laser transits with data-loggers, and other computer hardware and software (e.g., GIS)—made it possible for George Crothers's teams in Mammoth Cave during the 1990s to implement and expand upon Redman's suggestion (Crothers 2001). Scanning electron microscopes enable detailed analyses of anthropogenic versus nonanthropogenic sediments in cave sites, resulting in quantities of new information about prehistoric human activities in and near them (Goldberg and Sherwood 2006; Sherwood 2008; Simek et al. 1997). Accelerated mass spectrometry (AMS) dating of pictographs (Diaz-Granados 2008), laser transit mapping, and digital photography of pictographs and petroglyphs provide chronological information as well as minute particulars concerning techniques used by ancient cavers to create the images (e.g., Simek and Cressler 2008, 170–71). Analyses of ancient hormones and of human and nonhuman DNA in paleofecal deposits are revealing a new array of data about prehistoric human and nonhuman individuals and their specific environments (Sobolik et al. 1996; LeBlanc et al. 2007; Poinar et al. 2001).

At a broader methodological level, two other trends are now apparent. One is represented by the Cave Archaeology Research Team (CART), established in 1995 at the University of Tennessee under the direction of Jan Simek. CART is systematically surveying all known Tennessee caves for evidence of prehistoric human presence, something that should be done in all the other caverniferous states of the United States. According to a recent summary (Simek 2008, 266–68), 1,000 caves of the approximately 9,000 listed by the Tennessee Cave Survey have been investigated by CART. Of that 1,000, 250 contain prehistoric archaeological remains. Of those 250, 195 preserved artifacts of various kinds; eighty-eight caves contain only cane-torch fragments and/or charcoal wall smudges, suggesting exploration as the sole activity; sixty-two were mortuary caves or pits; forty-seven (now sixty-seven; Simek and Cressler 2009) contain cave art; and only fourteen reveal evidence of chert, clay, and/or mineral mining, mineral mining being especially rare with only four sites known so far. Thus, dark-zone exploration—eighty-eight caves out of 250 examined—is a major category of prehistoric cave use in Tennessee (see also Douglas 2008).

Simek makes the important general point that subterranean cultural resources must be included in Cultural Resource Management (CRM) surveys if we are to understand the prehistoric human past in karstic regions like the US Midwest, Midsouth, and Southeast. And of course many caves also contain significant *historic* archaeological remains (Blankenship 2008; Crothers 1983; Duncan 1997; Matthews 2006; Mickelson 2008; Munson and Munson 1990; Smyre and Zawislak 2007; Taylor and Nicola 2007; Trader, Ward, and Switzer 2008).

The other general methodological trend is, in a sense, the inverse of that just noted. The CRF Archeological Project and others demonstrated the value to Americanist archaeology of following ancient cavers into the world underground. By the 1980s and 1990s several archaeologists and cavers significantly advanced knowledge of prehistoric activities in cave dark zones. Now a vigorous and enthusiastic community of speleoarchaeologists collaborates with cavers skilled in cave cartography, cave photography, and other relevant areas of expertise. These teams may be so happy and successful belowground, however, especially in renowned karst regions with many deep pits and multiple-mile-long caves, that aboveground archaeology and its relation to cave use may be neglected. I certainly stand guilty in the case of Jaguar Cave: fourteen trips to Aborigine Avenue over a period of 10 years but virtually no attention paid to the surrounding surface archaeology. Happily, however, Jay Franklin (2002) recently completed an archaeological study of Fentress County where Jaguar is located. Moreover, most karst states maintain good site files, and most speleoarchaeologists in those places are far more familiar with local prehistoric and early historic archaeology than am I, a refugee from West Asian prehistory. Hence, I am optimistic that this last problem is on its way to solution. Getting federal, state, county, and municipal CRM regulations altered to include survey and mitigation procedures for caves and sinkholes will require a more prolonged campaign, however.

Finally, our biggest *theoretical* challenge now is to incorporate paleocognitive foci into interpretations of prehistoric activities in the dark zones of Eastern North American caves. This must be done extremely carefully because the evidence is sparse, difficult to locate and document accurately, and difficult to interpret. The great temptation is to construct overly elaborate formulations too complex and weighty for their frail, sometimes nearly invisible, evidential bases. Nevertheless, these efforts must be made. We have taken only the first few steps toward understanding this aspect of dark-zone cave archaeology in the Eastern Woodlands, but it is clear that This World and The World

Below were integral parts of a single cognitive universe for those ancient cavers we pursue into subterranean darkness.

ACKNOWLEDGMENTS

The following people provided valuable help, but are not to be blamed in any way for the use made of their contributions in this chapter. Thank you, Scott Nicolay and Craig Williams, for organizing the Society for American Archaeology symposium (Session 63) in which an earlier version of this chapter was presented on April 23, 2009 (the 74th Annual Meeting of the SAA, April 22–26, 2009, in Atlanta, Georgia). And thank you, Holley Moyes, session discussant, for inviting me to contribute a chapter to the present volume on cave archaeology. Thank you, Carol Diaz-Granados and Jerome Jacobson, for information regarding the Uktena being. Thanks are also owed to P. Willey for alerting me to the paper by Joe Douglas (2008); and to George Crothers for information about the Mammoth Cave Main Cave survey. I am deeply grateful to Paul Hauck for generously taking the time to send me, not only the latest manuscript maps, but also his current thoughts about aboriginal cavers moving around in the highly complex Unknown Cave/Crystal Cave/Smith Avenue region of the Flint Ridge Cave System. As to Joe Caldwell: I think he knew, prior to his untimely death in 1973, how much his help meant to me and the CRF Archeological Project. At any rate he kindly wrote the Preface for our first big report (Watson 1969, iii–iv), and was aware of subsequent results that were leading up to a second volume (Watson 1974). Be that as it may, I owe him more than I can say, first for his refusal to undertake archaeological work in Salts Cave, thus causing me to do it; second, for making sure the project would get off to a good start by giving us the vital field assistance of Bob Hall as well as funds for that first summer's work underground in 1963; and third, by ensuring publication of the Salts Cave monograph by the Illinois State Museum in 1969.

I gratefully acknowledge the permissions granted and other assistance generously offered through the decades by many National Park Service personnel at Mammoth Cave National Park. Finally, I owe unending gratitude to the officers, members, and joint venturers of the Cave Research Foundation who have—for half a century, and now into the second and third generations of archaeological research—provided unstinting support aboveground and below, along Kentucky's Green River and elsewhere in the world of caves and karst.

REFERENCES CITED

Anderson, David G., and Robert C. Mainfort, eds. 2002. *The Woodland Southeast*. Tuscaloosa: University of Alabama Press.

Barrier, Casey R., and Myrisa K. Byrd. 2008. "Gypsum Mining at Indian Salts Cave: An Examination of Early Woodland Subterranean Mineral Extraction." In *Cave Archaeology of the Eastern Woodlands*, ed. David Dye, 79–96. Knoxville: University of Tennessee Press.

Blankenship, Sarah A. 2008. "Cagle Saltpetre Cave in Van Buren County, Tennessee: The Archaeology of Nineteenth-Century Caves in the Midsouth." In *Cave Archaeology of the Eastern Woodlands*, ed. David Dye, 219–33. Knoxville: University of Tennessee Press.

Browman, David L., Gayle J. Fritz, Patty Jo Watson, and David J. Meltzer. 2009. "Origins of Food-Producing Economies in the Americas." In *The Human Past*, ed. Chris Scarre, 306–49. London: Thames and Hudson.

Brucker, Roger W., and Richard A. Watson. 1976. *The Longest Cave*. New York: Alfred A. Knopf.

Carstens, Kenneth C. 1980. "Archaeological Investigations in the Central Kentucky Karst." PhD dissertation, Department of Anthropology, Washington University, St. Louis, MO.

Chapman, Jefferson, and Patty Jo Watson. 1993. "The Archaic Period and the Flotation Revolution." In *Foraging and Farming in the Eastern Woodlands of North America*, ed. Margaret Scarry, 27–38. Gainesville: University Press of Florida.

Creswell, Bradley. 2007. "Phase I Archaeological Survey of Caves and Rockshelters within the Proposed Corridor of the Knoxville Parkway (SR 475) in Anderson, Knox, and Loudon Counties, Tennessee." Archaeological Research Laboratory, University of Tennessee, Tennessee Department of Transportation Project 98012-1264-04, Knoxville.

Crothers, George M. 1983. "Archaeological Investigations in Sand Cave, Kentucky." *National Speleological Society Bulletin* 45: 19–33.

Crothers, George M. 2001. "Mineral Mining and Perishable Remains in Mammoth Cave: Examining Social Process in the Early Woodland." In *Fleeting Identities: Perishable Material Culture in Archaeological Research*, ed. Penelope Drooker, 314–34. Center for Archaeological Investigations, Occasional Paper 28. Carbondale, IL: Southern Illinois University Press.

Crothers, George M. 2012. "Early Woodland Ritual Use of Caves in Eastern North America." *American Antiquity* 77 (3): 524–541.

Crothers, George M., Charles H. Faulkner, Jan F. Simek, Patty Jo Watson, and P. Willey. 2002. "Woodland Cave Archaeology in Eastern North America." In *The Woodland Southeast*, ed. David Anderson and Robert Mainfort, 502–24. Tuscaloosa: University of Alabama Press.

Crothers, George M., and P. Willey. 2009. "Mortuary Caves and Sinkholes in the Interior Low Plateau and Southern Appalachian Mountains of the Eastern United States." Paper presented at the 17th International Speleological Congress, Kerrville, Texas, July 19–26.

Davis, Daniel B. 1996. "A Preliminary Report on the Mud Glyphs in 15Wa6, Warren County, Kentucky." *Current Archaeological Research in Kentucky* 4: 332–53. Kentucky Heritage Council, Frankfort.

Diaz-Granados, Carol. 2008. "Picture Cave: The Study, Dating, and Gating of a Rare Prehistoric American Indian Site." In *Cave Archaeology of the Eastern Woodlands*, ed. David Dye, 203–15. Knoxville: University of Tennessee Press.

DiBlasi, Philip J. 1996. "Prehistoric Expressions from the Central Kentucky Karst." In *Of Caves and Shell Mounds*, ed. Kenneth

C. Carstens and Patty Jo Watson, 40–47. Tuscaloosa: University of Alabama Press.

Douglas, Joseph C. 2008. "Under the Edge of This World: A Preliminary Investigation of Deep Cave Exploration on the Eastern Highland Rim Escarpment, Tennessee. Selected Abstracts from the 2008 National Speleological Society Convention, Lake City, Florida." *Journal of Cave and Karst Studies* 70: 177.

Douglas, Joseph C., Brian Roebuck, and Lynn Roebuck. 2008. "Torches in the Dark: Late Mississippian Exploration of Hubble Post Office Cave." In *Cave Archaeology of the Eastern Woodlands*, ed. David Dye, 157–67. Knoxville: University of Tennessee Press.

Duncan, M. Susan. 1997. "Examining Early Nineteenth Century Saltpeter Caves: An Archaeological Perspective." *Journal of Cave and Karst Studies* 59: 91–4.

Dye, David, ed. 2008. *Cave Archaeology of the Eastern Woodlands*. Knoxville: University of Tennessee Press.

Faulkner, Charles H. 1986. *The Prehistoric Native American Art of Mud Glyph Cave*. Knoxville: University of Tennessee Press.

Faulkner, Charles H. 1988. "A Study of Seven Southeastern Glyph Caves. *North American Archaeologist* 9 (3): 223–245.

Faulkner, Charles H. 2008. "Cavers and Archaeologists: The Study of Mud Glyph Cave." In *Cave Archaeology of the Eastern Woodlands*, ed. David Dye, 193–201. Knoxville: University of Tennessee Press.

Franklin, Jay D. 2002. "The Prehistory of Fentress County, Tennessee: An Archaeological Survey." PhD dissertation, Department of Anthropology, University of Tennessee, Knoxville.

Franklin, Jay D. 2008. "Big Cave Archaeology in the East Fork Obey River Gorge." In *Cave Archaeology of the Eastern Woodlands*, ed. David Dye, 141–67. Knoxville: University of Tennessee Press.

Freeman, John P., Gordon L. Smith, Thomas L. Poulson, Patty Jo Watson, and William B. White. 1973. "Lee Cave, Mammoth Cave National Park, Kentucky." *National Speleological Society Bulletin* 35: 109–25.

Fritz, Gayle J. 1990. "Multiple Pathways to Farming in Precontact Eastern North America." *Journal of World Prehistory* 4 (4): 387–435. http://dx.doi.org/10.1007/BF00974813.

Goldberg, Paul, and Sarah C. Sherwood. 2006. "Deciphering Human Prehistory through the Geoarchaeological Study of Cave Sediments." *Evolutionary Anthropology* 15 (1): 20–36. http://dx.doi.org/10.1002/evan.20094.

Gremillion, Kristen J. 2002. "The Development and Dispersal of Agricultural Systems in the Woodland Period Southeast." In *The Woodland Southeast*, ed. David Anderson and Robert Mainfort, 483–501. Tuscaloosa: University of Alabama Press.

Hall, Robert L. 1967. "Archaeology by Lamplight: An Exploration of Salts Cave, Kentucky." *The Living Museum* (March 1967): 84–85. Illinois State Museum, Springfield.

Haskins, Valerie A. 1988. "The Prehistory of Prewitts Knob, Kentucky." MA thesis, Department of Anthropology, Washington University, St. Louis, MO.

Hemberger, Jan M. 1989. "Kentucky Cave Archaeology: A Cultural Resource Management Perspective." MA thesis, Interdisciplinary Studies, University of Louisville, Louisville, KY.

Horton, Elizabeth T. 2003. "Investigation of Perishable Materials Associated with Fawn Hoof, a Desiccated Burial in Short Cave, Kentucky." MA thesis, Department of Anthropology, Washington University, St. Louis, MO.

LeBlanc, Steven A., Lori S. Cobb Kreisman, Brian M. Kemp, Francis E. Smiley, Shawn W. Carlyle, Anna N. Dhody, and Thomas Benjamin. 2007. "Quids and Aprons: Ancient DNA from Artifacts from the American Southwest." *Journal of Field Archaeology* 32 (2): 161–75. http://dx.doi.org/10.1179/009346907791071610.

Marquardt, William H., and Patty Jo Watson, eds. 2005. *Archaeology of the Middle Green River Region, Kentucky*. Institute of Archaeology and Paleoenvironmental Studies, Monograph 5. Gainesville: University Press of Florida.

Martin, Susan R. 1999. *Wonderful Power: The Story of Ancient Copper Working in the Lake Superior Basin*. Detroit: Wayne State University Press.

Matthews, Larry E. 2006. *Big Bone Cave*. Huntsville, AL: National Speleological Society.

Mickelson, Andrew M. 2008. "Mammoth Cave's Nineteenth-Century Saltpeter Works: Analysis of the Hydraulic System." In *Cave Archaeology of the Eastern Woodlands*, ed. David Dye, 235–60. Knoxville: University of Tennessee Press.

Munson, Patrick J., and Cheryl A. Munson. 1990. *The Prehistoric and Early Historic Archaeology of Wyandotte Cave and Other Caves in Southern Indiana*. Indianapolis, IN: Indiana Historical Society.

Munson, Patrick J., Kenneth B. Tankersley, Cheryl A. Munson, and Patty Jo Watson. 1989. "Prehistoric Selenite and Satinspar Mining in the Mammoth Cave System, Kentucky." *Midcontinental Journal of Archaeology* 14: 119–45.

Poinar, Hendrik, Melanie Kuch, Kristin D. Sobolik, Ian Barnes, Artur B. Stankiewicz, Tomasz Kudor, W. Geoffrey Spaulding, Vaughn M. Bryant, Alan Cooper, and Svante Pääbo. 2001. "A Molecular Analysis of Dietary Diversity for Three Archaic Native Americans." *Proceedings of the National Academy of Sciences* 68: 4317–4322.

Pritchard, Erin. 2008. "Deep Cave Mining: Archaeological and GIS Investigations of a Prehistoric Gypsum Mine at Hubbards Cave." In *Cave Archaeology of the Eastern Woodlands*, ed. David Dye, 97–116. Knoxville: University of Tennessee Press.

Redman, Charles L., and Patty Jo Watson. 1970. "Systematic Intensive Surface Collection." *American Antiquity* 35 (3): 279–91. http://dx.doi.org/10.2307/278339.

Robbins, Louise R., Ronald C. Wilson, and Patty Jo Watson. 1981. "Paleontology and Archeology of Jaguar Cave, Tennessee." *Proceedings of the Eighth International Congress of Speleology Proceedings, Bowling Green, Kentucky*, ed. Barry Beck, 377–80. Americus: Georgia Southwestern College.

Sherwood, Sarah C. 2008. "Increasing the Resolution of Cave Archaeology: Micromorphology and the Classification of Burned Deposits at Dust Cave." In *Cave Archaeology of the Eastern Woodlands*, ed. David Dye, 27–47. Knoxville: University of Tennessee Press.

Sherwood, Sarah C., and Jan F. Simek, eds. 2001. "Cave Archaeology in the Eastern Woodlands." *Midcontinental Journal of Archaeology* 26 (2): 135–267.

Simek, Jan F. 2008. "Afterword: Onward into the Darkness." In *Cave Archaeology of the Eastern Woodlands*, ed. David Dye, 261–70. Knoxville: University of Tennessee Press.

Simek, Jan F., and Alan Cressler. 2005. "Images in Darkness: Prehistoric Cave Art in Southeastern North America." In *Discovering North American Rock Art*, ed. L. Loendorf,

C. Chippindale, and D. Whitley, 93–113. Tucson: University of Arizona Press.

Simek, Jan F., and Alan Cressler. 2008. "On the Backs of Serpents." In *Cave Archaeology of the Eastern Woodlands*, ed. David Dye, 169–91. Knoxville: University of Tennessee Press.

Simek, Jan F., and Alan Cressler. 2009. "Prehistoric Cave Art in Southeastern North America." 15th International Congress of Speleology, Kerrville, TX, July 19–26.

Simek, Jan F., Alan Cressler, and E. Pope. 2004. "Association between a Southeastern Rock Art Motif and Mortuary Caves." In *The Rock-Art of Eastern North America: Capturing Images and Insight*, ed. C. Diaz-Granados and J. R. Duncan, 159–73. Tuscaloosa: University of Alabama Press.

Simek, Jan F., Charles H. Faulkner, Todd Ahlman, Brad Creswell, and Jay D. Franklin. 2001. "The Context of Late Prehistoric Southeastern Cave Art: The Art and Archaeology of 11th Unnamed Cave, Tennessee." *Southeastern Archaeology* 20: 142–53.

Simek, Jan F., Charles H. Faulkner, Susan R. Frankenberg, Walter E. Klippel, Todd M. Ahlmann, Nicholas P. Herrmann, Sarah C. Sherwood, Renee B. Walker, W. Miles Wright, and Richard A. Yarnell. 1997. "A Preliminary Report on the Archaeology of a New Mississippian Cave Art Site in East Tennessee." *Southeastern Archaeology* 16: 51–73.

Simek, Jan F., Jay D. Franklin, and Sarah C. Sherwood. 1998. "The Context of Early Southeastern Prehistoric Cave Art: A Report on the Archaeology of 3rd Unnamed Cave." *American Antiquity* 63 (4): 663–75. http://dx.doi.org/10.2307/2694114.

Smith, Bruce D. 2002. *Rivers of Change*. Washington, DC: Smithsonian Institution Press.

Smith, Bruce D., and Richard A. Yarnell. 2009. "Initial Formation of an Indigenous Crop Complex in Eastern North America at 3800 B.P." *Proceedings of the National Academy of Sciences of the United States of America* 106 (16): 6561–6. http://dx.doi.org/10.1073/pnas.0901846106. Medline:19366669.

Smyre, John L., and Ronald L. Zawislak. 2007. *Big Bone and the Caves of Bone Cave Mountain*. Rock Island, TN: Rocky River Press.

Sobolik, Kristin D., Kristen J. Gremillion, Patricia L. Whitten, and Patty Jo Watson. Oct 1996. "Sex Determination of Prehistoric Human Paleofeces." *American Journal of Physical Anthropology* 101 (2): 283–90. http://dx.doi.org/10.1002/(SICI)1096-8644(199610)101:2<283::AID-AJPA10>3.0.CO;2-W. Medline:8893089.

Tankersley, Kenneth, Cheryl Munson, Patrick Munson, Nelson Shaffer, and R. Leiniger. 1990. "The Mineralogy of Wyandotte Cave Aragonite, Indiana, and Its Archaeological Significance." In *Archaeological Geology of North America*, ed. N. Lasca and J. Donahue, 219–30. Geological Society of America, Centennial Special Volume 4. Boulder, CO: Geological Society of America.

Tankersley, Kenneth, Cheryl Munson, Patrick Munson, Nelson Shaffer, Samuel Frushour, and Patty Jo Watson. 1997. "Archaeology and Speleothems." In *Cave Minerals of the World*, ed. Carol Hill and Paolo Forti, 266–70. Huntsville, AL: National Speleological Society.

Taylor, Peter L., and Christos Nicola. 2007. *The Secret of Priest's Grotto*. Minneapolis: Kar-Ben Publishing.

Trader, Patrick D., Robert Ward, and Ronald R. Switzer. 2008. "Peeling Back the Layers of Time: Nels C. Nelson and the Mammoth Cave Vestibule." In *Cave Archaeology of the Eastern Woodlands*, ed. David Dye, 49–62. Knoxville: University of Tennessee Press.

Walthall, John A., and D. L. DeJarnette. 1974. "Copena Burial Caves." *Journal of Alabama Archaeology* 20: 1–59.

Watson, Patty Jo, ed. 1969. *The Prehistory of Salts Cave, Kentucky*. Illinois State Museum Reports of Investigations 16. Springfield, IL: Illinois State Museum.

Watson, Patty Jo, ed. 1974. *Archeology of the Mammoth Cave Area*. New York: Academic Press.

Watson, Patty Jo. 1976. "In Pursuit of Prehistoric Subsistence: A Comparative Account of Some Contemporary Flotation Techniques." *Midcontinental Journal of Archaeology* 1: 77–100.

Watson, Patty Jo. 1986. "Prehistoric Cavers of the Eastern Woodlands." In *The Prehistoric Native American Art of Mud Glyph Cave*, ed. Charles Faulkner, 109–16. Knoxville: University of Tennessee Press.

Watson, Patty Jo. 1997. "The Shaping of Modern Paleoethnobotany." In *People, Plants, and Landscapes: Case Studies in Paleoethnobotany*, ed. Kristen Gremillion, 13–22. Tuscaloosa: University of Alabama Press.

Watson, Patty Jo. 1999. "From the Hilly Flanks of the Fertile Crescent to the Eastern Woodlands of North America." In *Grit-Tempered: Early Women Archaeologists in the Southeastern United States*, ed. Nancy M. White, Lynne P. Sullivan, and Rochelle A. Marrinan, 286–97. Gainesville: University Press of Florida.

Watson, Patty Jo, Mary C. Kennedy, P. Willey, Louise M. Robbins, and Ronald C. Wilson. 2005. "Prehistoric Footprints in Jaguar Cave, Tennessee." *Journal of Field Archaeology* 30 (1): 25–43. http://dx.doi.org/10.1179/009346905791072440.

Watson, Patty Jo, and Richard A. Yarnell. 1969. "Conclusions: The Prehistoric Utilization of Salts Cave." In *The Prehistory of Salts Cave, Kentucky*, ed. Patty Jo Watson, 71–78. Illinois State Museum Reports of Investigations 16. Springfield. IL: Illinois State Museum.

Willey, P., Judith Stolen, George Crothers, and Patty Jo Watson. 2005. "Preservation of Prehistoric Footprints in Jaguar Cave, Tennessee." *Journal of Cave and Karst Studies* 67: 61–8.

Willey, P., Patty Jo Watson, George Crothers, and Judy Stolen. 2009. "Holocene Human Footprints in North America." *Ichnos* 16 (1–2): 70–5. http://dx.doi.org/10.1080/10420940802470839.

Yarnell, Richard A. 1969. "Contents of Human Paleofeces." In *The Prehistory of Salts Cave, Kentucky*, ed. Patty Jo Watson, 41–54. Illinois State Museum Reports of Investigations 16. Springfield, IL: Illinois State Museum.

Yarnell, Richard A. 1974a. "Intestinal Contents of the Salts Cave Mummy and Analysis of the Initial Salts Cave Flotation Series." In *Archeology of the Mammoth Cave Area*, ed. Patty Jo Watson, 109–12. New York: Academic Press.

Yarnell, Richard A. 1974b. "Plant Food and Cultivation of the Salts Cavers." In *Archeology of the Mammoth Cave Area*, ed. Patty Jo Watson, 113–22. New York: Academic Press.

13

A New Overview of Prehistoric Cave Art in the Southeast

Jan F. Simek, Alan Cressler, and Joseph Douglas

This chapter is designed to serve as an introduction to a prehistoric cave-art tradition that has only come to light over the past two decades in the Appalachian Plateau uplands of Southeastern North America. First identified by archaeologists in 1980, this cave art represents a widespread, complex, and long-standing aspect of indigenous prehistoric culture, one with local origins and development and one intrinsically linked to the evolution of prehistoric Southeastern religious iconography. There has been a small series of overviews of this cave art (Simek and Cressler 2001, 2005), but as our efforts to discover new caves continue, the number of known sites grows dramatically and at a rapid rate. Our last review, published in 2005, examined a cave-art record that included twenty-six known sites. This chapter, written only a few years later, will consider a sample of forty-nine sites. Although we have now examined more than 1,000 Southeastern caves in hopes of finding prehistoric art, there are more than 8,500 caves in Tennessee alone, with thousands more in Alabama, Georgia, and the Upper South. There is a great deal of survey work still before us, and there will certainly be more caves to consider in the future. Our discussion here will follow quite closely our earlier overviews in format, employing our larger samples to expand on what we have presented already, based on fewer sites. We believe that this will best allow the reader to compare what patterns we have seen over time as sample size and variation increase.

Dark-zone cave art (decoration in the areas of caves beyond the reach of external light) was actually known among a small group of cavers in the Southeast from the 1950s. Engravings that were thought to be prehistoric by those cavers who saw them, were identified at the mouth of 12th Unnamed Cave. (Because of potential vandalism, we use a numerical designation system rather than a cave's common or registered names; see Simek et al. [1997] for a description of this system.) The site remained a relative secret, unknown to archaeologists, until Charles Faulkner of the University of Tennessee was taken there in the 1980s. Faulkner had begun the first archaeological study of a Tennessee cave-art site, Mud Glyph Cave, in 1980, and he had made inquiries among the caving community about the possibility of other prehistoric cave-art sites in the region (Faulkner 1986). Mud Glyph Cave itself was discovered in 1979, when a recreational caver explored a narrow subterranean stream passage and saw images incised into the wet clay lining the stream banks. The caver, in turn, alerted an archaeologist friend who told Faulkner about these images. Upon seeing the site, Faulkner quickly recognized that the art was prehistoric, and he initiated a documentation project. Mud Glyph Cave art resembled that found on Mississippian ceremonial objects (Muller 1986) and therefore Faulkner believed it was linked to the wider Mississippian iconography labeled by Waring and Holder (1945) as the Southeast Ceremonial Complex, or

SECC. Other sites began to come quickly to light. By 1988, Faulkner could document seven cave-art sites, including Mud Glyph and 12th Unnamed caves (Faulkner 1988). His was the first overview in the series that we continue in the present chapter.

Since the discovery of Mud Glyph Cave, dark-zone art has been recorded in forty-eight other caves in the karst regions of Tennessee, Kentucky, Virginia, West Virginia, Alabama, and Georgia. Chronological data from these sites (Simek and Cressler 2001; Simek, Franklin, and Sherwood 1998) demonstrate a long-term regional tradition of cave art unrecognized before the 1980s. As Faulkner observed, some of the imagery can be understood in terms of other prehistoric iconography, as its association within the SECC might imply (Muller 1989), but some has less obvious connection with such symbolic representation. It is clear that the existence of a major prehistoric cave-art tradition in the Southeast is no longer at issue. We can now turn our attention to trying to understand this art, what it meant to those who made it, and its role in complex, prehistoric Southeastern symbolic and ceremonial behavior.

THE SITES

We consider here only forty-one of the forty-nine known Southeastern cave-art sites. Sites not included here either contain artwork of uncertain integrity (possible fakes), or were discovered so recently that we have not yet been able to document them in even rudimentary detail. As we have noted before (Simek and Cressler 2005), Southeastern cave-art sites occur in a variety of environmental contexts. We still find no patterned relationship between specific or characteristic site environments and the presence or nature of cave art. Some art caves are long (twenty-five in our sample of forty-one have more than 500 meters of passageways); some are short (sixteen examples are less than 500 meters). Fifteen sample caves have flowing water near the area where art assemblages are found; twenty-six have no water in the vicinity of the artwork. Twenty-eight caves are located on or in the Appalachian Plateau physiographic province, while thirteen are in ridge and valley contexts. Eighteen caves are in a major river valley, while twenty-three are located in smaller tributary stream valleys. Thus, while most sites seem to be associated with regional karst terrain, no other obvious location determinants are apparent. We are still unable to predict where cave-art sites will be within the more than 20,000 known caves of Southeastern North America.

THE NATURE OF SOUTHEASTERN CAVE ART

Cave art in the Southeast comprises engraved petroglyphs in stone (Faulkner 1988; Simek and Cressler 2001; Simek, Frankenberg, and Faulkner 2001), painted pictographs of mineral pigments, charcoal (see DiBlasi 1996), and clay (Simek et al. 1997), and perhaps the region's "signature" art form, mud glyphs in damp clay (Cressler et al. 1999; Faulkner 1986; Faulkner and Simek 1996a; Faulkner and Simek 1996b; Faulkner and Simek 2001; Simek 1996; Simek et al. 1997). There is variation in where these different art types can be found: pictographs and petroglyphs are also found on exterior rockshelter walls and bluff faces (Faulkner 1996; Faulkner, Simek, and Cressler 2004), while mud glyphs are found exclusively inside caves (Faulkner and Simek 2001). Most often, only one kind of art is found in a given cave. There are, however, some exceptions to this. Mud glyphs and petroglyphs are occasionally found in the same cave, but one or the other form is always numerically dominant. Pictographs are often found in association with other art types, but they are rare and sample sizes are too small to identify clear patterns of association.

As has been noted, much of the subject matter of prehistoric Southeast cave art seems related to the SECC, and this is not too surprising given what we know of its chronology (see below). Many images reflect the central tenets of Mississippian religion—ancestors, nature, warfare, and transformation—but prior to the Mississippian, subject matter is different. In early sites, geometric shapes, lines, and representational figures are present that have no reference in the SECC (Cressler et al. 1999; Simek, Franklin, and Sherwood 1998). Many of the pictographs in our sample are representational images, although more-abstract pictographs are known from a number of sites (Simek and Cressler 2001). Petroglyphs also commonly depict religious icons, animals, or anthropomorphs. Mud glyphs are equally variable and include winged anthropomorphs (Faulkner and Simek 1996b), animals and even insect effigies, abstract shapes, and linear figures. Masses of meandering lines (Simek et al. 1997) are common in mud glyph panels, and these create difficulties in deconstruction and interpretation.

There is a great deal of variability in the archaeological contexts of Southeast cave art, and this, in part, reflects the complexity of prehistoric cave use more generally in the region (Simek 1998). In 1986, Patty Jo Watson defined four types of prehistoric cave use in the Eastern Woodlands (Watson 1986), including exploration (documented by torch remnants and footprints), mining (with evidence for industrial extraction of some raw materials), burial (the presence of human remains), and ceremonial caves (primarily exemplified by the presence of cave art). In fact, prehistoric cave art in our sample is associated with all of these uses. Nearly every cave-art site has evidence showing that prehistoric explorers examined the entire cave, often

FIGURE 13.1 Avian effigy images from Southeast Mississippian sites. (a) Woodpecker heads engraved on a shell gorget from Tennessee. (b) Petroglyph engraving of a turkey on the wing from 7th Unnamed Cave, Tennessee.

visiting many miles of passageways, not just where the art was produced. Fifteen of the sites in our sample of forty-one are (or were) burial caves. None of these burial caves is very long, although lightless reaches are present in many of them. Cave-art sites as burial contexts, therefore, may have something of an attribute focus. A smaller number of caves (seven) show evidence of cave art in association with clay, chert, or mineral mining. These caves can be quite extensive, requiring long and arduous treks to where the mining and art are located. In at least one case, art, mining, and burial were all performed in the same cave (Simek et al. 2001).

Of the twenty-six nonburial sites, fourteen contain one or very few prehistoric glyphs that are produced in only one medium and are highly localized within the cave, and there is no evidence for activities other than art production. These simple sites (with only a few glyphs) are widely distributed geographically, but are most common in Tennessee. This may be partly an artifact of our own survey zone and partly due to the fact these sites are rather difficult to identify because they contain few, often faint images. The remaining twelve cave art sites have many glyphs (sometimes hundreds) present in the art assemblage. Most of the cave-art sites in Kentucky and Virginia, and many sites in other states, are of this art-rich type, making it the most widespread and diverse class. Curiously, there do not seem to be "middle ground" sites with glyphs scattered here and there through the cave but not present in either small or large numbers.

CHRONOLOGY

Wherever in the world cave art is found, two major approaches are used to place its images into temporal context. One is stylistic dating, in which cave-wall images are compared to similar images found in other contexts with better chronological control, such as on artifacts from buried archaeological horizons. Chronometric age determination is a second approach and is performed either directly on cave art where possible or on artifacts associated with the images, like torch charcoal fragments from the floor below the images. We consider each of these methods in turn.

STYLE

As has been noted, our classification of sites or specific images as Mississippian (ca. 1100 years BP) has often been based on characteristic icons identified in other, firmly dated archaeological contexts (cf. Muller 1989). For example, bird effigies are known from a variety of Mississippian open-site contexts (figure 13.1a) and from caves (figure 13.1b). Thus, some Mississippian parietal works can be given temporal provenience in light of their subject matter or method of depiction. It should be noted that radiocarbon age determinations associated with Mississippian icons confirm the stylistic attributions in nearly every case.

Stylistic dating of cave art from the Woodland (ca. 2900–1100 years BP) and Archaic (ca. 10,000–2900 years BP) periods, that is, before the SECC, is more difficult. Cave

FIGURE 13.2 Petroglyph of a face effigy with a "Toothy Mouth" from 11th Unnamed Cave, Tennessee.

art from these periods is well known (Cressler et al. 1999; Crothers et al. 2002). However, earlier art is less elaborate and less representational than for the Mississippian and often includes images for which there are no SECC referents. Woodland period sites in the Southeast do contain elaborately decorated ceramics (Broyles 1968; Williams and Elliott 1998), some decorated stone, bone, and shell artifacts that seem to anticipate Mississippian religious paraphernalia, and evidence for connections with artistically rich cultures like the Hopewell. As we have argued elsewhere (Cressler et al. 1999; Simek et al. 2001; Simek et al. 1997), pottery decoration motifs are sometimes illustrated in mud-glyph cave art, both in the Woodland period and later. Patterned use of specific symbols, symptomatic of a true iconography during Mississippian times (and therefore a source of stylistic data), is not present for the Woodland Southeast. Symbolic representations in the Archaic are very rare, and nothing like an iconography has been recognized for Archaic cultures. In effect, style is not particularly helpful in dating pre-Mississippian cave art.

CHRONOMETRIC DATES

Table 13.1 presents more than ninety chronometric age determinations associated with Southeast dark-zone cave art. Several things are worthy of note. There are as yet no Paleoindian dates in this series (earlier than 10,000 years BP), so we have no evidence to indicate that cave art was a cultural facet of the first settlers in the region. A number of determinations show that artwork in deep caves was produced during the Archaic period, although all Archaic ages fall rather late in that phase in our region. Archaic ages have been obtained in association with parietal artwork from very deep cave contexts, including mud glyphs from Adair Glyph Cave in Kentucky with a radiocarbon determination of 3560±110 BP (DiBlasi 1996). In 3rd Unnamed Cave, Tennessee, dates on hearth charcoal recovered more than a kilometer underground also indicate a Late Archaic occupation. The fireplaces illuminated flintknapping in a chert deposit in this deep-cave context (Simek, Franklin, and Sherwood 1998). On the ceiling above, petroglyphs were incised, including a sun, chevrons, and other more enigmatic symbols (see illustrations in Simek, Franklin, and Sherwood 1998). It seems likely, therefore, that Archaic hunter-gatherers were the first to produce parietal art in Southeast caves, and that at least some art production accompanied deep-cave mining.

The Woodland period has the greatest number of age determinations for cave visitations in the Eastern Woodlands (Kennedy 1996; Watson 1969, 1974, 1986). But cave-art sites are few, given the scale of Woodland cave use. Woodland period age determinations come from Mud Glyph and 2nd, 5th, 6th, and 25th Unnamed Caves in Tennessee; Crumps Cave in Kentucky; and 19th Unnamed Cave in north Alabama. Three of these are burial caves, and 19th Unnamed Cave is within the Copena culture area, partly defined by cave burial (Walthall and DeJarnette 1974). These observations suggest Woodland mortuary use of cave-art sites.

The most frequent chronometric determinations for cave art are with the Mississippian period. Within that period, a cluster of radiocarbon determinations is evident between 800 BP and 600 BP (Faulkner and Simek 1996b; Simek and Cressler 2001). In particular, mud-glyph caves have age determinations during this period; yet even this form of cave art has its origins in the Archaic and Woodland periods (Cressler et al. 1999; Faulkner and Simek 1996b, 2001). Nine Mississippian ages have been obtained from perhaps the most complex cave art site of all, 11th Unnamed Cave in Tennessee, where pictographs, engraved petroglyphs, and mud glyphs have all been found in association with other rather enigmatic dark-zone activities, including clay mining and burial (Simek et al. 2001). Thus, the Mississippian period seems to be the culmination of Southeastern cave-art production.

In addition, five presently known burial caves have Mississippian age associations, including a number of mass-burial sites. As we argue elsewhere (Simek, Cressler, and Elayne 2004), Mississippian burials in caves are often associated with a rather particular artistic image, the "Toothy Mouth" (figure 13.2). If this association holds up with more research, an important clue to the interpretation of at

TABLE 13.1 Uncalibrated radiocarbon age determinations for Southeastern cave-art sites. Dates are unreported or from Cressler et al. 1999; DiBlasi 1996; Faulkner 1986, 1988, 1996; Faulkner and Simek 2001; Haskins, personal communication, 1997; Simek and Cressler 2001; Simek et al. 1997; Simek, Franklin, and Sherwood 1998.

Lab No.	Analysis	RC Age	Site Name	Art Type
Archaic Period				
	Standard	3560±110	Adair, KY	Mud glyphs
Beta-126038	AMS	3320±70	3rd UC, TN	Petroglyphs
Beta-126041	AMS	3310±60	3rd UC, TN	Petroglyphs
Beta-134992	AMS	3180±40	3rd UC, TN	Petroglyphs
Beta-96624	AMS (LLNL)	3080±50	3rd UC, TN	Petroglyphs
ISGS-4234	standard	3060±70	3rd UC, TN	Petroglyphs
ISGS-4232	standard	3050±70	3rd UC, TN	Petroglyphs
Beta-134987	AMS	3020±60	3rd UC, TN	Petroglyphs
Beta-114172	AMS	2990±40	3rd UC, TN	Petroglyphs
Beta-114173	AMS	2980±40	3rd UC, TN	Petroglyphs
Beta-96623	std, ext ct	2980±110	3rd UC, TN	Petroglyphs
Beta-134989	AMS	2900±40	3rd UC, TN	Petroglyphs
Woodland Period				
Beta-142931	AMS	2430±40	25th UC, TN	Mud glyphs
Beta-142930	AMS	2360±40	25th UC, TN	Mud glyphs
Beta-106695	AMS (LLNL)	2000±50	5th UC, TN	Petroglyphs
	AMS	1980±60	Crumps, KY	Mud glyphs
Beta-126040	AMS	1970±60	3rd UC, TN	Petroglyphs
Beta-134990	AMS	1970±40	3rd UC, TN	Petroglyphs
Beta-142934	AMS	1950±40	13th UC, TN	Petroglyphs
Beta-134991	AMS	1890±40	3rd UC, TN	Petroglyphs
Beta-116408	AMS	1880±80	Crumps, KY	Mud glyphs
Beta-109675	AMS	1850±50	6th UC, TN	Petroglyphs
	AMS	1800±60	2nd UC, TN	Mud glyphs
Beta-126044	AMS	1730±60	19th UC, AL	Mud glyphs
Beta-126036	AMS	1710±60	20th UC, TN	Mud glyphs
		1485±60	36th UC, TN	Mud glyphs
Beta-142929	AMS	1400±40	12th UC, TN	Petro, mud glyphs
Beta-142933	AMS	1400±40	13th UC, TN	Petroglyphs
Beta-142927	AMS	1360±40	12th UC, TN	Petro, mud glyphs
Beta-106698	AMS (Kiel)	1350±40	7th UC, TN	Petroglyphs
Beta-142926	AMS	1340±40	12th UC, TN	Petro, mud glyphs
Beta-137899	AMS	1330±40	7th UC, TN	Petroglyphs
Beta-142928	AMS	1330±40	12th UC, TN	Petro, mud glyphs
Beta-153230	AMS	1310±50	31st UC, TN	Pictographs
Beta-144277	AMS	1280±40	12th UC, TN	Petro, mud glyphs
Beta-137898	AMS	1230±30	7th UC, TN	Petroglyphs
Beta-137900	AMS	1230±40	7th UC, TN	Petroglyphs
Beta-142923	AMS	1180±60	12th UC, TN	Petro, mud glyphs
Beta-126043	AMS	1180±60	19th UC, AL	Mud glyphs
Beta-83404	std, ext ct	1130±120	Little Mountain, VA	Mud glyphs

continued on next page

TABLE 13.1—continued

Lab No.	Analysis	RC Age	Site Name	Art Type
Mississippian Period				
Beta-144276	AMS	1050±40	12th UC, TN	Petro, mud glyphs
Beta-13937	standard	1030±90	11th UC, TN	Petro, picto, mud glyphs
Beta-151847	AMS	1030±40	30th UC, AL	Pictographs
Beta-83405	std, ext ct	1020±120	Little Mountain, VA	Mud glyphs
AA-15811	AMS	970±60	2nd UC, TN	Mud glyphs
	AMS	955±75	Williams, VA	Mud glyphs
Beta-153232	AMS	950±40	31st UC, TN	Pictographs
Beta-134982	AMS	940±60	11th UC, TN	Petro, picto, mud glyphs
Beta-142924	AMS	940±50	12th UC, TN	Petro, mud glyphs
Beta-13936	standard	940±60	12th UC, TN	Petro, mud glyphs
Beta-137901	AMS	930±40	7th UC, TN	Petroglyphs
Beta-151846	AMS	930±40	30th UC, AL	Pictographs
	AMS	920±65	Williams, VA	Mud glyphs
Beta-134034	AMS	910±50	22nd UC, TN	Pictographs
Beta-134034	AMS	910±50	22nd UC, TN	Pictographs
Beta-134983	AMS	910±50	22nd UC, TN	Pictographs
	AMS	890±70	Williams, VA	Mud glyphs
Beta-83403	std, ext ct	860±110	Little Mountain, VA	Mud glyphs
Beta-151845	AMS	830±40	21st UC, AL	Petroglyphs
SI-5098B	standard	795±60	36th UC, TN	Mud glyphs
Beta-134981	AMS	780±40	11th UC, TN	Petro, picto, mud glyphs
Beta-126032	AMS	770±60	11th UC, TN	Petro, picto, mud glyphs
Beta-134984	AMS	760±40	39th UC, TN	Petroglyphs
	standard	750±45	36th UC, TN	Mud glyphs
Beta-126042	AMS	720±60	18th UC, AL	Petroglyphs
SI-5098A	standard	715±60	36th UC, TN	Mud glyphs
Beta-126033	AMS	670±60	11th UC, TN	Petro, picto, mud glyphs
Beta-141458	AMS	660±40	11th UC, TN	Petro, picto, mud glyphs
	standard	635±50	36th UC, TN	Mud glyphs
Beta-131221	AMS	630±60	11th UC, TN	Petro, picto, mud glyphs
Beta-136491	AMS	630±40	11th UC, TN	Petro, picto, mud glyphs
Beta-126039	AMS	620±60	3rd UC, TN	Petroglyphs
Beta-13938	std, dbl ct	620±150	11th UC, TN	Petro, picto, mud glyphs
	standard	615±60	36th UC, TN	Mud glyphs
ISGS-A-0141	AMS	603±44	36th UC, TN	Mud glyphs
Beta-13935	standard	590±80	12th UC, TN	Petro, mud glyphs
Beta-83406	std, ext ct	530±90	Little Mountain, VA	Mud glyphs
Beta-142932	AMS	460±40	25th UC, TN	Mud glyphs
Beta-153233	AMS	450±40	1st UC, TN	Mud glyphs
Beta-153234	AMS	430±40	1st UC, TN	Mud glyphs
Beta-103531	AMS (LLNL)	420±50	1st UC, TN	Mud glyphs
Beta-153235	AMS	400±40	1st UC, TN	Mud glyphs

continued on next page

Lab No.	Analysis	RC Age	Site Name	Art Type
Beta-106697	AMS (LLNL)	370±50	6th UC, TN	Petroglyphs
Beta-134993	AMS	320±60	20th UC, TN	Mud glyphs
	standard	345±65	36th UC, TN	Mud glyphs
Beta-151844	AMS	270±40	21st UC, AL	Petroglyphs
AA-15810	AMS	260±50	1st UC, TN	Mud glyphs
Beta-134988	AMS	190±40	3rd UC, TN	Petroglyphs
	standard	190±80	36th UC, TN	Mud glyphs
Beta-142925	AMS	160±60	12th UC, TN	Petro, mud glyphs
Beta-126035	AMS	140±60	1st UC, TN	Mud glyphs

least one art motif may be forthcoming. This itself points out the importance of contextual analysis in the interpretation of prehistoric cave art.

Based on our current chronological information, it is evident that cave art in the Southeast clearly has a relatively great time depth, spanning more than 3,000 years. Over this time span, the context of the art comprises a great deal of ecological and cultural variability, spanning as it does the last stages of hunter-gatherer economies in the region, the domestication of plants, and the adoption and elaboration of complex agricultural societies. This contextual complexity, in fact, makes interpretation of Southeast cave art rather difficult.

THE PROBLEM OF MEANING

Perhaps the most difficult aspect of the archaeology of Southeastern cave art is its interpretation. Unlike many areas of the world where cave art is found (e.g., Africa, Australia, California, and Mesoamerica), there are no historical records or references concerning its production and/or use. Moreover, the recent discovery of this corpus of underground ceremonial imagery has meant that it has not been considered in analyses of Southeast symbolism, which studies have been based on decorated artifacts and contexts exclusively outside cave environments (Brown 1989; Galloway 1989; Kneberg 1959; Lankford 2004; Power 2004; Waring and Holder 1945). Under these circumstances, the temptation is strong to employ ethnographic—that is, analogical—means for interpreting cave art, and several scholars have taken that path for the Southeast data (Diaz-Granados and Duncan 2004; Duncan and Diaz-Granados 2004; Hall 1989). Such an approach is not surprising, as this has been the case for rock-art studies in general in North America.

We have grave reservations about using ethnographic documents as a direct source of interpretation for prehistoric rock art generally, but especially for the Southeast, which is characterized by a long and complex history of human migration, diasporas, interaction, and population collapse, with evidence for this complexity coming from both the archaeological record (Anderson 1994; papers in Anderson and Mainfort 2002; papers in Nassaney and Sassaman 1995; papers in Sassaman and Anderson 1996; Scarry 1996; Smith 2002) and from molecular biology (cf. Bolnick and Smith 2003; Malhi et al. 2002). This is particularly the case for the Appalachian uplands, where most of the Southeastern cave art sites are located (papers in Sullivan and Prezanno 2001).

Our reservations have their source in two places. One is the long debate in Americanist archaeology about how ethnographic data are to be linked to the archaeological record in interpretation. Central to this debate has been the need for explicit analytic procedures that warrant the use of specific ethnographic data, and a lot of effort and thought has gone into formalizing such procedures over the history of American archaeology. The second is the senior author's career in Paleolithic archaeology, where a healthy suspicion of ethnography in interpreting any aspect of the archaeological record has led to the general methodological view that "art is artifacts," no different in the way it is to be approached than harpoons or fireplaces. In the latter context, art is viewed as a strictly archaeological problem, requiring rigorous scientific analysis in order to infer meaning.

In North America, two main avenues for warranting the use of ethnographic data in archaeological inference have been developed, and both have evolved as a result of extensive methodological discussion. One was the "direct historical approach," the intellectual forerunner of today's NAGPRA-mandated concept of "lineal affiliation," which presumes an historical connection between people and artifacts in a region. The second was use of ethnographic data as sources for indirect inferences about the archaeological record through analogical reasoning, that is, "ethnographic analogy."

The direct historical approach has a long and distinguished history in American archaeology, with its first formal applications in the Southwest by Nels C. Nelson, Alfred V. Kidder, Alfred L. Kroeber, and others before the First World War. In 1942, Julian Steward articulated its methodological approach to using comparative ethnographic information: "to start with historic sites and, through stratigraphy, or seriation, or both, to carry sequences backward beyond the point where the trails of known, historic peoples faded out" (Steward 1942, 338). For Steward and others, this was the *only* warrant for using ethnographic data to interpret archaeological data directly: a demonstrable, empirical, lineal affiliation. Lacking such verifiable connections, archaeologists were left with simple taxonomic schemes to structure the archaeological record, and, for Steward, "the result is a set of timeless and spaceless categories" that he explicitly viewed as rather arbitrary (ibid., 339).

For Steward and his colleagues, historical connectivity was not a simple product of geographical location. Even in circumstances where the requisite elements were in place for undertaking direct historical correlations between the ethnographic and prehistoric pasts, such correlations were not automatic. In 1941, for example, Robert Heizer attempted to connect the three taxonomically derived phases composing the Late Culture in central California. As was required for the direct historical approach, the phases were stratigraphically superimposed in numerous sites and entailed an historic Phase 3 (identified as the post–European Contact period), a protohistoric Phase 2 (chronologically post-Contact but not materially so), and a prehistoric Phase 1 with many similar material traits to the later phases.

To address the interpretation of Phase 1 in ethnographic and historical terms, Heizer examined unpublished primary historical documents in the Bancroft Library at the University of California at Berkeley and consulted ethnographic accounts for the regions where archaeological work was concentrated. What should have been a straightforward interpretive process was not. Heizer found four major problems with the data: "(1) the ethnographic record was highly imperfect; (2) the historical documents might help to fill *some* of the lacunae; (3) the geographic location of certain native groups was a matter of relatively recent standing; and (4) a widespread cultural alteration had ensued in the valley following the establishment of Spanish missions on the coast" (Heizer 1941). In the end, history and ethnography could not be used directly. Instead, these documentary sources only pointed up the fact that novel and unsuspected interpretations were needed. It should be noted that rock art was part of the archaeological record being considered in Heizer's exercise, and he was careful in this situation not to posit meanings for the art. Steward noted similar problems with interpreting even the most recent archaeological phases in the Plains, Southwest, and, in particular, the Southeast (Steward 1942). Bassie-Sweet has expressed reservations similar to Steward's for Late Classic Maya cosmological reconstructions, even though historical continuity can be demonstrated, because of probable population shifts and culture change in the region (Bassie-Sweet 1996, 5). Thus, even the most rigorous method for warranting ethnographic interpretation of archaeological data is problematic at best. Using ethnographic information in the absence of warranting arguments is obviously a dangerous methodological leap.

A second means for interpreting archaeological data using ethnographic information, ethnographic analogy, is among the oldest forms of archaeological inference. One of its first uses was during the Renaissance, when the superintendent of the Vatican Botanical Gardens, Michael Mercati (1541–1593), wrote *Metallotheca,* in which he attempted to explain prehistoric implements he found in rural Italy by reference to the growing ethnographic collection of stone tools curated at the Vatican (Clarke 1968). Ethnographic analogy is a comparative technique based on similarities and differences in characteristics of the items being compared. Over time, it became standard practice for archaeologists to interpret what they found in the ground based on ethnographic materials of known use and similar appearance and manufacture. By its very nature, ethnographic analogy is a process that depends on an investigator's familiarity with ethnography and material culture, and archaeologists began to seek, sometimes in ad hoc fashion, elements in ethnography that were similar to what they wanted to explain archaeologically. Researchers interpreted the archaeological record—stone tools, fireplaces, cave art— in terms of the ethnography they had read or by reference to such resources as the Human Relations Area Files. The process was not formal, and over time dissatisfaction arose with a perceived subjectivity in the interpretive approach (Binford 1967; Clarke 1968).

This dissatisfaction culminated, during the rise of the New Archaeology, in a debate about the merits of ethnographic analogy and how it should be structured for scientific use. Lewis Binford (1967) defined one set of requisites for proper ethnographic analogy in his classic paper, "Smudge Pits and Hide Smoking: The Use of Analogy in Archaeological Reasoning." In that paper, he laid out a program for formal assessment of the fit between archaeological and ethnographic data being compared. Based on examination of several philosophical considerations of the process of analogy, Binford argued (1967, 2) that there are two characteristics of successful analogies: (1) similarities between archaeological and ethnographic objects must be such that the known properties of the latter would account for the former, and (2) the more numerous, detailed, and comprehensive the similarities are, the more likely the ethnographic case can account for the archaeological one. But perhaps most telling in Binford's view was the notion that analogy was not to be a source of direct interpretation, but instead should be used to generate testable hypotheses for other aspects of the archaeological record associated with the object being considered (1967, 11). Scientific testing of analogic interpretations was required to warrant their ultimate authority. Similarity in form was not sufficient; context had to be known and demonstrated similar as well. These were difficult requirements; it was not how analogy had been used, nor is it how analogy is used today.

Does this mean that analogy has no place in archaeology generally or in rock art studies specifically? No, it does not mean that; the method continues to be widely applied today (e.g., Whitley 2000), particularly as those interested in agency and the role of individuals in the past strive for the means to support their inferences (Van Reybrouck 2000). The debate over methodology and efficacy, however, remains essentially unchanged by this recent work. Alison Wylie (1985) has noted that archaeologists are and have always been ambivalent about the use of analogy, primarily because of its inherent unreliability and inconclusiveness. She believes that analogy to ethnographic data does have a place in archaeological inference, if a precise series of formal considerations are met. Analogical reasoning must be first and foremost guided by relevance. For Wylie, relevance is "a function of knowledge about underlying principles of connection between source and subject," and relevance implies that attributes observed as similar or different in the source (ethnography for our purposes) were caused in the same way by the same attribute relationships in the subject (archaeological) case. The relationships are causal processes rather than formal properties (Wylie 1985). And, as Binford observed, they can be tested against the archaeological record in a formal, scientific fashion.

In prehistoric-art studies, this concern with process and scientific testing is often replaced by a view that ethnography can provide meaning rather than explanation. In some areas of the world, this may be a reasonable proposition when direct historical relations can be documented. Diaz-Granados and Duncan interpret Missouri rock art in terms of cosmological constructs recorded for Osage people who occupied the region historically (Diaz-Granados and Duncan 2004; Duncan and Diaz-Granados 2004). David Whitley argues that for some California rock art, the ethnic affiliation of the art is known and the art can thus be interpreted in reference to the religious practices and beliefs of those ethnographically known groups (Whitley 2000, 71–103). However, even here caution must be exerted, because ethnography itself can be made up of distortion and because population and culture flux can occur over even short periods of time (Bassie-Sweet 1996; Bury 1999). Most problematic in our view are situations where general or universal ethnographic similarities are gleaned from across a continent or more, melded into a kind of *uber*-cosmology that is not based in a culture as usually conceived but is used to interpret specific cases of prehistoric imagery without presenting warranting arguments of connection or relevance. The fact that ancient Egyptians, Maya, and Navaho all make reference to a bird man in their myths does not mean that those groups tell us anything about the bird images from Appalachian Plateau Mississippian sites (Strong 1989).

Obviously, a great deal must be understood about how form and function relate in the source of the analogy. In our case, this implies that we know at a minimum how cave art was produced in the ethnographic case we wish to use as a source for analogical inference, and in what contexts and for what purposes. As the reasoning process entails all attributes of the phenomena being examined, it is not enough to consider oral traditions that were current in a given region at the time of contact, or similarity between iconographic representations found in sites and elements of specified oral traditions. The functional connections between oral tradition, iconography, and cave-art production must be shown to be relevant in specific instances if the analogy is to be logically drawn. And they ideally should be shown to explain the specific archaeological case under consideration by direct, falsifiable hypothesis testing. In short, ethnographic analogy, properly done, is every bit as demanding in its terms and consequences as is the direct historical approach. Neither of these archaeologically derived methodologies has seen much proper application in cave-art interpretation, and in great measure this is because the formal criteria for their use are very difficult to meet.

We offer an example of this difficulty from prehistoric cave art from the Southeast. At Mud Glyph Cave, Faulkner observed a number of images that appeared similar to iconography found on Mississippian artifacts from outside of caves in the same region, artifacts that have received a great deal of study and interpretation by Mississippian iconographers over the years (Brain and Phillips 1996; Power 2004). A winged anthropomorph, frequently bearing weapons, is one such image (figure 13.3a). Details of the garb of these winged humans, like hairstyles and artifact associations, have been interpreted as reflecting warrior or even chiefly attire, often based on analogy (usually implicit) to burial

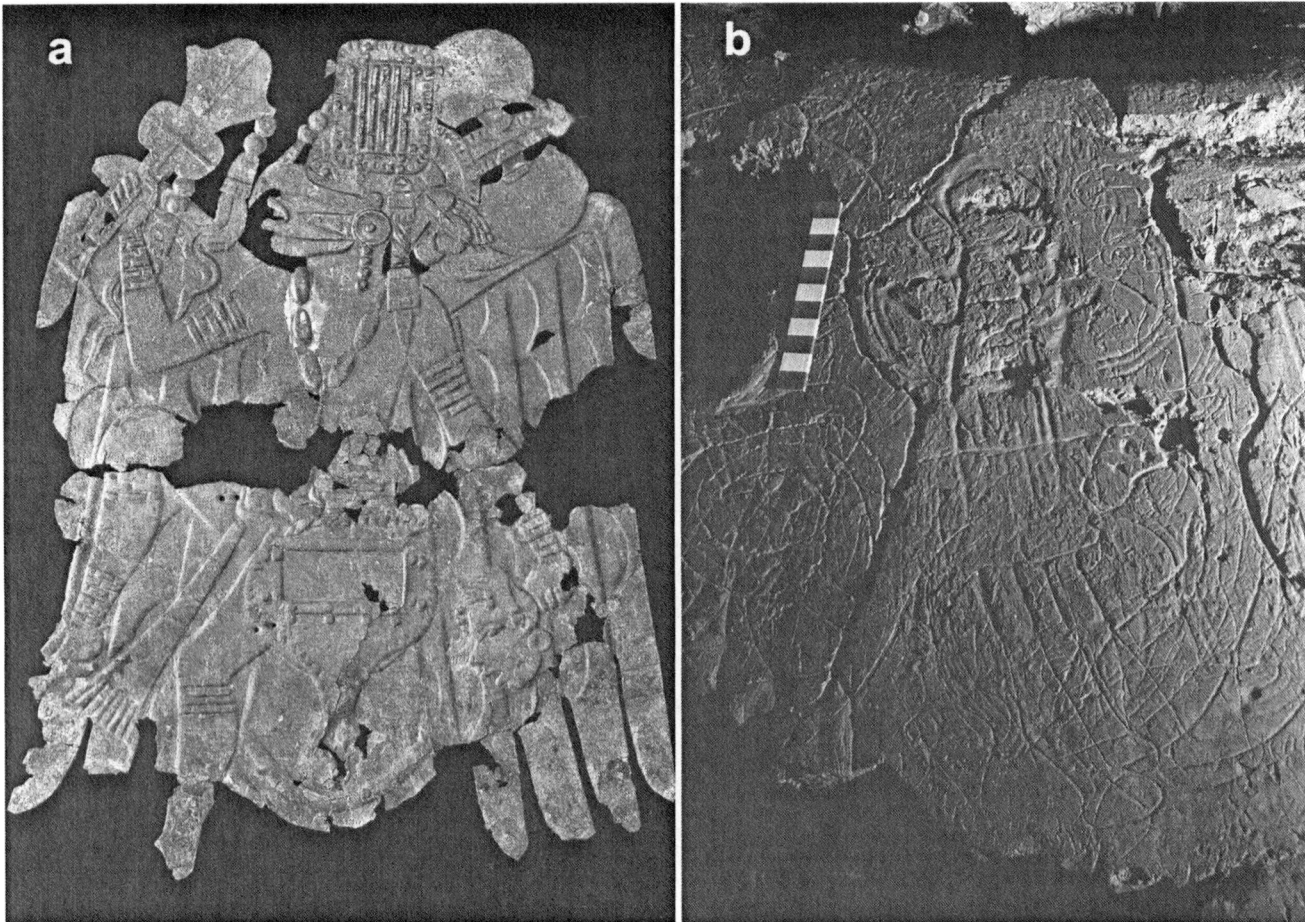

FIGURE 13.3 Winged-warrior effigies from Southeast Mississippian sites. (a) Embossed copper plate, Etowah, Georgia. (b) Mud glyph from Mud Glyph Cave, Tennessee.

associations (Strong 1989). Winged warriors are identified by a number of Mississippian iconographers in quite specific terms as dancers, bird-impersonators, Thunderers, and even specific mythical personalities, usually by reference to ethnographic sources from a variety of historic tribes (Hall 1989). Moreover, these depictions are assigned roles and locations in reconstructed Mississippian "cosmologies," wherein they exemplify connections between the human world and a posited "Upper World" encompassing a dense celestial symbolism (Lankford 2004). All of this is usually based on loose analogous reference to various Southeast Native American ethnographies or to conversations with living native peoples (Hall 1989). Typically, these interpretations are unconstrained by the criteria of the direct historical approach, wherein a lineal relationship must be established with the ethnographic sources being employed.

The problem is that we see similar images quite frequently in dark-zone cave contexts, far from the "Upper World." At Mud Glyph Cave (figure 13.3b), for example, at least one anthropomorphic image has trailing lines behind it, suggesting feathers or wings, and talons instead of human feet. The Mud Glyph Cave specimen might look very much like the "Falcon Warrior" icon, but there are others that are less similar, such as the Mississippian avimorph from 11th Unnamed Cave (figure 13.4), where primarily avian morphological characteristics are associated with weapons and human haberdashery (Simek et al. 2001). This image is associated with weapons combined with human heads. Thus, even in the Classic Mississippian period, we have presumptive "Upper World" characters found in underworld contexts, and in this distinctive context, their form and subject matter vary quite dramatically when compared to the outside images. This represents a lack of logical connection between source and subject, a lack that denies a warrant for inference by ethnographic analogy to these same sources.

Further complicating interpretation of this winged anthropomorph is time depth. Winged humans are evident in petroglyph art from 12th Unnamed Cave, which was produced late in the Woodland period in Middle Tennessee (ca. 1200 BP). In this cave, avian images are the dominant figures, along with a variety of anthropomorphs. On one panel deep in the cave, three figures are placed in a group (figure 13.5). A bird unlike any of the many others found in the site is shown flying upward on the wall (figure 13.6a). Next to the bird is a phallic male human figure (figure 13.6b); this person bears no weapons or symbols of warrior class, and indeed, there are no representations of military paraphernalia or weaponry anywhere in the cave. Right next to these images is an avian/human figure that may represent a blend of the other elements in the panel (figure 13.6c). Twelfth Unnamed Cave provides many examples of such panel compositions, including a number of scenes grouping human and "box anthropomorphs" in scenes of interaction. One of these (figure 13.7) shows a box/human group with the box giving birth to a human child. Thus, the imagery in this Early Mississippian cave

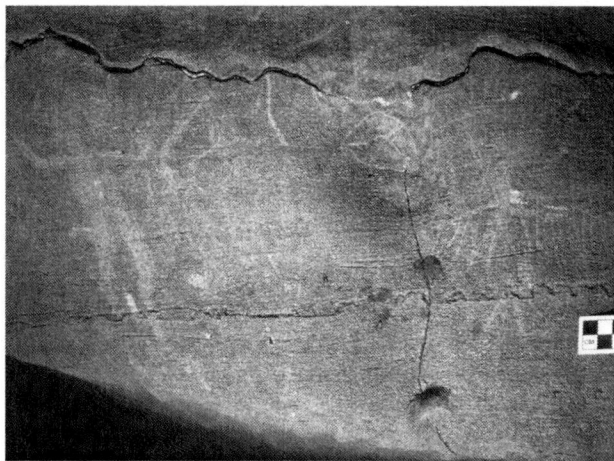

FIGURE 13.5 Panel of three petroglyphs from 12th Unnamed Cave, Tennessee.

suggests sexual rather than military symbolism, including the human in the bird/human panel. Given this, how can we refer to prevalent iconographic interpretations for this material, and if we cannot do so here, where is there sufficient warrant in any other rock-art context?

If not by ethnography then how do we interpret prehistoric rock art in the Southeast? If we acknowledge that rock art is artifacts, then we can conceive of its study as a strictly archaeological problem. In Binford's terms (Binford 1983), we must concentrate on artifacts and their relationships. Our attention is turned to matters of chronology and structure, spatial patterning, and composition. These are not easy issues of course (chronology in particular), but archaeological approaches simply require that we devote our resources to them. This was, in fact, the approach taken from early on in Europe, where first Breuil (Breuil 1979) and then Leroi-Gourhan (Leroi-Gourhan 1971) were always concerned with the chronology of Paleolithic art and its context. This led to extensive mapping programs, materials analyses, and concern with the other artifacts found with art. In the end, Leroi-Gourhan (1971) and many others (e.g., Aujoulat 2004; Clottes 2001) defined spatial and stratigraphic patterns in Paleolithic cave art that show its complexity and evolution without need for external ethnographic enrichment.

We suggest that a similar approach will prove informative in the Southeast, and will close with a brief illustration. Faulkner undertook a mapping project while studying Mud Glyph Cave and was able to show that specific images were not randomly distributed through the cave. We have continued this analytic approach and have now completely mapped a number of cave-art sites. None has a random array of images; all are characterized by spatial clustering of like figures along the cave walls. Composition

FIGURE 13.4 Avian effigy with human-warrior characteristics, including a single head feather, weeping eye, and ceremonial maces, from 11th Unnamed Cave, Tennessee.

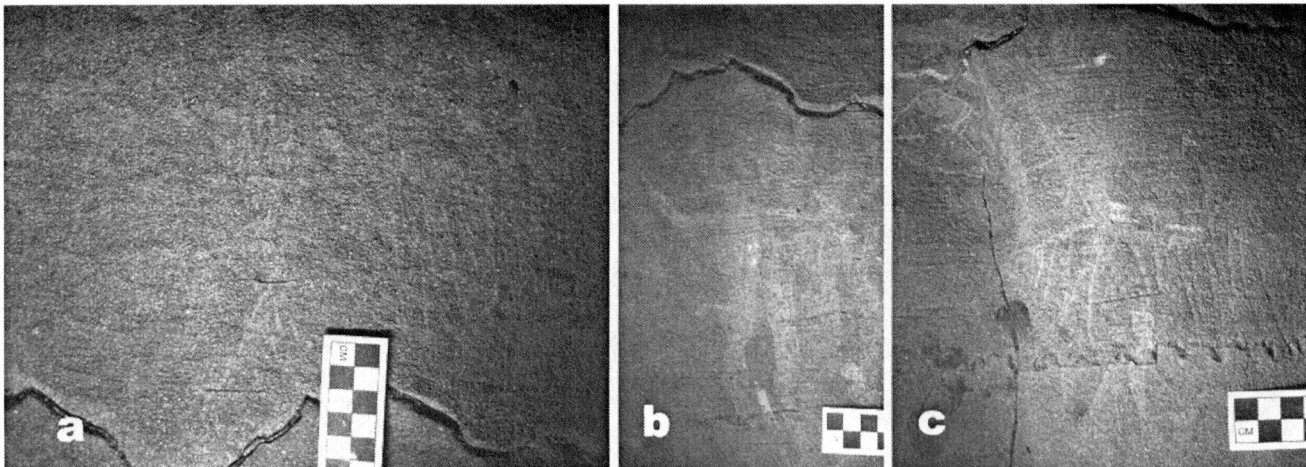

FIGURE 13.6 Elements of panel composition shown in figure 13.5. (a) Bird effigy shown ventrally and pointing upwards with wings extended to sides and a triangular tail pointing down. (b) Phallic male human image with elaborate hair/headdress, shown in profile. (c) Human figure with similar hair as in (b) and with bird wings extended laterally as in (a).

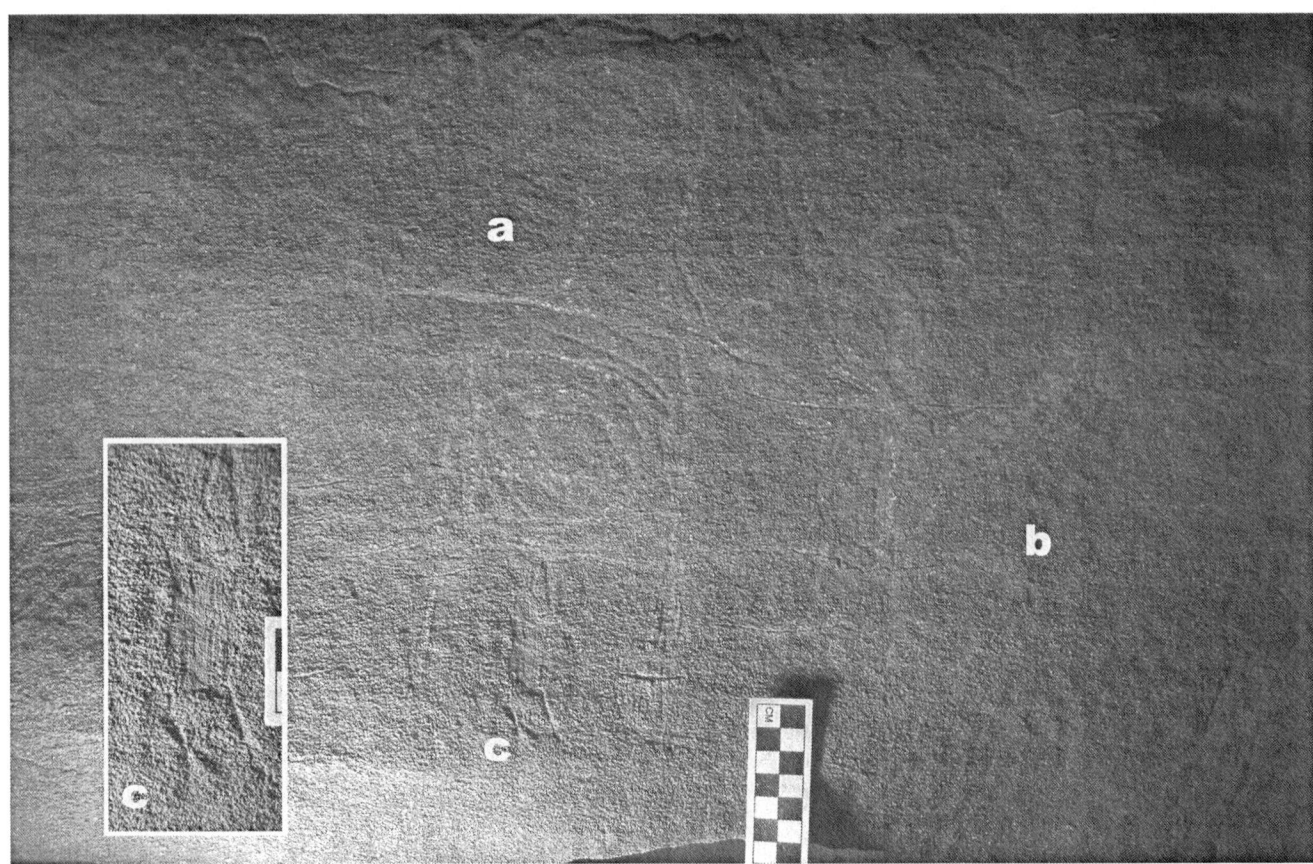

FIGURE 13.7 Triptych panel from 12th Unnamed Cave showing (a) a box-shaped anthropomorph, (b) a human figure, and (c) an infant human emerging from between the box creature's legs (enlarged in inset).

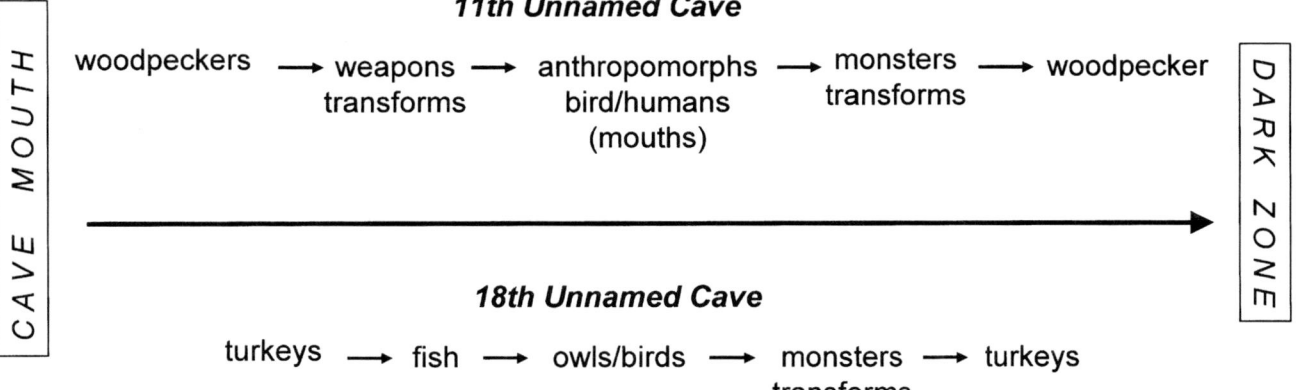

FIGURE 13.8 Models for the spatial structure of four Mississippian cave-art sites in the Southeast.

on a sitewide scale is evident. Comparing four mapped Mississippian cave-art sites (figure 13.8), we see remarkable consistency in structure: arrays begin and end with birds, and representative images—anthropomorphs, weapons, transformational creatures—become less mundane, more unearthly, as the cave deepens. There seems to be a transcendental grammar of cave-art composition. We suggest that this may be related to ritual use of these caves for processional ceremonies.

The prehistoric cave-art sites of Southeastern North America have great time depth and span the region's culture history from Late Archaic hunter-gatherers, through the origins of agriculture, and culminate with the large-scale regional militaristic polities that characterize the last, Mississippian phases of prehistory. Almost certainly, Southeastern cave art is an indigenous phenomenon, as it has its origins in ancient and simple examples of the practice within the region itself. Inside the Southeast's caverns, the origins and development of the complex iconographic system referred to as the SECC may be illuminated by controlled chronological sequencing of sets of images. There are interesting geographical questions to be addressed—for example, why Southeastern cave-art sites are located so far away from the areas of primary prehistoric urban habitation. It may be that this simply reflects the distribution of arable land as opposed to karst landscapes, or it may reflect a more complex influence of ceremonial concepts on landscape. In short, there is much to learn about content and structure of Southeastern cave-art sites by concentrating on them as archaeological sites. Ethnographic interpretations alone, especially if poorly warranted, will not provide a particularly useful or enriched understanding of this newly elaborated prehistoric cave art tradition.

ACKNOWLEDGMENTS

The authors wish to thank Todd Ahlman, Paul Aughey, Joanne Bennett, Stuart Carroll, Charles Faulkner, Jay Franklin, J. Bennett Graham, Nick Herrmann, Gerald Moni, Marion O. Smith, Sarah Sherwood, Patty Jo Watson, and Richard Yarnell, who have all lent advice and assistance in the task of identifying and documenting these cave-art sites. David G. Anderson commented on an earlier draft of the chapter. The National Science Foundation, the Dogwood City Grotto, SERA, the Lucille S. Thompson Family Foundation, the National Geographic Society, the

Tennessee Valley Authority, the Tennessee Historical Commission, and the University of Tennessee, Knoxville, SARIF Fund all contributed funding for the work described here.

REFERENCES CITED

Anderson, David G. 1994. *The Savannah River Chiefdoms: Political Change in the Late Prehistoric Southeast*. Tuscaloosa: University of Alabama Press.

Anderson, David G., and Robert C. Mainfort. 2002. *The Woodland Southeast*. Tuscaloosa: University of Alabama Press.

Aujoulat, Norbert. 2004. *Lascaux: Le Geste, L'Espace et le Temps*. Paris: Seuil.

Bassie-Sweet, Karen. 1996. *At the Edge of the World*. Norman: University of Oklahoma Press.

Binford, Lewis R. 1967. "Smudge Pits and Hide Smoking: The Use of Analogy in Archaeological Reasoning." *American Antiquity* 32 (1): 1–12. http://dx.doi.org/10.2307/278774.

Binford, Lewis R. 1983. *Pursuit of the Past*. London: Thames and Hudson.

Bolnick, Deborah A., and David G. Smith. 2003. "Unexpected Patterns of Mitochondrial DNA Variation among Native Americans from the Southeastern United States." *American Journal of Physical Anthropology* 122 (4): 336–54. http://dx.doi.org/10.1002/ajpa.10284. Medline:14614755.

Brain, Jeffrey P., and Philip Phillips. 1996. *Shell Gorgets: Styles of the Late Prehistoric and Protohistoric Southeast*. Cambridge, MA: Peabody Museum Press.

Breuil, Henri. 1979. *Four Hundred Centuries of Cave Art*. Montignac, France: Centre d'Etudes et de Documentation Prehistoriques.

Brown, James A. 1989. "On Style Divisions of the Southeastern Ceremonial Complex: A Revisionist Perspective." In *The Southeastern Ceremonial Complex: Artifacts and Analysis*, ed. Patricia Galloway, 183–204. Lincoln: University of Nebraska Press.

Broyles, Bettye J. 1968. "Reconstructed Designs from Swift Creek Complicated Stamped Sherds." *Proceedings of the 24th Southeastern Archaeological Conference* 8: 49–73.

Bury, Rick. 1999. "Too Many Shamans: Ethics and Politics of Rock Art Interpretation." *American Indian Rock Art* 25: 149–54.

Clarke, David L. 1968. *Analytical Archaeology*. London: Methuen.

Clottes, Jean, ed. 2001. *La Grotte Chauvet: L'Art des Origines*. Paris: Seuil.

Cressler, Alan, Jan F. Simek, Todd M. Ahlman, Joanne L. Bennett, and Jay D. Franklin. 1999. "Prehistoric Mud Glyph Cave Art from Alabama." *Southeastern Archaeology* 18 (1): 35–44.

Crothers, George, Charles H. Faulkner, Jan F. Simek, Patty Jo Watson, and Patrick Willey. 2002. "Woodland Period Cave Use in the Eastern Woodlands." In *The Woodland Southeast*, ed. David G. Anderson and Robert Mainfort, 502–524. Tuscaloosa: University of Alabama Press.

Diaz-Granados, Carol, and James R. Duncan. 2004. "Reflections of Power, Wealth, and Sex in Missouri Rock Art Motifs." In *The Rock-Art of Eastern North America: Capturing Images and Insight*, ed. Carol Diaz-Granados and James R. Duncan, 145–58. Tuscaloosa: University of Alabama Press.

DiBlasi, Philip J. 1996. "Prehistoric Expressions from the Central Kentucky Karst." In *Of Caves and Shell Mounds*, ed. Kenneth C. Carstens and Patty Jo Watson, 40–47. Tuscaloosa: University of Alabama Press.

Duncan, James R., and Carol Diaz-Granados. 2004. "Empowering the SECC: The 'Old Woman' and Oral Tradition." In *The Rock Art of Eastern North America: Capturing Images and Insights*, ed. Carol Diaz-Granados and James R. Duncan, 190–215. Tuscaloosa: University of Alabama Press.

Faulkner, Charles H., ed. 1986. *The Prehistoric Native American Art of Mud Glyph Cave*. Knoxville: University of Tennessee Press.

Faulkner, Charles H. 1988. "A Study of Seven Southeastern Glyph Caves." *North American Archaeologist* 9 (3): 223–46. http://dx.doi.org/10.2190/U6DQ-Q24V-WGRF-V27H.

Faulkner, Charles H. 1996. "Rock Art of Tennessee: Ceremonial Art in This World and the Underworld." In *Rock Art of the Eastern Woodlands*, ed. Charles H. Faulkner, 111–18. San Miguel, CA: American Rock Art Research Association.

Faulkner, Charles H., and Jan F. Simek. 1996a. "1st Unnamed Cave: A Mississippian Period Cave Art Site in East Tennessee, USA." *Antiquity* 70 (270): 774–84.

Faulkner, Charles H., and Jan F. Simek. 1996b. "Mud Glyphs: Recently Discovered Cave Art in Eastern North America." *International Newsletter on Rock Art* 15: 8–13.

Faulkner, Charles H., and Jan F. Simek. 2001. "Variability in the Production and Preservation of Prehistoric Mud Glyphs in Southeastern Caves." In *Fleeting Identities: Perishable Material Culture in Archaeological Research*, ed. Penelope B. Drooker, 335–356. Carbondale: Southern Illinois University Press.

Faulkner, Charles H., Jan F. Simek, and Alan Cressler. 2004. "On the Edges of the World: Prehistoric Open Air Rock Art in Tennessee." In *The Rock-Art of Eastern North America: Capturing Images and Insight*, ed. Carol Diaz-Granados and James R. Duncan, 77–89. Tuscaloosa: University of Alabama Press.

Galloway, Patricia. 1989. *The Southeastern Ceremonial Complex: Artifacts and Analysis*. Lincoln: University of Nebraska Press.

Hall, Robert L. 1989. "The Cultural Background of Mississippian Symbolism." In *The Southeastern Ceremonial Complex: Artifacts and Analysis*, ed. Patricia Galloway, 239–78. Lincoln: University of Nebraska Press.

Heizer, Robert F. 1941. "The Direct Historical Approach in California Archaeology." *American Antiquity* 7 (2): 98–122. http://dx.doi.org/10.2307/276058.

Kennedy, Mary C. 1996. "Radiocarbon Dates from Salts and Mammoth Caves." In *Of Caves and Shell Mounds*, ed. Kenneth C. Carstens and Patty Jo Watson, 48–81. Tuscaloosa: University of Alabama Press.

Kneberg, Madeline. 1959. "Engraved Shell Gorgets and Their Associations." *Tennessee Archaeologist* 15 (1): 1–39.

Lankford, George E. 2004. "World on a String: Some Cosmological Components of the Southeastern Ceremonial Complex." In *Hero, Hawk, and Hand*, ed. Richard F. Townsend, 207–17. New Haven, CT: Yale University Press.

Leroi-Gourhan, Andre. 1971. *Prehistoire de l'Art Occidental*. Paris: Mazenod.

Malhi, Ripan S., Jason A. Eshleman, Jonathan A. Greenberg, Deborah A. Weiss, B. A. Schultz Shook, Frederika A. Kaestle, Joseph G. Lorenz, Brian M. Kemp, John R. Johnson, and David G. Smith. 2002. "The Structure of Diversity within New World Mitochondrial DNA Haplogroups: Implications for the Prehistory of North America." *American Journal of Human Genetics* 70 (4): 905–19. http://dx.doi.org/10.1086/339690. Medline:11845406.

Muller, Jon. 1986. "Serpents and Dancers: Art of the Mud Glyph Cave." In *The Prehistoric Native American Art of Mud Glyph Cave*, ed. Charles H. Faulkner, 36–80. Knoxville: University of Tennessee Press.

Muller, John. 1989. "The Southern Cult." In *The Southeastern Ceremonial Complex: Artifacts and Analysis*, ed. Patricia Galloway, 11–26. Lincoln: University of Nebraska Press.

Nassaney, Michael S., and Kenneth E. Sassaman, eds. 1995. *Native American Interactions: Multiscalar Analyses and Interpretations in the Eastern Woodlands*. Knoxville: University of Tennessee Press.

Power, Susan. 2004. *Early Art of the Southeastern Indians*. Athens: University of Georgia Press.

Sassaman, Kenneth E., and David G. Anderson, eds. 1996. *The Archaeology of the Mid-Holocene Southeast*. Gainsville: University Press of Florida.

Scarry, John F. 1996. *Political Structure and Change in the Prehistoric Southeastern United States*. Gainesville: University of Florida Press.

Simek, Jan F. 1996. "1st Unnamed Cave: CSA Cooperative Research on a New 'Mud Glyph' Cave in East Tennessee." *Journal of the Cumberland Spelean Association* 3 (1): 12–23.

Simek, Jan F. 1998. "Prehistoric Use of Caves." In *Tennessee Encyclopedia of History and Culture*, ed. Carol Van West, 749–50. Nashville, TN: Rutledge Hill Press.

Simek, Jan F., and Alan Cressler. 2001. "Issues in the Study of Prehistoric Southeastern Cave Art." *Midcontinental Journal of Archaeology* 26 (2): 233–50.

Simek, Jan F., and Alan Cressler. 2005. "Images in Darkness: Prehistoric Cave Art in Southeastern North America." In *Discovering North American Rock Art*, ed. Lawrence Loendorf, Christopher Chippendale, and David Whitley, 93–113. Tucson: University of Arizona Press.

Simek, Jan F., Alan Cressler, and Elayne Pope. 2004. "Association between a Southeastern Rock Art Motif and Mortuary Caves." In *The Rock-Art of Eastern North America: Capturing Images and Insight*, ed. Carol Diaz-Granados and James R. Duncan, 159–73. Tuscaloosa: University of Alabama Press.

Simek, Jan F., Charles H. Faulkner, Todd Ahlman, Brad Cresswell, and Jay D. Franklin. 2001. "The Context of Late Prehistoric Southeastern Cave Art: The Art and Archaeology of 11th Unnamed Cave, Tennessee." *Southeastern Archaeology* 20 (2): 142–53.

Simek, Jan F., Charles H. Faulkner, Susan R. Frankenberg, Walter E. Klippel, Todd M. Ahlman, Nicholas P. Herrmann, Sarah C. Sherwood, Renee B. Walker, W. Miles Wright, and Richard Yarnell. 1997. "A Preliminary Report on the Archaeology of a New Mississippian Cave Art Site in East Tennessee." *Southeastern Archaeology* 16 (1): 51–73.

Simek, Jan F., Susan R. Frankenberg, and Charles H. Faulkner. 2001. "Towards an Understanding of Southeastern Prehistoric Cave Art." In *Integrating Appalachian Highlands Archaeology*, ed. Lynne Sullivan and Susan Prezanno, 49–64. Knoxville: University of Tennessee Press.

Simek, Jan F., Jay D. Franklin, and Sarah C. Sherwood. 1998. "The Context of Early Southeastern Prehistoric Cave Art: A Report on the Archaeology of 3rd Unnamed Cave." *American Antiquity* 63 (4): 663–75. http://dx.doi.org/10.2307/2694114.

Smith, Marvin T. 2002. *Coosa: The Rise and Fall of a Southeast Mississippian Chiefdom*. Gainesville: University of Florida Press.

Steward, Julian H. 1942. "The Direct Historical Approach to Archaeology." *American Antiquity* 7 (4): 337–43. http://dx.doi.org/10.2307/275399.

Strong, John A. 1989. "The Mississippian Bird-Man Theme in Cross-Cultural Perspective." In *The Southeastern Ceremonial Complex: Artifacts and Analysis*, ed. Patricia Galloway, 211–38. Lincoln: University of Nebraska Press.

Sullivan, Lynne P., and Susan C. Prezanno. 2001. *Archaeology of the Appalachian Highlands*. Knoxville: University of Tennessee Press.

Van Reybrouck, David. 2000. "Beyond Ethnoarchaeology: A Critical History of the Use of Ethnographic Analogy in Contextual and Post-Processual Archaeology." In *Verg Leichen als Archaologische Methode: Analogien in der Archaologien,* ed. Alexander Gramsch, 39–52. BAR International Series 825. Oxford: Archaeopress.

Walthall, John A., and David L. DeJarnette. 1974. "Copena Burial Caves." *Journal of Alabama Archaeology* 20 (1): 1–62. http://dx.doi.org/10.2190/MDEP-VM2K-YB2Q-L1D0.

Waring, Antonio J., Jr., and Preston Holder. 1945. "A Prehistoric Ceremonial Complex in the Southeastern United States." *American Anthropologist* 47 (1): 1–34. http://dx.doi.org/10.1525/aa.1945.47.1.02a00020.

Watson, Patty Jo. 1969. *The Prehistory of Salts Cave, Kentucky*. Springfield: Illinois State Museum.

Watson, Patty Jo. 1974. *Archaeology of the Mammoth Cave Area*. New York: Academic Press.

Watson, Patty Jo. 1986. "Prehistoric Cavers of the Eastern Woodlands." In *The Prehistoric Native American Art of Mud Glyph Cave*, ed. Charles H. Faulkner, 109–16. Knoxville: University of Tennessee Press.

Whitley, David S. 2000. *The Art of the Shaman*. Salt Lake City: University of Utah Press.

Williams, Mark, and Daniel T. Elliott. 1998. *A World Engraved: Archaeology of the Swift Creek Culture*. Tuscaloosa: University of Alabama Press.

Wylie, Alison. 1985. "The Reaction against Analogy." In *Advances in Archaeological Method and Theory*, vol. 8, ed. Michael B. Schiffer, 63–111. New York: Academic Press.

14

Reevaluating Cave Records

The Case for Ritual Caves in the Eastern United States

Cheryl Claassen

In his study of migration legends of the Creek Indians, Albert Gatschet of the US Bureau of Ethnology recorded that, in 1781, Chief Milfort led 200 Creek warriors on a pilgrimage to their ancestral caves—"from which the nation had issued in bygone times"—located in a forest along the Red River some 150 leagues above its junction with the Mississippi River. On their approach, bison, wild oxen, and wild horses fled from within the cluster of caves. The men overwintered there and in the early spring returned to their village with abundant food (Gatschet 1884, 230).

Caves and rockshelters in the minds of archaeologists have historically been cast in the role of temporary shelters and camps. In this chapter I suggest that caves and at least some rockshelters, including several archaeologically well-known locales, were regarded in the past as places where the ancestors as well as spirits responsible for water and game could be contacted, as Gatschet's account indicates. They were places then, not for habitation but for conducting rituals and leaving offerings. Here I reconsider the archaeological records of the Mammoth/Salts Cave complex (in Kentucky), Newt Kash Hollow Shelter (also in Kentucky), several Woodland Period mortuary caves, and the older Russell Cave (Alabama), Rodgers Shelter (Missouri), Dust Cave (Alabama), and Austin Cave (Tennessee). Most of the sites mentioned in the text can be found in figure 14.1.

NORTH AMERICAN CAVES AND COSMOLOGY

Ethnohistoric records make it abundantly clear that natives of North America moved through a ritualized, sacred landscape (Milne 1994). Springs, stone outcrops, waterfalls, sinkholes, hot springs, and caves were important loci for the opportunities these features afforded individuals and communities to glimpse the powers and sentiments of supernaturals. Both the visual elements of these geological features—their shapes and colors, and the effervescent spume and spray of any associated waterfalls and streams—and their audible aspects—their echoes, groans, and whistles (Milne 1994)—contributed in great measure to the sacred experience.

In the eastern United States, the recorded accounts of the origins of numerous groups involved their emergence into the surface world from caves. The Alibamu (Neshoba County, Mississippi) and the "Muskohgeh" (Muskogee Creeks) are two examples. The Caddo relate that an elder brought fire, a pipe, and a drum from the Below World, while his wife brought corn and pumpkin seeds, but before all the rest of the Caddo could emerge, the hole closed. The Tunica believed they originated in the hot springs of central Arkansas. The Six Nations of the Iroquois trace their origins to six families who emerged from a cave on the Oswego River, as commanded to do by the "Holder of the Heavens" (Gatschet 1884, 218).

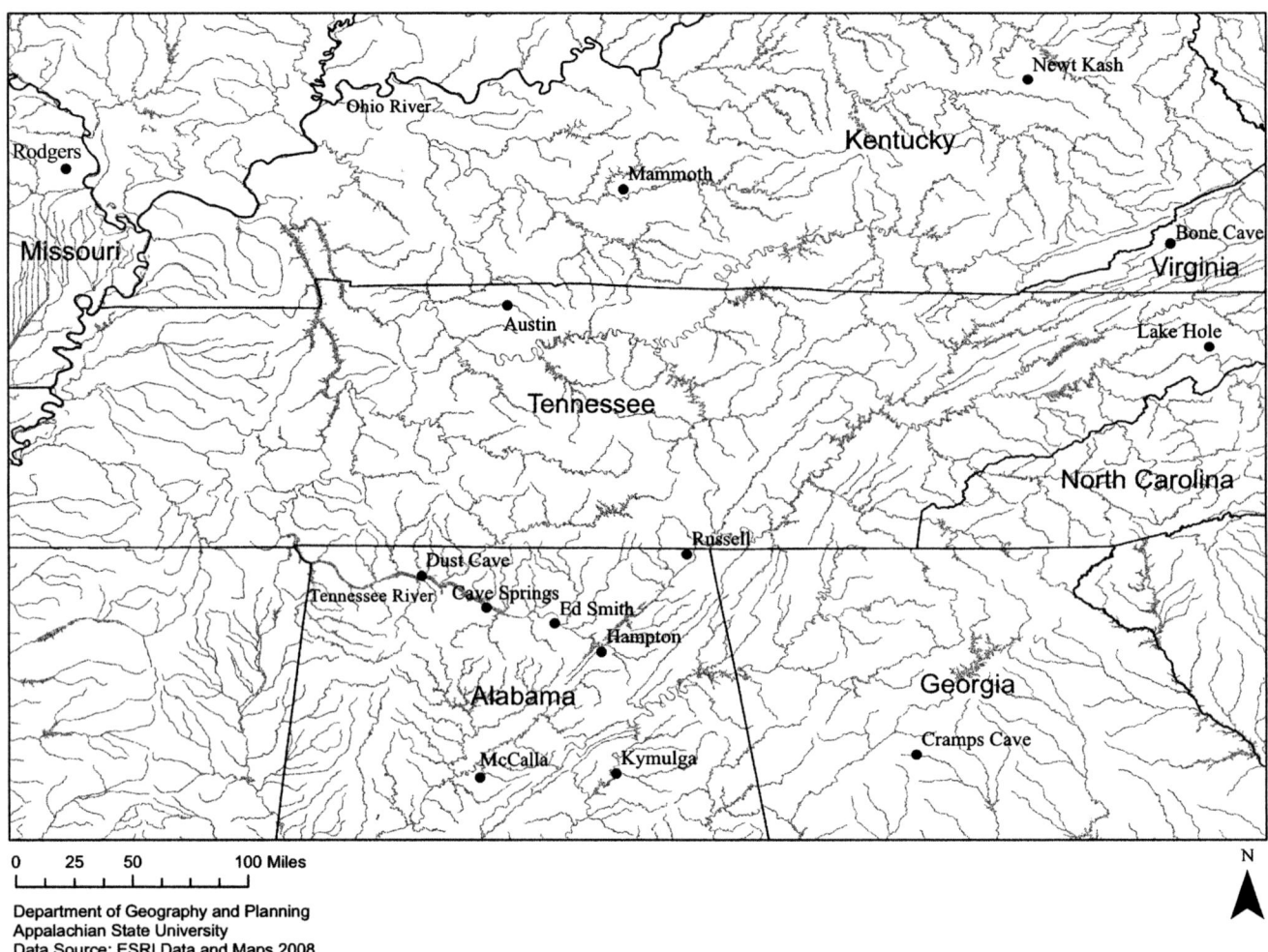

FIGURE 14.1 Sites mentioned in the text. (Map created by Andi Cochran, Appalachian State University.)

Similarly, the Cha'hta (Choctaw) say that

> a *red man* came down from above, and ... threw up a large mound or hill ... Then he caused the red people to come out of it, and when he supposed that a sufficient number had come out, he stamped on the ground with his foot ... [S]ome were partly formed, others were just raising their heads above the mud, emerging into light, and struggling into life. (Gatschet 1884, 106, italics in original; quoting the *Missionary Herald*, 1828, 181)

"The idea that their forefathers issued from caves was so deeply engrafted in the minds of these Indians, that some of them took any conspicuous cave or any country rich in caves to be the primordial habitat of their race" (Gatschet 1884, 234).

In addition to emergence from a troubled underworld into this world through caves, caves were home to monsters, the Good Spirit, and passageways to the Other World. For instance, the Tunica say the monster Mogmothon who brought sickness and hunger to people was thrown into a cave at Hot Springs, Arkansas, whereupon the mountain folded in on it. The Tonkawa of Texas revere Enchanted Rock, a dome outcrop with caves, creeks, and valleys, as the doorway to the Other World (Milne 1994). The Cherokee believe in an early sustenance mountain, with a cave that once contained all the game. The Cree revere the cave of Gitchi Manitou Ouitch-chouap as the house of the Great Spirit and of hairy-faced dwarfs, and La Colline Blanche Cave as House of the Rabbit (Milne 1994, 16). The Seneca believe that the Good Spirit lives in the Cave of the Winds near Niagara Falls (Milne 1994, 20). Crazy Horse, the Lakota leader, had a vision in which he went toward an arrow-shaped cave and had his body punctured with seven small stones that gave him messages from the Wakan Tanka (Milne 1994, 33). The Jicarilla Apache believe that the Great Spirit lived in a particular cave at Manitou Springs,

Colorado, which they never entered for fear of angering the Great Spirit (Milne 1994, 44). The Yavapai goddess Kamalapukwia, known as "grandmother of the supernatural," lives in a cave in Sedona, Arizona (Milne 1994, 66).

These specific accounts of emergence from caves and life forces which dwell in caves are suggestive of a much more ancient reverence for caves. It is the task of this chapter to show the time depth to these beliefs and to a sacred landscape that included reverence for caves. In the following pages I offer evidence that rituals were conducted in some caves as far back as the Paleoindian period.

WOODLAND PERIOD RITUAL CAVES

The Woodland period (3000 to 1000 BP) has the greatest number of radiocarbon determinations for cave use and was a time when caves were mined for a variety of minerals, including selenite, gypsum, and aragonite. Making art in eastern caves and mining minerals from the walls apparently were activities of male ritual specialists as early as 3,000 years ago. Both activities have been the focus of numerous published and unpublished papers (e.g., Crothers et al. 2002, Simek and Cressler 2005). Cave burials also occurred, and probably involved larger social groups during the Woodland period. I offer that all three of these cave activities—mining, art making, and burial—were ritualized. In the search for evidence of ritual in caves, it is instructive to start with the burial caves of the Woodland period in Tennessee, Georgia, Kentucky, and Virginia to examine the fauna, artifacts, and conditions of bodies.

WOODLAND MORTUARY CAVES

Thirty to forty mortuary caves are known in Georgia, including a few Copena culture caves (Walthall and DeJarnette 1974, 51), and twenty-three mortuary caves are known in Virginia (Hubbard and Barber 1997). Little information about artifacts and features is available from either of these two regions for looting has been extensive, but several records from Virginia are available.

From two small squares dug near the entrance of Bone Cave, Virginia, came human skeletal fragments. Six individuals had marine shell beads, pottery, cut mica, and thousands of faunal remains indicative of Late Woodland use. The bodies of at least one fetal-newborn, one 1–3-year-old child, one 4–6-year-old child, one late adolescent, and two adults were identified and had apparently been placed on the ground inside the cave (Kimball and Whyte 1995, 9). There is some evidence that all bodies were primary deposits rather than redeposited bundle burials (Boyd and Boyd 1997, 20). The human bone was highly fragmented although in good condition.

At Bone Cave the faunal materials were mixed with the human bone; all were greatly gnawed and fragmented, and some were burned. Freshwater snails and bivalve shells were common. Because the faunal remains were assumed to be *natural* additions to the cave, only a sample of bones was analyzed. The numerous taxa included deer, turkey, dog, woodchuck, pond turtle, box turtle, opossum, cottontail, snakes, raccoon, mink, gray squirrel, toad, deer mouse, shrew, salamander, mole, vole, woodrat, duck, and songbird (Kimball and Whyte 1995, 38–40).

Fifteen mortuary caves are known in eastern Tennessee and are thought to date from the Middle Woodland to Early Mississippian periods. The most intensively studied site, Lake Hole Cave, was severely disturbed by the time professional archaeological attention began (Whyte and Kimball 1992). Human and animal bones, and freshwater mollusks were mixed in the deposits and many had been partially burned (Whyte and Kimball 1992, 68). Approximately 100 individuals were carried into this cave, apparently as primary interments.

Dozens of species were recovered from the cleanup excavations at the Lake Hole mortuary cave. The NISP (based on six-millimeter screening) sorted into 14 fish (5 taxa), 38 amphibian (4 taxa), 97 bird (11 species), 631 reptile (5 taxa), and 5,200 nonhuman mammal bones (24 species). Snakes (garter snake, black racer, indeterminate racer/coachwhip, ratsnake, kingsnake, and poisonous snakes) were present, as were box turtles, lizards, songbirds, and ducks. Opossums, woodchucks, mice, rats, and raccoons are the best-represented mammalians, in that order. Other mammals present were beaver, rabbit, deer, squirrels, and bear. Given that the entrance to this cave was about 1 meter by 1 meter, and that the investigators suggest it may have been closed with rock during and after its use as a mortuary cave, it is difficult to imagine how the larger creatures could have wandered into this crevice.

There is no question that Lake Hole Cave was a mortuary cave rather than a habitation site. Nevertheless, twenty-five arrow points, two perforators, one drill, one *piece esquille*, one preform, and sixty-seven flakes were recovered in the cleanup excavation, as were 136 Middle Woodland grit-tempered sherds and over 6,000 shell beads. Many of the arrow points were broken and possibly embedded in the bodies brought into the small two-chambered cave.

Six Copena culture mortuary caves are known in Alabama. Cramps Cave in Blount County has dry interior rooms where bodies were found in long wooden troughs or canoe-shaped coffins (Walthall and DeJarnette 1974). Accompanying the bodies were copper urns, marine shell cups, wooden bowls, and trays. Bodies wrapped in bark or cane matting were bound with withers or bark.

Hampton Cave, near Guntersville, deemed uninhabitable by excavators, had charred human bone 4 feet deep in one small room. Human bone was calcined, as were all grave goods—copper reel gorgets, cut copper sheets, beads, earspools, marine-shell cups and beads, galena nodules; a pearl bead, and stone points. These items were rare and therefore were presumably accorded special status, strongly suggesting that the humans they accompanied were also of a special status.

McCalla Cave had twenty-six bodies occurring as burials or resting on the cave floor either in the entrance to the cave or near the back of the cave. The majority of the bodies were cremated elsewhere, brought to the cave in baskets, and placed in basin-shaped pits or in corners of interior rooms. Several burials were covered with puddled clay. Marine shell cups, 400 disk beads, a pearl bead, basketry, mats, fabric-impressed sherds, a huge copper celt, copper reel gorgets, copper beads, and much galena were retrieved (Walthall and DeJarnette 1974)—these were "expensive" items not typically included with the dead.

The Ed Smith Cave in the Huntsville area had bodies located at the back of the cave. The remains of fifty to 100 individuals had been dropped through a slit in the roof. Grave goods consisted of three shell cups, four copper beads, and a siltstone cup.

Cave Springs near Decatur, on the south side of the Tennessee River, was yet another Copena mortuary cave. It has a year-round spring flowing as a creek through the main passageway and into the Tennessee River (Walthall and DeJarnette 1974). Eighteen bodies were placed in three spots a quarter of a mile inside the cave, just before the point at which the passageway branched. One group of bodies was on a ledge above the main corridor. In preparing the resting area, clean sand was brought from a stream and spread over the area, and a burial bound in two layers of split cane or bark was placed on the cave floor. Wet clay was walled around and over burial. Only two of these bodies had goods: a bow and five cane arrows, and a blob of red ochre. Many feet of passageways lay beyond the burial areas and discarded cane-torch material indicates that people ventured down them. Kymulga Cave, on the Coosa River, had one group of bodies placed on an inner ledge. The one infant was placed on the floor and covered with puddled clay.

RITUAL ELEMENTS IN WOODLAND MORTUARY CAVES

Rituals have rarely been envisioned in the archaeological record from caves and rockshelters. All vertebrate remains tend to be explained as entrapments, prey, or stomach contents, not as grave goods, offerings, or feasting evidence. Only the artifacts in contact with the bodies are thought to be ceremonial in origin and then only if they were "ornaments" or recognized ritual items such as copper cutout or carapace rattles. "Domestic items" in the grave are usually interpreted as the tool kit of the deceased or for the journey to the land of the dead. Only the immediate area of human burials is considered to be a ceremonial area, while the place of burial, a cave, is afforded no ritual significance. For instance, Walthall and DeJarnette said about the Copena caves, "we can first define a burial cave as a cave or a segregated portion of a cave spatially removed from contemporary living areas" (1974, 46). Even when the evidence for habitation is scant, a need for shelter is assumed to be the reason the person was present in the cave when death occurred. Most archaeologists imply or state that artifacts and ecofacts found apart from bodies, in caves, are mundane in origin.

The preceding brief survey of cave use suggests that several elements of ritual can be found in Woodland period cave mortuaries.

1. Infants appear as primary placements, often above ground. Burning is rare.
2. When bodies are present, they often come from all life stages and in groups of four or five bodies.
3. Human and animal bones may be mixed and highly fragmented, and some may be burned.
4. A great variety of taxa are present, including many small taxa. Ritually important animals such as deer, snakes, waterbirds, and songbirds are found.
5. Vertebrates typically occur as incomplete skeletons, such as crania, or the bones of one side, particularly the left side, may be found.
6. Vertebrate taxa are typically represented by very few individuals.
7. Aquatic invertebrates are often present in unmodified as well as modified forms.
8. Textiles and weaving equipment often occur.
9. Arrows and bifaces are common.
10. Burned objects are common.

It does appear that human bodies of all ages and sexes were deposited as primary burials on the floor of these caves. Some cremations were also evident (Boyd and Boyd 1997, 165) and fire-reddened soils were encountered in some caves (e.g., Lake Hole Cave). Different elements of Woodland ritual are the inclusion of bodies in wooden troughs and the mounding of puddled clay over bodies lying in the ground. Unique to Copena cave-mortuary sites are platform pipes, siltstone cups, and freshwater pearl beads. I also draw attention to the occurrence of what I think was a ritually important combination of bodies seen in Bone Cave. Five individuals from different stages of life—newborn, child, adolescent, and adult—were found just inside the entrance, possibly a ritualized combination of ages (see Claassen 2010 for more examples and further development of this idea).

Items of flint or chert have much ritual significance in later times. Several groups believe that stone was the substance from which the oldest people were made or into which they were turned (Furst 1997). Arrow offerings placed in caves and rockshelters were prevalent among historic Plains tribes (Sundstrom 2000). Stories of Thrown Away/Spring Boy indicate that arrows were used to lure deities and spirits out of caves/dens. I think that the presence of chert items in these caves indicates that similar beliefs and practices were followed much earlier in time.

As ritual locations, these caves might have been located near village sites. Mg7, a habitation site, and Leeman Mound are within 2 miles of Cave Springs and Rockhouse Spring Cave. Ross Mound is located near Hampton Cave and Ed Smith Cave is but a few miles to its west. In both situations radiocarbon dates from the mounds or villages indicate the possibility that they were used simultaneously with the caves.

Are there grounds for arguing the ritual use of other caves during the Woodland Period apart from the obvious mortuary caves? Seeman (1984) has presented evidence that Mammoth/Salts Cave was used for ritual purposes. Here I argue that the primary role for this cave system was ritual in nature.

Mammoth/Salts Cave

Organic artifacts and feces in the Salts and Mammoth Caves complex have been dated to the interval 1200 to 200 cal BC (Crothers 2012:525). That human bone and glyphs were found in these caves has almost been overshadowed by the mummies, domesticated squash and gourd, and fecal specimens, not to mention the grand size of the cave system.

Faunal material was recovered primarily from the vestibules of these two caves. Curiously, the vestibule material in Salts Cave was a mixture of fragmented nonhuman and human bones that clearly had the same depositional history, for they had the same appearance and were equally fragmentary. "Together with the remains of game animals are many broken, splintered, and sometimes charred pieces of human bone, giving one the strong impression that the vestibule dwellers were at least part-time cannibals" (Watson 1974, 83). Recently, Mensforth (2001) reaffirmed these data as evidence of cannibalism.

The child known as Little Al, found inside the cave, was in good health at the time of his death and was placed in a flexed position after death. It is possible that he died from a blow to the chest. Robbins (1974, 159) concluded that the mummies found in the cave passages were placed in this cave (except for Lost John, the accident victim) without grave goods, clothing, or grave preparation. Mummies were venerated in caves as oracles by the Wixarika (Schaefer 2002) and other Mesoamerican groups, as well as by Aleuts (Laughlin 1980, 102) and throughout Andean societies. I suspect the same practice occurred in the United States.

At least forty-three individuals (3 fetuses, 5 infants, 10 children, and 23 adults) were recovered as highly fragmented bones, many burned or with butcher marks from numerous deep levels of the Salts Cave vestibule excavations. Butcher marks appear in places that suggest defleshing and scalping but also random cutting. Most of the subadult bone had not been burned. Evidence of crushing and fracturing of bones was frequently observed. In Trench J, Level 6 and below, there was a noticeable increase in the amount of bone from fetuses, infants, and children. A number of awls fashioned from human bone were also recovered. I have suggested elsewhere that strata or clusters of infant burials may indicate rituals having to do with rain calling and site dedication rites (Claassen 2010).

Robbins (1974, 159) made an extensive search of other skeletal collections and the literature and concluded that the skeletal remains in these two connected caves were unique with regard to their fragmentation, burning, population characteristics, and lack of whole skeletal burials. The parts of the human skeleton most common in the collection from Salts Cave are the skull, long bones, and ribs. Burial collections from older open-air Archaic shell heaps in the vicinity often had individuals lacking long bones, hands, feet, and skull. These missing elements have been interpreted as trophy parts (Mensforth 2001). Since it is these same elements most commonly found in the Salts vestibule, it would seem that this cave was an appropriate place to deposit/offer such trophy parts later in time.

Within the 2,000-plus bones recovered were elements of thirteen nonhuman species and an MNI of fifty-five creatures from the three horizons exposed in the Salts Cave vestibule. A large part of the unidentified bone was bird bone. Freshwater bivalve shells were also found in the deposits, some of which were burned. Shells are commonly found in caves and rockshelters and in historic times symbolized renewal and rebirth as well as being specifically associated with infants, women, warriors, and initiates (Claassen 2008, 2010). Bird bones in unusual quantities and proportions are what one would expect in ritual offerings.

One pocket of concentrated turkey bones and another of concentrated human bone was encountered in the Salts vestibule excavation (Watson 1974, 94). Feature 7A contained the proximal end of a right ulna of raccoon, a thoracic vertebra of an immature deer, a deer rib, large mammal bones, bones from a small bird, and a turkey rib. Feature 7D contained the right distal humerus of a turkey, fifty-seven large mammalian bones, and two bird bones. Feature 7F had six large mammal bone fragments. Just past the vestibule, in the Iron Gate vicinity and on the surface, were found a turkey and a groundhog, and beyond that, a catfish ceratohyal, turkey bones, and deer-bone fragments. This list of animals includes those that could be predicted to die accidentally in the vestible—mice, rats, and bats, for instance (Duffield 1974, 130). However, the range of one rat, the hispid cotton rat, does not include Kentucky today, and the pack rat, which is ubiquitous to area caves, was absent from the excavated remains—both observations suggesting that the faunal collection was not from natural deaths. Fish, particularly catfish and bass, were recovered from the deepest horizon and fish scales were found in some feces. Raccoons were represented predominantly by skull fragments. "There is a surprisingly small quantity of post cranial elements of these animals present" (Duffield 1974, 128). While there is evidence that several turkeys were brought into the cave whole, "most of the identified turkey bones are from the anterior portion of the bird" (1974, 128). The other taxa present have few individuals—striped skunk, red fox, gray fox, snakes, and so forth—and probably were not accidentals, says the analyst, because their skeletons are incomplete. A sample of faunal material recovered from the vestibule of Mammoth Cave by Nelson (1917) adds black bear, opossum, porcupine, brown bat, turtle, elk, and a crane to the list.

About the remains in both caves, Duffield concluded that hunting was of little importance (Duffield 1974, 132) to these Early Woodland peoples, in marked contrast to the peoples living elsewhere at the time. But, if we discard the notion that the vestibules served as campgrounds and consider them instead to be the staging area for rituals where offerings were left, then both the paucity and the variety of animals take on new significance. As indicated in the list of characteristics of offerings, the variety of taxa, the low MNIs, the presence of small species, and the occurrence of isolated skeletal parts and anterior parts strike me as material for offerings. The features suggest renewal offerings/requests specifically placed inside of this portal to the underworld.

In addition to the unworked bone and small quantities of chert flakes and tools, ground-stone and bone tools were recovered from excavation units in the vestibule. Cores, chips, projectile points, celts, and mostly used flakes amounted to 131 pieces of chipped stone. Two whole pestles and two fragments, eight chipped celts, five atlatl weights, six awls, a needle, and worked antler pieces were also among the finds in the Salts Cave vestibule. All artifacts and many flakes were utilized and the majority of celts, pestles, and atlatl weights appear to have been in a cache.

Seeman pointed out that the lithic and worked-bone industries here "seem impoverished and inconsistent with a view of the site as a camp" (1984, 568). There were also weaving and sewing tools. In a unique study of weaving among Wixarika women, Schaefer (2002) documents the intimate association between weaving and hunting, marked by the deposit of weaving equipment and weavings at hunting shrines typically located in rockshelters. In this light, then, textiles and awls are also appropriately considered offerings.

There are other aspects of the cave not emphasized in the two reports that are relevant to a ritual-use interpretation. For example, a handful of glyphs in Mammoth Cave are found at some distance from any entrance. It is my assumption that glyphs in dark zones are part of ritual practice. This is also a cave system with significant water features. Underground water, in the form of cold springs, hot springs, or a stream, was revered by many (or perhaps all) North American groups in the historic period (Milne 1994). In addition, waterfalls were also power points on the landscape (Milne 1994). The Mammoth/Salts Cave system contains several spectacular water features that no doubt elicited awe from viewers.

The paleofeces were found in greatest density in the area of the mirabilite that occurs less than a quarter of a mile before there is a dramatic water spout. Here water falls in a tight stream from the ceiling and forms a small lake on the floor. Remembering later beliefs that caves are the origin of water, and thus that the water in them is the purest of all water, it makes perfect sense that the pilgrim would purge his system (all fecal specimens tested successfully for amino acids have been indicative of male hormones) with the mirabilite—which works very quickly as a laxative—before approaching the water spout.

Finally, let us reconsider the diet of the Mammoth/Salts Caves users. Diet was recovered in the paleofeces and in the intestinal contents of a desiccated cadaver of a 9-year-old boy found inside. In his intestine were found "Iva seeds, hickory nutshell, evidence of animal protein, pieces of pre-adult insect cuticle, and fragments of carbonized material" (Yarnell 1974, 109). By weight, 73.4 percent of the processed material consisted of hickory nutshell and 26 percent of Iva and chenopod seeds. The twenty-seven paleofecal specimens examined from Mammoth Cave (Marquardt 1974, 194) contained hickory nutshell, chenopod seeds, maygrass seeds, sunflower achenes, plant and fruit skin, charcoal, sumpweed, squash, blackberry/raspberry, strawberry, grape seeds, and animal parts, in that order by weight. Charcoal was the most ubiquitous element followed by chenopodium. Animal remains were in seventh place and included snail shell.

Robbins cites the lack of animal parts and the infrequent evidence of animal consumption in her support of the cannibalism hypothesis. By all other comparisons and expectations, these feces reveal an *unusual* diet. Who eats charcoal, hickory nutshell, fish scales (but not fish bones), sunflower hulls, snail shells, and ectoskeletons of insects, a point first raised by Seeman (1984)? And who do we expect to eat a vegetarian diet in the Late Archaic and Early Woodland periods? If we grant this cave system the symbolic significance I am arguing for then it is appropriate to reconsider the dietary evidence as evidence of *ritual* diet, not habitual diet and the individuals found inside of the cave as ritual practitioners.

The original interpretation of human activities at Salts/Mammoth Cave was that a group of gatherer-hunters dwelled in the cave vestibule and because of a protein-poor diet resorted to cannibalism (Watson 1974). By 1996, however, the artifacts and bones located in the vestibule of Salts Cave were being interpreted as evidence for prehistoric habitation and/or mortuary use (Kennedy 1996, 52) and the mortuary-ritual cave idea had been argued by Mark Seeman (1984) a decade earlier. Furthermore, other caves with comparably aged human use differed in important ways from Salts/Mammoth, suggesting that Salts/Mammoth had a unique place in the cultural landscape.

Instead of a picture of nomadic campers, a strong case can be made for the staging of rituals in the vestibule of Mammoth/Salts cave that included human sacrifices, trophy-part disposal and meat consumption, and petitions for world renewal. The implication then, is that the mining and the people found as desiccated cadavers were also part of ritualized activities inside of this cave system.

PALEOINDIAN AND ARCHAIC RITUAL CAVES

Evidence for older ritual caves and caves rituals can be found as well. Several caves with older dates are known for their glyphs—Jaguar Cave and 3rd Unnamed Cave (both in Tennessee) and Lee Cave (in Kentucky), for example, and are discussed elsewhere in this volume (see Simek, Cressler, and Douglas, chapter 13; Watson, chapter 12). I want to look at other caves with potential evidence for ritual use that are much older than those: Russell Cave, Rodgers Shelter, Dust Cave, and Austin Cave. They may allow us to push back the symbolic significance of caves and aspects of a sacred landscape even further in time.

Russell Cave

Much of the surface water on the lower edge of the Cumberland Plateau is captured by limestone fissures and tube caves moving the water underground for miles until it exits through holes in the bluff face, usually as springs (Hack 1974). At Russell Cave, the roof of a tube-cave system collapsed before 9000 BP, exposing the captured stream, forming a sinkhole, and providing a cross-section of the tube fissure (figure 14.2). The tube at this point in the mountain was double-barreled, exposing two rockshelter-type rooms: a front and lower room, and a back and upper room. In the lower room, the underground tube continues draining the water into the room. The sinkhole also captures a surface stream that likewise drains from the lower room into the tube fissure. The upper room is dry and had cultural material 14 feet deep. When excessive rain falls, the room floods, the sink fills, and water spills downhill—no doubt an impressive sight. For the following observation, I rely on the report by John Griffin (1974), conducting one of three excavations in Russell Cave.

If this sinkhole was actually a sacred place, then the material deposited in the upper room may constitute offerings and ritual debris rather than habitation debris, as was assumed by excavators. The artifactual material indicates a heavy use of the sink during the Early and Middle Archaic periods and during the Middle and Late Woodland periods. Layer G, the deepest, is Early Archaic, with one burial of an infant aged 20–24 months and dated 10,215 to 8790 cal BP. Layer F is Middle Archaic and had one infant, one child, one adolescent, and two adults (one male and one female)—the combination of ages and the greater number of adults that I suggested was a ritually important configuration at Bone Cave. None of the burials had grave goods.

Several differences are apparent in the assemblage of items from the two gross time periods at Russell Cave. During the earlier Archaic period, but not later, burials were put into the upper room and a great number of broken projectile points, unifacial tools, and utilitarian ground-stone tools were left in the room. The Woodland peoples left more ornamental stone items than utilitarian, but bone awls, needles, and pins were the most frequent types of bone tools for both time periods. Shell ornaments and perforated teeth were most commonly found in Woodland levels. Limestone-tempered sherds vastly outnumbered any other temper type, suggesting that a ritual involving ceramics—perhaps like the Mayan annual breakage of cave-water vessels—was particularly important during the Late Woodland period.

Over 30,000 pieces of bone were recovered in this one excavation that sorted into at least sixty-six species, including an extinct peccary. "Russell Cave . . . appears in some respects similar to that of Dust Cave . . . small terrestrial mammals are represented in greater or equal proportions to deer in both early and Middle Archaic levels" (Goldman-Finn 1994, 219). Mammals and birds dominated the species list at this site. At least twenty turkeys

FIGURE 14.2 Russell Cave. (Photograph by the author.)

and 155 gray squirrels were retrieved from Layer G. Deer were present in all layers but could be said to be uncommon in relation to other sites. Some deer were killed in the fall or winter months. The bones were highly fragmented. Black bear was present in all layers except the later Middle Archaic. Porcupine occurs here quite south of its modern range. Dog remains were rare. Thirteen species of birds were recovered in just the excavations by Griffin. All passenger pigeons present were adults and must have been taken during migration. Loons, teal, wood duck, red-tailed and red-shouldered hawks, barred owl, and red-bellied woodpecker were also recovered from the excavations in the upper room, all with symbolic and ritual associations. Amphibians and reptiles were numerous as well and at least twelve fish species were present, with their largest number in Layer C. Drum and catfish were the most common species. Freshwater snails and bivalves brought from the Tennessee River six to seven miles distant, amounted to 4,710 specimens. The greatest variety of species was attributed to the Woodland period visits. Again, a pattern consisting of incomplete bodies, coupled with a great variety in taxa but low numbers of individual animals, is highly suggestive of ritual activities.

Dust Cave

Dust Cave is, like Russell Cave, part of a solution-tube cave system created by underground water flow in karstic limestone (figure 14.3). It has been described as "unimposing with a small, low entrance and floor-to-ceiling height in most areas of less than 50 cm" (Goldman-Finn and Driskell 1994, 1). Altogether there are 100 square meters of exposed cave floor and more in passageways. The entrance chamber has been tested and the passageway explored until it pinches out. In 1994 it was suspected that much more of the cave lay beyond the constriction. The density of artifacts at the site is reported to be relatively low, which I take to favor the ritual-use hypothesis over the habitation hypothesis.

FIGURE 14.3 Dust Cave. (Photograph by Jessica Vavrasek.)

The deposits here span Paleoindian to Late Archaic cultures and were screened with ¼-inch mesh. Concentrations of ash, charcoal, and burnt clay are found throughout the sequence. There are medium- and small-sized pits filled with charcoal, burnt bone, shell, and sometimes heat-altered limestone. Large concentrations of burnt aquatic periwinkle shells, in lenses and in pits, also occur in these deposits.

Paleobotanical remains were dominated by acorn and hickory nutshell, with hickory increasing through time. "Dust Cave does not support the general patterns of Archaic period nut exploitation inferred by Yarnell and Black from their compendium of Eastern Woodlands archaeo-botany" (Gardner 1994, 209). Larger samples might change that impression.

A preliminary analysis of the Dust Cave fauna showed that small-animal species dominated the 5,500-year record. Large quantities of fish bone and aquatic mollusks came out of the Early and Middle Archaic levels. The relative proportion of deer bone remained low throughout the Archaic sequence. As already mentioned, this pattern is like that at Russell Cave but is unexpected. "This pattern [of low deer proportion] defies conventional wisdom on the Archaic, and clearly contrasts with data from other important sites in the Mid-south" (Goldman-Finn 1994, 219). Other characteristics of the Dust Cave fauna were a large quantity of ducks in the earliest deposits, and a general increase in aquatic-mammal bones through time. Four dog burials were found and may have come from the same source of dogs that are so prolific at the Perry shell mounds less than 3 miles away. Of great relevance to the thesis of this chapter, one analyst asked, "Is Dust Cave an unusual site type whose faunal assemblages are not indicative of overall subsistence strategies?" (Grover 1994, 131–32). I offer that the answer is yes. Dust Cave was a ritual cave for at least a portion of its history.

In the entrance trench, two pestles were found in Middle Archaic Seven Mile Island phase deposits. Ninety-five percent of the 130 stone tools recovered were made from blue-gray Fort Payne chert famously used in the overly large Benton cache blades. None of the remaining tools or the 21,000 pieces of debitage employed the fossiliferous Fort Payne chert found in the walls of the cave. The debitage was largely indicative of later stages in the manufacturing process in all the components. Only 143 bone tools and three shell ornaments had been found by 1994, most coming from the most recent component. These were awls (81), "worked objects" (11), beads/tubes (9), needles (7), and miscellaneous items like perforated teeth, tine segments, edges, and spatulas.

Nineteen individuals were apparently buried as corpses in Dust Cave and parts of eighteen others were recovered (Turner 2006). A probable 5-year-old child was the initial burial, in the Kirk Stemmed level, reminiscent of the initial infant burial at Russell Cave. The dead sorted into eighteen adults, one juvenile, nine children, two subadults, and seven infants. One dog burial seemed to accompany the juvenile.

Thirty-two percent of the dead in this cave had violent deaths and another 16 percent probably did (Turner 2006, 81). Six had cranial-depression fractures (Turner 2006, 130). The incomplete skeletons are not surprising, given the record at Salts Cave, but they are poorly annotated. I suspect that dog burials were part of a ritual for rebalancing the community, an idea explored in Claassen (2010).

Rodgers Shelter

Features similar to those detailed at Mammoth/Salts also were recorded inside Rodger's Shelter, Missouri. Feature 8233 in the Middle Archaic Horizon 8 included one finely flaked point; a human humerus and tibia; a bison tooth; a large bird bone; a terrapin shell fragment; cottontail parts; squirrel humerus, calcanium and radius fragments; and a pharyngeal fragment from a drum. Six inches away sat a hematite-processing slab. The quantity of hematite was remarkable. In Middle Archaic Horizon 7, there were two hematite-grinding areas showing large quantities of powdered hematite, hematite-stained grinding slabs, bits and pieces of ground hematite, and hearths. Kay points out that the complex supports the "idea that chunks of hematite were purposely fired both to enhance the color and make the hematite softer" (Kay 1982, 571). Hematite's red color has long been found associated with burials as old as Paleoindian times.

A second such feature contained the pelvis and sacrum of deer; one bison phalanx; rabbit teeth, ulna, and radius; terrapin shell; turkey ulna and corocoid; *Canis* premolar; and a squirrel radius. A Dalton-aged feature contained most of the skeleton of a trumpeter swan (Kay 1982). It appears to me that these Archaic-aged features derive from offerings of thanksgiving/propitiation to an earth spirit that could be contacted through these portals, with specific requests for the continuation of humans and at least seven other animals.

Three possible "structures" were identified by Kay in the Horizon 7 Middle Archaic levels inside Rodgers Shelter. Structures 1 and 2 were rings of rock 5 feet in diameter. Structure 2 had three pieces of hematite, one hammerstone, five cores, two biface performs, three projectile points, one scraper, four utilized flakes, one tooth, and one piece of galena. Structure 3, which was 6.7 feet in diameter, had two ground-stone fragments, five cores, one biface preform, and one projectile point. Kay allowed that these rock clusters might be remains of ceremonial structures. (A circle of large stones was also uncovered inside nearby Graham Cave.) I propose that they are either altars or shrines. There may be sweat lodges inside caves as well.

Austin Cave

Austin Cave is located on a tributary of the Cumberland River in Tennessee and is a double-entrance tube cave (figure 14.4). It has been severely looted. However, excavations were conducted in the midden outside the mouth of the cave and on the bank above the cave (Barker 1997). Over 60,000 artifacts indicating Paleoindian as well as Early and Middle Archaic activities were recovered, including more than 300 points and hide-processing tools. Over 9,000 bone pieces were also recovered in screens.

While the excavator considered this material to constitute "an open habitation site" and "base camp occupied throughout the year," the remains strike me quite differently. The midden was at and around the mouth of the cave and was 140 centimeters deep. The ritually important Fort Payne chert and a local substitute, Saint Louis formation chert, predominated. Four contiguous test units placed above and immediately north of the cave and totaling 4 square meters yielded 51,428 lithics from three strata. Blank flakes were 64 percent of the total. Other than flakes, blanks, scrapers, points, and knives, there was a single banded-slate bannerstone.

Fauna recovered sorted into 144 individuals of 22 mammalian, 15 avian, 2 amphibian, 9 reptilian, and 4 fish taxa (Barker 1997). Ninety percent of the 8,693 pieces came from the bottom stratum of the four units. Nineteen percent were burned. The birds present were turkey, passenger pigeon, and the very ritually significant sandhill crane and trumpeter swan, as well as ducks and geese. Water turtles outnumber land terrapins. Small mammals represent 25 percent of the meat weight and they, along with deer, account for most of the meat in evidence. Altogether these species indicate year-round activities at the cave. Body

FIGURE 14.4 Austin Cave. (Photograph by and with the permission of Gary Barker.)

parts present and number of individuals are not given in the research paper, and the excavation undertaken was not sufficient to identify the features necessary to support the interpretation of a base camp.

I think it is far more likely that these deposits around the exterior of this cave resulted from ritual activities, in which the stone artifacts played a prominent role. Stone housed the spirits of humans and deities throughout the Americas (e.g., Furst 1997; Irwin 1994; Milne 1994), and the Aztecs referred to children as "the chips" or "the flakes" (Furst 1997, 175). I suggest that the flakes at Austin Cave were part of ritual offerings and petitions for fertility. Furthermore, flintknapping releases lightning and many groups believed lightning issued from caves and the sound of clashing stones mimicked thunder. These materials were found at the *mouth* of the cave, also suggesting that there was hesitation in entering, appropriate when the cave housed a lightning deity. The fauna here meet some of the expectations for offerings in the high diversity yet low number of individuals, in the presence of ritually important species, and in the high number of small species. Were the flintknappers of Austin Cave priests who were calling out the rain and petitioning for renewal?

THE CASE FOR RITUAL ROCKSHELTERS

There is also sufficient evidence to press the interpretation of some rockshelters as places where women retreated during menstruation and birthing and where groups (medicine societies?) organized initiation ceremonies during the Woodland period, if not millennia earlier. Newt Kash Hollow Shelter of eastern Kentucky is famous for the cache of *Chenopodium berlandieri* ssp. *jonesianum* and abundant *Iva annua* seeds recovered there during excavations in 1935, and dating to approximately 3,400 BP (Webb and Funkhouser 1936), but archaeologists also recovered hundreds of pieces of fabric, string, textiles, cordage, large fabric beds, a cradleboard, shell spoons and containers, nutting stones, gourd containers, hunting tools, and wood-shaving tools. Animal bones, freshwater mussels, antler points, awls, needles, pottery, gourds, arrowheads, a large number of fecal specimens, pits, and postholes were retrieved as well. There are also dozens of species of plants represented in abundance. The authors remarked on the paucity of hunting equipment and animal bones. The low variety and numbers of artifacts and the high variety of meat, though from few individuals, do not meet expectations for a family camping for an extended stay. Instead of either scenario, this rockshelter assemblage gives strong indication that it was a place where women passed time, processing plant materials, making string, fabric, and nut oil.

Women in many historic native groups removed themselves for about 4 days during menstruation, according to historic records. Creek Indian women of Georgia and Alabama retreated for 4 days to a menstrual structure where they used unique utensils for food preparation and consumption, ate no meat from large animals, and, before leaving, bathed and changed clothing. In at least one North Carolina group, women were reportedly absent some 40 days after giving birth. A rockshelter is an obvious and convenient place to pass the time.

At Newt Kash, the beds, the cached edible seeds, the buried and discarded textiles, with evidence of nuts, seeds, and small-mammal consumption answer directly to the test implications of an historic women's menstrual retreat. So do the numerous pieces of bottle gourd, a natural container useful for liquids, the shell spoons and dishes, and the pottery—all of which kept the powers of the menstruating and postpartum woman apart from the larger community.

The evidence for group ritual activities can be gathered from other aspects of the setting and the remains found here. This rockshelter is 150 feet below the mesa top and 50 feet above the floor of the ravine, making it somewhat secluded. The shelter is large (225 feet long and 55 feet deep) and dry, giving ample space for a group to assemble. Inside of the shelter, much of the rockfall from the roof is positioned at the drip-line edge, providing seating in a natural theater that faces inward.

Also suggestive of ritual activities are the groupings of pits. Eight equally spaced large pits were in a line against the back wall, with the three largest pits in the middle and at the two ends. Five additional pits form a quincunx approximately in the center back of the shelter. The quincunx was associated with earth creation and earth renewal and was present in the Ohio Valley at least by 1,700 years ago (Hall 1997). A third group of three small pits and numerous small postholes are to be found in the back center of the shelter. The postholes enclose a space that suggests either a sweat lodge or platform. This grouping of pits is separated from the quincunx pits by two boulders that could have served well as altars or benches for idols, offerings, ritual objects, or individuals staging a ritual. An infant was buried between these two boulders.

Plants with medicinal properties abound in the debris of this shelter and the taking of medicine would surely have been associated with all the possible rites conducted here for menstruation, pregnancy, and "women's problems." What we may be seeing is a pharmacy: laid-up stores of potentially important medicines. While the various barks were present for cordage needs, they also were useful in treating numerous types of maladies. Wood, seeds, florets, roots, quids, leaves, and mosses recovered amounted to two potential abortatives, twelve gynecological and venereal disease aids, twelve gastrointestinal aids, ten kidney and urine aids, ten skin and burn aids, one sedative, and several disinfectants, among numerous other categories of medicines (sources consulted were Boone 2000; Gillespie 1986; Jones 1936; Krochmal, Walters, and Doughty 1971; Westbrooks 1989). Only the rattles of a rattlesnake were recovered, but even those have gynecologically useful properties and symbolic associations with women (Denig 1930). Quids (chewed or beaten masses) of compass plant (*Silphium laciniatum*) were abundant here and were used historically by the Winnebago as an emetic in ceremonial cleansing and by the Chippewa for "female trouble" and back pain (Densmore 1929, 293, 340). The button snakeroot, although primarily found as fabric and cordage in this shelter, also has a place in historic cleansing and renewal ceremonies (Ethridge 1979).

I propose then that Newt Kash Hollow Shelter was used as a menstrual seclusion and birthing locus for women who removed themselves from a nearby village for periods of 4 days to numerous weeks at a time. While women were secluded at this rockshelter, they cached seeds for later consumption; produced nut oils and dyes, cordage, and possibly fabrics; slept and ate; combed the surrounding area for food, medicinal plants, bark, and grasses; and took ritual baths. I also propose that this shelter was a birthing retreat and a staging place for rituals expressing earth-renewal beliefs and possibly involving sweat baths, the oiling of the body and hair, and probably the shedding and renewal of clothing. (This argument is much more fully developed in Claassen 2011 along with numerous other rockshelter examples.)

CONCLUSIONS

Caves have been sacred elements in the landscape for many North American groups, east and west. It is certain that some caves were also special loci during Mississippian and earlier Woodland times. But there is little recognition of uses other than as mortuaries or for mining during the Woodland period. Based on the mortuary caves, a list of criteria for ritual activities has been offered, and on the basis of this list, some Early Archaic period cave records also seem to indicate ritual use.

If these caves and probably many rockshelters were primarily ritual places, and the features and debris excavated from them were left as offerings or the remains of rituals, we must reconsider how these materials and places have been interpreted. For one, we have been looking at points in a sacred landscape that we can now begin to connect and to fill out with true habitation locations. The cosmovision of many modern native groups in North America is structured around significant topographical loci; surely this was so in the past. Second, the use of paleofecal samples for generalized dietary information from Mammoth Cave and Newt Kash Hollow Shelter may be wrong. Instead, we have samples of the diet of several male ritual specialists in Mammoth Cave and from menstruating women living in seclusion at Newt Kash. The domesticated seeds may have been domesticated in seclusion locations for seclusion needs or they may have been transported to the shelter from the women's lowland village gardens. Either interpretation requires that we rethink what has been said about these early domesticates.

This chapter is a call not only for the reconsideration of previously excavated cave collections but for greater attention to be given to sacred landscape and to ritual practice in the past. Numerous recent Society for American Archaeology symposia on ritual caves in the United States and Mesoamerica signal greater awareness on the part of professional archaeologists of the role of caves and rockshelters in such a landscape in the Americas. To identify markers of ritual more securely, it will be necessary to examine village midden, mound, and cave osteological debris for details of species, species proportions, fragmentation, burning, body parts (including side of body from which bones originate), and age. I suspect that the enumerated characteristics will be indicative of rituals and offerings, whatever the setting. It is clearly a mistake to consider cave art as separate from cave fauna, as has nonetheless been done by so many archaeologists, and to assume that fauna in cave assemblages are always only entrapments or stomach contents. Art, fauna, human bones, and artifacts are integral aspects of ritual use of caves.

The sacred landscape began to take shape as soon as people entered the eastern United States. Some caves and sinkholes apparently were identified very early as especially potent places. By the Middle Archaic, humans began creating ritual locations such as seen in the shell mounds of the southern Ohio Valley and earthen mounds of the Gulf Coastal Plain, but it seems that at least the shell mounds may have been founded with respect to important caves. I suspect that several of the famous Archaic shell-mound mortuaries in the karstic regions of the southern Ohio Valley were associated with specific caves. I have noted the geographical proximity of Wyandotte and Squire Boone Caves to Miller and other shell mounds in southern Indiana; the Perry shell mound and Dust Cave in northwestern Alabama: Widows Creek and Russell Cave in northeastern Alabama: the Ervin shell mound and Cheek Bend Cave in central Tennessee; and Mammoth/Salts Caves as well as Carlston Annis and other shell mounds downriver on the Green River in Kentucky. These karstic regions are filled with powerful natural places and archaeological sites that we have misunderstood and even overlooked.

REFERENCES CITED

Barker, Gary. 1997. "Upland Middle Archaic Adaptation in Tennessee's Western Highland Rim, a View from the Austin Cave Site." *Tennessee Anthropologist* 22 (2): 177–223.

Boone, Rebecca. 2000. *Native Medicinal Plants of Shenandoah Valley*. Blacksburg, VA: Pocahontas Press.

Boyd, Cliff, and Donna Boyd. 1997. "Osteological Comparison of Prehistoric Native Americans from Southwest Virginia and East Tennessee Mortuary Caves." *Journal of Caves and Karst Studies* 59 (3): 160–5.

Claassen, Cheryl. 2008. "Shell Symbolism in North America." In *Early Human Impact on Megamolluscs*, ed. Andrzej Antczak and Roberto Cipriani, 37–43. British Archeological Reports S1865. Oxford: Archaeopress.

Claassen, Cheryl. 2010. *Feasting with Shellfish in the Southern Ohio Valley: Sacred Sites and Rituals*. Knoxville: University of Tennessee Press.

Claassen, Cheryl. 2011. "Rock Shelters as Women's Retreats: Understanding Newt Kash." *American Antiquity* 76 (4): 628–641.

Crothers, G. M., C. H. Faulkner, J. F. Simek, P. J. Watson, and P. Willey. 2002. "Woodland Cave Archaeology in Eastern North America." In *The Woodland Southeast*, ed. D. G. Anderson and R. C. Mainfort Jr., 502–24. Tuscaloosa: University of Alabama Press.

Crothers, George. 2012. "Early Woodland Ritual Use of Caves in Eastern North America." *American Antiquity* 77(3):524–541.

Denig, Edward. 1930. *Indian Tales of Upper Missouri*. Washington, DC.: Government Printing Office.

Densmore, Frances. 1929. *Chippewa Customs*. Washington, DC: Government Printing Office.

Duffield, Lathel. 1974. "Nonhuman Vertebrate Remains from Salts Cave Vestibule." In *Archeology of the Mammoth Cave Area*, ed. Patty Jo Watson, 123–33. New York: Academic Press.

Ethridge, Robbie. 1979. "Button Snakeroot Symbolism among the Southeastern Indians." *Tennessee Anthropologist* 4 (2): 160–6.

Furst, Jill. 1997. *The Natural History of the Soul in Ancient Mexico*. New Haven, CT: Yale University Press.

Gardner, Paul. 1994. "Carbonized Plant Remains from Dust Cave." *Journal of Alabama Archaeology* 40: 192–211.

Gatschet, Albert. 1884. *A Migration Legend of the Creek Indians*. Brinton's Library of Aboriginal American Literature, No. 4. Philadelphia: D. G. Brinton.

Gillespie, William. 1986. *Wild Foods of Appalachia*. Morgantown, WV: Seneca Books.

Goldman-Finn, Nurit. 1994. "Dust Cave in Regional Context." *Journal of Alabama Archaeology* 40: 212–31.

Goldman-Finn, Nurit, and Boyce Driskell, eds. 1994. "Dust Cave in Regional Context." *Journal of Alabama Archaeology* 40: 1–255.

Griffin, John, ed. 1974. *Investigations in Russell Cave*. Washington, DC: National Park Service.

Grover, Jennifr. 1994. "Faunal Remains from Dust Cave." *Journal of Alabama Archaeology* 40: 116–34.

Hack, John. 1974. "Geology of Russell Cave." In *Investigations in Russell Cave*, ed. John Griffin, 16–28. Washington, DC: National Park Service.

Hall, Robert. 1997. *An Archaeology of the Soul: North American Indian Belief and Ritual*. Urbana: University of Illinois Press.

Hubbard, David, and Michael Barber. 1997. "Virginia Burial Caves: An Inventory of a Desecrated Resource." *Journal of Caves and Karst Studies* 59 (3): 154–9.

Irwin, Lee. 1994. *The Dream Seekers: Native American Visionary Traditions of the Great Plains*. Norman: University of Oklahoma Press.

Jones, Volney. 1936. "The Vegetal Remains of Newt Kash Hollow Shelter." In *Rock Shelters in Menifee County, Kentucky*, by William Webb and W. Funkhouser, 147–65. University of Kentucky Reports in Archeology and Anthropology, Vol. 3(4). Lexington, KY: University of Kentucky.

Kay, Marvin, ed. 1982. "Holocene Adaptation within the Lower Pomme de Terre River Valley, Missouri." Report submitted to the US Army Corps of Engineers, Kansas City District.

Kimball, Larry, and Thomas Whyte. 1995. *Archaeological Investigations at Bone Cave (44Le169), Lee County*. Virginia. Appalachian State University Laboratories of Archaeological Science, Technical Report No. 4. Boone, NC: Department of Anthropology, Appalachian State University.

Krochmal, Arnold, Russell Walters, and Richard Doughty. 1971. *A Guide to Medicinal Plants of Appalachia*. Washington, DC: US Government Printing Office. USDA 400 USGPO.

Laughlin, William. 1980. *Aleuts: Survivors of the Bering Land Bridge*. New York: Holt, Rinehart, and Winston.

Marquardt, William. 1974. "A Statistical Analysis of Constituents in Human Paleofecal Specimens from Mammoth Cave." In *Archeology of the Mammoth Cave Area*, ed. Patty Jo Watson, 193–203. New York: Academic Press.

Mensforth, Robert. 2001. "Human Trophy Taking in Eastern North American during the Archaic Period: Its Relationship to Warfare and Social Complexity." In *Archaic Transitions in Ohio and Kentucky Prehistory*, ed. O. Prufer, S. Pedde, and R. Mendl, 110–45. Kent, OH: Kent State University Press.

Milne, Courtney. 1994. *Sacred Places in North America: A Journey into the Medicine Wheel*. New York: Stewart, Tabori and Chang.

Nelson, Nels C. 1917. *Contributions to the Archaeology of Mammoth Cave and Vicinity*. Kentucky Anthropological Papers 22, Part 1. New York: American Museum of Natural History.

Robbins, Louise. 1974. "Prehistoric People of the Mammoth Cave Area." In *Archeology of the Mammoth Cave Area*, ed. Patty Jo Watson, 137–62. New York: Academic Press.

Schaefer, Stacy. 2002. *To Think with a Good Heart*. Salt Lake City: University of Utah Press.

Seeman, Mark. 1984. "Adena 'Houses' and Their Implications for Early Woodland Settlement Models in the Ohio Valley." In *Early Woodland Archeology*, ed. Ken Farnsworth, 564–80. Kampsville, IL: Center for American Archaeology.

Simek, Jan, and Alan Cressler. 2005. "Images in Darkness: Prehistoric Cave Art in Southeast North America." In *Discovering North American Rock Art*, ed. Lawrence Loendorf, Christopher Chippendale, and David Whitley, 93–113. Tucson: University of Arizona Press.

Sundstrom, Linea. 2000. "Blind Encounters: Archaeologists and Sacred Sites in the Northern Plains." Paper presented at the annual meetings of the Plains Anthropological Conference, Saint Paul, MN.

Turner, James. 2006. "An Investigation of Violence-Related Trauma at Two Sites in the Pickwick Basin: Dust Cave and the O'Neal Site." MA thesis, Department of Sociology, Anthropology, and Social Work, Mississippi State University, Starkville, MS.

Walthall, John, and David DeJarnette. 1974. "Copena Burial Caves." *Journal of Alabama Archaeology* 20 (1): 1–55.

Watson, Patty Jo, ed. 1974. "Prehistoric Cultural Debris from the Vestibule Trenches." In *Archeology of the Mammoth Cave Area*, ed. Patty Jo Watson, 83–96. New York: Academic Press.

Webb, William, and W. Funkhouser. 1936. *Rock Shelters in Menifee County, Kentucky*. University of Kentucky Reports in Archeology and Anthropology, Vol. 3(4). Lexington, KY: University of Kentucky.

Westbrooks, Rebecca. 1989. *Medicinal Plants of Western North Carolina: As Used by the Cherokee Indians*. Columbia: University of South Carolina.

Whyte, Thomas, and Larry Kimball. 1992. "Archaeological Investigations of Lake Hole Mortuary Cave in the Southern Appalachians." Draft report submitted to Cherokee National Forest, Cleveland, TN.

Yarnell, Richard. 1974. "Intestinal Contents of the Salts Cave Mummy and Analysis of the Initial Salts Cave Flotation Series." In *Archeology of the Mammoth Cave Area*, ed. Patty Jo Watson, 109–13. New York: Academic Press.

15

Ceremonial Use of Caves and Rockshelters in Ohio

Olaf H. Prufer and Keith M. Prufer

Caves and rockshelters represent highly specialized environments within broader cultural systems. Their occupation can be found in Asia during the Middle Pleistocene of China, and throughout Europe and North America. Though such locales can provide protection from the vicissitudes of the environment, many have more enigmatic functions as loci of ritual. It should be noted that dark zones of deep caves both in the Americas and in the Old World were not actually "occupied" in the mundane sense of the word; they are too dark and could only be lit by artificial means. To our knowledge prehistoric humans never used cave dark zones for habitation, though secular activities related to exploration and general curiosity can certainly leave ambiguous materials markers. In these spaces, the human fascination with subterranean environs frequently enters the realms of ritual and religion. By contrast, rockshelters, overhangs, and cave entrances frequently served more mundane purposes of residence and shelter, though they too served as spaces for ritual activities. As far as Upper Paleolithic caves in Europe and prehistoric caves in Mesoamerica are concerned, ceremonial interpretations have been legion. However, globally speaking, there is obviously no interpretive scheme that can be uniformly applied.

As such, we will not generalize on cave and shelter utilization but we focus instead upon ceremonial activities traced in the prehistoric records of a specific well-researched region. From the outset, one thing is clear: while ceremonial activities of various kinds were carried out at many such sites that were occupied, our problem is how to interpret the often tantalizingly fragmentary evidence. For this discussion we must first broadly define the difference between real caves and mere rockshelters or overhangs. Real *caves* such as Mammoth Cave in Kentucky or Lascaux in France are caverns hidden in extensive limestone massifs and plunged in perpetual darkness; *rockshelters,* on the other hand, are more or less extensive overhangs with access to light. Cognitive distinctions may not always be clear; some rockshelters are entrances to caves, and some caves have no overhang.

THE PREHISTORIC EVIDENCE

The present chapter deals with test cases from Ohio, which abounds in rockshelters as well as a few poorly investigated caverns. Our sample consists of more than 500 shelters and two caves that have been investigated in modern times. All of these are known to us; most of them yielded no unambiguous evidence of ceremonial activities of any kind. We have restricted this brief discussion to no more than thirty-eight sites which were extensively excavated by Olaf Prufer and his associates over a period of some 50 years (figure 15.1). In addition, there are many more or less anecdotal and completely outdated nineteenth-century as well as

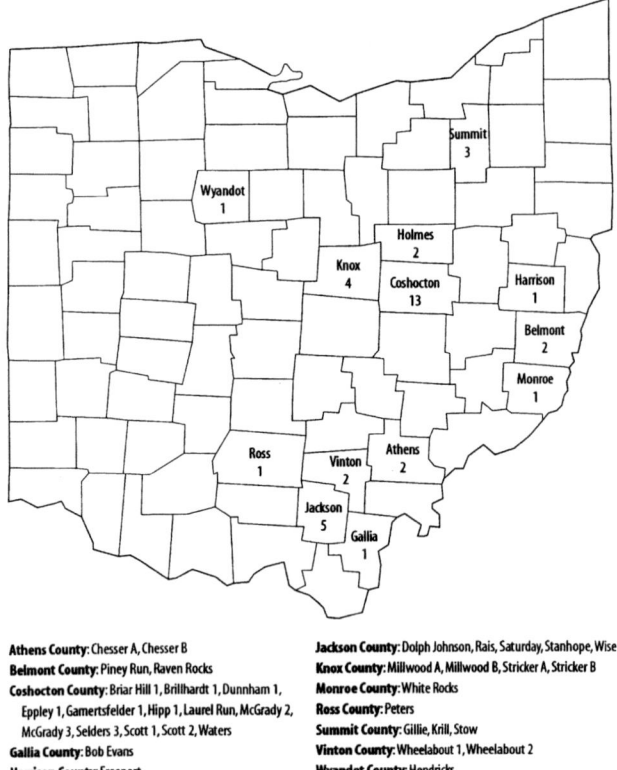

FIGURE 15.1 Distribution of Ohio caves and rockshelters.

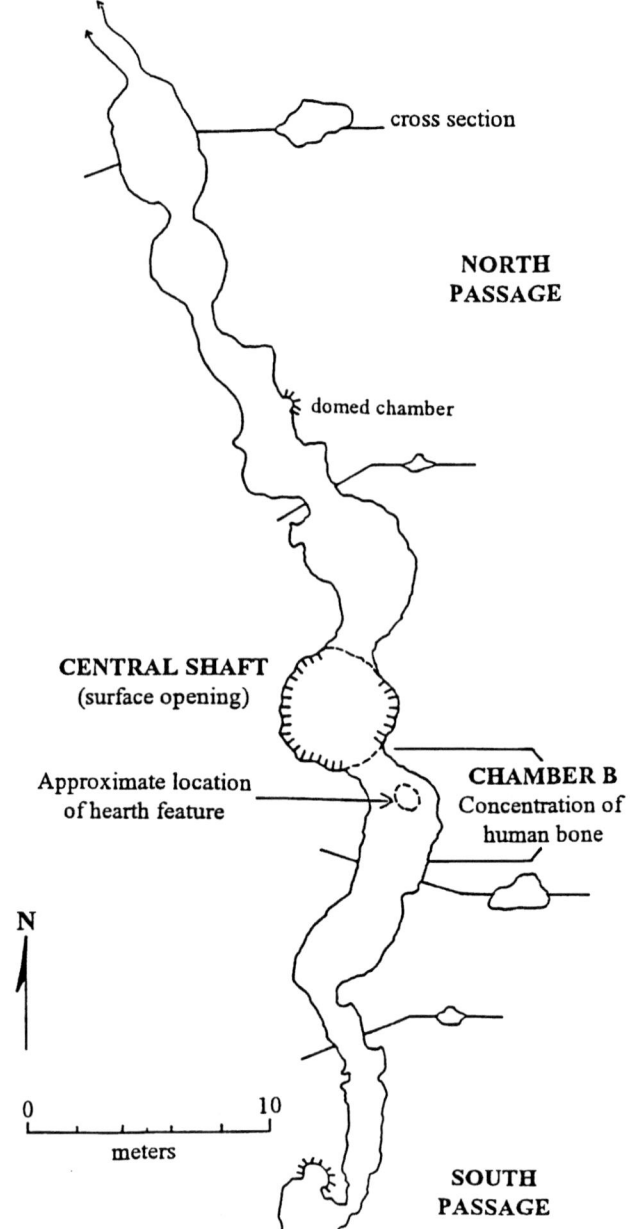

FIGURE 15.2 Floor Plan of Hendricks Cave.

later amateur reports of "cave explorations." These tend to be garbled, referring to, among other things, human mummies and textile remains associated with burials. Although some of these remains have been preserved, their nature is unclear, although we venture to guess that they represent some form of ceremonial activity. It should be noted that such cases are rare and that this vague "evidence" defies interpretation.

With one exception—Hendricks Cave—all localities represent a chronological range of domestic occupations spanning the period from Late Paleoindian to historic times. Winter and summer occupations dominate, and the data for intensive domestic shelter utilization tend to be massive. Artifacts and other debris often count in the tens of thousands. At first glance evidence of ceremonial activities appears to be rare.

Mortuary Practices

Most of the ceremonialism associated with the disposal of human remains in Ohio caves and shelters seems to date from Late Archaic times (3500 to 1500 BC). Several dubious reports by looters and nonprofessionals allude to late prehistoric mortuary activities, but these cannot be verified. In the Archaic sample we can distinguish two patterns of disposal of skeletal remains: isolated dismembered bodies, bundles if you will, and mass burials of fragmentary groups of individuals thrown more or less haphazardly into the archaeological deposits. These materials are well dated.

The most startling case derives from Hendricks Cave (Pedde and Prufer 2001), a deep cavern, actually a sinkhole in northwestern Ohio (figure 15.2). Here, in a dark chamber characterized by a fireplace, the floor was littered with 137 human skeletal elements representing at least fourteen individuals; some of the bones may have been altered (fig-

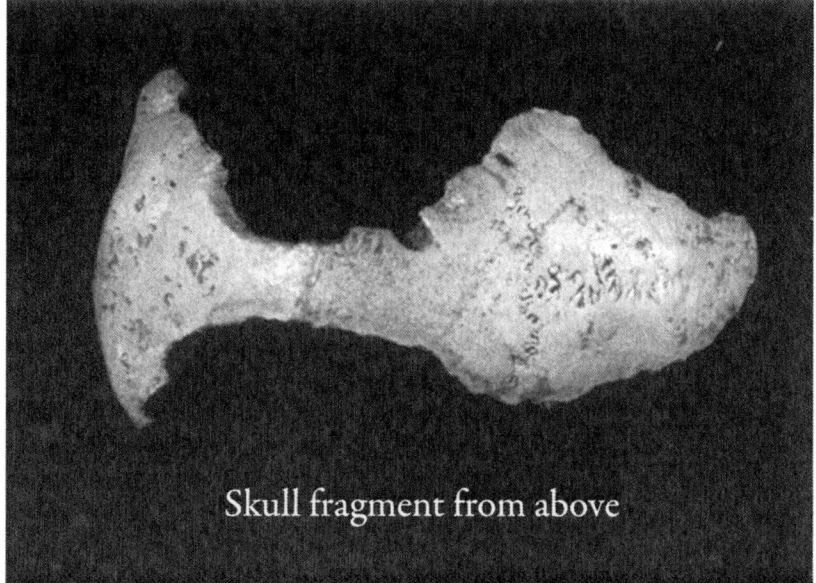
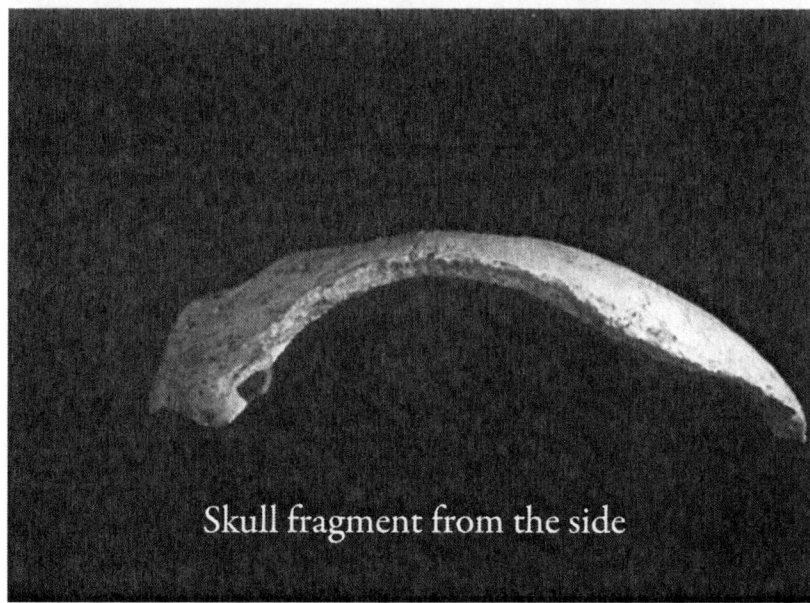

FIGURE 15.3 Hendricks Cave: (Left) possibly altered human cranial bone and (above) a Late Archaic Laurentian projectile point.

ure 15.3). The only artifact was a Late Archaic Laurentian projectile point in the fireplace that has been radiometrically dated to 2503 +/– 220 BC, placing this mortuary deposit squarely into the Late Archaic. Among the 137 skeletal elements, leg bones (31), cranial elements and mandibles (33), and ribs (22) dominate the assemblage. Adults and juveniles as well as males and females are represented. It should be stressed that Hendricks Cave, located some 25 feet below the surface of the land, is plunged in complete darkness and was only made accessible in 1964 when the landowner cleared the sinkhole that had plugged the entrance to this cave system.

A startlingly similar case of mass disposal of disarticulated, randomly strewn human skeletal remains was discovered at Stanhope Rockshelter in southern Ohio (Spurlock and Prufer 2002). This was an overhang, almost a small real cave, which had been extensively used through time from the Archaic right up to the end of prehistory. In the furthest recesses, well below the post-Archaic/Early Woodland occupation, the fragmented remains of at least eight skeletons were found distributed in the deposits sealed by later occupations (figure 15.4). The original tally sheets of the raw bone conducted in 1966 are no longer extant, and the bone material has disappeared. Suffice it to say that at least 100 skeletal elements were represented. Archaic artifacts abounded. The population included one infant, three children, one adolescent, and three adults; the three adults were females. The well-preserved cranium of

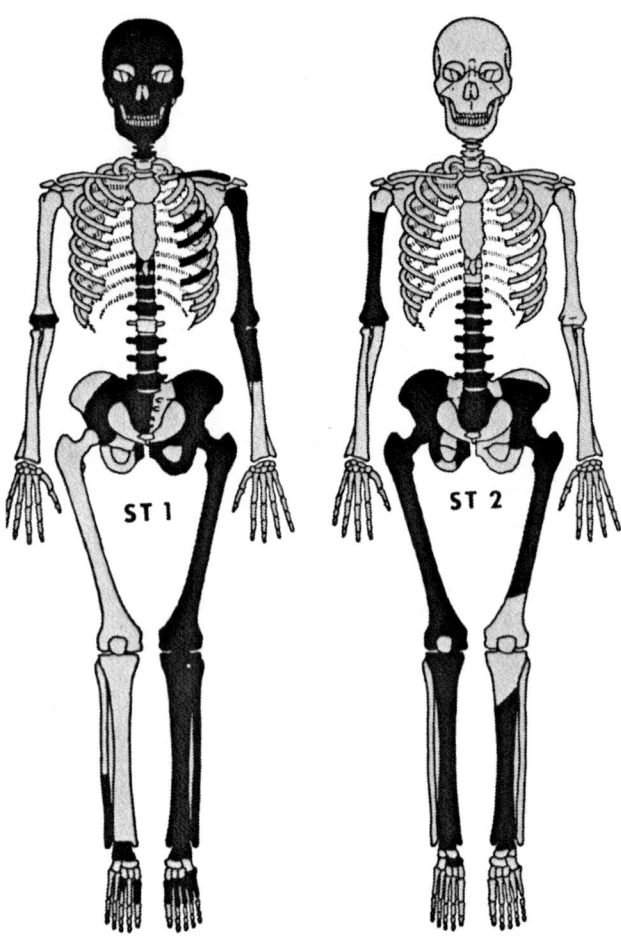

FIGURE 15.4 Stanhope Rockshelter: Completeness chart of two skeletons. Portions rendered in black represent the bones present.

one of these adults had been shot three times with deer-antler projectile points into the right temporal bone of the skull, obviously causing her death (figure 15.5).

Yet another case of mass disposal of human skeletal remains has been noted at Krill Cave in north-central Ohio (Prufer, Long, and Metzger 1989). As in the instances already cited, this rockshelter produced large numbers of randomly disposed human remains, including one especially placed fragmentary cranium strewn with red ocher and the deliberately and anatomically placed lower leg bones of two adults. There were no traces of any other skeletal elements that could be related to these individuals. The bones were also pigmented with ochre. Anatomically it is noteworthy that the majority of the bones from this mess consisted of hand and foot digits, whereas crania, ribs, vertebrae, and so forth were conspicuously rare. The total tally of skeletal elements is in excess of 150. The minimum number of individuals is estimated at fifteen, including three males and two females. The total breakdown amounts to four infants, four children, two adolescents, and five adults. As far as cultural placement is concerned, we know that Krill Cave is characterized by a rich Late Archaic assemblage radiocarbon dated to 1390 +/−65 BC and 2030 +/−130 BC. The original investigators of Krill Cave, Olaf Prufer and Robert Mensforth, opined that the curiously skewed distribution of skeletal elements may argue for either the massive off-site disposal of the human remains or cannibalism. Clearly such mass hecatombs appear to represent a specific Archaic pattern of ceremonial interment.

In addition, we know from personal experience of at least three rockshelters—Wheelabout, Rais, and Dolph Johnson—all in southern Ohio which, in addition to the usual domestic cultural debris, yielded fragmented and disarticulated bones of single individuals in what may be styled bundle burials. These remains were found in Archaic contexts and may represent a variation on the mass-burial theme already discussed. Five adults and one infant were present in the assemblage, but gender could be determined for only one male. We note that in none of the cases discussed is there any evidence of grave goods directly associated with the human remains. It is obvious that these Archaic burials represent a form of sacred ceremonialism that would appear to be quite complex and well patterned. The Archaic period generally lacks comparable examples of similar burials, making interpretation difficult beyond our observations above.

One of the more tantalizing bits of presumed ceremonial evidence comes from White Rocks, a large rockshelter in southeastern Ohio that yielded a very substantial archaeological assemblage including vast numbers of faunal remains (Ormerod 1983). During screening, this site revealed the presence of three ossicles of the inner ear; at minimum one individual is represented. Without screening, these tiny bones would not have been recovered by conventional excavation. What is interesting about this find is that there is no evidence of any burial at the site. Clearly these ossicles fell out of dry skulls that had been maintained by the inhabitants. One can speculate that the evidence represents the remnants of trophy skulls which were subsequently moved to some other location. Meager as this information is, it would seem to be powerful evidence for some ritual activity connected with the disposal of the dead. The age of this material is uncertain although it would appear to be of late vintage.

Caches

Ohio rockshelters occasionally have yielded evidence of deliberately placed ceremonial deposits of artifacts. A most important such deposit was recovered in 1955 by one of Olaf Prufer's associates at the Stow Rockshelter between

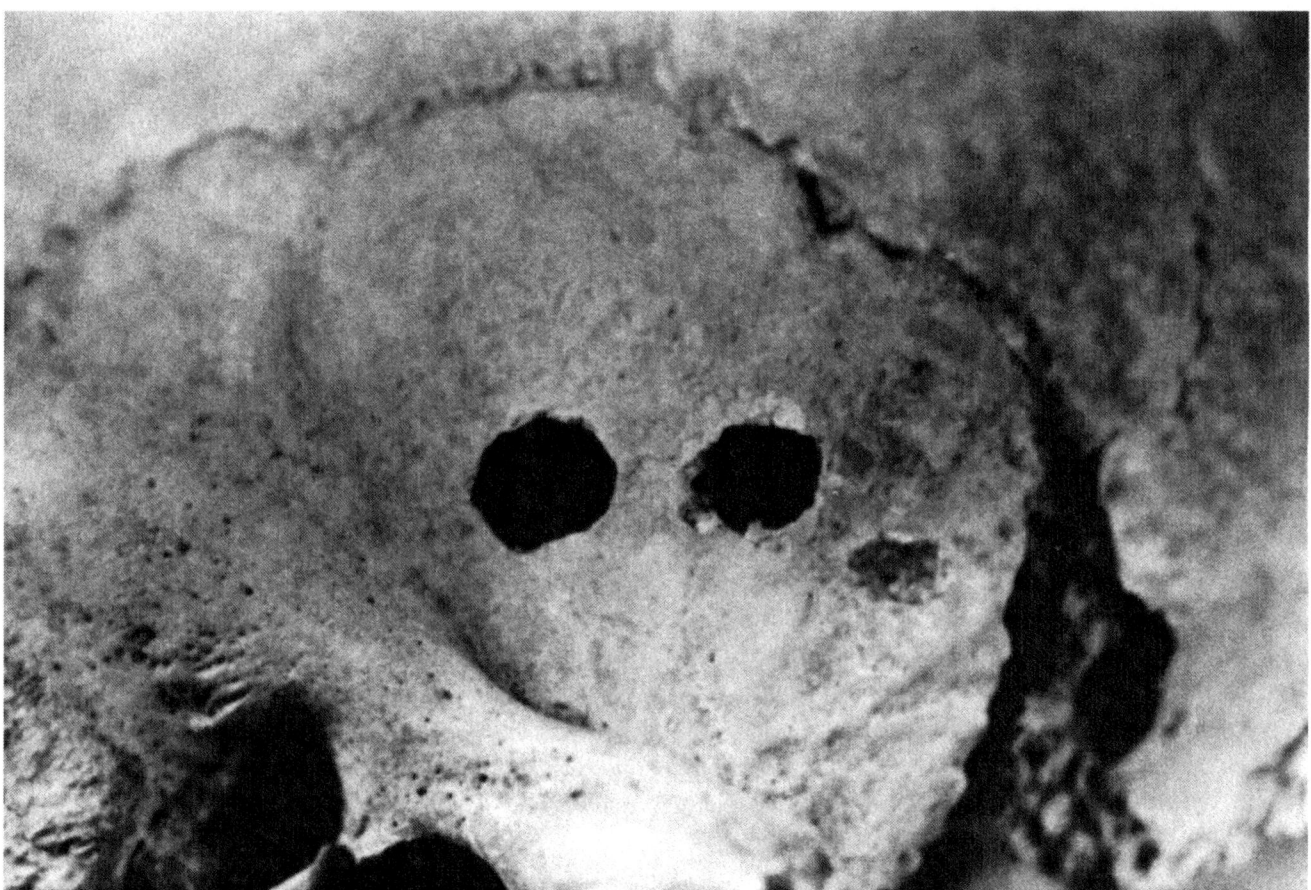

FIGURE 15.5 Stanhope Rockshelter: Female skull with three penetration impact wounds. The area shown is the temporal bone, above the zygomatic arch.

Akron and Cleveland (Pedde and Prufer 2001). This site, although in an urban area, had escaped the all-pervasive looting by amateurs. It contained primarily a very late prehistoric occupation with a sprinkling of Archaic lithics. The excavator, at a depth of 24 feet below the surface, discovered, under a large rock, a cache consisting of two discoidal stones (so-called chunkeys), a beautiful late prehistoric (skin-processing) beamer, a variety of bone tools, and a triangular projectile point. There is no question that this deposit was purposefully placed (figure 15.6). Perhaps it represents a medicine bundle of some sort. What is most interesting about this cache is that it is composed of artifacts foreign to the region. Discoidal stones are usually associated with the Southeastern United States, ranging rarely into extreme southern Ohio. They are commonly associated with Mississippian cultures. As far as northern Ohio and western Pennsylvania are concerned, we are reliably aware of only one other specimen, from northwestern Pennsylvania. Similarly, the perfect bone beamer does not fit easily into northern Ohio prehistoric assemblages. The remaining artifacts of the cache, although in perfect condition, are culturally indifferent except for the index fossil of the very late triangular projectile point. The meaning of this unique deposit is difficult to fathom, but it clearly represents a very special situation that, at a minimum, we would interpret as part of a private form of ceremonialism rather than the result of some collective group rite.

Another curious cache was recovered from Stricker Rocks in central Ohio (Reymond 1973). Here one of the component rockshelters of a complex system of adjacent and nearby overhangs yielded the usual sequence of domestic debris, including literally tens of thousands of artifacts mainly representing flint-manufacturing debitage. The usual cultural periods are well represented. The vast flint assemblage consists almost exclusively of locally derived Upper Mercer flint for which the area is famous. This material is easy to identify and can in many cases be pinpointed to specific quarries. Toward the entrance of the shelter a roughly circular pit was discovered. It contained some 1,600 densely packed flint chips and two deliberately

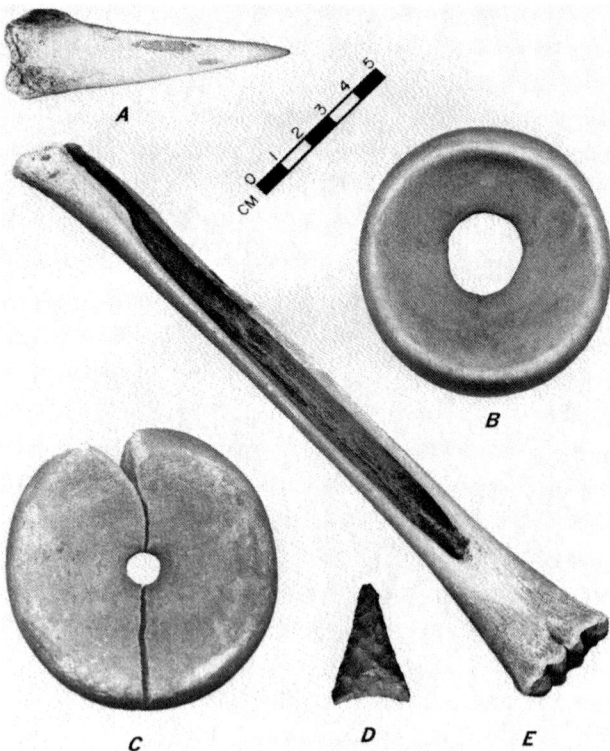

FIGURE 15.6 Stow Rockshelter cache.

FIGURE 15.7 Late Archaic cache from Rais Cave, showing Archaic Perkiomen projectile points made of light-colored exotic flint of unknown origin. (Ritchie 1961, 42–43.)

placed classic Early Woodland cache blades. What makes this deposit interesting is not only the deliberate placement of this material but that it consists of a distinctive brown raw material that is utterly foreign to the area. As in the case of the Stow Rockshelter caching of the discoidals, it would appear to have been the product of an intentional behavioral action not related to any known secular activity. The date of this material should be somewhere around 100 BC.

Another cache of flint tools was found in 1966 by O.C. Shane, deeply buried, at Rais Cave, a rockshelter in southern Ohio (Prufer Archives, file 32). They consist of more than twenty Transitional Archaic Perkiomen projectile points (Ritchie 1961, 42–43) made of some light-colored exotic flint of unknown origin (figure 15.7). The cache was strewn over an area of about 2 square feet. It may have been anciently disturbed by rodents. In the immediate vicinity a Transitional Archaic lugged, gray steatite bowl-rim sherd was recovered. Two roughly associated radiocarbon dates of 2805 +/– 100 BP or 855 BC (GX 1454), and 2970 +/– 220 BP or 1020 BC (GX 1247) should date this material.

Once again we return to Stanhope Cave in Southern Ohio. Here, during his major excavations in 1966, Olaf Prufer discovered at the very rear of this almost-cave a complete, upright, very large ceramic vessel (figure 15.8). It had been carefully placed into the sandy topsoil. The discovery of such a vessel in such a context is unique. Deep below its location the Stanhope disarticulated human skeletons were found. The vessel in question however is of very late vintage. It is typical of southern Ohio late prehistoric assemblages; it was found in the context of a radiocarbon assay of 1205 +/– 85 BP or AD 745 (GX-966). It is unclear whether this pot was associated with the domestic occupation of the site or whether its placement has some ceremonial significance.

Petroglyphs

In general, cave paintings so startlingly common in European deep caves do not tend to be preserved in rockshelters and overhangs in Ohio. Therefore the point of whether such paintings were made in the Eastern Woodlands of Ohio is moot. However, the issue of pecked petroglyphs is another matter. These enigmatic and often chaotic depictions of clearly mythological content abound in the Ohio Valley. A major inventory of such material was published some years ago by James Swauger (1974) of the Carnegie Museum in Pittsburgh. Not only did he list virtually all known instances but he also subjected them to a thematic analysis. Further he noted that caution is advised in attributing all pictographs on rock ledges to prehistoric times; many are modern fabrications sometimes imitating famous motifs copied from the real article. Genuine pictographs, such as that on Kelly's Island in Lake Erie, or Leo in southern Ohio, present a bewildering array of fantastic images and suggestive symbols clearly in the domain of mythology. It is curious to note that they most commonly are not on walls of caves or shelters but simply on freestanding rocks or rock ledges. Is there any evidence for the

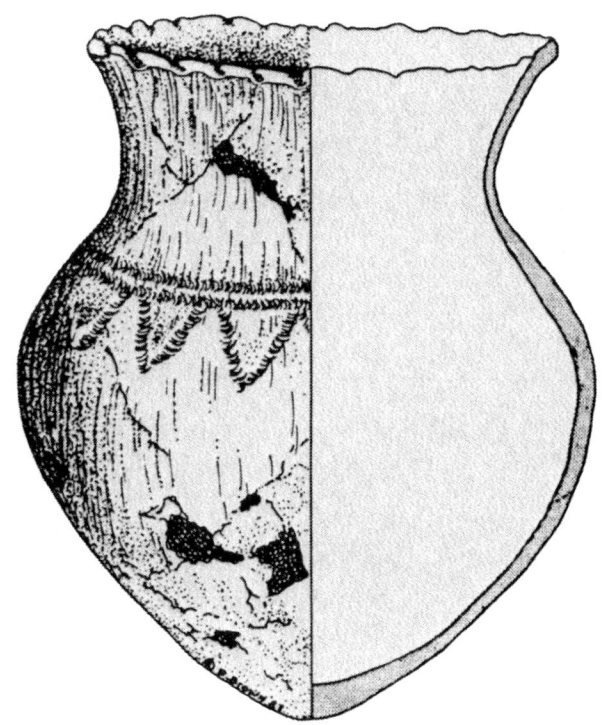

FIGURE 15.8 Ceramic vessel from Stanhope Rockshelter.

presence of such petroglyphs within our shelter sample? We know of only three instances, and the authenticity of one of these is in doubt.

One of the unambiguously genuine petroglyphs came to light on a sandstone rock wall at Gillie Rockshelter between Akron and Cleveland, Ohio (figure 15.9). This site was excavated in the 1970s and yielded a predominantly late prehistoric assemblage (Bernhardt 1973). Here, upon excavating layer by layer of the deposits, a brilliant petroglyph was discovered on the vertical wall of the shelter. Before excavation it had been completely covered by the accumulation of prehistoric debris. The image appears to represent a turkey foot, a motif found on many other petroglyphs in the state. Its meaning is elusive but we assume that it may be related to some form of hunting magic. Another case not too far from Gillie Rockshelter, likewise located along the stream known as Tinkers Creek, has had its authenticity called into doubt (Murphy 1973a). On stylistic grounds, we are reasonably certain that this image is genuine. It comes from a place romantically known as Poets Cave and was engraved by pecking on a large float block, or boulder, that had collapsed from the shelter roof. At the time of its discovery in the 1960s, it was covered by moss and lichen. It consists of two elements: a birdlike figure on the run—perhaps a turkey—and an amorphous circular amoeba-like design. Neither of these elements is out of line with genuine prehistoric petroglyphs. Here again we suggest that (if the petroglyph is genuine) we are confronted with some evidence of hunting magic.

A most interesting petroglyph from Tycoon Lake Rockshelter in Gallia County, located in southern Ohio, has been described and illustrated by Murphy (1979, 17–18). This find was pecked into the rockshelter wall. The small shelter yielded a predominantly Late Woodland occupation characterized by mixed shell- and limestone-tempered ceramics identical with those recovered from the nearby Bob Evans Rockshelter (Murphy 1973b), with a presumed date range between AD 720 and 1200, based on stylistic similarity to other dated materials. The petroglyph represents an outstretched human hand with a circular design in the palm. The picture measures about 10 inches in length. It clearly reflects one of the classic themes of the so-called Southeastern Ceremonial Complex as exemplified by the "hand-and-eye" motif frequently encountered in the art of late prehistoric assemblages often associated with the "Southern Cult" of the Southeastern United States (Fundabark and Foreman 1957). The equivalent cultural entity in Ohio would be Fort Ancient. This is clearly a sacred design.

More ambiguous and elusive as far as ritualism is concerned is the curious evidence of Raven Rocks in southeastern Ohio. This spectacular overhang, located in a deep, canyon-like, truly dark and spooky ravine (figure 15.10), produced a rather curious though meager tool assemblage

FIGURE 15.9 Gillie Rockshelter petroglyph, perhaps representing a turkey foot.

FIGURE 15.10 Raven Rocks, general view (circa 1892).

spanning the period between Late Archaic and late prehistoric times (Prufer 1981). The use of the site is also very curious. It yielded a very large faunal assemblage (some 20,000 bones) characterized by completely skewed distributions of bone elements. Typically what was expected to be found under normal circumstances was not there—we note the almost complete absence of deer crania. In contrast, however, was the presence of large numbers of small birds. It looks as if the Raven Rocks inhabitants performed some very strange practices at this site, presumably shortly before its abandonment. Certainly the overall evidence does not conform to the usual pattern of mere economic exploitation of rockshelters. Whether this can be indirectly related to ritual activities such as deer ceremonialism and/or the collection of bird feathers for some unknown purpose is unclear. In any event there is no direct evidence—only a suspicion that Raven Rocks may have been involved in something other than mere mundane domestic activities.

Finally, quite a few sites, such as White Rocks, yielded virtually identical freshwater shell pendants with marginal drill holes, though in no particular context (figure 15.11). Stylistically the pendants are very uniform and would seem to date from late prehistoric times. Whether they are mere ornaments or whether they reflect some sort of magic talismans is open to debate. (For examples see Mortine and Randles 1997; Ormerod 1983; Spurlock and Prufer 2002.)

HISTORIC EVIDENCE

It would be a mistake to dichotomize cave and rockshelter utilization into disconnected prehistoric and historic units of analysis. In fact, virtually every site examined for this chapter yielded potent evidence of recent historic activities. The earliest of these date back to about the Civil War. Why there is no reliable evidence for earlier historic visitations is not known. Most of the activities reflected by historic artifacts relate to hunting and camping activities. They are represented by large numbers of gun shells and food consumption (picnic) debris. On a less than licit economic level, quite a few remote shelters, such as Wheelabout in Vinton County, yielded remains of the products of alcoholic distilleries. However there is also potent evidence for undoubted ceremonial activities in the domains of both the sacred and the secular.

The historic information is important on three counts. First, and unlike Mesoamerican rockshelters where the preponderance of use is ritual, the same cannot always be said for the Eastern Woodlands. Second, understanding the material patterning of a range of cave and rockshelter uses can assist archaeologists in defining and interpreting archaeological contexts, and lead to better discussions of function. Third, dichotomies between prehistoric and his-

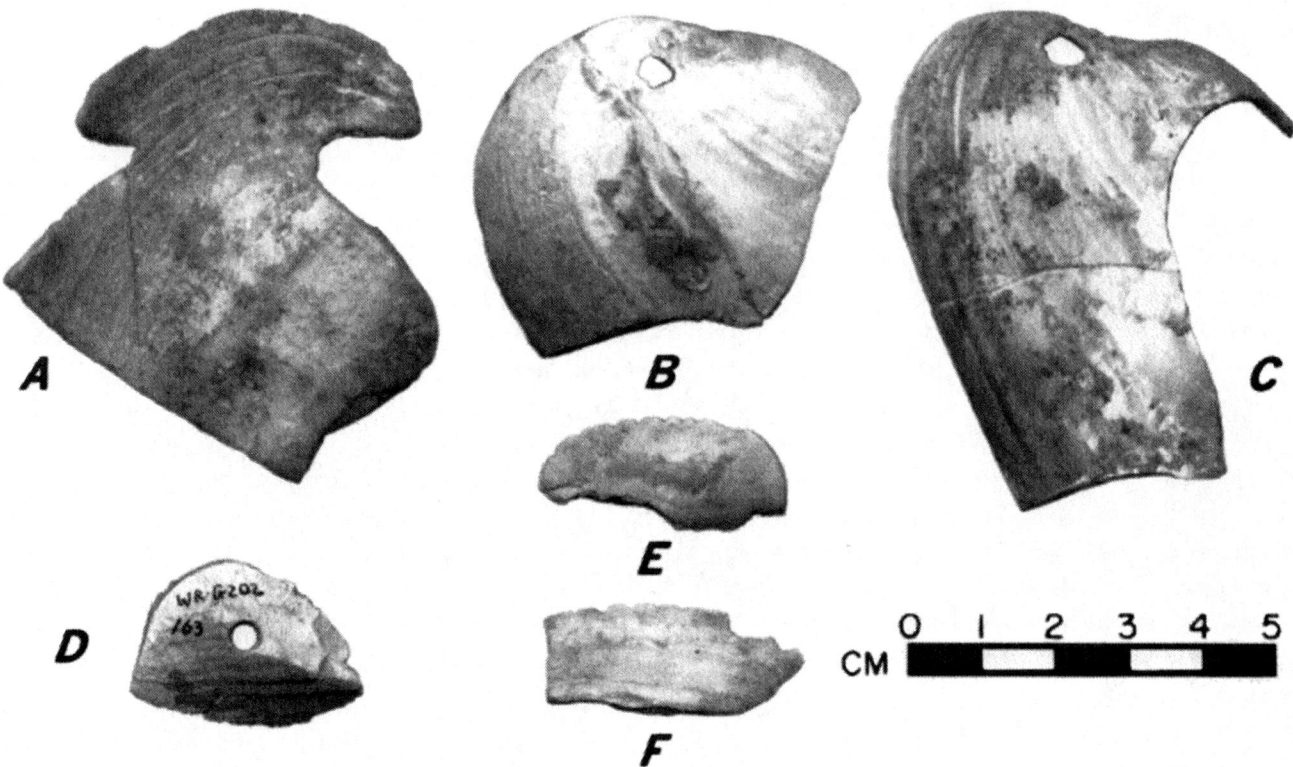

FIGURE 15.11 White Rocks shell pendants.

toric occupations can frequently be spurious. These sites were used by humans at all times.

In these Ohio cave and rockshelters, the historic uses of least significance are the numerous, often dated graffiti that adorn the shelter walls. They usually consist of either paired initials or names (as in "John loves Jane"). We suppose that at a pinch these scribblings could be considered part of secular rituals of trysting couples. Such graffiti, often deeply incised into the rocks are ubiquitous.

Of major significance is the use of certain rockshelters for clearly ritual activities. Thus, from Krill Cave, between Cleveland and Akron, we have a large photograph dating from the 1930s showing some fifty people at a formal feast crammed into the limited space of the shelter (figure 15.12; Prufer Archives, file 7). Upon research it became apparent that the site was used by descendents of soldiers of the Grand Army of the Republic of Civil War fame. The setting is quite formal; the participants all wore white dress. No females were present. Further inquiry revealed that such ritual meetings of the group took place periodically over many years. Clearly this is a case of social ritual. Interestingly, from an archaeological point of view, there is no material evidence that would permit us to infer such activities.

As far as modern sacred activities are concerned, the case of Gillie Rockshelter, again between Akron and Cleveland, is instructive. At the time of excavation in the early 1970s, the flat parapet of the rockshelter was used by a fundamentalist church for Sunday outdoor services. These services were actually advertised by the roadside and attracted numerous people; they appear to have included wedding ceremonies. These activities tended to interfere with the archaeological operations. Clearly the spot was chosen because of the immediately adjacent rockshelter which formed a backdrop to this sacred tableau.

In addition, during the 1960s and until 1972 many caves, particularly Peter's Cave in Ross County (Prufer and McKenzie 1966), were used for formal smoking of marijuana, extensively so, and with ceremony. Indeed one of the caves in the Peter's Cave system was known as the Dope Den, with all the necessary paraphernalia. The actors in these modern ceremonies included both crew members on the archaeological project and locals. These activities could not be traced archaeologically. Rumor also has it that during the Great Depression of the 1930s an old woman lived in Raven Rocks, Belmont County; some chronologically appropriate copper pennies and gnawed-over chicken bones seem to confirm these tales.

Other, perhaps quasi-ceremonial events include Boy Scout overnight excursions to rockshelters, often involving considerable travel distances from home base; the senior

FIGURE 15.12 Krill Cave, ceremonial feast of male descendents of veterans of the Grand Army of the Republic (ca. 1938).

author participated in such an event at Raven Rocks, Belmont County, in 1971. The distance from home in Cleveland, Ohio, to the shelter measures approximately 150 miles. Modern cave and shelter occupations that do not fit into the neat patterns of sacred and secular activities fall into the realm of tourism and public relations, often as part of state-sponsored projects. Thus, the spectacular shelters in the Appalachian Hocking Valley State Park, maintained by the government, are annually visited by hordes of tourists arriving by the busload. It is interesting to note that their activities leave virtually no archaeologically traceable remains, because the state authorities methodically and regularly clean up the detritus left behind by these visitors.

CONCLUSIONS

In summarizing this chapter we want to stress these points. First, it is overwhelmingly clear that the most important ritual activities relate to the disposal of the dead and are therefore in the realm of the sacred. Although not all of the mortuary data are Archaic in age, most appear to date from that period, involving fragmented and disarticulated bodies sometimes interred *en masse*. Deposits of caches and petroglyphs are rare. We do, however, have some limited evidence of late prehistoric ritual from the Rais and Stanhope caves.

On the whole, and in contrast to, say, the intensive ritual utilization of caves and shelters in Europe and Mesoamerica, the evidence for ceremonialism in Ohio is quite meager. However, the examples described clearly indicate that caves were used throughout prehistory for ceremonial purposes. It remains that most of the sites simply represent a wide range of ordinary economic activities, although one can only guess what kinds of ceremonial activities, untraceable in the archaeological record, may have occurred. While it remains possible that such data are irretrievable, additional research in this area will undoubtedly produce a wider body of evidence for the ritual use of Ohio caves and rockshelters.

Note: All references to the Prufer Archive files in the text refer to a formal archive maintained at the University of New Mexico by Keith Prufer.

REFERENCES CITED

Bernhardt, John. E. 1973. "Gillie Rockshelter: A Late Woodland Phase in Summit County, Ohio." MA thesis. Kent State University, Kent, OH.

Fundabark, Emma L., and Mary D.F. Foreman. 1957. *Sun Circles and Human Hands*. Luverne, AL: Emma Lila Fundabark.

Mortine, W. A., and D. Randles. 1997. "The Laurel Run Rockshelter." *Ohio Archaeologist* 47 (2): 4–7.

Murphy, James L. 1973a. "Daniel Boone's Button." *The Explorer*, Cleveland Museum of Natural History 16 (2): 12–7.

Murphy, James L. 1973b. "A Polissoir in Geauga County, Ohio." *Ohio Archaeologist* 2394: 21–22.

Murphy, James L. 1979. "A Probable 'Hand and Eye' Petroglyph, Gallia County, Ohio." *Ohio Archaeologist* 29 (30): 17–8.

Ormerod, Dana E. 1983. *White Rocks: A Woodland Rockshelter in Monroe County, Ohio*. Research Papers in Archaeology 4. Kent, OH: Kent State University.

Pedde, Sara E., and Olaf H. Prufer. 2001. "Hendricks Cave, Rockshelters, and Late Archaic Mortuary Practices in Ohio." In *Archaic Transitions in Ohio and Kentucky Prehistory*, ed. Olaf H. Prufer, Sara E. Pedde, and Richard S. Meindl, 328–54. Kent, OH: Kent State University Press.

Prufer, Olaf H. 1981. *Raven Rocks: A Specialized Late Woodland Occupation in Belmont County, Ohio*. Kent Research Papers in Archaeology 1. Kent, OH: Kent State University.

Prufer, Olaf H., Dana A. Long, and Donald J. Metzger. 1989. *Krill Cave: A Stratified Rockshelter in Summit County, Ohio*. Kent Research Papers in Archaeology 8. Kent, OH: Kent State University Press.

Prufer, Olaf.H., and Douglas H. McKenzie. 1966. "Peters Cave: Two Woodland Occupations in Ross County, Ohio." *Ohio Journal of Science* 66(3): 233–53.

Reymond, G. 1973. "Stricker Rocks: A Multicomponent Rockshelter Occupation." MA thesis, Kent State University, Kent, OH.

Ritchie, W. A. 1961. *A Typology and Nomenclature for New York Projectile Points*. Bulletin 384. Albany: New York State Museum and Science Service.

Spurlock, Linda B., and Olaf H. Prufer. 2002. "Stanhope Cave: A Multicomponent Site in Jackson County, Ohio." *Ohio Archaeologist* 52 (1): 4–16.

Swauger, J. L. 1974. *Rock Art of the Upper Ohio Valley*. Graz, Austria: Akademische Druck- und Verlagsanstalt.

16

The Ritual Use of Caves and Rockshelters in Ozark Prehistory

George Sabo III, Jerry E. Hilliard, and Jami J. Lockhart

Caves and rockshelters are common features of the Ozark uplands in the American mid-South (figure 16.1). The dry sediments of these sites contain abundant materials left by pre-Contact American Indians, including an extraordinary range of perishable items usually not found in other archaeological contexts. Scientific investigations began in the nineteenth century and continue to the present, but archaeologists have only recently considered the ritual use of these sites.

In this chapter we demonstrate the utility of a landscape approach in studies of prehistoric ritual spaces. We begin by briefly reviewing the history of Ozark cave and rockshelter investigations. Next, we summarize evidence pertaining to the ritual use of these sites. Finally, we provide an example of our current research, in which we reevaluate previous interpretations of rockshelters, placing these sites within a regional social and environmental context. We suggest that rockshelters with unique characteristics served as elite mortuary spaces.

A BRIEF HISTORY OF OZARK CAVE AND ROCKSHELTER INVESTIGATIONS

Ozark caves and rockshelters drew the attention of some our country's first professional archaeologists. For example, excavations by Charles Peabody and Warren K. Moorehead at Jacob's Cavern in Missouri sparked an early debate concerning the antiquity of American Indians in the region (Chapman 1948; Peabody and Moorehead 1904). Discoveries of perishable remains preserved in the dry sediments of these sites also attracted archaeologists working for prestigious eastern institutions, such as the Phillips Academy of Andover, Massachusetts, and the United States National Museum in Washington, DC. Much of their work was undertaken to acquire examples of basketry and other items for museum exhibits.

The first investigations directed toward producing a coherent understanding of regional culture history were conducted in the 1920s by Mark R. Harrington of the Museum of the American Indian-Heye Foundation in New York. Harrington excavated several dry rockshelters in the upper White River drainage of northwest Arkansas and southwest Missouri in 1922 and 1923, retrieving abundant and well-preserved materials. Harrington attributed most of the remains he excavated to a so-called Ozark Bluff-Dweller culture (Harrington 1960, 147). We now know that this "culture" actually represents the material residues of several discrete upland manifestations associated with more extensive settlement patterns (e.g., Brown 1984). Important for our purposes is the evidence Harrington provides concerning a specialized mortuary program at several of the sites he investigated.

Dismayed over the removal to eastern institutions of spectacular archaeological materials from Arkansas sites,

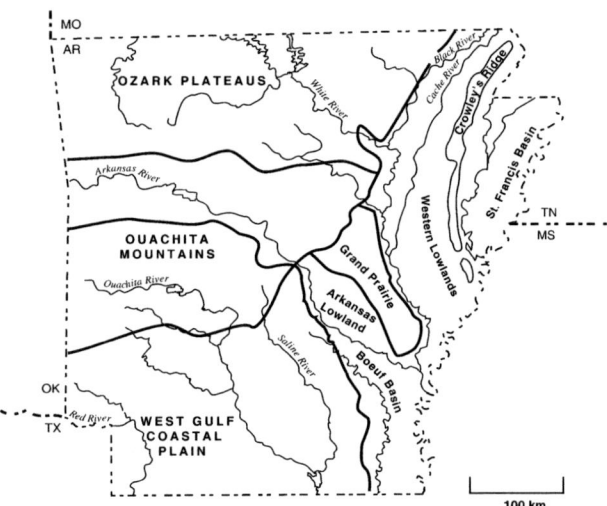

FIGURE 16.1 Physiographic regions in Arkansas.

Samuel C. Dellinger, then director of the University of Arkansas Museum, organized a large-scale effort to excavate additional dry rockshelter sites in 1928 (Dellinger 1928; see also Mainfort 2008). Field crews under his direction excavated eighty-five sites over a 7-year period. This work produced an extensive collection of artifacts and human skeletal remains still preserved in what is now the University of Arkansas Collection. Unfortunately, no site reports or major summaries of this work were produced, though Dellinger and other specialists with whom he collaborated issued reports on some of the more interesting materials, including ceramics (Dellinger and Dickinson 1942), baby cradles (Dellinger 1936), and human skeletal remains (Wakefield and Dellinger 1936, 1940; Wakefield, Dellinger, and Camp 1937). Melvin R. Gilmore studied preserved plant materials collected by Harrington and by Dellinger's crews to produce one of the first scientific studies of ancient Indian subsistence practices in eastern North America (Gilmore 1930).

The Dellinger excavations were a product of their time and the field techniques used then fall short of modern archaeological practices. Dellinger's crews were nonetheless meticulous in their record-keeping habits, and as a result, modern scholars have been able to extract much useful information from the collections. Important contributions to Ozark prehistory come from more recent studies of animal remains (Cleland 1965); cordage, netting, basketry, and fabrics (Horton 2010; Kuttruff 1988, 1993; Scholtz 1975); marine-shell beads (Hilliard and Harcourt 1997); and plant remains (Hilliard 1986; Fritz 1984, 1986, 1997; Fritz and Smith 1988).

Many additional studies of Ozark caves and rockshelters have been undertaken since the 1940s (see Sabo et al. 1988, 15–33, for a summary review). Major efforts at Rodgers Shelter (Kay 1982; Wood and McMillan 1976) and Graham Cave (Klippel 1971) in Missouri, along with work by the Arkansas Archeological Survey (e.g., Cande 2000; Guendling 2008; Raab 1976; Trubowitz 1980) produced major advances in our understanding of Ozark prehistory. Regional cultural sequences are now based on improved radiocarbon chronologies and we have a much better understanding of the evolution of human land-use practices and cultural adaptations to regional changes. These advances provide a useful context for modern efforts to reexamine older materials such as those collected by Harrington and Dellinger, and to address poorly studied topics, including the ritual use of Ozark caves and rockshelters.

CAVES, ROCKSHELTERS, AND THE ARCHAEOLOGY OF RITUAL

The Southeastern Ceremonial Complex (SECC) is a rather unsatisfactory term that has been used to refer to a set of artistic motifs that occur on decorated ceramic, embossed copper, engraved shell, and carved-stone objects found at sites across eastern North America but that are largely concentrated at the Etowah site in Georgia, Moundville in Alabama, the Lake Jackson site in Florida, and the Spiro site in Oklahoma (Galloway 1989; King 2007). Archaeologists now believe that this distinctive artistic tradition developed between AD 900 and 1000 in the Cahokia area of the American Bottoms, from which it spread to adjacent regions, where local stylistic variations emerged during subsequent centuries (Brown 2004, 2007; Brown and Kelly 2000). The current view held by many regional specialists is that SECC imagery reflects myths and associated beliefs concerning the spirit realm embraced by Mississippi period (AD 900–1500) communities across eastern North America (Knight 2006; Knight, Brown, and Lankford 2001).

The discovery in 1979 of SECC imagery incised into clay deposits deep inside Mud Glyph Cave in Tennessee focused new attention on caves and their dark zones as sites where ancient ritual activities were conducted (Faulkner 1986). The antiquity of cave rituals has since been pushed back into the Archaic era (Simek, Franklin, and Sherwood 1998), and associations at several Southeastern caves connect the production of art (in the form of pictographs, petroglyphs, and mud glyphs) with contemporaneous mortuary activities (Simek, Cressler, and Pope 2004). Pictographs and petroglyphs depicting SECC motifs also occur at the Gottschall Rockshelter in Wisconsin (Salzer and Rajnovich 2001) and at several rockshelters in Arkansas (Sabo and Sabo 2005) and Missouri (Diaz-Granados and Duncan 2000; Diaz-Granados et al. 2001).

These images have been interpreted as representations of ancient mythologies and cosmological traditions. Clarion calls for the archaeological study of ancient religion in eastern North America (Brown 1997; Hall 1997) are also stimulating new efforts to investigate associated ritual uses of caves and rockshelters.

RITUAL USES OF OZARK CAVES AND ROCKSHELTERS

Several lines of evidence reflect the performance of ritual activities in Ozark caves and rockshelters. First, many of these sites contain rock art in the form of pictographs and petroglyphs. As indicated previously, some of this art represents SECC iconography, and much of it appears to be associated with the performance of ritual activities that express the mythological and cosmological beliefs of local Mississippian communities (Diaz-Granados and Duncan 2000, 214–40; Duncan and Diaz-Granados 2001).

Second, there is much evidence of mortuary rituals conducted in Ozark rockshelters. The best evidence comes from sites investigated by Harrington and Dellinger. We now understand that many of the burials they excavated reflect a specialized mortuary program dated to the Mississippi period. Below we provide a reexamination of some of this evidence.

A third line of evidence may be represented by the skeletal remains of American Indians who died exploring cave dark zones in Arkansas. To date we do not have an accurate inventory of such remains, which by themselves do not specifically reflect ritual activity. The awareness of dark zones indicated by these remains, however, suggests that further study of the ancient use of caves and their dark zones may yield additional information concerning the performance of ritual activities.

A LANDSCAPE APPROACH TO THE STUDY OF CAVE AND ROCKSHELTER RITUALS

Our approach to the archaeology of ritual begins with the recognition that material evidence for ritual activities is expressed at several levels of spatial resolution, ranging from specific features within sites to interconnections among sites distributed across localities and regions. Our ability to recognize and interpret this evidence is enhanced when we work back and forth across these different levels of spatial resolution. For example, we may be able to advance our understanding of rituals performed at residential or special-purpose sites if we examine relationships connecting those sites to community ceremonial centers where different but related rituals took place. In the same way, our understanding of the ritual functions of ceremonial centers may be advanced through comparison with evidence for household rituals and rituals performed at special-purpose sites. Finally, we believe that it is necessary to examine ritual places within the context of encompassing cultural landscapes that include other site types along with natural features associated with constructed elements (Bradley 2000). The underlying premise of this approach is that rituals are often part of larger activity complexes (that may include nonritual elements) connecting separate places and temporal phases in the ongoing life of the community (Bell 1997, 171).

In keeping with this perspective, our study of the ritual use of Ozark caves and rockshelters includes analysis at three levels of spatial resolution. At the broadest or "macro" level, we examine the environmental relationships of contemporaneous sites comprising discrete cultural landscapes. Using Geographic Information System (GIS) approaches, we construct models that identify natural features associated with the locations of different site types. These models can be used to study the influence of natural features as well as cultural factors in site-location choices. At the "meso" level, our focus shifts to specific localities where demonstrable relationships among sites can be interpreted in relation to specific ritual complexes. Finally, at the "micro" level, we examine in greater detail the evidence of ritual activities performed at specific sites.

AN ARKANSAS EXAMPLE

The Arkansas Archaeological Survey's Automated Management of Archeological Site Data in Arkansas (AMASDA) database system provides access to information concerning approximately 45,000 documented archaeological sites in Arkansas (Hilliard and Riggs 2000). With up to 150 data fields for each site, the database can be accessed in a variety of ways. We began this study by querying the database for six Mississippian site types (caves, rockshelters, rockshelters with rock art, rockshelters with burials, mounds, and residential sites) possessing high-accuracy location coordinates within a twenty-county study area comprising the Ozarks and adjacent Arkansas River Valley (table 16.1). We reviewed the original report forms for each site and corrected erroneous data entries prior to our analysis. We also point out that two of our site types—mound centers and rockshelters with burials—are represented by comparatively few examples, so interpretation of statistical measures for these sites must proceed with caution.

Macro Level Analysis

GIS data layers for our study area were created for ten environmental variables (Table 16.2). The sources of

TABLE 16.1 Mississippian site lists used in this study.

Mississippian Site Types	Number of Sites
Caves	148
Rockshelters	1,169
Rockshelters with art	116
Rockshelters with burials	27
Mound centers	32
Residential sites (>100 square meters)	647

TABLE 16.2 Environmental-data layers created for GIS analysis.

GIS Data Layer	Source	Scale/Resolution
Elevation	USGS NED	30 meters
Slope	USGS NED derived	30 meters
Aspect	USGS NED derived	30 meters
GAP vegetation	CAST, Thematic Mapper	30 meters
National landcover data	MRLC Consortium, TM	30 meters
Soils	NRCS STATSGO	1:250,000/100m
Watersheds	NRCS 8-digit Hydro. Basins	100m
Small-scale hydrography	USGS State of Arkansas	1:500,000/250m
Geology	USGS State of Arkansas	1:500,000/250m
Physiographic subdivisions	USGS State of Arkansas	1:500,000/250m

US Geological Survey (USGS)
Center for Advanced Spatial Technologies (CAST)
National Elevation Dataset (NED)
Multi-Resolution Land Characteristics (MRLC)
Natural Resources Conservation Service (NRCS)
State Soil Geographic Database (STATSGO)

information for these data layers are summarized in the following paragraphs.

Arkansas is divided into eight physiographic subdivisions. Subdivision boundaries for this data layer were digitized from the 1:500,000-scale United States Geological Survey (USGS) State of Arkansas base map. Geological unit boundaries were digitized from the 1:500,000-scale Geologic Map of Arkansas (GMA) prepared by the USGS and the Arkansas Geological Commission. The GMA is adapted from the USGS State of Arkansas base map. These maps employ the same Lambert conformal conic projection used for USGS 7.5-minute quadrangles on which archaeological site locations are plotted. Soils data are from the Soil Conservation Service (SCS) State Soil Geographic Database (STATSGO), compiled by generalizing classifications on more detailed soil-survey maps. The vegetation-data layer is derived from a digital classification of Landsat Thematic Mapper (TM) satellite imagery. National Land Cover Data (NLCD) are also derived from Landsat TM imagery. This data set consists of twenty-one categories projected in Albers conic equal area at a 30-meter horizontal resolution. The resulting data layer is an unsupervised classification in which similar spectral signatures are clustered.

Elevation data are from the USGS National Elevation Database (NED), UTM Zone 15 North. This digital elevation model (DEM) has a horizontal resolution of 30 meters and a vertical resolution of 1 meter within each 30-meter cell. Elevations in our study area range from 49 to 837 meters above mean sea level (amsl) and are divided into five equivalent elevation ranges for purposes of analysis. The slope data set is derived from the elevation-data layer and shares the same projection, datum, and resolution. For this analysis, the slope data are categorized into nine 5-degree classes. Aspect data are also derived from the elevation-data layer, and are categorized into eight 45-degree increments plus a "no aspect" category for flat terrain.

Watersheds are derived from the National Resources Conservation Service (NRCS) Watershed Boundary Dataset for Arkansas. Hydrography for primary streams was digitized from the USGS 1:500,000-scale State of Arkansas base map. The distance-to-streams data set was constructed from the hydrography-data layer using 300-meter buffer increments. The 7.5-minute USGS quadrangles on which archaeological site locations are plotted were produced using the 1927 North American datum (NAD27), so we converted location coordinates for each of our data layers to that datum.

These environmental-data layers were then used to produce site-occurrence reports for each site type, yielding a total of sixty reports (table 16.3). High chi-square values indicate potentially significant associations (positive or negative) between sites and specific properties of their locations. For this study, we adopted a conservative approach and examined site associations that included at least ten sites with double-digit chi-square scores. Here is what these reports show:

Residential sites and mound centers exhibit high positive associations with flat terrain (no aspect; 0–5 percent slopes), alluvial geological settings that sustain agriculturally productive soils, and location in the larger river valleys. Both site types are also highly associated with modern agricultural vegetation. Residential sites generally occur within 1,200 meters of a stream or river; mound centers are typically located less than 300 meters distant. These results are not surprising, even considering the low frequency of mound centers in our sample.

Rockshelters show significant associations with west-facing aspects, steeper terrain (11–35 percent slopes), and

TABLE 16.3 Example site-occurrence table, aspect for rockshelter sites with art. Classes with more than ten (actual) sites and double-digit chi-square scores are boldfaced.

Aspect Increment	% cover	Expected Sites	Actual Sites	Chi Square	Degrees of Freedom
No aspect	35.3	40.9	7	28.113	1
1–45 degrees	7.5	8.7	4	2.533	1
46–90	8.1	9.3	0	9.347	1
91–135	8.5	9.8	2	6.255	1
136–180	7.6	8.8	9	0.003	1
181–225	7.6	8.8	14	3.004	1
226–270	**8.5**	**9.8**	**28**	**33.684**	**1**
271–315	**9.0**	**10.4**	**37**	**67.916**	**1**
316–360	8.0	9.3	15	3.503	1
Totals	100.0	116.0	116	154.359	8

distance-to-stream measures of less than 900 meters. There are also high-positive associations with limestone, sandstone, and shale geological units supporting unproductive upland soils. These locations also show significant association with modern forest land cover and vegetation.

Rockshelters containing rock art share some properties with undecorated rockshelters, including aspect, slope, soils, and modern land cover, but there are some interesting differences as well. For one, the rock-art sites generally occur farther away from water. This is the result of a pattern we observe in the field where many of these sites are located in out-of-the-way places that are more sheltered from view and harder to reach than other sites. Small, isolated shelters may have been used for private rituals such as vision quests. This hypothesis gains support from the fact that we seldom find habitation debris at these sites. There is also a significant association with sandstone geological units, in keeping with observed preferences for rock-art decoration of durable sandstone surfaces in contrast to more fractious limestone exposures.

Rockshelters with burials (the other site type, in addition to mound centers, with a low frequency of cases) exhibit what might be a significant association with the distance-to-water category of less than 300 meters. One other high correlation is with very steep terrain (16–35% slope values). In other words, these sites are noteworthy for their location on visually prominent landforms lying close to major streams. Finally, cave sites show high positive associations with west-facing aspects, distance-to-stream values of less than 300 meters, and steep slope values (16–35%).

To facilitate the visualization of these patterns, each GIS-data layer was reclassed to produce a binary "environmental similarity" data layer. We assigned a score of "1" to each unique combination of environmental variable and site type (e.g., aspect and rockshelter) where ten or more sites had double-digit chi-square scores. Then we combined the derived-data layers for each site type (that is, we added up the numbers—one or zero—assigned to each grid cell for all ten variables) to produce a general environmental similarity model for that site type. The resulting models display the range of low to high coincidences between site types and environmental variables. The environmental similarity models for each site type are shown in figure 16.2.

The rockshelter model exhibits the most striking pattern, in which locations (grid cells) possessing very high aggregate similarity scores occur across much of the interior Ozark region (i.e., Springfield Plateau physiographic subdivision). Interestingly, locations possessing high aggregate similarity scores for residential sites and, to a slightly lesser degree, mound centers, are distributed *around* this primary rockshelter area. This is the result of concentrations of residential sites and mound centers in major river valleys (especially the Arkansas, White, and Illinois rivers) surrounding the interior Ozark region. Mississippian communities located in those surrounding river valleys used rockshelters (and other sites) in the interior Ozark uplands for a variety of ritual and nonritual purposes.

What about caves and rockshelters containing rock art and burials? The environmental similarity models for these sites show no concentrations of grid cells with high scores. On the basis of our field surveys of these sites, we suggest that this "negative" pattern is a reflection of a pronounced tendency for these sites to occur at specific and often widely separated locations possessing distinctive features, including vibrant rock colors, visually striking geological formations, special acoustical properties, and spectacular views of the surrounding terrain. Such features are not captured in standard environmental-data layers such as the ones used to produce these models. In other words, these sites—at which much of our evidence for ritual activities occurs—tend to be located in "special" places that possess unique combinations of features.

Meso Level Analysis

Several localities within our study area were occupied by Mississippian communities whose land-use patterns produced distinctive cultural landscapes. These community landscapes were organized around mound centers with associated residential sites that were distributed along river valleys where fertile soils supported limited agricultural production. Ozark mound centers were mostly used as vacant civic-ceremonial centers, that is, as special places where people gathered for the performance of periodic ceremonies. Mortuary rituals scheduled in relation to a

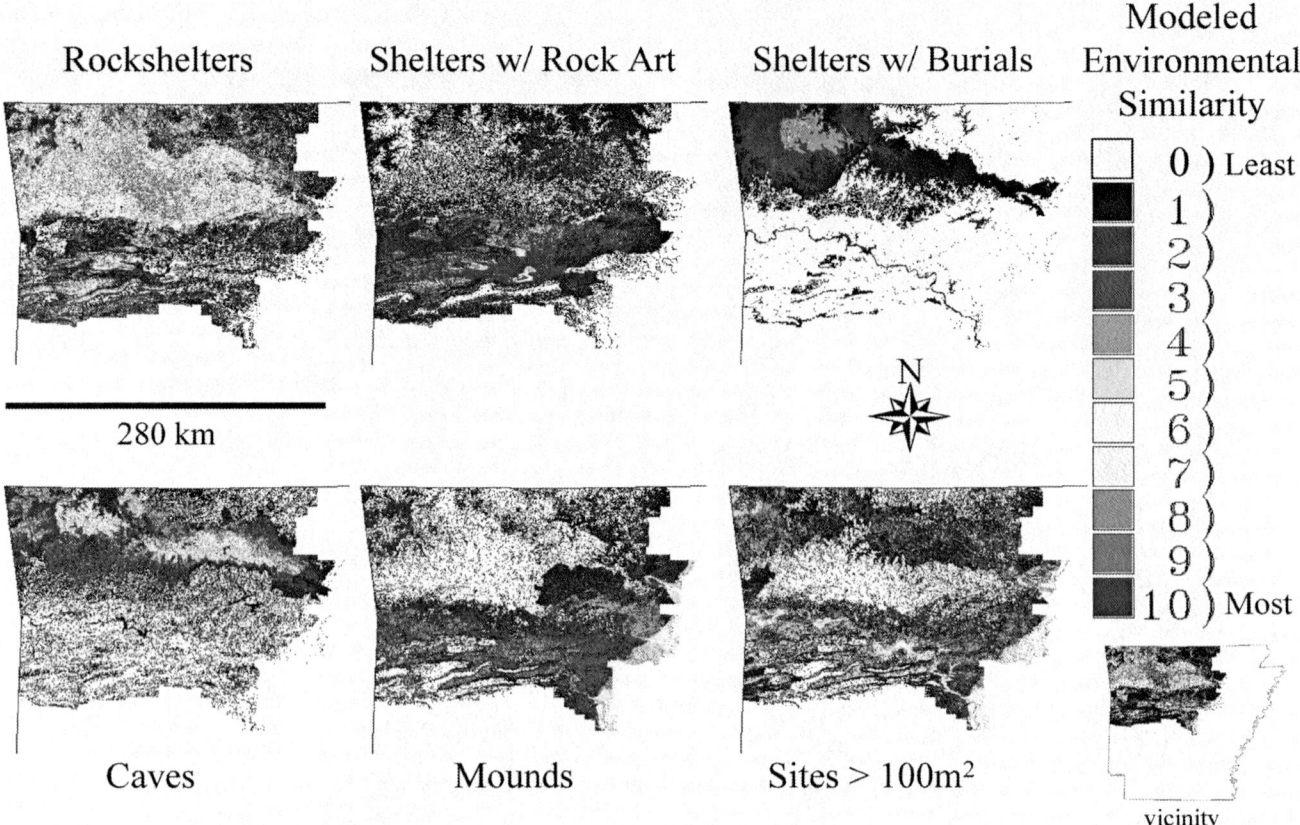

FIGURE 16.2 Environmental similarity models for six archaeological site types.

seasonal calendar were one of the major ceremonial functions served by these sites. These landscapes also included special-purpose sites located in a wide variety of environmental settings. Caves and rockshelters were used for a variety of purposes, including temporary habitation, storage of nut and grain crops, and burial of the dead (Sabo et al. 1988, 97).

Our best information on the ritual organization of these communities comes from excavations at several mound sites located in the Grand (Harlan, Norman), Illinois (Goforth-Saindon), and White (Huntsville) river basins in northwest Arkansas and northeastern Oklahoma. These sites—all satellites of the Spiro site—produced evidence of a distinctive mortuary pattern, radiocarbon dated to calibrated AD 1000–1300, involving the ritual destruction and rebuilding of "Harlan-style" charnel houses built on platform mounds. Human remains initially stored in the charnel houses were reinterred in separate, accretional burial mounds (Kay and Sabo 2006).

Harlan-style charnel houses exhibit several distinguishing features. They are square structures with walls of small-diameter upright posts and large interior posts that supported grass-thatched roofs. In contrast to similar residential structures, the charnel houses lack interior hearths but retain evidence of multiple benches constructed to support human remains. Another distinctive feature of these structures is a long, narrow entryway (which residential structures do not possess) that faces the southwest and is oriented to the winter solstice sunset. Residential structures, in contrast, are differentially oriented in relation to seasonal sunlight patterns for purposes of maintaining comfortable interior conditions (Kay and Sabo 2006, 35–38).

The mortuary ritual involving these structures began with intentional burning of earlier structures, often built on a natural rise that formed the core for subsequent platform-mound construction. The function of these initial structures, along with evidence bearing on the presence or absence of entryways, was destroyed by the manner in which they were burned. Next, a new mantle of sediments was added to form a low platform mound. The Harlan-style charnel house was then constructed in a shallow pit excavated into the platform-mound surface. After service as a mortuary storage facility, its contents of human remains and associated funerary offerings were removed and reburied in nearby accretional burial mounds that also grew in size as additional sets of remains were added. The emptied charnel-house interior was then cleaned and, if necessary, repairs were made to the clay-plastered floors. The entryways were blocked with a small clay pedestal and in most cases a post was set into the center of the pedestal to block entrance into (or exit from) the interior. The structure was then burned and the remains were covered over with a new layer of sediments. Another structure—nearly identical in construction, position, and orientation—was then erected on the new mound surface or within a newly excavated pit and the mortuary program was repeated. The nature of the funerary offerings, which include marine-shell beads and such examples of SECC sacra as a copper long-nose god mask (Bell 1972, plate 10a), indicates that this program was associated with the deaths of elite members of the local communities (Bell 1972, 1984).

Kay and Sabo interpret this mortuary program in relation to written accounts of beliefs concerning the afterlife held by Caddoan-speaking Hasinai, Wichita, and Pawnee groups who, during the historic era, occupied the Plains region immediately west of our study area (Kay and Sabo 2006, 39–42). In brief, these groups believed that the souls of the dead traveled to the west, where they gathered together to await passage to a spirit realm located in the southern or southwestern sky (Hatcher 1927, 162; cf. Lankford 2007). Fire plays an important role in this belief system. Fire in its controlled state is a symbol of the continuity of life, whereas uncontrolled or accidental fires (such as an accidental house burning) were associated with death. Smoke issuing from ceremonial fires and dissipating into the air is regarded as an *axis mundi* connecting the world of the living with the spiritual realm of the sky. Following this logic, smoke from a burning charnel house can be interpreted as a way of transporting the souls of the dead to the spirit realm.

Formal elements of this mortuary program, including directional orientation, periodic gathering of the remains of the dead for ritual treatment aimed at assisting transportation to the spiritual realm, and the use of fire, have parallels in a different but possibly related mortuary program that can be reconstructed, if only partly, from evidence produced by the Harrington and Dellinger rockshelter excavations.

Micro level Analysis

Many Ozark rockshelters contain one or two burials. These display a wide range of mortuary treatments presumably corresponding to status variations and the location, timing, and circumstances of death. Associated habitation debris (including living surfaces with associated features and middens) suggests these burials were an element of more-extensive site usage. Fewer sites contain multiple burials in larger numbers, and these are noteworthy for their much closer adherence to a distinctive mortuary program evidently restricted to local elites. The sites at which these multiple burials occur sometimes had been occupied previously but it appears that such occupation ceased when the sites were converted to use as mortuary facilities. These sites also feature visually distinctive qualities and they are all located very close to—indeed, directly overlooking—major Ozark waterways. Many of these sites are also decorated with rock art.

Five rockshelters with multiple burials located along a segment of the upper White River in northwest Arkansas, all excavated by Harrington or by Dellinger's crews, provide evidence of Mississippian mortuary practices that can be compared with the previously discussed mound centers (Harrington 1960; Dellinger Field Books, University of Arkansas Museum).

The first site, 3WA4, is a long, south-facing, sheltered ledge with an area of desiccated sediments extending from the rear wall to a line of fallen slabs. Here, eighteen burials and a large number of artifacts (most of uncertain association with the burials) were excavated. Radiocarbon assays obtained for preserved organic materials associated with these burials produced dates in the calibrated AD 1000–1300 range (Fritz 1986, 74–75).

The excavator's field notes indicate that seventeen of the burials were single interments; there were also multiple interments containing two and four individuals. Infants, juveniles, and adults are represented. Fourteen of the burials are described as cremations based on the extent to which the bones were burned. Excavators also note considerable amounts of ash and partially burned wood, suggesting in situ cremation. A few fragments of woven fabric and basketry used to cover the burials escaped consumption by fire, along with several bone and shell beads. Two noncremated burials were oriented toward the west. Finally, there was one rather elaborate burial in which two individuals wearing beads were interred on a cedar-pole framework. These individuals had been covered with woven fabric and cane matting.

Harrington excavated three burials at 3BE1, including one—of an adult male and a female plus a juvenile—in a pit that had been lined with a thick layer of grass, a feather robe, and finally a large deerskin, on which the bodies had been laid (Harrington 1960, 76). Feathered robes are frequently depicted in SECC motifs associated with the well-known "Birdman" theme, and a carved-stone Birdman statue wearing a feathered robe was also found at the Spiro site. Feathered robes were among the most revered symbols of elite status in Mississippian communities (Kuttruff 1993).

Dellinger's crews excavated seventeen adult, juvenile, and infant burials at 3BE6. The burials were found in small niches or crevices at the rear of the shelter, and some crevices contained multiple, overlapping burials, suggesting sequential interment. Twelve burials were cremated. At least two burials were laid to rest on cedar poles. Fabric and cane mat fragments were preserved in several burials, and one individual had been wrapped in a feathered robe. Eight burials were oriented toward the west. Beads manufactured from the columella and walls of marine whelk shells were found with some of these burials (Hilliard and Harcourt 1997). Radiocarbon assays on organic materials associated with these burials produced dates in the calibrated AD 900–1300 range (Fritz 1986, 74–75).

Another set of multiple burials was excavated by Harrington and by Dillinger's crews at 3BE18, consisting of a series of closely spaced, southwest-facing rockshelters. Radiocarbon assays on maygrass stems from one of the shelters yielded a date range of calibrated AD 631–813 (Late Woodland period), but many of the artifacts found with excavated burials suggest a Mississippian temporal placement (Fritz 1986, 74–75).

Harrington identified a burial area in the rear portion of one of the shelters behind a deposit of "great fallen slabs." Here, seven individuals were interred, including two adults, four children, and two infants. At least one of the children had been cremated. One infant was covered by a textile wrap and wore a bead necklace. The other infant was buried in a woven-cane cradle (Harrington 1960, 28–31). The spatial association of these burials is similar to that of the crevice burials at 3BE6, once again suggesting sequential, accumulative burial processing.

The last site in this series, 3BE189, possessed a noteworthy feature that Harrington described in the following words: "a cold spring issues from the bluff, bringing with it, in the summertime at least, a blast of cold air from some subterranean cavern so strong that it makes a continual rushing sound" (Harrington 1960, 26). So while the other sites described here are distinguished by striking visual features, this site is noteworthy for its unusual acoustic properties. Harrington excavated six burials in a dry area at one end of the shelter, near the cave opening that produces the cold air blast. One of the burials was an infant interred in a woven cane cradle laid on "cedar twigs and bits of wood." Another burial contained the remains of an infant wrapped in a tanned deerskin along with the bundled remains of an adult wrapped in a feathered robe (Harrington 1960, 40–43).

To summarize, we have identified a series of rockshelters containing elaborate, multiple burials along impressive, south-facing bluff lines overlooking the upper White River in the Arkansas Ozarks. Several of these sites are decorated with rock art and all occur on distinctive landforms. As a group, the sites display features that would prompt extraordinary sensory experiences. Interments of adults, juveniles, and infants were placed in crevices along the rear walls of these shelters or in areas behind large rockfalls. Several individuals were interred with beads and other small ornaments, some made from exotic marine shell. A few were buried with feathered robes. Others were covered with woven fabric or woven-cane mats. Some infants were buried in cradles. A few individuals were laid to rest on cedar-pole frameworks, some of which were also covered with woven cane mats. Several burials were interred with heads oriented toward the west, and many were subjected to in situ cremation. These dispositions were presumably reserved for elite members of the local community.

Points of correspondence between these rockshelter burials and the mortuary program identified at nearby mound centers include the apparent significance of site and burial orientation to the west, southwest, and south; the use of fire as a medium to transport souls of the dead to the spirit realm; and the periodic "gathering" of remains in specialized facilities as part of program of sequential, accumulative mortuary processing. Both mortuary programs also focus on the remains of elite members of local communities and they clearly were manifestations of a single conceptual system.

SUMMARY AND CONCLUSIONS

The analysis presented here suggests that a specialized mortuary program in selected Ozark caves and rockshelters shares important features with funeral ceremonies performed at nearby mound centers. Both programs involved the selection of sites relative to specific natural landscape features, the locations of nearby residential sites, and cultural concepts concerning relationships between ritual performance and special qualities attributed to natural landscape features.

It is now clear that these mortuary programs were part of a larger ritual complex that ties mound centers and rockshelters to other sites and natural features—some possessing culturally charged attributes—within integrated cultural landscapes. It is perhaps worth reiterating, in closing, that we might not have discovered these relationships if we had studied these sites as independent entities. The integrated "landscape" perspective that frames our research and the process of working back and forth across multiple levels of spatial resolution played an important role in developing our interpretations of the ritual use of Ozark caves and rockshelters.

REFERENCES CITED

Bell, Catherine. 1997. *Ritual: Perspectives and Dimensions*. New York: Oxford University Press.

Bell, Robert E. 1972. *The Harlan Site, Ck-6: A Prehistoric Mound Center in Cherokee County, Eastern Oklahoma*. Oklahoma Anthropological Society Memoir, No. 2. Oklahoma City, OK: Oklahoma Anthropological Society.

Bell, Robert E. 1984. "Arkansas Valley Caddoan: The Harlan Phase." In *Prehistory of Oklahoma*, ed. Robert E. Bell, 221–40. New York: Academic Press.

Bradley, Richard. 2000. *An Archaeology of Natural Places*. London: Routledge.

Brown, James A. 1984. *Prehistoric Southern Ozark Marginality: A Myth Exposed*. Missouri Archaeological Society Special Publications, No. 6. Columbia, MO: Missouri Archaeological Society.

Brown, James A. 1997. "The Archaeology of Ancient Religion in the Eastern Woodlands." *Annual Review of Anthropology* 26 (1): 465–85. http://dx.doi.org/10.1146/annurev.anthro.26.1.465.

Brown, James A. 2004. "The Cahokian Expression: Creating Court and Cult." In *Hero, Hawk, and Open Hand: American Indian Art of the Ancient Midwest and South*, ed. Richard F. Townsend, 105–23. New Haven: CT: The Art Institute of Chicago in association with Yale University Press.

Brown, James A. 2007. "Sequencing the Braden Style within Mississippian Period Art and Iconography." In *Ancient Objects and Sacred Realms: Interpretations of Mississippian Iconography*, ed. F. Kent Reilly III and James F. Garber, 213–45. Austin: University of Texas Press.

Brown, James A., and John E. Kelly. 2000. "Cahokia and the Southeastern Ceremonial Complex." In *Mounds, Modoc, and Mesoamerica: Papers in Honor of Melvin L. Fowler*, ed. Steve Ahler, 469–510. Illinois State Museum, Scientific Papers, Vol. 28. Springfield: Illinois State Museum.

Cande, Kathleen H. 2000. *Spradley Hollow Habitations*. Arkansas Archeological Survey Research Series, No. 56. Fayetteville, AR: Arkansas Archeological Survey.

Chapman, Carl H. 1948. "A Preliminary Survey of Missouri Archaeology, Part IV: Ancient Cultures and Sequences." *Missouri Archaeologist* 10: 133–64.

Cleland, Charles E. 1965. "Faunal Remains from Bluff Shelters in Northwest Arkansas." *Arkansas Archeologist* 6 (2–3): 39–63.

Dellinger, Samuel C. 1928. "Preserving Ancient Relics for Study in the University Museum." *Arkansas Alumnus* 5 (6): 7–9.

Dellinger, Samuel C. 1936. "Baby Cradles of the Ozark Bluff-Dwellers." *American Antiquity* 1 (3): 197–214. http://dx.doi.org/10.2307/275143.

Dellinger, Samuel C., and Samuel D. Dickinson. 1942. "Pottery from the Ozark Bluff Shelters." *American Antiquity* 7 (3): 276–311. http://dx.doi.org/10.2307/275484.

Diaz-Granados, Carol, and James R. Duncan. 2000. *The Petroglyphs and Pictographs of Missouri*. Tuscaloosa: University of Alabama Press.

Diaz-Granados, Carol, Marvin W. Rowe, Marian Hyman, James R. Duncan, and John R. Southon. 2001. "AMS Radiocarbon Dates for Charcoal from Three Missouri Pictographs and Their Associated Iconography, a Report." *American Antiquity* 66 (3): 481–93. http://dx.doi.org/10.2307/2694246.

Duncan, James R., and Carol Diaz-Granados. 2000. "Of Masks and Myths." *Midcontinental Journal of Archaeology* 25 (1): 1–26.

Faulkner, Charles H. 1986. *The Prehistoric Native American Art of Mud Glyph Cave*. Knoxville: University of Tennessee Press.

Fritz, Gayle J. 1984. "Identification of Cultigen Amaranth and Chenopod from Rockshelter Sites in Northwest Arkansas." *American Antiquity* 49 (3): 558–72. http://dx.doi.org/10.2307/280360.

Fritz, Gayle J. 1986. "Prehistoric Ozark Agriculture: The University of Arkansas Rockshelter Collections." PhD dissertation, University of North Carolina, Chapel Hill.

Fritz, Gayle J. 1997. "A Three-Thousand Year Old Cache of Crop Seeds from Marble Bluff, Arkansas." In *People, Plants, and Landscapes: Studies in Paleoethnobotany*, ed. Kirsten J. Gremillion, 42–62. Tuscaloosa: University of Alabama Press.

Fritz, Gayle J., and Bruce D. Smith. 1988. "Old Collections and New Technology: Documenting the Domestication of Chenopodium in Eastern North America." *Midcontinental Journal of Archaeology* 13: 3–28.

Galloway, Patricia. 1989. *The Southeastern Ceremonial Complex: Artifacts and Analysis*. Lincoln: University of Nebraska Press.

Gilmore, Melvin R. 1930. "Vegetal Remains of the Ozark Bluff-Dweller Culture." *Papers of the Michigan Academy of Science, Arts, and Letters* 14: 83–102.

Guendling, Randall L., ed. 2008. "Brown Bluff: Modern Excavations and Reanalysis of 1932 Collections at a National Register Bluff Shelter (3AWA10), Washington County, Arkansas." Final Report submitted to the Arkansas Highway and Transportation Department, Arkansas Archeological Survey, Fayetteville.

Hall, Robert L. 1997. *An Archaeology of the Soul: North American Indian Belief and Ritual*. Urbana: University of Illinois Press.

Harrington, Mark R. 1960. *The Ozark Bluff-Dwellers*. Museum of the American Indian, Indian Notes and Monographs No. 12. New York: Heye Foundation.

Hatcher, Mattie Austin, trans. 1927. "Description of the Tejas or Asinai Indians, 1691–1722." *Southwestern Historical Quarterly*, 30: 206–18, 283–304; 31: 50–62, 150–80.

Hilliard, Jerry. 1986. "Selection and Use of Acorn Species by Late Prehistoric Ozark Inhabitants." In *Contributions to Ozark Prehistory*, ed. George Sabo III, 81–85. Arkansas Archeological Survey Research Series, No. 27, 81–85. Fayetteville, AR: Arkansas Archeological Survey.

Hilliard, Jerry, and James Harcourt. 1997. "Marine Shell Beads from the University of Arkansas Museum Bluff Shelter Excavations." *Arkansas Archeologist* 36: 35–45.

Hilliard, Jerry, and John Riggs. 2000. *AMASDA Site Encoding Manual, Version 3.0*. Arkansas Archeological Survey Technical Paper, No. 1. Fayetteville, AR: Arkansas Archeological Survey.

Horton, Elizabeth T. 2010. "The Ties that Bind: Fabric Traditions and Fiber Use in the Ozark Plateau." PhD dissertation, Washington University, St. Louis, MO.

Kay, Marvin. 1982. *Holocene Adaptations within the Lower Pomme de Terre River Valley, Missouri*. Springfield: Illinois State Museum Society.

Kay, Marvin, and George Sabo III. 2006. "Mortuary Ritual and Winter Solstice Imagery of the Harlan-style Charnel House." *Southeastern Archaeology* 25 (1): 29–47.

King, Adam, ed. 2007. *Southeastern Ceremonial Complex: Chronology, Content, Context*. Tuscaloosa: University of Alabama Press.

Klippel, Walter E. 1971. *Graham Cave Revisited: A Reevaluation of Its Cultural Position during the Archaic Period*. Missouri Archaeological Society Memoir, No. 5. Columbia, MO: Missouri Archaeological Society.

Knight, Vernon James, Jr. 2006. "Farewell to the Southeastern Ceremonial Complex." *Southeastern Archaeology* 25 (1): 1–5.

Knight, Vernon James, Jr., James A. Brown, and George E. Lankford. 2001. "On the Subject Matter of Southeastern Ceremonial Complex Art." *Southeastern Archaeology* 20 (2): 129–41.

Kuttruff, Jenna T. 1988. "Textile Attributes and Production Complexity as Indicators of Caddoan Status Differentiation in the Arkansas Valley and Southern Ozark Regions." PhD dissertation, Ohio State University, Columbus.

Kuttruff, Jenna T. 1993. "Mississippian Period Status Differentiation through Textile Analysis: A Caddoan Example." *American Antiquity* 58 (1): 125–45. http://dx.doi.org/10.2307/281458.

Lankford, George E. 2007. "The 'Path of Souls': Some Death Imagery in the Southeastern Ceremonial Complex." In *Ancient Objects and Sacred Realms: Interpretations of Mississippian Iconography*, ed. F. Kent Reilly III and James F. Garber, 174–212. Austin: University of Texas Press.

Mainfort, Robert C., Jr. 2008. *Sam Dellinger: Raiders of the Lost Arkansas*. Fayetteville: University of Arkansas Press.

Peabody, Charles, and Warren K. Moorehead. 1904. *The Exploration of Jacobs Cavern, McDonald County, Missouri*. Department of Archeology, Bulletin No. 1. Andover: Phillips Academy.

Raab, L. Mark. 1976. *Pine Mountain: A Study of Prehistoric Human Ecology in the Arkansas Ozarks*. Arkansas Archaeological Survey Research Report, No. 7. Fayetteville, AR: Arkansas Archeological Survey.

Sabo, George, III, Ann M. Early, Jerome C. Rose, Barbara A. Burnett, Louis Vogele Jr., and James P. Harcourt. 1988. *Human Adaptations in the Ozark and Ouachita Mountains*. Arkansas Archaeological Survey Research Series, No. 31. Fayetteville, AR: Arkansas Archaeological Survey.

Sabo, George, III, and Deborah Sabo. 2005. *Rock Art in Arkansas*. Arkansas Archeological Survey Popular Series, No. 5. Fayetteville, AR: Arkansas Archeological Survey.

Salzer, Robert J., and Grace Rajnovich. 2001. *The Gottschall Rockshelter: An Archaeological Mystery*. Rev. ed. St. Paul, MN: Prairie Smoke Press.

Scholtz, Sandra C. 1975. *Prehistoric Plies: A Structural and Comparative Analysis of Cordage, Netting, Basketry, and Fabric from Ozark Bluff Shelters*. Arkansas Archaeological Survey Research Series, No. 9. Fayetteville, AR: Arkansas Archeological Survey.

Simek, Jan F., Alan Cressler, and Elayne Pope. 2004. "Association between a Southeastern Rock-Art Motif and Mortuary Caves." In *The Rock-Art of Eastern North America: Capturing Images and Insight*, ed. Carol Diaz-Granados and James R. Duncan, 159–73. Tuscaloosa: University of Alabama Press.

Simek, Jan F., J. D. Franklin, and S. C. Sherwood. 1998. "The Context of Early Southeastern Prehistoric Cave Art: A Report on the Archaeology of 3rd Unnamed Cave." *American Antiquity* 63 (4): 663–75. http://dx.doi.org/10.2307/2694114.

Trubowitz, Neal L. 1980. *Pine Mountain Revisited: An Archeological Study in the Ozarks*. Arkansas Archaeological Survey Research Reports, No. 23. Fayetteville, AR: Arkansas Archaeological Survey.

Wakefield, Elmer G., and Samuel C. Dellinger. 1936. "Diet of the Bluff Dwellers of the Ozark Mountains and Its Skeletal Effects." *Annals of Internal Medicine* 9: 412–8.

Wakefield, Elmer G., and Samuel C. Dellinger. 1940. "Diseases of Prehistoric Americans of South Central United States." *CIBA Symposia (New York)* 2: 453–62.

Wakefield, Elmer G., Samuel C. Dellinger, and John D. Camp. 1937. "Study of the Osseous Remains of a Primitive Race Who Once Inhabited the Shelters of the Bluffs of the Ozark Mountains." *American Journal of the Medical Sciences* 193: 223–31.

Wood, W. Raymond, and R. Bruce McMillan. 1976. *Prehistoric Man and His Environments: A Case Study in the Ozark Highland*. New York: Academic Press.

Part III
Case Studies in Ritual Cave Use

17

The Prehistoric Funerary Archaeology of the Niah Caves, Sarawak (Malaysian Borneo)

Graeme Barker and Lindsay Lloyd-Smith

The prehistory of cave use in Island Southeast Asia is commonly summarized as a first phase of domestic use by Late Pleistocene and Early Holocene foragers followed by a second phase of funerary use by Neolithic and Metal Age farmers (Anderson 1997). The sequence was exemplified by the major program of excavations conducted in the 1950s and 1960s by Tom and Barbara Harrisson in the Niah Caves in Sarawak in northern Borneo (figure 17.1). Their remarkable discoveries in the West Mouth of Niah Great Cave included, in a deep sounding cut at the front of the cave termed the Hell Trench, a human skull (the so-called Deep Skull) in deposits that yielded a radiocarbon date of circa 40,000 BP (years before the present), making it the earliest modern human in southeast Asia (Brothwell 1960; T. Harrisson 1958). At higher levels in the same part of the cave they found evidence for intensive habitation and occasional burials dating to the Late Pleistocene and Early Holocene. Further into the interior they identified a cemetery of about 200 burials of broadly Neolithic date and character, yielding radiocarbon dates from circa 5000 BP to circa 2500 BP (Brooks, Helgar, and Brooks 1977; B. Harrisson 1967; T. Harrisson 1965, 1970). They also conducted excavations in several other entrances to the cave complex, finding evidence for small-scale Pleistocene occupation in Gan Kira, Terminal Pleistocene/Early Holocene occupation in Lobang Angus, and further possible Neolithic burials in Gan Kira. In Kain Hitam, the so-called Painted Cave a few hundred meters east of the Gan Kira entrance, they found bodies buried in wooden boats dated to about 1,000 years ago, together with wall paintings of boats and dancing figures that were thought likely to be associated with the boat burials. The Niah Caves remain unique in the region for the length of the sequence of human activity found and the wealth of the material culture associated with it.

However, there have always been major uncertainties about the Harrissons's findings, for three reasons (Bellwood 1985, 1997; Solheim 1977a, 1977b, 1983; Zuraina 1982). First, although numerous interim reports and specialist papers were published, there was never a final comprehensive report. Second, the excavation was in horizontal spits, a method ill suited to the typically complex and frequently dipping deposits of caves. Third, the various radiocarbon dates obtained were very early in the development of the method, and methodologies have of course transformed in precision and accuracy since then. In an attempt to resolve these uncertainties, since 2000 an interdisciplinary team of archaeologists and environmental scientists has undertaken further fieldwork in and around the caves, integrated with detailed study of the substantial archive of records and finds from the previous excavations (Barker 2005; Barker et al. 2000, 2001, 2002a, 2002b, 2003, 2007). The scope of the present chapter is to discuss the evidence, old and new, for the complexity of prehistoric funerary behavior in the cave.

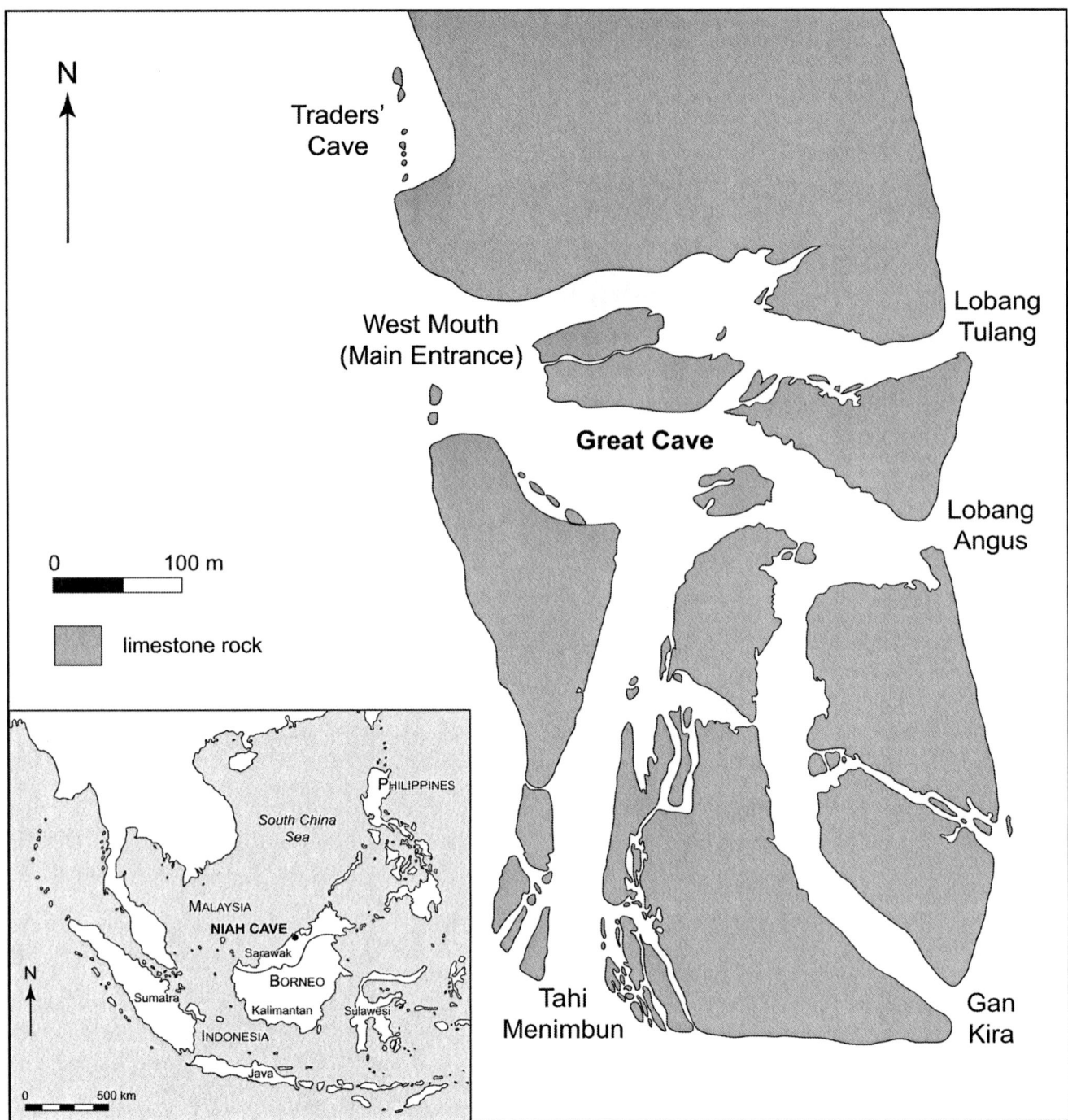

FIGURE 17.1 Plan of the Niah Caves complex, Sarawak. The main excavations by Tom and Barbara Harrisson were in the West Mouth, Lobang Tulang, Lobang Angus, and Gan Kira.

PLEISTOCENE BURIAL IN THE WEST MOUTH

The West Mouth of Niah Cave is a truly monumental setting (figure 17.2). Formed by a confluence of two massive (cathedral-like) cave passages, the entrance measures over 150 meters across and over 75 meters in height. Even though the entrance is so large, however, a series of massive speleothem pillars, as well as large trees and the hanging jungle vegetation around the cave's edges, mean that much of the cave's immediate interior is shielded from bright sun-

FIGURE 17.2 The West Mouth of Niah Great Cave, measuring about 150 meters across and 75 meters in height. (Photograph: Graeme Barker.)

light. The main focus of its use by Pleistocene foragers was in one of the light and airy parts of the entrance in front of a small rockshelter or overhang at its northwest corner (figure 17.3), in a natural basin formed between, on the one side, the rocks of the cave lip or rampart and, on the other, the bat and bird guano deposits that slope down toward the cave entrance from the cave interior. The Hell Trench is located where the basin was situated.

The geomorphological studies of our project have shown that, in the later Pleistocene, water flowed down episodically from the cave interior into this basin, and then flowed across it parallel to the cave lip into the rockshelter, where it exited down a sinkhole (Gilbertson et al. 2005). Sediment buildup from stream flow led to the formation in this basin of red silts, classified as Lithofacies 2 in the project's stratigraphic sequence. Although skeptics have argued that the Deep Skull might be the reworked and redeposited remains of a human skull from one of the numerous Neolithic inhumations located in this same part of the West Mouth, our studies have provided strong collaborative evidence that the original assessment and dating of the Deep Skull were largely correct (Barker et al. 2007). The Harrissons found the Deep Skull in red silts, immediately below a "pink and white" deposit that was thought to result from a steady stream of (pink) sediment and (white) pebbles falling from the cave roof, but we have demonstrated that the latter deposit was in fact a "mudslip" of wet guano that flowed down from the cave interior, probably over a few particularly wet seasons (Gilbertson et al. 2005). A series of radiocarbon dates from the new excavations demonstrates that human occupation in the cave certainly dates back to about 50,000 years ago (calibrated BP), and a stone tool found 50 centimeters below the basal dated sediments implies that initial occupation is earlier still. U-series dates on a fragment of the Deep Skull indicate an age of around 37,000 years ago. The skull (of a teenage girl) was in fact associated with other human remains likely to be of the same individual.

Tom Harrisson reported that, within the red silts, the Deep Skull was associated with plentiful evidence of human occupation in the form of fragments of ash, charcoal, occasional stone tools, and numerous fragments of

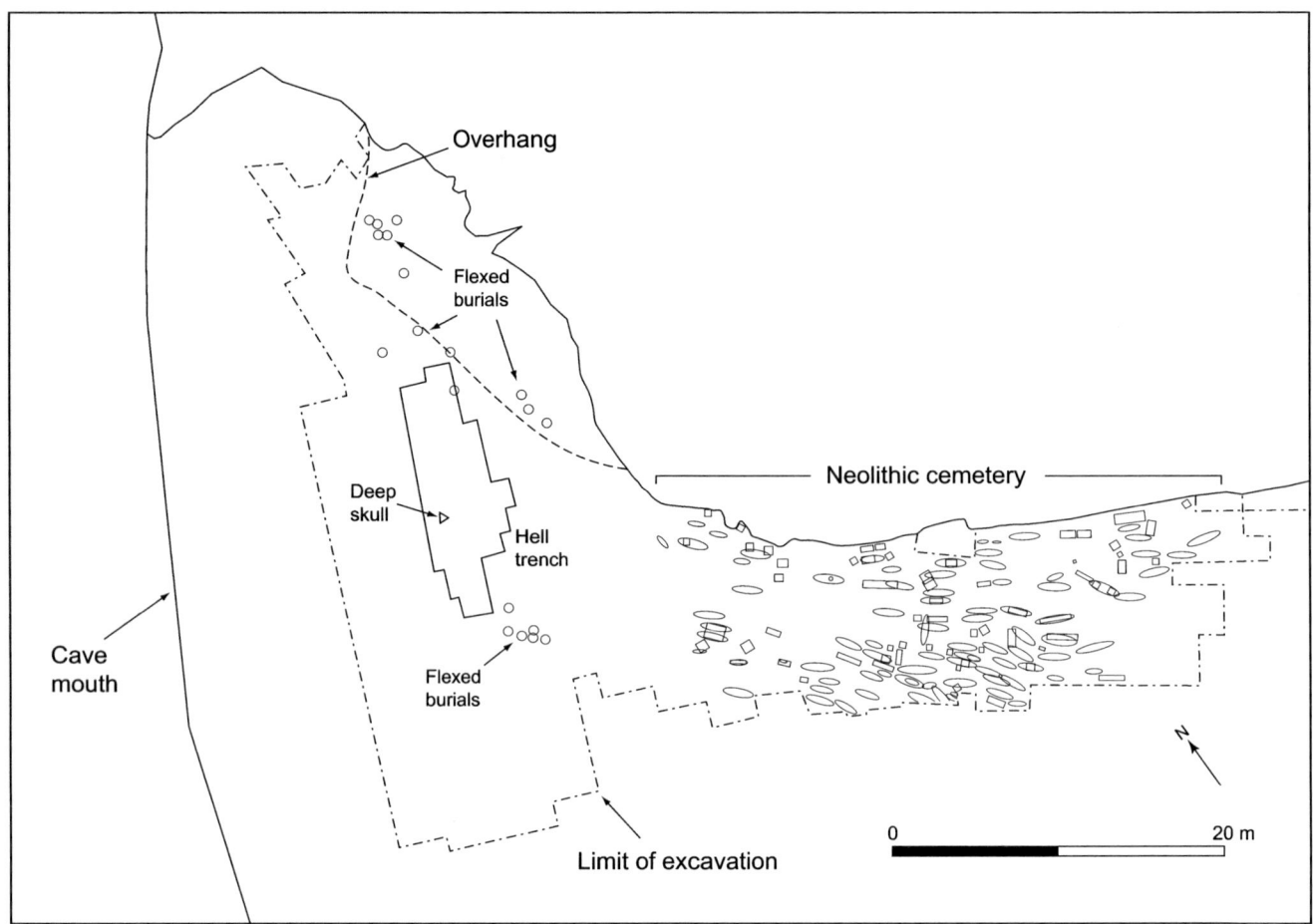

FIGURE 17.3 The archaeological zone of the West Mouth of Niah Great Cave, showing the location of the rock overhang, the Hell Trench, and the Neolithic cemetery. (Plan: Lindsay Lloyd-Smith.)

animal bone. He termed this the "bone under ash" layer, though it was probably in fact a palimpsest of short temporary occupations rather than a single long-lived occupation implied by the term *layer*. Careful examination of their excavation records reveals that, although they were excavating in arbitrary horizontal spits, the Harrissons in fact tracked this cultural deposit carefully across the front of the cave. Our excavations of a surviving balk in the Hell Trench, HP6, revealed a series of archaeologically rich surfaces within colluvial sediments sloping down from the cave lip into the basin (figure 17.4), suggesting that the preferred zone of occupation for the first human visitors to the cave was probably at the cave lip, though some human activity also took place in the basin. The faunal material tells the same story: much of it consists of small fragments that had probably slipped down from where they had been dumped at the cave lip, but there are also clusters of articulated or related bones from the same animal, almost certainly butchered in situ in the basin (Rabett and Barker 2007; Rabett, Piper, and Barker 2006). In many respects the Deep Skull and the fragmentary human limb-bones found near it resemble these "in situ butchery events," but there are indications that they may have been buried in a pit rather than being the remains of a body dumped at the cave lip that then slipped down into the basin along with other cultural debris (Hunt and Barker, n.d.).

The West Mouth was used repeatedly by human foraging groups between about 35,000 cal BP and the end of the Pleistocene about 11,500 cal BP. The faunal material hints at the separation of the main living areas, where primary butchery took place, from a main zone of refuse dumping in and immediately in front of the rock overhang. In the latter, the Late Pleistocene animal bones lack burning and are often abraded, suggesting that they were lying on the surface exposed to the elements and not subject to trampling. Given the enormity of the Great Cave, it is note-

FIGURE 17.4 Excavating a surviving balk in the Harrissons' Hell Trench, in 2002. The balk consists of a succession of colluvial layers and layers rich in ash, charcoal, and archaeological debris, such as fragments of butchered animal bone, all sloping down from the exterior of the cave (to the right) into the stream basin (to the left), where they interleave with the red silts in which the Deep Skull was found in 1958. (Photograph: Graeme Barker.)

worthy that exactly same location used for the discard of food refuse by the Late Pleistocene foragers also appears to have been one of the few locations in the cave system where they chose to deposit their dead. The fact that both human remains and food refuse were placed together on the periphery of the human domestic space could be taken to imply that these Pleistocene foragers believed in the existence of a close association between the living and the dead, or at least that the dead should be kept "close" to, rather than at a distance from, their camp's social center. Burials within habitation deposits in caves in central Maluku in eastern Indonesia (Latinis and Stark 1998) and Papua (Pasveer 2003) suggest similar close linkages between the domains of the living and the dead in Pleistocene cave use. It may be that Pleistocene foragers also reserved some caves specifically for rituals: painted handprints have been found in a remote cave high in the Gunung Marang mountains in east Kalimantan (Indonesian Borneo), and provisional dates of stalagmite covering them indicate a date older than 10,000 years (Causse and Plagnes 2001).

EARLY HOLOCENE AND NEOLITHIC BURIAL PRACTICE AT NIAH

The Niah Caves continued to be visited by foragers, and the West Mouth used as a place of burial, through the Early Holocene until about 8000 cal BP. The burial record indicates the repeated use of the cave for periods of several centuries, rather than sporadic occupation over the millennia. The Harrissons found a series of crouched burials of Early Holocene date in and immediately in front of the rock overhang, one of them with a rhinoceros leg-bone "pillow" placed above the head (T. Harrisson 1957; Figure 17.5). Burial practices included flexed inhumations and the secondary burial of body parts, sometimes cremated, the former suggesting that some bodies were buried "opportunistically" if a death occurred during foragers' visits to the cave, and the latter that the remains of selected individuals who had died elsewhere were brought to the cave for burial. Flexed bodies were placed on the inward side of the main occupation and burial zone in the West Mouth. Some of the Early Holocene burials were placed in a seated position,

FIGURE 17.5 An Early Holocene crouched human burial excavated by the Harrissons in front of the West Mouth rockshelter. (Photograph reproduced by the kind permission of the Sarawak Museum.)

in pits over fires lit at the time of burial, and a pair of bodies was buried back to back, bound in the flexed position, and decapitated.

There then appears to be a gap in the burial sequence, from about 8000 cal BP to about 4000 cal BP. The start date of the occupation hiatus coincides with the mid-Holocene marine transgression, when intertidal mangrove vegetation spread around much of the Niah Cave massif, making the outcrops effectively offshore islands (Hunt and Rushworth 2005, 648). The mid-Holocene climate also favored the expansion of dense dipterocarp lowland rainforest from its Pleistocene refugia, another factor that presumably made the general locality unattractive for foragers, a phenomenon noted in other parts of the region.

The West Mouth began to be used once more as a place of burial in the second millennium BC. A large series of radiocarbon dates between about 5000 cal BP and about 2500 cal BP was obtained on collagen from human bone from the Neolithic cemetery (Brooks, Helgar, and Brooks 1977), but these dates are now regarded as unreliable because of the increased and variable diagenesis of bone in wet tropical environments (Spriggs 1989). However, new radiocarbon dates obtained by the Niah Cave Project on bamboo, wood, and cremated bone (thirty-four dates, from thirty-three burials) securely confirm the probable date range for the use of the Neolithic cemetery at Niah as circa. 4000–3500 cal BP to circa 2200 cal BP.

The main burial zone was behind the Pleistocene occupation zone, extending into the cave for over 50 meters (figure 17.3). The gigantic size of the West Mouth, though, means that the cemetery area is not in complete darkness, and as one's eyes adjust to the half-light of the cemetery zone, it is possible to see far back into the cavernous interior of the Great Cave, beyond which it is pitch black (figure 17.6). The location of Neolithic graves in the other entrances is much the same: a "twilight" zone between the light entrances and the dark interiors is a location conceivably symbolizing some kind of liminal or boundary zone between life and death. In spite of the wet tropical conditions, the high ammonia content of the bird and bat

FIGURE 17.6 Looking eastwards from the cave entrance into the archaeological zone of the West Mouth of Niah Great Cave. The nearest 2-meter ranging pole and the middle one (a few meters into the cave to the left) are located by balks containing evidence of the Pleistocene occupation. The 2-meter ranging pole in the distance marks the beginning of the main suite of burials of the Neolithic cemetery. The plank boxes to the right of that ranging pole protect burials that were exposed but not excavated in the Harrissons' excavations. (Photograph: Graeme Barker.)

guano in which the bodies were interred has preserved a wide variety of organic materials alongside the human skeletal remains, stone tools, and ceramic jars: wooden coffins, bamboo and rattan baskets, leaf and plant "pillows," textiles, and artifacts including carved wooden sticks, vegetable and seed beads, and shell and bone tools.

The detailed analysis of the Neolithic cemetery by Lindsay Lloyd-Smith has indicated that it divides spatially into a central burial group surrounded by four smaller satellite groups (Lloyd-Smith 2009; figure 17.7). Within these groups, pairs and rows of extended burials can be identified. Barbara Harrisson classified the approximately 200 Neolithic burials she excavated into a broad chronological sequence. The earliest graves were extended inhumations, the bodies being placed in wooden coffins fashioned from hollowed-out logs or crude planks. Later, bodies were placed in large ceramic vessels or jars, sometimes being partially cremated first. The small-scale excavations we have conducted in selected zones of the cemetery, and the new radiocarbon-dating program, have confirmed the broad validity of this sequence, but also greatly amplified it and given it greater chronological precision. The cemetery began with a few dispersed flexed burials. Between about 3300 cal BP and 3000 cal BP, a formalized cemetery was laid out, consisting of rows of extended burials, mostly of individuals in wooden coffins, though some were simply wrapped in a shroud (figure 17.8). Grave goods included pots, stone axes and grinders, beads, basketry, and textiles. The first jar-burials date to this period. The main rite in the period of about 3000–2700 cal BP consisted of secondary burials of bodies previously buried elsewhere. Some of the human bones have distinctive weathered and exfoliated surfaces, suggesting prolonged periods of exposure, so in some instances perhaps flesh was removed at initial burial rites and then a selection of bones was reinterred in a secondary burial ritual. The bones were placed in a

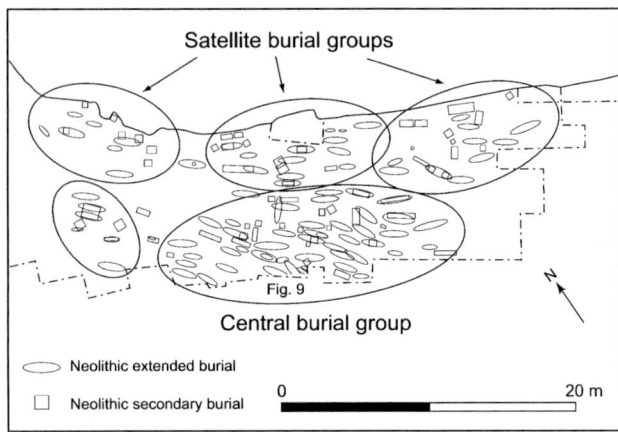

FIGURE 17.7 Spatial patterning in the Neolithic cemetery in the West Mouth of Niah Great Cave: a large central cluster, and four satellite groups. (Plan: Lindsay Lloyd-Smith.)

FIGURE 17.8 A Neolithic inhumation burial (B211) excavated by the Niah Cave Project in 2003. Note the possible grave marker post protruding from the pelvic area. Scale: 2 meters. (Photograph: Graeme Barker.)

variety of containers as well as in big jars—in bamboo caskets, for example. Cremation became the dominant way of dealing with the dead in the period of about 2700–2400 cal BP, but there was then (ca. 2400–2200 cal BP) a reversion to nonburnt secondary burial, and finally to primary extended burial, with coffins being reopened for later burials in some cases.

The complexity of the funerary archaeology is well illustrated by our excavation within the central burial group of a cluster of overlapping burial episodes, all probably dating to within a few generations of one another (figure 17.9). The oldest burial, not excavated, was Burial 217, probably an extended inhumation of a single adult wrapped in matting. Burial 210, severely truncated by Burial 216, consisted of a relatively shallow scoop without human remains or coffin wood. Burial 216 was a coffin burial of a young (0–2-year-old) child, the coffin wood yielding radiocarbon dates of 2632 +/− 28 bp or 2729–2784 cal BP (OxA-14027), and 2640 +/− 40 bp or 2722–2844 cal BP (OxA-14010). Red staining was visible around the head, and a piece of ochre was in the burial, as well as a pig bone. (The association between human burials, pigs, and ochre was also noted by Barbara Harrisson in her excavations in Upiusing Cave about 10 kilometers from the West Mouth: Barbara Harrisson 1965.) The bones were roughly in the order that

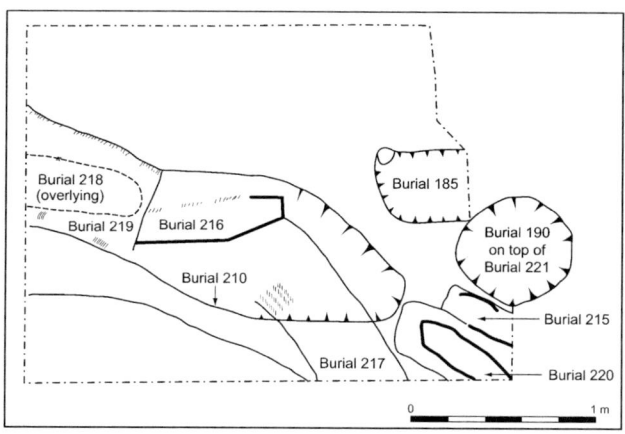

FIGURE 17.9 Plan of intercutting burials in part of the Neolithic cemetery, Niah Great Cave (see text for description). (Plan: Lindsay Lloyd-Smith.)

FIGURE 17.10 Niah Great Cave Neolithic cemetery: rattan matting on which a 3-year-old child was laid (Burial 219). The matting was radiocarbon dated to 2847 +/− 27 BP or 1120–920 cal BC (OxA-14028). Scale: 30 centimeters. (Photograph: Graeme Barker.)

would have been expected of an articulated skeleton but were not actually articulated; they may have slipped or been disturbed after deposition, or conceivably they were carefully reinterred from elsewhere. Burial 219 consisted of the remains of a 3-year-old child, the skull stained red, interred on top of well-preserved rattan matting (figure 17.10) that provided a radiocarbon date of 2847 +/− 27 bp or 2873–3062 cal BP (OxA-14028). Both Burials 217 and 219 appeared to have been staked or flagged with grave markers. Burial 218, uppermost in the sequence, contained a few disarticulated, possibly cremated, bones of an adult and some pottery fragments in a wood coffin dated to 2680 +/− 45 bp or 2742–2865 cal BP (OxA-14011).

On the eastern side of the trench was an extended burial, Burial 185, possibly containing two individuals in a wood coffin, a fragment of which was dated to 4216 +/−29 bp or 4629–4851 cal BP (OxA-14026). This was cut by two jar-burials, Burials 221 and 190 (figure 17.11). Burial 221 consisted of a paddle-made jar encased in basketry, containing the remains of a single subadult. Burial 190, another jar encased in basketry placed directly on top of Burial 221 and crushing it, contained an adult male, a subadult, an older child, a young child, and a neonate, conceivably a family or kin group. Burnt wood from this burial yielded an AMS date of 2308 +/− 35 bp or 2159–2362 cal BP (OxA-11548).

FIGURE 17.11 Niah Great Cave Neolithic cemetery: a Neolithic jar-burial (B190) placed directly on top of an earlier Neolithic jar-burial (B221). The base of the small vertical scale rests on the earlier jar-burial and the top of it is level with the bottom of the later burial. Both of them cut through an earlier inhumation burial, marked by a baggy pot on the right and some limb bones at bottom right. The larger scale measures 30 centimeters, the small scale 10 centimeters. (Photograph: Graeme Barker.)

In the cemetery as a whole, the oldest burials appear to have been in the central burial group and the satellite cluster to its west. Subtle differences in the arm positions of the extended burials in these and the other clusters in the cemetery appear to reflect a combination of the group or family in which a body was buried, and the gender of the person. Isotope analyses of the body chemistry (strontium/lead ratios) indicate that a few people, females especially, were nonlocal (Valentine, Kamenov, and Krigbaum 2008). A possible interpretation is that different lineages with distinct ancestral traditions used different parts of the cemetery over time, and that marriage exchange was a feature of these societies. Further family-like clusters can also be identified in the secondary burials.

WERE THE NEOLITHIC PEOPLE AT NIAH FARMERS?

Although Neolithic people in Island Southeast Asia have traditionally been assumed to be immigrant Austronesian farmers on the basis of their pottery and polished-stone tools (Bellwood 1985, 1997, 2004), it is not in fact clear whether the Neolithic people buried in the West Mouth Neolithic cemetery lived as foragers or whether they practiced agriculture to a greater or lesser extent. The current evidence is ambiguous. Some paddle-made Neolithic pottery was excavated by the Harrissons in the upper 24 inches of cave sediment under the rock overhang. None of that deposit remains, but we found similar Neolithic sherds in the Lobang Angus entrance associated with butchered bone of wild terrestrial and riverine species and riverine mollusks indicative of a forest-foraging strategy. Starch grains adhering to stone tools and in sediments suggest that both Pleistocene and Neolithic people at Niah relied heavily on tubers such as yam, taro, and sago for their carbohydrates (Barton 2005; Paz 2005). There are rare occurrences of bones of domestic pigs and dogs in the Harrisson fauna (Clutton-Brock 1959), but those bones are Metal Age rather than Neolithic. Stable-isotope analyses of Neolithic skeletons from the West Mouth cemetery

TABLE 17.1 Simplified burial sequence in the West Mouth of Niah Great Cave. (After Lloyd-Smith 2009.)

Phase	Approximate date range (calibrated years BP)	Description
1	37,000	Deep Skull burial.
2	11,500–8000	Flexed inhumations and some secondary burial, including of burnt bones.
3	3500–3300	Dispersed and sporadic flexed burial in the cemetery area.
4	2300–2900	Establishment of a formalized cemetery with rows of extended burials.
5	2900–2700	Widespread transition to nonburnt secondary burial.
Hiatus?	ca. 2800	Possible hiatus, of unknown duration, in burial activity in the cave.
6	2800–2500	Widespread appearance of cremation burial; spatial reorganization of the cemetery.
7	2500–2200	Reversion to nonburnt secondary burial; reappearance of primary extended burials.
Hiatus?	ca. 2200	Abandonment of Neolithic cemetery. Possible hiatus, of unknown duration, in burial activity at the site.
8	ca. 2200–1500?	Loosely flexed primary burials; continuation of secondary burial including skull burial.

(Krigbaum 2005) indicate that the people buried in the cave in the period of about 11,500–8000 cal BP consumed a diet extracted from a predominantly closed-canopy landscape by—on the evidence of the food refuse in habitation deposits—a mix of hunting, fishing, and plant gathering. The Neolithic people buried in the cave in the period of about 4000–2200 cal BP have isotopic signatures of an open-canopy landscape, taken by Krigbaum to indicate the practice of (rice?) farming, but those Neolithic burials now securely dated to the end of the first millennium BC in fact have closed-canopy isotopic signatures, implying a return to foraging. Pollen sequences indicate small-scale clearances near the caves at the time of the main phase of the Neolithic cemetery, and rice pollen occurs in these sequences (Hunt and Rushworth 2005), but the identification of the pollen grains as of domesticated species is ambiguous and the first evidence for significant forest clearances dates from the Metal Age.

It is striking, too, that some aspects of the Neolithic burial rites at Niah are reminiscent of the "animistic" or naturalistic ideologies of prehistoric hunter-gatherer societies in other parts of the world, such as the use of red ochre to cover the bodies (to signify blood, fertility, etc.?) and the use of bones and teeth of prey animals for necklaces and other items of body decoration. (In animist belief systems, nonhumans and humans are indivisible as persons who share and are part of a sentient, conscious universe.) These "natural" (i.e., untransformed) objects are found with other items of the burial repertoire—such as pottery, polished-stone axes, and grindstones—that are artifacts transformed by human actions from their original state. Such artifacts are common elements in the grave goods of early agricultural societies (in Europe and Southwest Asia, for example) whose ideologies are commonly thought to have included a greater emphasis on ancestry and theism ("sky-gods" separate from and controlling the human world) (Barker 2006).

CONCLUSION

The reanalysis of the immaculate field notes made by Barbara Harrisson from her 1950s and 1960s excavations of hundreds of pre-Neolithic and Neolithic burials in the West Mouth of Niah Great Cave, augmented by further targeted excavations and a new radiocarbon-dating program, have yielded a remarkably nuanced history of burial practices (table 17.1).

The Pleistocene and Early Holocene foragers who visited the Niah Caves appear to have deliberately placed their dead, like their food refuse, close to but separate from their living spaces. The careful preparation and treatment of the dead were features of Early Holocene burials. Some of these were primary interments of the recently dead, but secondary burial was also practiced, whereby body parts were brought to the cave for burial of selected individuals who had died, and were likely treated with other funerary rites at that time, elsewhere.

The use of the caves for burial ceased about 8000 cal BP, coinciding with the mid-Holocene high sea level when the sea invested the Subis mountain massif in which the caves are situated. When burial activity resumed after about 4000 cal BP, the Neolithic people carefully separated the zones of the living and the dead, both within and between the various entrances of the Niah Caves complex. According to current orthodoxy, Neolithic people in coastal Borneo were immigrant Austronesian rice and pig farmers from the north (ultimately from Taiwan: Bellwood 1990, 1996, 1997, 2001, 2004). However, the Neolithic skeletons of the West Mouth cemetery are morphologically of the same physical type as the Late Pleistocene and Early Holocene foragers buried in the cave (Krigbaum and Manser, in press). It is clear that the locations of the earlier burials were known and respected (perhaps there were burial marker posts, as some later burials have: see figure 17.8), and indeed they formed the focus for the Neolithic burials. The earliest Neolithic burials were flexed, like pre-Neolithic flexed burials, and were placed in a sporadic or informal fashion, but during the second half of the second millennium BC a formalized cemetery was established, with rows of extended primary burials laid out in discrete clusters. By about 3000 cal BP the dominant burial rite was secondary burial of unburnt bones, cremation becoming more common after about 2700 cal BP. There was then (ca. 2400 cal BP) a reversion to unburnt secondary burial, alongside the reappearance of the practice of primary inhumations of extended bodies. The variability in burial practices between and within grave groups, augmented by isotope evidence that the population was a mixture of local and not-local people (Valentine, Kamenov, and Krigbaum 2008), suggest that the West Mouth cemetery was used by distinct Neolithic lineages linked by intermarriage.

There are indications of different but similarly complex structuring in the domestic and funerary domains of pre-Neolithic and Neolithic people elsewhere in Island Southeast Asia. In east Kalimantan in Indonesian Borneo, for example, Neolithic communities seem to have systematically divided caves at different altitudes in limestone cliffs into separate domains: large dry rockshelters at the foot of rock outcrops were preferred as dwelling places, and small tunnel caves high up in those outcrops were used for burials and for wall painting, the latter consisting of both hand stencils and human stick figures (Chazine 1995, 2000; Fage and Chazine 2009). Caves in mainland Malaysia such as Gua Cha seem to have been used as both dwelling and burial sites (Haji Taha 1991), but the unusual wealth of pottery in others suggests that some caves may have been sacred places for burials and other rituals (Tweedie 1953). In southern Thailand, Neolithic societies tended to use coastal caves as foci of habitation, and inland caves for burials (such as Tham Lang Rongrien, which contained about twenty extended inhumations in wooden coffins or in unlined pits). Those societies also adorned certain caves that were located on the shore edge, or that were partially submerged, with wall paintings, commonly of human figures, fish, and birds (Anderson 1990, 1997). The painted caves frequently include cultural deposits (pottery, shellfish, animal bones) that may be residues of ritual activities associated with the paintings. At the regional scale, there are many similarities in the material culture used by Neolithic communities in Peninsular and Island Southeast Asia, but the way that material culture was employed in burial rites was markedly different. The rich ambiguities and complexities of the Niah pre-Neolithic and Neolithic funerary archaeology are very difficult to reconcile with a model of Neolithic Austronesian colonists (Barker and Richards 2012).

ACKNOWLEDGMENTS

We would like to thank the Chief Minister's Department of Sarawak for permission to undertake the fieldwork at Niah, and the staff of Sarawak Museum, especially its Director, Sanib Said and, subsequently, Ipoi Datan, for their continued support and encouragement of the Niah Cave Project. The project has been funded principally by the UK's Arts and Humanities Research Council, whose generous support is acknowledged, as well as the British Academy's Committee for Southeast Asian Studies and the UK's Natural Environment Research Council. We would also like to thank Barbara Harrisson for her enthusiasm and support of our renewed interest in the prehistoric burials in the Niah Caves. This chapter draws on the research of many scholars collaborating in the Niah Cave Project, whose contributions are gratefully acknowledged, especially Huw Barton, Franca Cole, Patrick Daly, David Gilbertson, Chris Hunt, John Krigbaum, Sue McLaren, Victor Paz, Phil Piper, Ryan Rabett, Tim Reynolds, and Mark Stephens.

REFERENCES CITED

Anderson, Douglas. 1990. *Lang Rongrien Rockshelter: A Pleistocene, Early Holocene Archaeological Site from Krabi, Southwestern Thailand*. University Museum Monograph 71. Philadelphia: University Museum.

Anderson, Douglas. 1997. "Cave Archaeology in Southeast Asia." *Geoarchaeology* 12 (6): 607–38. http://dx.doi.org/10.1002/(SICI)1520-6548(199709)12:6<607::AID-GEA5>3.0.CO;2-2.

Barker, Graeme. 2005. "The Archaeology of Foraging and Farming at Niah Cave, Sarawak." In *The Human Use of Caves in Peninsular and Island Southeast Asia*, ed. Graeme Barker and David Gilbertson, 90–106. Asian Perspectives 44 (1). Honolulu: University of Hawai'i Press.

Barker, Graeme. 2006. *The Agricultural Revolution in Prehistory: Why Did Foragers Become Farmers?* Oxford: Oxford University Press.

Barker, Graeme, and Martin Richards. 2012. "Foraging-Farming Transitions in Island Southeast Asia." *Journal of Archaeological Method and Theory*. http://dx.doi.org/10.1007/s10816-012-9150-7.

Barker, Graeme, Huw Barton, Paul Beavitt, Simon Chapman, Michael Derrick, Chris Doherty, Lucy Farr, David Gilbertson, Christopher Hunt, Wayne Jarvis, John Krigbaum, Bernard

Maloney, Sue McLaren, Paul Pettitt, Brian Pyatt, Tim Reynolds, Garry Rushworth, and Mark Stephens. 2000. "The Niah Caves Project: Preliminary Report on the First (2000) Season." *Sarawak Museum Journal* 55 (n.s. 76): 111–49.

Barker, Graeme, Dana Badang, Huw Barton, Paul Beavitt, Michael Bird, Patrick Daly, Patrick, Christopher Doherty, David Gilbertson, Ian Glover, Christopher Hunt, Jessica Manser, Sue McLaren, Victor Paz, Bryan Pyatt, Tim Reynolds, Jim Rose, Garry Rushworth, and Mark Stephens. 2001. "The Niah Cave Project: the Second (2001) Season of Fieldwork." *Sarawak Museum Journal* 56 (n.s. 77): 37–119.

Barker, Graeme, Huw Barton, Paul Beavitt, Michael Bird, Patrick Daly, Christopher Doherty, David Gilbertson, Christopher Hunt, John Krigb`aum, Helen Lewis, et al. 2002a. "Prehistoric Foragers and Farmers in Southeast Asia: Renewed Investigations at Niah Cave, Sarawak." *Proceedings of the Prehistoric Society* 68: 147–64.

Barker, Graeme, Huw Barton, Michael Bird, Franca Cole, Patrick Daly, David Gilbertson, Christopher Hunt, John Krigbaum, Cynthia Lampert, Helen Lewis, Lindsay Lloyd-Smith, Jessica Manser, Sue McLaren, Francesco Menotti, Victor Paz, Philip Piper, Bryan Pyatt, Ryan Rabett, Tim Reynolds, Mark Stephens, Gill Thompson, Mark Trickett, and Paula Whittaker. 2002b. "The Niah Cave Project: the Third (2002) Season of Fieldwork." *Sarawak Museum Journal* 57 (n.s. 78): 87–177.

Barker, Graeme, Huw Barton, Michael Bird, Franca Cole, Patrick Daly, Allan Dykes, David Gilbertson, Christopher Hunt, John Krigbaum, Cynthia Lampert, Helen Lewis, Lindsay Lloyd-Smith, Jessica Manser, Sue McLaren, Francesco Menotti, Victor Paz, Philip Piper, Bryan Pyatt, Ryan Rabett, Tim Reynolds, Mark Stephens, Gill Thompson, and Mark Trickett. 2003. "The Niah Cave Project: the Fourth (2003) Season of Fieldwork." *Sarawak Museum Journal* 58 (ns 79): 45–119.

Barker, Graeme, Huw Barton, Michael Bird, Patrick Daly, Ipoi Datan, Allan Dykes, Lucy Farr, David Gilbertson, Barbara Harrisson, Tom Higham, Christopher Hunt, et al. 2007. "The 'Human Revolution' in Lowland Tropical Southeast Asia: The Antiquity and Behavior of Anatomically Modern Humans at Niah Cave (Sarawak, Borneo)." *Journal of Human Evolution* 52:243–61. http://dx.doi.org/10.1016/j.jhevol.2006.08.011. Medline:17161859.

Barton, Huw. 2005. "The Case for Rainforest Foragers: The Starch Record at Niah Cave, Sarawak." In *The Human Use of Caves in Peninsular and Island Southeast Asia*, ed. Graeme Barker and David Gilbertson, 56–72. Asian Perspectives 44 (1). Honolulu: University of Hawai'i Press.

Bellwood, Peter. 1985. *Prehistory of the Indo-Malaysian Archipelago*. Sydney: Academic Press.

Bellwood, Peter. 1990. "Foraging towards Farming: A Decisive Transition or a Millennial Blur?" *Review of Archaeology* 11 (2): 14–24.

Bellwood, Peter. 1996. "The Origins and Spread of Agriculture in the Indo-Pacific Region: Gradualism and Diffusion or Revolution and Colonization?" In *The Origins and Spread of Agriculture and Pastoralism in Eurasia*, ed. David Harris, 465–98. London: UCL Press.

Bellwood, Peter. 1997. *Prehistory of the Indo-Malaysian Archipelago*. 2nd ed. Honolulu: University of Hawai'i Press.

Bellwood, Peter. 2001. "Early Agriculturalist Population Diasporas? Farming, Languages, and Genes." *Annual Review of Anthropology* 30 (1): 181–207. http://dx.doi.org/10.1146/annurev.anthro.30.1.181.

Bellwood, Peter. 2004. *First Farmers: The Origins of Agricultural Societies*. Oxford: Blackwell.

Brooks, Sheilagh, Roger Helgar, and Richard Brooks. 1977. "Radiocarbon Dating and Palaeoserology of a Selected Burial Series from the Great Cave of Niah, Sarawak, Sarawak, Malaysia." *Asian Perspective* 20: 21–31.

Brothwell, Don. 1960. "Upper Pleistocene Human Skull from Niah Caves, Sarawak." *Sarawak Museum Journal* 9 (ns. 15–16): 323–50.

Causse, Christiane, and Valerie Plagnes. 2001. "Peintures Rupestres à Bornéo; de la Radiométrie á la Datation." *Journal du CEA-Saclay* 14: 3.

Chazine, Jean-Michel. 1995. "Nouvelles Perspectives Archéologiques à Bornéo, Kalimantan." *L'Anthropologie* 99 (4): 67–70.

Chazine, Jean-Michel. 2000. "Découverte de peintures rupestres à Bornéo." *L'Anthropologie* 104 (3): 459–71. http://dx.doi.org/10.1016/S0003-5521(00)80006-0.

Clutton-Brock, Juliet. 1959. "Niah's Neolithic Dog." *Sarawak Museum Journal* 9 (ns 13–14): 143–5.

Fage, Luc-Henri, and Jean-Michel Chazine. 2009. *Bornéo: La Mémoire des Grottes*. Lyon: Fage Éditions.

Gilbertson, David, Michael Bird, Christopher Hunt, Sue McLaren, Richard Mani Banda, Brian Pyatt, Jim Brian, and Mark Stephens. 2005. Past Human Activity and Geomorphological Change in a Guano-Rich Tropical Cave Mouth: Initial Interpretations of the Late Quaternary Succession in the Great Cave of Niah, Sarawak." In *The Human Use of Caves in Peninsular and Island Southeast Asia*, ed. Graeme Barker and David Gilbertson, 16–41. Asian Perspectives 44 (1). Honolulu: University of Hawai'i Press.

Haji Taha, Adi bin. 1991. "Gua Cha and the Archaeology of the Orang Asli." *Bulletin of the Indo-Pacific Prehistory Association* 11 (2): 363–72.

Harrisson, Barbara. 1967. "A Classification of Stone Age Burials from Niah Great Cave." *Sarawak Museum Journal* 15 (ns 30–31): 126–99.

Harrisson, Tom. 1957. "The Great Cave of Niah: A Preliminary Report on Bornean Prehistory." *Man* 57: 161–6. http://dx.doi.org/10.2307/2795279.

Harrisson, Tom. 1958. "The Caves of Niah: A History of Prehistory." *Sarawak Museum Journal* 8 (ns 12): 549–95.

Harrisson, Tom. 1965. "50,000 Years of Stone Age Culture in Borneo." *Smithsonian Institution Annual Report* 964: 521–30.

Harrisson, Tom. 1970. "The Prehistory of Borneo." *Asian Perspectives (Honolulu)* 13: 17–45.

Hunt, Christopher, and Garry Rushworth. 2005. "Cultivation and Human Impact at 6000 cal. yr. BP in Tropical Lowland Forest at Niah, Sarawak, Malaysian Borneo." *Quaternary Research* 64 (3): 460–8. http://dx.doi.org/10.1016/j.yqres.2005.08.010.

Hunt, Christopher, and Graeme Barker. N. d. "Missing Links, Cultural Modernity and the Dead: Anatomically Modern Humans in the Great Cave of Niah (Sarawak, Borneo)." In *East of Africa: Southern Asia, Australia and Modern Human Origins*. Cambridge: Cambridge University Press.

Krigbaum, John. 2005. "Reconstructing Human Subsistence in the West Mouth (Niah Cave, Sarawak) Burial Series Using Stable Isotopes of Carbon." In *The Human Use of Caves in Peninsular and Island Southeast Asia*, ed. Graeme Barker and David

Gilbertson, 73–89. Asian Perspectives 44 (1). Honolulu: University of Hawai'i Press.

Krigbaum, John, and Jessica Manser. In press. "The West Mouth Human Remains." In *The Archaeology of Niah Caves, Sarawak: Excavations 1954–2004*, ed. Graeme Barker, David Gilbertson, and Tim Reynolds. McDonald Monographs. Cambridge: McDonald Institute for Archaeological Research; Kuching, Sarawak: Sarawak Museums.

Latinis, David Kyle, and Ken Stark. 1998. "Prehistory, Subsistence and Arboriculture in Central Maluku." In *Old World Places, New World Problems: Exploring Issues of Cultural Diversity, Environmental Sustainability, Economic Development and Local Government in Maluku, Eastern Indonesia*, ed. Sandra Pannell and Franz von Benda-Beckmann, 34–65. Canberra: Centre for Resource and Environmental Studies, Australian National University.

Lloyd-Smith, Lindsay. 2009. "Chronologies of the Dead: Later Prehistoric Burial Practice at the Niah Caves, Sarawak." PhD dissertation, University of Cambridge, Cambridge.

Pasveer, Juliette. 2003. *Djief Hunters: 26,000 Years of Lowland Rainforest Exploitation on the Bird's Head of Papua, Indonesia*. Groningen: STIP Stencilwerk, Leeuwarden, and Rijksuniversiteit Groningen.

Paz, Victor. 2005. "Rock Shelters, Caves, and Archaeobotany in Island Southeast Asia." In *The Human Use of Caves in Peninsular and Island Southeast Asia*, ed. Graeme Barker and David Gilbertson, 107–18. Asian Perspectives 44 (1). Honolulu: University of Hawai'i Press.

Rabett, Ryan, and Graeme Barker. 2007. "Through the Looking Glass: New Evidence on the Presence and Behaviour of Late Pleistocene Humans at Niah Cave, Sarawak, Borneo." In *The Human Revolution Revisited*, ed. Paul Mellars, Ofar Bar-Yosef, and Chris Stringer, 411–24. Cambridge: McDonald Institute Monographs.

Rabett, Ryan, Philip Piper, and Graeme Barker. 2006. "Bones from 'Hell': Preliminary Results of New Work on the Harrisson Faunal Assemblage from the Deepest Part of Niah Cave, Sarawak." In *Uncovering Southeast Asia's Past: Selected Papers from the 10th International Conference of the European Association of Southeast Asian Archaeologists*, ed. Elisabeth Bacus, Ian Glover, and Vincett Pigott, 46–59. Singapore: National University of Singapore Press.

Solheim, Wilhelm. 1977a. "The Niah Research Program." *Journal of the Malaysian Branch of the Royal Asiatic Society* 51: 28–40.

Solheim, Wilhelm. 1977b. "Tom Harrisson and Borneo Archaeology." *Borneo Research Bulletin* 9 (1): 3–7.

Solheim, Wilhelm. 1983. "Archaeological Research in Sarawak, Past and Future." *Sarawak Museum Journal* 53: 35–58.

Spriggs, Matthew. 1989. "The Dating of the Island Southeast Asian Neolithic: An Attempt at Chronometric Hygiene and Linguistic Correlation." *Antiquity* 63 (1): 587–613.

Tweedie, Michael. 1953. "The Stone Age in Malaya." *Journal of the Malaysian Branch of the Royal Asiatic Society* 26 (2): 1–90.

Valentine, Benjamin, George Kamenov, and John Krigbaum. 2008. "Reconstructing Neolithic Groups in Sarawak, Malaysia, Through Lead and Strontium Isotope Analysis." *Journal of Archaeological Science* 35 (6): 1463–73. http://dx.doi.org/10.1016/j.jas.2007.10.016.

Zuraina Majid. 1982. "The West Mouth, Niah, in the Prehistory of Southeast Asia." *Sarawak Museum Journal* 31 (ns 52): 1–200.

18

Recognizing Ritual in the Dark

Nakovana Cave and the End of the Adriatic Iron Age

Timothy Kaiser and Stašo Forenbaher

Nakovana Cave overlooks the Adriatic Sea from just below the crest of a 400-meter-high ridge near the tip of the strategically important Pelješac peninsula, 100 kilometers north of Dubrovnik on Croatia's Dalmatian coast (figure 18.1). In the distance, the sea stretches out to the neighboring islands of Mljet, Korčula, Hvar, and Vis. These were some of the most important Adriatic sea-lanes in antiquity.

The entrance to the cave is obscured by a screen of trees growing on a terrace immediately in front of it, and cannot be seen from the plateau below. From the terrace, though, the cave looks like a slit cut at a shallow angle back into the limestone. The entrance chamber is 20 meters wide but only 2 meters high at the front. Its ceiling slopes down to meet a rubble-strewn floor some 15 meters away, where the cave seems to end.

We began our investigation of Nakovana Cave in July 1999, when it was already well known as the type-site for the eastern Adriatic Early Copper Age (Forenbaher 2000; Petrić 1976). During five excavation seasons, we exposed a total area of 78 square meters. Initially we focused on a deep sounding located in the entrance chamber (Sector 1), where prehistoric cultural deposits are about 4 meters thick and cover the entire local post-Mesolithic sequence. Eleven occupation phases and subphases span 6,000 years, from the Early Neolithic to the Illyrian Iron Age (Forenbaher and Kaiser 2001, 2003).

None of these deposits contains anything unusual. Neither the features nor the assemblages of various classes of artifacts, fauna, mollusks, and so on hint at any special activities taking place in the entrance chamber. We should hasten to point out that this is a comparative assessment. For while it is certainly true that all caves are in some sense special places, as Richard Bradley (2000) reminds us, we would add that some caves are more special than others.

Examples are close at hand. Nakovana faces another famous cave, Grapčeva, located across the channel on the steep south slopes of the island of Hvar (Novak 1955). There, an extreme abundance of pottery (much of it highly decorated), faunal remains consistent with conventional feasting, and the deposition of disarticulated and probably defleshed human skeletal elements, suggest that Grapčeva was the site of ritual behavior(s) of some kind during the Late Neolithic (fifth millennium BC) (Forenbaher and Kaiser 2000, 2008; Forenbaher, Kaiser, and Frame 2010).

The entrance chamber of Nakovana Cave shows no comparable anomalies. Instead, for century after century, prosaic activities and uses (shelter, cooking, penning domestic animals, concealment, etc.) were more common than was symbolically charged, ideologically motivated behavior. That, at least, was the impression gained from the evidence recovered from our deep sounding in Sector 1.

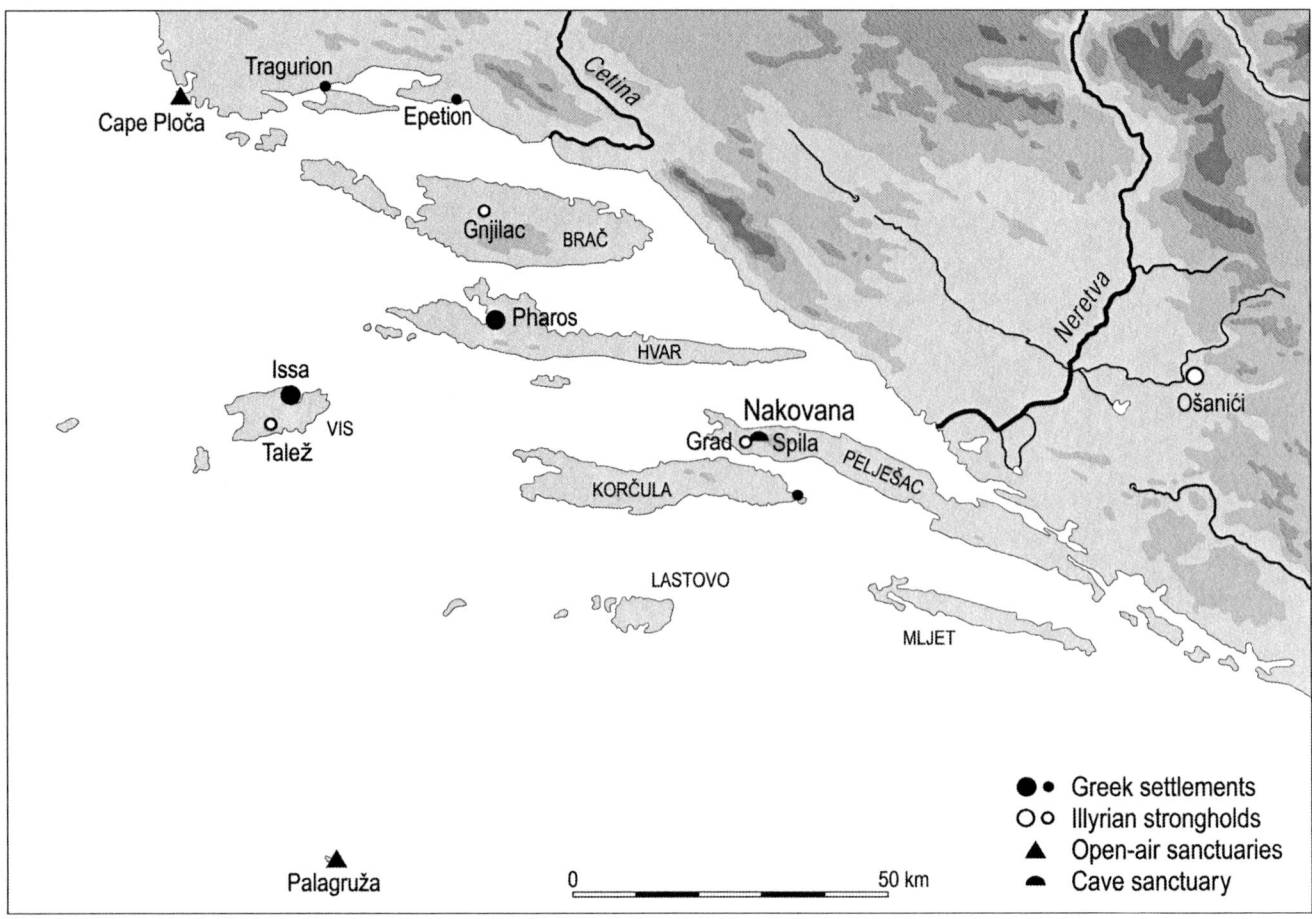

FIGURE 18.1 Central Dalmatia, showing the location of Nakovana Cave and other sites discussed in the text.

DISCOVERY OF A HIDDEN CHANNEL

Early in the excavation of this sector, our experience of cave morphology led us to suspect that the channel might continue beyond the point where the rubble met the downward curve of the ceiling. Wondering whether there was anything more to the cave, toward the end of our first season we started to look for a possible entrance to a (then-hypothetical) hidden channel. Our suspicions were borne out. We found that the rubble choked a wide, low passageway, less than half a meter high, with stalactites suspended from the ceiling. This passage slopes slightly downward into the dark for almost 10 meters. Then the cave opens up, revealing a long, high-ceilinged channel that widens to form two fairly spacious chambers (figure 18.2). On our first visit to the hidden channel, a stalagmitic crust covered parts of the surface, forming thick layers in some parts and a light glaze in others. Close inspection of the crust showed that it was undisturbed. Clearly, the channel was choked a long time ago, intentionally, sealing off the back of the cave.

Nakovana's middle chamber drew our immediate attention (figure 18.3). Fragments of many pottery vessels were lying on the surface, most of them Hellenistic Greek finewares, dating to the last four centuries BC. They were exceptionally well preserved, relatively large, and, judging from their associations, appeared for the most part to have been left where they were broken. The densest cluster of pottery was found in front of the chamber's dominant feature, a single, relatively large (0.65-m high) stalagmite. Taken together, the ceramic assemblage, the distribution of finds, and the setting itself suggested that this might be a ritual site of special significance, a sanctuary.

Moreover, Nakovana Cave was an undisturbed site. The nature of the site's discovery is a rare one in archaeology, since it is almost never the case that archaeologists are the first to enter a sealed cave. Over the course of two seasons, we excavated the middle chamber's Hellenistic layer in Sector 2, exposing 47 square meters of its surface and removing about 3 tons of cultural deposit. This layer was rarely more than a few centimeters thick, and it petered out

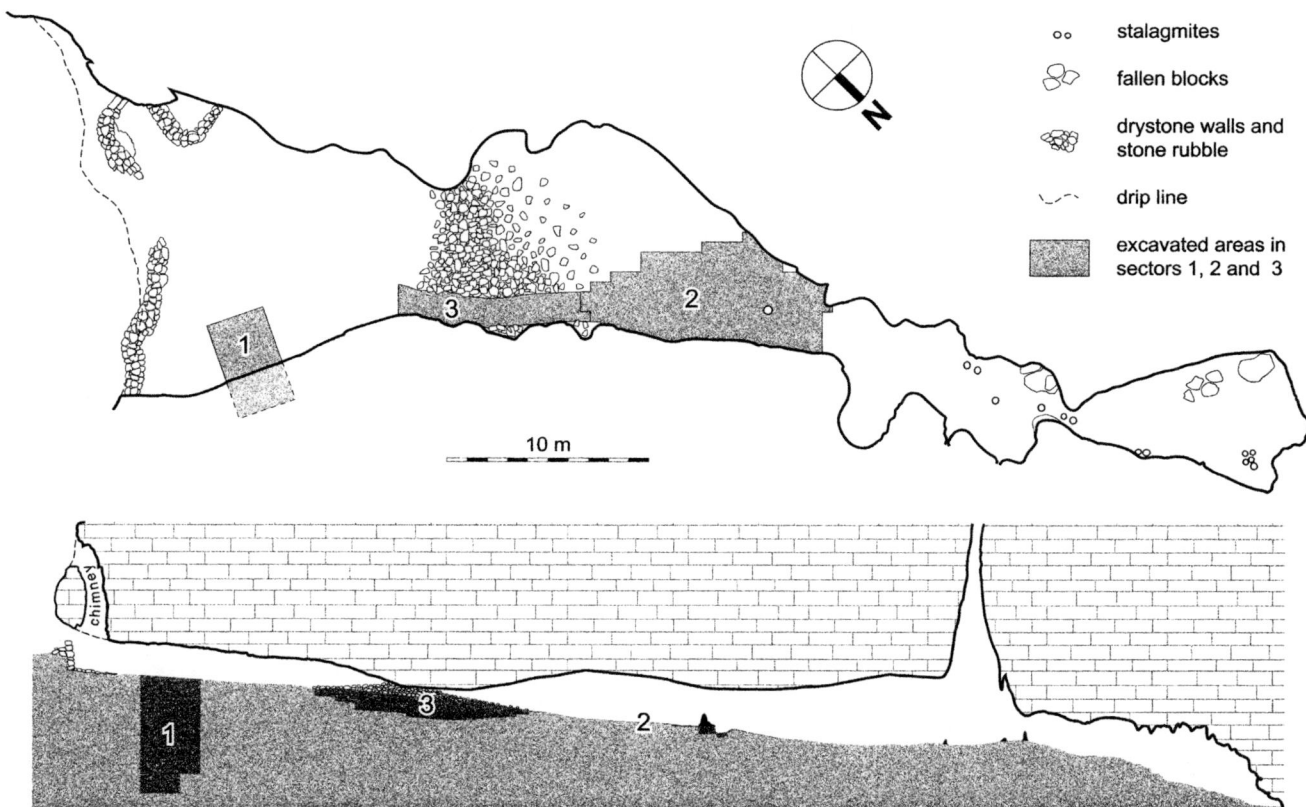

FIGURE 18.2 Plan and section of Nakovana Cave, showing excavated areas.

completely beyond the excavated area. The extremely high density of unusually well-preserved finds embedded in a matrix of very plastic wet clay called for particularly careful recovery methods. Excavation proceeded in half-meter squares, and all the excavated sediment was transported to the field laboratory where it was wet-sieved on tables with 3-millimeter meshes, aided by a high-pressure water gun. We should point out that not a single artifact was recovered from the cave interior that could be dated to a time any later than the first century BC.

Nakovana Cave thus provides us with a rare opportunity to investigate an undisturbed ritual site. In this chapter, we discuss what it is that persuades us that this cave was an Illyrian sanctuary, what sorts of ritual activities took place there, and what aspects of a wider context help us understand why the cave suddenly became part of a sacred landscape, and why it just as suddenly dropped out of the picture.

FOCUSING ATTENTION: A SPECIAL SPACE

Ritual activities tend to be carried out at locations with unusual natural characteristics, in places that can contain the participants, focus their attention, and veil them in mystery (Renfrew 1985, 18). At Nakovana, the middle chamber fits this bill perfectly. It is the largest, most comfortable space in the interior part of the cave. With a relatively smooth, slab-like, angled ceiling and an almost straight vertical wall forming its long axis on the right, there is enough room here for a small group. Access to this space is tightly controlled, however. To gain entry, one must crawl through the long, low passage.

The chamber is almost completely dark, except for a pale beam of daylight that penetrates through the passage, faintly illuminating the single large stalagmite. This formation sits on the edge of a break in the cave floor's slope, beyond which a high, vaulted corridor descends into the mountain, setting the stalagmite against a dark background. When the light is on it, a dramatic visual effect is created, enhancing the impression of size, and establishing the overriding visual focus.

The stalagmite bears no signs of having been carved. Instead, nature has worked an uncanny piece of mimicry. The stalagmite strongly resembles a phallus, right down to a pair of basal protuberances that look like testicles. One should regard this observation with some caution, however,

FIGURE 18.3 The middle chamber of Nakovana Cave.

since the stalagmite is still active and we do not know exactly what it looked like more than two millennia ago.

Since there were no stalagmites of comparable size in the middle chamber, we wondered whether this one could have formed somewhere else, only to be moved to its present prominent location. In an attempt to resolve questions about its history, we dug a small sounding immediately next to it (figure 18.4). The stalagmite rested on top of a series of superimposed prehistoric layers, including hearth remains associated with Early Copper Age pottery, dated by radiocarbon to the mid-fourth millennium BC (4870 ± 40 bp, 1-sigma range: 3700–3635 cal BC [Beta-156934, wood charcoal], and 4570 ± 40 bp, 1-sigma range: 3490–3120 cal BC [Beta-156933, wood charcoal]). A direct radiocarbon date on the base of the stalagmite suggests that it began to grow about 3,600 years ago or later (3630 ± 85 bp, 1-sigma range: 2140–1880 cal BC [Z-3024, calcium carbonate]). Therefore, whether the stalagmite grew in this spot, or whether it was moved there from elsewhere, remains an open question. The layer containing the Hellenistic pottery ran up against the stalagmite, which must therefore predate the fourth century BC.

The stalagmite sits between two artificial features, a shallow transversal trough and a deeper pit, both dug in Hellenistic times. The pit is a kettle-like feature dug into the cave floor immediately behind the stalagmite. A meter in diameter and half a meter deep, we found it empty, but we surmise that it used to fill with water trickling from the nearby rock wall. The evidence for this is a thick stalagmitic crust that covers one side of the pit, created by a long, slow flow of drip water. One can only hypothesize that this pit may have been used for ritual cleansing, or it might have been a lustral basin used to divine the supernatural.

PARTICIPATION AND OFFERING: SPECIAL THINGS

Thanks to the fact that the cave's deeper recesses were sealed soon after the sanctuary was abandoned, the evidence of what people did there during the last few centuries BC is unusually well preserved. Unlike general-purpose cave sites, the evidence is highly structured and clearly suggests ritual behavior. In this section we discuss various aspects of that structure.

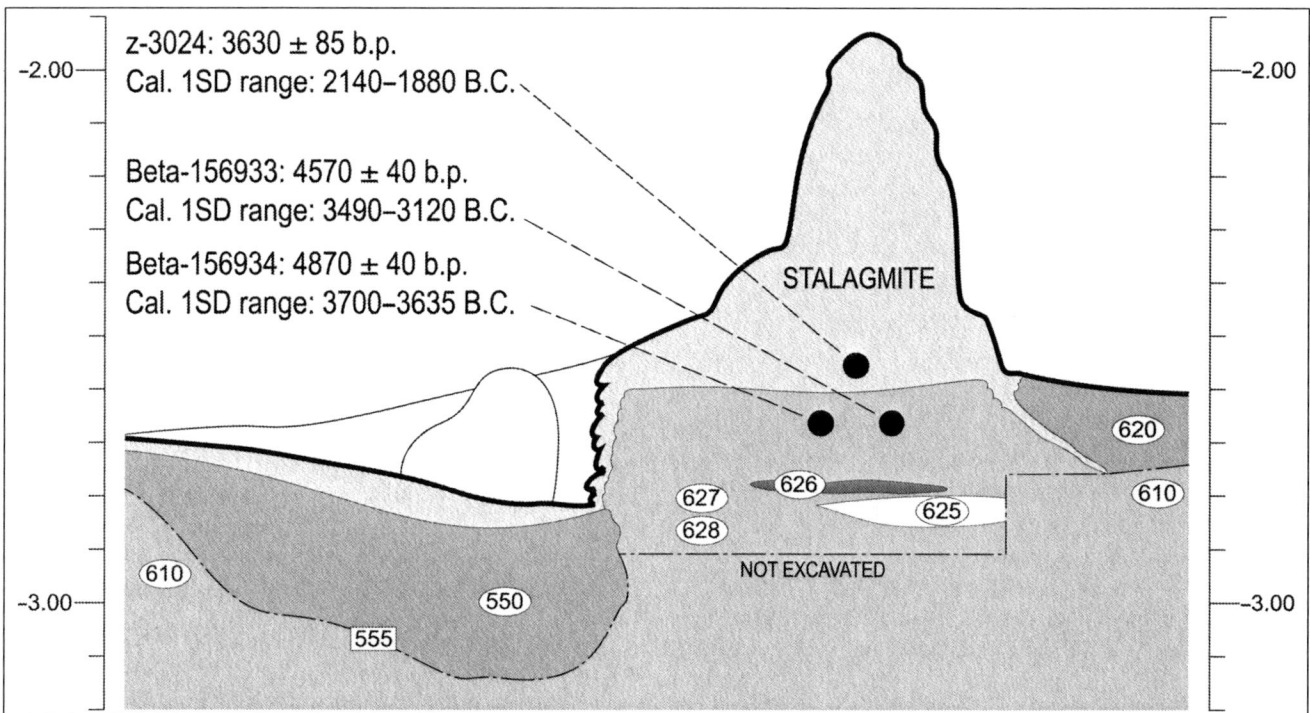

FIGURE 18.4 Stratigraphic context and dating of the stalagmite: 620 = main Hellenistic layer; 550 = fill of Hellenistic pit; 555 = cut of Hellenistic pit; 627 and 628 = Early Copper Age layers; 625 and 626 = Early Copper Age hearths; 610 = Early Copper Age (?) layer. Relative elevation from arbitrary datum in meters.

	n	n %	weight (kg)	weight %
Handmade pottery	2,182	23.3	29.2	31.7
Hellenistic finewares	6,168	65.9	27.9	30.3
Hellenistic coarsewares	817	8.7	2.8	3.0
Amphorae	180	1.9	31.8	34.6
Unclassified	10	0.1	0.4	0.4
TOTAL	9,357	100.0	92.1	100.0

TABLE 18.1 Pottery recovered from the middle chamber of Nakovana Cave.

Pottery provides us with an initial set of clues. Many of the almost 10,000 sherds recovered from the Hellenistic layer were refitted to form well over 100 nearly complete vessels. More than 6,000 sherds, amounting to almost exactly two-thirds of the total assemblage (table 18.1), were finewares dating from the mid-fourth to the early first century BC. Various types of cups—*skyphoi* and *kantharoi* especially—were the most numerous, followed by plates, bowls, and single-handled juglets. Also present were occasional pitchers, miniature amphorae, and other miniature vessels. Hellenistic coarse wares and amphorae together contributed just over 10 percent of all sherds. The sheer dominance of finewares in the pottery assemblage is very unusual and strongly suggests that this was not a general-purpose site.

The Hellenistic finewares in the Nakovana assemblage were not produced locally, but came from a variety of sources. Most of the polychrome painted Gnathia and black-gloss wares were probably produced in workshops at the Greek colony of Issa, located 65 kilometers west of Nakovana on the island of Vis (Kirigin 1996, 132–133). It is possible that some other Greek outpost in Dalmatia also produced some of the fineware vessels that were ultimately deposited at Nakovana (Brusić 1990; Kirigin, Hayes, and Leach 2002). Even more distant workshops are represented in the Nakovana assemblage as well. A small number of Gnathia and black-gloss vessels probably came from Greek colonies in southern Italy (Forti 1965). A few vessels of Alto-Adriatico style came from the head of the Adriatic, possibly from Spina or Adria (Kirigin 2000). Still others came from the Greek mainland (Athens and Corinth), and a few faience body sherds may have come from distant Egypt.

Small amounts of fine Greek or Hellenistic ceramics do appear at a number of settlements in Dalmatia that were occupied by native Illyrian communities, such as Talež on the island of Vis (Gaffney et al. 2000, 189) or Gnjilac on the island of Brač (Stančič et al. 1999, 158–59). Such sites, however, never yield ceramic assemblages that are heavily dominated by imported finewares. A substantial amount of fine Hellenistic ceramics (mainly fragments of Gnathia cups and a few pitchers) was found at the major Illyrian stronghold of Ošanići, some 70 kilometers away in the mainland interior. Interestingly, the greatest part of that assemblage was recovered from a structure that its excavator called a "temple (?)" (Marić 1973, 177–78, plates 10–26). If, however, one looks for assemblages as heavily dominated by imported finewares as the one from Nakovana Cave, the closest parallels are those from Palagruža and Cape Ploča, both of which are demonstrably ritual sites (Kirigin 2003, 2004; Kirigin and Čače 1998).

Fine Hellenistic vessels were systematically deposited in front of the stalagmite in the middle chamber. Their spatial distribution clearly shows that this was indeed the focus of attention. By far the highest concentration—up to 7 kilograms per square meter—is right in front of the stalagmite in an area only about 1 meter across (figure 18.5). This, plus the fact that fragments are usually grouped, indicates that vessels were not smashed and scattered around, but were either left complete or deliberately crushed on the spot.

Over 2,000 sherds from the middle chamber, amounting to almost a quarter of the total assemblage, come from handmade pots (table 18.1). These are products of a traditional prehistoric technology and were made from local clays, fired at low to moderate temperatures using simple bonfires or pit fires. Their scattered distribution, as well as the occasional diagnostic piece, suggest that most of these sherds may be much older residual finds that were incorporated into the disturbed layer along the entrance passage, or that slid down slope into the middle chamber from the outside, or that were kicked up to the surface from the directly underlying Bronze Age and earlier layers. A likely exception is seen in the fragments of a dozen or more very roughly made small vessels that were recovered from within the main concentration of Hellenistic finds in front of the stalagmite. Several are fully reconstructed small conical bowls or miniature cup-shaped and dish-shaped vessels. These are probably contemporaneous with the Hellenistic finewares.

Clusters of vessels show that pottery was left in groups near the stalagmite, possibly as discrete episodes of deposition (figure 18.6). Three such groups are very clearly defined, with another half-dozen groups more hazily apparent. Given the manner in which the fine ceramics were deposited, it seems reasonable to infer that offerings were being made here. Half a dozen Greek or Latin graffiti, scratched onto the vessels, support this inference.

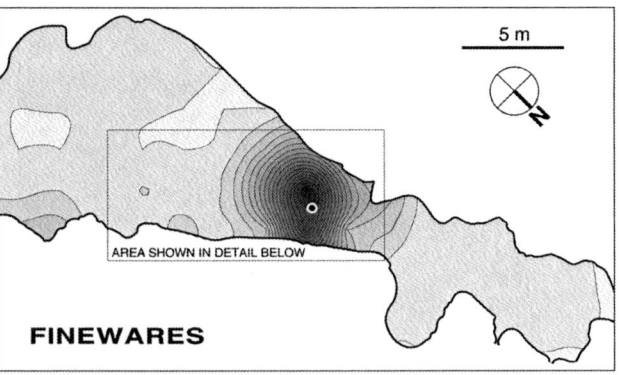
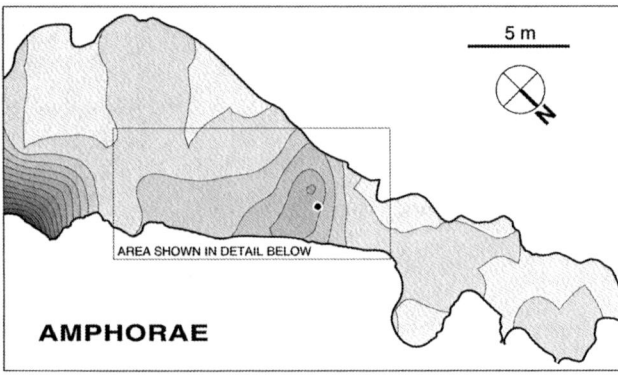
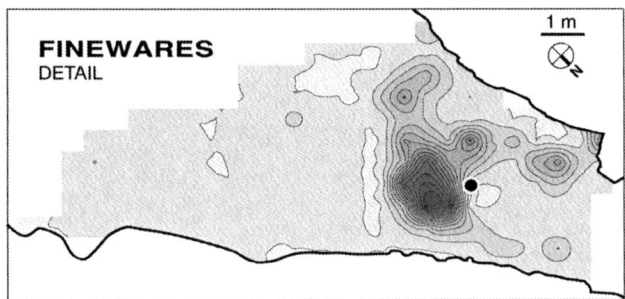
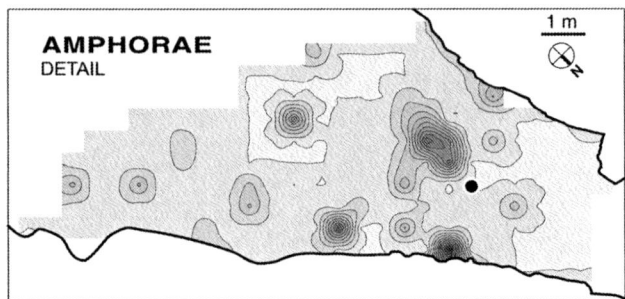

FIGURE 18.5 Weight-density distribution of Hellenistic finewares and amphorae in the middle chamber of Nakovana Cave, based on (top) a 2-meter grid and (bottom) a 0.5-meter grid within Sector 2. Black dot marks the position of the stalagmite.

Breakage and dispersal may also be explained by postdepositional factors. The sanctuary was in use for about three centuries, which means that the earlier offerings may have been damaged or removed during the later episodes of

FIGURE 18.6 A cluster of Hellenistic cups and plates in situ, next to the stalagmite in the middle chamber of Nakovana Cave.

ritual activity. There is some supporting evidence in that the remains of older vessels tend to be less complete than the younger ones. Natural agents that may have caused ceramic vessels to topple and break include various small animals, such as dormice, weasels, and snakes, which frequently come into the cave to drink, as well as massive earthquakes, several of which have hit the region in recent times.

Dealing with the supernatural is usually considered dangerous and so requires that rules of behavior be strictly observed. As a result, ritual behavior tends to be highly formalized and conservative, resulting in redundancy within all classes of archaeological evidence (Renfrew 1985, 19). Such redundancy seems to exist in our case, with the same narrow repertoire of ceramic-vessel types being deposited in the same way, in the same place, during several episodes of activity, stretched over a period of about three centuries.

The ceramic assemblage consists mainly of drinking and serving vessels. Cups are the most common class, followed by plates; several jugs and a pitcher were also recovered. This is consistent with feasting behavior. The analysis of the relatively small faunal assemblage cannot unequivocally demonstrate that ritual feasting was taking place in the cave, nor can it preclude that possibility (Wilson 2002; see Appleby and Miracle, chapter 19, this volume, for a detailed consideration of Nakovana's faunal remains). Since organic residues on the pottery have not yet been recovered, we can only hypothesize that the drinking vessels probably contained wine, which was brought up to the cave in amphorae. These ancient "cheap containers" were not treated with the same care as were the finewares. Their fragments were scattered more evenly across the full length of the chamber, even though they were much heavier (see figure 18.6). Their main concentration is in the entrance passage, but we also find them outside, marking a 200-meter-long trail down the hillside.

It is bad form to offer cheap stuff to the gods. Most of the finds recovered from the middle chamber of the cave can be regarded as valuable items. Most ceramic offerings were imported finewares, including special vessels made for ritual use, such as a gray ware relief-molded shallow libation vessel (*phiale*) with figural motifs (figure 18.7) produced most probably in Italy in the third century BC (Bonomi 1995, figures 5 and 6; Sanesi Mastrocinque 1986, 95, figure 555). Other offerings include various miniature vessels.

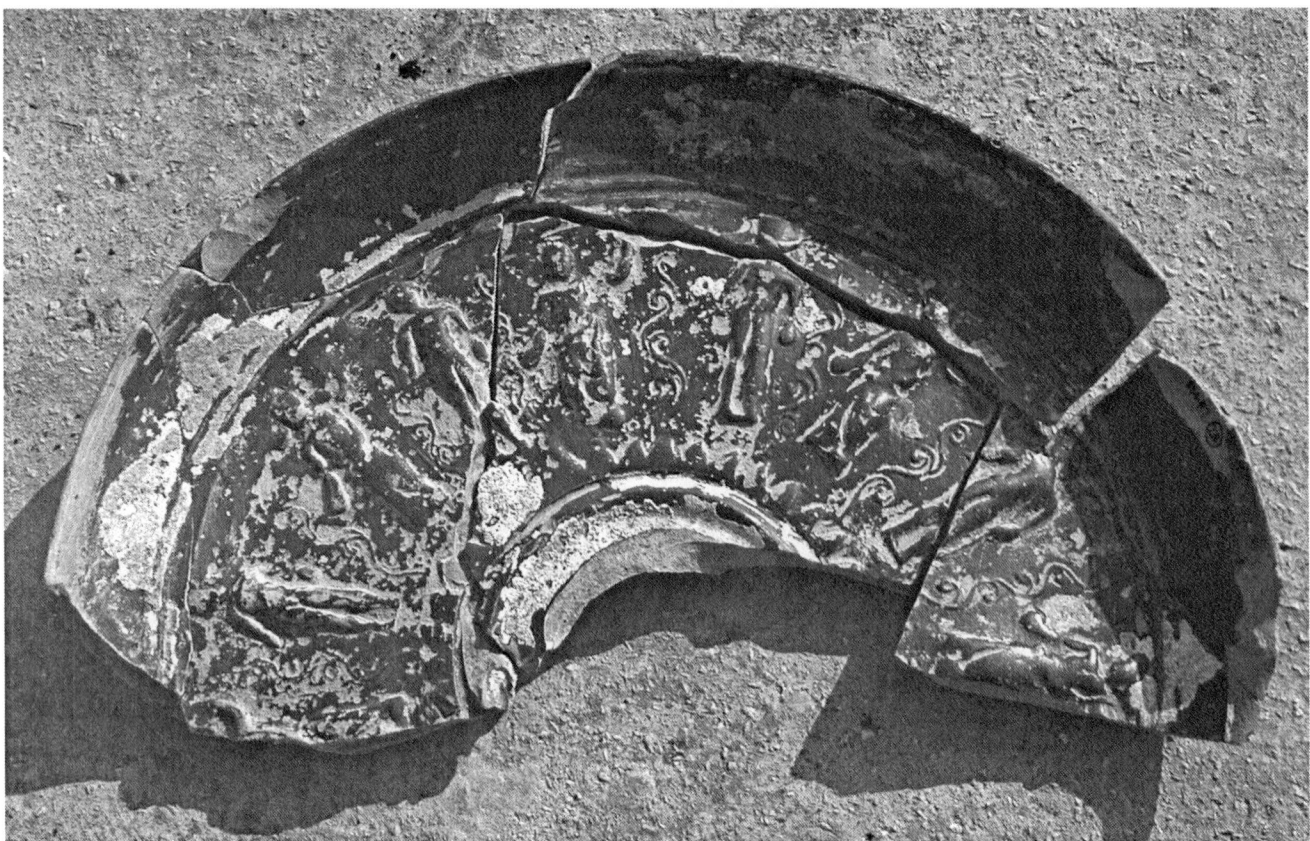

FIGURE 18.7 Partially reconstructed gray ware relief-molded *phiale* with figurative motifs.

The votive nature of these deposits is further underscored by the (admittedly rare) graffiti dedications. The acquisition of such vessels—whether by trading or raiding—must have involved considerable investment. Another hint that these objects were highly esteemed is the unusually high frequency of mending holes bored through the potsherds. Apparently, efforts were made to keep these vessels functional as long as possible.

PRESENCE OF THE DEITY

Religious ritual is a communion between human participants and a transcendental power. The presence of this power is often symbolized by an image. In our case, the focus of attention—the phallic stalagmite—may be interpreted as such an image, with obvious iconographic associations of masculine fertility, potency, and other traditional male-related qualities such as warrior strength and prowess. While we do not rule out the participation of females in whatever celebrations took place at the cave, we note that, out of the four names that appear on the pottery graffiti, two are male and the other two indeterminate.

It is highly tempting, given all the Hellenistic pottery, to draw on classical Greek sources in order to understand the cult at Nakovana Cave. In the Greek world, and in the world of their neighbors, votive offerings were a customary ritual practice in the sanctuaries (Burkert 1985). Among the most important offerings was alcohol, especially wine. The ritual consumption of alcoholic beverages was an important symbolic act, often associated with gatherings at ceremonial or cult sites. The association of copious alcoholic consumption with a phallic monument suggests the possibility of Dionysian behavior, with all the orgiastic excesses the term connotes (Bruit Zaidman and Schmitt Pantel 1992, 198–207, 218–22). Similar qualities of hypervirility are associated with other mythological figures as well, from Pan to Priapus. Of course, these were not the only Greek deities with a potential claim on the attention of the Nakovana celebrants. One partial graffito inscription, consisting of four letters ("ITES"), is consistent with several possible Greek names, including that of Aphrodite.

One should bear in mind, though, that Nakovana Cave was not controlled by the Greeks (this issue is discussed below in some detail). It was located well within the territory of a relatively strong and well-defined local Illyrian community. In the centuries that followed, the most popular deity in Roman Dalmatia was Sylvanus, a Roman interpretation of Pan, often worshiped in caves. Rendić-Miočević (1955, 10–11) has argued convincingly that, in Dalmatia, an important Illyrian deity lurked behind Sylvanus's numerous depictions. It is quite possible that the stalagmite at the ritual focus of Nakovana Cave represented that same Illyrian deity.

It would be incautious to assume that Illyrians were using Greek things in a conventional (Greek) fashion. Indeed, the sanctuary in Nakovana Cave yielded some clear evidence of non-Greek behavior. The mending holes on the finewares represent a departure from Greek practice, where votive offerings were previously unused objects not meant ever to be removed from the offering place (Burkert 1985). Equally suggestive is the absence of several classes of finds that one would expect to encounter in a classical sanctuary. The Greeks, and later the Romans, used characteristically shaped ceramic lamps. In cave sanctuaries in Greece proper, such lamps are common finds (Francis et al. 2000). By contrast, we did not find a single ceramic lamp fragment at Nakovana Cave. The local people did not use them, and light must have been provided by other means. We also found no coins, weapons, or jewelry, all of which are common in Greek sanctuaries of the period (Burkert 1985).

Both wine and the gear needed to drink wine were expensive. Their use among the Illyrians was an act of conspicuous consumption, as it was for other Iron Age Europeans (Dietler 1990; Stipčević 1989, 70). Drinking exotic, imported alcohol set the elite apart from everyone else. Alternatively, wine made for a significant reward for services rendered to a chief, who could use gifts of wine to build or cement a following. Finally, wine made for a very special offering, imbuing any ritual occasion with importance.

WHO WERE THE CELEBRANTS?

The rare graffiti on ceramics, three of which apparently display Greek names, indicate that non-Illyrians sometimes may have been allowed to participate in the ritual. A few Greek graffiti do not mean, however, that the sanctuary was under Greek control. Other important, indisputably Illyrian sites have also yielded sherds with Greek graffiti—the mostly Hellenistic amphorae from the mainland stronghold of Ošanići, for example, do not alter that site's Illyrian identity (Marić 2004). At Nakovana, all other evidence suggests that local people, Illyrians therefore, were the celebrants in the cave.

Nakovana Cave does not sit in a vacuum. Our survey of the surrounding microregion provides a sound basis for discussion of the celebrants' identity (Forenbaher, Kirigin, and Vujnović 2001). A short walk downhill from the cave brings one to the base of a towering hill fort. Grad, as it is called, dominates the western end of the Pelješac peninsula (Petrić 1978). From the ridge immediately above the cave entrance, the hill fort sits in plain view, only 1 kilometer away to the southwest. Our intensive surface survey of Grad produced a large pottery assemblage consisting of a mixture of local handmade wares and Hellenistic coarse wares and amphorae. While only a handful of black-gloss fineware fragments were recovered, these were identical to some of the finds from the cave sanctuary. Structural remains visible at the surface of the hill fort are consistent with local, indigenous dry-stone building traditions, and there is a telling absence of classic Greco-Roman building materials such as roof tiles or plaster.

The hill fort is surrounded by cemeteries consisting of more than fifty burial cairns. None of them has been systematically excavated, but many were looted in antiquity or in more recent times (Petrić 1981). What remains in and around the looted cairns provides some basic information about their original contents. The character of the funerary rite is unquestionably Illyrian (Marijan 2000, 119–23). Each cairn contained one or several inhumation burials in tombs that are lined with stone slabs or dry-stone walls. Grave goods that the looters overlooked include locally made Iron Age jewelry, handmade pottery, and—fairly often—fragments of fine Hellenistic ceramic vessels, identical to those from the cave.

It follows from the above that Grad hill fort was intensively occupied while the cave sanctuary was in use; that the local Illyrians controlled the area at that time; and that the Illyrian elites from the hill fort had access to exotic goods such as fine Hellenistic ceramics. Trade with the rest of the Mediterranean world was a critical factor in the political economy of the Illyrian polities (Wilkes 1992). Illyrians imported Greek and Italic goods and used them as prestige objects in their most significant social transactions (Batović 1984; Čović 1987, 472; Marijan 2000, 95–100). By the same token, trade with their "barbarian" neighbors was a significant activity for the Greeks, for it provided Greece and its colonies with raw materials, slaves, and other commodities.

Archaeological indicators of power and wealth from the hill fort and the surrounding cairn cemeteries suggest that, during the Late Iron Age/Hellenistic period, western Pelješac was a significant Illyrian stronghold. Geography supplies much of the explanation (see figure 18.1). The channels on either side of the peninsula were used by ships sailing north to the head of the Adriatic, or by those bound for the mouth of the Neretva River and thence the Balkan interior (Čače 1999, 68–69). Perched on their naturally defended hilltop, and with watchtowers on nearby promontories, the people at Grad could intercept some of the richest cargoes of the day. Ancient chroniclers repeatedly report that trading and raiding were important segments of the coastal Illyrian economy (Wilkes 1992, 168, 171, 224–25). Piracy, in the eyes of some, good business to others, it contributed to a constant flow of wealth.

The limited number of pottery groups left in the Nakovana sanctuary over a 300-year period may be taken to indicate that the offerings made there were not routine events. Rather, they suggest that special times called for special events, perhaps once a generation. Maybe the benevolence of supernatural forces had to be secured by a feast and the deposition of offerings before departure on some risky escapade at sea or on land. Perhaps the Illyrian leaders of Grad felt it necessary to secure the firm support of their followers by giving them gifts of high-status food and drink, served in appropriately classy gear. Maybe such festivities were held in gratitude after exceptionally successful trading ventures or pirate raids. Why not all of these together? In any event, part of the wealth that was acquired was left behind in the dark recesses of the cave, marking ancient celebrations.

Based on pottery typology, Nakovana Cave began to function as a sanctuary at some point during the second half of the fourth century BC, or, roughly the time of Alexander the Great. It ceased to function in the first century BC, at the outset of the Roman Imperial period. These two dates neatly bracket an unusually dynamic period in the eastern Adriatic, the unsettled centuries beginning with the Greek colonization of the central Dalmatian islands of Vis and Hvar, and culminating in the Roman conquest of the area (Kirigin 1996, 2004; Novak 1961; Wilkes 1969, 1992). The legends surrounding the Illyrian Queen Teuta notwithstanding, these were times when masculine power and warrior prowess would have been held in high esteem.

Realistic representations of the human form are quite rare in the pre-Roman Illyrian iconography of the Dalmatian coast and its hinterland. There are, however, several examples from the wider region (the west Balkans and the east Alpine foothills) that provide suggestive depictions. A couple of sketchy examples from the territory of the Japodes (an Illyrian group of western Bosnia and parts of southern Croatia) feature male human figures equipped with helmets—that is, warriors—in a state of sexual excitement (Čremošnik 1959, plates 1:2 and 2:3). Farther to the west, depictions of sexually aroused warriors engaged in ritualized combat adorn a bronze belt-sheath and a bronze bucket (Kastelic 1962, plates 32 and 36).

The almost exclusive presence of imported Hellenistic goods in an Illyrian sanctuary raises important questions. Ancient Greek custom was quite elaborate with respect to drinking rituals, prescribing the use of certain kinds of vessels when making particular offerings or dedications. Were the Illyrians faithfully adopting Greek customs as well as Greek goods, or were the local traditions only being embellished by the addition of novel cultural items? The answer is not likely to be found in the historical sources.

The Illyrians were thoroughly disliked by most of the classical historians. The Greeks, who supply us with the first accounts, regarded Illyrians as pirates and brigands, formidable opponents who came to play a significant role in the balance of power in the Adriatic and the Balkans. The Romans took an even more disparaging view. They did not understand the Illyrians very well, and had little interest in writing unbiased accounts of Illyrian ritual customs. Nakovana Cave provides a rare glimpse of the Illyrian spiritual world, which, although obviously incomplete, has not been distorted by the lens of a classical chronicler.

ABANDONMENT AND CLOSURE

The Illyrian lands finally fell under Roman control after a long and grim series of campaigns, beginning with the First Illyrian War of 229 BC. Almost 200 years later, Octavian (soon to become the first Roman emperor, Augustus) decided to subdue the Illyrians once and for all. His military campaigns lasted 8 years, from 35 to 27 BC, and encompassed almost the entire eastern Adriatic and much of its hinterland (Wilkes 1992: 196–97). During the first year of operations, the Roman army massacred the native populations of the islands of Korčula and Mljet. The Roman historian Appianus refers to the inhabitants of these islands as outlaws who were totally destroyed because they pillaged maritime commerce (Wilkes 1969, 50). Adult men were executed and the rest were sold into slavery. Historical sources do not say whether the Illyrians on the Pelješac peninsula were caught up in the disaster, but even if they were not involved directly, the slaughter in their immediate neighborhood must have made a major impact.

Although we lack a specific historical account, it seems that the Nakovana area met a particularly bad end. Our survey of the microregion found virtually no traces of occupation during the Early Imperial or Late Roman periods. This is an unusual situation in Dalmatia, where those periods often account for the bulk of archaeological remains. Apparently, the conquering Romans could not tolerate a native stronghold at such a key strategic position. The local population was either exterminated or forced to move to the mainland.

Soon after the Grad hill fort was abandoned, the sanctuary at Nakovana Cave was sealed. The evidence does not allow us to say whether this was done by some Illyrian at the moment of the hill fort's abandonment, or whether the cave was sealed some time later, perhaps by a shepherd who wanted to keep his animals from getting lost in the dark interior of the cave. Whoever filled the passage with rubble preserved the contents of the sanctuary for posterity, providing us with a remarkably eloquent set of archaeological assemblages. For that act, we offer thanks.

ACKNOWLEDGMENTS

The Nakovana Cave Project was funded by a generous gift from Audrey and David Mirvish and the Royal Ontario Museum Foundation, Toronto, Canada. This project was sponsored also by the Ministry of Science, Education and Sports of the Republic of Croatia (project no. 196-1962766-2740). Our work at Nakovana would not have been possible without the major engagement of John Hayes and Branko Kirigin, whose frequent counsel was invaluable.

REFERENCES CITED

Batović, Šime. 1984. "Contribution aux études de la céramique Corinthienne sur la côte orientale de l'Adriatique." *Vjesnik za arheologiju i historiju dalmatinsku* 77: 37–62.

Bonomi, Simonetta. 1995. "Adria nel secoli IV e III a. C." In *Concordi e la X Regio*, ed. P. Croce Da Villa and A. Mastrocinque, 263–365. Padova: Zielo editore.

Bradley, Richard. 2000. *The Archaeology of Natural Places*. London: Routledge.

Bruit Zaidman, Louise, and Pauline Schmitt Pantel. 1992. *Religion in the Ancient Greek City*. Cambridge: Cambridge University Press.

Brusić, Zdenko. 1990. "Resnik kod Kaštel Novog: Helenističko pristanište." *Arheološki pregled* 29: 117–19.

Burkert, Walter. 1985. *Greek Religion*. Cambridge, MA: Harvard University Press.

Čače, Slobodan. 1999. "Manijski zaljev, Jadastini i Salona." *Vjesnik za arheologiju i historiju dalmatinsku* 90–91: 57–87.

Čović, Borivoj. 1987. "Srednjodalmatinska grupa." In *Praistorija jugoslavenskih zemalja*, vol. 5, ed. S. Gabrovec, 422–80. Sarajevo: Akademija nauka Bosne i Hercegovine.

Čremošnik, Irma. 1959. "Spomenik sa japodskim konjanicima iz Založja kod Bihaća." *Glasnik Zemaljskog muzeja (arheologija)* new series 14: 103–11.

Dietler, Michael. 1990. "Driven by Drink: The Role of Drinking in the Political Economy and the Case of Early Iron Age France." *Journal of Anthropological Archaeology* 9 (4): 352–406. http://dx.doi.org/10.1016/0278-4165(90)90011-2.

Forenbaher, Stašo. 2000. "'Nakovana Culture': State of Research." *Opuscula archaeologica* 23–24: 373–85.

Forenbaher, Stašo, and Timothy Kaiser. 2000. "Grapčeva spilja i apsolutno datiranje istočnojadranskog neolitika." *Vjesnik za arheologiju i historiju dalmatinsku* 92: 9–34.

Forenbaher, Stašo, and Timothy Kaiser. 2001. "Nakovana Cave: An Illyrian Ritual Site." *Antiquity* 75: 677–8.

Forenbaher, Stašo, and Timothy Kaiser. 2003. *Spila Nakovana: An Illyrian Sanctuary on the Pelješac peninsula*. Zagreb: V.B.Z.

Forenbaher, Stašo, and Timothy Kaiser. 2008. *Grapčeva Špilja: Pretpovijesni stan, tor i obredno mesto (Rezultati arheološkog istraživanja 1996. godine)*. Split: Kniževni krug.

Forenbaher, Stašo, Timothy Kaiser, and Sheelagh Frame. 2010. "Adriatic Neolithic Mortuary Ritual at Grapčeva Cave, Croatia." *Journal of Field Archaeology* 35 (4): 337–54.

Forenbaher, Stašo, Branko Kirigin, and Nikša Vujnović. 2001. "Terenski pregled Nakovanske visoravni (poluotok Pelješac)." *Obavijesti Hrvatskog arheološkog društva* 33(2): 46–49.

Forti, Lidia. 1965. *La ceramica di Gnathia*. Napoli: Gaetano Macchiaroli.

Francis, Jane, Simon Price, Jennifer Moodz, and Lucia Nixon. 2000. "Agiasmati: A Greek Cave Sanctuary in Sphakia, SW Crete." *Annual of the British School at Athens* 95: 427–71.

Gaffney, Vince, Branko Kirigin, John Hayes, Timothy Kaiser, Peter Leach, and Zoran Stančič. 2000. "The Adriatic Islands Project: Contact, Commerce and Colonization 6000 BC–AD 600." In *Extracting Meaning from Ploughsoil Assemblages: The Archaeology of Mediterranean Landscapes*, vol. 5, ed. R. Francovich and H. Patterson, 185–98. Oxford: Oxbow.

Kastelic, Jože, ed. 1962. *Umetnost alpskih Ilirov in Venetov*. Ljubljana: Narodni muzej.

Kirigin, Branko. 1996. *Issa, grčki grad na Jadranu*. Zagreb: Matica Hrvatska.

Kirigin, Branko. 2000. "Alto-Adriatico Vases from Dalmatia." In *Adriatico tra IV e III sec. A.C., vasi Alto-Adriatici tra Piceno, Spina e Adria*, ed. M. Landolfi, 131–37. Rome: L'Erma Di Bretschneider.

Kirigin, Branko. 2003. "Palagruža godine 2002: Preliminarni izvještaj s arheoloških iskopavanja." *Opuscula archaeologica* 27: 367–78.

Kirigin, Branko. 2004. "The Beginning of Promontorium Diomedis Preliminary Pottery Report." *Hesperia* 18: 141–50.

Kirigin, Branko, and Slobodan Čače. 1998. "Archaeological Evidence for the Cult of Diomedes in the Adriatic." *Hesperia* 9: 63–110.

Kirigin, Branko, John Hayes, and Peter Leach. 2002. "Local Pottery Production at Pharos." In *Greek Influence along the East Adriatic Coast*, ed. Nenad Cambi, Slobodan Čače, and Branko Kirigin, 241–60. Split: Književni krug.

Marić, Zdravko. 1973. "Arheološka istraživanja na gradini u Ošanićima kod Stoca 1963 godine." *Glasnik Zemaljskog muzeja (arheologija)* new series 27–28: 173–235.

Marić, Zdravko. 2004. "Grafiti sa grčkih posuda iz razorenog ilirskog grada Daorsona iznad sela Ošanića kod Stoca u Hercegovini." *Godišnjak: Centar za balkanološka ispitivanja* 33/31: 185–94.

Marijan, Boško. 2000. *Željezno doba na južnojadranskom području (istočna Hercegovina, južna Dalmacija)*. *Vjesnik za historiju i arheologiju dalmatinsku* 93: 7–221.

Novak, Grga. 1955. *Prethistorijski Hvar*. Zagreb: Jugoslavenska akademija znanosti i umjetnosti.

Novak, Grga. 1961. "Stari Grci na Jadranskom moru." *Rad Jugoslavenske akademije znanosti i umijetnosti* 322: 145–221.

Petrić, Nikša. 1976. "Prethistorijske kulture Pelješca." *Pelješki zbornik* 1: 295–313.

Petrić, Nikša. 1978. "Gradina Grad u Nakovani na Pelješcu." In *Novija i neobjavljena istraživanja u Dalmaciji*, ed. Željko Rapanić, 35–48. Split: Hrvatsko arheološko društvo.

Petrić, Nikša. 1981. "Nakovana, Pelješac: Ilirski tumul." *Arheološki pregled* 22: 44–45.

Rendić-Miočević, Duje. 1955. "Ilirske predstave Silvana na kultnim slikama s područja Delmata." *Glasnik Zemaljskog muzeja u Sarajevu (arheologija)* new series 10: 5–40.

Renfrew, Colin. 1985. *The Archaeology of Cult: The Sanctuary at Phylakopi*. London: British School at Athens.

Sanesi Mastrocinque, Lucia. 1986. "La ceramica a vernice nera." In *Gli Etrusci a nord del Po,* ed. R. DeMarinis, 92–96. Udine: Campanotto.

Stančič, Zoran, Nikša Vujnović, Branko Kirigin, Slobodan Čače, Tomaž Podobnikar, and Josip Burmaz. 1999. *The Archaeological Heritage of the Island of Brač, Croatia*. British Archaeological Reports, International Series 803. Oxford: Archaeopress.

Stipčević, Aleksandar. 1989. *Iliri: Povijest, život, kultura*. 2nd ed. Zagreb: Školska knjiga.

Wilkes, John J. 1969. *Dalmatia*. London: Routledge & Kegan Paul.

Wilkes, John J. 1992. *The Illyrians*. Oxford: Blackwell.

Wilson, J. 2002. "Sacred Spaces, Sacred Species: An Analysis of the Faunal Remains from the Iron Age Shrine in Nakovana Cave." BA thesis, Department of Archaeology, University of Cambridge, Cambridge.

19

Sacred Spaces, Sacred Species

Zooarchaeological Perspectives on Ritual Uses of Caves

Joanna E.P. Appleby and Preston T. Miracle

During recent years, the role of animals in structuring and mediating social relations has been increasingly recognized within the discipline of zooarchaeology. In addition, animals and food are being recognized as rich in symbolism and as often-critical components of ritual and religious behavior (O'Day, van Neer, and Ervynck 2003). However, such approaches have been slow to filter through to the analysis of faunal remains from cave sites. Rather, caves continue to be seen predominantly as sites for habitation, where animal bones represent food refuse or raw materials for toolmaking activity, and where zooarchaeological research agendas are still predominantly driven by ideas of resource exploitation. In this chapter, we seek to illustrate that such approaches to faunal remains from caves are necessarily impoverished by their failure to address questions of symbolism, ritual, and religious action, and that the nature of caves as places makes them particularly amenable both to symbolic human behavior and to the zooarchaeological analysis of such behavior.

Caves as locations are far more than places of habitation or temporary refuge. Their nature makes them stand out from other places within the landscape, physically situated within but separate from the wider world. Often perceived in historical cultures as a boundary between the world above and the world below (Bradley 2000), there are few places so well suited to the idea of liminality (van Gennep 1981). It is thus not surprising that caves form some of the earliest known locations for human symbolic behavior (Bahn 1999), and have been associated with ritual and religious practices throughout prehistory and history (e.g., Emery 2003; Galik 2003; Rutkowski 1986). Caves form architectural spaces that have particular impacts upon the senses, being associated with particular kinds of sights, sounds, and smells that would have had an impact upon the ways in which they would have been used by humans.

Before proceeding to discuss the possibilities of using faunal remains to discuss symbolic and ritual behavior in caves, it is first necessary to give a brief description of what we mean by *ritual* in this case. Ritual can often be overused in archaeology as a convenient catchall explanation for aspects of depositional behavior that cannot be easily understood in a functional sense (Hill 1996). That is not what is meant in the present case. Rather, ritual is seen as a structured set of actions, related to traditions and beliefs. It may be related to religious activity but can also refer to certain kinds of secular actions. Bell (1997, cited in O'Day, van Neer, and Ervynck 2003, xii) defines *ritual* as "a complex sociocultural medium variously constructed of tradition, exigency and self-expression; it is understood to play a wide variety of roles and to communicate a rich density of over determined messages and attitudes." It may be embedded within daily actions or occur at specific special times or places. Symbolic behavior may be related to ritual behavior, but also refers to the social meanings encoded within the categories of animals and material culture.

ANIMALS, SYMBOLISM, AND SOCIETY

In human societies, animals are never just animals. Rather they are always imbued with symbolic and metaphorical significance (Russell 1999). Animals may be used to represent particular behavioral characteristics (e.g., the cunning fox, the brave lion), they may be associated with particular groups of people as totems or mascots (e.g., the Michigan Wolverines), with particular kinds of people (witches' cats), or they may be associated with deities (the Lamb of God). Such meanings of animals are culturally specific and influence the ways in which they can be used and manipulated in human social action (Douglas 1984).

In addition to meanings embedded within cultural traditions, animals (and thus faunal remains) are an important food resource. The relative inefficiency of raising livestock and the unpredictability of hunting means that the consumption of meat is about far more than relative numbers of calories. Fiddes (1991) has suggested that for this reason meat can be seen as having a universal social value. This leads to meat being exploited by individuals who are attempting to increase their social standing, particularly in the arena of feasting (Dietler 1996, 2001; Hayden 1996, 2001). Animals and their products are thus a fundamental means by which individuals can assert or contest status.

Caves are a prime location in which faunal remains may represent the result of ritualized behavior. Their special nature as a place aside from day-to-day life marks them out as somewhere for special events, in particular ritual activity (cf. Renfrew's "attention focusing devices" [1994]), while their specific architecture marks them out as phenomenological spaces. Although animal bones recovered from cave sites have often been analyzed merely in terms of everyday consumption and animal exploitation, they may represent the results of more complex behavior.

INTERPRETIVE STRATEGIES FOR IDENTIFYING RITUAL AND SYMBOLIC BEHAVIOR IN CAVES

The investigation of ritual uses of caves through the study of faunal remains does not require the development of major new types of zooarchaeological analysis, nor does it need the application of a "shopping list" of particular techniques. Rather, existing methodologies need to be employed to answer new kinds of questions, and they should be tailored to the research questions suggested by particular sites. Specifically, it is the practices directly leading to bone deposition, rather than more general day-to-day human-animal interactions, that need to form the focus of analysis. Of particular interest are the relationships between ideology and the use of animals, the possible use of animal sacrifice, and the presence and meaning of feasting behaviors. Relationships between faunal remains and other types of artifacts must also be considered. These questions then need to be tied in to the particular physical character of the cave via spatial analyses and considerations of the cave form.

Ideology and symbolism have formed the basis of much archaeological thought in the past 20 years; however, they have been relatively late to be adopted by faunal specialists (O'Day, van Neer, and Ervynck 2003). In historic cases, the symbolic meanings of animals are often known, and it is the ways in which animal remains are used to manipulate these meanings that are of interest. In prehistoric settings, the questions that need to be asked are more basic, as the symbolic meanings of animal remains are not known from other sources. In such contexts, the patterns of deposition of faunal remains, and their juxtaposition with other types of artifact, can be used to elucidate symbolic meanings.

One form of ritual behavior that has been associated with caves is animal sacrifice (Rutkowski 1986). This is something amenable to being studied by zooarchaeologists, both through analysis of butchery patterns and subsequent treatment of the carcass (e.g., Hamilakis and Konsolaki 2004). However, the form of sacrifice varies cross-culturally, preventing a "shopping list" approach to its identification.

A related behavior that may occur in caves is feasting. Characteristics of feasts that may be reflected in faunal remains have been well established (Albarella and Serjeantson 2002; Hayden 2001; Kelly 2001; Miracle 2002). As feasts tend to involve communal consumption, the amounts of meat required for a feast can be large. In addition, notions of generosity and excess often associated with feasts mean that more meat may be provided than can actually be consumed by the people present. Thus it may be assumed that large amounts of food waste will be produced in a single event. Zooarchaeologically, this may be represented by large numbers of particular kinds of animals in bone dumps (Hayden 2001; Kelly 2001) or by many articulated elements (Albarella and Serjeantson 2002; Hayden 2001). Particular species may be reserved for feasts, and this may be represented in caves by the presence of animals not usually found in habitation sites of an area.

In addition to identifying *which* species were present on a site, it has been suggested that *how* animals were processed may be an important means by which feasting can be identified zooarchaeologically. Two main factors are often cited in support of this. The first of these refers to the parts of the carcass that are eaten in feasts. As feasting behavior is supposed to be characterized by overabundance, some researchers have postulated that the meat-rich parts of the carcass (such as upper limb-bones and the axial skeleton) should be overrepresented in feasting debris. Measures such as Binford's Meat Utility Index (MUI) and Food Utility Index (FUI) may therefore be able to be used to analyze whether such a pattern is present within a faunal assemblage (Miracle 2002). In addition, feasting may involve a different mode of consumption than is seen in everyday food (Russell 1999) and this may lead to differences in cooking practices (Kelly 2001; Knight 2001; Wiessner 2001).

Caves have particular advantages and disadvantages when it comes to analyzing faunal remains. First, unlike many open-area excavations, modern cave excavations tend to operate using a grid-based system. This allows faunal remains to be easily situated in time and space, and can aid interpretation of depositional practices. Second, caves represent distinct, bounded areas that would have retained many physical characteristics from prehistoric and historic periods. The location of animal bones within a cave may be a direct reflection of the processes that have gone on there—in the absence of manipulation by carnivores subsequent to deposition, this means processes of human behavior. Differential deposition of bones in particular parts of the caves may cast light on ritual action. For example, it may be that bones are deposited near the cave entrance, or at its deepest darkest point; particular species may also be deposited in specific locations, as with the bear skulls placed on ledges within Chauvet Cave (Bahn 1999). A major disadvantage of caves is that activity is spatially constrained, and there is thus a tendency for archaeological deposits to form a palimpsest of material from different time periods, which may be difficult to separate stratigraphically. In addition, they form suitable habitats for a wide range of animals, many of which may interfere with archaeological deposits.

In order for the approaches outlined above to work, a rigorous approach to taphonomic factors must be maintained. Zooarchaeologists must be very certain that particular patterns of remains represent human behavior rather than weathering, gnawing, transportation by natural agents, or other such factors. For ritual behavior to be analyzed, it must be known which parts of an assemblage represent human deposition, which carnivore accumulation or disturbance, and which natural sedimentological processes. For example, where caves have a "chimney" shape and entry is possible only from above, the remains of animals that have fallen into a cave and suffered natural deaths must be distinguished from those faunal remains that have been put there deliberately. This can be particularly difficult where other taphonomic factors have moved faunal remains from their original positions (Galik 2003). An understanding of any changes in the configuration of caves is essential when making archaeological inferences (Farrand 2001).

NAKOVANA CAVE

Nakovana Cave is located on the tip of the Pelješac Peninsula of southern Croatia and contains deposits resulting from ritual behavior within a relatively inaccessible inner chamber (figure 19.1, and see Kaiser and Forenbaher, chapter 18, figure 18.1, this volume). Roof fall probably occurring after the mid–first century BC means that deposits of animal bone have survived intact.

Given the obviously special nature of the deposits from the inner chamber at Nakovana Cave, it was important that the study of the faunal remains should contribute as much as possible to the understanding of the events associated with the deposition of the Hellenistic wares at the end of the Iron Age. It was important to investigate not only what kinds of animal were represented by the sample, but also how animals were used to create and mediate particular kinds of meanings. Thus there were two distinct fields of investigation. First, we set out to establish the pattern of deposition of animal remains, and the relationship between the deposition of animal bones and ceramics. In this way, we hoped to elucidate the ways in which animals and objects differently structured the rituals that took place in Nakovana Cave. Second, we used the analysis of the faunal assemblage itself to investigate the practices that were occurring, their periodicity, and their possible meanings.

Investigations by Kaiser and Forenbaher (Forenbaher and Kaiser 2003; Kaiser and Forenbaher, this volume), have established that fine ceramics were preferentially deposited in front of the central stalagmite. Many of the ceramics were imported Greek vessels, some of considerable workmanship. The relationship between these and the stalagmite suggested that they had been deposited as the result of some ritual, possibly connected to feasting (Forenbaher and Kaiser 2003; Kaiser and Forenbaher, this volume). Thus it was of interest to know whether the animal-bone remains were the result of the same ritual depositional processes, or whether they represented a separate practice.

Animal remains from an excavation and collection area of 40 square meters in the inner chamber at Nakovana were analyzed. All sediment was wet-sieved using 1-millimeter mesh, and all bone was saved. The results discussed below are from study of a systematic 50-percent sample (alternating fifty-centimter by fifty-centimeter squares were analyzed). A total of 2,652 fragments were recovered, of which 904 were identifiable to element and/or taxon.

Taphonomic analysis of the sample suggested that it was unlikely to have been much disturbed by nonhuman

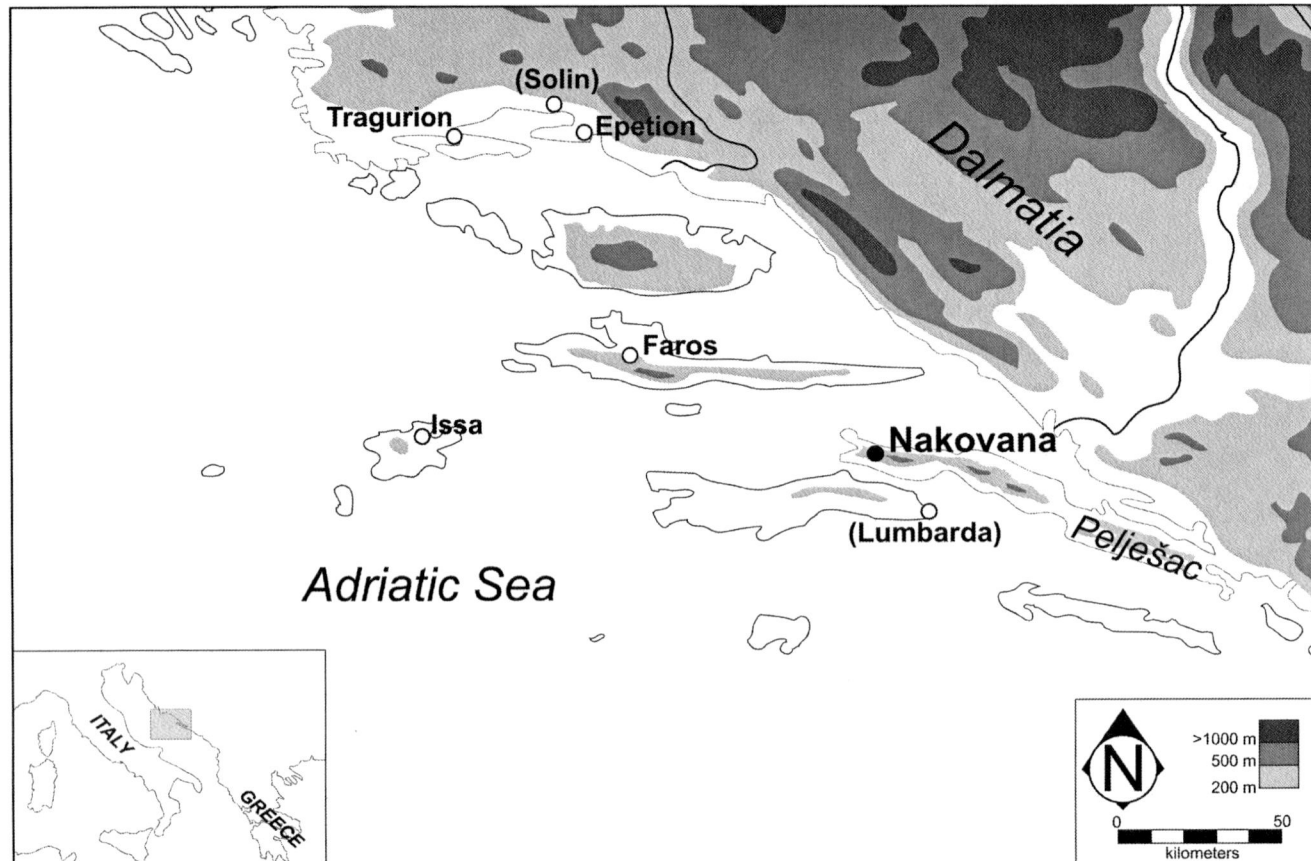

FIGURE 19.1 Location of Nakovana Cave and other major sites with Hellenistic pottery in Dalmatia.

postdepositional factors. Levels of carnivore gnawing were extremely low (4 percent of the total sample), and there was a lack of weathering processes, suggesting that the bones were unlikely to have been moved around other than by human action (Wilson 2002). This meant that it was possible to make direct comparisons between the faunal remains and the ceramic assemblage.

The distribution of faunal remains as recorded in the excavation grid was plotted in Arcview and superimposed onto an outline of Nakovana Cave (figure 19.2). Both weights and numbers of remains from the excavated area were investigated. Each showed a distinct concentration in a single area of the cave. Interestingly, this was not directly in front of the stalagmite, as was the case for the fine ceramics, but to one side, although at the same distance into the cave. This distribution was similar to that of the coarse wares and amphorae, of which the distribution of the latter is plotted in figure 19.2.

There are several possible explanations for the differences seen in the distribution of ceramics and faunal remains in Nakovana Cave. Faunal remains may have been deposited either separately or in the same events as ceramics. The faunal data do not allow us to distinguish between these two possibilities, as, although ceramics and faunal remains are commingled, this could have occurred subsequent to the initial event.

There are thus two possible explanations for the spatial patterning of faunal remains at Nakovana. It is possible that animal remains were deposited to one side of the stalagmite due to the limited amount of available space. A second possibility, that animal remains were removed from around the stalagmite and redeposited along the cave wall, is perhaps more interesting. This interpretation is supported by the large degree of dry-bone breakage in the Nakovana sample (table 19.1), which is consistent with the movement of animal bones some time after their initial deposition.

The faunal assemblage from Nakovana Cave was heavily dominated by sheep and goat (table 19.2). These are also the most commonly represented taxa on Croatian domestic sites of this period (Wilkes 1992). Thus the use of sheep and goat does not represent anything very unusual. In

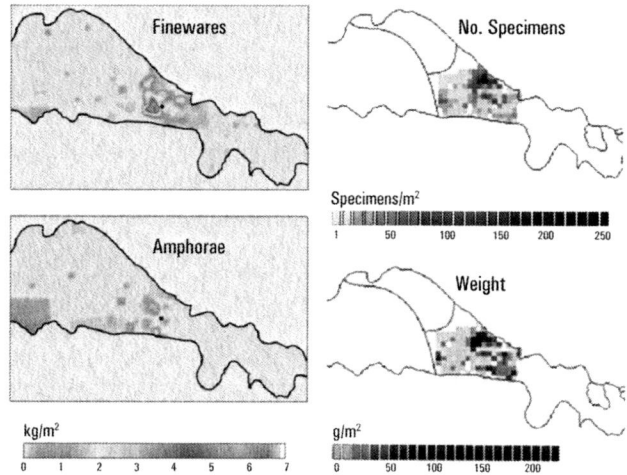

FIGURE 19.2 Distribution of (left) fineware ceramics and amphorae and (right) faunal remains in Nakovana Cave.

contrast, the ceramics were mostly finewares (73 percent) and were almost all imported Greek vessels (Forenbaher and Kaiser 2003). These would have been obtained either through piracy or trade with the Greek colonies on the neighboring islands of Issa and Hvar, and would have represented exotic and expensive luxuries. This suggests that there may have been two distinct spheres of ritual action going on within the cave.

The ceramics would have been visually appealing and exotic, and would have presented a spectacle to people entering the cave. They would have acted as a continuing reminder of the wealth of their donors, and of their ability to enter into exotic spheres of action. In contrast, although the ability to sacrifice animals would have required a certain amount of wealth, such sacrifices would have involved only local spheres of interaction. In such cases, the important point would be the death and consumption of the animal itself—there would have been no lasting visual display. This may have led to the clearing away of the debris of animals in order to create new space for a more lasting display of ceramics and would explain the high frequency of dry-bone breakage in the Nakovana assemblage. An additional factor in support of this hypothesis is that some animal remains were found in front of the stalagmite, possibly representing the final meal or animal sacrifice before the cave chamber was blocked.

If the species representation is not unusual, is there any evidence suggesting an extraordinary treatment of animals (and their remains) in the inner chamber? For a start, the faunal remains from the inner chamber at Nakovana differed significantly from those retrieved from the cave entrance. Bones from the entrance area showed a relatively high degree of burning and frequent breaks characteristic of fresh bone (see table 19.1). This would indicate that the bone from the cave entrance represents the result of an everyday mode of food consumption. In contrast, the bone from within the chamber shows few green-bone breaks, and there is very little sign of burning (only 1.6 percent of the bone is burned). This suggests that the inner chamber was the locus of carcass manipulation and deposition

TABLE 19.1 Relative frequency of burning and fracture type in the faunal assemblages from the cave entrance and inner chamber at Nakovana Cave.

	Burning		Fracture types			
	N	% burned	N	% dry-bone	% fresh-bone	% unbroken
Prehistoric, cave entrance	987	9.1	816	15.8	57.4	6.1
Hellenistic, inner chamber	688	1.6	548	35.4	13	27.4

TABLE 19.2 Minimum Numbers of Individuals (MNI) for the faunal assemblage from Nakovana Cave.

Species	Element used in MNI calculation	MNI*
Sheep/goat (*Ovis aries/Capra hircus*)	right M_3, right calcaneus (neonate)	11 (3)
Red deer (*Cervus elaphus*)	right humerus	1
Pig (*Sus scrofa*)	axis, left femur (neonate)	2 (1)
Cow (*Bos taurus*)	left femur, dp_2 (neonate)	2 (1)
Hare (*Lepus* sp.)	first phalange	1
Dog (*Canis* sp.)	central tarsal	1
Total		18 (5)

*Numbers shown in parentheses indicate the number of neonates

different from that of the day-to-day practices at the cave entrance.

Having established the patterning of deposition of animal remains, it remains to be seen what specific practices this material represents. Is it the result of sacrificial feasting, as has been suggested preliminarily by Kaiser and Forenbaher (2001)? This would certainly fit with some recent models of Iron Age political systems proposed by Dietler (1990, 1996, 2001), among others, and could have been an important means of reinforcing political authority (Hayden 2001). Evidence of feasting-related depositional patterns of faunal remains in the assemblage was therefore investigated.

One of the critical factors in identifying archaeologically the existence of feasting is the abundance of animal remains. Unfortunately, the Nakovana sample size is small, with only about 1,000 bones coming from the identified sample. This has resulted in a low MNI and a low intensity of deposition, with a minimum total of only eighteen animals (of which eleven are sheep/goat) dating to the whole 300 years during which ritual activity seems to have occurred at this site. This low level of faunal abundance may be a result either of real patterns of deposition or the taphonomic processes that the assemblage has been exposed to. Although carnivore gnawing and weathering had minimal impacts, the sample was highly fragmented, with almost 40 percent of the sample being less than 10 percent complete. This will inevitably have decreased the identifiability of the assemblage and have led to underestimation of the number of individual animals. However, even taking this into account, it is unlikely that rituals would have occurred very frequently or have involved very large numbers of animals.

Given the low level of deposition, could feasting have occurred at Nakovana Cave? While animals were deposited in small numbers at the site, the presence of relatively large numbers of head and lower-limb fragments suggests that the cave was the site of death for these animals (or at least that animals would have been brought to the cave whole, as it is unlikely that heads and feet would have been brought to the cave without the intervening body parts). This would fit with the general thesis that Nakovana Cave was a sacrificial site, but would not necessarily support the idea that feasting was occurring there. However, as it is not possible to slaughter only selected portions of animals, each individual animal sacrifice would have produced a reasonably substantial amount of meat for consumption. This means that despite a low intensity of deposition, feasting could have occurred at Nakovana. Significantly, the numbers of people taking part would have been limited if the numbers of animals represented in the faunal sample are representative of the actual intensity of activity at the site. The probability of feasting going on at Nakovana is therefore related to whether the animal remains are seen as representing multiple small sacrificial events or larger, rarer events.

Sacrificial calendars retrieved from Archaic and Classical Greek inscriptions record that sacrifices would have been of single animals in most cases (van Straten 1995, 172). However, while there is obviously some overlap between Greek religious practice and rituals occurring at Nakovana in terms of material culture (Greek pottery and Greek inscriptions on offerings at Nakovana), these cases are separated in space and time. While the rites taking place at Nakovana Cave would have been situated in wider understandings of the world, including knowledge of Greek religious practice, they were not one and the same thing. Rather they must be seen as locally situated and constructed within these wider logics. Thus the literary evidence cannot be used to demonstrate the scale of ritual events taking place. This paves the way for two possible interpretations of sacrificial rituals at Nakovana. In the first scenario, a number of animals would have been slaughtered contemporaneously, producing a large availability of meat for consumption. If this was the case, then sacrificial rites must have been extremely rare, perhaps only occurring every 40 to 50 years, but would have provided a substantial amount of material for feasting. In the second scenario, sacrificial rituals would have taken place more often (although still relatively rarely) and would have involved only single animals, thus reducing the quantity of meat available. A point to be emphasized here is that while pottery sherds are present in much larger numbers than are animal bones, they still represent a generally low level of deposition (around one complete pot for every 3 years of use). However, rather than uncontroversially suggesting regular small events, three distinct "sets" of contemporary ceramic material have been identified (Forenbaher, personal communication). This indicates that the rituals occurring in Nakovana cave may have been rarely occurring "exceptional" events.

While the small sample size may or may not have indicated feasting, a more direct measure of ritual practices at Nakovana is in the analysis of the cuts of meat used and patterns of consumption. Kaiser and Forenbaher (2001) have suggested from observations made in the field that the faunal remains from Nakovana Cave represent consumption of the best cuts of sheep and goat. This would also be an expected result of feasting behavior (Hayden 2001). If this were to be the case, then the elements most commonly represented in the Nakovana identified sample could be expected to be those representing the parts of the animal carrying the most meat: the upper fore- and hindquarters and the ribs (Binford 1978). Thus upper limb-bones, ribs, and pelvis might be expected to be common in the sample

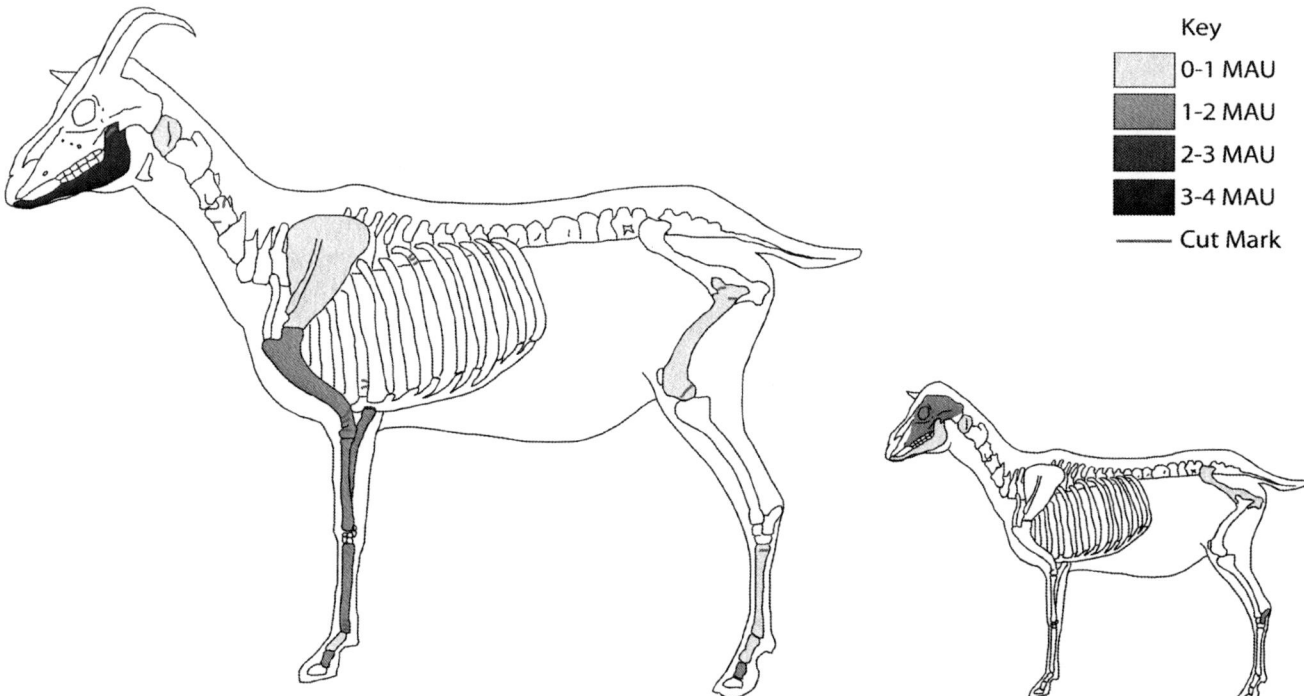

FIGURE 19.3 Minimum Animal Units (MAU) and distribution of cut marks for the Nakovana sample.

in comparison to lower limbs and heads. In order to examine this proposition, Minimum Animal Unit (MAU) values have been calculated (after Binford 1981, 1984) for the sheep/goat remains from the Nakovana identified sample. This allows the abundance of each element to be examined relative to its frequency within the skeleton (Lyman 1994). The elements present in the greatest numbers in the sample were mandibles and maxillae, with a slightly increased number of phalanges (figure 19.3). Meat-poor lower legs and feet are also present in greater quantities than are either the upper limbs or the abdomen. In addition, there is a lack of articulated bone remains from Nakovana Cave. Although great efforts were made during analysis to identify articulating units, only one lower leg (tibia, calcaneus, and astragalus) was recorded as definitely articulated. Thus it seems unlikely that the bones deposited inside the cave at Nakovana are themselves the debris of sacrificial feasts.

Consumption itself may be marked both by cut marks to the bones, indicating the butchery practices that have gone on (Binford 1978, 1981; Lyman 1994), and evidence of cooking (burning or other evidence of heating of bones). However only twenty-five specimens out of 904 identified remains from Nakovana display cut marks. These are clustered around major articulations and appear to be from skinning and early stages of carcass dismemberment and butchery (see figure 19.3). Were animals being consumed as part of feasting rituals, it might be expected that they would first have been cooked, thus burning the bones (Russell 1999). However, the incidence of burning on the bones in the sample is rare (only seventeen burned specimens from the identified assemblage and 193 burned specimens from the unidentified sample, equating to 0.8% and 6.5%, respectively). Such a low incidence of burning may indicate that deposited faunal remains have not been subjected to cooking. However, this need not necessarily be the case. Bones are not equally affected by cooking processes (Gifford-Gonzalez 1993; Montón Subías 2002; Speth 2000). Bones that have been cooked by boiling rather than roasting will not show signs of burning, and Gifford-Gonzalez (1989) has noted that where bones are roasted in a pit or earth oven, burning of surfaces can be virtually nonexistent. It is interesting that Outram (2002) has noted that boiling may lead to "old" looking fractures on fresh bones, fitting in with the dominant fracture pattern of the Nakovana assemblage. Cooking of any sort in the inner chamber of Nakovana Cave can almost certainly be discounted, as it is almost entirely sealed and would have quickly filled with smoke. However, there is a flat area immediately outside the cave suitable for a fire pit or earth oven (Forenbaher, personal communication).

One further point to note is that burning of bones was a common element in Greek sacrificial practices (Durand 1987; Isaakidou et al. 2002; van Straten 1995). The lack of evidence for burning is therefore a way in which the

Nakovana rites assert their independence from the Greek practices with which they share a common material culture.

DISCUSSION

The faunal remains from Nakovana Cave can be used to reconstruct a number of aspects of the ritual that took place there. First, there was a highly restricted idea of the species that were appropriate for sacrificial rituals, with very little representation of wild taxa. Second, portions of carcasses deposited in the cave were dominated by the head and lower limbs. Third, many of the remains were in a fragmentary condition, suggesting they may have been trampled during successive periods of use of the cave. Finally, evidence of consumption itself was essentially absent. From these characteristics, the use of Nakovana Cave as a shrine can be divided into two areas for interpretation. The first of these relates to the inside of the cave where surviving material allows inferences to be made about the practices that were going on; the second—what happened to material not represented in the sample?—must be more of a matter of conjecture.

The material deposited in the cave may have been deposited for the gods, the "divine portion" of the sacrifice (Price 1999; van Straten 1995). This seems to have been particularly focused on the head, although other portions were present. Rather than being left where deposited, as the ceramic material was, faunal remains may have been moved to the side of the stalagmite during successive reuse of the cave.

While evidence of consumption as opposed to deposition of animals at Nakovana Cave is extremely limited, this may have been partially a result of practical considerations. The lack of air flow inside Nakovana Cave would have meant that were portions of the carcasses to have been cooked in preparation for consumption, it would have had to take place outside the cave, something that could easily have taken place on the flat platform there. This would explain why certain portions (such as upper limb-bones, ribs, and other meat-rich parts of the carcass) were underrepresented inside the cave. Remains from meat consumed outside the cave would no longer be recoverable.

In similar terms, the numbers of animals sacrificed at the cave in any one event may have varied, and are difficult to gauge exactly, as some portions may have been removed from the cave. Yet they do not seem to have been very great in relation to the quantities of ceramics deposited—compare the deposition of a minimum of eleven sheep/goat carcasses to over 100 fully reconstructed Hellenistic pots. This is a reflection of the intentions of the users of the cave and may have been related to ideas of both aesthetics and value. While animal sacrifice may have been an important part of the rituals that were going on, it will not have made the same impact as the deposition and destruction of expensive imported goods. The use of such goods may have reflected a value placed upon esoteric knowledge of the distant (cf. Helms 1988), while sacrificial animals would have been a locally situated resource and valued for different reasons. The use of different kinds of material culture—because food is always material culture (Miracle 2002)—therefore followed different logics. In the case of the ceramic remains, the impact created would have been rooted in the physicality of the artifact itself: its color, shape, texture, and the ideas of the exotic that these would have invoked. Such properties would have been largely unchanging with time—despite the decomposition of any contents, the visual impact of the vessels themselves would have remained. In contrast to this, the effect produced by fauna can perhaps be seen as far more immediate and fleeting. The leading of an animal to sacrifice, and its death and subsequent disposal, would emphasize the performative *practice* rather than the continuing presence of material (cf. Schechner 1994).

Such contrasts in the visual appeal of different forms of material culture with time brings perhaps the most noticeable characteristic of Nakovana Cave to the fore: there are good reasons for supposing that the rituals at the cave were separated by quite long periods of time. An understanding of this, together with analysis of the faunal remains themselves from Nakovana, have combined to create an enigmatic picture of a site that, though it was used only infrequently, was obviously understood as an extremely special place. It is noticeable that despite the probable time gaps between each depositional event, the rituals had a highly normative character in terms both of the material used and the way in which it was deposited. Such a character implies a value placed upon maintenance of a practical knowledge of the rituals over a long time span.

CONCLUSION

Faunal remains have a great deal to contribute to the understanding of ritual action that takes place in caves. Despite the fact that there has often been a lack of confidence in using animal bones to answer more esoteric questions, this does not have to be a difficult process. Although an excellent understanding of taphonomic factors is necessary in order for explanations of ritual behavior to be worthwhile, no new or complex zooarchaeological methods are required. Rather, existing methodologies can be used to provide new insights into the minds of people in the past. The example of Nakovana Cave illustrates how the deposition of faunal remains can illustrate different aspects of ritual than the deposition of other artifacts, and that this can lead to richer understandings of ritual actions. Rather than just providing a locus for ritual action, the morphology of caves themselves has an influence on how rituals evolved, and this can be reflected in faunal remains.

REFERENCES CITED

Albarella, Umberto, and Dale Serjeantson. 2002. "A Passion for Pork: Meat Consumption at the British Late Neolithic Site of Durrington Walls." In *Consuming Passions and Patterns of Consumption*, ed. Preston T. Miracle and Nicky Milner, 33–49. Cambridge: McDonald Institute for Archaeological Research.

Bahn, Paul G. 1999. *Journey through the Ice Age*. London: Seven Dials.

Bell, C. 1997. *Ritual: Perspectives and Dimensions*. Oxford: Oxford University Press.

Binford, Lewis R. 1978. *Nunamiut Ethnoarchaeology*. New York: Academic Press.

Binford, Lewis R. 1981. *Bones: Ancient Men and Modern Myths*. New York: Academic Press.

Binford, Lewis R. 1984. *Faunal Remains from the Klasies River Mouth*. New York: Academic Press.

Bradley, Richard. 2000. *The Archaeology of Natural Places*. London: Routledge.

Dietler, Michael. 1990. "Driven by Drink: The Role of Drinking in the Political Economy and the Case of Early Iron Age France." *Journal of Anthropological Archaeology* 9 (4): 352–406. http://dx.doi.org/10.1016/0278-4165(90)90011-2.

Dietler, Michael. 1996. "Feasts and Commensal Politics in the Political Economy: Food, Power and Status in Prehistoric Europe." In *Food and the Status Quest: An Interdisciplinary Perspective*, ed. Polly Wiessner and Wulf Schiefenhövel, 87–125. Oxford: Berghahn Books.

Dietler, Michael. 2001. "Theorizing the Feast: Rituals and Consumption, Commensal Politics and Power in African Contexts." In *Feasts: Archaeological and Ethnographic Perspectives on Food, Politics and Power*, ed. Michael Dietler and Brian Hayden, 65–114. Washington, DC: Smithsonian Institution Press.

Douglas, Mary. 1984. *Food and the Social Order: Studies of Food and Festivities in Three American Communities*. New York: Russell Sage Foundation.

Durand, Jean-Louis. 1987. "Sacrifice et découpe en Grèce Ancienne." *Anthropozoologica Premier Numéro Spécial* 59–67.

Emery, Kitty F. 2003. "Animals from the Maya Underworld: Reconstructing Elite Maya Ritual at the Cueva de los Quetzales, Guatemala." In *Behavior behind Bones: The Zooarchaeology of Ritual, Religion, Status and Identity*, ed. Sharyn Jones O'Day, Wim Van Neer, and Anton Ervynck, 101–13. Oxford: Oxbow.

Farrand, William R. 2001. "Sediments and Stratigraphy in Rockshelters and Caves: A Personal Perspective on Principles and Pragmatics." *Geoarchaeology: An International Journal* 16 (5): 537–57. http://dx.doi.org/10.1002/gea.1004.

Fiddes, Nick. 1991. *Meat: A Natural Symbol*. London: Routledge.

Forenbaher, Stašo, and Timothy Kaiser. 2003. *Spila Nakovana: An Illyrian Sanctuary on the Pelješac Peninsula*. Zagreb: V.B.Z.

Galik, Alfred. 2003. "An Iron Age Bone Assemblage from Durezza Cave, Carinthia, Austria: Detecting Ritual Behavior through Archaeozoological and Taphonomic Analysis." In *Behavior behind Bones: The Zooarchaeology of Ritual, Religion, Status and Identity*, ed. Sharyn Jones O'Day, Wim Van Neer, and Anton Ervynck, 54–61. Oxford: Oxbow.

Gifford-Gonzalez, Diane. 1989. "Ethnographic Analogies for Interpreting Modified Bones: Some Cases from East Africa." In *Bone Modification*, ed. Robson Bonnichsen and Marcella H. Sorg, 179–246. Orono: Center for the Study of the First Americans, Institute for Quaternary Studies, University of Maine.

Gifford-Gonzalez, Diane. 1993. "Gaps in Zooarchaeological Analyses of Butchery: Is Gender an Issue?" In *From Bones to Behavior; Ethnoarchaeological and Experimental Contributions to the Interpretation of Faunal Remains*, ed. Jean Hudson, 181–99. Carbondale: Center for Archaeological Investigations, Southern Illinois University.

Hamilakis, Yannis, and Eleni Konsolaki. 2004. "Pigs for the Gods: Burnt Animal Sacrifices as Embodied Rituals at a Mycenaean Sanctuary." *Oxford Journal of Archaeology* 23 (2): 135–51. http://dx.doi.org/10.1111/j.1468-0092.2004.00206.x.

Hayden, Brian. 1996. "Feasting in Prehistoric and Traditional Societies." In *Food and the Status Quest: An Interdisciplinary Perspective*, ed. Polly Wiessner and Wulf Schiefenhövel, 127–47. Oxford: Berghahn Books.

Hayden, Brian. 2001. "Fabulous Feasts: A Prolegomenon to the Importance of Feasting." In *Feasts: Archaeological and Ethnographic Perspectives on Food, Politics and Power*, ed. Michael Dietler and Brian Hayden, 23–64. Washington, DC: Smithsonian Institution Press.

Helms, Mary W. 1988. *Ulysses' Sail: An Ethnographic Odyssey of Power, Knowledge, and Geographical Distance*. Princeton, NJ: Princeton University Press.

Hill, J. D. 1996. "The Identification of Ritual Deposits of Animals: A General Perspective from a Specific Study of 'Special Animal Deposits' from the Southern English Iron Age." In *Ritual Treatment of Human and Animal Remains*, ed. Sue Anderson and Katherine Boyle, 17–32. Oxford: Oxbow.

Isaakidou, Valasia, Paul Halstead, Jack Davis, and Sharon Stocker. 2002. "Burnt Animal Sacrifice at the Mycenaean 'Palace of Nestor,' Pylos." *Antiquity* 76: 86–92.

Kaiser, Timothy, and Stašo Forenbaher. 2001. "Nakovana Cave: An Illyrian Ritual Site." *Antiquity* 75: 677–8.

Kelly, Lucretia S. 2001. "A Case of Ritual Feasting at the Chahokia Site." In *Feasts: Archaeological and Ethnographic Perspectives on Food, Politics and Power*, ed. Michael Dietler and Brian Hayden, 334–67. Washington, DC: Smithsonian Institution Press.

Knight, Vernon James. 2001. "Feasting and the Emergence of Platform Mound Ceremonialism in Eastern North America." In *Feasts: Archaeological and Ethnographic Perspectives on Food, Politics and Power*, ed. Michael Dietler and Brian Hayden, 331–33. Washington, DC: Smithsonian Institution Press.

Lyman, R. Lee. 1994. *Vertebrate Taphonomy*. Cambridge: Cambridge University Press.

Miracle, Preston T. 2002. "Mesolithic Meals from Mesolithic Middens." In *Consuming Passions and Patterns of Consumption*, ed. Preston T. Miracle and Nicky Milner, 65–88. Cambridge: McDonald Institute for Archaeological Research.

Montón Subías, Sandra. 2002. "Cooking in Zooarchaeology: Is This Issue Still Raw?" In *Consuming Passions and Patterns of Consumption*, ed. Preston T. Miracle and Nicky Milner, 7–15. Cambridge: McDonald Institute for Archaeological Research.

O'Day, Sharyn, Wim van Neer, and Anton Ervynck. 2003. "Introduction." In *Behavior behind Bones: The Zooarchaeology of Ritual, Religion, Status and Identity*, ed. Sharyn Jones O'Day, Wim Van Neer, and Anton Ervynck, xi–xv. Oxford: Oxbow.

Outram, Alan K. 2002. "Bone Fracture and Within-Bone Nutrients: An Experimentally Based Method for Investigating Levels of Marrow Extraction." In *Consuming Passions and Patterns of Consumption*, ed. Preston T. Miracle and Nicky Milner, 51–63. Cambridge: McDonald Institute for Archaeological Research.

Price, Simon. 1999. *Religions of the Ancient Greeks*. Cambridge: Cambridge University Press.

Renfrew, Colin. 1994. "The Archaeology of Religion." In *The Ancient Mind: Elements of Cognitive Archaeology*, ed. Colin C. Renfrew and Ezra B. W. Zubrow, 47–54. Cambridge: Cambridge University Press. http://dx.doi.org/10.1017/CBO9780511598388.007.

Russell, Nerissa. 1999. "Symbolic Dimensions of Animals and Meat at Opovo, Yugoslavia." In *Material Symbols: Culture and Economy in Prehistory*, ed. John E. Robb, 153–69. Carbondale: Center for Archaeological Investigations, Southern Illinois University.

Rutkowski, Bogdan. 1986. *The Cult Places of the Aegean*. New Haven, CT: Yale University Press.

Schechner, Richard. 1994. "Ritual and Performance." In *Companion Encyclopedia of Archaeology: Humanity, Culture and Social Life*, ed. Tim Ingold, 613–17. London: Routledge.

Speth, John D. 2000. "Boiling vs. Baking and Roasting: A Taphonomic Approach to the Recognition of Cooking Techniques in Small Animals." In *Animal Bones, Human Societies*, ed. Peter Rowley-Conwy, 89–105. Oxford: Oxbow.

Van Gennep, Arnold. 1981. *Les rites de passage*. Paris: Picard.

Van Straten, Folkert T. 1995. *Hiera Kala: Images of Animal Sacrifice in Archaic and Ancient Greece*. Lieden: Brill.

Wiessner, Polly. 2001. "Enga Feasts in a Historical Perspective." In *Feasts: Archaeological and Ethnographic Perspectives on Food, Politics and Power*, ed. Michael Dietler and Brian Hayden, 115–43. Washington, DC: Smithsonian Institution Press.

Wilkes, John. 1992. *The Illyrians*. Oxford: Blackwell.

Wilson, Joanna E.P. 2002. "Sacred Spaces, Sacred Species: An Analysis of the Faunal Remains from the Iron Age Shrine of Nakovana Cave." Undergraduate dissertation, University of Cambridge, Cambridge.

20

Ritual Cave Use in the Bahamas

Robert S. Carr, William C. Schaffer, Jeff B. Ransom, and Michael P. Pateman

The caves of the Bahamas represent an important part of the archipelago's archaeological record. Cultural materials associated with Bahamian caves include human remains, pictographs, petroglyphs, faunal bone, botanical remains, and a variety of cultural material. Archaeological and ethnographic evidence indicates the importance of caves in Taíno mythology and cosmology throughout the West Indies. Recent excavations at Preacher's Cave on the island of Eleuthera have provided the best-documented Lucayan burials yet found in the Bahamas. Results of these investigations provide information on ritual mortuary practices that were used during cave use in the northern Bahamas and that ranged from as early as circa AD 700 through European Contact.

Archaeological studies in the Bahama archipelago (figure 20.1) have focused mainly on the cultural and technological adaptations of the Lucayans (AD 600–1500) to their environment (e.g., Berman and Hutcheson 2000; Carlson 1993; Hoffman 1967; Keegan 1982a, 1982c). Fieldwork has mainly focused on site surveys and large-scale village excavations (e.g., Bohon 1999; Keegan 1985; Vernon 2007; Winter 1978). Surveys and excavations of burial sites in the recent past tended to occur only when skeletal remains were found inadvertently. Limited human skeletal material from antiquity has been recovered in the Bahamas as a result of excavation and documentation in a scientific manner.

The cave systems throughout the archipelago have yielded a variety of artifacts that have not been preserved at open-air sites. Notably, this includes artifacts such as *duhos,* which are ceremonial seats reserved for the ruling elite. Caves also contain human remains not normally found in open-air sites. Caves exist in two forms: wet/submerged (including blue holes and caves entirely or partly below the water table) and dry caves. The wet caves can include complex underground caverns, making remains located within them difficult to access. Burials and associated artifacts in wet caves tend to be intact. In contrast, dry caves are generally more accessible but are usually highly disturbed by collectors and guano gatherers. It should be noted that distinctions between interments in dry caves and blue holes or wet caves have not been fully established.

CAVE MYTHOLOGY AND COSMOLOGY

Caves in the Bahamas are an integral part of Lucayan-Taíno mythology and cosmology. Lucayan-Taíno religion has it roots in the pre-Taíno migration of the West Indies and is structurally related to the mythology of Amerind people—particularly the people indigenous to Amazonia and the Orinoco River (Stevens-Arroyo 1988). Caves are a constant physical and mythical feature within the region's cosmic geography, occurring throughout the Circum-Caribbean and Mesoamerica.

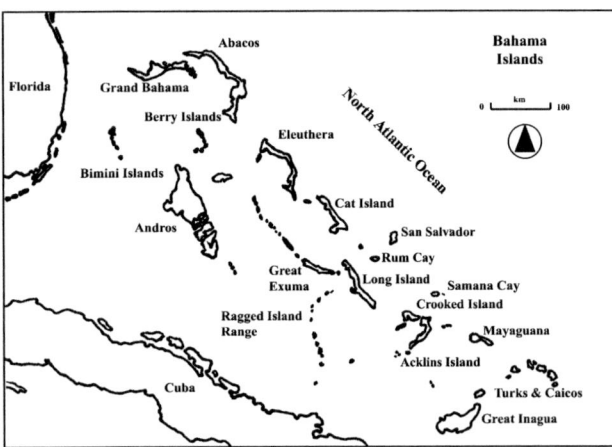

FIGURE 20.1 Islands in the Bahama archipelago, 21° to 27°30' N and 69° to 80°30' W. (Line art by William C. Schaffer, courtesy of Curran and White 1995.)

Caves were believed to be the place of origin or birthplace of humans in addition to the emergence of the sun and moon. In his 1497 account of the Taíno people on the island of Hispaniola, Hieronymite Friar Ramón Pané recounts their belief that people originated in two caves at the mountain known as Cauta. The ancestral Taínos emerged from one cave, Cacibajagua, and non-Taínos came from the other, Amayaúna (Pané 1999, 5–6). The sun and moon originated from a cave called Iguanaboina, where two highly regarded *zemis* (carved figurines of spirits), Boinayel ("Rain-Bearing Clouds") and Márohu ("Without-Clouds"), depicted individuals with their hands tied and apparently perspiring (Pané 1999, 17). This was a place to visit in order to request specific weather.

Caves play a significant role in the Taíno concept of a three-tier universe. The celestial vault above and the watery vault below ground, known as Coaybay, were the "house and dwelling place of the dead" (Pané 1999, 17–18). It is at the earth's surface that portals to the underworld are located (Beeker, Conrad, and Foster 2002; Seigel 1997). The importance of the underworld is that it is the home of the ancestral spirit, *opía,* and thus the placement of the dead into caves and blue holes facilitated their access to Coaybay (Pané 1999, 19).

PREVIOUS RESEARCH

The prehistoric significance of caves in the Bahamas is, in part, reflected by the history of archaeological investigations across the island chain. The first published account of archaeological remains in the Bahamas is a paper by W. K. Brooks (1888, 215–25) describing three crania from various cave sites. Two general surveys (De Booy 1912, 1913; Rainey 1941) documented numerous sites across the Bahamas and the Turks and Caicos, but most site assessments were cursory with the exception of Froelich Rainey's investigation of the Gordon Hill Caves on Crooked Island (Granberry 1955, 1978; Rainey 1934). He investigated seven caves in the Gordon Bluff group. Four of them had been previously disturbed to extract guano and were sterile, two caves contained human burials (Gordon Hill Burial Caves Nos. 1 and 2), and one cave contained other cultural material and human burials (Gordon Hill Dwelling Cave) (Granberry 1955, 160–68; Rainey 1934). Gordon Hill Burial Cave No. 1 produced two disturbed human graves. One skeleton was interred on a small rock shelf below the cave soil. A second was lying on the rock floor of the cave (Rainey 1934, 20–22). Gordon Hill Burial Cave No. 2 produced disturbed bones with the apparent articulation of a radius and ulna, suggesting at least a single grave near the mouth of the cave.

Rainey excavated 50 square meters of one cave that was about 120 square meters in area. The cave had a central chamber with two smaller side chambers. He determined that cultural material was buried within the first 25 centimeters and that the front and back of the cave had the highest concentrations of artifacts. Fire pits occurred across the cave replete with faunal bones and conch-shell refuse. Artifacts were common, including pottery sherds, a wooden fishhook, a wooden fireboard, as well as bone and shell artifacts (Rainey 1934, 23–26). Nearly 50 years passed before the human skeletal material housed at the Yale Peabody Museum from Rainey's excavations was analyzed and a descriptive inventory completed (Keegan 1982b). Unfortunately, most of the graves were too disturbed to allow for reconstruction of burial positioning and mortuary patterning.

Human remains have also been discovered at the Sanctuary Blue Hole on South Andros Island (Palmer 1997). The skeletal remains of seventeen individuals (eleven males, five females, and one subadult) were recovered by cave divers in 1990 and 1991. However, this recovery lacked provenience, and contextual information concerning the burials was not recorded. Descriptive inventories of these individuals are complete with analyses of oral-dental and gross skeletal pathology as well as stable isotopes (Mack and Armelagos 1992; Pateman 2007). Faunal remains include an alco (*Canis familiaris*), hutia (*Geocapromys ingrahami*), and a variety of birds (Aves), but no formal analysis has been conducted. A recent study revealed that this recovery at Sanctuary Blue Hole was incomplete, since at least five additional individuals have subsequently been located (Pateman 2007).

In 1995, a canoe was found in the Stargate Blue Hole, also on South Andros near the Sanctuary Blue Hole (Palmer 1997, 172). This canoe is believed to be ceremo-

TABLE 20.1 Documented Bahamian caves and burial sites.

Island	Keegan	Pateman	Aarons and Riggs
Abacos	(2)	3 (1)	14
Acklins Island	1 (1)	—	2
Andros	3 (1)	3 (3)	8
Berry Islands	—	1	—
Cat Island	—	—	1
Crooked Island	3	3	5
Eleuthera	3	2 (6)	6
Grand Bahama	(2)	—	3
Inaguas	1	—	6
Long Island	4	4	15
Mayaguana	—	1	—
New Providence	10	3	9
Rum Cay	1	3	9
San Salvador	2	3	13
Turks and Caicos	8 (1)	—	20
Subtotal	36 (6)	26 (10)	111
Total	42	36	111

Submerged cave/burial location in parentheses.

TABLE 20.2 Documented petroglyphs and pictographs in the Bahamas.

Island	Petroglyph Caves	Reference(s)
Crooked Island	2	Hoffman 1973; Winter 1978
Eleuthera	1[†]	Carr et al. 2006
Inaguas	1	Winter 1991
Long Island	1	Winter 1991
Rum Cay	1	Maynard 1890; Winter 1991
San Salvador	2	Winter 1991

[†] Pictograph

nial because it would not have been navigable at sea due to its size (less than 2 meters in length). Human remains were also located, though not recovered. It has been posited that the vessel may have been a burial canoe and loaded with offerings.

Keegan summarizes archaeological site types throughout the Bahamas and the Turks and Caicos (Keegan 1992, 70). He places caves and rockshelters in separate categories and distinguishes burial caves (wet and dry) from caves without documented evidence of human remains. Aarons and Riggs assembled an inventory of 111 cave sites (Keegan 1997, 33) but much of these data lacks specifics (i.e., wet vs. dry, cave vs. rockshelter) and is duplicated and redundant. Pateman (2007) provides the most current inventory reflecting a synthesis of data solely from burial caves (table 20.1).

Specific to problem-oriented skeletal research, few detailed reports exist concerning the prehistory of the Bahamas. Only until recently has the sizeable Lucayan assemblages been adequately inventoried (MNI = 71), and a biocultural approach used to look at variables such as health, nutrition, social status, and mortuary patterns (Pateman 2007).

Exclusive of the newly uncovered Preacher's Cave material, the existing inventories represent mostly surveys and only one substantial excavation. Poor preservation coupled with a lack of archaeological context has thus hindered our knowledge of mortuary behavior and related social organization.

Some social aspects can be interpreted through petroglyphs and pictographs, which have also been documented in association with Bahamian caves. John Winter (1991, 672–80) has written the best summary of Bahamian petroglyphs, noting that they occur in both caves and solution holes. He notes that they occur in both wide-mouth flank margin caves as well as narrow-mouth caves, such as solution holes. Winter identifies Bahamian petroglyphs as being of the Timehri type, an anthropomorphic design first classified by Williams (1985), who believes it functioned to maintain subsistence horticulture and has its origin in Amazonia. Winter notes that five of the principal islands have documented petroglyphs and these are presented in table 20.2.

Currently, evidence for only one pictograph has been reported in the Bahamas from Preacher's Cave on Eleuthera (Carr et al. 2006). The pictograph is highly eroded, but an anthropomorphic or zoomorphic face is still apparent. This could be the type of image suggested by Winter (1991), but given the fact that Preacher's Cave is a burial ground, it could possibly be a revered animal such as the bat or owl that inhabits caves, oftentimes suggestive in Taíno artifacts as resembling the spirits of dead humans (Garcia Arévalo 1984, 1997) Additional testing to substantiate this feature as being prehistoric has yet to be conducted.

PREACHER'S CAVE

Located on the northern part of Eleuthera adjacent to Jean's Bay, Preacher's Cave is situated just south of the reef system known as the Devil's Backbone (figure 20.2). Preacher's Cave is characteristic of a sea cave, lacking speleothems and mostly horizontal in origin with a grand vertical promenade at the entrance. A vertical intrusion reminiscent of a pit cave provides a skylight once in the interior of the formation. Freshwater interaction from

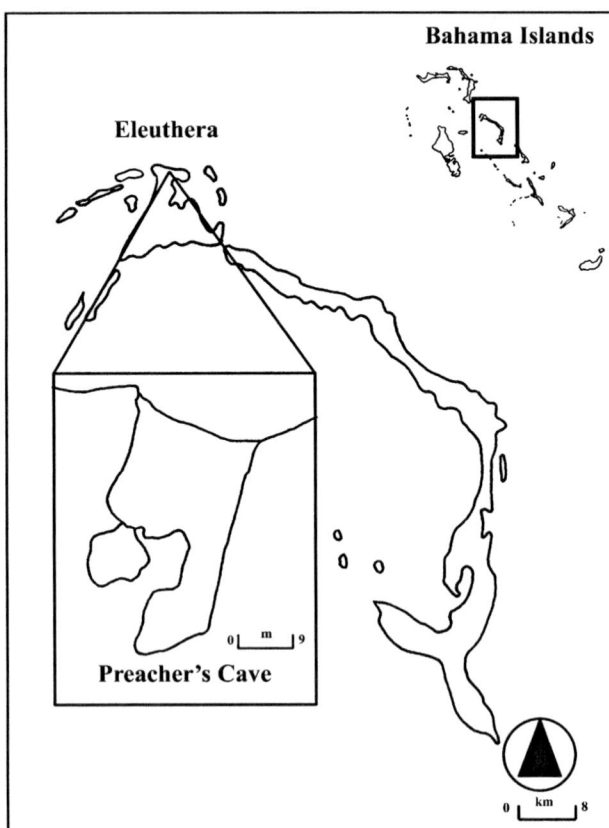

FIGURE 20.2 Plan view of Eleuthera Island with inset of Preacher's Cave.

precipitation is surely a factor in its formation, though it must be noted that the pit feature could have been at one point a breached flank margin cave, diagnostic of a high-level sea stand. The cave extends southeast into a narrow corridor, with many slender vertical shafts providing ample twilight. There are no true dark zones, where artificial light is essential for navigation during the daytime, as numerous of these shafts pierce the formation. However, the area with the least light infringement is the back corridor and this is where the bulk of prehistoric burials have been discovered.

Until recently, interest in the cave has traditionally focused on the saga of the first English settlers of the Bahamas, the Eleutherian Adventurers. They were Puritans in search of religious freedom that denounced King Charles I as the head of the Anglican Church, fled Bermuda, and shipwrecked in 1648. They sought refuge in the grotto for shelter and conducted sermons (Albury 1975; Craton 1986; Craton and Saunders 1992). The cave's archaeological potential was first recognized in 1992 during an archaeological survey of north Eleuthera, substantiating the veracity of historic accounts with the discovery of historic artifacts and European burials (Carr 1991; Carr, Day, and Norman 1993; Dickel 1993). These investigations also revealed a significant Lucayan component within the cave.

EXCAVATION RESULTS

Recent archaeological investigations have confirmed that Preacher's Cave was intensely used by the Lucayans, principally as a mortuary locale (Carr et al. 2006). These excavations have yielded the most complete Lucayan graves documented in situ by archaeologists in the Bahamas. Radiocarbon dating of materials associated with archaeological deposits was conducted using the AMS method by Beta Analytic, Inc., Miami, Florida. A culturally modified triton shell (*Charonia tritonis variegata*) found outside the cave dated AD 560–720 and shells buried with Individual 1E have a mean date of approximately AD 1290 (table 20.3). The triton-shell date range represents the earliest evidence of occupation in the northern Bahamas and suggests that the peopling of the archipelago may have taken place on the island of Eleuthera and the northern Bahamas 200–300 years earlier then previously believed (Berman and Gnivecki 1995; Berman and Pearsall 2000; Keegan 1992, 1997). The archaeological context and associated artifacts advocate that the human skeletal remains date to the broad Ostionoid period (AD 600–1500).

A total of twelve individuals have been uncovered in Preacher's Cave, of which six are Lucayans, five are historic, and one, currently undetermined. Individuals 1A and 1B, as well as a cremation-related deposit, were uncovered during a 1-week excavation session in March 2006. Individuals 1C–1E were subsequently discovered during a 2-month field season from January to March 2007 (figure 20.3). The six Lucayan individuals include three males, two females, and one of indeterminate sex. A subadult female (1A, 15–20 years) represents the youngest age category, followed by two young adult males (1D, 20–25 years and 1E, 25–30 years) and a young adult female (1C, 30–35 years) (table 20.4). Individual 1B was also likely a young adult male, yet remnants of this individual's remains were too scant for a more accurate assessment. The individual represented in the cremation-related deposit was of indeterminate sex due to fragmentation and partial calcification; however, skeletal elements suggest this individual was at least a young adult (20–34 years) at the time of death.

The bodies were interred either flat and extended, and sometimes semiflexed on the side. Individual 1D was the anomaly of the group, bound by cordage, and interred face down. Preservation and completeness was typically dictated by historical and modern disturbances. Most skeletal material was recovered from fine, moist beach sands. Preserved grave goods were found only with Individual 1E and are detailed below.

TABLE 20.3 Preacher's Cave radiocarbon samples.

Beta	Material	Location	Depth*	Cal. Date$
218509	Burnt shell	ST N110/E240	60 cmbs	AD 1460–1660
218512	Triton shell	ST 39 N207/E507	80 cmbs	AD 560–720
218517	Charred cob	Unit 9	0–20 cmbs	AD 1430–1530; 1560–1630
218518	Charcoal	Individual 1A	40 cmbs	AD 700–980
218519	Charcoal	Cremation deposit	10–20 cmbs	AD 1270–1320; 1340–1390
218520	Charcoal	Feature 44, Unit 16	16–20 cmbs	AD 1430–1650
220176	Charcoal	Cremation deposit	10–20 cmbs	AD 1460–1520; 1580–1630
242393	Tellin shell	Individual 1E	51 cmbs	AD 1190–1310
242394	Triton shell	Individual 1E	44 cmbs	AD 1270–1400

* cmbs, centimeters below surface
$ Calibrated to 2 sigmas (95% probability)

TABLE 20.4 Age and sex distribution of prehistoric graves from Preacher's Cave.

Individual	Sex	Age at death
1A	F	15–20
1B	M?	24–36
1C	F	30–35
1D	M	20–25
1E	M	25–30

Individual 1A was a subadult female in the mid-teens to early twenties (15–20 years) at or around the time of death. She was laid out extended in a pit, and her body subsequently formed to its concavity. The neck region affirmed this placement with curved posture in synch with the slope of the depression. The mandible (lower jaw) faced due south away from the mouth of the cave. Individual 1B was likely a young adult male (24–36 years) at the time of death and interred perpendicular to the head of Individual 1A. This individual was also laid out flat and extended, but the grave had been highly disturbed, purportedly by European occupation. Thus, most of the skeletal remnants are too fragmentary or simply absent for a more in-depth assessment of burial practice.

Individual 1C was a female in her early to mid-thirties (30–35 years) at the time of death. This individual was wrapped in a plaited mat and interred on the left side, the upper legs semiflexed and the lower legs flexed. The impression of the mat is well preserved on the left parietal, left zygomatic (cheekbone), and right clavicle (collar bone) (figure 20.4). Its pattern can be compared to a schematic of basketry-impressed Palmettan Ostionoid ware from the Pigeon Creek site on San Salvador (Berman and Hutcheson 2000).

Individual 1D was a male in his early twenties (20–25 years) at the time of death. This individual was fixed by cordage around the arms and hands, buried face down with the upper limbs semiflexed, with hands restrained and crossed in front of the waist. It appears that the lower legs had been separated from the upper legs. The skull and atlas (C1) were absent, though no visible signs in the skeleton suggest that this individual died from decapitation or strangulation. Most likely the skull was removed while still fleshed. Also, a fairly uniform horizontal incision breached the cortical surface and penetrated the trabecular content of the humeral head—possible evidence of sharp-force trauma to the right shoulder from capture or struggle. If it was a wound, the injury would have been sustained prior to death, as there is no sign of healing.

Individual 1E was a young adult male (25–30 years) at the time of death. This individual was also wrapped in a plaited mat, in the same manner as Individual 1C, but laid on the right side with the upper and lower legs semiflexed. A large (30 centimeter) culturally modified triton shell lay in front of the chest cavity. A cache of twenty-nine sunrise tellin (*Tellina radiata*) with a piece of red ochre (2 gram) and a fish-bone scarifier lay just behind the left shoulder. In addition, the neck and shoulder regions of an articulated sea turtle (*Chelonia mydas*, *Eretmochelys imbricate*, or *Caretta caretta*) that had been severed from the head and carapace lay at the foot of this individual.

DISCUSSION

The Spanish detailed aspects of social rank within Taíno society as having two components: division of labor and control of resources. Those who performed the brunt of

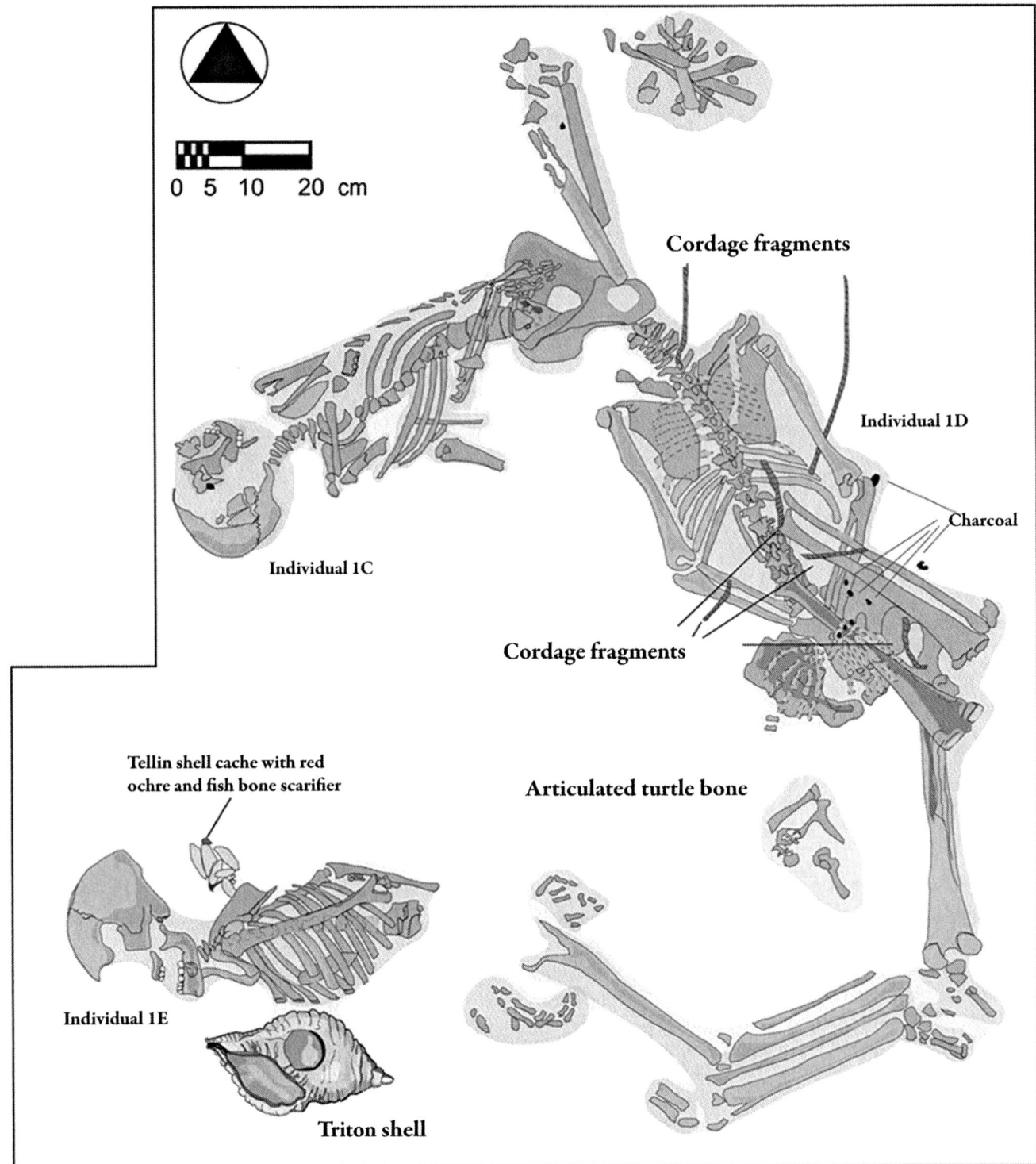

FIGURE 20.3 Plan view of Individuals 1C–1E. (Line art by William C. Schaffer.)

manual tasks associated with the production of food and textiles were known as the *naboría*. These workers relinquished the rights to the end result of their efforts, handing over produce and manufactured goods to the ruling *cacique,* or chieftain, and his constituency. *Caciques* were a ruling stock selected from a privileged class referred to as the *nitaíno*. Accounts of the Spanish do not provide a lucid depiction of the *nitaíno* as a whole, but they do present dis-

FIGURE 20.4 Basketry-impressed left zygomatic (cheekbone). (Photo by William C. Schaffer.)

parities between the commoners and *caciques* in terms of daily activities and even burial practices.

The surviving works of Christopher Columbus describe many funerary procedures, some with association to social rank and others with greater ambiguity. They discuss practices that include placing people in hammocks or net beds, burying people in caves with food and receptacles filled with water, burning of the dead, and even removing the heads of individuals. In fact, in Columbus's diary while on the northeast coast of Cuba, he recounts that his men found human skulls in baskets held on posts in Taíno houses. Yet some of the more provocative details lie in the treatment of the *caciques*. Their bodies were said to be exposed to fire and dried to be preserved completely intact.

Interpreting social rank through mortuary data and ethnohistoric evidence is oftentimes challenging, especially since at present the Preacher's Cave sample is the only viable case study. Oftentimes social rank can be expressed in terms of those who are buried with grave goods or not, or those buried with more valuable goods than others (Morbán Laucer 1979). In this case, the combination of burial hammocks and grave goods with evidence of interpersonal violence is sufficient to allow hypothesizing.

Since only Individual 1E was buried with grave goods and wrapped in a hammock, it seems that he may have been a member of higher status, either of the *nitaíno*, or more specifically, a *behique* (physician or shaman) or a ruling *cacique*. The triton shell may have held an offering of water, possibly associated with a libation ritual. Accordingly, the remains of a butchered turtle may be an offering of food. On the other hand, the sunrise tellin cache is one of even greater mystery. The twenty-nine shells in this cache may be completely random or a purposeful calculation. It may be mere coincidence that the average days in a full lunar cycle (synodic month) is identical to the number of shells within the cache, or a valid interpretation of the denomination. As aforementioned, Taínos believed that the moon originated from caves. This could be the symbolic manifestation of the lunar cycle that occurs during life as a tribute to restoring it to its celestial origin through death and interment within the cave. Two other artifacts were also situated within the cache: a fish-bone scarifier and a piece of red ochre. These items, along with the sunrise tellin shells, likely served as a body paint kit. Plants such as jagua (*Genipa americana*) and anchiote (*Bixa orellana*) both yield coloring by which the Taínos could mix with oil and decorate their bodies (Sauer 1966). It is logical to assume that any available coloring in the environment, such as red ochre, could accommodate the need for body art.

Based on our data, we suggest that after the death of Individual 1E, his body was wrapped in basketry and dried for a few days, possibly by the heat of flame. Immediately following his death, Individual 1D was sacrificed in his honor. Evidence of traumatic injury and cordage binding suggests that this person was an unwilling participant, possibly a nonlocal who may have been captured. No grave goods or basketry were associated with his skeleton, thus reinforcing this interpretation. He was the first in succession to be interred. His head was removed shortly thereafter and parts of his legs were removed and shuffled in order to fit Individual 1E in his resting place. It is unclear when Individual 1C was buried, but the close spatial proximity to Individual 1E suggests that they may be related. Since Individuals 1C and 1E were both wrapped in burial hammocks, they are likely of similar status. Individual 1C may have been a wife of Individual 1E.

SUMMARY AND CONCLUSIONS

Caves have long been used by the indigenous peoples of the Bahamas for shelter, processing of foodstuffs, and most importantly, burial of the dead. To date, Preacher's Cave is the only site that offers a detailed account of Lucayan ritual burial patterns associated with grave goods. The results of archaeological investigations at Preacher's Cave reinforce the significance of caves to Lucayan ceremonial practices and can be viewed in the broader context of the cosmology of caves for the ancestral Taíno throughout the greater West Indies. Ethnohistoric accounts of Taíno mythology by the Spanish provide some insight to caves as a portal between the natural and supernatural, specifically as a pivotal element within the indigenous mythology and cosmology of the Taíno people.

ACKNOWLEDGMENTS

We thank Jane S. Day (Research Atlantica Inc., Boca Raton, FL); Jock "Bandit" Morgan (North Eleuthera Historical Society) and his wife Caroline; Dr. Keith Tinker (Director of The National Museum of The Bahamas); Dr. Steven A. Symes, DABFA (Mercyhurst Archaeological Institute, Erie, PA); Dr. Richard Rozencwaig, MD, FACS, and Office Manager Nina Blier (Orthopedic Care Center, Aventura, FL), and radiologic technologists José Borges, Ursala Chen, and Nestor Cabrera; and the entire AHC Preacher's Cave crew of professional archaeologists and volunteers, especially Aaron Henry for his assistance in the excavation, documentation, and packaging of skeletal material. Also, we extend a very special thanks to Dr. Mary Jane Berman (Miami University, Oxford, OH) for her ideas and encouragement.

REFERENCES CITED

Albury, Paul. 1975. *The Story of the Bahamas*. London: MacMillan Caribbean.

Beeker, Charles D., Geoffrey W. Conrad, and John W. Foster. 2002. "Taíno Use of Flooded Caverns in the East National Park Region, Dominican Republic." *Journal of Caribbean Archaeology* 3: 1–26.

Berman, Mary Jane, and Perry L. Gnivecki. 1995. "The Colonization of the Bahama Archipelago." *World Archaeology* 26 (3): 421–41. http://dx.doi.org/10.1080/00438243.1995.9980285.

Berman, Mary Jane, and Charlene D. Hutcheson. 2000. "Impressions of a Lost Technology: A Study of Lucayan-Taíno Basketry." *Journal of Field Archaeology* 27 (4): 417–35. http://dx.doi.org/10.2307/3092720.

Berman, Mary Jane, and Deborah M. Pearsall. 2000. "Plants, People, and Culture in the Prehistoric Central Bahamas: A View from the Three Dog Site, an Early Lucayan Settlement on San Salvador Island, Bahamas." *Latin American Antiquity* 11 (3): 219–40. http://dx.doi.org/10.2307/972175.

Bohon, Kristine. 1999. "Excavation, Artifact Analysis, and Pottery Paste Characteristic at the Pink Wall Site, New Providence, Bahamas." MA thesis, Louisiana State University, Baton Rouge.

Brooks, W. K. 1888. "On the Lucayan Indians." *National Academy of Science Memoirs* 4: 215–33.

Carlson, Lisabeth A. 1993. "Strings of Command: Manufacture and Utilization of Shell Beads among the Taino Indians of the West Indies." MA thesis, University of Florida, Gainesville.

Carr, Robert S. 1991. "An Archaeological Survey of Spanish Wells and North Eleuthera, Bahamas." Report on file with the Archaeological and Historical Conservancy, Inc. Florida: Davie.

Carr, Robert S., Jane S. Day, and Sandra Norman. 1993. "Archaeological Investigations at Preacher's Cave North Eleuthera, Bahamas Phase II." Report on file with the Archaeological and Historical Conservancy, Inc. Florida: Davie.

Carr, Robert S., Jane S. Day, Jeff B. Ransom, William C. Schaffer, and John G. Beriault. 2006. "An Archaeological and Historical Assessment of Preacher's Cave, Eleuthera, Bahamas." Report on file with the Archaeological and Historical Conservancy, Inc. Florida: Davie.

Craton, Michael. 1986. *A History of the Bahamas*. Waterloo: San Salvador Press.

Craton, Michael, and Gail Saunders. 1992. *Islanders in the Stream: A History of the Bahamian People*, Vol. 2. Athens: University of Georgia Press.

Curran, H. Allen, and Brian White. 1995. "Introduction: Bahamas Geology." In *Geological Society of America Special Paper* 300: 1–3.

De Booy, Theodoor. 1912. "Lucayan Remains in the Caicos Islands." *American Anthropologist* 14 (1): 81–105. http://dx.doi.org/10.1525/aa.1912.14.1.02a00050.

De Booy, Theodoor. 1913. "Lucayan Artifacts from the Bahamas." *American Anthropologist* 15 (1): 1–7. http://dx.doi.org/10.1525/aa.1913.15.1.02a00020.

Dickel, David N. 1993. "Analysis of Human Skeletal Remains Recovered from Preacher's Cave." Report on file with the Archaeological and Historical Conservancy, Inc. Florida: Davie.

Garcia Arévalo, Manual Ant. 1984. "El Murciélago en la mitología y el arte taíno." *Boletín del Museo del Hombre Dominicano* 19: 45–56.

Garcia Arévalo, Manual Ant. 1997. "The Bat and the Owl: Nocturnal Images of Death." In *Taíno: Pre-Columbian Art and Culture from the Caribbean*, ed. Fatima Bercht, Estrellita Brodsky, John A. Farmer, and Dicey Taylor, 106–11. New York: The Monacelli Press and El Museo del Barrio.

Granberry, Julian. 1955. "Survey of Bahamian Archaeology." MA thesis, Department of Anthropology, University of Florida, Gainesville.

Granberry, Julian. 1978. "The Gordon Hill Site, Crooked Island, Bahamas." *Journal of the Virgin Islands Archaeological Society* 6: 32–44.

Hoffman, Charles A., Jr. 1967. "Bahama Prehistory: Cultural Adaptation to an Island Environment." PhD dissertation, University of Arizona, Tucson.

Hoffman, Charles A., Jr. 1973. "Petroglyphs on Crooked Island, Bahamas." In *Proceedings of the Fourth International Congress for the Study of the Pre-Columbian Cultures of the Lesser Antilles*, 9–12. Castries, St. Lucia: St. Lucia Archaeological and Hist6orical Society.

Keegan, William F. 1982a. "A Biological Introduction to the Prehistoric Procurement of *Strombos gigas*." *Florida Anthropologist* 35: 76–88.

Keegan, William F. 1982b. "Lucayan Cave Burials from the Bahamas." *Journal of New World Archaeology* 5: 57–65.

Keegan, William F. 1982c. "Lucayan Fishing Practices: An Experimental Approach." *Florida Anthropologist* 35: 146–61.

Keegan, William F. 1985. "Dynamic Horticulturalists: Population Expansion in the Prehistoric Bahamas." PhD dissertation, Department of Anthropology, University of California, Los Angeles.

Keegan, William F. 1992. *The People Who Discovered Columbus: The Prehistory of the Bahamas*. Gainesville: University Press of Florida.

Keegan, William F. 1997. *Bahamian Archaeology: Life in the Bahamas and Turks and Caicos before Columbus.* Nassau: Media Publishing.

Mack, Michael E., and George A. Armelagos. 1992. "Skeletal Analysis of the Sanctuary Blue Hole Remains: The Lucayan Taino." Report submitted to the Bahamian Department of Archives, Nassau, the Bahamas.

Maynard, Charles Johnson. 1890. "Some Inscriptions Found in Hartford Cave, Rum Cay, Bahamas." *Contributions in Science* 1: 167–71.

Morbán Laucer, Fernando. 1979. *Ritos funerarios: Acción del fuego y medio ambiente en las osamentos precolmbias.* Santo Domingo: Academia de Ciéncias de la República Dominicana.

Palmer, Rob. 1997. *Deep into Blue Holes.* London: Unwin Hyman.

Pané, Fray Ramón. 1999. *An Account of the Antiquities of the Indians.* Ed. José J. Arrom and trans. Susan C. Griswold. Durham, NC: Duke University Press.

Pateman, Michael P. 2007. "Reconstructing Lucayan Mortuary Practices through Skeletal Analysis." *Journal of the Bahamas Historical Society* 29: 5–10.

Rainey, Froelich G. 1934. "Diary Beginning January 22, 1934: Upon Arrival in Port-au-Prince." Manuscript on file at the Yale Peabody Museum, New Haven, CT.

Rainey, Froelich G. 1941. "Excavations in the Ft. Liberté Region, Haiti." *Yale University Publications in Anthropology* 23–24.

Sauer, Carl O. 1966. *The Early Spanish Main.* Berkeley: University of California Press.

Seigel, Peter E. 1997. "Ancestor Worship and Cosmology among the Taínos." In *Taíno: Pre-Columbian Art and Culture from the Caribbean*, ed. Fatima Bercht, Estrellita Brodsky, John A. Farmer, and Dicey Taylor, 106–11. New York: The Monacelli Press and El Museo del Barrio.

Stevens-Arroyo, Antonio M. 1988. *Cave of the Jagua: The Mythological World of the Taínos.* Albuquerque: University of New Mexico Press.

Vernon, Nicole. 2007. "Investigations at the Clifton Site: A Specialized Lucayan Site on New Providence Island, the Bahamas." Report on file with the Clifton Heritage Authority, Nassau, the Bahamas.

Williams, D. 1985. "Petroglyphs in the Prehistory of Northern Amazonia and the Antilles." *Advances in World Archaeology* 4: 335–87.

Winter, John. 1978. "Preliminary Work from the McKay Site on Crooked Island." In *Proceedings of the Seventh International Congress for the Study of the Pre-Columbian Cultures of the Lesser Antilles*, 237–242. Montréal: Centre de Recherches Caraibes.

Winter, John. 1991. "Petroglyphs of the Bahamas." *Proceedings of the Fourteenth Congress of the International Association for Caribbean Archaeology* 672–80.

Part IV
Ethnographic and Ethnohistoric Studies

21

Caves in Ireland

Archaeology, Myth, and Folklore

Patrick McCafferty

The underworld is prominent in Irish myths and folktales. It seems that, for millennia, people lived their lives on the surface of the land, aware that beneath their feet a separate world existed, a world that was both fascinating and fearful. Ancient tales recounted how the Tuatha De Danann, mythical gods of a bygone era, were defeated by the invading Sons of Míl, and were then given control of the world beneath the ground while the victors became rulers above ground (Curran 2000, 153). The megalithic tombs, dolmens, passage tombs, burial mounds, ringforts, and other archaeological ruins in the Irish landscape were thought to be portals to this strange underworld, so parents warned their children never to enter ringforts (early-medieval circular embankments) in case the fairies, the *sid*, or leprechauns stole them and took them underground, or punished them with illness. As Yeats (1888, 348) observed of ringforts: "The fairies have taken up their abode therein, guarding them from all disturbance. Whoever roots them up soon finds his cattle falling sick, or his family or himself." At *Samhain*, or Halloween, it was even thought that the barriers between the underworld and our world weakened, and that on this night, the dead, who had been buried underground, walked among the living (Curran 2000, 240).

Ireland is also a country with many caves. Could these caves have inspired the Irish picture of the underworld as a home of gods? To what extent did people in Ireland interact with caves? Were caves used for prehistoric rituals? How significant were caves in the Irish cultural landscape? This chapter examines various aspects of caves: references to caves in medieval manuscripts, caves in folklore, traditions associated with caves, and the archaeology of caves in Ireland. Although these cannot answer all questions, it is hoped that this multifaceted approach will shed some light on the hidden significance of caves.

IRELAND'S CAVES

Underlying roughly half of Ireland is a thick layer of Carboniferous limestone, perfect for forming caves. However, much of this limestone lies below other strata of rock or underneath the water table. In addition, enormous quantities of chalk and limestone once exposed on the surface were scraped off during various Ice Ages. As a result, Ireland has only two major cave systems: the impressive karst landscape known as the Burren in County Clare, and the system flanking the Arigna coalfield in Counties Fermanagh, Cavan, Sligo, and Leitrim (Drew, Jones, and O'Reilly 1977, 1). There are also some important individual caves in Counties Cork, Tipperary, Galway, Kerry, Kilkenny, Mayo, and Waterford and in the chalk cliff-faces of County Antrim (figure 21.1). In the Republic of Ireland, there are an estimated 689 caves totaling 147 kilometers in length (Drew 2004). These vary in size from small openings

FIGURE 21.1 Counties of Ireland and Northern Ireland. For more detailed locations of caves, see database of Irish Caves (Drew 2004 and Drew and Huddart 2006, 165).

in cliff faces to Pollnagollum Cave in Co. Clare with 15 kilometers of passages. Statistics for Northern Ireland are not as readily available, but caves in Fermanagh such as Marble Arch and Reyfad are at least 5 kilometers long.

FOLKTALES OF CAVES

Many of these caves feature in folktales. Some tales recount historical events. For example, Noon's Hole, Co. Fermanagh, was named after the unfortunate Dominic Noone who was accused of spying and then thrown down a shaft in 1826 (Jones et al. 1997, 23–26). At Captain Webb's Hole, Co. Mayo, twelve women were allegedly thrown into the hole by Captain Webb (Wilde 1887, 228). Many caves are named after animals, for example, Pollabrock and Legnabrocky (badger); Pollawaddy and Poulnamadda (dog); Pollnagapple and Legacapple (horse); Oweynagat and Pollnagat (cat); Pollnagollum (dove); Poulnamuck (pig); Sheep Pot; Spider Pot; and Legnaveagh (deer) (Jones 1974, 108–110).

Some cave animals are supernatural. In Co. Clare, a cave on a cliff face is known as Labbanaheanbo, the "bed of the one cow." Westropp (1910, 181) reports "in this bed, the Heanbo [one cow] will support the Leinster man who will win the freedom of Ireland in the last great battle." Kilcorney 1 Cave, Co. Clare, also known as "Cave of the Wild Horses," is thought to be a passage to the Antipodes (Shaw and Tratman 1969, 26). At Kilcorney, an enchanted bird was caught "which spoke like a human being" (O'Donovan and Curry 1997 [1928], 87). The cave was "famous in the eighteenth century for throwing out floods of water full of fish" (Westropp 1910, 181). One legend states that, "when the floods are out a fairy herd of white horses comes out of the cave. Many attempts were made to catch them and eventually one was captured and put to stud with the local horses to produce the famous strain of Clare horses" (Shaw and Tratman 1969, 26). One can easily imagine that such a rush of water from an aquifer could have inspired the legend of white horses but it is more difficult to explain a legend of a fairy trout in The Pigeon Hole, Co. Galway, or a tale of corn ground by fairies at Fairy Mills Cave, Co. Galway (Drew 2004), or the Faracat, "a monstrous cat having a crescent on its forehead and a sharp nail in its tail" (Westropp 1910, 180, 183, 479).

There are many tales associated with Keshcorran Cave, in Co. Sligo. In one, a woman emerged here, having entered the Hellmouth Cave, Co. Roscommon, 24 miles away, and traveled underground through the night, dragged by her unruly calf whose tail she held (Harbison 2002, 78). Another odd tale of a cave animal comes from Mitchelstown Cave, Co. Tipperary, once known as "Oonacaragreisha" (Cave of the Grey Sheep). In a local folktale, "a grey sheep came out of here and was reared by a local farmer. On his killing one of her offspring she gathered her lambs together and vanished again into the cave" (Coleman 1965, 18). This particular cave is also associated with Oisín, the son of Finn mac Cumhall, who spent 300 years in Tír na n-Óg, the land of eternal youth; apparently, he entered the otherworld through this cave (MacNeill 1989, 119).

In Vigo Cave, near Lough Inchiquin, Co. Clare, "the Quin chieftain found a beautiful woman asleep in a cave. She agreed to marry him provided he never allow an O'Brien to enter his castle at Inchiquin. A year or so later the feast celebrating the birth of their son was attended by one of the O'Brien family and the chieftain's wife leapt out of a window with their son and disappeared forever in the lough. The castle and the land passed to the O'Briens soon afterwards" (Davies, 1853, 436). In an associated tale, Lough Inchiquin was once a flourishing city that sank under water. "The dark spirit of its king, who ruled also over the surrounding country, resides in a cavern in one of the hills which border the lake, and once every seven years at midnight he issues forth on his white charger, and urges him at full speed over hill and crag, until he has completed the circuit of the lake, till the silver hoofs of his steed are worn out, when the curse will be removed, and the city reappear in all its splendour" (Davies 1854, 73).

It is said that the legendary Finn mac Cumhall and his followers, the Fianna, are asleep under a cave, waiting to emerge during Ireland's greatest hour of need. According to Lady Augusta Gregory (1970 [1905]):

> And one time a smith made his way into a cave he saw, that had a door to it, and he made a key that opened it. And when he went in he saw a very wide place, and very big men lying on the floor. And one that was bigger than the rest was lying in the middle, and the Dord Fiann [Finn's hunting horn] beside him; and he knew it was Finn and the Fianna that were in it.
>
> And the smith took hold of the Dord Fiann, and it is hardly he could lift it to his mouth, and he blew a very strong blast on it, and the sound it made was so great, it is much the rocks did not come down on him. And at the sound, the big men lying on the ground shook from head to foot. He gave another blast then, and they all turned on their elbows.
>
> And great dread came on him when he saw that, and he threw down the Dord Fiann and ran from the cave and locked the door after him, and threw the key into the lake. And he heard them crying after him, "You left us worse than you found us." And the cave was not found again since that time. (p. 393)

This theme, of an army sleeping in a cave or under a hill, is a common one. Near Ardee, it is said that Garret Early (a late medieval chieftain) and his 10,000 men lie enchanted under Dawson's Mount. If they rise, it is predicted that Garret and his men will slay many people until stopped by a red woman at a bridge. On two occasions, the army was nearly roused, once by a man who found his way into the fort and almost drew a sword, and the second time by a girl standing on a hill overlooking the fort (Jones 1908, 321–22).

Many aspects of these tales are quite fantastic and are not easy to reconcile with real caves. It is difficult to understand how caves could have inspired stories of gray sheep, underground armies, or the periodic emergence of a king on a white horse every seven years. The tales seem to contain a warning: any benefits accrued from entering caves are later removed. However, these tales may simply be the result of centuries of imagination, and therefore provide little insight into prehistoric cave rituals. To gain a better understanding than folktales from recent centuries can provide, we will next look at tales written in early medieval Ireland.

CAVES IN MEDIEVAL TALES

Ireland, an island situated off the west coast of Britain, has a landscape steeped in myth. Standing testament to its ancient past are hundreds of megalithic tombs erected during the Neolithic, and hundreds of stone circles and standing stones from the Bronze Age. A major challenge facing any attempt to understand these ancient structures is that written history does not begin in Ireland until the introduction of Christianity in the fifth century AD. Prior to this, it seems that Ireland's elite adhered to the practice ascribed by Julius Caesar to the druids of Gaul: "They are said to commit to memory a great number of verses . . . Nor do they judge it to be allowed to entrust these things to writing" (Koch and Carey 2000, 21–22).

If almost nothing was written in Ireland until the arrival of Saint Patrick, Irish society made up for this in subsequent centuries, producing an extensive corpus of manuscripts containing legal texts, annals, genealogies, poems, prose sagas, religious writings, translations of classical texts, and place-name lore. It is to these materials, particularly the prose tales that we turn to next.

The narrative tales, written in Old or Middle Irish, describe characters that supposedly lived many centuries earlier: the Mythological Cycle, describing the deeds of various gods, the Tuatha De Danann, is set in the Bronze Age, at the time of Troy. The Ulster Cycle describes heroic events set in the Iron Age, and the Finn Cycle describes the deeds of a legendary warrior chief in the third century AD. In these tales of Lugh, Cú Chulainn, and Finn mac Cumhall, caves and the underworld play an interesting role. A list of tales, many of which are now lost, includes the category *Uatha*, traditionally translated as "tales of caves" (O'Curry 1861, 835). More recently, these are translated as "tales of terror" (Toner 2000, 89), but significantly, the tale *Uath Beinne Etair* is set in a hag's cave on the Hill of Howth and describes the hag's betrayal of the young lovers, Diarmaid and Gráinne, who were hiding in her cave from Finn (Meyer 1890, 125–34; Ní Shéaghdha 1967, 130–37).

When Diarmaid, a handsome young warrior, eloped with Gráinne, the bride of the old chief-warrior, Finn mac Cumhall, they hid (and slept together) in caves, and ultimately settled near the cave of Keshcorran, Co. Sligo (Ní Shéaghdha 1967, 78–79). In the tale of the "Enchanted Cave of Keshcorran" (*Bruidhean Chéise Corainn*), Finn and his warriors were weakened and trapped by three hideous hags who sat outside the cave spinning. Finally, they were rescued by one-eyed Goll mac Morna of the flaming hair, who struck one of the three strongest blows ever experienced in Ireland (Ní Shéaghdha 1941). These stories suggest that the cave has associations with motifs of fertility and rejuvenation.

In some tales, the location of the cave is unspecified but it is described as the entrance to a mysterious, magical underworld. Finn mac Cumhall chased a hybrid pig/deer with moons in its side into a hill, where he encountered the Red Woman and a king in a magnificent shining palace (Gregory 1970 [1905], 274–77). In some medieval tales, access to the underworld was through a *síd*, or fairy-mound. These probably refer to passage tombs, constructed circa 3000 BC though, at times, the distinction between "caves" and "graves" is unclear. When the Vikings dug to raid the three huge passage tombs at Newgrange, Knowth, and Dowth in AD 863, the word used by the annalist was *uamh* (cave), rather than *uagh* (grave):

> U863.4 "The caves [*uamh*] of Achadh Aldai and of Conodba and the cave of the mound of Boadán above Dubad and the cave of the wife of Óengaba were searched by the foreigners (*Gaill*), which had never been undertaken before." (Mac Airt and Mac Niocaill 1983)

Both caves and passage tombs were regarded as entrances to the underworld. In the tale *Fled Bricrenn*, or "Bricriu's Feast," strange beasts emerge from the cave of Uaim na gCat or Oweynagat, Co. Roscommon, the "cave of the cat": "one night as their portion was being assigned to them, three cats from the Cave of Cruachan were let loose to attack them, i.e. three beasts of magic" (Koch and Carey 2000, 92). In another tale, "every year at Samhain time, a woman comes out of the hill of the Sidhe of Cruachan and brings away nine of the best out of every herd," and "three she-wolves come out of the Cave of Cruachan every year and destroy our sheep and our wethers" (Gregory 1970 [1905], 263–64). In yet other accounts, from this cave, "the Irish entrance to Hell," emerged the Morrígan, a goddess of battle, with pigs of magic, a triple-headed monster, and red birds that withered up everything they touched (Waddell 1983, 22). Another tale that attributes destructive elements to caves is the early medieval "Life of St. Maccrecius," which recounts that an enormous and ferocious badger emerged from Poul na Bruckee, its cave above Rath Lake, to devastate the country, slaying men and cattle (Scharff et al. 1906, 67).

It is difficult to connect such fiery, volcanic imagery with the quiet cave at Oweynagat. The images of flaming birds remind one of fireballs and meteors and may fit the suggestion that Iron Age Ireland occasionally experienced, and mythologized, major meteor storms (McCafferty and Baillie 2005, 116–17). If so, it would seem that, incredibly, the cave at Oweynagat was somehow regarded as the source of a meteor shower.

A possible explanation for this is that Irish monks may have felt the need to demonize or denigrate the previous pagan pantheon. One can see this process in tales of the gods of the Mythological Cycle, the Tuatha De Danann. *Lebor Gabála Érenn*, the "Book of Invasions of Ireland," recounts that they arrived in Ireland through the air (Macalister 1941, 109) and defeated the Fir Bolg, who had arrived in Ireland years earlier. These divine characters have clear celestial attributes, and it has been argued that Lugh of the Long Arm, who rises in the west with his face shining like the sun, could even be a comet (McCafferty and Baillie 2005, 44–50).

However, after their defeat by the Sons of Míl, who became ancestors of the Irish, the Tuatha De Danann were given control of the world below the ground, while the victors were awarded the earthly realm (Koch and Carey 2000, 145). As *Lebor Gabála Érenn* describes, "the Tuatha De Danann were demons of a different order, and that it is they who came from heaven along with the expulsion by which Lucifer and his demons came from heaven; having taken an airy body upon themselves to destroy and to tempt the seed of Adam." (Macalister 1940, 155–56).

Accordingly, pagan celestial deities could have become chthonic, falling like Lucifer from their original heavenly home to a Christian underworld associated with purgatory and hell. The cave of Oweynagat might thereby have become a locus for any manner of celestial deities, or strange, fiery beasts associated with hell. Indeed, it is said that each Halloween, at Oweynagat, "the gates of hell were opened, and humans were abducted into the fairy realms inside" (Lane 2007). These images of the cave may therefore owe more to Christianity than to pre-Christian ritual.

This observation raises a difficulty with the interpretation of Irish myths. It was thought for years that these tales were passed down orally from a pagan past until being written down by medieval monks. Irish tales were thereby seen as the last voice of Celtic druids, who survived on an island free from the influence of the Roman Empire. However, in recent decades, scholars have gained a greater appreciation of the contributions by the monastic authors of the tales (McCone 1990). Irish monks had access to a wide range of international literature, both religious and secular. It is now recognized that many motifs in Irish tales owe their origins to that literature.

As a result, medieval Irish tales can no longer be used reliably to gain insights into the practices of pre-Christian Ireland. Ironically, the survival of some pagan elements in folk traditions may offer a better insight into ancient practices than the mythical tales, written but sanitized by monks, and it is to these we next turn.

FOLK TRADITIONS: THE LUGHNASA FESTIVAL AT CAVES

There are reports of people gathering at the entrances to caves for ritual purposes. The month of August is called *Lughnasa* (pronounced "loonasa") in Ireland, and is named after the ancient Celtic god Lugh, who gave his name to towns across Europe, for example Lugo in Spain and Lyon (Lugdunum) in France. The last Sunday in July, known as Garland Sunday or Reeks Sunday, was once a major festival of Lughnasa across Ireland, when people made pilgrimages to "heights, natural features or water sites to pick bilberries and spend the day in rural festivities" (Coleman 1965, 56). Even today, on the last Sunday in July, people climb Croagh Patrick, a prominent mountain in Co. Mayo, barefoot.

In her study of sites associated with the Lughnasa festival, MacNeill noted only three caves—Polticoghlan (Co. Leitrim), Tory Cave (Co. Cavan), and Keshcorran (Co. Sligo) (MacNeill 1962, 121–23, 175, 185–87)—with possible connections suggested for Leafrin Hill (ibid., 144), Caher Roe's Den (ibid., 225–27) and Carrickbyrne Hill (228). In addition, Coleman listed Poulagaddy (Robber's Hole) and School Cave, Co. Sligo, as Lughnasa sites—these are part of the Keshcorran Cave system (Coleman 1965, 56). Marion Dowd has identified Poll na Bruidhne, Co. Limerick, as another possible Lughnasa site. This cave, known as the home of Donn Fírinne, may even be artificial (Dowd 2004; Drew 2004).

In recent times, these Lughnasa celebrations seem to have taken place outside caves. Perhaps this is because cautionary tales of the Lughnasa musician warned people not to enter caves. At Keshcorran Cave, Co. Sligo, which is associated with a divine harp, one tale explains that the Lughnasa festival "was started by a wandering fiddler" (Melia 1967, 369). Another legend tells of a fiddler who entered the Tory Hole to play a few tunes and never returned, "although his music is still heard sometimes from inside the cave" (ibid., 369). "What happens to him is not explained in any of the Irish stories, but the musician's fate is considered terrible enough to explain why no one enters the cave" (ibid., 365).

There are stories of sounds emanating from other caves. In Co. Cork, Carrigacrump Cave has a legend of a trumpeter (Oldham 1981, 5). Similarly, Reidh na h'Uanach and Piper's Cave, which supposedly connect the Islands of Inisheer and Inishmore in Co. Galway, have a legend of a piper (Mullan 2003, 242; Mullan and Boycott 2004, 147). Mac Neill has examined the widespread motif of the musician in the cave and, based on Lugh's skill as a musician, concluded that such sites were used for the celebration of Lughnasa (1989, 114).

So, even in Christian Ireland, people visited caves for the annual festival of Lugh. If this practice, like Lugh's name, is a continuation of a Celtic tradition, it offers an insight into a prehistoric cave ritual—implying that worshippers of Lugh, accompanied by a musician, celebrated at the entrance to a cave associated with him. We might even speculate that while the congregation remained outside, the musician entered the cave and added to the mood by playing music that resonated from the ground, or threatened to wake the subterranean god. If a tradition like this can provide an insight into ancient ritual, it may be worthwhile examining other Christian connections with Irish caves.

CAVES AND CHRISTIAN TRADITION

When barefoot pilgrims reach the top of Croagh Patrick on Reeks Sunday, they are almost certainly continuing a pre-Christian tradition. However, at the top of the mountain, they celebrate Mass. Like elsewhere in the world, one would not expect the adoption of Christianity in Ireland to have obliterated every aspect of pagan tradition. Instead, some traditions would have received a Christian veneer, beneath which they were allowed to continue. For example, the character of Saint Brigit is thought to contain elements of a fertility goddess.

Some caves were used for Christian ritual. Pollanaffrin, Co. Fermanagh, means "the hole of the Mass." It has a narrow, concealed entrance into a cavern with standing room, and in local tradition, was used for the celebration of Catholic Mass during the time of penal laws. There was also a Mass rock "in a sort of cave" at Carricknahorna, Co. Sligo (MacNeill 1962, 188). Bricklieve Cave (A) in Co. Sligo is a tunnel, 20 meters long. Also known as Chapel Cave, at least part of this cave seems to be artificial (Thorn, Drew, and Coxon 1990, 122).

The cave with the strongest association with Christianity is Saint Patrick's Purgatory on an island in Lough Derg, Co. Donegal. Saint Patrick supposedly fought a serpent at the lake and experienced a terrible vision. On an island in the lake there was thought to be a cave with a locked door and steps leading below—into Purgatory. With the arrival of the Anglo-Normans in the twelfth century AD, the island grew famous. Legends told of the adventures of Knight Owen in the cave, while Giraldus Cambrensis wrote of "nine Pits, in any of which, should someone dare to spend the night . . . he is immediately seized by evil spirits and is tortured all night with such heavy pains, and tormented so incessantly with so many grievous and unspeakable torments of fire and water, that with morning there is scarcely any or only the dregs of life surviving in his wretched body" (1795 [1200], Part II, chapter 5).

Such legends brought many noble pilgrims from across Europe and are even thought to have inspired Dante (Leslie 1932, xx–xxi). After fasting and praying for nine days, visitors to the lake would be locked into the hole overnight, naked, with a warning that previous pilgrims had vanished, overcome by the temptations of the Devil. Not surprisingly, many pilgrims reported hellish visions. The cave was closed in 1497, and destroyed in 1632, though pilgrimages continued. An act was passed in the reign of Queen Anne, 1704, prohibiting the pilgrimage, but it was repealed by Queen Victoria in 1871 (Leslie 1932, 86). Today, pilgrims spend two nights on a different island on Lough Derg, praying and fasting. So here we see that a cave became the inspiration for a place of Christian pilgrimage, though pilgrims do not actually enter any cave, and instead spend their time on a neighboring island.

There are good reasons to suspect that Lough Derg was the sight of a pre-Christian cave ritual. This lake was once called Lough Finn, after Conan, the son of Finn mac Cumhall, found a worm in his jaw and threw it into the lake:

> it grew so big within 24 Hours, that the whole Lake could hardly contain it. This Monster, called by the natives *Caoranach*, would suck Men and Cattle into its mouth at a Miles distance . . . When almost all the Cattel in Ulster were destroyed[, Conan] undertook to be avenged of the Monster, and taking a Dagger in his Hand[, was] swallowed up by it himself. When he was in *Caoranach*'s Belly . . . he cut his Way through it with his Dagger, and swam to the Shore, having lost his Skin and Hair by the Heat of its Entrails . . . The Monster immediately died, and *Conan* having cut off its Head, threw it upon the shore . . . The blood of the Body ran in so great a Quantity into the lake, that it was red for 48 Hours, and for this Reason it goes by the name of *Lough-Derg* [Red Lake] ever since. (Richardson 1727, 2–4)

This story of a naked human struggling to escape the belly of the worm may describe or mirror the journey of an initiate from a cave. If so, it suggests that the cave on the island in Lough Derg was a pre-Christian ritual site. It is even possible that many aspects of the later, Christian ritual (fasting for nine days, being naked) were in fact aspects of a much older ritual.

Saint Patrick is not the only saint to be associated with a cave. Lismore Cave, a 10-meter-long passage in Co. Waterford, is associated with Saint Carthage (Coleman 1965, 30). Saint Colman MacDuagh lived in a small cave in the Burren, Co. Clare, for 7 years (Shaw and Tratman 1969, 26), and Saint Coemgen "hid in the hollow of a cave" (Plummer 1922, 123). Saint Brendan spent a night of penance in a cave, which resulted in "hosts of angels going upwards to the heaven, and downwards to the earth over the cave till the morning" (ibid., 46). Though similar to the practice at Lough Derg, the tale contains no mention of Purgatory, suggesting that the particular element in Lough Derg is a later Christian addition to a more widespread cave ritual. These rituals of saints may therefore represent the continuation or adoption of a pre-Christian ritual.

In the tale *Do Faillsiugud Tána Bó Cuailngni* (Meyer 1905, 4–6), the chief poet of Ireland spent three days and nights at the grave of Fergus, communing with his ghost, and was told the forgotten story of the epic tale of Cú Chulainn, *Táin Bo Cúailnge*. This suggests that in pre-Christian Ireland, there was a ritual of communing with ancestors in graves or caves for inspiration. Whether that ritual involved a preparatory fast, as at Lough Derg, is impossible to say, but the irony is that the ostensibly Christian practice at Lough Derg may have had pagan or even shamanic origins.

CAVES AND ARCHAEOLOGY

Is there any archaeological proof that caves were used for rituals or for habitation in prehistory? Of all the caves in Ireland, almost eighty are thought to contain archaeological remains (Dowd 2005, 85; Drew 2004). According to the Irish caves database (Dowd 2004; Drew 2004), human remains have also been discovered in the following thirty-three caves in the Republic of Ireland: Robber's Den, Alice and Gwendoline Cave, Barntick Cave, Bat's Cave, the Catacombs, Elderbush Cave, and Poll Rannagh East in Co. Clare; Castletownroche Cave 7, Killavullen Caves 1–3, and Killura Cave in Co. Cork; Lisodigue Cave and Cloghermore Cave in Co. Kerry; Killuragh Cave and Red Cellar Cave in Co. Limerick; Kelly's Cave and Lady's Buttery in Co. Mayo; Knocknarea Cave (1–4) and Polldonin in Co. Sligo; Mitchelstown Cave in Co. Tipperary; Ballynamintra Cave, Brothers' Cave and Oonaglour, Carrigmurrish Cave, and Kilgreany Cave in Co. Waterford; and of course Dunmore Cave in Co. Kilkenny. Human remains have also been discovered in caves in Northern Ireland, for example at caves near Cushendall and Port Bradden in Co. Antrim (Coleman 1965, 77), and Pollnagollum of the Boats in Co. Fermanagh (Doughty 1995, 54).

Ireland does not have any caves with Paleolithic art. While humans were painting on cave walls in France and Spain, most of Ireland lay under a thick sheet of ice. It was hoped that some caves in the very south of Ireland may have been habitable during the Ice Age, especially when mammoth bones were discovered in Castlepook Cave in Co. Cork (Ussher 1905, 1–5). Kilgreany Cave in Co.

Waterford was found to contain bones from Pleistocene species (for example, Arctic lemming and fox), and upper layers of cave debris contained bones from domesticated species such as sheep, pig, horse, and dog (Jackson 1928, 151; Woodman, McCarthy, and Monaghan 1997, 129–59). When human bones were found in the deeper layers of the cave, along with bones of giant deer, it was initially thought that these might date to the Ice Age (Tratman 1929, 120) but they instead turned out to be Neolithic (Dowd 2002, 89; Movius 1935, 282).

In general, Irish caves are cold and damp and are not particularly appealing. In Dunmore Cave, Co. Kilkenny, "the temperature is always between eight and ten degrees Celsius whilst the water remains at nine degrees Celsius" (Drew and Huddart 1980, 14). In Ireland, air temperature rarely drops below freezing or rises above 20 degrees Celsius, so caves rarely provide refuge from extreme temperatures. Furthermore, from the evidence of bones found in caves, it would appear that some caves were the homes of bears and wolves (now extinct) and this would have added to their perception as uninviting, scary places. Some caves in Ireland do show evidence of temporary inhabitation, though it must be stressed that this was in the entrance to caves, in the light zone. Irish caves were not homes for the living.

Human bones found in caves have radiocarbon dates from the Mesolithic to the later Middle Ages. At Killuragh Cave, Co. Limerick, excavations suggested "ritual activity in the early Mesolithic, associated with two or more human bodies" (Woodman 1997, 67). The earliest dated bone, from Sramore Cave, Co. Leitrim, has been attributed to the Mesolithic–Neolithic transition (Dowd 2008, 306).

The Neolithic period appears to be the most significant period for cave burial, with dates for human bones from fourteen caves, and "a marked concentration of Irish cave dates between 3600 and 3400 BC, essentially around the transition between the Early and Middle Neolithic" (Dowd 2008, 306). Interestingly, "intact Neolithic *inhumation burials* have only been discovered in two Irish caves—Annagh Cave and Kilgreany Cave," where "individuals appear to have been placed directly on the cave floors" (Dowd 2008, 309). In Kilgreany Cave, "at least eight adults and an infant" were deposited (Dowd 2007b, 89). These sites are exceptions: most caves contain small numbers of bones. For example, Elderbush Cave and Alice and Gwendoline Cave both contained a preponderance of "hand- and foot-bones" (Scharff et al. 1906, 17–18, 63), consistent with a practice of excarnation or token deposition. In many cases, human remains were accompanied by the bones of animals or by artifacts. For example, at Kilgreany Cave, Co. Waterford, "a stone axe fragment, shell beads, perforated and worked animal teeth and a hollow scraper" were deposited in the cave during the Neolithic (Dowd 2007b, 89).

Even in Neolithic times, it seems that people preferred not to enter caves (Dowd 2008, 312). Caves in Cave Hill in Belfast, Co. Antrim, are thought to be artificial, perhaps rock-cut tombs (Chart, Evans, and Lawlor 1940, 53). Between 3400 and 3000 BC, many passage tombs were constructed. These essentially consist of a passage leading to a central chamber formed of megalithic orthostats, topped by a corbeled roof of large slabs, and then covered with an enormous quantity of stones. In the landscape, a passage tomb looks like a cave in a small hill, and the similarity between the words *uamh* and *uagh*, for "cave" and "grave," respectively, has already been noted. Dowd notes a similarity between passage tombs and caves chosen for burial: "the preferred cave type consisted of a simple long narrow passage such as Barntick Cave, Bat's Cave, Elderbush Cave, Killuragh Cave and Knocknarea Cave. It is possible that these passage-type caves were the most symbolic of a passage to another world and/or passage to the world of the dead" (2008, 311). By constructing passage graves as artificial caves, Irish people had new focal points for ritual and burial, and little need to enter real caves.

Even when they did place their dead in caves, they avoided the deepest parts. Dowd notes that "bodies or bones were placed at, immediately inside, or immediately outside cave entrances, and that material was subsequently washed or carried deeper into the caves" (2008, 311). Furthermore, caves may have been used only for the purpose of initial excarnation, with subsequent burial in a passage tomb. Bones from caves had few gnaw marks, suggesting that the entrances to the caves may have been temporarily blocked to prevent scavengers (Dowd, Fibiger, and Lynch 2006, 17).

Seven caves have been found with Bronze Age burials (Dowd 2007a, 37). Graves in caves in Knockane, Co. Cork, and Glencurran, Co. Clare, contained unburnt remains accompanied by personal adornments, including amber, and these have been categorized as "rich burials" (Grogan 2004, 61; Dowd 2009, 94). At Knockninny, Co. Fermanagh, the skeletal remains of up to nine individuals were found, along with two flint flakes. Potsherds from a food vessel were also found in the cave, along with charcoal, and an urn containing cremated remains was found enclosed in a small cist in a wall niche (Coleman 1965, 77; Plunkett 1870–1879, 465).

Glencurran Cave, Co. Clare, is the only cave in Ireland where a cairn or burial structure has been discovered. The cairn, located 13 meters from the cave entrance, was recently excavated by Dowd (2007a) and found to contain seventeen human bones, representing two adults. One bone was dated at 3035 ± 35 BP (UB-6660)—the Middle

Bronze Age. Excavation of the cairn revealed "charcoal, fragments of scallop shells, a shale axe, a rubbing stone, a copper-alloy object, a net-sinker, three bone beads, three perforated cowrie shells, a perforated and an unperforated periwinkle shell, and forty-two amber bead fragments with a few complete beads" (Dowd 2007a, 36). Glencurran Cave contained a further burial 32 meters deeper inside the cave. Here, nine unburnt bones of a 2–4-year-old child were found. One of these produced a date of 2536 ± 31 BP (UB-6661)—the Late Bronze Age. Beside the child's skull, which rested on a layer of grasses, were found several amber beads, pottery sherds and "85 perforated cowrie shells and perforated periwinkle shells," with the unburnt bones of five hares and the burnt bones of many neonatal animals (six lambs, four piglets, and two calves). Dowd (2007a, 38) has suggested that these apparently deliberate deposits were sacrificed animals, of sympathetic age to the child. Dowd also discovered a Viking necklace of seventy glass beads, with evidence of medieval occupation in Glencurran Cave.

In addition, "during the Dowris Phase of the Late Bronze Age, Kilgreany Cave became a focus for votive deposition" (Dowd 2007b, 89). Other caves found to contain Late Bronze Age hoards are Brothers' Cave, Co. Waterford, and Kilmurry, Co. Kerry (ibid, 90). An amber bead, bone implements, and two metal bracelets were found in Alice and Gwendoline Cave, Co. Clare (which also contained human bones) (Scharff et al. 1906, 68). A stone lamp and bronze pin were found in Bat's Cave, Co. Clare (ibid., 72). The Catacombs, Co. Clare, contained human bones and "a bronze strap, a buckle or brooch of bronze, plated in silver, and engraved with an interlaced pattern" (ibid., 70–71).

At Oweynagat, near the major royal or ritual center of Rath Croghan, the entrance was altered:

> a souterrain entrance 2 ft. high and 4 ft. wide, leads into a lintelled passageway with *Ogham* inscriptions on two lintels immediately inside the entrance. [Ogham stones are standing stones incised with scratches, where each group of incisions denotes a letter.] 6 ft. in the passage turns left and continues as a joint fissure 2 to 3 ft. wide (possibly partly quarried) and roofed with lintels for 40 ft. Crawling under a half wall built across the passage, the cave is a natural rift from here on, averaging 15 to 18 ft. high with a mud floor. This natural section is 130 ft. long to where the rift closes. (Coleman 1965, 68)

This alteration, when combined with the many stories of Oweynagat encountered earlier, suggests that it was an important ritual site, and one can imagine individuals entering the cave at Samhain, mindful of the magical beasts that lived inside. The alteration may have been carried out by Christians trying to control the site. Indeed, most evidence for habitation in Irish caves dates to the Early Medieval period, just after the introduction of Christianity.

In Midleton, Co. Cork, a cave had a black habitation layer containing numerous animal bones and marine shells, together with bone pins, a bone comb, a spindle whorl, whetstones, iron knives, parts of a bronze brooch, and a decorated bronze bar, thought to be "part of the mounting of a shrine" from the eighth century AD (Coleman 1942, 71–75). Some caves were modified to be more habitable: Dowd (2007a, 38–39) reports that at Glencurran Cave in Co. Clare, "a series of limestone blocks were fitted neatly across the cave entrance, and it is possible that they functioned as a plinth for a wooden door, particularly as an iron barrel padlock key was discovered inside the cave." She notes, "Glencurran cave is one of seventeen Irish caves that have produced evidence for early medieval occupation, possibly short-term in nature. The size of these caves suggests one occupant, possibly an itinerant, a shepherd or someone travelling away from home." However, these modifications may match stories of saints occupying caves on particular nights.

The arrival of Vikings in the ninth century may have revived the practice of cave burials. At Cloghermore Cave in Co. Kerry, a D-shaped enclosure, a feature typical of Viking sites, was built around a shaft leading into the cave. Inside the cave, fifteen subadults and fifteen adult humans were buried in two phases of burial: from early Christian Medieval Ireland and from the slightly later Viking age (Lynch 2005, 254). These were accompanied by many artifacts including worked bone, antler, and ivory; beads of amber, bone, stone, and glass; worked stone; whetstones; pottery; iron objects including an axehead, knife, shears, and saw; copper-alloy pins; bone combs; and a clay pipe (Connolly and Coyne 2005, 188–230). In some cases, the bones of individuals were deliberately disarticulated. The skull was apparently removed from one body before the flesh was completely decomposed—a grisly task (ibid., 54, 283–84).

In AD 928, "Godfrey, grandson of Imhar, with the foreigners of Ath Cliath demolished and plundered Dearc Fearna, where 1000 persons were killed in this year" (O'Donovan 1848–1851). This cave, Dearc Fearna, has been identified as Dunmore Cave in Co. Kilkenny, and the presence of the bones of forty-five humans and Viking coins has reinforced the tradition that these were victims of a massacre by Vikings (Drew and Huddart 1980). Recently, Connolly and Coyne (2005, 42) suggested that Dunmore Cave was "a place of Irish burial with the subsequent insertion of Scandinavian or Hiberno-Scandinavian burials," though Dowd (2007b, 16) has noted some problems with this interpretation.

Caves may also have been used for temporary shelter. Robert the Bruce hid in a cave in Rathlin Island, where he was inspired by a spider's repeated attempts to cast a silken anchor line for her web across the wall of the cave. Coastal caves are often associated with smugglers. A cave in Co. Clare was used to house an illicit "still" to distill alcoholic *poteen* (Shaw and Tratman 1969, 28–29). Caves were occasionally used as workplaces. In 1824, Croker reported that some of the caves of Killavullen were inhabited. In almost mythical tones, he notes that a smith occupied one cave, "the light from whose forge threw a broad and vivid reflection across the road, which lay in the solemnity of deep shadow" (Coleman 1965, 25).

Although the above list is impressive, one must be careful of concluding that cave burials in Ireland were commonplace. The above list represents the burial of perhaps two hundred individuals, a tiny fraction of all deaths in Ireland. In general, for the past millennium, Irish people avoided entering caves. In the past century, in almost every town, people constructed a grotto, in front of which they placed a statue of the Virgin Mary. Each December, shops erect a grotto to house a man dressed in red. In these ways, Irish people can worship the goddess or visit the old man in the cave, without ever venturing underground.

CONCLUSION

It is difficult to reconstruct the nature or extent of rituals in Irish caves. However, the approach of combining archaeology with folklore and myths has provided tantalizing glimpses of gods worshipped from outside, monstrous figures and mating couples in the dark, faint echoes of ancient music, and naked warriors struggling to reemerge from cavernous spaces. Ultimately, to appreciate the Irish relationship with caves, it has been necessary to speculate, to use the imagination. In a way, this process is in keeping with a long tradition of using the mind to fill the gaps in our knowledge of what lay underground.

The engagement between the Irish and caves is complex, and there appear to have been different phases. Until circa 3400 BC, they were used for burial, but it seems that people were never quite comfortable entering caves. Over the next 400 years, passage tombs acted as artificial caves, though caves may have been used for preparatory excarnation or token deposition (Dowd 2008, 309). Over subsequent centuries, caves were occasionally used for burials.

There are hints from medieval tales and later traditions that, during the Iron Age, those worshipping Lugh visited caves, accompanied by music, for his festival. Although most people may have stayed outside, it also seems likely that some individuals entered caves for rituals, possibly involving inspirational or shamanic trances. From tales of Diarmaid and Gráinne, one might speculate that caves were used for ritual mating between a sovereign male and female. From a reference to Oisín entering Tír na nÓg through a cave, one might conclude that some high-status individuals failed to return to the surface.

With the introduction of Christianity, one might expect an attempt to outlaw cave rituals. From the increased evidence for habitation at this time, it seems that Irish monks made a determined show of their power over cave sites: inhabiting caves would have disrupted the rituals of pagans who stubbornly continued ancient tradition. However, it also seems likely that some ancient practices were adopted and modified. The practice of visiting the exterior of caves at Lughnasa continued until recent centuries. In addition, at Lough Derg, the terrors experienced by those in a shamanic ritual in a cave became transformed into visions of Purgatory, and ultimately diluted to a ritual of penance on an island without a cave.

Since medieval times, there seems to have been increasingly less engagement with caves. Rituals were carried out only at the entrances to caves. In a land of fairies and leprechauns, caves became forbidden, liminal spaces, entrances to a realm of the dead, openings to a parallel underworld governed by the terrors of the human imagination. Much more than simply holes in the ground, Irish caves were the portals to Purgatory; the doorways to the dark psyche of the imagination; the cave, the grave, of terror; the *uamh*, the *uagh*, of *uath*.

ACKNOWLEDGMENTS

Thanks to Holley Moyes for her encouragement and patience, and to Marion Dowd for very useful advice. Thanks also to the Queens University Belfast Caving Club for helping me overcome my ancestral fears, and for introducing me to an amazing underground world.

REFERENCES CITED

Cambrensis, Giraldus. 1795 [1200]. *Topographia Hiberniae*. Dublin: A. Stewart.

Chart, D. A., E. Estyn Evans, and H. C. Lawlor. 1940. *A Preliminary Survey of the National Monuments of Northern Ireland*. Belfast: H. M. Stationery Office.

Coleman, Jack C. 1942. "Cave Excavation at Midleton, Co. Cork." *Journal of the Cork Historical and Archaeological Society* 47: 63–76.

Coleman, Jack C. 1965. *The Caves of Ireland*. Tralee: Anvil Books.

Connolly, Michael, and Frank Coyne, with Linda G. Lynch. 2005. *Underworld: Death and Burial in Cloghermore Cave, Co. Kerry*. Bray: Wordwell.

Croker, Thomas Crofton. 1824. *Researches in the South of Ireland*. London: John Murray.

Curran, Bob. 2000. *Complete Guide to Celtic Mythology*. Belfast: Appletree.

Davies, F. R. 1853. Legends of the County Clare. *Notes and Queries* 8 (210): 436 (5 November).

Davies, F. R. 1854. Legends of the Co. Clare. *Notes and Queries* 9 (222): 73 (28 January); reprinted in *British Caver* 13 (1945): 20.

Doughty, P. S. 1995. "The Vertebrate Fauna of Pollnagollum of the Boats." *Irish Speleology* 15: 54–60.

Dowd, Marion A. 2002. "Kilgreany, Co. Waterford: Biography of a Cave." *Journal of Irish Archaeology* 11: 77–97.

Dowd, Marion A. 2004. "Caves: Sacred Places in the Irish Landscape." PhD thesis, Department of Archaeology, University College Cork, Ireland.

Dowd, Marion A. 2005. "Caves." In *Archaeological Inventory of County Sligo*, Vol. 1: *South Sligo*, ed. Ursula Egan, Elizabeth Byrne, Mary Sleeman, et al., 85–86. Dublin: Government of Ireland.

Dowd, Marion A. 2007a. "Living and Dying in Glencurran Cave." *Archaeology Ireland* 21 (1): 36–9.

Dowd, Marion A. 2007b. "Recent Archaeological Discoveries in Dunmore Cave, County Kilkenny: Further Questions Regarding Viking Activity at the Site." *Old Kilkenny Review, Journal of the Kilkenny Archaeological Society* 59: 7–17.

Dowd, Marion A. 2008. "The Use of Caves for Funerary and Ritual Practices in Neolithic Ireland." *Antiquity* 82 (316): 305–17.

Dowd, Marion A. 2009. "Middle and Late Bronze Age Ritual Activity at Glencurran Cave, Co. Clare." In *From Bann Flakes to Bushmills: Papers in Honour of Peter Woodman*, ed. Nyree Finlay, Sinead McCann, Nicky Milner, and Caroline Wickham-Jones, 89–100. London: Oxbow Books.

Dowd, Marion A., Linda Fibiger, and Linda G. Lynch. 2006. "The Human Remains from Irish Caves Project." *Archaeology Ireland* 20 (3): 16–9.

Drew, David. 2004. *A Cave Database for the Republic of Ireland*. http://www.ubss.org.uk/irishcaves/irishcaves.php, accessed June 15, 2012.

Drew, David, and David Huddart. 1980. *Dunmore Cave: A Short Guide*. Dublin: National Parks and Monuments Service, Office of Public Works.

Drew, David, and David Huddart. 2006. "A Database of Caves in Ireland." *Irish Geography* 39 (2): 159–68. http://dx.doi.org/10.1080/00750770609555874.

Drew, David Philip, Gareth Llwyd Jones, and P. M. O'Reilly. 1977. *Caves and Karst of Ireland: Guidebook for the Speleological Congress 1977*. Sheffield: 7th I.S.C. Committee.

Gregory, Lady Augusta. 1970 [1905]. *Gods and Fighting Men: The Story of the Tuatha De Danaan and of the Fianna of Ireland, Arranged and Put into English by Lady Gregory, with a Preface by W. B. Yeats*. 2nd ed. Gerrards Cross: Colin Smythe.

Grogan, Eoin. 2004. "Middle Bronze Age Burial Traditions in Ireland." In *From Megaliths to Metals: Essays in Honour of George Eogan*, ed. Helen Roche, Eoin Grogan, John Bradley, John Coles, and Barry Raftery, 61–71. Oxford: Oxbow Books.

Harbison, Peter. 2002. *Our Treasure of Antiquities: Beranger and Bigari's Antiquarian Sketching Tour of Connacht in 1779*. Bray: Wordwell.

Jackson, J. Wilfrid. 1928. "Report on the Animal Remains Found in the Kilgreany Cave, Co. Waterford." *Proceedings of the University of Bristol Spelaeological Society*, 137–153.

Jones, Bryan H. 1908. "Irish Folklore from Cavan, Meath, Kerry and Limerick." *Folklore* 19 (3): 315–23. http://dx.doi.org/10.1080/0015587X.1908.9719836.

Jones, Gareth Llwyd. 1974. *The Caves of Fermanagh and Cavan*. Enniskillen: Watergate Press.

Jones, Gareth Llwyd, Gaby Burns, Tim Fogg, and John G. Kelly. 1997. *The Caves of Fermanagh and Cavan*. Florencecourt: The Lough Nilly Press.

Koch, John T., ed., in collaboration with John Carey. 2000. *The Celtic Heroic Age: Literary Sources for Ancient Celtic Europe and Early Ireland and Wales*. Oakville, CT, and Aberystwyth: Celtic Studies Publications.

Lane, Raymond M. 2007. "To Hell and Back: In Search of the Irish Underworld." *Washington Post*, March 11.

Leslie, Shane. 1932. *Saint Patrick's Purgatory: A Record from History and Literature*. London: Burns Oates & Washbourne Ltd.

Lynch, Linda G. 2005. "Appendix 2: Human Skeletal Remains." In *Underworld: Death and Burial in Cloghermore Cave, Co. Kerry*, ed. Michael Connolly and Frank Coyne, with Linda G. Lynch, 231–288. Bray: Wordwell.

Macalister, Robert Alexander Stewart, ed. 1940. *Lebor Gabála Érenn: The Book of the Taking of Ireland*, Part III. Dublin: Irish Texts Society.

Macalister, Robert Alexander Stewart, ed. 1941. *Lebor Gabála Érenn: The Book of the Taking of Ireland*, Part IV. Dublin: Irish Texts Society.

Mac Airt, Seán, and Gearóid Mac Niocaill, eds. 1983. *The Annals of Ulster*. Dublin: Dublin Institute for Advanced Studies.

MacNeill, Maire. 1962. *The Festival of Lughnasa*. London: Oxford University Press.

MacNeill, Maire. 1989. "The Musician in the Cave." *Béaloideas* 57: 109–32. http://dx.doi.org/10.2307/20522334.

McCafferty, Patrick, and Mike Baillie. 2005. *The Celtic Gods: Comets in Irish Mythology*. Stroud: Tempus.

McCone, Kim. 1990. *Pagan Past and Christian Present in Early Irish Literature*. Maynooth: An Sagart.

Melia, Daniel F. 1967. "The Lughnasa Musician in Ireland and Scotland." *Journal of American Folklore* 80 (318): 365–73. http://dx.doi.org/10.2307/537415.

Meyer, Kuno. 1890. "Uath Beinne Etair." *Revue Celtique* 11: 125–34.

Meyer, Kuno. 1905. "Die Wiederauffindung der Táin Bó Cúalnge (Royal Irish Academy MS D 4 2, fo 49b 2)." *Archiv für Celtische Lexikographie* 3(1). Max Niemeyer, Halle an der Saale.

Movius, Hallam Leonard. 1935. "Kilgreany Cave, Co. Waterford." *Journal of the Royal Society of Antiquaries of Ireland* 65: 254–96.

Mullan, Graham, ed. 2003. *Caves of County Clare and South Galway*. Bristol: University of Bristol Spelaeological Society.

Mullan, Graham, and Tony Boycott. 2004. "Cave Notes, Co. Clare, Ireland." *Proceedings of the University of Bristol Spelaeological Society* 23 (2): 143–8.

Ní Shéaghdha, Nessa. 1941. "Bruighion Chéise Coruin." In *Trí Bruidhne*, ed. Nessa Ní Shéaghdha and Máire Ó Mhuirgheasa, 3–15. Dublin: Stationery Office.

Ní Shéaghdha, Nessa. 1967. "Uath Beinne Etair." In *Tóruigheacht Dhiarmada agus Ghráinne: The Pursuit of Diarmaid and Gráinne*, ed. Nessa Ní Shéaghdha, 130–37. Irish Texts Society, Vol. 48. Dublin: Irish Texts Society.

O'Curry, Eugene. 1861. *Lectures on the Manuscript Materials of Ancient Irish History*. Dublin: James Duffy.

O'Donovan, John, ed. and trans. 1848–1851. *Annala Rioghachta Eireann: Annals of the Kingdom of Ireland, from the Earliest Times to the Year 1616, by the Four Masters*. Dublin: Hodges and Smith.

O'Donovan, John, and Eugene Curry. 1997. [1928] *The Antiquities of County Clare: Letters Containing Information Relative to the Antiquities of County Clare Collected during the Progress of the Ordnance Survey in 1839*. Ed. Maureen Comber. Ennis: Clasp Press.

Oldham, Tony. 1981. *The Caves of Co. Cork*. Dyfed: Crymych.

Plummer, Charles, ed. and trans. 1922. *Bethada Náem nÉrenn: Lives of Irish Saints*. Vol. 2. Oxford: Oxford University Press.

Plunkett, Thomas. 1870–1879. "On the Exploration of the Knockninny Cave." *Proceedings of the Royal Irish Academy* 12: 329, 465–83.

Richardson, John. 1727. *The Great Folly, Superstition, and Idolatry of Pilgrimages in Ireland; Especially of that to Patrick's Purgatory*. Dublin: J. Hyde.

Scharff, R. F., Richard John Ussher, Grenville A.J. Cole, E. T Newton, A. Francis Dixon, and Thomas Johnson Westropp. 1906. "The Exploration of the Caves of County Clare." *Transactions of the Royal Irish Academy* 33B: 1–76.

Shaw, Trevor R., and Edgar Kingsley Tratman. 1969. "Mainly Historical." In *The Caves of North-West Clare, Ireland*, ed. Edgar Kingsley Tratman, 15–32. Newton Abbot: David & Charles.

Thorn, Richard, David Drew, and Catherine Coxon. 1990. "The Hydrology and Caves of the Geevagh and Bricklieve Karsts, Co. Sligo." *Irish Geography* 23 (2): 120–35. http://dx.doi.org/10.1080/00750779009478757.

Toner, Gregory. 2000. "Reconstructing the Earliest Irish Tale Lists." *Éigse* 32: 88–120.

Tratman, Edgar Kingsley. 1929. "Report on Excavations in Ireland." *Proceedings of the University of Bristol Spelaeological Society* 3: 109–52.

Ussher, Richard John. 1905. "On the Discovery of Hyena, Mammoth, and Other Extinct Mammals in a Carboniferous Cavern in Co. Cork." *Proceedings of the Royal Irish Academy* 25B: 1–5.

Waddell, John. 1983. "Rathcroghan: A Royal Site in Connacht." *Journal of Irish Archaeology* (1): 21–46.

Westropp, Thomas Johnson. 1910. "A Folklore Survey of County Clare." *Folklore* 21 (2): 180–99; (3): 338–49; (4) 476–87.

Wilde, Lady Francesca Speranza. 1887. *Ancient Legends, Mystic Charms, and Superstitions of Ireland*. London: Ward & Downey.

Woodman, Peter. 1997. "Limerick 1996: 242, Killuragh Cave." In *Excavations 1996: Summary Accounts of Archaeological Excavations in Ireland*, ed. Isabel Bennett, 67. Bray: Wordwell.

Woodman, Peter C., Margaret McCarthy, and Nigel Monaghan. 1997. "The Irish Quaternary Fauna Project." *Quaternary Science Reviews* 16 (2): 129–59. http://dx.doi.org/10.1016/S0277-3791(96)00037-6.

Yeats, William Butler. 2003 [1888]. *Fairy and Folk Tales of the Irish Peasantry, with Foreword by Paul Muldoon, as Irish Fairy and Folk Tales*. New York: Modern Library.

22

Caves in Black and White
The Case of Zimbabwe

Terence Ranger

Zimbabwe's granite plateau is a country of rockshelters, shallow caves, and overhangs. Most of them are millions of years old and existed long before there were any people, but many of these sites have a social history. Stone Age peoples lived, danced, and painted in them. Iron Age farmers buried their chiefs in them, took refuge in them in time of war, and venerated some of them as oracular rain shrines. Rhodesian whites were fascinated by them, feared them as sites of superstition and resistance, and disciplined them both by dynamite and science. In the late 1960s and 1970s, black and white ideas and uses of these sites came together during the guerrilla war. Since 1980 the "cave" has become for Zimbabweans a more important symbol of secret power and authenticity than ever before. I want to trace this social history here with particular reference to the Matopos hills of southwestern Zimbabwe, which contain a greater number of caves and rockshelters than anywhere else in the country.

UTILIZATION OF THE CAVES

Gilbert Pwiti's edited collection reflecting "Zimbabwean archaeology today" is entitled *Caves, Monuments and Texts* (Pwiti 1997). This reflects a sequence of research as well as a list of topics. Scientific Zimbabwean archaeology began in caves, and especially in the caves of the Matopos. Walker and Thorp's chapter in the book summarizes its results. Modern humans, they say, developed in the Middle Stone Age (MSA) and "southern Africa was at the forefront of this change." Excavations at Bambata cave in the Matopos unlaid MSA material dating back 40,000 years (Walker and Thorp 1997, 15). Late Stone Age (LSA) materials date back at least 20,000 years. At some during this period it seems that rock art began in "the painted caves" (Garlake 1987). "For the first time there is evidence for systematic ritual . . . People now adapted more closely to their environments[, . . .] fruits were important as a food source and in hilly terrain, such as the Matopos, people adopted strategies to exploit the smaller, more abundant animals, unlike more open settings where big game were more significant in the diet" (Walker and Thorp 1997, 19). They provide "a tentative chronology" for the LSA that "refers to the Matopos only" and is derived from excavations of rockshelters.

Indeed Walker's (1995) definitive study of the Matopos investigated 113 shallow caves and rockshelters dating from the Early Stone Age (ESA) to the Early Iron Age. Walker writes that "the large number of natural shelters is a feature of the Matopos. Many have formed under big boulders, but some have been sculpted out of the sides of hills" by a process of erosion. "Some sites have been growing at rates less than a meter every million years." Walker creates a morphological typology in which he refers to the largest shelters measuring between 20 and 75 square meters as "caves" (p. 55). However, none of these sites supports a dark zone; they are actually large rockshelters.

After careful descriptions of climate, fauna, and flora, Walker turns to the utilization of rockshelters. There are few places in the extensive granite range farther than 500 meters from a rockshelter. "The consequence was that the Later Stone Age people were able to incorporate these locations into their settlement patterns," though there were so many shelters that hunter-gatherers used less than a third of the number available. Larger shelters were used as "central places" surrounded by "smaller, satellite sites." Seven percent of the sites can be classified as shallow caves—"at least 75m² in area, which is about the minimal area needed for the hypothetical band of 25, plus some communal space." All LSA occupational sites show evidence of paintings, which are not limited to the caves but are more numerous there than at the shelters, and better preserved.

Walker's section on "the excavated sequences" in the Matopos moves from Nswatugi (one of the largest caves, deep and narrow, measuring 10 meters by 25 meters; p. 69); to the Cave of the Bees; to Pomongwe ("a fine, aspidal dome"; p. 127); to Bambata ("a large, perfectly shaped, hemispherical hollow"; p. 152). At Bambata, "the evidence from the upper levels suggests the kind of contact between foragers and farmers some 2,000 years ago that preceded the adoption of herding by some forager communities." Walker speculates that it was in the Matopos that this adoption took place before it spread southwards to the Cape (p. 168).

Walker summarizes the findings from these sites. By 9100 BP people were living all year round in the Matopos. After 4500 BP groups began to aggregate in larger bands, living in the larger sites. Around 2000 BP, livestock, pottery, and metal were introduced. It is likely that "agropastoralists entered the Matopos in the first few centuries AD. Clashes between the two economic systems followed. Some hunters were probably dispersed into the lowveld [and] others acquired stock and the art of pot making and moved further south." But Iron Age farmers took young San women, leading to the collapse of San society and the emergence of a genetically mixed population in the Matopos (pp. 241–255). This new population did not live in rockshelters.

AFRICAN PERCEPTIONS OF THE CAVES

San hunter-gatherers had lived in the shelters for many thousands of years and must have been intimately familiar with them. They covered the walls with paintings that have variously, and often fancifully, been interpreted as clues to their cosmology (Garlake 1997). But the people who used shelters did not represent them, or any other landscape feature, on their walls. We have no way of telling how they "saw" those spaces or what they "thought" of them. Farther south, scholars have laid emphasis on San rainmaking and its association with particular shelters. They stress the significance of snakes among the paintings—"snakes, particularly pythons, are associated with rain and are believed to be 'cool.' Rain medicines are sometimes stored in shelters as they are considered cool places. Cool snakes are thus linked with cool places that include caves... [A]rtists painted these snakes emerging from the walls of rock shelters" (Dowson 1998, 79–80). Such scholars speculate that San rainmakers and snake symbols became especially important when contact with rain-thirsty farmers began (Dowson 1998; Jolly 1998, 85, 263).

Among the Matopos shelter paintings, Walker lists five animal-headed snakes, or 1 percent of the subjects depicted (Walker 1996, 89). Garlake writes of "five large snakes with animal heads and thin tail ends" on the walls of the great Silozwane cave on the southern escarpment of the Matopos, and of "an enormous snake" with an animal head and open jaws in the small, domed cave of Gulubahwe (Garlake 1987, 89). But while Walker admits that "the animal-headed snakes might be linked with rain-making," he insists that "there is as yet no evidence... that people came from more arid places to make or request rain." If Matopos San society was, as it seems, focused intensely on the locality, then "it could be argued that the Matopos is not an area where rain-making would have been important" because of its perennial springs and abundant water (Walker 1996, 70, 71). As Walker knows, however, the Matopos—and especially its caves and shelters—became a renowned rainmaking site in Iron Age times (Walker 1996, 70). Nothing is known about the antiquity of the Matopos raincult, which later came to be focused on a number of oracular caves in the hills (Daneel 1970, 1998; Nthoi 2006; Nyathi 2003; Ranger 1999, 2007). Certainly nothing is known about whether it began with interactions between farmers and hunter-gatherers. By contrast with all the Stone Age archaeology in the Matopos, there has been little work and no excavation devoted to an Early Iron Age sites. No San or Early Iron Age myths or traditions have been collected in the Matopos. All we can say with certainty is that Iron Age people, who did not live in the caves, nonetheless developed a rich mythology about them.

This mythology has been most fully set out by the mission doctor, Herbert Aschwanden. In his *Karanga Mythology* (1990), Aschwanden describes the cosmology of the Karanga-speaking people, who live far to the east of the Matopos. Nevertheless the mountains and their caves are central to Karanga metaphysics. Aschwanden recounts myths in which the creation of the world takes place among the rocks, with the hills descending like rain clouds and then being split by the lightning arrows of Mwali into rocks and rivers and caves (pp. 12–16). He comments that "real rocks are meant here; the Karanga refer to the Matopo Hills where there are caves in which one hears the voice of God" (p. 13). In the caves are pools that contain snakes "sent by God to bring rain and fertility to the world."

In Aschwanden's interpretation, the caves and pools are highly sexualized. "The pregnant woman, carrying in her womb the new life and the amniotic fluid, is by the old Karanga associated with the . . . water in the cave" (Aschwanden 1990, 15). But there are male symbols too. "The rock in the sacred mountain becomes the man's scrotum because it contains the 'power' of begetting. From this sacred rock the snake (as source of fertility) originates" (p. 37). In the cave pools also live *njuzu*, water spirits. These njuzu, "sent from the Matopos to guard the water" (p. 137), now live in rivers, pools, subterranean caves, and swamps. They "live especially in waters where there is a cave . . . [C]aves containing water and pools on mountain tops are well known habitats of water-sprites."

At the Matopos "the cave with the pool from which God's voice can be heard is compared with a jar filled with water. As God's voice is heard from inside the cave he is called *mu-hari*, 'he who is in the jar'" (Aschwanden 1990, 206). Karanga elders believe that, angry with people's disobedience, Mwali withdrew from the world, taking the rain with him. But he took pity on his creation and "returned and from then on his voice was heard in the caves of the Matopo-mountains. He returns in nature's re-awakened fertility when he sews together the sky and the earth by the rain-clouds. God also appears in the woman's body where (in the amniotic fluid) the renewal of man takes place" (p. 217). So, the Karanga send messengers to the Matopos caves to ask for a good harvest, and their seed is "sprinkled with water from the cave." Barren women go to the caves and are rewarded with children (p. 219). Messengers ask for rain and are rewarded. There are Karanga myths about very dark underground caves in which live evil old women, who eat children and wither crops (p. 108). But overwhelmingly the idea of the cave summons up for them the life-giving cave shrines of the Matopos.

Aschwanden's work on the distant Karanga perception of the caves is echoed in Lynette Nyathi's study of their immediate environment in the Matopos. Lynette's family lives near Zhame cave shrine in the eastern hills, a "female" cave from which a possessed old woman speaks as the voice of Mwali. She has not collected any of the myths of origin and other cave stories given to Aschwanden but her thesis describes a highly gendered ritual landscape in which "male" and "female" caves are nodal points in a network of sacred groves and pools. The foundress of the Zhame shrine, Bachikutu, lies buried in its original cave at Shashe. "All social and environmental ills have to be reported" to her and "she has to be provided with drinking water annually but most specifically before the community goes out in preparation for the rain ceremonies" (Nyathi 2003, 52). Otherwise the cave shrines contain no graves or other man-made structures except fragile palisades at their entrances. They represent nature rather than culture and no ritual or symbolic significance is attributed to the paintings on their walls.

The cosmology presented by Aschwanden can be seen in action at the cave shrines today. The late Sitwanyana Ncube, the very dogged and much disputed priest at the senior shrine of Njelele, told me in 1988 that when he was inducted he spent "three months living with a lion, leopard, baboon, snake in Sizabana cave . . . where I was taught the traditions of the shrine. I was talking directly to a snake which is the one which showed me all the caves" (Ranger 1999, 23). In the early 1990s a prophetess, Mbuya Juliana, came from the Matopos cave pools into Karanga territory, aiming to seize back ritual control of the mountaintops from chiefs and Zionist churches. She spoke on behalf of the njuzu spirits of Dzilo cave shrine. She told the Swedish medical anthropologist, Gurli Hansson, in 1993 that she had herself been trained underwater by the njuzu. "The *Njuzu* takes you under water and it stays with you. You live down there just like the crocodiles do. There is everything down there—even bibles" (Ranger 1999, 284–5).

CAVES, POLITICS, AND VIOLENCE

The cave shrines were primarily concerned with rain and natural and human fertility. But one cave, Dula, "stood out as the only shrine associated with males both spiritually and physically" (Nyathi 2003, 57). Dula was associated with the making and ending of war. Inevitably the caves and the Mwali cult clashed with the successive state systems which established themselves near the Matopos. Cult narratives, which have been told for at least a hundred years, emphasize that the rise and downfall of regimes was foretold by the cave shrines and depended on the state's respect for Mwali (Ranger 1999). There are many stories of how the pre-Ndebele Rozwi kings tried to suppress the god's voice, blocking caves, blowing up rocks, and cutting down sacred trees. This led to their downfall at the hands of the invading Ndebele in the 1830s. The Ndebele kings settled near the Matopos, and Mzilikazi chose to be buried in a cave in the mountains, thereby asserting his spiritual control over them. But the caves continued to operate as rainmakers and witch-finders. (It was believed that Mwali detested the very smell of a witch and that anyone guilty of witchcraft would be blasted and die before they reached the caves. Under the Ndebele kings men and women accused of being witches could appeal away from the judgment of the diviner and make the trip into the Matopos to face the ordeal of the caves. If they reached the caves alive they were cleared of the charge of witchcraft.)

The fall of the Ndebele state in 1893 was also foretold by the shrines. But the first years of white rule were oppressive and were accompanied by drought, locusts, and disease. In 1896 first the Ndebele and then the Shona speakers to the east (including the Karanga) rose up against the whites. Dula, the cave shrine for war, was by now controlled by a leading Ndebele general, and whites believed that the whole revolt had been coordinated by the cave priests (Cobbing 1977; Nthoi 2006; Ranger 1967).

WHITE PERCEPTIONS OF CAVES: PENETRATION AND WAR

Even before the 1896 uprisings, white imaginations were possessed by caves. Maria Teresa Pinto Coehlo has reminded us that British "novels of empire," as they imagined the Zimbabwean interior, invoked the symbol of the cave. In both H. Rider Haggard's *King Solomon's Mines* and John Buchan's *Prester John* "the main characters discover a secret cave in the mountains where a treasure is hidden, and both caves have a secret entrance." Africans have forgotten the way in, the effete Portuguese have never discovered it, but these imperial heroes break in. "Once inside the cave," however, "the heroes get trapped because they can't open the secret door and have to find another and complicated way out, which they do due to their intelligence, endurance and physical capacities" (Coehlo 2000, 365).

The cave was a good metaphor for colonial penetration and extraction. But once inside Zimbabwe, the first missionaries, soldiers, and administrators found that caves were not so easy to claim for empire. No caves stuffed with secret treasures were found. Instead Africans seem to have laid imaginative claim to them. Missionaries thought of African divinities as diabolical manifestations of the underworld; caves and underground pools were an appropriate site for their worship. Thus in 1880 the Jesuits described an oracular shrine in the Matopos:

> This God lives in a subterranean cave in a labyrinth of rocks … In this cave is a deep, black well, the well of the abyss. From time to time dull sounds like thunder come forth from this well. The faithful, trembling with fear, place offerings on the edge of the abyss—wheat, corn, poultry, cakes and other gifts—to appease the hunger of the terrible God and to make him propitious … They seek information about hidden things … After a few moments of deep silence, they hear, in the midst of the subterranean noises, inarticulate sounds, strange words, broken and incomprehensible, which the accomplices of the makers of thunder explain to the credulous devotees. (Roberts 1979, 264–5)

To redeem this diabolic landscape the Jesuits themselves offered their first Mass in a cave in the Matopos. "There, with an altar of rock and the 700 foot pyramid as canopy, we offered to God the sacred sacrifice of Calvary. At that solemn moment it seemed that the mountain itself, together with the Holy Angels surrounding us, was trembling with joy and adoring the Eucharistic God" (Ranger 1999, 15).

There were sacred caves that challenged the whites in other parts of Zimbabwe. In the Mazoe Valley Charwe, the female medium of the great Nehanda spirit—believed by the whites to be the instigator of the "Shona" uprising in June 1896—owned a cave in which were stored ritual objects as well as, in 1896 and 1897, the property of whites killed in the uprisings. Nehanda's cave was dealt with not through a Mass but with dynamite. In September 1896 Horace McMahon reported on the process of "clearing the Granite Range in the Mazoe Valley"—"on our way up [the hills] we burnt several kraals and mined some important caves, [among which was] the cave of the famous witch doctoress, Nyanda, who was reported to be the cause of most of the discontent prevailing in the district." Nhenda was gone but McMahon recovered white property and was "determined to destroy [that cave] completely in order to show the natives that the white man had little respect for Nyanda's power" (Charumbira 2008, 7–8). Charumbira remarks that "the blasting of Nehanda-Charwe's cave was a concerted effort to desecrate African sacred places and spaces."

In 1896 the white army was not in sufficient command of the Matopos to make it possible to contemplate dynamiting the Mwali caves. But after the uprising was over, in January 1906, Native Commissioner Archie Campbell, asserting that "the whole country has been in secret communication" with the Mwali shrines, urged that "the caves from which these voices come be demolished by dynamite, the priests be imprisoned and their kraals and people scattered" (Ranger 1999, 45). This did not happen. By this time, perhaps, whites had come to realize—as the Rozwi kings had done—that you could not blow up a sacred cave. It was the spirit that made the cave sacred and the spirit could—and did—move from cave to cave. Today Nehanda mediums have a new ritual cave in Mazoe, and in the Matopos the voice of Mwali still speaks, even if from different caves. But however ineffective dynamite was in exploding religion, it was all too terribly effective in blowing up people. In 1896 Ndebele fighting men took refuge in caves in the Matopos. They lit their camp fires in caves so as to hide them from enemy scouts (Nobbs 1924, 43); they retreated into and fired from them when attacked. Experienced white imperialists described the Matopos as worse country to fight in than Afghanistan or Chitral in

Pakistan. Cecil Rhodes realized that the Ndebele would have to be negotiated with and initiated the famous *indabas* (meetings) that brought the Ndebele rising to an end. But the decentralized Shona rebels in central and eastern Zimbabwe were dealt with differently and here dynamite came into its own. A cartoon in the settler broadsheet, *The Nugget*, on July 12, 1897, showed a Janus-faced Rhodes showering beer and blankets on the Ndebele and casks of dynamite into Shona caves (Ranger 1967, 340).

The dynamite had terrible effects on the Shona fighters and their women and children who had taken refuge in the caves. The first effective use of dynamite was against Chief Manyepera in the Marendellas district. Manyepera and his people took refuge in the caves. There was room at the entry for only one man at a time. The whites could not rush them. But they noticed that "along the flat rock which formed the whole roof of the cave there was a narrow crack." First some seven-pound shells were dropped through, then a wagonload of dynamite arrived. After a guard was "skinned from top to toe," one case of the dynamite was lowered down against the entrance and touched off. About sixty women and children then came out, but the fighting men remained in the cave. In his reminiscences, Native Commissioner "Wiri" Edwards described what happened next:

> Next day several cases of dynamite were laid along the fissure on top of the caves and fuses timed so that they all went off at once. The fuse was fired and we retired to a safe distance. The explosion rent the cave from end to end. It was the end so far as the rebels in the cave were concerned. Two natives only escaped. (Ranger 1967, 76–77)

Thereafter dynamite was used systematically in attack after attack and against chief's cave after chief's cave, most famously to blast Chief Makoni and his people out of the great caves of Gwindingwi (Ranger 1967, 1985).

WHITE PERCEPTIONS OF CAVES: PEACE

It took some time for white Rhodesians to stop being alarmed by caves. But gradually, as Africans were disarmed and the white administration established itself, whites came to domesticate caves and even to love them. Cecil Rhodes himself gave the supreme example of how the symbols of rocks and caves could be captured by whites from Africans. During 1896 Rhodes had visited the cave grave of the first Ndebele king, Mzilikazi, in the eastern Matopos. It was because he was so impressed with the grandeur of this royal sepulchre that Rhodes determined that he would himself be buried in the Matopos, among the rocks and above a cave in which pre-Ndebele kings had been buried. After his death in 1902 Rhodes was installed as tutelary deity of the Matopos.

Other whites could not aspire to such grandeur. But they did come to make claims on the caves, first as sites of science and then as landscape. As we have seen, Rhodesian prehistory—which for a long time was the country's main claim to scientific originality—was mainly established through excavations in the Matopos caves (Walker 1995). The paintings on the cave walls became increasingly studied and displayed as a tourist attraction. The Matopos became a special landscape for Rhodesians, the site of walks, climbs, photographs, and paintings (Ranger 1999). Some whites became famous, even among Africans, for their love of the hills and caves. Native Commissioner H. N. Hemans (Hemans 1935) was nicknamed *Mathandidwala,* "he who likes bare granite hills." His son, Trevor, also a Native Commissioner, wrote in his memoirs that

> I inherited not only my father's [nick]name but also his love of hills and the lonely places . . . I was the first to record at least three beautiful caves with unique paintings . . . I also visited the known caves whenever I had the opportunity . . . Other caves were formed at the base of hills where giant boulders had settled leaving gaps between them extending so far in some cases that all natural light was excluded and one had to explore by torch light, with a string attached to one's belt to ensure safe return. (Hemans 1987, 20–1)

The Mwali oracular caves, particularly Njelele, exercised a particular fascination for whites, leading to many attempts to reach the shrine. One such was described in the Bulawayo *Chronicle* in February 1930. A group of whites requisitioned an African guide, "but being aware of the native superstitions we were careful not to mention the cave." Nevertheless the guide took them way off course and then abandoned them. They climbed the "steep, smooth rock," came upon "a perfect little wood," and then found "a pole fence." They moved some of the poles aside and went in. "In front of us were two large rocks, with a smaller one almost filling the opening between them. Near the rocks were three or four large earthenware pots. We climbed the small rock and crawled through a short dark tunnel and came into the real cave . . . just a small gloomy space between two big rocks leaning against each other." There were hoes and beer pots. This particular party did not take away any of the pots. But intrusions like this, and the belief that some whites had stolen ritual objects from the cave, were blamed by Africans for the eventual silence of Mwali's voice at Njelele (*Chronicle*, February 13, 1930). For their part, Rhodesian whites came to believe that the mountains and caves of the granite plateau were their own particular landscape, defining them as a people (Uusihakala 2008).

WHITES, BLACKS, AND THE CONTESTED CAVES

Things changed with the rise of African nationalism and especially with the guerrilla war of the late 1960s and 1970s. Africans began to use caves again in all sorts of ways. African leaders sought the advice and backing of the Matopos oracular shrines (Ranger 1999). Guerrillas hid in the Matopos caves. Incoming guerrillas were shown by elders and spirit mediums the cave hideouts that had been used in past wars. Scattered about the plateau, these caves were too numerous to make the dynamiting strategy again possible for Rhodesian whites, though some were bombed.

Guerrilla use of caves has been recorded by many researchers. Oliver Zvaba has described an oracular cave at Nyachiranga on the mountain frontier between northeastern Zimbabwe and Mozambique. From the cave is heard the voice of Dzivaguru, eastern Zimbabwe's High God. Zvaba writes:

> The structures inside the cave are very symbolic and have a bearing on agricultural fertility. In the cave is a stream which has its source in the cave, which flows into a ninga, or bottomless pit; a Baobab tree; a dome-shaped pillar; mifura trees with bee-hives; two expansive rock dwalas, one close to the entrance and the other at the far back of the cave. In the cave, scenery is attractive, full of life, biological as well as well social. (Zvaba 1985)

During the 1970s this "paradisial" place was put at the disposal of the guerrillas. They were allowed to camp in the cave. The High God's voice warned them of any impending Rhodesian attack, and the stream flooded to bar the way for the enemy (Zvaba 1988).

In Makoni district, where Chief Chingaira had been dynamited out of Gwindingwi cave in 1896, a guerrilla intelligence officer told me in 1981 that

> In 1978 I found that the guerrilla platoons had fall-back hide-outs. In Makoni detachment area there was Mugumabwemairi hill… The hill was honey-combed with caves and at one point a small crevice in the rock led into a large chamber where many could hide in safety. Our ancestors took refuge there in 1896… Then there was Matotwe mountain, the burial place of chief Makoni. Special ceremonies were carried out there by two mediums, an old man and an old woman, who had inherited their role. They allocated caves in the mountain to the comrades where they could not disturb the spirits… The enemy attacked where we had been and we were not there any more… We had been warned by the mediums at Matotwe. (Ranger 1985, 211)

By the 1970s Zimbabwean caves had become for whites a symbol of backwardness and savagery, and a source of danger. The division of the rural landscape emerges very clearly in the reminscences of the great Zimbabwean novelist and poet, Chenjerai Hove. In the 1970s Hove was teaching at Pamushana Secondary School. He recalls that

> The school is located on the side of a massive hill. There is a highway on the northern side and the caves and other hills are on the southern side. The highway side was as far as the Rhodesian soldiers could go… Beyond the mountain it was a no-go area… This is where we spent most of our week-ends, singing and dancing to those chimurenga songs. As we sat right there on the mountain top, huge boulders staring at us like hungry baboons… [T]he young [school] girls came back from behind the boulders and the caves, giggling on the arms of one or other commander. (Hove 2006)

Hove describes a Rhodesian helicopter attack on the caves, with the planes coming back over the school to drop on it the bodies of dead girls, shouting from the air that they were "whores of the terrorists" (Hove 2006).

CAVES AFTER INDEPENDENCE

In 1979 the deadly stalemate of the guerrilla war led to a political agreement that paved the way for Zimbabwean independence. The caves of the guerrillas had outlasted the helicopters of the Rhodesians. Caves have been more prominent in the Zimbabwean imagination than ever. Joshua Nkomo, leader of the Zimbabwe African People's Union (ZAPU), held his first election rally in 1980 at the foot of Njelele hill. The Matopos cave shrines have been declared part of a "national cultural landscape" (Ranger 1999, 2007); pilgrims come to them from all over southern Africa (Daneel 1998; Nthoi 2006); and delegations travel to them to consult not only on rain and on politics—as Joshua Nkomo and his allies did urgently during the Matabeleland repression of the 1980s—(Ranger 1999) but also on environmentalism and theology.

In 1990, for instance, a delegation of chiefs, war veterans, and spirit mediums went from Karanga country to the Mwali cave-shrine at Dzilo in the eastern Matopos. They went to seek Mwali's blessing on their tree-planting campaign. Martinus Daneel, the missiologist-anthropologist who accompanied them and has described their pilgrimage, emphasizes that the delegation's composition was "a clear departure from the old-age tradition" that only special messengers went from chiefdoms to the caves. "It was quite moving, during the 1990 visit, to observe the expectancy of chiefs as they arrived for the first time at the cult center… Their attitudes reflected awe, respect and mystification, as if they were about to probe the mystery of their origins, the very heart of Africa. From the secret depths of the shrine cave, the rocks of Mwari, they were to hear for the first time the voice of Africa's creator God." Daneel quotes a press report from the *Masvingo Provincial Star* for January 19, 1990, that described how "after a few speeches a hoarse voice answered from the cave. Everyone's backs were to the cave. It was a hair-raising experience." Daneel (1998, 106, 108, 170–78) himself describes the cave session in equally dramatic terms but adds a touch of white science when he transcribes his tape-recorded interviews with the god's voice!

By the 1990s the voice had long ceased to speak at Njelele. Control of the shrine was disputed between rival priests (Nthoi 2006) and local people were skeptical and disillusioned. But the national reputation of the Matopos shrines had boomed. When the cave at Njelele was fired—its wooden palisades burnt and the inside of the cave blistered with the heat—the *Herald* newspaper in Harare declared it an act of sacrilege against the nation. And this mystic importance of caves had come to affect even the way people thought of the Great Zimbabwe monument itself, after which the new nation was named. Great Zimbabwe has massive and impressive walls both on the hill and in the valley. The German geologist, Carl Mauch, who was the first white to record what he saw at Great Zimbabwe in 1871, stressed the "great walls built apparently in European style." He also mentioned dismissively "an obscure little cave" on the eastern end of the hill (Summers 1963, 10).

But this obscure cave has become central to the sacredness of Great Zimbabwe. In his book on the conservation of Great Zimbabwe, the archaeologist, Webber Ndoro analyzes interviews held with Africans living around the monument. "From the interviews it was clear that the Matopo (Matonjeni and Njelele) are far more sacred to the Shona than Great Zimbabwe. However even at Great Zimbabwe, the Hill Complex, particularly the cave, emerged as the most sacred part of the monument. It is here that the spirit used to speak through the rocks. Some speak of huge caves and underground passages in the Hill Complex" (Fontein 2006; Ndoro 2001, 99).

On May 10, 2003, a male spirit medium appeared at Great Zimbabwe accompanied by chiefs, officials, and war veterans. He proclaimed that he had come to "unlock the mystery [and] to perform a ritual ceremony to open up the underground [where] lie structures in which people lived and lie hidden treasures." He was turned away by the archaeologist custodians for fear he would "tamper with physical structures at the national shrine" (Ranger 2007, 147).

CAVES IN ZIMBABWEAN LITERATURE

Given all this, it is not surprising that Zimbabwe's novelists and poets have written profoundly about caves. Zimbabwe's great female novelist, the late Yvonne Vera, makes use of the cave symbol both in her first novel, *Nehanda* (Vera 1993), and in her last, *The Stone Virgins* (Vera 2002). In these books she brings together the story I have been telling. Vera describes how the Nehanda medium in 1896

> goes into the darkness of the cave and waits. Voices come to her from the earth, entrusting her with messages for her people, urging her. She dreams the futures of her people whom she sees walking in freedom on their ancient ground. Once again the people return. She stays in the darkness of the cave, and speaks to the people from within, out of their sight. Her voice is that of the departed. It comes from the beginning of time. The people stand at the mouth of the cave, calling, asking her to pass to them the voices of the departed. The voices come from within them, from the cave, from below the earth, from the roots of trees. The voice awakens the dead part of themselves . . . [P]urged of their fears, they are prepared to live and to die. (Vera 1993, 81)

Later, hotly pursued by the Rhodesians, she "goes into the cave and banishes her own shadow. In the cave is her second birth" (ibid., 92).

In *The Stone Virgins,* Vera's murderous protagonist, Sibaso, hides out as a guerrilla in the caves of the Matopos during the 1970s, and continues to live in them after independence in 1980, sallying out to murder civilians as a "dissident." These caves, however, do not bring about Sibaso's second birth or liberate him with ancestral voices. Instead they stunt and darken him:

> He finds himself in dark places, unlit sites, dark and grim. A shadow when he walks; a shadow when he sleeps . . . When he stands his head hits against something heavy—he discovers that history has its ceiling . . . He has to crouch and his body soon assumes a defensive attitude; the desire to attack. If he loses an enemy, he invents another. (Vera 2002, 74–75)

Living in the caves of Gulati among the bodies of dead guerrillas, Sibaso is also surrounded by the unfathomable past. On the walls of the cave are San paintings of women. As Sibaso presses his hands on the paintings he feels

> forty thousand years gather in my memory like a wild wind. It is true, everything else in Gulati rots except the rocks. On the rocks history is steady, it cannot be tilted forwards or backwards. It is not a refrain. History fades into the chaos of the hills but it does not vanish. In Gulati I travel four hundred years, then ten thousand years, twenty more. (Vera 2002, 214; see also Ranger 2002)

For Vera caves can be both liberating and repressive; they can evoke a history that can be both a cleansing voice from the beginning of time and 40,000 years of a wild wind. It is an ambiguity well expressed by the Zimbabwean poet, Zimunya:

> The day we shall know the way back
> To the caves of the ancestors
> The lion tongue of death will be licking
> The last gush of blood from our souls.
> (Mutswairo 1991, 107)

REFERENCES CITED

Aschwanden, Herbert. 1990. *Karanga Mythology*. Gweru: Mambo.

Charumbira, Ruramisai. 2008. "Nehanda and Gender Victimhood in the Central Mashonaland Rebellion, 1896–7: Revisiting the Evidence." *History in Africa* 35, 108–31.

Cobbing, Julian. 1977. "The Absent Priesthood: Another Look at the Rhodesian Risings of 1896–7." *Journal of African History* 18, 61–84.

Coehlo, Maria Teresa. 1997. "The Image of the Portuguese in the British Novel of Empire." In *Culture and Colonialism*, ed. Theo D'haen and Patricia Kriis, 357–69.

Daneel, Martinus. 1970. *God of the Matopo Hills: An Essay on Mwari*. The Hague: Mouton.

Daneel, Martinus. 1998. *African Earth Keepers*, Vol. 1: *Interfaith Missions in Earth-Care*. African Initiatives in Christian Mission 2. Prestoria: UNISA.

Dowson, Thomas. 1998. "Rain in Bushman Belief, Politics and History: The Rock-Art Rain-Making in the South-Eastern Mountains, Southern Africa." In *The Archaeology of Rock-Art*, ed. Christopher Chippindale and Paul Taçon, 73–85. Cambridge: Cambridge University Press.

Fontein, Joost. 2006. *The Silence of Great Zimbabwe: Contested Landscapes and the Power of Heritage*. London: University College London.

Garlake, Peter. 1987. *The Painted Caves: An Introduction to the Prehistoric Art of Zimbabwe*. Harare: Modus.

Hemans, H. N. 1935. *The Log of a Native Commissioner*. London: H.F. and G. Witherby.

Hemans, Trevor. Ca. 1987. *Those Were the Days*. Bulawayo, Zimbabwe [?]. http://www.archive.org/details/ThoseWereTheDays_290.

Hove, Chenjerai. 2006. *Small People, Big Wars: A Personal Memoir*. Uppsala: ICORN.

Jolly, Pieter. 1998. "Modelling Change in the Contact Art of the South-eastern San, Southern Africa." In *The Archaeology of Rock-Art*, ed. Christopher Chippindale and Paul Taçon, 247–64. Cambridge: Cambridge University Press.

Mutswairo, Solomon. 1991. "A Zimbabwean Poet Writing in English: A Critical Appreciation of Mwaemura Zimunya's *Thought Tracks*." *Zambezia* 18 (2): 105–118.

Ndoro, Webber. 2001. *Your Monument, Our Shrine: The Preservation of Great Zimbabwe*. Studies in African Archaeology 19. Uppsala: Department of Archaeology and Ancient History, Uppsala University.

Nobbs, Eric. 1924. *Guide to the Matopos*. Cape Town: Maskew Miller.

Nthoi, Leslie. S. 2006. *Contesting Sacred Space: A Pilgrimage Study of the Mwali Cult of Southern Africa*. Trenton: Africa World Press.

Nyathi, Lynette Sibonakaliso. 2003. "The Matobo Hills Shrines: A Comparative Study of the Dula, Njelele and Zhame Shrines and Their Influence on the Surrounding Communities." History Honours dissertation, University of Zimbabwe, Harare.

Pwiti, Gilbert, ed. 1997. *Caves, Monuments and Texts: Zimbabwean Archaeology Today*. Studies in African Archaeology 14. Uppsala: Department of Archaeology and Ancient History, University of Uppsala.

Ranger, Terence. 1967. *Revolt in Southern Rhodesia, 1896–7*. London: Heinemann.

Ranger, Terence. 1985. *Peasant Consciousness and Guerrilla War in Zimbabwe*. London: James Currey.

Ranger, Terence. 1999. *Voices from the Rocks: Nature Culture and History in the Matopos Hills of Zimbabwe*. Oxford: James Currey.

Ranger, Terence. 2002. "History Has Its Ceiling: The Pressures of the Past in *The Stone Virgin*." In *Sign and Taboo: Perspectives on the Poetic Fiction of Yvonne Vera*, ed. Robert Muponde and Mandi Taruvinga, 203–16. Harare: Weaver.

Ranger, Terence. 2007. "Living Ritual and Indigenous Archaeology: The Case of Zimbabwe." In *The Archaeology of Ritual*, ed. Evangelos Kyriakidis, 123–54. Cotsen Advanced Seminars 3. Los Angeles: Cotsen Institute of Archaeology, University of California.

Roberts, Ray. 1979. "Letter of 28 March 1890." In *Journey to Gubulawayo: Letters of Fr. H. Depelchin and C. Croonenberghs, S.J., 1879, 1880, 1881*, ed. Ray Roberts, 264–65. Trans. Moira Lloyd. Bulawayo: Books of Rhodesia.

Summers, Roger. 1963. *Zimbabwe: A Rhodesian Mystery*. London: Nelson.

Uusihakala, Katja. 2008. *Memory Meanders: Place Home and Commemoration in an ex-Rhodesian Diaspora Community*. Research Series in Anthropology. Helsinki: University of Helsinki.

Vera, Yvonne. 1993. *Nehanda*. Harare: Baobab, Weaver.

Vera, Yvonne. 2002. *The Stone Virgin*. Harare: Weaver.

Walker, Nicholas. 1995. *Late Pleistocene and Holocene Hunter-Gatherers of the Matopos: An Archaeological Study of Change and Continuity in Zimbabwe*. Studies in African Archaeology 10. Uppsala: Department of Archaeology and Ancient History, University of Uppsala.

Walker, Nicholas. 1996. *The Painted Hills: Rock Art of the Matopos*. Gweru: Mambo.

Walker, Nicholas, with Carolyn Thorp. 1997. "Stone-Age Archaeology in Zimbabwe." In *Caves, Monuments and Texts: Zimbabwean Archaeology Today*, ed. Gilbert Pwiti, 9–32. Studies in African Archaeology 14. Uppsala: Department of Archaeology and Ancient History, University of Uppsala.

Zvaba, Oliver. 1988. "Nyachiranga Regional Cult." PhD dissertation, Department of Religious Studies, University of Zimbabwe, Hahare.

23

Where the Wild Things Are

An Exploration of Sacrality, Danger, and Violence in Confined Spaces

Sandra Pannell and Sue O'Connor

In the war-torn and transformed landscape of Timor-Leste, culture is arguably one of the victims and survivors of the quarter-century of Indonesian occupation. In the post-Independence period, with the government and international aid agencies focused upon reinstating such fundamental amenities as health, housing, water, and sanitation, and on redeveloping local economies throughout the countryside, issues of heritage and identity appear to be overlooked or relegated to nonessential status. Yet, throughout Timor-Leste the issue of cultural sovereignty is emerging as one of the new domains of struggle and resistance. Out of the ashes of recent history, and liberated from their common identities as Indonesian citizens, various ethnic groups are increasingly demanding their own cultural space and moral authority within the fledgling nation-state.

In a landscape wracked by both natural and social forces, the assertion of sovereign authority by diverse cultural communities is also a struggle about "the appropriation of symbols, a struggle over how the past and present shall be understood and labeled, a struggle to identify causes and assess blame, a contentious effort to give partisan meaning to local history" (Scott 1985, xvii).

In the far eastern reaches of the island, these assertions are often conveyed and sustained through people's experience of *téi*. Throughout this Fataluku-speaking area, caves are often said to "be" or "have" *téi*. The concept of téi is often glossed in the literature as "sacred" or "taboo," (or *lulic*, in Tetum, Timor-Leste's other official language) and said to apply to a range of practices, objects, and spaces, such as agricultural fertility ceremonies, ceramic plates, and remnant forest groves (see Capell 1944; Forbes 1989; Gomes 1972; King 1963, McWilliam 2001, 2006; Traube 1986). As a number of these authors note, the experience of téi evokes a set of disparate attitudes that range from respect to awe, from fear to familiarity. As these comments suggest, and as we argue in this chapter, the notion of téi is positioned at the center of a discourse that explores the often perilous limits of sociality. Implicated in this discursive topography of violence, danger, and power, téi represents a peculiar or "uncanny" form of the sacred—a kind of "impure sacred" where cosmology and politics collide. In this context, caves not only confine local notions of power but also constitute focal elements of the Fataluku landscape that carry both the freight and weight of recent and more distant political histories. In the following sections, we focus upon three téi-ascribed places—Ili Kérékéré, Léné Ara, and Titiru—and associated events to illustrate more endemic cultural processes and perceptions relating to the proliferation of sovereign assertions in Timor-Leste. Two of these places, Ili Kérékéré and Léné Ara, are caves with painted rock art. Léné Ara is also an excavated cultural deposit of significant antiquity.

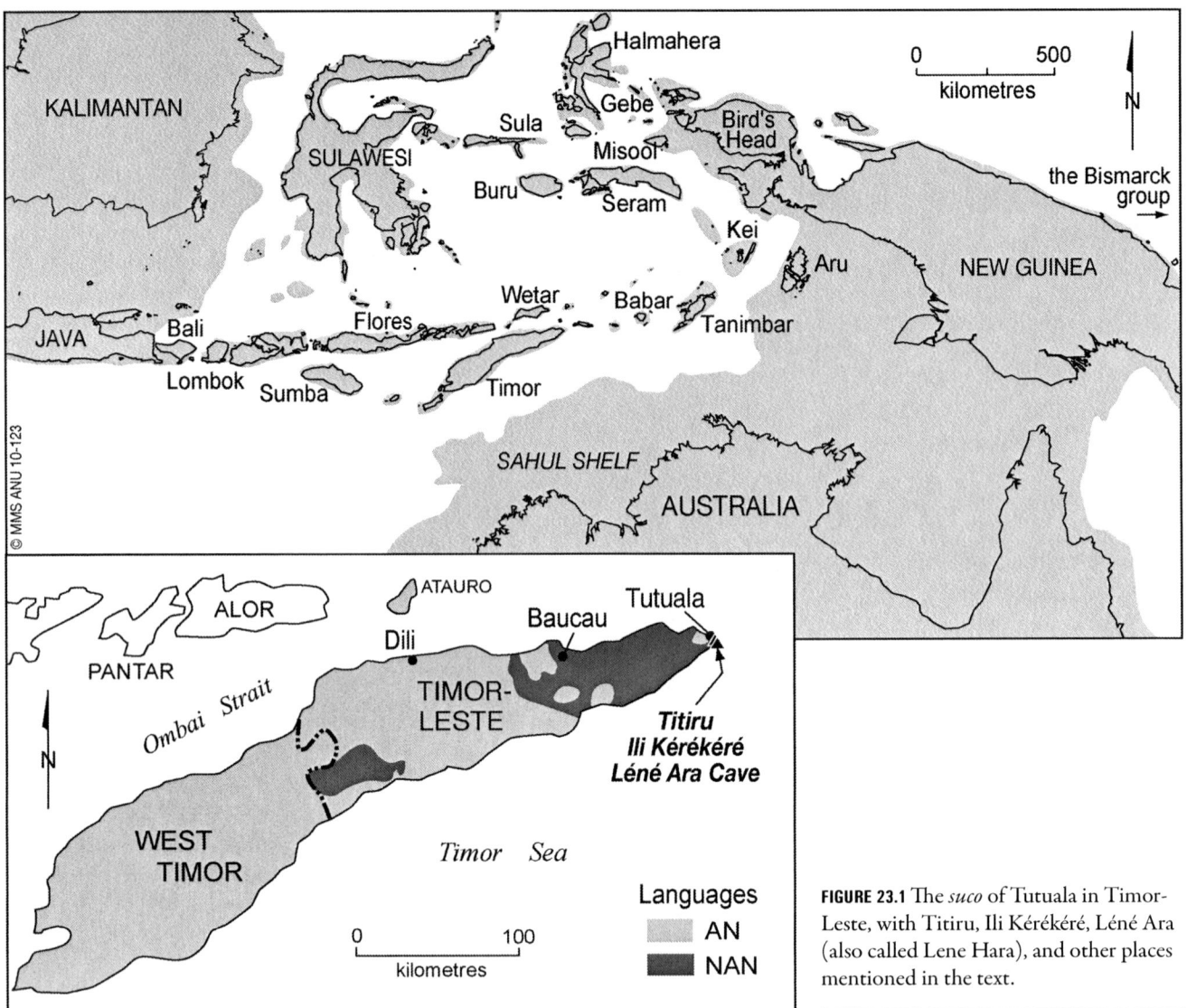

FIGURE 23.1 The *suco* of Tutuala in Timor-Leste, with Titiru, Ili Kérékéré, Léné Ara (also called Lene Hara), and other places mentioned in the text.

THE SETTING: THE *SUCO* TUTUALA

The *suco* (Tetum: "village") of Tutuala lies at the eastern tip of the island of Timor (figure 23.1). This suco consists of four hamlets (*aldeia*)—Pitileti, Vero, Ioro, and Chailoro—which are clustered around the main road between Tutuala and the regional center of Los Palos. This residential arrangement is a legacy of both Portuguese colonialism and more recent Indonesian occupation. The Tutuala region is fertile and well watered, supporting large expanses of primary- and secondary-growth rain forest. The forest is home to various species of game birds, together with deer, wild pigs, monkeys, civet cat, and cuscus, which are regularly hunted by local people. While people commonly engage in hunting and gathering activities, they are predominantly swidden agriculturalists, cultivating corn, various kinds of yams, and a range of vegetables. In addition, they raise pigs, buffalo, and chickens for both domestic consumption and sale. Buffaloes and domestic pigs also constitute an important form of currency in the local ritual economy involving mortuary and marriage prestations. With few exceptions, the residents of Tutuala are Fataluku speakers.

While Tetum and Portuguese are the two official languages of Timor-Leste, Fataluku is one of at least sixteen indigenous languages acknowledged in the constitution as a "national language valued and developed by the State." Fataluku is one of three Papuan languages belonging to the Trans–New Guinea phylum (the other two are Makassae and Bunak) spoken on the island of Timor today. Although the origin point of Fataluku and the other Papuan languages is unknown, they are completely unrelated to the Austronesian languages spoken throughout West Timor and much of the western half of Timor-

Leste (McWilliam 2007). Reports suggests that there are between 25,000 and 30,000 Fataluku speakers residing in the area from Tutuala, at the eastern tip of the island, west to the area of Lautem on the coast (McWilliam 2006; Wurm and Hattori 1981, 40). A small number of mostly senior Fataluku speakers in Tutuala also speak Lóvaia (also known in the linguistic literature as Maku'a). They identify Lóvaia as the original language spoken by their ancestors and state that over time, Fataluku, a later language arrival regarded by locals as an "easier" language to speak, replaced it. Tutuala people's beliefs and observations regarding the relationship between Lóvaia and Fataluku receive some support from linguists. While Capell (1972) and Wurm and Hattori (1981) identify Lóvaia as a Papuan language, more recent linguistic research suggests that Lóvaia is an Austronesian language. Specifically, Hull (1998a, 5) refers to Lóvaia as a "West Arafuric (South-West Moluccan) language" and believes it was originally introduced to Timor from the nearby Leti archipelago to the east. Wurm and Hattori are correct, however, in indicating that Lóvaia is specific to the Tutuala area (see also Ferreira 1951a, 1951b) and that the "speakers of Maku'a (Lóvaia) have been almost completely assimilated by those of Fataluku" (1981, 3). Indeed, as Fox and Soares point out, in this part of Timor-Leste it is clear that Papuan and Austronesian languages "have borrowed from and influenced one another over a considerable period of time" (2000, 5). In the Tutuala area, Lóvaia and other Austronesian language place-names and terms for social groups (for example, *ratu*, "clan group") are the more obvious evidence of this borrowing wherein the foreign is rendered familiar. As we discuss here, this interplay between the foreign and the familiar is a pervasive and recurrent theme in Fataluku beliefs and practices.

The name of the suco of Tutuala derives from an important mythological and art site (Tutuhala), situated some 50 meters below the cliff-top guest house built in Portuguese times on a former Fataluku village, also called Tutuhala. The large stone outcrop at Tutuhala is said to have "staked" and "secured" the first land to emerge from a cosmological world of water. People call this land Ili Kérékéré.

TÉI AND THE UNEXPECTEDNESS OF THE FAMILIAR

ILI KÉRÉKÉRÉ

Ili Kérékéré ("high rock with markings") is a large limestone gallery, located some 300 meters above sea level, on the uplifted Pleistocene reef terraces that characterize the northern coastline of this part of Timor-Leste (figure 23.2). In a society where precedence is inextricably tied up with identity and rights, Ili Kérékéré occupies an alpha position as a point of origins and beginnings. Not only is

FIGURE 23.2 Ili Kérékéré, showing the wall that separates the area known as *Otoulumuha* ("stomach") from that known as *Otoiriku* ("backside").

Ili Kérékéré said to be the first land in Timor, but it is also the first place the founding ancestors stepped foot upon when they descended from the sky and joined with the land. As such, it is also identified as the first village (*lata*) established by the autochthonous ancestors of Tutuala Ratu. The threefold social classifications that exist within this *ratu* are embedded in the geography of Ili Kérékéré. The most easterly section of the gallery is named Otochau ("place of the head"), the more northerly-facing section is called Otoulumuha ("place of the stomach"), while the entrance to the gallery is identified as the backside ("Otoiriku") of the entire complex. As these names suggest, Ili Kérékéré, like the entire island of Timor, is viewed as an embodied and, as we suggest below, animated social space. This Fataluku view of Timor as a human body, with Jaco Island as its head, contrasts with the mythic representation of the land mass, increasingly encountered in tourist brochures, government publications, and as part of the curriculum in local schools, as a "half-submerged crocodile" (Fox and Soares 2000, 1), with its head at Kupang, and its tail at Tutuala. Fataluku speakers believe that all humans, regardless of language and cultural differences, originated from the Tutuala region, begotten by an earthly human. Consequently, they dismiss the view that depicts humans as coming from a crocodile and they become angry at being placed at the tail end of an animal. Regarding this "crocodile history" and its promulgation as a national story under the Indonesian regime, Fataluku speakers are wary of any attempts to impose a new national history, particularly one they regard as a Tetum-centric account of the origin and order of things. Instead, they advocate recognition of local cultural histories, or perhaps more pertinently, their cultural history.

FIGURE 23.3 Painted panel of small anthropomorphs, holding objects above their heads, from Ili Kérékéré. The bodies of the figures are in a dark red-brown pigment. The faces and garments worn around the waist are painted in a lighter red pigment.

While at one level Ili Kérékéré can be regarded as a microcosm of Fataluku history and society, it can also be seen as a nexus for the entanglement of other historical and political processes. Seemingly positioned on the geopolitical margins of a number of colonial and postcolonial histories, Ili Kérékéré has long captured the imagination of occupying others, whether Portuguese archaeologists, Indonesian bureaucrats, UN personnel, and more recently, a trickle of Western tourists. Throughout the twentieth century, at least, these others have been drawn to Ili Kérékéré by the attraction of "primitive" art. During the Indonesian occupation, the government constructed a small car park, installed a series of concrete picnic tables, paved the path leading to the site, and erected a new "door" in their attempt to transform Tutuala into a largely domestic tourist destination. Prior to 1975, the Portuguese guest house in Tutuala provided some amenities to tourists and curious visitors. Both of these innovations still exist today, though in a somewhat dilapidated state.

Adorning the body of Ili Kérékéré, and reaching their highest concentration in the area known as Otoiriku, are hundreds of painted and drawn images. Many of the images are placed high on the vertical walls of the sea cliff, in places up to 5 meters above the ground, and we were only able to record them by constructing a long bamboo ladder. The images at Ili Kérékéré comprise mostly geometric forms, such as circles with outward emanating rays, and triangle and lattice motifs. Figurative motifs are numerically dominated by small anthropomorphs, usually portrayed as dancing or fighting, and holding weapons or other objects above their heads (figure 23.3). Many of these diminutive figures appear to be wearing feather headdresses. Boats are also well represented at Ili Kérékéré and at most other painted galleries in the Tutuala area. Animal

FIGURE 23.4 Pedro Morais (seated and partially visible at right), a group of children, and visitors at the newly replaced carved wooden post at the entrance to Ili Kérékéré. Peter Lape (University of Washington, Seattle) is at front right and Sandra Pannell is partially visible behind him with a field notebook.

depictions are less common and are restricted mostly to fish, birds, and horses. In terms of locational context, subject, and style, the Ili Kérékéré paintings conform with painted rock-art sites elsewhere in eastern Indonesia and the western Pacific, which have been grouped under the sobriquet the "Austronesian painting tradition" (Ballard 1992; O'Connor 2003).

Senior members of Tutuala Ratu, the traditional custodians of Ili Kérékéré, believe the rock art (excluding the boat motifs) to preexist humans, appearing at the same time that Ili Kérékéré emerged from the sea. For local people, the shapes and figures covering the walls of the gallery fall into five broad categories—depictions of water craft (*loiasu*); *lontar*-leaf baskets (*poko*), used for storing kapok fiber; various designs of horse-blinkers (*faria*) and images of horses (*kucha*); human forms (*maluwana*); and *rusu*, triangular shapes infilled with ochre. Stylized versions of the art of Ili Kérékéré appear in the architecture of traditional houses (*lé iya valu*), on concrete grave markers, and on the woven cloths (*sisiranlau*) of Tutuala Ratu. These cloths also contain other images associated with Ili Kérékéré, though not with the rock art, per se.

With the exception of the boat images, all of the other images mentioned above are identified by Fataluku as indigenous and as being *téi*. The boats depicted at Ili Kérékéré are said to belong to foreigners from other islands, who were attracted to Ili Kérékéré by the light emitted from a large beeswax candle, placed by the original occupants of Otochau. According to local narratives, upon landing at various sites along the coast in the vicinity of Ili Kérékéré, the boats of these new arrivals turned into stone and the occupants were summoned by the ancestors of Tutuala

Ratu and accorded a portion of land to settle upon. Today, the candle site in Otochau is marked by a raised, circular stone platform. A large carved wooden post (*saka* or *sikua*), said to be the candle at the center of the structure, was stolen in 1983 during the period of Indonesian governance. However, in 2004 following Independence a new carved wooden post was erected here.

The ubiquity and commonality of the use of the boat as a symbol throughout much of Mainland and Island Southeast Asia, and the use of real boats, boat replicas, or carved, painted, and woven representations of boats in mortuary contexts throughout eastern Indonesia and the western Pacific, perhaps belies such a utilitarian explanation for the proliferation of boat paintings in the art sites around Tutuala. For example, in the Tanimbar Islands of eastern Indonesia, large stone boats mark the physical and conceptual center of a village. At these stone arrangements, villagers met, danced, and made sacrifices to the ancestors (de Jonge and van Dijk 1995, 78–9; McKinnon 1988: 152–160).

Similarly, at the original landing sites (*iya mari tuliya*), the stone boats of the first arrivals to Tutuala are important markers of significant events in the cultural history of the respective ratu descendants. Members of the immigrant ratu regularly attend to these sites, making offerings and seeking protection from sickness and adversity from their respective ancestors. These sites, which appear to the casual observer as natural outcrops of limestone, are physically marked by the same structural elements found at a number of other sites in the landscape. However, unlike the stone boats, these latter sites are identified as original features of the landscape. Indeed, a number of stone boats are located near one of these preexistent sites. These original sites, and the elements that mark their presence, are identified as téi, as are the physical markers of the stone boats. In this respect, the landing sites of the immigrant ratu represent a spatial synthesis of a recurrent Fataluku cultural theme, whereby the foreign is rendered familiar through the presence and experience of téi. However, as we discuss shortly, while the presence of téi elements appears to indigenize these landing sites, these sites are not of the same order and being as the original téi places.

Entrance to the Ili Kérékéré gallery complex is afforded by the "door" (*lat'o*) to the village, a natural break in the limestone boulders. Located just inside the "village" is a platform of layered stones. When we first visited Ili Kérékéré in 2000, the central area of the platform was marked by a hole extending half a meter or so into the soft deposit of the cave floor. We were told that this hole had once contained a large carved wooden post that, like the one in Otochau, was said to have been "stolen by the Indonesians" some years before. This post was also replaced in 2004 and ceremonies were resumed at this ritual location (Figure 23.4). The entire structure is identified as téi. Each of the elements, either singly or together, are said to have been placed by the apical ancestors to indicate the presence of the being that inhabits the hole. This being, like all the other beings that occupy preexistent téi places within the Fataluku landscape, has a ritual name, considered "hot" and "dangerous" and known only by the *Liurai* (a tetum term for a customary elder or ritual leader) from Tutuala Ratu. Also spoken of as téi, the being at Ili Kérékéré is said to manifest itself in a number of phenomenal forms—an owl or a human-like figure with the torso of a snake (*aka*). Other téi adopt the shape of crocodiles, eagles, crows, horses, dogs, or multiheaded snakes. As this suggests, the term *téi* is equally used as a noun, an adjective, and sometimes, though less frequently, as a verb (see King 1963, 155).

The being at the entrance to Ili Kérékéré is said to guard the "village," and one finds similar téi structures at the entrance to past and present village sites throughout the Tutuala area. Téi sites are also encountered throughout the forests of Tutuala, where they are said to "guard" an area and the ratu members associated with that area from strangers and sickness (figure 23.5). Entering village sites, and other places marked by téi, without the custodial ratu member(s) and the appropriate introductions and exchange of "polite" words with the téi, is considered a dangerous thing to do, and certainly invites all manner of catastrophes.

The named being also offers protection from sickness or mortal adversity to the members of Tutuala Ratu and the custodians of Ili Kérékéré. When the appropriate ceremonies are conducted, the being can be directed to kill others or bring about sickness. These beings are not regarded as people's ancestors, nor are they said to have been made by human ancestral figures. Téi are seen as malevolent, animating forces in the landscape. They are the ultimate moral authority, located outside of local concepts of human ontology and the politics of ancestral precedence. Accordingly, humans are unable to create new téi places; they can only replace the physical indicators of the téi that are broken, rotten, or stolen.

It is perhaps misguided to think of téi as entities "set apart," as suggested by the Latin origin of the term *sacred* (from *sacrâre*, "to set apart, consecrate"). Téi require ongoing engagement and a degree of familiarity with their respective custodial ratu in order to avert calamity and bring about some form of tenuous certainty. The more obvious forms of engagement occur when the ratu members "feed" the téi with ritual offerings of rice, eggs, pig meat, and palm spirit. In this sense, téi are seen to possess fundamental human qualities and to require contact with

FIGURE 23.5 Agustu Mendes, senior spokesman from the group Sina Ratu, standing near the téi at Hiyo.

humans; they are even said to follow people when they relocate village sites. Like humans, téi are regarded as possessing different characteristics; for example, some are not so dangerous and apparently take "longer to kill people." While all téi are not alike, so is it the case that the physical markers of téi differ from site to site, though each site retains the basic elemental features as previously described.

Familiarity with humans and contact with human-made things is said to calm the téi. Thus, téi marked by upturned roots and forked branches, and unmodified by humans, are seen to be more dangerous and unpredictable than are téi marked by posts carved by human hands (see figures 23.4 and 23.5). A téi fed with food produced and consumed by humans is a satiated téi. When the téi is hungry or thirsty, it is said to emerge from its hole, and it is at this moment that it becomes a real threat to humans. Fundamentally, téi are wild at heart and their alleged actions at times blur the boundary between benevolent and malevolent, creating strange affinities between things. This is particularly evident in those situations in which the hole inhabited by the téi is exposed by the theft of the post, and the téi is akin to a genie out of its bottle, acting without any social constraint.

People attribute the premature death of the local Liurai at the time and talk about the sudden deaths of a number of construction workers as the action of the téi, angered by the tourist development undertaken by the Indonesians at Ili Kérékéré in the 1980s. One of the interesting ironies of this interpretation of events is that upon completion of their construction work, the Indonesians erected a sign that read "*Ili Kérékéré, Dilarang masuk mengunjunjungi tanpa seijin pemiliknya. Terima kasih*," which translates as "Ili Kérékéré. It is forbidden to enter and visit without the permission of the owner. Thank you." The interest of tourists in the art site and their willingness to pay for this experience has generated considerable dispute between members of the three named sections of Tutuala Ratu (i.e., Otochau, Otoulumuha, and Otoiriku) about which subgroup, or individuals within these divisions, is the "owner." Largely expressed as veiled allegations about certain individuals who secretly accompany tourists to the site and greedily pocket any payments, this talk is not just about the "who" of ownership but strikes at the very heart of the notion of proprietary, suggested by the sign. In this context, the novel events, surprising experiences, and the strange occurrences attributed to the power of the téi, form a moral critique of the idea that places and history can be the exclusive possession of any one individual. Fataluku accounts of the creation of their multiorigined society, together with local marriage and funerary practices, certainly rally against this perilous notion of sociality.

As the previous example suggests, téi have few if any binding allegiances to those ritually responsible for their well-being. Failure to uphold these responsibilities brings about adverse consequences. For instance, the theft of the carved post marking the presence of the téi at the entrance to Ili Kérékéré, and the failure on the part of the members of Tutuala Ratu to undertake the ceremonies to replace it, were identified by a number of people as the reason for the sudden death of the senior ritual custodian from Tutuala Ratu in 2003. Others attributed his death to a series of archaeological excavations that took place at Léné Ara in 1963 and later in 2000 and 2002.

Léné Ara

As the name suggests, Léné Ara (also called "Lene Hara" in the literature), is identified as the "first cave" to emerge and be occupied by the ancestors of Tutuala Ratu when they left Ili Kérékéré. As Glover (1986, 17) points out, there are two entrances to the cave system. Located in the northern entrance is what Glover describes as "an interesting structure, a forked wooden pole set in a low semicircle of stones, reminiscent of the spirit shrines of central Timor" (ibid.). While Glover notes that the rocky floor

FIGURE 23.6 Rafael Quimaraes, Liurai from the group Tutuala Ratu, addressing the téi at Léné Ara.

"ruled out the possibility of excavation here" (ibid.), our experience suggests that the problems posed by strata was certainly not the only constraining factor in the minds of local people. The structure that Glover described and photographed (see Glover 1986, 18) is a téi. Léné Ara is identified as a former village site, and thus the téi at the "door" is, like the one at Ili Kérékéré, the guardian of the village. The forked wooden pole that Glover reports has gone, though the other elements—the standing stone, the offering stone, and the base platform—are still present (figure 23.6). Members of Tutuala Ratu continue to approach the téi and seek ratu fertility and protection from illness.

Léné Ara is also a place that has generated continued interest among archaeologists. The Portuguese scholar Antonio Almeida dug two trenches in the cave in 1963 (Almeida and Zbyszewski 1967), which were still open at the time of Glover and Mulvaney's visit in 1966. Local people recall these visits, and particularly the excavations of Almeida. There is a widespread belief among members of Tutuala Ratu that permission to disturb the cave deposits was not sought from the Liurai at the time. If there was permission to excavate, it appeared to come from government officials.

In 2000, a team of archaeologists from the Australian National University (ANU) commenced excavations at Léné Ara. While this team sought permission and arranged for the Liurai to conduct the appropriate ceremonies with respect to the téi to "open" and "close" the earth at the beginning and termination of the excavation, it seemed that some local people were dissatisfied with the nature of these proceedings. Upon returning to Léné Ara in 2002 to undertake further excavations in the cave, team members heard about the death of the younger brother of the Liurai. For some local people, this event was linked to what they regarded as anomalies in the ritual process in 2000, for example, not sacrificing a pig to the téi at the end of the excavation. In 2003, when some of the members of the team again returned to Tutuala, they were saddened to learn of the death of the Liurai himself, only some 2 months earlier. The sudden death of such an important person generated considerable discussion and a number of local theories of causation. As previously mentioned, some linked his death to the failure to placate the téi at Ili Kérékéré by not replacing the stolen post, or by allowing paying foreigners to enter and view the art site. Others suggested that the disturbance of the téi at Léné Ara by archaeological excavations that spanned a period of nearly 40 years was to blame. A number of close relatives even suggested that as a result of these various disruptions and indiscretions, the Liurai was killed by the paramount téi at Titiru.

It is interesting to note here the role that the unexpected, the novel, and the strange play in each of these explanations. For Fataluku people, téi are familiar places and things that are linked to surprising events and experiences, which are ultimately explicable within the logic of téi. In this respect, téi are credited with creating what seems to be randomness and disorder, yet at the same time, they are also said to respond to these kinds of disruptions and bring about an unstable certainty. An example of this tension occurs when the téi caused the deaths of Indonesian construction workers and, in the eyes of local people, thus halted further development. The arrival of archaeologists, the theft of the carved téi posts, sudden deaths, Indonesian tourism developments—can all be viewed as unique events or random acts that are essential to the very notion of téi and the Fataluku conception of agency. While the purported operation of téi may give the impression of displacing human creativity and agency, in the end effective action derives from people's relationship with the familiar yet alien power of the téi. As the following discussion illustrates, this shared vision of agency, where agency is sought but not necessarily and exclusively claimed by people, is linked to a legacy of recent violence.

Titiru

Nearby the Ili Kérékéré carpark is located the "president" of all téi at Titiru (figure 23.7). This téi is further said to be the "biggest head and bones" (*téi ilafai chau hafa*) of all "the téi in Timor." At the center of the Titiru platform stand two stones, the larger of the stones is said to be the husband of the smaller one. While identified as "human," this téi is also able to change it shape. The language of statehood is further extended to a number of other nearby téi that are said to act as the "deputy" and the "commander" of Titiru. The belief among some Fataluku people that

FIGURE 23.7 Titiru, the president of all téi.

a former Liurai was said to have been killed by this téi, dressed in a khaki army uniform and carrying a briefcase, seems quite consistent with this particular idiom. While the identification of this téi as the "president" captures its paramount rank in the local order of téi, it also links it to other orders, in particular the New Order Government of Indonesia and the violence that characterized people's experience of this regime. The presidential status of this téi is further connected to the political struggles of the new nation-state of Timor-Leste.

For Fataluku speakers in Tutuala, the téi at Titiru is ultimately responsible for the defeat of the Indonesian military and various militia groups in the later part of 1999. A desperate resistance leader, Xanana Gusmao, is said to have personally requested assistance from the present Liurai to dispel the foreigners. Upon receiving this request, and with a photograph of the Falantil leader in hand, the Liurai sacrificed a pig at Titiru in September 1999 and requested the téi to emerge from its hole and take action against the Indonesians and others. Out of its hole, the téi started to "eat" the enemy, while Xanana is said to have been imbued with the thoughts and power of the téi, the two creating an unbeatable front to the Indonesian forces. When the Indonesians left, the Liurai returned to Titiru and sacrificed another pig to "calm" the téi down and entice it to enter its hole once again, satiated with food and drink as well as the "blood and flesh" of the enemy. The rest is history, though whose history is still up for grabs.

Perhaps, it is not so surprising that Timor-Leste was "saved" by the téi at Titiru, particularly given the Fataluku belief that their region and their ancestors are the source of all peoples and lands comprising the island. Nor is it so surprising that the fledgling state of Timor-Leste is absorbed into this original center of cultural sovereignty and moral authority. As a postscript to this observation, following the replacement of the missing téi posts at Ili Kérékéré the first president of Timor-Leste, Xanana Gusmao, attended the ensuing Fataluku rituals of local statehood.

THE ARCHAEOLOGY OF TÉI

The above discussion underlies one of the fundamental challenges to archaeology and cultural heritage management in attempting to reconcile contemporary social practice and its physical manifestations with archaeological methodology and the requirements of cultural heritage practice. As is apparent from the above discussion of téi at Ili Kérékéré and Léné Ara, it is not simply that caves are sacred but that these particular caves are not simply "caves." In the Fataluku classification they are also seminal "villages." This problem of classification is further exemplified by a stone structure recorded by the authors in a cave known as Ili Mimiraka, which, on the basis of its physical attributes and associations, would be absorbed within the archaeological class téi. However, it was not acknowledged as téi by the senior members of Tutuala Ratu. The reason was plain: it lacked agency. Here was a raised stone platform with neither a link to nor a relationship with people, and as such it did not exist—not as a téi anyway.

Compound structures comprising a stone platform and wooden or stone uprights that resemble *téi* structures are ubiquitous in the landscape of Timor-Leste. They have been recorded by the authors close to the capital, Dili, in the mountainous Maliana region, on the Baucau Plateau, and in the Com region to the west of Tutuala. Other and earlier writers have depicted or remarked on these structures, often referring to them by the Tetun word *lulik* (cf. Forbes 1989; King 1963; McWilliam 2001, 2006; Traube 1986; Vroklage 1953). For example, in an account of her travels in the Fatu Ló (i.e., Fataluku-speaking) district of Lautem, King describes visiting "new and varying kinds of *lulics*" (1963, 156), including:

> a man and a woman; sometimes a man, a woman and a dog; sometimes an ancient ceramic plate; a flat stone, a forked wooden pole, and, in the depth of one forest, an enormous stone altar. (ibid., 156)

Elsewhere in Island Southeast Asia similar structures have been recorded, although these are often glossed in the literature as "ancestor shrines" or sacrificial platforms for descent group "founder ancestors," "ancestral war leaders," or "male deities" (de Jonge and van Dijk 1995, 64). Like those in Timor-Leste, these structures take the general form of a raised stone platform with a central upright. In some cases, the upright is carved into a human form, but in others it is aniconic. In Luang and Leti the upright often had human-like features and was seated in a boat or on a boat-shaped construction. One photographed in Babar in 1913, which was placed in the former ritual center of the village (de Jonge and van Dijk 1995, 60–61, 64, photograph 4.18) with a stepped carving at its outer end, looks remarkably similar to many of the téi structures recorded by the authors in the Tutuala area. While there is scant detailed anthropological description regarding the cultural practices associated with these structures, what there is suggests that they were presented with offerings of rice, eggs, palm wine, betel nut, coconut, and cooked meat. De Jonge and van Dijk (1995, 64) state that on the islands of Leti, Babar, and Kisar, each "village had a ritual centre where the male deity was represented by a wooden stake or pole statue. . . . Here sacrifices were made to the gods and assistance was entreated." They note that the statues on the islands to the west of Babar were "often adorned with 'hunting trophies'" (de Jonge and van Dijk 1995, 64) but they do not specify whether these were carved representations or actual trophies.

FIGURE 23.8 Liurai Rafael Quimaraes (right), from the group Tutuala Ratu, and his son, Custodio Quimaraes (left), interacting with the téi at Lumuku. Lumuku téi has a wooden upright comprising an upturned tree root. It has a red cloth tied around its "neck" and sits on a long, well-constructed stone platform that is oriented east-west. This site was identified as a fertility site for Tutuala Ratu.

In Timor-Leste, téi structures are usually aniconic. They include unmodified, upturned tree roots (figure 23.8), shaped posts with geometric carvings or "steps" at the upper end (figures 23.4 and 23.5), stone uprights, and combinations of these forms (figures 23.7 and 23.9), but rarely are features represented, although the placement of cloth around the "neck" of some téi uprights may denote that some are conceived of as iconic. The authors have recorded a few iconic examples, including one stone upright in the Tutuala region with roughly carved, human-like facial features. The remnants of past sacrifices or offerings—the skulls of pigs and other animals—are often seen dangling from a rope or overhanging branches above them (figures 23.7 and 23.8).

An orthodox archaeological approach to these structures would be to classify them using physical and functional criteria. The structures would be described of them-

FIGURE 23.9 Téi structure combining a stone platform, an uncarved wooden upright, a forked stick, and a stone upright in an overhang formed in uplifted Pleistocene marine terraces at Mua Mimiraka. (From left to right) Fernando Rodriguez (of the Jenlai Ratu), Pedro Morais (Kwawatcha Ratu), Rafael Quimaraes (Tutuala Ratu), and Custodio Quimaraes (Tutuala Ratu).

selves and in their context. This would allow comparative assessment of each structure within the framework of the corpus of such structures. Context would include their placement within the physical landscape and associated cultural materials such as animal bones or macrobotanic remains.

This comparative approach would seek to address such questions as, Where did the structures come from, what were they used for, and how old are they? The widespread occurrence of such structures in Timor, and of similar structures in other parts of Island Southeast Asia, might be interpreted as indicating that they are the physical manifestation of a shared cosmology or belief system. The commonality of such structures over a large geographic region might be argued to indicate that this shared cosmology derives from a common ancestry. Rice, pigs, and chickens have been depicted as the cornerstones of the agricultural package brought by Austronesian-speaking migrants as they made their way from Taiwan and into Island Southeast Asia (Bellwood 1997). The link between téi and offerings of rice, pig and chicken eggs might, therefore, be argued to provide a timescale for the antiquity of the structures.

It would follow from this reasoning that the structures, cosmology, and social practice have their roots in the Austronesian homeland in Taiwan or in one of the first islands settled following Austronesian dispersal into Island Southeast Asia. On linguistic and archaeological grounds, this is argued to have occurred sometime between 4000 and 3500 BP (Bellwood 1997). Direct dating of these structures might be used to test some of these hypotheses.

Reasoning like this is commonly applied in reconstructing past anthropological, linguistic, and archaeological communities. A good example is the Comparative Austronesian Project whose stated aim is "to draw together anthropological, archaeological and linguistic approaches for the study of the Austronesian-speaking populations and to fashion a general framework for the mutual interpretation of the complexities of the Austronesian heritage" (Bellwood, Fox, and Tryon 1995, 6). Such phylogenetic studies seek to "discover" cultural "origins" and "homelands." They may be not only somewhat circular in their methodology but may also be used to derive or drive national and ethnic agendas (cf. Anderson 1991, 178–185; Ikawa-Smith 1999; Trigger 1984, 1989, 101–147). Archaeology can provide tangible evidence of the glorious past that can be used to enhance identity construction and assert legitimacy. For example, the Taiwanese have been quick to seize upon archaeological and linguistic research advocating Taiwan as the prehistoric "homeland" for some 350 million Austronesian language speakers, stretching from Madagascar in the west to Easter Island in the east (Bellwood 1997, 310–13). Hundreds of millions of dollars have been spent on museum exhibits and education programs which promote this "separate" identity from China (Frazier 2003, 2004). Needless to say, the "Taiwanese homeland" model is less popular in other parts of Island Southeast Asia, where it is seen as a type of cultural imperialism subsuming indigenous developments and creativity.

An archaeological narrative that suggested that téi were a symbolic outcome of a pan-Austronesian belief system with an origin in Taiwan would beggar belief for Fataluku people. It is doubtful if they would even comprehend the choice of attributes that the archaeologist would use. Radiometric dating would appear ludicrous, as it would relate only to the physical structures that humans rearrange and replace, and not to the animate beings that inhabit them. Our evidence suggests that Fataluku view téi as "social others" (Gell 1998, 222) with whom they have mutually dependent relationships that relate them to the landscape, both in the present and in the past, and that the attributes that they would highlight would emphasize these relationships and the agency and efficacy of téi.

IMPLICATIONS FOR CULTURAL HERITAGE MANAGEMENT

The implications of the above for archaeological cultural heritage management should be apparent. In a contemporary environment where the present government of Timor-Leste is seeking to consolidate and unify a national identify wrought from 25 years of struggle for independence, there may be little room for Fataluku to assert their collective cultural identity. Some indication of this political and cultural squeeze is evident in the government's management of forests in the Tutuala area where they have gazetted a large area of "traditional land" as Timor-Leste's first national park (the Nino Konis Santana National Park), thus limiting the rights of Fataluku with traditional tenure over this land to exploit resources within its boundaries (McWilliam 2003). Protected cultural heritage status for the rock-art galleries of Ili Kérékéré and Léné Ara (which lie within the park boundaries) is provided by the park, however this is in name only, as no framework for management or protection has thus been enacted that involves local people from Tutuala or considers their use of the sites in contemporary practice (O'Connor, Pannell, and Brockwell 2011).

This issue is dealt with in some detail by Byrne (2004, 1), who identifies it as one of the critical concerns facing cultural heritage managers in Southeast Asia today:

> a key consideration in everyday life is that these objects and places, in and of themselves, have efficacy. They can do things to you and, more importantly, they can do things for you. . . . Our own rational view of these same objects and places is that they are inert constructions of stone, metal, wood, pigment etc that are of historical and aesthetic value. In our view of things we manage and conserve old things and places. In the supernatural view . . . [t]hey are not . . . available to be managed, one has a dialogue with them. *These two views represent fundamentally different ways of understanding the world.* (emphasis added).

Archaeological or cultural heritage assessments that classify and assign significance primarily in terms of rational, scientifically observable criteria, such as antiquity, aesthetic quality, representativeness, uniqueness, completeness, rarity, and preservation, will potentially impede the relationships that give sites like Ili Kérékéré, Léné Ara, and the téi platforms their agency. Limiting access to such sites or controlling the activities that may be performed at or in them would rob them of the essence that makes them significant to Fataluku people. As Byrne (2004, 2009) points out, in Southeast Asia today many millions of people identify with the supernatural view of such sites and objects. The challenge for cultural heritage managers in the twenty-first century lies in accommodating this view rather than marginalizing it, as has been the wont of many archaeologists from Western nations up until now. The recent history of the use and abuse of the cave sites of Ili Kérékéré and Léné Ara also alerts us to the chilling fact that cultural heritage issues in many developing countries are circumscribed by histories of sovereign struggle and violence.

CONCLUSION

As the preceding discussion suggests, if the term *sacred* is to apply to téi, as some authors have suggested, then we need to look at the involvement of the sacred in local questions of power, violence, culture, and heritage. In this respect, téi are the ultimate mimetic operators in this nexus, impersonating and, at times, inverting Fataluku experiences at a number of levels. The violent qualities and outbursts ascribed to téi encode the tension of local social relations, capture regional histories of enmity, and reflect the national experience of political oppression. Like the state, local power here, as a regulatory moral authority, is backed by the threat and use of violence. On the other hand, the sociopolitical order is attributed to the strange and dangerous conjunction of force and téi-inspired fate, where nothing is left to chance. As this suggests, the experience of téi is linked to Fataluku notions of agency. In a strange twist, Fataluku people commemorate the violence and desecration wrought by outsiders by recasting the source of creativity and action, locating it in their own sacred-political order, where téi are positioned as a far superior moral authority. Fataluku people share in this sense of agency by maintaining familiar relations with téi, even though at times it seems that familiarity breeds contempt. The violence and destructive acts committed by téi can be seen not only as a manifestation of their existence, and as a counterpoint to the existence of alien others, but also as an assertion of the continued existence of the state of Fataluku culture, incorporating a sovereign polity founded upon ideas of origins and precedence and the power of indigeneity. In this respect, téi affirm the savage potency and pervasive powers of autochthony. Interestingly, the "wild humanity" (Taussig 1987, 77) and random powers attributed to téi by local people were also central to the typologies of the Portuguese and Indonesian colonizers. For example, in Indonesia, *orang asli* (native people) or *suku terasing* (isolated ethnic groups) continue to be "depicted as 'wild,' 'backward' and 'strange' in official development discourses" (Pannell 2003, 90). In many respects, the experience of téi as both familiar and unexpected, constitutes a dramatic reminder to Fataluku people that the Indonesian government failed to entirely absorb or displace local sources of sovereign authority in Timor-Leste. In this sense, the experience of téi can be seen as blurring the distinction between state categories and ancestral traditions or, as the example of Léné Ara suggests, the distinctions between scientific knowledge and Fataluku history.

Results from the recent excavations at Léné Ara, particularly the radiocarbon dates of between 38,000 and 35,000 BP for human occupation (O'Connor et al. 2010; O'Connor, Spriggs, and Veth 2002) have been readily embraced by people in Tutuala. To the surprise of the archaeologists, these dates, among the oldest dates of human occupation in Timor-Leste so far, are not so surprising to Fataluku people. Indeed, they confirm their own theory of knowledge about the origins of humans and the creation of Timor. In this respect, caves are not just the abode of téi, or good places to dig up the past. Their contents testify to the veracity of local histories and provide substance to Fataluku assertions of cultural sovereignty. Moreover, international publication of excavation results from Léné Ara, and the distribution of these articles to the Ministry of Culture, Youth and Sport in Dili, readily accords with Fataluku people's expansionist tendencies and their resistance to the imposition of what they regard as yet another nationalistic history. Moreover, if recent Internet reports that the Liurai have handed out copies of our archaeological articles to tourists are accurate, it seems that Fataluku people themselves are actively taking steps to extend the familiar into foreign hands and lands. While not quite culture wars yet, the small-arms fire of everyday struggle has begun, again.

ACKNOWLEDGMENTS

This study was supported by an Australian Research Council Large Grant, the Australian National University, and the Rainforest Cooperative Research Centre, James Cook University. In Timor-Leste, research was undertaken under the auspices of the Ministério da Educação (Ministry of Education) and we would like to extend our general thanks and appreciation to the Ministry staff. Particular thanks go to Cecília Assis and Virgílio Simith who arranged our permits and for their much-welcomed support. We would also like to acknowledge that without the support of the people of Tutuala this research would not be possible. In this regard, we are particularly indebted to Srs Rafael Quimaraes, Custodio Quimaraes, and Pedro Morais for their intellectual input, constant interest, and friendship while in the field.

REFERENCES CITED

Almeida, Antonio de, and G. A. Zbyszewski. 1967. "A Contribution to the Study of the Prehistory of Portuguese Timor—Lithic Industries." In *Archaeology at the 11th Pacific Science Congress*, ed. W. G. Solheim, 55–67. Asian and Pacific Archaeology Series 1. Honolulu: Social Science Research Institute, University of Hawai'i.

Anderson, Benedict. 1991. *Imagined Communities Reflections on the Origin and Spread of Nationalism*. New York: Verso.

Ballard, Chris. 1992. "Painted Rock Art Sites in Eastern Melanesia: Locational Evidence for an 'Austronesian' Tradition." In *State of the Art Regional Rock Art Studies in Australia and Melanesia*, ed. J. McDonald and I. Haskovec, 94–106. Occasional AURA publication no. 6. Melbourne: Australian Rock Art Research Association.

Bellwood, Peter. 1997. *Prehistory of the Indo-Malaysian Archipelago*. Rev. ed. Honolulu: University of Hawai'i Press.

Bellwood, Peter. James J. Fox, and Darrell Tryon. 1995. "The Austronesians in History: Common Origins and Diverse Transformations." In *The Austronesians Historical and Comparative Perspectives*, ed. P. Bellwood, J. J. Fox, and D. Tryon, 1–16. Canberra: Department of Anthropology, Australian National University.

Byrne, Denis. 2004. "Agency and Divine Heritage: The Issue of Agency in the Conservation of Divine Heritage." Paper Presented at the Australian Archaeological Association Conference, University of New England, Armidale, NSW, December 2004.

Byrne, Denis. 2009. "The Fortress of Rationality: Archaeology and Thai Popular Religion." In *Cosmopolitan Archaeologies*, ed. Lynn Meskell, 68–88. Durham, NC: Duke University Press.

Capell, Arthur. 1944. "Peoples and Languages of Timor." *Oceania* 14(3): 191–219; 14(4): 311–37; 15(1): 19–48.

Capell, Arthur. 1972. "Portuguese Timor: Two More Non-Austronesian Languages." In *Linguistic Papers*, I: *General*; II: *Indonesia and New Guinea*, 95–104. Oceania Linguistic Monograph No. 15. Sydney: University of Sydney.

De Almeida, A., and G. Zbyszewski. 1967. "A Contribution to the Study of the Prehistory of Portuguese Timor-Lithic Industries." In *Archaeology at the Eleventh Pacific Science Congress: Papers presented at the XI Pacific Science Congress, Tokyo, August–September 1966*, ed. W. G. Solheim II, 55–67. Asian and Pacific Archaeology Series. Honolulu: Social Science Research Institute, University of Hawai'i, Hawaii.

De Jonge, Nico, and Toos van Dijk. 1995. *Forgotten Islands of Indonesia: The Art and Culture of the Southeast Moluccas*. Singapore: Periplus.

Ferreira, Manuel. 1951a. "Tutuala I—Apontamentos etnográficos." *Seara* 3 (5): 211–17.

Ferreira, Manuel. 1951b. "Tutuala II—Apontamentos etnográficos." *Seara* 3 (6): 256–59.

Forbes, H. O. 1989. *A Naturalist's Wanderings in the Eastern Archipelago*. Oxford: Oxford University Press.

Fox, James. J., and Dionisio Babo Soares. 2000. *Out of the Ashes: Destruction and Reconstruction of East Timor*. Adelaide: Crawford House Publishing.

Frazier, David. 2003. "New View of Taiwan." *Far Eastern Economic Review* 166, no. 11 (March 20): 57.

Frazier, David. 2004. "Taiwan, the Homeland." *Far Eastern Economic Review* 167, no. 3 (January 22): 54–56.

Gell, Alfred. 1998. *Art and Agency an Anthropological Theory*. Oxford: Clarendon Press.

Glover, Ian. 1986. *Archaeology in Eastern Timor, 1966–67*. Canberra: Australian National University.

Gomes, Francisco de Azevedo. 1972. *Os Fataluku*. Lisboa: Instituto Superior de Ciencias, Socias e Politicia Ultramarina, Universidade Tecnica de Lisboa.

Hull, Geoffrey. 1998a. "The Languages of Timor 1772–1997: A Literature Review." In *Studies on Languages and Cultures of East Timor*, ed. Geoffrey Hull and Lance Eccles, 1: 1–38. Macarthur: Academy of East Timor Studies, University of Western Sydney.

Ikawa-Smith, Fumiko. 1999. "Construction of National Identity and Origins in East Asia: A Comparative Perspective." *Antiquity* 73 (281): 626–9.

King, Margaret. 1963. *Eden to Paradise*. London: Hodder and Stoughton.

McKinnon, S. 1988. "Tanimbar Boats." In *Islands and Ancestors: Indigenous Styles of Southeast Asia*, ed. J. P. Barbier and D. Newton, 152–69. Munich: Prestel-Verlag.

McWilliam, Andrew. 2001. "Prospects for the Sacred Grove: Valuing Lulic Forests on Timor." *The Asia Pacific Journal of Anthropology* 2 (2): 89–113.

McWilliam, Andrew. 2006. "Fataluku Forest Tenures and the Conis Santana National Park in East Timor." In *Sharing the Earth, Dividing the Land: Land and Territory in the Austronesian World*, ed. Thomas Reuter, 253–75. Canberra: ANU E Press.

McWilliam, Andrew. 2007. "Customary Claims and the Public Interest: On Fataluku Resource Entitlement in Lautem." In *East Timor: Beyond Independence*, ed. Damien Kingsbury and Michael Leach, 165–78. Melbourne: Monash Asia Institute Press.

O'Connor, Sue. 2003. "Nine New Painted Rock Art Sites from East Timor in the Context of the Western Pacific Region." *Asian Perspective* 42 (1): 96–128. http://dx.doi.org/10.1353/asi.2003.0028.

O'Connor, Sue, Anthony Barham, Matthew Spriggs, Peter Veth, Ken Aplin, and Emma St. Pierre. 2010. "Cave Archaeology and Sampling Issues in the Tropics: A Case Study from Lene Hara Cave, a 42,000 Year Old Occupation Site in East Timor, Island Southeast Asia." *Australian Archaeology* 71: 29–40.

O'Connor, Sue, Sandra Pannell, and Sally Brockwell. 2011. "Whose Culture and Heritage for Whom? Exploring the Limitations of National Public Good Protected Area Models in East Timor." In *Rethinking Cultural Resource Management in Southeast Asia: Preservation, Development and Neglect*, ed. John N. Miksic, Geok Yian Goh, and Sue O'Connor, 39–66. London: Anthem Press.

O'Connor, Sue, Matthew Spriggs, and Peter Veth. 2002. "Excavation at Lene Hara Establishes Occupation in East Timor 30,000–35,000 Years Ago." *Antiquity* 76: 45–50.

Pannell, Sandra. 2003. "Exploring the Narrative Terrains of Terror and Violence in the Spice Islands." In *A State of Emergency: Violence, Society and the State in Eastern Indonesia*, ed. Sandra Pannell, 77–104. Darwin: NTU Press.

Scott, James C. 1985. *Weapons of the Weak: Everyday Forms of Peasant Resistance*. New Haven, CT: Yale University Press.

Taussig, Michael. 1987. *Shamanism, Colonialism and the Wild Man: A Study of Terror and Healing*. Chicago: University of Chicago Press.

Traube, Elizabeth G. 1986. *Cosmology and Social Life: Ritual Exchange among the Mambai of East Timor*. Chicago: University of Chicago Press.

Trigger, Bruce. 1984. "Alternative Archaeologies: Nationalist, Colonialist, Imperialist." *Man* 19 (3): 355–70. http://dx.doi.org/10.2307/2802176.

Trigger, Bruce G. 1989. *A History of Archaeological Thought*. Cambridge: Cambridge University Press.

Vroklage, B.A.G. 1953. *Ethnographie der Belu in Zentral-Timor*. Leiden: E.J. Brill.

Wurm, Stephen A., and Shiro Hattori. 1981. *Language Atlas of the Pacific Area*. Canberra: Australian Academy of the Humanities.

24

Ritual Uses of Caves in West Malaysia

Joseph J. Hobbs

Many readers of this volume are accustomed to considering caves as sacred spaces exclusively in historical and archaeological terms. Others, archaeologists of the Maya in particular, are fortunate enough to brush shoulders regularly with people who still believe in the sanctity of caves. The beliefs and activities of the cave-reverent people of today are important in their own right, and there is an urgent need to document them before they, too, pass into history and archaeology. They are also important for their ethno-archaeological value. By understanding what constitutes sacred space around the world in modern times, it may be possible to acquire valuable tools for interpreting the past. Much research and theoretical consideration remain to be done to establish how and under what conditions the present may shed light on the past.

With the expectation that such efforts will be made, and with the conviction that present cave beliefs and rituals already do help shed light on the past, this chapter offers both emic and etic perspectives on modern cave ritual in one especially active region, West Malaysia. Arguably, the most diverse and vibrant ritual uses of caves anywhere in the world today are in the 50-kilometer stretch of tower karst (turmkarst) centered on Ipoh in Perak state, with an outlier farther south, at mainland Asia's southernmost karst tower near Kuala Lumpur in Selangor state (figure 24.1) (Allen 1961; Crowther 1978; Price 2001, 8, 10). In this area the author conducted open-ended interviews with cave visitors in June and July 2001.

The sacred caves visited in that survey number forty-four, including the nine Hindu cave sites of the Batu Caves complex near Kuala Lumpur; eleven Hindu cave temples around Ipoh; the Sai Baba cave temple near Ipoh; and twenty-three cave temples, cave monasteries, or undeveloped caves near Ipoh that may be described broadly as Buddhist and Taoist. A complete gazetteer of the region's caves, including those with sacred associations, is published in Price (2001; see also her website, cavesofmalaysia.com). None of Malaysia's cave-temple structures is very old. Except for a 400-year-old Buddhist cave temple, the oldest dates to about 1850. Several were founded in the 1890s and 1920s. There was a period of restoration and expansion in the early 1980s. But by far the greatest activity is going on today; it may be said that the "golden age" of ritual cave construction, rediscovery, reconsecration and use is the present. When this fieldwork was conducted, most of the major cave temples in the region were in the midst of multiyear renovations and additions that included excavation of new passages and construction of new shrines, while temples were being erected for the first time in many lesser caves. This chapter begins with a survey of the chief religious traditions behind these activities, and some of their characteristic temples and other material expressions.

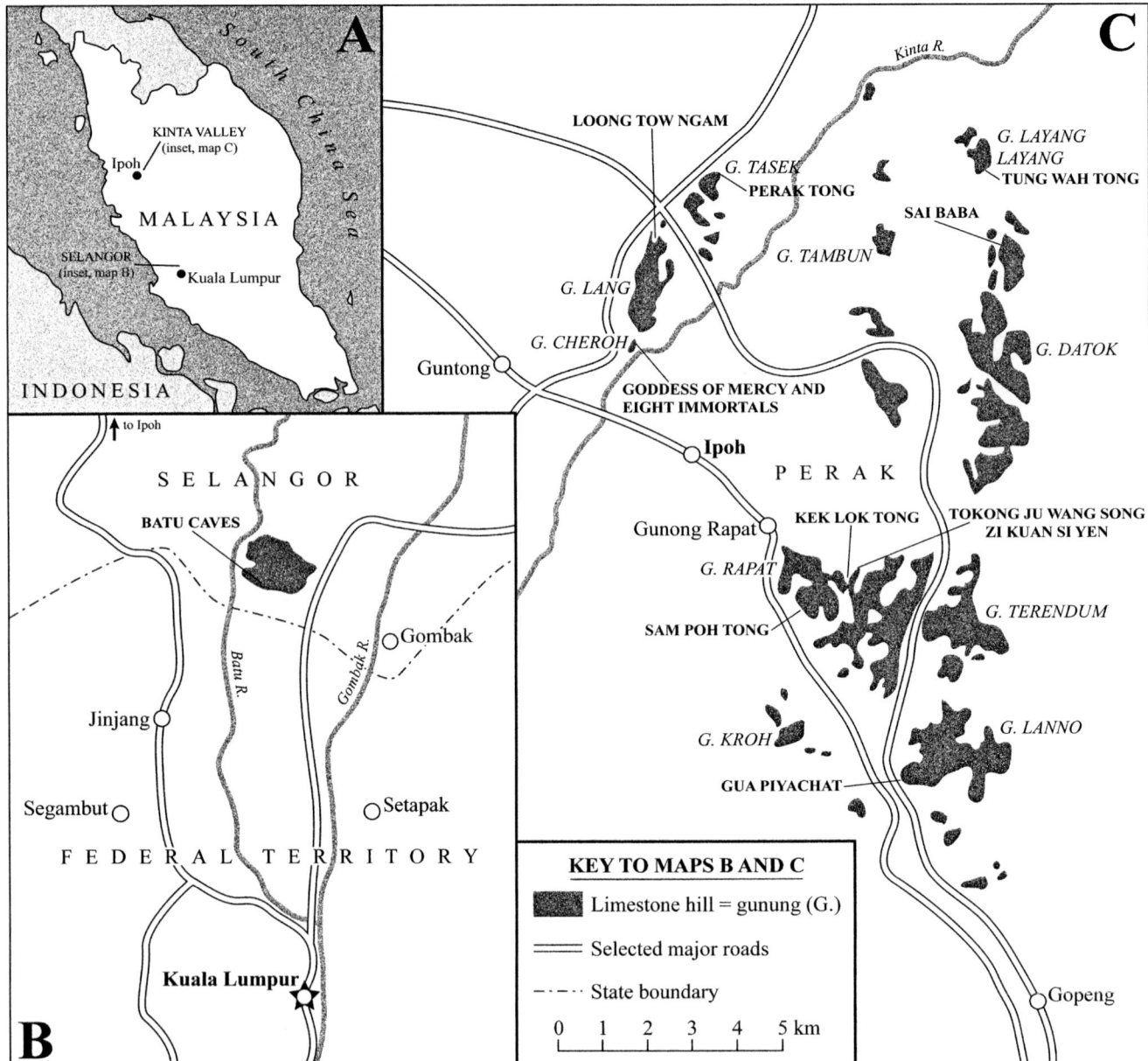

FIGURE 24.1 (A) Malaysia, showing karst regions and principal cave temples of (B) the Batu Caves, Selangor state, north of Kuala Lumpur, and (C) the Kinta Valley near Ipoh. (Cartography by Andrew Dolan, University of Missouri Department of Geography; after Crowther 1978, 200.)

THE SITES AND THEIR CONTEXT

Representing Malaysia's prosperous Chinese minority (24% of the country's population), the Buddhist presence is very strong, particularly in the Kinta Valley around Ipoh. Both the Therevada and Mahayana traditions are represented, but the Mahayana, with their rich admixture of beliefs and iconography, prevail. The most renowned Mahayanist site is Sam Poh Tong ("Three Buddhas Cave"; *tong* means "cave"), dating to 1890 and still serving as an active monastery. The archetypal Mahayanist cave temple imagery features a central figure of the Vairocana Buddha seated on a 108-petal lotus flower, delivering the Hwa Yen (Avatamsaka) Sutra (figure 24.2). He is flanked by the Bodhisattvas of transcendental wisdom and knowledge (Manjusri, seated on a lion) and universal virtue (Samantabbadra, seated on an elephant). Maitreya, the Buddha of the Future or the

FIGURE 24.2 The Vairocana Buddha, flanked by the Bodhisattvas of transcendental wisdom (seated on a lion) and knowledge and universal virtue (on an elephant), Kek Look Tong Temple, Ipoh.

laughing Buddha, is also prominent in these temples. So is Kwan Yin (the "Goddess of Mercy," the feminine version of Avalokiteshvara, the Bodhisattva of compassion (figure 24.3). Until its closure in 2003, one temple in Ipoh was in fact dedicated to a living figure many believe to be an incarnation of Kwan Yin, the Cliff Temple of Tokong Ju Wang Song Zi Kuan Si Yin. Residing mainly in Taiwan, the cave's namesake dignitary travels all over East Asia ministering to the sick and healing them miraculously. Locals explain that her curative power comes "from Buddha." She does bear an uncanny resemblance to the generic depiction of Kwan Yin statuary around the Ipoh temples. She was thronged by the faithful from as far away as Singapore when she visited this shrine in June 1999.

The Taoist tradition, in which caves are seen as receptacles of subtle energy, is very strongly interwoven with the Buddhist (Munier 1998, 37). Some of the cave temples, including Kek Look Tong and Tung Wah Tong, lean more strongly to Taoism, and are more ostentatious and lively than their rather serene Buddhist counterparts. Typically they contain central figures of Buddha and Bodhisattvas, but they can also have special chambers and altars dedicated to Taoist deities and heroes such as the Jade Emperor (Yu Huang), to the god of prosperity (Lu Xing), to the beneficent Emperor of Hell, who chose to remain there to help others get out, to the Three Pure Ones, or to Lao Tse himself (figure 24.4). There is also a single temple (Chee Chai Dudjom) representing the Bhutanese Lamaist tradition, close to Sam Poh Tong on Gunung Rapat.

In the Kinta Valley and just north of Kuala Lumpur are numerous Hindu cave temples. These represent the traditions of 80 percent of Malaysia's Tamils, who came to serve British interests in the rubber and tin industries, beginning in the nineteenth century, and who are West Malaysia's most underprivileged ethnic group. The greatest Hindu site is the complex in and around the Batu Caves (dating to 1891), 15 kilometers north of downtown Kuala Lumpur.

While the great majority of the region's sacred caves are identifiable as belonging in either mainstream Buddhist, Taoist, or Hindu traditions, a few represent offshoots from these, and some are notable for bridging faiths. Especially prominent is the cave temple dedicated to Sathya Sai Baba, who was born in India in 1926 and who would, he said, die at age 96 (he passed away in 2011). Claiming to be the incarnation of the nineteenth-century Sai Baba of Shirdi,

FIGURE 24.3 Statue of Kwan Yin outside the cave temple of Kek Look Tong, Ipoh.

and of Siva and Sakti, Sai Baba encouraged his followers to practice what he said are five fundamental and universal virtues (truth, righteousness, peace, universal love, and nonviolence). Said to have 6,500 congregations in 137 countries, he encouraged practitioners of all other faiths to participate, and used the Christian gospels in his message (Brooke 1979). This explains the extraordinary conjunction of icons and statuary in the Sai Baba temple and shrines around Ipoh: Buddhist, Hindu, Catholic, and figures of Sai Baba himself. But this convergence of distinct religious traditions is not restricted to Sai Baba's following. In numerous caves around Ipoh one may see the side-by-side placement and worship of Buddhist and Hindu icons. James Ong, an ethnic Chinese living in Ipoh, replied with enthusiasm to a question on whether Chinese and Hindu traditions could mix: "We have a temple with five religions in Ipoh!"

There are also "animistic" elements in the caves, although they are seldom manifested in shrines and statuary. In the Southeast Asian Buddhist traditions, cave spirits are associated with snakes, yaks, lions, tigers, and monkeys (Munier 1998, 170). Fieldwork for this chapter did not include interviews about these spirits. These beliefs are probably accessible only in oral accounts, and further work will be needed to document them. Longtime Malaysian cave explorer Liz Price reported that at a cave in Pahang state, she met a group of Indians who were to stay in the cave until they could successfully summon a spirit that would accompany home one of their members (personal communication, 2005).

Perhaps related to the animistic properties of the caves, and certainly part of the spirituality associated with them, is what may be called the "karst aesthetic" that is most prominent in the Buddhist traditions. The natural beauty and lyrical appeal of surface karst landscapes such as those around Guilin has long influenced Chinese art and literature, and inspired landscape manipulation with pavilions, fountains, and statuaries set around natural or artificial grottoes. Across Southeast Asia, this karst aethetic has even generated a unique "zen kitsch" of concrete and polymer karst sculptures, replete with pagodas, waterfalls, and tigers (figure 24.5). Appreciation of the counterpart subsurface features seems to have grown apace, imbuing vocabulary and image-making in the Chinese cave temple culture of

FIGURE 24.4 Taoist figures in the Goddess of Mercy and Eight Immortals Cave Temple, Ipoh.

West Malaysia. Natural formations within the caves are likened to dancing dragons, wriggling snakes, gushing waterfalls, pillars of beads, human silhouettes, and wild beasts (Kek Look Tong Temple 2001). Some speleothems, notably the striking elephant-like formation of the Kong Fook Ngam Cave Temple, have inevitably become identified with certain historic characters and deities (in this case, Sakka's vehicle, the three headed elephant Erawan). These associations, even with the wild beasts, are above all benign and comforting, and the cave faithful experience a sense of harmony with nature—a marked contrast with many other cultures' dread of the underground.

THE RITUALS

An extraordinarily diverse array of rituals and related activities takes place in these caves. In the category of "miscellaneous purposes," caves of Peninsular Malaysia serve as a Buddhist youth retreat, a Buddhist meditation center, as "art galleries" to relate the major events of the Ramayana and of a Tamil poet's life, as a crematorium, and as a columbarium, where the ashes of the deceased are reposed.

Mainly, however, the caves serve as places of worship, prayer, and meditation. In the daily *puja* at cave shrines and temples, Hindus make offerings to their deities (figure 24.6). Buddhists have no specified times or days for prayer, but the sites are especially busy on the ninth day of the lunar new year, on All Souls' Day, and on other special occasions. Hindus conduct rituals even in caves without temples. Prayers and offerings are made at natural speleothems in what wild caves—those that have not been converted into temples—there still are. In Perak's Gua Kelawar, for example, the faithful burn joss sticks and make offerings of soda and alcoholic beverages at the bases of stalagmites and other speleothems. Other wild caves are said to be favored sites for the divination of winning lottery numbers (discussed below), of foreign "new agers" who are, according to local observers, "seeking good vibes," and for drug taking. (Reportedly, an especially favored site for all of these activities was the Ramayana Cave at Batu Caves, before it became an "art gallery.")

Both votive and thanksgiving prayers and offerings characterize cave temple use. These rituals have a substantial material component that should be of interest to all

What is not self-evident is *why* people leave their offerings—that is, what their wishes are—but the author's interviews reveal some of their intentions. Here are a few representative explanations. The Goddess of Mercy has many manifestations in Buddhist cave shrines and temples, and these serve different needs. School children pray at the Goddess of Mercy for Education to succeed in their exams. Kwan Yin is also an object of votive offerings for better health. Some of the cave temples contain statues of the five deities, often associated with Chinese fortune telling, representing wood, gold, water, fire, and earth. A deity may have been offended, and if one is ill or has failed to find a spouse, one may pray and make offerings to identify and reconcile with that deity. Wishes for success and prosperity in business are very common—and very appropriate for the goal-oriented Chinese—who burn sometimes enormous (1-meter high) joss sticks, along with paper objects symbolizing cash, gold, automobiles, or homes. Devotees at

FIGURE 24.5 The karst aesthetic. This display of the popular Vietnamese miniature landscape artform known as *hòn non bộ* is outside a hotel in northern Vietnam.

who study cave offerings in other contexts. At Buddhist sites, people leave tins of vegetable oil, fruit, cakes, beer (especially Guinness), and cigarettes; and at the Hindu sites, of vegetarian food, flowers, incense, and sometimes blood from the ritual slaughter of animals (a practice introduced from Tamil Nadu) (Ferro-Luzzi 1977; Flood 1996, 208). These substances and artifacts accumulate so quickly that they often have to be removed on a daily or even more frequent basis. At one shrine in Perak Tong on All Souls' Day, incense sticks were being deposited so rapidly that the attendant had to remove them about every 10 minutes to make space for new ones (Liz Price, personal communication, 2005). At Sam Poh Tong, the release of turtles—as an offering meant to return good fortune—has grown out of control. Several pool surfaces are crowded with turtles desperately paddling in search of haulouts, or resting on dead turtles. Some of the faithful ignore signs reading "no turtle releases allowed now," presumably meant to address the overcrowding.

FIGURE 24.6 The Hindu faithful at Batu Caves, a temple complex centered on the worship of Murugan (Subramanium).

the Lamaist cave temple of Chee Chai Dudjom explained that their most common wish was for better health. In the annual Thaipusam ritual, Hindus carry to Batu Caves and other caves the miniature shrines called *kavadis*, which represent the burden of ignorance. The supplicant first carries the kavadi to make a wish, for example for recovery from illness, healthy delivery of a baby, or reconciliation within a family. He or she has made a pact that if the wish is fulfilled, he or she will return for three subsequent years bearing kavadis of thanksgiving. Buddhists also commonly respond to the fulfillment of votive prayers with thanksgiving offerings and prayers.

Also in the category of votive and thanksgiving rituals, what Malaysians call "white" and "black" magic must be considered. Both are increasingly common, mainly among Muslim Malaysians, and are of much concern to the Muslim government, which regards them as heretical or satanic. Both are frequently associated with caves. In the innocuous "white" magic, people pray and make offerings in caves to divine the four winning numbers of the national lottery, for example, or to bring rain, or to win a spouse. "Black magic" is the label attached to rituals that generally involve exorcism, and which all too often are associated with beatings and even murders in caves. Such rituals are not restricted to Muslim Malaysians. In 2002, Malaysian newspapers carried sensational accounts of an ethnic Chinese bride-to-be beaten by her brother, his girlfriend, and several other family members in order to free her of evil spirits. The venue chosen for this violent exorcism was a cave in Kuantan (Star Online News 2002).

Conspicuous by its absence is any "mainstream" tradition of cave ritual among Malaysia's majority Muslims. Caves certainly have an important place in Islam; the prophet Muhammad was meditating in the cave of Hiraa, outside Mecca, when God began transmitting the Koran to him in AD 622. However, there has never been a broader tradition of cave mosques or *masjids*. Islam disdains iconography, and the colorful pantheons of Malaysia's Hindu and Buddhist cave temples are anathema to the austerity of Muslim worship. Hindu informants related that many Muslims do not climb the stairs to the Cathedral Cave Hindu temples at Batu Caves because they would end up above the level of mosques in the area. Others said it was sacrilege for Muslims to visit any Hindu temples, and only "one percent" or "very liberal" Muslims do. It must be noted that there are very few temples in caves of the northeastern states of Kelantan and Terengganu, which are predominantly Muslim areas, and also very few in the states of Perlis and Kedah, where caves tend to be in areas inhabited mainly by Muslims (Liz Price, personal communication, 2005. In 2011 she observed a Muslim prayer room behind a dumpling factory at the mouth of an Ipoh cave).

Thaipusam is the only notable cave-related ritual in Malaysia that is associated with pilgrimage—and a major pilgrimage it is. Over a period of three days around the full moon in January or February, up to a million Hindus participate in it. This festival commemorates Parvati's giving of the "electric spear" or *vel* to the god Murugan (also called Subramanium) (Arasaratnam 1966). There are several Thaipusam festivals in the country, but the overwhelmingly largest—with up to a million participants—begins with the transfer of the image of the god Murugan by chariot from a temple in downtown Kuala Lumpur to the Batu Caves, 15 kilometers away. Chanting, music, drumming, and incense burning accompany the procession of tens of thousands, during which most of the pilgrims make offerings to the deity. These include fruit, milk, money, hair, roosters, and peacocks (the two animals most closely associated with Murugan; Clothey 1978, 180). At the foot of the mountain containing the Batu caves, aspirants achieve a trancelike state, and many mortify their flesh with skewers and hooks of various kinds. These symbolize the spear with which Murugan vanquished his enemy. Their kavadis are then outfitted with images of Murugan, milk, and other offerings. Amidst the masses, they ascend the 272 steps to the great Cathedral Cave and deposit their offerings within its main shrine, thus fulfilling the formal aspect of their vows (figure 24.7) (Arasaratnam 1966; Belle 1998; Cheam and Gwynne 1999, 116; Clothey 1978; Moore 1989, 59).

Another distinct set of cave rituals and other spiritual practices relates to Buddhist monasticism. Several caves around Ipoh are hermitages and monasteries representing the Lamaist, Mahayana, and Theravada traditions. The two monks residing at the Lamaist temple-monastery of Chee Chai Dudjom are renowned for their intervention on behalf of the sick. The Thai Therevada tradition is represented by a few monks and nuns who prefer caves in remote areas above all other places. In "Gua Piyachat," a cave in the hill of Gunung Lanno south of Ipoh, a Thai nun named Piyachat relocated from Had Yai to take up residence in 1999. She explained that she came originally to meditate but then began to administer to the spiritual and other needs of devout people who sought her out. Her reputation as a healer grew quickly and spread far (she gets visitors from Singapore), and she took on volunteer help to expand the cave's physical capacity. Each Sunday, several families from Ipoh assist Piyachat in widening and lengthening the cave's passageways, toiling with chisels, hammers, shovels, and wheelbarrows. Asked why she was going to all this effort, she was elusive. It is notable, however, that many monasteries in Southeast Asia originated when hermits and monks lived in caves, and people came to visit and feed them. As the caves' fame spread, still more monks came to live in them and ultimately they became monasteries

FIGURE 24.7 The stairway to Cathedral Cave, Batu Caves.

FIGURE 24.8 Sister Mae Chee Piyachat in her cave.

(Munier 1998, 159). That is how, according to locals, Sam Poh Tong originated. It is possible that Piyachat sees herself as a potential founder of such as establishment. There is also a broader Buddhist tradition of "improving" caves, especially by expanding them, as a meritorious act. King Li Thai of Sukhothai in AD 1345 wrote that one of the best epitaphs one might earn would be that "he accomplished good deeds, mainly . . . took care of his parents, respected elderly people, loved his brothers, other people, the monks and his masters [and] gave yellow robes, built stupas, fitted out caves, cells for monks, built monasteries" (Munier 1998, 165).

Piyachat is not evasive about the effectiveness of her mission. Responding to the question "Can you cure people?" she laughed and said "People come to this place every night and pray to Buddha. These are sick people." What kind of sicknesses do they have? "Number One is money, Number Two is family. I help them to see themselves . . . When you meditate, your mind and soul are composed and you achieve wisdom." This is a happy, whimsical place, made all the more pleasant by Piyachat's constant beaming visage (figure 24.8). Incidentally, she takes appointments by her cell phone, which works well at the mouth of the cave.

DISCUSSION

An overarching question that emerged in the course of this fieldwork was one that is central to this volume: "Why caves?" Why are these people of various ethnic and religious backgrounds so motivated to observe their beliefs and practice their rituals in caves? There are two ways to address this question, first the emic with what the people themselves say, and then the etic with social scientific interpretations.

Piyachat responded to the question of why she chose her cave. "I came first because it's quiet, and cool, and good for meditation." The monks of Chee Chai Dudjom also said they came to the cave here because it is a quiet place, but added they could use any quiet place, not just a cave, for the same spiritual effect. The proprietor at the cave temple of Kek Look Tong ("Cave of Great Happiness") said, "The name of this cave means happiness. The cave makes people feel happy, and you feel fresh in a cave." At Perak Tong, the

Chinese caretaker explained why this cave was chosen for a temple. The founder brought his ideas here from China in 1926: "In China there are a lot of caves, especially Taoist caves, that are temples; this is true of mountains, too. These Taoists recognize *fengshui* in mountains and caves, and because of those concepts the founder had the idea to convert this place to a temple and attract people." Another Chinese Buddhist did not share this diffusionist view. "Why are Buddhist temples in caves? Because caves are a place of seclusion, away from the crowd, a retreat, places with the beauty of nature. Attraction to caves has nothing to do with Buddha. It is a local tradition, local to Malaysia." A Chinese woman from Ipoh said, "Buddhists favor caves because there you divest yourself of homes and other material goods."

A young, educated Hindu man explained why the Batu Caves' main temple is situated where it is: "The temple is here because there is a mountain, and this is the only one that you have a cave within it, so it is a very special one. On top of a mountain and within a cave is very, very special." I then asked, "What is especially important about a cave?" to which he answered, "Most of our hermits and all of our saints used to meditate in them, and they are very special and peaceful . . . that is in the Tamil Nadu tradition specifically. So, this combination of factors makes Batu Caves an obvious site." A young Tamil woman who is not literate explained why the Murugan temple at Ipoh is located in a cave. "We believe he liked to stay in caves," she said. "The story is that in Palani, India, he [Murugan] had been in an argument with his brother Ganesh, and his parents Siva and Sakti sent him to a cave. So people like to make his temples in caves." Indeed, one of Murugan's names is *Guha*, "the One Who Dwells in the Cave" (Smith and Narasimhachary 1997, 227).

From social scientific perspectives, there are other explanations for the importance of caves in the West Malaysian traditions. It has been argued that, for Hindus, the cave and its natural superstructure constitute a natural temple. A human-made temple is an effort to reconstitute the mountain, while its chambers mimic the cave as a place of retreat and as the occasional habitation of the gods. Thus the cave is the original and archetypal temple of the Hindus—an obvious draw to them:

> In all Hindu temples the sanctuary is strongly reminiscent of a cave; it is invariably small and dark as no natural light is permitted to enter, and the surfaces of the walls are unadorned and massive. Penetration toward the image or symbol of the deity housed in this setting is always through a progression from light into darkness, from open and large spaces to a confined and small space. This movement from complexity of visual experience to that of simplicity may be interpreted by the devotee as a progression of increasing sanctity culminating in the focal point of the temple, the cave or "womb." Accompanying the penetration toward the cave is the ascent upwards to the symbolic mountain peak, whose summit is positioned over the center of the cave-sanctuary. This means that the highest point of the elevation of the temple is aligned with the most sacred part of the temple, the center of the inner sanctuary which houses the image of the god. Summit and sacred center are linked together along an axis which is a powerful projection upwards of the forces of energy which radiate from the center of the sanctuary. (Michell 1988, 68)

In the Buddhist context, it has been argued that mountains were the islands that emerged from the waters that flooded the previous world. On these mountains, and in the caves they contained, the Buddha rested while delivering people from their suffering (Munier 1998, 6). The Buddha was said to have frequently meditated in caves (although he made a point of the fact that he did not reach enlightenment in a cave), and so monks have preferred them for centuries in their spiritual quests. Munier points out that statues of the Buddha in meditation are more numerous in caves than in temples (1998, 165), and also discusses the exceptionally powerful conjunction of cave and mountain in the Buddhist context:

> Caves are often isolated from the world, sometimes dominating it, difficult to reach, mysterious and magic, secret and sacred places believed to be inhabited by angels or demons. After having first been occupied during prehistoric times, they became places where *rishis* [divinely inspired poets] and monks came to follow their spiritual quests.
>
> Being both closed and open spaces materializing the concept of interiority, caves seem to be more linked to human beings than rocks. While rocks are "objects" caves fit the idea of a "subject": be they womb-caves, from where we all are born, or cave-tombs, like those of the Tang emperors, or places where hermits meditate to transcend the cycle of life and death, caves have a universal appeal. When parts of sacred mountains they are mythical places where Immortals, *arahants*, *bodhisattas*, Buddhas and Pacceka Buddhas live, inaccessible to the non-purified ones. To find such caves is a proof of purity: one must overcome obstacles or else have a guide. (1998, 12)

The topographic conjunction of cave and mountain is thus highly meaningful for these cultures (as it is, coincidentally, for the ancient and modern Maya). The extensive crematoria of Sam Poh Tong and the related columbaria and stalls for venerating ancestors may well be explained by Munier's observation that the mountain and cave combine to form a huge reliquary or stupa: "The funerary value of mountains and caves are considered alive, as the relics, having been parts of those who transcended life and death, are not dead and burnt bones but seeds. The rocks and caves that contain them will thus attract people and become places for pilgrimage. The future is the very reason for the existence of the relics" (1998, 39). This author also underscores the natural architectural advantage of caves as places of Buddhist worship: caves are "made of" rock, and are superior sites in an environmental setting where wood succumbs to the elements (1998, 36).

Perhaps most significantly, cave temples and cave rituals serve important roles in expressions of ethnic solidarity and resilience in Malaysia. They reflect the economic and political fortunes of the country's Indian and Chinese communities. The Indians represent just 8 percent of Malaysia's population, and the Chinese 24 percent. As these minorities see it, the majority ethnic Malays are not willing to yield their political and cultural preeminence in national affairs, and are trying to build a greater Malaysian culture on Islamic principles. Malaysian political life has polarized into Muslim and non-Muslim spheres, with the Muslims dominant or ascendant. Unable to assert themselves politically, Indians and Chinese are increasingly asserting their identities and voices as Hindus and Buddhists in the religious realm (Ackerman and Lee 1988; Belle 1998). Caves are central in the religious traditions of both groups, so it is little wonder that there has been a recent boom in cave-temple construction and ritual visitation. In some instances, this construction may be designed to offset perceived Muslim destruction of other Buddhist and Hindu sites. Early in 2005, for example, the state government of Negeri Sembilan announced a plan to raze ten Buddhist and Hindu temples in the province (Star Online News 2005).

Some particular cave sites and events associated with them play an especially strong role in validating and invigorating these minority cultures. Thaipusam at Batu Caves serves both to advance the universal Hindu presence in Malaysia and to instill special pride and sense of place among the formerly lower caste, the historically disadvantaged Tamil Hindus. Murugan was originally a "folkish" deity, part of the "little tradition" brought to Malaysia by colonial era Tamil laborers (Belle 1998; Clothey 1978, 31; Ellmore 1984; Whitehead 1980). In Tamil Nadu, where Murugan originated, he was revered almost exclusively by the less educated, disadvantaged Tamils, while the educated Tamils and most other Indians followed Siva (Rasainthiran Menayah, personal communication, 2001). Today, Thaipusam at Batu Caves is the preeminent event of the Hindu year in Malaysia, and its protagonist Murugan has taken his place among the most revered of the Hindu deities for all spectrums of Hindu society in the country, and even draws some Sikhs, Sinhalese, and Chinese devotees (Belle 1998).

Ipoh's Perak Tong, acknowledged as the most popular cave-temple destination for Peninsular Malaysia's Chinese minority, plays an especially strong role in reinvigorating the solidarity of that ethnic community. Its standing was underscored by the temple's proprietor, Wong Soon Teck: "Perak Tong is the only *tong* in Malaysia where you can find all the Chinese cultural characteristics: the famous artists from Taiwan, China, Hong Kong created here. This is a place to maintain and continue Chinese culture."

Any threats to the cave-temples cultures of West Malaysia thus may threaten the cohesion of these minority groups. There are diverse dangers to the cave traditions. The tin and iron ore boom of Malaysia has passed into history, and along with it the high-impact tin mining that took place within numerous caves in the Peninsula (including the cave-temple site of Kek Look Tong), to be replaced by the even more destructive force of quarrying for marble and for cement. Gunung Cheroh and other karst hills around Ipoh are prized targets in the Kinta Valley's building boom, and in many cases quarrying concessions and activities extend to the very thresholds of the cave temples. There are also "secular" uses of caves that the faithful insist are dangerous, particularly drug taking. Another source of competition for cave use comes from poor squatters, mainly Tamil, who have taken up residence in numerous caves and rockshelters around Ipoh. Tragically, since the early 1970s rockfalls have taken many squatters' lives.

Some of the faithful also fear that money, even greed, often ostensibly linked to cave ritual, might undo the integrity of the cave traditions. Some of the temples are very wealthy. Endowment of the temples is an old tradition—governors, patriarchs, notables, and businessmen have all contributed (Munier 1998, 165)—but much of the wealth accumulates from the donations and admissions receipts from the everyday faithful. An ethnic Chinese couple in Ipoh scoffed at the Buddhist cave temple boom there: "The motive for the expansion of the Chinese caves is purely commercial. Why extend the Loong Tow Ngam ['Dragon Head'] cave, as they are doing? Maybe it's a form of doing good deeds. Maybe it's to get karmic points. Maybe it's for prestige. And maybe it's for money." Some of the Hindu faithful at Batu Caves complained that there is a "donation" charge for each shrine visited, making the temple very wealthy, and added that Thaipusam was immensely profitable for the temple. One said, "A lot of Hindus don't like the Batu Temple. The temple authorities provide no services—they just charge and sweep up. Just to say prayers on an ordinary day is 18 ringgits! [= $5 US]. They are so rich!" Another pointed to the planned 6.5 million ringgit ($1.7 million) development of the Batu Caves area that would include a park with shops and scenic attractions: "The Batu Caves Temple is fearful this will divert tourism away from the Batu Caves." The Batu Caves temple authorities had tried to acquire Dark Cave, presently a wild cave managed for nature tourism by the Malaysian Nature Society. With its entrance just opposite that of Batu's most important Cathedral Cave, Dark Cave would have made a fine location for a Vishnu Temple, the authorities thought. The Selangor provincial government blunted this effort, according to Malaysian Nature Society personnel, not such much to protect the wild status of the cave as slow the growing wealth and power of the Batu Temple.

A growing tide of mainly secular tourists also spends on donations, souvenirs, and services at the cave temples. Supplementing the longtime traffic of South Korean and Taiwanese visitors, a boom in tourism by wealthy Chinese since 1995 has brought a particularly large infusion of money into Ipoh's Buddhist cave temples.

At the larger temples throughout West Malaysia, all of these sources of revenue help to expand infrastructure, while smaller temples struggle to raise funds and compete for visitors with expansions of their own. To the outsider, Ipoh in particular may look like so many cave-temple theme parks jostling for business.

Pursuit of the almighty dollar—or in this case the almighty ringgit—certainly is partly responsible for this being the "golden age" of West Malaysian cave temples. Interviews with the faithful however, make it clear that caves are something far more meaningful than moneymaking meccas. Whether through their sacred shrines or the resources of the people like Piyachat who inhabit them, the caves help individuals who need help, and in turn encourage them to help others. They foster companionship and socialization; even monks and nuns visit every day with the faithful, including children, who feed them. They demand participation through ritual, and help build and reaffirm a sense of community. They bestow a strong sense of place that bolsters ethnic identity. Finally, they may even promote not just ethnic cohesion but also ethnic tolerance. Nowhere is this more evident than in an Ipoh cave shared by multiple faiths, where images of Kwan Yin, Hanuman, and Christ stand side by side.

ACKNOWLEDGMENTS

I am grateful especially to Liz Price, who gave so much of her time to sharing with me the cultural and natural wonders of West Malaysia's caves. Ms. Price also proofed this manuscript and updated the status of the temples through mid-2012. Rajan Menayah, Suja Yussof, Sister Mae Chee Piyachat, and Phang Kooi Yoong and her husband Ooi Sze Hwa kindly put me up in Ipoh for the duration of my stay. Lee Sooi Fong was generous in introducing me to the Long Tow Ngan Temple, and James Ong and David Chong also took time to show me several sites. Andy Dolan was patient and meticulous with his cartography. This research was made possible by funding by the University of Missouri Faculty Summer Research Program, the University of Missouri Department of Geography, the National Speleological Society, the Association of American Geographers, and by my mother, Mary Ann Hobbs-Frakes. I owe my life of fieldwork to her inspiration.

REFERENCES CITED

Ackerman, Susan E., and Raymond M. Lee. 1988. *Heaven in Transition: Non Muslim Religious Innovation and Ethnic Identity in Malaysia*. Honolulu: University of Hawai'i Press.

Allen, Betty Molesworth. 1961. "Limestone Hills near Ipoh." *Malayan Nature Journal* Special Issue: Nature Conservation in West Malaysia 1961: 68–73.

Arasaratnam, S. 1966. *Indian Festivals in Malaya*. Kuala Lumpur: Marican and Sons.

Belle, Carl Vadivella. 1998. "Tai Pucam in Malaysia: An Incipient Hindu Unity." Paper presented at the First International Conference Seminar on Skanda-Murukan, Chennai, December 28–31. http://murugan.org/research/belle.htm.

Brooke, Tal. 1979. *Sai Baba: Lord of the Air*. New Delhi: Vikas.

Cheam, Jeremy, and Jessamyn Cheam Gwynne. 1999. *Insight Guides: Malaysia*. Singapore: APA.

Clothey, Fred W. 1978. *The Many Faces of Murukan: The History and Meaning of a South Indian God*. The Hague: Mouton.

Crowther, J. 1978. "Karst Regions and Caves of the Malay Peninsula, West of the Main Range." *Transactions of the British Cave Research Association* 5 (4): 199–214.

Ellmore, W. T. 1984. *Dravidian Gods in Modern Hindusim*. New Delhi: Asian Educational Service.

Ferro-Luzzi, Gabriella Eichinger. 1977. "The Logic of South Indian Food Offerings." *Anthropos* 72 (3–4): 529–56.

Flood, Gavin. 1996. *An Introduction to Hinduism*. Cambridge: Cambridge University Press.

Kek Look Tong Temple. 2001. "The History of Kek Look Tong." Unpublished brochure of the Kek Look Tong Cave Temple, Ipoh, Malaysia.

Michell, George. 1988. *The Hindu Temple: An Introduction to Its Meaning and Forms*. Chicago: University of Chicago Press.

Moore, Wendy. 1989. *Malaysia*. Lincolnwood, IL: Passport Books.

Munier, Christophe. 1998. *Sacred Rocks and Buddhist Caves in Thailand*. Bangkok: White Lotus.

Price, Liz. 2001. *Caves and Karst of Peninsular Malaysia*. Kuala Lumpur: Gua Publications.

Smith, H. Daniel, and M. Narasimhachary. 1997. *Handbook of Hindu Gods, Goddesses and Saints Popular in Contemporary South India*. Delhi: Sundeep Prakashan.

Star Online News. 2002. *Girl Battered to Rid Her of Evil*. Star Online News, January 2. http://thestar.com.my

Star Online News. 2005. *MCA to Probe Demolition of Temples*. Star Online News, January 27. http://thestar.com.my.

Whitehead, Henry. 1980. *The Village Gods of South India*. Delhi: Summit Publications.

25

A Quantitative Literature Survey Regarding the Uses and Perceptions of Caves among Nine Indigenous Andean Societies

Nathan Craig

This chapter reports on a regional study of cave use among nine indigenous cultures of western South America that are located along the Andean mountain chain. In many respects, the Andean region is superlative. Broadly defined either in terms of the mountain range or human perceptions of settlement on and around these mountains, the Andes are renowned for precocious cultural developments and exceptional archaeological preservation. Spanning over 7,000 kilometers from north to south, the Andean Cordillera is the largest exposed mountain range in the world. Some of the earliest inhabitants of the New World are found at Monte Verde in eastern Chile (Dillehay 1989). The Chinchorro mummies from the coast of southern Peru and northern Chile are among the earliest mummified human remains in the world (Arriaza 1995). The earliest large architecture in the Americas is found during the Late Preceramic on the central coast of Peru (Haas, Creamer, Ruiz 2004; Shady Solís, Haas, and Creamer 2001). The Andes are the only place in the Americas where large animals, llamas and alpacas, were domesticated. About the first century AD, the Moche established a pristine state on the north coast of Peru that flourished for 700 years (Stanish 2001). Two major empires, the Wari (Schreiber 1992) and Tiwanaku (Kolata 1996), flourished during the Middle Horizon. A third empire, the Chimor, developed during the Late Intermediate Period. A fourth—larger—empire, the Inca, arose during the Late Horizon.

Cultural landscape analysis has been a central theme of Andean studies for over 50 years (Moore 2004, 84). Still, rather than approaching Andean cave sites as vivid and powerful elements of the human landscape, archaeologists have overwhelmingly treated them as little more than protective containers that allowed for the accumulation of stratified cultural deposits and good organic preservation (Dransart 1997). Andean archaeologists have been ready to recognize the social and symbolic nature of architecture. However, when it comes to interpreting cave deposits, recognition of the social nature of space has not been an emphasized theme. When asked about caves, many Andean cultural anthropologists have anecdotally reported that caves are vitally important landscape features for modern Indigenous peoples of the highlands. Still, when several Andean archaeologists from both Peru and the United States have been questioned on the issue of caves, they consistently remarked that ritual use of caves has not developed as a prominent theme in the archaeological literature of the region. Thus, it seems that Andean archaeologists have approached caves as places to excavate for developing chronologies—not as places to search for cosmologies.

The present quantitative literature survey of cave uses and perceptions was undertaken in an effort to reconsider the behaviors that one might expect to have contributed to cave deposits both in the Andes and other world areas. The development of the sample of societies began by searching the electronic Human Relations Area Files (eHRAF) for the words *cave* and *cueva* and by examining entries that are generally considered Andean societies. At the time the search was submitted (10-21-2004), it only produced two strictly Andean societies: the Kogi and the Aymara. A sample of two was deemed insufficient for evaluating patterning. To increase the size and range of social types represented in the sample, consideration was given to a broader range of western South American cultures that live along the Andean mountain chain.

USE OF THE TERM *CAVE* IN THE PRESENT LITERATURE SURVEY

The Oxford English Dictionary defines *cave* as "a hollow place opening more or less horizontally under the ground" and it lists the earliest use of the term at circa AD 1220 in a medieval bestiary. Archaeologists often distinguish between caves, which have dark zones, and rockshelters, which lack dark zones but may have twilight zones (see Moyes, Introduction, this volume). Caves with extensive dark-zone areas are generally, though not necessarily always, formed in karstic landscapes.

Karstic deposits are present in the Andes, but they are far less extensive when compared to regions like Mesoamerica. Because of this, large dark-zone caves are far less common in the Andes than they are in Mesoamerica, where use of dark zone caves for ritual purposes is well documented. Limestone caves are known north of Huarochiri near the town of Moya and to the west of Pariacaca. South of Huarochiri near Yauyos more limestone caves have been reported. A group of cavers exploring this area discovered a single human skull and some other unidentified bones in a cave called Sima Pumacocha 4 (http://members.shaw.ca/pumacocha/pumapages/caves.htm website visited: 7-9-12). Many other limestone caves are likely present but have yet to be reported. Though deep limestone caves are not common, there are myriad reports of surface collections and excavations in small caves and rockshelters throughout the Andes. Though some dark-zone caves are present in the Andean region, most of the accounts of cave uses and perceptions encountered in this literature survey referred to twilight-zone rockshelters and small caves.

CULTURE GROUPS

The present sample of societies is far from exhaustive. However, it represents the largest and most diverse systematic treatment of cave use that I am aware has yet been attempted for the South American continent. In alphabetical order, the cultures included in the sample are: Alacaluf, Chonos, Inca, Kogi, Ona, Puelche, Quechua/Aymara, Tehuelche, and Yahgan. Many more societies could, and probably should, have been included. The selection of societies was constrained by time and access to source material in either Spanish or English.

The Alacaluf, Chonos, Ona, Puelche, Tehuelche, and Yahgan are all forager societies of the southern cone of South America. These societies represent two-thirds of the sample. The reason for such a high sampling density in one fairly restricted region was that several of the key texts cross-reference cultural practices of more than one group, and though information is limited, these cultures represent the best-documented foraging societies available for study in western South America. Because a large fraction of Andean cave excavations have focused on Archaic hunter-gatherers, it is useful to have some societies in the sample that reflect this general economic mode even if there is some sampling bias. The Kogi, Inca, and Quechua/Aymara are all agropastoral societies. The Kogi are a transegalitarian society. The Inca represent the only empire in the sample. The modern Quechua/Aymara cultures have descended from pre-Columbian empires, but they are probably best described today as peasant societies. Regrettably, there is no classically defined chiefdom included in this sample.

FUEGAN AND PATAGONIAN HUNTER-GATHERERS

Historic and early ethnographic accounts of indigenous inhabitants from Tierra del Fuego and Patagonia form some of the few rare and important firsthand descriptions of South American hunter-gatherers. Though some of these societies persisted into the historic period, their cultural patterns cannot be considered pristine at the time of description. They had already been decimated by Contact-related diseases brought about by the formation of Salesian missions (Martin 1969; Skottsberg 1913, pl. XXXVI). Living ancestors of these historic groups remain to varying degrees, but their culture has been profoundly transformed through acculturation. Few, if in some cases any, native speakers remain alive today.

The Yahgan were maritime hunter-gatherers who inhabited the far southernmost portion of the Andes Mountains before this range descends into the sea at Cape Horn. The Alacaluf were maritime hunter-gatherers who inhabited the region around the Brunswick Peninsula archipelago of the Chilean coast, from the Gulf of Peñas to the islands west of Tierra del Fuego (Bird 1963). The Chono were maritime hunter-gatherers who occupied the Chonos archipelago of southern Chile (Cooper 1963a). The Ona inhabited Tierra del Fuego and they were primarily terrestrial hunters who relied heavily on guanaco.

The Alacaluf, Chonos, Ona, and Yahgan are treated separately in the *Handbook of South American Indians*

(Steward 1963). The Ona and Yaghan have been described as patricentric bilocal bands (Burton et al. 1996, 107). The Tehuelche are a Patagonian society who have been considered together with the Ona as forming the "Tehuelche Complex" (Siffredi 2002, 299). The Ona recognized two subgroups, the Haush and the Selk'nam, but they are treated here as one culture. The Puelche were Patagonian and pampa peoples who after Contact rode and hunted wild horses. The Tehuelche were Patagonian hunters who subsided largely on guanaco and rheas (Cooper 1963b, 141). Information on the Fuegan and Patagonian foragers comes almost completely from such historical sources as travelers' journals and missionary accounts. Some of these, like the works of Father Martin Gusinde, are marvelously detailed accounts. But his work is exceptional. In general, information on cave use had to be culled from lengthy texts devoted largely to other subjects.

Agropastoralists

With its capital in Cuzco, Peru, and spanning more than 5,500 kilometers of the Andes mountains, the Inca were the largest native state to arise in the Western Hemisphere and the largest ancient empire to ever develop in the Southern Hemisphere (Moseley 1992, 7). Scholars generally view the beginnings of the Inca polity sometime around AD 1200; imperial expansion began circa AD 1438 and lasted until the Spanish conquest in AD 1532 (Rowe 1963, 200). Three of many possible ethnohistoric sources on the Inca were consulted. The texts were selected because they reflect two radically different perspectives present in early historical writing in the Americas (Salomon 1999): native authors and priests. The texts consulted were the native chronicler Guaman Poma de Ayala (1978 [1615]), Father Bernabé Cobo (1990 [1653]), and Father Francisco de Avila (Anonymous 1998 [ca. 1597], 1873). These works were supplemented by modern synthetic archaeological and ethnohistoric research.

The Kogi are an extant agropastoral people who live in the Sierra Nevada of northern Colombia. The Kogi speak a Chibcha-related language and claim descent from the ancient Tairona people who occupied the northern and western flanks of the Sierra Nevada prior to European contact. The Kogi are among the few living indigenous peoples to make seasonal migrations between the coast and the highlands. In the past, this settlement pattern may have been far more widespread than today. Kogi cosmovision was meticulously documented by Gerardo Reichel-Dolmatoff. Unlike many of the other sources consulted in this survey, Reichel-Dolmatoff's work systematically investigated and documented Kogi cosmology.

The modern Quechua and Aymara were the most intensively sampled group. Quechua probably served as the *lingua franca* of the Inca Empire. It is spoken today by peoples from as far north as the central highlands of Ecuador to as far south as the northern Lake Titicaca Basin. Aymara is spoken from the northern Lake Titicaca Basin southward to Sucre, Bolivia. A large and accessible corpus of formal ethnographic literature exists for these two groups. Only a minuscule fraction of this literature was reviewed and quantified in the present study. However, classic ethnographies such as Catherine Allen's *The Hold Life Has* (1988) and June Nash's *We Eat the Mines and the Mines Eat Us* (1979) were consulted among others. In addition, the novel *Yawar Fiesta* (*Blood Feast*) by the renowned Quechua anthropologist José María Arguedas was examined as an example of emic fiction.

METHODS

In order to evaluate similarities and differences in the use and perception of caves among societies in the sample, major texts describing each culture were systematically perused. When use of a cave was mentioned for any reason, the nature of this use was noted, assigned to a category, and tallied in a table. The assignment of a textual reference to a use category tended toward "splitting" into specifics rather than "lumping" into generalities; if others feel that certain categories are redundant, they are free to aggregate them in the future. A goal of the study was to assess variation and patterning in the uses and perceptions of caves by Indigenous Andean peoples. To achieve these ends splitting was deemed more appropriate than lumping.

Once the table was compiled it was possible to quantitatively and graphically explore the results to look for patterning in the use and perception of caves. To detect for "universals" among the sample, percent totals of each category were computed for the pooled sample. Cross-cultural studies demonstrate that spiritual practice is a cultural universal, but economic mode strongly predicts the kind of spiritual practitioners that are present in a society (Winkelman 1986, 1990). Thus to test for the influence of economic mode on the nature of cave use by societies in the present sample, each culture was assigned to either a Forager or Agropastoral economic mode. Then percent totals of each use category were calculated for these two economically defined subgroups.

The paired-t, sign, Wilcoxon signed rank, and Mann-Whitney U tests were then applied to these subtotals to test for the possibility of significant differences in use categories between the two economically defined subgroups. Paired-t is a parametric test that assumes a normal distribution. The sign and the Wilcoxon signed-rank tests are both nonparametric. The sign test assumes that the samples are independent. The Wilcoxon signed-rank test assumes that the samples are dependent. The Mann-Whitney U test is nonparametric and assumes that the samples are independent. Whether or not the distributions are normal is an empirical question that cannot be assumed with confidence because the samples are very small. The independent or dependent nature of the samples could readily be contested based on differing interpretations of culture history—a complex issue not easily solvable with the empirical evidence at hand. However, from a conservative perspective one can argue that, given Galton's problem (Naroll 1965) and some prior knowledge of the cultures involved, it is probably most appropriate to say that the samples are nonrandomly distributed and dependent. Thus, the most appropriate comparative statistic is one that is designed for nonparametric dependent samples. That would be the Wilcoxon signed-rank test. Still, each of the comparisons described above is applied and reported to evaluate how the different assumptions about the samples might influence the possibility of significant differences between the economic subgroups.

Hierarchical clustering with the Ward's linkage method and nonparametric multidimensional scaling with Euclidean distance linkage were used as tools to explore the relationship between known similarities between the groups and trends in cave use/perception. Ward's method was employed because it minimizes within-group variance. Multidimensional scaling is applied to visualize the ranked differences in use categories among the societies represented in the sample.

RESULTS

The nine indigenous culture groups were found to make use or perceive of caves in a total of thirty-three different ways (table 25.1). Except for the Chonos, each society used or perceived of caves in multiple ways ($x = 9$, s = 8, min = 1, max = 21, median = 5). Only a handful of Chonos words entered the written record. Thus it is very likely that more kinds of cave uses and perceptions were present in this culture but not reported.

Burial of Dead/Ancestors in Cave occurred in seven of the nine societies, or 78 percent of the cases. Within the sample, this is the most frequently present use/perception category. Of the texts surveyed, only the Ona and Quechua/Aymara lacked specific mention of the practice of burying the deceased in caves. The next three highest ranked use/perception categories were Habitation in Twilight Zone, Dwelling Place of Powerful Natural Force, and Dwelling Place of Malevolent Anthropomorph. Each category was present in four of the nine societies sampled.

Twenty-seven of the use/perception categories are exclusively related to spiritual practice. Only six of the

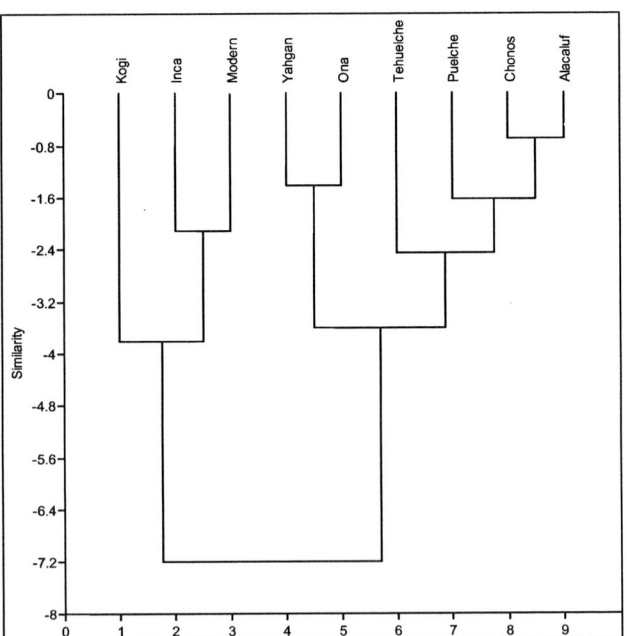

FIGURE 25.1 Results of hierarchical cluster analysis applying the Ward's linkage method. Modern = Quechua/Aymara.

use/perception categories could be interpreted as having a secular element. These are: Habitation in Twilight Zone, Fortified Location, Hiding Place During Contact, Hunt Animals in Caves, and Cave Accompanied by External Performance Space. At least 81 percent of the uses and perceptions of caves entail elements of spiritual practice.

When the sample of societies was subgrouped according to economic mode, the presence of use/perception categories exhibited significant difference according to the paired t-test ($t = -6.39$, $p < 0.001$), sign test ($r = 27$, $p < 0.001$), Wilcoxon signed-rank test ($W = 462$, $p < 0.001$), and the Mann-Whitney U test ($U = 121$, $p < 0.001$). Thus, differences are significant regardless of whether one assumes that the two samples have normal or nonnormal distributions, or whether the samples come from independent or dependent samples.

Hierarchical clustering (figure 25.1) and nonparametric multidimensional scaling (figure 25.2) both show that when the sample is considered as a whole, the use/perception of caves sorts according to economic mode. The seven forager groups are in general mutually propinquitous but distinct from the agropastoralists and vice versa. The specific patterns of category presence and absence identified by these techniques are discussed below.

DISCUSSION

Only three use/perception categories were exhibited by Foragers but not by Agropastoralists. These are: Emergence

TABLE 25.1 Abbreviations and textual references for each of the nine indigenous groups: F = foragers; AP = agropastoralists; Pl = pooled; Al = Alacaluf (Bird 1963, 73, 77; Gusinde 1960 [1937], 1037, 1054); Ch = Chonos (Gusinde 1960 [1937], 1037, 1054); In = Inca (Anonymous 1998 [ca. 1597], 36, 78, 94, 98, 103; Arguedas and Duviols 1966, 255; Bauer 1991, 18; Cobo 1990 [1653], 12–16, 45, 54, 74, 93; Hastorf 2003, 306; Poma de Ayala 1978 [1615], 24, 30, 44–45, 75, 237; Salomon 1991, 72; Salomon and Urioste 1991, 94, 103; Taylor 1987); Ko = Kogi (Preuss 1997 [1926], 122, 126; Reichel-Dolmatoff 1974, 297; 1978, 15, 24; 1987, 95, 107; 1997a [1949–1950], 29, 240, 262, 284–285; 1997b [1951], 44–46, 57, 143, 174, 268; 1997c [1990], 5); On = Ona (Gusinde 1960 [1937], 1157; 1996 [1931], 287); Pu = Puelche (Cooper 1963b, 166, 168; Fonck 1900, 5, 20); QA = Quechua/Aymara (Arguedas 1988 [1941], 14, 20; Delfino 2001; Flannery, Marcus, and Reynolds 1989, 144, 157, 169–170; Isbell 1978; Llanos and Osterling 1982; Nash 1979, 18–20; Perales, personal communication; Quispe 1969; Salomon 1998); Te = Tehuelche (Bórmida and Siffredi 1969–1970, 204; Cooper 1963b, 143, 166; Musters 1872, 1969 [1897]; Siffredi 1968; 1969–1979; 2002, 304); Ya = Yahgan (Cooper 1946 [1917], 85; Gusinde 1960 [1937], 8–9, 236, 376, 681, 1101–1012; Lothrop 1928, 175–6).

Culture Group	Al	Ch	In	Ko	On	Te	Pu	QA	Ya	F %	AP %	Pl %
Economic Mode	F	F	AP	AP	F	F	F	AP	F	%	%	%
Habitation in Twilight Zone	0	0	0	0	1	1	0	1	1	50	33	44
Do Not Live in Dark Zones	0	0	1	0	1	0	0	0	1	33	33	33
Habitation in Caves During a Mythic Past	0	0	1	1	0	0	0	1	0	0	100	33
Burial of Dead/Ancestors in Cave	1	1	1	1	0	1	1	0	1	83	67	78
Creative Emergence of an Ethnic Group	0	0	1	0	0	0	1	0	0	17	33	22
Emergence of a Ruling Individual or Class	0	0	1	0	0	0	0	0	0	0	33	11
Creative Emergence of Animals	0	0	0	0	0	1	0	1	0	17	33	22
Emergence of Great Creator after Battle with Family	0	0	0	0	0	1	0	0	0	17	0	11
Dwelling Place of Powerful Natural Force	0	0	1	1	0	1	0	1	0	17	100	44
Dwelling Place of Malevolent Anthropomorph	0	0	1	0	1	0	0	1	1	33	67	44
Dwelling Place of Anthropomorph	0	0	1	0	0	0	0	1	0	0	67	22
Dwelling Place of Malevolent Zoomorph	0	0	0	1	0	0	0	0	0	0	33	11
Fortified Location	0	0	0	0	0	0	1	0	0	17	0	11
Hiding Place During Contact	0	0	1	0	0	0	1	1	0	17	67	33
Hiding Place of Spiritual Creatures	0	0	1	1	0	0	0	1	0	0	100	33
Location of Adult Male Initiation Ritual	0	0	0	1	0	0	0	0	1	17	33	22
Location of Priestly Class Initiation Ritual	0	0	0	1	0	0	0	0	0	0	33	11
Hunt Animals in Caves	1	0	0	0	0	0	0	0	1	33	0	22
Cave as Metaphor of Residential Architecture	0	0	0	1	0	0	0	0	1	17	33	22
Cave as Uterine Orifice	0	0	0	1	0	0	0	0	0	0	33	11
Caves as Locations of Riches	0	0	1	1	0	0	0	1	0	0	100	33
Cave as Location of Rebirth/Rejuvenation	0	0	0	1	0	0	0	1	0	0	67	22
Caves as Locations of Genii Loci	0	0	1	1	0	0	0	1	0	0	100	33
Caves as Places of Agricultural Fertility Offerings	0	0	1	1	0	0	0	1	0	0	100	33
Place to Deposit Dangerous Magical Objects	0	0	1	1	0	0	0	1	0	0	100	33
Sealing of Caves to Contain Magical Forces	0	0	1	0	0	0	0	1	0	0	67	22
Cave as Conduit of Spiritual Energy	0	0	1	1	0	0	0	1	0	0	100	33
Cave Accompanied by External Performance Space	0	0	1	0	0	0	0	1	0	0	67	22
Mine/Cave Metaphors	0	0	1	0	0	0	0	1	0	0	67	22
Artificial Creation of Cave-Like Spaces	0	0	1	0	0	0	0	1	0	0	67	22
Cave as Pilgrimage Shrine	0	0	1	0	0	0	0	1	0	0	67	22
Cave as a Place where Water Emerges	0	0	0	0	0	0	0	1	0	0	33	11
Magical Lakes Located in Caves	0	0	0	0	0	0	0	1	0	0	33	11
Totals	2	1	20	15	3	5	4	21	7	—	—	—

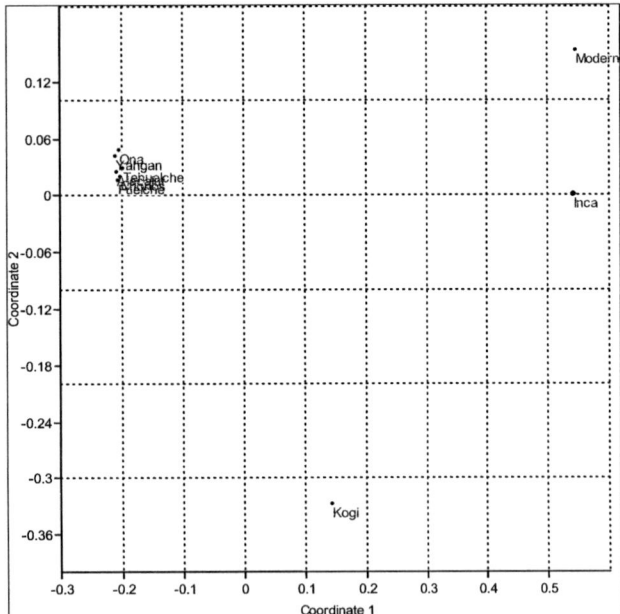

FIGURE 25.2 Results of multidimensional scaling applying the Euclidean linkage method. Modern = Quechua/Aymara.

of a Great Creator after Battle with Family (Tehuelche), Fortified Location (Puelche), and Hunt Animals in Caves (Yahgan). The Yahgan are maritime foragers who hunted seals by cornering them in caves. Reasons for the Forager exclusivity of the other two use/perception categories remains elusive. It seems likely that further sampling of historic literature is likely to yield agropastoral examples of using caves as a Fortified Location.

Twenty categories of use/perception are exhibited by Agropastoral groups but are not exhibited by Foragers. These are: Habitation in Caves During a Mythic Past (All AP); Creative Emergence of an Ethnic Group (Inca); Dwelling Place of Neutral Anthropomorph (Inca, Quechua/Aymara); Dwelling Place of Malevolent Zoomorph (Quechua/Aymara); Hiding Place of Spiritual Creatures (All AP); Location of Priestly Class Initiation Ritual (Kogi); Cave as Uterine Orifice (Kogi); Caves as Locations of Riches (All AP); Caves as Locations of Rebirth/Rejuvenation (Kogi, Quechua/Aymara); Caves as Locations of Genii Loci (Kogi, Quechua/Aymara); Caves as Places of Agricultural Fertility Offerings (All AP); Place to Deposit Dangerous Magical Objects (All AP); Sealing of Caves to Contain Magical Forces (Inca, Quechua/Aymara); Caves as Conduits of Spiritual Energy (All AP); Caves Accompanied by External Performance Space (Inca, Quechua/Aymara); Mine/Cave Metaphors (Inca, Quechua/Aymara); Artificial Creation of Cave-Like Spaces (Inca, Quechua/Aymara); Cave as Pilgrimage Shrine (Inca, Quechua/Aymara); Cave as Place where Water Emerges (Quechua/Aymara); and Magical Lakes in Caves (Quechua/Aymara).

The significant differences in the use/perceptions of caves that were detected by the Wilcoxon signed-rank test are likely due to the twenty categories that are absent among Foragers but present among Agropastoralists. These same twenty categories probably also produce the patterns of difference that are observed in the results of hierarchical clustering and multidimensional scaling.

Several of these use/perception categories do not occur among the Foragers because they are not associated with behaviors typical of foraging economies. Foragers, particularly bilocal bands like the Ona or Yahgan, do not tend to have priestly classes (Winkelman 1986, 1990); ergo, foragers in general are not going to perform priestly initiation rituals in caves. However, though shamanism is a common form of spiritual practice among hunter-gatherers, it is notable that no instances of shaman initiation in a cave were found among Foragers. Foragers do not tend to accumulate large quantities of material riches, thus it is no surprise that the use/perception of Caves as Locations of Riches is absent among Foragers in the sample.

There is no instance of Foragers having a use/perception category of Habitation in Caves During a Mythic Past but it is exhibited by all three Agropastoral groups. One hypothesis for this trend is that because agropastoral peoples live in more substantial architecture, Habitation of Caves During a Mythic Past forms part of an origin narrative of development that creates a difference from undomesticated "wild" or "natural" creatures. Foragers tend to lack substantial residential architecture. Thus it seems unlikely that Forager origin stories will emphasize a past in which ancestors lived in simpler structures. Therefore, the Forager perception of Habitation of Caves During a Mythic Past may not be exhibited. More intensive sampling of the literature on the Foragers included in the sample along with comparisons to other Forager societies from South America and other world areas are required to test this hypothesis further.

At least one type of cave use/perception that is absent among Foragers but present among Agropastoralists defies a simplistic argument that is based on the development of a broader array of cultural practices among more complex societies. Hunter-gatherers have rich and detailed cosmologies that include many spiritual creatures, yet none of the Forager accounts mentions caves as Hiding Places for Spiritual Creatures. Why is this the case? Is it a sampling error or a more robust pattern? Further investigation is again warranted.

Habitation in Twilight Zone has been observed for Quechua/Aymara peoples. This is because Quechua/Aymara people will use caves for temporary shelter either when herds are being pastured far from home or during long-distance caravans. Living in Dark Zones is not reported for any of the societies in the sample. As stated at the outset, relatively few dark-zone caves exist in the Andes. However, for three societies it has been observed that people explicitly Do Not Live in Dark Zones even if they exist (Inca, Ona, Yahgan). Given the negative evidence for habitation of dark zones and positive evidence indicating that some groups definitely do not live in dark zones when they exist, archaeological remains found in true cave darkzones are not likely to be secular residential refuse. Given the overwhelming proportion of spiritual cave uses and perceptions represented in this sample, there is at least an 80 percent chance that dark-zone refuse is directly related to some form of spiritual practice.

Considering that all of the societies surveyed, except the Chonos, for which there is very limited information, caves are used and perceived of in multiple ways, it seems safe to say that caves are polysemic or multivocal landscape features. In no case were uses and perceptions limited to only the six secular categories. Every society had some use or perception that involved spirituality. Thus, for the societies surveyed, caves are polysemic spiritual landscape features. Based on the sample, Agropastoralists used and perceived of caves in more ways than Foragers. With respect to caves, could this indicate that as cultures become, in the Durkheimian sense, increasingly complex, more "voices" enter into the referential chorus of polysemy? Perhaps the present trend is an artifact of sampling bias. Nonetheless, comparison of cave uses and perceptions with other world areas and similar studies with other landscape symbols could test this hypothesis.

CONCLUSION

Caves were universally used by all nine indigenous societies of western South America that were considered in this sample. However, there are some distinct differences in the nature of the uses and perceptions of caves that vary by group. Given that the sample derives from a single world area, it is difficult to determine to what degree these similarities may be due to trait sharing by association or common descent. Trait sharing across the economically defined subsamples is unlikely. A good portion of patterning within the two economic subgroups is most surely due to common descent and trait sharing. Most of the Foragers resided in adjacent territories. Though they spoke different languages and were considered distinct groups here, the degree of trait sharing among several of the groups was so great that many scholars have treated these groups as a common "cultural complex." Thus, one can a priori expect some common patterning in the use and perception of caves among Foraging groups in this sample. For the Agropastoral groups, the Inca occupied the entire Quechua/Aymara territory. Quechua was the *lingua franca* of the Inca Empire, thus trait sharing due to common descent can be expected.

It is compelling that the burial of the deceased is common to both subgroups of the sample. It is also compelling that more than 80 percent of the use/perception categories involved aspects of spiritual practice. Further, it seems very likely that the high frequency of burying the dead in caves is linked to the high proportion of spiritually related uses and perceptions of these spaces. Even if the deposits contain domestic refuse, archaeologists would be well served to keep this potential relationship in mind when crafting interpretations of cave-site assemblages. Even if the tendency or desire to excavate cave sites continues to stem from the fact that they contain well-preserved stratified remains—this survey concludes that spiritual practice is an overwhelming factor in the perception and uses of caves among the nine indigenous cultures surveyed. Therefore, in the quest for chronology it is important to remember that the remains encountered are bound to have resulted from the materialization of cosmology.

REFERENCES CITED

Allen, Catherine J. 1988. *The Hold Life Has: Coca and Cultural Identity in an Andean Community*. Smithsonian Series in Ethnographic Inquiry, No. 12. Washington, DC: Smithsonian Institution Press.

Anonymous. 1998 [ca. 1597]. *The Huarochirí Manuscript: A Testament of Ancient and Colonial Andean Religion*. Trans. F. Salomon and G. L. Urioste. Austin: University of Texas Press.

Arguedas, José María. 1988 [1941]. *Yawar Fiesta*. Lima: Editorial Horizonte.

Arguedas, José María, and Pierre Duviols. 1966. *Dioses y Hombres de Huarochiri: Narración Quechua Recogida por Francisco de Avila, 1598?* Lima: Instituto Francés de Estudios Andinos / Instituto de Estudios Peruanos.

Arriaza, Bernardo. 1995. *Beyond Death: The Chinchorro Mummies of Ancient Chile*. Washington, DC: Smithsonian Institution Press.

Bauer, Brian. 1991. "Pacariqtambo and the Mythical Origins of the Inca." *Latin American Antiquity* 2 (1): 7–26. http://dx.doi.org/10.2307/971893.

Bird, Junius. 1963. "The Alacaluf." In *The Handbook of South American Indians*, ed. J. Steward, 55–80. New York: Cooper Square Publishers.

Bórmida, Marcelo, and Alejandra Siffredi. 1969–1970. "Mitología de los Tehuelches Meridionales." *Runa* 12 (1–2): 199–245.

Burton, Michael L., Carmella C. Moore, John W.M. Whiting, Kimball A. Romney, David F. Aberle, Juan A. Barcelo, Malcolm M. Dow, Jane I. Guyer, David B. Kronenfeld, Jerrod E. Levy, et al. 1996. "Regions Based on Social Structure." *Current Anthropology* 37 (1): 87–123. http://dx.doi.org/10.1086/204474.

Cobo, Bernabé. 1990 [1653]. *Inca Religion and Customs*. Trans. R. Hamilton. Austin: University of Texas Press.

Cooper, John M. 1946 [1917]. *Analytical and Critical Bibliography of the Tribes of Tierra del Fuego and Adjacent Territory*. Washington, DC: Government Printing Office.

Cooper, John M. 1963a. "The Chono." In *The Handbook of South American Indians*, ed. J Steward, 47–54. New York: Cooper Square Publishers.

Cooper, John M. 1963b. "The Patagonian and Pampean Hunters." In *The Handbook of South American Indians*, ed. J. Steward, 127–68. New York: Cooper Square Publishers.

Delfino, Daniel D. 2001. "Of Pircas and the Limits of Society: Ethnoarchaeology in the Puna, Laguna Blanca, Catamarca, Argentina." In *Ethnoarchaeology of Andean South America*, ed. L. A. Kuznar, 116–37. Ethnoarchaeological Series 4. Ann Arbor, MI: International Monographs in Prehistory.

Dillehay, Tom D. 1989. *Mote Verde: A Late Pleistocene Settlement in Chile*. Smithsonian Series in Archaeological Inquiry. Washington, DC: Smithsonian Institution Press.

Dransart, Penny. 1997. "Rockshelters and Ritual Activities in the Atacama Desert of Northern Chile." In *The Human Use of Caves*, ed. C. Bonsall and C. Tolan-Smith, 667: 207–16. Oxford: BAR International Series.

Flannery, Kent V., Joyce Marcus, and Robert Reynolds. 1989. *The Flocks of the Wamani: A Study of Llama Herders on the Punas of Ayacucho, Peru*. San Diego: Academic Press.

Fonck, Francisco. 1900. *Viajes de Fray Francisco Menendez a la Cordillera: Publicados y Comentados por Francisco Fonck*. Valparaiso: Carlos F. Niemeyer.

Gusinde, Martin. 1960 [1937]. *The Yamana: The Life and Thought of the Water Nomads of Cape Horn*. Trans. F. Schütze. Die Feuerlan-Indianer II. New Haven, CT: Human Relations Area Files.

Haas, Jonathan, Winifred Creamer, and Arturo Ruiz. 2004. "Dating the Late Archaic Occupation of the Norte Chico Region in Peru." *Nature* 432 (7020): 1020–3. http://dx.doi.org/10.1038/nature03146. Medline:15616561.

Hastorf, Christine A. 2003. "Community with the Ancestors: Ceremonies and Social Memory in the Middle Formative at Chiripa, Bolivia." *Journal of Anthropological Archaeology* 22 (4): 305–32. http://dx.doi.org/10.1016/S0278-4165(03)00029-1.

Isbell, William. J. 1978. *To Defend Ourselves: Ecology and Ritual in an Andean Village*. Prospect Heights, IL: Waveland Press.

Kolata, Alan L. 1996. *Tiwanaku and Its Hinterlands: Archaeology and Paleoecology of an Andean Civilization*. Washington, DC: Smithsonian Institution Press.

Llanos, Oliverio, and Jorge P. Osterling. 1982. "Ritual de la Fiesta del Agua en San Pedro de Casta, Perú." *Journal of Latin American Lore* 8 (1): 115–50.

Lothrop, Samuel Kirkland. 1928. *The Indians of Tierra del Fuego*. New York: Museum of the American Indian.

Martin, Kay M. 1969. "South American Foragers: A Case Study in Cultural Devolution." *American Anthropologist* 71 (2): 243–60. http://dx.doi.org/10.1525/aa.1969.71.2.02a00040.

Moore, Jerry. 2004. "The Social Basis of Sacred Spaces in the Prehispanic Andes: Ritual Landscapes and the Dead in Chimú and Inka Societies." *Journal of Archaeological Method and Theory* 11 (1): 83–124. http://dx.doi.org/10.1023/B:JARM.0000014348.86882.50.

Moseley, Michael E. 1992. *The Incas and Their Ancestors: The Archaeology of Peru*. New York: Thames and Hudson.

Musters, George C. 1872. "On the Races of Patagonia." *Journal of the Anthropological Institute of Great Britain and Ireland* 1: 193–207. http://dx.doi.org/10.2307/2840953.

Musters, George C. 1969 [1897]. *At Home with the Patagonians: A Year's Wanderings over Untrodden Ground from the Straits of Magellan to the Rio Negro*. New York: Greenwood Press.

Naroll, Raoul. 1965. "Galton's Problem: The Logic of Cross-Cultural Analysis." *Social Research* 32: 428–51.

Nash, June. 1979. *We Eat the Mines and the Mines Eat Us: Dependency and Exploitation in Bolivian Tin Mines*. New York: Columbia University Press.

Poma de Ayala, Felipe Guaman. 1978 [1615]. *El Primer Nueva Corónica y Buen Gobierno*. Trans. C. Dilke. New York: E. P. Dutton.

Preuss, Konrad T. 1997. [1926]. *Journey of Exploration to the Cagaba*. New Haven, CT: Human Relations Area Files.

Quispe, Ulpiano M. 1969. *La Herranza en Choque Huarcaya y Huancasancos, Ayacucho*. Instituto Indigenista Peruano Monografía no. 20. Lima: Ministerio de Trabajo.

Reichel-Dolmatoff, Gerado. 1974. "Funerary Customs and Religious Symbolism among the Kogi." In *Native South Americans: Ethnology of the Least Known Continent*, ed. P. J. Lyon, 289–301. Boston: Little, Brown and Company.

Reichel-Dolmatoff, Gerado. 1978. "The Loom of Life: A Kogi Principle of Integration." *Journal of Latin American Lore* 4 (1): 5–27.

Reichel-Dolmatoff, Gerado. 1987. "The Great Mother and the Kogi Universe: A Concise Overview." *Journal of Latin American Lore* 13 (1): 73–113.

Reichel-Dolmatoff, Gerado. 1997a [1949–1950]. *The Kogi: A Tribe of the Sierra Nevada de Santa Marta, Columiba 1*. New Haven, CT: Human Relations Area Files.

Reichel-Dolmatoff, Gerado. 1997b [1951]. *The Kogi: A Tribe of the Sierra Nevada de Santa Marta, Columiba 2*. New Haven, CT: Human Relations Area Files.

Reichel-Dolmatoff, Gerado. 1997c [1990]. *The Sacred Mountain of Colombia's Kogi Indians*. New Haven, CT: Human Relations Area Files.

Rowe, John. 1963. "Inca Culture at the Time of the Spanish Conquest." In *The Handbook of South American Indians*, ed. J. Steward, 198–330. New York: Cooper Square Publishers.

Salomon, Frank. 1991. "Introduction Essay: The Huarochirí Manuscript." In *The Huarochirí Manuscript: A Testament of Ancient and Colonia Andean Religion*, trans. F. Salomon and G. L. Urioste, 1–38. Austin: University of Texas Press.

Salomon, Frank, and George L. Urioste, eds. and trans. 1991. *The Huarochirí Manuscript: A Testament of Ancient and Colonial Andean Religion*. Austin: University of Texas Press.

Salomon, Frank. 1999. "Testimonies: The Making and Reading of Native South American Historical Sources." In *The Cambridge History of the Native Peoples of the Americas*, ed. F. Salomon and S. B. Schwartz, vol. 3: *South America*, 19–95. Cambridge: Cambridge University Press.

Schreiber, Katharina. 1992. *Wari Imperialism in Middle Horizon Peru*. Anthropological Papers 87. Ann Arbor: University of Michigan, Museum of Anthropology.

Shady Solís, Ruth, Jonathan Haas, and Winifred Creamer. 2001. "Dating Caral: A Preceramic Site in the Supe Valley on the Central Coast of Peru." *Science* 292 (5517): 723–6. http://dx.doi.org/10.1126/science.1059519. Medline:11326098.

Siffredi, Alejandra. 1968. "Algunos Personajes de la Mitologia Tehuelche Meridional." *Runa* 11 (1–2): 123–32.

Siffredi, Alejandra. 1969–70. "Hierofanias y Concepciones Mitico-Religiosas de los Tehuelches Meridionales." *Runa* 12 (1–2): 247–71.

Siffredi, Alejandra. 2002. "Fragments of Southern Tehuilche Religiosity and Myths." In *Native Religions and Cultures of Central and South America: Anthropology of the Sacred*, ed. L. E. Sullivan, 299–312. New York: Continuum.

Skottsberg, Carl. 1913. "Observations on the Natives of the Patagonian Channel Region." *American Anthropologist* 15 (4): 578–616. http://dx.doi.org/10.1525/aa.1913.15.4.02a00030.

Stanish, Charles. 2001. "The Origin of State Societies in South America." *Annual Review of Anthropology* 30 (1): 41–64. http://dx.doi.org/10.1146/annurev.anthro.30.1.41.

Steward, Julian, ed. 1963. *Handbook of South American Indians*. New York: Cooper Square Publishers.

Taylor, Gerald. 1987. "Cultos y Fiestas de la Comunidad de San Damián (Huarochirí) Según La *Carta Annua* de 1609." *Bulletin, Institut Francais D'etudes Andines* 16 (3–4): 85–96.

Winkelman, Michael J. 1986. "Trance States: A Theoretical Model and Cross-Cultural Analysis." *Ethos (Berkeley, Calif.)* 14 (2): 174–203. http://dx.doi.org/10.1525/eth.1986.14.2.02a00040.

Winkelman, Michael J. 1990. "Shamans and Other 'Magico-Religious' Healers: A Cross-Cultural Study of Their Origins, Nature, and Social Transformations." *Ethos (Berkeley, Calif.)* 18 (3): 308–52. http://dx.doi.org/10.1525/eth.1990.18.3.02a00040.

26

Caves and Related Sites in the Great Plains of North America

Donald J. Blakeslee

The Great Plains are not known for spectacular caves, but caves and especially rockshelters are present. Many have been excavated, usually without regard to the possibility of ritual. In this chapter, I discuss ethnographic evidence for the cosmological significance of caves and equivalent sites. I also emphasize the larger context of caves, suggesting that many caves were parts of larger ritual precincts. Finally, I will discuss the implication of the cosmological themes identified ethnographically for the interpretation of archaeological remains in and near caves.

The first cave in this region to be mentioned in the historic literature is Carver's Cave in St. Paul, Minnesota. Jonathan Carver, a British fur trader, wrote the following in his journal in 1776:

> This day arrived to the great stone cave called by the Naudowessee Waukon Teebee, or in English the house of spirits.[Actually, "sacred house" would be a better translation.] . . . The mouth of the cave [was] about ten feet broad and three feet high [and] the room [was] upwards of thirty feet broad, and about sixty feet from the enterence of the cave [to] where I came to a lake. As 'twas dark I could not find out the bigness nor the form [of it]. The roof was about 20 feet high [and] the bottom clean white sand a little descending to the water from the mouth . . . I found many strange hieroglyphycks cut in the stone some of which was very a[n]cient and grown over with moss. (Parker 1976, 91–92)

Later visitors found the entrance intermittently covered by rockfall from the bluff above and it was repeatedly reopened. In 1826, the Indian agent wrote that the Dakota held a medicine dance above the "Big Stone Cave." (Taliaferro 1820s). In 1837, Joseph Nicollet visited the cave and mentioned petroglyphs near the entrance (Nicollet 1845, 72). Although his Dakota informants said they did not bury any of their dead in the cave itself, they did put scaffold burials on the bluff top above the cave entrance, and Woodland period burial mounds are found a short distance to the east. Nicollet also mentioned the presence of native trails and an abundance of productive maple groves and wild rice stands in the vicinity (Nicollet 1852, 97).

No formal excavation of the cave ever occurred. In the 1850s the cave floor was quarried for sand, and in the 1860s the Chicago and St. Paul Railroad cut back the bluff, removing about 20 feet of the front part of the cave, destroying the bulk of the petroglyphs.

Luckily, Theodore H. Lewis visited the cave and recorded his observations of what remained. He published drawings of four rattlesnakes carved into the roof of the cave. He also mentioned depictions of men, birds, fish, turtles, and lizards (Lewis 1901, 231–3). Details of this brief description of one cave resonate with some of the symbolic themes and associations common to caves and related sites all across the plains (figure 26.1).

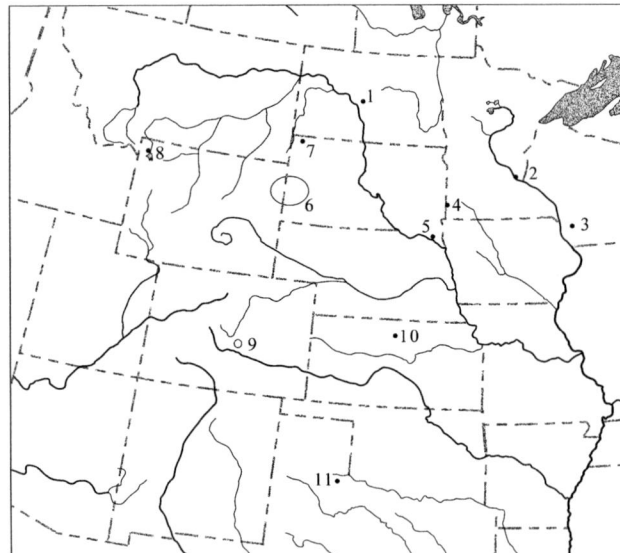

FIGURE 26.1 Location of sites in the Great Plains mentioned in the text: (1) *Paha wakan* (sacred hill); (2) Carver's Cave; (3) Gottschall Rockshelter; (4) Pipestone quarry; (5) Spirit Mound; (6) the Black Hills precinct; (7) Ludlow Cave; (8) Obsidian Cliff; (9) the Pikes Peak precinct; (10) Waconda Spring; and (11) Tule Canyon.

PLAINS CAVES WERE SELDOM USED FOR BURIAL

Unlike the pattern in other parts of North America, caves in the Great Plains were seldom used as places to bury the dead. While the Comanche and Apache residents of the Southern Plains often tucked the dead into crevices in the caprock, this seems to have been more a matter of convenience than of symbolic statement, as the number of bodies in any one spot almost never exceeds one. To find true burial caves, one has to go to central Texas, where Archaic period people regularly interred at least some of their dead in natural shaft tombs (Bement 1994). Thus Nicollet's comment about Dakota practices at Carver's Cave is typical for all of the plains.

CAVES ARE ENTRANCES TO THE UNDERWORLD

Natives of the Great Plains, like other residents of the New World, had a tripartite cosmology consisting of a sky world, this world, and an underworld. In this worldview, caves are obvious entrances to the underworld, but they are not the only ones. For the Cheyenne, any place where the deep underworld is exposed to the sky provides access to the underworld (Schlesier 1987, 6). Clefts in a rock face, high hills, places with upthrust rocks, cliffs, earthen bluffs—all could be the functional equivalents of caves. In some cases, isolated buttes or hills are imagined to have caves within them, with the entrance covered by a rock. For example, one Hidatsa myth refers to a time when all of the game animals were locked inside Dog Den Butte and the "entrance and smokehole were covered over" (Bowers 1965, 195–96). Gaps in a line of hills or through a cliff also functioned in ways similar to caves, as discussed below.

Water mediates between the worlds. It comes from the underworld at springs, rises as mist, forms clouds especially at some high peaks, and falls back to earth as rain. A cave that contains water or from which water flows is thus doubly significant. Water that occurs out of place is also sacred, such as a spring or pool at the top of a hill. Waconda Spring in Kansas, Manitou Springs in Colorado, and Sun-Mountain Spring (a Kiowa name) in Texas are three such places. Equally significant is the ability of still pools of water to reflect images of the bodies in the night sky—that is to say, the souls of the moon and stars.

Caves and other sites also relate to water via water vapor. Deep caves, such as Cave of the Winds near Pikes Peak, appear to breathe with changes in the weather—inhaling when a high-pressure system approaches and exhaling with the advent of a low-pressure system. When air moves out from a deep cave, it is usually very humid, and in cold weather it can form a vaporous cloud. Clouds also form at certain mountain peaks when weather conditions are right. One of the Pawnee names for Pikes Peak—Head Covered with Downy Eagle Feathers—appears to reflect this phenomenon (Blasing 1993, 2). The widespread association between some caves and the bison spirit may reflect the fact that on a cold winter's day a bison herd could be detected from a distance by the frozen vapor that collected high above the herd (Sundstrom 2004, 83). Similar clouds rise from springs and ponds. A Pawnee myth mentions the mist rising above Manitou Springs, as does a Shoshone myth (Murie 1981, 189; Ruxton 1950, 237–40).

Water in association with caves is also important because the underworld is an underwater world. It is ruled by a chimerical being—one with the features of various animal species. This earth monster is usually depicted with an alligator-like tail (figure 26.2). It may also have horns, antlers, or feathers on its head. Depictions of other denizens of the watery underworld are marked by very long tails, whether the spirit depicted is bison, panther, or other. This underwater realm is sometimes equated with the sky world below the southern horizon. The souls of dead Pawnees, for example, rise to the sky like sparks and then travel along the Milky Way until they reached the South Star (Canopus) below the southern horizon (Chamberlain 1982, 113).

CAVES PROVIDE CONNECTIONS WITH THE PRIMORDIAL ORDER

Many North American societies believed that their ancestors originated from either the underworld or the sky world. The Creek origin myth says that their ancestors emerged into this world at "cavernes" at the headwaters of the Red River (Gatschet 1884, 224–5). The reference is to the narrows of Tule Canyon, truly a spectacular spot although not a true cave.

The Awatixa division of the Hidatsas, by contrast, trace their origin to fiery arrows (meteors) that descended from the sky world at Charred Body Creek, North Dakota (Ahler, Thiessen, and Trimble 1991, 28).

The Pawnee were created at the Garden of Evening Star, which is the Garden of the Gods in Colorado, adjacent to the Cave of the Winds (Blasing 1993). Kiowas retain a tradition of the transformation of the world thanks to the courage of a young man who dived into the boiling water that issues from the Dragon's Mouth

FIGURE 26.2 The earth monster, as depicted at site 14OT4, Kansas.

FIGURE 26.3 The Dragon's Mouth, Yellowstone Park.

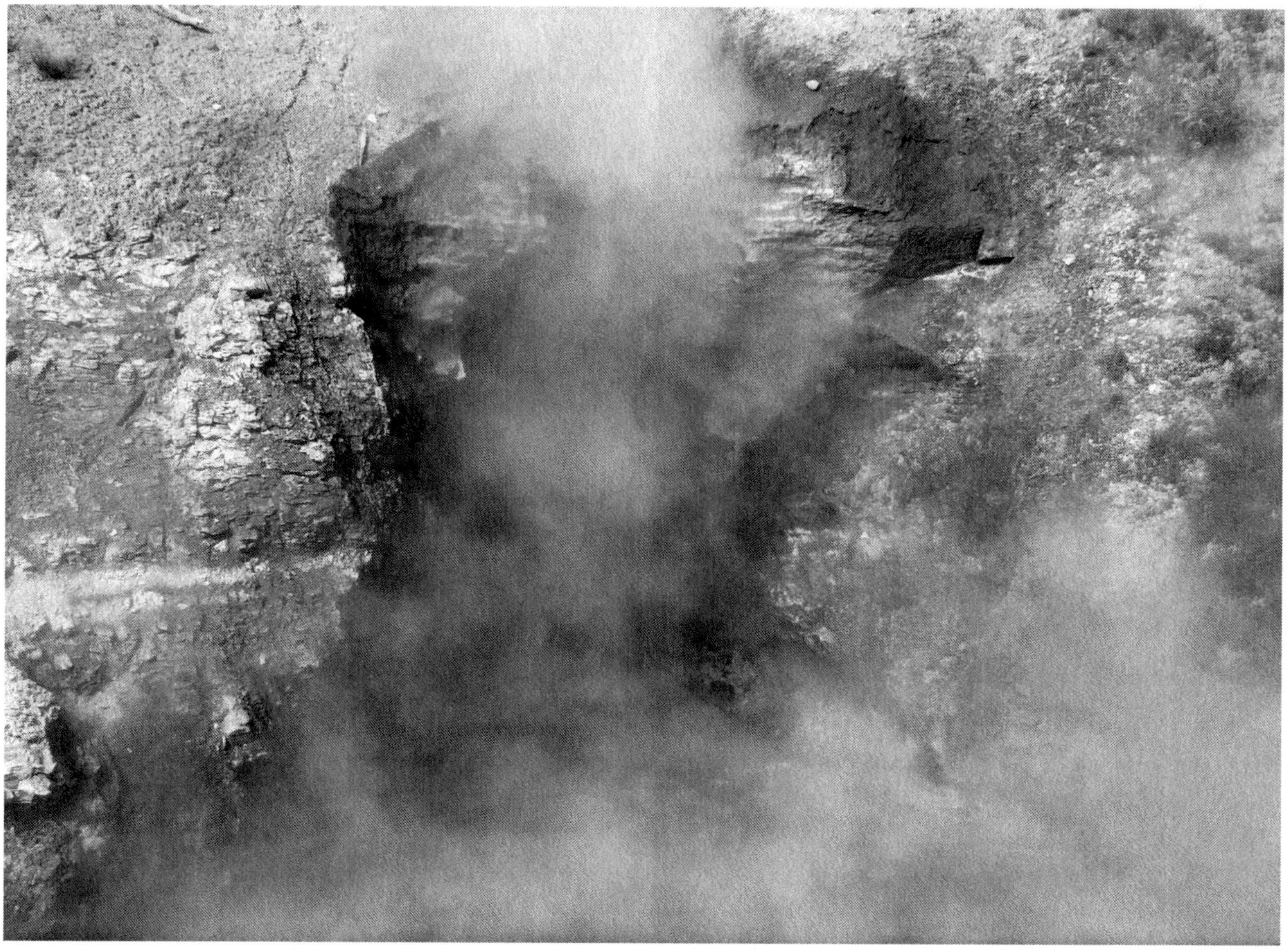

(figure 26.3), a cave in Yellowstone Park that emits waves of hot water, clouds of vapor, and intermittent roaring sounds (Nabakov and Loendorf 2004, 72–75). Gottschall Rockshelter in Wisconsin retains images of the Hochunk (Winnebago) culture hero Red Horn and the giants mentioned in his myth cycle (Salzer and Rajnovich 2000).

CAVES ARE SOURCES OF UNDERWORLD SUBSTANCES

Caves can be the sources of sacred minerals, paints, and crystals. Munson and Munson (1990) document the mining of chert and aragonite in the dark zone of Wyandotte Cave, Indiana, and have used trace-element analysis to show that the aragonite was used in the manufacture of sacred reel-shaped gorgets and pipes found in sites in Ohio, Tennessee, Illinois, and Iowa. The Flathead quarried red paint in the dark zone of a cave near Helena, Montana, that was said to open and close (Teit 1930, 340).

Quarries were the functional equivalents of caves in this respect; they were places in which (sacred) substances were taken from the underworld. The catlinite quarry in southwestern Minnesota where red pipestone was quarried is an important sacred site and is associated with a large amount of rock art (Hughes 1995). The removal of material from the underworld at these spots may have required rituals similar to rites of passage in that the material was being taken across a cosmological boundary. A hillside composed of eroding hematite at the Sunrise Mine in Wyoming was used as a source of sacred red paint since Paleoindian times. Numerous spear points were apparently thrown into the hillside as offerings (Stafford et al. 2003).

Clay for making pottery is another underworld substance, and knowledge of ceramics derives from underworld spirits. Thus Hidatsa potters kept their clay out of the sight of the sky and made pots with both the lodge door and the smokehole closed (Bowers 1965, 373–74). Flintknapping was another ceremonial activity done inside a closed lodge using light from the fireplace in place of daylight (Bowers 1965, 166). Unfortunately, both ceramics and flintknapping fell into disuse so early that we do not have comparable information for most Plains tribes.

CAVES ARE ASSOCIATED WITH HUNTING MAGIC

Spirits that animate all game animals dwell in the underworld. Humans enter caves to petition the spirits to ensure success in the hunt, and a great deal of rock art is related to this theme. Bison, deer, and other game animals are often depicted in association with weapons such as nets, atlatls, or bows and arrows, or with obvious wounds from weapons. Sites that are the functional equivalents of caves with respect to hunting magic include the objects known as ribstones on the northern plains. These are rocks located on high hills that have grooves pecked into them to represent the ribs and sometimes the spine of the bison. Such sites were visited prior to bison hunts in order to petition the bison spirit for success in the hunt (Fedirchuk and McCullough 1991; Wormington and Forbis 1965, 170).

Many ribstones also exhibit cup-shaped depressions (Fedirchuk and McCullough 1991, 13). The most revered ribstone on the northern plains is the Alberta meteorite (Fedirchuk and McCullough 1991). Natural depressions on the meteorite are similar to the artificial depressions on other ribstones. Meteorites have other symbolic connections to the bison spirit. For instance, figure 26.4 shows some of the petroglyphs at a site in southwestern Kansas, including a line of stars above what appears to be a ribstone. (I am indebted to Larry Loendorf for recognizing the ribstone motif at this site.) This site is near the Brenham meteorite field, where Hopewellians obtained meteoric iron (Blakeslee 2003; Wasson and Sedwick 1969).

CAVES ARE ASSOCIATED WITH CURING DISEASE

Humans entered caves to obtain the supernatural power needed to cure disease, power that was controlled by animal spirits residing in the underworld. Pawnees obtained it at places anthropologists call "animal lodges" (Parks and Wedel 1985). These spots had a number of attributes (see below), including a cave or similar feature. Pawnee narratives tell how doctors obtained curing power by visiting councils of animal spirits in the underworld. At Waconda Spring, Kansas, the spirits in the council included beavers, otters, wolves, dogs, bison, bears, jackrabbits, muskrats, and mud puppies (salamanders), along with species associated with the sky world, such as eagles and hawks (Murie 1981, 223). At Hidatsa sites like Dog Den Butte and Singer Butte, too, various animal spirits met in the underworld (Bowers 1965, 435).

CAVES RELATE TO ANIMAL AND HUMAN FERTILITY

Closely related to petitions for success in the hunt are prayers to ensure the fertility of game animals. The image of bison herds emerging from the underworld to feed humans occurs all across the plains (e.g., Brown 1992, 19; Marriott 1963, 12–23). In the southern plains, the narrows of Tule Canyon was one place where the bison and other animals were thought to emerge. Bison herds did winter in the well-protected canyons along the edge of the Llano Estacado,

FIGURE 26.4 Meteorite fall and ribstone at the Star Site, southwestern Kansas.

so their emergence in the spring from such places gave the religious belief an empirical underpinning. Other such spots include the Buffalo Gap in the Black Hills and the Buffalo Gap in the White Buffalo Buttes of central South Dakota (Sundstrom 2003, 276–77). Both are associated with caves from which the bison were thought to emerge from the underworld.

Depictions of pregnant game animals occur with some frequency. Examples include pregnant deer in a hunting scene in Tainter Cave in Wisconsin (Boszhardt 2003, 47–50) and the spectacular bison on a rock wall opposite Ludlow Cave in northwestern South Dakota.

> The bison cow, laboriously abraded into the rock to a depth of about an inch, is some seven feet long from nose to tail. She has strange lyre-like horns, an extraordinarily long tail, and ears between her horns. These features indicate that this is a spirit bison, associated with the underground world, rather than an ordinary one. Her lower back is humped in labor, and a line apparently representing the afterbirth extends from her hindquarters. Her calf stands directly under her belly, ready to nurse. Across the deeply recessed abdomen of the buffalo are five deeply incised buffalo tracks. Around the bison is an array of other rock art designs of varying types and ages, including more buffalo tracks and deeply incised vagina designs. A loop is also deeply incised just behind the bison cow's throat. This probably represents a snare. The snare is a Mandan and Hidatsa symbol of the power to take animals in any kind of trap—a bison jump or pound, a catfish trap, or an eagle-catching pit. In this case, it undoubtedly refers to bison trapping. This petroglyph is a visual prayer for the regeneration of the buffalo herds and success in hunting. (Sundstrom 2004, 81)

Strongly associated with the image of the female bison are ideas about human fertility. In the northern plains, there is a rock-art tradition that directly relates human fertility to that of animals. Called the track-vulva-groove style, because it equates the human vagina with the tracks of cleft-hoof animals, it appears to date from the Late Prehistoric into the Contact Period (Sundstrom 2004, 78–98). Associated with these motifs are numerous grooves worn in the rocks, apparently from the sharpening of women's bone tools, such as bone awls. At Ludlow Cave, offerings of awls and porcupine quills used to decorate clothing have been found as offerings inside the cave (Sundstrom 2004, figure 8.7). Thus the rituals performed there seem to have included broad ideas about women's productivity beyond biological fertility.

Other caves and hills had similar significance. For the Hidatsa, "The spirits destined to become human beings, like those that will become animals and birds, were believed to inhabit certain hills in their traditional territory. Women would put toys at the foot of these hills if they wanted children" (Bowers 1965, 126).

As mentioned above, some ribstones (e.g., Scapa, Viking, Trochu, and Endiang) are marked with cup-shaped depressions (Fedirchuk and McCullough 1991, 13), and some glacial erratics exhibit these depressions without the other ribstone imagery. Callahan (2000) has suggested that the cup-marked boulders of the northern plains may have been created by women seeking to become pregnant, as was the case among the Pomo and Shasta of California. The image of what appears to be a baby in a cradleboard in the dark zone of Tainter Cave (Boszhardt 2003, 38) is another obvious reference to human fertility in a cave setting.

DWARVES LIVE IN CAVES AND EQUIVALENT FEATURES OF THE LANDSCAPE

Dwarves, or little people, appear as a relatively minor motif in plains mythology, possibly because informants were reluctant to discuss them. Commonalities in the various stories about dwarves are that they live below the ground and are associated with arrows. The best-known spot where they are said to dwell is Arrow Rock, at Pryor Gap, Montana, so named because the Crow offered arrows to the little people who lived underground there (Lowie 1922, 428). The arrows were shot into a cleft in a rock face—reminiscent of the spear offerings at the Sunrise Mine. Crows thought the Little People made arrow points (Linderman 1962, 40; see also Mooney 1979, 411, for a Kiowa connection between dwarves and arrows), while Crees believed dwarves made the first ribstone (Wormington and Forbis 1965, 170–71). Lewis and Clark visited another lodge of little people—Spirit Mound—just north of present day Vermillion, South Dakota. They learned that the Omaha, Sioux, and Oto, and other nations all feared this spot (DeVoto 1997, 22).

CAVES PROVIDE CONNECTIONS TO THE SKY WORLD

This assertion seems counterintuitive, given the widespread idea that the spirits of the sky world are opposed to those of the underworld. Yet there are repeated instances in which the three worlds interconnect at caves and equivalent sites. The Comanche once kept a meteorite in a sacred cave on the slope of Santa Anna Mountain in Texas. When the cave collapsed, they dug out the meteorite and hauled it by horse travois to a small hill on the bank of the Red River (Harston 1963, 50, 111–16). In Tainter Cave is a rock-art panel divided by a natural horizontal crevice. Below the crevice is a hunting scene; above it are depictions of headless birds (Boszhardt 2003, 47–49). A set of sites in the Black Hills that are sacred to the Lakota are seen as the mirror images of a set of constellations in the sky (Goodman 1992, 9–19, 29). This brings us back to the sky world seen reflected in a pool of water, which in turn is an entrance to the underworld.

CAVES ARE OFTEN PARTS OF SACRED PRECINCTS

Blasing (1991, 1993) has performed fieldwork at the Pawnee animal lodges that can be located today. One of his conclusions is that they share a number of features that I list here in an amended form to take into account some of his later work: (1) A river or stream; (2) a native trail; (3) a vertical exposure of rock or earth; (4) a feature shaped like a Pawnee earthlodge; (5) a high point that provides an unobstructed view of the countryside; (6) a cave, spring, or hole that serves as an entrance to the underworld (which may be under water); and (7) healthy vegetation and game animal populations.

The implication of this list is that any cave that served as an entrance to the underworld might be surrounded by other sacred features. In some cases they are nearby, as at Guide Rock, known to the Pawnee as "Hill that Points the Way." Here, the Republican River has cut a bluff in the side of a high hill, and the earthlodge-shaped feature (figure 26.5) lies at the base of the hill, just east of the bluff. The Pawnee trail crossed the river immediately west of the bluff.

Similar complexes of features may have prompted other groups to identify certain caves as especially sacred. The trails, burial areas, ceremonial ground, and wild rice and sugar maples at Carver's Cave, itself a cave in a bluff beside a river and under a very high hill, are a case in point. As is the case at Guide Rock, all of these features lie close to one another.

The most important of the Pawnee animal lodges, identified by Blasing (1993) as the area around Pikes Peak, is not so compact (figure 26.6). Here the sacred features are scattered across a distance of 80 kilometers. The high hill is Pikes Peak, the entrance to the underworld is the Cave of the Winds, the vertical rock faces (plural; the Pawnee count four of them) are in the Garden of the Gods, while the springs are Manitou Springs, and the trail is Ute Pass trail (Blasing 1993, 3).

The Black Hills are another precinct, rich in sites sacred to many societies. From Buffalo Gap in the southeast to Devils Tower in the northwest is a distance of 160 kilometers. The Lakota timed their movements across this precinct to match the movement of the sun through various constellations in the sky (Goodman 1992, 11–14).

SACRED SITES ARE SHARED

Various sources say peace was supposed to reign at sacred sites. Carver (Nydahl 1950, 196) says as much about the catlinite quarry in Minnesota, and Ball (1941, 48) asserts the same for quarries in general. Other references are more indirect. In 1739, the Mallet brothers referred to the Solomon River at Waconda Springs as the *Rivière Aimable* (Blakeslee 1996, 85–93). Even such fierce enemies as the Pawnee and the Sioux worshiped at the same spot, called "Mound on the Water" by Pawnees and "Holy Hill" by Sioux (Gilmore 1929, 17).

The Black Hills in general and Bear Butte in particular were sacred to all of the peoples who passed that way. Sundstrom (2004, 128–32) documents a canyon in the

FIGURE 26.5 Animal lodge at Guide Rock, Nebraska.

FIGURE 26.6 Pawnee sacred precinct at Pikes Peak.

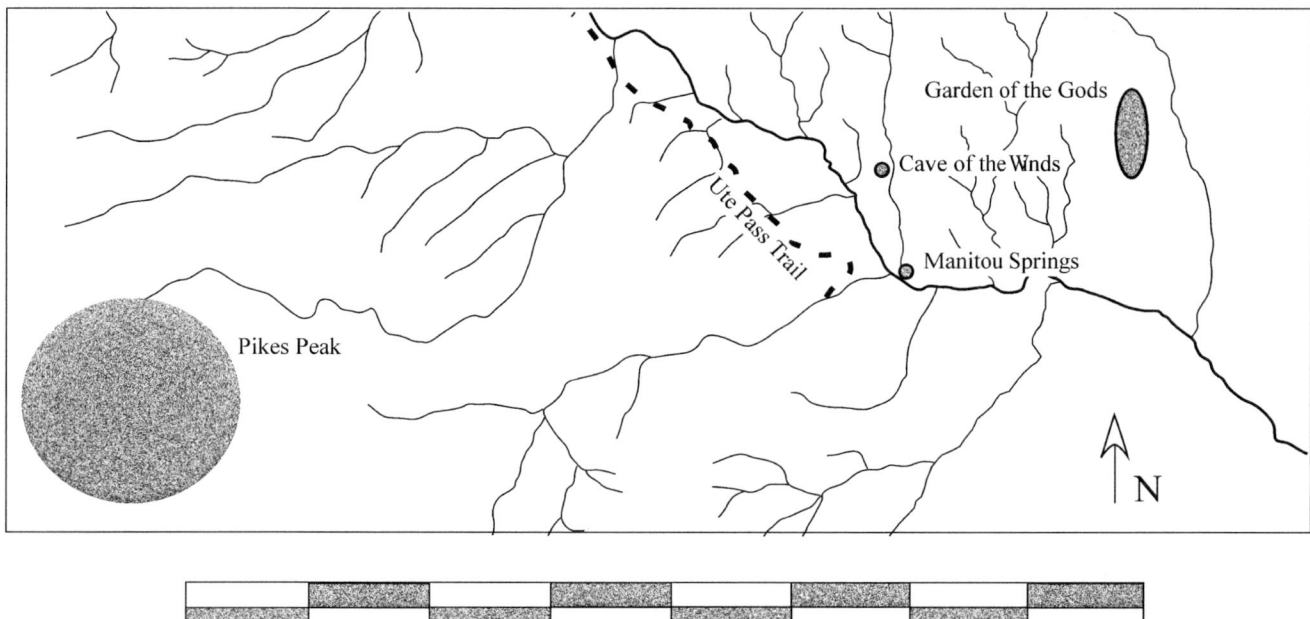

Black Hills that contains sacred images left by the Poncas, who were only in the region for a few years. Pikes Peak is another spot that was universally revered. Even the details of the beliefs are similar. The Ute held their Bear Dance there, which symbolizes the renewal of life on earth in the spring, while Pawnee spring-renewal ceremonies feature men who represent the standing rocks in the Garden of the Gods (Blasing 1993, 3). For the Pawnee, the Ute Pass Trail was the route by which the creator Tirawahat came to earth; for the Ute, "the Great Spirit stepped from the clouds to the mountaintop" (Fetler 1966, 28). The Pawnees believed that the Cave of the Winds was the home of the Thunders (Blasing 1993, 4); for the Jicarilla it was home to the Creator (Milne 1994, 44).

IMPLICATIONS FOR THE ARCHAEOLOGY OF CAVES

First, we can expect that caves and their equivalents contain ritual offerings, both within the cave proper and nearby. There is some regularity to the nature of the offerings described in various sources, whether the site is a cave, a ribstone, or a meteorite. They include items of shell, especially beads, as well as arrows, pipes, and tobacco. There is no accidental resemblance here. Tobacco smoke is one means for sending a prayer from this world to the sky world; so are arrows (e.g., Dorsey 1997, 63–64). In fact, pipes are symbolic weapons (Hall 1997, 107–23). Shell is an underwater/underworld substance, and it is no accident that in this region, marine-shell beads (and some fossil shell beads) were used primarily as grave goods for millennia (Blakeslee 1997). I would be remiss not to mention finds of certain Mississippian-style shell masks. Two came from a small, wet cave in Montana, the walls of which had been painted red. One mask yielded an AMS date of 520 +/– 70 BP (Jaynes 1997). The other came from a talus slope on the side of Bear Butte in South Dakota. The latter may have been made from fossil shell (Fosha 1997).

Nevertheless, few excavations of caves have been conducted with ritual in mind. For instance, Pictograph Cave in Montana, excavated in the 1930s and filled with over 100 pictographs in black, red, and yellow, located beside a spring and behind a fine grove of trees, was used more to develop a cultural sequence for the region than to interpret the religious behavior of its prehistoric visitors (Mulloy 1958). Mummy Cave in Wyoming is another example of a cave that has proven invaluable in delineating the cultural sequence of the region but which has been relatively silent in regard to ritual (Husted and Edgar 2002).

There are some exceptions. The huge collections of arrow points from Ludlow and Medicine Creek Caves are clear examples of ritual deposits (Sundstrom 2004, 132–37). And Sundstrom's (2004, 83–98) recognition of the connection between offerings of awls and porcupine quills with a petroglyph style is an important contribution. Also, the recent discoveries at Tainter Cave and Gottschall Rockshelter (Salzer and Rajnovich 2000) have publicized the presence of cave shrines to the archaeological community. Consider Tainter Cave with its rock art that echoes the themes of hunting magic, animal and human fertility, and references to the sky world. To what extent will the remains in the sediments on the floor of the cave, if excavated, relate meaningfully to these themes? What about deposits and other features outside the cave?

At Gottschall Rockshelter, the case for a shrine is even clearer. Here was found evidence for feasting and the construction of wooden platforms; offerings of points and rolls of lime-covered hides; fires used for nondomestic functions, including one used to illuminate a rock-art panel; piles of bone, pottery, and clay; and the manufacture in the cave of items with underworld connections, including a pot that was used and discarded in the cave, (limited) flintknapping, and the manufacture of shell beads. Even more impressive are the "anthroseds"—man-made soil layers of combined wood ash, powdered limestone, and mussel shells—and the creation of an apparent bas relief of a thunderbird in those sediments (Salzer and Rajnovich 2000).

Given the large number of caves and shelters that have been excavated previously and the uncertain prospects for both finding and excavating more of them, there is a need for a coherent review of the contents of caves and shelters that have already been reported. These, of course, were excavated in a variety of ways with widely differing modes of recovery and attention to provenience. Even so, one might expect to find some patterning in their assemblages that differs from those in normal habitation sites. A coherent review of the assemblages might shed light on the ages of the various symbolic themes discussed in this chapter. Some may well be older than others. In this attempt, a logical starting point would be the rock-art style sequences that have been developed (Francis and Loendorf 2002; Keyser 1977; Sundstrom 2004).

Here are two examples. Layer 30 at Mummy Cave, with a radiocarbon dates of 4090 to 4420 BP, yielded four tubular-bone smoking pipes along with shell beads from Tennessee and (probably) the Gulf of Mexico (Husted and Edgar 2002, 26, 66–67). The pipes are easily the oldest clear examples of smoking pipes found on the Plains, and they compare favorably in age with stone pipes found in the East. Are they part of a ritual deposit? Far more ancient are the Paleoindian spear points embedded in the red ocher slope at the Sunrise Mine. Here we have a parallel with the offerings of arrows made at places like Ludlow and

Medicine Caves, Arrow Rock, and the Wichita County meteorite in Texas. Will a review of Archaic assemblages from caves show continuity in ritual offerings of weapons from Paleoindian into the Historic Period?

REFERENCES CITED

Ahler, Stanley A., Thomas D. Thiessen, and Michael K. Trimble. 1991. *People of the Willows: The Prehistory and Early History of the Hidatsa Indians*. Grand Forks: University of North Dakota Press.

Ball, Sydney H. 1941. *The Mining of Gems and Ornamental Stones by American Indians*. Bureau of American Ethnology Bulletin 128, Anthropological Paper 13. Washington, DC: U.S. Government Printing Office.

Bement, Leland C. 1994. *Hunter-Gatherer Mortuary Practices during the Central Texas Archaic*. Austin: University of Texas Press.

Blakeslee, Donald J. 1996. *Along Ancient Trails: The Mallet Expedition of 1739*. Niwot: University Press of Colorado.

Blakeslee, Donald J. 1997. "The Marine Shell Artifacts of Kansas." *Central Plains Archaeology* 5 (1): 3–9.

Blakeslee, Donald J. 2003. "A Meteor, a Mirror, a Metaphor." In *Deep-Time Perspective Studies in Symbols, Meaning, and the Archaeological Record*, ed. J. D. Reynolds and M. L. Fowler. *The Wisconsin Archaeologist* 84(1–2).

Blasing, Bob. 1991. "Pawnee Animal Lodges Revisited." Paper Presented at the 13th Flint Hills Conference, Lincoln, NE.

Blasing, Bob. 1993. "A Possible Location for the 'Garden of the Gods' Described in Pawnee Stories." Paper presented at the 15th Flint Hills Conference, Wichita, KS.

Boszhardt, Robert F. 2003. *Deep Cave Art in the Upper Mississippi Valley*. St. Paul, MN: Prairie Smoke Press.

Bowers, Alfred W. 1965. *Hidatsa Social and Ceremonial Organization*. Bureau of American Ethnology Bulletin 194. Washington, DC: U.S. Government Printing Office.

Brown, Joseph Epes. 1992. *Animals of the Soul: Sacred Animals of the Oglala Sioux*. Rockport, MA: Element Press.

Callahan, Kevin. 2000. "Pica, Geophagy, and Rock Art: Ingestion of Rock Powder and Clay by Humans and Its Implications for the Production of Some Rock Art on a Global Basis." Paper presented at the Society for American Archaeology, Philadelphia.

Chamberlain, Von Del. 1982. *When Stars Came Down to Earth: Cosmology of the Skidi Pawnee Indians of North America*. Los Altos, CA: Ballena Press.

DeVoto, Bernard. 1997. *The Journals of Lewis and Clark*. Boston: Houghton-Mifflin.

Dorsey, George A. 1997. *Traditions of the Caddo*. Lincoln: University of Nebraska Press.

Fedirchuk, Gloria J., and Edward J. McCullough. 1991. "Prehistoric Art and Spiritualism: A Perspective from Pine Coulee." *Alberta Archaeological Review* 22: 11–9.

Fettler, John. 1966. *The Pikes Peak People*. Caldwell, ID: Caxton Printers.

Fosha, Michael. 1997. "Faces of Shell: Two Marine Shell Mask Gorgets from South Dakota." *Central Plains Archaeology* 5 (1): 69–71.

Francis, Julie E., and Lawrence L. Loendorf. 2002. *Ancient Visions: Petroglyphs and Pictographs of the Wind River and Bighorn Country, Wyoming and Montana*. Salt Lake City: University of Utah Press.

Gatschet, Albert S. 1884. *Migration Legend of the Creek Indians*. 2 vols. Philadelphia: D. G. Brinton.

Gilmore, Melvin R. 1929. *Prairie Smoke*. New York: Columbia University Press.

Goodman, Ronald. 1992. *Lakota Star Knowledge: Studies in Lakota Stellar Theology*. Rosebud, SD: Sinta Gleska University.

Hall, Robert L. 1997. *An Archaeology of the Soul: North American Indian Belief and Ritual*. Champagne: University of Illinois Press.

Harston, J. Emmor. 1963. *Comanche Land*. San Antonio: The Naylor Company.

Hughes, David. 1995. "Perceptions of the Sacred: A Review of Selected Native American Groups and Their Relationships with the Catlinite Quarries." Report to the National Park Service, Midwest Archaeological Center, Lincoln, NE.

Husted, Wilfred, and Robert Edgar. 2002. *The Archaeology of Mummy Cave, Wyoming: An Introduction to Shoshonean Prehistory*. National Park Service, Midwest Center and Southeast Archaeological Center, Special Report 4, Technical Report Series No. 9. Lincoln NE: Midwest Archaeological Center.

Jaynes, Stanley. 1997. "Marine Shell Mask Gorgets in Montana." *Central Plains Archaeology* 5 (1): 105–6.

Keyser, James D. 1977. "Writing-on-Stone: Rock Art on the Northwestern Plains." *Canadian Journal of Archaeology* 1: 15–80.

Lewis, Theodore H. 1901. "Sculptures in Caves at St. Paul, Minnesota." *De Lestry's Western Magazine* 6 (6): 229–33.

Linderman, Frank S. 1962. *Plenty Coups, Chief of the Crows*. Lincoln, NE: Bison Books.

Lowie, Robert H. 1922. *The Religion of the Crow Indians*. Anthropological Papers of the American Museum of Natural History, 25(2). New York: American Museum Press.

Marriott, Alice. 1963. *Saynday's People: The Kiowa Indians and the Stories They Told*. Lincoln: University of Nebraska Press.

Milne, Courtney. 1994. *Sacred Places in North America: A Journey into the Medicine Wheel*. New York: Stewart, Tabori and Chang.

Mooney, James. 1979. *Calendar History of the Kiowa Indians*. Washington, DC.: Smithsonian Institution Press.

Mulloy, William T. 1958. "A Preliminary Historical Outline for the Northwestern Plains." *University of Wyoming Publications (Laramie, Wyo.)* 22 (1): 1–235.

Munson, Patrick J., and Carol Munson. 1990. *The Prehistoric and Early Historic Archaeology of Wyandotte Cave and Other Caves in Southern Indiana*. Indianapolis: Indiana Historical Society.

Murie, James R. 1981. *Ceremonies of the Pawnee*. Ed. Douglas R. Parks. Washington, DC: Smithsonian Contributions to Anthropology.

Nabakov, Peter, and Lawrence Loendorf. 2004. *Restoring a Presence: American Indians and Yellowstone National Park*. Norman: University of Oklahoma Press.

Nicollet, Joseph N. 1845. "Report Intended to Illustrate a Map of the Hyrographical Basin of the Upper Mississippi River." Washington, 26th 3 Congress, 2nd session, S. Ex. Doc. no. 237 (H. Doc 52).

Nicollet, Joseph N. 1852. "Notices of the Natural Caves in the Sioux Country, on the Left Banks of the Upper Mississippi River." In *Information Respecting the History, Condition, and*

Prospects of the Indian Tribes of the United States, ed. Henry R Schoolcraft, 2: 95–99. Philadelphia PA: Lippincott, Grambo & Co.

Nydahl, Theodore L. 1950. "The Pipestone Quarry and the Indians." *Minnesota History* 31 (4): 193–208.

Parker, John. 1976. *The Journals of Jonathan Carver and Related Documents, 1766–1770*. Minneapolis: Minnesota Historical Society Press.

Parks, Douglas R., and Waldo R. Wedel. 1985. "Pawnee Geography: Historical and Sacred." *Great Plains Quarterly* 5 (3) (Summer): 143–76.

Ruxton, George A.F. 1950. Ruxton of the Rockies. Comp. Clyde and Mae Reed Porter. Ed. LeRoy R. Hafen. Norman: University of Oklahoma Press.

Salzer, Robert J., and Grace Rajnovich. 2000. *The Gottschall Rockshelter*. St. Paul, MN: Prairie Smoke Press.

Schlesier, Karl. 1987. *The Wolves of Heaven: Cheyenne Shamanism, Ceremonies, and Prehistoric Origins*. Norman: University of Oklahoma Press.

Stafford, Michael D., George C. Frison, Dennis Stanford, and George Zeimans. 2003. "Digging for the Color of Life: PaleoIndian Red Ochre Mining at the Powars II Site, Platte County, Wyoming, USA." *Geoarchaeology* 18 (1): 71–90. http://dx.doi.org/10.1002/gea.10051.

Sundstrom, Linea. 2003. "Sacred Islands: An Exploration of Religion and Landscape in the Northern Great Plains." In *Islands on the Plains: Ecological, Social and Ritual Use of Landscapes*, ed. Marcel Kornfeld and Alan J. Osborn, 258–300. Salt Lake City: University of Utah Press.

Sundstrom, Linea. 2004. *Storied Stone: Indian Rock Art of the Black Hills Country*. Norman: University of Oklahoma Press.

Taliaferro, Lawrence. 1820s. *Manuscript Journals*. St. Paul, MN: Division of Archives and Manuscripts, Minnesota Historical Society.

Teit, J. A. 1930. *The Salishan Tribes of the Western Plateau*. Annual Report of the Bureau of American Ethnology for 1927–1928. Washington, DC: Smithsonian Institution.

Wasson, J. T., and S. P. Sedwick. 1969. "Possible Sources of Meteoric Material from Hopewell Indian Burial Mounds." *Nature* 222 (5188): 22–4. http://dx.doi.org/10.1038/222022a0.

Wormington, H. Marie, and Richard G. Forbis. 1965. *An Introduction to the Archaeology of Alberta*. Proceedings of the Denver Museum of Natural History, 11.

Part V
New Approaches

27

Civilizing the Cave Man
Diachronic and Cross-Cultural Perspectives on Cave Ritual

Andrea Stone

Getting a handle on cave ritual in all of its multifaceted dimensions—origins, evolution, motivation, formal variation, social significance—is an overwhelming task in light of its extraordinary time depth and global distribution. If, for instance, cave burial can be considered a form of ritual, then evidence for it extends back to the Neanderthal world of 180,000 years ago (Clottes, this volume; Drew 2004). The birth of cave ritual, among the earliest expressions of ideologically motivated conventional human behavior, is an event so remote as to escape precise understanding beyond general recognition of its profound antiquity. At the same time, these primeval origins do not contradict the fact, attested by essays in this volume, that cave ritual has made sporadic appearances throughout human history in many kinds of societies found on every inhabited continent with accessible caves.

Cave ritual's endurance from the remote past to the present should not be taken as proof that it is a relic of "primitive" behavior preserved in the collective psyche, out of which it emerges in new disguises shaped by the vicissitudes of historical circumstance. Rather, it does show that cave ritual, like food or anything else ideally suited for satisfying critical human needs, serves a purpose that is fundamental and therefore is reimagined over and over again in different times and places. That purpose is to provide an effective medium for constituting and maintaining relationships between humans and a location in the environment—relationships that play a significant role in interpersonal and larger group cohesion. Put another way, social interaction is always mediated by spatial environment and temporal flow. More intimately, space and time are incorporated into the dialectical process of constituting social structure (Pred 1984). Likewise individual practices, understood as social agency, must play out through the medium of the material conditions of time and space (Giddens 1979, 54), as well as through physical objects, such as art, that occupy socially mediated space (Gell 1998). Interaction with objects, through their production and subsequent manipulation, transforms an ostensibly natural space (like a cave) into something humanly constructed.

The spatial milieu for these social processes is uniquely articulated by caves as penetrations in the earth, representing both shelter and the natural world's substrate. The conformation of cave-space is also reliably stable, thus having distinct advantages as a ritual setting, especially in prearchitectural eras. The cave's internal spatial stability perfectly meshes with ritual's characteristic invariance, discussed in greater detail below. Cave ritual's ability to strengthen social solidarity because it melds ideology with a unique spatial milieu is an enduring fact, as true in primordial as modern times. Humans live on the land, of course, and they have complex ideas about it, no matter what their form of social organization. The need to construct relationships between people and landscape is so compelling that cave ritual has emerged independently, at many points on the globe, in many types of societies; therein lies its durability.

Following this, the analytical interest of cave ritual should not be seen as a matter of relevance only to hunter-gatherer ways of life, as is often assumed. The potential contributions cave ritual can make to understanding religious experience, as well as social, political, and even economic development, are therefore not only substantial but also transcend ethnic, temporal, and subsistence-based contingencies.

It is unfortunate that cultural expressions found in caves, such as ritual, tend to be seen as properly belonging to an early developmental stage before humans embraced sedentary lifestyles. Assumptions of this sort are common, no less in the realm of artistic expression in caves. The Paleolithic art specialist, Ann Sieveking (1997, 25) makes the blanket statement that "the predilection for decorating a deep underground cave, unsuitable for habitation and seldom visited, is peculiar to the Palaeolithic." This is a highly questionable assertion. For instance, Bahn points out that dividing the roughly 300 Upper Paleolithic painting sites known today by their period of production—some 20,000 years—results in one cave being painted every 75 years. And since only half of these caves are truly deep, according to Bahn, the calculation yields one cave painted every 150 years. He goes on the say that "neither-cave dwelling nor cave-painting are truly characteristic of the Upper Palaeolithic" (Bahn 1997, 35).

Whether or not this is an accurate statement—something hard to confirm because of our tenuous grasp of the survival rate of Paleolithic paintings—it can also be pointed out that in far more recent times, in what is nonetheless "ancient" Mesoamerica, deep caves were decorated; however, the number of surviving examples is admittedly limited. Nevertheless, Olmec-style paintings are found three-quarters of a mile into Juxtlahuaca Cave, Guerrero, Mexico (Gay 1967), in all respects a place "unsuitable for habitation and seldom visited." To the south, the Maya produced an even larger corpus of cave art. The remoteness of several paintings at Naj Tunich, Guatemala, requiring a rope descent to reach after walking a half a mile into the cave, is unparalleled in Mesoamerica (Stone 1995). Elsewhere in the Americas, dark-zone cave art occurs in abundance in the Caribbean while sporadic examples can be found in North America. A cluster of about twenty such caves are located in the southeastern United States (Stone 2004). With the exception of some of the North American caves, much of this art, including the most deeply sequestered, was produced by sedentary agriculturalists. Tolan-Smith and Bonsall (1997, 217) state categorically that "The penetration of truly deep caves before the advent of modern speleology is reported from only three areas, Central America, Southwest Europe and the Urals." One must add to this the penetration of deep caves by ancient people in the southeast United States (see Claassen; Prufer and Prufer; Sabo, Hilliard, and Lockhart; Simek, Cressler, and Douglas; and Watson; this volume). In certain Mesoamerican cases, including the Maya and Aztec, these agriculturalists lived in state-level societies. We must get beyond the notion that cave art and cave ritual have an intrinsically important connection with hunter-gatherers, while examples from sedentary societies amount to little more than anachronistic oddities, marginal to an understanding of events of any significance. Indeed, much of what cave ritual has to offer as an effective mediator of social phenomena is as applicable to agriculturalists as to hunter-gatherers.

CAVES AS RITUAL SITES AND FORMS OF SOCIAL ORGANIZATION

Why would societies running the gamut from Paleolithic hunter-gatherers to village-dwelling agriculturalists, and even elites of state-level societies, find caves attractive as ritual spaces? For the Paleolithic period, it is well documented that caves were used for seasonal migrations resulting in a cycle of repeated visits. Periodic convergences fostered a process of forging emotional and ideological ties between migrating groups and particular caves (Tolan-Smith and Bonsall 1997, 217). Emphasis should be placed on "particular" since all caves were not equal in terms of the strength or even presence of such ties. This point is made in the survey in the present volume by Robin Skeates. His regional study of caves in southeast Italy shows that even during the Early Paleolithic, around 30,000 years ago, an archaeological distinction can be made between caves with a strict utilitarian function and caves having an added layer of cultural importance. Only certain caves contain "special artifacts," what Skeates interprets as nonutilitarian features of material culture, such as objects collected for their aesthetic attraction. The presence of artifacts that are not part of the toolkit of quotidian domestic life is generally considered archaeologically diagnostic of a ritual site. Skeates proposes an intriguing model of the evolution of caves from seasonal aggregation sites to ritual sites. As he sees it, unrelated social groups converging on a selected cave needed to communicate. This was accomplished through material objects manipulated in a performative context, acting as mediators of social agency. Through an accretion of these performances over time, certain caves assumed a deepening cultural identity that formed the basis of increasingly complex ritual behaviors. Skeates sees this progression unfolding chronologically in the archaeological record of his Italian study area in the following behavioral sequence:

first the curation of objects, then burials, and finally the creation of parietal art and more elaborate examples of mobiliary art.

Tolan-Smith and Bonsall (1997, 217) see the types of cave rituals that would have developed during the Paleolithic as falling into two categories: caves as theaters of ritual, evidenced archaeologically by the presence of cave art or votive deposits, and caves as burial chambers, which can be assumed to have had their own suite of associated ritual behaviors. The development of either genre of cave ritual in the archaic past would have been fostered by the unique benefits caves offered as permanent shelters, thus contributing to ritual's tendency for invariance. Like no other spatial setting available at that time, caves preserved material reminders of the collective experiences of a social group that could be repeatedly accessed: animal bones, lithics, objects of aesthetic interest, and the remains of deceased members of those groups (Gamble 1999, 75). Caves were, in effect, repositories of the material correlates of group identity and experience. The ability to return to these significant remains at a consistent location, a service which caves rendered especially well because of their imperviousness to environmental disturbance, created a logistical and structural framework for ritual behavior. Above all, the fixity of caves in space was an armature for structured behavior, the basis of ritual, which by definition is structured.

Let us pause for a moment to consider ritual in greater depth. On a basic level, ritual entails a customary set of actions typically occurring in a prescribed format using a distinct means of communication. The repetition and precision of ritual are singularly important. Bell (1997, 150) subsumes these qualities under the term *invariance*. A corollary of this is that ritual involves conventional actions occurring within a given space—hence the integral nature of space in the ritual process—whose character bears on the unfolding events. Through this structured behavior, rituals reify symbolic values and group ethos, thus providing a mechanism of socialization and potentially affecting the individual psyche through catharsis or emotional intensity (Bell 1997, 89).

While some authors emphasize the communicative aspect of ritual (Bloch 1974), others suggest that actions and performance are key (Bell 1997, 159–164; Bradley 2005, 34). A distinction has also been drawn between secular and religious ritual. According to Rappaport (1971, 29), "Religious rituals always include, in addition to messages of social import, implicit or explicit references to some idea, doctrine, or supernatural entity." For the sake of clarity, the kind of cave rituals we are discussing can be understood as religious ritual. The fact that ritual entails repetition—of actions occurring in a prescribed manner—made caves attractive as ritual theaters because they fixed the material focus of ritual so that critical actions could be repeated, over substantial periods of time, in relation to them. Caves, thus, contributed to the invariance of ritual by their own inherent characteristics of permanence and stability.

As permanent enclosures, caves afforded opportunities for social interaction with exceptional levels of privacy, no small matter for folks living in small bands where face-to-face contact is difficult to avoid (Wilson 1988). Caves provided arenas of performance for social occasions or, what Gamble (1999, 75) calls in the case of Paleolithic societies of Europe, a "place." Indeed, he considers caves the quintessential "place" of what might be called Europe's prearchitectural era. Gamble notes the importance of sensory associations in terms of inculcating emotional ties to caves. Perhaps not all, but many caves do offer uniquely striking visual experiences: dramatic lighting in semidaylight areas and, in the dark zone, an enclosed landscape of rock and water that can be spectacularly beautiful. Acoustical effects, unique to the cave environment, likely factored into the totality of this experience (Waller 1993).

Should the relationship between topographic features, considered sacred or having some extra-utilitarian function in the context of preagricultural populations, be seen as wholly different from this same relationship in respect to sedentary agriculturalists? Scholarly opinion has varied widely in this matter. Among others, Wilson (1988, 30) and Ingold (1986), echoed by Bradley (1997, 6) and Tilley (1994, 36–39), have argued that hunter-gatherers have a fundamentally different relationship to landscape than do sedentary agriculturalists because of the way they utilize and inhabit the land. The argument goes that hunter-gatherers view the landscape in terms of discrete or delineating features that, in a manner of speaking, give it personality and provide concrete access points for key interactions. These include paths, tracks, and landmarks embedded within or coextensive with natural topography. It is claimed that hunter-gatherers personally identify with individual features that mediate their interaction with the land. Land ownership is seen more in terms of controlling these critical paths and landmarks than as ownership of a bounded territory. The land is also taken as a given, "as is" so to speak, rather than as something to be tamed or transformed. As a result, hunter-gatherer myths and beliefs are woven into the landscape as it exists on its own terms (Wilson 1988, 50). Hunter-gatherers create mental maps of the landscape that locate where things of interest actually *are*—for instance, where foodstuffs can be collected and sacred sites visited (ibid., 153–54).

Conversely, domestic folk, who relate to the land in terms of broadly circumscribed plots as an outgrowth of their agricultural activities, have a territorial rather than a feature-oriented view of the land. Their cosmological models are strongly influenced by the structures they build, especially the houses they inhabit, architectural models which they impose on the cognized landscape and which emerge in their symbolic systems. In contrast to the maps of hunter-gatherers, which locate existent cynosures, those dwelling in houses and working land plots create diagrams, which are models of where things *ought* to be (Wilson 1988, 154).

Confirmation of the latter is not difficult to find in the archaeological record. Modeling not just the landscape but caves themselves in terms of architecture is well documented among complex societies of the ancient New World. In Prehispanic Mesoamerica the model of the house, in the sense of a chthonic house inhabited by gods and spirits, is a principal though not an exclusive symbolic role of caves (Stone 1995, 35–36). The term *stone house* appears in a number of Mayan languages to refer to "cave," and extensive ethnographic and ethnohistoric evidence links caves to houses. We see, for instance, in the sixteenth-century K'iche epic myth, the *Popol Vuh*, a reference to the House of Bats as a thinly veiled allusion to a cave. Caves are depicted in Classic Maya art and architecture in architectonic terms (see Moyes and Brady, figure 10.4, this volume; Stone 2003). Mesoamericans also physically altered the land to put caves where they *ought* to be in terms of cosmological models. Artificial caves were dug at many sites in the Maya area, typically in soft volcanic ash (Brady and Veni 1992; Moyes and Brady, this volume). This practice, in effect, brought natural topography into architectural centers and created a kind of ideal landscape (Stone 1992). Even the immense cave under the Pyramid of the Sun at Teotihuacan is not natural.

Architectonic models for caves can also be seen in the high Andes among the Inca whose origin myth centers on three caves at a place called Pacariqtambo. The myth echoes a belief, prevalent among indigenes in the Valley of Cuzco, in an ancestral place of origin, or *paqarina*. The Inca's royal paqarina at Pacariqtambo provides an intriguing study of how, as elsewhere in the world, ruling elites supported their claims of exalted status by affiliating themselves with phenomena outside the normal social order (Bauer 1991). Here Pacariqtambo is "exotic" because of its location outside the Valley of Cuzco. The origin myth describes three ancestral brothers and their sister-consorts emerging from a group of three caves in a hill called Tambotoco. Bauer (1991) tracked down several potential locales which may have been the original Pacariqtambo, all located in a region south of Cuzco. One site is a real cave; however, the others consist of architectural or sculptural remains that arguably would have been construed as caves.

FIGURE 27.1 Detail of drawing by sixteenth-century Quechua author, Pachacuti Yamqui, depicting the three caves at Pacariqtambo: (center) Capactoco, (right) Sutitoco, and (left) Marastoco. The caves resemble windows, which would conform with the Inca view of caves as the windows of a mountain. (After Cummins 1994, figure 9.)

The chief ancestor is Manco Capac, who formed a union with his sister-consort, Mama Oclla. From this couple the Inca emperor traced his lineal descent. Their emergence place at Tambotoco is the central cave in the group of three. A cave-hill complex today bearing the name Tambotoco is a potential site of Pacariqtambo (Bauer 1991, figure 6). The caves are called Capactoco, Sutitoco, and Marastoco. The –*toco* (*t'oqo*) suffix means "window" (Urton 1990, 20), as the caves were seen as windows resting at the base of a mountain. As sketched by the indigenous Quechua author Pachacuti Yamqui, the three caves do resemble windows (figure 27.1). However, we must keep in mind that Inca windows are trapezoidal in shape and that these graphic forms closely resemble standard textile patterns, as well as following a general tendency for geometric abstraction prevalent in Andean design (Cummins 1994, 202). Yet, Pachacuti Yamqui's caves are an abstraction possibly with an architectonic twist. Indeed, the nested rectangles recall the recessed double-jamb windows and doors of Inca architecture.

While the above seems to support drawing a hard line between the hunter-gatherer and the agriculturalist in terms of their cognized models of caves, and consequently their ritual use, other authors see commonalities in the uses of caves for rituals by groups at different sociopolitical levels. Something along these lines is implicit in a study by Bradley (2000) that finds common ground, at least on this issue, among egalitarian Saami hunters of northern Scandinavia and agriculturalists from Bronze Age Crete, the latter described as at the "early developmental stage of the state." Information on Saami beliefs and use of topographic shrines comes from a wealth of contemporary ethnohistoric sources spanning the past centuries. They tell us that Saami caves were one of several types of distinct, unaltered topographic locales called *siejdde*, used for petitioning specific gods through offerings, generally to ensure a good hunt. They were often associated with a sacred tree and an unusual, often humanoid-looking, rock formation. Ukonsari Cave in Finland is cited as one cave *siejdde*.

Information about Bronze Age Crete's ritual cave use is scant, but some ideas can be gleaned from knowledge of related phenomena, such as the use of hilltop shrines found in Classical Greece, descriptions of which come from observant Hellenistic writers such as Pausanius. In Greece, caves were places of the origin and emergence of the ancestral gods. Zeus was thought to have been born in a Cretan cave. This may seem a far cry from the Saami *siejdde*, where hunting was the central focus, but Bradley (2000, 28) makes the general point that in both regions topographic shrines were associated with specific supernatural beings and were geographically transitional, joining different kinds of terrain, usually the meeting of sea and mountain or earth. By invoking Eliade's (1954) notion of sacred and profane, wherein the sacred expresses cosmic order and rituals at sacred sites are geared to reinforce that order, the comparison is further extended. In both regions topographic shrines—such as caves, or, in Classical Greece, hilltop shrines or fissures, such as the one used by the Oracle of Delphi—were marginal, indeed liminal, places where different cosmological layers converged and where humans could communicate through those layers with the divine.

Bradley (2000, 29), unfortunately, ultimately explains this similarity through a shared substrate of "shamanic cosmology" both in the Aegean and in northern Scandinavia. However, I see other universal features of socioreligious experience, such as a concern for origins and ancestor worship, as an equally plausible foundation upon which comparable beliefs and rituals would emerge. Evidence for associating ancestors with topographic shrines is as prevalent among agriculturalists as hunter-gatherers, and could be as easily extrapolated into the past as shamanism. In the former case we can point out evidence from ancient Mesoamerica and the Andes, as noted above. Certainly there is ample evidence from the hunter-gatherers of Australia to support this same conclusion. We simply have a lack of information about the role of ancestors and kinship as it relates to Paleolithic cave ritual. Claiming shamanic models as *the* substrate is arbitrary and limits the full scope of religious experience that may have been important. Notwithstanding all of this, I do applaud Bradley's attempt to find common ground in ritual cave use among groups at distinct sociopolitical levels. I also concur with the explanation that these similarities can be traced to shared functions on the most general level.

In conclusion, this chapter has argued that studies of cave ritual should embrace examples from later agricultural periods, even those of state-level societies. What caves can tell us about mediating social interaction is not diminished by levels of social complexity, and, indeed, understanding this role is enriched by seeing it in all possible dimensions. For instance, the best vantage point from which to study cave ritual's capacity to reify the mythic charter of political power is in the context of state-level, or at least agricultural, societies. Beyond that, productive comparisons can be made between cave ritual practices of both sedentary and nonsedentary groups, an exercise that may highlight similarities as well as differences in their cognized maps of the land. As argued here, caves are effective spatial mediators of social interaction and are especially suited for ritual because of their unique physical and geographic properties. As permanent shelters with stable internal conformations, caves supported ritual's need for structure and invariance, while the sensory experiences they offered were ideal for heightening ritual's emotional and psychological content. Viewing cave ritual as an artifact of a primordial psychology that can be recovered in hunter-gatherer lifeways denies its relevance in constructing meaningful relationships between people and landscape no matter what era or place, as the critical nature of this has never become obsolete.

REFERENCES CITED

Bahn, Paul. 1997. "Dancing in the Dark: Probing the Phenomenon of Pleistocene Cave Art." In *The Human Use of Caves*, ed. C. Bonsall and C. Tolan-Smith, 35–37. BAR International Series 667. Oxford: British Archaeological Reports.

Bauer, Brian. 1991. "Pacariqtambo and the Mythical Origins of the Inca." *Latin American Antiquity* 2 (1): 7–26. http://dx.doi.org/10.2307/971893.

Bell, Catherine. 1997. *Ritual: Perspectives and Dimensions*. Oxford: Oxford University Press.

Bloch, Maurice. 1974. "Symbols, Song, Dance, and Features of Articulation: Is Religion an Extreme Form of Traditional Authority?" *European Journal of Sociology* 15 (1): 54–81. http://dx.doi.org/10.1017/S0003975600002824.

Brady, James, and George Veni. 1992. "Man-made and Pseudo-Karst Caves: The Implications of Subsurface Features within Maya Centers." *Geoarchaeology* 7 (2): 149–67. http://dx.doi.org/10.1002/gea.3340070205.

Bradley, Richard. 1997. *Art and the Prehistory of Atlantic Europe: Signing the Land*. London: Routledge.

Bradley, Richard. 2000. *An Archaeology of Natural Places*. London: Routledge.

Bradley, Richard. 2005. *Ritual and Domestic Life in Prehistoric Europe*. London: Routledge.

Cummins, Tom. 1994. "Representation in the Sixteenth Century and the Colonial Image of the Inca." In *Writing without Words: Alternative Literacies in Mesoamerica and the Andes*, ed. Elizabeth Boone and W. Mignolo, 188–219. Durham, NC: Duke University Press.

Drew, David. 2004. "Burials in Caves." In *Encyclopedia of Caves and Karst Science*, ed. John Gunn, 167–69. New York: Fitzroy Dearborn.

Eliade, Mircea. 1954. *The Myth of the Eternal Return*. London: Arkana.

Gamble, Clive. 1999. *The Palaeolithic Societies of Europe*. Cambridge: Cambridge University Press.

Gay, Carlo. 1967. "Oldest Cave Paintings of the New World." *Natural History* 76 (4): 28–35.

Gell, Alfred. 1998. *Art and Agency: An Anthropological Theory*. Oxford: Clarendon Press.

Giddens, Anthony. 1979. *Central Problems in Social Theory: Action, Structure and Contradiction in Social Analysis*. Berkeley: University of California Press.

Ingold, Tim. 1986. "Territoriality and Tenure: The Appropriation of Space in Hunting and Gathering Societies." In *The Appropriation of Nature: Essays on Human Ecology and Social Relations*, ed. Tim Ingold, 130–64. Iowa City: University of Iowa Press.

Pred, Allan. 1984. "Place as Historically Contingent Process: Structuration and the Time-Geography of Becoming Places." *Annals of the Association of American Geographers: Association of American Geographers* 74 (2): 279–97. http://dx.doi.org/10.1111/j.1467-8306.1984.tb01453.x.

Rappaport, Roy. 1971. "The Sacred in Human Evolution." *Annual Review of Ecology and Systematics* 2 (1): 23–44. http://dx.doi.org/10.1146/annurev.es.02.110171.000323.

Sieveking, Ann. 1997. "Cave as Context in Palaeolithic Art." In *The Human Use of Caves*, ed. Clive Bonsall and Christopher Tolan-Smith, 25–34. BAR International Series 667. Oxford: British Archaeological Reports.

Stone, Andrea. 1992. "From Ritual in the Landscape to Capture in the Urban Center: The Recreation of Ritual Environments in Mesoamerica." *Journal of Ritual Studies* 6 (1): 109–32.

Stone, Andrea. 1995. *Images from the Underworld: Naj Tunich and the Tradition of Maya Cave Painting*. Austin: University of Texas Press.

Stone, Andrea. 2003. "Principles and Practices of Classic Maya Cave Symbolism." Paper presented at the Society for American Archaeology, Milwaukee, WI.

Stone, Andrea. 2004. "Cave Art in the Americas." In *Encyclopedia of Caves and Karst Science*, ed. John Gunn, 91–94. New York: Fitzroy Dearborn.

Tilley, Christopher. 1994. *A Phenomenology of Landscape: Places, Paths and Monuments*. Oxford: Berg.

Tolan-Smith, Christopher, and Clive Bonsall. 1997. "The Human Use of Caves." In *The Human Use of Caves*, ed. Clive Bonsall and Christopher Tolan-Smith, 217–18. BAR International Series 667. Oxford: British Archaeological Reports.

Urton, Gary. 1990. *The History of a Myth: Pacariqtambo and the Origin of the Incas*. Austin: University of Texas Press.

Waller, Steven J. 1993. "Sound Reflection as an Explanation for the Content and Context of Rock Art." *Rock Art Research* 10 (2): 91–95.

Wilson, Peter J. 1988. *The Domestication of the Human Species*. New Haven, CT: Yale University Press.

28

Caves and Spatial Constraint
The Prehistoric Implications

Ezra B.W. Zubrow

> Art in Nature is rhythmic and has
> a horror of constraint.
>
> Robert Delaunay

> And the arbitrariness of the constraint serves
> only to obtain precision of execution.
>
> Igor Stravinsky

The purposes of this chapter are to introduce "spatial constraint theory" to archaeology and to suggest that it is relevant to understanding prehistoric adaptations to caves and rockshelters. In the 1960s when I was first introduced to archaeology and anthropology, I read works of the Kulturkreislehre School (Kluckhohn 1936) as historical documents. Being of a mathematical bent, I was fascinated also by some of the work of Graebner (1911) and its archaeological counterparts. I sat in on a seminars by visiting professors Robert MacArthur (1984; MacArthur and Connell 1966; MacArthur and Wilson 1967) and George Gaylord Simpson (1965, 1967) at the University of Arizona in the late 1960s. I read E. C. Pielou (1969, 1977, 1991), and was greatly influenced by Peter Haggett's and Richard Chorley's articles and books on locational analysis and spatial modeling (Haggett 1965; Haggett and Chorley 1970; Chorley 1973; Chorley and Haggett 1968, 1970). The quantitative geographers and ecologists were also important in shaping my thinking about the location of both cultural and natural sites. Many years later (the spring and summer of 1996) I had a chance to spend several months with Peter Haggett at the Institute for Advanced Study in Bristol where he was the director. My interests in such topics were reawakened.

SPATIAL ANALYSIS

The early work from the 1960s has been built upon and superseded by new developments through the last decades emphasizing statistical characteristics, choice, temporal changes, and autocorrelation (Bartlett 1975; Cliff and Ord 1973; Cormack and Ord 1979; Golledge and Rushton 1976; Rogers 1974). Others focused on quantitative methods (Fischer and Getis 1997; Fotheringham, Brunsdon, and Charlton 2000; Fotheringham and Rogerson 1994). In 2001, a summary article by Manfred M. Fischer brought many of these together in a single table reprinted here (table 28.1). Since 2001, exploratory analysis, Bayesian statistics, and their applications to such areas as ecology, traffic, crime, and urban planning have become important (Andrienko and Andrienko 2006; Fortin and Dale 2005; Longley and Batty 2003; MacNab 2004; Majumdar, Ochieng, and Noland 2004).

Time is fundamental as well as space. A good summary of the analytical relationships among spatial and temporal issues is provided by Emilio Casetti (2001). Many studies analyze, model, or reconstruct changes across both space

TABLE 28.1 Popular techniques and methods in spatial data analysis.

Object data	Exploratory Spatial Data Analysis	Model-Driven Spatial Data Analysis
Point pattern	Quadrat methods	Homogeneous and heterogeneous Poisson process models and multivariate extensions
	Kernel density estimation	
	Nearest neighbor methods	
	K-function analysis	
Area data	Global measures of spatial associations: Moran's I, Geary's c	Spatial regression models
	Local measures of spatial association: G_i and G_i^* statistics, Moran's scatter plot	Regression models with spatially autocorrelated residuals
Field data	Variogram and covariogram	Trend surface models
	Kernel density estimation	Spatial prediction and kriging
	Thiessen polygons	Spatial general linear modeling
Spatial interaction data	Exploratory techniques for representing such data	Spatial interaction models
		Location-allocation models
	Techniques to uncover evidence of hierarchical structure in the data such as graph-theoretic and regionalization techniques	
		Spatial Choice and Search Models

and time. Frequently, they rely upon diffusion, osmosis, migration processes, and flows. One may analyze space from the perspective of time or time from the perspective of space. So Casetti divides spatiotemporal analysis into canonical models that emphasize the spatial variation of temporal change and compartmental models where interactions such as flows "link sub models referring to spatial entities such as regions or countries" (2001, 14837).

Many of these developments are the result of a huge GIS industry. From a series of small university laboratory innovations in the late 1950s and early 1960s, the GIS industry has grown to a technology that is seen in almost every country in governmental and business enterprises. It was estimated to be worth more than 4.4 billion US dollars by the end of 2010 (http://gislounge.com/gis-industry-trends/). Early proponents of using spatial analysis and GIS included Duane Marble, Richard Tomlinson, and Hugh Calkins (Marble 1967; Marble and Anderson 1972; Marble and Bowlby 1968; Marble et al. 1984; Tomlinson, Calkins, and Marble 1976). A good historical overview from 1960 through the first decade of the twenty-first century is the Centre for Advanced Spatial Analysis's time line of GIS. It may be found at (http://www.casa.ucl.ac.uk/gistimeline/).

Today, GIScience complements GISystems in many arenas. The former emphasizes theory, methods, and solutions to particular problems, including such examples as spatial interpretation and interpolation, discontinuous and patchy data, geometric and temporal modeling, topological equivalency, boundary recovery, and tetrahedralization, to name a few. The latter seems to be dominated by three large software systems. ESRI's ARC focuses mostly on end-user applications and is a favorite of academics for research. INTERGRAPH appears frequently in very large scale and infrastructure developments. Both are commercial with high-end, expensive systems. GRASS is open-access software and is favored by those who prefer to do their own programming.

SPATIAL ANALYSIS IN ARCHAEOLOGY

Archaeology has always had a strong spatial component. It derives from several sources. One has been the long-term recognition of the importance of provenience. Even before the eighteenth century, the spatial locus of prehistoric and historic finds were thought to be important. Provenience verified reality and authenticity. Later, it was understood that context and provenience could provide dating, reconstruction, and the answers to the questions of what, when, where, and why as archaeology moved through stages of evolutionism, diffusionism, cultural historicism, processualism, and postprocessualism (Trigger 2006; Willey and Sabloff 1980).

Another direction was from ethnoarchaeology—examining activity areas (Kent 1984, 1987) and domestic space (Gamble and Boismier 1991; Kent 1990; Ogundele 2005) as well as cultural landscapes both secular and religious (Ceruti 1999; Rossignol and Wandsnider 1992).

Seminal works include Binford's (1978, 1991) studies in the arctic and temperate areas.

A third direction would be from archaeological cognition (Renfrew and Zubrow 1994), which supplements and reinforces ethnoarchaeology, and vice versa. This direction is concerned with how prehistoric individuals thought, not from a postprocessualist interpretation, but from a more behavioral and neuroscientific view of cognition. Such studies as Andre Costopoulos's on the spatial impact of changing memory capacity (2001), Françoise Audouze on food sharing or education (1999; Audouze and Enloe 1991), Jason Shapiro's spatial grammars after Glassie (Shapiro 2005; Glassie 2000), and Shannon Plank's architectural and linguistic integration (2004) would be examples. Indeed, it would be nice to be able to take the work of David Mark with the Hopi and Zuni or the cross-cultural classification of types of terms used for different landscapes and features and move it backward through time (Mark, Turk, and Stea 2007).

However, more particularly, spatial analysis has had a long history in archaeology. General studies date back to the 1970s and 1980s (Clarke 1977; Hodder 1978; Hodder and Orton 1976). There were early modeling studies (Paynter 1982) and analyses of inter- and intra-spatial relationships (Hietala and Larson 1984). Although earlier studies exist, beginning slowly in the 1970s the interest in the spatial characteristics of the prehistoric landscape rapidly increased through the 1980s and 1990s and continues up through the present with what seems to be an inexhaustible range of prehistoric and archaeological landscape studies. A very small, typical but nonrepresentative (in any statistical sense) sample can be cited here: Attema and Rijksuniversiteit te Groningen 2002; Barker 1981; Barker, Hodges, and Clark 1995; Cherry, Davis, and Mantzourani 1991; Cremeens and Hart 2003; Grinsell and Fowler 1972; Hauser 2007; Kelso and Most 1990; Metheny 2007; Mithen 2001; Reeves-Smyth and Hamond 1983; Taylor, Everson, and Williamson 1998; Trément, Pasquinucci, and POPULUS 2000; Trinkley et al. 1992; Ucko and Layton 1999; Wagstaff 1987; and Wiseman and Zachos 2003.

As in the case of geography, Geographic Information Science and Geographic Information Systems have had a major impact on the discipline (Richards 1998). The changes in two decades have been very significant from the early introductions in the late 1980s and early 1990s (Allen, Green, and Zubrow 1990) to the state of the art today (Aldenderfer and Maschner 1996; Conolly and Lake 2006). Two processes should be noted. One is as the software improved and became easier to use, as well as cheaper, the use of GISystems as part of the standard toolkits and procedures for excavations and surveys became de rigueur.

Concomitantly, the use of GISystems diffused from specialists to almost all field and analytical archaeologists (Bintliff, Kuna, and Venclová 2000; Doolittle, Neely, and Adams 2004; Gaffney and Stančič 1991). The second process, which has been only slightly slower, has been the use of GIScience to determine spatial relationships that were indiscernible in the prehistoric record, such as interpolated land-ownership patterns and religious viewsheds or soundsheds (Estrada-Belli 1999; Galloway 2006; Lock and Stančič 1984). A large number of predictive models for site type and site location have revolutionized contract archaeology in the past decade (Henry and Armstrong 2004; Mehrer and Wescott 2006). In short, spatial analysis is an important part of the historical arts and sciences (Galloway 2006; Knowles 2002).

SPATIAL CONSTRAINTS: THEORY AND PRACTICE

Generally, spatial constraint theory has developed in computer science and cognitive science departments, but it also builds on a considerable literature from geography (Frank 2006), querying strategy (Goldstein 1996), databases (Gaede 1996; Kuper and Wallace 1996), artificial cognition (Allen 2007; Loula, Gudwin, and Queiroz 2007), reverse engineering (Menon, Desai, and Buckey 1997), spatial layout (Baykan 1991), dynamics flows, and temporal problems (Chin, Karl, and Wilsky 1992; Schott 1989; Zhao and Badler 1989).

As Frank (2006) has pointed out, the relationships between extended objects—that is non-point-like objects—need to be created as extensions of the relations among points. Peuquet and Zhan suggest visual interpretation that is essentially a conic system (Peuquet and Ci-Xiang 1987). Another by Papadias and Sellis (1992) is based upon bounding rectangles that are related to GIS buffering. Similarly Frank has suggested the sets of spatial relationships illustrated in figure 28.1.

Spatial constraints may be qualitative, quantitative, and/or material (Gross-Amblard and de Rougemont 2006). One way to conceive of spatial constraints is to consider them from the perspective of spatial reasoning. One may conceive of a spatial constraint network—that is, a qualitative graph—where the nodes represent objects and the arcs represent spatial relations. Inserting a new object or a new relationship between two objects in the network impacts not only the original objects but, because of the composition, the insertion yields additional constraints (Frank 2006). One might think about a simple prehistoric example in which one node is individuals, another fire pits, and another middens, and then imagine what happens if a new object such as a cave wall is inserted.

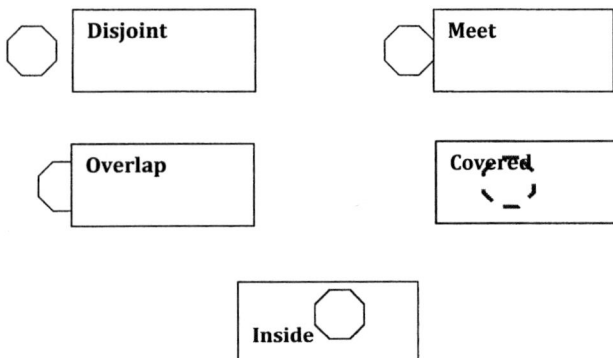

FIGURE 28.1 Spatial relationships redrawn from Frank (2006).

Others augment these generalities, working downward from the broader to the more specific. In general, the greater the constraints the more precise is the execution and the better the predictability. This is because there are fewer choices. Some constraints will slow motion or create a change in direction. Others, such as a cave wall, will block motion completely. In a three- or four-dimensional system, spatial constraints may be the result of the ability of the actor to move in only two or three dimensions.

Constraints are based on the ability of the mover to sense the constraint or, conversely, for the constrainer to sense the mover. In some sense, constraints are based upon the signals of the constraining phenomenon that it is, indeed, constraining. Furthermore, frequently it is necessary for the phenomenon doing the constraining and the phenomenon being constrained to signal each other. Namely, signals must be sent that the one is constraining and that the other is approaching the constraining phenomenon. In addition, there are issues of reducing constraints. To what degree are the "once constrained" able to figure out ways to "unconstrain" themselves?

Movement is not a uniform phenomenon under constraining systems. In some cases the amount of constraining resistance will vary, creating preferred directions. There will be preferred movements—for example, in a cave situation there may be general rules that people will prefer to move away from the dark to the light. In general, if one is unable to go directly to the goal, it is preferable to move parallel to the general direction of the goal than in any other direction. In some cases moving in one direction will be more difficult than moving in the opposite direction, even over the same spatial transect—for example, going uphill on skis, in contrast to downhill. Sometimes moving to the goal will be more difficult if one leaves the path, for there may be greater constraints to returning to the path than there may be to getting to the original goal.

Constraints may change over time. They may be periodic in space, in time, or both. Furthermore, they may evolve singularly or together. The constraints themselves may change in a periodic manner. For example, a cave may show periods of deposition or erosion. Or, there may be sequences of depositing and eroding that occur with a periodicity. For example, sequences of deposition and erosion that result from wave action could be related to the constraining factor of the tide. Or the spatial-constraint networks may evolve over time until a threshold is reached and then there is a fixed pattern indefinitely (Condotta et al. 2006).

Constraints may be realized proactively or reactively. Constraints may be junctive or disjunctive, by which is meant that when there are two or more criteria that are creating the constraints, they may be junctive ("and") or disjunctive ("or"). These constraint systems are far more general than simply human motion. For example, assume that a type of lithic production (Levalloisian) is a process in which strikes are created using a mallet, a core, and an intervening bone or horn tool. The production tools should satisfy the following two criteria: first, they should be able to withstand the forces they are going to be subject to, and second, the tool shapes should be such that no tool parts interfere in the striking process. These would be junctive constraints in that both of the two criteria (durability *and* non-interfering shape) need to be met.

Now I turn to some constraining conditions regarding people who use caves. People move in and are compliant in all directions. However, there are preferred and nonpreferred directions of motion at a given time point. Caves create spatial constraints on human movement physically, perceptually, and culturally. These may include issues with light and dark, the sacred and profane, and simply pressure. They may act as a box in which the human activity is similar to Brownian motion. The smaller the box or, correlatively, the faster the movers are moving, the greater the pressure.

SIMULATION AND ANALYSIS

In order to examine the impact on spatial constraint on prehistoric cave users, I have created a set of experiments. A number of simulations were done. Sets of caves of three shapes were created: an arc, an extended arc, and a flat arc. They were conceived as being a more or less standard large-mouthed cave, a much deeper large-mouthed cave, and something more similar to a shallow rockshelter than a true cave. Other shapes could be created—a small-mouthed, large-bodied cave, for one example.

Into each cave, the same numbers of people were introduced, in the same manner, and for the same length of time. These people then moved in a periodic manner.

TABLE 28.2 Location by figure number of the results from the simulations shown in this chapter's figures. u = upper diagrams and l = lower diagrams, such that "2u" should be read as "Figure 28.2, upper diagrams," and "3l" should be read as "Figure 28.3, lower diagrams."

Direction/Cave type	Arc	Extended Arc	Flat Arc
Vertical-South/North	2u, 3u, 5u	6u	7u, 7l
Horizontal/West-East	2l, 3l, 5l	6l	7u, 7l
Combined/All Directions	4		

One type of periodic movement was that they could move toward the inside of the cave or toward the mouth of the cave. That is, they would move back or forth along a north-south axis. A second type of periodic motion was moving back and forth along a west-east axis. The third form would comprise movement in both directions, north-south and west-east.

When one wants to determine existing temporal phenomena, one uses such dynamic methods as Fourier series, auto- and cross-correlation, and trend or decomposition analysis to tease out the processes and the equations that best describe the dynamics of the temporal phenomena. However, as in this case, when one wants to create dynamic and periodic movement within a constrained space, it is a much easier process. Similarly, determining recursive phenomena is more difficult than creating it. Thus, in all of the following simulations, periodic movement was created with the use of spatial and temporal sine and cosine functions. Recursive functions were created by nesting and, if self-reifying, by fractals. Results are found in table 28.2.[1]

Figure 28.2 (upper diagrams) shows the locations of people as they move periodically north to south and back north again, and then north-south again. The upper-left and the upper-right diagrams have identical periodicity functions, but in the case of the upper-left simulation the entry domain is linear while in the case of the upper-right simulation the entry domain is bimodal. In other words,

---

1. A brief glossary of terms is provided for clarity. *Periodicity* is a measure of the degree of recurrence at regular intervals. *Oscillation* is the repetitive variation around a central value spatially or temporally or both. *Recursion* is repetition in a self-similar way. Frequently, it is reiterative. It can be at the same scale or different scales. Fractals are a group of mathematical equations that show self-similarity at different scales and frequently have dimensions that exist between integers. *Bimodality* is a continuous process with two different modes that appear as distinct peaks [or depressions] in the distribution—for example, the height of the tide every day. *Linearity* relates to a straight line in which y is a direct function of x where both have exponents of one. A change in x will make a proportional change in y.)

the two simulations have slightly different characteristics as the population first enters the cave area but then they are essentially similar in following the same periodic movements in and out of the internal area of the cave. The lower graphs are similar except the periodic motion of the people is from west to east and then from east to west, and back again. The entry domain is linear in the lower left and bimodal in the lower right.

The results are interesting. For all four diagrams, clear patterns are created. For the upper- and lower-left graphs, a line of circles appears across the entrance of the cave, with a larger circle below and then some outliers. The circles are bilaterally symmetrical around a north-south axis. The upper graph is slightly more patterned than the lower graph in that there are slightly fewer outliers in the deepest part of the cave and along the edge. For the upper- and lower-right graphs, the only clear pattern is the bilateral symmetry around the north-south axis. For both there is a clear line of activity around the entrance of the cave and, in the lower, a central activity area. Conclusions that might be fairly reached are that linear entry provides more repetitive organization than the bimodal, that all combinations of periodicity and entry provide significant activity at the entrance to the cave, and that there are round activity areas near the entrance of the cave for both north-south and west-east periodic motions.

Figure 28.3 shows the results of four more complicated periodic movement patterns in the same caves as figure 28.2. The movement patterns are more complicated in the sense that the periodic movement consists of the combination of two interacting periodic movements acting at the same time in the same oscillating direction within the cave. A strong degree of activity at the entrance to the cave continues in three of the four simulations—the exception is that the distribution along the cave mouth is less pronounced in the upper-right diagram, where the patterning is oriented around four circles. The two upper simulations show people making use of the entire cave, while the two lower indicate that most of the cave use is toward the mouth.

The upper- and lower-right graphs, with bipolar entry in common, are still primarily patterned in bilateral symmetry around the north-south axis. However, in the right upper, it is far more focused along the walls and internal depth of the cave. Finally, in figure 28.3 compared to figure 28.2, it is clear that north-south motions result in considerably more activity deeper within the cave than do west-east motions.

The fourth figure consists of four periodic movements in which the periodic movement is in both directions simultaneously. All four figures (left and right, upper and lower) show significant patterning. The upper results are

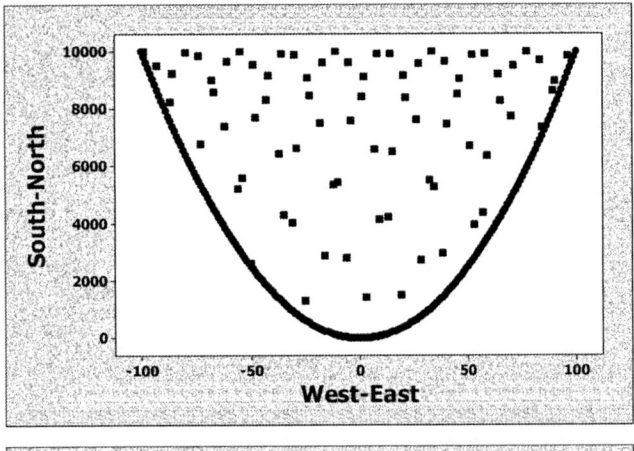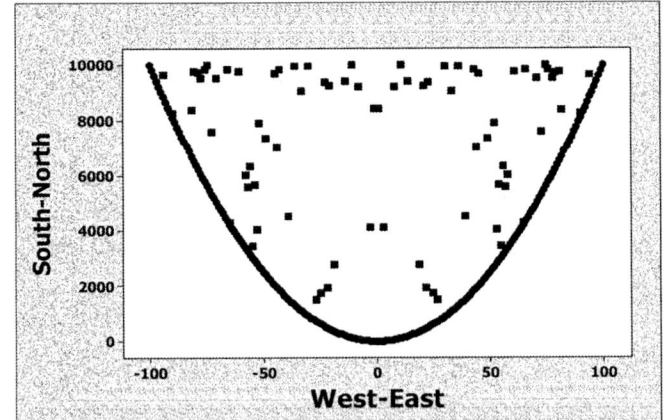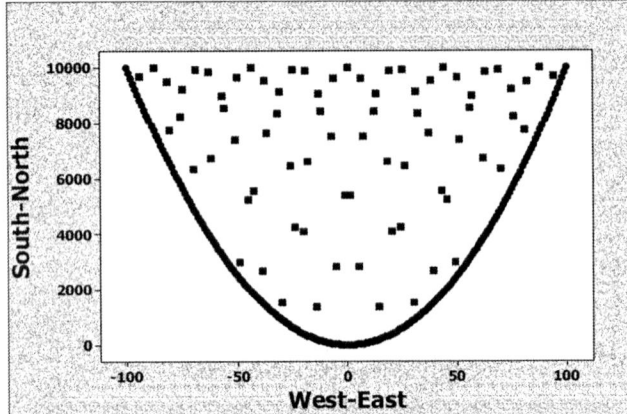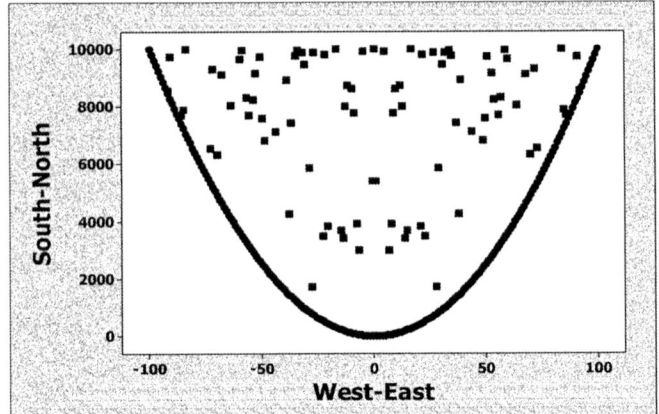

FIGURE 28.2 Four simple periodic movement patterns. Upper graphs: north-south motions. Lower graphs: west-east motions. Left graphs: linear entry domain. Right graphs: bimodal entry domain.

simple, single combinations of the north-south and west-east periodic motions. The lower two add recursive motion. For these upper pictures, the previously heavy activity at the mouth of the cave has now moved farther north and is actually in front of the cave mouth. The circular patterning moves relative to the entrance such that there is more activity outside the entrance and less activity at the entrance itself. In the middle of the upper-left figure (and thus in the middle of the hypothetical cave) are three circular patterns. In the upper-right graph a large circle is bisected west-east at about the entrance. The lower figures, both left and right, are the result of both north-south and west-east movements created recursively. By *recursive* is meant is that the function is self-defined, which results in a repetition in a self-similar way. It is nested. An easily understood example is a room or elevator that has mirrors on opposite walls, so as one looks into one mirror one sees the reflection of the other one, and vice versa, going on to infinity. This is a recursive function. Figure 28.4 (lower left and right) shows the caves with both north-south and east-west periodic movements combined and defined so that they are recursive. The result is that the interaction is moved far more into the interior of the cave in the lower-left example. The linear entry (lower left) is far more laterally patterned (that is, along the cave walls) than the bipolar entry (lower right). The constraints are more symmetrical in the lower left than the lower right. In short, both the single combinations and the recursive combinations change the locus of the interactions (outside the mouth and into the center of the cave.)

Figure 28.5 shows the distributions of the results of the periodic motions if the motions are both nested and self-reifying—that is, if they are fractals (Zubrow 2007). The two images at upper left and right are north-south oscillating motions based upon fractals, while the lower left and right graphs are west-east oscillating movements. The entrance of the cave is where the motions begin again for all four images. The entrance of the upper-left cave has nine circular activity areas, if the partial circles on the sides of the cave are counted. There is also a pattern in the center of the cave that consists of three nested elongated ellipses

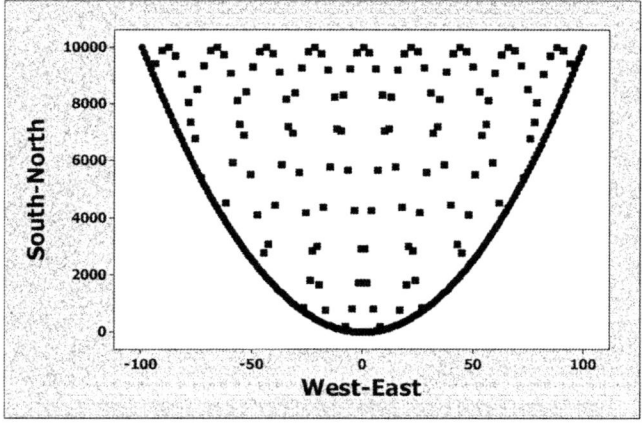
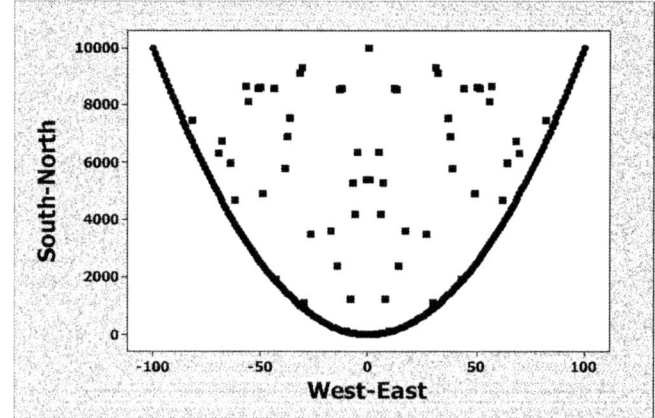
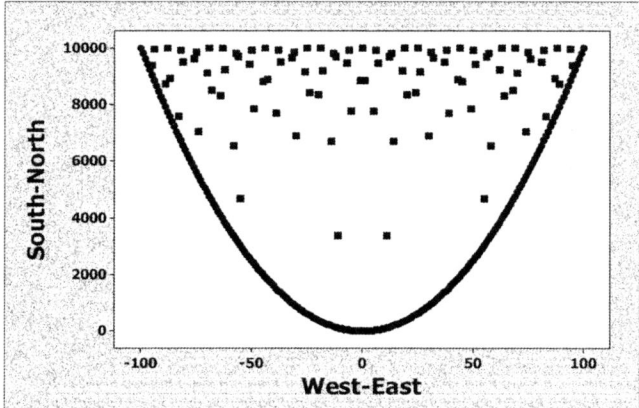
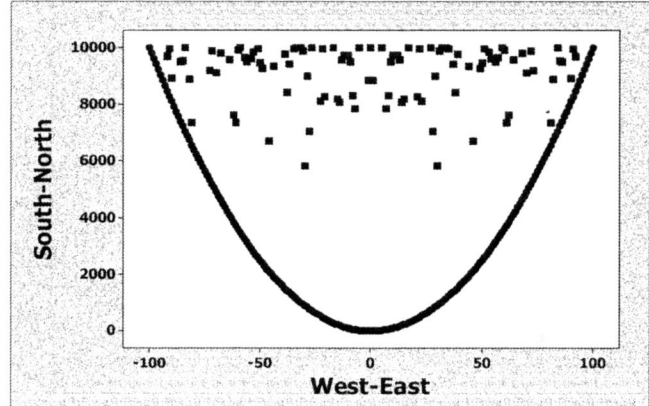

FIGURE 28.3 Four more-complicated periodic movement patterns created by the combination of two interacting periodic movements acting at the same time in the same oscillating direction. Upper graphs: north-south motions. Lower graphs: west-east motions. Right graphs: bimodal entry domain.

whose axis is east-west. The bipolar entry (upper right) continues to be less patterned, and bilaterally symmetrical around the north-south axis. It also does not completely utilize the entire depth of the cave, stopping all motion about two-thirds of the way into the cave. The lower figures, both with west-east motion, are generally similar to their north-south counterparts. However, a difference is noted. The lower-right (west-east) figure shows more use of the deeper parts of the cave than the upper-right (north-south) figure. Furthermore, in comparison to the line of circular activity areas at the front of the cave, there are two distinct circular areas in the north central part of the cave in the lower-right diagram, and overall there is a far greater concentration of motions at the front of the cave and in the center than in any other of the diagrams in figure 28.5.

Figure 28.6 shows the result of extending the cave walls—that is, making much larger caves. In addition, the periodic motions are extended to reflect the larger size. The diagram at upper left shows a familiar pattern. There is a concentration in the entrance, with six-plus activity circles. In the center and depth of the cave are three nested circular activity areas. In the upper-right diagram, the three nested circular activity areas have extended to take up almost the entire cave.

However, what is far more surprising takes place in the lower figures, where the west-east periodic motions are taking place. In these cases, both the lower-left and lower-right graphs, all the activity is taking place in the deepest part of the cave. The diagram on the left, with the linear entrance domain, shows activity that is very patterned. In contrast, the lower-right diagram, with a bimodal entrance domain, displays less patterning but does have three small circular activity areas in the deepest part of the cave.

Figure 28.7 shows extended activities. In the upper diagrams, two simultaneous motions take place: two north-south oscillating motions (upper left) or two west-east motions (upper right). Considerable activity for each of these takes place in front of the caves—more than in

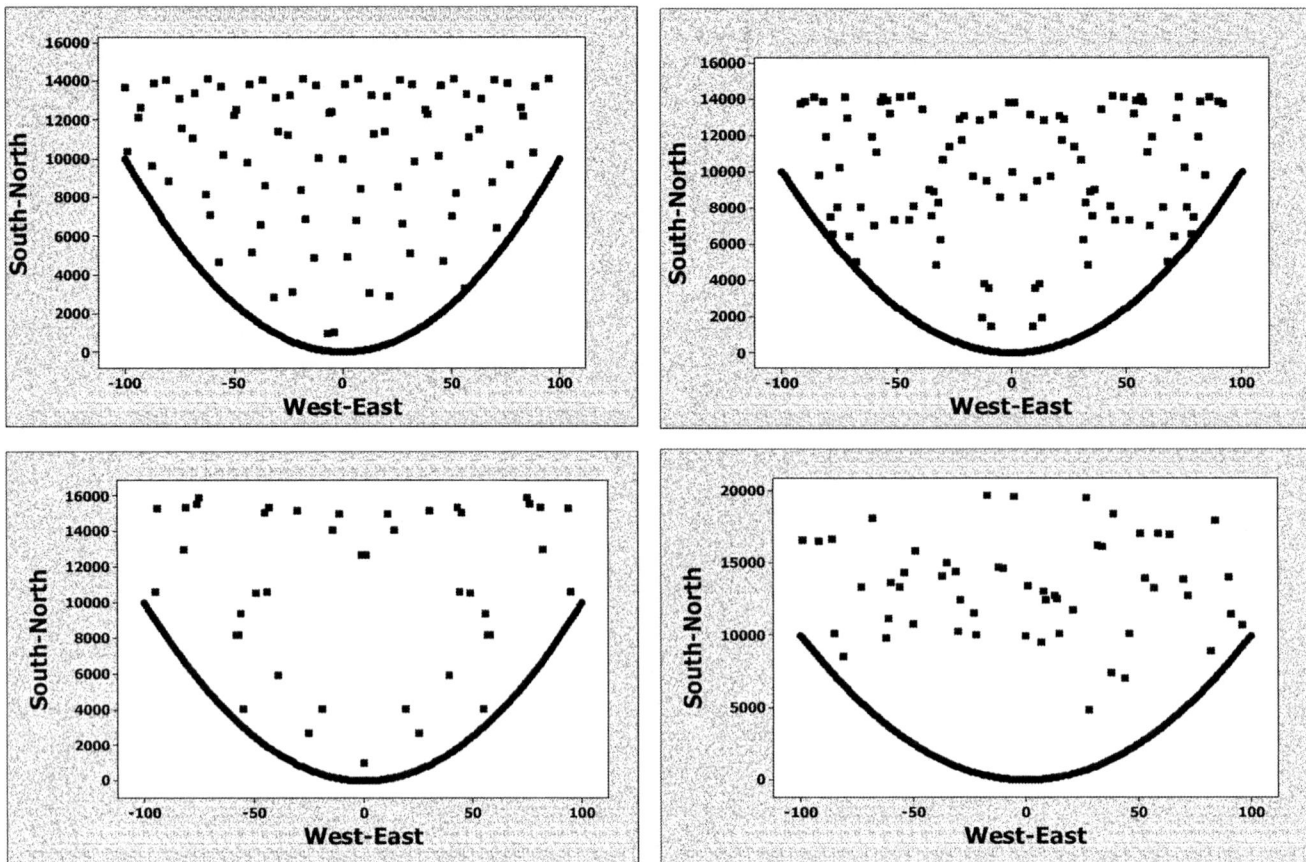

FIGURE 28.4 Four more-complicated ("two oscillating directions") periodic movement patterns. The periodic movement is in both north-south and west-east directions simultaneously. The lower two diagrams add recursive motion. (Upper graphs: north-south motions. Lower graphs: east-west motions with recursive motions. Left graphs: linear entry domain. Right graphs: bimodal entry domain.)

any previous diagram. On the upper left there really is not any pattern in the same sense as we have seen before, while the upper-right diagram has a clear if complicated pattern. There appear to be two circular activity areas spanning the mouth of the cave and one slightly more rectangular one deeper into the cave.

In the lower diagrams, nested and self-reifying fractal motions take place in both directions at the same time. Both show increased activity at the mouth of the cave, with diminishing activity as one moves outside or inside the mouth. Furthermore, most of the activity is concentrated in the center of the mouth and is represented by diminishing numbers of elements as the radius from the center becomes larger.

The simulation shows in general that linear entry creates more patterned interaction than does bipolar entry. North-south motions generally are more patterned than west-east motions. There are generally more changes in the amount of cave used within the cave in west-east movements than north-south. The combination of west-east and north-south movements, whether with or without recursion, changes the amount of cave used both inside and outside the cave significantly, as does extending the walls or changing the shape. Changing the motion to a fractally based motion also has a significant impact.

CONCLUSIONS

This chapter has reviewed both the history and present use of spatial analysis as well as its use in archaeology. It has introduced the rapidly developing field of spatial constraint theory and suggested some uses in archaeology. In particular, it has argued for spatial constraint theory's relevance to understanding prehistoric use and adaptation to caves and rockshelters. A simulation study was undertaken, using used different types of (1) entry to caves, (2) directions of periodic oscillating motions (north-south, west-east, and in combination, (3) different shaped caves, and (4) dif-

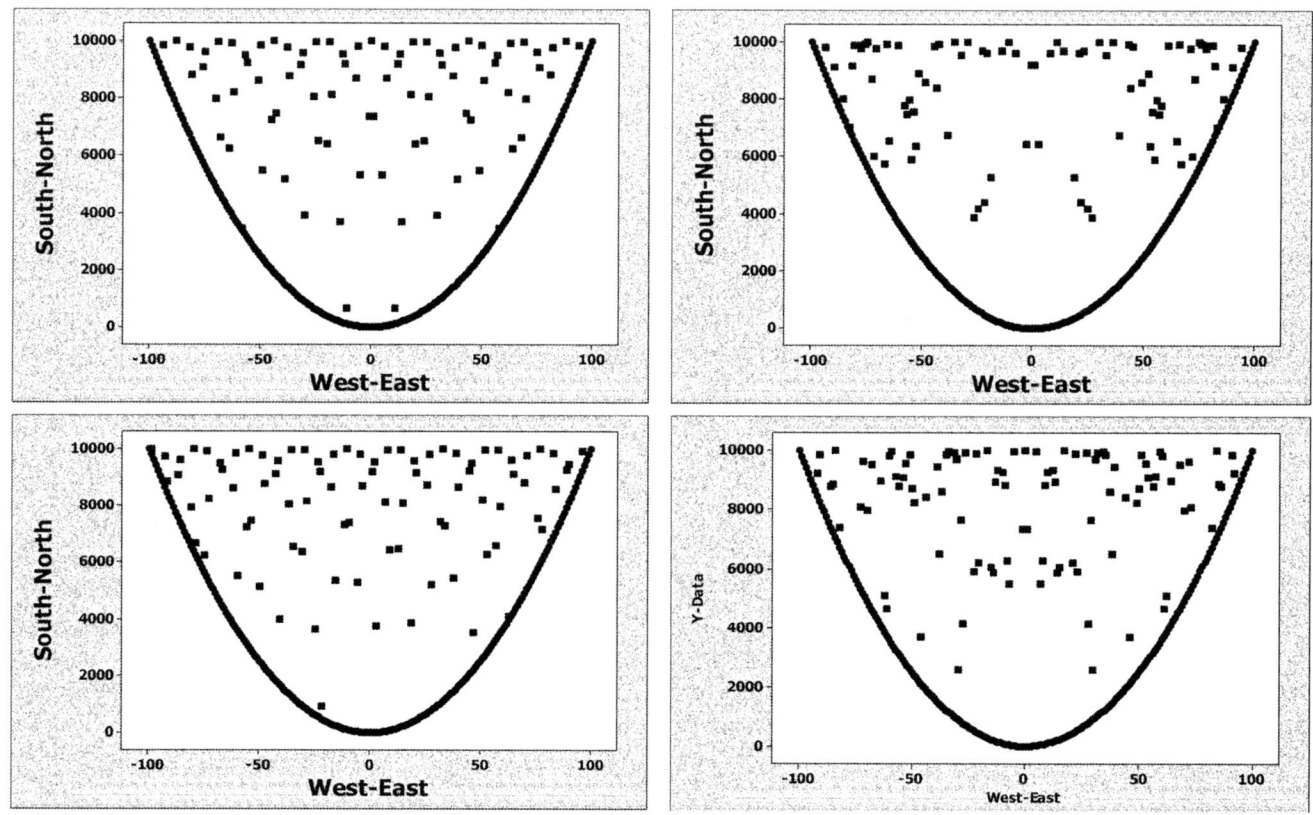

FIGURE 28.5 Four fractal periodic movement patterns, nested and self-reifying, and spatially constrained by cave walls.

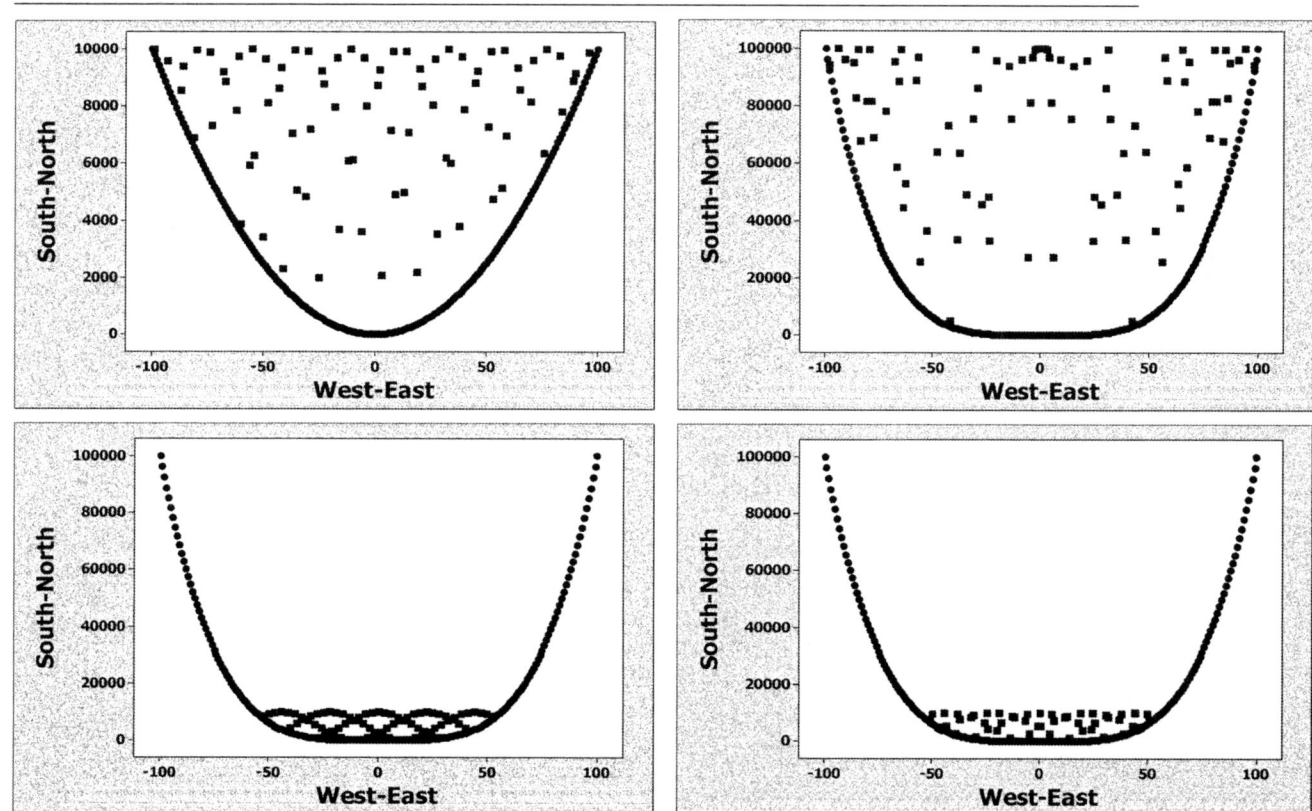

FIGURE 28.6 Four extended-function periodic movements with larger extended caves.

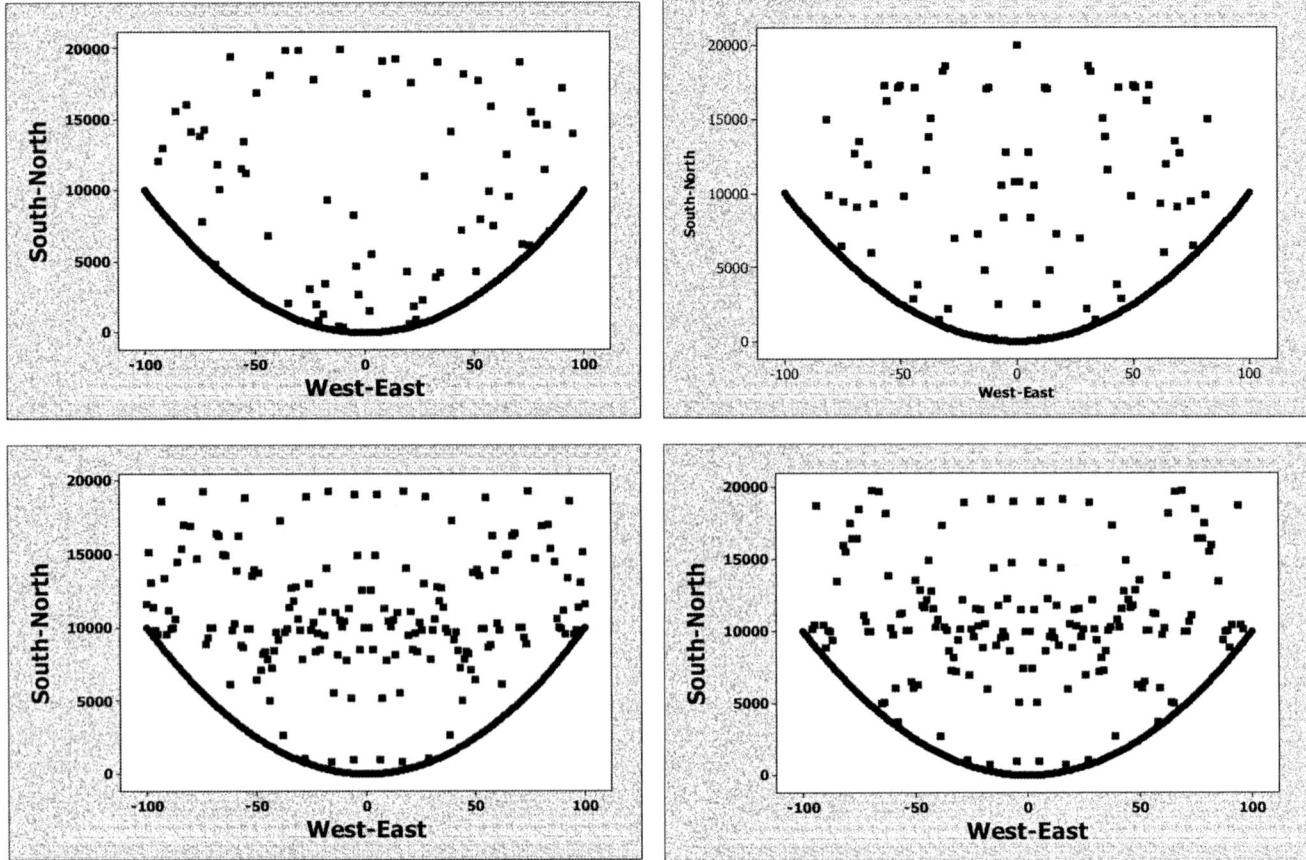

FIGURE 28.7 Four extended activities reflecting periodic movements for caves with multiple functions. The upper diagrams are (left) two simultaneous north-south oscillating motions and (right) two simultaneous west-east oscillating motions. The lower diagrams are nested and self-reifying fractal motions taking place in both directions at the same time.

ferent types of oscillating periodic motions based upon simple, extended, fractal, and recursive functions. The simulation shows significant differences in patterning caused by type of entry and increased patterning in interactions created by periodic movements that are perpendicular to the cave mouth (north-south). Oscillating periodic movements that are parallel to the cave mouth (west-east) vary the amount of cave use both inside and outside the front of the cave, as do oscillating movements resulting from the combination of directions, without or with recursion.

If nothing else, this chapter shows that to understand the distribution of artifacts within and around caves, the constraint of human movement by the shape of the cave will need to be understood. The use of spatial constraint theory should help. Obviously, ritual frequently requires constrained periodic spatial movement. For example, one might think about people attending a Christian Church as each leaves his or her seat and moves forward to receive Communion and Holy Sacrament. One could use spatial constraint theory to see what primary and ancillary interactions are possible. This could be done with other ethnographically more relevant examples. I also believe that one might be able to look at the distribution pattern of the artifacts and the cave boundaries and probably infer backward to the spatial constraints. Both of these, however, raise a series of theoretical and methodological problems that cannot be dealt with in this relatively short chapter.

REFERENCES CITED

Aldenderfer, Mark S., and Herbert D.G. Maschner. 1996. *Anthropology, Space, and Geographic Information Systems.* New York: Oxford University Press.

Allen, Gary L. 2007. *Applied Spatial Cognition: From Research to Cognitive Technology.* Mahwah, NJ: Lawrence Erlbaum Associates.

Allen, Kathleen M.S., Stanton W. Green, and Ezra B.W. Zubrow. 1990. *Interpreting Space: GIS and Archaeology.* Bristol, PA: Taylor & Francis.

Andrienko, Natalia, Gennady Andrienko, and SpringerLink (online service). 2006. *Exploratory Analysis of Spatial and Temporal Data: A Systematic Approach.* New York: Springer.

Attema, Peter A.J. and Rijksuniversiteit te Groningen. 2002. *New Developments in Italian Landscape Archaeology: Theory and Methodology of Field Survey, Land Evaluation and Landscape Perception, Pottery Production and Distribution.* Oxford: Archaeopress.

Audouze, Francoise. 1999. "New Advances in French Prehistory." *Antiquity* 73 (279): 67–75.

Audouze, Francoise, and James G. Enloe. 1991. *Subsistence Strategies and Economy in the Magdalenian of the Paris Basin, France.* Research Report, Council for British Archaeology 77: 63–71.

Barker, Graeme. 1981. *Landscape and Society: Prehistoric Central Italy.* New York: Academic Press.

Barker, Graeme, Richard Hodges, and Gillian Clark. 1995. *A Mediterranean Valley: Landscape Archaeology and Annales History in the Biferno Valley.* New York: Leicester University Press.

Bartlett, Maurice Stevenson. 1975. *The Statistical Analysis of Spatial Pattern.* New York: Chapman and Hall.

Baykan, Can. 1991. "Formulating Spatial Layout as a Disjunctive Constraint Satisfaction Problem." PhD dissertation, Department of Architecture, Carnegie Mellon University, Pittsburgh.

Binford, Lewis Roberts. 1978. *Nunamiut Ethnoarchaeology.* New York: Academic Press.

Binford, Lewis Roberts. 1991. *Cultural Diversity among Aboriginal Cultures of Coastal Virginia and North Carolina.* New York: Garland.

Bintliff, John. L., Martin Kuna, and Natalie Venclová. 2000. *The Future of Surface Artefact Survey in Europe.* Sheffiled, UK: Sheffield Academic Press.

Casetti, Emilio. 2001. "Spatial-Temporal Modeling." In *International Encyclopedia of the Social and Behavioral Sciences*, ed. Neil J. Smelser and P. B. Baltes, 14837–14840. Amsterdam: Elsevier. http://dx.doi.org/10.1016/B0-08-043076-7/02517-1.

Centre for Advanced Spatial Analysis. 2008. http://www.casa.ucl.ac.uk/gistimeline/ (July 21, 2008).

Ceruti, María Constanza. 1999. *Cumbres sagradas del noroeste argentino: avances en arqueología de alta montaña y etnoarqueología de santuarios de altura andinos.* Buenos Aires: Editorial Universitaria de Buenos Aires.

Cherry, John F., Jack L. Davis, and Eleni Mantzourani. 1991. *Landscape Archaeology as Long-Term History: Northern Keos in the Cycladic Islands from Earliest Settlement until Modern Times.* Los Angeles: UCLA Institute of Archaeology.

Chin, Toshio M., William Clement Karl, and Alan S. Wilsky. 1992. "Sequential Optical Flow Estimation Using Temporal Coherence." *IEEE Transactions on Image Processing* 346: 42. Cambridge, MA: Center for Intelligent Control Systems, MIT.

Chorley, Richard J. 1973. *Directions in Geography.* London: Methuen.

Chorley, Richard J., and Peter Haggett. 1968. *Models in Geography.* London: Methuen.

Chorley, Richard J., and Peter Haggett. 1970. *Frontiers in Geographical Teaching.* London: Methuen.

Clarke, David L. 1977. *Spatial Archaeology.* New York: Academic Press.

Cliff, Andrew D., and J. Keith Ord. 1973. *Spatial Autocorrelation.* London: Pion.

Condotta, Jean-Francois, Gerard Ligozat, Mahmoud Saade, and Stavros Tripakis. 2006. *Ultimately Periodic Simple Temporal Problems (UPSTPs).* Thirteenth International Symposium on Temporal Representation and Reasoning, Budapest, 69–77. IEEE.

Conolly, James, and Mark Lake. 2006. *Geographical Information Systems in Archaeology.* New York: Cambridge University Press.

Cormack, R. M., and J. Keith Ord. 1979. *Spatial and Temporal Analysis in Ecology.* Fairland, MD: International Co-operative Publishing House.

Costopoulos, Andre. 2001. "Evaluating the Impact of Increasing Memory on Agent Behaviour: Adaptive Patterns in an Agent-Based Simulation of Subsistence." *Journal of Artificial Societies and Social Simulation* 4 (4). http://jasss.soc.surrey.ac.uk.

Cremeens, David L., and John P. Hart. 2003. "Geoarchaeology of Landscapes in the Glaciated Northeast." *Proceedings of a Symposium Held at the New York Natural History Conference VI.* University of the State of New York, State Education Department, Albany, NY.

Doolittle, William Emery, James A. Neely, and Karen R. Adams. 2004. *The Safford Valley Grids: Prehistoric Cultivation in the Southern Arizona Desert.* Tucson: University of Arizona Press.

Estrada-Belli, Francisco.1999. *The Archaeology of Complex Societies in Southeastern Pacific Coastal Guatemala: A Regional GIS Approach.* Oxford: British Archaeological Reports.

Fischer, Manfred M. 2001. "Spatial Analysis in Geography." In *International Encyclopedia of the Social and Behavioral Sciences*, ed. Neil J. Smelser and P. B. Baltes, 14752–14758. Oxford: Elsevier. http://dx.doi.org/10.1016/B0-08-043076-7/02489-X.

Fischer, Manfred M., and Arthur Getis. 1997. *Recent Developments in Spatial Analysis: Spatial Statistics, Behavioural Modelling, and Computational Intelligence.* New York: Springer.

Fortin, Marie-Josée, and Mark R.T. Dale. 2005. *Spatial Analysis: A Guide for Ecologists.* New York: Cambridge University Press.

Fotheringham, A. Stewart, Chris Brunsdon, and Martin Charlton. 2000. *Quantitative Geography: Perspectives on Spatial Data Analysis.* Thousand Oaks, CA: SAGE Publications.

Fotheringham, A. Stewart, and Peter Rogerson. 1994. *Spatial Analysis and GIS.* London: Taylor & Francis.

Frank, Andrew. 2006. "Twenty Years of Reasoning with Spatial Relations." In *Classics from IJGIS Twenty Years of the International Journal of Geographic and Information Science and Systems*, ed. T. Fisher, 341–46. Boca Raton, FL: CRC Press.

Gaede, Volker. 1996. *Constraint Databases and Applications: Second International Workshop on Constraint Database and Systems.* CDB '97, Delphi, Greece, January 11–12, 1997, CP '96 Workshop on Constraints and Databases, Cambridge, MA, August 19. New York: Springer.

Gaffney, Vincent L., and Zoran Stančič. 1991. *GIS Approaches to Regional Analysis: A Case Study of the Island of Hvar.* Ljubljana: Znanstveni inštitut Filozofske fakultete.

Galloway, Patricia Kay. 2006. *Practicing Ethnohistory: Mining Archives, Hearing Testimony, Constructing Narrative.* Lincoln: University of Nebraska Press.

Gamble, Clive, and W. A. Boismier. 1991. *Ethnoarchaeological Approaches to Mobile Campsites: Hunter-Gatherer and Pastoralist Case Studies.* Ann Arbor, MI: International Monographs in Prehistory.

Glassie, Henry H. 2000. *Vernacular Architecture.* Philadelphia: Material Culture; Bloomington: Indiana University Press.

Goldstein, Jonathan. 1996. *Using Constraints to Query R*-Trees*. Madison, WI: University of Wisconsin–Madison, Computer Sciences Department.

Golledge, Reginald G., and Gerard Rushton. 1976. *Spatial Choice and Spatial Behavior: Geographic Essays on the Analysis of Preferences and Perceptions*. Columbus: Ohio State University Press.

Graebner, Fritz. 1911. *Methode der ethnologie*. Heidelberg: C. Winter.

Grinsell, Leslie V., and P. J. Fowler. 1972. *Archaeology and the Landscape: Essays for L. V. Grinsell*. London: J. Baker.

Gross-Amblard, David, and Michel de Rougemont. 2006. "Uniform Generation in Spatial Constraint Databases and Applications." *Journal of Computer and System Sciences* 72 (4): 576–91. http://dx.doi.org/10.1016/j.jcss.2005.09.008.

Haggett, Peter. 1965. *Locational Analysis in Human Geography*. London: Edward Arnold.

Haggett, Peter, and Richard J. Chorley. 1970. *Network Analysis in Geography*. New York: St. Martin's Press.

Hauser, Kitty. 2007. *Shadow Sites: Photography, Archaeology, and the British Landscape, 1927–1955*. New York: Oxford University Press.

Henry, Mark, and Leslie Armstrong, and the United States National Park Service. 2004. *Mapping the Future of America's National Parks: Stewardship through Geographic Information Systems*. Redlands, CA: ESRI Press.

Hietala, Harold J., and Paul A. Larson. 1984. *Intrasite Spatial Analysis in Archaeology*. New York: Cambridge University Press.

Hodder, Ian. 1978. *The Spatial Organisation of Culture*. Pittsburgh: University of Pittsburgh Press.

Hodder, Ian, and Clive Orton. 1976. *Spatial Analysis in Archaeology*. New York: Cambridge University Press.

Kelso, William M., and Rachel Most, and the Thomas Jefferson Memorial Foundation Inc. 1990. *Earth Patterns: Essays in Landscape Archaeology*. Charlottesville: University of Virginia Press.

Kent, Susan. 1984. *Analyzing Activity Areas: An Ethnoarchaeological Study of the Use of Space*. Albuquerque: University of New Mexico Press.

Kent, Susan. 1987. *Method and Theory for Activity Area Research: An Ethnoarchaeological Approach*. New York: Columbia University Press.

Kent, Susan. 1990. *Domestic Architecture and the Use of Space: An Interdisciplinary Cross-Cultural Study*. New York: Cambridge University Press.

Kluckhohn, Clyde. 1936. "Some Reflections on the Method and Theory of the Kulturkreislehre." *American Anthropologist* n.s. 38 (2): 57–196.

Knowles, Anne Kelly. 2002. *Past Time, Past Place: GIS for History*. Redlands, CA: ESRI Press.

Kuper, Gabriel, and M. Wallace. 1996. "Constraint Databases and Applications." *Esprit Wg Contessa Workshop, Friedrichshafen, Germany, September 8–9, 1995: Proceedings*. New York: Springer.

Longley, Paul, and Michael Batty, and the University College London, Centre for Advanced Spatial Analysis. 2003. *Advanced Spatial Analysis: The CASA Book of GIS*. Redlands, CA: ESRI Press.

Loula, Angelo, Ricardo Gudwin, and João Queiroz. 2007. *Artificial Cognition Systems*. Hershey, PA: Idea Group.

MacArthur, Robert H. 1984. *Geographical Ecology: Patterns in the Distribution of Species*. Princeton, NJ: Princeton University Press.

MacArthur, Robert H., and Joseph H. Connell. 1966. *The Biology of Populations*. New York: Wiley.

MacArthur, Robert H., and Edward O. Wilson. 1967. *The Theory of Island Biogeography*. Princeton, NJ: Princeton University Press.

MacNab, Ying C. 2004. "Bayesian Spatial and Ecological Models for Small-Area Accident and Injury Analysis." *Accident Analysis and Prevention* 36 (2004): 1019–28.

Majumdar, Amab, Washington Yotto Ochieng, and Robert B. Noland. 2004. "Spatial and Temporal Analysis of Safety-Belt Usage and Safety-Belt Laws." *Accident Analysis and Prevention* 36 (2004): 551–60.

Marble, Duane Francis. 1967. *Three Papers on Individual Travel Behavior in the City*. Evanston, IL: Transportation Center, Northwestern University.

Marble, Duane Francis, Hugh W. Calkins, and Donna J. Peuquet. 1984. *Basic Readings in Geographic Information Systems*. Williamsville, NY: SPAD Systems.

Marble, Duane Francis, and Bruce Anderson. 1972. *LANDUSE: A Computer Program for Laboratory Use in Economic Geography Courses*. Washington, DC: Association of American Geographers.

Marble, Duane Francis, and S. R. Bowlby. 1968. "Shopping Alternatives and Recurrent Travel Patterns." In *Geographic Studies of Urban Transportation and Network Analysis*, ed. Frank E. Horton, 42–75. Northwestern University Studies in Geography 16. Evanston, IL: Northwestern University.

Mark, David, Andrew Turk, and David Stea. 2007. "Progress on Yindjibarndi Ethnophysiography." *COSIT* 207: 1–19.

Mehrer, Mark, and Konnie Wescott. 2006. *GIS and Archaeological Site Location Modeling*. Boca Raton, FL: Taylor & Francis.

Menon, Jai, Ranjit Desai, and Jay Buckey. 1997. *Constraint-Based Reverse Engineering from Ultrasound Cross-Sections*. Yorktown Heights, NY: IBM T. J. Watson Research Center.

Metheny, Karen Bescherer. 2007. *From the Miners' Doublehouse: Archaeology and Landscape in a Pennsylvania Coal Company Town*. Knoxville: University of Tennessee Press.

Mithen, Steven J. 2001. *Hunter-Gatherer Landscape Archaeology: The Southern Hebrides Mesolithic Project, 1988–1998*. Cambridge: McDonald Institute for Archaeological Research.

Ogundele, Samuel Oluwole. 2005. "Ethnoarchaeology of Domestic Space and Spatial Behaviour among the Tiv and Ungwai of Central Nigeria." *African Archaeological Review* 22 (1): 25–54. http://dx.doi.org/10.1007/s10437-005-3158-2.

Papadias, Dimitris, and Timos Sellis. 1992. *Spatial Reasoning Using Symbolic Arrays*. Pisa: Springer-Verlag.

Paynter, Robert. 1982. *Models of Spatial Inequality: Settlement Patterns in Historical Archeology*. New York: Academic Press.

Peuquet, Donna J., and Zhan Ci-Xiang. 1987. "An Algorithm to Determine the Directional Relationship between Arbitrarily-Shaped Polygons in the Plane." *Pattern Recognition* 20 (1): 65–74. http://dx.doi.org/10.1016/0031-3203(87)90018-5.

Pielou, Evelyn Christine. 1969. *An Introduction to Mathematical Ecology*. New York: Wiley-Interscience.

Pielou, Evelyn Christine. 1977. *Mathematical Ecology*. New York: Wiley.

Pielou, Evelyn Christine. 1991. *After the Ice Age: The Return of Life to Glaciated North America*. Chicago: University of Chicago Press.

Plank, Shannon E. 2004. *Maya Dwellings in Hieroglyphs and Archaeology: An Integrative Approach to Ancient Architecture and Spatial Cognition.* BAR International Series 1324. Oxford: John and Erica Hedges Ltd.

Reeves-Smyth, Terence, and Fred Hamond. 1983. *Landscape Archaeology in Ireland.* Oxford: BAR.

Renfrew, Colin, and Ezra B. W. Zubrow. 1994. *The Ancient Mind: Elements of Cognitive Archaeology.* Cambridge: Cambridge University Press.

Richards, Julian. 1998. "Recent Trends in Computer Applications in Archaeology." *Journal of Archaeological Research* 6 (4): 331–82. http://dx.doi.org/10.1007/BF02446083.

Rogers, Andrei. 1974. "Statistical Analysis of Spatial Dispersion: The Quadrat Method." In *Monographs in Spatial and Environmental Systems Analysis.* London: Pion.

Rossignol, Jacqueline, and LuAnn Wandsnider. 1992. *Space, Time, and Archaeological Landscapes.* New York: Plenum Press.

Schott, Jean-Pierre. 1989. "Three-Dimensional Motion Estimation Using Shading Information in Multiple Frames." PhD dissertation, MIT Artificial Intelligence Laboratory, Cambridge, MA.

Shapiro, Jason S. 2005. *A Space Syntax Analysis of Arroyo Hondo Pueblo, New Mexico: Community Formation in the Northern Rio Grande.* Santa Fe, NM: School of American Research Press.

Simpson, George Gaylord. 1965. *The Geography of Evolution: Collected Essays.* Philadelphia: Chilton Books.

Simpson, George Gaylord. 1967. *The Meaning of Evolution: A Study of the History of Life and of Its Significance for Man.* New Haven, CT: Yale University Press.

Taylor, Christopher, Paul Everson, and Tom Williamson. 1998. *The Archaeology of Landscape: Studies Presented to Christopher Taylor.* Manchester: Manchester University Press.

Tomlinson, R. F., H. W. Calkins, and Duane Francis Marble. 1976. *Computer Handling of Geographical Data: An Examination of Selected Geographic Information Systems.* Paris: Unesco.

Trément, Frédéric, Marinella Pasquinucci, and POPULUS project. 2000. *Non-Destructive Techniques Applied to Landscape Archaeology.* Oxford: Oxbow.

Trigger, Bruce G. 2006. *A History of Archaeological Thought.* New York: Cambridge University Press.

Trinkley, Michael, Natalie Adams, and Debi Hacker. 1992. *Landscape and Garden Archaeology at Crowfield Plantation: A Preliminary Examination.* Research Series (Chicora Foundation) 32. Columbia, SC: Chicora Foundation.

Ucko, Peter J., and Robert Layton. 1999. *The Archaeology and Anthropology of Landscape: Shaping Your Landscape.* New York: Routledge.

Wagstaff, J. Malcolm. 1987. *Landscape and Culture: Geographical and Archaeological Perspectives.* New York: Blackwell.

Willey, Gordon R., and Jeremy A. Sabloff. 1980. *A History of American Archaeology.* San Francisco: W. H. Freeman.

Wiseman, James, and Konstantinos L. Zachos. 2003. *Landscape Archaeology in Southern Epirus, Greece I.* Princeton, NJ: American School of Classical Studies at Athens.

Zhao, Jianmin, and Norman I. Badler. 1989. *Real Time Inverse Kinematics with Joint Limits and Spatial Constraints.* Philadelphia: University of Pennsylvania, School of Engineering and Applied Science, Department of Computer and Information Science.

Zubrow, Ezra B.W. 2007. "Remote Sensing, Fractals, and Cultural Landscapes: An Ethnographic Prolegomenon Using U2 Imagery." In *Remote Sensing in Archaeology*, ed. J. R. Wiseman and Farouk El-Baz, 219-35. New York: Springer Verlag. http://dx.doi.org/10.1007/0-387-44455-6_9.

29

Why Dark Zones Are Sacred

Turning to Behavioral and Cognitive Science for Answers

Daniel R. Montello and Holley Moyes

According to legend, the monstrous Minotaur—half-man, half-bull—made his home in the Labyrinth at Knossos on the Mediterranean island of Crete. The cave-like Labyrinth—large, dark, complex in layout, but homogeneous in appearance—was built by Daedulus for King Minos. To repay the Athenians for the slaying of his son, Minos exacted tribute of fourteen Athenian youths every nine years. This lasted until the Athenian hero, Theseus, decided to assume the role of one of the sacrificial youths, travel deep into the Labyrinth, and slay the Minotaur. But how was Theseus to find his way out of the confusing passages once the deed was done? The answer came from Ariadne, daughter of Minos. She gave Theseus a ball of string and the idea to unwind it as he traveled toward the monster. Theseus entered the Labyrinth, unwinding the string as he went along. After plunging his sword into the Minotaur, Theseus followed the string safely back out to the surface world. For her cleverness and willingness to betray her father for love, Ariadne was abandoned by Theseus on the island of Naxos during his homeward voyage.

The story of the Labyrinth at Knossos suggests the power caves have had to capture the human imagination; they are places of fear, mystery, gloominess, weirdness, and wonder. The legend of the Minotaur and his home, the Labyrinth, has been exceptionally widespread and influential in many parts of the world, showing up in art, architecture, folklore, and symbolism in many cultures for thousands of years. The Minotaur himself is a concrete personification (terrification?) of the essence of dread and strangeness induced by the cave. The psychological power of caves is reflected in many other stories and symbols besides the Minotaur, such as the attitude many people in many cultures have had about the bat as denizen of the underworld or just "bat out of hell" (Lawrence 1993).

It can hardly be accidental that dark zones of caves have so often been important sacred or mythological spaces in the ritual and ideological lives of humans. The chapters in this volume have all documented and described the roles that caves have played in the past and continue to play today among diverse human groups in terms of symbolism, cosmology, myth, and ritual. Traditions of ritual cave use have originated at different times in widely separated geographic areas and may be traced back to the earliest modern humans. The long temporal spans and deep antiquity witnessed in the archaeological record allows us to appreciate the pervasiveness of the phenomenon over time and space. The pattern argues against a solitary model of cultural diffusion and points toward the independent development of similar conceptual formulations of caves. What could explain independently occurring cave constructs?

In this chapter we address how places dynamically arise as meaningful locations by exploring the case of ritual cave use as a cross-cultural phenomenon. The phenomenological approach detailed by Alfred Schutz (1967) and adapted for environmental studies by Timothy Auburn and Rebecca Barnes (2006) provides a framework that helps explain how human–environmental interactions may produce shared constructs. The phenomenology of Schutz is based on the Husserlian observation that people fundamentally accept that a material world exists independent of themselves and that this world is the same for others. Schutz was interested in how people lived with and renewed their assumptions about the world and how this influenced the production of social order. He proposed his general thesis of the alter ego (1962) as a basis for intersubjectivity. Here Schutz posited that an encounter takes place within a "common communicative environment" but that people are aware of their subjective experiences. They are able to overcome their subjectivity and reach mutually shared constructs, or what he refers to as a "We-relationship," based on two properties of human thought that constitute his general thesis of the reciprocity of perspectives. The first, the idealization of the interchangeability of standpoints, maintains that people assume that if they change places with one another, another's "here" becomes theirs. The second, the idealization of congruency of the system of relevances, maintains that people assume, until faced with counter-evidence, that they interpret objects and features in an identical manner to others. In the We-relationship, participants are aware of each other in face-to-face encounters that are experiential and interactive, and it is through this mutual experience that they negotiate shared ideas. The relationship is not static but continues to evolve, establishing and maintaining a commonly understood world of objects, events, and motivations that constitute knowledge constructions (types, categories) and ultimately orderliness (social constructs).

Auburn and Barnes (2006, 43) point out that what is important for studies of place is that the We-relationship is not only a social relationship but a located relationship. The common communicative environment in which human interactions occur is not only a social space but an environmental one as well. We-relationships are constituted by the mutual orientation of the participants not only to each other but also to the setting in which the encounters occur.

This is a useful framework from which to understand how dark zones of caves may become socially constructed ritual spaces and idealized places. Phenomenology suggests that the shared human experience of the cave is a major factor establishing and maintaining typological designations and meanings. What it does not address is why the concept arises over and over again in various cultures throughout time and space. What is it specifically that produces this pattern?

We suggest that a shared human cognitive and emotional response to dark zones of caves is at the core of the development of similar conceptualizations, which in turn lends these spaces to mythic constructions and ritual use. In the case of long cultural traditions of ritual cave use such as those found in Paleolithic Europe (Clottes, chapter 1, this volume), the ancient and modern Americas (chapters 10, 11, 12, this volume), or Neolithic and Bronze Age Greece (Tomkins, chapter 4, this volume), similar perceptual-environmental interactions would be expected to reinforce conceptual formulations and facilitate cultural transmission by providing a relatively fixed environmental referent in the form of stable geographic features. Several authors have suggested that caves also provided the referents for later ritual architecture (see this volume, Moyes and Brady, chapter 10; Skeates, chapter 2; Smith, chapter 7; Stoddart and Malone, chapter 3; and Yorke and Ilan, chapter 6), thus reinforcing the environmental stimulus in the built environment.

Our stance requires that we reject Cartesian notions of mind–body duality in favor of modern theories of embodied knowledge such as experiential realism. This theory of the mind developed by George Lakoff and Mark Johnson (1999) is a philosophical stance that asserts that mental models of the world come from one's experience with it. Even though the mind cannot experience the world "directly," the indirect experiences of the world are shaped in consistent ways by its physical nature, by the physical nature of our individual senses, and by the physical nature of our own bodies and how they interact physically with the world. More recently, Vittorio Gallese (2005) has joined Lakoff in further developing this theory by reviewing evidence from neuroscience. Both argue that the formulation of concepts cannot be divorced from sensory-motor regions of the brain and are thus grounded in material reality and experience. This agrees with Gerald Edelman's (1992) theory of neuronal group selection (TNGS), which argues that minds become structured not on a genetically specified schedule but by the building of certain neural firing patterns reinforced by experience.

These theories suggest that events in the mental and physical development of individuals occur in physical environments, and the course of these developments depends to a great extent on the nature of the environments in which they occur. This holds true for many human characteristics—our need for water and particular nutrients, the sensitivity of our sensory systems to particular types of energy and not others, our anatomical and morphological characteristics, and so on. It also holds true for human characteristics that are behavioral and cognitive—what attracts our attention, how we remember certain kinds of information, how we reason and make decisions, what actions we tend to take in particular situations, and so on.

In this chapter, we consider the physical properties of caves as environments, including their structure and appearance. This has particular implications for human psychological responses that include perceptions, cognitions, emotions, and behaviors. To gain insight into human psychological responses to the physical environments of caves, we look to the behavioral and cognitive sciences and to environmental design fields. Spatial cognition studies conducted in a variety of disciplines attempt to describe and explain human perception and cognition in diverse environments, including built/natural environments and indoor/outdoor spaces. This literature includes work that we believe can aid in explaining why caves are often used as sacred spaces by distinct cultures separated in time and space. In particular, literature on spatial orientation points to physical factors that contribute to the ease or difficulty of maintaining orientation within environments. These factors include visibility (including the lengths of vistas or sightlines), differentiation of appearance, and structural layout complexity. Empirical and evolutionary considerations suggest a special status for three-dimensional environments in human psychology. In addition, studies on perceptual and cognitive aspects of environmental aesthetics point to culturally universal characteristics of human-environment interaction, such as "legibility" and "mystery," that can help explain emotional responses to various places.

Our chapter applies behavioral and cognitive science research to examine the responses of diverse human populations to the notion of "cave" as well as to actual psychological responses to cave environments. In this chapter, we examine literature found in such disciplines as environmental psychology, perceptual and cognitive psychology, behavioral and cognitive geography, planning, and architecture that explicitly considers the influence of the physical environment on mind and behavior. Among the interesting outcomes of analyzing caves in terms of the spatial-cognition literature is that different types of caves can be compared in terms of their structure and geological character in a way that helps explain their differential tendency to serve as sacred spaces.

ORIENTATION AND DISORIENTATION IN CAVES

A good example of a psychological response for which the physical environment of caves is relevant is spatial orientation. To be oriented is to "know" where you are, in some sense (Montello 2005). You can be oriented to various degrees in a variety of ways, with respect to spaces at different scales, and to varying degrees of conscious awareness. Knowing where you and your destinations are on the Earth's surface is *geographic orientation*. Geographic orientation involves some combination of knowledge about your location and about your heading or course—your facing and traveling directions, respectively. Knowledge of location and direction, like any spatial information, are always defined relative to some baseline locations or directions, called *reference systems*. These may be defined with reference to some combination of one's former body location or heading, the locations or headings of local features or landmarks in the environment, or the locations or headings of global features of the environment, the Earth, or the celestial sphere. The last type of reference system, based on global features that are stable and may be perceived over large areas, is known as an *abstract allocentric* or *absolute* system. Because such a system transports easily from place to place as one moves about (in cases such as the latitude-longitude system, it transports all around the Earth), it is often the most flexible and powerful reference system. Thus, to many animals, including humans, aligning one's sense of body heading or course to the orientation of an absolute system at a particular place can be key to maintaining geographic orientation.

Whether carried out formally or informally, maintaining orientation while moving about is called *updating*. Updating occurs by some mixture of two processes: landmark-based and dead reckoning. *Landmark-based* updating, also known variously as piloting or position-fixing, is updating based on recognizing external features. This recognition requires either an internal memory of the feature or an external memory, such as a cartographic map or chart. It is noteworthy that landmarks typically aid orientation in an indirect way. Sometimes they act as "beacon" destinations that can be directly oriented to, as when one knows where the cave opening is because it can be seen. But in so many situations, a recognized landmark does not directly indicate where a target destination is; instead, it functions to "key" one's perceived surroundings to an internal or external representation—a cognitive or cartographic "map"—that contains the nonperceived target destination. For example, recognizing a particular distinctive stalactite or rock cairn probably does not mean you have found your ultimate destination, but it does mean you know where you are within your representation of the portion of the cave containing that distinctive feature.

In contrast to landmark-based updating, *dead reckoning* does not involve recognition of features in the environment, so it does not require internal or external memory for any features. Dead reckoning is inferring or calculating your location after movement, based on information about your original location and about your velocity or acceleration of movement; as vector quantities, velocity and acceleration include directional information. Because dead reckoning can be thought of as essentially integrating directed motion relative to travel time, in the sense of integral calculus (even if it is not carried out by a mechanism that actually does calculus), it is often called *path integration*. Dead reckoning is based on internal (*idiothetic*) signals, such as vestibular sensing, or external (*allothetic*) signals, such as optic flow in the visual field. The key aspect of dead reckoning, however, is that it does not involve specific recognition of features or places, even if it is based on visual information like optic flow. Notice that unlike landmark-based updating, dead reckoning only tells you your new location relative to your original location. Furthermore, errors accumulate with dead reckoning, so that a small misorientation soon becomes a large misorientation. Such error must be dealt with by taking periodic fixes (landmark-based updating), and if error accumulates quickly, fixes must be taken frequently.

The processes by which people maintain orientation vary in the demands they place on limited attentional resources. That is, some processes of orientation happen outside of consciousness and do not "fill up" working memory capacity; because they are nonconscious—people are not aware they are going on and cannot tell you how they are doing them (though they certainly may tell you all about their personal theories of how they do it, mistaking that for direct access to their cognitive processing). Other processes are very much a part of conscious experience; they fill working memory and falter if a person is distracted in some way. People are aware of what they are thinking about during such processing and can tell you validly what that is. Finally, a variety of processes can be seen to be intermediate between the extremes of very implicit and very explicit, and of course, acts of orientation and disorientation typically incorporate various component processes that vary in attentional demand.

On one extreme are relatively *automatic* processes that do not require much attention and provide people with a "sense" of where they are as they turn or locomote over short distances. For example, you can probably maintain a sense that you have turned by 90° as you walk around the corner of a building without paying much conscious attention at all. People differ a great deal in their ability to automatically update in this way (Hegarty et al. 2002; Loomis et al. 1993) and in any case, such automatic updating cannot be relied on for very long distances. Exactly how long is an important research question, but it appears to be no more than several meters.

Updating while traveling over highly familiar terrain becomes automatized. For example, most people can walk or drive to work without paying much attention and not get lost. In fact, such a trip probably never becomes completely automatic; a person's attentional resources are likely to be somewhat engaged at the moment they must choose within a branching path structure, even when they have traveled the route many times. Again, there is more research to be done on the question of how attentional resources are marshaled during trips of varying familiarity.

In contrast, people often maintain a sense of orientation only with conscious effort. This is typically the case when traveling in unfamiliar environments, when lost and trying to reestablish orientation, and when giving verbal directions (the museum guard giving instructions to the bathroom for the umpteenth time provides an automatized exception). An important instance of effortful, attention-demanding orientation processes occurs when controlled, explicit *strategies* are applied. For example, children and adults can be taught the look-back strategy wherein a traveler stops, turns around, and explicitly takes a "mental snapshot" of the view going in the other direction (Cornell, Heth, and Rowat 1992). People can also intentionally retrace their steps or branch out back and forth from a familiar base point while attempting to reorient.

The converse of orientation is disorientation. Geographic disorientation—"being lost"—occurs when a person is uncertain about where he or she is or where he or she needs to go to get to some destination (Montello and Lemberg 1995). A critical aspect of this definition is that one must have a destination, a place where one wants to be or go, in order to be lost. A recreational caver who enters a cave to walk around and have a look at the cave structures is not necessarily going anyplace. People engaged in such goal-free travel cannot reasonably be said to be lost, even though they may not know where they are, because they do not care where they are or where they are going. As soon as the caver decides to end her walk and return to the entrance, however, she becomes lost when she realizes she is unsure of the way back.

This points to a further issue that is important when thinking about geographic disorientation. Being disoriented is a subjective state, not an objective state. You are lost when you *believe* you are unsure about your location or your destination. When you are lost, you may or may not actually be where you think you are or be heading in the correct direction of your destination. In fact, people rarely if ever have a complete and precise understanding of their actual location on the Earth relative to all possible features, reference systems, and so on. Likewise, people are sometimes right where they intend to be, possibly standing in front of their destination, but are unaware of it. People in such a state are lost. We may distinguish "disorientation" as a subjective state from "misorientation" as the state of being objectively mislocated, of not being where you think you are, or not knowing where you are but not caring.

Caves are clearly among the most disorienting of all environments. In the next section, we discuss characteristics of these natural labyrinths that lead to the psychological response of disorientation, as well as other responses. Caves are dark, without normal external cues like the sun, moon, or stars. The walls and features of many caves have a "sameness" or undifferentiated appearance that is infamous for its ability to confuse human navigators, dependent as they are on recognizable landmarks. The obstructed and constrained vistas of most caves restrict visibility even in the path of a flashlight beam. It is the rare cave that allows the kind of view that would support apprehension of the cave's overall structure. And this structure is usually exceedingly complex, much more than in a built environment. The web-like pathways provide numerous choice points and an irregular structure that exploits our disorientation in oblique layouts. There is no regular grid pattern here. Furthermore, the average cave has no respect for the "planar" nature of human spatial cognition—in caves we are dealing with true three-dimensional environments, not "pseudo" three-dimensional environments like high-rise buildings. Pathways that can branch off in any direction from one's body present an unusual and difficult situation for humans. Compounding these difficulties, traveling through caves requires great physical effort (try crawling on your stomach through a small passage for a hundred meters) and is often accompanied by anxiety or even claustrophobia.

When taken to the extreme, the reduction in sensory stimulation found in many caves provides some of the conditions similar to isolation experiments. Especially in the remote dark zones of many caves, there is little or no light, sound, or air movement. One may also be alone, lacking communication or social contact with others. Such conditions have been shown to produce a characteristic set of symptoms to accompany this *sensory deprivation* (Goldberger 1966; Zubek 1969). For brief periods, sensory deprivation can produce relaxation and introspection, like a meditative state. For longer periods, it can lead to more radical psychological states, including delusion, hallucination, anxiety, increased suggestibility, or a variety of cognitive deficits such as memory loss.

PHYSICAL CHARACTERISTICS OF ENVIRONMENTS RELEVANT TO PSYCHOLOGICAL RESPONSES

It is apparent that human psychological responses in various environments, including caves, can be understood better by considering physical characteristics of those environments. Physical characteristics of environments include their ambient lighting, the appearance of their surfaces (textures, colors, and surface reflectivity), the geometric structure of their chambers and path networks, their temperature and humidity, the ruggedness and ground support of their terrain, their flora and fauna, and so on. Many people (e.g., Hartig and Evans 1993) have attempted to summarize variations in the physical characteristics of environments in terms of the distinction between built and natural environments. *Built* environments are created by humans; *natural* environments are created relatively freely of human agency. There are many intermediate cases, of course, and the very concept of "natural" is complex and, to some extent, culturally constructed (Proctor 1998). There do seem to be a few general differences between natural and built environments. On average, natural environments like caves tend to contain fewer straight lines, right angles, and other regular shapes such as perfect triangles or circles; they also tend to contain fewer regularly repeating, evenly spaced, pattern elements. As a built structure, King Minos's Labyrinth had more straight and regular elements than the typical natural cave. Natural environments also tend to contain more vague and less clearly demarcated boundaries and transitions. However, this difference does not always hold; depending on the geology of their formation, for example, caves may contain very straight stalactites or smooth straight passages. The appearance of natural environments like caves does tend to vary over space "logically," with contiguous areas likely to be quite similar and transitions likely to be gradual or at least comprehensible within a larger situational context. In contrast, the appearance of built environments can vary capriciously (e.g., in color, height, materials) in ways that violate this natural logic. Alternatively, and perhaps unfortunately for the people in them, the appearance of built environments sometimes lacks variation of any kind. Natural environments also tend to contain a greater density and heterogeneity of edges, lines, textures, shadings, and fractal patterns. At some point, however, the complexity of natural environments, understood in information-theory terms, is so great that it creates a visual homogeneity, ending up being less *psychologically* complex than more minimalist built environments (Kaplan, Kaplan, and Wendt 1972).

Whatever the utility of distinguishing natural from built environments, there is clearly considerable variation among environments, all of which are natural or all of which are built. Caves, in particular, differ quite a bit from many other natural environments. Caves also differ from each other in potentially important ways, depending on the material that composes them, the history of their formation, their exposure to moisture, and their exposure to flora and fauna (including humans). Given the conceptual difficulty of the built–natural distinction and the wide variations within, as well as between, environments of each type, we think it is more fruitful to consider the influences of environmental characteristics on psychological responses independently of whether the environments are built or natural. The visual and structural characteristics of environments like caves facilitate or impede various activities of people, and they alter the experience people have in them, both cognitively and emotionally. Of course, people (especially sighted people) find it difficult to act in the dark, and they can find it difficult to walk or crawl over watery or rock-strewn cave floors. However, we find it more interesting that different environments afford different information for the people in them, information that is useful for anticipating resources and dangers and finding one's way. Different information allows different wayfinding strategies, and it makes the strategies easier or harder to apply effectively. Different information tells people what to expect ahead or keeps them uncertain. In some environments, information misleads people about what to expect. Knowing or not knowing what to expect can certainly lead to emotional responses such as calmness, anxiousness, happiness, or fear.

FOUR PHYSICAL CHARACTERISTICS

Weisman (1981) and Gärling, Böök, and Lindberg (1986) proposed a typology of environmental characteristics that is very useful for understanding how physical characteristics of environments affect psychological responses to those environments. These authors discuss the role of physical factors on spatial orientation and "legibility" within the environment, but we think the factors are very likely to be relevant to a host of psychological responses, including anxiety, uncertainty, and aesthetics. The authors also focus on understanding built environments, but their typology clearly applies to natural environments too, including caves specifically. The typology includes the factors of differentiation of appearance, visual access, and complexity of layout. Both authors also consider the role of sign systems in the psychology of environments; although typically not very relevant in cave systems, we do consider sign systems briefly in what follows.

DIFFERENTIATION OF APPEARANCE

Environments differ in the degree to which their parts are homogeneous or heterogeneous in appearance. They differ with respect to size, shape, color, architectural style, and so on. As we discussed above, natural environments are often more differentiated than built environments, but of course some natural environments are much less differentiated than others. Generally, people find differentiated environments easier to comprehend and wayfind in because the differentiated parts are more distinct and memorable—differentiation creates better landmarks (Appleyard 1969, Lynch 1960). At some point, however, environments may be so differentiated that they appear chaotic and would be disorienting. But it is important to remember that differentiation cannot be assessed solely as an objective physical variable. It is a subjective variable, too: what we see (what we notice) depends in part on our expectations, our interests, our training, and our state of mind. To take one relevant example, geologists who are cave specialists will see greater differentiation in caves than nonspecialists will. To the untrained eye, natural environments, in particular, can look quite undifferentiated. Gladwin (1970) tells the fascinating story of the navigators of the Pulawat Islands of Micronesia (other South and West Pacific peoples have similar traditions). They pick up a great deal of useful information from the sky and water, which are richly differentiated to those trained to perceive it. This information supports technologically unaided boat trips of up to several hundred miles or more over open ocean. The information includes air and water color, wave and swell patterns, sun and star patterns, and identified bird species and their known ranges.

VISUAL ACCESS

The second relevant physical characteristic of environments is their visual access, the degree to which different places and feature in an environment can be seen from various vantage locations. Conversely, it also concerns the locations *from* which people can see particular places and features, including locations where they were previously standing, locations to which they are headed, and various key landmarks or structural features. To what degree is the overall layout of an environment visible from a single vantage point? People have a greater sense of comprehension and can maintain their spatial orientation more easily when visual access is high. Greater visual access will decrease mystery and uncertainty; in a complex or unfamiliar environment, it will tend to reduce excessive stress, while in a simple or familiar environment, it will tend to reduce acceptable stress to boredom. Of course, visual access of, or from, some locations will be more informative than of, or from, other locations.

Planners and architects have systematically studied visual access, typically in interior spaces, under the guise of *isovist analysis* (Benedikt and Burnham 1985); geographers, surveyors, forest managers, and others have studied it in outside landscapes under the guise of *viewshed analysis* (Llobera 2003). Since caves are interior spaces, we use the term *isovist* for the collected spatial extent of all views, or vistas, from a single location within a cave. It is commonly assumed that the vistas are two-dimensional and 360° around a vantage point. For analyzing caves, both of these assumptions should probably be altered, as the three-dimensional structure of cave spaces is unusually important, and the dark interior illuminated by a unidirectional headlamp is less like a 360° experience than fully lit spaces would be. Large unobstructed chambers in caves have large isovists that are fairly symmetric around locations near the center of the chamber. Narrow winding cave passages have small isovists that are very asymmetric, depending on whether you face across or along the passage. Several theorists believe that isovist characteristics of environments will relate to the psychological responses the environments engender, including ease of orientation, sense of privacy, stressfulness, and aesthetic judgments. Many different physical properties of the isovist could be relevant, such as total size, symmetry, maximum length, and so on. But so far, only a little work has systematically tested these properties; for example, Sadalla and Oxley (1984) found that a rectangular room appears larger from the center than a square room of the same floor area. No one has yet applied isovist analysis to caves.

Complexity of Layout

Although it is difficult to define and measure layout complexity formally, it certainly has important implications for human psychology. Exactly what constitutes a "complex layout" in a psychological sense is a question for ongoing research. A more articulated space, broken up into more different parts, is generally more complex, though the way the different parts are organized is critical. It is clear that certain patterns of path networks are more or less psychologically complex; for example, oblique turns are more disorienting than orthogonal turns (Montello 1991). However, defining psychological complexity is difficult because humans organize information into meaningful units in a way that reduces complexity in an information-theory sense to relative simplicity in a psychological sense. A case in point is the fact that the overall shape or "gestalt" of a path layout can determine whether a particular element is disorienting. In many built environments, for example, the road network consists entirely of simple rectilinear grids or symmetric radial patterns. But a grid pattern may be disorienting if its axes do not run north-south and East-West—at least for those people who incorporate cardinal directions into their wayfinding. A curved path is more complex than a straight one, but curved paths are understood better when they fit within a radial network pattern, as long as that radial pattern is in fact apprehended. Layouts may be said to vary in their closeness to a "good form"; comprehending a layout is easier when the layout has an overall pattern that can be apprehended as a single simple shape. A square is easier than a rhombus; a circle is easier than a lopsided oval. People tend to understand and remember layouts as good forms, and when the layout does not have such a form, knowledge distortion results (e.g., Tversky 1992). Kevin Lynch (1960) mentions that people interviewed by his research team were confused by the Boston Common because they tended to assume it was a square, when it is actually an irregular pentagon.

Cave layouts vary from each other, of course, but in general, they are among the most complex layouts that humans ever encounter. Few buildings, if any, have layouts anywhere near the complexity of the average cave structure. Caves are large and extremely articulated, with chambers and corridors varying greatly in size and shape. Caves may branch off into any number of corridors, sometimes with little apparent physical logic. Their corridors are never restricted to orthogonality, moving in any direction with nearly equal probability. That is, caves have a unique property that one rarely finds in other environments: a nearly true three-dimensional structure. Not only does the floor rise and fall haphazardly in caves, as might be true in any rugged natural terrain, but corridors can branch off above and below dramatically, leaving people to wonder what happened to their normal world with a horizontal terrain surface. Our sense of balance and uprightness normally depends critically on visual information about the horizon, the sky, and the ground (Gibson 1979). In some caves, people must depend on less reliable and robust proprioceptive sensations of gravity (from the utricle and saccule of the inner ear) to maintain a sense of up and down. High-rise buildings and underground construction involve three-dimensional environments, too, but the vertically arrayed spaces of such built environments are layered in a "2.5-dimensional" manner. Caves need not obey such layering; they can go from three partially overlapping layers to two layers to one layer and back again, smoothly or discontinuously (not that a person in one of the layers is likely to be aware of the vertical arrangement). It appears that people have special difficulty in comprehending three-dimensional environmental layouts, as humanity evolved on what is essentially a two-dimensional Earth surface (Montello and Pick 1993). The three-dimensional structure of caves also makes effective cave mapping quite a challenge (Moyes 2002), a challenge that is only partially solved by the standard practice of showing map readers both plan and cross-sectional views of cave chambers and corridors.

We clearly need more research on how to define and measure layout complexity so we can predict and explain how different environmental layouts, including cave layouts, lead to disorientation and other responses. We can further observe that the distinction between "unicursal and multicursal mazes or labyrinths can apply to caves" (Matthews 1970). *Unicursal* labyrinths have no branching or looping structure. Their layout consists essentially of one path from the "start" location to the "goal" location; the path may or may not turn or curve, and it may have any number of side paths attached that do not ultimately lead to a goal location. In contrast, *multicursal* labyrinths have one or more branches or loops. The distinction between unicursal and multicursal has implications for the effectiveness of particular strategies for finding one's way out of a cave, and it likely has implications for the state of disorientation that people would experience in them. However, no systematic and comprehensive analysis exists to explain how cave layouts affect psychological responses. One promising analytic approach is provided by *space syntax* analysis (Hillier and Iida 2005).

Sign systems

A fourth physical factor relevant to psychological responses in built environments is the nature of sign systems. Sign systems are "semiotic artifacts" intentionally designed and placed in environments to provide information and otherwise communicate messages to people. Signs incorporate words, pictures, maps, and graphical "gestures" such as arrows. The design and placement of signs in the environment clearly influences the behavior and experience of people in that environment (Arthur and Passini 1992). Caves, like other natural environments, do not generally have sign systems; we do not consider unintentional landmarks in caves to be sign systems. However, natural environments that have been "manicured" by humans do sometimes have sign systems put in place. Many caves are not entirely untouched by human activity, and sign marks, paintings, or petroglyphs are sometimes placed on cave walls, or rock cairns or other features are built at key nodes in cave networks. In general, sign systems can facilitate orientation and reduce uncertainty, but they can also impede orientation and increase confusion, either intentionally or unintentionally, when they are poorly designed or placed. And no matter how well sign systems are designed or laid out, they cannot entirely ameliorate negative psychological effects resulting from the other three physical-environmental factors.

PHYSICAL CHARACTERISTICS AND ENVIRONMENTAL AESTHETICS

Another body of behavioral- and cognitive-science research that may shed light on the sacredness of caves involves environmental aesthetics. Why do people find some environments more aesthetically pleasing than others? Starting in the 1950s, a branch of psychological research called experimental aesthetics attempted to offer a scientific analysis of aesthetics based primarily on formal syntactical qualities of images or patterns. Specifically, Berlyne's (1960) principle of stimulus complexity proposes that aesthetic responses to stimuli depend on their so-called collative properties. *Collative properties* are those qualities that generate perceptual conflict, eliciting curiosity, interest, and a tendency to explore. They include complexity, mystery, surprisingness, and incongruity. According to Berlyne, an optimal aesthetic response is generated when a stimulus elicits an intermediate balance between the motivation to explore and the motivation to avoid novelty.

Other psychologists (Mehrabian and Russell 1974; Wohlwill 1976) extended experimental aesthetics to environmental scenes, starting the field of environmental aesthetics. A general relationship between collative properties and aesthetic preference was found, although typically the stimulus scenes that were tested were not high enough in collative properties to inspire the downturn in aesthetic preference predicted by the principle of stimulus complexity. As we mentioned above, natural scenes generally do not reach a level of subjective complexity that some built scenes can achieve. But more than questioning the range of collative properties represented by environmental scenes, researchers came to realize that formal stimulus properties like complexity will not, by themselves, provide an adequate explanation of environmental aesthetics. That is, early attempts to apply experimental aesthetics to environmental scenes were criticized for focusing too much on "syntactic" qualities and ignoring "semantic" qualities—scene content. For example, people from different cultures will generally express aesthetic preference for natural scenes over urban scenes. Similarly, people rate environmental scenes more highly if they contain water or green vegetation, aside from their collative properties.

This result has inspired researchers to consider environmental aesthetics within a biological evolutionary framework. Kaplan and Kaplan (see Kaplan 1992), for example, were inspired by Gibson's (1979) concept of environmental "affordances" to look at environments functionally. They theorized that humans evolved preferences for particular places or environments because of the functional advantage of preferring some and avoiding others. The environments in which early humans evolved functioned to facilitate or impede such adaptively important activities as stealth and hiding, hunting and gathering, wayfinding, and social organization and communication. Accurate information processing would have been important, the Kaplans theorized, but so would quick information processing. These conditions would have favored the evolution of rapid, preconscious, and relatively automatic responses, including affective responses, to various environmental characteristics. Based on this reasoning, Kaplan and Kaplan introduced their *informational model* of environmental psychology. According to this model, predictors of environmental preference result from the interaction of two human needs—"making sense" and "involvement"—with two amounts of cognitive processing—"immediate" and "inferred (or future)" (see Hartig and Evans 1993). Four concepts derive from crossing the two levels of human needs with the two levels of processing: coherence, legibility, complexity, and mystery. These are reminiscent of Berlyne's collative properties but were developed from explicit evolutionary reasoning.

Evolutionary thinking about environmental aesthetics has probably reached its greatest application in various versions of the *savannah hypothesis*. Assuming that humans evolved on the African savannah, the hypothesis conjectures that environments with savannah-like properties will be maximally aesthetic to people across cultures. Evidence for this hypothesis has come from studies of landscape preference among children and adults (Balling and Falk 1982) and studies of tree-shape preference among Japanese gardeners (Orians and Heerwagen 1992). Appleton (1975) introduced a version of the savannah hypothesis called *prospect-refuge theory*. It proposes that people evolved to prefer the control over visual access provided by savannah environments—their prospect, or opportunities for large vistas, and refuge, or cover. In other words, people will find environments appealing that afford seeing without being seen. In this way, prospect-refuge theory explicitly connects evolutionary theories of environmental aesthetics with information-based theories, such as the Kaplans's.

Arthur Stamps (2005) recently developed *permeability theory*, which like the savanna hypothesis and prospect-refuge theory has at its core the evolutionary advantage of safety as an explanatory framework for evaluating environmental preferences. In permeability theory, the environment influences safety, and these influences may be evaluated by limiting perception or motion. A limitation might be complete, such as a brick wall, or partial, such as a fog bank. It might differ for locomotion and sensation. For example, one could hear through a thin wall but not see through it, move through dense fog but not see through it, or see through a window but not move through it. Distance also figures into the safety equation. If one can perceive danger at a greater distance, the chances of escape increase. Survival could also depend on knowing how accessible regions of safety might be. In permeability theory, mystery is related to preference because mystery indicates compromised perception. Stamps's experiments were conducted in both urban and natural settings and investigated the properties that most influenced impressions of mystery—occlusion, depth of view, and light. His findings suggest that mystery may primarily be a function of light levels, which is of interest when thinking about cave environments.

UNDERSTANDING CAVE USE FROM AN ENVIRONMENTAL PERSPECTIVE

Surveys of prehistoric and historic cave use suggest that cave morphology largely determines how cave space is used. Archaeologists have long noted that cave habitation occurs almost solely in the mouth of caves or in rockshelters (for discussion see Introduction, this volume), a point that has been reiterated throughout the essays of this volume. These sites tend to be relatively open and, in some cases, cave mouths may be quite large (see Barker and Lloyd-Smith, chapter 17, this volume), well lit, and have open access so that they were not likely to entrap their inhabitants. When we think of these characteristics in terms of the interplay between human cognition and the environment, archaeological findings begin to make sense. For instance, ideas about environmental aesthetics such as the savannah hypothesis, prospect-refuge theory, and permeability theory all suggest that humans will feel safer in open, well-lit environments or in environments in which they may view the surrounding area without being seen. Many cave mouths or rockshelters are situated in high places, affording large vistas, and may have increased feelings of security. In these cases, isovist or viewshed analysis would be expected to aid in understanding why certain sites were chosen for habitation over others (see Sabo et al., chapter 16, this volume).

In studies of environmental aesthetics, cave dark zones would score very highly with respect to collative or informational properties, such as mystery and complexity. From an evolutionary perspective, they would have been unusual environments, lacking in revealing vistas or vegetation, and therefore not preferred for habitation. This leads us to believe that due to their morphology and low-light conditions, dark zones would not be highly preferred habitation sites insofar as they would generate too much uncertainty, and lack cohesion and legibility. It also suggests that as the quality of light dims, perceptions of mystery and danger should increase. It may account for the almost total lack of habitation in dark zones and explain why they are only inhabited under overriding or desperate conditions such as extreme cold (see Taçon et al., chapter 9, this volume).

The very conditions that make caves inhospitable habitations render them useful for other purposes. One might expect that because cave interiors are hostile environments for humans, they may be considered "fugitive lairs" suitable for antisocial behavior (see Leicht and Tolan-Smith 1997, 125), or provide a protective barrier for those wishing to conceal themselves (see Ranger, chapter 22, this volume; Stone 1997, 202). When inhabited dark zones are discovered in the archaeological record, one should ask what overriding conditions were present in this choice of environment.

Consider cave environments from the Gibsonian perspective of "affordances." In Gibson's (1979) view, human and nature are not separate but are in an intertwined reciprocal relationship. To Gibson, it is a mistake to separate a cultural from a natural environment, or to distinguish mental products from the world of material products. We are created by the world we live in, while at the same time we are consistently changing, modifying that world. The Earth and its environments offer affordances. Affordances are properties of environmental entities that may include geographic features, rocks, minerals, air, animals, or any other material entity that, from a human perspective, may provide a means to fulfill real or perceived needs. In this sense, affordances may be seen as dynamic and changing, insofar as our needs are dynamic and changing, or fixed and universal, insofar as our needs are fixed and universal. In this sense, affordances defy classification. While a stone may be used as a projectile, it may also be a paperweight, a bookend, or a plumb bob. Human creativity is a major factor in designating affordances and is thus dynamic and highly variable, but all affordances are ultimately defined in reference to an observer while not deriving from the experiences of the observer. That is, affordances are not subjective values such as feelings of pleasure and pain but are, rather, the ways in which an entity may be employed.

According to Gibson, the habitat of a given animal contains places. Places are not neutral and have affordances that may be positive, such as a berry patch, or negative, such as the edge of a cliff. What caves offer humans is an environment that lacks light and is morphologically complex. These qualities offer special affordances for caves, both negative and positive, relative to human needs. In many caves, interior passages do not allow upright mobility, while they also require increased physical effort, special equipment, or technical knowledge to traverse them. Wayfinding is difficult, and even with modern equipment one is easily disoriented in the dark and often relatively unfamiliar environment. Cave interiors may also be enclosed spaces in which one can become trapped. For these reasons, cave dark zones do not offer high-quality affordance for habitation, but they do offer high-quality affordance for hiding and secrecy. Caves offer a shadowy environment that is different from the surface world, an environment of mystery. In addition, due to sensory deprivation, dark zones of caves can help produce meditative states or stimulate otherworldly experiences, such as hallucinations that are characteristic of many shamanic practices (see Williams 2002 for a thorough discussion).

While these properties are not conducive to habitation, dark zones stimulate human imagination and encourage "imaginary geographies," as described by Gallese and Lakoff (2005, 9). Because of this property, we suggest that cave dark zones offer *transcendental affordance*. While Gibson never discussed the notion of symbolic places, this extension is in keeping with his ideas that affordances straddle the material world and the world of the mind. It is telling that some of the first known ritual practices and art of early humans (see Clottes, chapter 1, this volume) occurred in deep caves in Europe during the Paleolithic period, as indicated by painted cave walls and the use of the spaces for burials. While there is little doubt that earlier forms of portable art existed, and that these cave remains are an artifact of differential preservation, it is also possible that the caves themselves offered an affordance not presented elsewhere. The human-cave interaction may have worked reciprocally to facilitate and encourage symbolic or ritual behaviors. In other words, these early expressions may have been as much about the caves themselves as what occurred within them.

CONCLUSION

This chapter examined why cave dark zones are the subject of myths and stories and are so often used as ritual spaces. Part of our approach is quasi-phenomenological; we find that phenomenology is useful in defining patterns and can help us understand the active role of environments in the development of shared ideas. But phenomenology offers no explanatory power for why humans interpret some environments in similar ways.

We suggest that the physical properties of caves have particular implications for human psychological responses, and to understand these responses, we turned to studies of spatial cognition in the behavioral and cognitive sciences, and in the environmental behavior and design fields. Our review of the literature suggests that there is a correlation between types of environments and human perceptions that are important in inferring how caves were used in the past. The literature suggest that a number of factors such as low-light or no-light conditions, and three-dimensional complex morphology, lead to a general perception of cave dark zones as dangerous, mysterious, and illegible, rendering them useless for all but temporary habitation. By framing our discussion in terms of Gibson's affordances, we have come to understand that the very qualities that prevent caves from "affording" habitation are the very qualities that make them attractive as transcendent or imagined spaces that may be incorporated into myth and used in ritual. Although we have elected to focus on broad patterns of cave usage, we expect that our approach will be useful for analyses of single sites as well as intersite studies.

REFERENCES CITED

Appleton, Jay. 1975. *The Experience of Landscape*. London: Wiley.

Appleyard, Donald. 1969. "Why Buildings Are Known." *Environment and Behavior* 1 (2): 131–56. http://dx.doi.org/10.1177/001391656900100202.

Arthur, Paul, and Romedi Passini. 1992. *Wayfinding: People, Signs, and Architecture*. Toronto: McGraw-Hill Ryerson.

Auburn, Timothy, and Rebecca Barnes. 2006. "Producing Place: A Neo-Schutzian Perspective on the 'Psychology Of Place.'" *Journal of Environmental Psychology* 26 (1): 38–50. http://dx.doi.org/10.1016/j.jenvp.2006.03.002.

Balling, John D., and John H. Falk. 1982. "Development of Visual Preference for Natural Environments." *Environment and Behavior* 14 (1): 5–28. http://dx.doi.org/10.1177/0013916582141001.

Benedikt, Michael, and Clarke A. Burnham. 1985. "Perceiving Architectural Space: From Optic Arrays to Isovists." In *Persistence and Change: Proceedings of the First International Conference on Event Perception*, ed. W. H. Warren and R. E. Shaw, 103–14. Hillsdale, NJ: Lawrence Erlbaum Associates.

Berlyne, Donald E. 1960. *Conflict, Arousal, and Curiosity*. New York: McGraw-Hill. http://dx.doi.org/10.1037/11164-000.

Cornell, Edward H., C. Donald Heth, and Wanda L. Rowat. 1992. "Wayfinding by Children and Adults: Response to Instructions to Use Look-Back and Retrace Strategies." *Developmental Psychology* 28 (2): 328–36. http://dx.doi.org/10.1037/0012-1649.28.2.328.

Edelman, Gerald M. 1992. *Bright Air, Brilliant Fire: On the Matter of the Mind*. New York: Basic Books.

Gallese, Vittorio. 2005. "Embodied Simulation: From Neurons to Phenomenal Experience." *Phenomenology and the Cognitive Sciences* 4 (1): 23–48. http://dx.doi.org/10.1007/s11097-005-4737-z.

Gallese, Vittorio, and George Lakoff. May 2005. "The Brain's Concepts: The Role of the Sensory-Motor System in Conceptual Knowledge." *Cognitive Neuropsychology* 22 (3): 455–79. http://dx.doi.org/10.1080/02643290442000310. Medline:21038261.

Gärling, Tommy, Anders Böök, and Erik Lindberg. 1986. "Spatial Orientation and Wayfinding in the Designed Environment: A Conceptual Analysis and Some Suggestions for Postoccupancy Evaluation." *Journal of Architectural and Planning Research* 3: 55–64.

Gibson, James J. 1979. *The Ecological Approach to Visual Perception*. Boston: Houghton Mifflin.

Gladwin, Thomas. 1970. *East Is a Big Bird*. Cambridge, MA: Harvard University Press.

Goldberger, Leo. 1966. "Experimental Isolation: An Overview." *American Journal of Psychiatry* 122, 7 (Jan): 774–82. Medline:5321573.

Hartig, Terry, and Gary W. Evans. 1993. "Psychological Foundations of Nature Experience." In *Behavior and Environment: Psychological and Geographical Approaches*, ed. T. Gärling and R. G. Golledge, 427–57. Amsterdam: North-Holland. http://dx.doi.org/10.1016/S0166-4115(08)60053-9.

Hegarty, Mary, Anthony E. Richardson, Daniel R. Montello, Kristin Lovelace, and Ilavenil Subbiah. 2002. "Development of a Self-Report Measure of Environmental Spatial Ability." *Intelligence* 30 (5): 425–47. http://dx.doi.org/10.1016/S0160-2896(02)00116-2.

Hillier, Bill, and Shinichi Iida. 2005. "Network and Psychological Effects in Urban Movement." In *Spatial Information Theory*, ed. Anthony G. Cohn and David M. Mark, 475–90. Berlin: Springer. http://dx.doi.org/10.1007/11556114_30.

Kaplan, Stephen. 1992. "Environmental Preference in a Knowledge-Seeking, Knowledge-Using Organism." In *The Adapted Mind: Evolutionary Psychology and the Generation of Culture*, ed. Jerome H. Barkow, Leda Cosmides, and John Tooby, 581–98. New York: Oxford University Press.

Kaplan, Stephen, Rachel Kaplan, and John S. Wendt. 1972. "Rated Preference and Complexity for Natural and Urban Visual Material." *Perception & Psychophysics* 12 (4): 354–6. http://dx.doi.org/10.3758/BF03207221.

Lakoff, George, and Mark Johnson. 1999. *Philosophy in the Flesh: The Embodied Mind and Its Challenge to Western Thought*. New York: Basic Books.

Lawrence, Elizabeth Atwood. 1993. "The Sacred Bee, the Filthy Pig, and the Bat Out of Hell: Animal Symbolism as Cognitive Biophilia." In *The Biophilia Hypothesis*, ed. Stephen R. Kellert and Edward O. Wilson, 301–41. Washington, DC: Island Press.

Leicht, Roger, and Christopher Tolan-Smith. 1997. "Archaeology and Ethnohistory of Cave Dwelling in Scotland." In *The Human Use of Caves*, ed. Clive Bonsall and Christopher Tolan-Smith, 122–26. BAR International Series 667. Oxford: Archaeopress.

Llobera, Marcos. 2003. "Extending GIS-Based Visual Analysis: The Concept of *Visualscapes*." *International Journal of Geographical Information Science* 17 (1): 25–48. http://dx.doi.org/10.1080/713811741.

Loomis, Jack M., Roberta L. Klatzky, Reginald G. Golledge, Joseph G. Cicinelli, James W. Pellegrino, and Phyllis A. Fry. 1993. "Nonvisual Navigation by Blind and Sighted: Assessment of Path Integration Ability." *Journal of Experimental Psychology General* 122, 1 (Mar): 73–91. http://dx.doi.org/10.1037/0096-3445.122.1.73. Medline:8440978.

Lynch, Kevin. 1960. *The Image of the City*. Cambridge, MA: MIT Press.

Matthews, W. H. 1970. *Mazes and Labyrinths: Their History and Development*. Mineola, NY: Dover.

Mehrabian, Albert, and James A. Russell. 1974. *An Approach to Environmental Psychology*. Cambridge, MA: MIT Press.

Montello, Daniel R. 1991. "Spatial Orientation and the Angularity of Urban Routes: A Field Study." *Environment and Behavior* 23 (1): 47–69. http://dx.doi.org/10.1177/0013916591231003.

Montello, Daniel R. 2005. "Navigation." In *The Cambridge Handbook of Visuospatial Thinking*, ed. P. Shah and A. Miyake, 257–94. Cambridge: Cambridge University Press.

Montello, Daniel R., and David S. Lemberg. 1995. "The Minotaur's Revenge: Geographic Disorientation in Caves." Paper presented at the International Conference on Spatial Analysis in Environment-Behaviour Studies, Eindhoven, The Netherlands.

Montello, Daniel R., and Herbert L. Pick. 1993. "Integrating Knowledge of Vertically-Aligned Large-Scale Spaces." *Environment and Behavior* 25 (3): 457–84. http://dx.doi.org/10.1177/0013916593253002.

Moyes, Holley. 2002. "The Use of GIS in the Spatial Analysis of an Archaeological Cave Site." *Journal of Caves and Karst Studies* 64 (1): 9–16.

Orians, Gordon H., and Judith H. Heerwagen. 1992. "Evolved Responses to Landscapes." In *The Adapted Mind: Evolutionary Psychology and the Generation of Culture*, ed. J. H. Barkow, L. Cosmides, and J. Tooby, 555–79. New York: Oxford University Press.

Proctor, James D. 1998. "The Social Construction of Nature: Relativist Accusations, Pragmatist and Critical Realist Responses." *Annals of the Association of American Geographers. Association of American Geographers* 88 (3): 352–76. http://dx.doi.org/10.1111/0004-5608.00105.

Sadalla, Edward K., and Diana Oxley. 1984. "The Perception of Room Size: The Rectangularity Illusion." *Environment and Behavior* 16 (3): 394–405. http://dx.doi.org/10.1177/0013916584163005.

Schutz, Alfred. 1962. *Collected Papers I: The Problem of Social Reality*. Ed. M. Natansen. The Hague: Martinus Nijhoff.

Schutz, Alfred. 1967. *The Phenomenology of the Social World*. Trans. G. Walsh and F. Lehnert. London: Heinemann Educational Books.

Stamps, Arthur E., III. 2005. "Visual Permeability, Locomotive Permeability, Safety, and Enclosure." *Environment and Behavior* 37 (5): 587–619. http://dx.doi.org/10.1177/0013916505276741.

Stone, Andrea. 1997. "Pre-Columbian Cave Utilization in the Maya Area." In *The Human Use of Caves*, ed. Clive Bonsall and Christopher Tolan-Smith, 201–6. BAR International Series 667. Oxford: Archaeopress.

Tversky, Barbara. 1992. "Distortions in Cognitive Maps." *Geoforum* 23 (2): 131–8. http://dx.doi.org/10.1016/0016-7185(92)90011-R.

Weisman, Jerry. 1981. "Evaluating Architectural Legibility: Way-Finding in the Built Environment." *Environment and Behavior* 13 (2): 189–204. http://dx.doi.org/10.1177/0013916581132004.

Williams, David Lewis. 2002. *The Mind in the Cave: Consciousness and the Origins of Art*. New York: Thames and Hudson.

Wohlwill, Joachim F. 1976. "Environmental Aesthetics: The Environment as a Source of Affect." In *Human Behavior and Environment*, vol. 1, ed. I. Altman and J. F. Wohlwill, 37–86. New York: Plenum.

Zubek, John P., ed. 1969. *Sensory Deprivation: Fifteen Years of Research*. New York: Appleton-Century-Crofts.

Contributors

Mark Aldenderfer, Department of Anthropology, University of California, Merced, USA

Joanna E.P. Appleby, Department of Archaeology, University of Cambridge, Cambridge, UK

Graeme Barker, McDonald Institute for Archaeological Research, University of Cambridge, UK

Donald J. Blakeslee, Department of Anthropology, Wichita State University, USA

James E. Brady, Department of Anthropology, California State University, Los Angeles, USA

Wayne Brennan, Burramoko Archaeological Services, Katoomba, Australia

Robert S. Carr, Archaeological and Historical Conservancy, Inc., Davie, Florida, USA

Andrew T. Chamberlain, University of Manchester, UK

Cheryl Claassen, Appalachian State University, USA

Jean Clottes, Conservateur général du Patrimoine (honoraire), France

Nathan Craig, Department of Anthropology, Pennsylvania State University, USA

Alan Cressler, United States Geological Survey, Atlanta, GA, USA

Joseph Douglas, Department of History, Volunteer Community College, Gallatin, TN, USA

Stašo Forenbaher, Institute for Anthropological Research, Zagreb, Croatia

Jerry E. Hilliard, Arkansas Archeological Survey, University of Arkansas, USA

Joseph J. Hobbs, Department of Geography, University of Missouri, Columbia, USA

David Ilan, Hebrew Union College–Nelson Glueck School of Biblical Archaeology, Jerusalem, Israel

Timothy Kaiser, Department of Anthropology, Lakehead University, Canada

Matthew Kelleher, KN Consulting, Sydney, Australia

Lindsay Lloyd-Smith, McDonald Institute for Archaeological Research, University of Cambridge, UK

Jami J. Lockhart, Arkansas Archeological Survey, University of Arkansas, USA

Caroline A.T. Malone, School of Geography, Archaeology and Palaeoecology, Queen's University, Belfast, UK

Patrick McCafferty, Irish and Celtic Studies, Queens University of Belfast, Ireland, UK

Preston T. Miracle, Department of Archaeology, University of Cambridge, Cambridge, UK

Daniel R. Montello, Departments of Geography and Psychology, University of California, Santa Barbara, USA

Holley Moyes, Department of Anthropology, University of California, Merced, USA

Scott Nicolay, Independent Scholar, New Mexico, USA

Sue O'Connor, School of Culture, History, and Language, Australian National University, Canberra, Australia

Sandra Pannell, consultant anthropologist, Australia

Michael P. Pateman, School of Planning, University of Cincinnati, Cincinnati, Ohio; The National Museum of The Bahamas, Nassau, New Providence, Bahamas

Dave Pross, Amaroo Aboriginal College, Kariong, Australia

Keith M. Prufer, University of New Mexico, Albuquerque, USA

Olaf H. Prufer, Kent State University, Ohio, USA

Terence Ranger, Oxford, UK

Jeff B. Ransom, Office of Historic and Archaeological Resources, Miami, Florida, USA

Yorke M. Rowan, The Oriental Institute, University of Chicago, USA

George Sabo III, Arkansas Archeological Survey, University of Arkansas, USA

William C. Schaffer, Center for Bioarchaeological Research, School of Human Evolution and Social Change, Arizona State University, USA

Jan F. Simek, Department of Anthropology, University of Tennessee, Knoxville, TN, USA

Robin Skeates, Department of Archaeology, University of Durham, UK

Stuart Tyson Smith, University of California, Santa Barbara, USA

Simon K.F. Stoddart, Department of Archaeology, Cambridge University, UK

Andrea Stone, Department of Art History, University of Wisconsin, Milwaukee, USA

Paul S.C. Taçon, Chair in Rock Art Research, PERAHU, School of Humanities, Griffith University, Gold Coast Campus, Australia

Peter Tomkins, Département d'Archéologie et d'Histoire de l'Art, Université Catholique de Louvain, Belgium

Patty Jo Watson, Distinguished University Professor Emerita, Archaeology at Washington University in St. Louis, USA

Ezra B.W. Zubrow, Department of Anthropology, University at Buffalo, New York, USA and Honorary Fellow, Department of Archaeology, University of Cambridge, UK

Index

Page numbers in italics indicate illustrations.

abandonment ritual, 65; Nakovana Cave, 272–73
Aborigines: cave and rockshelter use, 136, 137–47
aboveground caves, 46; in Malta, 47–49, *49*, 51–52
abstract designs, Upper Paleolithic, 31, 32
Abu Hamid, 102
Abu Matar, 100
Abu Simbel, Ramses II temple at, 120–21, *121*
Abydos, 116, *118*
Acatzingo Viejo, 157
Actun Tunichil Muknal, 159, 160, 161, *162*, 163
Adair Glyph Cave, 190; images in, 188–89, 198
Adeimah, 89
Adriatic Sea, 2; Copper and Iron Age in, 263–73
Aegean region, 67; agriculture, 61–62; Neolithic and early Bronze Age, 60, 64, 66, 69–71
aesthetics, 392–93
Africa, 5, 9. *See also* Egypt; Zimbabwe
agriculture, 32, 34, 61–62, 88, 368; rituals, 161, 176
agropastoralists, Andean, 345, 348–49
Ajanta, 129
Akhet, 111; representations of, *119, 120*, 121
Alabama, 223; cave art, 195, 196, 198; Woodland-Mississippian caves in, 190, 211, 213–14
Alacaluf, 344
Alberta, 356
alcohol, ritual consumption of, 270, 271
alcohol distilleries, 232, 305
Alepotrypa, 71
Alibamu, 211
Alice and Gwendoline Cave, 302, 303, 304
Allen's Cave, 143
All Souls' Day, Hindu ritual on, 335, 336
Altxerri, 20
atlatls and darts, in caves, 175, 176
altars, *132*, 220; cached, 178–79
Altun Ha, 158
Amayaúna, 286
Am Duat, 111, 113, 115, 117, 118
American Southwest, 2; architecturally modified caves in, 5, 173–74, *174*; artifact deposits in, 174–75; cave use in, 171–72, 178–80; hunting ritual, 175, 175–76; sandals in caves, 177–78; witchcraft, 176–77
Amnisos, 68
Amud, 87
Amun, *113*
Amun-Re, 118, 120, 121
ancestor veneration, West Malaysian cave temples, 339–40
Ancestral Beings, Australia, 137, 146
Ancestral Puebloans, 173; altar caches, 178–79
Andean region, cave use, 343–49, 368
animal bones. *See* faunal remains
animal lodges, Pawnee, 356, 358–59
animals, 69, 160, 175, 298, 300, 334; Australian depictions of, 137, *138*, 140–41, *141, 144*; domesticated, 62–63; in Great Plains cosmology, 354, 356–58; Ili Kérékéré rock art, 320–21; in Upper Paleolithic Europe depictions, *18*, 20, *21, 22*, 24, 32; in Southeastern US cave art, 196, *197*; symbolism of, 275–83
animism, West Malaysia, 334
Annagh Cave, 303
Anne, Queen, 302
Antipodes, 298
Antrim County, 297, 302, 303
Anubis, *117*, 118
Apache, 354
Apesokari tholos, 72
Apophis, 110, 114, 120
Appalachian Hocking Valley State Park, 234
Appalachian Plateau, 196
Apulia region, 2, 7, 9; Bronze Age, 39–41; Copper Age in, 38–39; Neolithic in, 32–38; Upper Paleolithic in, 27–32
aquatic invertebrates, in Eastern US caves, 214, 219
aragonite mining, 356
archaeobotanical remains, 161; Eastern Woodland caves, *186, 187*, 190, 215, 219, 221, 222
archaeozoology. *See* faunal remains
Archaic period: American Southwest, 175–76, 177, 178, 179; Andean region, 344; Eastern US, 187–89, 197–98, 217–21, 226–30; Great Plains, 361; mortuary caves, 226–28
Archalochori, 72
architecturally modified caves, 5, 304; American Southwest, 173–74, *174*; Apulia region, 39–40, 41; West Malaysia, *333*, 337–38, 340

architecture, 48; Mesoamerican caves associated with, 157–58, 368
Arguedas, José María, 345
Ariadne, 385
Arizona, 171, *173*, 176, 178–79
Arkansas: archaeology in, 237–38; GIS studies in, 239–44; places of emergence in, 211, 212
Arnezano, 37
Arnhem Land, 137, 138, *139*
Arrow Grotto of Feather Cave, 172, *173*, 176, 178
Arrow Rock, 358
arrows, 179; as offerings, 358, 360. *See also* bows and arrows
artifact deposits, 62, 92, 93, 185, 213, 348, 366–67; American Southwest, 172, 174–78, 179–80; Apulia region, 31, 33, 35; Crete, 65, 67, 68–69, 72, 74; Eastern US, 185, 221, 228–30; Great Plains, 356, 358, 360; Maltese, 52–53; Mayan, 159–60, *160*, 161; Nahal Mishmar, *94*, 94–95. *See also* offerings
artificial caves, 36–37, 109, 118, 348; Chalcolithic, 90, 96–99, 102–3; in Ireland, 303, 305; Mesoamerican, 154, 157, 368
Aschwanden, Herbert, *Karanga Mythology*, 310–11
Asterousia region, 72
astronomy, Egyptian, *112*, 113
Aswan, 116
Atlas de Duran, 153
Auel, Jean, *The Clan of the Cave Bear*, 3
Aurignacian period, 19
Austin Cave, 211, 220–21, *221*
Australia, 2, 17, 136, 369; Cloggs Cave in, 138–39; northern, 137–38; Pleistocene in, 16, 135, 138–39, 143–45
Austronesia: cosmology, 327; painting tradition, 321
Avila, Francisco de, 345
Awatovi, 173
axes mundi, 68, 154, 243
Ay, 120
Ayios Antonios, 71, 73
Ayios Ioannis, 66, 67, 68, 70
Ayios Nikolaos, 66, 71–72
Aymara, 344, 345, 346, 348–49
Azor, 98, 99
Aztecs, 154, 366

Ba, representations of, 120, 123
Babar, 326
Bab edh-Dhraᶜ, 89
Bachikutu, 311
Bahamas: Lucayan burial, 288–89; Lucayan-Taino mythology in, 285–86; Preacher's Cave, 2, 285–92; Taino social organization, 289–91
Balankanche, 160, 161
Ballawinne, 145–46
Ballynamintra Cave, 302
Bambata cave, 309, 310
Bara-Bahau cave, 23
Bar Kokhba Revolt, 101
Barntick Cave, 302, 303
basalt vessels, Chalcolithic, 92, *95*, 96, 97, 102

base camps, Early Upper Paleolithic, 27–28
Bat Cave (New Mexico), 179–80
Bat's Cave (Ireland), 302, 303, 304
Bats'ub Cave, 162
Batu Caves, 331, *332*, 333, 335, *336*, 337, *338*, *339*; development of, 340–41
beamers, bone, 229, *230*
Bear Butte, 359, 360
Bear Creek Cave, 172, *173*
bears, 218; cave, 15, *24*, 277; and Neanderthal burials, 7, 17, 18; power of, 22–23
Bédeilhac, 18, 21
Beersheba Valley, 100–101
bees, rock-nesting 137
Bégoüen, Henri, 20
Belize, 17, 156, 157, 158, 159, *160*, 163, 164; rockshelter burials in, 161–62
Belize Valley, 164
benches, in Chalcolithic caves, 98
Bene Berak, 98, 99
Ben Shemen, 97–98, 99, 102
Bernifal, 19
Bhutanese Lamaist tradition, 333
Big Bone Cave, 189, 190
Bigeh Island, 118
Binford, Lewis, on ethnographic analogy, 202–3
Birdman motif, Mississippian, 203–5, 243–44
birds: in Southeastern US, 215, 216, 218, 219, 220; in cave art, *197*, 203–4, *204*, *205*, *207*
Bir es-Safadi, 97, *100*, 102
birthing sites, Newt Kash Hollow Shelter as, 222
bison, underworld emergence of, 356–57
Black Hills, 357, 358, 359–60
boats, 320, 321, 322
Bob Evans Rockshelter, 231
Bocca Cesira, 31
Bodhgaya, 130
Bodhisattvas, 332, *333*
Boinayel, 286
Bolivia, 345
Bolonchen, 155
Bon, 128–29
Bone Cave (Tasmania), 145
Bone Cave (Virginia), 213, 214–15
Bonita Creek (Arizona), Pueblo altar cache in, 178–79
Book of Caverns, 113, 114–15, 116
Book of Discipline, 129
Book of Gates, 113, 114–15, 116
Book of Going Forth by Day, 111, 115, 116, 117, 123
"Book of Invasions of Ireland," 300
Book of the Earth, 113, 116
Book of the Secret Chamber, 111, 112, 113–14, *114*, 115, 118
Book of the Two Ways, 117
Borneo, 7, 16; Late Pleistocene–Early Holocene, 250–54; Neolithic, 254–59; Niah Cave, 2, 249
boundary markers, 154, 189
bows and arrows, 175, 176, *177*, 179
boxes, ossuary, 89, *91*, 99
Boy Scouts, 233–34

Braidwood, Robert, "cave stage," 4
breathing, of caves, 354
Brendan, Saint, 302
Brenham meteorite field, 356
Breuil, Henri, 19, 20
Bricklieve Cave (Chapel Cave), 301
"Bricriu's Feast," 300
Brigit, Saint, 301
Britain: archaeological data in, 81–82; prehistoric cave burials, 82–85
British, in Zimbabwe, 312–13
Brochtorff Circle (Xaghra), 45, 51, 52, *53*, *54*, 55, 56
Bronze Age, 2, 9, 64, 69, 89, 90, 95, 102, 299; Aegean, *61*, 62–63; Apulia region, 39–41; Crete, 59, 67, 68, 71–73, 368, 369; Irish cave burials, 303–4
Brooks, W. K., 286
Brothers' Cave, 302, 304
Bruidhein Chéise Corainn, 299–300
Bruniquel cave, *17*, 25
Buchan, John, *Prester John,* 312
Buddha, 130; West Malaysian images of, 332–33, *333*
Buddhism: pilgrimage and, 130–32; Tibetan, 125, 127, 128–30
Buddhist traditions: *gnas,* 5, 129; Malaysian shrines, 2, 331, 332–41
Buffalo Gap (Black Hills), 357, 359
Buffalo Gap (White Buffalo Buttes), 357
burial chambers, 89; Egyptian, 110–18
burial mounds, Mississippian, 242–43
burials, 2, 15, *50*, 62, 197, 220, 286, 346, 353, 354, 367; American Southwest, 176, 178; Apulia region, 29, 34, 37, 38–41; British, 81, 82–84; Chalcolithic, 88–100, 102; Crete, 59, 71–73; Ireland, 303–4; Lucayan-Taino, 288–92; Malta, *53*, 55; Mayan, 154–55, 161–63; Nahal Mishmar, 94–95; Neanderthal, 7, 17–18; Niah Caves, 249, 251–60; Ozarks, 239, 243–44; Tibetan plateau, 128–29; Upper Paleolithic Europe, 24–25; Woodland-Mississippian, 190, 198–99; Zimbabwe, 312, 313
Bur Mghez, *50*
Burren, 297, 302

caches, 52, 159, 291; American Southwest, 176, 178–79; Ohio rockshelters, 228–30
Cacibajagua, 286
Caddoans, 211, 243
Caher Roe's Den, 301
Cahokia, 238
cairns, burial, 303–4
California, 175, 358
Campbell, Archie, 312
cane cigarettes, 171, 174, 176
cannibalism, 215, 217, 228
canoes, in Bahamian caves, 286–87
canyons, as emergence places, 356–57
Capactoco, 368
Cape Ploča, 268
Cappadocia, 5
Captain Webb's Hole, 298
captives, sacrifice of, 163

caravan routes, 122
cardinal directions, 154
Caribbean, 2, 366
Carlsbad Caverns, 178
Carlston Annis shell mound, 223
Carmel range, Mt., 90
Carrigmurrish Cave, 302
Carrickbyrne Hill, 301
Carricknahorna, 301
Carrigacrump Cave, 301
CART. *See* Cave Archaeology Research Team
Carthage, Saint, 302
Carver, Jonathan, 353
Carver's Cave, 353, 358
Casa Malpais, 178
Casal Sabini, 38
Castlepook Cave, 302
Castletownroche Cave, 7, 302
Catacombs (Ireland), 302, 304
Cathedral Cave (Batu Caves), 337, *338*
Catherwood, Frederick, 155
Catholic Church, in Ireland, 301
cattle, in Aegean caves, 69
Cauta, 286
Cavan County, 297, 301
Cave Archaeology Research Team (CART), 191
cave art, 7, 8, 366; chronology of, 197–201; interpretation of, 201–7; Southeastern US, 195–207. *See also* paintings; rock art
cave bears, 15; and Neanderthal burials, 7, 17, 18; Upper Paleolithic use of, 22–23, *23, 24*
cave cults, 36, 172
"Cave Dwellings of the Old and New Worlds, The" (Fewkes), 4
Cave Hill (Belfast), 303
Cave Hunting (Dawkins), 3
cavemen, cave dweller, stereotypes of, 3–4, 61, 136
Cave of Cruachan, 300
Cave of Sokar, 114, 118
Cave of the Bats (Dos Pilas), 156
Cave of the Bees, 310
Cave of the Glowing Skulls, *162*
Cave of the Subjugation of Mara, 129
Cave of the Treasure (Nahal Mishmar), 92, *94*, 94–95, 97, 102
Cave of the Warrior, 102
Cave of the Wild Horses, 298
Cave of the Winds (Colorado), 354, 359, 360
Cave of the Winds (Niagara Falls), 212
Cave I (Kinboko Canyon), 176
Cave Research Foundation (CRF), 185–86
caves: definitions of, 5–6, 151, 172–73, 225, 344; destruction of, 9, 52–53; layouts of, 391–92
Caves Branch Rock Shelter, 161–62
cave spirits, West Malaysian, 334
Cave Springs (Alabama), 214, 215
"cave stage," 4
Cellino San Marco, tombs in, 38–39
Celts, 300, 301
cemeteries, 7, 190, 271; Chalcolithic, 89, 101, 102; Neolithic Borneo, 2, 249, 254–58. *See also* burials; human remains

cenotes, 153, 163
censers (incense burners), Maya, 158, 159, 161
centrality, in landscape, 68–69
ceramics, 92, 176, 356; Chalcolithic, 89, *91, 96*, 97, 99; Crete, 66, 67, 68, 69, 72, 73, 74; Mayan, 153, *154*, 158, 159–60, *160*, 161, 164; in Nakovana Cave, 266, 267–70, *270*, 277, 278; Neolithic Aegean, 64, 65, 70; Neolithic Apulia region, 33, 34, 38; in Stanhope Cave, 230, *231*; Woodland, 198, 217
Ceremonial Cave (Hueco Mountains), 177
Chac (Chaak), 153–54, *154*, 155
Chaco Canyon shrines, 173
Chailoro, 318
Chalcolithic, 16; burial caves, 2, 87–88, 102–3; caves use during, 90–99; mortuary practices, 88–90. *See also various sites*
Chalcotzingo, El Rey monument from, *153*
chalk caves, 90, 96–99, 102, 297
Chang Tang, mortuary and village sites, 128–29
Chapel Cave (Bricklieve Cave), 301
Chapelle de la Lionne, 18
Charente, 15
Cha'hta (Choctaw), 212
charnel houses: Kissufim, 99–100; Mississippian, 242–43
Charwe, 312
Chauvet Cave, 22; art in, 19, 20, *21*; cave bears in, *23, 24*, 277
Chavez Cave, 173; "Tlaloc" effigies from, *174*, 180
Chechem Ha Cave, 156, *160*, 161, 164
Cheek Bend Cave, 223
Chee Chai Dudjom, 333, 337, 338
Cherokee, 212
chert, mining of, 17, 143, 189, 190, 215, 220, 356
Cheyenne, 354
Chiapas, 153, 158
Chichen Itza, 163
Chicomostoc (Place of the Seven Caves), 153, 155, 157
Chihuahuan Desert, 178
children, 163, 220, 304; initiation ceremonies, 20–21; in Woodland mortuary caves, 214–15, 216
Chile, hunter-gatherers in, 344–45
China, 339
Chinese, and Malaysian cave temples, 337, 340
Chippewa, 222
Chokhopani, 126
Chonos, 344, 346, 349
Christ, 87
Christianity, Irish, 83, 301–2, 304, 305
chronometric dates, Southeastern US cave art, 198–201
churches, as constructed caves, 9
cities of the dead, 46
Clan of the Cave Bear, The (Auel), 3
clans: Mayan, 154; Tibetan deities, 129
Clare, County, 297, 298, 302, 303, 304, 305
clay, 17, 214, 356
Cliff Temples, 333

climate, speleothem studies, 164
Cloghermore Cave, 302, 304
Cloggs Cave, 138–39
cloud blowers, 174, 176
clouds, and caves, 354
Coahuila, burial caves in, 178, 179
Coaybay, 286
Cobo, Bernabé, 345
Coemgen, Saint, 302
coffins, in Niah Cave burials, 255, *256,* 257
Coffin Texts, 111, 116
Colman MacDuagh, Saint, 302
Colorado, springs and caves in, 354
Colorado Plateau, 175, 212–13
Coliboaia painted cave, 19
Columbus, Christopher, 291
Comanche, 354, 358
comets, in Irish mythology, 300
communities, 8; Mesoamerican, 157–58
Conan, 302
constructed/cultural caves, 5, 9, 46, 157, 301; Apulia region, 36–37; Malta, 45, 47–51, 53–54, *55*, 55–56; at Teotihuacan, 155–56; Tibetan plateau, 125, 127–28
consumption, ritualization of, 65
Contact Period (Plains), 358
context, ritualization through, 64–65
Copena culture, 190, 198, 213–14
copper, 8; from Levant caves, *95*, 96
Copper Age, 36; Apulia region, 38–39; Nakovana Cave, 263, 266
Coralline limestone, construction using, 49, 50–51
cores, engraved, 31
Cocijo, 153
Comparative Austronesian Project, 327
Copan Valley, 161, 164
Copper Age, in Adriatic, 263, 266
Cork, County, 297, 301, 302, 303, 304
Correo Snake Pit, 176, 177, 180
cosmology, 72, 203, 317, 354; Austronesian, 327; Egyptian, 2, 9, 109–10, *111*; Fataluku speakers, 319–20; Lucayan-Taíno, 285–86; Mesoamerican, 154, 165; Maltese, 46, 52
Cosquer, 19, *20*, 21, 23
Cougnac, 24; finger markings and paintings in, 21, *22*
Covalenas, 20
Cowboy Cave, 177, 179
Cramps Cave, 213
Crazy Horse, 212
Cree, 212, 358
Creek Indians, 211, 221, 355
cremations, 213, 214, 256
Crete, 2, 4, 8, 368; Bronze Age, 9, 71–72, 369; cave use in, 62–63, 65–67; defining ritual in, 63–64; Labyrinth on, 385, 389; liminality, 67–68, 73; material culture deposits, 69–70; Minoan sites, 59, *60*
CRF. *See* Cave Research Foundation
Croagh Patrick, 301
Croatia, Copper and Iron Age in, 263–73
Crooked Island, 286
Crow, 358
Crumps Cave, 189, 198

Crystal Cave (Kentucky), Archaic period exploration, 187–88, *189*
Crystal Maiden, *162*, 163
Crystal Onyx cave, 190
Cú Chulainn, 299, 302
Cueva de la Candelaria, 178, 179
Cueva de Sangre, 163
cult objects, Chalcolithic, 94
cult sites, 6, 72, 120, 310; Nakovana, 270–71
cultural heritage management, Timor-Leste, 327–28
Cumberland Plateau, 217
Cumberland River, 220
Cussac cave, 15, 19; burials in, 24–25
custodians, of Timor-Leste caves, 323, *324*, 325
cyst burials, 176

Daedulus, 385
Dakota, 353
Dalmatia, 267–68, 271, 272
Dark Cave (Malaysia), 341
Darkingjung, 141–42
darkness, quality of, 136
dark zones, 6–7, 62, 123, 129, 136, 159, 173, 191, 356; Andean region, 344, 349; art in, 195, 366; Mammoth/Salts Caves, 185–86; sacredness of, 385–94; Upper Paleolithic use of, 18–25
Darug, Wollemi Caves, 141–42
Dawkins, W. Boyd, *Cave Hunting*, 3
Dawson's Mount, 299
dead reckoning, 387–88
Dead Sea, 89
Dearc Fearna (Dunmore Cave), 304
deep-cave symbolism, in Egypt, 109
Deep Skull (Niah Cave), 249, 251, 252
deer, 7, 17, *21*, 36, 160, 218
Deir el-Bahari, 118
Deir el-Medina, Pashed's tomb at, *117*
Dellinger, Samuel C., 238
demons, 130, 300
Dendara, 118
Derg, Lough, pilgrimage to, 301–2, 305
desecration, destruction: of artifacts and speleothems, 8, 23–24, *24*, 65; of caves, 9, 312, 313, 158; of space, 52, *53*, 56
Devil's Lair, 144–45
Devil's Tower, 359
Diarmaid, 299, 305
diets, ritual, 216–17, 222
Diné, witchcraft sites, 176
Dingo's Lair, 140–41, *143*, 144
direct historical approach, 201, 202
discoidal stones (chunkeys), 229, *230*
diseases, curing, 356
disorientation, 388–89
ditched settlements, Apulia region, 32, 41
divine, contact with, 87
Djara (Rohlfs Cave), 122
DNA analysis, paleofecal material, 191
Dog Den Butte, 354, 356
dogs, in Paleoindian and Archaic contexts, 219, 220
dolmens, Levant, 89
Dolores Cave, 176

Dolph Johnson rockshelter, 228
Dome of the Rock, 87
domestic space, 72; ritualization of, 64–65
Domingo Garcia, 19
Donn Firinne, 301
Dordogne Valley, 5, 7, 15, 23, 24
Dos Pilas, Cave of the Bats, 156
Dowth, 300
Dragon's Mouth (Yellowstone), *355*, 355–56
Dreamtime Beings, 142
Drenpa Namkha, 129
Dresden Codex, 153
drought, and Maya cave ritual, 164
druid, Celtic, 300
Duat, 110–11, 116, 117; representations of, *119*, *120*, 121, 123
Dula cave, warfare and, 311, 312
Dunmore Cave, 303, 304
Durán, Diego, 154
Dust Cave, 211, 217, 218–20, 223
dwarves, 212, 358
Dzijo cave shrine, 311
Dzilo, 314
Dzivaguru, 314

Eagle Ancestor, depictions of, *142*
Eagle's Reach, 140, *141*, 142
Early Classic Period, Maya cave shrines, 156
Early Dynastic Period, temples, *119*
Early Holocene, 7, 82; Australia, 136, *139*; Borneo, 249, 253–54, 259
Early Stone Age (ESA), Zimbabwe, 309–10
earth, as animate, 152
earth deities, 189; Mesoamerican, 154, 161
earth monster, 153, 354, *355*
earth-serpent/water-panther/long-tailed-monster, 189
Eastern Keres Pueblos, 180
Eastern United States, 2, 4, 8, 16, 211, *212*; Archaic period, 187–89; cave art, 195–207, 366; cave use, 185–87, 232–34, *234*; Woodland-Mississippian period, 189–90
East Timor. *See* Timor-Leste
Ed Smith Cave, 214, 215
Edwards, "Wiri," 313
Egypt, 8; cosmology of, 2, 9, 109–10, 121–23; Underworld/Netherworld in, 6–7, 110–18
Eighteenth Dynasty, 117
18th Unnamed Cave, *207*
Eilat, 102
Eileithyia cave, 62, 66, 67, 68, 71, 72
Elderbush Cave, 302, 303
electrum, in Nahhal Qanah Cave, 92
Elephantine Island, Temple of Satet, 118–19, *119*, 122
Eleuthera, Preachers Cave on, 285, 287–91
11th Unnamed Cave, *198*, 204, *205*, 207
elites, 158, 160, 161, 214, 291, 299
Ellenes, 72
Ellenospilia, 67, 69, 70, 71
Ellora, 129
emergence, places of, 16, 211–12, 286, 346, 348, 355–56, 368
emergence shrines, 179, 180
Emperor of Hell, 333

Emu Cave, 141, *145*
"Enchanted Cave of Keshcorran," 299–300
Enchanted Rock, 212
enclosure ditches, 36–37
En Gedi, 94
engraved caves, 18, 195
engravings, 15; in Australian caves, 144, 146; portable, *18*, 30, 31
environments: aesthetics of, 392–93; cave, 393–94; perception of, 386–87; psychological responses to, 389–92; spatial orientation in, 387–89
Enlène, 18, 22
Erawan, 335
Ervin shell mound, 223
Esquipulas, 157
Etcheberri-ko-karbia, 19
ethnoarchaeology, spatial analysis, 372–73
ethnobotanical remains. *See* archaeobotanical remains
ethnography, 1, 2, 4, 8; archaeological use of, 201–3; in prehistoric art studies, 203–4
Etowah (Georgia), 238
Etruria, 46
Etruscans, 46
Europe, 3, 5, 15, 47, 366, 367. *See also various named caves; countries; sites*
Europeans, in Zimbabwe, 312–14
excarnation, 71, 303
exorcisms, 337
exploration, 366; Eastern Woodland, 187–88, *189*, 190, 196–97

face-pots, Apulia region, 34
Faillsiugud Tána Bó Cuailngni, Do, 302
Fairy Mills Cave, 298
fairymounds, 300
Faracat, 298
Fataluku speakers, 317, 318; cultural sovereignty, 328, 329; and téi, 319–25
faunal remains, 2, 22, 30, 34, 72, 160, 252, 303; in Australian caves, 139, 144; Bahamian caves, 286, 289; in Eastern US, 213, 214, 215–16, 217–18, 219, 220–21, 232; Levant caves, 87, 92; Nakovana Caves, 277–83; Neolithic Crete, 69, 71; symbolic and ritual behavior, 275–83
feasts, feasting: animal remains, 276–77; historic, 233, *234*
Feather Cave, 178; Arrow Grotto, 172, *173*, 176; "Tlaloc" effigy from, *174*
feather robes, in Ozark burials, 243–44
fending sticks, 175, 176, *177*
fengshui, Taoism, 339
Fergus, 302
Fermanagh County, 297, 298, 301, 302, 303
fertility, animal and human, 356–58
fertility rites, 161, 270, 348; American Southwest, 174, 175, 176, 179
fetuses, burials of, 89, 215
Fewkes, J. Walter, 172; "The Cave Dwellings of the Old and New Worlds," 4
Fianna, 299
fiery beasts, in Irish mythology, 300
Fifth period, 126, 128

5th Unnamed Cave, 198
figurines, 34, 64, 99, 286; Cretan, 63, 70, 74; split-twig, *175*, 179; witchcraft-associated, 176–77
finger marks, 20; European Upper Paleolithic caves, 20–21, 23; Koonalda Cave, 17, 143–44
Finland, shrines in, 368–69
Finn, Lough, 302
Finn Cycle, 299
Finn mac Cumhall, 298, 299–300, 302
Fir Bolg, 300
fires, 15, 18, 243
first-fruit rites, 161
fish, 52, 216, 218
Fisher Ridge Cave, 188, 190
fishhooks, on Crete, 65–66
fissures, shrines in, 173
Flathead, 356
Fled Bricrenn, 300
flint, 23, 92, 143, 215, 229–30
Flint Ridge Cave system, 188
floors, in Cretan caves, 67
flowstone, mining of, 190
Floyd Collins Crystal Cave, 187
folktales, Irish, 298–99
folk traditions, Irish, 2, 301
Fondo Focone, 31
Fontanet, 19, 20, 22
food, 276; preparation and consumption of, 65, 69, 71, 280–81
Footprint Cave (Belize), 17
footprints, 15, 20, 188, 190
Fort Ancient culture, 231
fortifications, caves as, 346, 348
48th Unnamed Cave, 187
Fourth period, 126, 128
Foz Côa, 19
fragmentation, as ritual performance, 65. *See also* desecration, destruction
France, 5, 7, 17, 18, 22, 24
fundamentalist church, in Gillie Rockshelter, 233

galleries, Upper Paleolithic, 18–25
Galway County, 297, 298, 301
Gambier, Mt., 143, 145
gaming equipment, American Southwest, 174–75
Gan Kira, 249
Garden of the Evening Star (Garden of the Gods), 355, 359, 360
Gargano uplands, 34
Gargas, 18, 19, 20, 24
Garrett Early, 299
gateway communities, on Crete, 69
Gebel Uweinat, 122
gender, of caves, 311
Geographic Information Systems (GIS), 8, 372, 373; Ozark rockshelter and cave study, 239–44
geographic orientation, 387
geomancy, Tibetan, 130
Georgia, 195, 196, 213
Gerani cave, 62, 66–67, 69, 70

Gerar, 88
Ggantija, 45, *48*
Ggantija phase, 51
Ghar Dalam, 48
Ghassul, 89
Ghassullian culture, 93
giants, on Great Plains, 356
Gilat, 88, 89, 96
Gilf Kebir, 122
Gillie Rockshelter, 231, *232*, 233
Giraldus Cambrensis, 301
GIS. *See* Geographic Information Systems
Gitchi Manitou Ouitch-chouap, 212
Giv'at ha-Oranim, 95, 96–97, 102
Giv'at Ha-Radar (Hadera), 98
Giv'atayim Caves, *98*, 99
Giza, 111–12
Glencurran Cave, 303–4
Globigerina bedrock, in Malta construction, *49*, 50–51
glyphs, in Eastern Woodland caves, 188–89
gnas, 5, 129, 130, 132, 133
gnas-chen: creation of, 129, 130, 133; pilgrimage to, 130–32
Gnathia wares, 267, 268
goats, in Nakovana Cave, 278–82
Goddess of Mercy. *See* Kwan Yin
Goddess of Mercy and Eight Immortals Cave, 335
God's voice, from Matopo Hills caves, 311, 314
gold, in Naha Qanah Cave, 92
Goll mac Morna, 300
Good Spirit, Great Spirit, in caves, 212–13
Gordon Hill Caves, 286
Gordon's Cave 3, 161
Gottschall Rockshelter, 238, 356, 360
gourds, *186*, 190
Gozo, 48
Grad hill fort, and Nakovana, 271–73
graffiti, in Nakovana Cave, 270, 271
Gragano promontory, 39
Graham Cave, 238
Gráinne, 299, 305
Gran Can Cave, 17
Grand Army of the Republic, meetings of, 233, *234*
Grand Canyon, 179; split-twig figurines, *175*
Grand Quivira, and Surratt Cave, 174
Grapčeva, 263
grave circles, Levant, 89
grave goods, 161, 289; American Southwest, 176, 179; in Apulia region burials, 29, 37, 39, 40; British cave burials, *83*, 83–84; Chalcolithic burials, 90, 92, 97, 98–99, 101, 102; Irish caves, 303, 304; Minoan Crete, 72, 74; in Neanderthal burials, 7, 17–18; Niah Cave burials, 255–56; in Woodland period caves, 213–14
Gravettian period, 18, 19, 20, 22, 24
Great Britain. *See* Britain
Great Lakes region, latticework, 189
Great Plains, 2, 8, 353; archaeology, 360–61; hunting magic and fertility in caves, 356–58; sacred precincts, 358–60; as underworld entrance/border, 354–56

Great Pyramid, 111
Great Spirit, in caves, 212–13
Great Zimbabwe, 315
Greece, 71, 267, 272, 280, 369
Griffiths, D. W., *Man's Genesis,* 3
Grotta Cappuccini, 38
Grotta di Cala Colombo, 37
Grotta del Cavallo, 27
Grotta della Tartaruga, 40
Grotta della Zinzulusa, 38, 40
Grotta delle Mura, *33*
Grotta delle Venere, 32
Grotta delle Veneri, 29
Grotta di Occhiopinto, 34, *35*
Grotta di Porto Badisco (Grotta dei Cervi), 35–36, 37
Grotta di Santa Croce, 35, 36
Grotta di Uluzzo, 33
Grotta Paglicci, *29*, 30, 31
Grotta Romanelli, 31
Grotta Santa Maria di Agnano, 29, *30*
Grotta Scaloria, 34, 35, 36
Grottone di Manaccora, 39–40, *40*
Gruta de Chac, 161
Grymani, 67, 72
Gua Cha, 260
Gua Kelawar, 335
Gua Piyachat, 337–38
Guadalupe Mountains caves, 177
Guatemala, 154, 156, 157, 161, 163, 164, 366
Guerrero, 366
guerrillas, 314
Guide Rock, animal lodge at, 358, *359*
Gulubahwe, 310
Gunug Rapat, 333
Gunung Cheroh, 340
Gunung Lanno, 337
Gunung Marang mountains, 253
Guru Rinpoche Caves, 129, 130
Gusinde, Martin, 345
Gwindingwi caves, 313
gypsum, 158, 189, 190

habitation, 4, 48; Aegean caves, 61–62; Andean caves, 346, 348–49; Apulia region caves, 37, 38; Irish caves, 304–5; Niah Caves, 251–53; in rockshelters, 6, 18; Tibetan chambers, *127*, 127–28, *128*
Haderah, 98
Hagar Qim, 45, 52, 53, 54
Haggard, H. Rider, *King Solomon's Mines,* 312
Hal Saflieni, 45, 53; hypogeum at, *49*, 51, 54
Hampton Cave, 214, 215
hand-and-eye motif, 231
Handprint Cave (Actun Uayazha Kab), 161, 162
handprints, 253; Australian rock art, *142*, 145–46; Upper Paleolithic Europe, 20, 30
hand stencils, Upper Paleolithic Europe art, 20, 23
Hapy, 109, 118
Harrington, Mark R., 237
harvest rites, 161
Hasinai, 243
Hathor, 8, 18; temples to, 118, 120, 121

Hatsheptsut, 118
Haush, 345
Hautes-Pyrénées, 18
Hayonim Cave, 87
Head Covered with Downy Eagle Feathers (Pikes Peak), 354
hearths, 34, 35, 67
Heizer, Robert, direct historical approach, 202
Hellmouth Cave, 298
Hemans, H. N. (Mathandidwala), 313
Hemans, Trevor, 313
hematite, 220, 356
Hendricks Cave, *226, 227*
He'patina, 180
hermitages, hermits, 87, 128, 132, 337
Hidatsa, 354, 355, 356, 357, 358
hiding places, caves as, 304–5, 346
hill forts, 271
hilltop shrines, Bronze Age Crete, 72, 369
Himalayas, clan deities, 129
Hindu cave temples, 2, 331, 333, 335, *336,* 336–37, 339
Hindu traditions, 334, *336,* 340
Hiraa, 337
Historia de los Mexicanos por sus pinturas, 152
historical connectivity, 201, 202
hoards, *94,* 304
Hohokam, 174, 179, 180
Holocene, 2, 146. *See also* Early Holocene
Holy Hill, 359
Homo heidelbergensis, in Sima de los Huesos, 18
Honduras, 153, 161, *162*
hòn non bô, 336
Hopevale area, 137
Horbat Castra, 98
Horbat Govit, 102
Horemheb, 120
Hornos de la Peña, 24
Horus, 110, *114*
Horvat Beter, 97
Horvat Hor, 97
Hot Springs (Arkansas), 212
Hough, Walter, 172
House of Bats, 368
House of the Rabbit, 212
houses, 47, 65, 368; as materialized metaphor, 45–46
Hove, Chenjerai, 314
Howth, Hill of, 299
Huarochiri, 344
Hubbards Cave, 189, 190
Hueco Mountains caves, 177
Huichol, 179
human remains, 18, 62, 87, 101, 127, 137, 190, 344; in Bahamas, 286, 287; in Britain, 82–85; Chalcolithic, 90–92, 97; Cretan, 67, 70–73; in Eastern US, 213–14, 215–17, 226–28, *228, 229*; Irish, 302, 303; Mayan, 161–63; in Niah Caves, 249, 251, 253–60; secondary treatments of, 89–90, 99–100, 255–56; stable isotope studies, 258–59. *See also* burials; ossuaries
hunter-gatherers: Andean, 344–45, 346; landscape and, 367, 369
hunting, 232; in Andean caves, 345, 348

hunting blinds, 158
hunting magic, Great Plains, 356, 357
hunting ritual, 160, 216, 231, 356; American Southwest, 174, *175,* 175–76, 179
hurricanes, 158
Hvar Island, 263
hypogea: Bronze Age, 40–41; Late Neolithic, 36–37; Malta, *49,* 51, 53, 54, 55–56
Hypogeum of the Bronzes, 41

Iberian Peninsula, 19
iconography, 136, 272; Chalcolithic, 94–95, 96, 103; of Chicomostoc, 155, 157; Maya, 161, 163; Southeast Ceremonial Complex, 195–96, *197*; Southeastern US, 203–7
Ida, Mount, 68
Idaean Cave, 67, 68, 69, 72
Ignatievskaya, 19
Iguanaboina, 286
Ili Kérékéré, 317, *318, 319,* 319–23; paintings in, *320,* 320–22; téi in, 322–23
Ili Mimiraka, 326
Illyrians: ceramics, 267–70; deities, 270–71; and Nakovana hill fort, 271–72
imperialism, British, 312–13
Incas, 16, 344, 345, 348, 368
Inchiquin, Lough, 298, 299
Indiana, 186, 189, 223, 356
Indian Salts Cave, 189, 190
Indonesia, 320, 323, 325. *See also* Timor-Leste
Inene, 112
infants, 89, 214, 215, 217
Inishmore, 301
initiation ceremonies, 20–21, 36
Ioro, 318
Ipoh, 337, 341; cave temples in, 331, 333–34, 340
Ireland, 2, 83; archaeology in, 302–5; folk and Christian traditions in, 301–2; folktales, 298–99; Medieval tales, 299–301; underworld myths, 6, 297
Iron Age, 2, 305, 310; Adriatic, 263–73; faunal remains, 277–83; metaphorical houses, 45–46
Iroquis, 211
Isfet, representations of, 110, 120, 121
Islam, 337, 340
islands, cosmology of, 52
Island Southeast Asia, 249, 322
isovist analysis, 390–91
Israel, 89, 90, 92–93, 102
Issa, 267
Italy, 2, 366–67; burial caves, 7, 9; Neolithic cave use, 48, 56; Upper Paleolithic in, 27–32
Iuktas, Mount, 68, 69

Jacob's Cavern, 237
jade, in Maya burials, 161
Jade Emperor (Yu Huang), 333
Jaguar Cave (Tennessee), 185, 187, 188, 190, 217
Japodes, 272
Jemez Cave, 179
Jemez Pueblo shrines, 179, *180*
Jesuits, on Matopos shrines, 312

Jicarilla Apache, 212–13, 360
Jolja Cave, 158
Jordan, 90
Judean Desert, 102
Judea-Samaria-Galilee Anticline, 90
Juxtlahuaca Cave, 366

Kailash, Mt., 130
Kain Hitam Painted Cave, 249
Kakadu National Park, rock art in, *137, 138*
Kaligandaki Valley, 126
Kalimantan, 16, 260
Kamalapukwia, 213
Kamares cave, 64, 69, 70, 72
kancab (red earth), 158
Kansas, 354; meteorites and ribstones in, 356, *357*
Kapovaya, 19
Kaqchikel Maya, 151
Karanga mythology, 310–11
Karlie-ngoinpool Cave, 17
karst aesthetic, *336*
karstic caves, 125, 151, 196, 287, 344; Chalcolithic use of, 90–96, 102
karst landscapes, West Malaysia, 331, 334–35
karst towers (turmkarst), 331
Kastellos, 67
Katsambas, 68
Kebara, 87
Keep River, 136
Kek Look Tong, *333, 334,* 338, 340
Kelly's Cave, 302
Kempe, David, *Living Underground,* 4
Kentucky, 185, 190, 196, 211, 223; cave art in, *197, 198*; mud glyph caves in, 188–89
Kerry County, 297, 302, 304
Keshcorran Cave system, 298, 299, 301
Khafre's pyramid, *112,* 116
Khepri, 111, 114
Khufu's pyramid, *112*
kick balls and sticks, in American Southwest, 174, 175
Kilcorney I Cave, 298
Kilgreany Cave, 302–3, 304
Kilkenny County, 297, 303, 304
Killavullen Caves, 302, 305
Killura Cave, 302
Killuragh Cave, 302, 303
Kilmurry, 304
Kimberley, 138
Kinboko Canyon scalp, 176
kings, in Egyptian Underworld, 111–18
King Solomon's Mines (Haggard), 312
K'in Krus rites, 154
Kinta Valley, *332,* 333, 340
Kiowa, 354, 355–56
Kissufim, *91,* 92, 96, 99–100
Knockane, 303
Knocknarea Cave, 302, 303
Knockninny, 303
Knossos, 65, 66, *68,* 69, 70, 385, 389
Knowth, 300
Kogi, 344, 345, 348
Kong Foo Ngam Cave Temple, 335
Koonalda Cave, 17, 143–44, *145*

Koumarospilio, 66, 67, 71
Krill Cave, 228, 233
Kuala Lumpur, 331, 333, 337
Kuantan, 337
kurkar, 90, 98–99
Kusinara, 130
Kutikina Cave, 145
Kwan Yin, 333, *334,* 336
Kymulga Cave, 214
Kyparissi, 72

Labastide, 18, 21, 22
Labbanaheanbo, 298
Labouiche, 18
Labyrinth (Crete), 385, 389
labyrinths, 391–92
La Colline Blanche Cave, as House of the Rabbit, 212
Ladakh, 130
Lady's Buttery, 302
La Garma, 21
Laguna Pueblo, scalp storage, 176
Lake Hole Cave, 213, 214
Lake Jackson site (Florida), 238
Lakota, 359
Lamaist traditions, 333, 337
Lamayuru, 130
landmarks, caves associated with, 68–69, 72
landscape(s), 8, 9, 88, 129, 317, *336,* 343, 373; Australian sacred, 137, 141; centrality of caves in, 68–69; Mesoamerican, 154, 156; Ozark cave and rockshelter rituals, 239–44; Pawnee animal lodges, 358–59; ritualized, 211–12; role of caves in, 48, 154; social organization and, 367–68
land titles, Mesoamerican caves and, 154
land tenure, 367–68
Lao Tse, 333
La Pailita (Guatemala), 154
Lapchi, 129
Lascaux, 19, 20
Las Cuevas (Belize), 156
Las Monedas, 24
Late Classic Period (Maya), 163, 164, 202
Lateglacial Interstadial, burials, 82, *83*
Late Holocene, Australian rock art, 138
Late Prehistoric period, 358
Late Stone Age (LSA), Zimbabwe, 309, 310
Laterza, rock-cut tombs at, 38–39
latticework, symbolism of, 189
La Vache, 18
lava tubes, 179
Leafrin Hill, 301
Lebor Gabála Érenn, 300
Le Cheval at Arcy-sur-Cure, 19
Lee Cave, 185, 188, 217
Leeman Mound, 215
Legacapple Cave, 298
Legnabrocky Cave, 298
Legnaveagh Cave, 298
Leitrim County, 297, 301, 303
Léné Ara (Lene Hara), 317, *318,* 323–24, 328–29
Le Portel, 22
Lera, 66, 69

Leroi-Gouthan, André, 19
Les Trois-Frères, 18, 19, 20, 21
Leti shrines, 326
Le Tuc d'Audoubert, 19, 20, 21, 22
Levant, Chalcolithic burials, 2, 87–99, 101–2
Lewis, Theodore H., 353
Lhasa, caves near, 125–26
life rituals, 48
lightning, 221, 310
lightning sticks, 175
light zone, 6, 123
Limerick, County, 301, 302
limestone caves, Australia, 137, 143–44
liminality, 65; Cretan Neolithic caves, 67–68, 73
lineages, and caves, 154–55, 162
Lismore Cave, 302
Lisodigue Cave, 302
Li Thai, King, 338
Little People, 358
liturgical furniture, 52–53
Liurai, 323, *324,* 325, *326*
Living Underground (Kempe), 4
Llano Estacado, canyons on, 356–57
Lobang Angus, 249
lobster, in Cretan caves, 69
loess, 90; structures excavated into, 5, 99–101, 102
Loire Valley, 5
Long, Abijah, 178
Loong Tow Ngam, 340
Lóvaia (Maku'a), 319
Lower Mammoth Cave, 188
Lower Pecos region, 178, 179
Lower Salts Cave, 185, 189; Archaic exploration of, 187–88; botanical remains, *186, 187*
Luang shrine, 326
Lubbock, John, *Pre-historic Times,* 3
Lucayan-Taíno, 287; burial, 288–89, *290;* mythology and cosmology, 285–86
Ludlow Cave, 357, 358, 360
Lugh, 299, 301, 305
Lughnasa festival, 301, 305
Lugh of the Long Arm, 300
lulic, 317
Lumbini, 130
Lu Xing, 333

Ma'abarot, 98, 102
Ma'at, 110, 121
Macal Valley, 158
Madonna di Grottole, 41
Madonna di Loreto, 41
Madrid Codex, 153
Magdalenian period, 18, 19, 20
magic, Plains hunting, 356, 357
magical objects, 348, 356
Mahayana traditions, 332, 337
Maitreya (Buddha of the Future), images of, 332–33
maize rituals, 174, 177, 179
Maize God (Mayan), 153
Makoni, 313, 314
Malay, 340
Malaysia, 2, 260. *See also* West Malaysia

Malaysian Nature Society, 341
Malta, 45; above-ground caves, 47–49, *49;* cave infilling in, 52–53; construction processes, 50–51, 55–56; monument construction, 46, 48–50; natural and constructed caves in, 46–52; Neolithic temples, 9, 51–52
Mama Ocllo, 368
Mammoth Cave complex, 185, 186, 188, 211, 223; paleofecal deposits, 190, 222; ritual cultural deposits in, 215–17
Mammoth Cave National Park, 185–86
Manco Capac, 368
Mandan, hunting magic, 357
Manfredi hypogeum, 9, 36–37
manger, as cave, 87
Manitou Springs, 354; caves at, 212–13
man-made caves, 2, 5, 46, 51. *See also* constructed caves
Man's Genesis (Griffith), 3
Manyepera, 313
Marastoco, 368
Marble Arch Cave, 298
Marendellas district, 313
marijuana smoking, 233
marine travel, Aegean, 69
Márohu, 286
Marpa, 130
Mas d'Azil, 21
masks, shell, 360
Massat, 19
mastaba, 116
Matonjeni, 315
Matopos Hills, 309; in Karanga mythology, 310–11; post-independence use, 314–15; white imperialism and, 312–13
Mauch, Carl, 315
Maya, 8, 9, 16, 17, 46, 151, 202, 366, 368; burials, 161–62; cave use, 4, 16, 157; lineages, 154–55, 162; mining in caves, 158–59; rain and caves in, 153–54, 156
Maya Mountains, 157
Mayo Conty, 297, 298, 302
Mazoe Valley, 312
Mbuya Juliana, 311
McCalla Cave, 214
McMahon, Horace, 312
meat consumption, social context of, 65, 69
Mebrak, 126
Mebrak phase, mortuary chambers, 126–27
medicinal plants, 222
medicine bundles, 176, 229
Medicine Creek Cave, 360
medicines, 24, 222
Medieval era, Ireland, 299–301, 304
Medinet Habu, temple of Ramses III, 118, *120*
meditation caves, 130, 335
Mediterranean, Neolithic cave cults in, 36
Melos, obsidian from, 69
memory prompts, Australian rock art as, 142
men, fertility rituals, 270
Mendes, Agustu, *323*
Menkaure's pyramid, 112
menstruation, rockshelters as retreats from, 221–22

mental models, 386
Merneptah, tomb of, *115*, 115–16
Mesara, 67, 72
Meskine, 67
Mesa Karteros, 68
Mesoamerica, 2, 4, 6, 8, 16, 165, 174, 175, 215, 366, 368; architecture-cave associations in, 157–58; constructed caves in, 9, 46; cultural construction of caves in 151–55; pre-settlement cave use, 156–57
Mesolithic, 65–66, 82, 303
metal objects, 72; Chalcolithic, 88, 94–95, 97
metaphor: of cave infilling, 52–53; construction process as, 50–51; houses as, 45–46; physical constraint as, 51–52
metamorphisis, symbols of, 90
meteorites, 356, *357*, 358
meteor storms, in Irish mythology, 300
metonyms, caves as, 46
Mexico, 153. *See also* Mesoamerica; *various named caves, sites*
Mg7, 215
Miamou, 66, 67, 69, 72
Middle Kingdom, private tombs, 116–17
Middle Stone Age (MSA), Zimbabwe, 309
Mid-Holocene, Australian rock art, 138, *139*, 143, 146
Midleton, 304
Miller shell mound, and Squire Boone Cave, 223
Mimi spirits, 137
minerals: from caves, 7–8, 19, 23–24, 356; iron-oxide, 27–28
mines, as burial sites, 39
miniature objects, 160, 175, 176
mining, 7–8, 356; in caves, 17, 23, 220; Eastern Woodland, 189, 190, 197, 198; Maya, 158–59
Minnesota, 353, 359
Minoan period: on Crete, 59, *60*, 66, 67–68, 72–74; ritual evidence, 63–64
Minos, King, 385
Minotaur, 385
Mishi Bizi, 189
missionaries, European, 312
Mississippian culture, 190, 198–99, 213, 222; in Arkansas, 241–43; chunkeys, 229, *230*; Southeast Ceremonial Complex, 195–96, *197*, 203–5, *205, 206*
Missouri, 190, 203, 220, 237, 238
Mitchelstown Cave, 298, 302
Mixco Viejo, 157, 163
Mixtec, 153
Mnajdra, 45
modified caves, 34–35, 36, 37, 39–40, 41, 304. *See also* architecturally modified caves
Mogollon, 174, 178, 179
Mogmothon, 212
Mohammed, 87
monasteries, monastic communities, 129; in Tibet, *127*, 127–28, 130, 132; in West Malaysia, 331, 337–38
monks, Irish, 300
monsters, in caves, 212
Montana, 356, 358, 360

Monte d'Accoddi, 46
Monte Sannace, 38
Montespan, 19, 22
Montezuma Canyon, Spirit Bird Cave in, 173, *174*
monuments, Maltese construction of, 46, 47–50
moonmilk, 23, 24
Moorehead, Warren K., 237
Montu Temple, 118, *119*
Morrígan, 300
mortuary caves/rockshelters, 2, 7, 84, 178, 211; Apulia region, 29, 36–37, 38–41; Eastern US, 190, 198–99, 213–17, *226–28*, 239, 241; Levant, 89–99; Malta, 45, 52. *See also* burials
mortuary chambers, Tibetan plateau, 126–27
mortuary practices, 34, 102; Levant, 88–90, 99–100; Mississippian, 241–43; Niah Caves, 253–58; Tibetan plateau, 128–29
Mound on the Water, 359
Moundville (Alabama), 238
mountains, 46, 130; and caves, 68, 72, 153, 154; as center places, 68, 69; Crete, 68, 72; pyramids as, 9, 156
Moya, 344
Mud Glyph Cave, 16, 186, 189, 190, 198; mapping of images in, 205, 207; Mississippian art in, 195–96, 203–4, *204*, 238
mud glyphs, 196, 198. *See also* finger marks
Muhammad, 337
Muktinath Valley, 126
mummies, Woodland mortuary caves, 215, 216
Mummy Cave (Wyoming), 360–61
Murugan, 337, 339, 340
Museum of the American Indian–Heye Foundation, 237
music, musicians, and Irish caves, 301
Muskohgeh (Muskogee Creeks), 211
Muslim Malaysians, 337
Mwali (Mwari) cult, 310, 311; shrines of, 312, 313, 314–15
Mythological Cycle (Irish), 299, 300
mythology, 137, 270, 348; Great Plains, 354–56; Irish, 6, 297; Karanga, 310–11; Lucayan-Taíno, 285–86; Mesoamerican creation, 152–53
Mzilikazi, 311, 313
Nablus-Tell Balatah region, 89
Nabta Playa, 122
Nahal Hemar, 87
Nahal Mishmar (Cave of the Treasure), 92, *94*, 94–95, 97, 102
Nahal Qanah Cave, 96, 101; artifacts from, *93, 95*, 97; use of, 90–92, *92*
Naj Tunich, *155*, 157, 158, 159, 161, 162, 366
Nakovana Cave, 2, 263; abandonment and closure of, 272–73; description of, 264–65; faunal remains in, 277–83; as sanctuary, 265–72
Namorodo, *137*
Nancy Patterson site, 173
Naqada period, 122
Nardò, 27
Naropa, 130

Natufian burials, 87
Navajo witchcraft, 176
nawamis grave circles, 89
Ndebele, 311–12, 313
Neanderthals, 3, 7, 17–18, 25
Nefertari, 121
Negev Desert, 89, 121; loess caves and chambers in, 90, 99, 100–101, 102
Nehanda (Vera), 315
Nehanda's cave, destruction of, 312
Neolithic, 2, 45, 122, 303; Aegean, *61*, 62–63, 66; Apulia region, 32–38; Borneo, 249, 254–59; Britain, 82–83; Crete, 4, 59, *60*, 67–71; Levant, 101–2; Malta, 9, 46, 53–54
Neolithic Wet Phase, 122
Nerja, 19
Nerokourou, 69
Netherworld, Egyptian, 6–7, 120
nets, in American Southwest, 175, 176
Neube, Sitwanyana, 311
New Archaeology, 202–3
Newberry Cave, 175
Newgrange, 300
New Kingdom: rock-cut temples, 120–21; Underworld symbolism, 111, 112–14, 117–18; Valley of the Kings, 109, 123
New Mexico, 172, 174, 175. *See also various named caves, sites*
New South Wales, 139–40
Newt Kash Hollow Shelter, 211, 221–22
Ngari, 127
Niagara Falls, Cave of the Winds at, 212
Niah Caves, 2, 7, 249–50, *250*; Early Holocene and Neolithic burials in, 253–58, *258*; Late Pleistocene use of, 251–53; Neolithic lifeways at, 258–59
Niah Great Cave, 249; Early Holocene and Neolithic burials in, 253–58, *258*; West Mouth, *251*, 251–53, *253*
Niaux, 18, 19, 20, *21*
Nicollet, Joseph, 353
Nile River, 118, 120
Nile Valley, 110
19th Unnamed Cave, 198
Nino onis Santana National Par, 328
Njelele, 311, 313, 314, 315
njuzu spirits, 311
Nkomo, Joshua, 314
Noon's Hole, 298
Northern Territory, *139*
Nubia, 120–21, 122
Nullarbor plain, 135, 143
Nunamira Cave, 145
Nswatugi, 310
Nyachiranga, 314
Nyanda, 312
Nyathi, Lynette, 311

Oaxaca, 153, 161
objects, 56, 132; deposition of, 52, 54, 65, 159–60, *160*; Early Upper Paleolithic, 27–28; portable art, 27–28, 30, 31–32; Upper Paleolithic deposition of, 21–22, 29
O-Block Cave figurines, 176

O'Brien clan, and Vigo Cave, 298–99
obsidian, Neolithic Crete, 69–70
ochre, 29, 102, 137, 256
Octavian, 272
offerings, 8, 39, 74, 119, *132*, 154, 216, 348; American Southwest, 175, 176, 177–80; Chalcolithic, *93, 94*; in Eastern US, 220–21; Great Plains, 356, 358, 360; Mayan, 158, 159–60, *160*, 161; Nakovana Cave, 267–70, *270*; Neolithic Apulia, 36, 38; Saami shrines, 368–69; Upper Paleolithic, 21–22, 31–32; West Malaysian temples, 335–37
Ohio, 2, 225, 356; caches in, 228–30; historic cave and rockshelter use in, 232–34, *234*; mortuary caves in, *226*, 226–28; petroglyphs, 230–32
Oisín, 298, 305
Oklahoma, 242
Old Kingdom, 109, 116, 118–19, *119*
Olmec, 366
Omaha, 358
Ona, 344, 345, 346, 348
Oonacaragreisha (Cave of the Grey Sheep), 298
Oonaglour, 302
opía, 286
Oracle of Delphi, 369
oracles, 87, 155, 215, 369; in Zimbabwe, 310, 311, 312, 313, 314
Orchestra Shell Cave, 144
orientation, 387–88
Osage rock art, 203
Ošanići, 268, 271
Osirion, *116*
Osiris, 110, 111, 118; and private tombs, 116–17; representations of, 113, 114, 115, *121*
ossuaries, 161; Levant, 89–93, 95–100, 102
Ostionoi period, 288
Oswego River, 211
other world, access to, 16, 87, 212, 298
Oto, 358
oversized objects, 160
Owen, Knight, 301
Oweynagat Cave (Uaim na gCat), 298, 300, 304
Ozark Bluff-Dweller culture, 237
Ozarks, 2, 8, 237–38

Pacariqtambo, 368
Pachacuti Yamqui, 368
Padmasambhava (Guru Rinpoche), 130
Pahang state, 334
pahos (prayer sticks), 171, 174, 176, 178, 179
Painted Cave (Kain Hitam), 249
painted pebbles, 179
paintings, 160, 310, 313; Ili Kérékéré, *320*, 320–22; sacred Australian, 137–38; Neolithic Apulia region, 35, 36; Timor-Leste caves, 317, *320*; Upper Paleolithic, 18–25, 30–31. *See also* pictographs
Paiute Cave (northeastern Arizona), 179
Paiute Cave (Arizona Strip), 179
Pak Che'n, 161
Palagruža, 268
paleofecal deposits: Eastern Woodland Caves, 190, 191, 222; ritual diets, 216–17

Paleoindians, 360; Eastern US, 217–21
Paleolithic, 2, 4, 7, 9, 15, 87, 205, 366, 367
Palestine National Authority, 89, 102
Palewardia Walana Lanola, 145
Palmahim Cave, 97, *98*, 99
palygorskite (blue pigment clay), 158–59
Pan, 271
Pané, Ramón, 286
Partira, 66, 72
Parvati, 337
Pashed, tomb of, *117*
passage tombs, Ireland, 300, 303
pastoralism, Aegean, 62–63
Patagonia, 344–45
pathways, 161
Patrick, Saint, 302
Pawnees, 243, 354, 355, 360; animal lodges, 356, 358–59
Peabody, Charles, 237
peace, at sacred precincts, 359–60
Peak District, *85*; cave burials, *83, 84*
pebbles, engraved, 31
Pech-Merle, 20
Pelekita, 65–66, 67, 68, 69, 70
Pelješac peninsula, 271–72, 277
Pennsylvania, 229
Peqi'in, 89, 97, 101; ossuaries in, *91*, 92–93, 102
Perak state, 331, 335
Perak Tong, 336, 338–39, 340
performance: Andean cave use, 346, 348; ritualization through, 64–65
Pergouset, 19
Perkiomen points, *230*
permeability theory, 393
Perry shell mound, 219, 223
Peru, 345
Peter's Cave, 233
Petras Kephala, 69
Petroglyph Cave (Belize), 159, 160
petroglyphs, 122, 287; Eastern Woodland, 189, 190, 230, 231–32; Great Plains, 353, 356, 357–58; Maya, 160, 161; Southeastern US, 196, *197*, 197–98, *198*, 204, *205, 206*
Pfeiffer, John, 20
phallic images, 32, 70; Nakovana Cave, 265–66, *266*, 270, 271
Phillips Academy, 237
Phuzdeling, 126
Pictograph Cave (Montana), 360
pictographs, 160, 196, 230, 360; American Southwest, 175, 176; Eastern Woodland, 189, 190, 191. *See also* paintings
Picture Cave (Missouri), 190
Piedras Negras, 158
Pigeon Hole, 298
Pikes Peak, 354; as sacred precinct, 358–59, *359*, 360
Pileta, 19
pilgrimages, 173, 178, 211, 337, 348; Ireland, 302, 305; to Matopos cave shrines, 314–15; Mayan, 157, 158, 164; Tibetan religious, 125, 129, 130–32
Pima, 180
Pinson Cave, 190

Piper's Cave, 301
pipes, Plains smoking, 360
Pitileti, 318
Pit of the Skulls (Kentucky), 190
pits, 34, 45; in Eastern US caves, 221–22, 229–30
Piyachat, Mae Chee, 337–38, *338*
Piyang, *127*, 127–28, *128*
Pizzone, 38
places, 67, 394; of emergence, 16, 211–12, 286, 346, 348, 355–56, 368; meaningful, 385–86; perceptual-environmental interactions in, 386–87; of power, 2, 129, 130; sacred, 135–36, 367
Plains Indians, 8, 215. *See also various tribes*
Plakias region, 65
plants. *See* archaeobotanical remains
plaques, Australian carved, 145
plaquettes, 18
Platyvola, 66, 70
Pleistocene, 2, 7, 65, 358; Australia, 135, 136, 138–39, 143–45; Borneo, 249, 251–53, 259; Irish caves, 302–3; Tasmania, 145–46. *See also* Paleolithic
poets, Zimbabwe, 315
Poets Cave, 231
politics, 9, 317; and Mayan ritual, 157–58; Timor-Leste, 320, 323, 325
Pollabrock Cave, 298
Pollanaffrin, 301
Pollawaddy Cave, 298
Polldonin, 302
pollen studies, in Niah Cave Neolithic burials, 259
Poll na Bruidhne, 301
Pollnagapple Cave, 298
Pollnagat Cave, 298
Pollnagollum Cave, 298
Pollnagollum of the Boats, 302
Poll Rannagh East, 302
Polticoghlan Cave, 301
Poma de Ayala, Felipe Guaman, 345
Pomo, 358
Pomongwe, 310
Ponca, 360
Popol Vuh, 8, 157, 368
portable art, Paleolithic, 15, *18*, 29, 30, 31–32
Portugal, 19
posts, poles: in Ili Kérékéré, *321*, 322, 323; Léné Ara, 323, *324*; Timor-Leste ritual, 326, *327*
Potala Palace, 130
pottery. *See* ceramics
Pottery Neolithic, 90
Poulagaddy Cave, 301
Poul na Bruckee, 300
Poulnamadda Cave, 298
Poulnamuck Cave, 298
prayer(s), 154, 335–36
Preacher's Cave, 2, 285; burials in, 288–89, *290, 291*; description, 287–88
Preclassic Period (Maya), 161, 164
Pre-historic Times (Lubbock), 3
Prester John (Buchan), 312
projectile points, in caches, 229, *230*
prospect-refuge theory, 393

Pryor Gap, 358
psychological response, to environment, 389–94
Psychro, 63, 72, 73
Ptah, 121
Pueblo Bonito, and Threatening Rock Fissure, 173
Pueblo Creek (Soccorro County), 172
Pueblo V (Gran Quivira), 174
Pueblo VI, 179
Pueblos, 173; cave cults, 171, 172; ritual artifacts, 174–75; warfare and hunting ritual, 175–76
Pueblo II period, 179
Puelche, 344, 345, 348
Purgatory, on Lough Derg, 301–2
Pyramid of the Sun (Teotihuacan), cave under, 46, 155–56, 157, 368
pyramids, 161; Egyptian, 9, 109, 111–12, *112*; as gate to Underworld, 111–12, *112*
Pyramid Texts, 111
Pyrenees, 22
Pyrgos, 72
pyrite, in Maya burials, 161

Qafzeh, 87
Qana Cave, 87
quarries, 143, 159
Quechua/Aymara, 344, 345, 346, 348–49
Queensland, 137
Quest for Fire (Rosny), 3
Quimaraes, Custodio, *326*
Quimaraes, Rafael, *324, 326*
Quin chieftain, 298
quincunx, in Newt Kash Hollow Shelter, 221–22
Quintana Roo, 161
Qulah, 99
Quleh, 99, 102

rabbit sticks, 175, 176
radiocarbon dates, 24, 38, 82, 191, 244, 288, 303, 360; Léné Ara, 328–29; Niah Cave burials, 249, 251, 254, 257; of Ohio cave artifacts, 228, 230; for Southeast US cave art, 198–201
rain, 153
rain ceremonies, 163, 174, 175–76, 179, 310
rain deities, Mesoamerican, 153–54, 161
Rainbow Serpent, 137, *138*
Rainey, Froelich, 286
rain houses, caves as, 153
Rais Cave, 228; cache from, *230*
Ramayana Cave, 335
Ramses II, Abu Simbel temple, 120–21, *121*
Ramses III, temple of, 118, *120*
Ramses VI, tomb of, *113*
Rath Croghan, 304
Rathlin Island, 304–5
Raven Rocks overhang, 231–32, *232*, 233, 234
Re: cosmology of, 109–10, 118, 120; Underworld journey, 6–7, 113–14, *114*, 115–16
Re-Atun, 111
rebellion, 312
rebirth, symbolic, 130
Red Cave, 173, 175, 179
Red Cellar Cave, 302

Red Horn, 356
red paint, 356
Red River, 355
Red Sea Hills
Re-Horakhti, 111, *113*, 121
rebirth, 90
Red Bow Cliff Dwelling, 173
Red Woman, 300
reference systems, 387
refuge, caves as, 6, 304–5, 312–13, 314, 346
Régourdou, Neanderthal burials in, 7, 17–18, 25
Reichel-Dolmatoff, Gerardo, 345
Reidh na h'Uanach, 301
reification, of boundaries, 154
Rekhit, 120
religious traditions, 2, 25, 171, 233, 367; Tibetan plateau, 128–32. *See also various sects; traditions*
renewal rites, Maya, 160
Republican River, Pawnee animal lodge at, 358
Réseau Clastres, 19
Reyfad Cave, 287
Rey monument, El, *153*
Rhodes, Cecil, 313
Rhodesia. *See* Zimbabwe
ribstones, 356, *357*, 358
Rinpoche (Padmasambhava), 130
ritual: definitions of, 7–8, 15–16; prehistoric Crete, 63–65
ritual deposits, 6, 348; in Malta caves, 52–53; in Nakovana Cave, 277–83
ritualization, 73; of food preparation and consumption, 69, 71; performance and context of, 64–65
ritual objects, storage/deposition of, 52, 54
Robber's Den (Ireland), 302
Robert the Bruce, 304–5
rock art, 15, 16, 122, 160, 179, 317; Australian, 136, *137*, 137–47; human and animal, 357–58; Ili Kérékéré, *320*, 320–22; Ozark caves and rockshelters, 239, 241; Upper Paleolithic, 18–25
Rockhouse Spring Cave, 215
rock-marking, in Australia, 136
rock platforms, Sydney region, 136
rockshelters, 2, 4, 15, 16, 18, 125; American Southwest, 172, 176; Australian, 136, 138, *139*, 146–47; as caves, 5–6; definition of, 151, 225; Mayan, 161–62; as menstrual retreats, 221–22; Ohio, 227–35; Upper Paleolithic, 19, 27–28, 31; Zimbabwean, 309–10
Rodgers Shelter, 211, 220, 238
Rohlfs Cave (Djara), 122
"Role of Caves in Maya Culture, The" (Thompson), 4, 158
Rome, Illyrians and, 272
Roscommon, Cave, 298
Rose, Valle delle, 38
Ro-Setau, 113, 114, 115, 116, 117, 118
Rosny, J.-H., *Quest for Fire*, 3
Ross Mound, and Hampton Cave, 215
Rouffignac, 19, 20
Rozwi kings, 311
Rumania, 19

Russell Cave, 211, 217–*18*, 222
Russia, 19

Saami, topographic shrines, 368–69
sacred precincts, Great Plains, 358–60
sacrifices, 34; animal, 220, 276, 280–82; human, *162*, 163, 217
Sahara, 122
sahkab (white earth), 158
Sai Baba cave temple, 331, 333–34
Saint Patrick's Purgatory, 301–2
St. Paul (Minn.), Carver's Cave in, 353
saints, Irish, 301, 302
Sakyamuni, 130
Salts Cave, 185, *186*, 211, 223; ritual cultural deposits in, 215–17; Woodland-Mississippian period use, 189, 190
Samhain, 304
Sam Poh Tong (Three Buddhas Cave), 332, 333, 336, 338, 339
San, rockshelter use, 310
San Bartolo, 153
sanctuaries, 20, 60; Bronze Age, 68, 69; Chalcolithic, 94, 96; Nakovana Cave as, 265–73
Sanctuary Blue Hole, 286
sandals, American Southwest, 176, 177–78
Sand Dune Cave, 176
sandstone caves, Australia, 137, 139–40
Santa Anna Mountain (Texas), 358
Saqqara, 118
Sarawak, 249
Sardinia, Monte d'Accoddi, 46
Sarnath, 130
Satet Temple, 118–19, *119*, 122
Sathya Sai Baba, 333–34
savannah hypothesis, 393
Scaloria Alta, 37
Scaloria Bassa, modification of, 34–35
scalps, and rain ritual, 175–76
School Cave (Ireland), 301
seals, Crete, 63
SECC. *See* Southeast Ceremonial Complex
secondary burials, 89–90, 99–100; Niah Caves, 255–56. *See also* ossuaries
2nd Unnamed Cave, 198
Sedona, 213
Selk'nam, 345
Seneca, 212
Senonian chalk, excavated caves in, 90, 96–98
sensory stimulation, reduction in, 389
Serabit el-Khadim, 121
Seti I temple, 116, *118*
7th Unnamed Cave, art in, *197, 207*
sexual art/symbolism, 32, 311
shamanism, 19, 179, 369
Shahe, 311
Shasta, 358
sheep, in Nakovana Cave, 278–81
Sheep Pot, 298
shells, 29, 215, 360; in Ohio caves, 232, *233*
shell mounds, 219, 223
shelters, Irish caves as, 304–5. *See* rockshelters
Shiqmim, 88, 89, 92, 97, 99, 101, 102
Shoham, *91*, 93, 95–96, 97, 99, 102

Shona, 312, 313, 315
Short Cave, 190
Shoshone, 354
shrines, 2, 6, 63, 94, 129, 156, 220, *326*;
    American Southwest, 173, 174, 175, 176, 177–78, 179, 180; Malta, 49, 53; Matopo Hills, 311–12, 313, 314–15; Saami, 368–69
Shumla Caves, 178
Sicily, 48, 51, 56
Sidhe of Cruachan, 300
Siega Verde, 19
sign systems, 392
Silozwane cave, 310
Sima de los Huesos, *Homo heidelbergensis* bones in, 18
Sima Pumacocha, 344
Sinai, 8, 89
Singer Butte, 356
sinkholes, 151, 153, 190, 217
Sioux, 358, 359
sipapus, shipap, caves as, 173, 180
Siva, 340
Six Nations, 211
Sixth period, 126
6th Unnamed Cave, 198
Skaphidhia, 67, 71
skeletons. *See* human remains
Skhul, 87
Skorba, 49
Skoteino, 72
skulls, trophy, 87, 228
sky world, caves and, 354, 358
Sligo County, 297, 298, 299, 301, 302
snakes, 52, 310
Soda Dam, shrine beneath, 179, *180*
Sokar, 113, *114*, 115
solar cycle, Egyptian, 120
Solutrean period, 19, 23
Songsten Gampo, 130
Sons of Míl, 300
sorcery, 155, 176
South America, 343. *See also* Andean region
South Andros Island, 286–87
South Dakota, 357, 358, 360
Southern Cult, 231
Southeast Asia, 249, 322, 334. *See also various countries; regions*
Southeast Ceremonial Complex (SECC): Birdman theme in, 243–44; cave art related to, 195–96, *197*, 207, 231, 238–39
Southeastern United States. *See* Eastern United States
space, 2, 8; definition of, 365–66; infilling and destruction of, 52–53
Spain, 7, 18, 19, 22, 24
spatial analysis, 371–73
spatial cognition studies, 387
spatial constraint theory, 2, 371, 373; simulation and analysis of, 374–80
spatial orientation, 387–88
spatiotemporal analysis, 372
spears, as offerings, 356, 360
speleothems, 35, 335; Maya use of, 159, 160, 164; in Nakovana Cave, 265–66, 271; Upper Paleolithic use of, 23–24, *24*

Spell of Twelve Caves, 116
Spider Pot, 298
Sphinx (Hor-em-Akhet), *112*
Spirit Bird Cave, 173, *174*
Spirit Mound, 358
spiritual danger, 16
Spiro site, 242
split-twig figurines, *175*, 179
springs, 48, 151, 158, 211, 212, 244, 354
Squire Boone Cave, 223
Sramore Cave, 303
stable isotope studies, Niah Cave, 258–59
stalagmites, 35, 122, 164; Nakovana Cave, 265–66, 271; Upper Paleolithic breakage and removal of, 23–24, *24*
stalactites, removal and decoration of, 31
standing stones, Bronze Age, 299
Stanhope Cave/Rockshelter, 230; human remains in, 227–28, *228*, 229
Stargate Blue Hole, 286–87
Star Site, *357*
Stela Cave, 158
stelae, 97, 99, 158
Stephens, John Lloyd, 155
Steward, Julian, 202
stone circles, 89
Stone Virgins, The (Vera), 315
storage, 52, 54, 176
Stow Rockshelter, cache from, 228–29, *230*
stratigraphy: in Malta temples and hypogea, 54–55; as metaphor, 52–53
Stravomyti cave, 62, 67, 68, 70
Stricker Rocks rockshelters, cache from, 229–30
subterranean chambers/features, *68*; Chalcolithic, 99–101; Mesoamerica, 155–56; Negev Desert, 100–101; Tibetan plateau, 125, 127–28
Sukhothai, 338
sulfate minerals, 190
Sunflower Cave, 178
Sun-Mountain Spring, 354
Sunrise Mine, 356
supernatural beings, Great Plains, 353, 358, 360
supernatural powers, 346, 348, 356
Surratt Cave, 173, 174, 176
Sutitoco, 368
Sutlej (Langchen Kebab) River, 127
sweat baths, in Maya caves, 161
Sydney region, 136
Sylvanus, 271

tables, stone offering, 63
tablitas, 174, 176, 178
Tabun, 87
Táin Bo Cúailnge, 302
Taíno: mythology and cosmology, 285–86, 291–92; social rank and, 289–91
Tainter Cave, 357, 358, 360
Tairona, 345
Taiwan, and Austronesian culture, 327
Taiyiba, et-, 97; ossuary from, *91*
Talocan, 158
Tambotoco, 368
Tamil Nadu, 336, 340

Tamils, 333, 339, 340
Taos Pueblo, 180
Taoist traditions, 339; Malaysian shrines, 2, 331, 333, 334, *335*
Tarxien, 45, 52, 53, *55*, 56
Tasmania, 6, 137, 145–46
Tas Silg, 56
Tavoliere plain, 32, 34, 36
Taybeh, 102
Tehuelche, 344, 345, 348
Tehuelche Complex, 345
téi, 317; archaeology of, 326–27; cultural heritage management, 327–28; Ili Kérékéré, 322–23; Titiru, 324–25
Tel Aviv, 98
Tel Ifshar, 98
temples, 9, 156; Egyptian, 113, 118–21, 123; in Malta, 46, 48, 51, 52, 53–54; pilgrimage caves and, 131–32; Tibetan Buddhist, 127, 130; West Malaysia, 331, 332–41
Tennessee, 185, 186, 191, 195, 198, 356; Archaic Period, 187, 220–21; Woodland and Mississippian periods, 189–90, 211, 213
Tennessee River, 214
Teotihuacan, 46, 155–56, *156*, 157, 368
Terminal Classic period, 158
Terra di Corte hypogea, 40–41
Tetum, 317, 318
Texas, 177, 178, 354, 358
Thailand, 260, 337
Thaipusam ritual, 337, 340
Tham Lang Rongrien, 260
theory of neuronal group selection (TNGS), 386
Theravada tradition, 332, 337
Theseus, 385
Third period, 126
3rd Unnamed Cave, 185, 187, 188, 189, 190; Archaic period use of, 198, 217
tholoi, 72, 73
Thompson, J. Eric S., "The Role of Caves in Maya Culture," 4, 158
Thor's Cave, *85*
Thoth, 114
Threatening Rock Fissure, 173
3BE1, 243
3BE6, 244
3BE18, 244
3BE189, 244
Three Pure Ones, 333
3WA4, 243
Thrown Away / Spring Boy, 215
Thutmose I, 112
Thutmose III, *114*
Tibet, 127; religious traditions, 128–30
Tibetan plateau, 2, 125–26; habitation caves, *127*, 127–28, *128*; pilgrimage on, 130–32
Tierra del Fuego, 344–45
Tikal, 151, 163
Timehri petroglyphs, 287
Timna, 121
Timor, as human body, 319
Timor-Leste, 2, 9, 10, 317; cultural heritage management in, 327–28; téi, 320–29; villages, 318–19

Tipperary County, 297, 298, 302
Tirawahat, 360
Tír na n-Óg, 298, 305
Titicaca Basin, Lake, 345
Titiru, 317, *318*, 324–25, *325*
Tito Bustillo, 18
Tlaloc, 153, 154, 161, 163, *174*, 180
Tlaltecuhtli, 152
tobacco, as offering, 360
Tokong Ju Wang Song Zi uan Si Yin, 333
tomb chapels, Old Kingdom, 116
tombs, 47, 299; Egyptian, 9, 109, 110–18; Apulian rock-cut, 37, 38–39, 40; Irish passage, 300, 303; Maltese rock-cut, 48, 51; in Mayan caves, 161, 162; Minoan Crete, 72, 74
Tonkawa, 212
Toothy Mouth symbol, 198, 201
torches, in Eastern US caves, 188
Tory Cave (Tory Hole), 301
totemism, 146
tourism, 313, 320, 323, 341
track-vulva-groove style, 357–58
Trans-Pecos region, 179
Traostalos, Mount, 68, 69
Trapeza, 63, 67, 70, 71, 73
treasures, *94*, 94–95, 132, 348
Trisong Detsen, 130
trophies, human remains as, 215, 217, 228
Troubet, 22
Tuatha De Danann, 299, 300
tubs, ossuary, 89, *91*, 99
Tularosa Cave, 176
Tule Canyon, 355, 356–57
tumuli, Chalcolithic, 89
Tunica, 211, 212
Tung Wah Tong, 333
tunnels, 5, 155, 159
Turkey, 5
turkeys, Woodland period, 216, 217
turquoise mining, 8
turtles, at Sam Poh Tong, 336
Tutankhamen, 113
Tutuala, 318–19, 328; boat symbolism, 321–22
Tutuala Ratu, 324; and Ili Kérékéré, 321–23
12th Unnamed Cave, 195, 196; petroglyphs in, *205*, *206*
25th Unnamed Cave, 198
twilight zones, 6, 123, 146, 346, 348–49
Twin Falls Creek rock art, *139*
Tycoon Lake Rockshelter, 231
Tzinacapan, 158
Tzotil Maya, 153, 154

Uaim na gCat (Oweynagat), 300
Uatha (tales of caves), 299
U-Bar Cave, 173, *174*, 175, 176
Ubirr, *137*
Ukonsari Cave, 369
Uktena, 189
Ulster Cycle, 299
Unas, Pyramid of, *111*
Underworld, 6, 8, 39, 165, 188, 286, 297; bison emerging from, 356–57; Egyptian, 109, 110–18, 121–22; Great Plains caves, 354–56; Maya conduits to, 16, 158; witchcraft and, 176, 177
United States. *See* American Southwest; Eastern US; Great Plains
universe, Taino concept of, 286
Unknown Cave, Archaic period exploration, 187, 188, *189*
updating, spatial orientation and, 387, 388
Upiusing Cave, 256
Upper Crouchway (Crystal Cave/Unknown Cave), 187, 188, *189*
Upper Gila River Valley, 172
Upper Mustang District, 126–27
Upper Paleolithic, 2, 87, 366; in Apulia region, 27–32; in Europe, 18–25
Upper Salts Cave, 185, 188, 189
Urals, 19, 366
Utah, 173
Utatlan, 157
Ute Pass Trail, 360
Utes, 360
Uxbenká, 156

Vairocana Buddha, 332, *333*
Valley of the Kings, 109, 111, 112–13, *113*, *115*, 123
Vera, Yvonne, novels by, 315
vessels, stone, 65, 70, 92, *95*, 96, 97, 102
Valle Sbernia, 39
Ventana Cave, 179
Vero, 318
Vietnam, miniature landscapes, *336*
Vikings, 300, 304
Victoria (Australia), Cloggs Cave in, 138–39
Victoria, Queen, 302
Vigo Cave, 298–99
Vilhonneur, 15
villages, 5, 215, 318; Timor-Leste caves as, 319–26
Vinya Pitaka, 129
violence, and téi, 324–25
Virginia, 190, 196, 197, 213
visitation rates, 19
visual access, 390–91
votive objects, 8, 176; for Kwan Yin, 336–37; Minoan Crete, 63, 72, 73; Nakovana Cave, 269–70; West Malaysian caves, 335–36
vulva symbols, 32

Waconda Spring, 354, 356, 359
Wakan Tanka, 212
warfare, 6; rituals of, 157–58, 174, 175–76, 179; Zimbabwe, 311, 312–13, 314
Wargata Mina (Judd's Cavern), 145, 146
Warreen Cave, 145
warriors, winged, 203–4, *204*
water, 48, 52, 151, 155, 161, 196, 216, 354, 348; cults related to, 38, 179; Mesoamerican cosmology and, 154, 156, 158
Waterford County, 297, 302–3, 304
Water of Wernes and Osiris, 113
water-sprites, 311
weaving, 216
Webb, Captain, 298
wells, caves as, 155

Western Australia, 144–45
West Malaysia, 331; cave temples, 332–41
West Virginia, dark-zone art, 196
Wheelabout rockshelter, 228, 232
White, Jim, 178
White Buffalo Buttes, Buffalo Gap, 357
White Dog Cave, net from, 176
White River drainage (Arkansas), 237, 243–44
White Rocks rockshelter, 228, 232; shell pendants from, *233*
whites. *See* Europeans
Wichita, 243
wind chambers, 47
wine, ritual consumption of, 270, 271
winged anthropomorphs (birdmen), in Mississippian art, 203–5, 243–44
Winnebago, 222, 356
Wiradjeri, Wollemi caves, 141–42
Wisconsin, 238, 356, 357
witchcraft, 155, 176–77, 311–12
Wixarika, 215, 216
Wollemi region, caves, 139–43, *143*, 146
womb, cave as, 136
women's rituals, 8, 358; menstruation and birthing retreats, 221–22
Wong Soon Teck, 340
Woodland Period, 189–90, 211, 222, 231; cave art, 197–98; mortuary caves, 213–17
Wyandotte Cave, 186, 189, 190, 223, 356
Wyandotte Pillar of the Constitution, 190
Wyoming, 356, 360

Xaghra: Brochtorff Circle at, 45, 51, 52, *53*, *54*, 55, 56; hypogeum at, *49*
Xanana Gusmao, 325
Xemxija, 48

Yahgan, 344, 345, 348
Yalahau region, 155, 156, 161
Yarlung Tsangpo Valley, 129
Yauyos, 344
Yavapai, 213
Yellowstone National Park, Dragon's Mouth at, 355–56
Yiali, obsidian from, 69
York, Cape, 137
Yorkshire Dales, *83*
Yucatan Peninsula, 155, 161, 163. *See also* various sites
Yu Huang, 333

Zapotecs, 153
Zebbug, 48
Zebbug period, 51
Zeus, 369
Zhame cave shrine, 311
Zimbabwe, 2; cave shrines, 311–12; cave use, 309–10; literary descriptions of, caves, 315–16; mythology, 310–11; post-independence cave use, 314–15; white imperialism in, 312–14
Zinacantecan, 154
zooarchaeology. *See* faunal remains
Zuni, 177, 180; Scalp Dance, 175–76